THE OXFORD HANDBO

NEO-LATIN

THE OXFORD HANDBOOK OF

NEO-LATIN

Edited by
SARAH KNIGHT
and
STEFAN TILG

OXFORD
UNIVERSITY PRESS

OXFORD
UNIVERSITY PRESS

Oxford University Press is a department of the University of
Oxford. It furthers the University's objective of excellence in research,
scholarship, and education by publishing worldwide.

Oxford   New York
Auckland   Cape Town   Dar es Salaam   Hong Kong   Karachi
Kuala Lumpur   Madrid   Melbourne   Mexico City   Nairobi
New Delhi   Shanghai   Taipei   Toronto

With offices in
Argentina   Austria   Brazil   Chile   Czech Republic   France   Greece
Guatemala   Hungary   Italy   Japan   Poland   Portugal   Singapore
South Korea   Switzerland   Thailand   Turkey   Ukraine   Vietnam

Oxford is a registered trademark of Oxford University Press
in the UK and certain other countries.

Published in the United States of America by
Oxford University Press
198 Madison Avenue, New York, NY 10016

© Oxford University Press 2015

First issued as an Oxford University Press paperback, 2018

Library of Congress Cataloging-in-Publication Data
The Oxford handbook of Neo-Latin / edited by Sarah Knight and Stefan Tilg.
pages cm — (Oxford handbooks)
Includes bibliographical references.
ISBN 978-0-19-994817-8 (hardback) — ISBN 978-0-19-088699-8 (paperback) —
ISBN 978-0-19-998420-6 (online file)   1. Latin literature, Medieval and
modern—History and criticism.   2. Latin language—History.   I. Tilg, Stefan.
II. Knight, Sarah, 1975– III. Series: Oxford handbooks.
PA8015.O96 2015
870.9'004—dc23
2015000185

Contents

Notes on Contributors   ix
Abbreviations   xvii

    Introduction   1
    Sarah Knight and Stefan Tilg

PART I. LANGUAGE AND GENRE

1. Classical Latin—Medieval Latin—Neo-Latin   13
   Keith Sidwell

2. Neo-Latin's Interplay with Other Languages   27
   Demmy Verbeke

3. Lyric Poetry   41
   Victoria Moul

4. Narrative Poetry   57
   Florian Schaffenrath

5. Epigram and Occasional Poetry   73
   David Money

6. Comedy   87
   Stefan Tilg

7. Tragedy   103
   Gary R. Grund

8. Oratory   119
   Marc van der Poel

9. Political Advice   135
   Erik De Bom

10. Historiography   151
   Patrick Baker

11. Letters   167
    Jan Papy

12. Fiction   183
    Mark T. Riley

13. Satire   199
    Ingrid A. R. De Smet

PART II. CULTURAL CONTEXTS

14. School   217
    Robert Black

15. University   233
    Sarah Knight

16. Philosophy   249
    Guido Giglioni

17. Science and Medicine   263
    Brian W. Ogilvie

18. Contacts with the Arab World   279
    Dag Nikolaus Hasse

19. Biblical Humanism   295
    Andrew Taylor

20. Catholicism   313
    Jason Harris

21. Protestantism   329
    Irena Backus

22. Political Action   345
    Marc Laureys

23. Gender   363
    Diana Robin

24. Social Status   379
    Françoise Waquet

PART III. COUNTRIES AND REGIONS

25. Italy   395
    DAVID MARSH

26. France   411
    PAUL WHITE

27. The British Isles   427
    ESTELLE HAAN

28. The German-Speaking Countries   445
    ROBERT SEIDEL

29. Iberian Peninsula   461
    ALEJANDRO COROLEU AND CATARINA FOUTO

30. The Low Countries   477
    DIRK SACRÉ

31. Scandinavia   493
    ANNIKA STRÖM AND PETER ZEEBERG

32. East-Central Europe   509
    CRISTINA NEAGU

33. Colonial Spanish America and Brazil   525
    ANDREW LAIRD

34. North America   541
    JEAN-FRANÇOIS COTTIER, HAIJO WESTRA, AND
    JOHN GALLUCCI

35. Asia   557
    NOËL GOLVERS

General References   575
    SARAH KNIGHT AND STEFAN TILG

Index   581

NOTES ON CONTRIBUTORS

Irena Backus is Titular Professor at the University of Geneva (Institut d'histoire de la Réformation), and a specialist in the reception of the church fathers and of the New Testament Apocrypha in the fifteenth and sixteenth centuries. She has also worked on the history of biblical exegesis in the sixteenth century. Select publications include *The Disputations of Baden (1526) and Berne (1528): Neutralizing the Early Church* (Princeton University Press, 1993); *La patristique et les guerres de religion en France* (Institut d'Etudes Augustiennes, 1993); and (as editor) *The Reception of the Church Fathers in the West: From the Carolingians to the Maurists* (Brill, 1996).

Patrick Baker is Senior Research Associate at Humboldt-Universität zu Berlin. His work focuses on Renaissance humanism and the reception of the classical tradition. He is the author of *Italian Renaissance Humanism in the Mirror* (Cambridge University Press, 2015) and co-editor of *Christianity, Latinity, and Culture: Two Studies on Lorenzo Valla* (Brill, 2014).

Robert Black is Emeritus Professor of Renaissance History at the University of Leeds. His principal publications in the field of Renaissance education include *Studio e scuola in Arezzo durante il medioevo e il rinascimento* (Accademia Petrarca di Lettere, Arte, e Scienze, 1996), *Humanism and Education in Medieval and Renaissance Italy* (Cambridge University Press, 2001), and *Education and Society in Florentine Tuscany* (Brill, 2007).

Alejandro Coroleu is Institució Catalana de Recerca i Estudis Avançats (ICREA) Research Professor at the Universitat Autònoma de Barcelona. His main research areas are the role of Latin in early modern cultural history, and the study of the classical tradition in Renaissance Catalunya. He is the author of *Printing and Reading Italian Latin Humanism in Renaissance Europe, ca.1480–ca. 1540* (Cambridge Scholars Publishing, 2014).

Jean-François Cottier is Professor at the University of Paris-Diderot and Associate Professor at the University of Montreal. He has published on medieval and Neo-Latin and on the humanist interpretation of the Bible. In particular, he is the editor of Erasmus of Rotterdam's *Paraphrases* of the Gospels in the *ASD* series. Over the last few years, he has also developed an interest in the Latin heritage of New France.

Erik De Bom is a postdoctoral research fellow at the Institute of Philosophy of the Katholieke Universiteit Leuven (KU Leuven), Belgium, and a senior researcher at LECTIO (Leuven Centre for the Study of the Transmission of Texts and Ideas in Antiquity, the Middle Ages and the Renaissance) and Leuven Centre for Global

Governance Studies (GGS). He specializes in early modern political thought and contemporary political philosophy. Currently, he is editing with Harald E. Braun *A Companion to the Spanish Scholastics*, to be published by Brill.

Ingrid A. R. De Smet, FBA, is Professor of French and Neo-Latin Studies at the University of Warwick. She was educated at the Universities of Leuven and Cambridge and formerly held a Prize Fellowship and British Academy Postdoctoral Fellowship at Magdalen College, Oxford. Specializing in the intellectual culture of late sixteenth-century and early seventeenth-century France and the Low Countries, she is the author of *Menippean Satire and the Republic of Letters, 1581–1655* (Droz, 1996); *Thuanus. The Making of Jacques-Auguste de Thou (1553–1617)* (Droz, 2006); and *La Fauconnerie à la Renaissance: Le* Hieracosophion *de Jacques Auguste de Thou (1582/84)* (Droz, 2013). The present chapter on satire was written during her Leverhulme Major Research Fellowship (2011–2014), which also laid the groundwork for her project on "Secrets and Their Keepers in Late Renaissance France."

Catarina Fouto is Lecturer in Portuguese Studies at King's College, London. She took a D.Phil. at Oxford University with a study of Portuguese Neo-Latin. Her interests include medieval and early modern Portuguese literature (vernacular and Latin) and its cultural context, humanism and the Counter-Reformation, censorship and history of the book, and critical edition and translation.

John Gallucci is Professor of French at Colgate University (Hamilton, New York). He has published on seventeenth-century French literature and the Latin writings of the French Jesuit missionaries. His translation of the *Castorland Journal*, which documents a group of French émigrés settling in New York State in 1793–1797, appeared in 2010 (Cornell University Press).

Guido Giglioni is the Cassamarca Lecturer in Neo-Latin Cultural and Intellectual History at the Warburg Institute, School of Advanced Study, University of London. He has published books on Jan Baptiste van Helmont (Milan 2000) and Francis Bacon (Rome 2011), and has edited a volume of manuscript papers of Francis Glisson (Cambridge 1996). He works on the intersections of medicine and philosophy in the early modern period.

Noël Golvers is a Senior Researcher in the Department of Sinology at KU Leuven. He studies Latin sources for the Jesuit mission in China (the early Qing period), and is particularly interested in astronomy, the circulation of books, and the communication networks between Europe and China. His 2003 study, *Ferdinand Verbiest and the Chinese Heaven* (Leuven University Press), won the Royal Academy of Belgium's 2004 award, and his publications on *Libraries of Western Learning for China* have appeared in the series *Leuven Chinese Studies* between 2012 and 2014.

Gary R. Grund is Professor of English Literature at Rhode Island College in Providence, Rhode Island. Since receiving his Ph.D. from Harvard University in 1972, he has pursued his research interests in Renaissance literature and the intellectual history of the period, publishing monographs, articles, and reviews. Two of his more recent full-length works are his editions and translations of *Humanist Comedies* (2005) and *Humanist Tragedies* (2011), both published by Harvard University Press as part of its I Tatti Renaissance Library series.

Estelle Haan is Professor of English and Neo-Latin Studies at The Queen's University of Belfast. She is the author of book-length studies of the Neo-Latin poetry of Milton, Marvell, Phineas Fletcher, Dillingham, Addison, Gray, and Bourne. Having recently published *Both English and Latin: Bilingualism and Biculturalism in Milton's Neo-Latin Writings* (American Philosophical Society, 2012), and her edition of Milton's Latin poetry for Vol. 3 of *The Complete Works of John Milton* (Oxford University Press), she is currently completing an edition of Milton's Latin letters, and a book entitled *"That Puissant City": John Milton's Roman Sojourns 1638–1639*.

Jason Harris is a lecturer in early modern history in the History Department at University College Cork. Since 2008, he has been Director of the Centre for Neo-Latin Studies at UCC. His research focuses on late medieval and early modern intellectual culture, with particular interests in the Low Countries and northwest Germany during the Reformation, and in Irish Latin writing of the period. He has co-edited *Making Ireland Roman: Irish Neo-Latin Writers and the Republic of Letters* (with Keith Sidwell, Cork University Press, 2009) and *Transmission and Transformation in the Middle Ages: Texts and Contexts* (with Kathy Cawsey, Four Courts Press, 2007).

Dag Nikolaus Hasse is Professor in the History of Philosophy at the University of Würzburg. His publications include *Avicenna's* De anima *in the Latin West* (Warburg Institute, 2000) and *Latin Averroes Translations of the First Half of the Thirteenth Century* (Olms, 2010). He is currently completing a book on the reception of Arabic sciences and philosophy in the Renaissance.

Sarah Knight is Professor of Renaissance Literature in the School of Arts, University of Leicester. Her editions and translations include Leon Battista Alberti's *Momus* (with Virginia Brown, I Tatti, 2003), John Milton's *Prolusions* (Oxford University Press, forthcoming), and the accounts of Elizabeth I's visits to the University of Oxford for the new edition of John Nichols's *Progresses* (Oxford University Press, 2014).

Andrew Laird is Professor of Classical Literature at Warwick University. His publications on Greek and Roman literature and on Latin humanism in Renaissance Europe and colonial Spanish America include *Powers of Expression, Expressions of Power* (Oxford University Press, 1999), *Oxford Readings in Ancient Literary Criticism* (Oxford University Press, 2006), and *The Epic of America* (Duckworth, 2006).

Marc Laureys is Professor of Medieval Latin and Neo-Latin Philology and Founding Director of the Centre for the Classical Tradition at the University of Bonn. Along with Karl August Neuhausen, he is the founding editor-in-chief of the *Neulateinisches*

Jahrbuch and the *Noctes Neolatinae*. He has published on early modern historiography and antiquarianism, particularly in Italy and the Low Countries, and polemical discourse in Renaissance humanism.

David Marsh (Ph.D., Harvard, 1978), Professor of Italian at Rutgers, is the author of *The Quattrocento Dialogue* (Harvard University Press, 1980), *Lucian and the Latins* (University of Michigan Press, 1998), *Studies on Alberti and Petrarch* (Ashgate, 2012), and *The Experience of Exile as Described by Italian Writers* (Mellen, 2013), as well as the translator of Alberti's *Dinner Pieces* (Medieval and Renaissance Texts and Studies, 1987), Vico's *New Science* (Penguin, 1999), Petrarch's *Invectives* (I Tatti, 2003), and *Renaissance Fables* (MRTS, 2004).

David Money teaches Neo-Latin literature at the University of Cambridge, for the Faculty of Modern and Medieval Languages; he is a fellow of the Academia Latinitati Fovendae, and an active Latin poet; he has published widely on Neo-Latin, especially on British verse of the sixteenth to eighteenth centuries. He is the author of *The English Horace: Anthony Alsop and the Tradition of British Latin Verse* (Oxford University Press, 1998), and has edited and translated the verses delivered to Elizabeth I by Eton scholars in 1563 for the new critical edition of John Nichols's *Progresses* (Oxford University Press, 2014).

Victoria Moul is Lecturer in Latin Language and Literature at King's College, London. She has published widely on the early modern reception and translation of classical poetry (especially Horace, Virgil, and Pindar) and on Neo-Latin verse, of which she is a regular translator. She is the editor of *A Guide to Neo-Latin Literature* (Cambridge University Press, 2017).

Cristina Neagu holds a doctorate from the University of Oxford and specializes in the literature and arts of the Renaissance. Her publications include *Servant of the Renaissance: The Poetry and Prose of Nicolaus Olahus* (Peter Lang, 2003) and contributions in the essay collections *Humanism in Fifteenth-Century Europe* (Medium Aevum, 2012), and *The Perils of Print Culture: Theory and Practice in Book, Print and Publishing History* (Palgrave Macmillan, 2014). Currently, Dr. Neagu is in charge of Special Collections at Christ Church Library, Oxford.

Brian W. Ogilvie is Associate Professor of History at the University of Massachusetts, Amherst. His research focuses on history of science and cultural history in Europe from the Renaissance to the Enlightenment. He is the author of *The Science of Describing: Natural History in Renaissance Europe* (University of Chicago Press, 2006). His current book project examines the role of insects in European art, science, and religion from the Renaissance to the Enlightenment.

Jan Papy is Professor of Latin and Neo-Latin Literature at KU Leuven. His research focuses on Italian humanism, humanism in the Low Countries, intellectual history and Renaissance philosophy in the Low Countries. He is a member of the editorial board of *Humanistica Lovaniensia, Erasmus Studies* (formerly *Erasmus of Rotterdam Society Yearbook*), and *Lias: Journal of Early Modern Intellectual Culture and Its Sources*.

Marc van der Poel is Professor of Latin at Radboud University, Nijmegen, The Netherlands. His area of expertise lies at the crossroads between Latin philology and ancient rhetoric and its history until the present day. He is working on a new edition of Rudolph Agricola's *De inventione dialectica*, and is the current editor of *Rhetorica: A Journal of the History of Rhetoric*.

Mark T. Riley is Emeritus Professor of Classics at California State University Sacramento. He is the editor of John Barclay's *Argenis* (Van Gorcum, 2004) and *The Mirror of Minds or John Barclay's Icon Animorum* (Leuven University Press, 2013), in addition to articles on ancient philosophy and scientific thought.

Diana Robin is Professor Emerita of Classics at University of New Mexico. She is a Scholar-in-Residence at Newberry Library (Chicago). Her books include *Publishing Women: Salons, the Presses, and the Counter-Reformation in Sixteenth-Century Italy* (University of Chicago Press, 2007), *Francesco Filelfo. Odes* (Harvard University Press, I Tatti Renaissance Library, 2009), and *Filelfo in Milan* (Princeton University Press, 1991).

Dirk Sacré, Ph.D. (1986) in Classics, is Professor of Latin and Neo-Latin Literature at the KU Leuven. He is general editor of the journal *Humanistica Lovaniensia* and vice-president of the Academia Latinitati Fovendae (Rome). He co-authored part two of the *Companion to Neo-Latin Studies* (Leuven University Press, 1998) and has published on a variety of Neo-Latin poets from the sixteenth to the twentieth centuries.

Florian Schaffenrath is the director of the Ludwig Boltzmann Institute for Neo-Latin Studies in Innsbruck and teaches Classics at Innsbruck University. He is interested in narrative poetry and has written about Petrarch, Sannazaro, and other epic poets. He has published and translated an edition of Ubertino Carrara's epic *Columbus* (1715; Weidler 2006).

Robert Seidel is Professor of German Literature at the Goethe University, Frankfurt am Main. His research focuses on the literature and culture of the early modern period. Publications dealing with Neo-Latin subjects include a monograph about the later humanist, Caspar Dornau; various editions of texts (for instance, humanist lyric poetry from the sixteenth century and Martin Opitz's Latin works); as well as edited volumes on lyric poetry, drama, and the technique of *parodia*.

Keith Sidwell is Emeritus Professor of Latin and Greek, University College Cork, and Adjunct Professor, University of Calgary. He works on Greek drama, Lucian, and Irish Neo-Latin. Major Neo-Latin publications include *Making Ireland Roman: Irish Neo-Latin Writers and the Republic of Letters* (Cork University Press, 2009; with Jason Harris) and *The Tipperary Hero: Dermot O'Meara's* Ormonius *(1615)* (Brepols, 2011; with David Edwards).

Annika Ström is Associate Professor of Latin and currently Professor of Rhetoric at Södertörn University. She has specialized in the seventeenth-century literature of Sweden, especially rhetoric, occasional poetry, epistolography, and dissertations. She is the author of *Lachrymae Catharinae: Five Collections of Funeral Poetry from 1628* (Almqvist & Wiksell, 1994) and *Monumental Messages: Latin Inscriptions on Tombstones and Church Bells in Medieval Sweden* (Sällskapet Runica et Mediaevalia, 2002).

Andrew Taylor is Fellow, Lecturer, and Director of Studies in English at Churchill College, Cambridge. He publishes on Neo-Latin writing, biblical and literary translation, and humanism in the sixteenth century, and has recently edited (with Philip Ford), *Early Modern Cultures of Neo-Latin Drama* (Leuven University Press, 2013), (with Sarah Annes Brown) the Modern Humanities Research Association (MHRA) *Ovid in English 1480–1625* (2013), and *Neo-Latin and Translation in the Renaissance* (*The Canadian Review of Comparative Literature/Revue Canadienne de Littérature Comparée*, 2014).

Stefan Tilg is Professor of Latin at the University of Freiburg. Before that, he was the first director of the Ludwig Boltzmann Institute for Neo-Latin Studies in Innsbruck. His main publications are from the fields of Jesuit drama and ancient fiction: *Die Hl. Katharina von Alexandria auf der Bühne des Jesuitentheaters* (Niemeyer, 2005), *Chariton of Aphrodisias and the Invention of the Greek Love Novel* (Oxford University Press, 2010), and *Apuleius' Metamorphoses: A Study in Roman Fiction* (Oxford University Press, 2014).

Demmy Verbeke is Head of the Arts Library at KU Leuven. His research interests include Renaissance humanism, the history and future of the book, and scholarly communication. He has authored *Latin Letters and Poems in Motet Collections by Franco-Flemish Composers (ca. 1550–ca. 1600)* (Brepols, 2010) as well as articles in, among others, *Renaissance Studies*, *International Journal of the Classical Tradition*, *Paedagogica Historica*, and *Humanistica Lovaniensia*.

Françoise Waquet is *directrice de recherche* at the *CNRS* (Centre national de la recherche scientifique). Her work focuses on the history of the learned world up to the modern and contemporary periods. Her principal works are *Le Latin ou l'empire d'un signe, XVIe–XXe siècle* (Albin Michel, 1998), *Parler comme un livre: L'oralité et le savoir, XVIe–XXe siècle* (Albin Michel, 2003), *Les Enfants de Socrate: Généalogie intellectuelle et transmission du savoir, XVIIe–XXIe siècle* (Albin Michel, 2008), and *Respublica academica: Rituels universitaires et genres du savoir, XVIIe–XXIe siècle* (Presses Universitaires Paris–Sorbonne, 2010).

Haijo Westra is Emeritus Professor of Latin and Greek at the University of Calgary. A specialist in late antique and medieval Latin, he is also interested in Neo-Latin and vernacular texts concerning the history of Canada. His emphasis here is on the relationship of these texts to classical sources.

Paul White, Lecturer in Comparative Literature at the University of Leeds, works on French Renaissance humanism, and has published articles and book chapters on poetry, scholarship, and print culture in Latin and vernacular contexts; and co-edited books on topics in early modern thought and culture. He is the author of books on the French reception of Ovid (Ohio State University Press, 2009) and on the Parisian printer-scholar Josse Bade (Oxford University Press, 2013).

Peter Zeeberg, Ph.D., is Senior Editor of the Society for Danish Language and Literature, Copenhagen. His main research areas are Danish Neo-Latin poetry and historiography. Major publications and projects include *Erasmus Laetus' skrift om Christian IVs fødsel og dåb*, with Karen Skovgaard-Petersen (C.A. Reitzels, 1992), *Tycho Brahes Urania Titani* (Museum Tusculanums forlag, 1994), and the online resource *Renaessancens sprog i Danmark* (http://renaessancesprog.dk, 2009). He is co-editor of the collected works of Ludvig Holberg (http://Holbergsskrifter.dk).

Abbreviations

ACNL   *Acta conventus Neo-Latini.* Various editors, places, and publishers. 1973–.

ASD   *Opera omnia Desiderii Erasmi Roterodami recognita et adnotatione critica instructa notisque illustrata.* Various editors. Amsterdam: North-Holland Publishing Company; Elsevier; Brill 1969–.

CNLS   Jozef IJsewijn and Dirk Sacré. *Companion to Neo-Latin Studies.* 2 vols. Leuven: Leuven University Press 1990–1998.

CWE   *Collected Works of Erasmus.* Toronto: University of Toronto Press 1974–.

ENLW   Brill's *Encyclopaedia of the Neo-Latin World.* Edited by Philip Ford, Jan Bloemendal, and Charles Fantazzi. 2 vols. Leiden: Brill 2014.

HWR   *Historisches Wörterbuch der Rhetorik.* 10 vols. Tübingen: Niemeyer 1992–2012.

NLL   *A Guide to Neo-Latin Literature.* Edited by Victoria Moul. Cambridge: Cambridge University Press 2017.

INTRODUCTION

SARAH KNIGHT AND STEFAN TILG

WHAT IS "NEO-LATIN"?

WHEN we talk about "Neo-Latin," we refer to the Latin language and literature from around the time of the early Italian humanist Petrarch (1304–1374) up to the present day, focusing particularly on its period of greatest intellectual and social relevance: from the fifteenth to the eighteenth centuries. For this reason, the term is often used synonymously with "Renaissance Latin" or "early modern Latin." During these four centuries or so, Neo-Latin contributed significantly to the history of Europe, but also to that of other continents, as our chapters on the Americas and Asia show.

That said, the term "Neo-Latin" is convenient but should be used with careful awareness of the questions it raises and how far it extends. First, no early modern author would have described himself or herself as writing "Neo-Latin." Like many terms we readily use now to delineate phases of artistic expression or cultural activity— "Renaissance," "humanism," and so on—the term "Neo-Latin" is a late invention. Its origin seems to lie in Germany, where the poet and philosopher Johann Gottfried Herder speaks of *Neulatein* and *neulateinischen* poems and poets in a number of works from the 1760s onwards. The term first appears in a title in the *Neulateinische Chrestomathie* (*Anthology of Neo-Latin Texts*, 1795), a textbook assembled by the Silesian teacher Ernst Gottlob Klose. In the early nineteenth century, a scholar from Liège in Belgium, Johann Dominicus Fuss, used the phrase *poetis neolatinis* in his *Dissertation on Neo-Latin Poetry and Poets* (1822; see Verbeke 2014; *CNLS* 1:27–28). From this Greek-Latin formation, or from the German (or both), the word was adopted into other European languages, and at the first congress of the International Association for Neo-Latin Studies in 1973, "Neo-Latin" was officially sanctioned as the name of a budding discipline.

Second, while Neo-Latin can be defined in terms of chronology, the term also often connotes a more stylistically ambitious and more self-consciously "classical" form of Latin, as opposed to what we might think of as "medieval" or "scholastic" Latin. But while this dichotomy has proved useful in many respects, not least for understanding the project of humanists like Valla and Erasmus in "purifying" the Latin language, readers should bear in mind that there are many exceptions, and that there is no such thing as a linear and uniform development from "medieval Latin" to "Neo-Latin." Several chapters in this handbook show the crucial role that scholastic Latin and scholastic thought continued to play in intellectual life until the seventeenth and eighteenth centuries; and, more generally, the complicated tensions between scholasticism and humanism that often inform our idea of "Neo-Latin" are a common thread running throughout this volume.

Finally, to the majority of researchers active in the subject today, "Neo-Latin" means much more than a particular phase of artistic and linguistic expression, relating mainly to poets and literary prose writers. Neo-Latin has increasingly been seen as a foundation of all early modern culture in the Western world and its areas of influence. Accordingly, we extend our parameters more widely: we not only focus on concertedly "literary" works but are also interested in, for instance, philosophical writing, scientific treatises, rhetorical manuals, and so on. Moreover, although all chronological periods have their share of turbulence, the ideological upheavals that shaped this era factor so directly into the history of Neo-Latin expression that we thought it artificial to separate writings from their historical context. The Ottoman conquest of Constantinople in 1453, for example, forced out Greek intellectuals into Italy, where their teaching and scholarship underpinned the comparative textual studies in Latin and Greek undertaken by contemporary humanists. From the 1510s onwards, the impact of the Protestant Reformation reverberated throughout Europe and beyond: reformers like Martin Luther worked to make vernacular versions of the scripture available, so that priestly mediation of God's (Latin) Word was no longer paramount; while Philipp Melanchthon and his colleagues established a rigorously schematized Latin pedagogy, which influenced the European school system for centuries. The Catholic Church reacted forcefully, reclaiming and reasserting the Latin of Vulgate Bible and liturgy with which their denomination had been so intimately associated for so long. Gathering momentum from the mid-sixteenth century onwards, and given fresh purpose by the Catholic Counter-Reformation, the Society of Jesus became one of the most conspicuous forces in Latin education, drama, and rhetoric, as well as the most mobile, as it extended its theological mission and pedagogical system as far as colonial North and South America to the west, and China and Japan to the east.

In addition to these close associations between historical circumstance and composition, another difficulty if we try to disentangle Neo-Latin writing from its context is the fact that many of these works defy tidy categorization in their transgression of our modern delineations of genre and scholarly discipline. Thomas More's *Utopia* (1516), for example, is one of the few Neo-Latin works regularly taught on English literature, history, and politics courses; at the time of writing, one can buy a paperback copy (in translation) either as a Penguin Classic, a Norton Critical Edition (listed on the Norton website both as "British Literature" and as "Political Theory"), and as a Cambridge Text in the History of Political Thought. Students, scholars, and, more recently, publishers writing marketing copy have clearly struggled to define the discipline into which *Utopia* fits. Referring to two of the most distinguished early modern Latin writers, Anthony Grafton reminds us that

Leibniz was an historian and linguist and Newton was an alchemist and biblical inter-preter (Grafton 2009, 2): in the early twenty-first century, we might more readily praise these men's roles in inventing the calculus and dramatically advancing our understanding of physical laws, but to their contemporaries, their innovations in the mathematical and physical sciences were only a part of their contribution to scholarship. A similarly gifted multi-tasker, Thomas More, trained as a lawyer at Lincoln's Inn in London, lectured on Saint Augustine, worked as a diplomat, advised Henry VIII, translated the Greek satirist Lucian, and acted as Lord Chancellor, as well as authoring *Utopia*. More, Leibniz, and Newton are not isolated examples: the history of Neo-Latin writing is peopled by such rig-orous and creative thinkers who astonish us in our own world of academic specialism by their extraordinary command of several disciplines at once.

Many of the authors discussed in this book not only move impressively between scholarly disciplines but also balance (often with acute self-awareness) expression in their mother tongues against their use of Latin. During the early modern period, Latin was both model and competitor for emerging vernacular languages and literatures, but it was also the only truly international language—spoken, written, and read all over Europe and beyond. To take just one example, the primacy of Latin and the complexity of its linguistic relationships with modern vernaculars prompted one historian of edu-cation and ideas earlier in the twentieth century to despair of producing any kind of his-tory of Neo-Latin. The American Jesuit Walter J. Ong (1912–2003) began his 1958 study of the charismatic, controversial scholar Pierre de la Ramée (Petrus Ramus, 1515–1572) by establishing the centrality of Latin to the world Ramus inhabited, but Ong's assess-ment does not apparently augur well for a new study of Neo-Latin (Ong [1958] 2004, 10):

> there exists no general history of modern Latin literature, from the fourteenth
> to the eighteenth century, for the good reason that such a history is simply too
> vast to think about. It would cover all Europe and America, and weave in and out
> of the history of every vernacular literature from Portuguese to Hungarian, and
> from Italian to Icelandic, and be simply the history of the Western mind.

What we would perhaps call *early* modern Latin literature—Neo-Latin—was "too vast" a topic for Ong because of its global scope and its absolutely formative position in insti-tutions, education, and a majority of learned communication in this period. Ong called it a "universal language," a claim substantiated by the existence of a republic of letters, a community of learned exchange conducted largely in Latin and discussed by many contributors to this book. He was right to state that a history of early modern Latin runs in parallel to "the history of the Western mind," and we should keep in mind, too, his point that early modern Latinity is intimately entangled with contemporary vernacular languages, to the east as well as the west, and that most of these languages were forming literary canons of their own during the same period. This book does in fact consider how early modern Latin relates to Ong's deliberately far-flung choices of Portuguese, Hungarian, Italian, and Icelandic, but also to the vernaculars of Arabic, Dutch, English, French, German, Mandarin, Romanian, Spanish, Swedish, and many more.

Deciding whether to write in Latin or the vernacular was a genuine dilemma for many of the authors discussed here, and we have already seen how the wish to reach out to the wider republic of letters might prompt a writer to choose Latin over the vernacular.

The adoption of movable type in Europe from the mid-fifteenth century onward resulted in another important question for early modern authors, one that their classical or medieval counterparts had not faced: should they circulate their works in manuscript—still a viable option for many, especially those working in locations that did not have advanced print technology or a wide distribution network—or opt for print? As a consequence, in paratexts and letters of the period particularly, we sometimes read about authors' anxieties, not only about their choice of linguistic medium, but also about their decision to publish their works commercially. In the preface to his wide-ranging, erudite *Anatomy of Melancholy* (first printed in 1621, and continually revised throughout his lifetime), for instance, the Oxford scholar Robert Burton worried about the implications of his choices (Burton 1989–2000, 1:2):

> It was not mine intent to prostitute my Muse in *English*, or to divulge *secreta Minervae* [Minerva's secrets], but to have exposed this more contract in *Latin*, If I could have got it printed. Any scurrile Pamphlet is welcome to our mercenary Stationers in *English*, they print all . . . but in *Latine* they will not deale.

Over three centuries earlier, Dante had written *De Vulgari Eloquentia* (*On Eloquence in the Vernacular*, ca. 1304–1305) to argue for the rhetorical potential of his native Tuscan, but Burton's assertion that writing in English is a form of prostitution aligns the vernacular with "vulgar" in our contemporary sense of crass and money-grabbing, rather than with Dante's more neutral usage. An author's rejection of Latin meant that he cared more about the commercial gains accruing from a vernacular readership than about using a more elevated idiom better suited to the goddess of wisdom's secrets and more elegantly concise ("contract") mode of expression. But he represented himself as fatally inhibited from choosing the loftier linguistic option because "mercenary Stationers," greedy for the next best-selling "scurrile Pamphlet," vetoed writing in Latin. Burton's complaint neatly captures that the history of the book, whether manuscript or printed, is just as difficult to disentangle from the history of early modern Latin writing as is the history of vernacular literatures or the history of the Reformation.

THE DEVELOPMENT OF NEO-LATIN STUDIES AND REFERENCE WORKS

From the start, like the works of many of its most able practitioners, Neo-Latin studies have been unavoidably interdisciplinary in nature. We have seen that scholars have conceived of Renaissance and early modern Latin as a definite phase of linguistic and literary development from the late eighteenth century onward, but the contours of Neo-Latin as an expressly defined and self-aware discipline were not decisively traced until the 1970s, when the International Association of Neo-Latin Studies was established (1971) and the first edition of the Leuven Classics professor Jozef IJsewijn's *CNLS* appeared (1977; see De Smet 1999). The significance of Neo-Latin in the early modern period has not always been appreciated in modern scholarship, for Neo-Latin has long been marginalized, eclipsed by the study of its classical predecessor—ancient, pre-medieval Latin literature—on the one hand, and by the study of vernacular modern languages on the other. We can still safely state that Neo-Latin literature is the least known and least systematically studied of Europe's major literatures: James Hankins, initiator of the renowned *I Tatti Renaissance Library*, describes it as a "lost continent," while Walther Ludwig, doyen of German Neo-Latin studies, has called it "terra incognita" (Hankins 2001; Ludwig 1997, 324).

That said, over the last few decades, the momentum of Neo-Latin studies has increased. A number of Neo-Latin research centers have been founded across Europe and North America, while disciplines such as Classics, history, English and other modern languages have increasingly adopted Neo-Latin studies into their undergraduate and postgraduate curricula. Learned societies like the International Association of Neo-Latin Studies, the British Society for Neo-Latin Studies and Cambridge Society for Neo-Latin Studies, and the German Deutsche Neulateinische Gesellschaft promote the discipline through conferences, workshops, publications, and postgraduate-targeted events. The number of editions of Neo-Latin texts, monographs, and articles grows yearly. This growth of Neo-Latin studies has been mapped and discussed in various contributions on the current state of the discipline (e.g., De Smet 1999; Helander 2001; Ludwig, Glei, and Leonhardt 2003). The publication of companions, encyclopedias, and similar reference works is a logical step in this development.

The classic reference work, cited by many contributors to this handbook, is Jozef IJsewijn and Dirk Sacré's *Companion to Neo-Latin Studies* (*CNLS*) in two volumes—the second edition of IJsewijn's pioneering *Companion* of 1977, mentioned above. The first part, by IJsewijn, is entitled "History and Diffusion of Neo-Latin Literature" and focuses on the development of Neo-Latin literature in individual countries; the second part, by IJsewijn and Sacré, is entitled "Literary, Linguistic, Philological and Editorial Questions" and considers individual genres. The *Companion* proved fundamental in establishing terms of enquiry within the discipline. IJsewijn and Sacré take an encyclopedic approach to the subject, which they dissect into numerous small parts. In the first volume, for instance, thirty countries or other larger geographical areas are dealt with one at a time. In the second volume, Neo-Latin literature is divided into some hundred genre-based subdivisions. Some space is devoted to almost every aspect of Neo-Latin, but little to any one specific element. Larger interpretative issues are somewhat neglected, to prioritize a broad survey of the field. It is impressive to see that only two individuals—in fact, IJsewijn wrote the first volume alone—were able to achieve this survey, but given the vastness of material and the complexity of the issues, any new reference work of this sort must be an intellectual collaboration between many experts in the discipline.

We did not have new reference works until very recently. But then, astonishingly, and suggesting contemporary interest in Neo-Latin, 2014–2017 saw not one, not two, but three related books commissioned by major publishing houses. These are this handbook, *Brill's Encyclopaedia of the Neo-Latin World* (*ENLW*) in two volumes, and the *Guide to Neo-Latin Literature* (*NLL*). The *Encyclopaedia* is a comprehensive and complex work building on the encyclopedic approach of IJsewijn and Sacré's *Companion*. It has sixty-six longer and 145 shorter articles, including many specialized subjects such as "coins and medals" and "the typography of Renaissance humanism." The *Guide to Neo-Latin Literature* has a narrower focus. The word "literature" in its title signals the book's emphasis on the literary form and aesthetic potential of major Neo-Latin genres; close readings of individual passages are central to its coverage. Our own handbook is meant to be more compact than the *Encyclopaedia*, while placing a more concerted emphasis on cultural and historical contexts than does the *Guide to Neo-Latin Literature*. As well as at dedicated Neo-Latinists and Renaissance scholars, we aim at a broad, international, and diverse readership—to include those interested in early modern languages and literatures; classicists working on early modern reception and the shifting characteristics of post-classical Latin language and literature; political, social, and intellectual historians; and readers working on particular geographical areas of interest. We hope that this handbook will also provide a clear and helpful point of access to those readers new to Neo-Latin studies who want to learn more about the discipline before taking their own research forward.

Inevitably, as the discipline has grown, it has also become more methodologically contentious and more self-aware. The variety of approaches adopted by contributors to this handbook reflects this development, and we believe that the chapters, taken in their entirety, are representative of the state of the subject today (for recent accounts of Neo-Latin methodology, see, e.g., Van der Poel 2014; Verbeke 2014; Van Hal 2007). To identify just a few examples, some of our contributors have focused on detailed critical readings of individual Latin works; considering, for instance, the nuanced decisions made by poets about diction and meter (e.g., Chapter 5, "Epigram"); other contributors explore the ideological engagement of Neo-Latin writing, analyze their authors' discourse, and consider both in historical context (e.g., Chapter 22, "Political Action"); others still adopt a more cultural-historical approach, examining Latin's contribution to sociological and intellectual formation across a broad chronological span of time (e.g., Chapter 24, "Social Status"). The division of the handbook into three discrete sections has facilitated this variety of approach: the first thirteen chapters, "Language and Genre," combine philological discussion with literary criticism and rhetorical analysis, and, in most cases, consider these aspects within an author's or work's historical context. The following eleven chapters in the "Cultural Contexts" part focus—with some overlap—on pedagogy and education, academic disciplines, and confessional and sociological categories (such as gender and class). In the final eleven chapters, the "Countries and Regions" part, we have tried to expand our coverage as broadly as possible, proceeding roughly (and without implying any ranking) from the countries that generated a conspicuous amount of Neo-Latin writing throughout the early modern period (such as

Italy, France, and the German-speaking countries) to the countries that produced far fewer Latin works in terms of quantity, but where composition in Latin was still fundamental to the self-definition, development, and ideological purpose of those writing it (as in the Americas and Asia).

EDITORIAL PRINCIPLES AND PRACTICES

A multi-author project like this handbook raises numerous editorial issues, and it may be helpful to explain some of the more significant decisions we made. First and foremost, we wanted to make the volume as accessible to a varied readership as possible. Our selection of chapters cannot, of course, encompass every single aspect of and context for Neo-Latin writing, but aims instead to introduce key forms, topics, and geographical areas of activity to a diverse audience. Nor should complete coverage be expected from the individual chapters: written by leading specialists in the field, they represent distinctive scholarly approaches and perspectives while introducing specific topics. There are no footnotes: references are provided in the text, and supported by a "Suggested Reading" section at the end of each chapter, which gives some direction for further study, as does the annotated bibliography we have included at the end of the volume. All contributions are in English, today's successor to Latin as the international *lingua franca*. All Latin (including titles) and other foreign-language citations have been translated into English (with a few exceptions concerning proper names, Latin words whose meaning is self-evident, and titles clearly paraphrased in the immediate context).

A particular difficulty was the presentation of Latin citations. Although Neo-Latin is fundamentally the same language as classical Latin, it often *looks* slightly different: in early modern manuscripts and printed texts, we see, for instance, "unclassical" spellings like *lachryma* (for *lacrima*, "tear") and *amicitie* (for *amicitiae*, "of friendship"). Printed texts frequently adopt digraphs and an accent system meant to mark out certain grammatical forms: indeclinable forms, for example, often carry a grave accent (such as the adverb *latè*, "widely"); the circumflex distinguishes vowel lengths (the nominative *rosa* ["rose"] is distinct from the ablative *rosâ*; Steenbakkers 1994). Other features like punctuation are affected by early modern usage (which often differs from its modern equivalent) as well as by the purpose of the text itself: an oration to be delivered to an audience, for example, may be differently punctuated from a treatise intended to be privately read. Scholars often fall into two factions when editing Neo-Latin texts (cf. Deneire 2014, who includes further references to this debate; and Rabbie 1996): one group wishes to retain all or most of these early modern features, while the other advocates standardization according to classical and modern conventions. We opted for standardization, because as editors of a multi-contributor volume (rather than a single-author or single-work scholarly edition), we had to work with very divergent material across the chapters. After all, thirty-nine different contributors across thirty-five chapters cite Latin passages from both manuscripts and printed works, written across several centuries by many authors (who are themselves often inconsistent) in a variety of different genres. Therefore, we have agreed on some basic principles of standardization. We use classical spellings except when spelling has a particular significance for meter, meaning, or interpretation (but we have not standardized titles if this would create difficulties for readers wanting to find out more about specific works, which tend to appear with the idiosyncrasies of the early modern Latin). For clarity, we distinguish between "u" and "v," so forms like *Vua* or *Uua*, both found in early modern printed works, become *Uva*, "grape"); "j" becomes "i" (*jacio* is rendered *iacio*, "throw"); and "ae" (as in *laetus*, "happy") and "oe" (as in *poena*, "punishment") are preferred to "e" (*letus, pena*). We drop all accents and resolve all digraphs (*ae*, not *æ*). We expand the ampersand (using *et* not *&*), and we expand abbreviations whose meaning would not otherwise be clear. Punctuation is modernized where necessary, and we do not mimic early modern print characteristics like the long *s* ("ſ").

The spelling of personal names will be important to readers researching a particular author or group of individuals. Here again we had the choice of two contrasting approaches: we could either "classicize" all names following Latin and Greek practice, as many authors did themselves and as IJsewijn and Sacré tend to do, for instance, in their *CNLS*; or we could use only vernacular name forms. Again, we aimed for clarity and practicality: adhering absolutely to either of these two approaches would, we think, become jarring and even confusing. Few people today speak of Leonardus Brunus or Coluccius Salutatus, for example, rather than Leonardo Bruni or Coluccio Salutati, and even fewer would recognize Joris van Lanckvelt more easily than by his much more commonly used humanist name Georgius Macropedius. When in doubt, a variety of national library catalogs and especially *CERL* (Consortium of European Research Libraries; http://www.cerl.org/resources/cerl_thesaurus/main) proved helpful tools in making editorial decisions. For personal names from classical antiquity, we relied on the *Oxford Classical Dictionary* (which has, for example, "Virgil" and not "Vergil").

Our general editorial style follows *The Chicago Manual of Style* (16th ed., 2010), but we departed from that model in several details. Where *Chicago*, for instance, distinguishes in English translations of foreign titles between published and unpublished translations and accordingly uses uppercase and italics for the former (e.g., *The Praise of Folly*) and lowercase and Roman type for the latter (e.g., Experiments and exercises), we thought this would overcomplicate presentation and opted for consistent use of the "published" model (e.g., *Experiments and Exercises*). A final word on references to classical authors: these are usually given without indication of a particular edition and page numbers, as is usual in the discipline of Classics, but with reference to book and line or section number; e.g., Virgil, *Eclogues* 1.2 (Book 1, line 2), or Cicero, *Tusculan Disputations* 4.5 (Book 4, paragraph 5).

This book has profited from the advice and support of many people. In particular, we would like to thank Stefan Vranka from Oxford University Press (OUP) for commissioning the volume, for the interest with which he followed the project, and his patience when delays were inevitable. We also thank the anonymous OUP readers for their constructive comments on the handbook's structure and contents at proposal stage, and Sarah Pirovitz and Heather Sieve at OUP for their help with the volume. Philip Ford encouraged the project from its start and always expressed the idea that a handbook like this was a desideratum: his death in 2013 was a profound loss to Neo-Latin scholarship. Moreover, Stefan Tilg is grateful to the Ludwig Boltzmann Institute for Neo-Latin Studies in Innsbruck, Austria, which provided an excellent environment for working on the book. Discussions with its team, especially Martin Korenjak, Farkas Kiss, Florian Schaffenrath, Lav Subaric, and Valerio Sanzotta, constantly yielded valuable ideas. Sarah Knight would like to thank several friends and colleagues for fruitful conversations that took place while editing the handbook: at the University of Leicester, Gordon Campbell, John Coffey, Mary Ann Lund, and especially Philip Shaw; and for advice early on, Michael Davies and Greg Walker. She is also grateful to past and present officers and members of the British Society for Neo-Latin Studies, particularly Ingrid De Smet, Philip Ford, Jacquie Glomski, Brenda Hosington, Gesine Manuwald, Ann Moss, Victoria Moul, Elizabeth Sandis, and Andrew Taylor, for valuable discussion.

—S.T. and S.K.
Freiburg and Leicester
August 2014

References

Burton, Robert. 1989–2000. *The Anatomy of Melancholy*. Edited by Thomas C. Faulkner, Nicolas K. Kiessling, and Rhonda L. Blair. 6 vols. Oxford: Clarendon Press.

Deneire, Tom. 2014. "Editing Neo-Latin Texts: Editorial Principles; Spelling and Punctuation." In *ENLW* 2:959–62.

De Smet, Ingrid A. R. 1999. "Not for Classicists? The State of Neo-Latin Studies." *Journal of Roman Studies* 89:205–9.

Grafton, Antony. 2009. "A Sketch Map of a Lost Continent: The Republic of Letters." *Republics of Letters: A Journal for the Study of Knowledge, Politics, and the Arts* 1:1–18. http://arcade.stanford.edu/rofl/sketch-map-lost-continent-republic-letters.

Hankins, James, ed. 2001. "The Lost Continent: Neo-Latin Literature and the Rise of Modern European Literatures; Catalog of an Exhibition at the Houghton Library, 5 March–5 May 2001." *Harvard Library Bulletin* 12:1–92.

Helander, Hans. 2001. "Neo-Latin Studies: Significance and Prospects." *Symbolae Osloenses* 76:5–102.

Ludwig, Walther. 1997. "Die neuzeitliche lateinische Literatur seit der Renaissance." In *Einleitung in die lateinische Philologie*, edited by Fritz Graf, 323–56. Stuttgart: Teubner.

Ludwig, Walther, Reinhold Glei, and Jürgen Leonhardt. 2003. "Klassische und Neulateinische Philologie: Probleme und Perspektiven." *Rheinisches Museum* 146:395–424.

Ong, Walter J. (1958) 2004. *Ramus, Method, and the Decay of Dialogue*. Chicago: University of Chicago Press.

Rabbie, Erwin. 1996. "Editing Neo-Latin Texts." *Editio* 10:25–48.

Steenbakkers, Piet. 1994. "Accent-Marks in Neo-Latin." *ACNL* 1994, 925–34.

Van der Poel, Marc. 2014. *Neo-Latin Philology: Old Tradition, New Approaches.* Leuven: Leuven University Press.

Van Hal, Toon. 2007. "Towards Meta-Neo-Latin Studies? Impetus to Debate on the Field of Neo-Latin Studies and Its Methodology." *Humanistica Lovaniensia* 556:349–65.

Verbeke, Demmy. 2014. "History of Neo-Latin Studies." In *ENLW* 1:905–20.

PART I

LANGUAGE AND GENRE

CHAPTER 1

....

CLASSICAL
LATIN — MEDIEVAL
LATIN — NEO-LATIN

....

KEITH SIDWELL

*Tres illi tanquam triumviri ... Donatus, Servius, Priscianus quibus ego
tantum tribuo ut post eos quicunque aliquid de Latinitate scripserunt bal-
butire videantur: quorum primus est Isidorus, indoctorum arrogantissimus,
qui quum nihil sciat, omnia praecipit. Post hunc Papias, aliique indoctio-
res, Ebrardus, Huguitio, Catholicon, Aymo et ceteri indigni qui nominentur,
magna mercede docentes nihil scire, aut stultiorem reddentes discipulum
quam acceperunt.*

The three famous triumvirs (so to speak) ... Donatus, Servius and
Priscian, to whom I attribute so much that after them anyone writing
a word about Latinity appears to be stammering. First among whom is
Isidore, the most arrogant of the unlearned, who teaches everything
though he knows nothing. After him come Papias and others even less
learned, Everard, Hugutio, the *Catholicon* [of Johannes Balbus], Aymo
and others unworthy to be named, who at great expense teach their pupils
to know nothing or make them more stupid than when they took them in.

(Lorenzo Valla, *Elegantiae Latinae linguae* [*Elegances of the Latin
Language*] Vol. 2, preface: Garin 1952, 602)

THE Italian Renaissance had highly practical roots. The appropriation of materials
first developed for audiences in Republican Rome as aids toward the political and
ethical organization of the free *communi* of the Northern Italian *regnum* in the thirteenth century—especially Padua (Witt 2012, 438–71)—and the insistence of Petrarch
(1304–1374) upon the moral utility of these same materials are both indications of that
trend. But the decision to reclaim this corpus through the medium of the language in
which it was couched, the Latin we call "classical" (CL), which has been traced back to the
work of classicizing Latin writers such as Lovato de' Lovati (Witt 2012, 457–67), though

not necessarily the only logical choice (e.g., the *volgare* was more in evidence for these purposes in late thirteenth- and early fourteenth-century Florence), led directly to the last great change in the history of Latinity—a history rife with claims of "renewal" and "purification." This change, bypassing and downgrading the medium—Medieval Latin (ML), developed in response to such revolutions in the real world as the introduction of Christianity and the rise of regal and clerical bureaucracies—was to be of profound significance for the development of Western thought and culture. The close linguistic patterning that arose from this movement can be argued to have led both to the difficulty of continuing to express medieval political ideas in it and to a deep level of comfort with ancient pagan society that encouraged easy comparison and even reformulation of the idea of society itself in terms of the ancient model (Moss 2003; Witt 2012).

By the mid-fifteenth century, scholars such as Lorenzo Valla (1406–1457) were beginning to codify classical usage by close examination of ancient grammars and texts. As the citation at the start of this chapter shows, these "humanists" (as they called themselves) had a fairly clear idea that between the seventh century and their own day, anything written about Latinity was more or less gibberish and should be ignored. They sought *elegantia*, following the prescriptions they read in the newly discovered rhetorical works of Cicero (compare, e.g., the phrase *Latine loquendi accurata et sine molestia diligens elegantia*; "The careful and unfussily diligent elegance of Latin speech" in *Brutus* 143). The true arbiters of this *elegantia* were the ancient pagan writers and the grammarians who had written before the onset of the corrupt *media tempestas* ("Middle Ages")—though even these were not to be trusted above their evidence of actual usage. Not unnaturally, since this attitude implied a direct link between correct grammatical teaching alongside deep knowledge of classical texts and correct (and elegant) writing, the humanists dismissed the Latin writing of the Middle Ages with contempt. It is the purpose of this chapter to deal with three questions: First, what is classical Latin and what did the humanists think it was? Second, what characterizes ML? Finally, how—and how well—did the humanist enterprise manage to respond to the challenge it had set itself: to return to the pristine language of the classical period?

Classical Latin

> CL [Classical Latin] is defined by the characteristics common to literary authors in the period *c.* 90 BC–*c.* AD 120. It is a highly artificial construct which must be regarded linguistically as a deviation from the mainstream of the language, namely VL [Vulgar Latin].
>
> (Coleman 2012, 796)

The first of these statements is unequivocal and useful, inasmuch as it was a view shared by at least some of the humanists themselves (e.g., Valla; Tunberg 1988, 22–23).

The second is problematic and represents one of many ways in which linguists have attempted to explain the following sets of data:

(1) that comparative evidence from Romance languages and reconstruction backwards of its history leads to a language, VL (Proto-Romance), that does not have the (full) characteristics seen in CL (Palmer 1954, 148–80), and that Romance languages, though spread over widely distant geographical areas, nonetheless share a common analytical syntax (where word order is the crucial determinant of syntactical relationships), as opposed to the thematic one (where the relationships between words are determined by information embedded in the endings of the words) of CL (Adams 2007, 729);

(2) that CL fights to purify itself of syntactical aspects common in Archaic Latin, such as the use of *quod* and *ut* for introducing indirect statements (e.g., Terence, *Hecyra* 145) and the use of prepositions to support case-usage (Palmer 1954, 125), which recur with added intensity in Late Latin authors such as Egeria (or Aetheria) and then in ML.

Both Latin and Romance philologists have struggled with this dilemma. The fact that the written evidence is all in Latin, regardless of how much it may diverge from a supposed classical norm, makes it impossible to trace in it specific movements towards Romance languages (Adams 2007, 726). Väänänen provides a useful division of the debate about language breakdown into two opposed camps: those who favor the "unitary thesis"— that Latin stayed unvaried until very late (Väänänen 1983, 481)—and those who favor the "differential thesis"—that Latin began to have local varieties "from the imperial period" (Väänänen 1983, 490). But both polarities (at least thus articulated) have recently been shown to be unacceptable: "metalinguistic evidence . . . makes nonsense of the unitarian thesis, and the differential thesis as formulated by Väänänen . . . is itself not satisfactory, because the regional diversity of the language can be traced back at least to 200 BC" (Adams 2007, 684). It might be simpler, in fact, rather than insisting upon a constructional relationship of CL to VL or to continue with one or another model of syntactical collapse from Latin to VL, to suggest that the two languages had always been different from each other (a position espoused by some Italian humanists of the fifteenth century, e.g., Bruni and Valla: Ramminger 2010, 8), VL being formed by creolization from CL, perhaps (or vice-versa, even?), at an early date, though because they had shared the same sociocultural space for such a long time, their lexis had become fused, and by the time our written metalinguistic evidence begins, they were regarded as essential parts of a single system called *lingua Latina* (Sidwell 1997). In this model, the "vulgarisms" that intruded into the elite register (CL) and had to be contained by effective and detailed education and discipline, will have been the natural—and sometimes (as in Roman comedy) the artificial and intended—results of cohabitation with VL (Proto-Romance). In this way, conditions will have been propitious for the breakup of VL into the Romance languages, once the systems of imperial control that held VL in stasis had collapsed, while the upper register (CL) continued to be the controlling idiom of a replacement empire, that of the Christian Church, and thus retained—sometimes with difficulty and always by processes of educational stringency—its integrity.

We cannot know for certain the truth of this matter, but we can say for sure that the imperialist nature of Roman power ensured that its language (or languages) was imposed as soon as possible upon the newly conquered provinces, from Spain (197 BCE) to Dacia (106 CE), and that this was a matter of policy (Pliny, *Natural History* 3.5.39). The specific way in which the Romans acquired the loyalty of the native elites—that is, by allowing them a share in the power of government, both local and central—must soon have meant that many of them learned the high-level oral and written register we call CL (Tacitus, *Agricola* 21). Later, even an emperor's sister might be a learner, as was, apparently, Septimius Severus's sibling, a native speaker of Punic and so little versed in Latin speech that her brother sent her home from Rome (*Historia Augusta, Septimius Severus* 19.9: Adams 2007, 260). The reflex of the need to inculcate, enforce, and maintain a system for CL that was as far as possible standard in grammar and vocabulary can be seen in the grammatical literature of the empire, of whose precepts Lorenzo Valla took most account. That there was even an attempt to standardize pronunciation seems clear from the teachings of these treatises (Allen 1978, 95–100) and anecdotes about rustic deviations from a perceived norm (see, e.g., Suetonius, *Vespasian* 8.22). The general rules of this system are those taught in modern handbooks, and this is not the place for a detailed treatment of them. It must be noted, however, that even the rigorous systematization evidenced by the grammatical treatises did not prevent all sorts of divergence in practice, divergences that were thus readily available for imitation by anyone who paid stricter attention to the texts than to the grammarians.

MEDIEVAL LATIN

Ciceronianus es, non Christianus: nam ubi thesaurus tuus, ibi et cor tuum.

You are a Ciceronian, not a Christian: where your treasure is, there is also your heart.

(Jerome, *Epistles* 22.30.4 = *Patrologia Latina* 22.665)

Christianity is the great and encompassing fact that explains the longevity of CL and its transmutation into ML. The Roman Empire's language policy was still functioning when Christianity became the official religion at the end of the fourth century under Theodosius, and the church in the West naturally continued using the CL standard (with notable variations in vocabulary and grammatical usage) already adopted for its liturgy, its sacred book, and all the other manifold purposes required by an international organization. We do not know precisely when (or even whether) Latin ceased to be a language learned at one's mother's knee, but as has been said above, in any case the spread of Roman power had eventually necessitated the construction of an educational system across the empire that facilitated the acquisition of the standard tongue for those intending to play public roles. Christianity had a different colonial goal—conversion of the pagans—which nonetheless had a similar effect on the spread of the official language (and this applied equally to Greek in the East). The mission sent to Ireland by Pope Celestine I under Bishop Palladius in 421, for example, must have begun the process of establishing Latin education there among a Celtic-speaking people; and in 669, the arrival of Theodore of Tarsus and Hadrian in Canterbury at Pope Vitalian's bidding heralded the successful reintroduction of Latin (and Greek) education in Britain, this time among the Anglo-Saxons. This education was focused on Christian objectives and operated, until the Carolingian reforms of the late eighth and early ninth centuries, from monasteries. In time, it spawned its own series of grammatical aids, which dealt with matters of orthography, morphology, vocabulary, and metrics in ways specifically adapted to local conditions, though it seems these were used alongside late classical grammars, especially Donatus, which had the effect of keeping a role for pagan authors (poets, especially), since many of the examples cited in these texts were from the works of Virgil and Horace.

Highly educated Christian writers of the fourth century, such as Augustine and Jerome, commented that conversion required also a linguistic conversion, since the liturgy and especially the Latin translations of the Bible (the so-called *Vetus Latina* that remained in use until Jerome's fifth-century *Vulgata* became the official version during the reign of Charlemagne) were marked by aspects of "translationese" (the *Vetus Latina* was made from the Greek Septuagint) and by "vulgarisms" (under the influence of VL = Proto-Romance?) and were not in the high register taught still in the schools. But the continued pull of the CL pagan texts is graphically illustrated by the superscript to this section, from Jerome's dream of being called to account before God's tribunal and found wanting for his too-eager adherence to the words of Cicero. Irregularities—or deviations from CL standards dubbed "vulgarisms"—are found in a number of Late Latin texts, such as the fourth-century *Peregrinatio Aetheriae* (or *Egeriae; Pilgrimage of Aetheria/Egeria*), written by a nun from "the territory spanning the Gallo-Iberian border" (Adams 2007, 352–53). For example (24.1): *Nam presbyteri bini vel terni ... singulis diebus vices habent simul cum monazontes* ("For groups of two or three priests ... on individual days take turns together with the monks"). Here the preposition *cum* is used with the accusative, rather than the ablative, reflecting perhaps a situation in which Aetheria, who probably spoke Proto-Romance (VL), which had no ablative case, did not have a solid enough education in *grammatica* to allow her to recall the correct case following *cum* in the written language (CL).

While this sort of morphological error is relatively short-lived—it continued to be found especially in Merovingian texts and was due to the combined effects of the interference of Proto-Romance syntax and the collapse of the educational system of the Roman Empire, but more or less disappeared after the Carolingian reforms—other, more broadly syntactical, vulgarisms had a more lasting impact, probably because syntax was not so rigorously taught in the grammars as morphology. The most important of these—the use of *quod* and *ut* (joined by other words considered synonyms, such as *quia, quoniam, quomodo, qualiter,* and *quatenus*) to introduce indirect statements, which, as we have seen, were visible in Roman comedy but repressed in CL—reemerged, possibly as reflexes from Proto-Romance, in Christian texts such as the Bible translations and continued to be used (sometimes even alongside the accusative and infinitive) throughout the Middle Ages. For example, Bede in *Ecclesiastical History* 2.1 writes: *Dicunt quia die quadam . . . et ipsum Gregorium inter alios venisse* ("They say that one day . . . Gregory himself also had come among others"). Here the writer's reflex is to insert the conjunction after the verb of speech, but, possibly distracted by the two lines of intervening subordinate clauses he employs to fill in the background, when he gets to the reported statement, he reverts to accusative and infinitive. More commonly, the clause has a finite verb, indifferently indicative or subjunctive, as in this instance from the early twelfth-century *Gesta Francorum* (7.18): *Audientes itaque nostri quod humassent mortuos suos Turci* ("Our men, having heard that the Turks had buried their dead").

As can be seen from this latter example, correct morphology and case-usage often sit alongside misapprehensions about basic rules of syntax: here, the use of the reflexive adjective *suus* to refer to the subject of the subordinate noun-clause (*Turci*) rather than to that of the main clause (*nostri*). Slippage of this kind occurs everywhere in ML, but one of the main areas where CL standards were most regularly subverted was in the use of conjunctions. For example, *dum* ("while") becomes a regular substitute for *cum* and even takes the subjunctive with this meaning. The conjunctions for final clauses (*ut* and *qui* + subjunctive in CL) are joined by *quod, quatenus, qualiter,* and *quemadmodum,* and *ut non, ut nullus* are used as negatives instead of *ne, ne quis.* In consecutives, we see the same phenomenon, with *quod* (and very occasionally *quatenus*) being used for *ut,* and indifference being shown as to the mood of the verb (e.g., Petrus Alfonsi, *Disciplina clericalis* 19: *et tunc defecit illis cibus ita quod non remansit eis quicquam;* "And then their food ran out so that they had nothing left"). One isolated morphological development of Late Latin that was generalized in ML was the use of the ablative ending *–i* instead of *–e* in comparative adjectives (*a priori*) and in present participles (*praesenti*).

These substitutions are not, strictly speaking, linguistic developments, despite the longevity of their use. Latin during the Middle Ages was no longer a natural language, but a *Traditionssprache,* a "traditional language." It needed to remain fixed, since it served the purpose of an international medium of communication as well as encapsulating in its unchanging form the sacred books, liturgy, and collected interpretative analysis of these that formed the framework of the religious life whose language it was. It was guided by an established repertory of unchanging grammatical lore, where, however, sometimes subtleties remained unexpressed by the grammars (as, e.g., in the niceties of the sequence of tenses or the proper use of reflexive pronouns and adjectives). But sometimes even these works were inaccessible in the individual writer's poorly stocked monastery library: sometimes they were accessible, but not read by the writer or not well enough absorbed to be replicated. Hence, though we do find during the Middle Ages a good deal of Latin that deviates considerably from CL norms, we also find highly wrought texts that show minimal evidence of what we tend to think of as characteristics of all ML.

Another area in which VL may have had a serious influence on ML is in the emergence of *rhythmus,* poetic composition based on numbers of syllables and a stress accent (e.g., *éxiit dilúculo/rústica puélla*: three, four, three, and another three syllables, the first three with stress on the third from the end, the last one with stress on the second from the end), rather than on syllable quantity, as in CL. If VL was, like its Romance derivatives, a stress-based language, then the assimilation of Latin poetry to the vernacular style is as understandable as the difficulty many ML poets who were writing in the classical forms had in maintaining the correct quantities, which need to be learned individually and were very often at variance with the VL stress patterns in similar lexical items (e.g., CL *muliĕrem* with a short *e* and stress on the *i*, as opposed to VL *muliére*, with the stress on the *e* tending to lengthen the vowel, as in Spanish *mujer*).

The continued health and utility of Latin, then, depended solidly upon the level of the individual's education, as was recognized clearly in the style of the Carolingian reforms of the late eighth century in the Frankish realms. They were motivated by a fear that mishandling the language of the sacred texts and liturgy would be detrimental to the health of the kingdom, and they were supported by an influx of learned individuals from Lombardy, England, and Ireland, whose grasp of correct Latinity was well established and who proceeded to reimpose the standards of, essentially, CL morphology and, insofar as the grammars allowed, orthography, style, and syntax. Latin needed, nonetheless, to be able to develop in at least one direction: its vocabulary had to be constantly adapted to evolving circumstances. Thus the lexicon of ML expanded, first taking in the newly wrought language of Christianity, and later adapting to the needs of law, medicine, and technology, and at the same time providing geographical terms for settlements established outside the boundaries of the ancient world or for new ones within them. These new words, appearing in every corner of the world that used ML, were sometimes CL words given new meanings (e.g., *rotulus*: CL "little wheel"; ML "roll"), sometimes new words based on CL roots (e.g., *impeccantia*, "sinlessness"), sometimes Greek words (e.g., *baptizo*, "I baptize"), and sometimes borrowed directly from vernacular languages (e.g., *shopa*, "shop"; *wantus*, "glove", cf. French *guant*), though the latter group were generally confined to low-level administrative texts and tended to be kept out of—or at arm's length, if within—more literary productions. The resulting medium, in which imitation of ancient pagan models was not the central concern, served the purposes of both secular and ecclesiastical organizations for the better part of a millennium.

Neo-Latin

"Quatenus" autem significat "in quantum," sicut "eatenus" "in tantum."
Cicero in Laelio: videndum est quatenus amicitiae tribuendum est.

Quatenus, however, means "to what extent," just as *eatenus* means "to such an extent." Cicero in *Laelius* [cf. 61 *quatenus amicitiae dari venia possit*]: "We must see to what extent this should be attributed to friendship."

(Lorenzo Valla, *Elegantiae linguae Latinae* 2.42)

Unlike the Carolingian project, which had been needed to pull Latin back from the brink of unintelligibility, humanism set its sights on restoring the Latinity of the classical period. What this meant was never clearly fixed. Valla preferred to follow the practices of oratory from Cicero to Quintilian (Tunberg 1988, 32–33). But the desire to access comic and satirical registers tempted many writers, even of prose, to add the Roman comic poets Plautus and Terence to their imitative stockpile (Erasmus, *De ratione studii, ASD* 1.2:115–16); while in the seventeenth century, the works of Ammianus, Macrobius, and Martianus Capella could also readily amplify a writer's *copia* (O'Meara 2011, 42–43).

Nonetheless, the desire to approximate more closely the elegance in the syntax and style of writers whose works fell within the limits of antiquity (Christian and pagan) led directly from the early Quattrocento to the creation, by close study of the actual practice of ancient Latin writers, of tools that would allow this goal to be achieved. Valla's *Elegantiae*, quoted in the superscript to this section, in six books, finally finished in 1449, was the first and one of the most fundamental and influential works in the recovery of "sound" Latinity. In it, the scholar presented in the form of small articles, such as the one cited (*De Quandoquidem, Quando, Quatinus, Quatenus*), his findings about the ways in which his target group of writers (and others, such as Virgil and Horace) used items of Latin. Rather than bother to advert to the intervening traditions of usage, which he excoriates in the preface to this book, Valla silently passes over the fact that *quatenus* in ML had been dragooned into doing service as a conjunction introducing final and even consecutive clauses. He merely states that such and such is the way our classical writers use it. His *De reciprocatione* sui *et* suus *Libellus* (*Pamphlet on the Reflexive Use of* se *and* suus) takes a different tack, explaining in detail, for example, in chapter 9 *causa cur* eius, ipsius *et* illius *abutamur pro* suus ("the reason why we mistakenly use *eius, ipsius* and *illius* instead of *suus*"). The method of philological enquiry initiated by Valla had enormous success per se (Marsh 1979) and, along with other systematic enquiries into ancient usage (e.g., the *Cornucopiae* [1489] of Niccolò Perotti [1429–80], ostensibly a commentary on the poems of Martial, but in fact a dissertation on the ancient Latin language), paved the way for a renunciation of the ML continuum and its replacement by a variety of approaches that aimed at more closely following the linguistic norms of CL.

In his own writing, Valla shows a distinct preference for usages of the "Silver Age." Examples are: *quam pro* after a comparative, meaning "than befits" (not found before Livy in prose), indicative in clauses introduced by *quippe* (found in Sallust, but common in Silver Latin prose), and *quamvis* with the indicative (Tunberg 1988, 35–41). He was not able, however, to eradicate completely traces of ML usage, such as the use of *habere* for *debere*, the indicative for subjunctive in indirect questions, the use of *dum* for *cum*, and irregular treatment of tense sequence (Tunberg 1988, 41–51), the latter perhaps reflecting, in the absence of fully articulated grammatical rules, a tendency to pattern usage upon the vernacular (Horster 2011, 162; but see also Tournoy and Tunberg 1996).

One path trodden by Latin writers of the fifteenth and the sixteenth centuries was to replace a larger canon (narrower in Valla's case, broader in that of Erasmus) by close imitation of a single model, Cicero ("Ciceronianism"). Those who took a strict line— that only Ciceronian language should be used in writing prose—were satirized in

Erasmus's dialogue *Ciceronianus* (*The Ciceronian*, 1528). These included Christophorus Longolius, a native of Mechelin, who spent five years reading only Cicero and apparently "made it his rule never to use a word not found in Cicero" (Tunberg 1997, 15). But in the absence of later Ciceronian guides such as Mario Nizzoli's *In M. T. Ciceronem Observationes* (*Observations on M. T. Cicero*, 1552), even a strict Ciceronian such as Longolius includes in his Ciceronian orations syntactical structures not used by Cicero (e.g., *ut/ut ne* for a positive fear; *dum* for *cum; quando* meaning "since" + subjunctive); as well as adverbs, nouns, adjectives, verbs, and prepositions not found in his works (Tunberg 1997, 19–44). Nonetheless, even with the absence of fully controlled imitation, Longolius's style "gives a Ciceronian 'impression' by a tendency to amplitude . . . and the persistent use of Ciceronian tags and phrases" (Tunberg 1997, 45). This type of "Ciceronian impression" was one that had some longevity in Neo-Latin writing, as the highly successful Ciceronian reworking of the medieval Giraldus Cambrensis's writing on Ireland by Richard Stanihurst in his *De rebus in Hibernia gestis* (*Great Deeds in Ireland*, 1584) testifies (Barry 2004; Barry and Morgan 2013, 33–39). Cicero was, however, not the only author chosen for imitation: Lipsius, for instance, preferred Tacitus and Seneca (Helander 2004, 67).

With the triumph of humanism in the school systems of Europe, however, the greatest irritant for the Latinist was the constant aura of sharp criticism within which he had perforce to operate. Now that "usage" was the accepted criterion of good Latinity, other humanists might easily couch resentments that had other causes in terms of attacks on a writer's Latin. Erasmus, himself highly critical of Ciceronianism, as we have seen, and preferring himself to use and argue for a more eclectic style, nonetheless said of Colet: *Cum enim esset et natura et eruditione facundus, ac dicenti mira suppeteret orationis ubertas, tamen scribens subinde labebatur in his quae solent notare critici. Et hac, ni fallor, gratia a libris scribendis abstinebat . . .* ("For although he was eloquent both by nature and by training, and was amazingly fluent in speech, nonetheless, when he wrote he would repeatedly make slips in those areas that critics usually set black marks against. Unless I am mistaken, it was for this reason that he would abstain from writing books. . .": Thomson 1970, 118). Writers of Latin continued to live in the shadow of the fear of error—and of the ridicule of others arising from it (e.g., Dermot O'Meara in his prefatory *Letter to Thomas Butler*, ll. 49–53: O'Meara 2011, 85)—and while this nervousness may not have affected the very best, it is nonetheless clear that despite the triumph of classicism, the way in which Latin was generally learned (as a spoken *patois* used in schools perforce and then in universities) contributed to the survival, alongside the classicizing written form, of a simpler register much nearer to the ML standard, which now and then would peek out from beneath its classical trappings. Erasmus, at any rate, was still capable of using *quod* as conjunction introducing a consecutive clause (Thomson 1970, 133) and, a century later, O'Meara of employing it to introduce indirect statement (O'Meara 2011, 41).

Writing of poetry meanwhile returned to a more fully classical use of the CL quantitative system (which had still been employed throughout the Middle Ages) and set aside *rhythmus*, once writers such as Lovato de' Lovati had pointed the way by their own efforts and poured scorn on the medieval form (Witt 2012, 457–58). Here, in contrast to the world of prose, there were no pitched battles about correct style. An epic poet might make use of Virgil and Claudian in the same composition (O'Meara 2011, 32–34 and 580–81). To be sure, there were struggles with quantity—O'Meara seems to have been firmly convinced that the genitive singular of fourth declension nouns had a short –*u*–, for example (*Ormonius* 1.98: *furibundi caetŭs asylum*, "the refuge of the maddened band"). But the ease with which writers quickly moved to compose in the complex lyric meters of Horace's *Odes*—for instance, Ariosto (1474–1533; Ariosto 1947 and 2014)—demonstrates well both the power of the classicizing movement and its success.

In morphology (with the odd exception, such as the continued use of the ablative in –*i* with comparative adjectives and present participles), as also in syntax and in general aspects of lexical style, written Neo-Latin succeeded in affecting a classical appearance. But, as with ML, the exigencies of the contexts within which the language was deployed insisted, despite the strictures of card-carrying Ciceronians, on the development of the vocabulary stock to track social, political, economic, and technological change. Already Valla had accepted the necessity of using the word *bombarda* for "cannon" (Marsh 1979, 107), and Erasmus, always eclectic, was not above the use of *halbardacha* ("halberd": Thomson 1970, 129) or *billa* ("note," "bill": Hoven 2006). There continued to exist in the various different parts of Europe a vocabulary that specialized in terms from its own locale. For example, in the kingdoms of Britain and Ireland, the title "Earl" was variously glossed as *Satrapas* and *Comarchus* (O'Meara 2011, 406–8 and 546–47). Genre was paramount in determining vocabulary choice and the acceptable style of invention. Literary works tended to prefer a more purist approach, but this generally meant only that new formulations had to be correctly constructed on a classical base: new agent nouns in –*tor*, abstract nouns in –*tio*, diminutives in –*lus/-la*, and adverbs in –*im* are common (Helander 2004, 65–66). In any case, the range of available choice from ancient Latin vocabulary was never, except for the strict Ciceronians, restricted: everything from Plautus (or roughly contemporaneous archaic authors such as Ennius) to Jerome's *Vulgate* was fair game (Helander 2004, 66–67; Thomson 1970, 124–29). Moreover, it needs to be remembered "that in studying Neo-Latin vocabulary we are dealing with four hundred years of literature that mirrors all aspects of the growth and development of Early Modern Europe" (Helander 2004, 65). Specialized vocabulary (sometimes directly from ML, sometimes appropriated from CL with a new meaning) was in any case always essential in the areas of politics, warfare, academia, the church, industry, flora and fauna, and foodstuffs (CNLS 2:386–87). Sometimes even a classicizing poet, such as Sir Thomas Nugent (d. 1715), would be constrained by the desire for clarity of reference to introduce a barbarism (as in *Billa Exclusiva* at *Poema de Hibernia* 1.361, for the *Exclusion Bill* of 1679, aimed at the Catholic Duke of York, Charles II's brother), though, indeed, one he might have used Erasmus's authority for (Hoven 2006, headword *billa*). Johann Friedrich Nolte in his *Antibarbarus* (*Anti-Barbarian*, 1744) notes the special danger of attempting to substitute classicizing periphrases for actual titles (Helander 2004, 68):

Stultum est, ut placeas nonnullis grammatistis, qui cum cura Latinitatis rectum de rebus iudicium propter hebetem mentis aciem coniungere nequeunt, principibus displicere malle, et horum laedere maiestatem, ne Prisciani dignitatem laesisse videaris.

It is a foolish notion, in order to please a few grammarians, who because of impaired mental vision cannot link correct judgment of the real world with their care for Latinity, to prefer to displease princes and to injure their majesty, so as not to appear to have injured the honour of Priscian.

Of crucial importance, especially in the seventeenth and eighteenth centuries, but in fact for as long as academic literature was written in Latin, was the growth of the sciences and the consequent need to coin new terminology to keep pace with the vast growth in knowledge. New words were produced by adding suffixes to or making compounds from CL words (e.g., *ventricularis*, "pertaining to a ventricle"; *integrifolius*, "with complete leaves") or by the ascription of a new technical meaning to an existing CL word (e.g., *inertia*, "inactivity," used by Galileo and then Newton to signify "inertia"); by the use of Greek words (e.g., *phonologia, barometrum*); and by "retrograde formation" from modern languages (e.g., *ingeniarius*, "engineer"; Helander 2004, 68–72).

Conclusion

Quo magis infelicia superiora tempora fuere, quibus homo nemo inventus est eruditus, eo plus nostris gratulandum est, in quibus (si paulo adnitamur) confido propediem linguam Romanam vigere plus quam urbem, et cum ea disciplinas omnes iri restitutum.

The more unfortunate were earlier periods, when no learned man could be found, the more we must congratulate our own, in which I am confident that, if we only try a little, the Roman tongue will have more vigour than the city of Rome, and with it every branch of learning will be restored.

(Lorenzo Valla, *Elegantiae linguae Latinae* 1, preface: Garin 1952, 598)

Perhaps we should be astonished by the presumptuousness of Valla, in his assertion that the Latin of the ancients could be retrieved and made to serve the purposes of a general revival of learning. The later history of Latin in Europe and the New World tells us, however, that he was not wrong, and this is more astounding by a considerable degree. That a correct Latinity, continually looking back to and interacting with its classical sources, functioned as the agent of the early modern world's intellectual history and lasted in such a role in the face of the belligerent claims of national vernaculars well into the nineteenth century, is, however, a fact. It is also, regrettably, true that we do not know nearly enough about this idiom. Few studies exist of the Latinity of even the most important humanist scholars. While the Latin works of the major Italian humanists of the fifteenth century have always been of interest to students of the Renaissance and are now being made more widely available to the English-speaking world through the *I Tatti Renaissance Library* series in particular, the same is not generally true of those of later periods and of other geographical locations. Furthermore, no attempt has been made, as was done in the first third of the twentieth century for ML, to establish scientifically based national or international projects to compile a lexicon of Neo-Latin (though this is not to say that useful progress has not been made in this area: see, e.g., the *Instrumentum Lexicographicum* of the journal *Humanistica Lovaniensia*, Hoven 2006, and Ramminger's *Neulateinische Wortliste*). The neglect is a consequence of the reordering of the intellectual landscape in the nineteenth-century universities, as a result of which the classical languages and their literatures were separated from the modern languages and their literatures, history and the sciences were parcelled off into discrete compounds, and the world of the *Respublica Litterarum* disappeared into a hinterland of institutional oblivion. It will remain difficult to speak comprehensively of the history of Neo-Latin until this situation—which reflects, not its lack of historical importance, but the mere contingency of political forces—is ameliorated, and some way is found of reintegrating the study of Latin into all the disciplines that deal with the transition from the medieval to the early modern world, and from the early modern to the modern: history, history of science, history of art, history of ideas, comparative literature, and all the various modern languages and literatures that shared their space for so long with, and were for so long overshadowed by, their eloquent and cosmopolitan elder sister.

Suggested Reading

On CL, Palmer (1954) is the most accessible and readable account. For ML grammatical and orthographic "deviations," see Sidwell (1995, 362–75), and for general accounts of the history of ML, the introductory materials in Sidwell (1995) or Norberg (1968, 13–91; in French). For more detailed information, Stotz (1996–2004) is indispensable. On Latin and Romance, see Wright (1982 and 2002), though his theories about the nature of ML before the Carolingian reforms are still highly controversial; and for the development of French, Banniard (2010). For Neo-Latin, the mandatory starting-point is *CNLS* 2:377–433, a guide to language, style, the relations between Latin and the vernaculars, and prosody. Specialized studies on the language of Valla (Tunberg 1988) and Erasmus (Thomson 1970) provide useful further steps in understanding the details of the process of rehabilitating CL. Among the most useful general introductions to the history of Latin as a whole are Janson ([2002] 2004), Stroh (2007), and Leonhardt (2009).

References

Adams, James N. 2007. *The Regional Diversification of Latin 200 BC–AD 600*. Cambridge: Cambridge University Press.
Allen, William S. 1978. *Vox Latina: A Guide to the Pronunciation of Classical Latin*. 2nd ed. Cambridge: Cambridge University Press.

Ariosto, Ludovico. 1947. *Poesie Latine*. Edited by Aldo Capasso. Florence: Fussi.

———. 2014. *Carmina: Ariosto's Lyric Poems*. Edited and translated by Dennis Looney and Mark Possanza. Cambridge: Harvard University Press.

Banniard, Michel. 2010. "Du latin tardif (IIIe–VIIe siècle) au protofrançais: Vers un nouveau paradigme." *Diachroniques: Revue de Linguistique Française Diachronique* 1:39–58.

Barry, John. 2004. "Richard Stanihurst's *De Rebus in Hibernia Gestis*." *Renaissance Studies* 18:1–18.

Barry, John, and Hiram Morgan. 2013. *Great Deeds in Ireland: Richard Stanihurst's* De Rebus in Hibernia Gestis. Cork: Cork University Press.

Coleman, Robert G. 2012. "Latin Language." In *Oxford Classical Dictionary*, 4th ed., 796–98. Oxford: Oxford University Press.

Garin, Eugenio. 1952. *Prosatori latini del Quattrocento*. Milan: Riccardo Ricciardi.

Helander, Hans. 2004. *Neo-Latin Literature in Sweden in the Period 1620–1720: Stylistics, Vocabulary and Characteristic Ideas*. Uppsala: Uppsala Universitet.

Horster, Camilla P. 2011. "Perotti's Use of the Subjunctive: Semantic Ornamentation in the Latin *Genus Sublime*." *Renaessanceforum* 7:147–62.

Hoven, René. 2006. *Lexique de la prose latine de la Renaissance—Dictionary of Renaissance Latin from Prose Sources*. 2nd ed. Leiden: Brill.

Janson, Tore. (2002) 2004. *A Natural History of Latin*. Oxford: Oxford University Press.

Leonhardt, Jürgen. 2009. *Latein: Geschichte einer Weltsprache*. Munich: C.H. Beck.

Marsh, David. 1979. "Grammar, Method and Polemic in Lorenzo Valla's *Elegantiae*." *Rinascimento* 19:91–116.

Moss, Ann. 2003. *Renaissance Truth and the Latin Language Turn*. Oxford: Oxford University Press.

Norberg, Dag. 1968. *Manuel pratique de Latin médiéval*. Paris: Picard.

O'Meara, Dermot. 2011. *The Tipperary Hero: Dermot O'Meara's* Ormonius *(1615)*. Edited and translated by David Edwards and Keith Sidwell. Turnhout: Brepols.

Palmer, Leonard R. 1954. *The Latin Language*. London: Faber and Faber.

Ramminger, Johann. 2010. "Humanists and the Vernacular: Creating the Terminology for a Bilingual Universe." *Renaessanceforum* 6:1–22.

———. *Neulateinische Wortliste: Ein Wörterbuch des Lateinischen von Petrarca bis 1700*. Available at http://ramminger.userweb.mwn.de.

Sidwell, Keith. 1995. *Reading Medieval Latin*. Cambridge: Cambridge University Press.

———. 1997. "Languages and Power in the Roman Empire." In *Living Language: Aspects of Linguistic Contact and Identity*, edited by Anne Gallagher, 1–7. Maynooth: Language Centre; National University of Ireland.

Stotz, Peter. 1996–2004. *Handbuch zur lateinischen Sprache des Mittelalters*. 5 vols. Munich: C.H. Beck.

Stroh, Wilfried. 2007. *Latein ist tot, es lebe Latein! Kleine Geschichte einer grossen Sprache*. Berlin: List.

Thomson, Douglas F. S. 1970. "The Latinity of Erasmus." In *Erasmus*, edited by Thomas A. Dorey, 115–37. London: Routledge and Kegan Paul.

Tournoy, Gilbert, and Terence O. Tunberg. 1996. "On the Margins of Latinity? Neo-Latin and the Vernacular Languages." *Humanistica Lovaniensia* 45:134–75.

Tunberg, Terence O. 1988. "The Latinity of Lorenzo Valla's *Gesta Ferdinandi Regis Aragonum*." *Humanistica Lovaniensia* 37:30–78.

———. 1997. "Ciceronian Latin: Longolius and Others." *Humanistica Lovaniensia* 46:13–61.

Väänänen, Veikko. 1983. "Le problème de la diversification du Latin." In *Aufstieg und Niedergang der römischen Welt*, vol. 2.29.1, *Sprache und Literatur (Sprachen und Schriften)*, edited by Wolfgang Haase, 480–506. Berlin: De Gruyter.

Witt, Ronald G. 2012. *The Two Latin Cultures and the Foundations of Renaissance Humanism in Medieval Italy*. Cambridge: Cambridge University Press.

Wright, Roger. 1982. *Late Latin and Early Romance in Spain and Carolingian France*. Liverpool: Cairns.

———. 2002. *A Sociophilological Study of Late Latin*. Turnhout: Brepols.

....

CHAPTER 2

NEO-LATIN'S INTERPLAY
WITH OTHER LANGUAGES

....

DEMMY VERBEKE

IN the early years of the fourteenth century, Dante Alighieri (1265–1321) wrote *De vulgari eloquentia* (*On Eloquence in the Vernacular*, ca. 1302–1305), a manifesto propagating the use of the vernacular but published in Latin in order to be understood by a wide audience. Leon Battista Alberti (1404–1472) discussed the demise of Latin in the preface to the third book of his *Della famiglia* (*On the Family*, ca. 1432) but resorted to the classical language when writing his *Momus sive de principe* (*Momus, or The Prince*, ca. 1444–1450) a couple of years later. Erycius Puteanus (1574–1646), professor of Latin language and eloquence at the University of Leuven, incorporated praise of the vernacular tongue in his inaugural speech *Iuventutis Belgicae laudatio* (*In Praise of Belgian Youth*, 1607); as did Jacob Grimm (1785–1863) in his first (Latin) oration as professor at the University of Göttingen, entitled *De desiderio patriae* (*On the Love of the Fatherland*, 1830). Dissenting voices were heard as well: staunch supporters of the classical language produced a stream of treatises and speeches defending the use of Latin as a literary, scholarly, or universal language, a phenomenon that lasted well into the nineteenth century (De Santis 1995; IJsewijn and Sacré 1993), including texts by Romolo Quirino Amaseo (1489–1552), Carlo Sigonio (1522/3–1584), Johann Gottfried Herder (1744–1803), and Arthur Schopenhauer (1788–1860). These few examples illustrate that the discussion about which language to choose—Latin or the vernacular?—was a prominent one for more than half a millennium.

In the previous chapter, Keith Sidwell discussed the several phases that can be distinguished in the spread of Latin as a supranational medium of communication before the early modern period. Not only Romance languages, but also Germanic and other vernaculars went through a slow process of standardization and gained enough prestige to compete with Latin in several spheres of life from the thirteenth century onward. Focusing on texts favoring the use of the vernacular, such as those mentioned above, or the even more famous *Deffence et illustration de la langue françoyse* (*The Defense and Illustration of the French Language*, 1549) by Joachim Du Bellay (ca. 1522–1560), some scholars have argued that the *questione della lingua* ("linguistic question") was settled in favor of the vernacular by the seventeenth century, resulting in an irreversible marginalization of Latin, which would only continue to "vegetate as a university jargon" (Blumenthal and Kahane 1979, 188). Others have stressed that Latin continued to be used to quite a substantial degree well beyond the early modern period, partly because it was often the only tool of communication that people from different language groups had in common. This led, for instance, to Latin translations of vernacular works. Peter Burke has counted more than 1,100 such translations, published between 1500 and 1799, indicating that this practice reached its peak in the seventeenth century and only gradually disappeared, by the second half of the eighteenth century (Burke 2007, 65; see also Grant 1954). A revealing fact is that a Latin translation of a vernacular text was often reprinted or commented upon more frequently than the original version (Waquet 1998, 108–9; Pantin 2007, 170) and regularly acted as the intermediary for other versions— as is the case with Jakob Locher's Latin translation of Sebastian Brant's *Narrenschiff* (*Ship of Fools*, 1494; Metzger-Rambach 2008). Latin also continued to be used as the language of administration, legislation, and justice, especially in political entities that united several groups, each with its own language, under one central government. This was, for instance, the case in seventeenth-century Hungary (Béranger 1969) or in the Holy Roman Empire, which upheld Latin as the official language until its disintegration in 1806 (Licoppe 2003, 44). The classical language furthermore remained the preferred vehicle of official documents and prestigious or festive forms of communication, which demanded a language that was considered to be both eternal and universal, as is evidenced in the *querelle des inscriptions* ("dispute about inscriptions") in seventeenth-century France concerning the question of whether inscriptions on public monuments should be written in Latin or the vernacular (Denecker 2013), or in doctoral degrees bestowed *honoris causa*, which are, to this day, still written in Latin at many universities across Europe. Moreover, this continued use of Latin was certainly not limited to the "Old World": it was also, for instance, used by Jesuit authors from New Spain constructing a Mexican legacy (Laird 2012, Chapter 33).

It is therefore important to do justice to the linguistic diversity, and sometimes confusion, in the early modern world, where Latin, as the supranational language, coexisted for several centuries with the various national languages in any number of cultural spheres. One needs to avoid the pitfall of focusing on the opposition between the classical language and modern vernaculars, which is the particular domain of linguistic theory and controversy, and instead try to respect literary and linguistic reality by considering what Grahame Castor and Terence Cave have termed "the interpenetration of Neo-Latin and the vernacular" (Castor and Cave 1984, xii). The early modern world was very much a polyglot one, in which all intellectuals mastered Latin besides their native tongue and possibly other vernaculars or ancient Greek (Frijhoff 2010; Van Hal 2011). In literature, this clearly led to a mutual enrichment, as is exemplified in the work of John Milton (1608–1674; e.g., Hale 1997). It also gave authors the opportunity to switch languages as they saw fit: Thomas More (1478–1535), François Rabelais (ca. 1494–1553), Jean Calvin (1509–1564), Galileo Galilei (1564–1642), Thomas Hobbes (1588–1679),

René Descartes (1596–1650), and numerous others published in Latin as well as in their native tongues in order to reach different and broader audiences. When studying this code-switching, one finds indications that Latin and the vernaculars were regularly connected to specific situations or topics. A famous example is Martin Luther's *Tischreden* (*Table Talks*, 1566), delivered in German and Latin, wherein Latin seems reserved for the discussion of intellectual matters, especially theological ones (Stolt 1964). One also encounters instances of friction, when the dividing line between the vernacular and Latin is put into question. An interesting example is found at universities, traditionally seen (together with the Roman Catholic Church, see Waquet 1998) as bulwarks for the classical language. Despite this traditionalist context, some early modern academics criticized the preponderance of Latin as the language of science and scholarship because they were concerned about the commercial success of their work (Knight 2006).

POLYGLOT PUBLICATIONS

A particular category of sources, namely "polyglot publications"—used in this context as the overarching name for all books that contain more than one language, regardless of their organization, structure, or particular use—serves as an important testimony of the linguistic world of early modern Europe and offers vital information for the study of the social and cultural histories of the various languages involved. At the outset, it is important to identify different categories of polyglossia—for instance, on the basis of James Noel Adams's distinction between "mixed-language" and "multilingual" texts (Adams 2003). Mixed-language texts combine two or more languages in the same discourse (for example, an English text peppered with occasional Latin quotes), while multilingual texts basically repeat the same message in two or more languages so that there always is a certain element of repetition between different text sections (for example, an edition of a Latin text with a facing translation into English). The fact that early modern authors were already aware of this distinction is evidenced by the *Poematum Liber* (*Book of Poems*, 1573) of Richard Willes (1546–1579?; see also Binns 1990, 50–60). This *Poematum Liber* is a remarkable collection of one hundred poems, followed by a disputation about poetry and a commentary written by Willes himself. The book was intended as a defense of the art of poetry and as a sort of introduction to various verse forms. The hundred examples include acrostics, anagrams, chronograms, and visual poems, but also a number of poems that combine several languages. Interestingly enough, Willes makes more or less the same distinction as Adams would more than four hundred years later. On one hand, he identifies poems as *linguis diversis* (poems whose content is repeated "in several languages," which Adams calls "multilingual texts"); on the other, there are poems with a *linguarum mixtio* (so "mixed-language" texts). Willes explains that the interplay between the different languages in multilingual poems adds a certain charm, whereas mixed-language poems lift less distinguished languages to a higher level because they are paired with more prestigious ones.

MACARONICS

A particular category of mixed-language texts, which became popular during the Renaissance, are so-called macaronics—a disputed term, with fuzzy boundaries, for texts composed of material from more than one language (Demo 2014). When defined most strictly, macaronic texts are written in dactylic hexameters, offering a mixture of Latin with another language for humorous purposes. The term is used a bit less strictly to denote poems in which two languages are mixed, so that as a result words and expressions of one language are forced into the grammatical (and sometimes idiomatic) framework of the other, principal language—typically Latin, into which vernacular words or groups of words are inserted and superficially Latinized (Sacré 2006). However, the term "macaronics" is also—most broadly, and, some would argue, erroneously—used to denote any type of text mixing several languages. The flexibility of the term is, in any case, illustrated in the 1813 collection *Carminum rariorum macaronicorum delectus* (*Anthology of Remarkable Macaronic Poems*), which contains only one "real" macaronic poem according to the strict definition, but several other mixed-language and multilingual texts, bringing together Latin and English on the printed page (Demo 2014, 96–97).

The mixture of languages in macaronics provides an opportunity to make a witty play on the social status of the languages involved. Some macaronic texts thus undermine the use of Latin as "a device to maintain the power of the clergy and other professional men such as doctors, lawyers and of course academics" (Burke 1987, 2), by making fun of pseudo-intellectuals who use (pig) Latin in an effort to distinguish themselves from the common herd. Famous examples of this are found in George Ruggle's *Ignoramus* (1614), which is a merciless attack on legal jargon (Tucker 1977; Kallendorf 2003; Ryan 2013) and in the final scene of Molière's *Le malade imaginaire* (*The Imaginary Invalid*, 1673), satirizing the pomposity surrounding the medical profession.

OTHER FORMS OF POLYGLOSSIA

Besides the distinction between multilingual and mixed-language texts, further non-exclusive subcategories can be identified in the overarching group of polyglot publications, based on differences in their function and appearance (Verbeke 2013a). In what follows, attention will be paid to polyglossia used for didactic reasons, as well as to polyglossia as a literary device, leaving aside what one could call "accidental polyglossia," which is, for instance, found when an author's portrait accompanied by some laudatory verses in one language is reprinted in another publication in a different language. An example of this is provided by *A Discourse of the Conference Holden before the French King at Fontaine-Belleau, betweene the L. Bishop of Eureux, and Monsieur du Plessis L. of Mornay, the 4. of May 1600* (1601), an English edition of a French text, with numerous

Latin quotes printed in the margin. The main text is preceded by an engraved portrait of Philippe de Mornay (1549–1623), accompanied by a Dutch poem, and it can be surmised that both the portrait and the poem were reprinted from an earlier (further unrelated) Dutch publication.

Polyglot Publications for Linguistic Instruction

An intentional and obvious form of polyglossia involving Latin and one or more vernaculars is found in publications used for linguistic instruction. This category contains, besides dictionaries and grammars, also phrasebooks and collections of dialogues or other texts enabling the user to compare the version in the language he or she knows with the version in the language he or she is trying to learn. A survey of these didactic publications informs us that Latin continued to play a role, both as the universal language that can be used as a common basis by individuals from separate language groups, and as a language that should be taught not only as a literary but also as a practical medium of communication. Some of these publications, in other words, do not approach Latin as an artificial language confined to the sphere of high culture, but treat it on the same level as the vernacular, to be used as a means of communication in daily life. A telling example of the role of Latin in didactic publications of this kind is found in the various editions of the *Vocabulare* (*Vocabulary*, 1527) of the Antwerp schoolmaster Noël de Berlaimont (d. 1531). The original *Vocabulare*, printed in Antwerp in 1527, was a bilingual Dutch-French course book, including a number of dialogues, a word list, and a survey of pronunciation rules (van der Sijs 2000). It was aimed at Dutch speakers who wanted to learn French through private study. The book enjoyed remarkable success and was revised and expanded over and over again to include other languages such as English, Breton, Polish, Malaysian, Czech, Spanish, Portuguese, Italian, German, and Latin. More than 150 editions of these multilingual revisions appeared between 1527 and 1759, and de Berlaimont's work thus evolved into a truly international language manual used for more than two hundred years. The supranational status of Latin is proved by the fact that it frequently serves as the entry language in the reprints, while the entry language in the original edition was Dutch. We find, for instance, a bilingual Latin-French edition printed in Antwerp in 1576, omitting the Dutch original altogether and simply replacing it with a Latin translation, whereby the user was expected to learn French on the basis of his or her knowledge of Latin. A similar thing happens in a version with eight languages printed in the Dutch city of Vlissingen in 1613, in which Latin is clearly the dominant language, expected to be common to all possible users. The title page of this edition offers Latin first, in capitals and a large font, which is followed by the title in French and Dutch in smaller print. Moreover, all preliminary texts are written in Latin, and the Latin version of the dialogues is printed in the first column. This was probably done with the international marketing of this book in mind: as Latin was the universal language, it seemed logical to reserve the first place for it, so that it could be sold everywhere without having to change the title page or the structure of the book. The position of Latin is different in yet another revision of de Berlaimont's work that was especially aimed at the English market. This *English, Latine, French, Dutch, Schole-Master* was printed in London in 1637 and was intended—according to its subtitle—as *An Introduction to Teach Young Gentlemen and Merchants to Travell or Trade*. Contrary to the previous example, this particular revision does not accord a privileged place to Latin at all. The title page and the preface are both exclusively in English, and the Latin version of the dialogues is printed in the last column, with the Dutch original in the first. Instead of assuming that the user already knows Latin, the editor of this particular version of de Berlaimont's manual presents the classical language as a modern one that should be mastered by English-speaking merchants and other travelers in the same way as they should master Dutch or French. This practical application of Latin is also stressed in the preliminary poems—one in each of the four languages of the book—which advertise this publication as an ideal tool to acquire the expected linguistic skills, as is exemplified by the English one (de Berlaimont 1637, A2r):

> If thou Foure uarious Languages would'st know,
> Grudge not my price; For I to thee will show.
> Their seuerall Dialects, with which you may,
> Through spacious Europe trauell any way.

A related category of polyglossia is found in translations that print the Latin source text together with its vernacular rendition. This frequently happens with a didactic purpose in mind. Research over the last two decades has brought to light the many formats of bilingual presentation translators (or editors of translations) had at their disposal (Henkel 1995; Taylor 2006; Verbeke 2013b and 2015). Besides the (now common) *mise-en-page* (page placement) of printing the source text with its translation in parallel columns or on facing pages, we also find early printed books in which the source text is combined with an interlinear translation, mirroring medieval usage in, among others, biblical and liturgical texts (Hellgardt 1992). Such an interlinear version offers a vernacular equivalent for each individual Latin word, printed directly beneath or above it. It should thus be read vertically, as a word-for-word correspondence between the two versions, rather than horizontally (since the translation is not a syntactically coherent text when read horizontally). A variant offering sentence-by-sentence (instead of word-by-word) correspondence between the Latin original and its vernacular translation is, for example, found in bilingual phrasebooks based on Terence, such as the *Vulgaria quaedam abs Terentio in Anglicam linguam traducta* (*Common Phrases Taken from Terence and Translated into English*, first published in 1483 and reprinted six times up to 1529). This phrasebook was published in the same year and by the same printer as the *Compendium totius grammaticae* (*Compendium of All Grammar*, 1483) of John Anwykyll (d. 1487), schoolmaster of Magdalen College School in Oxford, and was thus most probably intended to be used with his grammar in the classroom. In the first couple of editions, each English phrase is followed by its Latin equivalent. The fact that the English comes first indicates that this was the entry language; the Latin, however, derives prominence from being printed in a larger font. But this layout changes in the editions of 1510 and 1529, in which the interlinear presentation is preserved, but the English and the Latin trade places: the Latin now comes first, while the English is printed in a larger font. The switch suggests that the intended use of these reprints was different from that of the original version. The English-Latin version was probably intended mainly to teach the students how to speak and write better Latin, starting from the English expressions and translating them into Latin. The Latin-English versions, on the other hand, start from the Latin and thus seem to be primarily designed to help students to translate Latin into English.

A more extreme example of a polyglot publication illustrating contemporary educational practice is provided by the bilingual schoolbooks printed according to the method of parsing, developed (and patented) by the linguist and physician Joseph Webbe (d. ca. 1630). The intention of Webbe's method is to enable students to see immediately the links between Latin sentences and their English equivalents without having to refer to any grammatical explanation (Salmon 1961a and 1961b). The result is a complex typographical system using clause numbers, horizontal and vertical lines, and various symbols to indicate which parts of a certain Latin sentence correspond with which parts in its English translation, without altering the original word order of either of the two versions. Other formats of bilingual presentation of a translated text clearly serve less didactic purposes, as is exemplified by an anonymous English rendition of the *Andria* (*The Girl from Andros*) of Terence printed in Paris in 1520, which literally marginalizes the Latin text in the layout. This type of *mise-en-page* had previously been used for annotated texts, with the text in the center of the page and the glosses in the margin, and was later copied by the translators of the same texts (Molins 2007). The dominance of the vernacular in this particular edition of the *Andria* is perhaps explained by the translator's desire to stress the (relatively) recently acquired status of the English language as a valid medium for literature. In a long preliminary poem, he argues that, thanks to the efforts of English poets such as Geoffrey Chaucer (ca. 1340–1400) and John Lydgate (ca. 1370–1449/50?), the English language is "amplyfyed so / That we therin now translate as well may / As in eny other tongis other can do" (Terence 1520, A1v).

POLYGLOSSIA AS A LITERARY DEVICE

A very diverse and large category of polyglot publications consists of multilingual and mixed-language texts that use polyglossia as a literary device (such as the macaronic texts already mentioned). In other words, Latin occurs in these texts together with one or more vernaculars to highlight the linguistic and literary abilities of the author or to add particular charm or humor to the text. A first example is the ballad *Amantium irae amoris redintegratio est* (*A Lovers' Tiff is the Renewal of Love*) printed in 1625, in which six verses of English are each time followed by a refrain in Latin (a facsimile together with a modern recording of the ballad is found as "no. 30011" in the *English Broadside Ballad Archive*). This refrain is the proverb *Amantium irae amoris redintegratio est*, whose origin can be traced to Terence (*Andria*, line 555). The presence of a classical language seems quite remarkable, since ballads were aimed at a broad audience and their content and style were therefore supposed to be kept simple. The use of Latin does not seem to fit that picture, but it is perhaps explained by the author's desire to elevate a popular genre as well as its vehicle—the vernacular—to a higher level, thus providing an example of Richard Willes's explanation of mixed-language texts.

A more elaborate use of various languages is, for instance, found in the single-sheet print *Ad Serenissimam Elizabetham Angliae Reginam* (*To the Most Noble Elizabeth, Queen of England*) from 1588, signed by the French Protestant humanist Théodore de Bèze (1519–1605). This publication, celebrating the defeat of the Spanish Armada, contains verses in eight different languages: Latin, English, Dutch, Spanish, Hebrew, Greek, Italian, and French. Each section more or less repeats the content of the verses in the other languages, except for the last, anonymous, French poem, which is addressed to de Bèze. A translator is identified by his initials above the Spanish version, but there is no indication of other translators, which seems to suggest that all the other sections were written by de Bèze himself. This print is a clear example of propaganda. It is known that de Bèze was trying to secure English support in the war against Savoy (Geisendorf 1967, 291 and 377) and consequently flattered Elizabeth I as the protector of all European Protestants and particularly those living in France, the Low Countries, and Italy—for instance, in the dedicatory epistle of his commentary on Job (of which the English translation was printed in London around 1589), in which he called Elizabeth the "nourcing mother to the French, Duch, and Italians, exiles for the profession of Christ, and the victorious defendresse of the whole true Christian religion" (de Bèze 1589, A2r). This might explain the inclusion of verses in French, Dutch, and Italian, but they in each case also serve, along with the five other languages used, to confirm the celebrated linguistic skills of Elizabeth I (Knight 2015) and obviously advertise the linguistic and poetic talents of de Bèze himself as well.

Another example of a polyglot publication illustrating the linguistic abilities of a particular author is found in the *Bausme de Galaad pour la guerison d'un coeur navré* (*The Balm of Gilead for the Healing of a Grieving Heart*) of the Dutch preacher Daniel Souterius (1571–1634), a volume written for the consolation of Elizabeth Stuart (1596–1662) at the time of the death of her eldest son, Henry Frederick, Elector Palatine, who drowned in 1629. The book is divided into four parts, each with its own title page and separate pagination, and each written in a different language (English, French, Dutch, Latin). An inadvertent reader would at first assume that the four parts are interchangeable translations, but it becomes clear upon closer inspection that the situation is somewhat more complex. The Latin section does not correspond at all with the vernacular ones, while the French and Dutch parts are more or less expanded versions of the English text, offering the same arguments in a different sequence (and therefore cannot be described as real translations either). The volume thus offers an interesting compilation that can only be enjoyed fully when the user reads all four sections (and so needs to master all four languages in order to be able to enjoy the collection as a whole).

Commemorative volumes of this sort form a genre in which polyglossia is frequently found, especially if the poems are written by various authors. For instance, the collections *Epicedium Cantabrigiense* (*Cambridge's Poem of Lament*) and *Iusta Oxoniensium* (*Oxford's Funeral Rites*), produced at the Universities of Cambridge and Oxford on the occasion of the demise of another Henry Frederick (1594–1612), the Prince of Wales, consist mainly of Latin poems, but both also include poems in ancient Greek and French, with additional verses in English and Italian in the Cambridge compilation, and in Hebrew in the Oxford one.

Emblem Books

Latin is also frequently combined with one or more vernaculars for literary reasons in polyglot emblem books, which Leonard Forster called "one of the characteristic literary products of the sixteenth and seventeenth centuries" (Forster 1970, 20). A famous example is *Silenus Alcibiadis, sive Proteus* (*The Silenus of Alcibiades, or Proteus*) of the Dutch poet and politician Jacob Cats (1577–1660), perhaps better known under the title *Sinne- en Minnebeelden* (*Portraits of Morality and Love*). This collection of emblems first appeared in 1618 and offered fifty-one emblematic images accompanied by mottos, poems, and quotations in Dutch, French, and Latin. Many revised and expanded editions appeared, including one in the same year offering additional explanations in Dutch and Latin prose (for a critical edition with a full discussion of the various editions of Cats's emblem book, see Cats 1996). As far as we know, the Dutch, French, and Latin texts in the original edition were written by Cats himself. The use of three languages paralleled the tripartite structure of the volume: the collection is structured in three parts mirroring the three Ages of Man (youth, maturity, and old age) and offers interpretations of the images on three levels; namely, amorous, moral, and religious. The division of labor between the three languages is both multilingual and mixed-language: certain sections are repeated in all three, whereas others are only available in one or two languages. Cats's emblem book thus not only offers an interplay between text and image, but also between the various languages.

A similar case is the polyglot expansion of the *Emblemes ou Devises Chrestiennes* (*Emblems or Christian Mottos*) of Georgette de Montenay (1540–ca. 1581). This emblem book first appeared in a monolingual French edition in 1571 but was later reprinted with additional verses in Latin, Spanish, Italian, German, English, and Dutch. De Montenay was not responsible herself for these additional verses, which are not simply translations of the original French, but offer new information. Like the previous examples, the resulting emblem book thus demands of the reader a mastery of all languages involved in order fully to enjoy the collection as a whole (A. Adams 2002, 2003). Other polyglot emblem books are less demanding; for instance, when the sections in different languages are, essentially, interchangeable translations of the same text. A case in hand is the *Lychnocausia sive moralia facum emblemata* (*Lychnocausia or Moral Emblems of the Light*, 1638) by the obscure Scottish poet Robert Farley (fl. 1624–1638). The bilingual character of this collection of emblems is already evident from the title page and other paratexts. There are two dedicatory epistles: one in Latin, addressed to Robert Ker (1578–1654), first Earl of Ancram; and a second one in English, addressed to Anne Ker (*née* Portman), the second wife of Robert. With this division between Latin for the male dedicatee and English for the female dedicatee, Farley draws a linguistic line between the sexes, which has also been observed in sixteenth-century Danish culture (Skafte Jensen 1991). Farley's dedicatory epistles are followed by several preliminary poems, both in English and in Latin. One of these, written by a certain Thomas Beedom, comments on the bilingual character of the collection and is—despite the fact that the poet is writing in English himself—not very complimentary toward the vernacular (Farley 1638, A6v, lines 9–14):

> So in this Midwifery of wit, by Thee
> Delivered, two lights, two Subjects be.
> Thy nobler Roman stile to day-borne men
> Children of Arts, directs thy Latin pen.
> And that the duller ignorant might see,
> They have a Mother-Moone begot by Thee.

This belittlement of the public for the English version of the text does not alter the fact that both languages are treated more or less equally in the collection. Each *pictura* (illustration) has a Latin and an English motto, and each has a Latin and an English poem, which are in essence reasonably trustworthy translations of each other. There is one exception: Emblem 57 has only an English explanation. It is thus clear that readers do not need to read all the verses in the different languages—as was the case in the polyglot editions of de Montenay and Cats. Instead, they can limit themselves to either the Latin or the English, and the division was probably intended to run along the same lines as the dedicatory epistles: men were supposed to read the Latin verses; women, the English.

Conclusion

One could state that mixed-language and multilingual texts from the early modern period acted as "ambassadors of Babel," as eloquent emissaries of the polyglot world that was early modern Europe (and beyond). Latin was clearly still an important part (or perhaps even the most important part) of the linguistic tapestry of this polyglot world and continued to be used in a wide variety of contexts. It coexisted and interacted with the modern languages in any number of ways. Sometimes it was the dominant partner, used when the occasion called for a certain dignity, longevity, and international appeal that the vernaculars in the opinion of most still lacked. Sometimes Latin was just one of the many languages in a piece of linguistic *bravura*, used either as an element within a polyglot piece of art or in order to address a certain segment of the reading public. On other occasions, the continuing practical application of Latin prevailed. The examples discussed in this chapter thus illustrate the flexible status of Latin during this period. The classical language was used differently from context to context, from publication to publication, and from author to author. And while the rise of the vernaculars cannot of course be denied, the study of polyglot publications proves that this was a slow process in which Latin continued to play a role in many guises, and interacted with the various national languages in numerous ways.

SUGGESTED READING

Forster (1970) offers a concise survey of multilingualism in literature, which still acts as a very readable introduction to this field of study. Haynes (2003) provides a more detailed overview of different sorts of multilingual books and the interference of Latin with English literature, while Janson ([2002] 2004) discusses the use of Latin terminology in the sciences and technical subjects, as well as loan words and neologisms. Playful bilingualism is treated in Jeanneret (1987), as is the sociolinguistic status of post-medieval Latin in Burke (1993). More recently, the online journal *Renæssanceforum* has devoted two special issues to Latin and the vernaculars in early modern Europe (Hass and Ramminger 2010) and the role of Latin in linguistic identity and nationalism from 1350 to 1800 (Coroleu, Caruso, and Laird 2012), which contain numerous interesting case studies.

REFERENCES

Adams, Alison. 2002. "Georgette de Montenay in the 1619 Polyglot Edition." In *Female Saints and Sinners: Saintes et Mondaines (France 1450–1650)*, edited by Jennifer Britnell and Ann Moss, 147–62. Durham: University of Durham.

———. 2003. "The Dutch Version of Georgette de Montenay's *Emblemes ou devises chrestiennes* in the 1619 edition." In *The Stone of Alciato: Literature and Visual Culture in the Low Countries; Essays in Honour of Karel Porteman*, edited by Marc van Vaeck, Hugo Brems, and Geert H. M. Claassens, 751–66. Leuven: Peeters.

Adams, James N. 2003. *Bilingualism and the Latin Language*. New York: Cambridge University Press.

Béranger, Jean. 1969. "Latin et langues vernaculaires dans la Hongrie du XVIIᵉ siècle." *Revue Historique* 242:5–28.

De Berlaimont, Noël. 1637. *The English, Latine, French, Dutch, Schole-Master*. London: A. G[riffin] for Michael Sparke.

De Bèze, Théodore. 1588. *Ad Serenissimam Elizabetham Angliae Reginam*. London: George Bishop and Ralph Newbery.

———. 1589. *Iob expounded by Theodore Beza, partly in manner of a commentary, partly in manner of a paraphrase*. London: John Legatt for Abraham Kitson.

Binns, James W. 1990. *Intellectual Culture in Elizabethan and Jacobean England: The Latin Writings of the Age*. Leeds: Francis Cairns.

Blumenthal, Henry, and Renée Kahane. 1979. "Decline and Survival of Western Prestige Languages." *Language* 55:183–98.

Burke, Peter. 1987. "Introduction." In *The Social History of Language*, edited by Peter Burke and Roy Porter, 1–20. Cambridge: Cambridge University Press.

———. 1993. *The Art of Conversation*. Ithaca: Cornell University Press.

———. 2007. "Translations into Latin in Early Modern Europe." In Burke and Hsia, 65–80. Cambridge: Cambridge University Press.

Burke, Peter, and Ronnie Po-Chia Hsia, eds. 2007. *Cultural Translation in Early Modern Europe*. Cambridge: Cambridge University Press.

Castor, Grahame, and Terence Cave. 1984. "Introduction." In *Neo-Latin and the Vernacular in Renaissance France*, xi–xvii. Oxford: Clarendon Press.

Cats, Jacob. 1996. *Sinne- en minnebeelden*. Edited by Hans Luijten. 3 vols. The Hague: Constantijn Huygens Instituut.

Coroleu, Alejandro, Carlo Caruso, and Andrew Laird, eds. 2012. *The Role of Latin in the Early Modern World: Linguistic Identity and Nationalism 1350–1800*. Special issue of *Renæssanceforum: Journal of Renaissance Studies*. Available at http://www.renaessanceforum.dk/rf_8_2012.htm.

Demo, Šime. 2014. "Towards a Unified Definition of Macaronics." *Humanistica Lovaniensia* 63:83–106.

Denecker, Tim. 2013. "Joannes Lucas SJ, *De monumentis publicis Latine inscribendis oratio* (Paris, 1677): Introduction, Analysis of Assumptions about Language, and Annotated Edition." *Humanistica Lovaniensia* 62:523–81.

De Santis, Carla. 1995. "Latin versus the Vernacular in Renaissance Italy: The Development of the Controversy with Special Reference to Carlo Sigonio's *De latinae linguae usu retinendo* (1556)." *Rinascimento* 35:349–71.

English Broadside Ballad Archive. Available at http://ebba.english.ucsb.edu/.

Farley, Robert. 1638. *Lychnocausia sive moralia facum emblemata*. London: Thomas Cotes for Michael Sparke.

Forster, Leonard. 1970. *The Poet's Tongues: Multilingualism in Literature*. London: Cambridge University Press.

Frijhoff, Willem. 2010. *Meertaligheid in de Gouden Eeuw: Een verkenning*. Amsterdam: Koninklijke Nederlandse Akademie van Wetenschappen.

Geisendorf, Paul F. 1967. *Théodore de Bèze*. Geneva: Jullien.

Grant, W. Leonard. 1954. "European Vernacular Works in Latin Translation." *Studies in the Renaissance* 1:120–56.

Hale, John. 1997. *Milton's Languages: The Impact of Multilingualism on Style*. Cambridge: Cambridge University Press.

Hass, Trine A., and Johann Ramminger, eds. 2010. *Latin and the Vernaculars in Early Modern Europe*. Special issue of *Renæssanceforum: Journal of Renaissance Studies*. Available at http://www.renaessanceforum.dk/rf_6_2010.htm.

Haynes, Kenneth. 2003. *English Literature and Ancient Languages*. Oxford: Oxford University Press.

Hellgardt, Ernst. 1992. "Lateinisch-deutsche Textensembles in Handschriften des 12. Jahrhunderts." In *Latein und Volkssprache im deutschen Mittelalter 1100–1500*, edited by Nikolaus Henkel and Nigel F. Palmer, 19–31. Tübingen: Max Niemeyer.

Henkel, Nikolaus. 1995. "Printed School Texts: Types of Bilingual Presentation in Incunabula." *Renaissance Studies* 9:212–27.

IJsewijn, Jozef, and Dirk Sacré. 1993. "The Ultimate Efforts to Save Latin as the Means of International Communication." *History of European Ideas* 16:51–66.

Janson, Tore. (2002) 2004. *A Natural History of Latin.* Oxford: Oxford University Press.

Jeanneret, Michel. 1987. *Des mets et des mots: Banquets et propos de table à la Renaissance.* Paris: Corti. Translated by Jeremy Whiteley and Emma Hughes as *A Feast of Words: Banquets and Table Talk in the Renaissance.* 1991. Chicago: University of Chicago Press.

Kallendorf, Hilaire. 2003. "Exorcism and the Interstices of Language: Ruggle's *Ignoramus* and the Demonization of Renaissance English Neo-Latin." In *ACNL 2003*, 303–10.

Knight, Sarah. 2006. "It was not mine intent to prostitute my Muse in English: Academic Publication in Early Modern England." In *Print and Power in France and England, 1500–1800*, edited by David Adams and Adrian Armstrong, 39–51. Aldershot: Ashgate.

———. 2015. "Texts Presented to Elizabeth I on the University Progresses." In *A Concise Companion to the Study of Manuscripts, Printed Books, and the Production of Early Modern Texts*, edited by Edward Jones. Oxford: Wiley-Blackwell.

Laird, Andrew. 2012. "Patriotism and the Rise of Latin in Eighteenth-Century New Spain: Disputes of the New World and the Jesuit Construction of a Mexican Legacy." In Coroleu, Caruso, and Laird, op. cit. 231–61.

Licoppe, Guy. 2003. *Le latin et le politique: Les avatars du latin à travers les âges.* Brussels: Musée de la Maison d'Erasme.

Metzger-Rambach, Anne-Laure. 2008. *"Le texte emprunté": Étude comparée du Narrenschiff de Sebastian Brant et ses adaptations (1494–1509).* Paris: Champion.

Molins, Marine. 2007. "Mises en page: Les efforts conjugués des traducteurs et des imprimeurs." *Camenae* 3. Available at http://www.paris-sorbonne.fr/la-recherche/les-unites-de-recherche/mondes-anciens-et-medievaux-ed1/rome-et-ses-renaissances-art-3625/revue-en-ligne-camenae/.

Pantin, Isabelle. 2007. "The Role of Translations in European Scientific Exchanges in the Sixteenth and Seventeenth Centuries." In Burke and Hsia, op. cit. 163–79.

Ryan, Cressida. 2013. "An Ignoramus about Latin? The Importance of Latin Literatures to George Ruggle's *Ignoramus*." In *The Early Modern Cultures of Neo-Latin Drama*, edited by Philip Ford and Andrew Taylor, 159–74. Leuven: Leuven University Press.

Sacré, Dirk. 2006. "Macaronic Poetry." In *Brill's New Pauly Online*, edited by Hubert Cancik and Helmuth Schneider. Leiden: Brill. Available at http://referenceworks.brillonline.com/entries/brill-s-new-pauly/macaronic-poetry-ct-e1502450.

Salmon, Vivian. 1961a. "Joseph Webbe: Some Seventeenth-Century Views on Language-Teaching and the Nature of Meaning." *Bibliothèque d'humanisme et renaissance* 23:324–40.

———. 1961b. "An Ambitious Printing Project of the Early Seventeenth Century." *The Library* 16:190–96.

Skafte Jensen, Minna. 1991. "The Language of Eternity: The Role of Latin in 16th-Century Danish Culture." In *ACNL 1991*, 41–61.

Stolt, Birgit. 1964. *Die Sprachmischung in Luthers Tischreden: Studien zum Problem der Zweisprachigkeit.* Stockholm: Almqvist och Wiksell.

Taylor, Barry. 2006. "Iberian-Latin Bilingual Editions, Fifteenth-Eighteenth Centuries." In *Latin and Vernacular in Renaissance Iberia, II: Translations and Adaptations*, edited by Barry Taylor and Alejandro Coroleu, 149–69. Manchester: Manchester Spanish and Portuguese Studies.

Terence. 1520. *Andria*. Paris: Phillipe le Noir.

Tucker, E. F. J. 1977. "Ruggle's *Ignoramus* and Humanistic Criticism of the Language of the Common Law." *Renaissance Quarterly* 30:34–50.

Van der Sijs, Nicoline. 2000. *"Wie komt daar aan op die olifant?" Een zestiende-eeuws taalgidsje voor Nederland en Indië, inclusief het verhaal van de avontuurlijke gevangenschap van Frederik de Houtman in Indië*. Amsterdam: L. J. Veen.

Van Hal, Toon. 2011. "A Man of Eight Hearts: Hadrian Junius and Sixteenth-Century Plurilinguism." In *The Kaleidoscopic Scholarship of Hadrianus Junius (1511–1575). Northern Humanism at the Dawn of the Dutch Golden Age*, edited by Dirk Van Miert, 188–213. Leiden: Brill.

Verbeke, Demmy. 2013a. "Polyglotte publicaties in de vroegmoderne tijd." In *De Tuin der Talen: Taalstudie en taalcultuur in de Lage Landen, 1450–1750*, edited by Toon Van Hal, Lambert Isebaert, and Pierre Swiggers, 71–91. Leuven: Peeters.

———. 2013b. "Cato in England: Translating Latin Sayings for Moral and Linguistic Instruction." In *Renaissance Cultural Crossroads: Translation, Print and Culture in Britain, 1473–1640*, edited by Sara Barker and Brenda Hosington, 139–55. Leiden: Brill.

———. 2015. "Types of Bilingual Presentation in the English-Latin Terence." In *Bilingual Europe: Latin and Vernacular Cultures, Examples of Bilingualism and Multilingualism c. 1300–1800*, edited by Jan Bloemendal, 73–82. Leiden: Brill.

Waquet, Françoise. 1998. *Le latin ou l'empire d'un signe: XVIᵉ–XXᵉ siècle*. Paris: Albin Michel.

CHAPTER 3

···

LYRIC POETRY

···

VICTORIA MOUL

DEFINING NEO-LATIN LYRIC

THE first obstacle encountered in any study of Neo-Latin lyric is one of terminology: in classical criticism, lyric poetry is, strictly speaking, poetry, whether Latin or Greek, written in the collection of meters designed for songs accompanied by the lyre. The bulk of this ancient lyric is Greek, and Pindar (ca. 518 to after 446 BCE) the single most influential poet. The only major classical Latin author of lyric poetry is Horace (65–8 BCE), though Catullus (ca. 84 to after 54 BCE) also wrote a handful of poems in Latin adaptations of the Greek lyric meters, plus some pieces in hendecasyllables and scazons that are often treated as lyric. Among later classical authors, the lyric choruses of Seneca (ca. 1–65 CE), and some Christian poets such as Prudentius (348–after 405 CE) have particularly influenced the Neo-Latin lyric tradition. Among all these writers, sapphics and alcaics are the most common stanza forms, followed by the various types of Asclepiad meter.

Epodic meters (used in Horace's *Epodes*) and elegiac couplets (a dactylic hexameter followed by a pentameter) are not strictly lyric: that is, they are not originally designed for song. But both Horace's *Epodes* and the Latin elegists treat themes typical of ancient Greek lyric, such as love, mythology, and political praise. This blurred boundary between lyric and elegy is inherited by Neo-Latin poetry (Schmitz 1994, 173–75): authors may describe, for instance, a solemn poem written in elegiac couplets as an "ode," and similarly we find pieces in lyric meters included in principally elegiac collections, as in the 1551 *Elegiarum liber* (*Book of Elegies*) by Petrus Lotichius Secundus.

A further strand of Neo-Latin lyric is introduced by the gradual conflation during the course of the Renaissance of classical lyric poetry—especially in its most high-flown and inspired forms, associated with the mythical poets Orpheus and Amphion—and the songs of the biblical psalms, attributed to King David. Countless Renaissance texts combine these elements when describing and situating their own lyric work: George Herbert's (1593–1633) fine ode *De musica sacra* (*Sacred Music*) is constructed around a series of first mythological and then scriptural references that form the spine of the poem and lead us from Deucalion (a perhaps surprising starting point, analyzed further below) to Orpheus, Amphion, the Graces, Moses, and then the psalms of David.

For the purposes of this volume, I have in general avoided lengthy discussion of dedicatory or descriptive verse keyed to specific occasions, as well as short poems upon named individuals, stock characters, or moral qualities, which are most naturally considered epigrams (on these aspects of Renaissance Latin poetics, see Chapter 5). All the same, this is an essentially artificial distinction: Arthur Marotti's magisterial study of English lyrics of the Renaissance makes "The Occasional Character of Renaissance Lyric Verse" his very first sub-heading (Marotti 1995, 2). Several of Horace's grandest odes, especially from his fourth book, are keyed to imperial victories; and the epinician odes of Pindar, traditionally the most sublime of all lyric poetry, not only respond to specific occasions (athletic victories), but were commissioned to commemorate them. Similarly, some markedly "occasional" Neo-Latin poems are clearly lyric, both in their form and in their poetic ambition—for instance, the ambitious alcaic ode on the Spanish Armada, probably by Theodore de Bèze (1519–1605), preserved in a single manuscript, and now made available by Dana Sutton (de Bèze 2007).

LYRIC FORMS I: HORATIAN AND PINDARIC ODES

The story of Horatian lyric meters in Neo-Latin poetry begins with Petrarch, one of whose verse letters to ancient authors is addressed to Horace, and composed in the first asclepiad meter. That important poem of the mid-fourteenth century is well discussed by Ludwig (1992) and Houghton (2009, 161–72), but Petrarch's appropriation of Horatian meter remained an isolated experiment until its wholescale adoption around a century later by Francesco Filelfo (1398–1481). Filelfo's fifty Latin odes in five books offered for the first time versions of all of Horace's meters, although the shaping of the books as a kind of verse autobiography (Filelfo 2009, xiv) is quite different from anything we find in Horace, and his poetry has been criticized as unmusical and lacking in literary merit. Many of the early Italian humanists of the fifteenth century, including Landino, Campano, Pontano, Marullus, and Navagero, composed a handful of odes in Horatian meters, usually in sapphics or alcaics, and often in the form of hymns.

In a departure from his Horatian model, nine of Filelfo's odes incorporated a change of meter mid-poem, with ode 3.8 displaying more than thirty different meters within a single poem. Polymetric lyrics of this sort, dubbed "mixed" odes by Maddison (1960, 332), are a feature of many later Neo-Latin poets—the Latin songs included in John Barclay's hugely successful Latin novel, *Argenis* (1621), for instance, are of this "mixed" type.

Latin odes could be "Pindaric" in two ways. First, and most obvious, are long Latin poems that attempt to imitate Pindaric meters: that is, poems with complex strophes of irregular line length, sometimes (though not always) arranged in triads of strophe, antistrophe, and epode. Latin Pindarics of this sort are a humanist invention—the first fully formed triadic examples seem to be those of Benedetto Lampridio (d. 1540), whose metrical invention perhaps inspired Julius Caesar Scaliger's prodigious project of metrical classification and experiment. Scaliger's *Poetics* (1561) illustrated every known ancient meter, both Greek and Latin, and his own poetry demonstrates many of them: his *Poemata Sacra* (*Sacred Poems*; 1600) includes two triadic Pindaric birthday odes, one for Christ and one for the Virgin Mary. One of the latest odes in this tradition is Milton's remarkable Latin Pindaric ode to John Rouse (1646; published 1673). Evidently, this kind of verse had become a school exercise by the seventeenth century: Cambridge University Library MS Dd 5.77 preserves a Pindaric ode presented to the Dean of Westminster upon his return from the country to London, one of a selection of Westminster school exercises of the 1680s.

But Latin odes could also be "Pindaric" in a smaller-scale—that is, more Horatian—manner. Typically composed in alcaic stanzas, such poems evoke Pindaric grandeur *via* Horace's major odes of Pindaric imitation (especially, ironically, Horace's less-than-wholly-sincere claim to *eschew* Pindaric style in *Odes* 4.2). Poems in this tradition are generally concerned with serious themes, often of religious praise. Revard (2001) offers a fine guide to what she terms the Renaissance "hymn-ode," and her companion volume (Revard 2009), though focused largely upon vernacular rather than Neo-Latin poetry, expands the discussion to the widespread adoption of this form, modeled on Horace's fourth book as well as Pindar himself, for more worldly panegyric. Casimir Sarbiewski's (1595–1640) poem to Pope Urban VIII, for instance, names Pindar directly (*ter Urbanum Camoenae / Pindaricis cecinere plectris*, "Three times have the Muses sung of Urban, in the Pindaric style," *Lyrica* 1.3.51–52). Ben Jonson's (1572–1637) knowing *Ode to Himself*, based closely on Horace, *Odes* 4.2, was translated by his admirer Thomas Randolph into Latin Pindarics, and circulated surprisingly widely in this form: the Latin poem, with or without the English original, is preserved in twelve extant manuscript miscellanies (Moul 2010, 202–6).

The grand Horatian ode of political praise was familiar enough as a sub-genre—both from Horace himself, and from popular Neo-Latin imitations of those poems, such as those by Sarbiewski—to allow for pastiche and ironic reappropriation: Abraham Cowley's (1618–1667) witty sapphic ode *Viola*, spoken by the violet flower herself, appropriates the language of the Horatian victory ode to describe a triumph over *fervidos hostes*, the dreadfully "seething enemy" (37–44):

> *Fervidos hostes minimo tumultu*
> *Exigo sensim sine clade victrix*
> *Corpus haud sentit placide peracti*
> *Vulnera belli.*
> *Cedit, et cessisse rubescit herbae*
> *Ad coronamenta epulasque natae,*
> *Virium atque irae nimium potentis*
> *Conscia febris.*

> Gently I expel the feverish enemy with the least possible disturbance—I am a victor without a rout; the body scarcely feels the wounds of this war that is carried out so calmly. Fever gives way, and blushes to have given ground to a herb born for crowns and banquets—but give way she does, aware of the herb's power and the force of her anger.

Each stanza is marked by Horatian allusion: here the phrase *sine clade victrix* is borrowed from Horace *Odes* 4.14.32 (*stravit humum sine clade victor*, "he covered the soil, a victor without a rout") where it describes Tiberius's victory over the Rhaeti. But the hostile forces of Cowley's poem turn out to be, not political enemies, but fever itself: as discussed in Moul (2012), the entire piece is an *aide-memoire* for the anti-pyretic powers of the violet.

Cowley's poem is a particularly marked example of the didactic appropriation of Horatian lyric, but the project is not in itself unusual: Jakob Balde's (1604–1668) moving ode *Ad Sabinum Fuscum Tyrolensem* (*To Sabinus Fuscus, a Tyrolean*), for instance, urges his friend Fuscus to climb the mountains with him, and offers a panoramic survey both of the constellations of the night sky—all of which are imagined as contributing to the heavenly chorus of harmony—and of the political landscape of Europe. The ode is dense with reminiscences of Horace, both the political odes and (in its opening section) the symposium pieces celebrating friendship, relaxation, and the springtime, although the overall effect—and especially the climactic hymn of praise, at the moment at which the power of poetry can carry the poet no further, and *alata virtus* ("winged virtue," 110) must continue the journey—is quite unlike anything in Horace.

Modern students and scholars tend not to think of Horace as a particularly religious poet, but the *Odes* include many hymns (nos. 10, 21, 30, 32, and 35 in Book 1 alone). Moreover, many of the great Christian hymns of the early church were themselves indebted to Horatian forms and models: Prudentius's *Cathemerinon* (*Hymns for the Day*) and *Peristephanon* (*Crowns of the Martyrs*) both employ lyric forms imitated from Horace, Catullus, and Seneca. This precedent encouraged the adoption of Horatian lyric for Christian religious verse: we find examples from the very beginnings of Neo-Latin poetry. The hymn to Diana by Landino (1424–1504), for instance (*Laudes Dianae* [*Praise of Diana*]), is in sapphics, the second most common meter in Horace's odes; in the following century, Quintianus Stoa of Brescia (1484–1557) experimented with presenting Christian—rather than pagan—devotion in Horatian meters, a project to which Jesuit Latin poets of the sixteenth and seventeenth centuries were to return enthusiastically. In Jacob Monavius's *Ipse faciet* (*He Will Act*, 1581; the title quotes Psalm 36.5) we find an entire appendix devoted to largely religious imitations of a single Horatian ode, 4.3 (De Landtsheer 2006).

The religious grandeur of the Horatian and Pindaric voice at its most prophetic, combined with the tendency to adopt Horatian and Pindaric lyric forms for religious verse of various kinds, created an early link between lyric and the translation of the Psalms. Early modern writers regularly associated the divinely inspired verse of the greatest classical poets with the Psalms of David and Solomon's *Song of Songs*. In *The Arte of English Poesie* (1589, 23), George Puttenham claims that hymns were the original form of poetry among both the Greeks and the Hebrews; fifty years later, François Gomaer, a Dutch

Calvinist theologian and Hebrew scholar, offered a detailed comparison of Pindar and the Psalms in his *Davidis Lyra* (*David's Lyre*, 1637).

As a result, we find a plethora of psalm translations, rendered both in Horatian meters (though often in stylistic imitation of Pindar, or at least of Horace at his most Pindaric) and in various Latin versions of Pindaric form (Gaertner 1956). Two of the most interesting examples are the psalm versions of Marcantonio Flaminio (1498–1550) and of George Buchanan (1506–1582): Flaminio's paraphrases of the Psalms, published in 1548, adopt not only Horatian meters but also his poetic style; Maddison describes how he "elaborates David's brief images into typical Horatian vignettes" (Maddison 1960, 128). George Buchanan (1506–1582), a major Scottish poet writing at around the same time, published his Psalm translations in 1565, with many subsequent editions. In recent years, they have attracted interesting commentary by R. P. H. Green in particular (Ford and Green 2009, Buchanan 2011, Harrison 2012). Not all Psalm translations, however, made use of Horatian meters: Pope Urban VIII's Latin "paraphrase" of Psalm 136, first published in his *Poemata* of 1631, uses elegiac couplets, the subject of the next section (for Psalm paraphrases of the seventeenth century in general, see Leblanc 1960).

LYRIC FORMS II: ELEGY

The elegiac couplet was the single most popular meter for Neo-Latin verse. It has been used for poems of almost all forms and lengths and is, as a result, the most difficult form to delimit for the purposes of this chapter; in particular, I have excluded from consideration here long poems that have more in common with didactic or epic verse, and short pieces that are best understood as epigrams—though this is a difficult distinction to make consistently and usefully. An important influence upon this range is the variety of genres in which Ovid wrote in elegiac couplets, including the verse letters of the *Heroides* (*Heroines*) and *Tristia* (*Sorrows*), the *Fasti* (*Calendar*) and the comic didactic of the *Ars Amatoria* (*Art of Love*) and *Remedia Amoris* (*Remedies for Love*), as well as the books of love elegies, *Amores* (*Loves*). Following *CNLS* 2:80, I focus here upon medium-length poems that deal in particular with strong emotions, whether of love (as in Ovid's *Amores*, as well as those of Propertius and Tibullus), grief, or praise.

Collections of *Amores* are found among the earliest Neo-Latin verse, including the *Cinthia* of Enea Silvio Piccolomini (1405–1464, later Pope Pius II; on this, see Charlet 1997). This genre was so popular that most major Neo-Latin authors produced at least one collection of this sort—examples from that enormous field include Pontano (1429–1503) and Poliziano (1454–1494) among many others in Italy, Du Bellay in France (1522–1560), Konrad Celtis in Germany (1459–1508), Klemens Janicki in Poland (1516–1542), Johannes Secundus in the Low Countries (1511–1536) and John Milton in England (1608–1674). Such collections are typically focused upon a single mistress, given a classicizing and anonymizing name—such as Piccolomini's Cinthia and Landino's Xandra—in imitation of the Cynthia, Delia, and Lesbia of the classical poets, although the details and narrative coherence of these collections vary: Pontano in his *De amore coniugali* (*Conjugal Love*), for instance, is one of several Renaissance elegists to celebrate his love for his lawful wife, while the four books of Celtis's *Amores* (1502) are each dedicated to a different love affair and a different region of Germany (Robert 2003 on Celtis; Pieper 2008 on Landino's *Xandra* and its generic context; Parker 2012 on the genre in general).

The sheer familiarity of the genre and its conventions invites pastiche and knowing misappropriation. Tito Strozzi (ca. 1425–1505) begins a typical piece by imagining Cupid, carelessly asleep and unarmed beneath a tree (*Eroticon* 2.16.1–2):

> *Materna caperet dum forte sub arbore somnum*
>   *Armaque securus deposuisset Amor. . .*

> While he [Cupid] happened to be taking a nap beneath his mother's tree
>   And had set down his weapons without the slightest concern. . .

Coming upon him in this vulnerable state, Diana does her best to extinguish his torches and break his arrows before Venus comes to the rescue of her son. The motif—of Cupid disarmed—is a familiar one, and ripe for playful variation. More than a century later, we find what seems at first a similar scene in the fourth elegy of Thomas Campion's *Poemata* (*Poems*, 1595), *De Mellea Lusus* (*Mellea, a Sport*, 1–3):

> *Pulchra roseta inter mea Mellea pulchrior illis*
>   *Dum legit umbroso mollia fraga solo:*
> *Venit Amor, qui iam pharetra positisque sagittis. . .*

> While in a fair rose-garden my Mellea, fairer still,
>   Was picking tender strawberries from the shady ground.
> Cupid arrived, and now, his quiver and arrows set aside. . .

There are several points in common here: the scene-setting with *dum*, the pastoral shade, the presence of Cupid, the erotic connotations—in Strozzi's piece, the boy Cupid is implicitly vulnerable, like those he wounds with love; in Campion, we imagine immediately at line 3 that Cupid himself has fallen in love with Mellea and so been "disarmed." In fact, Campion puts his own spin on the scene, as the poem continues (4–6):

> *gestitat ignivomo ferra forata cavo*
> *Pulvis agit sine voce pilas ubi concipit ignem,*
>   *Et nivis in tacito pulvere candor inest.*

> He [Cupid] was wielding bored-out irons with fire-belching muzzles.
> Soundlessly, his powder propels balls when it takes fire,
>   And there is a snowy whiteness to this silent powder.

The forceful alliteration of line four and the crude vividness of *ignivomo* (not a classical word) is part of the surprise: Campion's Cupid is not *dis*armed but *extra* armed, having upgraded his classical bow and arrows for an early modern firearm. The technology itself attracts some of the sort of sensuous descriptive attention we expect to be lavished upon the beloved, and also confounds our expectations: the gunpowder is miraculously silent (*sine voce; tacito*) but also beautiful, shining white like snow (*nivis . . . candor*): ordinary gunpowder is black, and muskets of course were noisy. The reversal of our expectations contributes to the dramatic setting because the silence of the gun allows Cupid to surprise Mellea, while the set of attributes and associations (fire and snow; bright beauty and silence) echo the tropes of erotic description.

Neo-Latin elegiac collections are by no means confined to love poetry: collections of *Amores* often included poems of mourning or political praise, influenced perhaps particularly by the varied components of Propertius's fourth book. For all his knowing manipulation of the tropes of love elegy, Campion opened the *Book of Elegies* contained in his *Poemata* with a poem that turns from the tropes of love elegy to the political and poetic blessings of England: the English poet can afford to invoke Cupid (and his genre) because the peace under Elizabeth I allows room for the *militia amoris*. The poem ends: *Alme puer, teneris adsit tua gratia musis, / Paces sive deae, seu tua bella canunt* ("Gentle child, may your grace attend our tender Muses, whether they sing of the goddess's [Venus's] peace, or your own wars"; Elegy 1.41–42).

The reference to Cupid and Venus here strikes us as a generic, rather than genuinely religious, feature, but many Neo-Latin poets composed religious elegies, whether of devotion (e.g., to saints or the Virgin Mary) or, in imitation of the *Heroides*, from one sacred character to another: the *Heroidum Christianarum epistolae* (*Letters of Christian Heroines*, 1514) of the German poet Helius Eobanus Hessus (1488–1540) even includes a verse letter from Christ to his mother Mary, and her reply (on which see Manuwald 2017). And, in addition to the many elegiac poems of mourning, there is a distinct sub-genre of the "exile" poem, in which the poet mourns for himself. That form is indebted of course to Ovid's exile verse, but interpreted with varying degrees of reality: Johannes Secundus (1511–1536) is merely homesick in his Elegy 3.11; John Milton (1608–1674) was probably simply spending a university vacation back in London in his first elegy, a highly self-conscious and ironic appropriation of Ovid, in which it is Cambridge, not London, that takes on the bleak barrenness of Ovid's Black Sea; whereas the elderly Danish astronomer Tycho Brahe (1546–1601) was enduring a real exile in Prague when he wrote his famous *Elegy to Denmark* (see Skafte Jensen 2009). The range of possibilities for Neo-Latin elegy is almost limitless: Houghton (2013) offers a lively overview.

Lyric Forms III: Short Lyrics (Catullan and Anacreontic)

Although Catullus wrote ambitious long poems (including the epithalamia 61 and 62, and the epyllion 64) as well as his shorter poems of praise, invective, and eroticism, his Renaissance rediscovery generally preferred the shorter pieces. Brief lyrics in a Catullan style—and often in hendecasyllables, a meter associated strongly with Catullus—are found in thousands of Neo-Latin poets from Giovanni Pontano (1429–1503) onwards. The most important work on the Renaissance reception of Catullus in general, and on Pontano in particular, is by Julia Haig Gaisser, whose comments stand behind many of my remarks in this section. She describes this craze for the hendecasyllable as follows (Haig Gaisser 1993, 197):

> So too, in its style, diction, subject matter, and affect, the Catullan hendecasyllable provided the language for a certain type of Renaissance lyric; and even as the tradition acquired new and non-Catullan (or even anti-Catullan) elements, it identified itself—often explicitly—as Catullan, and the poets—even at their farthest from the Catullan sensibility—saw themselves as devotees of Catullan poetry.

Giovanni Pontano's three Catullan collections, *Pruritus* (*[Erotic] Itch*, 1449), *Parthenopeus sive Amores* (*The Neapolitan, or Loves*, 1457), and *Hendecasyllabi sive Baiae* (*Hendecasyllables, or Baiae*, dating from around 1500) offer quite different perspectives upon his central model—*Pruritus* is often obscene, *Parthenopeus* combines recognizably Catullan material with poems more readily characterized as odes or love elegies, while the *Hendecasyllabi* helped to establish the principally Catullan associations of the hendecasyllable, as described by Haig Gaisser.

Several features are characteristic both of Pontano's Catullan imitations and the hundreds of poems composed across Europe in a similar vein in the following centuries. One is a self-conscious engagement with Catullus's programmatic tropes, especially of the relative insignificance of his small-scale genre (described as *nugae*, "trifles," at 1.4) and the capacity of the poet to remain chaste himself, while writing titillating or even frankly indecent material (an idea indebted in particular to Catullus 16). Specific images are also very widely imitated: none more so than the "many kisses" of Catullus 5 and 7 (in fact, Campion's fourth elegy, discussed above, incorporates this Catullan feature at lines 13–20) and the ambiguous sparrow, beloved of Lesbia and mourned after its death, of Catullus 2 and 3. Martial famously interpreted that sparrow as Catullus's penis in 11.5, and in *Parthenopeus* 1.5, Pontano followed Martial's reading, insisting that his "dove" is for the pleasure only of his girlfriend, not "boy catamites."

Both Catullus's kisses and his dead sparrow won a long poetic life. The nineteen *Basia* (*Kisses*, 1541) of Johannes Secundus were enormously influential upon love poetry, both Latin and vernacular, across Europe: Ben Jonson's well-known and much circulated lyrics *To Celia*, for instance, from his play *Volpone* (1606), are indebted both to Catullus and to Secundus. As for Catullus's sparrow, we find a myriad of Latin "bird" poems: early in the eighteenth century, the French Jesuit poet Noël Étienne Sanadon published *In mortem passeris* (*On the Death of a Sparrow*) in his 1715 collection of Latin verse (*Carmina* 3.2):

> *Lugete, o Charites, Ioci, Lepores,*
> *Et quantum est volucrum venustiorum,*
> *Et quantum est iuvenum pudentiorum.*

Weep, o Graces, o Pleasures, o Charms,
And as many of the lovely birds as may,
And as many of the chaste young men.

The poem is in hendecasyllables, and imitates Catullus in its imagery, structure, and vocabulary at many points. Catullus 3 begins *Lugete, o Veneres Cupidinesque* ("Weep, o Venuses and Cupids"), and the second line of Sanadon's poem is lifted almost verbatim from Catullus 3.2, altering only the fourth word: Catullus's *hominum* ("men") has become *volucrum* ("birds"), although the missing *hominum* is perhaps echoed in the *iuvenum* ("young men") of line 3.

Sanadon's version of Catullus retains the suggestion of an erotic context: this sparrow belonged to Thyrsis, and was for him, as for Lesbia, a source of pleasure (*innocens voluptas*, "innocent pleasure," line 4; Catullus uses the more erotically charged term *deliciae*, "delight" at 3.4). Moreover it was killed, it turns out, not by a hawk or a cat, as we might expect, but at the hands of Cupid, that *ales/implumis* ("bird without wings," ll. 11–12). The poem implies a complicated scenario: Thyrsis loved the bird and played with it, but in their games the bird was joined by Cupid, intent upon attack (ll. 15–20):

Ipse est pessimus alitum Cupido,
Milvis improbiorque, felibusque,
Qui colludere passeri solebat,
Atque una pueri in sinum volabat,
Et circum petulante vectus ala
Quaerebat tenerum ustulare pectus.

That's Cupid, the worst of all birds,
More wicked than sparrow-hawks, than cats:
He would play alongside the sparrow,
And fly with it into the boy's lap,
Carried around on the bird's bold wings,
He'd try to scorch his [Thyrsis's] tender breast.

Finally Cupid killed the bird in a fury *quum posset domino nihil nocere*, "because he could not wound its master" (l. 23).

The poem's speaker is never identified, but the piece itself is an artful appropriation—and, in a sense, a rejection—of the Catullan tradition: the virtuous Thyrsis is impervious to Cupid, and as such blithely innocent, too, of the obscene interpretation of his own pet sparrow. The lyric's edge relies upon our readerly *lack* of innocence: that is, upon our knowledge of that tradition. We understand why Cupid is in this poem, even if Thyrsis does not.

Related to this general fashion for short lyrics in the Catullan tradition is the widespread sixteenth and seventeenth century adoption of anacreontics: a meter of even shorter and more rapid lines than the hendecasyllable (Tilg 2014). The trend was inaugurated by Henri Estienne, who published the *Carmina Anacreontica* (*Songs of Anacreon*) in 1554: fifty previously unpublished poems by a number of ancient authors posing as the archaic Greek poet Anacreon (but in the early modern period generally seen as Anacreon's work), in a meter previously found only in a handful of Greek and Latin lyrics, including the *Greek Anthology* and a hymn of Prudentius (*Cathemerinon* 6; Laurens 2003). Estienne's work triggered almost immediately a great wave of imitations, first in France, and then across Europe (O'Brien 1995 and Laurens 2003). One example among many is the *Amphitheatrum Gratiarum* (*Amphitheater of Graces*, 1613) of the German poet Caspar von Barth (7.18.1–12):

> *Gremio meae Neaerae*
> *Suave dormitabam.*
> *– Quid somniatus ergo*
> *Es, amabilis Rosille?*
> *– Apis fui Matina,*
> *Suxi favum e labello,*
> *Florem extuli ex ocellis*
> *Et purpuram ex genellis,*
> *Ut inde mel liquarem,*
> *Mel dulce, mel suave,*
> *Condiret unde Carmen*
> *Anacreon venustum.*

> Upon my Neaera's lap
> I dreamt a sweet dream.
> – What did you dream,
> My dear Rosillus?
> – I was a Matine bee,
> I sucked the lip's honey,
> I took the eyes' bloom
> And the cheeks' purple,
> And strained from them honey,
> Sweet honey, fine honey,
> From which Anacreon constructs
> A charming song.

Poems of this sort draw upon recognizably Catullan elements. Like Lesbia's sparrow (compare Catullus 3.8), the speaker of this poem loves to rest in the lap (*gremio*, l. 1) of his mistress; the mistress's name is Neaera, most famous as the love interest of Johannes Secundus's Catullan *Basia*. But the meter here is anacreontic, and the poem is identified as belonging to Anacreon at line 12. The poetic lineage is further nuanced when the speaker reveals himself to be a "Matine bee": an image of poetic composition on a small scale in Horace, *Odes* 4.2.27–32, where the allusion to the mountain Matinus in Apulia refers to Horace's native land. However, the erotic connotations of the bee, who sucks nectar from Neaera's lip (and ends the poem by leaving his sting [*aculeum* in line 15] in her lap) are not Horatian.

Imitation and Allusion

As the extract from von Barth's poem demonstrates, Neo-Latin lyric is marked almost without exception by dense intertextuality, especially with the classical authors, but also with other Neo-Latin poets. The convoluted impression of a "patchwork of quotations," amounting in some cases to something approaching a cento, is one of the features of Neo-Latin verse for which it is most often criticized. But these techniques, which include the imitation of theme, structure, and style as well as specific reminiscences, can also be a source of creativity and emotional force. Any one of a host of Neo-Latin poems might demonstrate this point: I offer here a brief reading of just one—a poem that has to my knowledge attracted no previous sustained attention.

George Herbert's poem *De musica sacra*, mentioned above, is composed in an Horatian meter (alcaics), and its first stanza closes with a borrowing from Horace:

> *Cur efficaci, Deucalion, manu,*
> *Post restitutos fluctibus obices,*
> *   Mutas in humanam figuram*
> *   Saxa supervacuasque cautes?*

> Why, Deucalion, did you use your hand's power,
> After the waves were once more barred,
>   To transform into human shape
>   Rocks and useless crags?

The last line of the stanza, *supervacuasque cautes*, replicates in its structure and metrical position the final phrase of *Odes* 2.20, *supervacuos honores*, the last ode of Horace's second book. The Horatian poem describes the poet's metamorphosis into a mellifluous, white bird capable of ranging as far as the boundaries of the empire. The final phrase, *supervacuos honores*, describes the "empty honors" of the tomb that Horace dismisses as irrelevant to him in his new form. The transformation is an emblem, albeit a self-conscious and perhaps mildly ironic one, of the poet's power and immortality.

Herbert's poem begins with a phrase borrowed in part from the *end* of Horace's second book of odes. But the opening evocation of the story of Deucalion and Pyrrha, the only human couple to survive a deluge sent by Zeus, is also Horatian. *Odes* 1.2 also begins with a flood, in that case a devastating storm in Rome, which is at once compared (ll. 5–6) with the mythical flood survived by Pyrrha and her husband. The parallel is again a significant one, because Horace's poem, like Herbert's, is concerned with the interaction between the human and the divine, and in particular the punishment of and atonement for human sin. In Horace, the sin is that of the Roman civil war, and the central question is to which of the gods Jupiter shall assign the role of atonement. Horace suggests Apollo, Venus, Mars, and finally Mercury, in the guise of a human youth: that is, Octavian himself, with whose victory over the Parthians the poem ends (*te duce, Caesar,* "with you as leader, Caesar," l. 52). The presiding "sin" of Herbert's ode is the failure to respond to music, here described—partly by the structural parallel with the Horatian poem—as a central mode of communication between the human and the divine. Both poems are structured by a series of characters. Just as Horace's list combines mythical (Pyrrha, Proteus), divine, and historical figures, so Herbert's poem moves from classical myths and divinities to biblical rulers: Deucalion, Orpheus, Amphion, the Graces, the Muse, Moses, and David.

This is not to occlude the differences between these odes, the most significant of which is that Horace's ode looks to a particular person—Octavian—as well as a specific activity—successful war against foreign (rather than internal) enemies—as the mode of Rome's redemption. Herbert's ode, by contrast, identifies no specific modern savior, and the central activity is the making of music, not war. For all its celebration of music, Herbert's ode ends, as it began, with an attack upon the Puritans for their noisy but unharmonious failure to appreciate the power of musical praise and celebration: the movement of the ode, unlike Horace's, is circular, with the positive celebration in the center of the poem (ll. 21–37) rather than at the end.

Moreover, that celebration of music's power includes phrases quite alien to Horace's Latin: *Ramenta coeli, guttulaeque / Deciduae melioris orbis!* ("Flakes of heaven, and the falling / Droplets of a better world," ll. 35–36). The imagery here, at once so concrete (*ramenta, guttulae*) and so removed from worldly experience (*coeli, melioris orbis*) is characteristic of Herbert; unthinkable in Horace. One aspect of the poem's force, as in so many Neo-Latin lyrics, lies in the counterpoint between its Horatian structure, meter, and specific allusion and the un-Horatian—Christian, and in this case markedly metaphysical—imagery with which the heavenly power of music is described.

CONTEXT, SEQUENCE, AND
THE POETRY BOOK

The passage quoted from George Herbert's *De musica sacra* strikes us as not only quintessentially lyric (in this case, Horatian) in its form and tone, but also partly *about* lyric, insofar as it works carefully to conflate poets and musicians (Amphion, Orpheus, David, Horace himself) in its mythological canon. But in fact, the poem is one of a sequence, *Musae responsoriae* (*Responsorial Muses*), written in response to a theological controversy, and more specifically to a long and vituperative poem by the theologian Andrew Melville (1545–1622), attacking Anglican ritual practices and the refusal by the Universities of Oxford and Cambridge to abandon these features of their worship. Both Melville's poem and Herbert's sequence in response are certainly "occasional"; moreover, Herbert's wide-ranging sequence of forty short poems, in a variety of meters, several addressed to Melville himself (and most of the rest on the various aspects of Anglican rite that Herbert seeks to defend), are easily categorized as epigrams. But were we to encounter number 23, *De musica sacra*, in isolation—whether in a published anthology, a manuscript miscellany, or as a single loose leaf in an assortment of papers—we would quite naturally read these thirteen alcaic stanzas as primarily a Latin ode.

Herbert's is a fine example of an Horatian lyric that is partly about the function of such lyric itself; but its larger purpose can only be understood in the context of the sequence—of occasional epigrams on a theological controversy—of which it is a part. The role of sequence and context in our interpretation of Neo-Latin lyric is of particular importance: while relatively few editions exist of complete collections by Neo-Latin poets, the reader of Neo-Latin lyric will continue to encounter many poems for the first time in an anthology or appendix, just as so much Neo-Latin lyric poetry was preserved and circulated in early modern published anthologies or manuscript miscellanies and commonplace books. It is true of shorter poems in particular that the chief esthetic effect may be created by cumulative reiterations of a given image or idea over a large number of pieces that are relatively minor in themselves; similarly, a collection of love elegies, which invites the reader to reconstruct the sequence of a love affair over time, reads quite differently from an individual piece taken in isolation. This is, if anything, still more true of Neo-Latin collections, which may incorporate a mix of poems that would be confined to separate collections (e.g., eclogues, odes and elegies) in a classical context.

CONCLUSION: WHY READ OR WORK ON NEO-LATIN LYRIC?

Neo-Latin lyric poetry is a vast field, and one that makes considerable demands upon the modern reader: not least in its variety of meters, the daunting reliance upon classical allusion and complex intertextual relationships with Neo-Latin predecessors, and the alien social and political institutions—of patronage, dedication, and political and religious controversy—in which it arose. Those demands are increased by the difficulties of accessing this material, so much of which remains unedited, or inadequately so. All of this makes the field tempting territory for scholars, and a great deal of work remains to be done in editing and explicating the most important of these texts, their literary form and significance, and their relationship to other literature, both Latin and vernacular. Work of this sort has benefits for classicists and Classics departments as well as scholars of Renaissance culture: several classical texts that are routinely taught as if a single extant author is more or less the sum of their Latin genre—such as Horace's *Odes* and *Epodes*, or Martial's *Epigrams*—can only benefit from a greater awareness of the riches of post-classical Latin literature, and the enormous variety of ways in which these texts were interpreted, challenged, and rewritten in the changing contexts of medieval, Renaissance, and early modern societies.

Ignoring Neo-Latin lyric, moreover, distorts to a great extent our appreciation and understanding of the work of Renaissance and early modern poets: Petrarch and Milton are examples of major poets who wrote in both the Latin and the vernacular, and they are also rare examples of authors whose eminence is so great that both sides of their poetic personality have attracted critical attention (albeit unevenly). But a host of accomplished Latin authors continue to be taught and studied as if they wrote only in the vernacular, and many others are effectively excluded from the canon because they were primarily Latin poets. There is historical as well as literary importance in attending more carefully to the Latin literary tradition.

But the first and best reason for reading and thinking about Neo-Latin lyric must always be that so much of it is good poetry: beautiful, precise, and evocative; poetry that extends our sense of what Latin verse can be and can do.

SUGGESTED READING

Laurens (2004) (introduction and parallel translations in French) is currently the only readily available paperback anthology of Neo-Latin lyric. Of those no longer in print, Arnaldi, Gualdo Rosa, and Monti Sabia (1964) offers excellent coverage of fifteenth-century Italian authors; Laurens (1975) is the most complete; McFarlane (1980) is slight but with a good representation of erotic elegy. Nichols (1979) has parallel translations in English. The anthologies of Jesuit verse by Mertz, Murphy, and IJsewijn (1989) and Thill, Fumaroli, and Banderier (1999) print many odes. Kühlmann, Seidel, and Wiegand (1997) is an accessible introduction to German Neo-Latin lyric. Raven (1965) is an accessible and easily available guide to Latin meter.

As in all questions of Neo-Latin literature, readers should begin by consulting *CNLS* (2:79–99). The fine overview offered by Haig Gaisser (2017) concentrates on odes and Catullan lyric, permitting a fuller discussion of those forms than is possible here, and with different emphases. On Horatian imitation, see Ludwig (1992), Maddison (1960); (for German poets) Schäfer (1976); and (for English poets) Binns (1990). Revard (2001) discusses Latin Pindarics. On Catullan imitation, see Haig Gaisser (1993). On erotic elegy, see, most recently, Braden (2010), Parker (2012), and Houghton (2013); Ludwig (1976) also remains informative. Recent collections of essays focusing upon elegy are Chappuis Sandoz (2011), Cardini and Coppini (2009), and Catanzaro and Santucci (1999). The *NeoLatina* series has produced several monographs on individual elegiac poets. The most significant recent monograph on Neo-Latin elegy is Pieper (2008). On psalm translations, see Gärtner (1956). The chapters on elegy and lyric in *NLL* supplement this account.

REFERENCES

Arnaldi, Francesco, Lucia Gualdo Rosa, and Liliana Monti Sabia, eds. 1964. *Poeti latini del Quattrocento*. Milan: Ricciardi.

De Bèze, Theodore. 2007. "Ad Serenissimam Elizabetham Angliae Reginam." Edited and translated by Dana Sutton. *The Philological Museum: Library of Humanistic Texts*. Available at http://www.philological.bham.ac.uk/beza/.

Binns, James W. 1990. *Intellectual Culture in Elizabethan and Jacobean England: The Latin Writings of the Age*. Leeds: Francis Cairns.

Braden, Gordon. 2010. "Classical Love Elegy in the Renaissance (and After)." In *The Oxford Handbook of the Elegy*, edited by Karen Weisman, 153–69. Oxford: Oxford University Press.

Buchanan, George. 2011. *Poetic Paraphrase of the Psalms of David (Psalmorum Davidis paraphrasis poetica)*. Edited and translated by Roger P. H. Green. Geneva: Droz.

Cardini, Roberto, and Donatella Coppini, eds. 2009. *Il rinnovamento umanistico della poesia: L'epigramma e l'elegia*. Florence: Polistampa.

Catanzaro, Giuseppe, and Francesco Santucci, eds. 1999. *Poesia umanistica latina in distici elegiaci: Atti del convegno internazionale, Assisi, 15–17 Maggio 1998*. Assisi: Accademia Properziana del Subasio.

Chappuis Sandoz, Laure, ed. 2011. *Au-delà de l'élégie d'amour: Métamorphoses et renouvellements d'un genre latin dans l'antiquité et à la Renaissance*. Paris: Classiques Garnier.

Charlet, Jean-Louis. 1997. "Éros et érotisme dans la *Cinthia* d'Enea Silvio Piccolomini." In *Eros et Priapus: Erotisme et obscénité dans la littérature néo-latine*, edited by Ingrid De Smet and Philip Ford, 1–19. Geneva: Droz.

De Landtsheer, Jeanine. 2006. "Parodies on Religious Themes of Horace, *Carm.* IV.3 as an Appendix to Jacob Monavius's *Ipse faciet*." In *Pietas Humanistica: Neo-Latin Religious Poetry in Poland in European Context*, edited by Piotr Urbański, 287–301. Frankfurt: Lang.

Filelfo, Francesco. 2009. *Odes*. Edited and translated by Diana Robin. Cambridge: Harvard University Press.

Ford, Philip, and Roger Green. 2009. *George Buchanan: Poet and Dramatist*. Swansea: Classical Press of Wales.

Gaertner, Johannes A. 1956. "Latin Verse Translations of the Psalms, 1500–1620." *Harvard Theological Review* 49:271–305.

Haig Gaisser, Julia. 1993. *Catullus and His Renaissance Readers*. Oxford: Clarendon Press.

———. 2017. "Lyric", in *NLL*, 113–30.

Harrison, Stephen. 2012. "George Buchanan: The Scottish Horace." In *Neo-Latin Poetry in the British Isles*, edited by Luke B. T. Houghton and Gesine Manuwald, 155–72. London: Bristol Classical Press.

Houghton, Luke B. T. 2009. "Two Letters to Horace: Petrarch and Andrew Lang." In *Perceptions of Horace: A Roman Poet and His Readers*, edited by Luke B. T. Houghton and Maria Wyke, 161–81. Cambridge: Cambridge University Press.

———. 2013. "Renaissance Latin Love Elegy." In *The Cambridge Companion to Latin Love Elegy*, edited by Thea S. Thorsen, 290–305. Cambridge: Cambridge University Press.

Kühlmann, Wilhelm, Robert Seidel, and Hermann Wiegand, eds. and trans. 1997. *Humanistische Lyrik des 16. Jahrhunderts*. Frankfurt: Deutscher Klassiker Verlag.

Laurens, Pierre, ed. 1975. *Musae reduces: Anthologie de la poésie latine dans l'Europe de la Renaissance*. 2 vols. Leiden: Brill.

———. 2003. "Une situation de rivalité linguistique: La réussite tardive d'un Anacréon latin." In *La Poésie grecque antique: Actes du 13e colloque de la Villa Kérylos*, edited by Jacques Jouanna and Jean Leclant, 203–221. Paris: De Boccard.

———, ed. 2004. *Anthologie de la poésie lyrique latine de la Renaissance*. Paris: Gallimard.

Leblanc, Paulette. 1960. *Les paraphrases françaises des Psaumes à la fin de la période baroque (1610–1660)*. Paris: Presses Universitaires de France.

Ludwig, Walther. 1976. "Petrus Lotichius Secundus and the Roman Elegists: Prolegomena to a Study of Neo-Latin Elegy." In *Classical Influences on European Culture A.D. 1500–1700*, edited by Robert R. Bolgar, 171–90. Cambridge: Cambridge University Press.

Ludwig, Walther. 1992. "Horazrezeption in der Renaissance oder die Renaissance des Horaz." In *Horace: L'oeuvre et les imitations—Un siècle d'interprétation*, edited by Hermann Tränkle and Walther Ludwig, 305–79. Geneva: Fondation Hardt.

Maddison, Carol. 1960. *Apollo and the Nine: A History of the Ode*. Baltimore: Johns Hopkins University Press.

Manuwald, Gesine. 2017. "Verse Letters." In *NLL*, 131–47.

Marotti, Arthur F. 1995. *Manuscript, Print and the English Renaissance Lyric*. Ithaca: Cornell University Press.

McFarlane, Ian D., ed. 1980. *Renaissance Latin Poetry*. Manchester: Manchester University Press.

Mertz, James J., John P. Murphy, and Jozef IJsewijn, eds. 1989. *Jesuit Latin Poets of the 17th and 18th Centuries: An Anthology of Neo-Latin Poetry*. Wauconda: Bolchazy-Carducci.

Moul, Victoria. 2010. *Jonson, Horace and the Classical Tradition*. Cambridge: Cambridge University Press.

———. 2012. "Horatian Odes in Abraham Cowley's *Plantarum Libri Sex* (1668)." In *Neo-Latin Poetry in the British Isles*, edited by Luke B. T. Houghton and Gesine Manuwald, 87–104. London: Bristol Classical Press.

Nichols, Fred J., ed. and trans. 1979. *An Anthology of Neo-Latin Poetry*. New Haven: Yale University Press.

O'Brien, John. 1995. *Anacreon Redivivus: A Study of Anacreontic Translation in Mid-Sixteenth-Century France*. Ann Arbor: University of Michigan Press.

Parker, Holt N. 2012. "Renaissance Latin Elegy." In *A Companion to Roman Love Elegy*, edited by Barbara K. Gold, 476–90. Malden: Wiley-Blackwell.

Pieper, Christoph. 2008. Elegos redolere Vergiliosque sapere: *Cristoforo Landinos* Xandra *zwischen Liebe und Gesellschaft*. Hildesheim: Olms.

Raven, David S. 1965. *Latin Metre*. London: Faber and Faber.

Revard, Stella P. 2001. *Pindar and the Renaissance Hymn-Ode: 1450–1700*. Tempe: Arizona Center for Medieval and Renaissance Studies.

———. 2009. *Politics, Poetics, and the Pindaric Ode: 1450–1700*. Tempe: Arizona Center for Medieval and Renaissance Studies.

Robert, Jörg. 2003. *Konrad Celtis und das Projekt der deutschen Dichtung: Studien zur humanistischen Konstitution von Poetik, Philosophie, Nation und Ich*. Tübingen: Niemeyer.

Schäfer, Eckart. 1976. *Deutscher Horaz: Conrad Celtis, Georg Fabricius, Paul Melissus, Jacob Balde—Die Nachwirkung des Horaz in der neulateinischen Dichtung Deutschlands*. Wiesbaden: Steiner.

Schmitz, Thomas. 1994. "L'ode latine pendant la Renaissance française: Un catalogue des odes publiées au seizième siècle." *Humanistica Lovaniensia* 43:173–219.

Skafte Jensen, Minna. 2009. "Tycho Brahe's Double Identity as a Citizen of Denmark and of the World." In *Syntagmatia: Essays on Neo-Latin Literature in Honour of Monique Mund-Dopchie and Gilbert Tournoy*, edited by Dirk Sacré and Jan Papy, 569–78. Leuven: Leuven University Press.

Thill, Andrée, Marc Fumaroli, and Gilles Banderier, eds. 1999. *La lyre jésuite: Anthologie de poèmes latins (1620–1730)*. Geneva: Droz.

Tilg, Stefan. 2014. "Neo-Latin Anacreontic Poetry: Its Shape(s) and Its Significance." In *Imitate Anacreon! Mimesis, Poiesis and the Poetic Inspiration in the* Carmina Anacreontea, edited by Manuel Baumbach and Nicola Dümmler, 163–97. Leiden: Brill.

CHAPTER 4

....

NARRATIVE POETRY

....

FLORIAN SCHAFFENRATH

VIRGIL AND OTHER MODELS

....

THIS chapter deals with narrative hexameter poetry, a vast, popular, and very prestigious strand of literature in the early modern period. Heroic and didactic poetry will be discussed together, because they have many common features and were often seen as a single generic canon, to the extent that in a letter dated October 8, 1530, the famous Italian humanist Pietro Bembo called Girolamo Fracastoro's didactic poem *Syphilis* (1530; Fracastoro 2011), which gave the venereal disease its name, a "heroic poem" ("poema eroico"). The authority of Virgil, his works, and his literary career were decisive for the close link often made between didactic and epic narrative poetry. When Marco Girolamo Vida comes to speak about Virgil in the third book of his didactic poem *De arte poetica* (*The Art of Poetry*, 1527), he describes him in words that sound downright hymnic (3.554–56 and 565–66; Vida 1976):

> *Virgilii ante omnes laeti super astra feremus*
> *carminibus patriis laudes; decus unde Latinum*
> *unde mihi vires, animus mihi ducitur unde.*
> *. . . decus a te principe nostrum*
> *omne, pater*

> Now let us in exultation praise Virgil above all poets, bearing his praises beyond the stars in the songs of his native land. From him flows the Latins' glory, from him my powers, from him my strength of mind . . . All our glory, father, is ours because you are our leader.

Vida mentions Virgil's three main works elsewhere in Book 3: the progression from pastoral to didactic, then epic, poetry, represented by Virgil's *Eclogues*, *Georgics*, and *Aeneid*, became an example followed by many Neo-Latin poets, whose veneration of the Mantuan poet hardly knew any limits. Vida himself, for instance, started writing didactic poems before he wrote his *Christias* (1535), a heroic poem about the life of Christ. A later example is Niccolò Partenio Giannettasio, who wrote several didactic poems (e.g., *Nautica* on sailing, 1685), before the ten books of his *Xaverius viator* (*Wanderings of Xavier*, 1721) about the travels of Francis Xavier appeared.

However, there were several other authors apart from Virgil who also served Neo-Latin narrative poets as models. This is illustrated neatly in a scene from the epic *Columbus* (1715; Carrara 2006) by the Jesuit Ubertino Carrara. In Book 4, the hero encounters the nymph Poësis, who is sitting under a tree completely covered in lines from famous epic poems. Among them are lines from Homer's *Iliad* and *Odyssey*, Lucan's *De bello civili*, Statius's *Thebais*, and the *Argonautica* by Valerius Flaccus. Naturally, the highest branch belongs to Virgil's *Aeneid* (*Columbus* 4.73–119). The titles of such canonical works also account for the titles conventionally given to Neo-Latin hexameter poetry: the endings *-is* (as in *Aene-is*) and *-ias* (as in *Il-ias*) are the most popular choices. Apart from these classical epics, some poems from late antiquity (especially Claudian) and some renowned contemporary poets were also important points of reference. Ovid's *Metamorphoses*, on the other hand, were seldom imitated as a whole, probably due to its lack of transparent organization and the difficulty of distinguishing a main hero in the work, although short episodes in the style of the *Metamorphoses* can be found in very many poems. As far as didactic poetry is concerned, although the authority of Virgil was overwhelming (Ludwig 1989), Neo-Latin poets also wrote Lucretian philosophical texts (e.g., Benedict Stay's *Philosophia versibus tradita [Philosophy in Verse]*, 1744), astronomical poems resembling Manilius, or imitated the minor Roman didactic poets like Oppian, such as Pietro Angèli da Barga's *Ixeuticon* (*Poem on Bird-Catching*, 1566).

The predominant Virgilian model explains why almost all examples of Neo-Latin hexameter narrative work with a certain repertoire of stock elements. Every epic poem begins with a proem, and the majority imitate the syntactic structure of the first seven lines of the *Aeneid*. Similes offer the educated reader intertextual references to the classical literary tradition. Speeches often make up substantial parts of epic poems, and like Aeneas in Books 2 and 3 of the *Aeneid*, characters in Neo-Latin epic poems often take on the role of an authorial narrator. Storms at sea, divine assemblies (in heaven and in hell), *aristeiai* (i.e., outstanding performances in battle), and athletic games are included in most epic poems. In didactic poetry, one often finds imitations of famous scenes from the *Georgics*; for instance, the self-sufficient old man of Corycus in his garden (4.116–48) or the epyllion of the beekeeper Aristaeus (4.281–566; Hofmann 1993b).

The Poets and Their Audience

Courts, the church, and institutions of learning were three crucial, sometimes intimately connected and often overlapping, contexts for the production of Neo-Latin narrative poetry. Hoping for protection and patronage, those endowed with literary talent often sought to get close to a powerful person within these domains. The first group of writers, those based at or on the periphery of a court, often first made a name for themselves by writing shorter or didactic poems that allowed them to be admitted into high society; on admission, they then served that society's interests with their literary compositions, either by legitimating their patrons through panegyric, or by composing polemics attacking their patrons' enemies. The Turks' capture of Constantinople in 1453, or the Gunpowder Plot in England in 1605, to take just two high-profile examples, occasioned numerous epic poems that were strongly polemical in tone. The dominant Virgilian model often brought with it a tendency among writers to produce a "poetry of power." Virgil, as poet of the Roman principate, had glorified the Emperor Augustus and created a national epic for imperial Rome, as Cristoforo Landino (1424–98), for one, observed (Kallendorf 1995, 51). But the *Aeneid* was not just a vehicle of panegyric for Augustus: it also implied the Roman Empire's larger ideological purpose. Most Neo-Latin epic poems share this characteristic with the *Aeneid*: they "sing" about rulers and sovereigns, defend the power of religion (whether the Olympian pantheon or the Christian church) against its enemies, or celebrate the founding heroes of cities, countries, and religious orders. Those in power were interested in poetry that legitimized and glorified them, while poets gained the financial stability and social position necessary to write their works, thanks to such patrons.

Often, the writers of epic poems were clergymen: our second group of poets, who wrote in the interests of the church or order to which they belonged, rather than for more personal reasons. If a religious order wanted to promote the canonization of one of its members, for example, corresponding propaganda often included an epic poem about the prospective saint: Saint Ignatius Loyola (1491–1556) alone, who founded the Jesuit order, inspired several lengthy epic poems. The reason why so many epic poems about the Virgin Mary exist is because, in their fight against Protestantism, early modern Catholics intensified the expression of Marian piety through such literary representations.

The third group of epic poets were the scholars who taught at schools or universities and composed their poems for a number of different reasons. Antoine Garissoles (1587–1651), for example, was professor of theology at the Huguenot University of Montauban when he composed the twelve books of the *Adolphis* (1649) about the deeds of King Gustavus Adolphus in the Thirty Years' War (Braun 2007, 436–68). Johann Engerd, a quarrelsome professor of poetry at the University of Augsburg in Bavaria tried to win the favor of the prince-bishops of Trento, Italy, who were members of the Madruzzo family, through his epic poem *Madrucias* (1583), hoping that he would no longer have to rely on his teaching position for income. In the early modern classroom, we can observe how stock elements of hexameter narrative formed part of many curricula: in the Jesuit schools, for example. A Jesuit manuscript featuring an extensive collection of epic speeches has survived in the archives of the Pontifical Gregorian University in Rome (no. 3051): the speeches are organized according to topics (such as "lamentation of the death of a relative") and were probably meant to provide models and subject matter for the students' own similar literary compositions.

The question of a readership for Neo-Latin narrative poetry requires some careful disentangling, and is difficult to answer specifically. In many cases, the patrons from whom poets expected financial support were the primary addressees who often received lav-ishly worked presentation copies, still crucial to modern-day editing of these texts: the poets acknowledged these copies as versions of the text that they could publish in good faith, and that they believed would allow them to realize their various aims. Whether or not the individual recipients of these presentation copies actually engaged with the text in detail will have differed from person to person: a well-known connoisseur of art like Pope Leo X (1475–1521), for example, would probably have read the poem more carefully than another patron more invested in military pursuits.

The literary community to which the poet belonged would typically engage more deeply with his text than his patron. We can sometimes retrace discussions among the members of these communities through letters, as in the case of Sannazaro's epic *De partu Virginis* (*On the Virgin Birth*; Sannazaro 1988, 87–108), published in Naples in 1526. Somewhat more frequently, shorter poems survive in which the writer refers to a contemporary's epic poem, as Propertius did about Virgil in his second book of elegies (2.34.65–66): "Stand back, Roman and Greek writers! Something greater than the *Iliad* is being born." In a similar vein, the Roman Jesuit didactic poets often explicitly mention each other in their works (Haskell 2003, 178–244).

Print history gives us some indication of the reception and popularity of Neo-Latin epic. Some such poems were treated by contemporary scholars with as much intellectual seriousness as their ancient models, demonstrated by the publication of commentar-ies on Renaissance works resembling commentaries on Virgil and Ovid written around the same time: Jakob Spiegel's commentary on Riccardo Bartolini's *Austrias* (1516), which was printed in Strasburg in 1531, is just one example of this phenomenon. In other cases, epic poets acted as their own commentators, providing an exhaustive apparatus for their works explaining numerous historical and intertextual references. The num-ber of re-editions and translations is also a meaningful indicator of a work's reception, given the fact that some texts were published in many editions, reprints, and even unau-thorized versions within a very short period of time. One such case is that of Francisco Javier Alegre's *Alexandrias*, preserved in a first manuscript version of 1749–1751, pub-lished in 1773 under a pseudonym, officially printed in 1776 under the author's name (appended to Alegre's edition of Homer's *Iliad*), then published in a final version in 1783 (Kerson 1988). Other poems were not printed at all during the lifetime of their authors, but were (perhaps) included in larger collections of poetry much later: Henrik Harder's (1642–1683) epic about the siege of Copenhagen by the Swedish king Charles X Gustav in 1658–1659 (*Hafnia liberata* [*The Liberation of Copenhagen*]), for example, did not appear until Frederic Rostgaard published his collection *Deliciae quorundam poetarum Danorum* (*The Charms of a Number of Danish Poets*) in 1693 (Skafte Jensen 2007).

Numerous references to epic poems that were conceived, but never written or com-pleted, might prompt the observation that Neo-Latin epic poetry was a "genre of failure" from its very beginnings. Ever since Petrarch (1304–1374), who failed to complete his *Africa* in spite of the constant efforts described in his letters; or, indeed, ever since antiq-uity (for even the *Aeneid* was not completely finished), poets have repeatedly overex-tended themselves in their aim to write an epic poem and have ultimately had to admit failure. External circumstances often caused poets to abort their plans, too: William Alabaster (1567–1640) had intended to celebrate Elizabeth I in a twelve-book epic entitled *Elisaeis*, but abandoned the idea after his conversion to Catholicism in 1597 (Bradner 1940, 38). Francesco Filelfo (1398–1481) projected twenty-four books for the *Sphortias*, a poem about the Sforza in Milan, but only managed to write eight (Lippincott 1989, 418–22). Tito Strozzi faced a different problem when writing about the Este family in Ferrara in his poem *Borsias*: he was repeatedly confronted with the death of his heroes while working on the poem. This widespread failure to complete an epic poem is due both to the long period of time required to write a poem in many books, and to political and personal circumstances often subject to changes beyond the author's control.

THE CORPUS OF POEMS AND THE CURRENT STATE OF RESEARCH

The prestige that narrative hexameter poetry enjoyed helps explain the large number of such works. No comprehensive overview yet exists, but recent secondary studies of epic poems yield a corpus of about 450 texts; of these, only a few have been systematically studied, and no doubt more texts still wait in archives and libraries to be rediscovered. The concerted geographical focus of some of this research has expanded and, to some extent, distorted our sense of this corpus: France, for example, is represented more than almost any other country because of Braun's (2007) pioneering work. It is fair to say that even less research has been conducted into didactic poetry, where about 350 poems have been recently identified (Haskell 2003, 4).

That said, a growing interest in Neo-Latin literature over the past few decades has also led to an increased engagement with narrative poetry. Four decades ago, in the introduction to his edition of the *Borsias* by Tito Strozzi (left unfinished at Strozzi's death in 1505), Walther Ludwig was right to claim that Neo-Latin narrative poetry was as yet uncharted and for the most part unknown (Strozzi 1977, 10). Two later publications tried to hack a first rough path through the jungle. *CNLS* 2:24–45 dedicates the beginning of its overview of Neo-Latin poetry to heroic and dicactic poems, lamenting the fact that only a few texts are available in modern editions. Heinz Hofmann (2001), who wrote an introduction to Neo-Latin epic poetry featuring the largest collection of material so far, faced the same problem. After these two studies were published, several editions of epic poems were printed: Pierre Laurens produced a new edition of books 1–5 of Petrarch's *Africa* (left unfinished, as we have seen, at Petrarch's death in 1374; Petrarch 2006); Keith Sidwell edited Dermot O'Meara's *Ormonius* (1615) about the tenth Earl of Ormond, Thomas Butler (O'Meara 2011); and Eva von Contzen, Reinhold F. Glei, Wolfgang Polleichtner, and Michael Schulze Roberg published a new edition of Vida's *Christias* (Vida 2013), just to name three important examples. But more editions are needed to create a solid foundation for more comprehensive studies of developments across the genre. The influence of ancient epic poetry on Neo-Latin epic poetry has frequently been studied, while research into the reciprocal influence Neo-Latin epic poems had on each other is still very rare (Hofmann 1993a), and work on the mutual influence of vernacular epic poetry or vernacular prose and verse novels and Latin narrative poetry is even more sparse. Among the few scholars who have dealt with this latter topic is Nikolaus Thurn (2002, 46–51), who has shed considerable light on the influence of chivalric romance, Dante's *Divina Commedia*, as well as other Italian texts, on Ugolino Verino's (1438–1516) *Carlias*, an epic about Charlemagne. For didactic poetry, studies exist of the three most important geographical and institutional contexts in which such texts were written: Italy in the fifteenth and sixteenth centuries (Roellenbleck 1975); the French court of Louis XIV (Monreal 2010); and the Jesuit order (Haskell 2003). The single largest collection of texts is still the three volumes of François Oudin's *Poemata didascalica* (*Didactic Poems*, 1749, second edition 1813).

A problem that editors of ancient hexameter narrative do not face, but that sometimes renders the editing of Neo-Latin works particularly arduous, is the fact that several versions of one text may be available, to the extent that entire episodes and even books vary markedly. Rafael Landívar's *Rusticatio Mexicana* (*Mexican Country Life*), for instance, which contains elements of both heroic and didactic poetry, is in ten books in its 1781 Modena edition, while the 1782 Bologna edition, published in fifteen books, does not simply add an extra five books, but also organizes the text in a completely different way (Laird 2006).

The corpus of approximately 450 epic poems previously mentioned displays a very uneven chronological distribution: around forty are from the fifteenth century, 200 from the sixteenth, 150 from the seventeenth, and fifty from the eighteenth. After that, production ceased almost completely, with only ten poems known after 1800. The most productive phase was therefore during the last third of the sixteenth century. To provide—despite the limited space available—at least some insight into the material, I have here selected one distinctive text from each century, from the fourteenth through to the eighteenth centuries, as an example, too, of one subgenre of narrative hexameter poetry: these include poems about ancient history, mythology, modern history, and Christian religious matters, as well as supplements (i.e., continuations of existing narratives) and short epics (*epyllia*). For reasons of space, burlesque epic and translations of vernacular epic into Latin cannot be included. Although I will focus on heroic poems, I will also mention where possible any didactic poems written by the author under discussion.

THE FOURTEENTH CENTURY: ANCIENT HISTORY IN PETRARCH'S *AFRICA*

Petrarch is generally associated with the beginning of Neo-Latin poetry, and his *Africa* (Petrarch 2006) can be considered the first Neo-Latin epic. One should be aware, however, of the fact that this poem remained unique for a very long time, until Maffeo

Vegio (1407–1458) published a number of epics in the 1420s and 1430s, which include, among other topics, a sequel to the *Aeneid* and a poem about the Egyptian hermit and monk Antonius. *Africa* is an example of a relatively small subgroup of Neo-Latin epic poetry featuring events from ancient history as its subject matter; another, late example is the Jesuit Francisco Javier Alegre's *Alexandrias* (1773), which deals with Alexander the Great's siege of Tyre (Kerson 1988). Adapting an epic poem set in antiquity to a Christian mindset posed a special challenge, which Petrarch met in *Africa*, for instance, by combining in his character Jupiter exterior traits of the ancient father of the gods with the actual nature of the Christian God (Visser 2005).

Petrarch describes the end of the Second Punic War beginning with Scipio's voyage to Africa in 206 BCE up to the Battle of Zama in 202 BCE and the destruction of Carthage (for a summary, see Warner 2005, 20–22). The fact that the poem Petrarch started writing in 1338 remained incomplete is indicated by gaps in the text. The first two books are dominated by what Scipio's uncle and father tell him in his dreams, using, among other sources, Cicero's *Dream of Scipio* in the *De re publica* as a model. This narrative allows Petrarch to span a time-frame far wider than the five years his poem ostensibly describes. Petrarch's references to his own historical moment and even to the process of writing *Africa* was imitated by many epic poets in his wake. In the dream vision of the second book, for instance, Scipio learns from his father about a future poet (Petrarch) who will celebrate his deeds (*Africa* 2.441–43):

> *Cernere iam videor genitum post secula multa*
> *Finibus Etruscis iuvenem qui gesta renarret,*
> *Nate, tua et nobis veniat velut Ennius alter.*

> I already seem to see that after many centuries in the region of Tuscany a young man will be born, who will tell your story, my son, and who will be for us like a second Ennius.

Although Petrarch's patron, King Robert of Naples (1278–1343), had never actually laid eyes on the *Africa*, the poem was still the reason why Petrarch was crowned poet in May 1341 on Rome's Capitoline Hill—setting the example for the modern coronation of poets, popular throughout the early modern period and still palpable in the "poets laureate" of our own time. Petrarch includes this event in the dedication of the *Africa* (1.56–70): he states that he is not yet ready to write an historical epic about Robert himself, because he prefers to pick softer leaves from a lower part of the tree first (which recalls the image of Carrara's tree of epic poetry we discussed at the start of the chapter). Petrarch promises to celebrate his patron at some point in the future, deploying all his literary talents to win the laurel wreath on the Capitoline Hill a second time, but Robert's early death in 1343 prevented the promised poem from being written. Before his death, Virgil had ordered the unfinished *Aeneid* to be burned, and Petrarch followed his lead in this respect, too, in relation to the unfinished *Africa* (*Secretum* 3.77; Petrarch 2013). Neither poet was granted his last wish.

Examples from the Fifteenth Century: Basinio Basini and Ancient Mythology

Mythological epic poems form a subgroup that—like those based on ancient histori-cal subjects—is rather small, but the work of Basinio Basini, who was born near Parma then was admitted into the court of Leonello d'Este (1441–1450) at Ferrara, is one fruitful example. Dedicated to the avid hunter Leonello, Basini's epic poem *Meleagris* (1447–1448) recounts the Calydonian boar hunt Meleager led in three books, adding up to a total of 2,425 lines of poetry (Basini 2002). As a reward, Basini received a teaching position in Ferrara and undertook diplomatic missions for his patron. He later moved to the court of Sigismondo Malatesta in Rimini, for whom he composed his larger epic poem, *Hesperis* (completed in 1453), describing Sigismondo's battles against King Alfonso V of Aragon and his dreamlike journey westward (hence the title derived from *Hesperus*, the "evening star," or the "West") beyond the boundaries of the real world.

Basini's most important source of material and plot for his *Meleagris* was the section of Ovid's *Metamorphoses* dealing with the hunt (8.260–546). In his first book, Basini describes the backstory, then the preparations for and start of the hunt, which is con-cluded in the second book, followed by a banquet in the hunting lodge of the host, Oeneus. The third and final book represents the torments of Meleager and his love inter-est, the huntress Atalante, the quarrel over the hunting trophies, and finally Meleager's death. Basini displays considerable intertextual erudition by incorporating scenes from the *Iliad*, the *Odyssey*, the *Aeneid*, and Apollonius's *Argonautica* into his poem. The proem (1.1–5) demonstrates, however, that Virgil is his primary stylistic model: he clearly imitates the beginning of the *Aeneid* both syntactically and in other respects:

> *Musa, ducemne canes, dirae qui matris ob iram*
> *Funeream pestem domitus maioraque solvit*
> *Supplicia et leto fatalem mersus in ignem?*
> *Multaque ob insanum iuvenis male passus amorem*
> *Immeritas saevae poenas dedit ille Dianae.*

> Muse, will you sing of the hero, who, having vanquished deadly ruin, suffered too great a punishment when he was immersed in fated fire in death because of the anger of his cruel mother? Much did the young man badly suffer for his insane love, giving undeserved atonement to the irreconcilable Diana.

Basini also followed Virgil in writing both heroic and didactic poetry. His *Astronomica* (*Astronomical Matters*, 1455; Roellenbleck 1975, 42–48), one of the earliest Neo-Latin didactic poems, is dedicated to Sigismondo Malatesta, and the main sources for its content were Hyginus (first century CE) and Aratus (third/second century BCE).

At the beginning and end of the poem, Basini casts light on his literary career with a reference to his earlier epic poem, which significantly varies the well-worn trajectory of pastoral-didactic-epic career progression exemplified by Virgil. The so-called "pre-proem" of the *Aeneid* (now considered spurious, but influential in the Renaissance) established this convention of constructing a literary career: the "pre-proem" prefaces the *Aeneid*'s famous first line (*arma virumque cano*, "I sing of arms and a man") with references to Virgil's earlier bucolic and didactic poetry.

We return to the heroic poem: although the subject of the *Meleagris* is firmly anchored in the world of Greek mythology, Basini still finds a way to include his native country, Italy. In his final lines (3.933–36), Basini promises his patron Leonello d'Este that he will soon (*mox*) sing of his glory in a whole poem dedicated to him, but this promise was never fulfilled. Also, Basini mentions a certain Faunus among the hunting party who comes from Italy and whose group outshines all others. The author writes that their descendants, the Romans, will still be able to pride themselves on such ancestors (1.232–45). In this Virgilian fashion, Basini is able to refer to his current patrons, and potential future patrons, at key moments in his poem.

Examples from the Sixteenth Century: Contemporary History and Christianity

One of the largest subgroups of Neo-Latin epic consists of poems based on contemporary history. Princes and royal houses, military campaigns and sieges, exceptional military commanders or rulers are the subjects of countless works. The *Austrias* (1516) by Riccardo Bartolini from Perugia, which celebrates Emperor Maximilian I (1459–1519), is a useful example (Füssel 1987). Following a career in theology in his hometown, Bartolini came into contact with the German emperor's court on a mission as legate. After presenting a copy of his epic, he was permanently accepted into courtly society, where he remained until Maximilian's death.

The subject of the *Austrias*, which is still not available in a modern edition, is the War of the Succession of Landshut, which Maximilian was able to end in 1504 in the battle at Wenzenberg near Regensburg. The Virgilian elements abound. On the model of Virgil's "pious Aeneas" (*pius Aeneas*), Maximilian is called the "pious Austrian scion" (*Austriades pius*). Not only does he have to fight his mortal opponent, Ruprecht of the Palatinate, but also the immortal goddess Pallas, whom he had angered once by desecrating her temple (1.211–68; which we can compare with Aeneas's opponents, the mortal Turnus and the immortal goddess Juno). A prophecy by Jupiter, however, guarantees that the House of Habsburg is destined to rule the world (similar to Jupiter's prophecy about the rule of the Romans in Book 1 of the *Aeneid*). And again, as Virgil does in the

Aeneid, Bartolini expands the poem's focus beyond the immediate military action by also including a great number of subplots, predictions, embedded narratives, and similar devices. His poem centers on the House of Habsburg's rise to power and its greatness, its mission and its purpose. For a number of scenes, as well as to the *Aeneid*, Bartolini is also especially indebted to Homer's *Iliad*, which influences the poem's overall composition, as in the depiction of the games after Maximilian's triumph at the end of the poem, comparable in its position within the poem's structure to the funeral games for Patroclus in the *Iliad* (Klecker 1994–1995, 635–36).

The integration of Christianity was almost always a concern in Neo-Latin hexameter narrative. Some poets turned directly to the Bible epics of late antiquity by Iuvencus, Sedulius, or Arator, and many versified Bible paraphrases that draw on this tradition. A well-known example would be Nicodemus Frischlin's *Hebraeis* (1598), a history of the people of Israel up to the destruction of Jerusalem. The real challenge for humanists, however, was to create a Christian epic that would bear comparison with the *Aeneid* and, while adhering to generic conventions, would ideally outshine its model. An excellent example of this rich subgroup is Vida's *Christias*. Vida was born in Cremona and later studied in Rome, where he attracted attention early on through his verse: his didactic poem *Scacchia ludus* (*The Game of Chess*, 1527; Vida 1979) is still well known today, as are the three books of his *De arte poetica*. Pope Leo X commissioned him to compose a Christian epic, but did not live to see its completion. Vida was instead able to present the manuscript of the *Christias* to Pope Clement VII (1523–1534) in 1532, who made him bishop of Alba. This beautiful presentation copy still survives today in the Biblioteca Nazionale in Florence (Conventi Soppressi C 8, 1177). The success of the *Christias* was enormous: it was first printed in Cremona in 1535, numerous editions appeared across Europe within a few years, it was translated into several languages, and Bartolomeo Botta wrote an extensive commentary as early as 1569.

The *Christias* (Vida 2013) retells Christ's life and death in six books, but not in chronological order. Book 1 reports Christ's entrance to Jerusalem, the second recounts how he is taken prisoner and led before Pontius Pilate. The third and fourth books consist of long narrations from Joseph and John to Pilate, in which they tell him about Christ's childhood and his activities as a preacher. Book 5 describes the Passion, before Christ frees poor souls from the underworld in Book 6, then ascends to heaven and asks his Father to send the Holy Ghost. Vida emulates the *Aeneid* in many respects: Virgil cut Homer's number of books in half (the twenty-four books of the *Iliad* and the *Odyssey* become twelve books in the *Aeneid*), and Vida divides the twelve books of the *Aeneid* into six. He also imitates Virgil by dividing his poem into two halves and by creating resemblances between certain books in important positions: the first books of the two halves of the work closely correspond with each other, for instance. While Vida adopted the emotional subjectivity of Virgil's narrator, though, his combination of epic and biblical elements is original and distinctively his own.

The future greatness of papal Rome, of great importance to Vida personally, plays a prominent role in the *Christias*. God himself predicts it (6.662–76) in imitation of the prophecy of the great men in Rome's future in Book 6 of the *Aeneid*. Jesus says that the center of Christendom will be transferred from Jerusalem to a city far away (1.580 *longe alia . . . urbe*), namely, Rome. While praising Catholic Rome, by contrast Vida sharply criticizes the followers of the Protestant Reformation (1.919–22; Vida 2009).

> *Si qua tamen paulatim annis labentibus aetas*
> *decolor inficiet mores versisque nepotes*
> *degeneres surgent studiis, per dura laboresque*
> *exercens lapsam revocabo in pristina gentem.*

And if in the course of years a lesser age will coarsen men's morals, if a degenerate progeny turns away from such pursuits, then I will impose harsh labors upon that fallen race and so recall them to their earlier piety.

Examples from the Seventeenth Century: Supplements

I now turn to supplements, a subgroup of Neo-Latin epics that entertain a much closer relationship with their ancient models than the texts discussed so far. Supplements were composed especially for the *Aeneid*, but also for other epic poems, and served to close supposed "gaps" (as at the end of Lucan's incomplete *De bello civili*) or to round off an unsatisfactory ending (as with the *Aeneid* itself—see further below). The earliest example, Maffeo Vegio's additional thirteenth book of the *Aeneid* (1428), has already been mentioned. Thomas May's seven-book supplement to Lucan, published in 1639 and extending the plot of the *De bello civili* up to Caesar's death, also achieved a fair degree of popularity (May 2005). A number of didactic poems were composed to cover subject matter left out of classical works. Giovanni Pontano's *Urania sive de stellis* (*Urania, or The Stars*; written between 1475 and 1502), for example, supplemented five books on astronomical issues that were not treated by Manilius's *Astronomica* (*Astronomical Matters*; first century CE). Pontano's source was Firmicus Maternus, who wrote about astrology in the fourth century CE. One of the most famous Neo-Latin didactic poems, René Rapin's *Horti* (*Gardens*, 1665; Monreal 2010, 23–188) accomplishes in four books what Virgil only adumbrates in *Georgics* 4.116–48: garden care. The model of the *Georgics* is manifest in many details, but also in the number of four books itself, here dedicated to flowers, woods, water features, and orchard cultivation, respectively.

In 1698, C. Simonet de Villeneuve published his *Supplement to the Aeneid* (*Supplementum ad Aeneida*; Oertel 2001), which adds 827 lines to the end of Virgil's epic. The dark ending of the *Aeneid* with Aeneas's merciless killing of his arch-enemy, Turnus, and no clear resolution of the story, has always left readers puzzled. In Villeneuve's addition, Aeneas contemplates what to do with the dead body and decides to return it to Turnus's people. This is followed by peace negotiations with King Latinus, who promised his daughter, Lavinia, to Aeneas in *Aeneid* 7, but was then drawn into war by Turnus.

Now, in the supplement, Latinus is happy to give Lavinia to Aeneas in a magnificent wedding celebration. After some military intermezzi, the ending of the supplement shows us Aeneas busy rebuilding his cities, Laurentum and Lavinium, when he receives the report that Dido's sister, Anna, has hurled herself into the nearby river, Numicus (compare with Ovid's *Fasti* 3.599–660 and Silius Italicus's *Punica* 8.65–201). When Aeneas arrives there, he is betrayed by one of his companions and himself drowns in the river. The supplement ends with Aeneas being set among the stars, as alluded to by a number of ancient sources.

Not much is known about de Villeneuve. He served at the court of Duke Philippe of Orléans (1640–1701) and dedicated his poem to the duke's son, Philippe of Chartres, who succeeded his father in 1701. De Villeneuve commemorated his own name in a remarkable part of his supplement: shortly before the wedding celebration begins, King Latinus presents Aeneas's son, Ascanius, with a book containing the annals of his people, including future events. This book asserts that at some point, a certain Virgil will sing about the fight between Aeneas and Turnus, but that the events after Turnus's death will be sung about by "Villanova," the Latinized name of the author (*Supplementum* 215). These kinds of self-references are reminiscent of Petrarch's *Africa*, where the author similarly attempted to immortalize his name. Literary history places de Villeneuve's supplement within the context of the quarrel of the Ancients and the Moderns, as he criticizes Virgil in his preface for having left out quite an amount of material in the *Aeneid*, which it is now his task to supply. Technically speaking, de Villeneuve closes the gap between the end of the *Aeneid* and the episode about Anna in the *Fasti* of Ovid and the *Punica* of Silius Italicus.

An Example from the Eighteenth Century: Iturriaga's Epyllion *Californias*

Let us leave Europe and turn to a Mexican Jesuit priest. José Mariano de Iturriaga (1717–1787) joined the Society of Jesus in 1733 in Mexico City. His short epic, *Californias*, published in 1740, depicts the Jesuits' activities as missionaries in California (Iturriaga 1979). The hero of this epyllion of 804 lines is Juan María de Salvatierra (1648–1717), who worked as a missionary in Mexico before founding the first Jesuit settlement in California.

At the beginning of the poem, Salvatierra is taken up to heaven, and an angel shows him California, which is still firmly in the hands of the Devil, causing Salvatierra to pity its inhabitants. God calls an assembly in heaven, and following advice from Mary, its members then decide to entrust the Jesuit priest with the duty of converting the region. Meanwhile the Devil gathers all his forces to fight against the Society of Jesus. Salvatierra only manages to convince the Viceroy of New Spain (of which California was a part at the time) of his undertaking after the viceroy is ordered in a dream to give his consent. On his travels the priest endures a storm at sea, but finally lands safely in California, where he receives a warm welcome.

The poem glorifies the Jesuit order and its achievements in the New World. The praise for the order that Mary articulates in God's presence is not just panegyric, but also legitimizes and defends the activities of the Society. Not least because of its missionary activities, the order faced an increasing number of difficulties in Spain in the middle of the eighteenth century, before Pope Clement XIV finally suppressed it in 1773: written amidst this tumult, the *Californias*, in its relentless exposure of the viceroy's faulty decisions, becomes a political statement about the conflict between the Jesuit order and the Spanish government.

Given the fact that many elements of the *Californias*, such as the storm and the prophecies uttered during an assembly of the gods, are also essential components of the first book of the *Aeneid*, it seems likely that Iturriaga had originally planned to continue the poem in several more books. He also added three elegiac couplets at the end that classify what he wrote so far as an early work, a labor that old age (*senecta gravis*) now prevented him from completing. Like so many other Neo-Latin epic works, the *Californias* was apparently too ambitious in its scope to be completed during its author's lifetime.

Suggested Reading

An initial general introduction is provided by *CNLS* 2:24–45, while Hofmann (2001) presents more material. Recommended overviews of specific subgroups of heroic and didactic writing include: epic poetry about Columbus (Hofmann 1993a), the narrative poetry of the courts of Northern Italy in the fifteenth century (Lippincott 1989), and the Christian epic poetry of sixteenth-century Italy (Faini 2008–2010). Haskell (2003) discusses Jesuit didactic poetry; Monreal (2010) didactic poetry at the court of Louis XIV. Selected texts can be found in the anthology by Perosa and Sparrow (1979: 4–8 are about Petrarch; 154–58 about Sannazaro; 238–41 about Fracastoro; 255–59 about Vida). Some epic poems, especially from the early Italian Renaissance, have been published in the *I Tatti* series of Harvard University Press; other editions have also recently been printed as part of the series *Bochumer Altertumswissenschaftliches Colloquium*.

[*Translated from the German by Katharina Xenia Epstein.*]

References

Basini, Basinio. 2002. *Die* Meleagris *des Basinio Basini.* Edited and translated by Andreas Berger. Trier: Wissenschaftlicher Verlag Trier.

Bradner, Leicester. 1940. *Musae Anglicanae: A History of Anglo-Latin Poetry 1500–1925.* New York: Modern Language Association of America.

Braun, Ludwig. 2007. *Ancilla Calliopeae: Ein Repertorium der neulateinischen Epik Frankreichs (1500–1700)*. Leiden: Brill.

Carrara, Ubertino. 2006. *Columbus: Carmen epicum (1715)*. Edited and translated by Florian Schaffenrath. Berlin: Weidler.

Faini, Marco. 2008–10. "Heroic Martyrdom Unsung. Some Reflections on the Tradition of Christian Epic in Renaissance Italy and the European Context." *Wolfenbütteler Renaissance-Mitteilungen* 32:135–52.

Fracastoro, Girolamo. 2011. *La Syphilis ou le mal français: Syphilis sive morbus gallicus*. Edited and translated by Jacqueline Vons. Paris: Belles Lettres.

Füssel, Stephan. 1987. *Riccardus Bartholinus Perusinus: Humanistische Panegyrik am Hofe Maximilians I*. Baden-Baden: Koerner.

Haskell, Yasmin. 2003. *Loyola's Bees: Ideology and Industry in Jesuit Latin Didactic Poetry*. Oxford: Oxford University Press.

Hofmann, Heinz. 1993a. "*Adveniat tandem Typhis qui detegat orbes*: Columbus in Neo-Latin Epic Poetry." In *European Images of the Americas and the Classical Tradition*, edited by Wolfgang Haase and Meyer Reinhold, 420–656. Berlin: De Gruyter.

———. 1993b. "Variations on an Ending: Scipio, Aristaeus, and the Dream of Columbus." *Res publica litterarum* 16:227–38.

———. 2001. "Von Africa über Bethlehem nach America: Das Epos in der neulateinischen Literatur." In *Von Göttern und Menschen erzählen: Formkonstanzen und Funktionswandel vormoderner Epik*, edited by Jörg Rüpke, 130–82. Stuttgart: Steiner.

Iturriaga, José M. de. 1979. *La Californiada*. Edited and translated by Alfonso Castro Pallares. Mexico City: Universidad Nacional Autónoma de México.

Kallendorf, Craig. 1995. "From Virgil to Vida: The *Poeta Theologus* in Italian Renaissance Commentary." *Journal of the History of Ideas* 56:41–62.

Kerson, Arnold. 1988. "Francisco Javier Alegre: A Mexican Latinist of the Eighteenth Century." *Nova Tellus* 6:221–33.

Klecker, Elisabeth. 1994–95. "Kaiser Maximilians Homer." *Wiener Studien* 107–8:613–37.

Laird, Andrew. 2006. *The Epic of America: An Introduction to Rafael Landívar and the* Rusticatio Mexicana. London: Duckworth.

Lippincott, Kristen. 1989. "The Neo-Latin Historical Epics of the North Italian Courts: An Examination of 'Courtly Culture' in the Fifteenth Century." *Renaissance Studies* 3:415–28.

Ludwig, Walther. 1989. "Neulateinische Lehrgedichte und Vergils *Georgica*." In *Litterae Neolatinae: Schriften zur neulateinischen Literatur*, edited by Ludwig Braun, 100–27. Munich: Fink.

May, Thomas. 2005. *Das* Supplementum Lucani. Edited and translated by Birger Backhaus. Trier: Wissenschaftlicher Verlag Trier.

Monreal, Ruth. 2010. *Die* Hortorum libri IV *von René Rapin S.J. und die* Plantarum libri VI *von Abraham Cowley: Zwei lateinische Dichtungen des 17. Jahrhunderts*. Berlin: De Gruyter.

Oertel, Hans-Ludwig. 2001. *Die Aeneissupplemente des Jan van Foreest und des C. Simonet de Villeneuve*. Hildesheim: Olms.

O'Meara, Dermot. 2011. *The Tipperary Hero: Dermot O'Meara's Ormonius (1615)*. Edited and translated by David Edwards and Keith Sidwell. Turnhout: Brepols.

Perosa, Alessandro, and John Sparrow, eds. 1979. *Renaissance Latin Verse: An Anthology*. Chapel Hill: University of North Carolina Press.

Petrarch, Francesco. 2006. *L'Afrique*. Vol. 1. Edited and translated by Pierre Laurens. Paris: Belles Lettres.

———. 2013. *Secretum meum: Mein Geheimnis*. Edited and translated by Bernhard Huss and Gerhard Regn. 2nd ed. Mainz: Dieterich.

Roellenbleck, Georg. 1975. *Das epische Lehrgedicht Italiens im fünfzehnten und sechzehnten Jahrhundert*. Munich: Fink.

Sannazaro, Jacopo. 1988. *De partu Virginis*. Edited by Charles Fantazzi and Alessandro Perosa. Florence: Olschki.

Skafte Jensen, Minna. 2007. "Treacherous Danes or Greedy Swedes? Two Latin Epics of the 17th Century." In *Miraculum eruditionis: Neo-Latin Studies in Honour of Hans Helander*, edited by Maria Berggren and Christer Henriksén, 81–100. Uppsala: Uppsala Universitet.

Strozzi, Tito. 1977. *Die* Borsias *des Tito Strozzi*. Edited by Walther Ludwig. Munich: Fink.

Thurn, Nikolaus. 2002. *Kommentar zur* Carlias *des Ugolino Verino*. Munich: Fink.

Vida, Marco G. 1976. *The* De arte poetica *of Marco Girolamo Vida*. Edited and translated by Ralph G. Williams. New York: Columbia University Press.

———. 1979. *Schachspiel der Götter: Scacchia Ludus*. Edited by Walther Ludwig and translated by Johann J. I. Hoffmann. Zurich: Artemis.

———. 2009. *Christiad*. Translated by James Gardner. Cambridge: Harvard University Press.

———. 2013. *Christias*. 2 vols. Edited by Eva von Contzen, Reinhold F. Glei, Wolfgang Polleichtner, and Michael Schulze Roberg. Trier: Wissenschaftlicher Verlag Trier.

Visser, Tamara. 2005. *Antike und Christentum in Petrarcas* Africa. Tübingen: Narr.

Warner, J. Christopher. 2005. *The Augustinian Epic: Petrarch to Milton*. Ann Arbor: University of Michigan Press.

CHAPTER 5

···

EPIGRAM AND
OCCASIONAL POETRY

···

DAVID MONEY

A perfect woman; the marriage fixed in "super-glue"; the soldier who died in his chair; the curious incident of the dog which did not bark: read on, to meet them all, and more. Welcome to the people's Latin verse. Many thousands wrote epigrams, and read them; good, bad, and indifferent, they are almost unavoidable. The elegiac couplet is by far the most popular form; others, such as the hendecasyllable, regularly appear. Martial, Catullus, the *Greek Anthology* are the principal models. It was always difficult to define an epigram precisely; you know one when you see it: a very short work, ideally making a quick, effective point. That most influential of commentators, Julius Caesar Scaliger (1484–1558), took a broad view of the genre; it could include most topics and methods, with an attempt at *argutia* ("sharpness; wit") being highly desirable (Beer, Enenkel, and Rijser 2009, 16–22). The Dutch scholar and theologian Gerardus Vossius (1577–1649) also discussed the matter. Brevity can be a limitation, too; even some of the most memorable ancient epigrams are open to objections (Money 2012, 45). Length can be stretched (how far? opinions differ), and there is obvious overlapping with, for example, the (longer) love elegy. The third of the Dutch poet Johannes Secundus's famous *Basia* (*Kisses*, 1539) might well, at six lines, be called an epigram, and a very fine one, too. Liminary verses (poems "on the threshold," introducing a book) are a significant sub-genre, "a characteristic and specific literary phenomenon of humanism" (Binns 1990, 165). They could preface all kinds of books—thus allowing poetry to intrude into the realms of prose—and place Latin alongside the vernacular.

Most of the big names of Renaissance poetry engaged with the genre, to varying degrees. Angelo Poliziano (1454–94) and Giovanni Pontano (1429–1503) were prolific in this, as in other forms. Ludvig Holberg (1684–1754), revered in Norway and Denmark, was a keen epigram-writer, as well as Latin novelist and vernacular playwright. Thomas More's *Epigrammata* (*Epigrams*, 1518) initially brought him more attention abroad than his *Utopia*; they were an important part of his self-promotion, an "inherently social" genre with addressees and audience a vital part of the process

(McCutcheon 2003, 353); an antisocial one too, stirring up quarrels. Thomas More versus the French humanist Germain de Brie (1490–1538) was one such battle, but there were many others, from the start: "the fifteenth-century humanist was an irascible being, and the general run of Latin epigrams then written savor more of Martial than the Anthology" (Hutton 1935, 43). There was disagreement about obscenity: can a Christian follow the ancients there? Religious poets fought back in large numbers, pouring out verse on pious themes. Teachers strove to inculcate the less noxious forms of wit; Jesuit education on the Continent gave epigrams an honored role, as did large Protestant schools in England and elsewhere. Printed collections, such as *Lusus Westmonasterienses* (*Westminster* [*School*] *Games*, 1730–50), could showcase precocious skills. Numerous anthologies reprinted major poets of all nations. My intention here is to widen the focus, including some of the "little people" too, as representatives of a very widespread literary culture.

A typical epigram-book was a mixed bag. In one mid–seventeenth-century Catholic example, we can find some side-splitting casual sexism: woman (*mulier*), more mule than *mollis* ("gentle"), eh? Ho, ho. What is a heretic poet like? *Obscaenus, tumidus, protervus, audax* ("filthy, puffed-up, shameless, impudent"); and a grudging admission that Dutch Protestant poetry can be good, even if *Batava fides* ("Dutch faith") is not (Lindanus 1656). Otherwise combative epigrammatists can also surprise readers with intensity of feeling: More's collection ends with an unusually personal poem on his own marriages, indelicate perhaps, and perhaps profound (McCutcheon 2003, 359). Although, like all early modern Neo-Latin, writing epigrams was primarily a male activity, some learned women could and did participate as readers, writers, and recipients of praise. Sometimes the commendatory verses could outweigh the woman's own work, as in an eighteenth-century edition of Tarquinia Molza, with four of her Latin epigrams (Molza 1750, 85–86), and a few Italian ones, alongside a flood of tributes (Molza 1750, 26–35, 87–92). An Englishwoman in Prague, Elizabeth Weston, was prolific in elegiacs herself, her skills celebrated by sympathetic male circles (Weston 2000, 376–437).

Epigram writing spread wherever Latin did. In North America, the early colonist Peter Bulkeley (1583–1659) left short elegiac poems on an earthquake, on his birthday, on his old age, and an epitaph for John Cotton, Puritan divine, formerly vicar of Boston, England, and a founder of its American namesake (Kaiser 1984, 24–26). Michael Wigglesworth (1631–1705) wrote on his own misery with "simple and direct art": *Ira premit, peccata gravant, afflictio frangit* / . . . *Obruor adversis: succedunt imbribus imbres,* / *Meque simul feriunt ventus et unda minax* ("Anger oppresses me, sins weigh me down, affliction breaks me . . . I am overwhelmed by adversities, rainstorms come one upon another, and the wind and menacing wave strike me together"; Kaiser 1984, 29–31): a bleak picture of a man dismayed by metaphorical, and no doubt also literal, hurricanes of misfortune. Its despairing nobility is reminiscent of Greek tragedy, as in the great chorus of Sophocles's *Oedipus at Colonus* (ll. 1211–48), with its comparison of man to a coast tormented by wind and wave. Samuel Sewall (1652–1730) was a judge at the notorious trials of alleged witches at Salem, Massachusetts, in 1692, a distinction he lived long enough to regret; his letterbook preserves scraps of Latin verse penned on numerous occasions, more impressive perhaps in quantity than quality, testimony to his facility in rapid composition, and the naturalness of the medium for him (Kaiser 1984, 38–39).

How should it be done? Liminary verses by Walter Hawghe to Bishop John Parkhurst's *Ludicra* (*Amusements*, 1573) suggest some useful aims: use familiar vocabulary for clarity (*perspicuum*), seek to be amusing (*facetum*): *virtus praecipua est in hoc voluptas* ("pleasure is the chief virtue in this business"; Binns 1990, 32). This was not confined to books. Painted on a pillar of the south aisle in Norwich cathedral, near to the organ, is this distich in memory of an organist, William Inglott: *Non digitis Inglotte tuis terrestria tangis / Tangis nunc digitis organa celsa poli* ("Your fingers, Inglott, do not touch earthly things, you now touch with your fingers the high organs of heaven"). A visitor to most old churches will observe some Latin (and sometimes Neo-Latin verse), on brass or stone. At St. Bartholomew's, Corsham, Wiltshire, is a plain tablet. The lettering, all capitals, neat but not fancy, suggests a local stonecutter: *Quae per femineum sparsa est perfectio sexum / Lector in hac una tota sepulta iacet* ("The perfection that is scattered through the female sex, reader, is all buried here in this one woman"). More lines would dilute the effect. How, exactly, was she perfect? Better not to know. The prose below fills twice the space, with necessary but dry information: *Edw[ardus] Rede ar[miger] hoc distichon in memoriam Annae uxoris suae ex inclyta familia Baynardorum de Lecham oriundae hic incidi curavit, quae obiit August[i] 23 1615* ("Edward Rede, bearer of [a coat of] arms arranged for this couplet to be carved here in memory of his wife Anne, from the celebrated family of the Baynards of [Old] Lackham [House], who died on August 23, 1615"). Who cares for the Baynards now, except possibly their descendants? But Edward's versified cry of pain can still pierce the heart.

To Bark or Not to Bark? A Canine Case-Study

How should one assess an epigram, judge its neatness? Interpretations can be very subjective. One may miss the point, or get it, but find it flat. A poem may work for you, but not for me. I would like to look in detail at an epigram which seems to me to work. It is very short: one elegiac couplet, eleven words. The author is a Frenchman in Rome, Joachim Du Bellay (1522–1560; McFarlane 1980, 34):

> *Latratu fures excepi, mutus amantes:*
> *Sic placui domino, sic placui dominae.*

> I received thieves with barking, but lovers in silence; that's how I pleased my master—and that's how I pleased my mistress.

Neatness of form is the first thing to notice: besides the very obvious repetition in the second line, the first line has a carefully controlled economy of words, relying on the single verb in the center to be understood with both ends of the line, in subtly different senses. In the perfect tense, the verb *excipio* produces three long syllables, a weighty central word. Its meaning is fairly fluid. It can mean "catch" (appropriately for the thieves); but also "make an exception of," as the dog seems to do in the case of lovers favored by its mistress. The five-word hexameter could seem quite heavy (*latratu* is three long syllables, like *excepi*; and *fures*, which is two longs), but gains a lightness of touch from this concision. And while, in a longer poem, the facility with which the pentameter can fall into two matching dactylic halves sometimes seems too facile a trick, it is ideally suited to so short an epigram. Each half of the line is virtually identical, differing only in the gender of the noun. But how much difference is there in the sense! Thoroughly correct canine behavior on the one paw; on the other, the silent dog is complicit in adultery.

So the epigram is not so innocent or simple, not just a commemoration of a virtuous and useful creature. We feel that frisson of impropriety that is at the heart of so much of the best epigram writing. We are encouraged to enjoy it: to sympathize with the dog, to congratulate it for managing to satisfy all parties, except the unworthy thieves. But are not the lovers (plural) just as unworthy? Is it not a betrayal of his master to admit them so easily? The author appears to be taking rather a lax moral position, condoning the behavior of the dog, and by implication, also the mistress. But perhaps he is merely luring the reader into such a response, leaving us to question ourselves afterwards. Which of these participants do we really sympathize with? Is the master in fact only concerned with his wealth, in which case the dog is doing all the guarding required: and the master deserves an unfaithful wife? And how close is the poet to the action? Does he not only sympathize with the *amantes*, but become one of them, in a situation familiar to any reader of the ancient elegists? And, as the lover often has to placate a servant to get access to a mistress (as in Ovid, *Amores* 2.2, for example), so here he must convince the dog that he falls into the category of lover rather than thief. The mistress is *domina* in more than one sense.

In a situation rich with dramatic ambiguities, what do we really know from these two lines? We read that there are lovers, plural, which there do not have to be, for metrical reasons, as *amantem* (singular) would have fitted just as well. The plural makes a neater verbal parallel to *fures* (thieves). And it makes a difference, perhaps, to our attitude to the characters. The dog does not have to deal only with a single, long-term lover, but a whole sequence of them. One misplaced bark, and his mistress might be lost. What do we know of the dog? Is the dog male or female? Male, the masculine adjective *mutus* reveals; and this is required by the meter, if the line is to end with a word like *amantes*, starting with a vowel. Does this gender give the dog a special affinity with his mistress, as another, more innocent, *amans*; and a masculine rigor in standing up to intruders on his master's behalf? Probably it is mainly a matter of the poet's convenience, as making a female dog *muta* would create difficulties in choosing the right word to follow it. *Mitis* ("gentle") might have done, though, and preserved another ambiguity (as that form could be either gender).

Are we so sure that we have the sense the right way around: the master's money and the wife's lovers? That would be the most obvious reading, certainly in a sixteenth-century context. But it is quite reasonable for a wife to fear thieves; and also for a master to have lovers creeping around the house (of either sex—and *amantes* is ambiguous in gender:

the Latin is sufficiently flexible to be interpreted as "Thus [silently] I pleased the master, thus [barking] I pleased the mistress"), with added confusion for the dog. Some things a translator must probably pin down, but others can be left ambiguous; here is an English version of Du Bellay's poem, printed in the collection *Sales epigrammatum* (*The Wit of Epigrams*, 1663) edited by James Wright (McFarlane 1980, 35): "The Lover I let passe, the Thief did seize; / So I both Master did, and Mistresse please." This version in fact relies on a chiasmus, to get the more "obvious" reading, "Lover"/"Mistresse" and "Thief"/"Master": if we read it without a chiasmus, we come away with the alternative interpretation. *Excepi* becomes two verbs in English here; and the order of the first line is inverted to allow the vigorous rhyme "seize"/"please." An English line finds it more difficult to handle the repetition, and "did" may appear awkward. But perhaps it is worth making the reader wait for the word "please," and making us think about whether the dog "did" really do so. The master is only pleased while he remains in ignorance of the full story.

The title of Wright's anthology employs a key word for the epigram, *sal* ("salt," literally, but "wit" in this sense), not quite definable, but recognizable when it is there, and when it is not, both in people and in poems (compare the *mica salis*—"grain of salt"—of a girl's attractiveness in Catullus 86, l. 4). Judgements of both will differ: one person's deliciously biting wit can be over-salted, to another's taste, and virtually inedible. For me, at least, Du Bellay judges the salt just right in this little epigram. It is not only a matter of being clever, neat, and amusing: thought-provoking, too, and potentially problematic. Ambiguities intended by the author, or open to creation by a reader, are part of the problem, and of the charm. The more one looks, the more uncertainties there are. Are the dog's master and mistress necessarily husband and wife? Some other family relationship, father and daughter, for example, or son and mother, would offer a different dynamic, without the tension of adultery, though with other reasons for dog and human to tread carefully. And the dog's situation may not be enviable, in any scenario: the moment the master finds out that he has been letting in lovers, he is in for a beating, or removal as a guard dog; while as soon as he makes the mistake of barking at a lover and risking his mistress's safety, he may find that poison in his food prevents recurring embarrassment. His successful pleasing, we may note, is in the perfect tense; the title of the epigram is *Epitaphium cuiusdam canis* (*The Epitaph of a Certain* [*unnamed*] *Dog*). What we do not know, may in fact be the crux of the story. Did the dog die of natural causes? Many Neo-Latin epitaphs were actually put up on tombs, or could have been. This, however, falls into the genre of the impossible epitaph: its writing condemns the master to ridicule, the mistress to worse. So only an enemy could propose its erection over the grave of a real dog. Most likely, of course, it was all a fiction; but the existence of possible realities adds depth to the reading of a poem that is extremely short, yet by no means as slight as it may at first appear.

There is further artificiality in giving a voice to the dog, which cannot think and speak in quite this way, in any language, but which can indeed make a noise, or refrain from doing so, an ability central to this epigram. One may compare a tiny vernacular poem, from two centuries later, Alexander Pope's *Epigram: Engraved on the Collar of a Dog Which I Gave to His Royal Highness*: "I am his Highness' Dog at Kew; / Pray tell me Sir, whose Dog are you?" (Pope 1963, 826). If dogs could only speak and answer, this is a perfectly civil question, from one dog to another. When a human reads the collar, it becomes something very different, a sharp critique of the reader's role in society: Whose dog, metaphorically speaking, am I, after all? Am I a supporter of the Prince of Wales ("His Highness"), who is on bad terms with the king? A balancing act as clever as that of Du Bellay's dog may be required, in order to please everyone whose power can make or mar a career. Or is one, like the poet, perhaps, independent enough to be no one's dog, just at the moment? Pope's little couplet is suitable for a real collar, while Du Bellay's is not fit for a real tomb; it can be enjoyed on a trivial level, and also seen to have political or philosophical implications. Du Bellay, too, may make us think about the behavior of humans in society: are courtiers a little like this dog, always trying to please, in a dangerous world of shifting and incompatible priorities?

We saw with Du Bellay's dog that sexual matters can be raised in a fairly subtle way, becoming more shocking the more one considers the implications. But there is also a strong strain of crudity in the Neo-Latin epigram, following in the classical tradition and taking advantage of the freedom of a "learned" language to use obscenities (though, as we have seen, not without controversy). This can sometimes involve clever wordplay, as in an epigram of another sixteenth-century Frenchman, Théodore de Bèze, where a girlfriend responds to the poet's various endearments, including the diminutive *corculum* ("little heart"), with a fresh diminutive of her own: *Salve, inquit, mea mentula* ("Hello, she said, my little mind")—except that *mentula*, we know, is not a diminutive for "mind" but a popular obscenity indicating the penis (Summers 2001, 272). How clever of the girl to refer to him by the part that she really appreciates. Poems of this sort are better seen as literary jokes, than as a reflection of the real linguistic skills of poets' girlfriends; one may speculate that most of the educated women of the time who were capable of getting the joke would not have liked it much. In his later life as a leading Protestant theologian, de Bèze found it necessary to defend such youthful exuberance (Summers 2001, xxviii–xxxiv). It is interesting to find the very same *corculum/mentula* joke in a Latin writer active into the twenty-first century (whether arrived at independently, or in conscious or unconscious echo of the earlier example), the Austrian Gerd Allesch; he makes quite neatly, in three lines of iambics, the point that de Bèze takes eight hendecasyllables to expound. Here is the modern poet (Allesch 2000, 43): *Nuper saluto sic meam puellulam: / "sis salva, mens mea atque corculum meum!" / et illa: "have, meum cor atque mentula!"* ("Here's how I recently greeted my little girl, 'hello, my mind and little heart', and she replied 'hi, my heart and little mind/penis' "): a simple chiasmus of the diminutives (*cor/corculum; mens/mentula*), and a nice little risqué joke.

FAT BOOKS AND THIN BOOKS

One of the biggest names in the culture of the early modern epigram was John Owen, or Audoenus (ca. 1563/4–1622?), a schoolmaster from Wales. He is arguably the most influential writer Wales has ever produced, though little known today. Unlike such other major figures as More, Erasmus, Secundus, or Poliziano, he concentrated solely on the epigram. He worked within a flourishing (Latin and vernacular) British tradition, but transcended it to achieve international popularity, foreign editions outnumbering British by three to one (Poole-Wilson 1989). His works traveled widely, under many aliases or variant spellings, and despite Catholic prohibitions: in Spanish translation even "Ivan Oven"—who sounds as if he ought to have presented a cookery show in the old Eastern bloc—or the rather more Hispanic "Juan Ouen." Ironically, or perhaps appropriately, given the fondness of Neo-Latin for recycling and refashioning, one of Owen's best-known lines, *Tempora mutantur, nos et mutamur in illis* ("Times are changed, and we are changed with them") appears not to be original to him. Owen borrowed ideas, like almost everyone; his own impact on other, more local, epigram-writers was considerable. So prolific an author could not be consistent; he was admired and translated in Germany and France, some called him a second Martial, but *perperam* ("wrongly"), according to his scholarly French editor Renouard, *multa enim profert aut mediocria, aut etiam lectu parum digna* ("for he offers much that is mediocre or even not worth reading"; Owen 1794, v). Who does not, among epigrammatists of all ages? Still, it was worth his editor's while to prepare the neat, fat little volume, signing his preface *scribebam Parisiis, die 20 mensis florealis, anno reipublicae secundo* ("written at Paris, 20 Floréal, Year Two of the Republic"; Owen 1794, xii). The Flowery month of spring, the Terror at its height: time could still be found for Owen.

Printed collections of epigrams could fit the pocket, or the gentleman's study. They could get quite fat (even if in tiny print) as the "centuries" of short poems marched on, line by line, page by page, quip by clop. Some made a point of seeking relief, not only in short verses but in mini-volumes. *Cum fieri soleant ingentes carminum acervi, / Miraris, quod sim tam brevis? opto legi* ("Since poems usually come in great heaps, are you surprised I'm so short? I'd like to be read"): thus the little book to the reader, *Libellus ad lectorem*, speaking through the pupil of the Cologne Jesuit gymnasium, Arnold Birckman (*Poemata varia* 1631, 2). *Conviva est lector* ("the reader is a dinner-guest"), asserts his fellow-student Jacobus von Rottkirchen: *Non omnes acidis gaudent, non dulcibus omnes, / Dulcia multa coci, multa coquunt acida* ("not everyone likes sharp tastes, not everyone likes sweets; cooks prepare many sweets and many sour dishes"; *Poemata varia* 1631, 3). Small is beautiful, if that's the sort of thing you like. And they do mean small: the volume of *Various Poems* (*Poemata varia*) is no bigger than twelve by seven centimeters, forty-eight pages, thin enough for any pocket, at about half a centimeter, even bound cheaply but neatly in marbled boards. The space is sufficient to show off many of the skills of Jesuit education, with anagrams and emblems to the fore.

As in the case of church monuments, emblem books combined the literary and the visual. The classic case is Andrea Alciati (or Alciato), Italian lawyer and poet (1492–1550), whose sometimes mysterious mixture of image, motto, and epigram fascinated readers throughout Europe. "Even if Alciato is not quite habitually unpointed, it is difficult sometimes to locate where the point is" (Cummings 2007, 206). That clearly did not matter much, and if one idea proved hard to grasp, it was easy to move on to the next. Emblem bibliographies emphasize Alciati's bestseller status, among hundreds of other titles in a popular vernacular, as well as Neo-Latin, genre; in the Low Countries, for example, we have Antwerp editions in 1565, 1566, 1567, 1573, 1577, 1581, 1622, 1676, 1692; in Leiden in 1584, 1591 (twice), 1599, 1608, 1610 (Landwehr 1988, 42–47).

PRIVATE AND PUBLIC, SAD AND HAPPY: VERSE FOR ALL OCCASIONS

On November 15, 1616, the wedding bells rang out for Damian Botner, a Silesian pastor, and "the most chaste virgin" Barbara; the booklet of congratulatory poems was printed, with a blank space to be filled in by hand with a horoscope *ad tempus aestimatum copulationis novorum coniugum* ("at the estimated time of coupling of the newly-weds"; *Foederi novo coniugiali* 1616, A1v: it is duly completed in my copy). Eleven of the bride's cousins and friends had contributed verses; there are chronograms, Greek elegiacs, extended anacreontics in Greek and Latin (*Foederi novo coniugiali* 1616, A2v–A3v, with Georg Ritter repeatedly using the word *corculum* that we met above in a different kind of epigram). No German vernacular, however; these are graduates of the University of Leipzig, after all. There is genuine affection and enthusiasm for the match, forcefully expressed by Johannes Zeidler, bachelor of philosophy: *Coniugio melius nil; vita caelibe peius / Nil est* ("nothing is better than marriage, nothing is worse than a bachelor's life"; *Foederi novo coniugiali*, A4r): elsewhere, one might find that first *nil*, a monosyllable after the caesura, too awkward; here, its unexpected force perhaps serves to stress the point. Johannes's relative, Michael Zeidler, calls on God to favor a pair: *Quos castus firmo glutine iungit amor / . . . fac te duce tempore nullo / Cesset amor suavi languidus, oro, toro* ("whom chaste love joins with strong glue . . . under your guidance may love never become languid and cease on their sweet bed, I pray"; Leipzig 1616, A2r). Zeidler's lines might also possibly be read as "may languid love never cease," if we take *languidus* in a less negative sense ("unhurried," rather than "failing"), which creates an interesting erotic ambiguity. The tone is intimate, pious, passionate; though the wedding was naturally celebrated publicly in church, the poetry is essentially private, of interest to a small group of people in a limited locality. Yet it lasts rather well as a poignant example of what Neo-Latin can do.

"Occasional" verse covers a wide range. Metrically, it embraces more forms than the epigram usually does; Horatian lyrics could be surprisingly popular—and indeed many of Horace's great odes were addressed to friends on some occasion or other. Occasional verse was produced in immense quantities (*CNLS* 2:100–3, including a wedding at Tallinn in 1643). Some educational institutions seized every opportunity to showcase their collective talents. The scholars of Eton College, near to the royal residence of Windsor Castle, presented manuscript verses to Queen Elizabeth in 1560 and 1563; more poets contributed to the earlier volume, but the scope of their offerings is less ambitious (in no case exceeding twenty-eight lines). There is considerable metrical variety, and in

1563 the acrostic is a popular technique, deployed with great inventiveness to spell out phrases in Latin or English from letters at the beginning, middle, or ends of lines. In 1563 the word *epigramma* is used as a standard description for all poems, including one historical narrative based on Livy that extends to hundreds of lines. These "epigrams" may push the boundaries of the genre farther than is comfortable, and contain some errors born of youthful enthusiasm, but there is no doubting the commitment of the students and their teacher to Neo-Latin creativity (Nichols 2014).

Later in Elizabeth's reign, these commemorative collections moved from manuscript to print at Oxford and Cambridge (England's only two universities at the time), and began a tradition that was to last for about two hundred years, only petering out in the 1760s. As far as I know, this was a particularly English phenomenon: while many individuals and groups at Continental institutions poured out Neo-Latin during this period, I am not aware of such a formalized method, with regular volumes in a similar format, taking root elsewhere. Mostly, these books marked grand public occasions, royal births, marriages and funerals; less often, the deaths of people of more local significance to the universities. When a book was to be produced, a substantial proportion of the university's senior and junior members would be involved, often working at great speed. The results are a good reflection of Neo-Latin occasional poetry as a whole: varied in form and quality, sometimes rising remarkably well to the challenge of writing on a set subject, sometimes not so well. I will examine in some more detail one of these books, Cambridge's *Threnodia* (*Song of Lament*, 1670) on the death of General George Monck, Duke of Albemarle (b. 1608); Oxford also produced its *Epicedia* for Monck, and both universities also lamented Henrietta, Charles I's daughter (b. 1644), in the same year, Henrietta Maria, his widow (b. 1609), in the previous year, and Anne, Duchess of York (b. 1637), in 1671: a sad but busy time for the composers. As the man chiefly responsible for the restoration of Charles II in 1660, Monck's status in public life was very high; having fought for Charles I, then for Parliament, and for Cromwell, before seeking his own advantage and the nation's in a restored monarchy. He had changed loyalties several times, rising from modest gentry origins to great wealth, and just avoided becoming a scapegoat for the various disasters of 1665–1667, which included the Fire of London (1666) and the Dutch raid up the River Medway (1667) during the second Anglo-Dutch War.

More than a hundred Cambridge poets wrote in Latin on Monck's death; a few also in Greek, and fourteen in English at the end of the volume. Several note the curiosity of his dying not in bed, but in a chair; not in fact very heroic: it had been his habit since the winter of 1667–1668 to sleep propped up in a chair, unable to do so lying down. He expired from dropsy on January 3, 1670, aged sixty-one. So, for James Jackson, M.D. (d. 1686), fellow of Clare Hall (now Clare College), *Non cecidit, per quem spes Carolina stetit* ("he did not fall, through whom Charles's hope stood firm"); and for Henry Paman, M.D. (1623–95), fellow of St John's College, *Nec tamen ignave occubuit, cum stare nequiret, / Acriter in cathedra dimicat, et moritur* ("but he did not sink listlessly, when he could not stand: he strives keenly in his chair, and dies"; *Musarum Cantabrigiensium Threnodia* 1670, B4v). William Makernesse of Emmanuel College (d. 1680) does not stint in describing the ravages of disease, and also notes the seated demise, as a route straight to the stars *absque soloecismo* ("without solecism" [or impropriety?], a rather bold, if rather odd, piece of phrasing; *Musarum Cantabrigiensium Threnodia* 1670, G4v).

There are a few examples in the 1670 Cambridge volume of the irregular inscription, an interesting Neo-Latin genre in itself; a sort of prose-poetry, modelled on the epitaphs that might grace a real tomb, but often more expansive. Joseph Carr (bap. 1650/1), commoner (student) of St John's College, offers a vigorous *Carmen lapidarium* (*Lapidary Poem*, alluding to inscribing on stone) for the hero: *Cuius virtute resurrectionem vidimus / regiminis monarchici: / sanctus Georgius, Hercules Anglicanus, / Hydram fanaticam, / Beluam multorum capitum / Interfecit, obtruncavit* ("through whose courage we saw the resurrection of monarchical rule; a St. George, an English Hercules who killed and beheaded the fanatic hydra, many-headed beast"); following it with a fascinating explanation in more conventional verse (twelve elegiac lines), *Carminis soluti apologeticum* (*Defense of Free Verse; Musarum Cantabrigiensium Threnodia* 1670, H4v–I1r):

> *Forma meos neglecta decet (dux magne) dolores,*
> *   Agnoscit nullos nenia nostra modos.*
> *Intumuit flumen, toto spatiatur in agro:*
> *   Cum norunt suetas flumina parva vias...*
> Aestuat infelix angusto limite *Musa,*
> *   Compedibus metri dum iacet implicita.*

> Neglected form befits my grief, great duke; my dirge recognizes no meters. The river has swollen and spreads over the whole countryside, when little streams knew their accustomed ways ... My muse "rages unhappily in a narrow limit" while it lies bound in the restrictions of meter.

In his use of italics (here, roman type), Carr calls our attention to his borrowing from Juvenal's *Satire* 10.169, on Alexander the Great (a compliment to the general's career, a greater leader even than Monck), who *aestuat ... limite mundi*, famously "rages at the world's narrow limits," with nothing left worth conquering. This is proverbial arrogance, and all too soon he must be content with a narrow sarcophagus. Monck may not have been an Alexander, but he was better aware of human limitations, and played his cards very astutely. The young poet can thus comment neatly on his own creative ambitions, temporarily released from the meter (which he can naturally handle as well as most), as well as the fates of great men. Juvenal's moralizing is savage: just before Alexander, Hannibal is also dismissed as a madman, whose Alpine endeavors are merely *ut pueris placeas et declamatio fias* ("to please boys and make yourself a stock topic for rhetoric"; l. 167). If Monck, too, becomes a subject for future student exercises, as he well might, they will probably be in a more sympathetic vein.

Another apology ends the Latin part of the collection. James Duport (1606–79), vice-chancellor, Master of Magdalene College, and dean of Peterborough Cathedral, explains that sickness at Cambridge has hindered the preparation of the book (*Musarum Cantabrigiensium Threnodia* 1670, S1r):

Conflictata diu est letali Academia morbo,
  Abstulit illustrem cum mala Parca ducem.
Senserat infelix tanti praeludia fati,
  Tum quasi patrono commoritura suo.
Necdum convaluit geminato vulnere mater,
  Et morbo simul et funere pressa gravi.
Ignoscas ergo, petimus, si divite vena
  Nec fluit, et genium non habet iste liber.
Aegra manus calamum regit, et penus arida vatum,
  Et repit tardo languida Musa pede.

The university was long struck with a deadly plague, when evil fate took away the illustrious duke. It had felt unhappily the prelude of so great a death, being almost about to die alongside its patron. Nor had the mother (*alma mater*: the university) recovered from the double wound, oppressed by disease and the painful funeral at the same time. Therefore, we ask forgiveness, if the book has not flowed from a rich vein, and lacks genius. A sick hand guides the pen, and a meagre store of poets, and the muse creeps sluggishly on slow feet.

One might think there was no need for apology: Duport's own contribution was far from sluggish: twenty-three Greek hexameters and a further twenty-six lines of Latin elegiacs at the end of the volume, not to mention his opening fanfare comprising six Latin poems (five elegiac, one iambic) spread over five pages. There is little evidence of weakness elsewhere, among fellows or students, though doubtless even more contributions were indeed prevented in that unhealthy Fenland winter. What is notable is that Duport and his colleagues cared very much about the quality of what they were doing—whether the king himself read as far as the end is another matter. Neo-Latin occasional poetry mattered to the university: it was an important part of its collective public image, and the self-presentation of individual members as loyal and learned citizens. Duport himself was one of the leading Latin and Greek poets of the age, a master of biblical paraphrase; much of his output could be described as epigrams or occasional verse, including three books (almost 400 pages) of *Sylvae*, miscellaneous poems, besides those allocated to the specific categories of congratulation, lament, university ceremonies, or sacred epigrams; not just a young man's amusement, but a lifelong passion: *Nec res mira tamen senex poeta* ("an old man writing poetry is no surprise"; Duport 1676, 22).

The works of Anthony Alsop (ca. 1669/70–1726), born within a few days of the death of General Monck, provide many examples of the use of Horatian lyrics for occasional poetry, both public and private. Numerous odes addressed to friends are full of gently humorous, and sometimes sharply pointed, comment on events in their lives. When a slightly younger friend, the lawyer Joseph Taylor, sought to enter Parliament in 1722, he was warned that the election process could be dirty and expensive (Money 1998, 196–97, 320–21):

Sed per immensum oceanum et liquores
Mille sulcanda est via; multa fumi

Nubila erumpent fluitansque rivo
  Alla perenni.

But you must cleave your way through a great ocean of liquor, many clouds of smoke must pour out, and a perpetual river of ale must flow.

That year, Taylor withdrew from the contest. A much younger Alsop, in 1695, had celebrated the wedding of his Scottish friend David Gregory, Oxford professor of astronomy, in a poem that is open to very different readings, in different manuscript versions. In abbreviated form, it concentrates on what marriage will mean for a scientist, in mildly risqué fashion: *Mox qua mamillarum via lactea / Ducit, pererras improbula manu* ("Soon you wander with your wicked little hand where her breasts' milky way leads on"). But additional stanzas in some manuscripts focus on the political hopes shared by poet and bridegroom, for the restoration of the Stuart dynasty, once again exiled: *En! tempus instat, en! veniet dies, / Cum rursus in Coelum caput efferet / Nomen Stuartorum* ("Look, the time is at hand, look, the day will come, when the name of Stuart will again raise its head to heaven"; Money 1998, 135–42, 284–6). Queen Mary had just died; William's throne looked uncertain—these seditious thoughts were widely shared, appeared realistic, and while obviously unpublishable, even half a century later, they must have circulated among Latinate sympathizers. Neo-Latin reflected modern life, and political divides, like religious ones, could produce impassioned verse. Latin appealed to educated people on all sides; it found favor with many Jacobites (supporters of the exiled James II and his descendants) as a means of private expression. A master of the Jacobite political epigram was the Scottish poet and doctor Archibald Pitcairne (1652–1713), unrelenting in his hatred for William, who died in 1702: *Occidit Imperii Populatrix hydra Britanni* ("The hydra that laid waste the British Empire has fallen"; Pitcairne 2009, 225–27). Alsop's private occasional poetry, like Pitcairne's, could reach a wider audience than his own circle, whether through manuscripts or the occasional broadsheet: his satirical exposé of a pair of Oxford busybodies was printed (with or without his permission), taken up in someone else's book, and imitated in English (Money 1998, 106–34). Jokes about foolish individuals, in the early modern period just as in ancient epigrams, cannot always be fully appreciated by later readers. But enough often remains to reimagine a world in which Neo-Latin wit flowed back and forth as the rivers of ale were consumed.

As the century was ending, a Croatian in Rome, Rajmund Kunić (1719–1794), prolific epigrammatist, was translating Theocritus into Latin; for comparison, and for the epigrams he failed to complete, Kunić's editor supplied versions by Hugo Grotius and Daniel Heinsius (Kunić 1799). The genre was still alive, incorporating old and new. Indeed, it was one of the forms of Neo-Latin that lasted best into the nineteenth, twentieth, and twenty-first centuries, individually the slightest, but collectively perhaps the largest. Fascinating and frustrating, easy to attempt, hard to perfect, epigrams could never satisfy everyone. Sometimes, though, they made their mark.

Suggested Reading

On epigrams in general, see Beer, Enenkel, and Rijser (2009); Laurens (1989). Useful general anthologies, with good numbers of epigrams are Perosa and Sparrow (1979); McFarlane (1980). Thorough lists of poets (for Italy, France, Netherlands), focusing on Greek models are Hutton (1935 and 1946). On English university collections: Binns (1990, 34–45); Money (1998, 229–49); Money (2009). For some other British case-studies, see Houghton and Manuwald (2012). For other work related to the contents of this chapter, see Fara and Money (2004), Money (2006), and Money (2008).

References

Allesch, Gerd. 2000. *Epigrammatum libellus*. Vienna: Edition Praesens.

Beer, Susanna de, Karl Enenkel, and David Rijser, eds. 2009. *The Neo-Latin Epigram: A Learned and Witty Genre*. Leuven: Leuven University Press.

Binns, James W. 1990. *Intellectual Culture in Elizabethan and Jacobean England: The Latin Writings of the Age*. Leeds: Francis Cairns.

Cummings, Robert. 2007. "Alciato's Illustrated Epigrams." *Emblematica* 15:193–228.

Duport, James. 1676. *Musae Subsecivae*. Cambridge: Hayes.

Fara, Patricia, and David K. Money. 2004. "Isaac Newton and Augustan Latin poetry". *Studies in History and Philosophy of Science* 35:549–71.

Foederi novo coniugiali ... Damiani Botneri ... et castissimae virginis Barbarae ... Hartranfts ... ex alma universitate Lipsiensi gratulantur sponsae patrueles et amici. 1616. Leipzig: J. Hermann.

Houghton, L. B. T., and Gesine Manuwald, eds. 2012. *Neo-Latin Poetry in the British Isles*. London: Bristol Classical Press.

Hutton, James. 1935. *The Greek Anthology in Italy to the Year 1800*. Ithaca: Cornell University Press.

———. 1946. *The Greek Anthology in France and in the Latin Authors of the Netherlands to the Year 1800*. Ithaca: Cornell University Press.

Kaiser, Leo M. 1984. *Early American Latin Verse: An Anthology*. Chicago: Bolchazy-Carducci.

Kunić, Rajmund. 1799. *Theocriti idyllia et epigrammata*. Parma: Regium Typographeum.

Landwehr, John. 1988. *Emblem and Fable Books Printed in the Low Countries, 1542–1813: A Bibliography*. Utrecht: HES.

Laurens, Pierre. 1989. *L'Abeille dans l'ambre: Célébration de l'épigramme de l'époque alexandrine à la fin de la Renaissance*. Paris: Belles Lettres.

Lindanus, Ludovicus. 1656. *Epigrammata in haereticos*. Mechelen: Robert Jaye.

McCutcheon, Elizabeth N. 2003. "Laughter and Humanism: Unity and Diversity in Thomas More's *Epigrammata*." In *ACNL* 2003, 351–59.

McFarlane, Ian D., ed. 1980. *Renaissance Latin Poetry*. Manchester: Manchester University Press.

Molza, Tarquinia. 1750. *Opuscoli*. Printed and bound with Francesco M. Molza, *Poesie*. 2 vols., 1–94. Bergamo: Pietro Lancellotti.

Money, David K. 1998. *The English Horace: Anthony Alsop and the Tradition of British Latin Verse*. Oxford: British Academy.

Money, David K. 2006. "Eclogues in the English Universities". In Philip Ford and Andrew Taylor, eds. *Neo-Latin and the Pastoral: Canadian Review of Comparative Literature* 33:172–93.

———. 2008. "The Edge of War: how some poets (and preachers) reacted to Oudenarde and Lille". In *1708: Oudenarde and Lille*, edited by David Money, 122–36. Cambridge: Bringfield's Head Press.

———. 2009. "Neo-Latin and University Politics: The Case of Henry Sacheverell." In *Syntagmatia*, edited by Dirk Sacré and Jan Papy, 723–39. Leuven: Leuven University Press.

———. 2012. "Latin Poems Written in America, 2010 and 2011." *The Classical Outlook* 89.2:44–49.

Musarum Cantabrigiensium Threnodia in obitum incomparabilis herois ac ducis illustrissimi Georgii Ducis Albaemarlae. 1670. Cambridge: Hayes.

Nichols, John. 2014. *The Progresses and Public Processions of Queen Elizabeth I: A New Edition of the Early Modern Sources*. Edited by Elizabeth Goldring et al., 5 vols. Oxford: Oxford University Press.

Owen, John. 1794. *Epigrammata*. Edited by Antoine A. Renouard. Paris: P. Didot the elder.

Perosa, Alessandro, and John Sparrow, eds. 1979. *Renaissance Latin Verse: An Anthology*. London: Duckworth.

Pitcairne, Archibald. 2009. *The Latin Poems*. Edited and translated by John and Winifred MacQueen. Assen: Van Gorcum.

Poemata varia, opera ac studio iuventutis academicae in Gymnasio novo Trium Coronarum Coloniae Agrippinae. 1631. Cologne: Kinckius.

Poole-Wilson, P. N. 1989. "A Best-Seller Abroad: The Continental Editions of John Owen." In *Theatrum orbis librorum*, edited by Ton Croiset van Uchelen, Koert van der Horst, and Gunter Schilder, 242–49. Utrecht: HES.

Pope, Alexander. 1963. *The Poems of Alexander Pope*. Edited by John Butt. London: Methuen.

Summers, Kirk M. 2001. *A View from the Palatine: The Iuvenilia of Théodore de Bèze*. Tempe: Arizona Center for Medieval and Renaissance Studies.

Weston, Elizabeth J. 2000. *Collected Writings*. Edited by Donald Cheney and Brenda Hosington. Toronto: Toronto University Press.

CHAPTER 6

....

COMEDY

....

STEFAN TILG

PRELIMINARIES

....

In this chapter I give a survey of Latin comedy from ca. 1400 to 1750, with a particular emphasis on its originality in comparison with ancient comedy. I start, however, with a working definition of "comedy" and with some remarks about my corpus.

A clear-cut definition of "comedy" is impossible. If this is true in general, it is even truer for the early modern period, which discovered the potential of comedy for serious matters such as religious education, and loved mixed types such as "tragicomedy" or "comicotragedy." Yet, in most cases, a certain comic mode, intended to make an audience laugh, is sufficiently discernible from a tragic mode intended to make the audience feel pity and fear. As a rule of thumb, I have included plays with a general note of cheerfulness and liveliness and plays oriented towards established comic traditions like Roman comedy or vernacular farce. The various early modern poetics dealing with comedy do not provide a uniform and systematic framework, and practice can be a far cry from theory. But there is an almost universally accepted basic consensus in early modern views of Latin comedy: the qualities particularly associated with comedy are the use of familiar language and a certain realism in the representation of common life and the exploration of moral values. This harks back to a phrase transmitted in Donatus's late antique commentary on Terence (Donatus 1902, 22) and attributed to Cicero: it says that comedy is *imitatio vitae, speculum consuetudinis, imago veritatis* ("imitation of life, mirror of custom, image of truth"). This definition is quoted and paraphrased over and over in early modern prefaces and poetics (see, e.g., my discussion of Gnapheus's *Acolastus*, below).

As to the corpus, a good starting point is still provided by Leicester Bradner's "list of original Neo-Latin plays printed before 1650," attached to his general essay on Renaissance Latin drama (Bradner 1957). Bradner's list is certainly incomplete and, as its title states, it excludes manuscript evidence and plays published after 1650. But the list does give a more or less representative sample of the production up to 1650, which includes the main periods and manifestations of Neo-Latin theater until the point when Jesuit theater was left (almost) alone on the Latin stage. Bradner lays out his material alphabetically by authors and lists all prints and editions available to him. If we are interested in the sheer number of plays, we have to adjust the list for duplications of the same play (e.g., in various editions or in collections) and do a count. I came out at roughly 450 plays. To establish a corpus of comedies from these plays, I did my best to examine each play myself (which, thanks to mass digitization of early books, works reasonably well today). My result was a corpus of about 150 comedies. Comedies, then, make up about a third of all listed plays. In terms of periods, the most productive period for printed Neo-Latin comedies seems to have been the sixteenth and early seventeenth centuries. As far as geographical distribution is concerned, the greatest share of plays falls to the German lands, followed by the Low Countries, England, Italy, France, and a number of other countries. This meshes with the generally strong production of Latin literature in the German lands and the Low Countries, which combined a vibrant intellectual culture with the relatively weak position of the vernaculars. England is prominently present because of its lively theater culture at the Universities of Oxford and Cambridge.

Prehistory

Roman comedy was not unknown to the Middle Ages. Plautus (i.e., his eight plays then known to be extant; the other twelve were only rediscovered in 1429) and particularly Terence were widely read. However, they were not read as playwrights, but as masters of language and morality—hence the preference for Terence, whose language was easier and whose characteristic aphorisms were mined endlessly. Knowledge about performance and meter was largely lost. The plays were usually read as though they were prose dialogues. They inspired only a small and limited original production. In the tenth century, the canoness Hrotsvitha of Gandersheim wrote dialogue plays in rhythmic prose about the lives of Christian legendary heroes and martyrs, characterized by herself as an antidote to the immoral Terence for the young people. More secular, and picking up on the love interest of Roman comedy, a genre of literature called "elegiac comedy" dramatized characters and situations partly drawn from Plautus and Terence in narratives and dialogues cast in elegiac distichs. A closer and more programmatic resuscitation of Roman comedy came only in the Renaissance. Petrarch (1304–1374) seems to have been the first to try his hand at a comedy modeled on Plautus and Terence. Unfortunately, this text is lost, and all we have from self-references in Petrarch's later work (e.g., *Epistolae familiares* 2.6–7) is a title, *Philologia*, two more names, Philostratus and Tranquillinus, as well as an aphorism: *maior pars hominum expectando moritur* ("the majority of people die waiting"). The name of the main character, Philologia, has led scholars to believe that Petrarch's comedy was allegorical and perhaps indebted to Martianus Capella's late antique encyclopedic work *The Wedding of Philology and Mercury* (*De nuptiis Philologiae et Mercurii*). Whatever we may think of that, allegory was clearly *en vogue* at Petrarch's time, and the kind of educational allegory suggested by the name *Philologia* can be found in numerous later Neo-Latin comedies across Europe. Two examples from different periods would be Leon Battista Alberti's *Philodoxus* (*Lover of Fame*, after the eponymous protagonist; ca. 1424) and the anonymous Cambridge comedy *Stoicus vapulans* (*The Stoic Scourged*, 1618), which stages characters like Ira ("Anger") or Ratio ("Reason"). If Petrarch's *Philologia* really were allegorical, this would also anticipate a more general and fairly normal characteristic of later Neo-Latin comedies, that they are rarely "just" imitations of Plautus and Terence, but add other literary and intellectual elements of contemporary relevance.

THE ITALIAN QUATTROCENTO

After Petrarch's *Philologia*, it took another seventy years or so for Italian humanist comedy to take off (Grund 2005). More often than in later periods, Italian humanist drama was closet drama, a literary *jeu d'esprit* of authors wishing to work in a rediscovered genre. Here belongs, for instance, the Plautine comedy *Chrysis* (1444; named after an eponymous prostitute) by Enea Silvio Piccolomini, later Pope Pius II. Some pieces were also acted or recited in schools or universities, as were a number of comedies by Tito Livio Frulovisi in the 1430s. This is the typical context of production and reception in later periods. As subject matter, the context of education also informs the first recorded example of humanist comedy, Pier Paolo Vergerio's *Paulus* (ca. 1390). Set in the milieu of an Italian university town, the play revolves around a lazy student called Paulus. Some characters, like the cunning slave, and some plot elements, like the love interest of the young hero, suggest Roman comedy, but overall the *Paulus* is fairly unclassical by modern standards. It ends with sexual adventure and deceit, atypical of the happy ending in marriage known from Roman comedy. Setting and characters are contemporary. There is no division into acts, and the verse is in fact pseudo-verse, rhythmic prose in imitation of the iambic senarius (the typical verse of Roman comedy, consisting of six iambic feet). Partly this unclassical appearance is due to the state of philology at the time: the manuscripts of Plautus and Terence did not contain a division into acts (and in fact Plautus and Terence probably did not divide their plays into acts at all—while attempts at act division began as early as the first century BCE, the consistent five-act structure familiar to us and often seen in later Neo-Latin drama was introduced only by Renaissance editors; see Duckworth 1952, 98–101). Nor did most manuscripts preserve the meter of Roman comedy. Although some early humanists suspected verse behind the seeming prose, they could not work out the complicated rules of the iambic senarius. As a consequence, most Neo-Latin comedy of the fifteenth century is in prose or pseudo-verse. As far as setting, characters, motifs, and plot are concerned, we must keep in mind that classical comedy was just one model of humanist comedy, which was also strongly influenced by vernacular traditions like farce and the *novella*: on one hand, there was a strain of more or less pure farce, small and informal low-life comedy like Ugolino

Pisani's *Coquinaria confabulatio* (*Kitchen Talk*, 1435), which centers on a mock degree award for a bad cook; on the other hand, numerous plays, like Antonio Cornazzano's *Fraudiphila* (*Lover of Fraud*, ca. 1450) combine elements of Roman comedy with material from Boccaccio's *Decameron* (7.7) and other novellas. The influence of Roman comedy grew over time, however, particularly in the wake of the first printed editions of Terence (1470) and Plautus (1472). Near the end of the century, in 1483, Tommaso Mezzo was able to write a truly "Roman" comedy, the *Epirota* (the title designates the provenance of a leading character from the Greek region Epirus). This play is set in ancient Syracuse and imitates Terentian characters and plots very closely. At about the same time, the Accademia Romana, a circle of learned men in Rome around the central figure of Pomponio Leto (1428–1498), driven by enthusiasm for Roman antiquity and an antiquarian spirit, attempted to reconstruct ancient performance practices and brought Plautus and Terence on stage. Performance became an even greater concern with the first edition of Vitruvius's *De architectura* (*On Architecture*, 1486), which, among other things, also describes stage buildings.

FROM LATIN INTO ITALIAN "COMMEDIA ERUDITA" AND BACK INTO LATIN

The classicizing form of Italian humanist drama could be seen as its *telos*, but it might also be argued that it stifled further development. In any case, humanist drama in Italy (before Jesuit drama) came to a comparatively early end at the beginning of the sixteenth century. With very few exceptions, that was the end of all Latin drama in Italy before the Jesuits. The tradition of humanist comedy was picked up by the vernacular *commedia erudita*, the more learned and literary counterpart to the simpler and partly improvised *commedia dell'arte*. "Erudite comedies" were written by prominent authors such as Niccolò Machiavelli (1469–1525), Ludovico Ariosto (1474–1533), Pietro Aretino (1492–1556), and Giambattista della Porta (1535–1615). These and other authors successfully combined the Roman models with contemporary Italian life and manners. The *commedia erudita* also appealed to a large audience outside schools and universities, to the extent that it soon became itself a model for European theater, including a segment of the Latin productions. This can be seen in individual examples such as four comedies by the Spanish humanist Juan Pérez, who was professor of rhetoric at the Collegium Trilingue in Alcalá de Henares (Pérez 2012). Based on Italian *commedie erudite* by Ludovico Ariosto and Alessandro Piccolomini, Pérez performed his Latin adaptations with his students in around 1540. A more systematic transformation of *commedia erudita* into Latin comedy takes place in English university drama (editions in Spevack and Binns 1981–1991). While comedy was rarer in early university drama (which started in the 1540s), it began to dominate around 1600, with the rule of James I. This was also due to the success of models from the Italian *commedia erudita*, which by the 1590s had become *the* single most important source for comedies produced in Oxford and Cambridge. A famous example is England's best-known university comedy, George Ruggle's satire on an ignorant lawyer, *Ignoramus*, performed in Cambridge in 1614 and based on Giambattista della Porta's *La Trappolaria* (*Comedy of Trappola*, a speaking name meaning "trap"; 1596). The success of this play was such that the name of its anti-hero was adopted as a common noun in the English language.

BETWEEN DIALOGUE, FARCE, AND ROMAN COMEDY—CLASSICISM AND ITS UNDERCURRENTS

When Italian humanist drama crossed the Alps around 1500, it did not come as a ready-made literary form. It was more of a vague idea about the rebirth of Latin theater. Authors had to find their own ways of realizing that idea, and in the beginning they often picked up on established forms like dialogue and farce. A prominent French example is Ravisius Textor's (1492–1522) *Dialogi aliquot* (*Several Dialogues*, posthumously published in 1530), short allegorical and farcical plays of about 200–300 lines, partly in verse, partly in prose. Textor performed these pieces with his students at the Collège de Navarre in Paris, where he taught grammar and rhetoric. None of his plays is anywhere near the models of Plautus and Terence, and when he called one of his prose farces *comedia*, he chose this word simply as a then widespread translation of French *farce*. Textor's example shows that Latin comedy does not necessarily mean Roman comedy, which had to compete with more traditional forms north of the Alps just as in the Italian Quattrocento. The complex relationship between vernacular farce and classical comedy can be further illustrated by a much admired play that set standards for further Neo-Latin comedy, but was based on a French farce: Johannes Reuchlin's *Henno*, performed in 1497 by students in Heidelberg and published in 1498 (Reuchlin 1970). The *Henno*, often seen as the first "regular"—that is, classicist—comedy north of the Alps, was a huge success and saw thirteen editions in the thirty-five years after its first publication. Prominent later comic playwrights such as Georgius Macropedius explicitly acknowledged Reuchlin's influence. But in terms of plot and characters, the *Henno* had little do to with Roman comedy. Adapting the then-popular French *Farce de Maître Pathelin* (*Farce about Master Pathelin*), it tells the story of a slave who cheats first his master, then a draper, and finally a lawyer out of their money, the latter two by answering all questions with a sheep-like sound and thus feigning insanity (ll. 332–37 and 364–75).

The classicism of this farcical play lies in its form, although even here Reuchlin constructs a classicism of his own devising. For the first time north of the Alps, we have a five-act structure. This structure was underlined by the insertion of choruses between acts, a procedure probably inspired by Senecan tragedy, for Roman comedy did not have choruses. In addition, Reuchlin introduces the iambic trimeter to comedy, again an element taken from tragedy, to add formal strictness—arguably the trimeter seemed to him more regular and "classical" than the malleable iambic senarius characteristic of Roman comedy. With these innovations, as emerges from the prologue, Reuchlin wished to create a model comedy to establish classical school drama (15: *auctore se Germaniae schola luserit / Graecanicis et Romuleis lusibus*). That he carried out this plan by dramatizing the *Maître Pathelin* farce, however, demonstrates that even programmatic classicism could embrace contemporary vernacular culture. This happy symbiosis between farce and classicism is further emphasized by the fact that a free Latin translation of the French *Maître Pathelin* was published by a certain Connibert under the title of a *Novel Comedy* (*Comedia nova*) in Paris in 1512. Although this translation does not have a five-act structure, it is written in iambic verse (here trimeter and dimeter) and draws heavily on the language of Roman comedy.

Farce and other contemporary "low" material continued to influence Latin comedy also later when classicism was an easy option. The Dutchmen Georgius Macropedius around 1540 and Cornelius Schonaeus around 1600, two of the most famous Latin playwrights of their time, also wrote, beside religious drama, low-life farces about drunken peasants and tamed shrews. The Spanish humanist Juan Lorenzo Palmireno wishes to distinguish his prose comedy of 1574, *Aenaria* (the name of a Danish princess in the plot; Palmireno 2002–2004), from Roman comedy and prefaces it with the genre name of *fabella Atellana aut Milesia* (*Atellan or Milesian Fable*). The ancient categories of Roman Atellan farce and of the low-life fiction of the *Milesian Tales* are then filled with a fantastic plot drawn from chivalric romance. In his colophon, Palmireno says that he preferred this "Spanish farce" (*farsa hispanica*) to the "seriousness of Terence" (*Terentii gravitas*) because it appeals to a larger audience. Moreover, the dialogue of Palmireno's *Aenaria* switches back and forth between Spanish and Latin, a feature often seen in Spanish Neo-Latin drama. To a lesser extent, pieces of vernacular language may also appear in other comedies, such as the Italian and French spoken by a chimney sweep and a merchant chancing upon Caesar and Cicero in Nicodemus Frischlin's *Iulius redivivus* (*Julius Revived*, 1585; Frischlin 2003). Another kind of "low" material, folk tale, is dramatized in Martin Hayneccius's *Hansoframea* of 1581, which stages the folktale of the shoemaker and archetypical fault-finder Hans Pfriem (compare Grimm's Fairy Tales no. 178: *Master Pfriem*). When Hans comes by accident to heaven, he is told that he can only stay if he does not criticize anyone or anything. Of course this is impossible for Hans, but he routs all members of heaven wishing to deport him by drawing attention to their own faults. In the end he even defeats the innocent children by making them eat candies and thus exposing them as gluttons. English university comedy, especially in its later forms, teems with low-life elements such as the binge drinking and vomiting of two students so intoxicated that they believe themselves on board a ship in Abraham Cowley's *Naufragium ioculare* (*The Jocular Shipwreck*, performed in Cambridge in 1638). Even the Jesuits were no strangers to Latin farce: the English Jesuit William Drury, for instance, published a *Mors Comoedia* (1620; Herbrüggen 1991) in which both Death and the Devil are duped by a son, who engaged them to kill his rich but miserly father. When they appear to have done their job and demand the son's life and soul, they lose their case in court because of the sly conditions the son negotiated in their agreement. Drury's *Mors Comoedia* was printed three times and translated into English soon after its publication as *Death, A Comedie* (the manuscript, by one Robert Squire, is edited in Siconolfi 1982).

DRIVING FORCES AND SUBJECTS:
EDUCATION AND RELIGION

The adaptation and integration of farce and other low-life material in Latin comedy remained a constant undercurrent. But the most visible and important concerns fuelling Latin comedy from the sixteenth century onwards were more respectable, if still not derived from Roman comedy: education and religion. Both concerns were more relevant north of the Alps than they had been in Italy, where humanist education was more evolutionary than revolutionary and where Protestantism never gained a firm foothold. North of the Alps, however, the sudden implantation of humanism and the religious debates surrounding the Reformation and Counter-Reformation prepared the ground for countless plays participating in these larger discourses.

I turn first to education. Considering that we are dealing largely with school and university drama, the topic of education had the particular interest of bringing the normal social environment of authors and actors onstage. If comedy was generally thought of as a "mirror of life" (*speculum vitae*), then education was most suited to mirror the life of persons in the education business. Even the Latin language was a familiar and realistic element in this setting, given that Latin was the normal language spoken in school and higher education. The familiarity and intimate domesticity of this environment also implied that it could not normally be treated in tragedy, which requires grand subjects and larger-than-life characters, according to ancient and early modern poetics. Unsurprisingly, then, a list of all Latin comedies about education would have to be tediously long. In general, we could distinguish between school comedies about pupils and teachers, student comedies about students and professors, and allegorical comedies about grammar and other contents and values of education.

A prominent example for school comedy would be Macropedius's *Rebelles* (*Rascals*; Macropedius 1897), written ca. 1515 and published in 1535. *Rebelles* stages two nasty pupils led astray by the over-indulgence of their mothers and rescued by their teacher—normally school comedies of this type were written by teachers to emphasize their own importance. *Rebelles* was printed fourteen times in the sixteenth century, translated at least twice into German, and often imitated by other playwrights. The most successful Neo-Latin student comedy is Christoph Stymmelius's *Studentes* (Lachmann 1926). Stymmelius wrote this play in 1545 when he was a twenty-year-old student in Frankfurt on the Oder. In the preface, he explains that he wishes to depict contemporary reality just as ancient authors did in their time. Accordingly, Stymmelius provides a rich and convincing impression of student life, which focuses on three protagonists standing for diligent study on one hand and the temptations of money and sex respectively on the other hand. He also shows how students interact and fight with other townfolk like craftsmen, guards, and ordinary citizens. The reception of this play, first printed in 1549, was enthusiastic. Twenty-one editions were issued in the sixteenth and seventeenth centuries. Various translations include a Swedish one, and performances are recorded as far away as in Bergen in Norway. Finally, an example for grammar comedy would be Leonard Hutten's *Bellum grammaticale* (*Grammar War*), performed in 1581 in Christ Church, Oxford. Hutten, a student at the time, here adapted Andrea Guarna's popular comic narrative *Bellum grammaticale* of 1512. Guarna tells the story of how the irregularities of Latin grammar are really casualties suffered in a war between nouns and verbs, led by the king of nouns, Poeta ("poet"), and the king of verbs, Amo ("I love"). This mock-battle was brought onstage before and after Hutten, but his adaptation seems to be the first to appear in print. It crosses Guarna's tale with Roman comedy and introduces, for instance, two parasites called "Ille" and "Ubique." The Roman grammarians bringing the battle to an end in Guarna are supported and partly replaced on the stage by contemporary French and English grammarians. First published in 1635, Hutton's *Bellum grammaticale* had considerable success and appeared in five further editions, the last one as late as 1729.

Next let us address religion, a subject that at first sight may perhaps seem too serious for comic adaptations. But Latin playwrights found a number of ways to make religious comedy work. A turning point for the staging of religious subjects was Guilielmus Gnapheus's dramatization of the Prodigal Son narrative from Luke 15 in his *Acolastus* (*The Licentious One*, 1529; Gnapheus 1964). Before Gnapheus, religion was dealt with here and there, mostly in allegorical form, but it was not central to Neo-Latin drama. After the *Acolastus* it became a major force, not least because of Gnapheus's successful formula for religious *comoedia*, later often called "sacred comedy" (*comoedia sacra*). In his prologue, Gnapheus wonders why of all genres comedy is so little developed in his time and aims to become a new Menander and Terence himself. He argues that religion is a suitable subject even if it involves more "tragic outcries" (*tragicas exclamationes*) than classical laws may permit; in the end, the meaning and dignity of the subject outweighs such concerns—another testimony to the unclassical approach of Neo-Latin playwrights to dramatic genres. In the following play, Gnapheus tells the story of the Prodigal Son in Terentian language, characters, motifs, and scenes. As so often in Roman comedy, for instance, we have a father worrying about his son, hungry parasites, amusing servants, and a greedy pair of pimp and prostitute. This comic intimacy and familiarity in religious matters was much appreciated by the contemporary audience. By mapping a biblical subject onto Terentian comedy, Gnapheus set off a wave of Terentian-style religious plays with ripples felt until the first half of the seventeenth century. Gnapheus's most prominent successor, for example, his fellow Dutchman Cornelius Schonaeus, gained European fame under the name of "Terentius Christianus." Initially, this was the title of a pirated edition of 1591, which contained Schonaeus's first biblical plays. Surprised, but also flattered by this title, Schonaeus used the honorary attribute of "Terentius Christianus" himself from 1594 onwards for publishing most of his further religious and non-religious plays. Gnapheus's *Acolastus* and Schonaeus's religious comedies and tragicomedies were printed so often individually or in collections that it is difficult to keep track of their complete printing history (van de Venne 1983–1984). To supply just two figures: the *Acolastus* went through more than thirty editions in the sixteenth century alone, and Schonaeus's *Tobaeus* (another name for *Tobit*; edition in Verweij 1993), his single most successful play, was printed over fifty times, not including translations into many European languages.

The denominational significance of Bible plays like the *Acolastus* or the *Tobaeus* is disputed. If there is any, it is subtle. Because of the significance of grace in the father's forgiving, the *Acolastus*, for instance, was sometimes read as a Protestant play (e.g., Atkinson in Gnapheus 1964). Comedy is adapted more openly for confessional purposes in Protestant or Catholic attacks on each other. Here, however, we need to define comedy more generously. Take the case of Thomas Naogeorgus's celebrated *Pammachius* ([*The Pope*] *Who Fights Against Everything*, 1538; Naogeorgus 1975). This play is a satirical staging of the popes' rule throughout world history—yet the author calls it a tragedy, clearly because of what seems to him the growing Catholic evil, which only recently was opposed by Protestantism (the play ends with a close-up of contemporary Wittenberg). A performance of the *Pammachius* was given in Christ Church, Oxford, in 1545. This or the text itself no doubt inspired John Foxe to write his *Christus Triumphans* (*Christ Triumphant*), published in 1556. While Foxe treats world history from a similar anti-Catholic and satirical angle, he calls his work an "apocalyptic comedy" (*comoedia apocalyptica*). In these examples, comedy intersects with the aggressive attacks of satire and Greek Old Comedy, although it is unclear to what extent Aristophanes may have influenced the authors. On the Catholic side, personal attacks on Luther could be cited, such as the *Ludus ludentem Luderum ludens* (*Play Playing with the Playing Luther*, 1530) by Jan Horák, a Czech teacher of philosophy. Here, Luther is blamed for all his reforming ideas and finally burned. The author's debt to satire is made explicit in the concluding quotation from Horace (*Satires* 1.1.24–25): *Ridentem dicere verum? Quid vetat?* ("What prevents us from telling the truth while laughing?"). More notorious is the *Monachopornomachia* (*The Battle of Monks and Whores*, 1539; edition and translation in Mundt 1983) by the Swiss Simon Lemnius, published under the pseudonym of Lucius Pisaeus Iuvenalis. The last part of the pseudonym clearly refers to the Roman satirist Juvenal. This again confirms the relation of this kind of comedy to satire. Written completely in elegiac distichs to evoke love elegy, the play's only concern is to expose Luther, his fellow reformers, and their wives as fornicators—the *Monachopornomachia* is a treasure trove of obscene Latin vocabulary.

PLURALITY OF FORMS AND SUBJECTS

If Reuchlin's *Henno* is something like a model in form, and if education and religion are the most important subjects of Neo-Latin comedy, we must not forget that its range of forms and subjects is in fact much broader.

Regarding form, almost anything goes: we find comedies lacking a division into acts, or with a number of acts other than five. They may have choruses or not. They can be short sketches or run to thousands of lines. They can be in verse or prose—with the frequency of prose plays being significantly higher than in tragedy (rather than listing individual examples, I just refer to English university comedy, in which prose is a fairly regular feature). Prose could be suggested on one hand by the supposed realism of comedy as a "mirror of life," and on the other hand by the prosodic difficulties of Roman comedy, which prompted authors as late as the French Jesuit Gabriel Le Jay in 1727 (*Liber dramaticus* [*Book of Drama*], 447–48) to regard comic verse as particularly close to prose.

As far as subjects are concerned, I have already talked about an undercurrent of farce and other low-life elements. In addition, a number of pieces expose individual vices or characters. Melancholia, for instance, is at the center of Christian Bachmann's *Melancholicus* (*The Melancholic*, 1611; Bachmann 2003). Pedantry is satirized in Edward Forsett's *Pedantius* (*The Pedant*, 1581), just as is the haughty attitude of a would-be Stoic in the *Stoicus vapulans* of 1618. There are romantic comedies like Frischlin's *Hildegardis Magna* (*Hildegard the Great*, 1578; Frischlin 1995) and Friedrich Hermann Flayder's *Imma portatrix* (*Emma the Carrier*, 1625; Flayder 1925, 1–80), based on legends about the love life of wife and daughter of Charlemagne respectively. A similarly legendary tale, this time about the inseparable friendship of Titus and Gesippus, best known from Boccaccio's *Decameron* 10.8, found Latin adaptations in John Foxe's *Titus et Gesippus* of 1544/45 and Christoph Speccius's *De Titi et Gisippi amicitia* (*The Friendship of Titus and Gesippus*, 1623). I have mentioned above Palmireno's Latin-Spanish chivalric romance comedy, *Aenaria* of 1574. There are also intellectually more demanding strands: around 1600, Daniel Cramer combined the romance plot of his comedies *Areteugenia* (*Virtue Well Born*; about the legendary kidnapping of a knight and his sister) and *Plagium* (*Abduction*; about the historical kidnapping of two young princes in Saxony; Cramer 2009) with social criticism regarding the exploitation of farmers and charcoal burners. Some comedies even aspire to a comprehensive understanding of man and world: Matthew Gwinne's allegorical *Vertumnus sive annus recurrens* (*Vertumnus* [the god of the seasons], *or the Returning Year*, 1605) calls his protagonist "Microcosmus," and shows the four stages of his life (childhood, youth, adulthood, and old age) interacting with the four seasons of the year. Johann Valentin Andreae's *Turbo* of 1616 (translation in Andreae 1907) has been fittingly called a Latin Faust comedy because it stages the quest of the unquiet—hence "Turbo" ("Whirlwind")—protagonist for knowledge, which he eventually only finds in God.

JESUIT COMEDY

My survey so far has taken us up to the first half of the seventeenth century, with the inclusion of a few later examples. After that, Latin drama does not cease to exist, but is largely an affair of the Jesuits and other Catholic orders inspired by the Jesuit model.

Protestants, who authored the greater part of printed drama up to this point, abandoned school theater completely or switched to writing it in the vernacular. And in the Catholic world, the Jesuit school system (Grendler 2014) grew to such dominance by the seventeenth century that not many "private" schoolmasters were left.

Although Jesuit performances outnumbered Protestant and Catholic non-Jesuit plays by far, Jesuit drama was printed much more rarely. This is not necessarily due to an issue of quality, but to a certain view of drama as performative genre, not normally published as reading text. Most pieces are lost, therefore, although a considerable number are preserved in manuscript form, and we have many printed programs, so-called *periochae*, from ca. 1600 onwards. For these reasons, a survey of Jesuit comedy only on the basis of published texts would be misleading. It should be complemented by a comprehensive catalog of performances. Unfortunately, we have such a catalog for only one larger European area, the German-speaking countries, covered by Valentin 1983–1984 (note, however, that the German-speaking countries are the most prolific European arena of Jesuit drama). My following remarks, based on Valentin's catalog, should therefore be seen as a case study, not always fully representative of Jesuit drama in other areas (although I will add an example from France).

Valentin lists 7,650 performances given from 1555 to 1773, the year of the suppression of the Jesuit order. As with Bradner's list of printed plays, I went through all items of Valentin's catalog to determine what could be claimed for comedy—of course the margin of subjectivity here is even greater because for most plays I had to rely on mere titles or *periochae*. It becomes very clear, however, that comedy was not a favorite genre of Jesuit drama: my statistics show that only about 4 percent (some 250 pieces) of all titles were comedies. This chiefly results from the fact that the Jesuits preferred a more heroic concept of drama, with its most frequent protagonist being the Christian martyr, so Senecan tragedy was a far more important model than Roman comedy. My statistics also show an interesting distribution of comedies according to centuries—which is even more remarkable considering that the "sixteenth century" in this account starts only in 1555, and the eighteenth century extends only to 1773. While only 5 percent (ca. 415 pieces) of all Jesuit plays were performed in the sixteenth century, as many as 21 percent (ca. 57 pieces) of all Jesuit comedies fell within this century. The seventeenth century saw 39 percent of all plays (ca. 3,000 pieces), but only 23 percent (ca. 62 pieces) of all comedies. Finally, in the eighteenth century we have 56 percent of all plays (ca. 4,240 pieces), producing 56 percent (ca. 148 pieces) of all comedies. After a strong beginning in the first decades of Jesuit theater, then, comedy dropped out of favor in the seventeenth century, but it made a certain comeback in the eighteenth.

A look at forms and topics helps explain this development. Sixteenth-century Jesuit comedies are either more or less faithful adaptations of Roman comedies, or pick up the subject of education so popular in all Neo-Latin school drama. Jesuit comedy in these early stages was a means to catch up with the educational topics of Renaissance humanism. This concern is even seen in the title of one of the best-known Jesuit grammar comedies, Jacob Gretser's trilogy *Regnum humanitatis* (*The Rule of Humanist Education*, 1585–1590; Gretser 1897–1898; parts two and three edited in Dürrwächter 1912). In the seventeenth century, Jesuit drama was no longer so dependent on humanist models and focused on its own heroes, mostly martyrs and Christian rulers. Comedies about school and education became less important. Sporadically we get original pieces about certain vices like drinking and miserliness. An outstanding and well-known example is Jacob Masen's *Rusticus imperans* (*The Farmer as Ruler*, 1647; Masen 1988), an adaptation of the folk tale of the peasant prince, which is also treated by Shakespeare in his induction to *The Taming of the Shrew* (1590–1594). The comeback of Jesuit comedy in the eighteenth century seems due to institutional changes in the German-speaking countries. Around 1700, Jesuits in this area started to stage performances of individual school classes or certain groups of pupils and students in addition to the traditional performances including the whole school. The resulting multiplication and diversification of plays also brought new opportunities for comedy. Most importantly, the larger number of performances allowed more regular performances during carnival (before Lent), a privileged time of year for all Neo-Latin comedy. There is a taste for grotesque humor in some of these eighteenth-century Jesuit comedies. We have a group of *periochae*, for instance, which attest the staging of delusional characters who temporarily fall victim to their imagination: a man who believes he has lost his head (*Acephalus* [*The Headless*], 1736); a Christian hermit who believes he is an angel (*Joannes Brevis* [*John the Dwarf*], 1737); and a mayor who believes himself to be dead (*Stulti anastasis* [*The Resurrection of the Fool*], 1738). Other popular subjects can be seen from a printed collection of eleven comedies performed in Dillingen in around 1750 and edited by one of the most gifted Jesuit playwrights of all time, Anton Claus (Claus 1755; perhaps Claus also wrote a number of the pieces included himself). Most of these plays revolve around vices or topics of education. Meddlesomeness is the reason for the fall of a gooseherd previously risen to service at court in the *Vulpanser* (a playful combination of the protagonist's name, Vulpulus, and *anser*, "goose"); miserliness is satirized in the *Avaritia punita* (*Avarice Punished*). The largest group in the collection deals with education and school: with a mad student in *Passeres* (*Sparrows*; the student hears a bird in his head); with a rich student convinced that effort is only for the poor in the *Contemptus studiorum* (*Contempt of Study*); with a pupil partying through the night in the *Gymnasiasta Noctambulo* (*The Night-Walking Pupil*); or with a spoilt pupil in the *Poena neglectae educationis* (*The Punishment for Neglected Education*). Similar subjects occur in a French collection of prose comedies published in Paris at about the same time (1749). Its author is Charles Porée, Voltaire's teacher, and arguably the single most important French Jesuit playwright of the eighteenth century. Porée's comedies center on vices, father–son issues, and education. The *Paezophilus* (*The Lover of Playing*) warns against gambling. The *Pater nimio erga filium amore excaecatus* (*The Father Blind to His Son Because of Excessive Love*) stages, again, a spoilt son and his over-indulgent father; the *Misoponus* (*The Hater of Work*) an idler who, instead of studying, wants to open up an academy of idleness. In the *Liberi in deligendo vitae instituto coacti* (*The Children Forced in Their Choice of Life*), two sons rebel against their father because of the profession he has chosen for them; and the *Philedonus* (*The Lover of Pleasure*) shows us a dissipated young man who reforms after the death of one of his friends.

Concluding Observations

I would like to conclude this chapter with some observations on classicism and anticlassicism, comedy in relation to tragedy, and the scope of Neo-Latin comedy. Firstly, there is no simple linear development from non-classical to classical forms. Literary history sometimes creates the impression that, after unclassical early stages, Neo-Latin drama gradually finds its classical—that is, in comedy, its Plautine and Terentian—form (e.g., Ford and Taylor 2013, 7). While it is true that playwrights since the sixteenth century were perfectly able to write comedies in that style and many did so, we should keep in mind that many preferred or *also* exercised other options like farce, confessional satire, or dramatic romance. Even more important, authors often atomized, as it were, the language and motifs of Roman comedy and built something new from that, such as sacred comedies or comedies about contemporary student life. Rather than relying on classical definitions, I prefer to think of Neo-Latin comedy as diverse, hybrid, and innovative.

Secondly, the diversity, hybridity, and innovativeness of Neo-Latin comedy seems to me even more marked than that of tragedy. The contact with (sometimes even low-life) reality, so often emphasized in definitions of comedy as a "mirror of life," is a constant source of new forms and subjects. More specific cases in point would be the relatively frequent inclusion of passages in vernacular languages or the relatively frequent use of prose in Neo-Latin comedy. All this is much more rarely seen in tragedy, which generally aims at more abstract and uniform expression.

Finally, the scope of Neo-Latin comedy is much wider and more ambitious than that of Roman comedy. While the plots of Plautus and Terence may be entertaining, they are fairly predictable and somewhat remote from the Roman world (after all, they are all set in a timeless Greece). Neo-Latin comedy, by contrast, participates in a large variety of discourses of the early modern world (with education and religion being only the most important ones). It might be a paradoxical thing to claim, but Latin comedy of the early modern period, despite its use of an acquired language and its roots in schools and universities, often appears closer and more relevant to its own time than Roman comedy ever was.

Suggested Reading

Accounts of Neo-Latin comedy are usually found within larger discussions of Neo-Latin drama. The best general reference is Bloemendal and Norland (2013), which will lead readers to further secondary literature. Recommended shorter and still valuable introductions are Wimmer (1999), CNLS 2:139–64, and Bradner (1957). Edited volumes often contain a number of interesting case studies: recent examples include Glei and Seidel (2008), Bloemendal and Ford (2008), and Ford and Taylor (2013). For Roman comedy, see Duckworth (1952). Grund (2005) is an accessible collection of humanist comedies. Many English university comedies from Oxford and Cambridge are edited in Spevack and Binns (1981–1991). There are also a number of modern editions and translations of individual plays. I have given the citations in my text above when talking about individual authors and works. Jesuit theater across Europe (and beyond) is an extremely diverse subject, which no single study can adequately represent. Valentin's (2001) monograph on the German-speaking lands is the most thorough account of any European region (although, as is frequently the case in studies of Jesuit drama, the eighteenth century is absent).

References

Andreae, Johann Valentin. 1907. *Turbo oder der irrende Ritter vom Geist*. Translated by Wilhelm Süß. Tübingen: Verlag der Laupp'schen Buchhandlung.

Bachmann, Christian. 2003. *Melancholicus: Comoedia nova (1611)*. Edited and translated by Nicole Fabisch. Berlin: Weidler.

Bloemendal, Jan, and Philip Ford. 2008. *Neo-Latin Drama: Forms, Functions, Receptions*. Hildesheim: Olms.

Bloemendal, Jan, and Howard Norland. 2013. *Neo-Latin Drama: Contexts, Contents and Currents*. Leiden: Brill.

Bradner, Leicester. 1957. "The Latin Drama of the Renaissance (1340–1640)." *Studies in the Renaissance* 4:31–70.

Claus, Anton, ed. 1755. *Exercitationes theatrales a Societatis Iesu magistris inferiorum classium . . . exhibitae*. Augsburg: Wolff.

Cramer, Daniel. 2009. *Plagium*. Edited by Federica Masiero and translated by Bartholomäus Ringwaldt. Berlin: Weidler.

Donatus, Aelius. 1902. *Aeli Donati quod fertur Commentum Terenti*. Vol. 1. Edited by Paul Wessner. Leipzig: Teubner.

Duckworth, George E. 1952. *The Nature of Roman Comedy: A Study in Popular Entertainment*. Princeton: Princeton University Press.

Dürrwächter, Anton. 1912. *Jakob Gretser und seine Dramen: Ein Beitrag zur Geschichte des Jesuitendramas in Deutschland*. Freiburg: Herder.

Flayder, Hermann. 1925. *Hermann Flayders ausgewählte Werke*. Edited by Gustav Bebermeyer. Leipzig: Hiersemann.

Ford, Philip, and Andrew Taylor, eds. 2013. *The Early Modern Cultures of Neo-Latin Drama*. Leuven: Leuven University Press.

Frischlin, Nicodemus. 1995. *Hildegardis Magna—Dido—Venus—Helvetiogermani*. 2 vols. Edited and translated by Nicola Kaminski. Bern: Lang.

———. 2003. *Sämtliche Werke*. Vol. 3.1, *Priscianus vapulans (Der geschlagene Priscian)—Iulius redivivus (Julius Caesars Rückkehr ins Erdenleben)*. Edited and translated by Christoph Jungck and Lothar Mundt. Stuttgart: Frommann-Holzboog.

Glei, Reinhold F., and Robert Seidel, eds. 2008. *Das lateinische Drama der Frühen Neuzeit: Exemplarische Einsichten in Praxis und Theorie*. Tübingen: Niemeyer.

Gnapheus, Guilielmus. 1964. *Acolastus: A Latin Play of the Sixteenth Century*. Edited and translated by William E. D. Atkinson. London: Humanities Departments of the University of Western Ontario.

Grendler, Paul F. 2014. "Jesuit Schools in Europe: A Historiographical Essay." *Journal of Jesuit Studies* 1:7–25.

Gretser, Jakob. 1897–1898. *Jakob Gretsers De regno Humanitatis Comoedia prima.* Edited by Anton Dürrwächter. *Programm zum Jahresbericht über das Kgl. Alte Gymnasium zu Regensburg im Schuljahr 1897/98.*

Grund, Gary R. ed. 2005. *Humanist Comedies.* Cambridge: Harvard University Press.

Herbrüggen, Hubertus S. 1991. "La Danse macabre, the English Dance of Death, and William Drury's Mors Comoedia." In *ACNL* 1991, 645–53.

Lachmann, Fritz R. 1926. *Die* Studentes *des Christophorus Stymmelius und ihre Bühne: Als Anhang eine Übersetzung des Stückes.* Leipzig: Voss.

Macropedius, Georgius. 1897. *Rebelles und Aluta.* Edited by Johannes Bolte. Berlin: Weidmann.

Masen, Jacob. 1988. *The Jesuit Theater of Jacob Masen: Three Plays in Translation with an Introduction.* Edited and translated by Michael C. Halbig. New York: Lang.

Mundt, Lothar. 1983. *Lemnius und Luther: Studien und Texte zur Geschichte und Nachwirkung ihres Konflikts (1538/39).* 2 vols. Bern: Lang.

Naogeorgus, Thomas. 1975. *Sämtliche Werke.* Vol. 1.1, *Tragoedia nova Pammachius.* Edited with the translation of Johann Tyrolff by Hans-Gert Roloff. Berlin: De Gruyter.

Palmireno, Juan L. 1574 (2002–2004). "Palmyreni *Fabella Aenaria*: La *Farsa Enaria* de Palmireno (1574)." Edited by Julio Alonso Asenjo. *TeatrEsco* 0 (2002–2004). Available at http://parnaseo.uv.es/Ars/teatresco/Revista/Revista0.htm.

Pérez, Juan. 2012. *Teatro y universidad: Las comedias humanísticas de Juan Pérez (Petreius).* Edited and translated by María del Val Gago Saldaña. Madrid: Liceus.

Reuchlin, Johannes. 1970. *Henno.* Edited and translated by Harry C. Schnur. Stuttgart: Reclam.

Spevack, Martin, and James W. Binns, eds. 1981–1991. *Renaissance Latin Drama in England.* 32 vols. Hildesheim: Olms.

Squire, Robert. 1982. "Robert Squire's *Death, a Comedie*: A Seventeenth Century Translation of William Drury's *Mors.*" Edited by Michael T. Siconolfi. Ph.D. diss., Syracuse University. ProQuest (document ID 303249299).

Valentin, Jean-Marie. 1983–1984. *Le Théâtre des Jésuites dans les pays de langue allemande: Répertoire chronologique des pièces représentées et des documents conservés (1555–1773).* 2 vols. Stuttgart: Hiersemann.

———. 2001. *Les jésuites et le théâtre (1554–1680): Contribution à l'histoire culturelle du monde catholique dans le Saint-Empire romain germanique.* Paris: Desjonquères.

Van de Venne, Hans. 1983–1984. "Cornelius Schonaeus 1541–1611: A Bibliography of His Printed Works." *Humanistica Lovaniensia* 32:367–433 and 33:206–314.

Verweij, Michiel. 1993. "Het thema Tobias in het Neolatijnse schooltoneel in de Nederlanden in de 16de eeuw: De *Tobaeus* van Cornelius Schonaeus (1569) en de Tobias van Petrus Vladeraccus (1598)." Ph.D. diss., Leuven University.

Wimmer, Ruprecht. 1999. "Le théâtre néo-latin en Europe." In *Spectaculum Europaeum: Theatre and Spectacle in Europe*, edited by Pierre Béhar and Helen Watanabe-O'Kelly, 3–75. Wiesbaden: Harrassowitz.

CHAPTER 7

....

TRAGEDY

....

GARY R. GRUND

THE BACKGROUND

FROM the beginning, tragedy was a very unstable compound. In its earliest manifestation, sometime in the seventh century BCE, it was connected to the choral lyric, the dith-
yramb, which formed part of the religious worship of the god Dionysus. Later, "tragedy"
referred to narrative poetry. Aristotle, for instance, explicitly identified the *Iliad* and the
Odyssey as tragic genres in his *Poetics* (1448b–1449a), commending the former for its
pathetic finale and the latter for its retributive resolution whereby the hero received his
just rewards (1459a). Other tragic precepts of Aristotle, which influenced later poetics,
included his famous definition of tragedy as "an imitation (*mimesis*) of an action that is
serious, complete, and of a certain magnitude, adorned with elevated language" (1449b
24–26); his preference for heroic myth as subject matter; and his ideal protagonist who
is virtuous but who, through some flaw (*hamartia*) in him, falls precipitously from his
prosperity and good fortune to adversity, a reversal (*peripeteia*) that arouses in spectators the emotions of pity and fear (1453a). Thus, from the beginning, tragedy was about
great men and women who were forced to make decisions amidst impossible choices.
The purpose of tragedy's emotional arousal was to bring about a release, a cleansing
(*katharsis*), of these feelings that produced pleasure and represented a process unique to
this form of art. Although the concept of catharsis is well known today, it did not seem to
play an important role either for Aristotle himself or for his successors in poetics, until
the early modern period. As we shall see, however, most later discussions included an
emphasis on pitiable and pathetic events, especially in the resolution of the tragedy.

   Some important modifications to Aristotle's theory can be found in the late antique
grammarians Diomedes and Donatus, who were widely read in the medieval period.
Both authors emphasized the unhappy ending and extended the kinds of characters
suitable for tragedy to historical persons of high social status (Kelly 1993, 9–12). Implicit,
too, in their approaches to the tragic resolution was an acceptance of Aristotle's goal for
tragedy: to affect the emotions of the audience morally and aesthetically. There were

many definitions of tragedy formulated by other grammarians and rhetoricians during the late classical world and the Middle Ages. The writings of Lactantius (fourth century), Boethius (sixth century), Isidore of Seville (seventh century), Remigius (tenth century), and William of Conches (twelfth century), among many others, all testify to the ongoing readjustment, adaptation, and refashioning of the genre. The definition of tragedy was in a continuing state of flux and realignment, but it was precisely out of what seemed its permanently unsettled state that its adaptability emerged. Tragedy's very instability became the source of its utility in succeeding centuries. Later Neo-Latin dramatists would deploy tragedy as an instrument in propaedeutic and pedagogical instruction, in doctrinal and sectarian debate, and in historical orientation and national identity.

HUMANIST TRAGEDY

A critical turning point was reached, however, in the ongoing discourse regarding tragedy with the rediscovery of the eleventh-century Codex Etruscus of the tragedies of Lucius Annaeus Seneca (first century CE) at the Benedictine abbey of Pomposa, near Ferrara, in Italy by the Paduan scholar Lovato dei Lovati (1240/41–1309). This manuscript represented the earliest complete collection of Seneca's nine tragedies—*Hercules Furens, Troades, Phoenissae, Medea, Phaedra, Oedipus, Agamemnon, Thyestes,* and *Hercules Oetaeus*—and served as a fundamental text in the revival of tragedy. In fact, the history of Latin humanist tragedy in Italy during the Trecento and Quattrocento is largely the story of the imitation and adaptation of Seneca, with Padua and Lovati's learned circle providing an influential model (Witt 2000, 81–116).

Seneca's tragedies are filled with moral precepts. In addition, his moral essays and letters, which were well known in the Middle Ages, continued to exert an influence on humanist curricula as many educators mined Seneca's writings, including the tragedies, for their *sententiae* (Grendler 1989, 250–60). The plays tended to focus, too, "on the inner workings of the human mind, on the mind as *locus* of emotional conflict, incalculable suffering, insatiable appetite, manic joy, cognitive vulnerability, self-deception, irrational guilt" (Boyle 1997, 25). Seneca's inflated style—his long, declamatory speeches, his bombast, his *stichomythia*, his rhetorical characters (especially the *nuntius* ["messenger"])—had its core in Stoic wisdom and was never executed for ornamental display alone but was directed toward tragic characterization.

After Lovato's discovery of Seneca's plays at Pomposa and the establishment of Padua as the epicenter of Senecan scholarship, it was perfectly fitting that the first Senecan humanist Latin tragedy, the *Ecerinis*, would be written by Lovati's disciple Albertino Mussato (Locati 2006). The drama was written in 1314, and, though the *dramatis personae* are not made up of mythological characters, Mussato himself said that the title character in his *Ecerinis* reminded him of Seneca's *Medea* and *Thyestes*. The play is also like a Senecan drama in that it has five acts, a chorus, dialogue, and employs the dramatic iambic trimeter in its narrative passages. The central character was Ezzelino III da Romano (1194–1259), the "tyrant of Padua" as he was called, who as Frederick II's lieutenant was a central figure in the Guelf–Ghibelline conflicts of the thirteenth century. His Latinized name "Ecerinus" plus the epic sounding suffix *-is* accounts for the title *Ecerinis*. However, Mussato's historical narrative was a carefully crafted portrait of the Veronese tyrant Cangrande della Scala, who threatened Paduan sovereignty during Mussato's tenure as diplomat and soldier in the wars between Verona and Padua from 1312 to 1328. In short, the *Ecerinis* was written as a warning to Mussato's fellow Paduans.

Besides his use of Seneca's *Thyestes*, Mussato also drew on the pseudo-Senecan *Octavia*, a *fabula praetexta*. Such ancient dramas—and the *Octavia* is the only surviving example—dealt with historical subjects, in this case with the murder of Nero's ex-wife on her ex-husband's orders. Ezzelino played the same role in Mussato's tragedy as Nero did in the pseudo-Senecan play; they were both monsters, guilty of unspeakable atrocities, and destined to fall. And just as the Roman tragedy dealt with traditional nationhood and Roman identity, the *Ecerinis* prominently featured the Paduan citizenry in a leading role, clearly as the protagonist of the play, as the moral anchor in a tempestuous world. The play was so successful that Mussato was honored as poet laureate of the city-state on December 3, 1315, and a statute was passed that the play should be read to the public every Christmas to strengthen their patriotism. The dramatic convergence of history and myth discernible in the *Ecerinis* would have far-reaching consequences.

There were ten Latin humanist tragedies written during the Trecento and Quattrocento (for an accessible selection of texts, see Grund 2011), and in its treatment of Italian history, Mussato's *Ecerinis* influenced at least four of them: *The Misfortune of Cesena* (*De casu Cesene*, 1377) by Ludovico Romani da Fabriano; an unfinished tragedy (fifty-eight verses of the Chorus have survived) by Giovanni Manzini della Motta (1387) on the fall of Verona and of Antonio della Scala; the *Tragedy on the Captivity of Duke Giacomo* (*De captivitate ducis Iacobi tragoedia*, 1465) by Laudivio Zacchia da Vezzano; and the *Tragedy of Italian Affairs and the Triumph of Louis XII, King of France* (*De rebus Italicis deque triumpho Ludovici XII regis Francorum tragoedia*, 1499–1500) by Giovanni Armonio Manso (Stäuble 1991, 205–6). Mussato's choice of recent history as tragic subject matter, however, was not followed by his immediate successors; they chose instead to select episodes from ancient legend or history that Seneca had not used and to treat them as Seneca might have done. The goal, in short, was to "out-Seneca" Seneca.

Antonio Loschi, perhaps best known for his exchange of invectives with Coluccio Salutati regarding the wars between Florence and Milan from 1390 to 1401, wrote his *Achilles* sometime around 1387, a work that from its title would seem to indicate Loschi's source would probably be the same collection of Homeric heroic plots from which Seneca drew. Loschi's source, however, was not Homer but the late antique prose narrative *De excidio Troiae* (*The Destruction of Troy*) by pseudo-Dares the Phrygian, one of the most important agents in the transmission of Homeric legends to the Middle Ages. In its adaptation of Senecan dramatic convention, the *Achilles* followed Mussato's *Ecerinis*—both use dramatic meter and choruses, and both relied on the operation of the Senecan *lex talionis*, the law of retribution, to resolve the play—but Loschi's play presented two tragic protagonists, Paris and Achilles; two competing choruses, one Greek and the other Trojan; and insisted on a much more pagan (and Senecan) fortune than is found in Mussato's work: "All our acts depend on the turning stars, and the course of the heavens rules all things on earth. Not even a god himself can alter whatever is woven by the Fates on high" (ll. 937–40). In addition, love is made the vehicle of retribution, an idea that is neither Homeric nor Senecan (Herrick 1965, 13). The plot of the play is characterized by a constant oscillation between the two warring camps and the two overconfident heroes made vulnerable by love. Loschi's interest is in the melodrama of the love-intrigue. His obsession with the cruelty and treachery surrounding Achilles's murder by Paris will be repeated in a story of sexual desire and unimaginable horror, Gregorio Correr's *Procne* (ca. 1429), written when he was eighteen years old.

Correr's subject was also not drawn from the reservoir of Homeric plots but from the much more sensational *Metamorphoses* of Ovid where the story of Tereus, Procne, and Philomela is, perhaps, the most horrific of all (6.424–674). Accentuating the unspeakable nature of the action, characterized by rape, murder, and cannibalism, was Correr's choice to name his play, not after the victim of the *lex talionis* as Mussato and Loschi had done, but after its enforcer. The play was, furthermore, condensed into a few days of dramatic time so that the final banquet scene when Tereus eats the flesh and drinks the blood of his son Itys seems to come very quickly; the scene is also not reported but takes place onstage. Correr was very aware of the differences between simply narrating tragedy and theatricalizing it.

Like his predecessors, Leonardo Dati in his *Hiempsal* (ca. 1442) employed the same conventional Senecan devices but selected his plot neither from Homeric legend, Ovidian narrative, nor Italian history, but from Roman history, actually from an African episode in Roman history presented by Sallust in his *Jugurthine War* (ca. 41–40 BCE; Hiempsal was a rival of Jugurtha). Sallust was very concerned in his history of war in Numidia and the subsequent transference of power to express his own fear of the decline of Roman moral virtue. And like Mussato, who still clung to the traditions of medieval allegory by introducing Satan into his tragedy, Dati couched his entire play in the same moralistic context by having the subject (and character) of Envy frame the work along with Ambition, Modesty, Discord, and Perfidy. This reimagined morality play also functioned, we have come to learn, as Dati's submission to the second proposed *certame coronario*, a literary contest in Florence organized by Leon Battista Alberti (1404–1472) on the subject of envy. The contest never took place, but in the midst of a politically charged climate (Gorni 1972, 135–81) Dati's *Hiempsal* contextualized Florentine history and mirrored Sallust's method regarding ancient Roman history.

Humanist Neo-Latin tragedy in Italy had a much shorter shelf-life than comedy and apparently had little appeal for Renaissance readers. Thus, *Hiempsal* was never printed, *Procne* not until 1558, and *Ecerinis* and *Achilles* not until the seventeenth century. Some of the reasons may be obvious: tragedy was always concerned with larger-than-life men and women faced with impossible decisions, while humanist comedy dealt with the popular subjects known from Roman Comedy—love, sex, money, and manners. Tragedy was aristocratic, courtly, and rhetorical; comedy, everyday, ordinary, and conversational. Although the records of performances are scanty, comedy was acted before audiences more often and was found to be much more attractive to later vernacular dramatists.

By the end of the Quattrocento, the genre of tragedy had become further problematized by politics, and, although the final works in this period are negligible as drama, they maintained and transmitted the tradition that tragedy could deal with contemporary history. Both Carlo Verardi's *Historia Baetica* (*Andalusian History*, 1492), which concerned the conquest of Granada and the expulsion of the Moors by Ferdinand II of Aragon, and Carlo's nephew Marcellino Verardi's *Fernandus servatus* (*Ferdinand Preserved*, 1493), which dealt with an unsuccessful assassination attempt on Ferdinand, represent dramatic hybrids. They were vehicles of political propaganda set uneasily within the dimensions of Senecan drama. Both plays were performed before the newly elected pope, Alexander VI (1431–1503), and members of the papal court at the Palazzo Riario in Viterbo. The popularity of Ferdinand as an appropriate subject for drama may be partly explained by the recent election on August 11, 1492, of a Borgia pope, who was born in Valencia and whose uncle, Pope Calixtus III (1378–1458), was another Spaniard. Carlo advertised his play not even as drama but as history, while Marcellino called his work a *tragicomoedia* in its preface because, echoing Plautus's prologue to his *Amphitruo*, "the rank of the characters and the impious attack on his Majesty point to tragedy, while the happy ending belongs to comedy." While the *Fernandus servatus* represents an unusual compounding of history with epic myth (the play is written in dactylic hexameters), of ancient pagan drama with Catholic propaganda, and of medieval morality (Saint James, the patron saint of Spain, appears to Isabella) with theatrical spectacle, it does seem to have had some influence on later manifestations of historical tragedy.

For example, Jakob Locher, an ardent German humanist well known for his Latin translation of Sebastian Brant's *Das Narrenschiff* (*Ship of Fools*) in his 1497 *Stultifera navis*, probably came into contact with Verardi's *Historia Baetica* during his trip to Italy in 1493 because, two years later, Locher wrote and produced in Freiburg his *Historia de rege Franciae* (*History of the King of France*). This work, more documentary history than tragic drama perhaps, despite its use of Senecan conventions, dealt with the campaigns of Charles VIII against Naples in 1495. Apparently, the play achieved a measure of success, since Locher published two other tragedies: the *Tragedia de Thurcis et Suldano* (*Tragedy about the Turks and the Sultan*, 1497) and the *Spectaculum more tragico effigiatum* (*Spectacle, Written in the Form of a Tragedy*, 1502).

Another German humanist also influenced by Verardi, Johann von Kitzscher (d. 1521), studied in Rome and Bologna and composed his *Tragicocomedia de Iherosolomitana profectione illustrissimi principis Pomerani* (*Tragicomedy about the Famous Duke of Pomerania's Journey to Jerusalem*, 1501) on the pilgrimage to Jerusalem of Duke Bogislaw X. Hermann Schottenius's tragic prose drama on the Peasants' Rebellion, *Ludus Martius* (*War Play*), was published in 1525 and owes more to the medieval morality play— Bellona is opposed by Peace—than to Italian humanism. Still, the potent combination of contemporary history and Senecan dramatic convention continued to resonate well into the sixteenth century. Thus, as late as 1558, the Portuguese humanist Diogo de Teive composed his *Ioannes Princeps sive unicum Regni ereptum lumen* (*Prince John, or The Kingdom Bereaved of Its Only Light*) about the untimely death in 1554 of João Manuel, Prince of Portugal, the son of King John III who himself died in 1557. The play is gravely Senecan, laden with omens and a melancholy chorus, which expresses a dread of the extinction of the dynasty and the loss of independence (Frèches 1964).

It is clear that humanist tragedy was never confined to its birthplace in Italy, but as it moved north and west, its characteristic attributes were altered to meet many different cultural, political, and religious demands. In Spain, one of the earliest printed plays was the tragedy *Galathea* (1502; the title is from the eponymous heroine), composed by a Greek humanist who lived in Spain, Hercules Florus—a play that also looked back to the moral allegories of the Middle Ages in its use of such characters as Ratio (Reason), Occasio (Opportunity), and Ultima Necessitas (Ultimate Necessity) and warned in its sober conclusion that all earthly love leads to tragedy. The dramatic components of this tragic romantic pastoral, of course, call to mind another influential composition from the period, *La Celestina* by Fernando de Rojas, written in the vernacular in 1499. The influence of this work and the paucity of Neo-Latin tragedies outside of the schools suggest how firmly the vernacular would dominate later Spanish drama (Briesemeister 1985, 1–28).

THE INSTITUTIONALIZING OF NEO-LATIN
TRAGEDY AFTER 1500

It is fair to say that from the sixteenth century onwards, most Neo-Latin drama was written specifically for schools and universities across Europe. Seneca (as well as Plautus and Terence) continued to play an important role in pedagogy, both for his moral precepts and for his eloquence. "Since Cicero and Quintilian had both underlined the importance of enunciation (*pronuntiatio*) and memory (*memoria*) in the rhetorical training of the orator, the schoolmen were easily moved to promote school performances of the classical plays" (Parente 1987, 13–14). The early exuberance of humanist idealism, however, began to clash with the tenets of Christian orthodoxy, and this was especially the case as the sixteenth century wore on. Christian humanists like Konrad Celtis (1459–1508), Erasmus (1466–1536), Philipp Melanchthon (1497–1560), and Johannes Sturm (1507–1589) staunchly defended ancient drama, claiming, first, that classical grammar and rhetoric were essential for the contemporary theologian, for without this knowledge he would be unable to understand God's Word (Boyle 1997, 3–25), and, second, that ethical lessons could only be derived from a play, regardless of its genre, if the viewers were confronted with a choice between virtuous and evil behavior (Parente 1987, 20). Still, the unspeakable acts Senecan tragedy dealt with weighed uneasily on the minds of Christian schoolmasters. Though the works of Plautus, Terence, and Seneca continued to be performed in the schools, religious Neo-Latin plays outnumbered their secular counterparts, and both existed in a very uneasy alliance.

In Germany, and generally in Northern Europe, humanist drama was quickly adopted by the schools, although it would be quickly tempered by the religious concerns of the Reformation and Counter-Reformation, as we shall see below. Dutch and German schoolmasters regularly performed plays with their students, and the same was true at universities across Europe. Thus, George Buchanan, a Scotsman whose Latin erudition took him to teaching posts in Paris and Bordeaux, where one of his pupils, Michel de Montaigne, had acted in his plays, and finally to Coimbra, where he was imprisoned (along with Diogo de Teive) by the Inquisition, composed two tragedies for performance by his students, *Iephthes* (1554) and *Baptistes* (1577). So, too, Marc-Antoine Muret's only play, a Latin tragedy, *Julius Caesar* (1547), was presented at the college in Bordeaux, and in Paris, Claude Roillet published three tragedies in 1536, *Philanira, Petrus*, and *Aman*, to be acted by his pupils. Because of the wide availability of printing, universities could also import and export a variety of academic plays.

The enthusiasm of Continental humanists and reformers for the acting of classical plays as a method of educational training soon spread to academic circles in England (Boas 1914, 16). Oxford and Cambridge provide us with extensive records of performances of both religious and secular drama. The tragedies of Naogeorgus, Buchanan, and Roillet are duly represented in early Tudor years, and there can be no doubt that Continental Neo-Latin plays on biblical subjects influenced the work of the first Oxford dramatist, Nicholas Grimald (1519–1562), whose reputation in England is more closely attached to the lyric poems he contributed to Richard Tottel's *Miscellany* in 1557. Grimald wrote eight plays, six of which were in Latin, although only two have survived: *Christus redivivus* (*Christ Revived*, 1543) and *Archipropheta* (*Arch-Prophet*, 1548). The first play is indebted to a French humanist, Nicolas Barthélemy de Loches, whose *Christus xylonicus* (*Christ Triumphant Through the Cross*, 1529) ends with Christ on the cross and at the tomb, while Grimald's begins with his resurrection. Possibly the only trace of Senecan apparatus is to be found in the creation of the character Cacodaemon from Tartarus, a sort of pre-Miltonic Satan, who functions as an ally to the high priest Caiaphas. Nevertheless, the play seems to have exerted a strong influence on German school drama—it was also acted at Augsburg—and became absorbed in the German text used for the Passion play at Oberammergau until 1740 (Wilson 1969, 91). Grimald's *Archipropheta* also appears to have benefited from another Continental source, the *Ectrachelistis sive Ioannes decollatus* (*The Man with the Broken Neck or John Beheaded*, 1546) by Jakob Schöpper. Despite the fact that Grimald's rendering of the career of John the Baptist seems to beg for comparison to Buchanan's *Baptistes* (written during the 1530s but not published until 1577), Grimald's interweaving of romance and tragedy is far from the solemn austerity of Buchanan (Boas 1914, 41). At Cambridge, where the acting of comedy was more sought after, very little stands out except for, perhaps, Thomas Watson's *Absalon* (acted ca. 1540), until Thomas Legge's neo-Senecan tragedy *Richardus Tertius* (*Richard III*, acted in 1579), a play that has the distinction of being one of the first plays based on English history.

The overwhelming majority of tragedies written for schools and universities were on biblical themes. Of Old Testament stories, without question the most popular were those involving Joseph. "After Joseph the favorite figures were Adam and Eve, Isaac, David, Esther, and Susanna. ... Other subjects dramatized were Abel, Agag, Elijah, Deborah, Gideon, Jereboam, Jeremiah, Jonah, Job, Jephthah, Ruth, Saul, Samuel, Solomon, Sodom, Tobias, and Zedekiah" (Bradner 1957, 41–42). And because moral improvement was far more important than adherence to classical form, not only were school plays often only marginally Senecan, but they also tended to similarly blur the generic distinctions between tragedy and comedy. Tragicomedies—serious stories with happy endings—predominated and, indeed, seem to have contributed to the growth of tragicomedy as a genre in the later Renaissance (Herrick 1955).

Many plays that drew on narratives from the New Testament focused on the theme of the Prodigal Son and, of course, on events from the life of Christ. Those that dealt with his trial and crucifixion would appear to be ideal subjects of tragedy, and there was even some precedent in Italy post-1500 for such experiments: namely, the *Theoandrothanatos* (*God-Man-Death*, 1508) by Quintianus Stoa, who would also publish a tragedy in Paris six years later on the Last Judgment, the *Theocrisis* (*God's Judgment*), and the *Christus* (1556) by Coriolano Martirano (1503–1557). Stoa has the distinction of being the first to apply the style and structure of Senecan tragedy to a Christian subject. Of particular note because of its highly unusual adherence to classical precedent, in this case Aeschylean tragedy, was the much later *Parabata vinctus, sive triumphus Christi* (*Parabata* [i.e., *Lucifer*] *Bound, or The Triumph of Christ*, 1595) by Jacques-Auguste de Thou. Although de Thou's source was Aeschylus's *Prometheus Bound* (as well as one of Martirano's classical plays, the *Prometheus*), de Thou's Prometheus was replaced by Lucifer, Hephaestus by the Archangel Michael, and Oceanus and Io by Job, Elias, and John the Baptist. Plays on classical subjects were relatively scarce, but beginning in the middle of the sixteenth century, this pattern was reversed.

The translation, dissemination, and commentary on Seneca's tragedies reemphasized that tragedy could be adapted to didactic purposes; as we have seen, this was a principle adopted by early humanists like Erasmus and Melanchthon. Muret's *Julius Caesar* in 1552 may well have initiated the shift in taste since, in the next hundred years, at least forty plays on classical subjects appeared (Bradner 1957, 47). Many dealt with the events in the Virgilian epic, in Ovidian narrative, or ancient Roman history, such as Michael Virdung's *Brutus* (1596) and *Thrasea* (1609), Nicodemus Frischlin's *Dido* (1584), and Matthew Gwinne's *Nero* (1603), among many others (*CNLS* 2:145). Along with Gwinne at Oxford was William Gager, the author of three tragedies: *Meleager* (acted in 1582, printed 1592), *Dido* (acted in 1583), and *Ulysses Redux* (acted and printed in 1592). Perhaps the most gruesome of Senecan tragedies (and not even based on a classical story) performed at Cambridge was William Alabaster's *Roxana* (acted in 1592, printed 1632), which boasted such delightful elements as murder, suicide, incest, flagellation, poisoning, infanticide, and cannibalism. Even Gregorio Correr's *Procne*, which Alabaster was apparently familiar with, since an adaptation was performed on the same stage in 1566, had the decency to depict these unspeakable things offstage in appropriate Senecan fashion.

Reformation and Counter-Reformation Tragedy

From its early adoption in European schools and universities, religion was one of the dominating concerns of Neo-Latin drama. But its development in the context of religious controversy so pervasive in the sixteenth century deserves a section of its own. Although Protestants and Catholics sparred over the spiritual authority of the pope, the main objective of humanist religious drama in the sixteenth century was the dissemination of moral guidelines for the attainment of salvation (Parente 1987, 61). Clearly, of course, the theological differences were significant as the two sides argued over matters of faith and good works, but on the sixteenth-century stage, both Protestant and Catholic dramatists agreed on the basic possibility of salvation. Strangely, there was a good deal of cross-fertilizing. For example, at the Protestant Strasbourg gymnasium, founded in 1538 under the rectorship of Johannes Sturm (1507–1589), who was, perhaps, the most renowned educator associated with the Reformed Church, Gregorius Holonius's 1556 Catholic martyr-tragedy *Laurentias* was performed to great acclaim; in Jesuit schools as well, Protestant plays were performed rather regularly. The demands of pedagogy abrogated the polemics of theology. Thus, two anthologies of biblical plays printed in Basel by Brylinger (*Comoediae ac tragoediae aliquot ex novo et vetere testamento desumptae* [*Several Comedies and Tragedies Taken from the Old and New Testaments*], 1540) and Oporinus (*Dramata sacra* [*Sacred Plays*], 1547) included both Protestant and Catholic tragedies.

Instead of focusing on doctrinal differences, much Counter-Reformation tragedy engaged in attacks either on the legitimacy of the Protestant revolt or on its initiator, Martin Luther. For example, in the many tragedies of Hieronymus Ziegler (1514–1562), the Old Testament was the source of his condemnation of the Reformation, paralleling biblical events with the Lutheran schism. Andreas Fabricius also employed in his *Ieroboam rebellans* (1585) the rebellion of Jeroboam against the house of David in I Kings 12–14. Protestant responses were not lacking. Tales from the Bible were composed to mirror the conditions of the times, often with satirical intentions. We have already mentioned Thomas Naogeorgus, a fervent Lutheran pastor and important anti-Catholic polemicist, whose *Iudas Iscariotes* (1552) Creizenach (1918, 126) characterized as a drama of hate and anger. Judas is Naogeorgus's metaphor for those early converts to the cause of the Reformation who were now returning to Catholicism and undermining Lutheran advances. The conception of Judas is on one hand thoroughly medieval—the two allegorical figures of the Devil and Conscientia contend for the possession of Judas's soul—but Naogeorgus focuses on the emotional context of the betrayal and, on the other hand, casts Judas as a tragic figure in the Senecan mode with choruses punctuating each act. Two other plays, *Pammachius* ([*The Pope*] *Who Fights Against Everything*, 1538) and *Incendia* (*Fires*, 1541), are violent attacks on papal authority. When Naogeorgus turned his attention to biblical narrative as he did with *Iudas Iscariotes, Hamanus* (1543), and *Hieremias* (1551), he read the Bible as contemporary allegory; biblical drama and polemical drama were inseparable (Bradner 1957, 40). Although few editions of his Latin plays are extant, Naogeorgus's works were quickly and widely translated into vernacular languages across Europe.

Early in the sixteenth century, Neo-Latin religious drama was primarily an instrument in school curricula, designed for the inculcation and exposition of the articles of the new, reformed faith, and not as a weapon for evangelical change. The polemical potential of drama would be fully realized, however, with the advent of the Counter-Reformation. As we shall see, Jesuit school dramatists discovered that Christianizing classical drama was problematic, as students were increasingly drawn to the pleasures of pagan litera-ture; new restrictions would inevitably be placed on the use of ancient texts. At the same time, the humanist inheritors of Lutheran zeal, especially in the Netherlands, also con-fronted the dilemma of what Christ had to do with Apollo. A good deal of the consterna-tion was occasioned by the reinvention of Aristotle's *Poetics*.

Before 1498 when Giorgio Valla (1447–1500) published his Latin translation of the text, the *Poetics* was largely unknown. Despite the translation into Latin by William of Moerbeke in 1278 (only two manuscripts of that work have survived), Averroes's para-phrase translated from the Arabic by Hermannus Alemannus in 1256, or the publication of the Greek text in 1508 by Aldo Manuzio, the work was known only to a few scholars. It was only during the second half of the Cinquecento that Aristotle's text became more intelligible and influential; the surge of interest was stimulated by Francesco Robortello's commentary of 1548. Here, Robortello sees drama, and poetry in general, as having two ends: the pleasure and the instruction of the audience, much as Horace does in his *Ars poetica*. The instruction consists of the moral betterment of the audience through *exem-pla*, striking demonstrations, and *sententiae*. The rhetorical demands or expectations of the audience are the key.

Julius Caesar Scaliger (1484–1558) in his posthumous *Poetics* (1561) shared the beliefs of Robortello and others about the emotional effects of tragedy and, in fact, did more to reintroduce the Renaissance world to the rhetorical aspects of the genres of content (Francis Cairns in Grafton, Most, and Settis 2010, 391). Scaliger defined tragedy as an *oratio gravis, culta, a vulgi dictione aversa, tota facies anxia, metus, minae, exilia, mortes* ("a dignified oration, refined, distinct from vulgar diction, its entire form troubled, deal-ing with fears, threats, exiles, and deaths"; Parente 1987, 53), discarded the concept of catharsis from serious consideration, and adopted Seneca as his tragic epitome. Senecan violence and horrors, therefore, were the chief method of stimulating the appropriate responses from an audience. Despite the fact that Senecan tragedy turned on the seem-ingly Judeo-Christian idea of the *lex talionis*, the law of retaliation in kind, where crimes are punished according to their deserts in this life, Scaliger's vision was cynical, fatal-istic, and pessimistic, so it inevitably clashed with the Christian emphasis on history as soteriological, where God's divine justice and Christ's redemptive act prevailed. To forestall such potential doubts implicit in biblical tragedy, the tragedies of Hugo Grotius (1583–1645) and Daniel Heinsius (1580–1655) attempted to demonstrate that Christ's promise of salvation could turn tragic despair into Christian victory. Their experiments further problematized an increasingly uncertain genre. The growing amalgamation and syntheses of biblical Christianity and Senecan Stoicism in neo-Latin Reformation and Counter-Reformation tragedy represented the broad adaptability of the genre but underscored their uneasy alliance.

During the early Cinquecento, we should recall, Quintianus Stoa had composed his *Theoandrothanatos* (1508) on the Passion of Christ according to strict Senecan principles: a five-act structure, punctuated by vivid descriptions of the bloody torture of Christ, and a marked insistence on the inconsolable grief of the Virgin Mary expressed in long, declamatory speeches. Stoa had secularized a Christian subject, especially in emphasizing the Stoic fortitude of both Mother and divine Son; it was as if their suffering was an example of the immutable vicissitudes of fortune. When Grotius and Heinsius wrote their Christian tragedies, conversely they were acutely aware of the limitations of Senecan tragic theory. In *Adamus exul* (*Adam in Exile*, 1601) Grotius characterized Satan as the operator of the Senecan *lex talionis* who persuaded Eve through the use of Stoic arguments from the moral essays of Seneca. In other words, the Fall was brought about by a combination of Satanic revenge and the human weaknesses of Adam and Eve, and yet all would be made whole by the promise of a Redeemer: *Ipse veniet, ipse carnem sumet humanam Deus* ("He himself will come, God himself will take on human flesh"; Parente 1987, 58). In his later *Christus patiens* (*The Suffering Christ*, 1608) and in Heinsius's *Herodes infanticida* (*Herod the Infanticide*, written 1611, printed 1632) the Christianizing of Seneca continued by contrasting the victorious era of grace to the hopelessly limited vision of the pagan world. Heinsius, too, contributed in his *De tragoediae constitutione* (*The Nature of Tragedy*), a treatise published as a supplement to his 1611 edition of Aristotle's *Poetics*, to the ongoing codification of dramatic principles noted above, but in his work, seventeenth-century religious drama was put on an equal footing with secular theater. A similar respect for sacred content, thus, animated the work of many other humanist writers of biblical tragedy, including Rochus Honerdus in his *Thamara* (1611), which was dedicated to Grotius and Heinsius.

JESUIT TRAGEDY

Almost immediately after its founding by Ignatius of Loyola in the 1530s and the formal confirmation of the order by the papal bull of Paul III, *Regimini militantis ecclesiae* (*To the Government of the Church Militant*) in 1540, the Society of Jesus included dramatic activities in its astoundingly successful program of instruction. Like the Lutheran schools in Germany, Sturm at the Strasbourg gymnasium, Buchanan at Bordeaux, and the university drama in England, the Jesuit colleges recognized the pedagogical utility of Latin drama, an important component in Christian humanism, both as a means of perfecting eloquence in the ancient language, and as a way of exalting a devout life and inspiring the audience with the Christian virtues of humility and piety. Thus, in the hundreds of Latin Jesuit plays that have been printed (more than 100,000 may have been written) from its foundation until the temporary suppression of the order in 1773 by Pope Clement XIV, there was a decided concentration, first of all, on developing vocabulary fluency in Latin (*copia verborum*); and then on the resolution of the plot through the protagonists' piety and reward of heavenly bliss, or their tragic refusal to acknowledge God's Word. The Jesuit system of education, building on the curriculum devised by Renaissance humanists and recommending the inclusion of drama, was codified in the Society's curriculum, called *ratio studiorum*, of 1586, 1591, and (in its definitive form) 1599.

Jesuit drama was, of course, also propaganda drama. Many scholars have called attention to the timely coincidence of Ignatius's conversion and the spread of Reformation zeal. In any case, it may surely be stated that the Society of Jesus spearheaded the Counter-Reformation. The first recorded performance of a Jesuit play, in 1551, was an anonymous Latin tragedy staged at the Collegio Mamertino in Messina, Sicily, three years after the founding of this first Jesuit college. As the Reformation gained ground, the expansion of Jesuit colleges was dizzying: 33 in 1556, 150 by 1587, 300 in 1600, and more than 500 by 1700. Their mission stretched from Europe, Asia, and Latin America, with Jesuit drama adapting itself to local tastes and customs. Their plays were performed most regularly and successfully in Europe, but also in places as far away as the Jesuit college at Goa in India.

Although most authors of Jesuit drama were anonymous, in the case of a particularly gifted dramatist, we can identify the names of individual authors. Thus, we can point, for example, to the work of Pedro Pablo de Acevedo at Seville, a priest who wrote twenty-five plays from 1556–1572 and might have been the tutor of Cervantes; Stefano Tucci at Messina whose most popular tragedy, *Christus iudex* (*Christ as Judge*, 1569), achieved a prominence across Europe; Jakob Bidermann, surely the most successful of Bavarian dramatists, whose *Cenodoxus* (*Vainglorious*, the speaking name of the protagonist; first performed at Augsburg in 1602) attacked secular humanism, had his plays published posthumously in the collection *Ludi theatrales sacri* (*Sacred Dramatic Plays*, 1666); the Viennese Jesuit Niccolò Avancini (1612–1686) who wrote twenty-seven tragedies, many on ecclesiastical history; the Englishman Joseph Simons, who composed and performed his five tragedies at the English College at Saint-Omer between 1622 and 1631; and, lastly, Nicolas Caussin (1580–1651) who, along with Jean Surius and the Portuguese Luís da Cruz, published tragedies in the first decades of the seventeenth century in France. A number of tragedies were published in collections, some like da Cruz's *Tragicae comicaeque actiones* (*Tragic and Comic Plays*, 1605), Surius's two volumes of *Morata poesis* (*Poetry Adapted to Manners*, 1617–1618), and Caussin's *Tragoediae sacrae* (*Sacred Tragedies*, 1620) containing only each author's works, but there was also the well-known general collection *Selectae PP. Societatis Jesu tragoediae* (*Selected Tragedies of Fathers of the Society of Jesus*), published in Antwerp in 1634.

As far as subject matter is concerned, the Bible, of course, provided much useful material, but plots were usually—and differently from Protestant drama—selected from the lives of Christian martyrs and saints or, hence, from the early history of the church during its years of persecution by Rome. Some attention was also paid to topical matters of secular history, and, in the eighteenth century, to stories and heroes from classical antiquity. The most popular genre of play was tragicomedy, tragedy with a happy ending, as exemplified by the typical martyr play in which the hero triumphs in death. During a period of more than two centuries, from 1551 to 1773, the Jesuits acquired a remarkable repertory of tragic plays, which drew on such time-honored traditions as Senecan drama, biblical narrative, morality drama, and Catholic hagiography, all while fashioning their compositions to very distinctive national and cultural demands. At the heart of Jesuit tragedy is an insistence on individual responsibility and the exercise of free will, set within the overarching context of an omnipotent Providence. The difference from Luther's tenet of the bondage of the will (to translate the title of his famous treatise *De servo arbitrio* of 1525) was programmatic here. The dramatic ramifications of this endless struggle concerning the destiny of humankind were varied, but it is important to remember that many European writers looked back to the Jesuit school theater where they first came into contact with the stage as part of their schooling. We may point to Molière, Corneille, and Voltaire in France; Lope de Vega and Calderon in Spain; as well as to Protestant writers Joost van den Vondel, a later convert to Catholicism in Holland, and Andreas Gryphius in Germany (Schnitzler 1952, 289).

CONCLUSION

Both in theory and in practice, as we have seen, tragedy proved to be a very flexible, responsive, and fertile medium. The theoretical distance traveled from the speculations of Aristotle about the origins of tragedy to the realignment of Aristotelianism in the theories of Scaliger, for example, seems immense, almost exponential, spanning more than two millennia, and yet tragedy as a genre continued to have at its core an adaptability to the exigencies of cultural, social, political, and religious forces that determined its character.

Practice, of course, always precedes theory. The many Neo-Latin tragedies discussed in this chapter (of the countless written up to the eighteenth century) display a continuing awareness of changing cultural imperatives and, thus, were written to mirror not just the universal truths contained in ancient tragedy but the evolving struggles of contemporary life. The creation of the hybrid form of tragicomedy, the inclusion of historical subject matter, and the reliance on biblical themes represented the dramatic response to emerging societal needs. Thus, from this perspective, the thematic distance from Mussato's *Ezzelino* to Naogeorgus's *Judas* seems short: Paduan independence is as appropriate a subject for tragedy as German Reformation politics. The increasingly moral view of the genre, too, that employed classical, biblical, historical, and allegorical characters provided writers of drama in very different epochs with the opportunity to depict what will always be the central concern of tragedy, the endless struggle between the forces of destiny and human responsibility.

SUGGESTED READING

The subject of Neo-Latin drama is particularly extensive, largely because the genre was international, cross-cultural, and adapted to very different audiences throughout its history. The standard reference is now Bloemendal and Norland (2013). In addition, the *mise en scène* of neo-Latin tragedy has been the subject of many studies. For information on scenic design in Italian Neo-Latin theater, see Andrioli Nemola et al. (2000); on music and dance in Jesuit school drama Walsh (1954) and Devlin (1972). Regarding Jesuit drama, furthermore, the single most important book on Jesuit drama in any European region is Valentin's 1978 study of the German-speaking countries. Of the many European Neo-Latin entertainments, see Béhar and Watanabe-O'Kelly (1999), as well as more specialized national or cultural studies such as the study by Binns (1990) on Elizabethan Latin culture; for historical studies of Neo-Latin drama and its reception in Baltic countries, see Ekrem, Jensen, and Kraggerud (1996); for Nordic Neo-Latin theater, Jensen (1995); and on the subject of Neo-Latin historical drama, Lindenberger (1975) and Bloemendal and Ford (2008).

REFERENCES

Andrioli Nemola, Paola, Giuseppe A. Camerino, Gino Rizzo, and Paolo Viti, eds. 2000. *Teatro, scena, rappresentazione dal Quattrocento al Settecento*. Galatina: Congedo.

Béhar, Pierre, and Helen Watanabe-O'Kelly. 1999. *Spectaculum Europaeum: Theatre and Spectacle in Europe (1580–1750)*. Wiesbaden: Harrassowitz.

Binns, James W. 1990. *Intellectual Culture in Elizabethan and Jacobean England: The Latin Writings of the Age*. Leeds: Francis Cairns.

Bloemendal, Jan, and Howard B. Norland, eds. 2013. *Neo-Latin Drama: Contexts, Contents and Currents*. Leiden: Brill.

Bloemendal, Jan, and Philip Ford, eds. 2008. *Neo-Latin Drama: Forms, Functions, Receptions*. Hildesheim: Olms.

Boas, Frederick. 1914. *University Drama in the Tudor Age*. Oxford: Clarendon Press.

Boyle, Anthony J. 1997. *Tragic Seneca: An Essay in the Theatrical Tradition*. London: Routledge.

Bradner, Leicester. 1957. "The Latin Drama of the Renaissance (1340–1640)." and "List of Original Neo-Latin Plays Printed Before 1650." *Studies in the Renaissance* 4:31–54 and 55–70.

Briesemeister, Dietrich. 1985. "Das mittel- und neulateinische Theater in Spanien." In *Das Spanische Theater*, edited by Hans-Joachim Müller, 1–28. Darmstadt: Wissenschaftliche Buchgesellschaft.

Creizenach, Wilhelm. 1918. *Geschichte des neueren Dramas*. Vol. 2, *Renaissance und Reformation, 1. Teil*. 2nd ed. Halle: Niemeyer.

Devlin, Eugene J. 1972. "Music and Choreography on the Late Humanist Jesuit Stage." *The New Laurel Review* 2:28–34.

Ekrem, Inger, Minna S. Jensen, and Egil Kraggerud, eds. 1996. *Reformation and Latin Literature in Northern Europe*. Oslo: Scandinavian University Press.

Frèches, Claude-Henri. 1964. *Le théâtre neo-latin au Portugal (1550–1745)*. Paris: Nizet.

Gorni, Guglielmo. 1972. "Storia del Certame Coronario." *Rinascimento* 12:135–81.

Grafton, Anthony, Glenn Most, and Salvatore Settis, eds. 2010. *The Classical Tradition*. Cambridge: Harvard University Press.

Grendler, Paul F. 1989. *Schooling in Renaissance Italy: Literacy and Learning, 1300–1600*. Baltimore: Johns Hopkins University Press.

Grund, Gary R., ed. 2011. *Humanist Tragedies*. Cambridge: Harvard University Press.

Herrick, Marvin T. 1955. *Tragicomedy: Its Origin and Development in Italy, France, and England*. Urbana: University of Illinois Press.

———. 1965. *Italian Tragedy in the Renaissance*. Urbana: University of Illinois Press.

Jensen, Minna S. 1995. *A History of Nordic Neo-Latin Literature*. Odense: Odense University Press.

Kelly, Henry A. 1993. *Ideas and Forms of Tragedy from Aristotle to the Middle Ages*. Cambridge: Cambridge University Press.

Lindenberger, Herbert. 1975. *Historical Drama: The Relation of Literature and Reality*. Chicago: University of Chicago Press.

Locati, Silvia. 2006. *La rinascita del genere tragico nel Medioevo*. Florence: Cesati.

Parente, James A. 1987. *Religious Drama and the Humanist Tradition: Christian Theatre in Germany and the Netherlands, 1500–1600*. Leiden: Brill.

Schnitzler, Henry. 1952. "The Jesuit Contribution to the Theatre." *Educational Theatre Journal* 4:283–92.

Stäuble, Antonio. 1991. "L'idea di tragedia nell'umanesimo (con una bibliografia sulla tragedia umanistica)." In *Parlar per lettera: Il pedante nella commedia del Cinquecento e altri saggi sul teatro rinascimentale*, 197–219. Rome: Bulzoni.

Valentin, Jean-Marie, 1978. *Le théâtre des Jésuites dans les pays de langue allemande (1554–1680): Salut des âmes et ordre des cités*. 3 vols. Bern: Lang.

Walsh, John J. 1954. "Ballet on the Jesuit Stage in Italy, Germany, and France." Ph.D. diss., Yale University.

Wilson, Frank P. 1969. *The English Drama, 1485–1585*. Oxford: Clarendon Press.

Witt, Ronald G. 2000. *In the Footsteps of the Ancients: The Origins of Humanism from Lovato to Bruni*. Leiden: Brill.

CHAPTER 8

···

ORATORY

···

MARC VAN DER POEL

THE theory and practice of oratory were strongly intertwined in the Renaissance, as they had been in antiquity. In both Greece and Rome, the practice of public speaking went back to pre-literary times. In Greece, this practice was set down in theoretical rules around the fifth century BCE, and in Rome, the first handbooks of rhetoric were written as late as the first century BCE, although orators and writers were introduced to the Greek theory of eloquence long before that time. During the ten centuries or so when Greco-Roman rhetoric flourished, there was always a natural interplay between theory and practice: developments in the practice of eloquence owing to developments in culture and society were reflected in theory, and theoretical refinements introduced by teachers of rhetoric influenced the practice of public speaking. After the pagan civilization of ancient Greece and Rome gave way to Christianity, which used Latin as its *lingua franca* in what had previously been the Western part of the Roman Empire and in other territories that were Christianized, rhetoric continued its existence thanks to the teaching program of "liberal arts" (*artes liberales*), of which rhetoric formed the basis, together with grammar and dialectic. More specifically, rhetoric survived in the arts of prose composition (especially letters) and poetry, and in the art of preaching. In addition, public speaking on social and political occasions existed in the independent city states of late medieval Italy. Italian humanists continued the medieval tradition of the *artes liberales* and the cultivation of rhetoric that was part of it, but also turned their minds to antiquity, energetically rediscovering within the span of a few generations the bulk of the ancient texts that had lain hidden in monastic libraries, and thus acquiring more knowledge about ancient eloquence and rhetoric than had been current among medieval scholars. With this knowledge, they brought about a revolution in the cultivation of the Latin language and of both the oral and written forms of eloquence.

Rediscovery of the Classical Sources

Only a few classical sources for the study of rhetoric were known and used in the Middle Ages: the pseudo-Ciceronian *Rhetoric to Herennius* (first century BCE), Cicero's (106–43 BCE) *De inventione*, parts of Quintilian's (ca. 35–ca. 100 CE) *Institutio oratoria*, and, from the thirteenth century onwards, Aristotle's (fourth century BCE) *Rhetoric* in Latin translation. In the course of the fourteenth and fifteenth centuries, manuscripts of virtually all the surviving source texts for the knowledge of classical rhetoric became available one after the other. Besides the complete text of Quintilian's *Institutio oratoria*, the most important Latin texts are Cicero's *De oratore, Brutus, Orator, De optimo genere oratorum, Partitiones oratoriae*, and *Topica*; Tacitus's (ca. 60–ca. 120 CE) *Dialogus de oratoribus*; and the late antique minor Latin rhetoricians (*Rhetores Latini Minores*). Besides Aristotle's *Rhetoric*, the key Greek texts are the pseudo-Aristotelian *Rhetoric to Alexander* (fourth century BCE); Hermogenes's (second century CE) four treatises *On Invention, On the Modes of Proceeding in Legal Cases, On Forceful Speaking, On Types of Style*; and a number of works on literary criticism such as Dionysius of Halicarnassus's (ca. 60 BCE–ca. 10 CE) *On Literary Composition* and his other essays on literary criticism; Demetrius's (ca. 350–280 BCE) *On Style*; and pseudo-Longinus's (first or third century CE) *On Sublimity*. All these texts became available in print between 1465 (first edition of Cicero's *De oratore*) and 1554 (first edition of pseudo-Longinus's *On Sublimity*; Sandys 1908, 103–5). Many of these were translated, commented upon, or epitomized (Green and Murphy 2006). Additionally, speeches by famous orators such as Demosthenes and Cicero, and collections of declamations or summaries of declamations such as Seneca the Elder's *Controversiae et suasoriae*, pseudo-Quintilian's *Declamationes maiores* and *Declamationes minores*, or the Greek declamations of Libanius (fourth century CE), stimulated the study of Greco-Roman eloquence. Finally, the four Greek collections of *progymnasmata* or preliminary exercises (i.e., fourteen composition exercises to prepare the pupil for the composition of a full oration), were an important source of information and inspiration for the humanists. Theon's collection (second century CE) had been translated into Latin by Priscian (ca. 500 CE), and Aphthonius's (fourth century CE) collection was translated into Latin during the fifteenth century. The other two collections are attributed to Hermogenes (third/fourth century CE) and Nicolaus the Sophist (fifth century CE).

Renaissance Manuals of Rhetoric

Besides editions, commentaries, and translations of classical sources, many manuals of rhetoric were produced in the Renaissance following classical models. The catalog by Green and Murphy (2006) illustrates the quantity and print history of this material, sometimes published as late as the eighteenth and nineteenth centuries. We can also consult two early eighteenth-century surveys of the history of rhetoric by two famous professors of eloquence, Daniel Georg Morhof (1639–1691) and Balthasar Gibert (1662–1741; Van der Poel 1987, 156–57; *HWR* 7:1462), whose work offers a fascinating view of our subject from the inside. Both lived at a time when the culture of Renaissance humanism still existed and participated actively in that tradition: Morhof was professor of eloquence and poetry at the University of Kiel, while Gibert was professor of eloquence at the Collège Mazarin in Paris. Both regularly delivered academic orations, and their teaching of rhetoric concerned the practice of oratory: they trained students to write prose and poetry and to deliver these when appropriate. In his three-volume *Jugemens des savans sur les auteurs qui ont traité de la Rhétorique, avec un précis de la doctrine de ces auteurs* (*Judgements of the Learned on Authors who have Discussed Rhetoric, with a Summary of those Authors' Teaching*; 1713–1719), Gibert discusses chronologically and evaluates classical authors who wrote on rhetoric, and many early modern authors (until ca. 1650) who wrote on both secular and sacred rhetoric in Latin or the vernacular. Gibert also wrote his own rhetorical textbook, *Rhetorica iuxta Aristotelis doctrinam dialogis explanata* (*Rhetoric Explained Following Aristotle's Teaching, Set Out in Dialogues*, 1739; Messaoud 2005). Morhof based his *Polyhistor, sive de auctorum notitia et rerum commentarii* (*The Polymath, or Commentaries on the Knowledge of Authors and Subjects*, first complete edition 1708) on material collected for his courses, and surveys the contemporary status of scholarship across three separate sections: *Polyhistor literarius* (*The Literary Polymath*) deals with the humanities (philology, poetics, rhetoric); *Polyhistor philosophicus* (*The Philosophical Polymath*) with philosophy; and *Polyhistor practicus* (*The Practical Polymath*) with law and theology. Morhof saw printed only the first two books of the first part (1688); his collaborators published the others after his death, ultimately going through four editions between 1708 and 1747. Book 6 of the *Polyhistor literarius* deals exclusively with rhetoric: its four chapters cover ancient and early modern theorists writing in Latin (and a few in the vernacular); ancient (mainly Greek) orators; early modern orators; and finally, sacred orators and theorists of sacred eloquence (Morhof 1747, 1:941–1000). Morhof greatly admired Cicero's style, which shaped his judgments of contemporary prose writers and orators (Kapp 2000). Unlike Gibert's, Morhof's survey of early modern rhetorical authors is not strictly chronological, but geographical and hierarchical: he discusses, for instance, one Spanish author, a few Italian and German ones (singling out Johannes Sturm [1507–1589] as the most important German author), then focuses on the Jesuits. After these comes a group of four authors who "must be preferred even above those [the Jesuits]" (*et ante illos ponendi*; Morhof 1747, 1:951): Georgius Trapezuntius (1395–1486), Juan Luis Vives (1493–1540), Pedro Juan Núñez (1522–1602), and Gerardus Joannes Vossius (1577–1649). Gibert and Morhof both held rather traditional views on rhetoric, disapproving of rhetoricians who did not straightforwardly adopt classical rhetorical systems, such as Petrus Ramus (ca. 1515–1572).

The handbooks of rhetoric listed in Green and Murphy's catalog and discussed by Gibert and Morhof are all based on classical sources, but also necessarily adapt to contemporary contexts in which eloquence functioned. Therefore, in all of these surveys, we see a majority of works written in Latin, but also many vernacular works, as well as manuals focusing on secular rhetoric and manuals for writing and delivering sermons. Some manuals combine secular and sacred: *De eloquentia sacra et humana* (*On Holy and Human Eloquence*, 1619; twenty editions up to 1681), written by the Jesuit Nicolas Caussin (1583–1651), divides rhetoric into three branches—the epideictic, deliberative, and sacred. Most sermons were preached in the vernacular, so some Latin preaching manuals were translated, but vernacular preaching manuals translated into Latin also exist (Caplan and King 1949; Plett 1995, 44–69).

Some of the manuals of secular rhetoric closely follow the classical system with only minor necessary adaptations, while others deliberately do not. We can divide the manuals following the classical rhetorical system into two groups: academic works that discuss in detail this system for a scholarly and expert readership; and less learned works, usually aimed at students, that give a brief, practical survey. Gerardus Joannes Vossius (one of Morhof's four best contemporary authors on rhetoric) produced both kinds of book. His main rhetorical work intended for fellow scholars is *Oratoriarum institutionum libri sex* (*Six Books on the Training of the Orator*, 1606), first published when Vossius was only twenty-nine; but he continued to work on it throughout his life up to a fourth expanded edition in 1643 (Rademaker 1981, 75–77). *De rhetorices natura ac constitutione et antiquis rhetoribus, sophistis, ac oratoribus liber* (*Book on the Nature and System of Rhetoric, and on the Ancient Rhetors, Sophists, and Orators*, 1621) gives, besides theoretical background, a history of public speaking in antiquity and practical advice for the modern orator (Rademaker 1981, 177). Two other works are textbooks for students, *Rhetorices contractae sive partitionum oratoriarum libri V* (*Five Books of Rhetoric Abridged, or of the Divisions of Oratory*, 1621), which conveniently summarizes his *Oratoriae institutiones*, and *Elementa rhetorica oratoriis partitionibus accommodata* (*Elements of Rhetoric Adapted to the Divisions of Oratory*, 1626), which contains a survey of tropes and figures (Rademaker 1981, 177). In the early 1620s, Vossius was involved in writing the *Schoolordre* (*School Act*) issued by the provincial authorities of Holland and Westfrisia in 1625, which contains the standard humanistic school program discussed briefly below, and recommends the use of Vossius's two student textbooks on rhetoric (Kuiper 1958).

Many rhetorical manuals that deviate from the classical system adopt the ideas of Petrus Ramus, the French scholar and educational reformer who notoriously assigned the traditionally rhetorical stages of *inventio* ("invention"; that is, finding ideas suited to the subject of a speech) and *dispositio* (the "disposition" of a speech) to logic, and therefore limited rhetoric to the subsequent stages of *elocutio* ("expression") and *pronuntiatio* ("delivery"). His ideas about logic and rhetoric, soon translated into pithy, convenient textbooks, were hugely influential in early modern education, and his innovative theories, particularly on logic and dialectic, also contributed substantially to contemporary discussions of method; that is, the best ways to acquire and communicate knowledge (Gilbert 1960; Mack 2011, 136–63; Reid and Wilson 2011; Meerhoff and Moisan 1997 and 2005). Study of *loci argumentorum* (topics) fueled the debate on method, initiated by Rudolphus Agricola (1444–79) in his *De inventione dialectica* (*On Dialectical Invention*, 1479) and developed during the sixteenth century by scholars like Melanchthon, Johannes Caesarius, Johannes Sturm, and Ramus (Vasoli 2007; Mack 1993). The topics form a common ground between dialectic and rhetoric, and the humanists' dissatisfaction with how classical rhetoricians and late medieval dialecticians had treated the topics stimulated their thorough study of this subject.

There are various reasons why manuals offer only a partial treatment of rhetorical theory. Some manuals, for instance, discuss only *imitatio*, the method of using classical authors as models for writing Latin and acquiring a good individual style, which was an essential subject requiring considerable practice. Examples are the two practical textbooks written by Johannes Schefferus (1621–79), professor of eloquence at the University of Uppsala: *De stylo exercitiisque eius ad consuetudinem veterum liber* (*Book on Style and Practical Exercises for That, Following the Custom of the Ancients*, 1652–53) and *Gymnasium styli sive de vario scribendi exercitio ad exemplum veterum* (*The School of Style, or on Various Writing Exercises Following the Example of the Ancients*, 1657), which contain rules and examples for composition following the ancient *progymnasmata*, variously treating several elements of the parts of an oration such as the *narratio* (the narrative part of a speech), a *laudatio* ("praise"), or *vituperatio* ("criticism") of a person or a law, or a didactic anecdote about a famous person (*chreia*). Besides *imitatio*, other handbooks began to appear from the mid-sixteenth century onwards, when delivery became increasingly important in the culture of eloquence, which focused on the *actio* or *pronuntiatio*; that is, the proper use of voice and body when giving a speech. The first was Jodocus Willich's (1501–52) *Liber de pronunciatione rhetorica doctus et elegans* (*A Learned and Elegant Book on Rhetorical Pronunciation*, 1540). From this period onwards, the elegant delivery of prose or verse became an academic exercise in itself, related to dramatic performance in schools and colleges (Van der Poel 2007b, 276–80). Subsequently, by the beginning of the seventeenth century, Clemens Timpler (1563–1624) distinguished in his *Rhetoricae systema methodicum* (*Method-based System of Rhetoric*, 1613) three kinds of school exercises, the first being *exercitia declamatoria* ("exercises in delivery"). Another famous manual illustrating how important delivery had become in early seventeenth-century culture is Louis de Cressolles's *Vacationes autumnales, sive de perfecta oratoris actione et pronuntiatione libri tres* (*Autumnal Vacations, or Three Books on the Perfect Delivery and Pronunciation of the Orator*, 1620; Conte 2007). We can therefore see how substantial the variation was in the contents of Renaissance rhetorical handbooks. Modern editions of these works and secondary literature about them do not abound; although we now have Peter Mack's excellent *History of Renaissance Rhetoric*, the study of Renaissance handbooks of rhetoric remains preeminently a field in which it is necessary to acquire first-hand knowledge of the original texts and to build one's own work on the foundations of that knowledge.

ELOQUENCE IN RENAISSANCE CULTURE: THE EDUCATION PROGRAM OF THE HUMANISTS

The sheer number of manuals indicates how important rhetoric was, and in fact it forms the heart and soul of Renaissance humanism, for, although humanists were a very heterogeneous group, they all shared the claim that theirs was the pursuit of eloquence (Gray 1963, 498), collectively substantiating this aspiration through their reform of late medieval school education, and using as their main inspiration Quintilian's *Institutio oratoria*. Humanists adopted both the methods and the content of Quintilian's teaching program, copying Quintilian's version of the Ciceronian ideal of the orator as a *vir bonus* (Winterbottom 1964), and creating the humanistic arts curriculum (*studia humanitatis*), that focused on grammar, rhetoric, poetry, ancient history, and moral philosophy. It consisted on the one hand of detailed reading of classical orators, historians, and poets, along with analysis of these texts' structure and style; and, on the other hand, of continuous composition exercises in prose and verse. This curriculum culminated in the exercise of *declamatio*, which in principle meant an advanced pupil's writing and public delivery of a complete oration on a set theme, but in practice *declamatio* could vary considerably, and might involve, for instance, writing but not delivering an oration, or delivering an oration or poem that might not have been written by the pupil (Van der Poel 1987, 344–45, 348; Van der Poel 2007b, 276–77).

The humanists were convinced that young men thus trained would not only acquire the ability to reason and to express themselves elegantly and properly in all circumstances, but would also be equipped with refined sensibility and the will to live honestly. This ideal of the well-mannered, morally upright man of intellect is the Renaissance counterpart of the classical *vir bonus* (Gray 1963; Seigel 1968), and within the humanist education program, the *vir bonus* ideology is especially manifest in the union of eloquence and piety. More broadly, this ideology reflects Renaissance ideas about civility and courtesy: the *vir bonus*, well trained in the liberal arts and thereby culturally refined, represents perfected human nature and places his life at the service of his community and country (Kelso 1929). Baldassare Castiglione's (1478–1529) dialogue *Il libro del cortegiano* (*Book of the Courtier*; 1528) was a hugely influential work on this subject (Burke 1996; Richards 2003).

Countless pedagogical treatises written between the early fifteenth- and the mid-seventeenth centuries outlined the program and ideology of the *studia humanitatis*. Examples include four Italian Quattrocento humanists who wrote brief works on the subject—Pier Paolo Vergerio, Leonardo Bruni, Enea Silvio Piccolomini (the later Pope Pius II) and Battista Guarino (Kallendorf 2002)—which inspired sixteenth- and seventeenth-century authors of similar treatises in countries north of the Alps. Several seventeenth-century volumes compiled earlier treatises on the *studia humanitatis*, such as Thomas Theodor Crusius's compendium, *De philologia, studiis liberalis doctrinae, informatione et educatione litteraria generosorum adulescentum* (*On Philology, Studies* of High-Minded Knowledge, Instruction and Literary Education of Well-born Youths, 1696). Crusius's work contains several pedagogical treatises covering the entire *studia humanitatis*, such as *De studio litterarum recte et commode instituendo* (*On the Study of Letters to Be Taught Accurately and Conveniently*, 1527) by Guillaume Budé, and *De iuventutis instituendae ratione diatribe* (*Learned Discussion of the Plan for Teaching the Youth*) and the *Epistola de eloquentiae studio* (*Letter on the Study of Eloquence*) by the seventeenth-century Polish historian, poet, and philosopher Joachim Pastorius (1611–1681), as well as treatises that cover parts of it, such as the letters by Justus Lipsius (1547–1606) on the method of reading historiography and on the public recitation of literary texts. These compendia bear witness to the importance of rhetoric and the ideal of eloquence in Renaissance pedagogy and culture, and the different ways in which rhetoric was used.

Some pedagogical treatises also outline the actual humanistic arts curriculum. Probably the most influential treatise in this category was Erasmus's *De ratione studii ac legendi interpretandique auctores* (*On the Method of Studying, Reading and Interpreting Authors*, 1511), a brief work frequently reissued up to 1786 (ASD 1.2:111–51; CWE 24:666–91). Here, Erasmus discusses or epitomizes everything that gives the humanist educational treatise its identity: the idea that we need a command of language to achieve accurate knowledge and effective judgment; the principle that practice is more important than theory; the method of reading and analyzing texts alongside composition exercises, which become increasingly more difficult to match the pupil's age and ability (the core of Quintilian's teaching method, which ensures progress from simple to complex, and reinforces through repetition); awareness of the moral risks attached to reading pagan authors; and hence a focus on Christian interpretation of classical texts and on assigning contemporary subjects as well as ancient ones for composition exercises.

However, one important feature of the humanistic school curriculum as it developed in the later sixteenth century is missing from *De ratione studii*: namely, the focus on delivering speeches as the pinnacle of the pupil's training. Erasmus's aim was to teach students to speak Latin correctly daily and to develop their skill in reasoning alongside their personal writing style, and so he laid little emphasis on delivering Latin speeches at official gatherings following ancient rules of *actio*. In fact, he only emphasized the importance of training in *actio* for the sermon, because priests have to teach the gospel to believers and inspire them to live virtuously; to achieve this, Erasmus stressed the proper deployment of body and voice in the pulpit, which he sketched out in detail in his preaching manual *Ecclesiastes* (*The Preacher*, 1535), although here he focuses on sermons in the vernacular (Mack 2011, 98–103, 257–78). Erasmus criticized the practice of preaching sermons in Latin, such as those preached at the papal court (O'Malley 1979).

The influence of Erasmus's *De ratione studii* was most clearly visible in England. He wrote the treatise in the context of his correspondence with John Colet (1467–1519), Dean of St. Paul's Cathedral in London, who immediately put Erasmus's recommendations into practice in the school he founded there (Gleason 1989, 217–34). This foundation marks the beginning of Erasmus's influence on the English Renaissance school system. English grammar schools had a five-year curriculum and typically followed a set daily schedule (Abbott 1990). On the Continent, with the exception of Italy (Grendler [1989] 1991), several tight networks of humanist schools, from the elementary up to the university level, were established following the various Christian denominations (Van der Poel 1987, 346–48; Van der Poel 2007b, 274–76). Melanchthon (1497–1560), was the instigator of the Lutheran network, beginning in 1523 with the reform of the Arts Faculty in Wittenberg (Greschat 2010, 71–89; Stempel 1979). In 1538, the Lutheran Johannes Sturm brought elementary, secondary, and university level curricula together under one roof in the Strasbourg gymnasium (from 1566 onwards, the academical gymnasium; Schindling 1978). In some reformed Swiss cantons, schools were founded to train Zwinglian (later Calvinistic) clergymen, focusing on theology, rhetoric, and dialectic; John Calvin's (1509–64) Academy of Geneva, founded in 1559, provided a model adopted in other centers of Calvinism (Maag 1996). In Catholic countries and territories, the Society of Jesus, founded in 1540, developed a school network offering a rigorous liberal arts program at elementary, intermediate, and university levels, both in Europe and on other continents where the Jesuits settled. This program was standardized in the *ratio studiorum* (1599) and was used in Jesuit schools until the nineteenth century (Lukács 1986). These humanistically and denominationally determined networks of schools produced a more or less uniform education program in early modern Europe focused on teaching eloquence: no matter how Protestants and Catholics disagreed in matters of faith and dogma, all adopted the standard humanistic arts curriculum based on Quintilian and the Italian pedagogues, with a strong emphasis on uniting eloquence with piety.

Textbooks of Eloquence

Every school curriculum requires suitable teaching material. This was especially true for the humanist curriculum in its focus on the practice of reading and writing with minimal theorizing about grammar, dialectic, and rhetoric. Erasmus's *De ratione studii* sets out this principle in an exemplary way: he states that pupils, when learning a language, should receive only basic instruction in grammar, but should start speaking and reading Latin from the very beginning (*ASD* 1.2:114–15; *CWE* 24:667). At a more advanced stage of learning Latin, he suggests that pupils should study Valla's *Elegantiae linguae Latinae* (*Elegances of the Latin Language*, written in the 1440s) and the sections on Latin's virtues and vices in the grammars of Donatus and Diomedes (both fourth century CE), memorize the rules of poetry and its various meters, and gain a command of the basic rules of rhetoric, which are necessary both to evaluate the authors in the curriculum and to imitate them (*ASD* 1.2:116–17; *CWE* 24:670). Erasmus wrote a brief compendium of the basic rules of rhetoric for private use: the composition date of this *Compendium rhetorices* is unknown, and it was published posthumously in 1543 (Erasmus 1906–1958, 10:396–405). His lasting contributions to humanist education are the two textbooks he wrote offering practical advice and examples to develop the pupil's Latin writing skills: *De duplici copia verborum et rerum* (*On Copiousness in Both Words and Thoughts*, 1512) and *De conscribendis epistolis* (*On Writing Letters*, 1522; on both works, see Mack 2011, 80–96).

Erasmus began composing both these works in the 1490s as a private tutor in Paris, and both were frequently reprinted. In contrast to what is often suggested, *De copia* is not a manual to help writers acquire an overabundant style garlanded with flowers of speech; its goal instead is to provide the means to write intelligently, elegantly, and appropriately in any situation. To achieve this aim, Erasmus advises employing a number of techniques, primarily *variatio* through figures of style (which he supports with many examples showing how the same thing can be differently expressed), as well as ways of varying and developing thoughts, such as through using examples, providing additional details, inserting digressions, and so on. Unlike *De copia*, *De conscribendis epistolis* offers (besides a lot of practice material), a complete theory of eloquence: Erasmus describes the form of the letter's general characteristics in terms of classical rules of eloquence, such as the principle that every text must be adapted to the subject, occasion, and audience's character, or the theory that one must practice *imitatio* to learn to use all the registers of literary language. That said, despite Erasmus's close adherence to classical rhetorical theory, he nonetheless makes some interesting adaptations to the contemporary context; for example, classical strategies for argument in judicial cases are applied to letters in which one accuses or criticizes someone, or complains about something. A particularly interesting adaptation of classical theory occurs when Erasmus discusses letters written in the *genus deliberativum* (the "political" branch of oratory, which advises a future course of action), where he makes a distinction between encouragement or arousing by means of emotions, and persuasion or teaching by means of proof (*ASD* 1.2:315; *CWE* 25:73–74): he thereby mingles elements of demonstrative oratory and deliberative oratory, because, according to the Aristotelian system of *genera causarum* (the three kinds of speech), demonstrative oratory aims to please the audience by appealing to aesthetic and ethical feelings, whereas judicial and deliberative oratory tries to convince the audience by arguing for the validity of the orator's position in the case and refuting the adversary. In his discussion of the *genus demonstrativum*, on the other hand, Erasmus stresses that praise or blame for the sole purpose of giving pleasure, without using arguments, are seldom used in isolation (*ASD* 1.2:513; *CWE* 25:205–7).

Erasmus's examples in *De conscribendis epistolis* tend either to be brief letters or themes followed by suggestions for how the pupil may develop them, so his example of a letter of persuasion is therefore unusual because it offers a full-blown oration in the form of a letter on a contemporary topic. This is the famous "declamation in the deliberative genre in praise of marriage," previously published in 1518 in a collection of Erasmus's declamations: here, Erasmus sets out to persuade a well-born boy that it is better for him to marry the girl who loves him rather than opt for celibacy through religious scruples (*religio*) and grief about his mother's recent death (*ASD* 1.2:400; *CWE* 25:129–45). Conservative theologians who did not know anything about rhetoric read this balanced argument for the respectability of marriage as a direct attack on the doctrine that clerical celibacy is the only good form of Christian living, and attacked Erasmus violently, initiating a polemic that lasted from 1519 until 1532. The letter is a fine example of a contemporary argument developed entirely from classical rhetorical rules (Van der Poel 2000). *De conscribendis epistolis* may be Erasmus's finest work; written in his unique, often somewhat hasty but always engaging style, it reveals much of his wit and wisdom (qualities for which the conservative theologians hated him because they could not compete), and offers, despite its technical nature, many insights into early sixteenth-century culture.

Many other humanists wrote manuals of letter writing, usually intended for pedagogical use and offering the rules of rhetoric in a suitable form to be applied to contemporary society (Mack 2011, 228–56). Letter writing was probably the area in Renaissance life where rhetoric was most applicable and thus most practiced by the widest range of people, as Morhof's dedication of two full chapters to the subject of letter-writing attests (Morhof 1747, 1:270–320). Another highly popular kind of textbook in the Renaissance is the manual of rhetorical tropes and figures: these works tend to be based on classical descriptions of such devices, but their arrangement and modes of explanation vary considerably (Mack 2011, 208–27). Tropes and figures form a common ground between rhetoric and poetics, and so these textbooks helped pupils analyze and write not only Latin prose, but also poetry, while tropes and figures also functioned as an important channel through which vernacular poetry and prose could follow the quality and style of classical models (Vickers 1970 and 1988; Hildebrandt-Günther 1966; Lausberg 1998).

ELOQUENCE IN RENAISSANCE CULTURE: EPIDEICTIC ORATORY

As we have seen, rhetorical training through the humanist curriculum culminated in the *declamatio*, the composition and delivery of a speech (Van der Poel 1987), which goes back to Quintilian, in whose era declamations in the judicial and deliberative genres (*controversiae* and *suasoriae*) were not only showpieces through which teachers of rhetoric displayed their talents before large audiences, but also exercises for orators and students preparing to deliver speeches in the law courts and in the Senate and popular assemblies. Yet acknowledging the debt to classical practice must not make us forget that the functions of eloquence in Renaissance Europe were entirely different, because there was no place for orators in the administration of justice, but only for lawyers and advocates who had to conduct legislative procedures using written documents. Likewise, in state administration, the practice of free public debate in Latin during the meetings of representative bodies did not exist, for political matters were usually discussed behind closed doors in the vernacular tongue. So the practice of delivering speeches was confined to the epideictic genre—that is, speeches delivered to mark festive or solemn occasions, whether private or public, religious or secular (Van der Poel in *HWR* 5:68–70).

Renaissance scholars conducted much work on the theory of epideictic eloquence, in traditional handbooks, manuals of letter writing, and manuals of preaching (Van der Poel in *HWR* 5:63–68). They tend on the whole to discuss the treatment of the topics for praise and blame in more detail than classical handbooks did. Vossius's *Oratoriarum institutionum libri sex* (1606), offers a good case in point; by the third edition (1630), his discussion of epideictic oratory had come to cover sixty-nine pages, including a detailed survey of praising both pagan gods and the Christian God; the angels; human beings, human deeds; plants; inanimate things such as the sea, rivers, fountains, ports, regions, cities, villages, houses, schools, baths, gardens, farms, mountains, and bridges; arts and virtues; and citing both classical and early Christian examples.

Renaissance theorists often debated the epideictic genre's status. According to the classical system of rhetoric, this genre differs from the judicial and deliberative genres because it does not aim to steer listeners (whether judges or members of political bodies) towards making a decision about the case at hand, but rather to provoke their delectation through appealing to their aesthetic and ethical feelings. Some discussed whether or not an epideictic speech should contain arguments and counter-arguments: Trapezuntius and Agricola, for example, two important fifteenth-century theorists, held opposing views on this point (Van der Poel in *HWR* 5:64–65). In the sixteenth century, Melanchthon introduced an important development in the theory of the epideictic genre by distinguishing what he saw as its two functions: teaching and moving emotionally. In his *Elementa rhetorices* (*Elements of Rhetoric*, 1531), he invented a separate genus for the first function, the *genus didascalicum* or *didacticon* ("didactic genre"; Melanchthon 2001, 32, 40–54) and specified that this genre was especially suitable for the teaching of theological doctrine. Later, discussions of the role of *affectus* ("emotions") and how to play on them by means of *amplificatio* became prominent, such as in the Spanish Jesuit Cyprianus Soarez's (1520–93) *De arte rhetorica* (*On the Art of Rhetoric*, 1560; Flynn 1956 and 1957). In the baroque period, treatises dedicated to the *affectus* were not uncommon, such as the *Pathologia oratoria seu affectuum movendorum ratio* (*Study of the Passions, or the Method of Stirring Up Emotions*,1665) by the Lutheran theologian and professor of rhetoric Valentin Thilo the Younger (1607–1662).

WRITTEN FORMS OF ELOQUENCE

Letter writing as a form of eloquence was important, but in fact, just as in antiquity, all written literary forms fell within the boundaries of "rhetoric" during the Renaissance, since the theory of eloquence contained rules for the structure of texts (*inventio* and *dispositio*) and style (*elocutio*), and since writers learned their art by means of *imitatio*, which was always taught by rhetoricians. Many epideictic orations, particularly academic speeches, for example, were printed after they had been delivered, either because their content was considered significant, or to serve as stylistic models for the practice of *imitatio*. So all of the genres discussed in this book draw much of their theoretical basis from rhetoric, such as historiography, epistolography, fiction, satire, as well as the dialogue, a classical genre much deployed by both Latin and vernacular authors during the Renaissance for all kinds of subjects. The Italian humanist Carlo Sigonio (ca. 1524–1584) wrote a theory of the dialogue (*De dialogo* [*On the Dialogue*], 1552), which Morhof mentions in his chapter *De Rhetoribus atque Oratoribus* (*On Rhetors and Orators*), stressing that it "entirely pertains to eloquence" (*omnino ad eloquentiam pertinere*; Morhof 1747, 1:955). Renaissance literary dialogues tend to consist of either a combination of brief altercations or a mixture of longer and shorter speeches, and these are often of the epideictic kind. Within the field of epideictic oratory, too, the paradoxical encomium is an important genre: the praise of bad or unworthy things or persons (such as Erasmus's *Praise of Folly*) was very popular in Neo-Latin literature, especially in the sixteenth and seventeenth centuries. A very heterogeneous genre in form, content, and purpose, the paradoxical encomium can probably best be understood in relation to satire (Van der Poel 2001, 69–70).

Poetry was intimately linked to rhetoric in the Renaissance, as in antiquity and the Middle Ages (Walker 2000; Norden 1958, 2:883–908; Plett 1994, 12–13). To mention just one example, in Book 3 of his influential *Poetics* (1561), Julius Caesar Scaliger discusses the creative method poets follow using *inventio*—the finding of matter (*res*) by certain *topoi* of argument (*loci argumentorum*)—and *elocutio* (putting the *res* into suitable words, using figures of speech; Marsh 2004).

IMITATIO

Surveying all of this material, we can conclude that Latin oratory from the fourteenth up until the seventeenth century came in many forms and was practiced in many circumstances. Three considerations are particularly important: eloquence was taught and practiced both within educational contexts and in society more broadly; it was practiced in both oral and written forms; and both prose and verse texts arose from rhetorical training. What is common to all these forms of eloquence, though, and fundamental to its practice in all of these different contexts, is *imitatio*. From the moment Petrarch expressed his wish to follow the classical authors (especially Cicero) in his Latin writing, authors learning to write Latin faced the question of which models to follow. The general rule was that the best authors in each genre must be taken as models, and that writers should develop their own personal style through continuous practice; this creative process was usually represented by means of Seneca's metaphor of the bee, producing honey from pollen gathered everywhere (*Epistles to Lucilius* 84.3).

Many textbooks on *imitatio* were published that contained theoretical observations on *imitatio* and described various kinds of exercises to practice the technique, such as paraphrase, translation from Greek into Latin, or, in verse composition, the transposition of a classical poem into a different kind of meter. Many editions of the ancient *progymnasmata* appeared, especially Aphthonius, expanded by many contemporary examples (Kraus in *HWR* 7:159–91). For both prose and poetry, attention was paid to the structure of texts; the proper ways to present subject matter and to argue (that is, the use of the topics); and matters of style, such as attuning the style to the subject, the proper use of tropes and figures, and, in prose, the understanding of periodic sentence structure, including prose rhythm. Collections of adages and commonplaces, the fruit of intensive reading of classical authors, were either assembled and kept privately, or published to serve as treasure houses of knowledge and repositories of writing material. The great significance of *imitatio* for early modern Latin writing can be gauged from the fact that Morhof devotes four chapters to various aspects of it in his methodological Book 2 (*liber methodicus*): he allocates one chapter to the principles of *imitatio* in prose writing, including a discussion of important textbooks, complemented by related chapters that give examples of writing exercises and contain a collection of model letters based on Cicero's correspondence, taken from the works of Melchior Junius (1545–1604); and he devotes a second chapter to *imitatio* in poetry (Morhof 1747, 1:471–558).

Imitatio was not only an important practical subject in Latin schools, but also a central issue in Renaissance debates about style (Van der Poel 1997). There were two main opposing views on how one could best acquire a personal Latin style: purists (who were usually Ciceronians, like Pietro Bembo, 1470–1547) claimed that a writer should only imitate one author, to avoid a hybrid and impotent style; eclectics argued that one should follow a choice of authors to ensure the development of a truly individual style, a view well articulated by Gianfrancesco Pico della Mirandola (1469–1543) in his famous discussion with Bembo (Scott 1910, 1:22–23, 2:8–18; Dellaneva and Duvick 2007, 16–125). The difference between these views rests not so much on which Latin author possesses the best style, but rather on how the creative process of writing Latin functions: does one write better Latin by following one's own talent, or by choosing the best model? Erasmus's famous contribution to this debate in *Ciceronianus* (*The Ciceronian*, 1528; *ASD* 1.2:581–710) does not really describe his views on Latin style, but rather intends to brand the cult of Cicero by Italian, especially Roman, humanists like Bembo as a harmful kind of cultural elitism during a time that clamored for solidarity among intellectuals, which Erasmus saw as an important defense of the unity and moral integrity of the *res publica Christiana*. Erasmus's views on *imitatio*, expressed in his pedagogical works, are attuned to the classical virtues of style; namely *Latinitas* (grammatical correctness), *perspicuitas* (clearness), *ornatus* (embellishment by means of tropes and figures), and *decorum* (proper use of all the means of persuasion). The application of these rules would ensure the production of elegant, functional Latin by using the idiom of classical authors, but without rigidity (such as not refusing to use Christian words for Christian concepts, or new words for new things), and by mastering different kinds of style for different purposes. To this end, a reading program of many different authors in various genres was necessary, and this is exactly what the humanistic school curriculum offered throughout these centuries.

Suggested Reading

To study Renaissance rhetoric, one needs to know something about the history of eloquence in antiquity and the Middle Ages: Fuhrmann (2011) offers a good introduction to the system of rhetoric and the history of classical eloquence; see also Kennedy (1963 and 1972) for a detailed history of Greco-Roman eloquence; Martin (1974) for a full description of the system of rhetoric. For medieval rhetoric, see Murphy (1974), Camargo (1991), Kelly (1991), Koch on "Arenga" and "Ars Arengandi" (in *HWR* 1:877–89 and 1033–40), and Kienzle (2000). Green and Murphy (2006) is a useful bibliography.

References

Abbott, Don P. 1990. "Rhetoric and Writing in Renaissance Europe and England." In *A Short History of Writing Instruction from Ancient Greece to Twentieth-Century America*, edited by James J. Murphy, 95–120. Davis: Hermagoras.

Burke, Peter. 1996. *The Fortunes of the Courtier: The European Reception of Castiglione's Cortegiano*. University Park: Pennsylvania State University Press.

Camargo, Martin. 1991. *Ars dictaminis, Ars dictandi*. Turnhout: Brepols.

Caplan, Harry, and Henry H. King. 1949. "Latin Tractates on Preaching: A Book-List." *Harvard Theological Review* 42:185–206.

Conte, Sophie. 2007. "Louis de Cressolles: Le savoir au service de l'action oratoire." *Dix-septième siècle* 237:653–67.

Dellaneva, Joann, and Brian Duvick. 2007. *Ciceronian Controversies*. Cambridge: Harvard University Press.

Erasmus, Desiderius. 1906–1958. *Opus epistolarum*. Edited by Percy S. Allen et al. 12 vols. Oxford: Clarendon.

Flynn, Lawrence. 1956. "The *De arte rhetorica* of Cyprian Soarez, S.J." *Quarterly Journal of Speech* 42:356–76.

———. 1957. "Sources and Influences of Soarez' *De arte rhetorica*." *Quarterly Journal of Speech* 43:257–65.

Fuhrmann, Manfred. 2011. *Die antike Rhetorik: eine Einführung*. Mannheim: Artemis & Winkler.

Gilbert, Neal W. 1960. *Renaissance Concepts of Method*. New York: Columbia University Press.

Gleason, John B. 1989. *John Colet*. Berkeley: University of California Press.

Gray, Hanna H. 1963. "Renaissance Humanism: The Pursuit of Eloquence." *Journal of the History of Ideas* 24:497–514.

Green, Lawrence D., and James J. Murphy. 2006. *Renaissance Rhetoric Short-Title Catalogue 1460–1700*. Burlington: Ashgate.

Grendler, Paul F. (1989) 1991. *Schooling in Renaissance Italy*. Baltimore: Johns Hopkins University Press.

Greschat, Martin. 2010. *Philipp Melanchthon: Theologe, Pädagoge und Humanist*. Gütersloh: Gütersloher Verlagshaus.

Hildebrandt-Günther, Renate. 1966. *Antike Rhetorik und deutsche literarische Theorie im 17. Jahrhundert*. Marburg: N.G. Elwert.

Kallendorf, Craig W., ed. and trans. 2002. *Humanist Educational Treatises*. Cambridge: Harvard University Press.

Kapp, Volker. 2000. "Morhof und die Rhetorik." In *Mapping the World of Learning: The Polyhistor of Daniel Georg Morhof*, edited by Françoise Waquet, 121–38. Wiesbaden: Harrassowitz.

Kelly, Donald. 1991. *The Arts of Poetry and Prose*. Turnhout: Brepols.

Kelso, Ruth. 1929. *The Doctrine of the English Gentleman in the Sixteenth Century*. Urbana: University of Illinois Press.

Kennedy, George. 1963. *The Art of Persuasion in Greece*. Princeton: Princeton University Press.

———. 1972. *The Art of Rhetoric in the Roman World 300 B.C.–A.D.300*. Princeton: Princeton University Press.

Kienzle, Beverly M. 2000. *The Sermon*. Turnhout: Brepols.

Kuiper, Ernst J. 1958. *De Hollandse "Schoolordre" van 1625*. Groningen: J. B. Wolters.

Lausberg, Heinrich. 1998. *Handbook of Literary Rhetoric: A Foundation for Literary Study*. Leiden: Brill.

Lukács, Ladislaus, ed. 1986. *Ratio atque institutio studiorum Societatis Jesu (1586, 1591, 1599)*. Rome: Institutum Historicum Societatis Iesu.

Maag, Karin. 1996. *Seminary or University? The Genevan Academy and Reformed Higher Education, 1560–1620*. Aldershot: Scholar Press.

Mack, Peter. 1993. *Renaissance Argument: Valla and Agricola in the Traditions of Rhetoric and Dialectic*. Leiden: Brill.

———. 2011. *A History of Renaissance Rhetoric 1380–1620*. Oxford: Oxford University Press.

Marsh, David. 2004. "Julius Caesar Scaliger's *Poetics*." *Journal of the History of Ideas* 65:667–76.

Martin, Josef. 1974. *Antike Rhetorik: Technik und Methode*. Munich: Beck.

Meerhoff, Kees, and Jean-Claude Moisan, eds. 1997. *Autour de Ramus: Texte, théorie, commentaire*. Quebec: Nuit blanche.

———, eds. 2005. *Autour de Ramus: Le combat*. Paris: Champion.

Melanchthon, Philipp. 2001. *Elementa rhetorices. Grundbegriffe der Rhetorik*, edited by Volkhard Wels. Berlin: Weidler.

Messaoud, Samy B. 2005. "L'enseignement rhétorique de Gibert." *Recherches sur Diderot et sur l'Encyclopédie* 38:93–124. Available at http://rde.revues.org/299.

Morhof, Daniel Georg. 1747. *Polyhistor literarius, philosophicus et practicus*. 2 vols. 4th ed. Lübeck: Peter Böckmann.

Murphy, James J. 1974. *Rhetoric in the Middle Ages: A History of Rhetorical Theory from Saint Augustine to the Renaissance*. Berkeley: University of California Press.

O'Malley, John. 1979. *Praise and Blame in Renaissance Rome*. Durham: Duke University Press.

Plett, Heinrich F., ed. 1994. *Renaissance-Poetik*. Berlin: De Gruyter.

———. 1995. *English Renaissance Rhetoric and Poetics: A Systematic Bibliography of Primary and Secondary Sources*. Leiden: Brill.

Rademaker, Cornelis S. M. 1981. *Life and Works of Gerardus Joannes Vossius (1577–1649)*. Assen: Van Gorcum.

Reid, Steven J., and Emma A. Wilson, eds. 2011. *Ramus, Pedagogy and the Liberal Arts*. Farnham: Ashgate.

Richards, Jennifer. 2003. *Rhetoric and Courtliness in Early Modern Literature*. Cambridge: Cambridge University Press.

Sandys, John E. 1908. *A History of Classical Scholarship*. Vol. 2, *From the Revival of Learning to the End of the Eighteenth Century (in Italy, France, England, and the Netherlands)*. Cambridge: Cambridge University Press.

Schindling, Anton. 1978. *Humanistische Hochschule und freie Reichsstadt: Gymnasium und Akademie in Strassburg 1538–1621*. Wiesbaden: Steiner.

Scott, Izora. 1910. *Controversies over the Imitation of Cicero*. 2 parts (separately paginated). New York: Columbia.

Seigel, Jerrold E. 1968. *Rhetoric and Philosophy in Renaissance Humanism: The Union of Eloquence and Wisdom, Petrarch to Valla*. Princeton: Princeton University Press.

Stempel, Hermann A. 1979. *Melanchthons pädagogisches Wirken*. Bielefeld: Luther-Verlag.

Van der Poel, Marc. 1987. *De* declamatio *bij de humanisten*. Nieuwkoop: De Graaf.

———. 1997. "*Imitatio* in het Latijnse humanistenproza." In *Een kwestie van stijl*, edited by Caroline van Eck, Marijke Spies, Toos Streng, 65–77. Amsterdam: Historisch Seminarium van de Universiteit van Amsterdam.

———. 2000. "Erasmus, Rhetoric and Theology: The *Encomium matrimonii*." In *Myricae: Essays on Neo-Latin Literature in Memory of Jozef IJsewijn*, edited by Dirk Sacré and Gilbert Tournoy, 207–27. Leuven: Leuven University Press.

———. 2001. "Laudatio; Renaissance bis 18. Jh." In *HWR* 5:63–72.

———. 2007a. "Humanist Rhetoric in the Renaissance: Classical Mastery?" In *Latinitas Perennis*, edited by Wim Verbaal, Yanick Maes, and Jan Papy, vol. 1, *The Continuity of Latin Literature*, 119–38. Leiden: Brill.

———. 2007b. "Material for a History of the Latin Declamation in the Renaissance." In *Papers on Rhetoric VIII: Declamation*, edited by Lucia Calboli Montefusco, 267–91. Rome: Herder.

———. 2017. "Oratory and Declamation." In *NLL*, 272–88.

Vasoli, Cesare. 2007. *La dialettica e la retorica dell' umanesimo*. 2nd ed. Milan: Feltrinelli.

Vickers, Brian. 1970. *Classical Rhetoric and English Poetry*. London: Macmillan.

———. 1988. *In Defence of Rhetoric*. Oxford: Oxford University Press.

Walker, Jeffrey. 2000. *Rhetoric and Poetics in Antiquity*. New York: Oxford University Press.

Winterbottom, Michael. 1964. "Quintilian and the *vir bonus*." *Journal of Roman Studies* 54:90–97.

CHAPTER 9

··

POLITICAL ADVICE

··

ERIK DE BOM

ANY survey of early modern Neo-Latin political literature immediately stumbles upon various political traditions and a plurality of genres used to express political ideas. These genres ranged from theoretical manuals and orations to emblem books and didactic poems, and most partly depend on the political context in which they operated. One should have some sensitivity for this literary embeddedness: each genre was constituted by specific guidelines and well-chosen classical and medieval models, although a genre was not exclusively associated with a particular kind of political vocabulary, but was only the medium through which a political message could be disseminated and was chosen in the light of the purpose it had to serve. Broadly speaking, one could distinguish between two political contexts, republican and monarchical, which both relied on a set of preferred genres and subgenres. In this chapter, I will limit myself to the monarchical context. This is definitely not because the republican tradition is minor: on the contrary, building on medieval scholastic and rhetorical traditions, such distinguished Italian authors (often designated as "civic humanists") as Leonardo Bruni (1370–1444), Poggio Bracciolini (1380–1459) and Gasparo Contarini (1483–1542) brought republican discourse into full fruition in their Latin writings. This was such a powerful discourse that it passed from Italian city-states such as Florence and Venice to later generations in the early modern Dutch Republic, the seventeenth-century English generation of Oliver Cromwell, and even to colonial America (Pocock 1975). I will concentrate, however, on monarchical forms of government because they are even more prevalent than their republican counterparts and produced an even more influential discourse. As a case study, I will present an overview of princely advice literature, broadly understood, and its associated genres.

I will pay most attention to the *speculum principis* ("mirror for princes") tradition, although we should keep in mind that princely advice literature does not necessarily map onto *speculum principis* texts, being somewhat broader in its interests. The two main works the chapter explores are Desiderius Erasmus's *Institutio principis Christiani* (*Education of a Christian Prince*, 1516) and Justus Lipsius's *Politicorum sive civilis doctrinae libri sex* (*Six Books of Politics or Political Instruction*, 1589), since both works are among the best-known Neo-Latin works of political thought. However, they differ greatly from each other in some important respects. Lipsius not only renewed the *speculum principis* form in an almost revolutionary way, but he subjected the content, too, to major changes, although the broader frame of reference remained largely unaltered. As this chapter sketches out the evolution of this highly popular genre, it will become clear that Erasmus and Lipsius are only two, albeit very influential, names in a long and rich tradition.

Senecanism and Ciceronianism

The *speculum principis* genre was first and foremost practically oriented: its primary aim was to provide both general and specific guidelines for the conduct of the (ideal) prince. As such, the didactic and pedagogical intent is clear: instructed by the humanists' advice, the prince will guide the people as an exemplary figure and inspire them to lead a virtuous life, so princely virtues are at the core of these writings, which are not theoretically derived from general principles and are loosely connected rather than fully systematic. No distinct classical model for the *speculum principis* genre existed. It was fully developed by such Italian humanists as Bartolomeo Sacchi (also known as Platina) in his *De principe viro* (*On the First/Princely Man*, 1471); Diomede Carafa in *De regentis et boni principis officiis* (*On the Duties of a Ruler and Good Prince*, after 1473); Francesco Patrizi in *De regno et regis institutione* (*The Kingdom and the Education of the King*, after 1470); and Giovanni Pontano with his *De principe* (*The Prince*, 1468). From the Italian peninsula the genre spread throughout Europe, where it found such prominent spokesmen as Sebastián Fox Morcillo in *De regni regisque institutione* (*The Education of the Kingdom and the King*, 1556) and Juan de Mariana in *De rege et regis institutione* (*The King and the Education of the King*, 1599) in Spain, and Jakob Wimpfeling with his *Agatharchia* (*The Good Rule*, 1498) and Johannes Sturm with his *De educatione principum* (*The Education of Princes*, 1551) in Germany.

When Erasmus (1467/69–1536) composed his *Education of a Christian Prince* in 1515, he relied on the work of the Greek orator Isocrates (436–338 BCE), as he stated in the letter of dedication to Prince Charles: "I have taken Isocrates' work on the principles of government and translated it into Latin, and in competition with him I have added my own, arranged as it were in aphorisms for the reader's convenience, but with considerable differences from what he laid down" (*CWE* 27:204). The reference is, in fact, to Isocrates's *To Nicocles*, an oration addressed to King Nicocles of Salamis in which the author dwells on the duties of the monarch. This is, however, only one of the many sources which helped to form Erasmus's treatise. He likewise drew inspiration from the works of Plato, whose *Republic* and *Laws* he frequently cited, as well as from Aristotle's *Politics*, Xenophon's dialogue *Oeconomicus*, and Plutarch's essay *To an Uneducated Ruler* in his *Moralia* collection, to express his own ideas about politics. As well as these Greek sources, of equal importance were the Latin authors Seneca and Cicero, on whose *De clementia* (*On Mercy*) and *De officiis* (*On Duties*) respectively he heavily relied.

The continuous presence of such classical sources is a typical feature of Neo-Latin political works in general and *speculum principis* texts in particular. By renewing ancient paradigms of (political) life, early modern authors strove for a better understanding of contemporary political events and for a means to describe the best possible world. Ancient authors did not merely serve as a source of ideas, but were considered as equal interlocutors with their early modern counterparts in ongoing debate about new works: depending on the later authors' cultural backgrounds, their taste for different classical sources evolved over time and across various contexts. Among the many classical works featured in Erasmus's *Institutio*, we should dwell on Seneca's *De clementia* (55–56 CE) and Cicero's *De officiis* (44 BCE), since both works played a vital role in the development of the *speculum principis* tradition, and in fact Seneca's short work for the young Nero could be considered the oldest extant precursor of the genre. *De clementia* served as a mirror in which its author offered the young emperor an image of himself as he was at that moment—that is, as a good emperor—and thereby subtly urged Nero to live up to that high standard if he wanted to be seen as a good emperor by his subjects. The metaphor of the mirror proved a subtle and ingenious instrument to intermingle description and prescription so that the genre evolved from a mirror *of* princes to a mirror *for* princes (Truman 1999, 13).

Just as Seneca had relied on his rhetorical skills to offer Nero both a portrait and a model, so Erasmus presented a *speculum principis* to the Holy Roman Emperor Charles V (1500–1558) in which he depicted Charles already being the good prince whom the *Institutio* in fact was intended to bring forth. Therefore Erasmus created a process in which self-reflection and the typically Senecan idea of *cura sui* ("care for the self") both played a major role. By constantly and tacitly working out to what extent he embodies the qualities ascribed to him, the prince does not need anybody else to point him towards his responsibilities, which consequently makes the advice book superfluous, in a sense, but at the same time, the mirror becomes as much a model for future princes as it is for the current ruler. Erasmus makes this clear in the dedicatory letter of the *Institutio*: "I had the idea of setting forth the ideal of the perfect prince for the general good, but under your name, so that those who are brought up to rule great empires may learn the principles of government through you and take from you their example" (*CWE* 27:204).

Throughout the *Institutio*, Senecan imagery and thought frequently surface. Erasmus knew his subject: one year before the publication of the *Institutio*, he produced his first edition of Seneca's works, which remained the standard edition until it was replaced by Lipsius's masterful version of 1605 (Papy 2001). The basic philosophy underpinning the *Institutio* is that the education of the prince, and not the form of the political constitution, is more decisive for the well-being of the state. The *populus* ("people") is totally subjected to the *ius* ("law; rule") of the prince, who becomes, paradoxically, a real servant: "that is serving, not ruling" (Erasmus 1997, 41). By behaving thus, the prince is the true opposite of a tyrant who is the slave of his desires, since he is out of control of himself. Erasmus describes the prince under such honorific titles as *medicus reipublicae* ("physician of the state"), *pater patriae* ("father of the fatherland") and *apum rex* ("king of the bees"; Erasmus 1997, 92, 59, and 29). The prince for his state is as God for the universe. Among the many virtues in which he excels, mercy (*clementia*) is singled out as the most important and most human quality. Incarnating this and other princely virtues such as liberality, magnificence, and fidelity, alongside principal Christian virtues such as piety, charity, chastity, and modesty, and the cardinal virtues (fortitude, wisdom, moderation, and, above all, justice), which every private citizen should possess, the prince shows his true identity without wearing a mask and playing a role, a clear reference to the double meaning of the Latin word *persona* as both "person" and "mask."

Seneca's *De clementia* was very important for the *speculum principis* genre, but was not its only classical model. Besides many other classical authors, including those already listed, Cicero's *De officiis* exerted an even more lasting influence on *speculum principis* works from Petrarch onwards, as in that author's letter to Francesco da Carrara, hereditary lord of Padua at the time (*Seniles* 14.1, ca. 1370–73; Petrarch 1978). It might seem strange at first, as Peter Stacey (2007) has pointed out, that a clearly outspoken republican text (which depicts monarchy as tyranny) was appropriated for a princely context, but many themes in these Renaissance princely advice books can be traced back to *De officiis*, and the third book (on moral virtues and their relation to political success) proved particularly popular. Not only were Ciceronian ideas eagerly taken up, but Ciceronian style was also closely imitated by Petrarch and his followers. But let us focus first on the ideas.

One of Cicero's central preoccupations is an almost obsessive attentiveness to the Roman ideals of honor, glory, and fame, which should be attained through a life of virtuousness. In his letter to Carrara, Petrarch wrote: "You must lust after the treasure of virtue and win the fame of outstanding glory. This is a property that moths and rust cannot corrupt, nor can thieves steal it in the night" (Petrarch 1978, 61). By emphasizing the overarching role of virtue (*virtus*), Petrarch and later humanists embraced the idea that each person could overcome fortune's obstacles through his or her own efforts, and therefore rejected the medieval Augustinian view of fallen or corrupted human nature, turning their attention to the possibilities of the right education rather than the grace of God.

Although the humanists believed in man's own efforts and the cultivation of human virtue, they did not abandon Christian virtues. On the contrary, Christian virtues were synthesized with classical virtues. A potential problem presented itself when the demands of glory collided with those of virtuousness, but Petrarch and his fellow humanists solved this conundrum by turning to a famous passage in *De officiis* (3.30) stating that "nothing can be useful that is not at the same time just and honorable." This intrinsic bond between the useful and the honorable would become a *leitmotif* throughout these Renaissance mirrors for princes in particular, and early modern political literature in general. Another recurring theme was the question of whether it was better for a prince to be loved rather than feared: given the connection between the useful and the honorable, the answer should straightforwardly be "to be loved," and therefore to lead a virtuous life, since that was the sole guarantee of popular affection, itself the only guarantee of public security.

Generally speaking, the fifteenth- and much of the sixteenth-century *speculum principis* works take up many of these *topoi*, indebted as the tradition was to Cicero and

Seneca. However, we should add that many other classical authors were incorporated, too, as were the Bible and Roman law and its glossators. All of these sources helped to determine the outlook of the princely advice books, but clearly, the conceptual framework for these works was steeped in a Ciceronian and Senecan tradition.

TACITISM AND COMMONPLACING

By the end of the sixteenth century, both the form and content of the outlook traditionally adopted in the *speculum principis* genre had become substantially modified. Examining the work of the Southern Netherlandish humanist Justus Lipsius (1547–1606) helps us understand this change, although his renewal of the genre did not occur suddenly, but was rather anticipated by his previous work, as well as by that of other authors and a changing sociopolitical culture. However, it cannot be denied that Lipsius played a pivotal role in this development. It was not without pride that he presented his princely advice book, the *Politica* (*Politics*, 1589), with the following words: "For I have instituted an unusual kind of genre, in which I could truly say that everything is mine, and nothing. For although the selection and the arrangement [of the content] are mine, the words and phrases I have gathered from various places in the ancient writers" (Lipsius 2004, 231–33). In doing so, Lipsius embedded his mirror for princes in the genre of the "commonplace" book (Moss 1996 and 1998). He selected more than 2,650 aphorisms (*sententiae*) from no fewer than 116 authors (ancient, medieval, and contemporary alike) and gave each a specific place in one of the many chapters that functioned like the titles (*tituli*) in a commonplace book. It was his purpose, as in his philosophical manuals *Manuductio ad Stoicam philosophiam* (*Guide to Stoic Philosophy*, 1604) and *Physiologiae Stoicorum* (*Physical Theory of the Stoics*, 1604), to gather all statements and comments on politics—for just like any other humanist, he was convinced that all knowledge already existed and only needed to be rediscovered—and to present the material as clearly and efficiently as possible. This seems to have been one of the reasons why the *Politica* was such a popular manual for many generations (Enenkel 1985).

By presenting the *Politica* explicitly as a commonplace book, Lipsius offered his readers the opportunity to supplement his storehouse with even more quotations. The same technique underlies his mirror for princes for Archduke Albert VII (1559–1621) of the Spanish Netherlands, the *Monita et exempla politica* (*Political Advice and Examples*, 1605), which in fact was an illustration of the first two books of the *Politica*. The 1605 work offers an impressive collection of examples, also selected from ancient, medieval, and contemporary sources, arranged under similar *tituli* and closely following the structure of the *Politica*; Lipsius left it up to the reader to seek more examples, place them under other *tituli*, and read them according to either their original or new context, which turned his *Monita* (like the *Politica*) into an open-ended enterprise (Moss 2011). Such a structure does not facilitate interpretation, however, which becomes even more complicated by the fact that in the *Politica*, Lipsius links all the sentences to each other with his own words, therefore composing a strong discursive text that leaves it up to the reader to read it either as a loose amalgam of statements or as the exposition of a well-considered point of view. This makes the reader approach the text less as a commonplace book than as an extremely well-wrought product of the cento genre (Tucker 2011; Waszink 1997; Lafond 1981), which means that Lipsius's own ideas cannot be easily derived from it. Through selecting quotations, certain nuances in the original (con)text could be lost, whereas sentences could acquire additional or altered meanings when placed in the new text Lipsius created. Consequently, the perceived stance of the *Politica* has prompted various and sometimes contradictory interpretations.

Lipsius's choice of *sententiae* and *exempla* as his political advice books' main contents was symptomatic of a changing intellectual frame of reference. Absolutism's rise, which concentrated power in the hands of one individual and his small entourage of assistants and counselors, turned the art of politics into an isolated practice with its own patterns, so from now on one needed to be initiated in the *arcana imperii* ("mysteries of state") dominating political life. Arnold Clapmarius (1574–1604), a German professor of history and politics from Altdorf, devoted a whole treatise to this subject under the title *De arcanis rerum publicarum* (*On the Mysteries of State*, 1605). Consequently, the initiated opted for a political idiom characterized by brevity, which stimulated readers to think about its words' exact meaning and intention. These authors no longer wrote treatises that clearly and logically presented all relevant rules and guidelines (Viroli 1992), but offered instead concise articulations intended to prompt further thought. They no longer presented ready-made models to be imitated almost blindly, but rather included collections of examples, stories, and events from which the ruler had to select the most appropriate under his particular circumstances. The opening pages of Lipsius's *Monita et exempla politica* exemplify this idea: Lipsius advises the prince to proceed like the ancient Greek painter Zeuxis, who brought together the most beautiful girls from Agrigentum to produce a painting of the goddess Juno, combining the best qualities of each of these girls; similarly, the prince should turn to history and his predecessors and select the best of their individual qualities. The true master of this technique was the one who knew how to display the right quality at the right moment.

This predilection for *sententiae* and *exempla* meant a kind of rupture in the prevailing stylistic standards of the time, caused by changes both in literary models and in political vocabulary. Gradually, Cicero was replaced by the Roman historian Tacitus (56/57–after 117 CE), who dominated intellectual life from the end of the sixteenth century onwards (Tuck 1993), and Lipsius himself played a crucial role in this development. During Lipsius's stay in Rome from 1568 to 1570, Marc-Antoine Muret (1526–1585), professor of moral philosophy at the Sapienza University in Rome, and an expert classicist, introduced him to imperial Latin literature and roused his interest both in Seneca, and, above all, in Tacitus, who preoccupied Lipsius for the rest of his life. Soon after he returned from Rome, in 1574, Lipsius published his first highly influential edition of the Roman historian. Tacitus was identified as the new exemplar both of content and style because no one else got so acutely to the very heart of politics: writing under the early Roman Empire, he laid bare multiple court intrigues and cut through the complicated play of simulation and dissimulation, revealing as he went along the mysteries of state. His writings were especially valuable as an instrument for what Lipsius called the *similitudo temporum* ("similarity of historical periods"), and for that reason he quoted Tacitus more than any other author in the *Politica*. This turn to Tacitus had a more fundamental consequence for the dominant contemporary conception of history (Grafton 2007), which evolved from seeing history as the direct avenue to *virtus* to seeing it as leading to *prudentia*; or, as Lipsius put it, history became "the fountainhead of political prudence" (Lipsius 2004, 232). In this regard, *prudentia* lost its necessary connection with morality and was primarily related to political pragmatism.

This Tacitean turn altered not only the dominant political style, but also its intellectual frame of reference, as the *Politica* illustrates. In the first two books, Lipsius places *virtus* and *prudentia* in the heart of his exposition and discusses these in a traditional, Christian-Ciceronian way, mentioning, among other qualities, justice, mercy, reliability, modesty, majesty, generosity, and chastity. From the third book onwards, however, Lipsius questions this traditional framework by examining the many facets of *prudentia*, well aware that the morality of the prince alone was not a sufficient guarantee for the state's well-being, and showing the necessity in certain situations for the prince to take recourse to less orthodox and less morally exalted practice. So Lipsius introduces in the fourth book the concept of *prudentia mixta* that hints at "mixing the honorable with the useful" (*utilia honestis miscere*; Lipsius 2004, 508), which allows the ruler to use force and deceit to ensure the stability of the state. Equally important and no less controversial was Lipsius's plea for religious unity within the state, which demonstrated an unconventional respect for individual freedom of conscience; if citizens did not disturb the public peace, the prince was not allowed to interfere with their private beliefs, and only those who openly professed another religion were to be punished. In the last two books, Lipsius expounds on military *prudentia*, as a means to contend against other countries (Book 5) and as an instrument in civil war (Book 6). His decision to expound on this theme was telling, since the traditional Christian-Ciceronian mirrors for princes frequently reiterated that a prince should pursue his ends by virtue and never by (military) force.

Heralding a new tradition, Lipsius was probably one of the most successful authors who reshaped the traditional *speculum principis* genre in terms of its form and content. He tried to develop a politics that was both universal and abstract in design, and realistic and pragmatic in scope. His recourse to Tacitus prompted an entire historiographical movement and inspired many other authors: between 1600 and 1649, at least sixty-seven editions of Tacitus's *Annals* and *Histories* were printed, while between 1580 and 1700, more than 100 authors wrote commentaries on Tacitus, the majority of them political in nature. Some confined themselves to writing political observations and aphorisms in the margins, some commented extensively on certain passages, and others wrote systematic treatises in a Tacitean spirit. The form Lipsius had chosen for his *Politica* and *Monita et exempla politica*—as storehouses of *sententiae* and *exempla* respectively—influenced several contemporary political works, and Lipsius himself urged his readers to imitate this form. Examples of works of other authors who chose it include Lambert Daneau's

Politicorum Aphorismorum Silva (*Miscellany of Political Aphorisms*, 1583), Janus Gruterus's *Florilegium ethico-politicum* (*Ethical-Political Florilegium*, 1610–1612) and Balthasar Exner's *Valerius Maximus Christianus* (*The Christian Valerius Maximus*, 1620; the title refers to a Christianization of Valerius Maximus, the Roman writer of historical anecdotes of the first century CE). The most striking exemplar is Jean de Chokier de Surlet's *Thesaurus Aphorismorum Politicorum* (*Treasury of Political Aphorisms*, 1610), in which each chapter contains a section that quotes extensively from ancient authors and a section with a dozen or so examples to illustrate a point. Closely related to these political commonplace books is the genre of the political emblem book (Clements 1955; Peil 1986), in which the *sententia* becomes the "motto," also represented as an illustration and explained by an epigram. One of the best-known representatives of authors in this genre is the Spanish diplomat Diego de Saavedra Fajardo (1584–1648) who translated into Latin his own popular *Idea de un principe politico Christiano* (*Idea of a Christian Political Prince*, 1640).

Machiavellianism and Anti-Machiavellianism

The Tacitean movement in general and Lipsius's political writings in particular were, in fact, an attempt to come to terms with the legacy of the notorious Italian author and diplomat Niccolò Machiavelli (1469–1527). His *Il principe* (*The Prince*), originally written in the vernacular but soon translated into Latin, was steeped in the tradition of the mirror for princes genre as well (Skinner 1981), and caused a wave of indignation all over Europe. Two main reasons prompted this reaction. First, for Machiavelli, the goal of politics—acquiring honor, glory, and fame; maintaining the state—was the same as it had been for his predecessors, but the means to achieve this radically differed, since contrary to his fellow humanists, he no longer believed in the sole supremacy of virtue and consequently advocated violence if necessary. Second, he was prepared to sacrifice traditional Christian-Ciceronian virtues when circumstances demanded, and so took a far more realistic approach to politics that understood the discrepancy between how people ought to live and how they *actually* live.

Since *Il principe* was initially only available in manuscript and not printed until 1532, five years after its author's death, Machiavelli's ideas only gradually became known. Generally, other thinkers were enthusiastic about his political realism, but they did not sympathize with the means he suggested to implement it: it was not unusual for authors to be attracted to one aspect of his work and repelled by another, and although they were often eager to take up new topics he introduced, they usually situated these in more neutral contexts (Anglo 2005). Some of Machiavelli's arguments that troubled readers' minds include his breaking of the link between the useful and the honorable; his separation of prudence from wisdom; his advice that it is more expedient to *look* virtuous than to *be* virtuous; his advocation of fraud and force as exemplified by the metaphor of the fox and the lion, originally taken from Cicero's *De officiis* (1.41); and last but not least, the instrumental use of religion as a means for political manipulation.

As with the Tacitean writers, we cannot list all those who dealt with the Machiavellian legacy. The most outspoken thinkers were those who turned against his doctrines and are usually labeled as the "anti-Machiavellians" (Bireley 1990). As early as 1539, Reginald Pole (1500–1558), who went on to become archbishop of Canterbury in 1556, published his *Apologia Reginaldi Poli ad Carolum V* (*Apology of Reginald Pole for Charles V*) in which he inveighed strongly against Machiavelli's ideas. Among the most ferocious anti-Machiavellians were the Jesuits, whose "aggressive anti-Machiavellianism became virtually the Society's official doctrine" (Höpfl 2004, 86): these include the Italian Roberto Bellarmino, in *De officio principis Christiani* (*The Duty of the Christian Prince*, 1619); the Englishman Thomas Fitzherbert, in *An sit utilitas in scelere, vel de infelicitate principis Machiavelliani, contra Machiavellum et politicos eius sectatores* (*Does Crime Pay; or, On the Misfortune of the Machiavellian Prince, against Machiavelli and his Political Followers*, 1610); the Belgian Carolus Scribani in *Politico-Christianus* (*The Christian Politician*, 1624); and the German Adam Contzen in his *Politicorum libri decem* (*Ten Books of Politics*, 1621).

ARISTOTELIANISM

An interesting reaction to Machiavelli's doctrines came from the former Jesuit Giovanni Botero (1544–1617), who wrote an Italian political bestseller, *Ragione di stato*, which was soon translated into Latin. Botero was responsible for the dissemination for this recently coined term, translated as "reason of state" (*ratio status* in Latin), which had been in vogue for a while and was closely associated with Machiavelli's thinking. It is a complex term with no single meaning, and refers to politics as an autonomous art of governing according to its own laws, which are not necessarily strictly moral. A distinction was quickly made between "good" and "bad" reason of state, based on both the *end* being pursued (such as the common good *versus* self-interest) and the *means* employed to achieve that end, which might (or might not) be limited by justice, piety, God's law, and so on. For Botero, "good" reason of state was an instrument that helped him reconcile the duties of a true Christian with the requirements for being a successful politician, and these were not necessarily at odds. Importantly, "reason of state" thinking, together with Taciteanism, laid the foundation for the development of a real political "science." Political thinkers grew convinced that political conduct had its own rules, which could be revealed and laid down in scientific laws. In a common medical analogy, one sought to take care of the state's health as if it was a human body. Like a doctor, a politician had to analyze the state of public health, formulate appropriate counsel, and make sure that his instructions were turned into action. The typical style of the time, characterized, as we have seen, by brevity and in some ways by obscurity, helped penetrate into the listener's mind, incite him to further thinking, and, eventually, to act in a proper manner.

All in all, this kind of political "science" left considerable room for ambiguity and uncertainty. One influential way authors coped with this was to integrate humanist political thought within a wider Aristotelian framework. The *speculum principis* genre was subjected to systematization and situated within a wider intellectual context. Lipsius, again, offers a useful example when discussing the book's rationale and form in the *Politica*: "These authors [i.e., Plato and Aristotle] have written on all forms of government and the state in general; I, on the other hand, have selected for myself a part so to speak of this field to cultivate, that is, monarchy" (Lipsius 2004, 231). From the early seventeenth century onwards, monarchy was discussed as only one possible form of government, and discussion of the right form of government fitted within a larger exposition on the "science" of politics, an evolution that paralleled the development of the philosophical manual. Such manuals included summaries and elaborations of Aristotle's ideas, sometimes interspersed with others' thoughts. Aristotle's ideas had been continuously present in educated circles since the Middle Ages, of course, but from the sixteenth century onwards, the interest in him grew as his works were no longer read in Latin translation or filtered through a medieval commentator, but in their original Greek.

The way the mirrors for princes were integrated into an Aristotelian framework is beautifully illustrated by the *Institutiones Politicae* (*Political Principles*, 1623) of the Leuven professor of public eloquence and royal and imperial historiographer Nicolaus Vernulaeus (1583–1649). Vernulaeus states at the beginning that he will not embellish his work "with the words and sentences of many authors" (undeniably an attack on how Lipsius composed his political works), but he nonetheless neatly incorporates many parts of the *Politica* and the *Monita et exempla politica* within his political manual. In the preface, Vernulaeus emphasizes that an administrator of the state not only should possess certain virtues, but also needs to know the art of governing. In defending this thesis, Vernulaeus criticizes the morally oriented character of the *speculum principis* genre with its exclusive attention to virtues in general, and Lipsius's conception of politics in particular, and proposes instead a far more practical conception of political science. In the remainder of the preface, Vernulaeus gives a definition of politics that he elaborates according to Aristotelian method by means of material cause (*causa materialis*) and final cause (*causa finalis*). The *Institutiones Politicae* consists of four books, which touch on many of the topics also covered by Aristotle in the *Politics*: the first is devoted to the state in general; the second to counselors, diplomats, and other magistrates; the third to the materials of the state (e.g., religion, law, taxes, and public buildings); and the fourth to internal and external evils. The discussion of monarchy forms part of the first book, which contains, among other subjects, a lengthy treatment of the princely virtues.

Any overview of early modern political Aristotelianism is problematic, for two main reasons. First, a thinker could be indebted to Aristotle in such diverse and wide-ranging ways that it is difficult to define what counts as "Aristotelian." Political Aristotelianism tended to be elementary: it provided tools, but no clear-cut norms for the distribution of power or political action (Lindberg 2001), and usually Aristotle's ideas were supplemented by those of other philosophers. Second, Aristotelian philosophy was so firmly entrenched at universities across Europe that many tutors contributed to Aristotelian discourse through writing in such typical academic genres as lectures, disputations, orations, dissertations, and manuals. Special mention should be made of the German universities, where political Aristotelianism flourished and was explored by authors like Bartholomaeus Keckermann (ca. 1572–1609) and Johann Heinrich Alstedt (1588–1638) in often voluminous treatises.

Natural Law Discourse

Associated with, yet distinct from, humanist political thought is a less-studied but no less influential form of writing, on the subject of natural law (*ius naturale*); that is, the idea that there are rules for human behavior based upon objective, eternal norms that have been established by Nature and reason. This idea was indebted to humanism in its sensitivity to the linguistic renewal brought about by the humanists. It profited from ancient texts newly made available, which had been either unknown or barely read during the Middle Ages, and benefited from the humanists' emphasis on philological rigor. Far more important than natural law discourse's debt to humanism, however, was its reliance on Thomas Aquinas's great scholastic work, the *Summa Theologiae* (1265–1274). At the beginning of the sixteenth century, there was a great renewal of the Thomist tradition at the University of Salamanca in Spain, for example, where a range of scholars from different generations based their work on the *Secunda [pars] secundae [partis]* ("second part of the second part") of the *Summa Theologica*, which was devoted to the cardinal virtues. This part offered them the necessary tools to analyze and discuss contemporary theological and political problems. Such scholars would narrow down their exposition of the virtues to a treatment of justice, seen as the main virtue regulating the everyday contacts between people and between the prince and his subjects. They added to this discussion of justice many concepts taken from legal discourse, since law offered useful methods for capturing the significance of real actions. They therefore created a synthesis of ethics and legal right that offered an ideal way of approaching contemporary problems, and this close relationship was reflected in a title chosen for many of their works: *De iustitia et iure (On Justice and Right)*.

The writings of these Salamanca-based authors are usually called the "Second Scholastic" or, more specifically, the "Spanish Scholastic," and are far more technical than the humanist mirrors for princes. Their structure is typically scholastic, relying on technical jargon and tight argumentation. That said, their relationship with the mirror for princes genre is much closer than one would initially think. The many manuals entitled *De iustitia et iure* are just one product of authors who were moral theologians offering their readers concrete guidance for ethically ambiguous situations and representing themselves explicitly as moral counselors. The form in which they articulated such counsel, however, varied greatly. Individuals posed a moral question to them and they answered it; many of these answers were compiled and printed. They also composed confession books, to be used, for instance, by priests for whom they provided a storehouse of exemplary cases. In their writings *de iustitia et iure*, these moral theologians tried to develop a theoretical framework for the analysis of similar problems and cases. Taken as a whole, the "Second Scholastic" literature from Salamanca, including the more technical manuals, tried to offer concrete advice on a range of practical problems, many of which related to politics. And many of the people whom they advised were kings, sovereigns, and prominent politicians, so the similarity between these works and the humanist *speculum principis* becomes much more evident. It might come as no surprise, then, that Domingo de Soto (ca. 1494–1560), author of the first *De iustitia et iure* manual (1553; enlarged edition 1556), presented his work as a mirror for princes to Carlos, son of Philip II and Maria Manuela of Portugal (Decock 2013, 53). Invoking Xenophon's *Cyropaedia* (*Education of Cyrus*, early fourth-century BCE) de Soto called it a *Carolopaedia*.

The Spanish Scholastics' writing was simultaneously more abstract and more concrete than the humanists'. They developed a broad structure based on Aquinas's account of the virtues, particularly justice, and within this more abstract framework they analyzed various problems using more technical pedagogical aids like legal concepts. Yet they were more concerned with actuality than most of the humanists, providing princes and politicians with advice on specific cases and helping them solve problems related to real-world policies. The backbone of the Spanish Scholastics' theoretical frame of reference was a renewed interest in natural law discourse, which they lifted to a new height. An important figure is the Dominican Francisco de Vitoria (1483–1546), traditionally considered as a pioneer in Salamanca, who was taken up by his immediate successors and figured prominently in the Jesuits' thinking as the intellectual recipients of much of the work of the Spanish Scholastics. Among the many sixteenth and early-seventeenth century Spanish Scholastics and Jesuits, such prominent names stand out as Fernando Vazquez de Menchaca (1512-1569), Martin de Azpilcueta (also known as Doctor Navarrus, 1491-1586), Francisco de Toledo (1532-1596), Luis de Molina (1535-1600), Leonardus Lessius (1554-1623), and Francisco Suárez (1548-1617). Much of the thinking on natural law by the Spanish Scholastics and their successors was schematized in the *De iure belli ac pacis* (*On the Law of War and Peace*, 1625) of the Dutchman Hugo Grotius (1583–1645), whose work can be considered the culmination of the ancient tradition of natural law. Grotius in turn had a lasting influence on such thinkers as John Selden, whose *Mare clausum* (*The Closed Sea*, 1635) responded directly to Grotius's *Mare liberum* (*The Free Sea*, 1609, arguing that the sea was open to all nations for trade), Thomas Hobbes, whose main philosophical ideas are couched in his *De Cive* (*On the Citizen*, 1642), and Samuel Pufendorf in his *De officio hominis et civis* (*On the Duty of Man and Citizen*, 1675). In these authors, modern natural law theories found great advocates, but these were among the last who wrote about their political ideas in Latin.

Suggested Reading

For overviews of early modern political thought, see Burns and Goldie (1991); Lloyd, Burgess, and Hodson (2007); and Skinner (1978). Skinner (2002) also discusses the methodology of the history of political thought. The standard account of Renaissance republicanism is Baron (1955), and a recent overview is Hankins (2000). For early modern Dutch republicanism, see Haitsma Mulier (1980), and Van Gelderen and Skinner (2002) for a broader study. For Renaissance mirror for princes literature, see the first volume of Skinner (1978); Singer (1981); Müller (1985); Mühleisen and Stammen (1990); Truman (1999); Lipsius, forthcoming; and Stacey (2007) on the Senecan tradition. For Lipsius, the standard account remains Oestreich (1982 and 1989). *Prudentia* is analyzed in Morford (1993), while Van Houdt, forthcoming, offers a synthesis of Lipsius's political ideas and different interpretations in modern scholarship. For the Tacitean tradition, see Momigliano (1947 and 1990), Etter (1966), Schellhase (1976), Burke (1991), and Gajda (2009). On Machiavelli, see Skinner (1981) and Anglo (2005); Bireley (1990) and Zwierlein (2011) discuss anti-Machiavellianism; while for Jesuit political thinking (including anti-Machiavellianism), see Höpfl (2004). Much work on early modern political Aristotelianism needs to be done, but one can start with Dreitzel (1988), Blom (1995), and Lindberg (2001). No study is yet available that discusses the political thought of the Spanish Scholastics in detail, but for natural law discourse see Tuck (1979), Tierney (1997), and Scattola (2001). For discussion of the Spanish Scholastics on natural law, see Brett (1997). For other work related to the content of this chapter, see De Bom (2014).

References

Anglo, Sydney. 2005. *Machiavelli: A Dissection*. Oxford: Oxford University Press.
Baron, Hans. 1955. *The Crisis of the Early Italian Renaissance*. Princeton: Princeton University Press.
Bireley, Robert. 1990. *The Counter-Reformation Prince: Anti-Machiavellianism or Catholic Statecraft in Early Modern Europe*. Chapel Hill: University of North Carolina Press.
Blom, Hans W. 1995. "Causality and Morality in Politics: The Rise of Naturalism in Dutch Seventeenth-Century Political Thought." Ph.D. diss., University of Utrecht.
Brett, Annabel. 1997. *Liberty, Right and Nature: Individual Rights in Later Scholastic Thought*. Cambridge: Cambridge University Press.
Burke, Peter, 1991. "Tacitism, Scepticism, and Reason of State." In Burns and Goldie, 1991, 479–98.
Burns, James H., with Mark Goldie, eds. 1991. *The Cambridge History of Political Thought 1450–1700*. Cambridge: Cambridge University Press.
Clements, Robert J. 1955. "Princes and Literature: A Theme of Renaissance Emblem Books." *Modern Language Quarterly* 16: 114–23.
De Bom, Erik, Marijke Janssens, Toon Van Houdt, and Jan Papy, eds. 2011. *(Un)masking the Realities of Power: Justus Lipsius and the Dynamics of Political Writing in Early Modern Europe*, 97–114. Leiden: Brill.
———. 2014. "Political Philosophy." In *ENLW*, 641–48.
Decock, Wim. 2013. *Theologians and Contract Law: The Moral Transformation of the Ius Commune (ca. 1500–1650)*. Leiden: Martinus Nijhoff.
Enenkel, Karl A. E. 1985. "De Neolatijnse Politica—Justus Lipsius, *Politicorum libri sex*." *Lampas* 18:350–62.
Erasmus, Desiderius. 1997. *The Education of a Christian Prince*. Translated by Neil M. Cheshire and Michael J. Heath, and edited by Lisa Jardine. Cambridge: Cambridge University Press.

Etter, Else L. 1966. *Tacitus in der Geistesgeschichte des 16. und 17. Jahrhunderts*. Basel: Helbing und Lichtenhahn.

Dreitzel, Horst. 1988. "Der Aristotelismus in der politischen Philosophie Deutschlands im 17. Jahrhundert." In *Aristotelismus und Renaissance: In memoriam Charles B. Schmitt*, edited by Eckhard Keßler, Charles H. Lohr, and Walter Sparn, 163–92. Wiesbaden: Harrassowitz.

Gajda, Alexandra. 2009. "Tacitus and Political Thought in Early Modern Europe, c. 1530–1640." In *The Cambridge Companion to Tacitus*, edited by Anthony J. Woodman, 253–68. Cambridge: Cambridge University Press.

Grafton, Anthony. 2007. *What Was History? The Art of History in Early Modern Europe*. Cambridge: Cambridge University Press.

Haitsma Mulier, Eco O. G. 1980. *The Myth of Venice and Dutch Republican Thought in the Seventeenth Century*. Assen: Van Gorcum.

Hankins, James, ed. 2000. *Renaissance Civic Humanism: Reappraisals and Reflections*. Cambridge: Cambridge University Press.

Höpfl, Harro. 2004. *Jesuit Political Thought: The Society of Jesus and the State, c. 1540–1630*. Cambridge: Cambridge University Press.

Lafond, Jean. 1981. "Le centon et son usage dans la littérature morale et politique." In *L'automne de la Renaissance, 1580–1630*, edited by Jean Lafond and André Stegmann, 117–28. Paris: J. Vrin.

Lindberg, Bo. 2001. "Political Aristotelianism in the Seventeenth Century." In *Renaissance Readings of the* Corpus Aristotelicum, edited by Marianne Pade, 241–54. Copenhagen: Museum Tusculanum Press.

Lipsius, Justus. 2004. *Politica: Six Books of Politics or Political Instruction*. Edited and translated by Jan Waszink. Assen: Van Gorcum.

———. Forthcoming. *Monita et exempla politica (1605)*. Edited and translated by Marijke Janssens, Jan Papy, and Toon Van Houdt. Leuven: Leuven University Press.

Lloyd, Howell A., Glenn Burgess, and Simon Hodson, eds. 2007. *European Political Thought, 1450–1700: Religion, Law and Philosophy*. New Haven: Yale University Press.

Momigliano, Arnaldo. 1947. "The First Political Commentary on Tacitus." *The Journal of Roman Studies* 37: 91–101.

———. 1990. "Tacitus and the Tacitist Tradition." In *The Classical Foundations of Modern Historiography*, 109–31. Berkeley: University of California Press.

Morford, Mark. 1993. "Tacitean *prudentia* and the Doctrines of Justus Lipsius." In *Tacitus and the Tacitean Tradition*, edited by Torrey J. Luce and Anthony J. Woodman, 129–51. Princeton: Princeton University Press.

Moss, Ann. 1996. "Vision fragmentée et unitaire: Les *Politiques* et les recueils des lieux communs." In *Juste Lipse (1547–1606) en son temps*, edited by Christian Moucel, 471–78. Paris: Champion.

———. 1998. "The *Politica* of Justus Lipsius and the Commonplace-Book." *Journal of the History of Ideas* 59:421–36.

———. 2011. "The *Monita et exempla politica* as Example of a Genre." In De Bom, Janssens, Van Houdt, and Papy, op. cit., 97–114.

Mühleisen, Hans-Otto, and Theo Stammen. 1990. *Politische Tugendlehre und Regierungskunst: Studien zum Fürstenspiegel der Frühen Neuzeit*. Tübingen: Niemeyer.

Müller, Rainer A. 1985. "Die deutschen Fürstenspiegel des 17. Jahrhunderts: Regierungslehren und politische Pädagogik." *Historische Zeitschrift* 240:571–97.

Oestreich, Gerhard. 1982. *Neostoicism and the Early Modern State*. Edited by Brigitta Oestreich and Helmut G. Koenigsberger, and translated by David McLintock. Cambridge: Cambridge University Press.

———. 1989. *Antiker Geist und moderner Staat bei Justus Lipsius (1547–1606): Der Neustoizismus als politische Bewegung*. Göttingen: Vandenhoeck & Ruprecht.

Papy, Jan. 2001. "Erasmus' and Lipsius' Editions of Seneca: A 'Complementary' Project?" *Erasmus of Rotterdam Society Yearbook* 21:10–36.

Peil, Dietmar. 1986. "Emblematische Fürstenspiegel im 17. und 18. Jahrhundert: Saavedra—Le Moyne—Wilhelm." *Frühmittelalterliche Studien* 20:54–92.

Petrarch, Francesco. 1978. "How a Ruler Ought to Govern His State." Translated by Benjamin G. Kohl. In *The Earthly Republic: Italian Humanists on Government and Society*, edited by Benjamin G. Kohl, Ronald G. Witt, and Elizabeth B. Welles, 35–78. Manchester: Manchester University Press.

Pocock, John G. A. 1975. *The Machiavellian Moment: Florentine Political Thought and the Atlantic Republican Tradition*. Princeton: Princeton University Press.

Scattola, Merio. 2001. "Models in History of Natural Law." *Ius Commune* 28:91–159.

Schellhase, Kenneth C. 1976. *Tacitus in Renaissance Political Thought*. Chicago: University of Chicago Press.

Singer, Bruno. 1981. *Die Fürstenspiegel in Deutschland im Zeitalter des Humanismus und der Reformation*. Munich: Wilhelm Fink.

Skinner, Quentin. 1978. *The Foundations of Modern Political Thought*. 2 vols. Cambridge: Cambridge University Press.

———. 1981. *Machiavelli*. Oxford: Oxford University Press.

———. 2002. *Visions of Politics*. 3 vols. Cambridge: Cambridge University Press.

Stacey, Peter. 2007. *Roman Monarchy and the Renaissance Prince*. Cambridge: Cambridge University Press.

Tierney, Brian. 1997. *The Idea of Natural Rights: Studies on Natural Rights, Natural Law, and Church Law, 1150–1625*. Grand Rapids: Eerdmans.

Truman, Ronald W. 1999. *Spanish Treatises on Government, Society and Religion in the Time of Philip II*. Leiden: Brill.

Tuck, Richard. 1979. *Natural Rights Theories: Their Origin and Development*. Cambridge: Cambridge University Press.

———. 1993. *Philosophy and Government 1572–1651*. Cambridge: Cambridge University Press.

Tucker, George H. 2011. "Justus Lipsius and the *Cento* Form." In De Bom, Janssens, Van Houdt, and Papy, op. cit., 163–92.

Van Gelderen, Martin, and Quentin Skinner, eds. 2002. *Republicanism: A Shared European Heritage*. 2 vols. Cambridge: Cambridge University Press.

Van Houdt, Toon. Forthcoming. "Lipsius's Political Ideas." In *A Companion to Justus Lipsius*, edited by Jeanine De Landtsheer. Leiden: Brill.

Viroli, Maurizio. 1992. *From Politics to Reason of State: The Acquisition and Transformation of the Language of Politics 1250–1600*. Cambridge: Cambridge University Press.

Waszink, Jan. 1997. "*Inventio* in the *Politica*: Commonplace-Books and the Shape of Political Theory." In *Lipsius in Leiden: Studies in the Life and Works of a Great Humanist on the Occasion of His 450th Anniversary*, edited by Karl Enenkel and Chris Heesakkers, 141–62. Voorthuizen: Florivallis.

Zwierlein, Cornel. 2011. "Machiavellismus/Anti-Machiavellismus." In *Diskurse der Gelehrtenkultur in der Frühen Neuzeit*, edited by Herbert Jaumann, 903–51. Berlin: De Gruyter.

CHAPTER 10

HISTORIOGRAPHY

PATRICK BAKER

FROM THE MIDDLE AGES TO THE RENAISSANCE

ALL the typical historical genres of the Middle Ages—chronicle, hagiography, universal history, encyclopedia, compendium—lived on into the Renaissance. What is distinctive about Neo-Latin historiography, indeed, what makes it a proper chapter in the history of literature and scholarship, is not the death of something old but the birth of something new and its lasting impact. Like many novelties, the new historiography took shape in the longing for a bygone object of desire: in this case the self-conscious revival of classicizing Latin in the composition of historical works. Although Livy and especially Sallust were read and imitated throughout the Middle Ages (Smalley 1974, 19–20), it was in the fourteenth century that a massive effort began to recreate not only the forms and themes of the ancient Roman historians but also their syntax and diction (Witt 2000, esp. 139–56). This effort intensified in the fifteenth century as classical models were adapted, assimilated, appropriated—in a word, transformed—to satisfy the intellectual, political, and social needs of the present.

History was a major element in the classicizing literary movement and program for cultural renewal known as Renaissance humanism. As one of the *studia humanitatis*, along with grammar, rhetoric, poetry, and moral philosophy, it enjoyed a privileged place in the new education that swept Italy and then the rest of Europe in the fifteenth and sixteenth centuries (Kallendorf 2002). The lost or only partially available works of Livy, Tacitus, and Sallust were eagerly sought out (Billanovich 1981; Sabbadini 1967). Greek historians became the object of countless translation efforts, culminating in a massive project sponsored by Pope Nicholas V (1447–1455) which gave the world the first Latin version of Thucydides (by Lorenzo Valla), among others. Ancient historians, both Latin and Greek, received exhaustive commentary, ranging from marginal annotations to independent works of scholarship. The premium on classical historiography was so high that the Dominican scholar Annius of Viterbo was prompted to forge pseudo-*Antiquitates* (1498), posing as Berosus and Manetho, Cato and Fabius Pictor (Grafton 1991, 76–103).

GENERAL CHARACTERISTICS

The Latin historiography that grew out of this milieu differed from medieval historical writing in many respects (Gilbert 1965, 203–26; Cochrane 1981, 3–33). Not only was it classicizing in a way that would have seemed neither familiar nor urgent to medieval authors, but it paid greater heed to the principles of classical rhetoric, according to which history should both delight and teach the reader. Style was paramount. The narrative was decorated with rhetorical figures, elaborate periods, intricate descriptions of battles, and as many formal speeches demonstrating the historian's oratorical credentials as the matter would bear. At the same time, as Cicero had said, history was the *magistra vitae* ("teacher of life"), and thus it was akin to poetry and moral philosophy. As an ethical genre, history had to be useful—less, however, by elucidating the higher truths of human existence than by teaching the mundane truths of political experience. The context for this utility was, at first, emphatically civic. The earliest humanist historians intended to glorify the cities about which they wrote and to teach practical political lessons to their contemporaries.

In addition to these classical traits, humanist historiography evinces others that appear strikingly modern: it was distinguished by the emergence of a new sense of anachronism (or of historical perspective), of a more critical use of evidence, and of an enhanced preoccupation with causation (Burke 1969). As for the first, humanists perceived the past as distant and fundamentally different from the present; it had to be approached as something foreign. Second, the *auctoritates* that served as sources in the Middle Ages could not be trusted on the weight of their authority alone, or rather their authority depended on a critical evaluation. Ultimately this scrutiny would even be applied to the Bible and to Roman law, whose texts began, by the mid- to late fifteenth century, to be subjected to philological and historical analysis. Myths, especially founding myths, were dispelled on evidential grounds. Autopsy and reliable eyewitnesses were preferred to hearsay and unvetted testimony. And novel sources like archival documents and previously unknown histories, such as those in Greek that could now once again be read, began to be consulted. Causal relationships, finally, could no longer be affirmed generically but had to be minutely described and accounted for, nor could they simply be ascribed to a divine plan. Although the role of Providence was still universally recognized, historical events, periods, and developments were nevertheless fitted into secular frameworks and chains of human agency that gave only passing attention to the divine or the supernatural.

Now a caveat: the characteristics assembled here constitute in their entirety an ideal type. If most works of humanist historiography contained some or several of these modern traits, few manifested them all, and perhaps none did so consistently (Gilbert 1965, 219–23). The use of documentary sources, for example, would not become standard in Latin historiography for centuries, nor was it perceived widely as a sign of progress in the beginning. Humanist authors did not tend to sift various accounts but rather depended in general on one medieval or ancient source at a time, which they then rewrote according to the new fashion. Furthermore, the criticism of myths and legends could be as sporadic as it was impressive. Moreover, humanist historians were on the whole unapologetically partisan, nor were they averse to omitting or blatantly twisting the truth if doing so suited their rhetorical or moral exposition (to say nothing of the exigencies of their patrons; e.g., Ianziti 2012, 13–17; Kohl 2007). This motley practice resulted in part from an incongruity, namely, that the humanists who apprenticed themselves to discerning and discriminating ancient historians like Tacitus, Polybius, and Thucydides tended themselves to be either patriots or hired pens. But it is at least equally important that the humanists did not set out to be critical for criticism's sake, but rather that they saw that a critical approach could be useful when writing the history of entities and individuals that had broken with the two time-honored guarantors of political legitimacy: the empire and the papacy. Sometimes the best way to shatter the hold of tradition on an upstart republic like Florence, a *de facto* independent duchy like Milan, or a *parvenu* conqueror like Alfonso of Aragon was with a blow from the hammer of criticism. Thus, although humanist historiography has often been heralded as the beginning of modern, even of scientific, history (e.g., Ullman 1946; Fryde 1983, 3–31), it is more proper to view it as the habitat—classicizing, rhetorical, moral—in which modern critical historiography's various single-celled ancestors began to evolve.

THE MODEL OF LEONARDO BRUNI

The first great humanist historian, and long the measure for those aspiring to the title, was the Aretine Leonardo Bruni (1370–1444)—among the most famous, highly respected, and well-read humanists of the fifteenth century (Hankins 2003, 9–239). He was one of the first Italians of the Renaissance to learn Greek, served a long, successful tenure as papal secretary and then as chancellor of the city of Florence, and distinguished himself in numerous fields including moral philosophy, educational theory, oratory, epistolography, and, of course, history. Much of his historical work is heavily based on ancient Greek historians (Hankins 2003, 243–71; Ianziti 2012): the *Cicero novus* (*New Cicero*, 1413) was a revision of Plutarch's biography, recasting the Roman statesman and orator in a better light than the original comparison with Demosthenes had; Polybius served as the basis for the *Commentarii de primo bello Punico* (*Notes on the First Punic War*, 1418–1422), a history of the First Punic War meant to fill the lacuna of Livy's missing second decade; the *Commentarium rerum Graecarum* (*Notes on Greek History*, 1439) drew extensively from Xenophon's *Hellenica* (*Greek History*) to provide the readers of Bruni's day with knowledge of late classical Greece; and the *De bello Italico adversus Gothos* (*The Italian War against the Goths*, 1441) was essentially a redaction of Procopius that bridged a gap in Bruni's Latin audience's knowledge of late antique Italy. To the modern eye, such works appear as artful translations or even as acts of plagiarism, and indeed the former accusation (but not, apparently, the latter) was leveled in the fifteenth century. Yet Bruni maintained that these were bona fide histories (Ianziti 2012, 14–19). A translator is faithful to the sense, if not the letter, of his source, whereas an historian always follows his own will (*arbitratus*) regarding the order and arrangement of material and its artful presentation. The historian's primary function, Bruni argued, is to craft a narrative (*narratio*) in proper Latin out of the information available from extant sources, whatever and however many they be.

Bruni also wrote a memoir of the events that occurred in his own time, *De temporibus suis* (1440–1441), but it is his *magnum opus*, the *Historiae Florentini populi* (*History of the Florentine People*), that constitutes his greatest contribution to historiography. With this work, whose individual books began appearing at regular intervals in 1415 and which was completed in 1442, he effected a "shift of history writing from being present-focused in the service of the future, to being past-focused in the service of the present" (Ianziti 2012, 94; Fubini 2003, 93–194). Unlike the medieval chronicle tradition, which focused on bearing witness to one's own time and preserving authoritative knowledge about former ones, Bruni scrutinized the Florentine past—critically reviewing evidence and accepted stories, hazarding conjectures, and tapping new sources—to shape that past into a Livian grand narrative of the city's political and military history. The result had obvious propaganda value and by all appearances was effectively commissioned for this purpose by the city, but Bruni intended the *Historiae* to be more, namely, a guide to contemporary political decision-making (Hankins 2007). The statesmen of his own age were supposed to draw lessons and advice from the city's history, which Bruni traced from its origins down to the year 1402.

The import of the *Historiae*, however, transcends even the service it rendered to republican Florence and its governing citizens; for in this work Bruni revolutionized historiography (Bruni 2001, 1:ix–xxi). He exploded long-cherished myths about the city's past, including that it had been founded by Trojan exiles, destroyed by Attila the Hun, and refounded by Charlemagne. Instead he showed that it had been founded by veterans of the Roman general Sulla and had never been destroyed (although it had suffered at the hands of the Ostrogothic king Totila), thus bringing the city's origins out of a misty, epic past and into documented history—not to mention affiliating it with the Roman Republic and cutting ties with the empire. At the same time he broke with traditions in periodization. Abandoning the biblical scheme of the four kingdoms, which was based on the Book of Daniel and had been inscribed indelibly into European consciousness by Orosius (fourth–fifth centuries CE), Bruni envisioned the broader chronological horizon on which Florence was situated as divided into intervals of Etruscan, republican Roman, imperial Roman, barbarian, and German imperial hegemony, ending with the period of liberty that the city on the river Arno had by then indisputably enjoyed for a little over two centuries. Liberty, moreover, served as a protagonist in Bruni's vision of the *longue durée*, a kind of historical force whose presence or absence determined the character of peoples and accounted for change over time. The freedom of Etruria, republican Rome, and present-day Florence was the cornerstone of their greatness; the loss of liberty under the Roman Empire and its barbarian inheritors provided the explanation for periods of decadence. Furthermore, the division of time according to the index of freedom underlay a novel manner of partitioning European history in general, namely, dividing it into ancient, medieval, and modern periods. This new periodization, finally, implied a secular understanding of causation and historical change that can be seen throughout Bruni's work. There it is not divine providence but individuals, peoples, and their decisions that, in combination with contingent events, move history forward. To grasp Bruni's approach in a single comparison, one might consider that Guibert of Nogent (ca. 1055–1124) wrote the history of God *through* the Franks (*Dei gesta per Francos*, 1107–1108), but Bruni recorded the history wrought by the Florentine people.

Bruni had many imitators, emulators, and epigones (Cochrane 1981). In Florence itself, his humanist successors in the office of chancellor tried their hand at the new history (Wilcox 1969). Poggio Bracciolini penned a Sallustian continuation of Bruni's Livian monument entitled *Historia Florentina* (1455–1459), focusing on the theme of war in the century leading up to his own work. Bartolomeo Scala (1430–1497) intended to write an even more expansive work than Bruni had, but managed to finish only four of an envisioned twenty books before dying. Meanwhile the rest of Italy (Di Stefano et al. 1992) had been bitten by the Brunian bug: in the course of the fifteenth and sixteenth centuries, contemporary histories and histories *ab urbe condita* were assiduously written in all the major Italian powers, from Milan (Ianziti 1988), to Naples (Ferraù 2001), to Venice (Fabbri 1992), as well as in other important cities like Genoa, Siena, and Ferrara.

THE MODEL OF BIONDO FLAVIO'S ANTIQUARIANISM

Even when Italian humanist historians did not focus solely on princes and peoples—such as in Benedetto Accolti's account of the First Crusade, *De bello a Christianis contra barbaros gesto* (*The Christians' War against the Barbarians*, 1464)—politics and war were the leading themes of the day. Yet there was another major aspect of Quattrocento Italian humanist historiography that would go on to have enormous influence: antiquarianism. Here the founding figure is Biondo Flavio (1392–1463; Fubini 1968; Fubini 2003, 53–89; Flavio 2005, vii–xxvii). A friend of Leonardo Bruni's and, like him, a longtime member of the papal curia, Biondo wrote several enormous works of critical erudition dedicated to unearthing the Italian past. His *Roma instaurata* (*Rome Restored*, 1444–1446) attempted to reconstruct the physical appearance of the ancient city for his contemporaries, who were familiar mainly with its ruins and rubble. The goal of the *Roma triumphans* (*Rome Triumphant*, 1453–1460), on the other hand, was to make sense of ancient Roman religious, civic, and military institutions. In the *Italia illustrata* (*Italy*

Illuminated, 1448–1453) Biondo aimed to demystify the topography of the contemporary Italian peninsula, which had become hazy as a result of toponymic alterations brought about by the barbarian invasions and the development of the vernacular. Biondo "illuminated" Italy by going through its ancient provinces one by one, clarifying what was where, characterizing cities and regions, naming the most important individuals active there, and describing their political, military, and especially literary accomplishments (Clavuot 2002). In the process he provided a model for a genre, chorography, that would thrive especially beyond the Alps, and made a contribution to what we might now call "cultural history." Biondo's antiquarian interests also lay at the root of his major historical work, the *Historiarum ab inclinatione Romani imperii decades* (*Decades of History from the Decline of the Roman Empire*, 1439–1452), which has the distinction of being the first-ever history of medieval Europe (Hay 1988). In thirty-two books, the *Decades* run from the fall of the Western Empire, whose beginning Biondo placed at the Gothic sack of Rome in 410, to the year 1441, although the fifteenth century admittedly occupies a full third of the work. The scope is European, but the focus becomes increasingly Italian as Biondo nears his own day. In the great mass of humanist accounts of cities and principalities, the *Decades*, taken together with the *Italia illustrata*, was the closest thing to a history of Italy produced in the fifteenth century—and it would remain such until Carlo Sigonio's magisterial *De Regno Italiae* (*The Kingdom of Italy*, 1580).

Biondo's Latin did not quite meet the classicizing standards of his time, nor were his works as rhetorical as those of Bruni or of Bembo, who wrote a history of Venice. On the other hand, Biondo's method evinces many of the qualities that can make the new historiography appear so modern at times. He consulted a large number of written sources and critically compared them (Clavuot 1990). He pioneered the use of archaeological, numismatic, epigraphic, and cartographical evidence. He took advantage of extensive traveling to conduct research, although not as much as he leads his reader to believe (Cappelletto 1992, 181–89). And when travel proved impossible, he urged acquaintances to send him information, which many did, in some cases even providing polished reports. More important, although he could at times be nonchalant with evidence, he could just as often bring his critical acumen to bear on a whole range of sources, sifting and judging them in order to arrive at a complex picture of the truth that no single one of them contained by itself. It should be mentioned, finally, that by taking as clear a delight in excavating the facts of the past as he did in artfully arranging them and construing moral lessons from them, Biondo presaged the erudite history of the eighteenth century.

ITALIANS ACROSS THE ALPS

The influence of both Bruni and Biondo would be intensely felt as the new historiography made its way across the Alps. The initial carriers of this literary strain were Italians seeking employment abroad (Helmrath, Muhlack, and Walther 2002; Helmrath 2013, 189–212; Völkel 2002). Filippo Buonaccorsi (1436–1497) in Poland,

Paolo Emilio (d. 1529) in France, Antonio Bonfini (1427/1434–1503) in Hungary, Polydore Vergil (1470–1555) in England, Lucio Marineo Siculo (1444–1536) in Spain— all wrote grand narratives for their royal patrons, who sought a literary document that would both attest to a common national past and thereby act as a motor for fostering a sense of national identity. It is counter-intuitive that the first monumental histories of the emerging nations of Europe were written by foreigners, but the prestige of humanism was so great and the *auctoritas* of the Italians so undeniable that the latter even managed to beat out superior local competition, as when Paolo Emilio took the job that might otherwise have gone to Robert Gaguin (1433–1501). The marriage was not entirely harmonious. On the whole, rulers were pleased with the rhetorically polished works laid before them, but the Italians had a natural bias towards Rome that could grate on the descendents of the "barbarians" once brought under its yoke. Furthermore, the Italians could be insensitive to national honor in their application of critical standards to accepted truths. Polydore Vergil, for example, had little patience in his *Anglica historia* (*English History*, published in three different versions in 1534, 1546, and 1555) for the popular fables of English history and the revered Geoffrey of Monmouth, reserving particular scorn for King Arthur and the supposed Trojan founder of Britain, Brutus (Rexroth 2002, 423–29; Schlelein 2010). Antonio Bonfini, on the other hand, was more flexible in his *Rerum Ungaricarum decades* (*Decades of Hungarian History*, finished 1497, first printed 1543–1568; Baker 2012). He discarded some myths that seemed not to redound to national honor, but he retained others that would if properly massaged, such as the supposed Scythian origin of the Hungarians. Although one tradition equated the Scythians with *immanitas* ("barbarism"), Bonfini exploited another according to which they were noble savages, inhabitants of a simpler, purer Golden Age. With equal adroitness, he frankly admitted the ferociousness of the Huns, only to compare Attila to Romulus and then rehabilitate the whole people through its eventual conversion to Christianity under Saint Stephen. Finally, to substantiate the claims of his patron, Matthias Corvinus, to both the realm of Hungary and the Holy Roman Empire, Bonfini constructed a genealogy according to which the king was a descendent of the ancient Roman *gens* of the Valerii (and through them of the Sabines, and hence of the Lacedaemonians, and hence of the Heraclidae, and hence ultimately of Jove himself!). While this genealogy is patently false (and not only because of the mythical element), Bonfini substantiated it, in accordance with the critical norms developed by the humanists, with textual, numismatic, toponymic, and epigraphic evidence. Bonfini's success rested on his willingness to indulge local traditions, salute national pride, and abjure truth if it suited royal prerogative. But it owed just as much to the fact that he was writing for an international audience conditioned to salivate over a Ciceronian period, and not for the local audience that preferred its raw legends to Latin literacy. Perhaps this is why his history, finished only after Matthias's death, was solemnly shelved in the royal library and appears not to have been taken down again until its first three decades were printed in 1543; the work was first published in its entirety by Johannes Sambucus in 1568, when nostalgia was in the air for the era of Matthias (Almási 2009, 172–75).

CHOROGRAPHY

Italians were, of course, not the only ones to write the histories of lands beyond the Alps. As early as 1492, Konrad Celtis proclaimed the desideratum of a *Germania illustrata*, a work that was to remain a Platonic ideal but that would cast many worthy shadows (Muhlack 2002; Helmrath 2013, 213–78). The historical chorographies that appeared were influenced first and foremost by Biondo's *Italia illustrata*, but also by the rediscovery and publication of Tacitus's *Germania*, by Enea Silvio Piccolomini's trail-blazing geo-historical works *Historia Bohemica* (*Bohemian History*, 1458), *Historia Austrialis* (*Austrian History*, three redactions in 1453, 1455, and 1458), and *Europa* (1458), as well as by the sections on ancient Germany in Annius of Viterbo's *Antiquitates* (*Antiquities*). Celtis himself got only as far as a description of the city of Nuremberg, *De situ et moribus Norimbergae* (1502). More universal description of German lands was achieved in works such as Johannes Cochlaeus's *Brevis Germanie descriptio* (*Short Description of Germany*, 1512) and Sebastian Münster's *Germaniae atque aliarum regionum . . . descriptio* (*Description of Germany and Other Regions*, 1530).

Chorography also became a standard genre for geo-ethno-historical accounts of cities, principalities, ecclesiastical districts, and regions (Schirrmeister 2009; Brendle et al. 2001). Just a few of the countless examples, some of which crossed the line into panegyric and myth without compunction, are Albert Krantz's *Saxonia* (*Saxony*, 1520), which dealt with an area approximating the extent of the Hanseatic League, Ägidius Tschudi's *Alpina Rhaetia* (*Alpine Raetia*, 1536), and Johannes Bugenhagen's *Pomerania* (1517–1518). Autochthonous origins were at a premium in all such works (Borchardt 1971), but so were connections to Roman antiquity, however tenuous. Bugenhagen's text illustrates the clever mixture of the two (Helmrath 2013, 254–55; Kaiser 2009). Based on Helmold von Bosau's (ca. 1120–after 1177) *Cronica Slavorum* (*Chronicle of the Slavs*), epigraphic evidence, and oral traditions, Bugenhagen traced the *antiquitas* of the Pomeranians in Book 1 back to the ancient Veneti, or Wends. He then provided an extensive geographical description of their territory before relating, in Book 2, the people's eventual Christianization. Books 3 and 4, finally, dealt with the history of the reigning dynasty currently represented by Duke Bogislaw X (1474–1523), who had only recently reunited the various parts of Pomerania and, eager for a propaganda outlet, commissioned the work in question. But Bogislaw was not only the legitimate ruler of an ancient *natio*, he also presided, according to Bugenhagen, over a region through which Julius Caesar himself had marched. Indeed, as etymological kinship supposedly showed, the ducal residence Wolgast had begun as an army camp, *Iulia castra*.

This chorographic model spread outside of German-speaking lands as well, as evidenced by William Camden's *Britannia* (published in different versions from 1586 to 1606) and a blossoming of civic chorographies in the Netherlands (Esser 2005). It was also common for grand national narratives to start with chorographies. Thus began the *Historia* of Polydore Vergil and the *Decades* of Antonio Bonfini, as did, for example, Ubbo Emmius's *Rerum Frisicarum historia* (*History of Frisia*, 1616). Johannes

Pontanus's *Rerum Danicarum historia* (*History of Denmark*, 1631–1740) concluded with a substantial *Chorographica Daniae descriptio* (*Chorographic Description of Denmark*; Skovgaard-Petersen 2002, 143–69). It first briefly treats the name of Denmark. Then it provides a complete survey of the kingdom, characterizing the geography and culture of Danish towns, regions, and islands. Attention is given to landscape, buildings and monuments, history and famous incidents, and notable individuals. The *Descriptio* ends with a general overview of Denmark's government (in which the peculiar Danish mixture of hereditary and elective monarchy is described and defended), law, social classes, agriculture, national character, and learned traditions. It ends with a discussion of the Danish language and a catalog of the kingdom's learned men, from Saxo Grammaticus to the most recent university professors. What results is a picture of a stable, harmonious, cultivated kingdom, fertile and productive, buttressed economically by fishing and trade and militarily by a hardy sea-folk bent on conquest.

PRESTIGE, PROPAGANDA AND LEGITIMATION

The nationalist impulse (Hirschi 2005) behind the chorographies continued to drive the production of narrative histories, which after the initial Italian charge were now firmly in the hands of ultramontane authors. Both text types, the border between which is clearly fluid, served to lay bare the roots of a given people or place, to portray aspects of the European past that, because they had been recorded not by canonical ancient writers but by "benighted" medieval ones, could not yet be seen clearly on a horizon dominated by the tastes of humanism. Some histories were written in civic contexts. Others grew organically out of the programs of intellectual *sodalitates*. A particularly prolific context was provided by courts, whose products, even when critical in approach, had a clear propagandistic and political purpose (Völkel and Strohmeyer 2009). France, for instance, was treated in Robert Gaguin's *Compendium de origine et gestis Francorum* (*Compendium of the Origins and Deeds of the Franks*, 1495); Scotland in Hector Boece's *Scotorum historiae* (*History of the Scots*, 1526); and Poland in Martin Kromer's *De origine et rebus gestis Polonorum* (*The Origins and Deeds of the Poles*, 1555).

Political prestige and legitimacy depended not only on the distant past but also on the proper framing of contemporary rulers and events, and here, too, works of history could play an apologetic and even a polemical role. As a functionary of the *Consejo de Indias*, which oversaw the government of the colonies for the Spanish Crown, Pietro Martire d'Anghiera chronicled the discovery and exploration of the New World in his *De orbe novo* (*The New World*, first complete edition 1530). William Camden portrayed the reign of Elizabeth I as befitted the religious and political vision of James I, in his *Annales rerum Anglicarum et Hibernicarum regnante Elizabetha* (*Annals of English and Irish History under Elizabeth*, 1615–1625). The Schmalkaldic League employed Johann Sleidan to write an official history from the Reformed point of view, the *Commentarii de statu religionis et rei publicae Carolo V Caesare* (*Notes on the Situation of Religion and*

State under the Emperor Charles V, 1555), although Protestants were sorely disappointed in what they perceived as Sleidan's lack of partisanship (Kelley 1980; Kess 2008).

INSTITUTIONAL HISTORY

Partisanship was not lacking, however, in a new kind of ecclesiastical history poured from the crucible of confessionalization (Peters 2007; Scheible 1966; Zen 1994; Pullapilly 1975). If the Reformation turned primarily on arguments of a theological nature—*sola fides, sola scriptura*, the two swords—it was also animated by disputes over the historical nature of the early church and the development of Christian dogma and practice over time. Thus, on both sides, just as important as controversialist writings were works clarifying the history of Christianity; proper doctrine relied on proper historical knowledge. The Lutherans struck the first blow with the *Ecclesiastica historia* (*Church History*, 1559–1574). This work is commonly referred to as the *Magdeburg Centuries* because it was compiled by a group of scholars in Magdeburg and was divided into thirteen books, each devoted to one of the first thirteen centuries of Christian history (ending in 1298; materials treating the fourteenth to the sixteenth centuries remained in manuscript). The Centuriators were led by Matthias Flacius Illyricus, whose previous *Catalogus testium veritatis* (*Catalog of the Witnesses of Truth*, 1556) had used historical evidence to demonstrate that the medieval popes had continuously altered, that is, corrupted, the nature of the church. Now Flacius directed a research *équipe* to ferret out documents, and a team of writers to incorporate them into a full history of the demonic papacy's undermining of Christ's true *ecclesia*. Each of the thirteen volumes was divided into thematic chapters dealing with doctrine, ceremony, synods, and so on, as a whole producing a mountain of seemingly incontrovertible historical evidence for the Lutheran position. Meanwhile, Catholics had been preparing their own version of history. Onofrio Panvinio was prompted by Philip II to write a *Chronicon ecclesiae usque ad Maximilianum II* (*Chronicle of the Church until Maximilian II*, 1568). Pope Gregory XIII asked Carlo Sigonio to write a *Historia ecclesiastica* (*Church History*, 1579). But the definitive response to the Centuriators started coming in 1588, when Caesar Baronius issued the first volume of his *Annales ecclesiastici* (*Church Annals*, twelfth and final volume 1607). This massive, endlessly popular work traced the entire history of the church year by year and adduced, quoting at length whenever possible, the widest variety of sources: chronicles, hagiographies, letters, decrees, donations, documents of church councils, charters, inscriptions from catacombs, Roman imperial coins, and so on.

The adventitious result of these historical justifications of religious doctrine was a new kind of history writing: institutional. Traditionally, works dealing with aspects of history beyond the sphere of politics, peoples, rulers, and war were not narrative but rather took one of two basic forms. Universal histories, such as Jacopo Filippo Foresti's *Supplementum Chronicarum* (*Supplement to the Chronicles*, 1483), could contain anything the author wanted as long as the material was ordered chronologically from the Creation and subdivided geographically. The other option was to portray aspects of culture biographically, providing short descriptions of the achievements of a line of famous individuals in a manner familiar from Jerome's *De viris illustribus* (*Illustrious Men*, 392–393) or from Cicero's *Brutus*. Literary "histories" in this fashion include Johannes Trithemius's bio-bibliographical *Catalogus illustrium virorum Germaniae* (*Catalog of Illustrious Men from Germany*, 1495), an account of all German writers from the fourth century onward, and Erasmus's (1466–1536) *Ciceronianus* (1528), a dialogue satirically tracking the literary movement known as Ciceronianism. All aspects of culture—humanism, the visual arts, philosophy and medicine, politics and warfare—were represented in discrete sections of Bartolomeo Facio's *De viris illustribus* (1456). And Bartolomeo Platina's *De vita Christi ac omnium pontificum* (*The Life of Christ and of All the Popes*, 1479) was, taken in its entirety, a history of the papacy. Biondo Flavio had shown in his *Italia illustrata*, as did the flourishing chorography genre of the sixteenth and seventeenth centuries, how such biographical portraits could be combined with geographical description and historical information into a genre that we can recognize as a forerunner of cultural history. Now church history was coalescing in a similar manner, harnessing the global reach of the universal histories to the topical organizing principles of the collective biographies. By beginning, not with the Creation but with the Incarnation, by adopting a centuriate and annalistic approach, and by putting the primary focus on themes as opposed to individuals, the *Magdeburg Centuries* and the *Annales ecclesiastici* pulled back from eternity while simultaneously pushing beyond the popes (who nevertheless continued in their role as protagonists) to depict the church as an institution, as a body of doctrine, and as a community of believers. Incidentally, the history of literature would eventually be crystallized in a thematic narrative as well, but not until the eighteenth century and in a curious form: in 1759 Lorenzo Mehus's *Historia litteraria Florentina* (*Florentine Literary History*) appeared, an account of humanist literature spanning from Henry of Settimello to Ambrogio Traversari, appended to the *vita* of the latter author and prefixed to an edition of his letters (Mehus 1968).

Giovio, de Thou, Sigonio, and the Autumn of Latin Historiography

Finally, a word must be said about three figures indispensable to any survey of Neo-Latin historiography: Paolo Giovio (1483–1553; Zimmermann 1995), Jacques-Auguste de Thou (1553–1617; De Smet 2006), and Carlo Sigonio (ca. 1524–1584; McCuaig 1989). The first two wrote histories of their own times, which masterfully described the political circumstances, relationships, and events of the day in minute, breathtaking detail. The last fulfilled the promise of Biondo by writing the entire history of Italy, drawing for the task on an unprecedented treasury of histories, chronicles, *diplomata*, and archival sources of all kinds. What makes these writers so special is not only their acumen, historical sensibility, and excellent Latin, but also that they were unperturbed by political and ecclesiastical authority. The point is not that they acted independently of power—all moved in the higher orbits of princes spiritual and temporal—but that they exercised a precious independence of judgment regardless. Yet the contemporary history pioneered in Giovio's *Sui temporis historia* (*History of His Time*, 1550–1552) and perfected in de Thou's *Historiae sui temporis* (*History of His Time*, various versions, 1604–1617) had no major Latin legacy, and the magisterial histories by Sigonio—the *Historia de Occidentali Imperio* (*History of the Western Empire*, 1578), which traced the Late Roman Empire from Diocletian to Justinian, the *De Regno Italiae*, on Italy from the late sixth to the early thirteenth centuries, the *Historia Bononiensis* (*Bolognese History*, 1591)—were followed by a century-long void in historical writing of comparable quality (Cochrane 1980). This was in part fallout from the offense caused by their frank accounts. Yet more important was a change in the political climate, one that chilled the expression of independent thought (Bertelli 1973), as well as a definitive linguistic shift.

In a very important sense, de Thou and Sigonio sang the swan song of Latin historiography. After them we can no longer speak meaningfully of a widespread tradition with essential, recognizable characteristics. History continued to be written in Latin, of course, and without letup; one need think only of the Jesuits (Harney 1940–1941; Mungello 1985) and, more generally, of the rich heritage of Catholic ecclesiastical historiography, represented, for example, by Ferdinando Ughelli's *Italia sacra* (*Sacred Italy*, 1643–1662) and by the *Gallia Christiana* (*Christian Gaul*), initiated by Claude Robert (first edition, 1626) and enlarged successively into the late nineteenth century. Nevertheless, the major trends in historiography would be wrought, and written, in the vernacular. Admittedly, vernacular history had long run parallel to Latin, as a mere mention of the *Grandes Chroniques de France* (thirteenth to fifteenth centuries) or the *Anglo-Saxon Chronicle* (ninth to twelfth centuries) suffices to show. Yet until the end of the fifteenth century, Latin had enjoyed absolute pre-eminence as the literary language, with most vernacular authors not even pretending to stylistic or rhetorical distinction. Machiavelli and Guicciardini changed the stakes in Italy, as did Commines in France, and after another century the playing field was even if not tilted in Latin's disfavor. The great transformation of religious history-writing effected by the Centuriators and Baronius began in Latin because its reading public was initially ecclesiastic and learned, but it quickly shifted to Italian, German, and Polish once the masses became the target. In two cognate areas Latin did remain extremely important, if not dominant: discussions of historical method, or the *ars historica*, and the development of the auxiliary disciplines of modern historical scholarship among antiquarians and the learned. Otherwise, when new developments arose in historiography—the baroque style of the seventeenth century; empiricism and Pyrrhonism; the philosophical history practiced by Voltaire and Montesquieu; the "new science" (*nuova scienza*) of Vico; the "civil history" (*storia civile*) of Giannone; historicism—they did so overwhelmingly in the vernacular.

Suggested Reading

Other useful surveys of historiography, on which this account has drawn more often than citations can show, are Breisach (1994); Völkel (2006); Cochrane (1981); Kelley (1970); Zimmermann et al. (1999); and *CNLS* 2:180–217. Reynolds (1955) may also still be used with caution. For medieval historical genres that survived in the Renaissance, see Dale, Lewin, and Osheim (2007) for chronicles; Frazier (2005) for hagiography; Schürer (2010) for encyclopedias; and McLean (2007) for universal history. On the *ars historica*, see Cotroneo (1971); Kelley (1970); and Grafton (2007). On antiquarianism and erudite history, see Momigliano (1950); Knowles (1964); Cochrane (1958); and Rosa (1962).

References

Almási, Gábor. 2009. *The Uses of Humanism: Johannes Sambucus (1531–1584), Andreas Dudith (1533–1589), and the Republic of Letters in East Central Europe.* Leiden: Brill.

Baker, Patrick. 2012. "La trasformazione dell'identità nazionale ungherese nelle *Rerum Ungaricarum decades* di Antonio Bonfini." *Studi Umanistici Piceni* 32:215–23.

Bertelli, Sergio. 1973. *Ribelli, libertini e ortodossi nella storiografia barocca.* Florence: Nuova Italia.

Billanovich, Giuseppe. 1981. *La tradizione del testo di Livio e le origini dell'umanesimo.* Padua: Antenore.

Borchardt, Frank L. 1971. *German Antiquity in Renaissance Myth.* Baltimore: Johns Hopkins University Press.

Breisach, Ernst. 1994. *Historiography: Ancient, Medieval, and Modern.* 2nd ed. Chicago: University of Chicago Press.

Brendle, Franz et al., eds. 2001. *Deutsche Landesgeschichtsschreibung im Zeichen des Humanismus.* Stuttgart: Steiner.

Bruni, Leonardo. 2001. *History of the Florentine People.* Vol. 1. Edited and translated by James Hankins. Cambridge: Harvard University Press.

Burke, Peter. 1969. *The Renaissance Sense of the Past.* London: Edward Arnold.

Cappelletto, Rita. 1992. "*Peragrare ac lustrare Italiam coepi*: Alcune considerazioni sull'*Italia illustrata* e sulla sua fortuna." In Di Stefano et al. 1992, 1.1:181–203.

Clavuot, Ottavio. 1990. *Biondos* Italia illustrata: *Summa oder Neuschöpfung? Über die Arbeitsmethoden eines Humanisten.* Tübingen: Niemeyer.

——. 2002. "Flavio Biondos *Italia illustrata*: Porträt und historisch-geographische Legitimation der humanistischen Elite Italiens." In Helmrath, Muhlack, and Walther 2002, 55–76.

Cochrane, Eric. 1958. "The Settecento Medievalists." *Journal of the History of Ideas* 19:35–61.

——. 1980. "The Transition from Renaissance to Baroque: The Case of Italian Historiography." *History and Theory* 19:21–38.

——. 1981. *Historians and Historiography in the Italian Renaissance.* Chicago: University of Chicago Press.

Cotroneo, Girolamo. 1971. *I trattatisti dell'*ars historica. Naples: Giannini.

Dale, Sharon, Alison W. Lewin, and Duane J. Osheim, eds. 2007. *Chronicling History: Chronicles and Historians in Medieval and Renaissance Italy.* University Park: Pennsylvania State University Press.

De Smet, Ingrid. 2006. *Thuanus: The Making of Jacques-Auguste de Thou (1553–1617).* Geneva: Droz.

Di Stefano, Anita, Giovanni Faraone, Paola Megna, and Alessandra Tramontana, eds. 1992. *La storiografia umanistica.* 2 vols. Messina: Sicania.

Esser, Raingard. 2005. "Gelehrte in der Stadt im Spiegel niederländischer Chorographien des 17. Jahrhunderts." In *Funktionen des Humanismus: Studien zum Nutzen des Neuen in der humanistischen Kultur*, edited by Thomas Maissen and Gerrit Walther, 325–42. Göttingen: Wallstein.

Fabbri, Renata. 1992. "La storiografia veneziana del Quattrocento." In Di Stefano et al., op. cit., 1.1:347–98.

Ferraù, Giacomo. 2001. *Il tessitore di Antequera: Storiografia umanistica meridionale.* Rome: Istituto storico italiano per il Medio Evo.

Flavio, Biondo. 2005. *Italy Illuminated.* Vol. 1. Edited and translated by Jeffrey A. White. Cambridge: Harvard University Press.

Frazier, Alison K. 2005. *Possible Lives: Authors and Saints in Renaissance Italy.* New York: Columbia University Press.

Fryde, Edmund B. 1983. *Humanism and Renaissance Historiography.* London: Hambledon Press.

Fubini, Riccardo. 1968. "Biondo Flavio." *Dizionario Biografico degli Italiani* 10:536–59.

———. 2003. *Storiografia dell'umanesimo in Italia da Leonardo Bruni ad Annio da Viterbo.* Rome: Edizioni di Storia e Letteratura.

Gilbert, Felix. 1965. *Machiavelli and Guicciardini: Politics and History in Sixteenth-Century Florence.* Princeton: Princeton University Press.

Grafton, Anthony. 1991. *Defenders of the Text: The Traditions of Scholarship in an Age of Science, 1450–1800.* Cambridge: Harvard University Press.

———. 2007. *What Was History? The Art of History in Early Modern Europe.* Cambridge: Cambridge University Press.

Hankins, James. 2003. *Humanism and Platonism in the Italian Renaissance.* Vol. 1, *Humanism.* Rome: Edizioni di Storia e Letteratura.

———. 2007. "Teaching Civil Prudence in Leonardo Bruni's *History of the Florentine People*." In *Ethik: Wissenschaft oder Lebenskunst? Modelle der Normenbegründung von der Antike bis zur Frühen Neuzeit*, edited by Sabrina Ebbersmeyer and Eckhard Keßler, 143–57. Berlin: Lit Verlag.

Hay, Denis. 1988. "Flavio Biondo and the Middle Ages." In *Renaissance Essays*, 35–66. London: Hambledon.

Harney, Martin P. 1940–1941. "Jesuit Writers of History." *Catholic Historical Review* 26:433–46.

Helmrath, Johannes. 2013. *Wege des Humanismus: Studien zu Praxis und Diffusion der Antikeleidenschaft im 15. Jahrhundert.* Vol. 1. Tübingen: Mohr Siebeck.

Helmrath, Johannes, Ulrich Muhlack, and Gerrit Walther, eds. 2002. *Diffusion des Humanismus: Studien zur nationalen Geschichtsschreibung europäischer Humanisten.* Göttingen: Wallstein.

Hirschi, Caspar. 2005. *Wettkampf der Nationen: Konstruktionen einer deutschen Ehrgemeinschaft an der Wende vom Mittelalter zur Neuzeit.* Göttingen: Wallstein.

Ianziti, Gary. 1988. *Humanistic Historiography under the Sforzas: Politics and Propaganda in Fifteenth-Century Milan.* Oxford: Oxford University Press.

———. 2012. *Writing History in Renaissance Italy: Leonardo Bruni and the Uses of the Past.* Cambridge: Harvard University Press.

Kaiser, Ronny. 2009. "Caesar in Pommern: Transformation der Antike in Bugenhagens *Pomerania*." In *Retrospektivität und Retroaktivität*, edited by Marcus Born, 47–68. Würzburg: Königshausen & Neumann.

Kallendorf, Craig W., ed. and trans. 2002. *Humanist Educational Treatises*. Cambridge: Harvard University Press.

Kelley, Donald R. 1970. *Foundations of Modern Historical Scholarship: Language, Law, and History in the French Renaissance*. New York: Columbia University Press.

———. 1980. "Johann Sleidan and the Origins of History as a Profession." *The Journal of Modern History* 52:573–98.

Kess, Alexandra. 2008. *Johann Sleidan and the Protestant Vision of History*. Aldershot: Ashgate.

Knowles, David. 1964. *Great Historical Enterprises: Problems in Monastic History*. London: Nelson.

Kohl, Benjamin G. 2007. "Chronicles into Legends and Lives: Two Humanist Accounts of the Carrara Dynasty in Padua." In Dale, Lewin, and Osheim, op. cit., 223–48.

McCuaig, William. 1989. *Carlo Sigonio: The Changing World of the Late Renaissance*. Princeton: Princeton University Press.

McLean, Matthew. 2007. *The Cosmographia of Sebastian Münster: Describing the World in the Reformation*. Aldershot: Ashgate.

Mehus, Lorenzo. 1968. *Historia litteraria florentina ab anno MCXCII usque ad annum MCDXXXIX*. Edited by Eckhard Keßler. Munich: Fink.

Momigliano, Arnaldo. 1950. "Ancient History and the Antiquarian." *Journal of the Warburg and Courtauld Institutes* 13:285–315.

Muhlack, Ulrich. 2002. "Das Projekt der *Germania illustrata*. Ein Paradigma der Diffusion des Humanismus?" In Helmrath, Muhlack, and Walther, op. cit., 142–58.

Mungello, David E. 1985. *Curious Land: Jesuit Accommodation and the Origins of Sinology*. Stuttgart: Steiner.

Peters, Eckhart W., ed. 2007. *Die Magdeburger Centurien: Die Kirchengeschichtsschreibung des Flacius Illyricus*. 2 vols. Dößel: Stekovics.

Pullapilly, Cyriac K. 1975. *Caesar Baronius: Counter-Reformation Historian*. Notre Dame: University of Notre Dame Press.

Rexroth, Frank. 2002. "Polydor Vergil als Geschichtsschreiber und der englische Beitrag zum europäischen Humanismus." In Helmrath, Muhlack, and Walther, op. cit., 415–35.

Reynolds, Beatrice R. 1955. "Latin Historiography: A Survey, 1400–1600." *Studies in the Renaissance* 2:7–66.

Rosa, Mario. 1962. "Per la storia dell'erudizione toscana del '700: Profilo di Lorenzo Mehus." *Annali della Scuola Speciale per Archivisti e Bibliotecari dell'Università di Roma* 2:41–96.

Sabbadini, Remigio. 1967. *Le scoperte dei codici latini e greci ne' secoli XIV e XV*. Edited by Eugenio Garin. 2 vols. Florence: Sansoni.

Scheible, Heinz. 1966. *Die Entstehung der* Magdeburger Zenturien: *Ein Beitrag zur Geschichte der historiographischen Methode*. Gütersloh: Mohn.

Schirrmeister, Albert. 2009. "Was sind humanistische Landesbeschreibungen? Korpusfragen und Textsorten." In *Medien und Sprachen humanistischer Geschichtsschreibung*, edited by Johannes Helmrath, Albert Schirrmeister, and Stefan Schlelein, 5–46. Berlin: De Gruyter.

Schlelein, Stefan. 2010. "Gelehrte Fremde: Italienische Humanisten und die Transformation der europäischen Historiographie." In *Transformation antiker Wissenschaften*, edited by Georg Töpfer and Hartmut Böhme, 191–214. Berlin: De Gruyter.

Schürer, Markus. 2010. "Enzyklopädik als Naturkunde und Kunde vom Menschen: Einige Thesen zum *Fons memorabilium universi* des Domenico Bandini." *Mittellateinisches Jahrbuch* 45:115–31.

Skovgaard-Petersen, Karen. 2002. *Historiography at the Court of Christian IV (1588–1648): Studies in the Latin Histories of Denmark by Johannes Pontanus and Johannes Meursius*. Copenhagen: Museum Tusculanum Press.

Smalley, Beryl. 1974. *Historians in the Middle Ages*. London: Thames and Hudson.

Ullman, Berthold L. 1946. "Leonardo Bruni and Humanistic Historiography." *Medievalia et Humanistica* 4:45–61.

Völkel, Markus. 2002. "Rhetoren und Pioniere: Italienische Humanisten als Geschichtsschreiber der europäischen Nationen; eine Skizze." In *Historische Anstöße: Festschrift für Wolfgang Reinhard zum 65. Geburtstag*, edited by Peter Burschel et al., 339–62. Berlin: Akademie Verlag.

———. 2006. *Geschichtsschreibung: Eine Einführung in globaler Perspektive*. Cologne: Böhlau.

Völkel, Markus, and Arno Strohmeyer, eds. 2009. *Historiographie an europäischen Höfen (16.–18. Jahrhundert): Studien zum Hof als Produktionsort von Geschichtsschreibung und historischer Repräsentation*. Berlin: Duncker & Humboldt.

Wilcox, Donald. 1969. *The Development of Florentine Humanist Historiography in the Fifteenth Century*. Cambridge: Harvard University Press.

Witt, Ronald G. 2000. *"In the Footsteps of the Ancients": The Origins of Humanism from Lovato to Bruni*. Leiden: Brill.

Zen, Stefano. 1994. *Baronio storico: Controriforma e crisi del metodo umanistico*. Naples: Vivarium.

Zimmermann, T. C. Price. 1995. *Paolo Giovio: The Historian and the Crisis of Sixteenth-Century Italy*. Princeton: Princeton University Press.

Zimmermann, T. C. Price et al. 1999. "Historiography, Renaissance." In *Encyclopedia of the Renaissance*, edited by Paul F. Grendler, vol. 3, 165–84. New York: Charles Scribner's Sons.

CHAPTER 11

....

LETTERS

....

JAN PAPY

WRITING letters has been an art form since antiquity. Whereas the medieval *ars dictaminis*, a formulaic "art of letter-writing," had transformed the conversational patterns of ancient letter-writing into a more stereotyped style of expression (Camargo 1991), the discovery of Cicero's letters by Petrarch in 1345 and Coluccio Salutati in 1392 started the revival of the personal, private letter. From this moment on, the literary genre of the letter was firmly re-established and was central to all members of the republic of letters. New manuals defining the characteristics of different types of letters and offering a variety of models for imitation succeeded each other and found a wide readership (Henderson 1983a and 1983b). Letters, often perceived as a necessary but imperfect substitute for oral conversation, were at the heart of Neo-Latin literature, but they also served as a unique means of self-presentation and social identification. Beginning with Petrarch, Renaissance humanists—self-proclaimed men of letters—composed artistic prose letters or letters in verse, expressed friendship, communicated scholarly information, discussed business and family affairs, politics and religious conflicts, and in doing so, defined themselves as "littérateurs" (*litterati*), scholars, or scientists. In this respect, letters were much more than a literary composition reflecting and showing one's education and literary taste. Letters, and especially published letter collections, were a well-considered means to spread one's *persona*, one's often apologetic self-image as a man of letters or of science.

PETRARCH'S LATIN LETTERS: MIRRORING CICERO?

In order to grasp Petrarch's profound impact on this revival of humanist epistolography, it is important to understand first how his epistolary collection was conceived and why it evolved into its definitive form. Since the 1320s, Petrarch had kept a copy (the so-called *transcriptio in ordine*, "transcription in order") of every letter sent by him (the so-called *transmissiva*, "sent away," i.e., to his correspondent). Only after discovering Cicero's *Epistulae ad Atticum* in the Chapter Library of Verona in 1345 did he embrace the idea of editing his own letters into a coherent collection. Whereas his initial idea was to divide his collection of letters, then still called the *Epistularum mearum ad diversos liber (Book of My Letters to Different People)*, into twelve books, thus imitating the structure of Virgil's *Aeneid*, he came to favor a twenty-book model based on Seneca's *Letters to Lucilius* in the 1350s, and finally settled, by 1360, for twenty-four books in imitation of Homer's *Iliad* and *Odyssey* (Dotti 1987, 213–15; Rossi 1932). In line with his ancient models, Petrarch carefully selected, ordered, and prepared the 350 letters he finally chose to transcribe in the collection of *Familiarium libri XXIV (Twenty-Four Books of Familiar Letters)*. Some of them, especially the rhetorical set-pieces, were written specially for the collection; others were rewritten substantially, sometimes even more than once. As a consequence, the *Familiares* are to be considered as a literary and well thought-out composition. If Book 1, for instance, contains a number of fictitious letters (Billanovich 1947, 1–55), it was also an important programmatic opening of the collection offering a true "portrait of the artist as a young man" by the maturing artist and humanist intellectual Petrarch. Moreover, it has been observed that "many of these earlier letters, ostensibly dating back to the 1330s and 1340s, make considerable use of quotations from and references to classical texts not known to Petrarch until at least a decade later." In fact, "attitudes and sentiments attributed to one part of his life are often the fruit of Petrarch's later reflection, rewriting and editorial intervention," envisaging to order and enhance the fragments of his experience (Mann 1984, 24).

In molding these fragments into Latin private letters, all modeled after those of Cicero, Seneca, and Pliny (Clough 1976), Petrarch did find a form most suitable for his autobiographical ambitions. In apparently informal letters and "letter-essays," he was able to show his readers his multifaceted, colorful personality without the restraints imposed by the laws of the autobiographical genre. He could talk about his inner life, his wishes and ambitions, his doubts and preoccupations, his dreams and nightmares, his literary successes and the envious reactions they aroused, his travels and diseases, his pets and clothing, his friendships and welcome patrons, his intellectual enemies, his solitary walks and the social events he had to attend. The apparent spontaneity palpable in Cicero's letters is emulated by the humanist Petrarch. It is a spontaneity that is deliberately literary and that plays to the gallery, striving for fame with posterity, but also for tranquillity in the complexities of the inner self (Enenkel 2002, 367–84). As he put it in his opening letter dedicating the entire collection of his *Familiares* to his "Socrates" (i.e., the Limburg musician Ludovicus Sanctus of Beringen; Papy 2006, 13–30), Petrarch, imitating and emulating the great models of antiquity in all literary genres possible, clearly dreamt of becoming a second Cicero and Seneca (*Familiares* 1.1.47–48 in the edition of Petrarch 1933–42; translation from Petrarch 1975–85):

> *Dulce mihi colloquium tecum fuit, cupideque et quasi de industria protractum . . .*
> *Haec igitur tibi, frater, diversicoloribus, ut sic dicam, liciis texta dicaverim; ceterum,*

si stabilis sedes et frustra semper quaesitum otium contigerit, quod iam hinc ostendere se incipit, nobiliorem et certe uniformem telam tuo nomine meditor ordiri. Vellem ex his paucis esse, qui famam promittere possunt et praestare; sed ipse vi propria in lucem venies, alis ingenii subvectus nihilque auxilii mei egens. Profecto tamen, si inter tot difficultates assurgere potuero, tu olim Idomeneus, tu Atticus, tu Lucilius meus eris.

The discourse with you has been most pleasant for me and I have drawn it out eagerly and as though by design ... These letters, therefore, woven with multi-colored threads, if I may say so, are for you, brother. However, if I were ever to enjoy a steady abode and the leisure of time that has always escaped me, something that begins to appear possible, I would weave in your behalf a much more noble and certainly a unified web or tapestry. I should like to be numbered among those few who can promise and furnish fame; but you shall step forth into the light through your own merits. You shall be borne on the wings of your genius and shall need none of my assistance. If indeed, among so many difficulties I should manage to enjoy a measure of success, I shall make you my Idomeneus, my Atticus and my Lucilius.

Cicero's letters had shown the Roman orator's and politician's psychological unease with his own literary ambition and search for eternal fame, and his philosophical desire to escape, to withdraw to a more tranquil life of solitude so as to achieve liberty, self-possession, as well as peace of mind and body for study and spiritual advancement. Likewise, Petrarch's epistolary *oeuvre* provides a telling illustration of the humanist's evolutionary process and intellectual development. As such, Petrarch's letters are among the most important witnesses to and products of the elaboration of his self. Moreover, like all of his work, his epistles betray a recourse to classical models and at the same time a literary self-consciousness of having outshone his medieval and classical predecessors, especially when he addressed famous authors from antiquity such as Cicero, Seneca, Horace, Quintilian, Virgil, and Homer in a series of fictitious epistles in the twenty-fourth book of his *Familiares* (Cosenza 1910) and when he compiled his *Epistolae metricae* (*Verse Letters*), a selection of three books of letters written in hexameters after Horace (Wilkins 1956).

A central theme in Petrarch's "corpus" of letters, in which he collected "the dispersed fragments of his soul" so as "to be with himself as much as possible" (*Familiares* 13.4.7), is his search for conversion. Intending to correct the mistakes of the past and to reconstruct his life, he offers his readers a sort of "biography of the wise man amidst the storms of life and history" (Dotti 1987, 214). For Petrarch, his letters are a means to give himself—that *peregrinus ubique*, "a wanderer or pilgrim everywhere," as he often calls himself (Wilkins 1948)—a place from which he can draw lessons from his own history, from which he can judge his own time; a place, finally, where he can live according to his humanist program while searching for the Ciceronian *otium*, the contemplative life in solitude, be it the "transalpine Helicon" in Vaucluse while escaping from Avignon, Selvapiana in the Apennines while in Parma, or his hilltop home at Arquà near Padua.

Yet Petrarch's Latin letters also obviously transcend his models from antiquity, for they equally display a new fusion of classical, Christian, and medieval literary traditions. Founding an "Augustinian Socratism" (Trinkaus 1970, 18–19), echoing in his Italian lyric sonnets and his Latin epistolary dialogues alike, Petrarch taught himself, his readers, and posterity how to get to know oneself. Exiled in his youth from his own *patria,* Florence, and far removed from papal Rome—the only true center of the world and Christendom where ancient values and virtues should be revived—Petrarch found himself in papal Avignon, where he had the feeling that he had descended into hell alive. In a letter to his intimate friend Lello di Pietro Stefano dei Tosetti, whose name Petrarch classicized into "Laelius" in memory of Scipio Africanus's closest friend (third/second century BCE), it was precisely this *tumultus Babylonicus,* this "Babylonian confusion" that incited Petrarch to meditate upon his fate that exiled him from his fatherland Italy and brought him to Avignon, a place he could only survive thanks to the strenuous mental exercise never to feel as he did and never to allow ugliness into his mind. Forced to live near "neighboring Babylon which is called the Roman Curia" whereas "nothing is less Roman," Petrarch can only survive "the noise and smoke of the ungodly city" by "blocking his ears and eyes," in enjoying the pleasing idleness and desired solitude so as to become oblivious to and unmindful of urban cares (*Familiares* 15.8). Here, ancient values, practices, and ideas from antiquity had not only been re-established in Petrarch's humanist letters, but the exiled poet and humanist also formed a heroic image of the classical past which he believed to have returned in his own age. Moreover, his experience of a prestigious and mythical antiquity transformed and came to constitute his humanist and literary ego. It was this antiquity that mirrored the very image of what Petrarch aspired to become. In antiquity, Petrarch's creative genius discovered his own myth. This myth, so he wrote to Robert, king of Naples, on April 30, 1341, after he had been crowned poet laureate on the Capitoline in Rome in an almost unprecedented re-enactment of the classical past in the center of the classical world, he decided to live (*Familiares* 4.7.8):

> *Sane illos desperatio sua detrahat, nos impellat, et unde illis frenum ac vincula, nobis impetus ac stimuli accesserint, ut studeamus fieri qualem illi nullum opinantur, nisi quem antiquitas illustravit.*
>
> Doubtless the despair which holds them [i.e., some of his contemporary detractors] back motivates us, and the bridle and chains which affect them, are goads and spurs to us so that we try to become what they believe no one can become except one of the ancients.

The discovery of Cicero's "familiar" letters was a new encounter with antiquity that increasingly inspired Petrarch to the humanistic cult of literary immortality and glory. Yet, in his "Augustinian-Socratic" world, Petrarch also transcended pagan antiquity in his acute awareness that the very origin of writing itself is suspect, that all *negotium* is in fact a distraction from Christian contemplation and the ascent of man. This ambivalence would remain omnipresent in the works and letters of humanist writers after him.

QUATTROCENTO HUMANISM AND
THE LITERARY GENRE OF LETTER-WRITING

One of the first to follow Petrarch's idea of collecting his letters was the Florentine and Roman humanist scholar Poggio Bracciolini (1380–1459). Professionally, he devoted half a century to the official correspondence of five popes, but he also left his personal correspondence, some 700 letters to 192 friends, acquaintances, and public figures. Whereas Poggio Bracciolini originally mixed ten orations and some invectives with his first collection of 107 letters—thereby attesting to the fact that early humanist epistolography was closely connected to rhetoric—he finally selected ten books of letters in which he expended considerable effort to develop a coherent moral and social position for a learned layman such as himself. In this selection, one finds a most insightful witness of his remarkable age giving full play to his talent as chronicler of events, to his wide range of interests, and to his most acerbic critical sense (Poggio Bracciolini 1984–1988).

Likewise, the multifaceted literary *oeuvre* of the flamboyant Milanese humanist courtier Francesco Filelfo (1398–1481) included a vast collection of Latin and Greek correspondence in which he shaped and burnished the various layers of his social identity as a literary and scholarly author. Having served such heads of state as Pope Pius II, Cosimo de' Medici, and Francesco Sforza, his status as a humanist is that of the extraordinary but "marginalized" writer, the sharp-tongued brilliant but disillusioned scholar seeking patronage and recognition. He traveled to Constantinople and was enabled to acquire the most coveted humanist possession at that time, a scholarly knowledge of the Greek language—his unique knowledge of Greek enabled him to translate substantial portions of Aristotle, Plutarch, Xenophon, and Lysias. Since Filelfo's biography seems to consist of a record of the various towns in which he lectured, the masters he served, the books he wrote, the authors he illustrated, the friendships he contracted, and the wars he waged with rival scholars, his vast correspondence written both in Latin and Greek touches upon all important persons, events, and thoughts of the stirring times in which he lived. Repeatedly Filelfo had to balance his duties as a humanist writer in the service of mighty patrons such as Filippo Maria Visconti and Francesco Sforza, successive Dukes of Milan, with his arrogant temper and self-conscious personality. As a consequence, part of his *oeuvre* is filled with panegyrics and epics celebrating various princely patrons, encomiastic odes for birthdays and inflated epithalamia and funeral orations, rhetorical salutations greeting ambassadors and visitors from abroad or introducing one of his new courses at the start of the academic year, and political pamphlets taking sides in the great events of his country's history. Yet it is in Filelfo's letters that one can follow his literary and intellectual endeavors from within. In elegant and balanced phrases, they testify in a direct way to his paper warfare with his numerous enemies both in Florence and Rome; and his endless demands for payments, addressed to patrons and rulers, needed to fund his life of splendor and self-indulgence; his appealing intellectual journey between East and West; and his philosophical program—based on accurate, wide-ranging, but somewhat superficial erudition and untiring devotion to study—of uniting Plato's and Aristotle's views in a synthesis useful for his contemporaries. Filelfo took great care of his ever-growing collection of letters; one of the "final" stages of his Latin epistles, almost ready for print, is preserved integrally in the Codex 873 of the Milanese Biblioteca Trivulziana and has only very partially been published in three fifteenth- and sixteenth-century editions (Robin 1991, 11–30; De Keyser 2014). This Trivulziano codex is not only a special testimony to a "disturbing montage," to use the phrase of Diana Robin. When compared to its printed counterparts, it is also a unique source for the (development of) stylistics of early modern letter-writing, the Renaissance revival of letter-writing, the cultural encounter and exchange of knowledge between East and West, the sociocultural study of Renaissance patronage in Northern Italy, the sociological function of literary invectives in Renaissance Italy, the history of the coming of Platonism and Platonic ideas to the West and Western Renaissance philosophy, the history of the European–Ottoman relationships and the related views on the "Turkish threat."

Entirely different in scope are the *Illustrium virorum epistolae XII libris distinctae* (*Letters of Famous Men in Twelve Books*) by the poet-scholar Angelo Poliziano (1454–1494), the leading figure of the age of Lorenzo de' Medici, "Il Magnifico." This selection of 251 letters, posthumously published by the Venetian printer Aldo Manuzio, included both letters written by Poliziano and letters written by other illustrious scholars to him. Thus, the publication of the letters testified to Poliziano's central position and important role in the republic of letters. Medicean politics were not of interest to him; philology, scholarship, and literature were (Poliziano 2006).

Another clear "programmatic" use of letter-writing is palpable in the collection of *Familiar Letters* (*Epistolae familiares*) by Marsilio Ficino (1433–1499), one of the most influential humanist philosophers of the early Italian Renaissance, who also inspired artists such as Botticelli, Michelangelo, Raphael, Titian, and Dürer, and who attracted to him leading statesmen, scholars, and churchmen from all over Europe. As a reviver of Neo-Platonism, he was in touch with major academic thinkers and writers of his day, and was the first translator of Plato's complete extant works into Latin. While selecting his letters for posterity, he not only praised the unique intellectual talents of Cosimo de' Medici's grandson, Lorenzo, he also saw his collected correspondence—divided into twelve books and touching upon recurring topics such as music, acquaintances, patronage, books, moral exhortation, Neo-Platonic doctrines, daemons, the four Platonic frenzies (the lover, the creative artist, the priest, and the prophet), fortune and fate, Providence and astrology, the harmonization of Christianity and the Platonic tradition—as a practical extension of his "Platonic program." Letters discussing philosophical themes in a colloquial and accessible way were the perfect means to expound on his theoretical works and to propagate his new "Platonic" philosophy extolling man's dignity and divine origin (Ficino 1990–2010).

This Florentine Neo-Platonic revival, and especially the literature on the "dignity of Man" (*dignitas hominis*), was widely read in humanist circles in Paris and Lyon, and found its way into vernacular literature alike. Strikingly, however, the literary success of one of its most prominent advocates, Pico della Mirandola (1463–1494), was not due to his philosophical works. Whereas in the sixteenth century his now-famous *Oration on the Dignity of Man* was only printed twice (1530 and 1537), his *Golden Letters* (*Aureae epistolae*)—breathing Pico's "divine spirit," as Erasmus labeled it both in the preface to his collection of *Adages* of 1500 and in his *Ciceronianus* (*The Ciceronian*) of 1529—reached a much wider readership in twelve separate editions. Moreover, in the course of the early modern period, Pico's letters have been translated into French, English, and German; the *Oratio* remained untouched up to the twentieth century. After the cruel death of Charles VIII, the humanist, diplomat, historian, and minister Robert Gaguin (1433–1501), chancellor of the Sorbonne, threw himself into Pico's works. One thing that attracted his attention was one of Pico's letters to his nephew Gianfrancesco, which Gaguin translated under the title *Conseil profitable contre les ennuys et tribulations du monde* (*Profitable Advice against the Worries and the Tribulations of the World*, 1498). In the Low Countries, to give another example, interest in Pico's vast *oeuvre* was soon limited to his religious and pedagogical ideas, yet his *Aureae epistolae* remained central to humanist circles: several editions were published in Antwerp and The Hague, and Juan Luis Vives (1492–1540), living and working in Bruges and Leuven and well acquainted with Erasmus, considered Pico, along with a number of other humanist epistolographers, to be an ideal model for writing humanist letters (Laureys 1997, 632–33).

Erasmus's Letters: Italian Models and the Erasmian Program

As an heir of the Italian humanism, Erasmus thought and wrote in Latin, a language he mastered to such a degree that it became, effectively, his mother tongue. Moreover, as a humanist pedagogue, he wanted his contemporaries to write in a purer and more classical Latin, for he was convinced that only people mastering a proper language would be able to think clearly and lucidly, and thus become more humane. This is the reason why, following the lead of Italian humanists, Erasmus provided his contemporaries with manuals and examples to be imitated, such as dialogues, treatises, and orations. Yet he also wanted to show the way to the modern "alchemy of the word" in the art of letter-writing, the *ars epistolica*. If his *De conscribendis epistolis* (*On Letter Writing*) of 1521, chalking out his new epistolographical methodology on the basis of Cicero, Pliny, Jerome, and contemporary writers such as Enea Silvio Piccolomini, was highly influential (Gerlo 1971, 104–5, 111), Erasmus's own letters soon became true models of a unique flexibility and elegance of expression. It is important to stress that Erasmus himself never ceased to exercise and experiment in his "language laboratory" so as to mold his letters into a perfect medium—the letter being a medium that since antiquity had to be situated between conversation (*sermo*) and speech (*oratio*).

Still, Erasmus did not merely polish his style. Intending to publish his letters, he not only collected them, he also constantly rewrote and ordered his vast collection. If half of his days were filled with writing and answering letters—Erasmus testified that he had to deal with twenty, sixty, or even ninety letters a day—his careful collecting and rewriting proves that Erasmus recognized the value and possible impact of his published letter collections (Halkin 1983). Obviously, his letters were more than polite messages, "philological" essays, demands for manuscripts, or negotiations with booksellers and publishers. However important as such, his letters were equally more than personal comments on or discussions of political and religious issues. His collections of humanist letters were artistic works in their own right and constituted a fundamental part of Erasmus's literary *oeuvre* and autobiographical self-presentation, both to his contemporaries and to posterity (Jardine 1993, 147–74). Yet Erasmus's letter collections not only mirrored the aspects he wanted to emphasize; he also understood that within the network of the European republic of letters, his published correspondence, like that of Bruni, Filelfo, Piccolomini, and Poliziano, which he had read during his younger years as a novice in the monastery of Stein near Gouda, could function as an ideal medium to propagate and spread his humanist program, especially when published by first-rate publishers such as Dirk Martens and Johann Froben. In this way Erasmus's letter collections not only appear to be sophisticated autobiographical constructions, they are once again an extension and illustration of his *oeuvre* and humanist program.

Following the lead of Italian humanists such as Vittorino da Feltre, Guarino da Verona, Pier Paolo Vergerio the Elder, Poggio Bracciolini, and Lorenzo Valla, who all had their vision of what human beings should and could be, Erasmus also advocated a new education based on language training and Christian piety derived from ancient sources. Moreover, Erasmus's language training was, in his eyes, not unworldly or irrelevant, for he saw the fullest realization of man in the development of his reason (*ratio*), his thinking and speaking, and in the Stoic subjugation of passions such as hatred, envy, ambition, and lust. Education therefore had to have a double goal: to impart practical knowledge, yet also to train those being instructed by means of ancient literary models and philosophical precepts so as to combine knowledge with wisdom (*sapientia*) and piety (*pietas*), both fundamental to a person's ultimate self-fulfillment. Erasmus's letter of October 6, 1516, to Peter Gillis, in which he gives his good friend advice about how to live his life, and his letter of dedication to the German humanist Johann von Vlatten in his edition of Cicero's *Tusculan Disputations*, are both good examples, subtly balancing the words of pagan antiquity and those of Christianity to create a true osmosis resulting from the desire to modernize Christianity and provide strife-torn Europe with a new foundation for the unification of Christendom and *humanitas*. If this unity was a major obsession of Erasmus, a proper education aiming at virtue (*virtus*) was, for him, also a solid if not the sole basis for complete cultural, moral, and social development. Young princes, when educated properly within the framework of the new humanist studies (*studia humanitatis*), would be instilled with the examples of the "good letters" (*bonae litterae*) and the political ideals of antiquity. The only antidote against the prevailing tyranny, absolutism, nationalism, and colonialism of his day was a humanist education in which care for wisdom and piety fostered a proper care for human freedom and peace. Erasmus voiced this social and political program in several "open letters" to the prominent rulers of his day (Tracy 1978; Margolin 1973). His humanist ideas on education and his views on a revaluation of Pauline, evangelical faith, are all to be derived from the unity that Erasmus saw existing between grammar, rhetoric, and moral philosophy. Imitating words, especially in writing letters and prose compositions, was imitating the Word. Given the fact that he felt the need to educate young boys and princes with the aid of literary paradigms to be imitated so that pupils would acquire purity of expression, and also that these young intellectuals should be educated with examples from the ancients' history and moral philosophy in order to follow a pure moral life themselves, Erasmus consequently emphasized that the young Christian should meditate upon the Word, Christ himself. In this manner one could arrive at a pure faith with Christ and his Word at the center. This Christocentric program goes along with his cosmopolitan plea for peace and fraternity, as can be read in Erasmus's letter to Anton of Bergen (Erasmus 1906–1958, epistle 288, ll. 30–38; *CWE* 2:280):

> *Nobis qui Christi gloriamur cognomine, qui nihil nisi mansuetudinem et docuit et exhibuit; qui unius corporis membra sumus, una caro, eodem vegetamur spiritu, iisdem sacramentis alimur, eidem adhaeremus capiti, ad eandem immortalitatem vocati sumus, summam illam speramus communionem, ut sicut Christus et pater unum sunt, ita et nos unum cum illo sumus; potestne ulla huius mundi res esse tanti ut ad bellum provocet? rem adeo perniciosam, adeo taetram ut etiam cum iustissimum est, tamen nulli vere bono placeat.*

> For us, who boast of naming ourselves "Christians" after Christ who preached and practised naught save gentleness, who are members of one body, one flesh, quickened by the same spirit, nurtured upon the same sacraments, joined in union to a single head, called to the same eternal life, hoping for that supreme communion whereby, even as Christ is one with the Father, so we too may be one with him—how can anything in this world be so important as to impel us to war, a thing so deadly and so grim that even when it is waged with perfect justification no man who is truly good approves it?

This was one of the reasons why Erasmus, both in treatises and letters, pointed time and again to the internal discord and the corruption of political and religious rulers. Yet as soon as he became a central figure in the European intellectual network, he equally toned down the sharpness of his statements on nationalities: he finally became a cosmopolitan (*mundi civis*), yet even more the "disciple of Christ" of the Modern Devotion (*Devotio Moderna*)—the new spiritual movement to which both Erasmus and Thomas à Kempis (ca. 1380–1471) owed their education. In a period of crisis, of luxurious self-indulgence and corruption among the higher clergy and nobility, formalism, popular piety and superstition in society, decline and parasitism in the convents and abbeys, and empty theology, Erasmus found his own mission and his own words and style. Although opportunistic and personal motives guided his choices more than once, he definitely intended to transcend all nationalisms and confessions in a supra-national and supra-confessional humanism, bound together in a reciprocal dialogue of letters, so as to be a true example of his "philosophy of Christ" (*philosophia Christi*). His letters, and certainly his set-pieces, were meant to reinforce "the strong impression of textual *magnification*—the amplifying of key themes and ideas in the corpus as a whole" (Jardine 1993, 188).

Lipsius and the New Style

"Do you want to get to know me and others? Read my letters that depict us." With this inviting line, the humanist and classical scholar Justus Lipsius (1547–1606), described by his admiring correspondent Michel de Montaigne (*Essais* 2.12) as "one of the most learned men of his day" and regarded as the founding father of Neostoicism, introduces us (in his preface to the reader) to his world of letters. It is a fascinating world of scholars such as Ogier Ghislain de Busbecq, Carolus Clusius, Marc-Antoine Muret, Paolo Manuzio, Joseph Justus Scaliger, and many others, of expanding learning, communication and information, friendship and rivalry, and reputation and fame. Yet, however interesting Lipsius's vast and important letter collections may be for their first-hand information about the history of humanism and the sixteenth- and seventeenth-century world of learning, his humanist letters, published in separate collections of one hundred letters or *Centuriae* (De Landtsheer 1998), were certainly not only concerned with communicating *prima facie* information. Like the letter collection published in 1580 by Marc-Antoine Muret (IJsewijn 1985), Lipsius's printed letter collections were also endowed with a specific literary function. They were strategically molded by the writer as autobiographical and apologetic documents in accordance with the social conventions of the humanist milieu. Moreover, it is known that Lipsius, because of his controversial philosophical views and political theory, but also because of his intentional or unintentional shifts of loyalties, constantly had to defend his position. Therefore, like Cicero, who had his speeches revised for publication; and like Pliny, Petrarch, and Erasmus, who improved the artistic and dramatic effect of their letters before publication, Lipsius, too, deliberately touched up his portrait for the publication of his carefully selected correspondence. Of the 4,300 letters surviving to and from Lipsius, two-thirds were written by him. He himself saw to the publication of three *Centuriae* of letters, the first one being published at Leiden in 1586. Furthermore, he had prepared another *Centuria* for posthumous publication by his executor Johannes Woverius, to which Woverius and his fellow executors added a fifth *Centuria postuma* (Papy 2002). The remaining 3,800 letters have only recently been published in the ongoing series *Iusti Lipsi Epistolae*, initiated in print in 1978.

Lipsius's continuous adjustment of his public image and the careful selection of the evidence to be left for his future biographers were meant to enhance his posthumous fame with posterity. It should come as no surprise, then, that this deliberate attempt to establish his *persona* resulted successfully in the well-known and since then repeated image offered by his biographer Aubert Le Mire (1573–1640)—the icon Lipsius gifted with that unique humanist intellectual aura of a man who is free from the stain of worldliness and eminent by virtue of his gifts and constancy and his relentless dedication to study (Enenkel 1999).

From the first letter of his first *Centuria* onwards, a letter that, significantly, Lipsius addressed to his former professor Cornelius Valerius (1512–78), his *ductor doctorque meus in meliore hoc animi cultu* ("my leader and teacher in this better state of mind"), Lipsius echoes his doctrine of steadfastness and constancy, and emphasizes his "conversion" from philology and letters to Stoic philosophy harmonized with Christianity (Lipsius 1978, 159–60):

> *Vitae genus, quod a reditu elegeram, et indicavi praesens tibi, mi Valeri, et probavi: quietum istud, modestum, latens, remotum ab ambitu et a curis. Et iam ingressus serio eram cum (ecce subitam vim Fati) vereor ut subito id mutem. Nam tempora quae impendeant, vides, et quae tela improviso exorsa civilium bellorum.*

> The way of life which I had chosen from my return and which I showed in person, my dear Valerius, and of which I approved, is that quiet, modest and hidden life, removed from ambition and troubles. And though I had entered this way of life seriously, I fear that (behold the unexpected force of Fate) I will change it at once. For you see the times which are threatening us and the arms of the civil wars which have suddenly appeared.

Moreover, as the letter of dedication "To the Praetor, to the Consuls and to the Senate of Utrecht" of November 13, 1585, indicates, Lipsius was well aware of the fact that his first collection of letters was at the same time "a new and an ancient production of his genius: new by its disposition, and ancient by its composition." The publication of this first *Centuria* was indeed Lipsius's first *démarche* for a quasi-Senecan epistolary style in the republic of letters, taken in regard to an "eloquence of the heart" based on brevity (*brevitas*) and in which priority was given to self-expression (Fumaroli 1980). Years previously, Lipsius had decided not only on a conversion to Stoicism, but also to the application of the fluid and concise style proper to Stoicism. This movement towards the brevity of Tacitus and Seneca was certainly inspired by the care for an honest and graceful philosophical expression, but it was also, as Lipsius stated himself, because he wanted his writings to be like the paintings of the famous Timanthes (late fifth century BCE): there is always more that has to be interpreted than to be seen.

Still, Lipsius was first and foremost a humanist pedagogue. His choice of style—the letter as *speculum animi*, as "mirror of the soul"—was adapted to construct at the same time a philosophical discourse in the form of a "conversation," a *sermo* in the style of Seneca's *Epistles to Lucilius*. Like Erasmus, Lipsius wrote a new manual on letter-writing, the *Epistolica institutio* (*Principles of Letter Writing*, 1591; Lipsius 1996), but also illustrated his innovative views of epistolography and stylistics in his own letters. Lipsius has not only discovered a model of introspection in Seneca; the Roman Stoic is also his model of guiding his own pupils and friends, his Stoic *proficientes* ("those who are making progress"). In this respect, his first collection of published letters of 1586 was a deliberate move, a true manifesto of a humanist who was convinced that he had found in Senecan philosophy the consolation and solution for the public calamities he was enduring. Moreover, in his letters Lipsius tried to propagate his humanist program, and with it the perpetuation of his new *persona*. Because he met with real difficulties after the publication of the *De Constantia* (*On Constancy*, 1584), Lipsius saw himself obliged to prepare a second edition immediately, more "Christianized," so to speak, and to be published as early as 1585. Lipsius had enumerated the principal objections made against his views on "right reason" (*recta ratio*), destiny, and free will, and the problem of evil in an *Ad lectorem pro Constantia mea praescriptio* (*Preface to the Reader in Defense of my Constancy*), but equally counterattacked his detractors with the publication of his first *Centuria* of letters: not only does he explain step by step how his Neostoic program is adapted to and even reinforces the Christianity of Calvinists, Lutherans, and Roman Catholics, he also expounds by means of his letters how such a philosophy should be practiced. As Lipsius addressed Victor Giselinus (1543–1591) as the "doctor of both his body and soul" in the second letter of his collection, so he considered himself the predecessor and guide of his pupils and friends. For this reason, he wrote not only "letter-essays" on the value of country life (1.8), the place of philology compared to that of philosophy (1.16), the usefulness of traveling to Italy (1.22), and the opportunity of marriage (1.31), but also "Lucilian" letters, in which he chose an interior exile as Seneca himself did around 63 CE. Withdrawn into his Stoic fortress, Lipsius gave his recipe for happiness, his prescription for reason and interior liberty to fight the "mental diseases" of his contemporaries. Whereas he himself was sometimes poised between hope and fear, he persisted in encouraging others by furnishing them with his Stoic antidotes. In order to restore one's mental balance, he proposed a development of the self and a Stoic mental therapy against the chains of false opinion and eroded passions. As Seneca invited Lucilius to "be his own liberator," Lipsius transported his addressees and readers, either present or future, via a similar mental therapy.

Late Humanism and Beyond: From Literary to Non-Literary Letter Writing

As Lipsius's new style influenced baroque literature, his invention of publishing an anthology of one's correspondence (as in his *Centuriae*) was taken up by many after him. Not only his former student and successor at Leuven University, Erycius Puteanus (1574–1646), but also scholars, poets, diplomats, and polemical writers such as Joseph Justus Scaliger (1540–1609), Kaspar Schoppe (1576–1649), Gerardus Johannes Vossius (1577–1649), Hugo Grotius (1583–1621), Constantijn Huygens (1596–1687), and Johannes

Fredericus Gronovius (1611–1671) collected or had collected several selections of their own letters or the letters of important predecessors (posthumously). Besides, the humanist vogue of publishing letters of famous or learned men (often called *Virorum illustrium/doctorum epistolae*) similarly continued. As Lipsius had fashioned philological emendations and interpretations of difficult passages in classical authors as (fictitious) letters written to humanist masters, colleagues, and friends in his *Epistolicae quaestiones* (*Investigations in Letters*, 1577), so it became fashionable practice to publish "philological" letters, just as was the case with the publication of letters dealing with scientific and medical issues. In fact, correspondence advanced science, as in the field of astronomy, for instance, where we need only mention the *Epistolae astronomicae* (*Astronomical Letters*, 1596), a collection put together, annotated, and published by Tycho Brahe in order to distribute (and advertise) information about the stars and about the small island of Hven which the king of Denmark assigned to him to build an observatory. Likewise, the tradition of "medical letters" (*epistolae medicinales*) was longstanding, from earlier famous authors such as Giovanni Manardo (1521 and 1532); to Andreas Vesalius's *Epistola de radicis Chinae usu* (*Letter on the Use of China Root*, 1546) on the discovery and therapeutic use of the China root (*smilax chinae*) in the treatment of syphilis; to Conrad Gessner (1577), Balduinus Ronssaeus (1590), and Thomas Bartholin (who published his letters from 1663 onwards, with a posthumous volume in 1740). Scientific correspondence increasingly came to shape the scientific revolution. While most of the correspondence of the major scientists (Copernicus, Brahe, Kepler, Galileo, Descartes, Pascal, Hobbes, Huygens, and Newton) has been published and is well known, less studied and appreciated is the role of the major "intelligencers," serving as "secretaries" in the "Commonwealth of Learning." These individuals sent and received letters that were often copied, forwarded, circulated in groups, and read aloud at informal meetings, and their correspondence networks could be very complex and demanding: the "prince of erudition," Nicolas-Claude Fabri de Peiresc (1580–1637), for instance, once sent more than forty letters in a single day. He left some 10,000 to 14,000 letters after his death; they were addressed to nearly 500 correspondents throughout Europe. Although he was active in the fields of astronomy and optics himself, Peiresc's chief influence was mediating intellectual commerce across space, time, and theme. Thus he performed a "translation of learning" from Italy to France, Provence to Paris, humanism to science (Miller 2000). "Intelligencers" like Peiresc and Henry Oldenburg (1618–1677), secretary of the Royal Society from 1662 onwards, adapted the Renaissance ideal of a republic of letters to the realities of the new science. The number of correspondence networks grew; letters, perfectly suited to cut across traditional boundaries of space, time, language, class, and confessional domain, useful for organizing simultaneous observations of events and for spreading and comparing time-sensitive information from widely dispersed sites, functioned as journal articles or reviews, disseminating and discussing new findings, new philosophical views, and new discoveries. Letters had become a privileged medium, either in Latin or, in most cases now, in the vernacular, to convey scientific messages, and scientific controversies became communication events that were often made public in (open) letters and in public forums such as the *Philosophical Transactions of the Royal Society* (1660). The genre of the Latin private letter, especially those collected and selected for publication, moved into the medium of French, German, and English literature. There, the private letter found a new language and, also, a new function in epistolary novels such as Montesquieu's *Persian Letters* (1721), Goethe's *Sorrows of Young Werther* (1774), and Jane Austen's *Lady Susan* (1794).

SUGGESTED READING

Some material in my discussion of Petrarch is based on Papy (2011). A good analysis of Renaissance innovations *vis-à-vis* medieval practice is offered by Witt (1982). Fundamental for Neo-Latin epistolography is the seminal article of Clough (1976). Fumaroli (1978) surveys important shifts in literary and stylistic taste, while Bots and Waquet (1994) and Berkvens-Stevelinck, Bots, and Häseler (2005) contextualize literary and scientific correspondences within the literary and historical background of the republic of letters. Crucial to a correct understanding of the social function of letter-writing and letter collections is Van Houdt, Papy, Tournoy, and Mattheeussen (2002).

REFERENCES

Berkvens-Stevelinck, Christiane, Hans Bots, and Jens Häseler, eds. 2005. *Les grands intermédiaires culturels de la République des Lettres: Études sur les réseaux de correspondences du XVIᵉ au XVIIIᵉ siècles*. Paris: Champion.

Billanovich, Giuseppe. 1947. *Petrarca letterato: Lo scrittoio del Petrarca*. Rome: Edizioni di Storia e Letteratura.

Bots, Hans, and Françoise Waquet, eds. 1994. *Commercium litterarium: La communication dans la république des lettres (1600–1750)*. Amsterdam-Maarssen: APA-Holland University Press.

Camargo, Martin. 1991. *Ars dictaminis, ars dictandi*. Turnhout: Brepols.

Clough, Cecil H. 1976. "The Cult of Antiquity: Letters and Letter Collections." In *Cultural Aspects of the Italian Renaissance: Essays in Honour of Paul Oskar Kristeller*, edited by Cecil H. Clough, 33–67. Manchester: Manchester University Press.

Cosenza, Mario E. 1910. *Petrarch's Letters to Classical Authors*. Chicago: University of Chicago Press.

De Keyser, Jeroen. 2014. "Per un' edizione critica dell'epistolario di Francesco Filelfo." *Studi Umanistici Piceni* 34:69–82.

De Landtsheer, Jeanine. 1998. "Justus Lipsius (1547–1606) and the Edition of his *Centuriae Miscellaneae*: Some Particularities and Practical Problems." *Lias* 25:69–82.

Dotti, Ugo. 1987. *Vita di Petrarca*. Rome: Laterza.

Enenkel, Karl A. E. 1999. "Lipsius als Modellgelehrter: Die Lipsius-Biographie des Miraeus." In *Justus Lipsius, Europae lumen et columen*, edited by Gilbert Tournoy, Jeanine De Landtsheer, and Jan Papy, 47–66. Leuven: Leuven University Press.

———. 2002. "Die Grundlegung humanistischer Selbstpräsentation im Brief-Corpus: Francesco Petrarcas *Familiarium rerum libri XXIV*." In Van Houdt, Papy, Tournoy, and Matheeussen 2002, 367–84.

Erasmus, Desiderius. 1906–1958. *Opus epistolarum*. Edited by Percy S. Allen et al. 12 vols. Oxford: Clarendon Press.

Ficino, Marsilio. 1990–2010. *Lettere: Epistolarum familiarum liber I–II*. 2 vols. Edited by Sebastiano Gentile. Florence: Olschki.

Fumaroli, Marc. 1978. "Genèse de l'épistolographie classique: Rhétorique humaniste de la lettre, de Pétrarque à Juste Lipse." *Revue d'histoire littéraire de la France* 78:886–905.

———. 1980. *L'âge de l'éloquence: Rhétorique et* res literaria *de la Renaissance au seuil de l'époque classique*. Geneva: Droz.

Gerlo, Aloïs. 1971. "The *Opus de conscribendis epistolis* of Erasmus and the Tradition of the *ars epistolica*." In *Classical Influences on European Culture A.D. 500–1500*, edited by Robert R. Bolgar, 103–114. Cambridge: Cambridge University Press.

Halkin, Léon-E. 1983. *Erasmus ex Erasmo: Erasme éditeur de sa correspondance*. Aubel: Gason.

Henderson, Judith R. 1983a. "Defining the Genre of the Letter: Juan Luis Vives' *De conscribendis epistolis*." *Renaissance and Reformation* 7:89–105.

———. 1983b. "Erasmus on the Art of Letter-Writing." In *Renaissance Eloquence*, edited by James J. Murphy, 331–55. Berkeley: University of California Press.

IJsewijn, Jozef. 1985 "Marcus Antonius Muretus Epistolographus." In *La correspondence d'Erasme et l'épistolographie humaniste*, prepared under various editors, 183–91. Brussels: Editions de l'Université de Bruxelles.

Jardine, Lisa. 1993. *Erasmus, Man of Letters: The Construction of Charisma in Print*. Princeton: Princeton University Press.

Mann, Nicholas. 1984. *Petrarch*. Oxford: Oxford University Press.

Laureys, Marc. 1997. "The Reception of Giovanni Pico in the Low Countries." In *Giovanni Pico della Mirandola*. 2 vols., edited by Gian Carlo Garfagnini, vol. 2, 625–640. Florence: Olschki.

Lipsius, Justus. 1978. *Epistolae*. Vol. 1, *1564–1583*. Edited by Aloïs Gerlo, Marcel A. Nauwelaerts, and Hendrik D. L. Vervliet. Brussels: Paleis der Academiën.

———. 1996. *Principles of Letter-Writing: A Bilingual Text of* Justi Lipsi Epistolica institutio. Edited and translated by Robert V. Young and M. Thomas Hester. Carbondale: Southern Illinois University Press.

Margolin, Jean C. 1973. *Guerre et paix dans la pensée d'Érasme*. Paris: Montaigne.

Miller, Peter N. 2000. *Peiresc's Europe: Learning and Virtue in the Seventeenth Century*. New Haven: Yale University Press.

Papy, Jan. 2002. "La correspondance de Juste Lipse: Genèse et fortune des *Epistolarum Selectarum Centuriae*." *Les Cahiers de l'Humanisme* 2:223–36.

———. 2006. "Creating an 'Italian' Friendship: From Petrarch's Ideal Literary Critic 'Socrates' to the Historical Reader Ludovicus Sanctus of Beringen." In *Petrarch and His Readers in the Renaissance*, edited by Karl A. E. Enenkel and Jan Papy, 13–30. Leiden: Brill.

———. 2011. "Petrarch's 'Inner Eye' in the *Familiarium Libri XXIV*". In *Meditatio – Refashioning the Self: Theory and Practice in Late Medieval and Early Modern Intellectual Culture*, edited by Karl A. E. Enenkel and Walter Melion, 45–68. Leiden: Brill.

Petrarch, Francesco. 1933–1942. *Le Familiari*. Edited by Vittorio Rossi. 4 vols. Florence: Sansoni.

———. 1975–1985. *Letters on Familiar Matters*. Translated by Aldo S. Bernardo. 3 vols. Baltimore: Johns Hopkins University Press.

Poggio Bracciolini, Giovanni. 1984–1988. *Lettere*. 3 vols. Edited by Hélène Harth. Florence: Olschki.

Poliziano, Angelo. 2006. *Letters*. Vol. 1, *Books I–IV*. Edited and translated by Shane Butler. Cambridge: Harvard University Press.

Robin, Diana. 1991. *Filelfo in Milan: Writings 1451–1477*. Princeton: Princeton University Press.

Rossi, Vittorio. 1932. "Sulla formazione delle raccolte epistolari petrarchesche." *Annali della Cattedra Petrarchesca* 3:68–73.

Tracy, James D. 1978. *The Politics of Erasmus: A Pacifist Intellectual and His Political Milieu.* Toronto: University of Toronto Press.

Trinkaus, Charles. 1970. *In Our Image and Likeness: Humanity and Divinity in Italian Humanist Thought*. Chicago: University of Chicago Press.

Van Houdt, Toon, Jan Papy, Gilbert Tournoy, and Constant Mattheeussen, eds. 2002. *Self-Presentation and Social Identification: The Rhetoric and Pragmatics of Letter-Writing in Early Modern Times*. Leuven: Leuven University Press.

Wilkins, Ernest H. 1948. "Peregrinus ubique." *Studies in Philology* 45:445–53.

———. 1956. *The* Epistolae metricae *of Petrarch*. Rome: Edizioni di Storia e Letteratura.

Witt, Ronald. 1982. "Medieval 'Ars dictaminis' and the Beginnings of Humanism." *Renaissance Quarterly* 35:1–25.

CHAPTER 12

....

FICTION

....

MARK T. RILEY

NEO-LATIN prose fiction enjoyed an astonishing heyday from the sixteenth to the eighteenth centuries. Short stories, romances, fictional travel narratives (utopias and dystopias), prose or "Menippean" satires (for which see Chapter 13 in this volume), and long novels flourished to such an extent that they often outshone literary work in the continent's vernacular languages. Although France and Italy were the centers of production, outstanding works were also written by a host of superbly trained Latinists throughout Europe whose imaginations were pulled in one direction by the influence of the language and culture of their contemporaries, and in another by the Latin language and culture within which they studied and wrote. These writers imagined new worlds, addressed contemporary political and social problems, and satirized the great and the good in ways that their ancient counterparts could not have imagined. This freedom of imagination arose partly from the relative paucity of ancient models for prose fiction, and partly from the wave of discoveries in the New World, which encouraged Neo-Latin writers to set their creations in similarly exotic and unknown lands: the South Sea Islands, Peru, even a subterranean kingdom entered through a volcano.

The initial encouragement for Neo-Latin fiction came in the fifteenth century from the contemporary popularity of short stories in Italian. Indeed, the first prose Neo-Latin fictions were translations from Italian. During the next two centuries, such fiction became longer and more classical in language as the renewed humanist Latin spread throughout Europe. The last major Neo-Latin novel, Holberg's *Nicolai Klimii iter subterraneum* (*Niels Klim's Underground Journey*), was written in the eighteenth century by the founder of Danish-Norwegian literature. As the national languages developed their full resources, creativity in Latin declined, again first in Italy (although major works continued to be written in Rome), then in France, England, and Germany, with Scandinavia and Eastern Europe as the final actors (*CNLS* 1:44–49).

A few models for prose fiction came from antiquity; the most important are Heliodorus's *Ethiopian History* (third or fourth century CE; Latin translation 1556),

Petronius's *Satyricon* (probably first century CE), and Apuleius's *Metamorphoses* (second century CE). Heliodorus supplied the model for an intricate plot with mystery overtones; Petronius, an episodic plot with an errant protagonist; Apuleius, magic and fairy tale elements. However, More's *Utopia* and its imitators owe virtually nothing to these ancient novels. Even romances like John Barclay's *Argenis* (1621), while borrowing some elements, are focused on the contemporary world, its politics and problems. Of all the fictions mentioned here, the closest to an ancient model, Prasch's *Psyche Cretica* (*Cretan Psyche*, 1685), is nevertheless thoroughly Christianized and committed to the author's social and educational goals. The ancient novels' lack of influence arose partly from the fact that prose fiction was neither well developed nor respected in antiquity. Macrobius (fourth/fifth centuries CE), for example, scorned "frivolous" fiction in his commentary (1.2.6–8) on Cicero's *Dream of Scipio*, specifically mentioning Petronius and Apuleius. This attitude persisted into the Renaissance: Juan Luis Vives (1493–1540), the indefatigable writer of dialogues and colloquia for students, called such fiction worthless *fabulae licentiosae* ("licentious tales"). Petronius, Apuleius, and the authors of the Greek novels were so far out of the mainstream of high literature that there was no standard Latin name for the genre in which they wrote. Short stories were merely *fabulae* ("tales"); novels could be *mythistoriae* ("mythical history"), *fictae narrationes* ("invented narratives"), or *fabulae romanicae* ("romance tales"). For the most part, short stories and novels were considered to be teachers of immorality: at least one novel was written to denounce novels. In the *Gyges Gallicus* (*The Gallic Gyges*, 1658) of Friar Zacharie de Lisieux (who wrote under the pen name of Petrus Firmianus), the hero enters a Druid tomb and finds a ring of invisibility. Using this ring, he enters the palaces of Paris, where he confines himself to lamenting the wickedness and hypocrisy of the nobility—which he attributes to novel-reading! The friar undoubtedly had in mind the contemporary French novels of Honoré d'Urfé or Madeleine de Scudéry, but he would not have excluded from his condemnation Latin prose fictions such as Enea Silvio Piccolomini's *Historia de duobus amantibus* (*Story of Two Lovers*) or Barclay's *Argenis* (*CNLS* 2:241–42).

To overcome such disapproval, much Neo-Latin fiction endeavored to make itself uplifting. It must be remembered that prose fiction, viewed solely as entertainment, was rare in the Renaissance. Works of what we are calling "fiction" were at the time contributions to political theory, ethics, religion, and other areas of debate. Although Piccolomini's *Historia* is essentially an Italian novella written in Latin, the author presents his work as an instructive true story. More's *Utopia*, followed by countless others, contains serious discussions of real contemporary problems. Political discussions form a vital part of Barclay's *Argenis* and related works, which are not utopias but political romances. Satire was always a convenient method of attack, whether in short Menippean form or in longer novels such as Holberg's *Iter subterraneum*, which mocks European delusions of superiority, or John Barclay's *Euphormionis Lusinini Satyricon* (*The Satire of Euphormio from Lusinia*, 1605–1607), a satire on contemporary European education, religion, and politics—anything that the youthful author wished to attack.

ENEA SILVIO PICCOLOMINI, *HISTORIA DE DUOBUS AMANTIBUS*

Neo-Latin fiction began in Italy with translations of stories from Boccaccio's *Decameron* (ca. 1350). For example, Filippo Beroaldo (1453–1505), a noted scholar who wrote the first commentary on Apuleius's *Metamorphoses*, praised Boccaccio's *fabulosas historias* ("plot-filled tales") and translated two of them, the story of Tito and Gisippo (*Decameron* 10.8) and the story of Galeso (*Decameron* 5.1). The first and most successful original short story in Latin was the *Historia de duobus amantibus* (ca. 1440) of Enea Silvio Piccolomini, later Pope Pius II. As pope, the author repudiated his own story on moral grounds (see his letter in Piccolomini 1903, 63), but it was widely read, reprinted, and translated. While atypical because of its realism, the *Historia* nicely illustrates two forces driving Neo-Latin literature: the classical tradition and the vernacular.

Euryalus, a Bohemian noble in the service of Emperor Sigismund, is traveling with his master to Rome, where Sigismund is to be crowned as Holy Roman emperor. (The coronation occurred May 31, 1433; Piccolomini's story begins the previous summer). On the way, the imperial entourage stays several months in Siena, where Euryalus falls in love with Lucretia, the beautiful wife of Menelaus, an elderly Sienese grandee. Lucretia reciprocates his love, but of course the affair does not end well. Sigismund, attended by Euryalus, must leave Siena for Rome to be crowned. Lucretia desperately writes a letter, pleading "Take me with you." Euryalus replies that this is impossible: Lucretia's reputation would be ruined; their secret love would be revealed to all; the emperor would remove him from his post; but he will soon be returning to Siena. Unfortunately, Euryalus falls ill in Rome, is barely able to attend the coronation, and on his way back to Bohemia with the emperor, he merely rides through Siena without stopping. Lucretia wastes away and dies of love. Euryalus thinks only of Lucretia as he travels back to Bohemia, inconsolable until the emperor gives a beautiful noblewoman to him in marriage.

Since the *Historia* is in Latin, Piccolomini felt free to indulge his learning. Characters derive their pseudonyms from and are compared to figures in Greco-Roman history or mythology. Lucretia fears that she might be abandoned like Medea, Ariadne, or Dido. Euryalus cites men deceived by women: Troilus, Deiphobus, Ulysses's crew. The narrator addresses Amor as the ruler of all, one who can transform anyone, as Ovid implied when he wrote of men transformed into beasts, stones, and plants; and Virgil when he told of Circe's lovers changed into beasts (25; the page numbers in our discussion refer to Piccolomini 1903). Piccolomini uses conventional classical metaphors: at dawn Aurora leaves the saffron bed of Tithonus; Lucretia pines away like Laodamia for Protesilaus, like Dido for Aeneas, like Portia for Brutus (51). The author refers to classical philosophy as well. He has heard that some philosophers believe that fortune has no power over the wise man who delights in virtue alone, one who can be happy when poor or sick or even locked in Phalaris's bull—but he has not seen any such men, nor does he think any such exist. Fortune rules all (33–34).

Despite this classical veneer, the *Historia* is thoroughly contemporary. The action occurs in a real time and place; Euryalus could presumably be identified with one of Sigismund's attendants—deluded translators have identified several candidates. Piccolomini testifies to the story's veracity and utility: he prefaces the work with a letter to his friend Marianus Sozinus, in which the author claims that his story, which is an *historia*, not a *fabula*, will instruct young men not to enlist in love's army but stick to their studies (3, 42–43). The author in his own person comments on the morality of the lovers' actions and occasionally mentions the quirks of his Italian fellow citizens (37). He describes Euryalus's difficulties: a Bohemian nobleman, he does not know Italian—this hinders his lovemaking—but he learns it fast under love's impulse; he worries about his peers' reaction if they were to recognize him sneaking away from Lucretia's house (30). Lucretia's initial uncertainty is well presented: reluctant at first, fearful of her reputation, she then commits herself totally, even to death. She is clever, able to deceive her suspicious husband.

The other characters in the plot play conventional roles from Italian novellas or Roman comedy: the married lady who loves a stranger, the jealous husband, women who play tricks on their husbands (examples in *Decameron* 7.1–9). In addition the author's easy Latin style reminds one of the vernacular: sentences are short, non-periodic, straightforward, more medieval than classical. As in medieval Latin, many *sententiae* ("maxims") are scattered throughout the text, moral sayings and proverbs derived from literature or sermons. *Pars sanitatis est velle sanari* (10: "Part of health is the willingness to be healed"); *Heu! amor infelix qui plus fellis quam mellis habes* (45 [compare 52], a reminiscence of Juvenal 6.181; "Alas, unhappy love has more bile than bliss"). Animal metaphors from popular literature abound. Euryalus in love is compared to a war horse hearing the trumpet (8). In the same paragraph Lucretia is compared to a field of dry grass, which flares up at a spark (9). All nature is subject to the fires of love: white doves join with birds of other hues; timid deer battle each other; tigers, boars, lions, and sea monsters are inflamed by love (21).

The *Historia* represents the state of the Latin language prior to the great manuscript discoveries of (among others) Poggio Bracciolini, whose *Facetiae* (*Jokes*, 1438–1459), the shortest of short fictions, mock priests, monks, women, and rustics, and are similar to the *Historia* in their vernacular plots, characterization, and attitudes. Neo-Latin fiction soon became less dependent on vernacular models and more imaginative, comprising various combinations of utopia, fantastic voyage, satire, and romance. Previous to these manuscript discoveries, Latin writers had been educated with the usual medieval textbooks and readings from a narrow range of classical authors. Afterwards, students of the humanists, having read a wide variety of texts, learned to model their Latin on Roman writers, whether the periodic style of Cicero or the flamboyant style of Apuleius—thus the "revival of learning." Students practiced composition in prose and verse, developing the skills so visible in their literary productions (Baldwin 1944 describes humanist training in Latin). As a result, their Latin prose was more complex than that of Piccolomini; unlike him, they included a substantial amount of Latin verse in their novels.

THOMAS MORE, *UTOPIA* AND RELATED WORKS

Two generations after Piccolomini, after the spread of humanistic Latin education in Northern Europe, Sir Thomas More wrote the most influential piece of Renaissance Latin, his *Utopia* (1516). The book is a dialogue addressing some of the issues facing More as an under-sheriff of London and ambassador of Henry VIII in the Low Countries: the best system of justice, whether one should serve kings, private property versus social justice, are all discussed in Book 1 of *Utopia*. In Book 2, inspired by recent voyages of discovery and by his reading of Plato's *Republic*, More describes a polity, the island of Utopia, an imaginary island that provides to some extent answers to the problems outlined in Book 1. Book 2 was in fact written first; the "practical applications" in Book 1 were written later (More 1965, xv–xxiii). The people inhabiting the island of Utopia hold all property in common and use no money. They rotate jobs—every household farming for two years, then moving to the city to practice other crafts. They exchange houses every ten years. All wear the same type of garment. In short, every law or custom aims to reduce individual pride and promote national solidarity. The nation is like one big commune.

Several features of *Utopia* influenced the later developments of both Latin and vernacular fiction. First, More established the genre of utopian novel, thousands of which have been written over the centuries. "Utopia" has become a political as well as a literary term, and the writers of utopias are occasionally treated as political figures. It is no accident that the name of Tommaso Campanella (1568–1639), author of the utopian *Civitas Solis* (*City of the Sun*), is on a memorial obelisk in Moscow's Red Square as a precursor of the Communist revolution of 1917. More himself has been seen as a bourgeois rebel against feudalism, preparing the way for capitalism (Kautsky 1959) or as a Catholic thinker, protesting the excesses of his own time (Sturz in More 1965). Second, More made debate about serious political and social issues a legitimate part of fiction, no longer confining these issues to philosophy (Plato) or satire (Lucian). After *Utopia*, novelists from John Barclay to Dostoevsky and beyond have felt free to include political debates in their novels. Third, More popularized a method of attacking vice by satirically portraying virtue. However, since satire and irony can always be misinterpreted, the author's attitude towards his island has often been in question. Most books and articles about the concept of "utopia" view More's novel as a straightforward vision of an ideal commonwealth (Jameson 2005). The definitive Yale edition cites More as part of the humanist Christian revival; his utopia may not be achievable, but is still an ideal (More 1965, lxiv–lxxxi). Recent work has developed Heiserman's thesis that the island is not an ideal commonwealth, but is in fact the realm "opposite" to Europe (Heiserman 1963; Simpson 2009). This assumption that *Utopia* is semi-satirical, even playful, explains many odd details. The Utopians have abolished the death penalty for robbers, but have instituted it for slaves who accept money from free men. They abhor war in general, but readily begin colonial wars for *Lebensraum*. They practice euthanasia and slavery. More's imaginative names, derived from the Greek, reinforce this sense of oppositeness. Utopia is "Nowhere" (*ou*, "no," and *topos*, "place"); the narrator's name, Hythlodaeus, means "Idle Chatterer" (*hythlos*, "chatter"); the Utopian poet laureate is Anemolius, "Windbag" (*anemos*, "wind"); the main river of Utopia is the Anydrus, "No Water" (the negation *an-* and *hydōr*, "water"); the chief city and the meeting place of the Utopian senate is Amaurotum, "Fogtown" (*amauros*, "dim"). Even the serious discussions of Book 1 are undercut with such names: the best system of justice is found among the Polylerites, "Much Ravers" (*poly-*, "much," and *lēros*, "futility"); the most sensible foreign policy among the Achorians, "No Placers" (the negation *a-* and *chōros*, "land"). These names, and More's *jeu d'esprit* in general, suggest that the island does not exemplify his idea of a real solution to societal problems, but is instead a satirically written contrast with contemporary Europe and a meditation on how things could be different. More even invented a Utopian language and script, including in his dedication a poem in this script with its translation.

A close friend of Erasmus, More, it goes without saying, was a capable Latinist. His *Utopia* exemplifies the practical Latin style characteristic of dialogue: diction is straightforward, with some heightening of style by the use of rare or non-Latin words (*oligopolium* "oligopoly," *scopus* "goal," *morosophus* "idiot savant"), rhetorical questions, and metaphor. The syntax occasionally wanders (*enallage*), with changes from plural to singular, or second person to third. The narrator, Hythlodaeus, sometimes strays into thickets of syntax and obscurity (More 1965, 90–96, comments on a 900-word sentence). More does not attain the smooth, classical Latin style characteristic of seventeenth-century writers, but his language is far more elaborate and polished than Piccolomini's. More does not include any verse in his text, merely an introductory six-line poem supposedly by the Utopian poet Anemolius. More's grimly serious narrator Hythlodaeus has no poetry in his soul and would never stoop to verse—verse that More certainly could have written for a different narrator. His many Latin epigrams show his skills as a poet.

Other utopian writers took More's concept in different directions. The Englishman Joseph Hall's *Mundus alter et idem* (*Another World Yet the Same*, 1605; Hall 1981), a comic dystopia, continued More's playful satire but omitted his serious political discussions. Tommaso Campanella, the hero of Red Square, wrote *Civitas Solis*, the blueprint for an appalling totalitarian state. This work is a bizarre combination of astrology, technology, and futurology written in bad Latin (Campanella had not received a humanist education). His model is the monastic community writ large with all property in common and its communal life regulated in extreme detail. Other utopias include Antonius Legrand's *Scydromedia* (the name of the country described, 1669), a royalist utopia by a Franciscan friar working in England; and Caspar Stiblinus's *De Eudaemonensium Republica* (*On the Republic of the People of Eudaemon*, 1555), about an aristocratic republic located on the fictional island of Macaria. There were also Christian utopias. The Lutheran theologian Johann Valentin Andreae wrote *Christianopolis* (*The Christian City*, 1619), in which the narrator is shipwrecked and driven to an island, Caphar Salama, where an ideal Christian state has been established. The most developed of these Christian utopias is *Nova Solyma* (*New Jerusalem*, 1648; Morrish 2003), a romance by Samuel Gott set in a contemporary, seventeenth-century Jerusalem refounded by Jewish converts to Christianity. *Nova Solyma* contains long lectures on the educational practices appropriate for a Christian commonwealth.

Related to the utopias are travel narratives. A fine example in prose is *Icaria* (the name of a country, 1637) by the German Jesuit Johannes Bissel, a lightly fictionalized narrative of the author's 1632 tour of the Upper Palatinate (Oberpfalz) during the Thirty Years' War. In this work, the author deplores the corruption of true religion by the Protestants, who at the time were a large part of the region's population. The final chapters describe the terrible thunderstorm of April of 1624, which destroyed several buildings in Regensburg and which is treated as a symbol of the devastation wrought by the Swedish invasion and by religious strife (Wiegand 1997). The same author also adapted from a Spanish text his *Argonautica Americana* (*American Argonauts Story*, 1647), an adventure novel about a Jesuit's travels in Central America.

JOHN BARCLAY'S NOVELS AND RELATED WORKS

After More's *Utopia*, the best-known work of Neo-Latin fiction is John Barclay's *Argenis* (1621), which added romance and adventure to politics. In language, plot, and characterization, *Argenis* is the apex of Neo-Latin fiction, enjoying dozens of editions in Latin and multiple translations into all the major European languages (four into English, six into French). It was the best-selling novel of the seventeenth century. Barclay's writing is a testimony to the effectiveness of contemporary Latin education. Thoroughly classical in language, using clear, perspicuous syntax and vocabulary, his novels were models for later Neo-Latin writers and influenced the development of fiction both in Latin and in the European vernaculars (Salzman 1985, 148–76). John Barclay (1582–1621), the son of a Scottish father and a French mother, was educated in France, lived more than ten years (to 1615) in London at the court of James I, whom he knew personally, and spent the last six years of his life in Rome, where he was supported by Pope Paul V and by Cardinal Maffeo Barberini, later Pope Urban VIII. Thus Barclay had personal knowledge of the rulers and the issues current in the early seventeenth century. Throughout his travels, he wrote constantly: verse for the court, religious controversies, and most important, his apprentice novel, *Euphormionis Lusinini Satyricon* (1605–1607), a satire on contemporary society. Like its model, Petronius's *Satyricon* (the name originally meant "Satyr stories," but was often interpreted as "satire"), *Euphormio* is episodic, based on the protagonist's wandering from place to place, with prose and verse commentary on what he sees and experiences. *Euphormio* is important as the first major *roman à clef* in any language, beginning a seventeenth-century vogue for this type of novel. Its fictional characters were taken as portraits of real people, as the author presumably intended, judging from his use of anagrammatic names and transparent references. When Barclay wrote his much grander *Argenis*, he used a similar, though less satirical, method of character portrayal (Barclay 1973, xxix).

Argenis, set in an imaginary Greco-Roman antiquity, is a love story about the princess Argenis, daughter of King Meleander of Sicily, who is wooed by three suitors: Poliarchus, king of Gaul, the eventual victor; Archombrotus, heir to the throne of Mauretania; and Radirobanes, king of Sardinia. Poliarchus and Archombrotus, both high-spirited and noble, begin as fast friends, become hated rivals in love, then (by a plot twist) are restored to friendship when Archombrotus is discovered to be Argenis's half-brother. Radirobanes, after successfully helping King Meleander subdue rebellious noblemen, remains in Sicily to force his attentions on the princess, who (of course) loves another. This plot in five books, which are structured according to the five acts of Roman comedy, is developed with enough twists and turns, sieges, shipwrecks, storms, acts of treason, and battles that the novel has attracted readers for centuries. The poet William Cowper called it "The most amusing romance that was ever written." A few years later, Samuel Taylor Coleridge read "this great work" closely enough to suggest an emendation in the Latin text (Barclay 2004, 38–39). Adding to the interest aroused by the plot are the many passages in which characters debate contemporary issues troubling France, England, and Spain. For example, the problems arising from a king's love for unworthy favorites are discussed in a passage about the Overbury scandal of 1613 in London, and the murder in Paris of the favorite, Concini, by King Louis's guards in 1617. Other debates concern the best form of government, elective versus hereditary monarchy, the treatment of religious minorities, the validity of astrology, the dangers of standing armies, and the best method of taxation, among other topics. One character raises an issue and another responds respectfully, so that the speakers arrive at a reasonable conclusion.

Like his *Euphormio*, Barclay's *Argenis* is a *roman à clef*. The author explains his method in the novel itself. The poet Nicopompus, speaking for Barclay, is planning a "stately fable in manner of a history" which first will give advice in a pleasant, attractive, and palatable format, and second will change the novel from a source of mere entertainment into something more educational (Barclay 2004, 336). While portraying vices and virtues, not people, Nicopompus will ensure that some individuals can recognize themselves as in a mirror. Real-world characters portrayed include cardinals Maffeo Barberini and Ubaldini (both friends of Barclay in Rome), and John Calvin, whose followers, the Hyperephanii (Greek *hyperēphanos*, "arrogant"; the Huguenots), distress King Meleander's realm. Places include Mergania (an anagram of "Germania"), troubled by an elective Holy Roman emperor, and Sicily (representing France), immersed in religious and political conflict. Most editions of *Argenis* published after Barclay's death include keys, often fanciful and arbitrary, identifying characters with their real-world equivalents.

Barclay also introduced elements of the mystery novel into modern literature. In this he was inspired by the Greek novelist Heliodorus, whose *Aethiopica* (*Ethiopian History*), the story of two lovers' quest, begins *in medias res* and ends with a startling revelation.

Argenis begins in a similar manner; throughout the novel, the reader does not know who the chief characters really are. Poliarchus's origins, the fact that he is king of Gaul (France), are not revealed until Book 3. As for Archombrotus, the truth about his birth does not appear until the very end in Book 5. Why are Poliarchus and Archombrotus in Sicily at all? How did Poliarchus and the princess fall in love? The answers all come late in the story. Things are casually mentioned in the first pages (the "clues"), but they become significant only later. The term "mystery novel" should not be confined to modern genre fiction. Many serious novels—Dickens comes to mind—have a mystery at the heart of the plot.

Almost all Neo-Latin novels are adorned with verse. Barclay was an accomplished poet and scattered several thousand lines of verse throughout his two novels, imitating the ancient Menippean satires, which are largely prose with bursts of poetry. For example, the poet Nicopompus celebrates the defeat of Radirobanes by calling down a tempest on the retreating Sardinian fleet. Barclay's verse demonstrates a total command of classical meter, style, and metaphor; like his prose, it owes nothing to the vernacular (Barclay 2004, 618; translation by Thomas May, 1625):

> *Ite truces. Cuncti rapiant cava lintea venti.*
> *Ite rates. Sic aura fidem, sic aequora praestent,*
> *Ut vestri meruere duces. Simul ibit Enyo,*
> *Stridebitque comis, facibusque in concita missis*
> *Nubila, Tartareum deducet in aequora fulmen.*

> Go, treacherous ships; your sails all tempests drive.
> Such faith to you let winds and water give
> As you deserve. Enyo shall attend
> With frightful hair, and kindling with her brand
> The clouds, bring Stygian lightning on your fleet.

The seventeenth century was mad for *romans à clef,* and many contemporary novels, whether Latin or vernacular, attempted to satisfy this need. Very similar in plot to *Argenis,* and also showing the influence of Heliodorus, is *Austriana Regina Arabiae* (*Austriana, Queen of Arabia,* 1688) by Anton Wilhelm Ertl. Here the princess Austriana is wooed by Aurindus, the king of Arabia. Their union is delayed by their enemies Altomira and Tigrania, the latter of whom incites an attack on Austriana's capital by the king of India—but all turns out well in the end. Although Ertl supplied no key, the characters can be identified with figures in Habsburg history: Austriana is the ruling dynasty during the sixteenth and seventeenth century; her enemies are the kings of France, Louis XIII and XIV; the king of India represents the Turks and their siege of Vienna in 1683 (Tilg 2012). An extreme example of the Latin *roman à clef* is found in the *Peruviana* (*A Peruvian Tale,* 1645) of Claude-Barthélemy Morisot (1592–1661), a lawyer of Dijon who had read John Barclay carefully and had written a sequel to his *Euphormio.* This novel's intricate plot is set in Peru (France), whose king Manco Magnus (Henri IV) and queen Coya (Marie de Medici) have two sons, Yllapa (Louis

XIII) and Puma (Gaston d'Orleans), the hero of the novel. Morisot included a four-page key, without which the novel is virtually unintelligible.

LUDVIG HOLBERG'S *ITER SUBTERRANEUM*, AND OTHER LATE AUTHORS

Latin and the various European vernaculars mutually influenced each other throughout the seventeenth and eighteenth centuries. Many Neo-Latinists of the period were also known for their vernacular works, including some masters of French and English who were noted Latin poets: the Latin poems of Joachim Du Bellay (*Poemata*, 1558) and of John Milton (*Poemata*, 1645) have been widely admired. One prominent bilingual novelist is the founder of Danish-Norwegian literature, Ludvig Holberg (1684–1754), who wrote one of the last and perhaps the most entertaining (to modern tastes) of all the Latin novels. His *Nicolaii Klimii iter subterraneum* (1741) blends satire with a fantastic voyage and breathes the spirit of the eighteenth century. Other than its Latin language and passages of verse and prose adapted from classical authors, this novel is entirely modern in spirit. Its description of travel to exotic lands reminds one of his near-contemporary Jonathan Swift's *Gulliver's Travels* (1726), but with far more wit and humor; Holberg's narrator remains a lively and ambitious soul throughout the novel, rather than becoming an acerbic misanthrope like Gulliver, whose travels make him hate the human race. Holberg's notion of a hollow earth containing other habitable lands resembles Jules Verne's *Voyage au centre de la Terre* (*Voyage to the Center of the Earth*, 1864), but in a playful rather than a serious tone. Holberg's wit and sparkling humor, also on display in his autobiographical letters, have few parallels in Latin literature.

After graduating from the university in Copenhagen, the narrator Niels Klim returns to his home in Bergen. At loose ends, he decides to explore the mountains around Bergen, and while doing so, accidentally falls down an extinct volcano into the hollow center of our planet. Inside this hollow center is another spherical world about 900 miles in circumference on which our narrator lands. He sees a bull, is frightened, and climbs a nearby tree. He suddenly hears a voice (2.3):

> *qualis solet esse iracundae mulieris, moxque quasi palma excussissima colaphus mihi tanta vi inflictus est, ut vertigine correptus pronus in terram caderem. Ictu hoc iam quasi fulmine percussus ac terrore animam propediem agens, murmura undique audiebam et strepitus, qualibus resonare solent macella aut mercatorum basilicae, quando maxime sunt frequentes.*

> . . . like that of an angry woman, and I got at the same time a lively slap on my ear, which propelled me headlong to the ground. Here I lay as if struck by lightning, about to give up my spirit, when I heard around me a murmuring noise, such as is heard in the shops or at the Stock Exchange when a great crowd is assembled.

It turns out that he has rudely attempted to climb the mayor's wife. Seized by these ambulatory and clearly intelligent trees, he is taken to jail, where he is treated most humanely. He has landed on the planet Nazar near the city of Potu ("Utop-ia" backwards with the ending dropped), where he now must make his career. Because of his long legs (compared to trees') and superior mobility, he is appointed courier to the surrounding nations, and his travels give him the opportunity of describing strange customs: as the inhabitants of Quamboia age, they become more lascivious; in Cocklecu the women rule, the men are domestic servants; the people of Mascattia are all philosophers and as a result their nation is filthy, disordered, and violent. Indeed the Mascattians plan to vivisect Klim, who manages to escape and return to Potu with his dispatches. For variety, Holberg reports words, names, and phrases in the Potuan language.

The primary object of the novel's satire is the narrator Klim himself, who has conventional European attitudes. He is inordinately proud of his university diploma, even displaying it to ward off a giant griffin that menaces him during his descent to Nazar. He proudly informs the Potuans that his dissertation concerned the use of slippers among the Greeks and Romans. They laugh, offending Klim greatly. He considers his appointment as courier to be a shameful waste of his talents, since he is quick-witted and learns rapidly (4.19):

> *Nam animo continue oberravit ignobile, ad quod damnatus eram, ministerium, et indecorum ac turpe videbatur Ministerii Candidato ac Baccalaureo magni orbis vilem agere cursorem subterraneum.*

> The lowly office, to which I was condemned, constantly flashed before my mind, and it seemed disgraceful and shameful for a Bachelor of Arts and a Candidate for the Ministry in the larger world to act as a common courier in this subterranean world.

The Potuans, however, consider his mental quickness to be a defect and his speed of foot his only virtue. For their part, they prize slow reflection and even slower action and threaten *novatores* ("innovators") with death. They name Klim *Scabba*, "Hasty." Although Klim approves of some Potuan customs and laws, he nevertheless finds many practices of this subterranean world far inferior to the superior customs of our world, especially regarding the status of women. In an attempt to gain higher rank, he proposes a law making women second-class citizens. For this he is exiled to the *firmamentum*, the underside of our earth's crust. There he is welcomed by the Martinians, who look like monkeys. Here Klim is viewed not as hasty, but as slow-witted, and named *Kakidoran*, "Slow." The Martinians are avid for innovation, and seeing this, Klim makes his fortune by introducing wigs, which are enthusiastically adopted. Losing his position because of a false accusation, Klim lands on his feet in Quama, whose inhabitants are human beings, even if savages—although they are not cruel and barbarous like Swift's Yahoos. Klim "civilizes" them, begins to manufacture gunpowder, and succeeds in conquering the entire firmament. He becomes the Alexander of the subterranean world, a megalo-maniac who establishes a Fifth Monarchy (15.2):

> *Ex eo tempore novam in historiis epocham* [the editions have *nova ... epocha*] *sta-tui, et quinque Monarchiae numerari possunt, scil. Assyriaca, Persica, Graeca, Romana et Quamitica subterranea; et videtur novissima haec priores magnitudine ac potentia superare.*

> From this time I established a new period in history; now five Monarchies can be listed: the Assyrian, Persian, Greek, and Roman empires, and the Subterranean-Quamitic monarchy, this latter unquestionably exceeds them all in magnificence and power.

His subjects eventually rebel, he flees, and in his flight he falls through the same volcanic hole by which he had entered the subterranean world, thus returning to Norway twelve years after his original departure. He meets an old friend and tells him the strange story. Since Klim now needs to earn a living, his friend arranges for Klim to become an *aedituus*, a sacristan or custodian of the local church. From emperor to custodian in a few days! But, nothing daunted, Klim re-enters conventional life, marries happily, and has three sons—unlike Gulliver, who, after his travels and contact with Yahoos, cannot endure to sit at the same table with his wife.

Holberg was a true cosmopolitan, living for several years in Holland, England, France, and Italy. Returning to Copenhagen, he became famous as a writer of poems and comic dramas in Danish with the strong satirical streak that appears in his Latin works. He introduced themes from European literature into the then-insular Danish culture, and his comedies were popular. He used Latin for his entertaining autobiographical letters as well as for the internationally known *Iter subterraneum*. He also composed hundreds of Latin epigrams. His Latin is clear and easy to read, with short, non-periodic sentences. His vocabulary is large, well adapted for any description. He is fond of classical reminiscences. On visiting Cocklecu, where women rule, his narrator exclaims: *O terque quaterque beatam Europam nostram!* ("Thrice and four times happy is our Europe," adapting *o terque quaterque beati* from Virgil's *Aeneid* 1.94). The narrator often quotes verses from Virgil, Ovid, Juvenal, and Holberg's own epigrams, slightly adapting them to the context.

Other bilingual authors include Johann Ludwig Prasch (1637–1690), a prominent citizen who served as mayor of Regensburg in Germany. Prasch first wrote poetry, a history of the German language, and educational materials in Latin, but later turned his attention to the development and promotion of poetry in German. He attempted to reform the romance genre (typified by *Argenis*) in order to make it Christian. His wife, Susanna (1661–after 1693), had criticized novels as a corrupting influence on their readers, who learned from them only malice and vanity, and she had suggested that someone should write an uplifting story about the love between Christ and his bride, the faithful Christian soul (Morrish 2009). Her husband obliged with his novella-length *Psyche Cretica* (1685), one of the last major Latin fictions written in Germany. This work transforms Apuleius's narrative of Cupid and Psyche into a Christian story of devotion, temptation, and final salvation.

In Eastern Europe, the Hungarian author András Dugonics (1740–1818), a Piarist, prolific writer, and university professor of mathematics, wrote the first best-seller in Hungarian, the historical romance *Etelka*, and helped establish Hungarian as a literary language. But before *Etelka* and influenced by Barclay's *Argenis*, which Dugonics considered a masterpiece, he had written an immense novel (754 pages), *Argonautica* (*Argonauts Story*, 1778), retelling the adventures of Jason and the Argonauts (Tilg 2013). Portraying the Scythians as ancestors of the Magyars, Dugonics added episodes and characters such as the Scythian king Almus (Hungarian Álmos) to the Argonaut legend; these characters have been interpreted as representing Magyar national traits (Szörenyi 2006 164, 167). Like Holberg and Prasch, Dugonics applied what he had learned in his classical studies to his vernacular work, thus enriching his national language.

Holberg's *Iter* is the last significant Latin novel. Others have been published, even into the twenty-first century. Stephen Berard's *Capti* (*Captives*, 2011) is the most recent known to me. Translations from the vernacular continue to be published. Alexander Lenard's version of A. A. Milne's *Winnie the Pooh* (*Winnie Ille Pu*, 1960) was the only Latin book—and perhaps the only book in any foreign language—ever to become a New York Times best-seller, remaining on the list for 20 weeks. The same author translated Françoise Sagan's *Bonjour Tristesse* (*Tristitia Salve* [*Hello Sadness*], 1963). More recently Peter Needham has translated two Harry Potter novels: *Harry Potter and the Philosopher's Stone* (*Harrius Potter et Philosophi Lapis*, 2003) and *Harry Potter and the Chamber of Secrets* (*Harrius Potter et Camera Secretorum*, 2006). But it cannot be expected that the fires of Latin creativity will burn as brightly today as they did in the sixteenth to the eighteenth centuries.

Suggested Reading

Many Neo-Latin works are now available online, thanks to digitization, including most of those discussed in this chapter. The literature on *Utopia* is immense, covering literary, political, and psychological topics. On the latter two, see Mannheim (1949). Surtz and Hexter's Yale edition (More 1965) with its thorough introduction is definitive, but the best English translation is by Clarence Miller (More 2001). A good general discussion can be found in Davis (1981). The only good English translation of Campanella is Campanella (1981), from the original Italian, which is not always identical to the Latin text. Recommended editions and translations of other authors discussed are Piccolomini (1903), Hall (1981), Barclay (1973 and 2004), Begley (1902, who identified John Milton instead of Samuel Gott as the author of the anonymously published *Nova Solyma*), Prasch (1968), and Holberg (1970 and 1960). Holberg's letters and epigrams are in his *Opuscula Latina* of 1737. There are no published English translations of Prasch (the best study is Dachs 1957; an eighteenth-century German translation exists), Ertl (the only useful discussion is Tilg 2012), Morisot, or Dugonics. Work on the latter is in Hungarian except Szörényi (2006), Berényi-Révész (1962), and Tilg (2013). Recent literary and historical scholarship on the Neo-Latin novel (with particular emphasis on Barclay and Holberg) can be found in Tilg and Walser (2013).

Other original novels were written. These include a sequel to Barclay's *Argenis* by Gabriel Bugnot (1669) and Gian Vittorio Rossi's *Eudemia* (~ *Land of the Good People*, 1637), a satire on seventeenth-century Rome written in beautiful Latin. Short fictions include the Menippean satires, discussed in Chapter 13 of this volume, and the *Somnia* ("*Dreams*"), short stories addressing various issues: the *Somnia* of Juan Luis Vives (1520–1521) and Justus Lipsius (1581) concern the editing of ancient texts; the *Somnium* of Johannes Kepler (1634) tells of a rocket trip from the Earth to the Moon. Many collections of *Facetiae* exist; a theory of humor with many sample jokes can be found in Giovanni Pontano's *De sermone* (*On Conversation*, 1509).

References

Baldwin, William. 1944. *William Shakespere's Small Latine and Lesse Greek*. 2 vols. Urbana: University of Illinois Press.

Barclay, John. 2004. *Argenis*. Edited by Mark Riley and Dorothy Pritchard Huber. 2 vols. Assen: Royal van Gorcum.

———. 1973. *Euphormionis Lusinini Satyricon (Euphormio's Satyricon) 1605–1607*. Edited by David Fleming. Nieuwkoop: de Graaf.

Begley, Walter, trans. 1902. *Nova Solyma, The Ideal City; or, Jerusalem Regained: An Anonymous Romance Written in the Time of Charles I, Now First Drawn from Obscurity, and Attributed to the Illustrious John Milton*. New York: Charles Scribner's Sons.

Berényi-Révész, Maria. 1962. "Humanistische Anregungen bei den Anfängen des ungarischen Romans." In *Renaissance und Humanismus in Mittel- und Osteuropa: Eine Sammlung von Materialien*, edited by Johannes Irmscher, 95–103. Berlin: Akademie-Verlag.

Campanella, Tommaso. 1981. *La città del sole: Dialogo poetico—The City of the Sun: A Poetical Dialogue*. Translated by Daniel Donno. Berkeley: University of California Press.

Dachs, Karl. 1957. "Leben und Dichtung des Johann Ludwig Prasch (1637–1690)." *Verhandlungen des Historischen Vereins für Oberpfalz und Regensburg* 98:5–219.

Davis, James C. 1981. *Utopia and the Ideal Society: A Study of English Utopian Writing 1516–1700*. Cambridge: Cambridge University Press.

Hall, Joseph. 1981. *Another World and Yet the Same: Bishop Joseph Hall's* Mundus alter et idem. Translated by John Millar Wands. New Haven: Yale University Press.

Heiserman, Arthur R. 1963. "Satire in the *Utopia*." *Proceedings of the Modern Language Association* 78:163–74.

Holberg, Ludvig. 1737. *Opuscula quaedam Latina: Epistola I, epistola II, quinque libri epigrammatum*. Leipzig: Paulli Vidua.

———. 1960. *The Journey of Niels Klim to the World Underground*. Edited by James I. McNelis, Jr. Westport: Greenwood Press.

———. 1970. *Niels Klims underjordiske Rejse, 1741–1745*. Edited and translated (Danish) by Aage Kragelund. 3 vols. Copenhagen: Gad.

Jameson, Fredric. 2005. *Archaeologies of the Future: The Desire Called Utopia and Other Science Fictions*. London and New York: Verso.

Kautsky, Karl. 1959. *Thomas More and His Utopia*. New York: Russell & Russell.

Mannheim, Karl. 1949. *Ideology and Utopia*. New York: Harcourt, Brace, and Co.

More, Thomas. 1965. *The Complete Works of St. Thomas More.* Vol. 4, *Utopia.* Edited by Edward Surtz and Jack H. Hexter. New Haven: Yale University Press.

———. 2001. *Utopia.* Translated by Clarence Miller. New Haven: Yale University Press.

Morrish, Jennifer. 2003. "Virtue and Genre in Samuel Gott's *Nova Solyma.*" *Humanistica Lovaniensia* 52:237–317.

———. 2009. "Susanna Elisabeth Prasch, Neo-Latin Novels, and Female Characters in *Psyche Cretica.*" In *Women and the Divine in Literature Before 1700: Essays in Memory of Margot Louis,* edited by Kathryn Kerby-Fulton, 167–83 and 252–56. Victoria: University of Victoria Press.

Piccolomini, Enea S. 1903. *De duobus amantibus historia.* Edited by Joseph Dévay. Budapest: Heisler.

Prasch, Johann L. 1968. *Psyche Cretica.* Edited by Marie-José Desmet-Goethals in *Humanistica Lovaniensia* 17:117–56.

Salzman, Paul. 1985. *English Prose Fiction 1558–1700.* Oxford: Clarendon Press.

Simpson, James. 2009. "Rhetoric, Conscience, and the Playful Positions of Sir Thomas More." In *The Oxford Handbook of Tudor Literature,* edited by Mike Pincombe and Cathy Shrank, 121–36. New York: Oxford University Press.

Szörényi, László. 2006. "Dugonics' *Argonautica.*" *Camoenae Hungaricae* 3:161–68.

Tilg, Stefan. 2012. "Anton Wilhelm Ertl's *Austriana Regina Arabiae* (1687): A Little Known Latin Novel." In *ACNL,* 1109–18.

———. 2013. "The Neo-Latin Novel's Last Stand: András Dugonics' *Argonautica* (1778)." In Tilg and Walser, 161–71.

Tilg, Stefan, and Isabella Walser. 2013. *Der neulateinische Roman als Medium seiner Zeit: The Neo-Latin Novel in Its Time.* Tübingen: Narr.

Wiegand, Hermann. 1997. "Die Oberpfalz im konfessionellen Umbruch: Eine jesuitische Reisesatire aus dem Jahr 1632." In *Der Pfälzer Löwe in Bayern: Zur Geschichte der Oberpfalz in der kurpfälzischen Epoche,* edited by Hans-Jürgen Becker, 130–56. Regensburg: Universitätsverlag Regensburg.

CHAPTER 13

....

SATIRE

....

INGRID A. R. DE SMET

Amat Satyra ironias: etenim clam, et sub specie laudantis, cum risu mordere consuevit. Gaudet argumentorum varietate ("Satire loves irony, for it is wont to bite surreptitiously, whilst laughing and under the guise of praise. It delights in a variety of subject matter"), declared the Salamancan professor Juan González de Dios in 1739, in his commentary on the book of four Latin satires by his contemporary Francisco Botello de Moraes y Vasconcelos (1670–1747; Botello de Moraes y Vasconcelos 1739, 20). González continued with a summary of the criteria by which Latin (verse) satire should be judged:

> *In Satyra laudatur ingeniosa inventio, frequens et acuta sententia, vis et acrimonia: dicendi acumen, facetiae, urbanitates. In verbis expetitur proprietas, et elegantia: in versibus apta compositio, in acerbitate iocus. Satyra denique neque scurrilia, neque plebeia, neque obscoena quandoque verba reformidat.*

> In satire we praise clever topics, numerous pithy expressions, force and animosity, a pungency of speech, humor, wit. We seek out appropriate and elegant wording, skilled verse composition, tartness delivered with humour. Finally, from time to time satire does not shun scurrilous, vulgar, or even obscene terminology.

By Botello and González's time, Neo-Latin satire could already draw on a rich, if chequered, tradition. Neo-Latin satire was admittedly closely identified with Botello's chosen genre, known as "formal verse satire" or *sermo*, a poem in dactylic hexameters, modeled on the form favored by the Roman satirist Lucilius (ca. 180–102 BCE; hence also, and perhaps preferably, "Lucilian satire"), but for which Horace, Juvenal, and (in Botello's case) Persius provided the leading examples, often in some combined form but with shifting emphases according to the poet's preference (Pozuelo Calero 1994; Simons 2013).

However, Neo-Latin satire also manifests itself strongly as Menippean satire. Not formally defined as such in antiquity, this genre took its name from Varro's *Saturae Menippeae* (first century BCE), of which only titles and fragments survive, but which were known to mix prose with verse (hence also "prosimetric" or "Varronian satire").

The Menippean satire or *Menippea* has furthermore been linked to the reception of the equally lacerated, prosimetric *Satyricon* of Petronius (first century CE), the—much earlier—influence of Lucian's (second century CE) seriocomic stance (notably in satirical dialogues and the paradoxical *encomium*), and the medieval carnival, although scholars still debate just how flexible the category of Menippean satire should be (see the differing views of Blanchard 1995, De Smet 1996, or Weinbrot 2005). Last but not least, satire in its broadest, modern meaning of the use of sarcasm, irony, mimicry, scorn, and so on, to expose all kinds of vice, impropriety, foolishness, or evil, was as widespread and diverse in Neo-Latin as it was in vernacular literary traditions.

HESITANT BEGINNINGS: "SATYRA QUID?" ("WHAT IS SATIRE?")

If Horace, Persius, and Juvenal had been popular school texts during the Middle Ages, they were usually valued more as ethical writers (*ethici*) than as generic models; moreover, the Middle Ages applied the term *satyra* or *satura* rather freely, to poems in elegiac distichs or other meters, as well as to prose works. The Renaissance notion of satire thus started from a position of uncertainty: from the first humanist commentaries on the classical satirists onwards, such as Giovanni Britannico of Brescia's annotated edition of Persius (1481) or the assembled *praenotamenta* ("preliminary remarks") on all three Roman satirists in Josse Bade's commentary on Horace of 1500 (Debailly 2001), much ink flowed in the debate over the etymology and nature of *satura*, a variant spelling of *satira*, now believed to refer originally to "a mixture," "hodgepodge" or "farrago." Typically, humanists discerned between Lucilian or formal verse satire, on one hand, and an older, mixed form, which gradually came to be associated with Menippean satire, on the other. In addition, the misspelling of *satura* as *satyra* famously invited association with "satyrs," the petulant and uncouth hybrid woodland creatures of Greek mythology, and thus also with Greek satyr-plays (which the Renaissance not only linked to the coarse, extemporized "Atellan play" of ancient Italy, the *fabula Atellana*, but also compared to the French *soties*, morality plays and farces). Indeed, in Neo-Latin, the noun *satyrus* can also refer to "the satirist." The humanists' early attempts to reconcile the classical source material, however, remained largely inconclusive; rarely did they result in effective yardsticks for new productions. González's criteria, quoted earlier, thus usefully complement, say, Julius Caesar Scaliger's summation of satire as "a poem that is frank like the temperament of the satyrs and turns everything topsy-turvy, for the sake of a clever word. Therefore it needs neither introduction nor epilogue" (Scaliger 1994, 186; my translation). Meanwhile, the tripartite division of dramatic, isometric (with hexameter lines of equal length), and prosimetric satire also formed part of Daniel Heinsius's definition of the genre in his commentary on Horace's satires (1612). Modeling his concept on Aristotle's famous definition of tragedy, Heinsius specified, moreover, that satire's combination of serious or vitupera-tive intent with a style that varied from being simple and informal to harsh, sharp, or humorous and witty stirred emotive reactions of hatred, indignation, or laughter (De Smet 1996, 50).

Unsurprisingly, Neo-Latin authors sometimes applied the term *satyra* loosely, if not as a misnomer. The young Erasmus, for instance, named some of his early poems *satirae* before changing each of their titles to *elegia*, and seems not to have had a clear understanding of the *sermo* (Tournoy 1994, 99). Alternatively in 1607, Antonio Cerri, a little known humanist from Rimini, defined *satyra* "over and above its usual accep-tation" (*praeter tritam notionem*) as "just an accusatory way of speaking" (*satyram solum esse maledicum dicendi genus*), which he conceded was often mixed in nature. Cerri's *Satyrarum scholasticarum centuriae duae* (*Two Hundreds of Scholastic Satires*), in which this explanation occurs (Cerri 1607, *centuria prima*, 1r), consists of two sets of miscellaneous, if sharply critical, remarks in prose, that other humanists might have called *lucubrationes* ("nocturnal studies"). Likewise, the *Satyrae medicae* (*Medical Satires*, 1722) by Georg Franck von Franckenau (1643–1704) are not poetic, but con-tain the physician's sundry notes made during his extensive reading (Kivistö 2007). Somewhat more conformist is the late seventeenth-century chemist from Poitiers Just Bonin, who catered to his contemporaries' taste for pithy expression by parodying the medical profession's therapeutic principles in just twenty aphorisms, collectively labeled as a *Satyra in medicos quosdam de trivio* (*Satire on the Three Basic Remedies, against Some Doctors*; in Nicolas de Blégny's *Zodiacus Medico-Gallicus* [*French Medical Zodiac*, 1680]).

Although the Hellenist Isaac Casaubon (1559–1614) settled the etymological ques-tion in his authoritative *De satyrica Graecorum poesi et Romanorum satira* (*On the Greek Satyr-Play and Roman Satire*; 1605), goat-legged satyrs continued to form a popular motif on the illustrated title-pages of editions of both ancient and Neo-Latin satirical texts. The spurious explanation of satire's "satyr-like" origins was rehearsed until well into the eighteenth century, providing a seemingly authoritative justification for any bawdy content. Other enduring emblems of satire were the mirror (calling for self-knowledge), a lifted or torn-off mask (condemning hypocrisy), and the fool's cap (a sign that the satirist's irreverence must be endured, if not indulged).

Despite the widespread poetological comments, then, the Neo-Latins' actual writ-erly practice very much depended on a deliberate imitation of both ancient and more recent models: verbal, titular, and thematic echoes served as a self-imposed genetic imprint to create family resemblances that, as much as any formal traits, marked out a text as a particular type of satire. As for the satyr-play, Euripides's *Cyclops* (fifth century BCE) was, and is, the only fully extant example of its kind; notwithstanding some sixteenth-century experimentation with dramatic "satyr" in French or Italian such as Giambattista Cinzio's *Egle* (1545), the *Cyclops* itself did not yield any notable imitations, other than Florent Chrestien's Latin verse translation, published in 1605.

FORMAL VERSE SATIRE

The first verse satires emerged from the humanist milieu in northern and central Italy. An early witness was a satirical fragment (*satyra*) by Zanobi da Strada (d. 1361), criticizing a lawyer. In the fifteenth century, Gregorio Correr, Giovanni Michele Alberto Carrara, Gaspare Tribraco, and Lorenzo Lippi da Colle all left manuscript satires, published only in the twentieth century (Carrara 1967 and 1987; Correr 1973; Tribraco 1972; Lippi da Colle 1978). Better known are Francesco Filelfo's *Satirarum hecatostichon decades decem* (*Ten Decades of Satires of Hundred Lines*), ten books, each consisting of ten satires of precisely one hundred lines in length. Written between 1428 and 1448, they reflect the humanist's peregrinations from Florence to Siena, Bologna, and Milan. The complete set is preserved in eight principal manuscripts, with numerous others containing selections, whilst the first "decade" was printed in Milan in 1476 (Filelfo 2005). The collection's fanciful symmetry seems to go against the grain of the disorder associated with a hodgepodge genre. However, the satires cover various polemics; the opinions expressed in them are far from being in unison; and the tone ranges from virulent invective to a more poised, didactic stance. Although in 1503 the Modenese schoolteacher Francesco Rococciolo (ca. 1470–1528) only explicitly named Tribraco as a recent satirist in his *Satyrus* (a verse commentary on Juvenal; Haye 2008, 278–79), Filelfo was the only one of these early poets to exercise some enduring influence, even outside Italy; from the middle of the sixteenth century onward, however, his satires slipped into oblivion.

Also noteworthy are the two books of ten and twelve *sermones*, respectively, in Giovanni Aurelio Augurelli's collected poems of 1505; an earlier version survives in manuscript (Yale University, Beinecke Rare Book and Manuscript Library, Mellon MS 22). Augurelli (ca. 1456–1524) deliberately advocated a soft, Horatian approach to satire, preferring "gentle laughter" (*levi risu*) over outright, personalized denunciation (1505, 48b). A similar, gentle tone is evident in Tito Vespasiano Strozzi's *sermones*, published posthumously in Strozzi and his son's collected poetry (1513). If both Augurelli and Strozzi were criticized for their satires' lack of bite or bile (Simons 2013, 143), their approach heralded a strand of poetically accomplished, but rather toothless, moralizing verse that persisted until the eighteenth century.

More satirists emerged in the 1530s: the *Two Satires* (*Satyre due*, 1536) by the Paduan reformer Pietro Cittadella have yet to be investigated. The *Sermones* by the Ragusan Damjan Benešić (Damianus Benessa, 1477–1539), who enjoyed close ties with Italian humanist circles, remained in manuscript (Dubrovnik, Biblioteka Samostana Male Braće, MS 78, written before 1539). However, in 1531–32, the Neapolitan poet Giano Anisio (Ianus Anysius, ca. 1472–ca. 1540) published six books of verse satires (containing some fifty pieces in all, of varying length) as the second volume of his *Varia poemata et satyrae* (*Various Poems and Satires*). Anisio claimed that he had been composing satires from boyhood—ever since Juvenal (1.30: *difficile est saturam non scribere* ["it is difficult not to write satire"]), the satirical impulse was construed as irrepressible—and that he was the first to reintroduce satire to his homeland since antiquity (1531, 3r; 1532, fols. 75r, 76r). Mostly Anisio took a moderate attitude: "it is not safe to poke at every hole" (*Omnia non digito explorare foramina tutum est*; 1532, 26r). With nearly each satire addressing a different individual—Christ, popes Julius II and Leo X, several cardinals, poets such as his fellow Neapolitan Jacopo Sannazaro (1458–1530), two of the poet's brothers, and so on—the collection offers great insight into the satirist's milieu.

From the 1540s, Latin verse satire experienced a lull among the Italians: bar some exceptions such as the three admonishing *sermones* that Girolamo Faletti addressed to the young Alfonso II d'Este (Sacré 1992, 205), we have to wait for the Jesuit Giovanni Lorenzo Lucchesini (1638–ca. 1710) to berate various faultfinders as well as the corruption of youth in his *Specimen didascalici carminis et satyrae* (*Showcase of Didactic Poetry, and Satires*, 1672). Two decades later, the Roman official Lodovico Sergardi (1660–1726) directed his Juvenalian wrath against a fellow member of the Academy of Arcadia, Gian Vincenzo Gravina. Another late practitioner was the Ragusan nobleman Junije Antonio Restić (Junius de Restiis, 1755–1814), whose twenty-five verse satires appeared at Padua in the posthumous edition of Restić's *Carmina* (*Poems*, 1816).

Developments in Quattrocento Italy, in terms of editions of ancient satires and the first circulation in print of Filelfo's *hecatosticha*, encouraged an early spate of satire production in the Low Countries. The region was, moreover, characterized by a particularly strong humanistic interest in moral literature, which brought Persius and Horace to the fore—though less so Juvenal, thought to be obscene (Tournoy 1998). Following in the footsteps of Petrus Montanus (1467/8–1507), whose "twelve" (in fact eleven) satires appeared between 1501 and 1507, with part of the missing ninth published in 1529, Gerard Geldenhouwer (Gerardus Noviomagus, 1482–1542) addressed eight satires to "the truly religious" (*ad verae religionis cultores*; 1515), targeting ungodly priests and monks. In the 1540s and early 1550s, the historian and schoolmaster Lambertus Hortensius (1518–73) produced several "biting" satires, eight of which were published at Utrecht in 1552; a second, partial book of satires containing a further eight *satyrae*, numbered 5–13, survives in manuscript (Universiteitsbibliotheek Utrecht, MS 828). The Leiden statesman Janus Dousa the Elder (1545–1604) attacked his former friend "Fannius" (the German scholar Obertus Giphanius) for his alleged intentions to plagiarize in two satires, published in Dousa's début collection of poetry of 1569 (Heesakkers and Reinders 1993, 21–27). By the 1609 edition, however, Dousa's satires had increased to eight and dealt with a broader range of subjects, though some of them were evidently left unfinished. Jan van Havre's *Arx virtutis* (*Fortress of Virtue*, 1627; Laureys 2008), and the stern *Sermones familiares* (*Familiar Satires*) by the Antwerp magistrate Pieter Scholier (Petrus Scholirius, 1582–1635) reveal once more a moralistic tendency. Remarkably, Scholier's satires were assembled under the title *Diogenes Cynicus* (*Diogenes the Cynic*, 1635), a figure more often associated with the outlook of Menippean satire than with its Lucilian counterpart. Indeed, in the 1683 edition, with its extensive commentary by Albert Le Roy (1683), the satirist's portrait is tellingly flanked by the goddess of wisdom, Athena, and the scornful Cynic. In the Enlightenment, the Dutch physician Gerhard Nicolaas Heerkens (1726–1801) composed, whilst still a youth, four Latin satires, published in 1746 under the pseudonym "Curillus"; a later edition, in 1758, contained a further three satires (Haskell 2013).

Meanwhile, in the mid-sixteenth century, the Bavarian-born reformer Thomas Naogeorgus (1508–63) placed his *Satyrae* (1555) in the wake of Filelfo as well as the classical canon, claiming (not quite accurately!) that the satirical genre was hardly known or practiced in the German-speaking regions and that it generally suffered from a bad reputation for being offensive, brazen, and immodest. In the following decade, the Tübingen professor Nicodemus Frischlin (1547–90) launched eight satires against the Catholic convert Jacob Rabe (published in 1607). His contemporary Hannard van Gameren (Gamerius), who taught Greek at Ingolstadt, before moving to Tongeren and Harderwijk, supported the Lutherans' cause in his *Two Satires* (*Satyrae duae*), published first without an indication of year or place (possibly at Antwerp), and then at Munich in 1568. Probably the best-known German exponent of Neo-Latin verse satire is the Jesuit Jakob Balde (1604–68), whose nimble pen sang, amongst others, *The Glory of Medicine* (*Medicinae gloria*) and derided the emaciated appearance of philosophers (Freyburger, Lefèvre, and Schilling 2005).

The French no doubt also benefited from Filelfo, whose satires were reprinted in Paris in 1508 and 1518. Augurelli's *sermones* likewise circulated in France, but in a letter to Cardinal Du Bellay of 1547–1548, Salmon Macrin belittled Augurelli's supposed Horatian stance, which he thought strayed too far from its model (Scheurer and Petris 2008, 443). Among French Neo-Latin satirists feature the eminent names of Marc-Antoine Muret; Etienne de la Boétie, who addressed a lengthy verse satire to his friend Michel de Montaigne; and Chancellor Michel de L'Hospital, as well as occasional poets such as the physician Bonaventure Grangier. The expatriate Julius Caesar Scaliger (1484–1558), who was equally critical of Augurelli (Thurn 2008, 262), composed an unusual series of *Teretismata* (*Twitterings*), which appeared in his posthumous *Poems* from 1574 onwards. The first of these is a "satyra" that ironically questions the usefulness of writing in a world of depravity; then follow (partly autobiographical) pieces entitled *Poeta* (*Poet*), *Medicus* (*Doctor*), *Ego* (*I*), *Conviva* (*Table Companion*), *Pater* (*Father*), *Otium* (*Leisure*), and lastly *Machla*, a virulent satire on "a wanton woman."

On the Iberian peninsula, Botello had three significant precursors. The posthumous *Poetic Works* (*Opera poetica*, 1600) of Jaime Juan Falcó (1522–1594) contain nine formal verse satires: two attack gamblers (*aleatores*), whilst others target jurisprudents and the weaknesses of the law court—all of this mixed with moralist musings about contentment, the prevalence of man's soul, or the different stages in life. Curiously, Falcó also experimented with prosody: his seventh satire deliberately emulated Horace's first satire, but with each single line beginning and ending with a monosyllabic word. The three *sermones*, on the other hand, of Hernán Ruiz de Villegas (ca. 1510–after 1571), a former student of Vives at Leuven, remained in manuscript with the rest of his Latin poetry until 1734. The third representative is Francisco Pacheco (ca. 1540–1599), a canon from southern Spain, whose moralizing *Sermones* date from 1572–1573.

Elsewhere, it is harder to detect strong regional traditions. The British Isles, for instance, were not short of satirists, but verse satire adhered less closely to the classical canon. George Buchanan, famous for his anti-monastic *Franciscanus* (*The Franciscan*, composed in the 1530s), nonetheless left a *Satire against the Cardinal of Lorraine* (*Satyra in Carolum Lotharingium Cardinalem*), written in the wake of the Saint Bartholomew's Day Massacre (1572). In the next century, however, the Scot William Hog or Hogg (Gulielmus Hogaeus, ca. 1655–ca. 1702), translator of Milton, combined the popular exercise of a poetic paraphrase of the Old Testament Book of Ecclesiastes with the reproof of satire for his *Satyra sacra vanitatem* [*sic*] *mundi et rerum humanarum* (*Sacred Satire on the Vanities of the World and Human Affairs*, 1685). Last but not least, let us mention the Polish nobleman Antoni Poniński, whose *Sarmatides* (alluding to the ancient Sarmatians as the ancestors of the Poles), published under the pen name Jan Maximilian Krolikiewicz in 1741, expound on "nature," "religion," "education," "Polish affairs" and so on.

MENIPPEAN SATIRE

Alongside verse satire, polemicists found a versatile vehicle for reprehension and exposure in Menippean satire. Given the fragmented transmission of Varro, the Flemish humanist Justus Lipsius turned to Seneca's *Apocolocyntosis* (*The "Gourdification"* [*of the Divine Claudius*], 54 CE; the only example of this Varronian strand to survive more or less intact) as a model for his *Satyra Menippea: somnium, sive lusus in nostri aevi criticos* (*A Menippean Satire: The Dream, or Mockery of Contemporary Critics*, 1581), an attack on careless and unfounded interventions in textual criticism. Lipsius cast his satire as a dream set in ancient Rome, during which the narrator witnesses a senatorial debate featuring both ancient and more contemporary figures. The *Somnium* inspired a host of oneiric satires: in his acrimonious scuffle with the Catholic pamphleteer Kaspar Schoppe, for example, the Protestant Joseph Scaliger could count, not only on Daniel Heinsius's *Hercules tuam fidem* (*By Hercules!*, 1608) and *Virgula divina* (*Magic Wand*, 1609), but also on Caspar Barth's *Cave canem* (*Beware of the Dog!*, 1612) to defend his name. Other examples include Nicolas Rigault's *Funus parasiticum* (*Parasite's Funeral*, 1596–1601), Petrus Cunaeus's *Sardi Venales* (*Sardinians for Sale* [a proverbial tag meaning "worthless people"], 1612), and the anonymous *Monmori Parasitosycophantosophistae Apochytrapotheôsis* (*Casserolideification of Montmaur the parasite, sycophant and sophist*, ca. 1643).

In its longer incarnation, supposedly imitating Petronius's *Satyricon*, prosimetric satire allied itself closely with the novel, finding vernacular equivalents in the Spanish picaresque or the French *roman comique* (De Smet 1996; IJsewijn 1999): typically, a rather naïve protagonist finds himself wrapped up in a series of outlandish or quotidian adventures, which allow for humorous (and amorous) encounters, candid observation, the sampling of different philosophies, and much social criticism. If modern-day classical scholars question the wisdom of linking Petronius to the protean *Menippea*, it is important to remember that humanists considered the *Satyricon* a veiled anatomy of Nero's time. The principal innovator of the genre, John Barclay, and his detractors certainly thought of his *Euphormionis Lusinini satyricon* (*The Satire of Euphormio from*

Lusinia 1605–1607) as a satire, in which doctors, venal aristocrats, and the Jesuits, portrayed as the servants of "Acignius" (an anagram of "Ignatius [Ignacius]" of Loyola), run the gauntlet. Barclay's followers include the *Gaeomemphionis Cantaliensis satyricon* (*Satire of the Critic of the World from the Cantal*, 1628), attributed to François Guyet, the *Satyricon in corruptae iuventutis mores corruptos* (*Satire Against the Corrupt Morals of the Young*, 1631) by Leiden's maverick professor Jan Bodecher Benningh (who also wrote verse satires), and the *Misoponeri satyricon* (*Satire of the Hater of Evil*, 1617) attributed to Casaubon (1617). Noteworthy is also the *Eudemia* (*Land of the Good People*, 1637, enlarged 1647), partly modeled on Thomas More's *Utopia*, in which Gian Vittorio Rossi (Ianus Nicius Erythraeus) paints a detailed, if rather disjointed, portrait of Rome under the papacy of Urban VIII.

FLUID BOUNDARIES: OTHER FORMS OF SATIRIC WRITING

It is already amply clear that both isometric and prosimetric satire had fluid boundaries. The satirical spirit can certainly be found in other genres, such as the epigram, the pasquinade, mock-didactic verse (such as Friedrich Dedekind's *Grobianus* [*Boor*] of 1549), or joke collections such as the *Facetiae facetiarum* (*The Jokes of Jokes*, 1615) and *Nugae venales* (*Jokes for Sale*, 1642). Also popular is the epistolary form, as in Ulrich von Hutten's famous *Letters of Obscure Men* (Kivistö 2002; Bowen 2006), Théodore de Bèze's *Epistola magistri Passavantii* (*The Letter of Magister Passavant*, 1553; de Bèze 2004), or indeed some of the Greek verse epistles by Filelfo (Robin 1984). Several of Filelfo's satires are, moreover, conceived of as poetic letters, as was indeed Restić's tenth *satyra*, perpetuating the close ties between the two genres, that Pomponius Porphyrio (second-third century CE) already discerned in his scholia on Horace. Even Casaubon declared that "one should not tolerate those who think that [Horace's] books of *letters* ought to be excluded from the designation and number of *satires*" (*Ferendi non sunt, qui epistolarum libros satirarum appellatione ac numero censerint excludendos*), adding that even Lucilius had cast some of his satires as letters (Casaubon 1605, 292). Thus Pacheco's *Sermones* veer—despite their *sermones* label—between Juvenalian satire and Horatian epistle (Pozuelo Calero 1993 and 2000). Other examples where the distinction is blurred are Nathan Chytraeus's *Epistola satyrica contra pestem* (*Satirical Letter against the Plague*, 1578) and, above all, L'Hospital's posthumous *Epistolae seu sermones* (*Letters, or Satires*, 1585).

In the wake of their ancient models, verse satires often featured short dialogic exchanges between the poet and his reader or an imaginary adversary; some satirists, such as William King in his *Sermo pedestris* (*Pedestrian Conversation/Satire*, 1739), would exploit verse dialogue in full. Well before then, however, the rediscovery and Latin translations of Lucian produced a wealth of satirical dialogues in prose or prosimetrum, which have been well studied (Marsh 1998; Robinson 1979). Leon Battista Alberti's *Momus* (*Blame*, the name of the fault-finding protagonist, 1440s), with its exuberant plot and veiled allusions to the papacy of Eugene IV, is one of the best-known examples of this burgeoning trend, which also includes Giovanni Pontano's *Asinus* (*The Ass*, ca. 1488) and *Charon* (1467), or Willibald Pirckheimer's *Eccius Dedolatus* (*Eck Planed Down*, 1520), debunking Luther's opponent, the theologian Johannes Eck.

Neo-Latin satire also enjoyed close links with oratory. This is evident in the paradoxical encomium, which again relates to the Lucianic tradition, and of which Erasmus's *Praise of Folly* (1511) is the prime exponent: others wrote eulogies of animals such as the fly, ant, or ass; body parts such as the foot; and physical conditions or ailments such as gout, drunkenness, or fever—many of which were conveniently collected in Caspar Dornau's *Amphitheatrum sapientiae Socraticae ioco-seriae* (*Amphitheater of Seriocomic Socratic Wisdom*, 1619). Occasionally, humanists such as Juan Luis Vives, Petrus Nannius, or Francesco Benci took recourse to the Menippean mode for a public address, mostly in an academic context.

There is arguably kinship between satire and cento-writing; that is, the composition of a new poem by rearranging verse fragments from a chosen author (e.g., Homer, Virgil, Petrarch), because of the cento's inherent wit and parody, not to mention its jumbled nature. Few self-confessed satirists, however, truly experimented with this form, possibly because the Roman satirists' restricted number of lines did not offer sufficient scope for scrambled writing; still, Janus Dousa rose to the challenge with his *Centones aliquot Luciliani* (*Some Lucilian Centos*, 1597). Miscellaneous borrowings, however, are common, especially in Menippean satire, where theorists debated whether the poetic element of the prosimetric narrative ought to be original or not. The *Mercurius: satyra sive somnium* (*Mercury: Satire, or Dream*, 1618) by the Florentine Balduino de Monte Simoncelli actually indicated its sources in the margins, as many centos did. Later, Johan Bergenhielm (1629–1704) explicitly turned to the patchwork form for his *Cento satyricus in hodiernos motus septentrionis concinnatus* (*A Satirical Cento on the Present-Day Disturbances in the North*, 1700; Aili 1994). The pamphlet, which relates to the Great Northern War (1700–21), draws on (unacknowledged) prose and verse quotations from a broad range of authors; moreover, it takes the form of a play, not adhering at all to the traditional isometric manifestations of the cento form, but perhaps harking back to the elusive notion of dramatic satire.

Finally, macaronic poetry too, with its characteristic mix of languages, lent itself well to parodic and satirical purposes. Often using Latin (or dog Latin) as one of its components, macaronic poetry entered humanist culture in Northern Italy in the late fifteenth and early sixteenth centuries with Tifi Odasi (Odaxius, 1451–1492) and Teofilo Folengo (1491–1544), writing under the pseudonym "Merlinus Coccaius." However, it also found practitioners in other language areas. Thus Rémy Belleau's *Dictamen metrificum, sive de bello Huguenotico* (*Versified Writing; or, On the Huguenot War*, ca. 1562–1567) denounced the raiding bands of mercenaries tearing through France during the Wars of Religion. Prose or prosimetric equivalents include the *Themata medica de beanorum, archibeanorum, beanulorum et cornutorum quorumcunque affectibus et curatione* (*Medical Topics *on the Sufferings and Curation of Any Greenhorns, Arch-Greenhorns, Baby-Greenhorns, and the Horned*, 1626), a mock-medical treatise, no doubt authored by some German students, on the "ailments" befalling university freshmen or greenhorns (*beani* or *bejauni*, derived from the French *bec-jaune* ["yellow beak"] or, in German, *Gehörnte* ["horned ones"]).

"WHATEVER HUMANS DO . . . FORMS THE STUFFING OF OUR LITTLE BOOK"

Conscious of Juvenal 1.85–86 (*Quicquid agunt homines . . . nostri libelli farrago est*), Neo-Latin satirists took issue with the full range of shortcomings in human society: avarice, ambition, extravagance, and the many incommodities in life were readily carped at, whether as single topics or as part of a gamut of moral decay. Thus, the Bohemian scholar and poet Bohulslav Hasištejnský of Lobkovice (Hassenstenius; 1462–1510), who had been educated in Italy, denounced the sinking mores of the Bohemian aristocracy and people in his *Ad Sanctum Venceslaum Satira* (*Satire to St. Wenceslas*). The anonymous Menippean *Virtus vindicata, sive Polieni Rhodiensis satyra* (*Virtue Vindicated, or Satire of Polienus from Rhodes*, 1617) even took on "the depravity of the world's inhabitants" (*in depravatos orbis incolas*). In this, the satirist's outlook is variably that of a bewildered or amused observer, a belligerent champion of virtue, or a censorious judge who would like to distance himself from the theater of the world; yet he often finds himself a reluctant participant, compelled to admonish and correct.

Since Neo-Latin authors often prided themselves on their erudition, linguistic ability, and good judgement, attacks on ignorance and hollow displays of learning were also common. Thus, in the second of Antonio Codro Urceo's (1446–1500) two verse satires, the poet admits that his railing against ignorance might make him hateful, yet he feels compelled to write his satire (*coactus/haec scribo*): sheer indignation makes the Neo-Latin satirist break silence, just as it did his ancient precursor. Developing an idea already present in Horace (*Epistles* 2.1.117) and Juvenal (1.1–18), satirists eagerly targeted scribblers and penny poets: witness Pierio Valeriano's *De studiorum conditione sermo* (*Satire on the Condition of Studies*), published in his *Praeludia* (*Preludes*, 1509); Montanus's eighth satire *De poetis* (*On Poets*); Falcó's second satire *In malos poetas* (*Against Bad Poets*); or the anonymous *Satyra in poetastros O-c-enses* (*Satire against the O-c—ian Poetasters*, 1702), disparaging the poems on the death of William III and the succession of Queen Anne.

The imperative of imitation and the broad moral concern with virtue or happiness, however, did not stop Neo-Latin hecklers from exposing problems that were specific to their age: previous examples have already shown that, unsurprisingly, ecclesiastical misconduct and confessional differences are strongly present in Neo-Latin satire, on either the Protestant or the Catholic side. Pacheco, in a short but striking passage of his first *Sermo* (1.127–35), denounces slavery and the cruel torture that maintains it, whilst Balde decries excessive smoking (to which he himself was prone) in his *Satyra contra abusum tabaci* (*Satire Against the Abuse of Tobacco*). Nationalist traits, too, were grist to the satirist's mill. Around 1500, the Dutchman Kempo Thessaliensis, who studied in Paris for a while, denounced the scams of French tradesmen in his *De dolis Gallorum satyra* (*Satire on the Tricks of the French*, 1500) before inciting the French to a more virtuous life (Tournoy 1994, 107–8). In 1630–1636, Johann Lauremberg complained in his lengthy and multifaceted *Satyra qua rerum bonarum abusus et vitia quaedam seculi perstringuntur* (*A Satire Surveying the Abuses of Good Things and Certain Contemporary Vices*) about the encompassing vogue of all things French, whether it concerned affectation in language or in attitude (the *préciosité* emerging from witty seventeenth-century salon culture), clothing, or other pernicious customs, such as dueling (Lauremberg 1861, 91). And Heerkens weighed the respective merits (and demerits) of Paris and Frisia in his *Satyra de moribus Parhisiorum et Frisiae* (*Satire on the Customs of the Parisians and of Frisia*, 1750), once again at a time when the Dutch thought French was very much *à la mode* (Haskell 2013, 235).

We have already seen that the medical sphere likewise caused its fair share of ruffled feathers: attacks against incompetent doctors go back at least to medieval times. However, what particularly appealed to early modern satirists was the restorative concept of poetry, whereby the satirist is construed as an "anatomist," cutting, cauterizing, purging, and occasionally offering a sweetened pill in order to heal society, a notion that led to the frequent use of medical meta-language (Kivistö 2002). Yet therapeutic satire can slide into wounding invective: the *De morborum generibus* (*On the Kinds of Illnesses*) taken from a *satyra imprecatoria* ("cursing satire") by Montanus and published in the Strasbourg edition of Baptista Fiera's *Coena de herbarum virtutibus* (*Dinner, on the Virtues of Herbs*, 1529), is a virtuosic listing of all the illnesses the poet wishes upon greedy tax collectors.

Predictably, Neo-Latin satire is an overwhelmingly male affair. Despite the rediscovery in 1493 of a verse satire, which was wrongly ascribed to Sulpicia, the poetess of Pliny's day, but which the Renaissance thought genuine (Stevenson 2005, 558), the early modern period produced no satirists of note among its already scant female Neo-Latin writers, even if some of their vernacular counterparts (such as Louise Labé, Arcangela Tarabotti, Margaret Cavendish, or Madame Deshoulières) are now valued for their satirical wit. Nonetheless, it was said of Ann Baynard (1672–1697) that "having an eye to the saying of that Great Poet, *Semper ego Auditor tantum* ["Am I to be only a listener all my days?" Juvenal 1.1], she set herself to the Composing of many things in the Latine Tongue, which were rare and useful in their kind" (Prude 1697, 25), and indeed that she composed "some severe satyrs in the Latin Toung" (Stevenson 2005, 381–82; Cowper ca. 1700–1710, 193). Sadly, Baynard's writings are lost. Conversely, satirists viewed women themselves with great suspicion or according to stereotypes, as they did the institution of marriage: in the mid-fifteenth century, for instance, Cristoforo da Fano inveighed in one of his *satyrulae* (*Little Satires*, ca. 1455–1460) against "the many men who in marrying a woman consider only her beauty or the size of her dowry" (*Satyrula contra multos qui in ducenda uxore solam formam consyderant aut dotis quantitatem*); the Humiliati friar took inspiration from Juvenal's notorious misogynist sixth satire, but also from Jerome's treatise *Against Jovinian* (393 CE, advocating virginity and asceticism; Piacentini 2007).

This leaves the question of Latin and the vernacular. While critics have long shown that Neo-Latin and vernacular satire often developed in parallel or shared analogous concerns (Pagrot 1961; Hess 1971; Blanchard 1995), the cross-fertilization between the two is not yet fully understood. Neo-Latin verse satire certainly inspired few translations or adaptations, compared to Horace, Persius, or Juvenal, which from the sixteenth century onwards were much more readily rendered or emulated (the notions often overlap): in Italian by Ludovico Ariosto; in Spanish by Jerónimo de Villegas; in Dutch by Cornelis van Ghistele and "Emilius Elmeguidi" (Guilelmus de Mey [Ter Meer 1983]); in French by Mathurin Régnier, Vauquelin de La Fresnaye, or Nicolas Boileau-Despréaux; in English by Thomas Drant, Barten Holyday, or John Dryden—the list is woefully inadequate. Only from the late seventeenth century do sparse vernacular versions of Neo-Latin verse satire emerge: Sigmund von Birken's *Die truckene Trunkenheit* (*The Dry Drunkenness*, 1658) modeled itself on Balde's anti-tobacco satire. Another instance is *Santolius vindicatus* (1696), a poem by the Jesuit Jean-Antoine du Cerceau ridiculing Jean-Baptiste de Santeuil's inordinate pride in his Latinity, which du Cerceau himself "translated" as *Santeuil vengé* (*Santeuil Vindicated*). The original, however, is not a regular *sermo*, but alternates octosyllabic and dodecasyllabic verse. Similarly, in 1743, William Major appears to have been both the anonymous translator ("a Gentleman, Late of Balliol College Oxford") and hidden author of the *Four Satires* (*Satyrae Quatuor*), published in London in 1735 under the initials "D. G." and subsequently presented as a recently deceased "Native of Holland." Major's Latin satires, too, are irregular, since he uses elegiac couplets rather than just hexameters. More conventional is Girolamo Pallini's anonymous transposition, in the second half of the eighteenth century, of eight of Quinto Settano's (i.e., Sergardi's) satires in *terza rima*. The precedence and relative innocuousness of the classical texts, as well as the short-lived topical interest of many Neo-Latin satires, and a high degree of allusiveness and intertextual play, which sometimes descended into deliberate obscurity, are perhaps to blame for this meager traffic from Neo-Latin verse into the vernacular. Moreover, Neo-Latin mostly involves a deliberate linguistic choice. Evidently, some satirists also tested their bite in their mother tongue: Pacheco, for instance, penned a Spanish *Sátira contra la mala poesía* (*Satire Against Bad Poetry*) which survived in several manuscripts (Montera Delgado 1993).

There was greater latitude in the case of satirical prose or prosimetrum. The anonymous English "translator" of Lipsius's *Somnium* offset his own modest endeavor against that of highly acclaimed interpreters of the classics such as John Dryden in his preface to *The Parliament of Criticks* in 1702. The anti-Jesuit satire *Conclave Ignatii* (*Ignatius's Conclave*, 1610–1611), attributed to John Donne, appeared almost simultaneously in English (1611); within the next half-century, *Ignatius: His Conclave, or His Inthronisation in a Late Election in Hell* was reprinted no less than five times. Barclay's *Satyricon* knew four French adaptations—by Jean Tournet (1625), Sébastien (or Jean?) Nau (1626), Jean Bérault (1640), and Jean-Baptiste Drouet de Maupertuis (1712–13); in 1683, Nicolaas

Jachirides Wieringa produced a Dutch version. The *Comus, sive Phagesiposia cimmeria* (*Comus, or the Cimmerian banquet*, 1608) by the Leuven professor Erycius Puteanus gave rise to both a Dutch and a French version, whereas Bergenhielm's *Cento satyricus* sparked a version in Swedish verse and a German adaptation (Wittrock 1922).

Conversely, some vernacular satirical works proved so popular that a Latin translation was warranted: the late medieval satire by Sebastian Brant, *Das Narrenschiff* (*The Ship of Fools*, 1494), was translated into Latin by Brant's student Jakob Locher as *Navis stultifera* (1497). In the Parisian colleges, the satires and epistles of Boileau Despréaux (1636–1711) invited—rather ironically, given Boileau's dislike of modern Latin writers—various translations into Latin verse by Jean Maury (1669), Antoine Hennegrave (1710), Michel Godeau (1708, 1709, 1737), and Bénigne Grenan (1706), as well as an anonymous work pitting Juvenal rendered into French against a Latinized Boileau (1677; Briesemeister 1985, 209–10). Lastly, Traiano Boccalini's *Ragguagli del Parnaso* (*Reports from Parnassus*, 1612–1613) circulated in various vernacular translations as well as (partially) in Latin.

VEILED UNVEILERS

Satyram scribo, quod solent qui nomen suum nobilitare gaudent ("I write a satire, as those are wont who enjoy glorifying their name"), declared the unidentified author of *Amatus Fornacius: amator ineptus* (*Amatus Fornacius: The Clumsy Lover*, 1633), a good-natured lampoon of seventeenth-century social mores emanating no doubt from Leiden University's student milieu (De Smet 1989). As tongue-in-cheek as the statement is, the satirical vein has indeed inspired some of the most distinguished writers in Neo-Latin literature and humanist scholarship (Alberti, Filelfo, Erasmus, and Lipsius, to recall but a few); many others hid behind a pseudonym. Sobriquets were commonplace for the victims of satire and for toponyms, first, because this was thought to be in line with a number of ancient models; secondly, because of the monikers' satirical potential; and thirdly, because reprisals were not unthinkable. The satirists' avowed cautiousness no doubt partially explains why even in the age of print a good number of satires remained in manuscript. Condemnations could be long-lasting. Banned soon after publication, the Menippean satire *Nescimus quid vesper serus vehat* (*Little Do We Know What Late Evening Brings*, 1619–1620), written under the alias Vincentius Liberius Hollandus, but ascribed to the Venetian lawyer Niccolò Crasso (De Smet 1996, 201–8), remained on the Catholic Church's Index of Forbidden Books until the Index was abolished in 1966. So did Barclay's *Satyricon*. The same Index also listed Nicolas Chorier's pornographic dialogues, the *Satyra sotadica de arcanis amoris et Veneris* (*Sotadean* [alluding to Sotades, an obscene Greek poet of the third century BCE] *Satire on the Secrets of Love and Venus*, 1660), spuriously published under the name of the poetess Aloysia Sigaea (Luisa Sigea, ca. 1520–60; Martínez de Bujanda 2002, 103, 219, 254). It is ironic, however, that Crasso's satire, which goes back to the aftermath of the Venetian Interdict (1606–1607) and Venice's claims to jurisdiction over the Adriatic, contained within it a long section on book censorship: the satirist, after all, is the censors' censor, locked in a never-ending battle for the freedom to speak, for the greater good of his fellow man, and for the general reparation of society.

Suggested Reading

Satire is one of the most belabored literary concepts, but broader studies concentrating primarily on Neo-Latin satire are few: in this respect, IJsewijn's foundational articles (1975, 1976, 1999) remain the first port of call; new appraisals are provided by Porter (2014, prose) and Marsh (2014, verse). Pagrot (1961) is a thoroughly documented study on the theory of formal verse satire from antiquity to the eighteenth century, in Latin and the vernacular, but Debailly's (2012) study of Lucilian satire in France also traces the genre's characteristics. R. De Smet (1994) and Haye and Schnoor (2008) provide a range of studies devoted to (mostly) Neo-Latin satire, while Simons's analysis of the models claimed by verse satirists (2013) contains a wealth of up-to-date references. Blanchard (1995) and I. De Smet (1996) provide good starting-points for Menippean satire, but should be complemented with more recent work; for the Lucianic tradition, in particular, see Robinson (1979) and Marsh (1998). Kivistö (2009), on medical analogy in satire, offers an exemplary, well-integrated thematic approach.

References

Aili, Hans. 1994. "Swedish War Propaganda in Latin, German, and Swedish." In *ACNL* 1994, 271–83.

Anisio, Giano. 1531. *Varia poemata et Satyrae*. Naples: Sultzbach.

———. 1532. *Satyrae*. Naples: Sultzbach.

Blanchard, W. Scott. 1995. *Scholars' bedlam: Menippean Satire in the Renaissance*. Lewisburg: Bucknell University Press.

Botello de Moraes y Vasconcelos, Francisco. 1739. *Satyrae*. Salamanca: Nicolaus Josephus Villargordo.

Bowen, Barbara. 2006. "Obscure Men and Smelly Goats in Neo-Latin Satire." In *Laughter and Power*, edited by John Parkin and John Phillips, 19–36. Oxford: Peter Lang.

Briesemeister, Dietrich. 1985. "Französische klassische Literatur in neulateinischer Übersetzung." In *ACNL* 1985, 205–15.

Carrara, Giovanni M. A. da. 1967. *Opera poetica, philosophica, rhetorica, theologica*. Edited and translated by Giovanni Giraldi. Novara: Istituto Geografico de Agostini.

———. 1987. *Sermones objurgatorii*. Edited by Giovanni Giraldi. Milan: Pergamena.

Casaubon, Isaac. 1605. *De Satyrica Graecorum Poesi et Romanorum Satira*. Paris: Drouart.

[Casaubon, Isaac?]. 1617. *Misoponeri satyricon. Cum notis aliquot ad obscuriora prosae loca, et Graecorum interpretatione*. Leiden: "Sebastianus Wolzius".

Cerri, Antonio. 1607. *Satyrarum scholiasticarum centuriae duae*. Rimini: Simbenei.

Correr, Gregorio. 1973. *Liber Satyrarum*. Edited by Joseph R. Berrigan. *Humanistica Lovaniensia* 22:10–38.

Cowper, Sarah. ca. 1700–1710. *Miscellany* (MS). Hertford, Hertfordshire Archives and Local Studies. D/EP F44.

Debailly, Pascal. 2001. "La satire lucilienne et la poétique du blâme." In *Poétiques de la Renaissance: Le modèle italien, le monde franco-bourguignon et leur héritage en France au XVI* siècle, edited by Perrine Galand-Hallyn and Fernand Hallyn, 379–89. Geneva: Droz.

———. 2012. *La Muse indignée: La satire en France au XVI* siècle. Vol. 1. Paris: Garnier.

De Bèze, Théodore. 2004. *Le Passavant*. Edited by Jeltine L. R. Ledegang-Keegstra. Leiden: Brill.

De Smet, Ingrid A. R. 1989. "Amatus Fornacius, Amator ineptus (Palladii, 1633): A Seventeenth-Century Satire." *Humanistica Lovaniensia* 38:238–306.

———. 1996. *Menippean Satire and the Republic of Letters, 1581–1658*. Geneva: Droz.

De Smet, Rudolf, ed. 1994. *La satire humaniste*. Leuven: Peeters.

Filelfo, Francesco. 2005. *Satyrae*. Edited by Silvia Fiaschi. Rome: Edizioni di Storia e Letteratura.

Freyburger, Gérard, Eckard Lefèvre, and Robert Schilling, eds. 2005. *Balde und die römische Satire*. Tübingen: Narr.

Haye, Thomas. 2008. "Die Kommentierung Juvenals als Schlüssel zum persönlichen Erfolg: Der *Satyrus* des Francesco Rococciolo." In Haye and Schnoor, 2008, 275–99.

Haye, Thomas, and Franziska Schnoor, eds. 2008. *Epochen der Satire: Traditionslinien einer literarischen Gattung in Antike, Mittelalter und Renaissance*. Hildesheim: Weidmann.

Haskell, Yasmin A. 2013. *Prescribing Ovid: The Latin Works and Networks of the Enlightened Dr Heerkens*. London: Bloomsbury Academic.

Heesakkers, Chris L., and Wilma M. S. Reinders. 1993. *Genoeglijk bovenal zijn mij de Muzen: De Leidse neolatijnse dichter Janus Dousa (1545–1604)*. Leiden: Dimensie.

Hess, Günter. 1971. *Deutsch-lateinische Narrenzunft: Studien zum Verhältnis von Volkssprache und Latinität in der satirischen Literatur des 16. Jahrhunderts*. Munich: Beck.

IJsewijn, Jozef. 1975. "Neo-Latin Satire in Eastern Europe." *Živa antika* 25:190–96.

———. 1976. "Neo-Latin Satire: *Sermo* and *Satyra Menippea*." In *Classical Influences on European Culture, 1500–1700*, edited by Robert R. Bolgar, 41–55. Cambridge: Cambridge University Press.

———. 1999. "The Neo-Latin Satirical Novel in the 17th Century." *Neulateinisches Jahrbuch* 1:129–40.

Kivistö, Sari. 2002. *Creating Anti-Eloquence: Epistolae obscurorum virorum and the Humanist Polemics on Style*. Helsinki: Societas Scientiarum Fennica.

———. 2007. "G. F. von Franckenau's *Satyra sexta* (1647) on Male Menstruation and Female Testicles." In *The Trouble with Ribs: Women, Men and Gender in Early Modern Europe*, edited by Anu Korhonen and Kate Lowe, 82–102. Helsinki: Collegium for Advanced Studies. Available at http://hdl.handle.net/10138/25752.

———. 2009. *Medical Analogy in Latin Satire*. Basingstoke: Palgrave Macmillan.

Lauremberg, Johann. 1861. *Scherzgedichte*. Edited by Johann Martin Lappenberg. Stuttgart: Bibliothek des literarischen Vereins.

Laureys, Marc. 2008. "Zur Spätblüte der neulateinischen Satire in den Niederlanden. Johannes Havraeus, *Arx virtutis*." In Haye and Schnoor, op. cit., 301–16.

Marsh, David. 1998. *Lucian and the Latins: Humor and Humanism in the Early Renaissance*. Ann Arbor: University of Michigan Press.

———. 2014. "Satire." In *ENLW* 1:413–23.

Lippi da Colle, Lorenzo. 1978. *Satyrae V ad Laurentium Medicem*. Edited by Jozef IJsewijn. *Humanistica Lovaniensia* 27:18–44.

Martínez de Bujanda, Jesús. 2002. *Index des Livres interdits*. Vol. 11, *Index librorum prohibitorum 1600–1966*. Montreal: Médiaspaul.

Montera Delgado, Juan. 1993. "La *Sátira contra la mala poesía* del canónigo Pacheco: Consideraciones acerca de su naturaleza literaria." In *Estado actual de los estudios sobre el siglo de oro*, edited by Manuel García Martín, vol. 2, 709–18. Salamanca and Valladolid: Ediciones Universidad de Salamanca and Valladolid.

Pagrot, Lennart. 1961. *Den klassiska verssatirens teori: debatten kring genren från Horatius t. o. m. 1700-talet*. Stockholm: Almqvist and Wiksell.

Piacentini, Angelo. 2007. "Una *satyrula* di Cristoforo da Fano al giureconsulto bresciano Giovanni da Sale." *Aevum* 81:559–92.

Porter, David A. 2014. "Neo-Latin Prose Satire." In *ENLW* 1:323–34.

Pozuelo Calero, Bartolomé. 1993. "La oposición sermo/epístola en Horacio y en los humanistas." In *Humanismo y pervivencia del mundo clásico*, edited by José M. Maestre Maestre and Joaquin P. Barea, vol. 1, 837–50. Cadiz: Universidad de Cádiz.

———. 1994. "Méthodologie pour l'analyse des satires formelles néo-latines." In R. De Smet, op. cit., 19–48.

———. 2000. "De la sátira epistolar y la carta en verso latinas a la epístola moral vernácula." In *La epístola*, edited by Begoña López Bueno, 61–100. Seville: Universidad de Sevilla.

Prude, John. 1697. *A Sermon at the Funeral of the Learned and Ingenious Mrs. Ann Baynard*. London: D. Brown.

Robin, Diana. 1984. "Unknown Greek Poems of Francesco Filelfo." *Renaissance Quarterly* 37:173–206.

Robinson, Christopher. 1979. *Lucian and His Influence in Europe*. London: Duckworth.

Sacré, Dirk. 1992. "Le poète néo-latin Girolamo Faletti (†1564)." *Humanistica Lovaniensia* 61:199–220.

Scaliger, Julius Caesar. 1994. *Poetices libri septem*, edited by Luc Deitz. Vol. 1. Stuttgart: Frommann-Holzboog.

Scheurer, Rémy, and Loris Petris, eds. 2008. *Correspondance du Cardinal Jean Du Bellay*. Vol. 3, 1537–1547. Paris: Société de l'histoire de France.

Simons, Roswitha. 2013. "Der poetologischen Rekurs auf die römischen Vorbilder und das Selbstverständnis humanistischer Satirendichter." In *Norm und Poesie*, edited by Roswitha Simons and Beate Hintzen, 125–43. Berlin: De Gruyter.

Stevenson, Jane. 2005. *Women Latin Poets*. Oxford: Oxford University Press.

Ter Meer, Tineke. 1983. "Guilielmus de Meij (Willem de Mey), 'bij verspelding' Emilius Elmeguidi." *Voortgang* 4:73–81. Available at http://www.dbnl.org/tekst/_voo04198301_01/_voo04198301_01_0004.php.

Thurn, Nikolaus. 2008. "Die horazische Satire zwischen Augurelli und Ariost." In Haye and Schnoor, op. cit., 259–74.

Tournoy, Gilbert. 1994. "The Beginnings of Neo-Latin Satire in the Low Countries." In R. De Smet, op. cit., 95–109.

———. 1998. "Neo-Latin Satire in the Low Countries from an Italian Perspective." In *ACNL* 1998, 71–95.

Tribraco, Gaspare. 1972. *Satirarum liber, dedicato al duca Borso d'Este*. Edited by Giuseppe Venturini. Ferrara: SATE.

Weinbrot, Howard D. 2005. *Menippean Satire: From Antiquity to the Eighteenth Century*. Baltimore: Johns Hopkins University Press.

Wittrock, G. 1922. "Johan Bergenhielm." In *Svenskt biografiskt lexikon* 3, 459. Available at http://www.nad.riksarkivet.se/sbl/artikel/18575.

PART II

CULTURAL CONTEXTS

CHAPTER 14

....

SCHOOL

....

ROBERT BLACK

In the early modern period (ca. 1400 to ca. 1800), the principal influence on the
development of Latin language and literature was Renaissance humanism, a movement that began in Italy and then spread throughout the rest of Europe. Renaissance
humanists aimed to revive Latin culture as it had existed in antiquity. One of their principal activities was school teaching, but here their efforts to restore classical Latinity
were restricted by traditional pedagogical practices that had developed throughout the
Middle Ages. This chapter will first focus on the emergence of Renaissance humanism
in Italy, and then touch on its spread beyond the Alps: its primary theme will be the
encounter between medieval and humanist learning at the school level. "School" will
be defined, for the purposes of this chapter, as an institution of pre-university education, excluding university-level learning. There is early modern justification for distinguishing school from university. In the 1427 *catasto* (tax declarations) of Florentines and
their subjects, for example, there was a linguistic distinction between pupils who went
to school (*scuola*) and students who attended university (*studio*; Black 1996b, 197–98,
429–36; Black 2007, 469–527 *passim*), as there was between school (*scholae*) and university (*studium*) in the statutes of Forlì from the second half of the fourteenth century
onwards (Frova 1992, 181 n. 10).

   In the period from 1400 to 1800, the principal subject taught in European schools
was Latin: instruction was focused on the great Latin classics from Roman antiquity,
both prose and poetry, but also aimed at the acquisition of Latinity. By the fifteenth
century, outlines of school curricula appeared regularly in Italy. In Arezzo during the
1430s and 1440s, for example, there were three levels of teaching: the most elementary
class was for pupils "not yet reading Donatus" (for the meaning of this term, see below,
220–21); the second was for the Donatists; the third and most advanced was for the
study of Latin composition (*lactinare* [*sic*]) and literature (*auctores*; Black 1996b, 462,
479). This kind of division was typical throughout fourteenth- and fifteenth-century
Italy (Barsanti 1905, 115, 120; Manacorda 1914, 1:180–83; Rossi 1930, 14–15; Ortalli 1993,
16–17; Nada Patrone 1996, 42–45), and it held true for private tutors as well as for public elementary and grammar schools (Cherubini 1974, 397; Black 1996a, 391–92). In

some schools the curriculum extended to rhetoric: for example, in 1361, the town of San Gimignano appointed a teacher to "instruct and teach grammar and rhetoric and those wanting to learn the authors" (S. Gimignano Archivio storico comunale 125 [formerly NN 73], lxxiiii verso–lxxv verso: *legere et docere gramaticam et rectoricam [sic] et auctores quoslibet audire volentes*). A recent study of the school curriculum had as one of its aims the identification of manuscript schoolbooks surviving in Florentine libraries: it was possible to identify 110 theoretical grammatical or rhetorical works intended for school-level instruction (Black 2001, 426–27). All of these were Latin texts that aimed to teach only Latin. Similarly, 324 manuscripts of literary authors associated with school-level teaching and produced in Italy were identified: likewise, all these works were Latin texts (Black 2001, 386–425). This situation had not changed by the mid-sixteenth century. The progression from Latin grammar to Latin rhetoric, noted above in fourteenth-century San Gimignano, was still highlighted in 1542 by the humanist Marcantonio Flaminio, who declared: "One must teach a pupil grammar [i.e., Latin], and then get him used to eloquence [i.e., rhetoric]" (Trabalza 1908, 104 n. 2). At the school of San Lorenzo in Florence at the turn of the nineteenth century, the first discipline to be mastered was Latin grammar, which was divided into four classes (Florence Archivio di S. Lorenzo 2151, n. 155.ii, iii). The higher levels of the school consisted of "humanity" and "rhetoric." The lowest class concentrated on "principles of [Latin] grammar." The intermediate class learned Greek and Roman history, as well as biblical history and geography, while continuing their principal activity: the study of Latin. The superior grammatical class learned geography and ecclesiastical history; the principal focus was on classical texts in Latin (Ovid, *Tristia* 4; Phaedrus, *Fables* 1–2; Cicero, selected letters; Nepos, *Lives*, especially those of Cato and Pomponius Atticus). The class in "humanity" continued with geography, but otherwise focused entirely on the Latin classics (Virgil, *Eclogues*; Ovid, *Metamorphoses* 3–5; Cicero, *Pro Archia*; Caesar, *Gallic Wars*), with ancillary study of mythology and Roman antiquities. The rhetoric class covered rhetorical precepts as well as Greek history, but continued to concentrate on Latin classical texts: Terence, *Adelphoe*; Horace, *Odes* 3–4, *Ars poetica*, *Satires* 6–8 (book unspecified); Virgil, *Georgics* 4, *Aeneid* 7; Cicero, *Pro rege Deiotaro, De oratore* 2.1–12; Sallust, *Conspiracy of Catiline* 1–20 (Florence Archivio di S. Lorenzo 2151, n. 636). The overriding preoccupation with Latinity and Latin philology was lamented by the progressive Venetian educational reformer Gasparo Gozzi, writing in the 1770s (Brizzi 1981, 7):

> Not deserving mention are the most common and frequented schools, in which young people over the course of many years do the whole circuit of good literature. Would that they at least acquire common sense and civilized behaviour! Unending Latin grammar forms the basis of their studies, consuming the greater part of their young years in learning vocabulary and precepts that are useless for everyday life. And their memory is weighted down with rules and vain notions when one could garnish it with useful and important knowledge. From here one passes to the so-called humane studies, pedantically restricted to the explanation of assigned excerpts

of Latin orators, historians or poets, learning them by heart without any substantial thought. All reflection is consumed on vocabulary, figures, rhetorical colours. Every morning pupils are given practice in elaborating a useless subject, in preparing a composition extemporaneously and as quickly as the hand can write, without having first structured the topic in their brains, and in a pompous and unnatural style. The result is that it is necessary to forget all these lessons before one can write a personal letter with clarity. Such (or ones hardly dissimilar) are the exercises which occupy young people in schools up to the age of seventeen or eighteen; and one pretends that such activity serves as preparation for higher learning.

ELEMENTARY EDUCATION

The first textbooks were called *tabula* or *carta, salterium,* and *donatus.* The *tabula* or *carta* was a sheet of parchment or paper that began with the alphabet and concluded with syllables to sound out; it was fixed on a wooden board and took its name either from the parchment or paper (*carta*) or from the board (*tabula*; Lucchi 1978, 599; Grendler 1989, 142–46).

The next stage was reading words and phrases, accomplished in the later Middle Ages and the early modern period on the basis of the *salterium* (originally "psalter"), but the direction of the Italian curriculum here is clear: the Psalms were being replaced by common prayers and devotional texts, a process that was completed by the sixteenth century (Black 2001, 35–40). The use of Latin *salteri* for imparting basic reading skills remained standard practice in Italy until the later eighteenth century, when educators began to demand that pupils learn to read in Italian. Thus the *Compendio del metodo delle scuole normali per uso delle scuole della Lombardia* (*Handbook of the Method of the Normal Schools for Use in the Schools of Lombardy*), published in 1792 by the educational reformer Francesco Soave, insisted that "the first things that must be read by children ought to be Italian" (cited in Matarrese 1993, 32). The call for such reform became particularly importunate in the case of lower-class children, who had hitherto been taught to read, like the upper classes, using traditional Latin *salteri*. Now, however, the Lombard reformer Pier Domenico Soresi, in *Dell'educazione del minuto popolo* (*On the Education of the Common People*, 1775), called for "lower-class children to be excluded from schools of Latin and from its study," since their humble station did not allow them to "spend many years in the intricate study of Latin": "the less familiar the language, the more slowly will someone make progress in reading and writing, skills acquired with greater ease using Italian only" (cited in Matarrese 1993, 29 n. 7). Similarly, in Parma, the *Costituzione per i nuovi regi studi* (*Constitution for the New Royal Educational Institutes*) of 1768 envisaged teaching only Italian in the lowest school classes (reserved for pupils who would not go on to further study): "one would begin in the most elementary schools to teach good and correct Italian, which is needed every day" (cited in Matarrese 1993,

29). Such new methods seem to have been inspired by Enlightened contempt for useless Latinity and the corresponding wish to substitute a more practical form of elementary education. As Muratori wrote in *Della perfetta poesia italiana* (*On Perfect Italian Poetry*, 1706; cited in Matarrese 1993, 26–27):

> the highly praiseworthy but excessive zeal to instruct young people in the Latin language has as a result their inadequate familiarity with Italian, allowing them to leave state schools ignorant of their native tongue. Study of language is needed in the early years, and therefore the study of Latin must be joined to that of Italian, lest young people, through becoming learned in a foreign and dead language, always remain barbarians and foreigners in their own, living tongue.

Such ideas were incorporated into reform proposals for Lombardy submitted to Emperor Joseph II by the scientist Paolo Frisi, who argued that "one should not waste so much time on the Latin language and in such useless pursuits" (cited in Matarrese 1993, 30).

The final stages of elementary education in medieval and Renaissance Europe were presided over by Donatus. But it has long been recognized that, in Italy during the high and late Middle Ages, the principal textbook in elementary schools was not Aelius Donatus's *Ars minor* (*The Lesser Art* [*of Grammar*], as distinct from his *Greater Art* [*Ars maior*]) but the manual spuriously attributed to Donatus that Sabbadini christened *Ianua* (*Doorway*) after the first word of its verse prologue and that, as a parsing grammar, dominated the Italian manuscript tradition and early printing (Sabbadini 1896, 35, 42–44; Schmitt 1969, 43–80; Pinborg 1982, 65–67; Grendler 1989, 174–82; Gehl 1993, 82–106; Law 1986b, 138–41; Black 2001, 44–63). The parsing grammar was based on a traditional Roman teaching method preserved for posterity by Priscian in his *Partitiones* (*Divisions*), wherein the first verse of each book of the *Aeneid* was parsed minutely. This type of treatise takes the broad outline of Donatus's *Ars minor* as its starting point, divided as it is into sections on each of the eight parts of speech and cast in catechetical form. However, instead of general questions on the parts of speech as in the *Ars minor*, one word is chosen to represent each part of speech, and questions are asked about it in particular, providing a full exercise in parsing; general grammatical definitions are introduced in explanation of particular questions about an individual example (Law 1984, 211–16; 1985, 171–93; 1986a, 365–80; 1986b, 125–45). A distinctive text of *Ianua* first appeared in Italy and transalpine Europe by the twelfth century; this was a text laden with extensive theoretical material and examples, but by the fifteenth century it had been abbreviated: only condensed versions appear among later manuscript copies and early printed editions, and this was the version that was to prevail in early modern Italy. *Ianua* was first read phonetically without understanding the contents. The purpose here was to gain the skill of sounding out the syllables on the page phonetically. The second stage consisted of reading with understanding and memory. *Ianua* was read again, but now the emphasis was on meaning and particularly on memory: the text was actually memorized at this level. *Ianua* contained full paradigms of the nominal, adjectival, participial, and pronominal declensions, as well as of the regular and irregular verbal conjugations. Pupils could spend years memorizing *Ianua*, but, having accomplished the task, they were ready to progress to higher levels of grammatical study.

The Secondary Curriculum

The secondary curriculum in Italy was devoted, at the theoretical level, to learning to write in Latin. In the earlier Middle Ages, Latin syntax had been taught by what foreign-language teachers now call "total immersion." Latin was spoken exclusively in the classroom; the texts to be read were all in Latin. Eventually pupils began spontaneously to be able to write in Latin. This approach was admirable as long as pupils and parents were in no hurry to finish secondary school; it was a method ideally suited to monastic and ecclesiastical schools, with their leisurely pace and long duration, prevalent in the earlier Middle Ages. However, with the rise of the Italian communes in the eleventh and twelfth centuries came far greater pressure for rapid literacy. The burgeoning lay professional classes needed Latin to be able to pursue careers as lawyers, notaries, and physicians; merchants, too, needed Latin to be able to read simple legal and business documents; Latin was also necessary for the conduct of civic and public affairs. The pressure for rapid Latinity became even greater with the rise of the universities in the later twelfth and thirteenth centuries: Latin was a prerequisite for professional university courses in law and medicine, the principal subjects taught in Italian universities (Black 2001, 64–69).

The possibility of teaching Latin syntax rapidly and methodically was offered by developments in linguistic theory and logic that took place in French schools, particularly in Paris, during the twelfth century. A philosophical and scientific approach to language was responsible for the emergence of a comprehensive theory of Latin word order. The subject logically precedes the predicate (Thurot 1868, 240). This logical structure generated a necessary grammatical sequence of words: because the subject preceded the verb in logic, it followed that, grammatically, the subject preceded the verb in the order in which the words were spoken or written. This came to be known as the *ordo naturalis* ("natural order") of words (Thurot 1868, 342–43). Word order was thus conceived as a logical structure: the terminology *a parte ante* ("from the part before") or *ante se* ("before itself") and *a parte post* ("from the part after") or *post se* ("after itself"), used well into the Renaissance, appeared first in twelfth- and thirteenth-century grammatical writings to express a logical relationship (Thurot 1868, 384). Logically, the mover comes first, then the motion, and finally the destination of the motion. But grammatically this then becomes a formula for word order and, indeed, a convenient pattern for basic sentence structure. This concept of *ordo naturalis* rapidly found its way into school-level grammar textbooks. In Alexander of Villedieu's *Doctrinale* (*Textbook*, 1199; Alexander 1893), the treatment of syntax includes the natural or logical word order of the sentence (ll. 1390–96). Even more extensive is the treatment of natural word order by Pietro da Isolella da Cremona in his widely circulated *Summa* (1252–86; edited anonymously by Fierville 1886: see 57, 29–38, and 147; actual authorship discovered by Novati 1888, 72 n. 3).

Medieval textbooks such as Pietro da Isolella's *Summa*, the *Regule grammaticales* (*Grammatical Rules*, 1355–78) by the Pisan teacher Francesco da Buti, and especially Alexander's *Doctrinale* remained in wide manuscript circulation during the fifteenth century, and *Doctrinale* continued to be extensively used in schools well into the sixteenth century. In the early modern period, nevertheless, their place was gradually taken by new humanist textbooks. The most widely circulated fifteenth-century secondary grammars were by Guarino da Verona (ca. 1418) and Niccolò Perotti (ca. 1468). In terms of theory and content, these works are essentially indistinguishable from those of their Trecento predecessors. Guarino's *Regule grammaticales* has the same overall structure as Francesco da Buti's *Regule* and other fourteenth-century *summe*. Other common features among Guarino and fourteenth-century Italian secondary grammarians are: subdivisions of verbal types, followed by lists with vernacular equivalents; mnemonic verses; vernacular passages to be translated into Latin, called *themata*; a concentration on the declinable parts of speech; a preoccupation with syntax, as revealed by the usual scholastic syntactical vocabulary and a discussion of standard figures of construction such as prolepsis and zeugma; invented examples; and the concept of a natural word order, presupposed by the terms *ante se* and *post se*. Similarly, Perotti's *Rudimenta grammatices* (*The Rudiments of Grammar*) was thoroughly conservative in terms of syllabus, grammatical theory, and use of the vernacular, recalling not only Guarino's syllabus but also the normal secondary grammar course going back to the Italian prose *summe* of the thirteenth and fourteenth centuries, and ultimately to *Doctrinale*. Similarly conventional was Perotti's treatment of verbs divided into the usual syntactical categories, accompanied by vernacular translations, and he also included numerous invented sentences to illustrate grammatical points. He constantly employed the normal scholastic syntactical vocabulary. Particularly notable is the text's use of translation from Italian into Latin (*themata*), a Trecento practice indulged with little restraint by Perotti.

The school curriculum in medieval and Renaissance Italy was not limited to elementary reading and Latin grammar. At the end of the curriculum, attention shifted to style and rhetoric. Here the dominant textbook was Geoffrey of Vinsauf's *Poetria nova* (*The New Poetics*, 1208–1213), a work widely circulated in Italy until the end of the fifteenth century (Woods 2010). *Poetria nova's* treatment of style began with the distinction between natural and artificial word order (*ordo naturalis* and *ordo artificialis*). Although natural word order might have been thought appropriate for purely grammatical study, it was now considered sterile, and the artful approach was regarded as more felicitous. It is clear from Geoffrey's text that the work at this new, rhetorical and stylistic level of school education involved the kinds of exercises similar to those already encountered at the earlier secondary grammatical stage. Again the key term here was *thema*, but this had now come to mean the grammatically correct but plain Latin passage to which the pupil needed to apply his art; the theme was given in natural Latin order and wording, and it had to be rendered elegant and artificial (Black 2001, 342–49).

ITALIAN HUMANISM

The concept of *ordo artificialis* played a central role in Italian humanist schools, too. For example, in Niccolò Perotti's *Rudimenta grammatices* (1468), it is difficult not to be struck by the resemblance between Geoffrey's discussion of variation in word order to achieve greater elegance and the treatment in Perotti's section on epistolography. Just as in *Poetria nova*, in fact, much of Perotti's epistolography consists of listing alternative and more elegant ways of phrasing simple Latin statements.

Perotti's treatment of stylistics, coming as it did at the end of his best-selling *Rudimenta grammatices*, achieved an extensive circulation in the later fifteenth century, but there was another manual of Latin style that might have attained even greater popularity. This was the *Isagogicus libellus* (*Introductory Booklet*) by the Sienese humanist Agostino Dati, a work that came generally to be called *Elegantiolae* (*Little Elegances*). This short treatise, first published in Cologne in 1470 by Ulrich Zell and then soon afterwards in 1471 at Ferrara by André Belfort, received at least a further 112 incunabular printings and many more during the sixteenth century. Like Perotti's treatment, Dati's *Elegantiolae* have a striking overall resemblance to Geoffrey of Vinsauf's *Poetria nova*. Both texts are overwhelmingly preoccupied with teaching stylistic elegance. Like Geoffrey's distinction between natural and artificial style, Dati begins his treatment by contrasting grammatical and oratorical style. Both start where grammar leaves off: Geoffrey's point of departure is natural style, whereas Dati's is the terminology for the parts of the sentence developed by contemporary (medieval) grammarians. Just as the purpose of Geoffrey's work is to convert natural into artificial style, so Dati's aim is to turn the inelegant language of contemporary grammarians into eloquent prose. Geoffrey, as has been seen, makes continual reference to natural and artificial language, and Dati, too, distinguishes throughout between grammatical and rhetorical standards. Geoffrey had written from the point of view of the rhetorician, scoffing at the inelegance of so-called natural Latin (ll. 101–2), and Dati, too, ridicules grammatical style, not only calling it, as has already been seen, trite and vulgar, but referring as well to "many experts in the art of grammar also ignorant of Latin literature" (Dati 1471, 23r–v). Moreover, like Geoffrey Dati begins his treatment with word order, suggesting, as in *Poetria nova*, that it is more elegant to abandon the natural sequence of subject-verb-predicate. As in *Poetria nova*, variety is paramount, not only in phrases but also in individual words.

Dati's distinction between his treatise and the writings of grammarians confirms the point at which stylistics were treated in the school curriculum. The *Elegantiolae* presume a full knowledge of basic Latin grammar. In fifteenth-century Italy, it is clear that grammar was learned first, almost entirely divorced from stylistics and rhetoric. Once this basic grammar was mastered, the pupil's Latin was then gradually purified at the end of the syllabus through the study of stylistics and introductory rhetoric. This two-staged process followed medieval precedents, based on the distinction between natural and artificial language.

This perspective on the levels of discourse inherited from the Middle Ages has important consequences for evaluating the impact of humanist education at the rhetorical level in Renaissance Italy. Teaching the Latin language was the fundamental concern of all elementary and grammar schoolmasters, whether in medieval or Renaissance Italy. But it was universally assumed that language acquisition was a two-staged process, in which the pupil had first to master *ordo naturalis* before proceeding to *ordo artificialis*. The result was that humanist educators in Italy followed traditional methods in the earlier stages of Latin education. It has been seen that associated with *ordo naturalis* was a whole apparatus of methods for learning syntax, including the system of equating word order with syntactical functions of the parts of the sentence (*a parte ante* and *a parte post*). This system had been developed as a simple method of teaching Latin syntax to non-native Latin speakers. Hardly any Italian educators of the fifteenth century attempted to tamper with this eminently pragmatic system: a few purists might have been repelled by this unclassical approach, but almost every Italian grammar teacher ended up employing the educational practices inherited from the Middle Ages for teaching *ordo naturalis*.

It was another matter with *ordo artificialis*. Humanists saw themselves as the successors of Cicero, whose own discipline was not grammar but rhetoric. They might not have known how to replace medieval grammar in the educational syllabus, but no such problem existed with rhetoric. The ancient Romans left a series of eminently pragmatic rhetorical textbooks (e.g., the anonymous *Rhetoric to Herennius*, falsely ascribed to Cicero in the manuscript; Cicero's *De inventione*; Quintilian's *Institutio oratoria*) which provided the possibility for radical reform of rhetoric in a way that was entirely lacking in the discipline of grammar. Moreover, just as Geoffrey of Vinsauf had provided a quick route to eloquence and elegance according to medieval standards, so now Niccolò Perotti and Agostino Dati provided a comparable shortcut to Ciceronian prose in the later Quattrocento. The place in the syllabus occupied by simple handbooks of eloquence was the same as in the Middle Ages, but the content was entirely different. Ciceronianism replaced Geoffrey of Vinsauf's artificial system of stylistics (e.g., Geoffrey included no examples or citations from classical authors). At the grammatical level, Italian Renaissance education might have been "old wine in new bottles," but at the upper stages of school learning, when the preoccupation was more rhetorical than grammatical, it was doubtless "new wine in old bottles."

The final major task of pre-university schools was teaching Latin literature. Here the syllabus had been divided since the twelfth century into two groups of authors: the *auctores minores*, a cycle of late ancient pagan, early Christian, and medieval texts (ranging from *Disticha Catonis* to poems by Prudentius, Theodulus, and Henry of Settimello); and the *auctores maiores*, the Roman classics, mainly poetry (e.g., by Ovid,

Lucan, Horace, and Virgil) but also some prose texts (e.g., Sallust or Cicero; Black 2001, 173–74). Probably in the thirteenth century, another important text was added to the canon: Boethius's *Consolation of Philosophy*, a work that was normally seen to stand between the shorter texts by the minor authors and the longer Latin classics (Black and Pomaro 2000).

The development of the theoretical grammar curriculum had offered little room for intervention by the Renaissance humanists; they did, however, ultimately make a greater contribution in the study of Latin literature, although even here it would be inappropriate to speak of a "revolution in the classroom." The most radical change in the literary curriculum had already occurred between the twelfth and thirteenth centuries. Surviving manuscript schoolbooks from eleventh- and twelfth-century Italian schools show that the Latin classics continued to be read widely in the classroom. However, with the advent of the thirteenth century, the same kind of evidence indicates that there was a marked decline in school-level reading of the Latin classics. This waning of the Roman pagan authors in the thirteenth century provoked a reaction by the turn of the fourteenth century: in the Trecento, surviving manuscript schoolbooks demonstrate that the Latin classics were once again being read in the pre-university classroom (Black 2001, 182–218; Black 2006).

Fourteenth-century Italian schoolmasters deserve credit for restoring the traditional Roman school authors (Horace, Lucan, Ovid, Virgil) to the curriculum, as well as for introducing some new texts (such as Seneca's tragedies and Valerius Maximus's *Facta et dicta*; Black 2001, 200–18). But here there remained more room for humanist pedagogues to influence the curriculum. Although the classics were already being read widely at the school level by the fifteenth century, humanists did make some important changes to the literary syllabus: some texts previously at the center of the literary curriculum were now moved to the sidelines (such as Horace's *Ars poetica*, Lucan, Seneca's tragedies), whereas other authors previously little read (such as Terence, Juvenal, Persius) now assumed a key role. Most important here was the changed position of Cicero and Virgil. Cicero's shorter moral treatises (*De amicitia, De senectute, Paradoxa Stoicorum, De officiis*, and *Somnium Scipionis*) and Virgil had been read in the twelfth-century Italian classroom, but then dropped out of the syllabus during the thirteenth century, only to reassume a significant (if not predominant) position in the fourteenth century. But now, in the fifteenth century, Cicero's shorter moral treatises and Virgil's poetry became the most popular classical texts in the Italian school curriculum (Black 2001, 238–70).

Another accomplishment of humanist pedagogues was the eventual elimination of minor literary authors from the schoolroom, although this occurred less rapidly than was once thought. Surviving fifteenth-century schoolbooks show that, throughout the first half of the fifteenth century, the non-classical minor authors remained dominant at the early stages of the literary school curriculum (Black 2001, 225–38). Thereafter their position became increasingly tenuous, especially following the introduction of the printing press. Humanist editors occupied a central role in the production of schoolbooks, and so it is not entirely surprising to find that the minor authors figured less and less in the curriculum from the 1470s onwards (Black 2001, 270–73). Time-honored the-oretical grammar texts such as *Ianua* (Grendler 1989, 413–16) or Alexander's *Doctrinale* remained at the heart of the school curriculum in Italy in the age of the printing press, but traditional minor authors, not to mention Boethius's *Consolation*, went into a rapid decline in late fifteenth-century Italy.

Northern Humanism

The humanist school curriculum in Renaissance Italy did not signify a revolution-ary change, but rather constituted a hybrid of medieval and classical methods and sources, the product of a long evolution in which humanist pedagogues exercised a significant but uneven influence. At the most elementary level of learning to read, their contribution was almost nil: *tabula/carta, salterium,* and *Ianua* remained the standard introductory reading texts throughout the sixteenth century and beyond; the language of learning to read remained exclusively Latin; the traditional methods of phonics followed by memory/understanding continued in force. At the secondary level, where Latin grammatical composition was taught, textbooks by humanists such as Guarino and Perotti supplanted older manuals by the likes of Francesco da Buti or Pietro da Isolella da Cremona, gradually at first, and then rapidly after the advent of printing. However, this substitution hardly signified change either in content or in teaching methods: Guarino's and Perotti's manuals were traditional works, differing little from their medieval predecessors (Black 2001, 124–36). The humanists effected greater change in the study of Latin literature, although, even here, important qual-ifications must be made: the non-classical minor Latin authors remained in vogue until the late fifteenth century, and classical Roman texts had already been extensively reintroduced into the syllabus during the fourteenth century. It was at the final, rhe-torical level of Latin stylistics that the humanist pedagogues exercised the greatest influence. Although there had been a similar post-grammatical level concerned with refining style in Italian medieval schools, nevertheless the humanists now substituted Ciceronianism, normally learned from best-selling manuals such as Perotti's episto-lography or Dati's *Elegantiolae,* for the previous abstract system of stylistics contained in Geoffrey of Vinsauf's *Poetria nova,* also once a best seller, which went rapidly out of fashion in the late fifteenth century (and was first printed only in the eighteenth century).

It was in transalpine Europe that the advent of the humanist educational curriculum led to a radical, and even revolutionary, change. It has already been noted that the devel-opments in linguistic theory, originating in Parisian schools during the twelfth century, had profound effects on Italian grammatical education in the thirteenth and fourteenth centuries. In Italy, the emergence of a systematic, logical approach, based on Parisian theory, led to a streamlined and rapid system for teaching Latin composition, obviating the need for the slow traditional methods of total immersion previously employed. The result was a highly practical approach to grammatical learning, attuned to the utilitarian goals of Italian education: business or preparation for notarial, legal, or medical study. This system was developed for the urbanized world of Italian towns and cities, a social and economic context less prevalent in Northern Europe, where Latin school education was geared to prepare for university study, too, but where higher learning was dominated by faculties of theology, either absent or marginalized in Italian universities. Study in Northern universities was based on logical methods, uncharacteristic of Italian universities or at most limited there to specialized scientific disciplines; mainline subjects such as law, notarial studies, or rhetoric at Italian universities (Grendler 2002) were not pursued on the basis of Aristotelian logic, which, in contrast, was the very foundation of the philosophical and theological disciplines at the center of Northern universities (on Northern universities, see Renaudet 1953; Curtis 1959; Kearney 1970; Heath 1971; Nauert 1973, 1986, 1990; Kagan 1974; Fletcher 1981; Kittelson and Transue 1984; Overfield 1984; Cobban 1988).

Given this context, it is not surprising to discover that logical and philosophical methods penetrated the introductory subject of grammar in Northern schools, too. For example, the great verse grammars by Alexander of Villedieu and Evrard of Béthune (*Graecismus*, 1212; the name is owed to a chapter on derivations from the Greek), both written at the turn of the thirteenth century, circulated widely both north and south of the Alps, but their use reveals the difference between Italian and transalpine approaches. In Italy, these works served primarily as mines of mnemonic verses, used to help pupils memorize grammar rules and key examples. North of the Alps, on the other hand, the texts were memorized in their entirety (Black 2001, 84–85) and subjected to commentaries impregnated with logical and philosophical terminology and content. Thus, circa 1300, Jupiter (the pseudonym of a Dijonais grammar teacher named Jean [de Clacy?]) introduced a new style of commentary on Evrard's *Graecismus*, influenced by the latest fashions in speculative grammatical theory then current in the University of Paris Arts Faculty ("speculative" grammar was concerned with the search for a universal grammar underlying all languages and "mirroring"—from Latin *speculum*, "mirror"—reality; speculative grammar was also called "modistic" because the "modes of signifying" of individual parts of speech, i.e. the way they relate to reality, was a particular focus); in this connection, Jupiter was particularly beholden to Radulphus Brito and Michel de Marbais, two leading contemporary practitioners of speculative grammar (Grondeux 2000).

In view of the philosophical tendencies of Northern grammatical study, not just in universities but also at the school level, it comes as no surprise to discover that early Northern humanist pedagogues emerged as genuine radicals in a way inconceivable for their Italian humanist predecessors and counterparts. The Italian humanist curriculum represented a moderate, evolutionary, and gradual change of direction from traditional Italian medieval grammatical teaching methods, but when it was transplanted during the later fifteenth century as a whole into Northern Europe, with its philosophical and logical penchant for modistic and speculative grammar, Italian humanist education represented a truly revolutionary alternative.

The best-known humanist school in the German- and Dutch-speaking countries was St. Lebwin's in Deventer. With Alexander Hegius at the head from 1483 to 1498, it became the premier pre-university academy in the Netherlands, famous for its teaching of Latin. His school was possibly the first north of the Alps to offer Greek, and pupils there were encouraged to compose Latin poetry. He openly criticized modistic and speculative grammarians, then dominant in Latin teaching at both the school and university levels. For Hegius, studying language logically did not provide boys with a workable knowledge of grammar, and he rightly noted that Italian pedagogues did not, in his view, waste time teaching such idle and abstract topics. Other important German teachers, such as Wimpfeling or Dringenberg, were similarly hostile to modistic grammar (Post 1968; IJsewijn 1975; Nauert 1995). Italian humanist teachers such as Guarino and Perotti had similarly not taught speculative grammar (Percival 2004), but what is significant here is that neither had their important medieval Italian predecessors such as Pietro da Isolella da Cremona or Francesco da Buti (Black 2001; Percival 2004), whereas for Jupiter, a contemporary Northern grammar teacher of equal standing, modistic theory was at the heart of his pedagogical methods (Grondeux 2000; on Northern pre-university schools, see Simon 1969; O'Day 1982; Huppert 1984; Karant-Nunn 1990).

In Italy, therefore, teachers happily combined traditional and avant-garde methods and sources, whereas Northern European teachers had to choose between two alternate, fully developed systems: the traditional Northern speculative approach, or the non-philosophical, non-logical Italian humanist method. The latter method received the backing of the greatest reformers, including Luther, Melanchthon, and Calvin, and so it is not surprising that the humanist alternative displaced traditional methods and textbooks more thoroughly and more rapidly in Northern Europe than in Italy. This scenario can be illustrated by the printing history of Alexander's *Doctrinale* (see esp. Reichling's introduction to Alexander 1893): even over the first century of the press, *Doctrinale* continued in unabated use by Italian teachers and pupils. Until 1480, editions of the text were almost exclusively Northern Italian; at least forty-six Italian editions of the work were issued, half of these in Venice. Although some of these Venetian editions would have been prepared for the ultramontane (Grendler 1989, 337) and especially German market, nevertheless this cannot explain the *longue durée* of *Doctrinale* among Italian publishers. The text was subjected to relentless attack in Northern Europe and especially in Germany during the first decades of the sixteenth century, with the result that it ceased to be used in schools there by about 1520 (Heath 1971); the last German edition was produced in 1525, and two Paris publications (of 1526 and 1542) are the only ultramontane editions to appear after that date. On the other hand, *Doctrinale* continued to be printed in North Italy, with a final series of editions coming out at Brescia beginning in 1538 and continuing after 1550. The fact is that *Doctrinale*'s popularity in Italy grew, if anything, during the fifteenth century and sustained itself well into the sixteenth. Out of a total of 250 manuscripts, Reichling lists twenty-three manuscripts now in Italian libraries; on the other hand, out of a total 295 printed editions, 46 were published in Italy. It is a fact that, among all European countries, *Doctrinale* survived longest in Italy, with the last printing occurring there in 1588. As far as school education is concerned, Italy might have been the cradle of humanist pedagogy, but the new learning reached its fullest and purest form, at least as far as the pre-university level is concerned, in Northern Europe.

SUGGESTED READING

On the Latin curriculum in Italian schools, see Black (2001), Sabbadini (1896), Garin (1958), Lucchi (1978), Gehl (1993), and Percival (2004); on Italian schools and their organizational and institutional context see Zanelli (1900), Barsanti (1905), Mannucci (1910), Manacorda (1914), Chiuppani (1915), Grendler (1989), Frova (1992), Ortalli (1993), Nada Patrone (1996), and Black (2007). On the Latin curriculum in Europe as well as in Italy, see Law (1984, 1985, 1986a, and 1986b) and Woods (2010). For Latin at the school level in France, see Renaudet (1953), Huppert (1984), and Grondeux (2000); for Germany, Nauert (1973, 1986, 1990, and 1995), Overfield (1984), and Karant-Nunn (1990); for England, Simon (1969), Kearney (1970), and O'Day (1982); for the Netherlands, Post (1968) and IJsewijn (1975).

REFERENCES

Alexander of Villedieu. 1893. *Doctrinale*. Edited by Dietrich Reichling. Berlin: Hofmann.

Barsanti, Paolo. 1905. *Il pubblico insegnamento in Lucca*. Lucca: Marchi.

Black, Robert. 1996a. "New Light on Machiavelli's Education." In *Niccolò Machiavelli, politico, storico, letterato*, edited by Jean-Jacques Marchand, 391–98. Rome: Salerno.

———. 1996b. *Studio e scuola in Arezzo durante il medioevo e il Rinascimento: I documenti d'archivio fino al 1530*. Arezzo: Accademia Petrarca di lettere, arti e scienze.

———. 2001. *Humanism and Education in Medieval and Renaissance Italy: Tradition and Innovation in Latin Schools from the Twelfth to the Fifteenth Century*. Cambridge: Cambridge University Press.

———. 2006. "The Origins of Humanism." In *Interpretations of Renaissance Humanism*, edited by Angelo Mazzocco, 37–71. Leiden: Brill.

———. 2007. *Education and Society in Florentine Tuscany: Teachers, Pupils and Schools, c. 1250–1500*. Leiden: Brill.

Black, Robert, and Gabriella Pomaro. 2000. *Boethius's* Consolation of Philosophy *in Italian Medieval and Renaissance Education: Schoolbooks and Their Glosses in Florentine Manuscripts*. Florence: SISMEL.

Brizzi, Gian Paolo, ed. 1981. *La Ratio studiorum: Modelli culturali e pratiche dei gesuiti in Italia tra Cinque e Seicento*. Rome: Bulzoni.

Cherubini, Giovanni. 1974. *Signori, contadini, borghesi*. Florence: La Nuova Italia.

Chiuppani, Giovanni. 1915. "Storia di una scuola di grammatica dal medio evo fino al seicento (Bassano)." *Nuovo archivio veneto* n.s. 29:73–138, 253–304.

Cobban, Alan B. 1988. *The Medieval English Universities: Oxford and Cambridge to c. 1500*. Berkeley: University of California Press.

Curtis, Mark H. 1959. *Oxford and Cambridge in Transition, 1558–1642*, Oxford: Clarendon Press.

Dati, Agostino. 1471. *Isagogicus libellus*. Ferrara: André Belfort.

Fierville, Charles, ed. 1886. *Une grammaire latine inédite du XIIIe siècle*, Paris: Imprimerie Nationale.

Fletcher, John M. 1981, "Change and Resistance to Change: A Consideration of the Development of English and German Universities during the Sixteenth Century." *History of Universities* 1:1–36.

Frova, Carla. 1992. "Le scuole municipali all'epoca delle università." In *Vocabulaire des écoles et des méthodes d'enseignement au moyen âge,* edited by Olga Weijers, 177–90. Turnhout: Brepols.

Garin, Eugenio, ed. 1958. *Il pensiero pedagogico dello umanesimo*. Florence: Giuntine.

Gehl, Paul F. 1993. *A Moral Art: Grammar, Society, and Culture in Trecento Florence.* Ithaca: Cornell University Press.

Grendler, Paul F. 1989. *Schooling in Renaissance Italy*. Baltimore: Johns Hopkins University Press.

———. 2002. *The Universities of the Italian Renaissance*. Baltimore: Johns Hopkins University Press.

Grondeux, Anne. 2000. *Le Graecismus d'Evrard de Béthune à travers ses gloses: Entre grammaire positive et grammaire spéculative du XIIIe au XVe siècle*. Turnhout: Brepols.

Heath, Terrence. 1971. "Logical Grammar, Grammatical Logic, and Humanism in Three German Universities." *Studies in the Renaissance* 18:9–64.

Huppert, George. 1984. *Public Schools in Renaissance France*. Urbana: University of Illinois Press.

IJsewijn, Jozef. 1975. "The Coming of Humanism to the Low Countries." In *Itinerarium Italicum: The Profile of the Italian Renaissance in the Mirror of Its European Transformations,* edited by Heiko A. Oberman and Thomas A. Brady, 193–301. Leiden: Brill.

Kagan, Richard L. 1974. *Students and Society in Early Modern Spain*. Baltimore: Johns Hopkins University Press.

Karant-Nunn, Susan C. 1990. "Alas, a Lack: Trends in the Historiography of Pre-University Education in Early Modern Germany." *Renaissance Quarterly* 43:788–98.

Kearney, Hugh F. 1970. *Scholars and Gentlemen: Universities and Society in Pre-Industrial Britain, 1500–1700*. Ithaca: Cornell University Press.

Kittelson, James M., and Pamela J. Transue, eds. 1984. *Rebirth, Reform and Resilience: Universities in Transition, 1300–1700*. Columbus: Ohio State University Press.

Law, Vivien. 1984. "The First Foreign-Language Grammars." *The Incorporated Linguist* 23:211–16.

———. 1985. "Linguistics in the Earlier Middle Ages: The Insular and Carolingian Grammarians." *Transactions of the Philological Society* 83:171–93.

———. 1986a. "Late Latin Grammars in the Early Middle Ages." *Historiographia Linguistica* 13:365–80.

———. 1986b. "Panorama della grammatica normativa nel tredicesimo secolo." In *Aspetti della letteratura latina nel secolo XIII*, edited by Claudio Leonardi and Giovanni Orlandi, 125–45. Perugia: Regione dell'Umbria.

Lucchi, Piero. 1978. "La santacroce, il salterio e il babuino: Libri per imparare a leggere nel primo secolo della stampa." *Quaderni storici* 38:593–630.

Manacorda, Giuseppe. 1914. *Storia della scuola in Italia: Il medio evo*. 2 vols. Milan: Sandron.

Mannucci, Francesco. 1910. "I primordi del pubblico insegnamento in Sarzana." *Giornale storico della Lunigiana* 2:161–83.

Matarrese, Tina. 1993. *Il Settecento*. Bologna: Il Mulino.

Nada Patrone, Anna M. 1996. *Vivere nella scuola: Insegnare e apprendere nel Piemonte del tardo medioevo*. Cavallermaggiore: Gribaudo.

Nauert, Charles G. 1973. "The Clash of Humanists and Scholastics: An Approach to Pre-Reformation Controversies." *Sixteenth Century Journal* 4:1–18.

———. 1986. "The Humanist Challenge to Medieval German Culture." *Daphnis* 15:277–306.

———. 1990. "Humanist Infiltration into the Academic World: Some Studies of Northern Universities." *Renaissance Quarterly* 43:799–812.

———. 1995. *Humanism and the Culture of Renaissance Europe*. Cambridge: Cambridge University Press.

Novati, Francesco. 1888. *La giovinezza di Coluccio Salutati*. Turin: Loescher.

O'Day, Rosemary. 1982. *Education and Society, 1500–1800: The Social Foundations of Education in Early Modern Britain*. London: Longman.

Ortalli, Gherardo. 1993. *Scuole, maestri e istruzione di base tra Medioevo e Rinascimento: Il caso veneziano*. Vicenza: Pozza.

Overfield, James H. 1984. *Humanism and Scholasticism in Late Medieval Germany*. Princeton: Princeton University Press.

Percival, W. Keith. 2004. *Studies in Renaissance Grammar*. Aldershot: Ashgate.

Pinborg, Jan, ed. 1982. *Remigius, Schleswig 1486: A Latin Grammar in Facsimile Edition with a Postscript*. Copenhagen: Munksgaard.

Post, Regnerus R. 1968, *The Modern Devotion: Confrontation with Reformation and Humanism*. Leiden: Brill.

Renaudet, Augustin. 1953. *Préréforme et humanisme à Paris pendant les premières guerres d'Italie (1494–1517)*. 2nd ed. Paris: Librairie D'Argences.

Rossi, Vittorio. 1930. *Dal rinascimento al risorgimento*. Florence: Sansoni.

Sabbadini, Remigio. 1896. *La scuola e gli studi di Guarino Guarini Veronese*. Catania: Giannotta.

Schmitt, Wolfgang O. 1969. "Die Ianua (Donatus)." *Beiträge zur Inkunabelkunde* 3.4:43–80.

Simon, Joan. 1969. *Education and Society in Tudor England*. Cambridge: Cambridge University Press.

Thurot, Charles. 1868. *Notices et extraits de divers manuscrits latins pour servir à l'histoire des doctrines grammaticales au moyen-âge*. Paris: Imprimerie Nationale.

Trabalza, Ciro. 1908. *Storia della grammatica italiana*. Milan: Hoepli.

Woods, Marjorie C. 2010. *Classroom Commentaries: Teaching the* Poetria nova *across Medieval and Renaissance Europe*. Columbus: Ohio State University Press.

Zanelli, Agostino. 1900. *Del pubblico insegnamento in Pistoia dal XIV al XVI secolo*. Rome: Loescher.

CHAPTER 15

....

UNIVERSITY

....

SARAH KNIGHT

IF school turned a vernacular-speaking boy into a reader and translator of Latin, university fostered his ability to participate in scholarly disputation, perform in institutional drama if so inclined (a practice that began for many at school), and compose substantial, original literary or scientific works in Latin. And if, to cite three recent influential historians of Renaissance education, "every learned person became a classicist at school" (Grafton 2009, 2), then the university, where "Latin was the language of lecture hall, disputation and text" (Grendler 2002, 151), cemented those skills by a process during which students typically "spent six to seven years immersed in its mysteries for some four to five hours a day" (Brockliss 1996, 573). Along with lawyers, clergy, diplomats, doctors, and schoolmasters, university personnel were classed as "professional users of Latin" (*CNLS* 1:30), and for many, acquisition of this "professional" facility was enough to gain the competence and academic credentials necessary for a respectable career after graduation. But fortunately for the broader history of Latin literature, the early modern universities did not just churn out machine-tooled Latinists skilled in the jargon of their job, and many current and former students also wrote penetrating works about their experience of higher education between the fifteenth and the seventeenth centuries. This chapter will chiefly focus on those Latin literary works—often seen as inkhorn curios, dismissed as juvenilia, or neglected in favor of a famous author's later writing—rather than on the often more rigidly circumscribed Latin writing generated during the practical administration and regulation of the early modern universities (e.g., dissertations; statutes; student notebooks). Jacob Burckhardt famously argued that the Renaissance facilitated a peculiar strain of self-reflectiveness (Burckhardt [1860] 2004, 98–104), and if we agree, then it follows that a nation's hard-thinking young men based in its institutions of learning might be expected to demonstrate this tendency more than most. Anthony Grafton has called Erasmus and his like "a self-conscious avant garde of scholars bent on reforming the Church and the universities" (Grafton 2009, 4), and Richard Kirwan has argued that a "new elite" of early modern "university men" manifested "self-consciousness" in their "social behaviour, political actions and representational and symbolic practices"

(Kirwan 2013, 3). In addition, Walter Rüegg sees three powerful forces as shaping the early modern universities: "a desire for novelty, restlessness, a yearning for fame" (Rüegg 1996, 6), all of which helped to fuel the literary works produced there. Generally speaking, the universities' emphasis on argumentation fostered self-consciousness among its students, which led to the formation of group identity and the cultivation of fame for one's rhetorical abilities, both within the institution and in some fortunate cases outside its walls, too.

In what we might think of as a *speculum studiosi* (a "mirror for the studious" akin to the "mirror for princes" treatises discussed, for instance, in Chapter 9), one of the earliest humanist pedagogical writers, Pier Paolo Vergerio (1370–1444) called the *ratio disputandi* ("practice of disputation") the *discendi scientia sciendique disciplina* ("science of learning and the learning of science"), which *ad omne doctrinarum genus viam facile aperit* ("opens with ease the way to every kind of knowledge"; Vergerio 2002, 50–1). Arguing for or against a given thesis, following the conventional rules of argument while trying to demonstrate individual flair, was a main task demanded of students, and for a majority of early modern writers this strenuously argumentative mentality trained across a decade or more of formal education never left them. Authors working in Latin, the language of instruction and academic achievement, adhered even more closely to an intellectual habit hard-wired during their student careers. The educational primacy of *disputatio* also mapped neatly onto the natural competitiveness of high-achieving youths thrown together in a world that prized intellectual excellence: a rhetoric professor at Bologna and then Ferrara, Battista Guarino (1434–1513), son of one of the most famous humanist teachers, Guarino of Verona (1374–1460; Grafton and Jardine 1986, 1–28), argued that *aemulatio* ("a spirit of emulation") should be "kindled in them" (*quasi igniculis accendantur*; Guarino 2002, 266–67). The rhetorical habit of *disputatio* and the pedagogical fostering of *aemulatio* fundamentally shaped early modern Latin writing.

The number of literary works in Latin generated at the early modern universities is vast, and a short chapter obviously cannot do justice to them all, but a few examples that permit us to travel across three centuries and from Southern to Northern Europe show how richly idiosyncratic Latin writing at and about the universities could be. One side-effect of *disputatio* and *aemulatio* was that this writing was often oppositional in its rhetorical stance and authorial persona: writers often engaged critically with the pedagogical process they had undergone to define themselves against powerful formative influences, and, thereby, to assert their own distinctiveness of voice and originality of perspective. Starting with Leon Battista Alberti's (1404–1472) *De commodis litterarum atque incommodis* (*On the Advantages and Disadvantages of Letters*; late 1420s/early 1430s), written after school in Padua and university in Bologna, we will see how the study of *litterae*—"letters," "literature," "learning"—could be questioned as much as encouraged. A century later, the experience of studying and teaching in Paris described by the Scottish scholar George Buchanan (1506–1582), and the passionate debates over intellectual authority that arose around the contentious Petrus

Ramus (Pierre de la Ramée, 1515–1572) demonstrate impulses towards both innovation and tradition. We will finish in seventeenth-century England with a consideration of the Cambridge college tutor James Duport (1606–1679) and his better-known contemporary John Milton (1608–1674): both were celebrated as students for their Latin writing and went on to reflect on pedagogy later in their careers. I end in a century when many of the academic disciplines we take for granted today, such as history, geography, and science based on empirical observation rather than ancient authority, were changing, and the contours of the humanist republic of letters shifted to accommodate these new forms.

Whether satirically, polemically, or earnestly, each author in this chapter considered the institutional context that had formed him as an intellectual. Such formation often arose from the training offered by B.A. and M.A. degrees: the arts of the *trivium* (grammar, rhetoric, and logic) relate most directly to literary composition, and it was the B.A., especially, that "humanist critics most wanted to reform" (Nauert 1990, 800) during this period, since it was seen as the foundation of all other studies, taken by youths at a most intellectually formative moment. Alberti gained a doctorate in law in 1428, and Duport became a doctor of divinity in 1660; Ramus took his M.A. at Paris in 1536, Milton at Cambridge in 1632; Buchanan received one B.A. from St. Andrews in 1525 and was admitted for a B.A. at Paris two years later. More research on how authors who studied for higher degrees beyond the propaedeutic language arts went on to feed that more specialized learning into their literary endeavors would be welcome.

How these authors represent institutional contexts in their works varies, seeming at times to touch only glancingly on what we know verifiably happened within the institutions depicted, and to exaggerate or even invent events and individuals associated with the universities. Certainly, curricular and statutory reconstructions are important for learning what Renaissance students did and read (if they obeyed the rules), and over the last few decades, the systematic work of social, educational, and intellectual historians has profoundly advanced our understanding of the contexts inhabited by early modern students across Europe (e.g., Brockliss 1987, Feingold 1997, Grendler 2002). Pinpointing the subject and timing of a lecture given on a particular day of the week, for instance, identifying how many matriculants came from which village, and itemizing the books left in a tutor's will are all of pivotal importance for anyone studying the universities. And to learn about what individuals at those institutions considered important, to gain more insight into what they may have thought, we should also read what they wrote. Compared with statutes, registration lists, college account books, and inventories, literary works are elusive: ideas become refracted through rhetorical artifice and the conventions of genre; the tone might be sarcastic, idealized, chatty, hyperbolic, bawdy, erudite, intimate, or abstracted, while the form might be mock-epic, elegiac, satirical, tragic, philosophical, or panegyrical. But an author's strategies do not prevent us from considering which aspects of an educational experience mattered to him, based on what he chose to explore in literary form.

STUDENT EXPERIENCE AT THE EARLY
MODERN UNIVERSITIES

University marked the transition into the adult world of institutions (law, politics, the church, the academy itself). The Protestant Reformation's emphasis on unmediated access to scripture for all (that is, translated into modern mother tongues from the Vulgate) meant that from the early sixteenth century onwards, the growth of the European vernaculars as national literary languages accelerated, and some have argued that by 1600, the vernaculars had "already displaced" Latin "outside the university and the church" (Leonhardt [2009] 2013, 193). Latin was the universities' common denominator, but linguistic medium was not always an easy choice for alumni with wider complex aspirations: writing Latin might make you comprehensible to an international community, but opting for the vernacular could mean that you would reach a more demographically varied national readership. Even though schoolteachers were eager that their pupils speak Latin as often as possible, boys still often returned from school to a vernacular-speaking home—one famous exception was the young Montaigne, whose household was under strict instruction only to address him in Latin—so were not fully immersed in Latin (Janson [2002] 2004, 106–7; cf. Waquet [1998] 2001, 7–12). But at university, even though the youth would no doubt speak in the vernacular to friends, he had officially entered a world dominated by *Latinitas* where public and sometimes even private utterance of the vernacular tended to be forbidden by statute and frowned upon by many tutors. In an influential and provocative interpretation of over half a century ago, Walter Ong argued that no other earlier groups of learned men ever "achieved the close-knit, jealously guarded internal organization of the [early modern] university," which he attributes to Latin's dominance there as "a secret language to nourish their *esprit de corps*" (Ong 1959, 109), although this *esprit* might be counterbalanced or reinforced by the *disputatio* and *aemulatio* pushing students to perform rivalry in public. Contemporary conduct manuals for students emphasized the primacy of Latin. In his 1594 *Il giovane studente* (*The Young Student*), the Sienese humanist Orazio Lombardelli (ca. 1540–1608) stressed its importance: "so mainly," Lombardelli says to his imaginary student, "I would like you to become familiar with the Latin language" (*Principalmente dunque vorrei, che vi faceste familiare la lingua latina*; Lombardelli 1594, 39v; see also Davies 2013). In his "Rules for Students" (ca. 1660), which we will encounter again later, the Cambridge tutor James Duport urged his charges to "Speake Latine always in the Hall, if not else-where or at other times" (Duport ca. 1650, 8). Lombardelli's choice of Italian and Duport's of English suggests that students did not invariably stick to Latin, but despite their pragmatic selections of the vernacular, both men's insistence shows how important it was officially to be *seen* conversing in Latin as a student. To succeed academically, in any case, fluency in Latin was paramount: a reputation for the polished deployment of Latin might then lead to a prestigious "fast-track" career after graduation, even to becoming, in time, part of the scholarly establishment that could withhold or bestow its approval on other ambitious young men.

Across early modern Europe, the universities' religious affiliations, political conformity or heterodoxy, curricula, and personnel were subject to often micromanagerial governmental scrutiny and had a formative impact on their students. Although few tidy generalizations can be made, it is worth outlining some characteristics that many of these institutions shared. The fifteenth to the seventeenth centuries witnessed many reforms, but significant continuities with the medieval universities also existed: the basic faculty structures (Arts, Law, Medicine, Theology) remained the same (Brockliss 1996, 573; Denley 2013, 492); Aristotle continued to dominate disciplines such as logic, ethics, and, for much of the period, natural philosophy (Schmitt 1984; Lines 2002); and the Reformation and Counter-Reformation reanimated the closeness of the relationship between university and church. This religious factionalism affected existing institutions of learning, rendering them "strife-ridden but seldom boring" (Grendler 2004, 1), and caused new universities (especially Protestant ones in Northern Europe) to be constructed. The impact of the Reformation on higher education lasted decades, if not centuries, beyond Luther's first intervention at the University of Wittenberg (Grendler 2004), and directly affected academic staffing: in mid–sixteenth-century England, for example, depending on their denominations at a given moment, scholars at Oxford and Cambridge were alternately hired and fired by the Protestant Edward VI (r. 1547–53), his Catholic sister Mary I (r. 1553–58) and their more moderate Protestant sister Elizabeth I (r. 1558–1603). In the North, a growing need for secular professional training in law, medicine, and state administration modified the universities' medieval status as predominantly theological institutions, while in Italy, especially in the wake of the Counter-Reformation, theology found more space at universities that had previously focused on more secular disciplines (Kristeller [1944–1945] 1979; Grendler 2002, 353–92).

Many social and economic factors affected a youth's experience of university. Average matriculation ages varied (Houston 2002, 90–93), but students were typically much younger than the average now, and matriculated during their early teenage years. Status and family wealth were important: richer students often did not take a degree, while poorer ones often earned their board as servants; the twelve-year-old Ramus, for example, entered the Collège de Navarre as a *cubicularius* (chamber-boy; Nancel 1975, 177). Although the *peregrinatio academica* ("academic pilgrims' path") was perhaps not as well trodden as it had been in the Middle Ages, many students still chose to study abroad (see, e.g., Tervoort 2005; Woolfson 1998), either for religious reasons, as in the case of English Catholics or Italian reformers in exile; or because appropriate institutions had not yet been founded in their own nations; or simply out of intellectual curiosity. Accommodation and tutorial provision differed: the main systems, based on the practice of two of the oldest universities, were the *modus Parisiensis* ("method of Paris") of boarding in colleges (e.g., in England, France, and Spain), and the *modus Bononiensis* ("method of Bologna") of private accommodation (Italy, Eastern and Northern Europe; Müller 1996, 329; Denley 2013, 492–93). At institutions such as Padua and Paris, students were organized by geographical origin into *nationes* ("nations") living together (e.g.,

Davies 2009, 101–3, on Siena and Pisa), which affected both the extracurricular use of the vernacular and how students defined themselves against their peers. Even if *nationes* were not formally implemented, as at the English universities, students still often drifted into regional groups (e.g., Boutcher 1998). Registration numbers fluctuated across the period, but in the sixteenth century "the overall number of students . . . was very high everywhere, although the pace of the increase varied from country to country" (Di Simone 1996, 298–99). The phenomenon of higher registration numbers, changes in student demographics, and reforms of collegiate and other institutional structures, among other factors, prompted the social historian Lawrence Stone to identify an "educational revolution" at the English universities (Stone 1964), and related effects were also felt in other parts of Europe. All of these factors helped shape students' experience and are touched on in their writing.

"O Duram . . . Studiosorum Sortem!" Alberti and the Problems of Learning in Quattrocento Italy

"O cruel fate of studious men!" (Alberti 1976, 84; Alberti 1999, 36): Leon Battista Alberti was one of the first humanists to write about the life of a *litteratus*, a "lettered" or "learned" man—as a relentless barrage of misery. Alberti figures his *De commodis litterarum atque incommodis* as prompted by his experience at "Bologna, while I was engaged in literary studies there" (*apud Bononiam, dum in studiis litterarum illic versarer*; Alberti 1976). Few admissions tutors would push the treatise towards prospective students, since the *incommoda* tend to triumph, expressed in depressing aphorisms: " . . . the life of the studious man . . . is by far the most painful life, especially if he has any longing for the things that a young man of generous disposition is naturally somewhat inclined to want" (*istius vita studiosi . . . est longe acerbissima, eoque magis si quid inciderit cupiditatum ad quas ipsa duce natura omnis generosa iuventus admodum prona est*; Alberti 1976, 60; Alberti 1999, 24). Alberti starts with the central problem facing clever young men writing original Latin works: that no one could "say it better" (*melius dicere*) than *priscis illis divinis scriptoribus* ("those sacred ancient writers"; Alberti 1976, 38); this self-deprecating, candid figuring of *imitatio* as a burden rather than a sacred duty was picked up by later writers. Other, more personal, burdens also affected Alberti's student career: his father died after his son's first year as a student at Bologna; as an illegitimate son he inherited no property, and he seems to have suffered a physical breakdown (Grafton 2000, 7 and 33).

Devotion to study means that you will never be able to dance, marry, play sports, buy clothes, or even go on a country walk because *illico te inde incepta professio detorquet ad libros et litteras* ("the profession you have taken up will direct you from it to books and letters"; Alberti 1976, 61). Alberti's *professio* kept its classical sense of "public declaration" but also meant "profession" in a more modern sense: the *professio* of Alberti's *litteratus* stresses humanistic study, contrasted with what we would still call "the professions," law and medicine. Alberti's *alma mater* Bologna, the oldest university (with Paris) in Europe, was famous for its teaching of law: for 1426–1427, roughly when Alberti was studying there, twenty-five professors of canon law and twenty-eight of civil law taught, compared with only four professors of rhetoric and poetry (Grendler 2002, 8). Echoing this structure of the university he attended, Alberti opposes the fate of *grammatici, rhetores philosophique* ("grammarians, writers [or "teachers of rhetoric"], and philosophers"; Alberti 1976, 86; Alberti 1999, 37) with the fate of the *scriba, medicus ac iurisperitus* ("the scribe, the physician, and the lawyer"; Alberti 1976, 87; Alberti 1999, 38). Alberti refers to the latter three as *professiones* that are *non magis erudimentis claras . . . quam paupertate* ("not more known for their erudition . . . than for their poverty"; Alberti 1976, 86; Alberti 1999, 37): his point is that one can actually make money as a scribe, physician, or lawyer, which one cannot from teaching rhetoric, for example. The climax of the argument is that, ultimately, *sole . . . venales litterae in pretio sint* ("only venal learning is prized"; Alberti 1976, 87; Alberti 1999, 38). Alberti distinguishes between intellectual freedom and knowledge that generates money, arguing that true *litterati* should behave "with a proper distaste for ephemeral gain" (Grayson 1988, xxxv). At the same time, he paints a bleak landscape of the lonely scholar's life (see also Oppel 1989, 126).

De commodis looks askance at the professional emphasis of the Italian universities, and Alberti's distinction between different kinds of studies—those that generate income and those that do not—proved as influential as his account of scholarly misery. It is also worth mentioning two other important elements brought by Alberti into literary representations of university life. The first we might expect from the author of a treatise on the family: Alberti embeds his *litteratus* within a family structure similar to his own and conjures up a conversation with a father who regrets spending so much money on the legal studies of his *filius iurisconsultus plane litteratissimus* ("son, clearly a most learned lawyer"; Alberti 1976, 68). Ong characterizes the student as isolated by his Latinity from the vernacular domestic sphere (Ong 1959), but Alberti does not represent academic study as occurring in a vacuum: his *litteratus* is a son, a brother, and a friend as well as an isolated intellectual. The second element relates to the point made by Rüegg, and discussed at the start of this chapter, that a "yearning for fame" was formative for many students at the modern universities: Alberti questions this impulse wryly throughout his Latin works. The very title of his 1424 Plautine play *Philodoxus* (*The Lover of Fame*), and its eponymous youth who loves the character Doxia (Alberti 2005), for instance, recall the debates in *De commodis* over whether scholars are motivated by "the cause of knowing, or the pleasure of acquiring honour and fame" (*vel sciendi causa, vel honoris et famae adipiscendae gratia*; Alberti 1976, 44).

"CLAMITAS ESSE FUREM, SUPERBISSIMUM, INSANUM": SIXTEENTH-CENTURY PARIS AND THE CULTURE OF DISPUTATION

Such "fame," good or bad, was important at the universities. "You yell that he is a thief, too proud, mad": Petrus Ramus's characterization of his rival Adrien Turnèbe's (1512–1565) attitude towards him and other *logici* ("logicians") gives us a heady savor of the ferociously competitive world of Parisian higher education (Ramus 1556, 16v). Here *ad hominem* calumnies were commonplace as more and more scholars threw themselves into the intellectual scrum (Chartier 1976, 164). Mid–sixteenth-century Paris has been called "the most important centre of classical scholarship" of the period (Brockliss 1996, 574; Sharratt 1976, 4), but despite— or, perhaps, because of—this reputation for excellence, then as now, intellectuals enjoyed scoring points off each other and doggedly undermining each other's positions. Even by the standards of humanist pedagogical polemic, however, mid–sixteenth-century Paris was highly combative: Alberti had depicted scholarly isolation and questioned the zeal for fame, but the institutions of learning in Paris present us with quite a different view on the life of the *litteratus* inhabiting a febrile world powered by *aemulatio* and *disputatio*.

We have already mentioned the *modus Parisiensis*: for its hierarchy, coherence, and resilience the University of Paris has been called "a work of art" (Denley 2013, 495), and its "accepted order of precedence: theology, law, medicine, and a long way below the three 'higher' faculties, arts" (Brockliss 1987, 53–54) helped cement that clear structure (see also Tuilier 1994). But this rigid cohesion and domination was pedagogically complicated in the sixteenth century by the smaller *collèges* that sprang up around the university, as well as in the provinces (Barnard 1922, 286–87; Verger [1973] 2013, 71–72). Founded in the later Middle Ages as "boarding houses . . . which had gradually evolved into centers of instruction" (Ong 1958, 21), the *collèges*, where the language arts were taught, became by the early sixteenth century "the major venue for humanist influence" (Nauert 1990, 811). Two pedagogically-minded humanists of that century, George Buchanan and Petrus Ramus, started their academic careers teaching in the Collèges of Sainte Barbe and Du Mans respectively. Buchanan went on to teach Montaigne and oversee him in plays at the Collège de Guyenne in Bordeaux in the mid-1540s, worked at Coimbra, and returned to St. Andrews in the mid-1560s, occupying in the same period various political posts, getting into trouble with the Inquisition, and combining scholarship and politics as tutor to the future King James VI and I in the 1570s (Ford 1982, 4–11). Ramus progressed to the Collège de l'Ave Maria, thence to the Collège de Presles, becoming its head; promoted to Regius Professor in 1551, he was also one of the first professors at the recently founded Collège Royal. Falling out of favor largely due to his religious views, in the early 1560s Ramus traveled to Germany and Switzerland, where he clashed this time with Théodore de Bèze and others in Geneva, before finally returning to Paris. Buchanan and Ramus's lives were turbulent partly because of their religious affiliations; what we see in Ramus's career, especially, is the cross-pollination between iconoclastic attitudes he was perceived to voice towards classical authority and a seditious religious ideology imputed to him by his critics.

Buchanan's first elegy, written as a tutor at Sainte Barbe in the late 1520s and printed in 1567, offers a different perspective on the relationship between learning and life outside institutional walls we observed in Alberti. Its title, *How Wretched Is the State of Those Teaching Classical Literature in Paris* (*Quam misera sit conditio docentium litteras humaniores Lutetiae*), needs no explanation; its speaker's problem is not (in Alberti's terms) how to "say it better" than the ancient writers, but how to say anything at all, as he bids "farewell to the barren muses" (*sterilesque valete Camenae*, line 1; Buchanan 1715, 301). Things get worse: an "angry father" (*iratus . . . parens*) blames the tutor for his son's ignorance (ll. 77–80) and for wasting his money; the tutor "grieves" that he has "frittered away his youth in unworthy studies" (l. 105). What seems like elegiac lament is also humanist *imitatio*: leaning heavily on Juvenal's seventh satire, an account of authorial poverty very influential in the Renaissance, and where the Muses are "sad" rather than barren (*tristes . . . Camenas*, 7.2), Buchanan's tutor-speaker shows his learning even as he laments the pointlessness of a classical education (Knight 2017). His elegy raises interesting questions about the different aspects of scholarship in Paris: if part of that city's academic reputation was based on the work of scholars like Guillaume Budé, for instance, works like Buchanan's elegy show a different aspect of an intensely self-aware classicizing world. Such original Latin poems both cleverly demonstrate an intertextual debt to ancient authors like Juvenal and adapt those authors to new, specifically institutional, contexts. Certainly, when Montaigne came to write his essay on pedagogy *De l'institution des enfants* (*On the Education of Children*, 1. 26), he mentions Buchanan, "this outstanding poet" (*ce grand poete*), three times, and here the teacher apparently learned from the student: Montaigne mentions that Buchanan was also planning a pedagogical work "and would take mine as an exemplar" (*qu'il prenoit l'exemplaire de la mienne*). Having studied as a youth both at St. Andrews and at the University of Paris, then teaching at Parisian and provincial *collèges*, at a Portuguese university, and at court as a tutor to a young Scottish prince for the last decade of his life, Buchanan has one of the most interestingly varied higher-level educational careers among Renaissance pedagogues. His elegy on teaching Latin offers fresh ways of meditating on higher-level pedagogy, different from the systematic treatises humanists like Vergerio and Guarino, and later Erasmus and the Jesuits, wrote; as a poet-tutor Buchanan puts into practice—in his imitation of Juvenal, for instance—what such treatises could only outline in theory.

Like Buchanan, Petrus Ramus inspired devotion from accomplished pupils who went on to write about him, but in the crucible of mid–sixteenth-century Paris, his "revolutionary approach" (Brockliss 1996, 581) also provoked intense opprobrium (Ong 1958; Lewis 1998). We have already seen Ramus's *Admonitio* in reaction to Turnèbe's attacks on logicians; his long list of imagined insults to *logici* is an impressive example of rhetorical "copiousness" (*copia*) but also reads like an elaborate joke that goes on a little too long, delivered by a raconteur too infatuated with his own eloquence. As well as a mad arrogant thief, a parrot (*psittacum*), and an Augean stable (*Augiae stabulum*), Ramus ironically likens the *logicus* both to tragic actor (*tragoedum*) and to tragic monkey (*simiam tragicam*; Ramus 1556, 16v). The point is to itemize, control, and sarcastically belittle all of the insults leveled at a scholar like him, but Ramus in fact had cultivated a reputation as a kind of scholar-actor, packing out lecture theaters from his earliest days at the Collège de l'Ave Maria. Many of Ramus's contemporaries resented (and, perhaps, secretly envied) a man we now might think of as a scholarly celebrity for his mesmeric powers over students, and he was represented as a kind of overgrown student himself for his attacks on classical authority: Turnèbe lambasted him for *in eius parentes . . . furiose debacchatus esset* ("having madly raged against his parents") Quintilian, Cicero, and Aristotle (Turnèbe 1600, 72). The rector of the University of Paris, Pierre Galland (1510–59) wrote that Ramus's *nugas* ("trifles") were not read *ad fructum aliquem . . . capiendum* ("to extract some profit from them") but rather *veluti vernaculos ridiculi Pantagruelis libros* ("like the vernacular books about that ridiculous Pantagruel"), the brilliant, often bawdy works of François Rabelais (Galland 1551, 9v).

But while his contemporaries trivialized him in the 1550s, after he had converted to Protestantism and traveled to Geneva, the seditious power of Ramus's ideas was taken more seriously. For Théodore de Bèze, watching Ramus teach, the French scholar exemplified a *spiritus discordiae* ("spirit of discord") with the power "to disturb the churches" (*ad turbandas ecclesias*; de Bèze 1988, 30 and 216). As he was such a controversial figure in contemporary institutional life, several accounts attribute with vicious relish his violent death in the Saint Bartholomew's Day Massacre of August 1572 to his former students. Buchanan and particularly Ramus exemplify how pedagogy and politics could become intertwined in this turbulent period, and how Latin writing within an institutional context—far from remaining remote and desiccated—fed into ideological engagement.

"Be Frequent in Exercising Your Stile": Self-Promotion and Self-Reflection in Early Seventeenth-Century England

We have already seen how influential Juvenal's seventh satire was for Buchanan. The poem begins with the observation that the *spes et ratio studiorum* ("hope and incentive of studies") depend on *Caesare tantum* ("Caesar alone"; 7.1). The unpredictable favor of Caesar's successors, who might include royalty, the aristocracy, anyone wealthy, or powerful clergymen, is a constant refrain in the university writing of the time. In his encyclopaedic *Anatomy of Melancholy* (1621), the Oxford scholar Robert Burton glumly quotes Juvenal's line and then remarks "as he said of old, we may truly say now" (Burton 1989, 320) before slipping into an extended Latin complaint about self-aggrandizing scholars. As in Alberti's treatise, as we have seen, this became a familiar topos in university writing: the true *litteratus* looked inwards for intellectual development; the venal academic looked outwards for financial gain. But reality was much more complicated, of course, and the ethics of seeking preferment for one's academic prowess were murky. Institutional practice affected individual behavior: on high-profile occasions when a royal or aristocratic visitor was in town, the university authorities, like proud show business–minded parents, pushed their most gifted students into the spotlight shone onto the institution by that visiting worthy, and those students, understandably, hoped that a successful rhetorical performance in Latin on a conspicuous occasion might lead to preferment. Unfortunately, there were too many talented young men and too few opportunities for preferment: hopes of favor usually glittered more than actual outcomes.

An example from early seventeenth-century Cambridge illustrates the different trajectories promising student Latinists took in later life. In late September of 1629, Henry Rich (1590–1649), Earl of Holland and recently appointed chancellor of Cambridge, visited the university, and was greeted and praised with elaborate Latin speeches as Cambridge offered up its multilingual erudition and political conformity to this influential courtier. Two students each wrote two Latin "act verses" for the chancellor, poems that outlined the thesis and argumentation of a formal debate and were circulated among the audience (Knight 2010). The first student, James Duport, had perhaps the tougher task, writing two poems to accompany the debates in medicine on the unpoetic subjects "an annual purging as part of a health regime contributes to well-being" (*anniversaria evacuatio in regimine sanitatis confert ad salutem*) and "one should be allowed to practice medicine in the dog-days of summer" (*in diebus canicularibus licet medicari*; Duport 1676, 517–20). The second student, John Milton, wrote two poems to complement the philosophy debates, entitled "That Nature does not suffer decay" (*Naturam non pati senium*) and "On the Platonic Idea as understood by Aristotle" (*De idea Platonica quemadmodum Aristoteles intellexit*; Milton 2014, 184–91). Duport went on to become a well-liked tutor, priest, professor of Greek, and college head, writing some illuminating *Rules for Students* as well as many Latin poems suggesting their author's status high in the academic and ecclesiastical hierarchy and a series of occasional poems. Milton is the most famous bilingual English and Latin poet; although he participated in the official 1629 visit and wrote many poems on the death of university-affiliated worthies, he left Cambridge with decidedly mixed feelings towards his *alma mater*. As a B.A. and M.A. student at Christ's College between 1625 and 1632, Milton wrote the kind of Latin expected of a promising student (e.g., Hale 2005). His seven orations delivered in college and at the Public Schools, known as the *Prolusions*, cover a range of topics from Aristotelian philosophy (being, matter, generation) to knowledge versus ignorance and engage carefully with a range of ancient sources like Pythagoras, Hesiod, and the Orphic hymns, besides more curriculum-based analyses of Aristotle and Plato. Milton wrote a series of Latin poems as a student: as well as the two sets of act verses, which function to some extent as poetic versions of *Prolusions* by showing his skill in *disputatio*, his other poems dating from the mid-1620s variously commemorate the death of Cambridge-associated dignitaries like Lancelot Andrewes, bishop of Winchester (*Elegia tertia* [Third Elegy]); celebrate the advent of spring (*Elegia quinta* [Fifth Elegy]); attack the papacy and praise the monarchy (*In Quintum Novembris* [On the Fifth of November], a poem about the Gunpowder Plot to blow up the Houses of Parliament by Guy Fawkes and his co-conspirators in 1605); and demonstrate Ovid's influence by sneering at the university's rural provincialism to a similarly clever, urbane friend (*Elegia Prima* [First Elegy]). Milton's early English poems also reflect the diversity of university personnel, most famously in his threnody *Lycidas* (1637) for the drowned Christ's Fellow Edward King, but also in two 1631 poems on the death of Thomas Hobson, the university carrier who loaned out horses to staff and students. After leaving university, though, Milton frequently presented Cambridge in a highly skeptical light: he is very cutting towards student amateur theatricals in the tract *An Apology* (1642)—even though he wrote an Aristotelian college entertainment himself, starring *Ens* ("Being"), Quantity, Quality, and Relation (Milton 2014, 239–40); his two vernacular epics *Paradise Lost* (1667) and *Paradise Regained* (1671) look quizzically at disputation, as the fallen angels debate in hell, and Christ in the later poem rejects Athens and its various philosophical schools. In his pedagogical treatise *Of Education* (1644), having experienced the less formal institution of the Italian academies during the late 1630s (Haan 1998), Milton argued for a new kind of educational institution and seemed to distance himself from the way *Latinitas* was fostered at the university (Knight 2011). That said, at the end of his life, Milton oversaw the printing of various pedagogical works associated with his time at Cambridge, including his Ramist logic and the *Prolusions*.

Of the two young men who had entertained the Earl of Holland with their act verses, unlike Milton his more restless contemporary, James Duport stayed ensconced at Cambridge. The political fortunes of the two men were in stark contrast: during the 1650s, Milton worked as Latin secretary for Cromwell and wrote polemical prose tracts; in the same period, due perhaps to royalist sympathies, Duport lost some of his academic status, although he remained a fellow of Trinity (O'Day 2008). During that decade, Duport started work on his *Rules for Students*, which give us a vivid sense of how central the cultivation of Latin still was for institutional life, and outline conventions of university Latinity in a conversational, lucid list. The combative nature of a *Latinitas* honed by formal debate is key ("Vse often to dispute & argue"), as is the scaffolding of regulations that held it up ("Be sure you omitt no Acts nor Exercise, that either the statutes require, or your Tutor appoints you"), and the careful selection of rhetorical and poetic authorities ("Make choise of the best Authors in every faculty, as Demosthenes and Tully, for Oratory, Homer, and Virgil for poetrie and &c."; Duport ca. 1650, 8–9). At the same time, though, Duport urges his students to keep their writing fresh ("In your Speeches & Declamations, doe not use, or affect old Phrases"), to engage thoughtfully with their reading rather than doggedly plow through as many books as possible ("Thinke it not enough to read too much except you meditate on what you have read"), and to practice not only style but also new ideas, emphasizing competence in both classical languages as well as the vernacular ("Be frequent in exercising your stile, & invention in Greeke Latine, and sometimes in English"). Duport seems interested not only in getting students to pass their examinations efficiently, but also in encouraging them to develop their own intellectual habits, rhetorical talents, and literary voices. His *Rules* offer well-balanced guidance for students and point to an industrious but well-integrated experience of university. The reality of life at the early modern universities, as we have seen, though, was not always so harmonious: not all tutors were so humane, and not all former students remembered their time there with rosy nostalgia.

SUGGESTED READING

The chapters in De Ridder-Symoens (1996) provide a variety of perspectives on European universities. For readers new to the study of the universities, especially, Grendler (2010) is a very useful bibliography, and Houston (2002, 83–98) offers helpful brief orientation. For Italy, see Grendler (2002), Lines (2002) and Davies (2009); for France, Brockliss (1987), and Chartier (1976); for England, Stone (1964) still prompts debate, Feingold (1997) is a thought-provoking study of the humanities, and McConica (1986) and Morgan (2004) offer valuable discussion. Kirwan (2013, mainly on Italy) and Rundle and Petrina (2013) are two recent collections that include a number of different approaches to the universities.

REFERENCES

Alberti, Leon Battista. 1976. *De commodis litterarum atque incommodis*. Edited by Laura Goggi Carotti. Florence: Olschki.

——. 1999. *The Use and Abuse of Books*. Translated by Renée Neu Watkins. Prospect Heights: Waveland Press.

——. 2005. *The Play of Philodoxus*. In *Humanist Comedies*, edited and translated by Gary R. Grund, 70–169. Cambridge: Harvard University Press.

Barnard, Howard B. 1922. *The French Tradition in Education: Ramus to Mme Necker de Saussure*. Cambridge: Cambridge University Press.

Boutcher, Warren. 1998. "Pilgrimage to Parnassus: Local Intellectual Traditions, Humanist Education and the Cultural Geography of Sixteenth-Century England." In *Pedagogy and Power*, edited by Yun Lee Too and Niall Livingstone, 110–47. Cambridge: Cambridge University Press.

Brockliss, Laurence W. B. 1987. *French Higher Education in the Seventeenth and Eighteenth Centuries: A Cultural History*. Oxford: Clarendon Press.

——. 1996. "Curricula." In de Ridder-Symoens 1996, 563–620.

Buchanan, George. 1715. *Opera Omnia*. 2 vols. Edited by Thomas Ruddiman. Edinburgh: Robert Freebairn.

Burckhardt, Jacob. (1860) 2004. *The Civilization of the Renaissance in Italy*. Translated by Samuel G. C. Middlemore. London: Penguin.

Burton, Robert. 1989. *The Anatomy of Melancholy*. Edited by Thomas C. Faulkner, Nicolas K. Kiessling, and Rhonda L. Blair. Vol. 1. Oxford: Oxford University Press.

Chartier, Roger, Dominique Julia, Marie-Madeleine Compère, eds.1976. *L'Éducation en France du XVIᵉ au XVIIIᵉ Siècle*. Paris: SEDES.

Davies, Jonathan. 2009. *Culture and Power: Tuscany and its Universities*. Leiden: Brill.

——. 2013. "The Ideal Student: Manuals of Student Behaviour in Early Modern History." In Kirwan 2013, 21–38.

De Bèze, Théodore de. 1988. *Correspondance*. Vol. 13, *1572*. Edited by Hippolyte Aubert, Alain Doufour, and Béatrice Nicollier. Geneva: Droz.

De Ridder-Symoens, Hilde, ed. 1996. *A History of the University in Europe*. Vol. 2, *Universities in Early Modern Europe (1500–1800)*. Cambridge: Cambridge University Press.

Denley, Peter. 2013. "'Medieval', 'Renaissance', 'Modern': Issues of Periodization in Italian University History." In Rundle and Petrina 2013, 487–503.

Di Simone, Maria R. 1996. "Admission." In de Ridder-Symoens, op. cit., 285–325.

Duport, James. ca. 1650. "Rules for Students." Manuscript. Trinity College, Cambridge O 10A 33.

———. 1676. *Musae subsecivae seu poetica stromata*. Cambridge: John Hayes.

Feingold, Mordechai. 1997. "The Humanities." In *The History of the University of Oxford*, vol. 4, *Seventeenth-Century Oxford*, edited by Nicholas Tyacke, 211–358. Oxford: Clarendon Press.

Ford, Philip. 1982. *George Buchanan, Prince of Poets*. Aberdeen: Aberdeen University Press.

Galland, Pierre. 1551. *Pro schola Parisiensi contra novam academiam Petri Rami oratio*. Paris: Vascosan.

Grafton, Anthony. 2000. *Leon Battista Alberti: Master Builder of the Italian Renaissance*. London: Penguin.

———. 2009. "A Sketch Map of a Lost Continent: The Republic of Letters." *Republics of Letters: A Journal for the Study of Knowledge, Politics, and the Arts* 1:1–18. Available at http://arcade.stanford.edu/rofl/sketch-map-lost-continent-republic-letters.

Grafton, Anthony, and Lisa Jardine. 1986. *From Humanism to the Humanities: Education and the Liberal Arts in Fifteenth- and Sixteenth-Century Europe*. London: Duckworth.

Grayson, Cecil. 1988. "De commodis atque incommodis." *Modern Language Review* 83(4):xxxi–xlii.

Grendler, Paul F. 2002. *The Universities of the Italian Renaissance*. Baltimore: Johns Hopkins University Press.

———. 2004. "The Universities of the Renaissance and Reformation." *Renaissance Quarterly* 57:1–42.

———. 2010. *Universities*. In *Oxford Bibliographies Online: Renaissance and Reformation*. Oxford University Press. doi:10.1093/OBO/9780195399301-0033

Guarino, Battista. 2002. *A Program of Teaching and Learning*. In Kallendorf 2002, 260–309.

Haan, Estelle. 1998. *From* Academia *to* Amicitia: *Milton's Latin Writings and the Italian Academies*. Philadelphia: American Philosophical Society.

Hale, John. 2005. *Milton's Cambridge Latin: Performing in the Genres, 1625–1632*. Tempe: Arizona Center for Medieval and Renaissance Studies.

Houston, Robert A. 2002. *Literacy in Early Modern Europe: Culture and Education 1500–1800*. 2nd ed. Harlow: Longman.

Janson, Tore. (2002) 2004. *A Natural History of Latin*. Oxford: Oxford University Press.

Kallendorf, Craig W., ed. and trans. 2002. *Humanist Educational Treatises*. Cambridge: Harvard University Press.

Kirwan, Richard, ed. 2013. *Scholarly Self-Fashioning and Community in the Early Modern University*. Farnham: Ashgate.

Knight, Sarah. 2010. "Milton's Student Verses of 1629." *Notes and Queries* 255:37–39.

———. 2011. "Milton's Forced Themes." *Milton Quarterly* 45:145–60.

———. 2017. "How the Young Man Should Study Latin Poetry." In *NLL*, 52–65.

Kristeller, Paul O. (1944–45) 1979. "Humanism and Scholasticism in the Italian Renaissance." In *Renaissance Thought and Its Sources*, 85–105. New York: Columbia University Press.

Leonhardt, Jürgen. (2009) 2013. *Latin: Story of a World Language*. Cambridge: Belknap Press.

Lewis, John. 1998. *Adrien Turnèbe (1512–1565): A Humanist Observed*. Geneva: Droz.

Lines, David. 2002. *Aristotle's* Ethics *in the Italian Renaissance (ca. 1300–1650): The Universities and the Problem of Moral Education*. Leiden: Brill.

Lombardelli, Orazio. 1594. *Il giovane studente*. Venice: La Minima Compagnia.

McConica, James, ed. 1986. *The History of the University of Oxford*. Vol. 3. Oxford: Clarendon Press.

Milton, John. 2014. *Shorter Poems*. Edited and translated by Barbara Kiefer Lewalski and Estelle Haan. Oxford: Oxford University Press.

Morgan, Victor. 2004. *History of the University of Cambridge*. Vol. 2. Cambridge: Cambridge University Press.

Müller, Rainer A. 1996. "Student Education, Student Life." In de Ridder-Symoens, op. cit., 326–54.

Nancel, Nicolas de. 1975. *Petri Rami Vita*. Edited and translated by Peter Sharratt. *Humanistica Lovaniensia* 24:161–277.

Nauert, Charles G. 1990. "Humanist Infiltration into the Academic World: Some Studies of Northern Universities." *Renaissance Quarterly* 43:799–812.

O'Day, Rosemary. 2008. "Duport, James (1606–1679)." In *Oxford Dictionary of National Biography*. Oxford University Press. doi:10.1093/ref:odnb/8301

Ong, Walter J. 1958. *Ramus: Method, and the Decay of Dialogue; from the Art of Discourse to the Art of Reason*. Chicago: University of Chicago Press.

———. 1959. "Latin Language Study as a Renaissance Puberty Rite." *Studies in Philology* 56:103–24.

Oppel, John. 1989. "Alberti on the Social Position of the Intellectual." *The Journal of Medieval and Renaissance Studies* 19:123–58.

Ramus, Petrus. 1556. *Admonitio ad Turnebum*. Paris: Wechel.

Rüegg, Walter, 1996. "Themes." In de Ridder-Symoens, op. cit., 3–42.

Rundle, David, and Alessandra Petrina, eds. 2013. *The Italian University in the Renaissance*. Special issue, *Renaissance Studies* 27, 4:480–587.

Schmitt, Charles. 1984. *The Aristotelian Tradition and Renaissance Universities*. London: Variorum.

Sharratt, Peter, 1976. "Peter Ramus and the Reform of the University". In *French Renaissance Studies 1540-70*, ed. by Peter Sharratt, 4-20. Edinburgh: Edinburgh University Press.

Stone, Lawrence. 1964. "The Educational Revolution in England, 1560–1640." *Past and Present* 28:41–80.

Tervoort, Ad. 2005. *The* Iter Italicum *and the Northern Netherlands: Dutch Students at Italian Universities and Their Role in the Netherlands' Society (1426–1575)*. Leiden: Brill.

Tuilier, André. 1994. *Histoire de l'Université de Paris et de la Sorbonne*. 2 vols. Paris: Nouvelle Librairie de France.

Turnèbe, Adrien. 1600. *Opera*. Strasbourg: Zetzner.

Verger, Jacques. (1973) 2013. *Les Universités au moyen âge*. Paris: Presses Universitaires de France.

Vergerio, Pier Paolo. 2002. *The Character and Studies Befitting a Free-Born Youth*. In Kallendorf, op. cit., 2–91.

Waquet, Françoise. (1998) 2001. *Latin or the Empire of a Sign*. London: Verso.

Woolfson, Jonathan. 1998. *Padua and the Tudors: English Students in Italy, 1485–1603*. Toronto: University of Toronto Press.

CHAPTER 16

....

PHILOSOPHY

....

GUIDO GIGLIONI

BETWEEN the Middle Ages and the modern period, the fabric of philosophical Latin underwent a series of crucial transformations induced by historical events as well as intellectual reasons. To begin with, the translation activity from Greek into Latin carried out by several fifteenth-century humanists in Italy and their own reflection on that activity had a profound impact on the practice of philosophical writing, on both a stylistic and a conceptual level. In this context, Leonardo Bruni (1369–1444), Lorenzo Valla (1407–1457), and Giovanni Pico della Mirandola (1463–1494), to mention only a few, are perfect cases in point, but the debate about the style of philosophical Latin involved quite a number of humanists and schoolmen, continuing long after the sixteenth century. By injecting the germs of historicity, cultural relativism, and social constructivism into the body of metaphysical knowledge (a kind of knowledge viewed as stable and self-sufficient), humanistic reflection helped accelerate the crisis of philosophical Latin in the early modern period.

Closely connected to characteristically humanist discontents about the status of scholastic jargon was the renewed eagerness to provide Latin translations from Greek, Arabic, and Hebrew sources during the fifteenth and sixteenth centuries. While some of these works were in fact re-translations of previously translated texts, others were original versions of treatises that had never been translated before. The recovery of Platonic and Hermetic sources and Ficino's influential translations represent some of the most significant instances in this field. One should also add, however, the various editions of Aristotle's collected works supplied with Averroes's (ca. 1126–1198) commentaries, which, as was the case with the celebrated editions of the Venetian Giuntine press, came out with new translations and editorial contributions (Schmitt 1984b; Burnett 2013). Among the new translations of Averroes's works, his *Destructio destructionum* (*Destruction of Destructions*, refuting an earlier *Destruction of Philosophers* by the theologian Al-Ghazali) became certainly the most significant addition, first commented upon by Agostino Nifo (1470–1538) in a slightly revised version of the fourteenth-century translation by one Calonymos ben Calonymos of Arles, and later published in a new translation by a Neapolitan physician who also called himself Calonymos, in

1527, entitled *Subtilissimus liber Averois qui dicitur Destructio* (*The Most Subtle Book by Averroes Entitled Destruction*).

A third factor in the transformation of philosophical Latin was the increasingly more frequent appearance of cases of philosophical bilingualism, evident among authors who began to write in both Latin and the vernacular, such as Marsilio Ficino (1433–1499), Francesco Patrizi (1529–1597), Giordano Bruno (1548–1600), Francis Bacon (1561–1626), Tommaso Campanella (1568–1639), René Descartes (1596–1650), Thomas Hobbes (1588–1679), and Baruch Spinoza (1632–1677). Such a close proximity of Latin and the vernacular, besides signaling a growing tension between traditional institutional sites of Latin knowledge such as the university and milieus that were becoming more and more receptive to philosophical discussions in the vernacular (courts in the first place, but also academies, convents, chanceries, and salons), resulted in particularly creative phenomena of hybridization and cross-pollination between different linguistic currencies.

Finally, an important medium that more than any other reflects the early modern evolution of philosophical Latin is the genre of the Latin dictionary of philosophy, which became extremely popular between the sixteenth and the eighteenth century, as a by-product of a diffuse interest in lexica, glossaries, and other linguistic tools. Dictionaries were meant to handle and organize an increasingly unmanageable load of information that, between the fifteenth and sixteenth centuries, had poured out throughout Europe, as a result of the combined action of the printing press, geographical discoveries, technological progress, and a singularly vibrant culture of intellectual confrontation and debate. Among the various attempts to harvest and index philosophical information, the most significant case was Rudolph Goclenius's *Lexicon philosophicum* (1613) and *Lexicon philosophicum Graecum* (1615), but we should add Johannes Micraelius's *Lexicon philosophicum terminorum philosophis usitatorum* (*Dictionary of Terms Used by Philosophers*, 1653) and Étienne Chauvin's *Lexicon rationale, sive thesaurus philosophicus* (*Dictionary of Reason, or Philosophical Treasury*, 1692). Giordano Bruno compiled his own dictionary of philosophical concepts, *Summa terminorum metaphysicorum* (*Compendium of Metaphysical Terms*, 1609), probably devised as a teaching tool while he was lecturing in some German universities (Canone 1988; Bruno 1989). This tradition culminated with Bayle's vernacular *Dictionnaire historique et critique* (1697, 1702) and had its witty coda with Voltaire's *Dictionnaire philosophique*, published in 1764.

HUMANISM

Major linguistic turns have periodically affected the course of philosophical inquiries in Western Europe. In ancient Greece, the fifth-century sophists were able to question the idea of an original correspondence between reason and reality by emphasizing the inherently conventional and contractual nature of language. While doing so, they acted as powerful catalysts for both Plato's and Aristotle's responses in the domain of metaphysics. Likewise, the effort to test the boundaries that separate reality from its linguistic descriptions became a recurrent *leitmotif* in twentieth-century philosophy, in both Continental (Heidegger) and analytical traditions (Wittgenstein). The Renaissance represented another of these decisive linguistic turns. The fifteenth- and sixteenth- century debate concerning the relationship between reason and language took place on two different levels: one of a technical character (the nature of scholastic Latin), the other of a broader cultural significance (the issue of multilingualism).

With respect to the first level, it should be pointed out that, between the fifteenth and the eighteenth centuries, a large part of the philosophical output was still being written in scholastic Latin. Starting with Boethius in the sixth century CE and continuing for more than ten centuries, a momentous effort in translation and exegesis, marked by a sophisticated level of analytical precision and linguistic creativity, resulted in a formidable corpus of knowledge. Its constitutive language—scholastic Latin—was one of the principal reasons for its long-lasting success (Gregory 2006, 3; Dionisotti 1997). Precisely because of its aspects of raw artificiality, free from the strictures of idiomatic decorum, scholastic philosophical Latin turned out to be a most flexible tool for the exercise of thinking, open to all sorts of experiments with respect to both language and logic. Here I am deliberately using the oxymoronic label "raw artificiality." Within the field of philosophy, scholastic Latin was largely an artificial creation produced in the great translation laboratories of medieval Europe (in Spain, Sicily, and Provence) and remained characterized by a distinctive quality of unpolished immediacy that suited very well the task of thinking, and thinking outside the historical box. Due to particular circumstances, the encounter of scholastic Latin and philosophy was quite a unique episode in the history of Western culture, more so than in the fields of law and medicine, where the question of the relationship between verbal and nonverbal knowledge never managed to rise to the status of foundational issue, as had happened in metaphysics. During the seventeenth and eighteenth centuries, a number of philosophical innovators charged scholastic Latin with being a parasitical construction in relation to the free exercise of thought. In fact, that kind of Latin had long been an uncanny symbiosis of mind and word. As far as the second level is concerned—that is to say, the emergence of national vernaculars as legitimate media for literary pursuits of all kinds and orders—a generalized state of multilingualism at the beginning of the early modern period created the ideal conditions for the rise of original considerations on the nature of language.

The humanist revolt against the use of scholastic Latin in philosophy was fueled by discussions about the nature of translation. In *De interpretatione recta* (*On the Correct Way to Translate*), written around 1424 and designed as a manifesto stating the requisites for a good translation, Leonardo Bruni preferred to dwell on the technical aspects of the question rather than explore the speculative implications underlying the activity of thinking. Criticizing the medieval translator of Aristotle's *Nicomachean Ethics*, whom we know to be Robert Grosseteste (ca. 1175–1253), Bruni pointed out the "scholarly incompetence" (*imperitia litterarum*) of the latter—that is, both the naiveté with which he had undertaken a task well beyond his capabilities, and his obvious lack of literary taste, which had prevented him from reproducing the original flair of Aristotle's text (Bruni 1996, 152 and 160). In Bruni's opinion, the "efficacy" and "rationale" (*vis* and *ratio*) of a good translation lie in transferring the written form of a particular language into the form of another language. In order to do so, a translator needs to have a vast and confident knowledge of both languages, acquired through long and careful readings of different kinds of writing (*multiplex et varia ac accurata lectio omnis generis scriptorum*; Bruni 1996, 158). Being a transfer of forms more than an exercise in thinking, translation was first and foremost a reenactment of the original experience of literary enchantment and largely an aesthetic experience. This also applied to the field of philosophy, for, Bruni pointed out, Plato's and Aristotle's books were "replete with embellishments (*exornationes*) and elegance (*venustates*)" (Bruni 1996, 160 and 176). The best translator was therefore that artisan of the written word who was capable of transforming himself entirely—with both his mind and will—into the author he was translating (*sese in primum scribendi auctorem tota mente et animo et voluntate convertet*). Bruni argued that if a translator is not capable of recovering the spirit of the original, he cannot aspire to preserve its meaning (*sensus*). The skill lies in keeping the stylistic template of the original (*figura primae orationis*) and the verbal coloring (*verborum colores*). The model is therefore painting, not philosophy. More specifically, with respect to philosophical translation, the translator is supposed to combine knowledge of reality (*doctrina rerum*) with style (*scribendi ornatus*), for the ultimate aim behind all his efforts is to recover the life of the author's thoughts, their vividness (*splendor sententiarum*) and the naturally harmonic flow of the original (*tota ad numerum facta oratio*; Bruni 1996, 158 and 166).

A militant anti-philosophical attitude lingers in Valla's *Dialecticae disputationes* (*Dialectical Disputations*, composed in three different redactions, in 1439, 1448, and 1452). As in Bruni's *De interpretatione recta*, Valla's arguments were grammatical and aesthetic rather than philosophical (Valla 2012, 1:54–56; Dionisotti 1997). In focusing on the aspects of aesthetic and grammatical awkwardness among scholastic philosophers, Lorenzo Valla was close to Bruni's position. Like Bruni, he dismissed the scholastic tendency to reify adjectives and pronouns (sometimes even adverbs) into philosophical objects as an illegitimate and pointless practice, for they were abusing, as it were, the natural—grammatically correct—process of deriving abstract nouns from adjectives, such as *sanitas* ("health") from *sanus* ("healthy"). Contrary to the logic of historical languages, philosophers made instead *quiditas* ("whatness") out of *quid* ("what"), *perseitas* ("per se-ness") out of per se and *haecceitas* ("thisness") out of *haecce* ("this"), and this was all the more irritating because creations of this kind could not even be found in Aristotle's own works (*haec ab Aristotele non traduntur*). Most of all, Valla condemned the artificial decision of giving a name to the very essence of being, *entitas* (literally "being-ness," later entering standard English usage as "entity"), out of *ens*, which was a fictional present participle of the verb *esse* ("to be"), never used by Latin writers.

Giovanni Pico tackled the question of Latinate forms of philosophical expression by appealing to the ancient trope of contrasting nature with convention. In Pico's opinion, the effort to understand reality was always more pressing than finding the correct linguistic expression. Reworking in an original way the classical argument used to defend the power of language over freedom of thinking, he assigned a priority to philosophy over Latinity based on both nature and conventions. Addressing the Venetian scholar Ermolao Barbaro (1454–1493; Garin 1952, 804–23), he claimed that he was even ready to embrace the argument based on convention, which had always been the traditional prerogative of rhetoricians and sophists. If the foundations of any language were deemed to be conventional, Pico went on, then every linguistic community on earth was entitled to have its own laws (*normae dicendi*) and to philosophize in accordance with those laws. Indeed, it was precisely the thesis of the conventional, historical, and social origins of language, so often championed by the humanists, which, in Pico's opinion, made their charges of barbarism leveled at scholastic Latin irrelevant. However, he believed that anxieties about linguistic barbarism were even more out of place if the discussion pertained to the natural origin of meanings and words. If terminological correctness (*rectitudo nominum*) depended on nature, Pico went on, why should one turn to the rhetoricians to know more about the nature of this *rectitudo*, and not to the philosophers, "who alone have examined and clarified the nature of all things?" Formulated with a precise anti-rhetorical aim in mind, the tone of Pico's question was clearly rhetorical, for we know where Pico's allegiances lay (namely, for the philosophers and against the rhetoricians): "that which the ears reject as being too harsh, reason accepts as more in tune with reality (*utpote rebus cognatiora*)" (Garin 1952, 818–20). He was convinced that, by revealing the unsettling domain of things that could not be verbally articulated, the limits of language exposed reality in its more perplexing aspects. The need for philosophers to stretch the boundaries of the common use of words came, therefore, directly from a perceived rift between what could and what could not be said. "Why did the philosophers need to introduce innovations into the language and not to speak in Latin," Pico asked, "if they were born among Latins?" This time, the question was not rhetorical, and indeed was the most crucial question of all; for Pico, like Plato, was convinced that, ontologically speaking, there was an original surplus of meaning that no historic language could ever encompass (Garin 1952, 820), and even a language as nuanced as Latin was not equal to putting into words the full range of human ideas and experience.

Not only was reality ontologically richer than any description language could provide; it also evolved faster than historic languages. At a time when an overflow of new information demanded new words and new linguistic solutions, philosophers—whether metaphysicians, logicians, or natural and moral thinkers—did not have time to check their Latin grammars and repertoires of verbal *elegantiae*. In his *Dialogo delle lingue* (*Dialogue on Languages*, 1542), Sperone Speroni (1500–1588), one of the most illustrious members of the Paduan Accademia degli Infiammati, represented the contrast of convention (*arbitrio*) and nature (*natura*) by imagining a duel between the philologist Giano Lascaris (1445–1534) and the philosopher Pietro Pomponazzi (1462–1525). In this case, a curious reversal of roles occurred between nature and convention: Lascaris, who in the dialogue defended the need to be proficient in Greek and Latin in order to be able to practice philosophy, appealed to nature as a norm that could not be changed by social and cultural interventions; Pomponazzi, by contrast, resumed the well-rehearsed humanist argument about the conventional origin of languages in order to vindicate the right for every nation to philosophize in the vernacular (Speroni 1740, 193).

Stimulated by the broad linguistic turn that took place during the Renaissance and by individual contributions of humanist scholars (Schmitt 1984c), a good number of philosophers, including the most stylistically and linguistically alert, reached the conclusion that thinking required a deeper investment than simply relying on grammatical and rhetorical proficiency. The reason was that reality itself was "barbaric," alien, richer, and evolving more quickly than words. Thinking was also a more integral and wholesome experience than the one provided by correct descriptions of things, both grammatically and stylistically. Any verbal account of reality was inherently partial and effete compared to the freedom and poignancy of inner meditation. As Pico had pointed out to Barbaro, philosophers had always been in search of a language that could be close to reality as a whole, including the reality of the soul. In this sense, reasons of intellectual honesty made inward experience more valuable than linguistic proficiency: "Those who create a disagreement between the heart and the tongue are mistaken. However, aren't those who are all tongue (*toti sunt lingua*), precisely because they have no heart (*excordes*), simply dead dictionaries, as Cato says?" (Garin 1952, 820; Kraye 2007).

LATIN AND THE VERNACULARS

Starting with Dante's *Convivio* (*The Banquet*, ca. 1304) in Italy, French translations of Aristotle's *Nicomachean Ethics* and *Politics* in the fourteenth century, and a teeming output of mystical treatises in German (Meister Eckhart, active between the thirteenth and fourteenth centuries, being the most representative case), the use of the vernacular as a philosophical language was prompted by rhetorical, political, and religious motives, such as the need to extend the range of one author's readership, the will to reach social classes not directly involved in courtly or intellectual life, the urge to give immediate expression to lofty theological speculations, and a dearth of administrative and diplomatic personnel trained in the art of argumentation. And yet, in all these cases, there was still a link that connected the vernacular to the template of scholastic Latin. Even the rising of a philosophical discourse in German with strong mystical overtones emerged out of scholastic Latin (De Libera 1995). When Bernardo Segni (1505–1558), to give another example, translated and commented the *Nicomachean Ethics* into Tuscan (Segni 1550), the technical language remained highly Latinate and scholastic in origin. Giordano Bruno, to mention someone who was as linguistically creative in the vernacular as he loathed both scholastic obscurity and grammatical pedantry, fully recognized the speculative value of the scholastic tradition. Averroes, he famously retorted, knew his Aristotle better than any of his Greek readers (Bruno 1958, 306).

The relationship between Latin and the vernaculars in the domain of philosophical writing became increasingly more sophisticated during the early modern period. The practice of translating from Latin into the vernacular and the complementary trend to turn vernacular texts into Latin responded to different but parallel communicative strategies. While the move from Latin into the vernacular was largely aimed at expanding the social spectrum of the philosophical audience, the tendency to transpose vernacular texts into Latin made the most recent and innovative results in the field accessible to an international readership. To these general lines of exchange one should add individual cases of self-translation, in which authors, depending on their specific needs and rhetorical preferences, could switch from one medium to another and experiment with different linguistic resources. To mention a few examples of self-translation, Ficino turned his Latin *De amore* (*On Love*, 1469) and *De Christiana religione* (*On the Christian Faith*, 1474) into Tuscan; Campanella translated his *Città del sole* (*City of the Sun*, 1602), *Il senso delle cose* (*The Sense of Things*, 1604), and *Ateismo trionfato* (*Atheism Conquered*, 1606–1607) into Latin; while Hobbes provided a Latin version of the *Leviathan* (1651), with significant changes and additions to the English original (N. Malcolm in Hobbes 2012, 1:146–95). Translations into vernacular and Latin as well as self-translations were all ways of testing (and sometimes breaking) the limits of linguistic *rectitudo* and of demonstrating that the boundaries of reason in different contexts (between different languages, nations, and classes) were in fact porous. Leibniz advocated the need to start philosophizing in German (*Germanice philosophari*) and rejected a distorted use of Latin as a way of narrowing the social compass of philosophy by excluding laymen (*plebs*) and women (*feminae*) from its exercise (Leibniz 1875–1890, 4:144). It should also be noted that often the use of the vernacular ensured greater freedom of expression and a certain level of stylistic playfulness, which in particular situations could turn out to be refreshing and inspiring (Dionisotti [1960] 2004 13–14). Significantly, by the time Montaigne had written his *Essais*, "a type of philosophy had been created which was both colloquial and militant" (Zambelli [1994] 2012, 382).

Within the general debate about the philosophical potential of Latin in its relationship to both contemporary vernaculars and ancient languages (first and foremost Greek, but also Hebrew and Arabic), some technical points betrayed specific assumptions of a more theoretical order. A writer like Bruni, who believed that all languages could be translated into each other without losing any of the original meaning and style, was not interested in defending the special status of any particular historical language as better suited to the exercise of philosophical inquiry. His position differed from the one championed by such philhellenes as those depicted by Speroni in his dialogue (Giano Lascaris and Lazzaro Buonamici), who had no qualms about advocating the philosophical primacy of Greek, claiming that it had been no accident that philosophy had originally been written in Greek and that Greek should continue to be the model (philhellenism by the way, is a recurrent vogue in the history of Western philosophy, from Nicholas of Cusa to Heidegger). By contrast, even an admirer of the expressive potential of Latin and a firm believer in the superiority of both history and poetry over philosophy like Valla remained convinced that a number of philosophical concepts that had been originally elaborated in Greek could not find adequate expression in Latin and should not be translated at all costs: *multa belle dicuntur Graece quae non belle dicuntur Latine* ("many things can be said beautifully in Greek, but not in Latin"; Valla 2012, 1:6). Finally, a philosopher trained in the subtleties of scholasticism like Pomponazzi considered the question about what language was most suitable for writing philosophy as irrelevant and looked at philosophical discussions about the greater or smaller veridical import of historical languages as, ultimately, a waste of time (Paccagnella 2010). In addition, the thesis that one was allowed to philosophize in one of the available idioms represented a further argument against the dogmatic belief that there could only be one true description of the world. Speroni's recommendations "to philosophize in the vernacular (*filoso-far volgarmente*), without knowing Greek and Latin" (Speroni 1740, 193) were a sign that the time had finally come when people could write about philosophy in Italian, Spanish, English, French, Dutch, and German.

The philosophical potential of the vernaculars, being a question that was closely intertwined with issues of readership and communication, also bore on the problem of distinguishing between what was safe and not safe to say. Resuming a characteristically Platonic posture, Giovanni Pico did not miss the opportunity to describe the relationship between language and philosophy in terms of esoteric and exoteric communication. Philosophers, he argued in *De ente et uno* (*On Being and the One*, 1491), should "think as the few and speak as the many" (*sentire quidem ut pauci, loqui autem ut plures*), for people speak to be understood (*loquimur ut intelligamur*; Pico 1942, 1:396). This was another situation that required philosophers to strike the right balance between intellectual novelty and linguistic tradition. Since language represented the vehicle of conventional wisdom, thinkers were supposed to accept the rules of the linguistic game (with its attached social conventions) while skillfully circumventing the traps of linguistic pressure.

Keywords

Between the Middle Ages and the early modern period, the European Latin lexicon became enriched by new terms as a result of successive waves of Latin translations from Greek, Arabic, and Hebrew, from Boethius in the sixth century to Christian Wolff's Latinization of Leibniz's metaphysics in the eighteenth century. It would go well beyond the scope of this chapter to provide a complete record of even the most significant changes that affected the Latin philosophical vocabulary during the same period. Here I will confine myself to some representative specimens.

It should be noted, first of all, that some Latin keywords more than others marked the evolution of the early modern philosophical lexicon, such as *res* ("thing"), *subiectum* ("subject"), *obiectum* ("object"), *conceptus* ("concept"), *intentio* ("intention"), and *intentionalitas* ("intentionality"). Transliterations and calques from other languages, such as the Greek *entelechia* ("actualization") or the Arabic *colchodea* (the intellect as "giver of forms"), had already enjoyed a remarkable fate in scholastic Latin and continued to be the subject of heated debate among philosophers and humanists. Angelo Poliziano (1454–1494) devoted one of his essays in *Miscellaneorum centuria prima* (*First Hundred Miscellanea*, 1489) to clarify the many philological and philosophical issues involved in the discussion about the difference between *entelechia* (activity as fulfillment of a potentiality) and *endelechia* (activity as perpetual movement; Poliziano 1553, 1:224–28). If it is true that not as many transliterations from the Arabic became part of the technical lexicon of philosophical Latin as for mathematics, astrology, and alchemy (Burnett 2010, 41–42 and 44), the impact of the translations from Arabic during the Middle Ages and the Renaissance resulted in significant additions to the specific vocabulary of the internal senses ([*virtus*] *aestimativa*, i.e., animal instinct, and *cogitativa*, i.e., human reason, for instance). Some illustrious Greek transliterations also enjoyed a new life in the early modern period. This is the case, for example, of *energeia* ("energy") and *energeticus* ("energetic"), which, especially during the seventeenth century, began to be used with increasing frequency to denote the life and energy of matter and material beings. The English medical writer Francis Glisson is probably the most interesting case, with his *De natura substantiae energetica* (*The Active Nature of Substance*, 1672), a foundational work for modern physiology. New words were created by philosophers who felt the need to hone their expressive tools and expand the range of the available vocabulary. As an example, one may think of Campanella's *primalitas* (the primal attributes of being), *essentiatio* (the process of self-definition within being), *specificatio* (the process through which being divides itself into kinds), *corporatio* (the formation of bodies from the most abstract categories of being), and *toticipatio* (participation in the primal attributes of being; Giglioni 2006–2010).

In a discipline like philosophy, where words (*verba*) find themselves in a relationship of uneasiness with things (*res*) from the very beginning, it is precisely the use of barbarisms—in the technical sense of linguistic expressions contravening standards of good use and purity—that often facilitated the task of finding words for particularly vexing notions. Leonardo Bruni had recommended that translators avoid neologisms and new ways of expressing old things (*et verborum et orationis novitas*). Above all, a translator was supposed to shun nonsensical and outlandish terms (*inepta et barbara*). From a philosophical point of view, Bruni's strongest contribution was his idea that any language could be turned into any other, and that therefore Latin, too, had all the resources to say everything that had already been said in Greek (*nihil Graece dictum est quod Latine dici non possit*; Bruni 1996, 190). While concerned with the use of barbarisms in philosophy, others like the German metaphysician Goclenius (Rudolph Gockel, 1547–1628) displayed a more tolerant attitude. For instance, he described the use of the verb *vigorari* ("gain strength") in Jacopo Zabarella's commentary on Aristotle's *De anima* (published posthumously in 1605) as a form of barbarism, which was nevertheless necessary to explain the heightened condition undergone by the intellect when "invigorated" by the power of a forceful intelligible (i.e., object of understanding; *vehemens ac excellens intelligibile*; Goclenius 1613, 329). It is significant to note that by 1613, Goclenius, a scholastic philosopher by training and profession, had allowed certain latitude in the use of philosophical barbarisms. Among the "barbarians," Duns Scotus (1265–1308) had probably been one of the most creative, and Goclenius carefully surveyed his influence over the early modern lexicon of philosophical Latin. He noted that even Julius Caesar Scaliger's most refined Latin (*lautissima lingua*) entertained a conceptual closeness with Scotist ideas (Goclenius 1613, 19). Goclenius was so concerned with the influence that Latin barbarisms had exercised on the philosophical tradition that he added to his Greek dictionary of 1615 an appendix to the earlier Latin dictionary, entirely devoted to a meticulous analysis of all sorts of inappropriate ways of expressing philosophical notions in Latin, a *Sylloge vocum et phrasium quarumdam obsoletarum, minus usu receptarum, nuper natarum, ineptarum, lutulentarum, subrusticarum, barmi-barbararum, soloecismorum et hyposoloikōn* (*Collection of Some Words and Phrases That Are Obsolete, Less Ordinary, Recently Born, Improper, Impure, Uncouth, Including Barbarisms, Solecisms and Slight Solecisms*; Goclenius 1615, 282).

With respect to specific technical terms in philosophy, *res* can be considered one of the most important words in the lexicon of early modern philosophy. In his *Lexicon philosophicum*, Goclenius defined *res* as anything that can be conceived by our mind (*quodlibet conceptibile*) without involving a contradiction (*non includens contradic-tionem*), in the domain of both imagination (*ens rationis*) and reality (*ens reale*). He explained that in philosophy the word *res* could be taken in a "very general" sense (*com-munissime*), in a "general" one (*communiter*), and in the strictest one (*strictissime seu appropriate*). Combining Aristotle with Quintilian, and perhaps aware of Valla's sophis-ticated treatment of the matter in his *Dialecticae disputationes*, Goclenius identified *res* in the strictest sense with "substance" (*substantia*; Goclenius 1613, 983–84). Here it is crucial to point out that, while Goclenius reconfirmed the primacy of substance as the ontological marker of reality (and in this sense, *res* were *substantiae*), Valla had followed the opposite route and had brought *substantia* back to *res*, understood, in line with the rhetorical tradition, as that which can be said of a particular reality. By thus resolving "substance" into "thing," Valla, like other humanists at the time, had in fact deflated the ontological content of *res* by transforming it into any subject that could be conceptual-ized through words.

CONCLUSION

Among the most illustrious Latin words that entered a phase of remarkable decline dur-ing the early modern period, *actualitas* can be taken as a vivid example of a term with a glorious past in the sphere of philosophical learning, which, beginning in the fifteenth century, found itself heading towards extinction. Between the Middle Ages and the Renaissance, any professional philosopher trained in one of the many European uni-versities would have called reality *actualitas*. As recorded by Goclenius in his diction-ary, *actualitas prima*, the "first reality," was seen as the principal ontological requirement behind the existence of anything. In the twentieth century, the alleged process of reifi-cation (*actualitas*) through which the notion of being as activity (*energeia* in Aristotle) mutated into that of being as static presence (be that presence *subiectum* or *res*) was interpreted as the dominant event in the history of metaphysics. In an attempt to come to terms with the powerful consequences of René Descartes's philosophy and the way he polarized reality between the extremes of the "thinking thing" (*res cogitans*) and the "extended thing" (*res extensa*), the French neo-Thomist Étienne Gilson (1884–1978) dissected with painstaking precision the many layers accrued over the centuries by the principal categories of Western Latin ontology (*esse, ens, entitas,* and *essentia*), making a powerful case for the vitality and creativity of scholastic philosophy well into the seventeenth century. After all, Descartes's great accomplishment, in Gilson's opinion, lay in the way in which the French philosopher had taken advantage—both speculatively and linguistically—of scholastic lore, still fertile and productive at the time (Gilson 1912; Gilson 1952). The evolution of scholastic Latin in philosophy was also a source of speculative inspiration for Martin Heidegger (1889–1976), who secured his philosophical credentials by detecting in the process through which *energeia* became Latinized into *actualitas* the symptom of a lingering metaphysical malaise; that is, the gradual obfuscation of the true meaning of being (*Seinsvergessenheit,* the "oblivion of being").

Here it may be useful to point out that behind Heidegger's effort to reawaken our awareness of the *energeia* of being, there was no humanistic intent (as he clearly intimated in his *Brief über den Humanismus,* published in 1946). Indeed, the opposite was true for him. The legacy of scholastic philosophical Latin (and significantly Heidegger's first foray into the domains of philosophy had been a dissertation in 1916 on Duns Scotus's ontology) was clear and strong in his mind. Or perhaps, we might say that a peculiarly humanist urge underlay Heidegger's warnings about the "presentification" of being (*Gegenwärtigung*), in the sense that, like Lascaris and Buonamici, he thought that Greek was more suitable to metaphysical inquiries than Latin, for the ominous *Seinsvergessenheit* had already happened in the philosophical Greek of the pre-Socratics and therefore the truth had begun to hide itself (*Verborgenheit*) quite early on. In the specific domain of thinking, Greek was inherently philosophical and Latin was not, for Latin had helped disseminate the *Gegenwärtigung* of being. It was precisely by referring to Heidegger that in the 1990s Alain de Libera asked the crucial question: was Latin in fact a language suitable for philosophy? His answer to this question was unambiguously positive. He characterized the "multilingual *translatio* ["transfer"] of philosophy" (in particular its Latin transfer) during the Middle Ages and the Renaissance as a "linguistic event" that affected the development of modern thinking in a significant way (De Libera 1997, 8 and 21).

De Libera draws our attention to a moment in history "when Latin stops being a language of philosophy to become the language of philosophical taxonomy (not to say, taxidermy); in other words, a moment in which Latin moves from the status of a language that is philosophically alive to that of a language that is philosophically dead" (De Libera 1997, 1). That was not the case during the Middle Ages and the early modern period, which in fact were key periods in the transfer of learning prompted by translations (*translatio studiorum*), when Latin played a fundamental role in the "philosophical acculturation of Europe" (De Libera 1997, 3). And yet, from its very beginnings in Greece, Western philosophy has always had an extremely uncomfortable relationship with language. The act of thinking cannot help stumbling over words, especially written words. According to de Libera, the most fascinating aspect of scholastic Latin in the Middle Ages was the far-reaching linguistic experiment—an extremely successful one, it must be said—through which, in the translation and exegetical laboratories of European *studia* and universities, masters of arts and theologians forged a language suitable for philosophy, a privileged medium that allowed a trans-national, trans-linguistic, and trans-cultural discussion and transmission of ideas. So it happens that precisely the artificiality condemned by the humanists can today be seen as the major innovation and resource introduced by the philosophical Latin of the schools, for that raw and unreal Latin expanded the scope of the thinking exercise. In a way, Petrarch and Bruni failed to understand precisely this point.

Addressing Grosseteste, Bruni proudly declared himself to be part of a community of Latin writers and asserted his inability to make sense of Grosseteste's operation: *ego Latinus istam barbariem tuam non intelligo* ("as a Latin speaker I do not understand your barbarism"; Bruni 1996, 180). However, from a genuinely philosophical point of view, what Bruni did not understand was that the "barbarism" of not mastering a foreign language, with all its idioms and elegancies (which, in the final analysis, we should admit is a rather harmless form of barbarism) betrayed the scholastic philosopher's effort to come to terms with a much deeper kind of "barbarism"; that is, the remorselessly foreign and alienating experience of thinking of the other *qua* other. Giordano Bruno opposed the pseudo-philosophical obsession with linguistic decorum (an obsession that was for him the defining feature of "grammarians" and "pedants") to the genuinely philosophical sense of disorientation that derives from delving into the depths of the thinking process (*profondano ne' sentimenti*, Bruno 1955, 90; Bruno 1958, 1:258; Ciliberto 1979, xviii).

Perhaps, the most significant point we can make out of this whole discussion is that, more than in any other discipline, *novitas* ("novelty," the perplexing nature of what is unfamiliar) represents the very hallmark of philosophy. Reality is inherently "barbaric" because it is every time foreign and new to the human mind, and it challenges the mind's attempts to represent it. This sense of ontological "novelty" was clear to Giovanni Pico, who as a philosopher was equally open to reasons of linguistic perspicuity and philosophical inquiry. His was a subtle mediation between language (tradition) and thought (novelty). In *De ente et uno*, he praised Poliziano, "vindicator of a more elegant language," for allowing the use of "a few terms that were not entirely Latin, but necessary in any case because of the very newness of things [*ipsa rerum novitas*]" (Pico [1942] 2004, 1:389). The fact is that reality is for the most part brutally opaque, while language is often employed to confirm and reassert its opacity (through the use of rhetorical and literary devices, for instance), more than to shed light on it. The exercise of thinking, as an attempt to dissolve this resistance to interpretation, finds itself uneasily squeezed between a reality that is perceived as already given and the expressive resources made available by individual linguistic communities. The Latin of scholastic philosophy, precisely because of its artificiality and ugliness, was well equipped to cope with bouts of ugly reality, and it continued to do so well after the thirteenth century. To de Libera we should therefore add here Charles B. Schmitt: scholastic Latin was in good health during the sixteenth and seventeenth century, not just during the Middle Ages (Schmitt 1983, 64–88). Indeed, the taxonomical and taxidermic use of Latin, so much feared by de Libera, perhaps did not take place even in the eighteenth century, if we bear in mind that the imposing system of Leibnizian scholasticism Latinized by Wolff became the breeding ground for Immanuel Kant's so-called pre-critical production.

Suggested Reading

On the development of philosophical ideas in Latinate contexts from the later Middle Ages to the seventeenth century, see the section "Latin and philosophy" in *ENLW* 1:587–663 (essays by Garrod, Rees, Kraye, De Bom, and van Bunge). The close link between philology and philosophy in the Renaissance is examined by Kraye (1996). Finally, the Italian research institute Lessico Intellettuale Europeo has been publishing regular contributions to the study of philosophical Latin keywords in their developments from antiquity to the eighteenth century. Eleven volumes have been published so far (Florence: Olschki): *Ordo* (1979), *Res* (1982), *Spiritus* (1984), *Phantasia/Imaginatio* (1988), *Idea* (1990), *Ratio* (1994) *Sensus/Sensatio* (1996), *Signum* (1998), *Experientia* (2001), *Machina* (2005), and *Materia* (2011).

References

Bruni, Leonardo. 1996. *Opere letterarie e politiche*. Edited by Paolo Viti. Turin: Utet.

Bruno, Giordano. 1955. *La cena de le ceneri*. Edited by Giovanni Aquilecchia. Turin: Einaudi.

———. 1958. "De la causa principio e uno." In *Dialoghi Italiani*, edited by Giovanni Gentile and Giovanni Aquilecchia, vol. 1, 173–342. Florence: Sansoni.

———. 1989. *Summa terminorum metaphysicorum*. Edited by Tullio Gregory and Eugenio Canone. Rome: Edizioni dell'Ateneo.

Burnett, Charles. 2010. "The Enrichment of Latin Philosophical Vocabulary through Translations from Arabic: The Problem of Transliterations." In *Les innovations du vocabulaire latin à la fin du moyen âge: Autour du Glossaire du Latin philosophique*, edited by Olga Weijers, Iacopo Costa, and Adriano Oliva, 37–44. Turnhout: Brepols.

———. 2013. "Revisiting the 1552–1550 and 1562 Aristotle-Averroes Edition." In *Renaissance Averroism and Its Aftermath: Arabic Philosophy in Early Modern Europe*, edited by Anna Akasoy and Guido Giglioni, 55–64. Dordrecht: Springer.

Canone, Eugenio. 1988. "*Phantasia/Imaginatio* come problema terminologico nella lessicografia filosofica tra Sei-Settecento." In *Phantasia-Imaginatio*, edited by Marta Fattori and Massimo Bianchi, 221–57. Rome: Edizioni dell'Ateneo.

Ciliberto, Michele. 1979. *Lessico di Giordano Bruno*. 2 vols. Rome: Edizioni dell'Ateneo & Bizzarri.

De Libera, Alain. 1995. "*Sermo mysticus*: La transposition du vocabulaire scolastique dans la mystique allemande du XIVe siècle." *Rue Descartes* 14:41–73.

———. 1997. "Le latin, véritable langue de la philosophie." In Hamesse 1997, 1–22.

Dionisotti, Anna C. 1997. "Philosophie grecque et tradition latine." In Hamesse 1997, 41–57.

Dionisotti, Carlo. (1960) 2004. Introduction to *Prose e rime*, by Pietro Bembo, 7–54. Turin: Utet.

Garin, Eugenio. 1952. *Prosatori latini del Quattrocento*. Milan: Ricciardi.

Giglioni, Guido. 2006–2010. "Primalità (*primalitas*)." In *Enciclopedia bruniana et campanelliana*, edited by Eugenio Canone and Germana Ernst, vol. 1, 332–49. Pisa: Serra.

Gilson, Étienne. 1912. *Index scolastico-cartésien*. Paris: Alcan.

———. 1952. *Being and Some Philosophers*. Toronto: Pontifical Institute of Mediaeval Studies.

Goclenius, Rudolf. 1613. *Lexicon philosophicum quo tanquam clave philosophiae fores aperiuntur*. Frankfurt: Becker.

———. 1615. *Lexicon philosophicum Graecum . . . accessit adiicienda Latino lexico sylloge vocum et phrasium*. Marburg: Hutwelcker.

Gregory, Tullio. 2006. *Origini della terminologia filosofica moderna: Linee di ricerca*. Florence: Olschki.

Hamesse, Jacqueline, ed. 1997. *Aux origines du lexique philosophique européen: L'influence de la Latinitas*. Louvain-La-Neuve: Collège Cardinal Mercier.

Hobbes, Thomas. 2012. *Leviathan*, edited by Noel Malcolm, 3 vols. Oxford: Clarendon Press.

Kraye, Jill. 1996. "Philologists and Philosophers." In *The Cambridge Companion to Renaissance Humanism*, edited by Jill Kraye, 142–60. Cambridge: Cambridge University Press.

———. 2007. "Pico on the Relationship of Rhetoric and Philosophy." In *Pico della Mirandola: New Essays*, edited by Michael V. Dougherty, 13–36. Cambridge: Cambridge University Press.

Leibniz, Gottfried W. 1875–1890. *Die philosophischen Schriften*, 7 vols., edited by Carl I. Gerhardt. Berlin: Weidmann.

Paccagnella, Ivano. 2010. "La lingua del Peretto." In *Pietro Pomponazzi: Tradizione e dissenso*, edited by Marco Sgarbi. 285–314. Florence: Olschki.

Pico della Mirandola, Giovanni. 1942. "De ente et uno." In *De hominis dignitate, Heptaplus, De ente et uno, e scritti vari*, edited by Eugenio Garin, 101–65. 2 vols. Florence: Vallecchi.

Poliziano, Angelo. 1553. "Miscellaneorum centuria prima." In *Opera omnia*, 213–311. Basel: Nicholas Episcopius.

Schmitt, Charles B. 1983. *Aristotle and the Renaissance*. Cambridge: Harvard University Press.

———. (1984a). *The Aristotelian Tradition and Renaissance Universities*. London: Variorum.

———. (1979) 1984b. "Renaissance Averroism Studied through the Venetian Editions of Aristotle-Averroes (with Particular Reference to the Giunta Edition of 1550–2)." In Schmitt 1984a, chapter VIII [original pagination 121–42].

———. (1983) 1984c. "Aristotelian Textual Studies at Padua: The Case of Francesco Cavalli." In Schmitt 1984a, chapter XIII [original pagination 287–314].

Segni, Bernardo. 1550. *L'Ethica tradotta in lingua volgare fiorentina et comentata*. Florence: Torrentino.

Speroni, Sperone. 1740. "Dialogo delle lingue." In *Opere*, vol. 1, 166–201. Venice: Occhi.

Valla, Lorenzo. 2012. *Dialectical Disputations*. Edited by Brian P. Copenhaver and Lodi Nauta. 2 vols. Cambridge: Harvard University Press.

Zambelli, Paola. (1994) 2012. "From the *Quaestiones* to the *Essais*: On the Autonomy and Methods of the History of Philosophy." In *Astrology and Magic from the Medieval Latin and Islamic World to Renaissance Europe: Theories and Approaches*, 373–90. Farnham: Ashgate.

CHAPTER 17

··

SCIENCE AND MEDICINE

··

BRIAN W. OGILVIE

INTRODUCTION

"SCIENCE" as we know it did not exist in the period from 1400 to 1800. Rather, a number of disciplines, some centered on universities, others elsewhere, investigated distinct aspects of nature. Natural philosophy, which by 1400 was a fundamental element of the university arts curriculum, dealt broadly with the nature of matter and its changes, including local motion and the growth and decay of substances, including living bodies. Mathematics, including astronomy or astrology (terms that were often interchangeable), was also a university subject, though its connection to prognostication meant that it had a prominent place in court and in urban society (Westman 2011). Medicine was one of the three higher faculties of universities, along with theology and law, though much healing was done by apothecaries, "cunning folk," and others who had not studied at a university, if at all (Siraisi 1990). "Chymistry" (an early modern spelling meant to remind us that Renaissance authors did not distinguish alchemy from chemistry), on the other hand, was not a university subject at the beginning of the period; it would see its heyday ca. 1500–1700, when it became increasingly central to both medicine and natural philosophy (Principe 2013). Meanwhile, the study of animal, plant, and mineral species received slight attention in natural philosophy and medical lectures in the fifteenth century but would develop in the sixteenth into a new discipline, natural history, associated with university botanical gardens and collections of natural objects, but also with collections of curiosities, natural rarities, and exotic plants by rulers, aristocrats, and urban elites (Smith and Findlen 2001; Ogilvie 2006).

Latin was crucial to each of these subjects and the intellectual communities that engaged with them. It was the language of university instruction well into the seventeenth century, and the language in which lecture texts and commentaries were written. As an intellectual *lingua franca*, Latin permitted students and teachers who could not understand the local vernacular to communicate. It was far from being universal, even in universities, as university officials had to repeatedly admonish students to speak Latin, not a vernacular, and threaten fines for violations (Cobban 1999, 44). Outside universities, Latin texts vied with vernacular works bringing alchemy, astrology, medicine, and sometimes even natural philosophy to lay readers and practitioners.

And Latin speakers did not form a uniform community. There was a sharp divide in the fifteenth century in Italy, and in the late fifteenth and early sixteenth centuries in transalpine Europe, between scholastic philosophers, theologians, and jurists on one hand, and humanists on the other (Moss 2010). Scholastic Latin was a technical language whose syntax, vocabulary, and orthography differed substantially from its classical ancestor. The humanist revival of the stylistic ideal of classical Latin, and its attendant engagement with the meaning of Latin terms in their ancient Roman cultural context, threatened the stability and questioned the utility of the "barbarous" scholastic language. Both intellectual struggles and turf wars over students and resources characterized the relationship between these two latinophone communities (Rummel 1995).

By the second half of the sixteenth century, however, the humanist stylistic ideal was largely victorious. This was in part because theological controversy in the early decades of the Reformation required a form of argumentation that scholastic terminology could not provide (Moss 2010). But it was also due to the success of humanist-inspired primary and secondary education, including the Jesuit schools that proliferated after 1541 (Grendler 1989; Loach 2006; cf. Black 2001). Natural philosophy, medicine, chymistry, and other subjects continued to retain technical terminology, but they were increasingly expressed in a Latin that was, in broad terms, neoclassical in its vocabulary and syntax (see Fumaroli 1980, 116–230).

This linguistic homogeneity, albeit with national and regional variations, meant that the community of Latin speakers in the sixteenth century can usefully be thought of as a *respublica literaria* ("republic of letters"), a term that had its origins in the early fifteenth century but saw its heyday in the sixteenth and early seventeenth (Dibon 1978; Waquet 1989; Bots and Waquet 1997). As an imagined community, this *respublica* established norms of polite, reciprocal exchange for public benefit, as an antidote to the religious controversies of the age, though of course these norms, or regulative fictions, were frequently violated in practice (Ogilvie 2011). Insofar as we can consider "science" to be a coherent concept in the period ca. 1400–1800, it was as a loosely connected set of provinces within this *respublica* and the various vernacular traditions that partially displaced it, especially ca. 1650–1800, including the francophone *République des lettres* that partially re-created Latin's pan-European reach (Goodman 1994; Goldgar 1995).

This chapter provides an overview of Neo-Latin science, ca. 1400–1800. After examining broad trends over time and distinctions among disciplines, it turns to a more in-depth set of case studies, focusing on natural history and medical botany: modern works composed in Latin, translations from Greek to Latin, and translations from vernaculars to Latin. The conclusion examines the status of Latin in late eighteenth-century science and its persistence, particularly in biological taxonomy, to the present.

Broad Trends in Science and Medicine,
ca. 1400–1800

The late-medieval university curriculum in natural philosophy and medicine was based on classical texts, especially Greek, in Latin translation; Arabic commentaries on them and independent Arabic treatises, also in Latin translation; and a Latin commentary tradition on those works. The humanist movement of the late fourteenth and fifteenth centuries brought new ancient texts into this mix, especially newly rediscovered Greek works, as well as new Latin translations based on (often) more careful critical textual scholarship and expressed in the neoclassical style. Some of these new texts, such as Ptolemy's *Geography* (mid-second century CE) and much of Archimedes (third century BCE), were transformative. Other texts came to be better understood and more accurately translated, such as Dioscorides's work *De materia medica* (*On Medicinal Substances*, first century CE, discussed below), as old Latin translations were succeeded by new, although humanist scholars often "purified" these works of the medieval Arabic and Latin additions that could have important practical value.

In natural philosophy, new attention to Platonism, Epicureanism, and Stoicism in the late fifteenth century challenged the dominance of the Peripatetic school, especially in arts faculties dominated by humanists and outside of the university (Brown 2010). Chymical matter theory, based on a combination of practical experience and theoretical writings about salt, sulfur, and mercury, also posed a challenge to Peripatetics (Debus 1977; Newman 2004; Newman 2006). Though the iconoclastic medical chymist Paracelsus (Theophrastus Aureolus Bombastus von Hohenheim; 1493–1541) rejected Latin, writing and teaching in German to address a lay audience, other chymists continued to use the European *lingua franca*. The recently invented printing press allowed entrepreneurs to reach (and create) markets for books in both Latin and the vernaculars (and even Greek, though that remained a niche market for specialists). Writers on medical substances, plants, and animals published in Latin and the vernacular, and their works were frequently translated in both directions.

Vernacular works slowly grew in importance. In medicine, the vernacular was used by surgeons writing for those without a university education, such as Ambroise Paré's (ca. 1510–1590) French treatise on how to treat gunshot wounds (first published in 1545), and by physicians writing on topics such as baths that were of interest to lay clients. Mathematics, with its obvious practical use in gunnery and surveying, developed a vernacular tradition; Henry Billingsley translated Euclid's *Elements* into English (1570), with a preface by John Dee extolling the many uses of geometry. The seventeenth century was a watershed: after 1610, Galileo Galilei published almost exclusively in Italian, while René Descartes alternated languages, writing his *Discours de la méthode* (*Discourse on Method*; 1637) in French but his *Principia philosophiae* (*Principles of Philosophy*; 1644) and *Meditationes de prima philosophia* (*Meditations on First Philosophy*; 1641) in Latin. In England, Robert Boyle published his experimental natural philosophy in English; the *Philosophical Transactions of the Royal Society* were in English, and the *Journal des Sçavans* (*Journal of the Learned*), associated with the Royal Academy of Sciences in Paris, was in French. Yet the Royal Society in London published the works of Marcello Malpighi (1628–94) in Latin, and possibly the greatest work of seventeenth-century science, Isaac Newton's *Philosophiae naturalis principia mathematica* (*Mathematical Principles of Natural Philosophy*), appeared in 1687 in Latin, with subsequent editions in 1713 and 1726; the first English translation appeared only in 1729.

Latin continued to play an important, albeit diminished, role in eighteenth-century science. The *Acta Eruditorum* (*Transactions of the Learned*, 1682–1731), with its successor, the *Nova Acta Eruditorum* (*New Transactions of the Learned*, 1732–1776), was only one of several Latin periodicals addressing science, mathematics, and scholarship. Works of natural history and medicine appeared in Latin, though increasingly, vernacular works were given Latin titles to augment their scholarly cachet. The most obvious figure is Linnaeus (1707–1778), whose *Systema naturae* (*System of Nature*) and *Species plantarum* (*Species of Plants*) codified the use of Latin in botanical and zoological nomenclature, a role it has continued to occupy—though not exclusively—to the present. Even in 1800, Latin remained a language in which serious original scientific contributions were published.

LATIN IN THE SCIENTIFIC AND MEDICAL DISCIPLINES

The place of Latin varied among disciplines. Natural philosophy, which was firmly established in the university curriculum, involved a range of Latin texts. Translations of Aristotle were surrounded by layers of commentary intended to explain to students what "the philosopher" meant, and to explore the limitations or contradictions of his works (Lohr 1988). The fifteenth century saw a renewed interest in Platonism and Neo-Platonism, including Platonic natural philosophy, inspired in part by renewed intellectual contact between Italian humanists and Greek scholars from Byzantium (Hankins 1990). Epicureanism, Stoicism, and Hermetism were revived as alternatives to Aristotelian natural philosophy, generating translations of Greek works into Latin and a growing Latin literature of commentaries and treatises (Joy 1987). The competing "new philosophies" of the seventeenth century were, at the beginning, set out in Latin texts. Despite the increasing importance of the vernaculars in the late seventeenth century, 1687 saw the publication not only of Newton's *Principia* but also of Caspar Bartholin's Latin textbook *Specimen compendii physici* (*An Example of the Compendium of Physics*); a new edition of Wolferdus Senguerdius's natural philosophy; and Johann Heinrich Schweitzer's compendium of "Aristotelian-Cartesian" natural philosophy. Latin textbooks in the subject were published throughout the eighteenth century for students in the Latin schools of Central Europe.

Mathematics and astronomy drew upon a rich Greek heritage, largely known to Western scholars by 1300 but enriched in the fifteenth and sixteenth centuries (Rose 1975; Kaunzner 1987). In particular, Diophantus's *Arithmetics* (third century CE), Pappus's (ca. 290–ca. 350 CE) *Collection* and Apollonius's (ca. 262–ca. 190 BCE) treatise on conic sections became available in Latin in the sixteenth century (Grendler 2002, 413–14). The great sixteenth-century astronomical works of Copernicus and Tycho Brahe were written in Latin; despite Galileo's turn to the vernacular, Latin remained important in the seventeenth-century publications of Kepler and Hevelius. Ruđer Josip Bošković's five books on solar and lunar eclipses, written in Latin verse, appeared in 1760, with a sixth in 1779 (*CNLS* 2:330–31).

Latin occupied a more ambivalent position in chymistry. Like astronomers, chymists had knowledge that interested princes, aristocrats, and urban elites. But unlike astronomy, chymistry had no firm place in the university curriculum. Much chymical literature circulated in manuscripts, many of them vernacular. Furthermore, chymistry encompassed both "philosophical" chymists, interested in matter theory, and practitioners whose aims involved refining metals or distilling remedies (Newman 2004). The former often (though not always) wrote in Latin, while the latter were more likely to use their native tongue. Over the course of the sixteenth and seventeenth centuries, new alchemical texts came to outnumber the "historical canon" of ancient and medieval works. These texts were written both in Latin and in the vernaculars. Practitioners with a university background could read both, but a large cadre of "vernacular alchemists," illiterate in Latin, were restricted to the vernacular works (Nummedal 2011).

The study of living bodies, in medicine, anatomy, and natural history, showed a similar split between Latin and vernacular texts. Medicine was one of the three higher faculties of most early modern universities, and students flocked from all over Europe to the best-known medical schools in Padua, Montpellier, Basel, and (after its 1575 foundation) Leiden, as well as many smaller faculties. Medical professors lectured and wrote in Latin for this cosmopolitan audience. Several of the ancient Greek physician Galen's works had been used in the Latin Middle Ages; medical humanists added several more of his texts in their effort to remedy what they saw as medieval Arabic "corruption" (Nutton 1988). The study of anatomy through dissecting human cadavers was revived in the late Middle Ages, leading to the 1543 work *De humani corporis fabrica* (*On the Fabric of the Human Body*) by Andreas Vesalius (1514–1564), a physician from Brussels who taught in Padua before becoming a personal physician to the Holy Roman Emperor Charles V (O'Malley 1964). Latin remained an important language for medicine in the seventeenth and eighteenth centuries. William Harvey wrote his famous book *De motu cordis et sanguinis* (*On the Motion of the Heart and Blood*, 1628) and his monumental study *Exercitationes de generatione animalium* (*Exercises on the Generation of Animals*, 1651) in it, while Marcus Severinus's 1632 work on pathological anatomy was republished in 1732 (*CNLS* 2:347). But vernacular works and translations became increasingly numerous, especially in works intended to explain medicine to laypeople.

Like chymistry and medicine, natural history saw a proliferation of both Latin and vernacular titles in the sixteenth and seventeenth centuries, each with a distinct audience. Ancient Greek texts were translated into Latin, and works intended for university lectures or consultation by humanist scholars were composed in it. Humanist dialogues explained the methods and principles of the study of nature, as in Euricius Cordus's *Botanologicon* (~ *Botanical Dialogue*, 1534) and Antonio Musa Brasavola's *Examen omnium simplicium medicamentorum* (*Examination of All Simple Medicines*, 1537). But vernacular books were aimed at a lay audience interested above all in practical knowledge, especially of medicinal herbs; following in the tradition of the late-medieval *Gart der Gesundheit* (*Garden of Health*, 1485), Hieronymus Bock published his *New Kreütter Buch* (*New Herbal*, 1539) in German. The Portuguese physician Garcia da Orta (ca. 1500–1568) and the Spanish doctor Nicolas Monardes (1493–1588) published accounts of Asian and American medicinal plants in their native tongues.

Natural history thus provides an excellent set of case studies of the use of Latin in early modern science and its complex relationships with vernacular language communities. The next three sections draw on this new early modern discipline. After examining works composed in Latin through the example of Conrad Gessner, we will look at the role played by translation from Greek to Latin in science, and, finally, at a subject that is often overlooked: translations from European vernaculars into Latin.

NEO-LATIN NATURAL HISTORY WORKS

Conrad Gessner's *Historia animalium* (*History of Animals*, published in four volumes from 1551 to 1558, with a posthumous fifth volume in 1587) exemplifies Neo-Latin natural history. Gessner divided up the natural world according to categories established by Aristotle in his own *Historia animalium*: the first volume examined viviparous quadrupeds; the second, oviparous quadrupeds; the third, birds (including bats); and the fourth, fishes (including cetaceans). The title page of the first volume informed the prospective reader that it contained "not only the straightforward history of animals" (*non solum simplicem animalium historiam*) but also "copious commentaries and many corrections" (*commentarios copiosos et castigationes plurimas*) of ancient and medieval authors. The work was a compendium: when he wrote of animals he had seen himself, Gessner included his observations, but they were only a part of a much broader mass of information, drawn from dozens of authors, ancient and modern, and written in many languages. Gessner justified his decision to draw on all books, not merely the best, by quoting Pliny the Elder: "No book is so bad that it cannot provide something good" (*cum nullus tam malus sit liber, ex quo aliquid haurire boni liceat*; Gessner 1551–1587, 1:β1r).

Each of Gessner's alphabetical entries contained a range of material, arranged under eight headings (each identified by a capital letter A–H in the margins), along with at least one woodcut picture of the animal. The first contained the animal's

Latin, Greek, Hebrew, and vernacular names. These were followed by the creature's description, its region, and any differences among local varieties. Its physiology and mode of life followed in the third section, while the fourth contained its morals. The fifth discussed its use in general, while the sixth contained its use in food, and the seventh its use in medicine. The final section, H, contained "philology and its divisions" (*philologia eiusque partes*); this section, in turn, was subdivided according to the eight categories.

By "philology" Gessner meant not only grammar, but also the vast cultural lore associated with animals in antiquity. Section H.a., for instance, included less-common, dialectical, or poetic names, as well as the metaphorical use of the animal, things named after it, people's names that derived from animals, and the like; section H.d. reported on the lore connecting virtue and vice to animals. The final section, H.h., contained everything that did not fit elsewhere: true histories, fables, portents, religion, proverbs, and the symbolic or emblematic meaning of animals. The ideal article would be the *summa* of ancient and modern knowledge of every animal species. But this knowledge was not for everyone. The Zurich printer Christoph Froschauer, who published the work, included a note informing the reader that he planned to publish an epitome, "without the material pertaining to philology and languages" (*omissis scilicet iis quae ad philologiam et linguas pertinent*), for readers without the time or money for the complete version (Gessner 1551–89, 1:[α6]r). In fact, Froschauer issued two versions: a series of *Icones animalium* (*Pictures of Animals*) accompanied by the names in several languages, and a German translation of the work, with the "philology" severely curtailed. The Latin version of the work was for humanist scholars who might want to know, not only that binding a whole dormouse over warts would cure them, but also that Martial called dormice "drowsy" (*somniculosi*; Gessner 1551–1587, 1:622–23).

Gessner consciously related his Latin style to his subject, following a trope that equated eloquence with falsehood: "I have adopted a humble style without affectation . . . for in writings in which the knowledge of things is sought . . . what should be expressed is not the charm of splendid oratory, but unadulterated truth" (*Usus sum igitur dictione humili et minime affectata . . . Nam in his scriptis in quibus rerum cognitio quaeritur . . ., non luculentae orationis lepos, sed incorrupta veritas exprimenda est*; Gessner 1551–1587, 1:β2v). Once more, Pliny the Elder provided a justification: in words Gessner repeated, the ancient Roman encyclopedist explained that he reported the "sterile matter" (*sterilis materia* [*Natural History* 1, preface 12]) of life, not things that are meant to please the reader. Unvarnished style best suited the unvarnished truth; though Gessner's work was copious, it did not require Erasmian copiousness (*copia*) to describe.

The features of Gessner's Latin natural history were shared by his contemporaries and successors, including the massive, and mostly posthumous, series of zoological publications (1597–1642) by Ulisse Aldrovandi (1522–1605). Important works of natural history were composed in Latin in the seventeenth and eighteenth centuries: Francis Willughby and John Ray's *Ornithologia* (1676), Ray's *Historia plantarum* (*History of Plants*, 1686–1704), and of course the many editions of Linnaeus's *Systema naturae* and *Species plantarum*, to which we will return in the conclusion. But in the later seventeenth century, the material Gessner called "philology" disappeared from serious Neo-Latin natural history as well as from vernacular accounts (see Foucault 1970).

TRANSLATION FROM GREEK

Most serious ancient scientific works were written in Greek. The Latin tradition included some popular works and encyclopedias, such as Seneca the Younger's *Naturales quaestiones* (*Natural Questions*, 62–65 CE), Pliny the Elder's *Naturalis historia* (*Natural History*, dedicated to the Emperor Titus in 77 CE), Solinus's abridgement of Pliny, *Collectanea rerum memorabilium* (*Collection of Memorable Things*, compiled early third century CE), and a few medical texts such as Celsus's *De medicina* (*On Medicine*, first century BCE). But mathematics, astronomy, natural philosophy, geography, and medicine in the classical world were almost exclusively Greek. Despite the place of Greek in the humanist curriculum, only a minority of Renaissance and early modern readers could tackle these works in the original (Grafton and Jardine 1986, 99–125). Moreover, these works used difficult technical terms that required explanation. Hence, most early modern students of these disciplines approached them through Latin translations with commentaries.

The translation movement had of course begun earlier. A late antique translation of Plato's *Timaeus* had been an important part of early medieval natural philosophy (Sylla 2003, 175), while Dioscorides's work on medicinal substances was translated in the sixth century (Riddle 1980, 6). With the Norman conquest of Sicily and the contemporary *reconquista* in Iberia, an enormous number of scientific and medical texts were opened up to the Latin West. First via translations from Arabic versions into Latin, then directly from Greek, twelfth- and thirteenth-century translators produced versions of works by Aristotle, Galen, Ptolemy, Euclid, and other scientific, medical, and mathematical writers and their Arabic commentators (Burnett 2013; Goyens, de Leemans, and Smets 2008). Medieval Latin translations of Greek works often preserved the word order of the Greek original, replacing Greek particles with their closest Latin adverbial equivalents; hence, some Latin translations have served as witnesses to the lost Greek originals from which they were translated (Reynolds and Wilson 2014, 122).

In the fifteenth century, humanist manuscript hunters and Greek *émigrés* such as Bessarion added many new Greek scientific, mathematical, and medical works to those known in the Latin Middle Ages: Ptolemy's *Geography*, Theophrastus's works (ca. 370–ca. 287 BCE) on plants, much of Archimedes, and several works by Galen. As their medieval predecessors had done, fifteenth-century humanists produced Latin versions of these works: the *Geography* as early as 1406, while others had appeared by mid-century. Georgius Trapezuntius and Theodorus Gaza produced rival translations of Aristotle's *On Animals* and Theophrastus's *On Plants*. Though the latter was a newly discovered text, there were two medieval translations of the former. Nonetheless, humanists retranslated Aristotle to save him from the "barbarous Latin and muddled texts" of the scholastics, even as medieval translations continued to be used in university philosophy lectures.

When Greek scientific authors were published in Latin—usually well before the first Greek editions—publishers printed the manuscript to hand. The *editiones principes* of Aristotle's (1476) and Theophrastus's (1483) histories of animals and plants were based on Theodorus Gaza's translations (*Gesamtkatalog der Wiegendrucke*, nos. 02350 and M45920). On the other hand, the first printed edition of Aristotle's *De anima* (1472) was a medieval translation with Averroes's commentary (*Gesamtkatalog der Wiegendrucke*, no. 02349). Philosophers often resisted new humanist translations because they replaced familiar technical terms with new translations, and probably, too, because their Ciceronian periods made the texts harder for students to follow.

For texts that were not already entrenched in the curriculum, the new translations generally came to displace the old. A case in point is Dioscorides, *De materia medica*. The sixth-century Latin translation had been updated in the late eleventh or early twelfth century with new material from Arabic and reorganized in a loose alphabetical form, using only the first letter of each entry. Around 1300, Pietro d'Abano added a commentary. This "Dyascorides" with Pietro's commentary was published in 1478 (Riddle 1980, 7–8, 15–16, and 20–27). But humanist critics were deeply dissatisfied with this work. As Marcello Virgilio Adriani wrote in the preface to his translation, the old translation was written "with no attention to literary style" (*nullo bonarum litterarum cultu*); furthermore, it contained more from other authors than from Dioscorides himself (Dioscorides 1518, AAiiv). Though the latter might have made the book seem more practical to some, for humanists intent on purging Greek texts of their Arabic influences, it was a distinct drawback (Ogilvie 2006, 131; Touwaide 2008). In the 1480s or early 1490s, Ermolao Barbaro prepared a new translation but died before he could publish it. It saw the light in February 1516. Later that year, the humanist physician Jean Ruel published his own translation; Adriani's appeared two years later. Suddenly, readers had three different versions of Dioscorides from which to choose.

The new Latin Dioscorides translations were not all equally popular. Only one edition of Barbaro survives. Adriani's book saw five editions, including one with the Aldine Greek text (Riddle 1980, 29–30). Ruel's translation was far more popular: more than thirty editions were published before the end of the sixteenth century (Riddle 1980, 29–34). A dozen of those were accompanied by the commentary of Pietro Andrea Mattioli, who had originally published an Italian translation with commentary. In successive Italian and Latin editions, Mattioli's commentary grew to the point where it overwhelmed Dioscorides's original text; when university statutes in the later sixteenth and early seventeenth centuries called for "Dioscorides" to be the lecture text on medical botany, it was probably understood that Mattioli's commentary would be used.

But Ruel's Latin Dioscorides, with or without Mattioli's commentary, soon had competition. In 1530–1531, the Schott press in Strasbourg published the *Herbarum vivae eicones* (*Living Pictures of Plants*). As the name implies, the printer emphasized Hans Weiditz's woodcut illustrations of plants. The text was provided by the theologian and physician Otto Brunfels, who compiled it from ancient and modern sources. A torrent of other Latin herbals followed: some composed in Latin, others translated from the vernacular, such as Hieronymus Bock's *New Kreütter Buch*, rendered into Latin by David Kyber. But most of those authors continued to draw upon Dioscorides, even as they sought to render the Greek work obsolete.

Translation from the Vernacular

Kyber's translation of Hieronymus Bock's herbal draws our attention to another significant aspect of science in Latin: translations from the vernacular. Peter Burke has written that translations into Latin in the early modern period have drawn little attention (Burke 2007). But historians of science have been an exception. Even as the Western and Central European vernaculars grew in their technical vocabulary and their use in scientific works, Latin retained an important function to both legitimate scientific writing and to make it available to an international audience. The relationship between Latin and the vernaculars from 1400 to 1800 should not be considered merely as a displacement of the former by the latter. "The rise of the vernaculars" has been a recurring trope in early modern cultural history, yet it is more useful to think in terms of the interests and activities of linguistic communities (cf. Burke 2004). Already in the fourteenth century, the scholastic philosopher Nicole Oresme observed that in his day, French was to Latin as Latin had been to Greek for the ancient Romans: the former, the everyday language, and the latter, the technical language for philosophical specialists (Goyens, de Leemans, and Smets 2008, ix). Oresme translated from Latin to the vernacular to make Latin works accessible to the French court. As court and urban society took an increasing interest in the sciences in the sixteenth and seventeenth centuries, vernacular translations became more common—followed by scientific works composed in the vernacular.

With the printing press, vernacular works could reach, or even create, a new public. Galileo Galilei offers an example. After an ordinary career as a university mathematician, Galileo published his *Sidereus nuncius* (*Starry Messenger*), a 1610 Latin pamphlet trumpeting the astronomical discoveries he had made with the telescope, in order to make a career move into the court of the Medici grand dukes of Tuscany. The move was successful; Galileo was appointed court philosopher as well as professor of mathematics at the Tuscan university in Pisa (Biagioli 1993). Henceforth his publications appeared in Italian, not Latin, aimed at an audience of Italian courtiers and intellectuals rather than the broader *respublica literaria*. But many transalpine natural philosophers could not read Italian. Latin translations remedied the problem. Galileo's treatise on the proportional compass (a precursor to the slide rule) appeared in Latin in 1612. His 1632 *Dialogo sopra i due massimi sistemi del mondo* (*Dialogue on the Two Chief World Systems*), which led to his condemnation by the Inquisition and sentence of house arrest, appeared in Latin only three years later. His *Discorsi e dimostrazioni matematiche, intorno à due nuove scienze* (*Discourses and Mathematical Demonstrations on Two New Sciences*, 1638), meanwhile, appeared in Latin translation in 1699.

Other vernaculars were also translated into Latin for the international *respublica literaria*. Francis Bacon wrote the various works of his *Magna instauratio* (*Great Instauration*, first published in 1620) in English, but he had them translated into Latin for publication. The English originals were lost, so that those who wish to read Bacon's natural philosophy in English must rely on nineteenth-century retranslations (with a few exceptions). Even as French came to rival Latin as a European *lingua franca*, translations into Latin were made: René Descartes's *Discours de la méthode* (1637) appeared two decades later in Latin (1656; cf. Fumaroli [2001] 2010).

Even into the eighteenth century, Latin translations expanded the reach of the vernaculars, especially those spoken by small populations or in a limited area. Maria Sibylla Merian prepared two versions of her *Metamorphosis insectorum Surinamensium* (*Metamorphosis of the Insects of Surinam*, 1705): one with Dutch text for local connoisseurs, and a second in Latin for the international market. Earlier, Johannes Goedaert's *Metamorphosis naturalis* (*Natural Metamorphosis*, 1660–1669) and Jan Swammerdam's *Historia insectorum generalis* (*General History of Insects*, 1669) were published first in Dutch, but with Latin translations soon following. Swammerdam's masterwork, his *Bybel der natuure* (*Bible of Nature*), had also been written in Dutch. Though his sudden death in 1680 prevented its publication, the manuscript survived and was eventually acquired by the physician and professor Herman Boerhaave. When Boerhaave published the work in 1737–1738, it was in a bilingual edition: each page had two columns, one with Swammerdam's Dutch and the other containing the Latin version by Boerhaave's colleague, the professor of medicine and chemistry Hieronymus David Gaubius. The subsequent German (1752) and English (1758) translations drew chiefly on the Latin version, not Swammerdam's original. In this case, Latin provided a bridge that linked several vernaculars.

Conclusion: Latin Science in the Eighteenth Century and Beyond

Swammerdam's *Bybel der natuure* underscores the ambivalent position of Latin in eighteenth-century science. It was still a universal language, even in the age "when Europe spoke French" (Fumaroli [2001] 2010), but increasingly, science was being conducted in European vernaculars. Newton wrote his *Principia* in Latin but his *Opticks* (1704) in English—though again, a Latin translation appeared two years later. In the sixteenth century, writing in Latin meant aiming for the audience of university-educated scholars; in the eighteenth, choosing to write in Latin meant aiming for a *particular* audience of scholars, whereas choosing the vernacular meant appealing to a different, but no less scholarly, community. But the vernaculars were not equally important in every place and in every field. In the Holy Roman Empire, divided as it was into heterogeneous political and linguistic communities, Latin journals flourished until the eighteenth century's end; the language retained a unifying role (Waquet [1998] 2001, 84–85). In universities, Latin gradually ceded dominance: in Spain, Spanish and French slowly took its place (Rodríguez Ennes 2011). Yet it still retained a ceremonial function: even today, graduation exercises in Oxford and Cambridge are held in Latin.

Natural history, and in particular botany, appears to present the clearest exception to the general trend away from Latin in eighteenth-century science. Carl Linnaeus wrote in Latin because Swedish was scarcely known outside Scandinavia, and Latin allowed him to reach an international audience. His binomial nomenclature, in which every animal and plant species had a two-part name, a genus name and a "trivial" or species name, was popularized by his many publications, above all the *Systema naturae* (1735), whose tenth edition (1758–59) would become the basis of subsequent zoological nomenclature, and the *Species plantarum* (1753), which did the same for botany. In dry, telegraphic Latin, Linnaeus reformed botanical description. Earlier naturalists had written their descriptions in full sentences, choosing the appropriate case for nouns and employing a range of verbs to relate different parts. Linnaeus, on the other hand, wrote descriptions like lists, offering more precise definitions of terms and employing nominative case throughout (Stearn 1983, 34–39). In his and his followers' hands, Latin became a code that enabled naturalists to precisely and economically describe the salient biological features of living species. When the International Code of Botanical Nomenclature was adopted in Vienna in 1905, it required Latin descriptions of plants; this requirement was relaxed only in 2012, permitting either English or Latin (Válka Alves, José, Gonçalves da Silva, and Pereira 2012). In zoology, too, Latin long held sway: despite nationalistic calls in the early nineteenth century to grant scientific status to vernacular species names, the influential rules proposed by Hugh Strickland in 1838 and revised in 1842 retained Latin as the tongue in which beasts were named (McOuat 1996). However, zoologists were more relaxed than botanists about descriptions, permitting them in English, French, German, Italian, or Latin in the first formally adopted International Code of Zoological Nomenclature of 1905.

This last distinction, between creatures' names in Latin and their descriptions in a modern language, underscores the transformation of Latin as a scientific language from the mid-seventeenth century to the present. As a vibrant international language for university lecturing and scientific publication, it has been displaced in turn by French, German, and English (McNeill 1997). Yet it still retains its value as a sign: faced with the welter of mutually incomprehensible common names of plants and animals, and the myriad insects, fungi, and bacteria with no common name at all, biologists have stuck to Latin names, or at least names made to look Latin. They alone refer uniquely to a particular species—even to our own, *Homo sapiens sapiens*. In this regard, if not in others, Latin remains a universal scientific language in the twenty-first century.

Suggested Reading

Background on late-medieval and early modern science may be found in Lindberg (2007), Long (2011), and Dear (2009). Burke (2007) discusses translations into Latin, including scientific translations, while Longeon (1980) addresses the choice between Latin and the vernacular. A fuller though far from comprehensive account of important Neo-Latin scientific works, including modern critical editions, may be found in *CNLS* 2:324–52 (subdivided according to modern scientific disciplines). Modern botanical Latin and its development are addressed by Stearn (1983); though there is no analogous reference for zoological Latin, Nybakken (1959) examines scientific terminology in general. For understanding the contemporary use of Neo-Latin terms, including scientific terms, contemporary bilingual dictionaries are useful; Starnes (1954) provides an overview of Latin-English dictionaries. Schoeck (1980) offers an overview of using contemporary handbooks to better understand early modern disciplines.

References

Biagioli, Mario. 1993. *Galileo, Courtier: The Practice of Science in the Culture of Absolutism.* Chicago: University of Chicago Press.

Black, Robert. 2001. *Humanism and Education in Medieval and Renaissance Italy: Tradition and Innovation in Latin Schools from the Twelfth to the Fifteenth Century.* Cambridge: Cambridge University Press.

Bots, Hans, and Françoise Waquet. 1997. *La République des lettres.* Paris: Belin-De Boeck.

Brown, Alison. 2010. *The Return of Lucretius to Renaissance Florence.* Cambridge: Harvard University Press.

Burke, Peter. 2004. *Languages and Communities in Early Modern Europe.* Cambridge: Cambridge University Press.

———. 2007. "Translations into Latin in Early Modern Europe." In *Cultural Translation in Early Modern Europe*, edited by Peter Burke, and Ronnie Po-chia Hsia, 65–80. Cambridge: Cambridge University Press.

Burnett, Charles. 2013. "Translation and Transmission of Greek and Islamic Science to Latin Christendom." In *The Cambridge History of Science*, vol. 2, *Medieval Science*, edited by David C. Lindberg and Michael H. Shank, 341–64. Cambridge: Cambridge University Press.

Cobban, Alan B. 1999. *English University Life in the Middle Ages.* London: Taylor and Francis.

Dear, Peter. 2009. *Revolutionizing the Sciences: European Knowledge and Its Ambitions, 1500–1700.* 2nd ed. Princeton: Princeton University Press.

Debus, Allen G. 1977. *The Chemical Philosophy: Paracelsian Science and Medicine in the Sixteenth and Seventeenth Centuries.* New York: Science History Publications.

Dibon, Paul. 1978. "Communication in the *Respublica literaria* of the Seventeenth Century." *Res publica litterarum* 1:43–55.

Dioscorides. 1518. *De medica materia libri sex.* Florence: Haeredes Philippi Iuntae.

Foucault, Michel. 1970. *The Order of Things: An Archaeology of the Human Sciences.* New York: Pantheon Books.

Fumaroli, Marc. 1980. *L'âge de l'éloquence: Rhétorique et res literaria de la Renaissance au seuil de l'époque classique.* Geneva: Droz.

Fumaroli, Marc. (2001) 2010. *When Europe Spoke French.* Translated by Richard Howard. New York: New York Review of Books.

Gesamtkatalog der Wiegendrucke. 1925–. Compiled by the Staatsbibliothek zu Berlin. Stuttgart: Hiersemann. Available at http://www.gesamtkatalogderwiegendrucke.de.

Gessner, Conrad. 1551–1587. *Historia animalium.* 5 vols. Zurich: Froschauer.

Goldgar, Anne. 1995. *Impolite Learning: Conduct and Community in the Republic of Letters, 1680–1750.* New Haven: Yale University Press.

Goodman, Dena. 1994. *The Republic of Letters: A Cultural History of the French Enlightenment.* Ithaca: Cornell University Press.

Goyens, Michèle, Pieter de Leemans, and An Smets, eds. 2008. *Science Translated: Latin and Vernacular Translations of Scientific Treatises in Medieval Europe.* Leuven: Leuven University Press.

Grafton, Anthony, and Lisa Jardine. 1986. *From Humanism to the Humanities: Education and the Liberal Arts in Fifteenth- and Sixteenth-Century Europe.* Cambridge: Harvard University Press.

Grendler, Paul F. 1989. *Schooling in Renaissance Italy: Literacy and Learning, 1300–1600.* Baltimore: Johns Hopkins University Press.

———. 2002. *The Universities of the Italian Renaissance.* Baltimore: Johns Hopkins University Press.

Hankins, James. 1990. *Plato in the Italian Renaissance.* 2 vols. Leiden: Brill.

Joy, Lynn S. 1987. *Gassendi the Atomist: Advocate of History in an Age of Science.* Cambridge: Cambridge University Press.

Kaunzner, Wolfgang. 1987. "On the Transmission of Mathematical Knowledge to Europe." *Sudhoffs Archiv* 71:129–40.

Lindberg, David C. 2007. *The Beginnings of Western Science: The European Scientific Tradition in Philosophical, Religious, and Institutional Context, Prehistory to A.D. 1450.* 2nd ed. Chicago: University of Chicago Press.

Loach, Judi. 2006. "Revolutionary Pedagogues? How Jesuits Used Education to Change Society." In *The Jesuits II: Cultures, Sciences, and the Arts, 1540–1773*, edited by John W. O'Malley, Gauvin A. Bailey, Steven J. Harris, and T. Frank Kennedy, 66–85. Toronto: University of Toronto Press.

Lohr, Charles H. 1988. *Latin Aristotle Commentaries.* Vol. 2, *Renaissance Authors.* Florence: Olschki.

Long, Pamela O. 2011. *Artisan/Practitioners and the Rise of the New Sciences, 1400–1600.* Corvallis: Oregon State University Press.

Longeon, Claude. 1980. "L'usage du latin et des langues vernaculaires dans les ouvrages de botanique du XVIe siècle." In *ACNL 1980*, 751–66.

McNeill, John. 1997. "Latin, the Renaissance *Lingua Franca*, and English, the 20th Century Language of Science: Their Role in Biotaxonomy." *Taxon* 46:751–57.

McOuat, Gordon R. 1996. "Species, Rules and Meaning: The Politics of Language and the Ends of Definitions in 19th Century Natural History." *Studies in History and Philosophy of Science* 27:473–519.

Moss, Ann. 2010. "Other Latins, Other Cultures." In *Latinity and Alterity in the Early Modern Period*, edited by Yasmin Haskell and Juanita Feros Ruys, 19–34. Tempe: Turnhout; Arizona Center for Medieval and Renaissance Studies; Brepols.

Newman, William R. 2004. *Promethean Ambitions: Alchemy and the Quest to Perfect Nature.* Chicago: University of Chicago Press.

———. 2006. *Atoms and Alchemy: Chymistry and the Experimental Origins of the Scientific Revolution*. Chicago: University of Chicago Press.

Nummedal, Tara E. 2011. "Words and Works in the History of Alchemy." *Isis* 102:330–37.

Nutton, Vivian. 1988. *"Prisci dissectionum professores*: Greek Texts and Renaissance Anatomists." In *The Uses of Greek and Latin: Historical Essays*, edited by A. Carlotta Dionisotti, Anthony Grafton, and Jill Kraye. London: Warburg Institute.

Nybakken, Oscar E. 1959. *Greek and Latin in Scientific Terminology*. Ames: Iowa State College Press.

O'Malley, Charles D. 1964. *Andreas Vesalius of Brussels, 1514–1564*. Berkeley: University of California Press.

Ogilvie, Brian W. 2006. *The Science of Describing: Natural History in Renaissance Europe*. Chicago: University of Chicago Press.

———. 2011. "How to Write a Letter: Humanist Correspondence Manuals and the Late Renaissance Community of Naturalists." *Jahrbuch für Europäische Wissenschaftskultur* 6: 13–38.

Principe, Lawrence M. 2013. *The Secrets of Alchemy*. Chicago: University of Chicago Press.

Reynolds, Leighton D., and Nigel G. Wilson. 2014. *Scribes and Scholars: A Guide to the Transmission of Greek and Latin Literature*. 4th ed. Oxford: Oxford University Press.

Riddle, John M. 1980. "Dioscorides." In *Catalogus translationum et commentariorum*, edited by Ferdinand E. Cranz, vol. 4, 1–143. Washington, DC: Catholic University of America Press.

Rodríguez Ennes, Luis. 2011. "La progresiva sustitución del latín universitario por las lenguas vernáculas." *Boletin de la Real Academia de la Historia* 208:31–45.

Rose, Paul L. 1975. *The Italian Renaissance of Mathematics: Studies on Humanists and Mathematicians from Petrarch to Galileo*. Geneva: Droz.

Rummel, Erika. 1995. *The Humanist-Scholastic Debate in the Renaissance and Reformation*. Cambridge: Harvard University Press.

Schoeck, Richard J. 1980. "Renaissance Guides to Renaissance Learning." In *ACNL* 1980, 239–62.

Siraisi, Nancy G. 1990. *Medieval and Early Renaissance Medicine: An Introduction to Knowledge and Practice*. Chicago: University of Chicago Press.

Smith, Pamela H., and Paula Findlen, eds. 2001. *Merchants and Marvels: Commerce, Science, and Art in Early Modern Europe*. New York: Routledge.

Starnes, DeWitt T. 1954. *Renaissance Dictionaries: English-Latin and Latin-English*. Austin: University of Texas Press.

Stearn, William T. 1983. *Botanical Latin: History, Grammar, Syntax, Terminology and Vocabulary*. 3rd ed. Newton Abbot: David and Charles.

Sylla, Edith D. 2003. "Creation and Nature." In *The Cambridge Companion to Medieval Philosophy*, edited by Arthur S. McGrade, 171–95. Cambridge: Cambridge University Press.

Touwaide, Alain. 2008. "Botany and Humanism in the Renaissance: Background, Interaction, Contradictions." *Studies in the History of Art* 69:32–61.

Válka Alves, Ruy José, Nílber Gonçalves da Silva, and Jorge Fontella Pereira. 2012. "Latin Shaken, Not Stirred." *Taxon* 61:246.

Waquet, Françoise. 1989. "Qu'est-ce que la République des lettres? Essai de sémantique historique." *Bibliothèque de l'Ecole des Chartes* 147:473–502.

———. (1998) 2001. *Latin, or the Empire of a Sign: From the Sixteenth to the Twentieth Centuries*. London: Verso.

Westman, Robert S. 2011. *The Copernican Question: Prognostication, Skepticism, and Celestial Order*. Berkeley: University of California Press.

CHAPTER 18

CONTACTS WITH THE ARAB WORLD

DAG NIKOLAUS HASSE

ARAB people, the Arab world, and the Arabic language feature in many and important ways in Neo-Latin writings, especially in works of science, in grammars and vocabularies of the Arabic language, in travel reports, in historical accounts, in biographies of famous men, and in works of literature and religion. In the Renaissance period, which I shall focus on here, it was the scientists, in addition to Mohammad, who were the most famous Arabs in the Latin world. This finds an impressive reflection on the European book market: forty-five Arabic authors on sciences and philosophy were published in Latin translation before 1700, most of them before 1600. Averroes, Avicenna, Mesue, and Rhazes were the most frequently printed among them. Before 1700, 113 editions of Averroes, seventy-eight of Avicenna, seventy-six of Mesue, and sixty-eight of Rhazes appeared. The significance of these figures becomes even more evident if we compare the printing history of some medieval authors such as Peter Abelard or Roger Bacon, who received only one or two editions respectively.

As a result, every educated person of the Renaissance, even humanists who entertained prejudices against scholastic traditions, was surely acquainted with the names of the famous Arabic scientists. And everyone was aware that their works were mandatory reading at the faculties of medicine and philosophy at many European universities: Averroes's commentaries on Aristotle, Avicenna's *Canon of Medicine*, Mesue's pharmacological works, and Rhazes's pathology. Of course, the majority of these editions printed medieval Latin texts; that is, translations of Arabic authors produced between the eleventh and thirteenth centuries. But as recent research has shown, the humanist movement was involved to a considerable degree in the Latin textual tradition of Arabic authors in the Renaissance. Humanist scholars revised medieval Latin translations according to new stylistic ideals, and also produced new Neo-Latin translations of Arabic authors. Hence, Arabic scientific traditions in early modern Latin were much more than a medieval heritage: they formed an integral part of Renaissance Latin culture.

The Renaissance was a formative period for modern attitudes towards the Arab world. On one hand, some traditions of Arabic science reached the high point of their influence in Europe in the sixteenth century: Arabic medicine and pharmacology, astrology, logic, zoology, and (especially Averroes's) philosophy of the mind. On the other hand, the sixteenth century was also the time when European scientific culture gradually disconnected from its Arabic sources. The study of Averroes, Avicenna, and the other Arabic authorities declined in the decades around 1600, and the printing history of most of these authors phased out at about the same time. An important factor in this process was the polemics of hard-liner humanists against Arabic scientific traditions. Humanist prejudices against Averroes and his alleged irreligion go back to Petrarch, who had advised the addressee of a letter: "Be an enemy of Averroes, the enemy of Christ!" (*Epistolae seniles* 13.6). Later polemics extended beyond Averroes. In the last decades of the fifteenth century, a heated and long-lasting controversy arose over the value of Arabic sciences and philosophy. Many humanist writers called for a replacement of Averroes by the Greek commentators, of Avicenna and Rhazes by Hippocrates and Galen, of Mesue by Dioscorides, and of the astrologers Albumasar and Alcabitius by Ptolemy. People complained that the Arabic translations from Greek and the Latin translations from Arabic were unreliable and a great source of terminological confusion, and that the Arabs had stolen everything from the Greeks, as the botanist Leonhart Fuchs said: "The Arabs, many as they were, have not aimed at anything else than to consume, just as drones, the supplies of someone else's labor and to wear foreign and even stolen plumes" (Fuchs 1535, A6r). These polemics were not purely rhetorical. They formed part of a struggle about university curricula, academic positions, and intellectual leadership. In the present chapter, the focus will not be on the humanist polemics against Arabic scientific traditions, but on the other side of the coin: the great presence of Arabic traditions in Neo-Latin writings.

In addition to the rise and eventual decline of Arabic sciences, the Renaissance also witnessed other important changes with respect to the Arab world, which found various forms of expression in Neo-Latin writings. In the sixteenth century, the Arab world became the subject of philological and historical scholarship: Arabic manuscripts were collected, the Arabic language began to be taught at universities, grammars and lexica of Arabic were written, and the history and literature of the Arab world and of Islam were studied. A further development concerns travel, diplomacy, and commerce. In the sixteenth and seventeenth centuries, many more educated people traveled in Arab and Turkish countries, for religious, commercial, diplomatic, or scholarly reasons. As a result, there is a tangible increase in travel reports on the Middle East, which were written partly in the vernacular, partly in Latin. I shall pass by two further topics that also concern the relations between Occident and Orient: the religion of Islam, and the Ottoman Empire. Western attitudes towards both Islam and the Turks were also changing in the Renaissance period, but these developments are too complex to be covered adequately in this chapter as well. Also, I will not deal in any depth with works of literature and religion in the narrower sense. Instead, my survey will discuss, with respect to the Arab world and the Arabic language, the following genres of Neo-Latin texts: translations, scientific texts, biographies, works of Arabic scholarship, and travel literature.

TRANSLATIONS

Around 1300, medieval translation movements of Arabic to Latin, which had been very productive for more than two hundred years, ceased almost entirely, with very few exceptions. But after 1480, there set in a new wave of Latin translations of Arabic authors (Tamani 1992; Burnett 1999; Hasse 2006). Many of these translations were made from an intermediary Hebrew translation in Italy; others were made directly from Arabic in the Near East. This translation movement lasted about seventy years, from the first translations by Elia del Medigo until the death of the translator Jacob Mantino in 1549 (save for some excerpts from Avicenna's *Canon*, which were translated later). After Mantino, most translators were Arabist scholars motivated primarily by historical and philological rather than by scientific and philosophical interests. The Renaissance translation movement is characterized by two major projects: the translation of Averroes's commentaries on Aristotle that were not yet known in the Middle Ages, and the replacing of the medieval version of Avicenna's *Canon of Medicine* by a more reliable and more modern Latin text. The outcome of this translating activity is considerable: nineteen commentaries of Averroes were translated for the first time, in addition to the sixteen commentaries translated in the Middle Ages, and six new versions of Avicenna's *Canon* or of parts of it were produced (Siraisi 1987, 133–43). And apart from these two major projects, other authors, such as Alpetragius, Alhazen, or Albucasis, were translated as well.

The Latin competence of some of the translators from Hebrew was deficient in a way that affected the intelligibility of the texts. But others, and in particular the Jewish physician Jacob Mantino, had full command of the two languages involved. Mantino was the most competent translator of Averroes in the Renaissance. He served as personal physician to Pope Paul III, probably already before Paul's election in 1534. One of Mantino's translations is dedicated to Paul III, others to Pope Leo X and to Ercole Gonzaga, bishop of Mantua, who apparently promoted and probably also financed a considerable number of Mantino's translations of Averroes. In one of his dedications, Mantino criticizes the older—that is, medieval—translations as "unkempt and mutilated" (*inculta et mutilata*), and characterizes the older translations' style as "ugly, barbarous and obscure" (*foede, barbare, obscure*; Kaufmann 1893, 222). Mantino was concerned about the fact that many contemporaries condemned Averroes for the uncultivated style of his Latin versions. It is obvious that Mantino wanted to rescue Averroes for the humanist movement. Mantino's own Latin style is moderately classicizing, with respect to scientific vocabulary as well. In many cases, Mantino did not produce an entirely new translation, but worked with the wording of earlier versions, which he corrected against the Hebrew. Mantino's thirteen translations of Averroes and his single translation of Avicenna are major philological achievements, praised by the editors of the monumental Giunta edition of the combined works of Aristotle and Averroes of 1550–1552 and 1562, who speak of the "extremely lucid" (*dilucidissima*) and "golden" (*aurea*) translation of this "most learned" person (Aristotle and Averroes 1550–52, 1:9r, and 1562, 1:319r).

Other humanist scholars involved in the translation movement revised earlier Latin versions of Arabic texts without any access to the Arabic or Hebrew: these include Miguel Ledesma and Andrea Gratiolo, revisers of Avicenna's *Canon medicinae*; Jean Bruyerin Champier, a humanist physician in France, who produced a new version of Averroes's medical work *Colliget*; and Jacques Dubois (Jacobus Sylvius), the reviser of the pharmacological *Opera Mesue*. Ledesma's version of the Canon is a good example for illustrating the merits and limits of this approach. Miguel Jerónimo Ledesma, who died in 1547, was a major proponent of medical humanism in Spain. He was educated at a center of the humanist movement, the University of Alcalá. In the dedication to the Archbishop of Valencia, Ledesma praises Avicenna, in quintessentially humanist vein, for "always behaving as a translator of Galen," and he utterly deplores the fact that Avicenna had "a barbarous translator and even more barbarous commentators" (*nactus est barbarum interpretem barbarioresque multo enarratores*). Ledesma therefore promises to restore Avicenna to his "Arabic truth" (*ad Arabicam veritatem*). For this purpose, he says, he has used "an extremely old manuscript," which much differs from "the commonly used version" (Avicenna 1547, A2v). The text itself, however, does not bear any sign of the usage of Arabic sources. Rather, Ledesma translates Gerard of Cremona's medieval Latin translation into fluent humanist Latin and significantly shortens the text: he cuts information he finds repetitive or not essential to the argument. Ledesma's text is the most readable of all Latin versions of the *Canon*, but, due to the drastic cuts and syntactical rearrangements, it is not a good guide to what Avicenna meant, nor to the *Arabica veritas* that Ledesma promised.

Research into the influence of the newly translated Arabic works is still in its infancy. But it is already known that the new translations of Averroes's works about zoology and logic were much used and quoted by Paduan professors of the sixteenth century (Burnett 2013). The new versions of Avicenna's *Canon medicinae* also quickly found their readers, especially among Italian professors of medicine. And, very impressively, Jacques Dubois's revision of Mesue's works was reprinted twenty-one times and almost entirely replaced the medieval version on the print market.

MEDICAL, PHILOSOPHICAL, AND ASTROLOGICAL WORKS

Many traditions of Arabic medicine, philosophy, and astrology reached the high point of their influence in Europe in the fifteenth and sixteenth centuries. The basis for this successful reception in Renaissance Europe was the firm grounding of Arabic texts in university education and curricula. To be sure, many texts in this university tradition, even in the Renaissance, were still written in scholastic Latin. But humanist scholars, too, were engaged in the reception and development of Arabic sciences, especially in medical botany (*materia medica*), the philosophy of the mind, and various disciplines of astrology. Three examples may serve to illustrate this Neo-Latin current: Giovanni Manardo, the medical author; Francesco Vimercato, the Aristotelian philosopher; and Valentin Nabod, the astrologer and mathematician.

Giovanni Manardo (1462–1536) was a well-known protagonist of the Ferrara school of medical humanism (Nutton 1997). His teacher in Ferrara, Nicolò Leoniceno, had inaugurated a new trend in medicine with his book *De Plinii et plurium aliorum medicorum in medicina erroribus* (*The Errors of Pliny and Other Doctors in Medicine*), published successively from 1492 to 1507, in which Leoniceno attacked physicians without philological expertise, criticized their reliance on Arabic authorities, and called for a medicine based on Greek sources alone. Manardo continued the anti-Arab polemics of Leoniceno. He accused Avicenna of plagiarizing Greek authors and praised the ideal of the true medicine of antiquity (*antiqua et vera medicina*), cleansed of all barbarous additions. At the same time, however, Manardo did not shy away from Arabic sources. In particular, he composed a commentary *In Ioannis Mesue simplicia medicamenta* (*On Joannes Mesue's Simple Medicines*), which was first printed around 1521. Manardo gives for each drug a conspectus of the Greek and Arabic authorities who had also written on it, and then proceeds to comment on the specifics of Mesue's entry on the drug. By juxtaposing Mesue's doctrine with that of several other Greek and Arabic authorities on the issue, Manardo successfully links humanist and Arabic doctrines and vocabulary in the field of medical botany. The text pays much attention to textual correspondences and discrepancies between the different writers, but is not a philological commentary in the strict sense: its focus instead is on the value of the botanical and medical information. Manardo's empirical attitude is well captured in the following sentence: "It does not matter much, however, to know how it [i.e., the Arab plant *senna*] was called by the ancients, as long as we know its properties, which are without doubt noble and effective" (Manardo 1549, 548). Manardo, like his pupil Antonius Musa Brasavola, represents a pragmatic current within the movement of medical humanism. Other humanists of the sixteenth century, such as Jean Ruel and Leonhart Fuchs, entertained a more hostile attitude towards Arabic sources and tried to suppress Arabic medical traditions in Europe altogether. By the second half of the sixteenth century, it became clear that the hard-liner approach had lost the day against the Manardo-Brasavola tradition. Arabic *materia medica* had made too much progress over Greek science to be ignored (Hasse 2001).

Francesco Vimercato of Milan (d. ca. 1571), the Aristotelian philosopher and Greek philologist, is an example of a humanist reader of Averroes. Vimercato had studied at several Italian universities, but spent most of his academic career in Paris, where he became the first teacher of Greek and Latin philosophy at the Collège Royal. From the time of Paul of Venice in the early fifteenth century at least, Averroes, the Arabic commentator on Aristotle, had been of paramount importance for the teaching of philosophy at Italian universities. Vimercato prolonged this tradition by writing a commentary on Book 3 of Aristotle's *De anima*, in which he presented for each lemma the expositions not only of the Greek commentators, but also of Averroes. Vimercato was among the first, however, to systematically compare Averroes's long commentary with the Greek text of Aristotle's *De anima*. He was able to identify several passages in which Averroes's exposition was seriously hampered by a faulty translation or transmission, and complained about Averroes's understanding of the passages: *habuit textum a veritate Graeca . . . valde diversum* ("he has a text that differs much from the Greek truth"; Vimercato 1574, 19a). On the other hand, Vimercato did not challenge Averroes's most famous philosophical doctrine, which is that there is only one intellect for all human beings. Rather, Vimercato addressed the issue directly in another text, his *Peripatetic Dispute about the Rational Soul* (*De anima rationali peripatetica disceptatio*), first printed in 1543 in Paris. In this treatise, Vimercato occasionally quotes the Greek text, but the argumentation in general is philosophical rather than philological. By pondering the arguments of the Greek, Arabic, and Latin commentators on the nature of the human intellect, Vimercato arrives at several conclusions, among which is Averroes's "unicity" thesis (the doctrine that there is only one intellect for all human beings). Vimercato's reception of Averroes was not hampered by humanist prejudices, nor was it influenced by religious qualms. He was well aware of the problem of heterodoxy, and closed his treatise with the remark that Aristotle's doctrine of the rational soul does not accord with Christian faith and that the unicity thesis is absurd, but that there is no reason why he should refrain from freely presenting Aristotle's opinion. Vimercato thus clearly saw the Arabic philosophers as part of a Greek-Arabic-Latin tradition of Peripatetic philosophy, which he himself aspired to continue (Hasse 2004, 461–66; Hasse 2007).

A good example for the influence of Arabic astrology on Neo-Latin texts is a work by Valentin Nabod (1523–1593), professor of mathematics at the University of Cologne (Thorndike 1941, 6:119–23). In 1560, there appeared in print his *Description of the Elements of Astrology* (*Enarratio elementorum astrologiae*), which takes the form of a 472-page commentary on the *Introductory Book to the Art of Judicial Astrology* by Alcabitius (al-Qabīsī), a tenth-century Arabic author active in Syria. In the dedicatory letter, Nabod explains that he is going to compare throughout Alcabitius's astrological doctrines with those of Ptolemy and that he sets out to refute Alcabitius where his theories are in conflict with physics and hence are superstitious. Nabod cites Alcabitius's text in full, in its twelfth-century Latin version, and comments on almost the entire text in humanist Latin. He leaves out the last section of Chapter Four and most of Chapter Five—that is, the last part of Alcabitius's text—because he does not accept the Arabic astrological doctrine of the numerous lots (*partes*), of which Ptolemy had recognized only one, the lot of fortune (*pars fortunae*). Nabod is critical of many Arabic doctrines, especially of those that are in conflict with Ptolemy's astrology, but he still gives lengthy explanations of them. Such is the case, for instance, with the famous Arabic doctrine, originally of Sassanian-Persian origin, of the great conjunctions of Saturn and Jupiter in the sign of Aries, which happen every 960 or 800 or 784 years (depending on the figure of mean or real planetary motions used for calculation). These conjunctions, Arabic authorities such as Albumasar and Alcabitius claimed, signify great changes in religious and political history. Nabod discusses the doctrine in detail. To this end he even uses the new and more exact figures that Girolamo Cardano had proposed in 1547 for calculating great conjunctions (Nabod 1560, 354). But Nabod rejects the doctrine nevertheless, because he finds that it disagrees with Ptolemy and because he doubts that the time of the sun's entrance into Aries can be calculated with sufficient exactness. The doctrine of great conjunctions was often received critically in the Renaissance, as here by Valentin Nabod, but nevertheless enjoyed considerable success in the sixteenth and seventeenth centuries as the theoretical foundation for astrological historiography. Astrological authors from Girolamo Cardano to Johannes Kepler to Giambattista Riccioli in the mid-seventeenth century connected great conjunctions of Saturn and Jupiter with events of world history, especially with the foundation of Rome, the birth of Christ, and the *translatio imperii* under Charles the Great. In this sub-discipline of astrology as in others, Arabic sources substantially contributed to the boom of astrology in the early modern period.

BIOGRAPHIES

While interest in the biographies of Arabic authors was scanty in the Middle Ages, there was a significant rise of the biographical study of Arabic authors in the later fifteenth and sixteenth centuries. The founding text for this development was Jacopo Filippo Foresti da Bergamo's world chronicle *Supplementum chronicarum* (*Supplement to the Chronicles*, 1483), the first chronicle, as far as is now known, to give brief biographies of Arabic authors in several sections on illustrious scholars of the tenth to twelfth centuries. Foresti's work was to become the standard world chronicle of the Renaissance and considerably influenced later chronicles and biographical collections. As a result, many later sources, such as Hartmann Schedel's well-known *Liber chronicarum* (*Book of Chronicles*, 1493) and Symphorien Champier's *De medicine claris scriptoribus* (*Famous Authors of Medicine*, ca. 1506), included much material on Arabic authors, based on Foresti. There are several reasons for this rise of interest in the lives and works of Arabic authors: one being the general popularity of biographical writing and of treatises on famous men (*de viris illustribus*) in the Renaissance; another, the developing genre of histories of scientific disciplines, such as medicine or mathematics. Foresti, in fact, was apparently influenced by previous histories of medicine, and by Giovanni Tortelli's *Liber de medicina et medicis* (*Book of Medicine and Physicians*) in particular. Tortelli (d. 1466) inserted, between the ancient and the modern Italian physicians—that is, between Galen and Pietro d'Abano—a paragraph on two authorities of Arabic medicine, Rhazes and Avicenna. Foresti enlarged this group by discussing eleven Arabic authors. It seems that Italian pride in the continuous Greek-Arabic-Italian tradition in medicine was a motive for including the Arabs in such histories of science. A final factor in the rise of the biography of Arabic authors was their firm rooting in Renaissance university education, as described above.

Jacopo Filippo Foresti (1434–1520), was neither a man of letters nor a Latin scholar, but a friar of the order of the Eremites of Saint Augustine in the convent of Bergamo

(Cochrane 1981, 377–86; Krümmel 1991). His world chronicle is not yet a Neo-Latin or humanist work in the strict sense. It continues the tradition of medieval world chronicles, which do not aim at a narrative account of history, or at source critique. In another sense, however, Foresti was also a representative of the historiography of Italian humanism: he adopted some of its ideals, such as the usage of ancient sources and models, the inclusion of *viri illustres*, and a mildly classicizing Latin style. For his biographies of Arabic authors, Foresti could only draw on Western sources. Most of the material comes from internal evidence and cross-evidence in the Latin translations of Arabic authors. His biographies are therefore the result of a distinctly Western investigation into and imaginative rendering of the lives and works of Arabic scholars. His biography of Avicenna, for instance, is historically inaccurate on several points. While Avicenna was born in Buchara on the Silk Road, Foresti makes him an Andalusian, on the basis of a medieval ascription. He also relates fantastic legends about Avicenna, such as that he was poisoned by his rival Averroes (who, even if very critical of Avicenna, lived one century later and on the other side of the Islamic world). The murder story apparently is a reflection of the problematic Western image of Averroes as a heretical philosopher by their lights.

The biography of Avicenna (Siraisi 1987, 161–64) may serve to present two further examples of Neo-Latin biographies of Arabic authors, by the humanist scholars Franciscus Calphurnius and Jacob Milich. Franciscus Calphurnius of Vendôme, about whom not much is known, was part of the early phase of the humanist movement in France. Around 1517, he published a book with Neo-Latin epigrams. In 1522, he published a biography of Avicenna as part of a *Canon* edition printed in Lyon, possibly upon the request of the general editor, the physician Symphorien Champier (1471–1538). For this *vita*, Calphurnius drew on the Foresti-Schedel-Champier tradition of biographies and on a one-page *vita* of Avicenna that had been published by the editor Boneto Locatello in a *Canon* edition of 1505. The Locatello *vita* was doubtless based on original Arabic material, since it related authentic data about Avicenna's childhood as a *wunderkind* pupil in Buchara, and about his death resulting from a colic in 1037 CE— material that came from Avicenna's autobiography and the biography of his secretary. Calphurnius's biography of Avicenna is written in exquisite classical Latin style, and is based, purportedly, on proper source criticism. In truth, however, Calphurnius cared less about sources than about the standard humanist depiction of Averroes as an impious and villainous person. For he does not adopt the historical account of Avicenna's death from the Locatello *vita*, but concluded that the murder story must be true: that Averroes killed Avicenna with a poisonous drink.

A new level of historical precision in Latin biographies of Avicenna, even compared with the Locatello *vita*, was reached when the Venetian physician Nicolò Massa produced a Latin version of the combined autobiography-biography some time before 1544, when it was first published as part of a *Canon* edition. Massa had produced this text on the basis of an earlier Italian version of the Arabic sources by Marco Fadella. The result is not a translation proper, but rather a re-narration, with the addition of occasional remarks by the translators. It nevertheless transported much historically authentic material to the Latin world. Jacob Milich (1501–1599), my last example of a Neo-Latin author writing on the lives of Arabic scholars, was among the first readers of Massa's biography. Milich, a promoter of medical humanism, was the first professor of anatomy at the University of Wittenberg. In 1550, he published the nineteen-page *Oration on the Life of Avicenna* (*Oratio de Avicennae vita*) which was meant to incite the young students to study medicine and Avicenna in particular. Milich follows Massa's autobiographical account closely until Avicenna reaches the age of eighteen, but then continues with a completely fictitious biography, which brings Avicenna to study first with Rhazes in Alexandria and then with Averroes in Cordoba; back in Egypt, Avicenna studies the true Hippocratic and Galenic sources of medicine in Arabic translation and returns to his home country, where he writes his great book, the *Canon medicinae*. Milich certainly knew from Locatello's and Massa's biographies that Avicenna never traveled further West than Persia, but, from an educational viewpoint, it seemed preferable to let Avicenna "study with" two famous names of Arabic medicine, Rhazes and Averroes, that the students should know (but who were not, in fact, contemporaries of Avicenna), and to link him directly to the tradition of Greek medicine in Egypt. Milich ends his *Oratio* with Avicenna's advances over Greek medicine. Milich's *vita* thus bears witness to the high reputation of Arabic scientific authorities in the sixteenth century, and to the proud conviction of many scholars that Greek, Arabic, and Latin science belonged to one great international tradition of learning. In one sense, however, Jacob Milich was an exception in the biographical tradition on Arabic authors: other biographies were tendentious, but not unblushing fabrications like his biography of Avicenna. In all this, one has to keep in mind, of course, that there was a considerable imbalance between the great interest in the lives of Arabic scholars and the poverty of authentic material on them, even on Avicenna. This changed only in 1624, when Jacob Golius acquired a manuscript of Ibn Ḥallikān's celebrated thirteenth-century biographical dictionary (*The Obituaries of Eminent Men*) in Morocco.

Works of Arabic Philology

The sixteenth century saw the rise of Arabic studies in Europe. Chairs for the teaching of Arabic were founded in Paris in 1538 at the Collège Royal, at Leiden University in 1599, at Cambridge in 1631, and at Oxford in 1636. Scholars began to collect Arabic manuscripts systematically, and the collections in Rome, Heidelberg, and Leiden became centers of Arabic learning. Among the first humanists to own Arabic manuscripts were Giorgio Valla and Giovanni Pico della Mirandola. Johann Albrecht Widmanstetter and Guillaume Postel were important sixteenth-century collectors.

A crucial factor for the development of Arabic studies was the invention of printing with Arabic type. The first complete book in Arabic type was a prayer book, printed in 1514, probably in Venice (although the imprint gives Fano as the city of publication), upon commission by the pope, and destined for use by Christian Melkites in the Middle

East. Very influential was the second Arabic publication, a polyglot Psalter, which was published in 1516 in Genoa with annotations by Agostino Giustiniani (d. 1536). It prints, in facing columns, Hebrew, Greek, Aramaic, Arabic, and Latin versions of the Psalms and thus served many scholars of the sixteenth century as a textbook for learning Arabic. In 1584, there followed the founding of the Medici Oriental Press (*Typographia Medicea*) in Rome by Giovan Battista Raimondi.

Scholarly motivation for studying the Arabic language was manifold. Knowledge of Arabic was important for Christian scholars who wanted to convert Muslims. Also, it was a means to strengthen the ties with the Christian churches of the Middle East. From a theological point of view, the understanding of obscure Hebrew words in the Old Testament could be much improved by the study of other Semitic languages such as Aramaic, Syriac, and Arabic. And, finally, knowing Arabic gave one privileged access to the great Arabic scientists in medicine, philosophy, mathematics, and astrology (Fück 1955; Dannenfeldt 1955; Bobzin 1992; Bobzin 1995; Hamilton 2011, 297–313).

Among the many Neo-Latin texts that reflect this scholarly interest in the Arabic language, I shall mention three important examples written by the Arabists Guillaume Postel, Thomas Erpenius, and Jacob Golius. Guillaume Postel (1510–1581) was the first professor of Arabic at the Collège Royal and the author of the *Grammatica Arabica*, the first printed Arabic grammar, which appeared around 1540 in Paris. Postel's text is marred by misprints, in both Arabic and Latin, but it remains a remarkable achievement. In structure and vocabulary, the grammar is based on Arabic models, for which Postel used several Arabic grammar books current in Ottoman schools of the time. Postel successfully translated the traditional Arabic terminology of grammar into Latin. The book contains a programmatic *praefatio*, in which Postel stresses the scientific, missionary, and commercial benefits of knowing the Arabic language (Bobzin 1995, 430–47).

Postel's grammar was replaced in 1613 by the *Grammatica Arabica* of the Leiden professor of Arabic Thomas Erpenius (Thomas van Erpe, d. 1624). This text would remain the standard reference work until the early nineteenth century. In the presentation of the material, Erpenius follows Latin grammar, but he also transliterates and explains the most important technical terms of the venerable Arabic tradition of grammar. A precious document for the history of Arabic studies in Europe is Erpenius's two *Orations on the Arabic Language* (*Orationes de Lingua Arabica*) of 1613 and 1620, which were printed in 1621 together with a lecture on the Hebrew language. In the longer lecture on Arabic of 1620, Erpenius gives a brief history of the Arabs and of Islam, and then explains the good reasons for studying the language of the Arabs: the Arabs' great addiction to the arts and to learning; the unparalleled number of institutions of learning (*academiae*); the translation of the most important ancient authors into Arabic, so that "if the sciences of the Greeks were lost to us, they could be restored from the Arabic language"; and the many new things they had produced in all disciplines of learning. Erpenius also points to the great usefulness of Arabic for traveling in the Near East; for understanding the Old Testament; for European medicine ("you will be able to make the best use of the best known doctors: Avicenna, Mesue, Rhazes, and others"); law, philosophy (in particular: Averroes, "the other Aristotle"), mathematics, astrology, and history; and praises the delight one derives from Arabic poetry. Erpenius's oration thus testifies not only to the Western image of the Arab world, but also to the continuing fame of Arabic sciences and philosophy in Europe at the beginning of the seventeenth century (Erpenius 1621, 39–96, esp. 79–80; Jones 1986).

The Dutch Arabist Jacob Golius (Jacob Gool, d. 1667) was Erpenius's pupil and successor in 1624 at Leiden University. He was not a theologian, but a mathematician by training. Unlike Erpenius, who had learned his excellent Arabic from a Moroccan diplomat in Paris, Golius traveled extensively in the Near East: in Morocco, Syria, Mesopotamia and Turkey, where he got to know the great monolingual dictionaries of the Arabic language, but also Turkish and Persian lexica of Arabic. Based on these sources, Golius produced what would remain by far the best Arabic dictionary in Europe for two hundred years, the *Lexicon Arabico-Latinum*, which was first printed in Leiden in 1653 (Hamilton 1994, 68). Its successor, Georg Wilhelm Freytag's *Lexicon Arabico-Latinum*, of 1830–1837, was still in Latin, and only with Edward William Lane's *Arabic-English Lexicon* of 1863–1893 did the era of academic dictionaries of Arabic in Latin come to an end.

TRAVEL ACCOUNTS

The Ottoman Empire and Arab countries were the prime subjects of the flourishing genre of travel literature in the sixteenth century, even more so than the Americas or the Far East (Hamilton 2011, 13–103; MacLean 2004). Among the many texts produced, there was a considerable number written in Latin, especially by traveling scholars. A very popular travel account of the Renaissance period was the *Peregrinationes* by a German pilgrim to the Holy Land, Bernhard von Breydenbach (d. 1497), dean of the Cathedral of Mainz. This book, which was printed in Mainz in 1486, describes Breydenbach's journey to Palestine from April 1483 to January 1484 with a group of German pilgrims. After landing in Jaffa, he visited Jerusalem and then proceeded to Mount Sinai and St. Catherine's monastery, Cairo, and Alexandria. Breydenbach's account contains material from earlier pilgrim literature, but also his own observations on the customs of the different Christian, Jewish, and Muslim peoples he encountered, and, a novelty, woodcut illustrations by a fellow traveler. Among these illustrations are a panoramic view of Palestine and Jerusalem, an illustration of Arabic costumes, and a table of the Arabic alphabet, which here appeared in print for the first time (Hamilton 1994, 32–33).

An example of a sixteenth-century pilgrim to the Levant is Nuremberg patrician Christoph Fürer von Haimendorff (1541–1610), whose travel account was published in 1620–1621 under the title *Itinerarium Aegypti, Arabiae, Palestinae, Syriae, aliarumque regionum Orientalium* (*Itinerary of Egypt, Arabia, Palestine, Syria, and Other Oriental Regions*). He describes the cities and sites visited on a journey with another nobleman in 1565–1566, including Alexandria, Cairo, the Pyramids and the Nile, Mount Sinai, Jerusalem, Bethlehem, the Dead Sea, Damascus, and Tripoli. His report is enriched by many classical and biblical quotations, but also contains interesting contemporary material on Arab life and European diplomats in Egypt (Hamilton 2001, 38–39). Like many other travel reports of the later sixteenth and seventeenth centuries, it contributed to creating a new image of the Near East based on personal observation. It was also a forerunner to the "gentlemen traveler" literature of later centuries.

In addition to pilgrims' reports, there also exist travel accounts by missionaries, diplomats, merchants, and scientists. Among the scientists, a particularly productive group was the physicians and botanists (Brentjes 1999). An early example was Andrea Alpago (d. 1522), the well-known corrector of the Latin translation of Avicenna's *Canon of Medicine* on the basis of Arabic sources. Alpago was a descendant of an Italian noble family, and served for more than thirty years as physician to the Venetian embassy in Damascus. Apart from being a translator, he also composed the *Interpretatio Arabicorum nominum* (*Translation of Arabic Terms*, printed 1529) to Avicenna's *Canon*, a lexicon of 2,050 transliterated Arabic names of drugs, plants, minerals, and other items, as well as an index of Arabic drug names in Serapion's *Practica* (late ninth century), printed in 1550. Other sixteenth-century botanists also tried to improve Western knowledge of oriental drugs and plants; for instance, Pierre Belon, Leonard Rauwolf, and Prospero Alpini. Alpini (1553–1617) lived in Egypt for three years, from 1580 to 1583, where he served as a physician to the Venetian consul in Cairo; later, he became professor of medicine at the University of Padua and director of the botanical garden. His books *De medicina Aegyptiorum* (*The Medicine of the Egyptians*, 1591), *De plantis Aegypti* (*The Plants of Egypt*, 1592), and the posthumous *Res Aegyptiae* (*Egyptian Matters*, 1735) are major contributions to the Western knowledge of the medicine, botany, natural history, and customs of Egypt, based upon personal experience (Stannard 1970, 124–25). His *Res Aegyptiae* contains a detailed description of scientific life in Cairo and in the mosque Al-Azhar in particular, stressing that the education comprises almost all the disciplines: logic, natural philosophy, metaphysics, rhetoric, mathematics, medicine, magic, and, in particular, astrology (Brentjes 1999, 445–47).

The last book to be mentioned here comes from an Arab: Leo Africanus, whose original Arabic name was al-Ḥasan ibn Muḥammad al-Wazzān az-Zayyātī (Rauchenberger 1999; Davis 2006). Born in Granada, Spain, to a Muslim family, he traveled extensively as a diplomat and merchant to Istanbul, Timbuktu, Egypt, Sudan, and Mecca between 1507 and 1518, when he was captured by Christian pirates and given to Pope Leo X as a present. He converted to Catholicism in 1520 and took the name "Johannes Leo de Medicis." After the sack of Rome in 1527, he returned to Tunis and probably reconverted. In the years between 1518 and 1527, which he spent in Italy, Leo Africanus produced several works, the most famous of which was his *Descrittione dell'Africa* (*Description of Africa*), which was first printed in 1550, and was much read also in a Latin translation by the Dutch scholar Jan Blommaerts, first printed in 1556: *De totius Africae descriptione*. This work was a mine of information about Islamic Africa. It was the only major source on the contemporary Arab world that came from a native Arab. "Read Leo Africanus's book about Africa," Thomas Erpenius exhorted his students in the above-mentioned *Oration*, "and you will see that in that part of the world alone there were up to thirty famous universities" (Jones 1986, 18). Thus one single captive Arab was able to raise Western appreciation of Islamic civilization significantly.

SUMMARY

Neo-Latin writings testify amply to developments in the relationship between Europe and the Arab world that still influence the contemporary Western image of the Middle East: the rise of a new translation movement of Arabic sciences and philosophy; the intense reception of Arabic sources in Renaissance medicine, philosophy, and astrology; the great fame of Arabic scientists and philosophers in Europe, which is also expressed in many biographical writings; the fierce humanist polemics against Arabic scientific traditions, which run parallel to the attempts of other humanists to redress Arabic works in the classicizing Latin of the time; and, towards the end of the sixteenth century, the decline of Arabic traditions in European science. At the same time, new attitudes towards the Arab world emerged, demonstrated by the academic study of Arabic and of Islam, and eyewitness accounts by travelers to the Levant, who reported on its customs and intellectual life. Probably the greatest differences between the medieval Latin presentation of the Middle East and its Neo-Latin presentation are that the latter was more detailed and more visual. It was more detailed because of the dramatically increasing number of scholars and travelers who knew the language and who saw the countries. It was more visual, because of the many illustrations of the Arab world distributed in print. The most dramatic negative inheritance of the Renaissance clearly was the charge of plagiarism and barbaric style, which was voiced by humanist hard-liners against Arabic science. But the dominating Neo-Latin image of the Arab world, as surveyed in this chapter, was overwhelmingly positive.

SUGGESTED READING

For an introduction to the topic, see Burnett (1999); on the central figure of Avicenna and his reception in Renaissance medicine, Siraisi (1987); on Arabic philosophy in the Renaissance, Hasse (2007). A very informative survey of travel literature to the Middle East is given by Hamilton (2011, 13–103). The basic reference work on Arabic studies in Europe remains Fück (1955); for more recent literature, see Bobzin (1992). On the Renaissance study of the Koran, see Bobzin (1992) and Hamilton (2008); on Renaissance attitudes towards the Ottoman world, Meserve (2008) and Contadini and Norton (2013).

REFERENCES

Aristotle and Averroes. 1550–1552. *Aristotelis Stagiritae omnia quae extant opera . . . Averrois Cordubensis in ea opera omnes . . . commentarii.* 11 vols. Venice: Giunta.
———. 1562. *Aristotelis omnia quae extant opera . . . Averrois Cordubensis in ea opera omnes . . . commentarii.* 10 vols. Venice: Giunta.

Avicenna. 1547. *Prima primi Canonis Avicennae sectio Michaele Hieronymo Ledesma Valentino medico et interprete et enarratore*. Valencia: Johannes Mey of Flanders.

Bobzin, Hartmut. 1992. "Geschichte der arabischen Philologie in Europa bis zum Ausgang des achtzehnten Jahrhunderts." In *Grundriß der Arabischen Philologie*, vol. 3, *Supplement*, edited by Wolfdietrich Fischer, 155–87. Wiesbaden: Reichert.

———. 1995. *Der Koran im Zeitalter der Reformation: Studien zur Frühgeschichte der Arabistik und Islamkunde in Europa*. Stuttgart: Franz Steiner.

Brentjes, Sonja. 1999. "The Interests of the Republic of Letters in the Middle East, 1550–1700." *Science in Context* 12:435–68.

Burnett, Charles. 1999. "The Second Revelation of Arabic Philosophy and Science: 1492–1575." In *Islam and the Italian Renaissance*, edited by Charles Burnett and Anna Contadini, 185–98. London: Warburg Institute.

———. 2013. "Revisiting the 1552–1550 and 1562 Aristotle-Averroes Edition." In *Renaissance Averroism and Its Aftermath: Arabic Philosophy in Early Modern Europe*, edited by Anna Akasoy and Guido Giglioni, 55–64. Dordrecht: Springer.

Cochrane, Eric. 1981. *Historians and Historiography in the Italian Renaissance*. Chicago: University of Chicago Press.

Contadini, Anna, and Claire Norton, eds. 2013. *The Renaissance and the Ottoman World*. Farnham: Ashgate.

Dannenfeldt, Karl H. 1955. "The Renaissance Humanists and the Knowledge of Arabic." *Studies in the Renaissance* 2:96–117.

Davis, Natalie Z. 2006. *Trickster Travels: A Sixteenth-Century Muslim Between Worlds*. New York: Hill and Wang.

Erpenius, Thomas. 1621. *Orationes tres de linguarum Ebraeae atque Arabicae dignitate*. Leiden: Typographia Auctoris.

Fuchs, Leonhart. 1535. *Paradoxorum medicinae libri tres*. Basel: Bebel.

Fück, Johann. 1955. *Die arabischen Studien in Europa bis in den Anfang des 20. Jahrhunderts*. Leipzig: Harrassowitz.

Hamilton, Alastair. 1994. *Europe and the Arab World: Five Centuries of Books by European Scholars and Travellers from the Libraries of the Arcadian Group*. Dublin: Arcadian Group.

———. 2001. *Arab Culture and Ottoman Magnificence in Antwerp's Golden Age*. London: Arcadian Library.

———. 2008. *The Forbidden Fruit: The Koran in Early Modern Europe*. London: London Middle East Institute.

———. 2011. *The Arcadian Library: Western Appreciation of Arab and Islamic Civilization*. London: Arcadian Library.

Hasse, Dag N. 2001. "Die humanistische Polemik gegen arabische Autoritäten: Grundsätzliches zum Forschungsstand." *Neulateinisches Jahrbuch* 3:65–79.

———. 2004. "Aufstieg und Niedergang des Averroismus in der Renaissance: Niccolò Tignosi, Agostino Nifo, Francesco Vimercato." In *"Herbst des Mittelalters"? Fragen zur Bewertung des 14. und 15. Jahrhunderts*, edited by Jan A. Aertsen and Martin Pickavé, 447–73. Berlin: De Gruyter.

———. 2006. "The Social Conditions of the Arabic-(Hebrew-)Latin Translation Movements in Medieval Spain and in the Renaissance." In *Wissen über Grenzen: Arabisches Wissen und lateinisches Mittelalter*, edited by Andreas Speer and Lydia Wegener, 68–86 and 806. Berlin: De Gruyter.

——. 2007. "Arabic Philosophy and Averroism." In *Cambridge Companion to Renaissance Philosophy*, edited by James Hankins, 113–36. Cambridge: Cambridge University Press.

Jones, J. Robert. 1986. "Thomas Erpenius (1584–1624) on the Value of the Arabic Language, Translated from the Latin." *Manuscripts of the Middle East* 1:15–25.

Kaufmann, David. 1893. "Jacob Mantino: Une page de l'histoire de la Renaissance." *Revue des études juives* 26:30–60 and 207–29.

Krümmel, Achim. 1991. *Das* Supplementum Chronicarum *des Augustinermönches Jacobus Philippus Foresti von Bergamo: Eine der ältesten Bilderchroniken und ihre Wirkungsgeschichte.* Herzberg: Bautz.

Nabod, Valentin. 1560. *Enarratio elementorum astrologiae.* Cologne: Birckmann.

Nutton, Vivian. 1997. "The Rise of Medical Humanism: Ferrara, 1464–1555." *Renaissance Studies* 11:2–19.

MacLean, Gerald M. 2004. *The Rise of Oriental Travel: English Visitors to the Ottoman Empire, 1580–1720.* Basingstoke: Palgrave Macmillan.

Manardo, Giovanni. 1549. *In Ioannis Mesue Simplicia medicamenta.* Basel: Isengrin.

Meserve, Margaret. 2008. *Empires of Islam in Renaissance Historical Thought.* Cambridge: Harvard University Press.

Rauchenberger, Dietrich. 1999. *Johannes Leo der Afrikaner: Seine Beschreibung des Raumes zwischen Nil und Niger nach dem Urtext.* Wiesbaden: Harrassowitz.

Siraisi, Nancy G. 1987. *Avicenna in Renaissance Italy: The* Canon *and Medical Teaching in Italian Universities after 1500.* Princeton: Princeton University Press.

Stannard, Jerry. 1970. "Alpini, Prospero." In *Dictionary of Scientific Biography*, edited by Charles C. Gillespie, 1:124–25. New York: Charles Scribner's Sons.

Thorndike, Lynn. 1941. *A History of Magic and Experimental Science.* Vol. 6, *The Sixteenth Century.* New York: Columbia University Press.

Tamani, Giuliano. 1992. "Traduzioni ebraico-latine di opere filosofiche e scientifiche." In *L'Hébreu au temps de la Renaissance*, edited by Ilana Zinguer, 105–14. Leiden: Brill.

Vimercato, Francesco. 1574. *In tertium librum Aristotelis* De anima *Commentaria: Eiusdem de anima rationali peripatetica disceptatio.* Venice: Haeres Hieronymi Scoti.

CHAPTER 19

BIBLICAL HUMANISM

ANDREW TAYLOR

WITH the call *ad fontes*—"to the sources"—humanists pursued the values of ancient rhetoric and strove to rediscover and purify the texts of Greek and Roman antiquity. Before long, their growing philological and textual expertise began to be applied to biblical texts in their original languages. The Roman Catholic Church formally recognized the desirability of expertise in Hebrew, Syriac, Arabic, and Greek in the decree of the Council of Vienne (1311–1312), reissuing the recommendation at the Council of Basel in 1434. Biblical humanists found a model polyglot translator and exegete in Jerome (ca. 347–420; Rice 1985). Some humanists drew on local Jewish scholars to support their study of the Hebrew Bible and rabbinical commentaries, such as Rashi's (ca. 1100), which informed Nicholas of Lyra's extremely influential *Postilla litteralis super Bibliam* (*Literal Commentary on the Bible*, 1322–1331). Lack of formalized tuition in Greek made its acquisition more difficult in the West, especially north of the Alps, before the emergence of printed grammars and lexica from ca. 1500 (Botley 2010; Hankins 2003; Wilson 1992). In Italy, longstanding Greek communities, the rapprochement with the Eastern Orthodox Church attempted at the Council of Ferrara-Florence (1438–1445), and the learned refugees from fallen Constantinople (1453) all fostered Greek studies, and drew humanists to study there (Hankins 2003, 273–92). The medieval text of scripture in the Western Church was, however, the Latin Vulgate, which, although a translation (and the basis of all medieval translations of the Bible), was generally viewed by scholastic theologians as reliable, accurate, and immutable, despite the occasional issuing of corrections to counter corruptions; few considered revising the Vulgate in the thirteenth and fourteenth centuries.

Petrarch (1304–1374), who found the Vulgate's unclassical Latin unappealing, and, like Coluccio Salutati (1331–1406), lacked the biblical languages for philological study, returned to scripture through the Latin church fathers. He considered the younger, "Christian Cicero" Augustine (354–430 CE) of the *Confessions* and *The City of God* a model exegete, and in his *De sui ipsius et multorum aliorum ignorantia* (*On His Own Ignorance and That of Many Besides*, 1370) and elsewhere, Petrarch criticized the scholastic enterprise: it worshipped the pagan Aristotle; its dialectical method was opposed to the animation of a Christian *vita activa*; and its adversarial disputations were quibbling, contentious, and fundamentally un-Christian. As scholastic logic was relatively unestablished in Italy, humanism could, despite being no alternative philosophical system (Kristeller 1961), emerge there without confronting the powerful philosophical schools of Northern Europe, which would resist the application of humanistic textual and philological techniques to the Bible (Rummel 1995, 30–34).

Ambrogio Traversari led the reception of the Greek church fathers in Italy. Between 1415 and 1439, he translated works of Basil, Chrysostom, Athanasius, Gregory Nazianzen, and others (Stinger 1977; Stinger 1996, 486–87). Patristic commentary had previously been available mostly through such works as Thomas Aquinas's (1225–1274) continuous gloss on the four Gospels, *Catena Aurea* (Rex 2000, 57), a decontextualised "golden chain" of extracts from eighty authors (the Greeks often loosely translated), from which scholastics drew propositions to support lines of reasoning, rather than reading their fuller discourses in historical context. Likewise, Peter Lombard's (d. 1164) topical *Libri quatuor sententiarum* (*Four Books of Sentences*) offered biblical and patristic extracts for this dialectical meta-language of syllogism and inference based on late medieval logic. Paolo Cortese's (1465–1510) humanistic response, a brief commentary on Lombard, *Quatuor libri sententiarum* (1504), articulated patristic eloquence through presenting quotation in indirect speech (Moss 2003, 66, 72–73).

VALLA AND MANETTI

For the first master of classical usage, Lorenzo Valla (ca. 1407–1457), the Latin translation of the Greek New Testament required revision in order to be an authentic representation of the original text. He also underlined the corruption of the text and denied Jerome's authorship. Valla's philological expertise and acute critical spirit had led him to debunk the *Donation of Constantine* in 1439, Pseudo-Dionysius the Areopagite in 1457, and the spurious Seneca–St. Paul correspondence; he also exposed the Apostles' Creed as dating from the Councils of Nicaea (325 CE) and Constantinople (381 CE). In *De vero falsoque bono* (*On the True and False Good*, 1431), Valla stressed that God's word should appeal to the emotions and excite Christian virtue, and, like Petrarch, he saw the early church fathers as having kept theology uncontaminated by Aristotelian philosophy. He later attacked the ontological and logical categories of scholastic theology as opposed to the Christian teaching available in the text of scripture, in his *Repastinatio Dialectice et Philosophie* (*Replowing of Dialectic and Philosophy*) seeking to transform the formal study of logic into a rhetorical-grammatical dialectic (Nauta 2009, 1).

Valla's *Collatio Novi Testamenti* (*Collation of the New Testament*), a comparison of the Greek New Testament with the Vulgate, was begun in Naples between 1435 and 1448 (Valla 1970, xlvii), and redacted in Rome, probably sometime between 1453 and 1457, but possibly started as early as 1447, when his patron Nicholas V became pope (Wilson 1992; Trinkaus 1970, 2:571–78). Erasmus's discovery, editing, and publishing of the redacted version (known as the *Adnotationes in Novum Testamentum* [*Notes on the New Testament*]) in a manuscript copy he found near Leuven later brought the work to a far wider audience. Valla employed at least seven Greek and four Latin manuscripts (Celenza 1994), yet despite inaugurating the philological approach, he tended to neglect the possible effects of transmission on the Greek text, and so, like Giannozzo Manetti (1396–1459), Valla repeatedly conflated the Greek text from several manuscripts at the expense of the Latin tradition (Botley 2004, 95). One result of such *a priori* privileging of the Greek text over the Vulgate is shown by Valla's treatment of Matthew 6.13, "For thine is the kingdom and the power and the glory forever. Amen" (King James Version). Valla considered the Vulgate corrupted because it lacked this clause, whereas, as Erasmus (1466–1536) discussed in his own *Annotationes*, it was a later addition to the Greek New Testament drawn from liturgy, and was thus not found in any ancient Latin manuscripts or Fathers, except Chrysostom and Theophylactus (Bentley 1983, 151; Metzger 1975, 13–14). Valla was relatively restrained in his conjectural emendations to scripture, and only rarely sought variant readings in patristic commentaries, sources deeply mined by Erasmus. Groundbreaking, however, was Valla's grasp of the textual corruptions aris-ing from the laziness, ignorance, or incompetence of scribes, who, when faced with ambiguity or uncertainty, wrote out what they assumed should be there, or, during dictation, recorded words misheard, or misinterpreted homonyms. Scribes could also "improve" the text, or assimilate words or phrases from a similar verse nearby (on Luke 6.26 and Luke 6.22–23, see Bentley 1983, 42). In addition to purging medieval usages, Valla equated the Vulgate's rhetorical variety with potential loss of semantic clarity: for example, the Vulgate uses both *senior* and *presbyter* for the Greek *presbuteros* ("elder, priest"), and at Romans 4.3–8 offers *reputare*, *imputare*, and *accepto ferre* in its rendering of *logizomai* ("calculate, reckon, consider"; Bentley 1983, 52–53). In contrast, Manetti, although probably influenced by Valla in Rome (Botley 2004, 94–95), retained in his biblical translations some non-classical diction, and allowed context to determine usage (De Petris 1975, 15–32).

The pressure of theological orthodoxy may have governed both Valla's and Manetti's treatment of the *Comma Johanneum*, the passage (or Greek *komma*) at 1 John 5.7 con-taining the three heavenly witnesses—Father, Word (Son), and Holy Spirit—a proof-text for the Trinity. Present in most Vulgate manuscripts, it is now known to exist in only two Greek manuscripts copied in the Middle Ages, and in two others as the marginal additions of later scribes (Metzger 1975, 716–18). But Valla, who knew none of these four Greek manuscripts, nevertheless passed over the discrepancy between his Greek sources and the Vulgate in silence and retained the *Comma*. As Manetti also chose to include the *Comma* in his Latin translation of the Greek New Testament (the first since Jerome's), it was left to Erasmus, finding little authority in ancient Latin manuscripts, and none in the Greek, to act on the lack of a Greek witness and omit it from the Greek and Latin in his own edition of the New Testament, first entitled *Novum Instrumentum* (*New Instrument*, 1516).

Valla's emendation went beyond correcting corruptions and failed to respect the sen-tences on which doctrinal orthodoxy depended. When, in a series of four *Orationes in*

Laurentium Vallam (*Speeches against Lorenzo Valla*, 1452), the elderly and still querulous Poggio Bracciolini (1380–1459) attacked the unpublished *Collatio* as a threat to doctrine, Valla retorted that "if I emend anything, I do not emend Holy Writ, but the translations . . . strictly speaking, only what the saints themselves wrote in Hebrew and Greek is Holy Writ; for there is nothing in Latin" (Rummel 1995, 103). Although Valla's annotations are mostly restricted to grammatical points lacking in theological implication (Monfasani 2008, 24), the tripartite sacrament of penance (contrition, confession, satisfaction) was arguably at stake in the translation of *metanoia* ("repentance") at 2 Corinthians 7.10. Here Valla offered *mentis emendatio* ("amendment of mind") as its Latin equivalent, and distinguished it from *metamelomai* ("to feel regret") and that word's relationship to *poenitentia* ("moral grief"), *tristitia* ("sadness"), and a connection to the medieval doctrine (Valla 1505, XXXIIIIv). Equally, Valla found no justification for divine predestination, or its distinction from foreknowledge, in the Greek of 2 Corinthians 9.7, 8.19, and Philippians 3.14. Moreover, at 1 Corinthians 15.10, where St. Paul attributes his success to "the grace of God that is with me" (*hē charis tou theou hē sun emoi*), the Vulgate reads *gratia Dei mecum* ("the grace of God along with me"), which scholastic theologians understood as supporting *gratia cooperans* ("cooperating grace"); Valla stressed that all of Paul's success was owing to God's grace, and thus eroded the sense of a human contribution to achievements truly pleasing to God. Overall, the penetrating philological (rhetorical, linguistic, and historical) criticism of Valla's *Collatio* exposed sundry inadequacies of the Latin Vulgate as a translation of the Greek New Testament, and laid the foundations for both further textual and philological scholarship and a "rhetorical theology."

Giannozzo Manetti's expertise in Hebrew as well as Greek allowed him to defend the Christian understanding of scripture against Jewish criticism of the Greek Septuagint version of the Old Testament—the Septuagint was considered dependent upon, when not debased from, the integrity of the Hebrew manuscripts (Monfasani 2008, 19–20). He also understood the Septuagint translation in relation to its historical audience, an argument echoed by Erasmus, while his criticism of Jews constrained by a monoglot culture resonated with the humanistic commitment to an increasingly rich comparative setting of textual, philological, and then historical criticism.

Manetti's New Testament and polyglot Psalter were completed between 1455 and 1458. The influence of Leonardo Bruni's *De interpretatione recta* (*On Correct Translation*, ca. 1420) is evident in his *Apologeticus* (*Apology*, 1455–1456) appended to the Psalter: translation of philosophical and theological works should be neither too rigid (*ad verbum*) nor too free (*ad sensum*), and the text augmented or altered only where a want of clarity or the idiom required (Manetti 1981, 121, 128; Botley 2004, 80–82). Unlike humanists such as Brandolini and Barbaro who favored a rhetorically splendid translation fit for the church's grandeur, Manetti sought to translate the purer, humbler habit of the primitive origins of scripture by avoiding both the Vulgate's solecisms and the imposition of Valla's strict classicism. His more cautious approach anticipated the Complutensian Polyglot Bible (1514–1517; on which, see further below) and Sanctes Pagninus's *Veteris et Novi Testamenti nova translatio* (*New Translation of the*

Old and New Testament, 1528), the first complete Latin translation from the Hebrew and Greek; its literalness proved influential.

THE HEBREW OLD TESTAMENT

Following the piecemeal publication of the Old Testament (sometimes with rabbinical commentary), Joshua Solomon Soncino's *editio princeps* of the whole, vocalized, and accented Hebrew Bible appeared in 1488. The Hebrew Old Testament published in the Complutensian Polyglot (1520) was edited by Jewish converts working from ancient manuscripts and from finely printed biblical texts in both Hebrew and Aramaic available in Portugal, Spain, and Italy. Sebastian Münster's Hebrew-Latin Bible (1534–1535), the first edition of the *Biblia Rabbinica Bombergiana* (*Bomberg's Rabbinic Bible*, 1517; named after its printer, Daniel Bomberg), and Robert Estienne's editions (1539–1546) all depended on these early printed works. The *Biblia Rabbinica Bombergiana*, edited by Felice da Prato (d. 1539), broke new ground in 1516–1517 by including the Aramaic translations (*Targums*, or paraphrastic "interpretations," known as "Onkelos" and "Pseudo-Jonathan" for the Torah or Pentateuch), and several rabbinical commentaries. It was followed by the authoritative second edition in 1524–1525, edited by Jacob ben Hayyim and including his work on the Masorah (i.e., the history of textual transmission of the Hebrew Bible). The Hebrew grammars of Conrad Pellicanus (1478–1556) and Johannes Reuchlin (1455–1522) led to the more advanced treatises of the Jewish grammarian and lexicographer Elias Levita (1469–1549), whose works were made available in Latin translations by Münster and Paul Fagius (Kessler-Mesguich 2008). In 1538, Levita importantly argued that the vowel points of the Masoretic text were a seventh/eighth-century addition, an insight Catholics would use to defend the Septuagint (second century BCE) as witness to the original consonantal Hebrew text (Burnett 1996, 205–9).

The humanists' attitude to the Old Testament varied. Reuchlin's conviction in *De rudimentis Hebraicis* (*On the Rudiments of Hebrew*, 1506) that hearing the original words of God was theologically important, acquired a keener edge in the Swiss reformer Johannes Oecolampadius's confession in *In Iesaiam prophetam hypomnemata* (*Commentaries on the Prophet Isaiah*, 1525, α3v) that his understanding of the prophet depended on Hebrew commentaries. Earlier, Giovanni Pico della Mirandola's (1463–1494) sacred philology incorporated syncretic interests and the Jewish mysticism of the Kabbalah, influences developed by Reuchlin in his *De verbo mirifico* (*On the Miracle-Working Word*, 1494) and *De arte cabbalistica* (*On the Kabbalistic Art*, 1517). For Andreas Masius (1514–1573), reviser of the orientalist Johann Albrecht Widmanstetter's Syriac New Testament (1555) for the Antwerp Polyglot (1569–1572), the Kabbalah was but one part of a profound encounter with post-Christian Jewish learning (Dunkelgrun 2012, 364–81). Use of Jewish scholarship was met with charges of "Judaizing"—the *cause célèbre* of the "Reuchlin Affair" (1509 onwards; Price 2011), for instance—as rabbinical sources could supply both lexicographical information and an interpretive framework; in 1553, bonfires of Hebrew books blazed across Italy. Yet if Reuchlin, like Erasmus, was denounced as a forerunner of Martin Luther, Luther would later complain about Pagninus's and Münster's reliance on rabbinical learning. Agostino Steuco's apologetic, *Recognitio Veteris Testamenti ad veritatem Hebraicam* (*Examination of the Old Testament According to the Hebrew Truth*, 1529), expresses the fractured and contested field of such scholarship in precariously asserting the superiority of the Vulgate Old Testament over the Septuagint while also—as Erasmus wryly noted—making sundry emendations to it using Hebrew manuscripts and the *Biblia Rabbinica* (Delph 2008).

THE COMPLUTENSIAN POLYGLOT

The Complutensian's prime mover, Cardinal Francisco Ximénez de Cisneros (1436–1517), archbishop of Toledo from 1495, chancellor of the Kingdom of Castile, and primate of Spain, sought to reanimate faith, particularly in Iberia, by vigorously promoting biblical and patristic studies along text-critical and philological lines. The University of Alcalá de Henares (*Complutum* in Latin) was founded in 1498, and Cisneros attracted Greek and Hebrew scholars there to establish the Collegium Trilingue ("trilingual college") in 1508, ahead of the Collegium Trilingue at Leuven (1518), and François I's Collège Royal in Paris (1530). The Complutensian Bible edition consisted of six folios: the New Testament volume (fifth of the six folios) was completed in 1514, with the four-volume Hebrew Old Testament edition, including Aramaic, Greek, and Latin translations, undertaken between 1514 and 1517; the sixth volume contained materials for the study of the Hebrew Old Testament. The Complutensian was not officially published until 1520, when the license for 600 copies was approved. More is known about the scholars involved than about the manuscripts, some of which were lent by the Apostolic Library in Rome (Schenker 2008, 288; on the manuscript sources, see Welte 1999). For the New Testament, the most significant contributors were Antonio de Nebrija (1441–1522), Diego López de Zúñiga (Jacobus Stunica, d. 1531), and the Cretan Demetrius Ducas (ca. 1480–ca. 1527), inaugural professor in Greek at Alcalá (1508) following his work with Aldo Manuzio in Venice. Zúñiga probably led the editing of the Vulgate version, and would become its vociferous defender and a tenacious opponent of Erasmus. The Old Testament was handled by three *conversos* (converts to Catholicism from Judaism or Islam): Pablo Colonel, Alfonso the physician, and Alfonso de Zamora. Ducas and Hernán Núñez most probably edited the Greek Septuagint, and oversaw its Latin translation by Juan de Vergara and others (O'Connell 2006).

The printer Arnao Guillén de Brocar's *mise-en-page* (page layout) and typography are rightly celebrated. The lack of breathings and almost all accents in the Greek New Testament is defended in the Greek preface (probably Ducas's) as preserving the archaic majesty of the Greek originally used, an argument drawn from Poliziano's defense of the like printing of Callimachus's verses and the Sibylline Oracles; the Septuagint, being a translation, could, it was argued, be printed in the common manner (Lee 2005, 257 and 263). The edition of the Vulgate New Testament in the parallel column is similarly conservative, with the Vulgate's centrality in the Old Testament volumes conveyed by the flanking Masoretic Hebrew and the Greek Septuagint (with interlinear Latin). The Pentateuch's Aramaic paraphrase, with Latin translation, runs along the foot of the page.

The Complutensian editors engaged with the transmission of the Greek New Testament far more than Valla had done. Nebrija, however, sought more radical criticism of the Vulgate New Testament, and had earlier produced philological and textual notes, which had been confiscated by the Inquisitor General of Spain, Diego de Deza. When Cisneros succeeded Deza in 1507 and became cardinal, Nebrija was given freer rein, and dedicated to Cisneros his *Apologia* (*Apology*, 1516) in which he defended recourse to the Greek text of the New Testament, and the Hebrew of the Old Testament, to solve problems arising from discrepancies between manuscripts of the Latin Vulgate. In contrast, Zúñiga would later assert in his *Annotationes contra Erasmum Roterodamum* (*Notes Against Erasmus of Rotterdam*, 1520) that the Latin manuscripts were less corrupted than the Greek ones. Nebrija's collected notes (*Tertia quinquagena, The Third Fifty,* being the third redaction of fifty annotations on the text of the Old and New Testaments), which accompany the *Apologia*, display a critical expertise that rivals Valla's. However, his quitting of the project around the turn of 1514–1515, having arrived from his chair in grammar at Salamanca in 1513, limited his impact on the Complutensian. Moreover, it was Cisneros who insisted that emendation be justified by an early Latin witness and had prioritized the "optimizing" of the Vulgate's text on the basis of the Latin manuscript tradition.

Bending to preserve the Vulgate's authority and support Roman Catholic tradition, the Complutensian scholars seemingly failed to establish firm editorial principles. The *Comma Johanneum*, handled according to Aquinas's view that it had been suppressed by anti-Trinitarian heretics, was thus added to the Greek (the editors would not have seen any of the four Greek manuscripts possessing that passage; Bentley 1983, 95–97); yet the Lord's Prayer (Matthew 6.13) was approached more independently. The editors understood both the influence of Greek liturgy on the transmission of the Greek New Testament, and that the Greek scribes' familiarity with the liturgy, which led them unintentionally to distort the scriptural text towards it, had not had an impact on some Latin Vulgate manuscripts, which therefore preserved more faithfully the original, pre-augmented Greek (Metzger 1968). Although they appreciated how scribal errors had been introduced into the Latin manuscripts through, for example, the harmonizing of similar phrases and sentences, where New Testament Greek and early Vulgate manuscripts agreed and could have justified revision of the then-standard Vulgate reading, the Latin was sometimes left unaltered, while elsewhere emended on the authority of the Greek alone, with no warrant from the Latin tradition. Although inconsistency similarly marred the edition of the Septuagint, the quality of the manuscripts employed and the competence of individual editors offset the lack of editorial regulation.

ERASMUS

As Erasmus stated in his edition of Valla's *Adnotationes* (1505), "Queen Theology" should not begrudge the indispensable claims of her "humble attendant, Grammar," who perhaps "discusses trivial questions, but these have important corollaries," just as biblical translation was "clearly the task for the grammarian" (*CWE* 2:94). His *Novum Instrumentum* appeared in five editions between 1516 and 1535 as he refined and reinforced to differing degrees the work's three parts: the *editio princeps* of the Greek New Testament; his Latin translation (little reworked after mostly typographical correction for the retitled second edition, *Novum Testamentum* [*New Testament*], 1519); and his *Annotationes* commenting on and justifying his emendation of the Greek and his Latin translation. The *Annotationes*, which were as central as the *Paraphrases of the New Testament* (1517–1524) in the expression of Erasmus's exegetical commitments, grew as his scholarly labors continued and his opponents' objections mounted (Rummel 1986; Erasmus 1986 and 1990; Pabel and Vessey 2002). Unlike the *Paraphrases*, in which Erasmus recast the New Testament books in more classicized Latin to enhance their persuasiveness, he wrote the *Annotationes* in a far more accommodating, but also apologetic, form, which allowed him to respond to challenges to his interpretation of the Greek, and to win assent through his textual, philological, and rhetorical analysis.

Erasmus shared Valla's disdain for scribes' errors and his genius for correcting them, but went far further in amassing variant readings, which informed his understanding of how corruptions arose from homonyms, assimilation, negligence, or theological anxiety. His famous principle of the harder reading (*difficilior lectio potior*) resulted: "Whenever the ancients report variant readings, that one always seems to me more esteemed which at first glance seems more absurd, for it is likely that a reader who is either not very learned or not very attentive was offended by the spectre of absurdity and altered the text" (Rummel 1986, 117; Bentley 1978, 318–20). His keener understanding of the relative value of the manuscripts allowed his work on the Greek text to surpass that of Valla and the Complutensian editors (the Complutensian nevertheless helped improve Erasmus's fourth edition of 1527; Metzger 1968, 102). Erasmus also importantly related the corruptions in the Greek tradition to those in the Latin one, arguing that correction of each text could be informed by the other and not, therefore, privileging the Greek over the Latin, or *vice versa*. For example, where Valla, at 2 Peter 2.18, considered the Latin adverb *paululum* ("a little") in the Vulgate to be a corruption of *plane* ("clearly") approximating acceptably to the Greek *ontōs* ("actually"), Erasmus saw that *paululum* could instead correct the corrupted Greek to *oligōs* ("a little"; Bentley 1983, 149). The immense value of Erasmus's *Annotationes* lay in the clarity with which evidence in support of an emendation was discussed. Yet, despite professing merely to "correct what is corrupt" and "explain what is obscure," Erasmus blurred the distinction between grammarian and theologian, especially as he embraced issues of composition, authorship, and authenticity. Moreover, Erasmus's treatment of Revelation was less than rigorous: where Reuchlin's single Greek manuscript from which Erasmus worked lacked its final page, Erasmus simply translated the five missing lines into Greek from the Vulgate and added them to his *editio princeps*. When Erasmus came to address Revelation more carefully, he ended up making ninety revisions to the Greek text for the fourth edition.

Erasmus's Latin translation proved extremely controversial, despite his insistence that it was as provisional as any translation and was offered to support interpretation of the Vulgate. Nevertheless, his *Annotationes* worked to reduce the Vulgate from (in conservative eyes) an inerrant textual foundation of doctrine, to a representation of the Greek New Testament unflatteringly comparable to his own. Erasmus characterized the Vulgate's language as the common speech of late antiquity to argue that a translation should now conform more to the classicized Latin of its intended "common" readership. He aimed not for Ciceronian eloquence, unlike the "literary" version of Sebastian Castellio (1551), but achieved a lucid, literal translation of the *koiné* ("common") Greek that captured its colloquial idiom and rhetoric; this, according to Erasmus, minimized the need for the allegorical exegesis he criticized in some Fathers. Such literalness, however, acknowledged the need for a given Greek word to be translated by different Latin terms, depending on context, and this variation of scriptural vocabulary contributed to the destabilizing of a theology based on the repeated use of particular words.

The *Annotationes*, which included moral teaching and political comment, expanded into a full-scale commentary in response to critical pressures, continued collation, and the garnering, for the third edition onwards, of variant patristic readings; Erasmus, first to appreciate their value, edited Cyprian, Jerome, Lactantius, Ambrose, Athanasius, Chrysostom, Irenaeus, Augustine, and Origen. Thus Erasmus could use Cyprian's quotation of 1 Corinthians 13.7 as *omnia diligit* ("esteems all") to emend correctly the Greek *panta stegei* ("endures all") to *panta stergei* ("esteems all"; Bentley 1983, 144–45). Although the beleaguered Erasmus later retreated from some bolder interpretations and conjectural emendations, including those based on the sacred authors' "human error" (omitted from the 1527 and 1535 editions), he used the *Annotationes* to underline the lack of evidence for whatever he felt politically needed to be included. This was the case with the *Comma Johanneum*, which he included under some duress in the last three editions (De Jonge 1980).

To some, especially in Italy, Erasmus's rhetorical approach to the interpretation of scripture, together with his broader appeals to the laity and criticism of the church, had helped initiate the Lutheran revolt (Seidel Menchi 1987, 41–67). Erasmus's unsettling of time-honored texts made him seem to some a hydra of Arian, Pelagian, and Apollinarian heresies. His plight only worsened when evangelicals exploited his work to denounce the Roman Church, attack the Vulgate's authority, or endorse vernacular Bible translations. The collision between the scholastics' ontological preoccupation with the word and the humanists' rhetorical emphasis on discourse is captured in Erasmus's daring rendering of John 1.1 ("In the beginning was the Word") as *In principio erat sermo: sermo* for the Greek *logos* ("speech, account") pointed to a dialogue or conversation rather than a simple utterance; Jarrott 1964; Drysdall 2012). He was later accused of attacking the sacrament of marriage—Luther rejected it as unbiblical—because he was critical of the Vulgate's use of *sacramentum* to translate *mustērion* at Ephesians 5.31–32. *Gratia* also became a highly charged word, so when Erasmus chose to rewrite Gabriel's famous greeting of Mary in the Annunciation (Luke 1.28), the Vulgate's *Ave gratia plena* ("Greetings, one full of grace") to *Ave Gratiosa* ("Greetings, beloved one"), there was more than salutatory manners at stake. In rendering *kecharitōmenē* as "beloved one" or "one highly favored" (*gratiosa*) Mary is no longer necessarily the sinless repository of grace, but rather, as Erasmus remarks from Origen's *Homily on Luke*, a woman greeted in unfamiliar terms (Erasmus 1986, 154–55). The understanding of original sin—concupiscence inherited from Adam, whose state was transformed by the Fall—was likewise disturbed by Erasmus's rendering of Romans 5.12: the *Annotationes* states, "I consider this [propensity] arises more from example than from nature" (*CWE* 56:140), and the second book of *Hyperaspistes* (*Protector*, 1527) against Luther, "death . . . as referring to the sin by which we imitate Adam" (*CWE* 77:704). This implication that imitating Adam's fallen state seems willed rather than ineluctably destined, unsurprisingly prompted charges of Pelagianism from the conservatives Edward Lee and Franz Tittelmans (Bentley 1983, 210). Erasmus's interpretation of *metanoia* ("repentance") and its lack of support for the sacrament of penance, including confession to a priest and the penitential works of satisfaction, was seized upon by evangelicals: where the Vulgate has *Poenitentiam agite* ("do penance") at Matthew 4.17, Erasmus first suggested *poeniteat vos* ("repent") in 1516, and then, in 1519, *respiscite* ("change your mind, return to your senses"), further suggesting the non-sacramental interior act of the individual.

Zúñiga, who attacked the *Pauli epistolae* (*Epistles of Paul*, 1512) of the French humanist Jacques Lefèvre d'Etaples (ca. 1455–1536) in *Annotationes contra Jacobum Fabrum Stapulensem* (*Notes Against Jacques Lefèvre d'Etaples*, 1519), and denounced him as a Lutheran even before d'Etaples had commenced his vernacular Bible translation (1523–1530), unleashed six polemics against Erasmus between 1520 and 1524, branding him "the standard-bearer and Prince of the Lutherans" in *Erasmi Roterodami blasphemiae et impietates* (*Blasphemies and Impieties of Erasmus of Rotterdam*, 1522, Aiir-v); "either Erasmus Lutherizes or Luther Erasmusizes," cried Zúñiga in *Libellus trium illorum voluminum praecursor* (*A Little Book as Precursor of Those Three Volumes*, 1522, fols. Givv-Gvv; the title refers to three earlier attacks on Erasmus); and he tarred Reuchlin and Lefèvre with the same brush. He defended the Vulgate on philological grounds in the *Assertio ecclesiasticae translationis Novi Testamenti* (*Assertion of the Ecclesiastical Translation of the New Testament*, 1524), for example: scribes, not the translator, had introduced solecisms; philology and theology were to be kept separate; usage was fittingly literal or appropriately expressed Hebrew idioms of the *koiné* (Tittelmans and others advocated faithful preservation of any opacity in the original). Noël Béda (ca. 1470–1537), the conservative Paris theologian, in 1526 similarly associated Lefèvre's *Pauli epistolae* and Erasmus's *Paraphrases of the New Testament* with the Lutheran challenge, condemning "these theologizing humanists" for attempting to explain all sacred matters through profane learning and languages (Rummel 2002; Crane 2010). In his *Annotationes* (1526) against d'Etaples and Erasmus, Béda set the scholastic authority of

Peter Lombard, William of Auxerre, Alexander of Hales, Albertus Magnus, Aquinas, Bonaventure, Richard of Middleton, Ockham, and Peter Paludanus, many of whom had written commentaries on Lombard's *Sentences*, against that of the humanists' Greek and Latin Fathers, the "poets" Origen, Tertullian, Basil, Hilary, Chrysostom, Ambrose, Jerome, and their like (Aa1v); Erasmus termed them "grammarians" (*CWE* 4:49). Béda's colleague Pierre Cousturier (Petrus Sutor), in his *De tralatione bibliae* (*On the Translation of the Bible*, 1525), rejected wholesale any tampering with the faultless Vulgate as blasphemous, perverted heresy, the product of madness or stupidity, conceited self-interest, shocking audacity, and so on, as he emptied his polemical scattergun. For him, if not for Béda, Jerome's version was divinely inspired, just as the Septuagint had been, with Jerome's distinction between prophet and translator, commonly restated in the apologies (*apologiae*) of humanists' biblical works, betokening only the church father's modesty.

What was to be considered old or new was violently contested: for conservatives, scholastic tradition and the Vulgate had superseded "the sources"; for others, a return to classical Latin would redeem true discourse, as opposed to the barbarous innovations of scholastic terminology and the peculiar form of language through which philosophy and theology were pursued. In his *Ratio seu methodus compendio perveniendi veram theologiam* (*Plan or Method for a Compendious Arrival at True Theology*, 1518), Erasmus stressed that scripture was not intelligible without the original biblical languages. Scholastics, who possessed the higher university degrees and training authorizing theological inquiry, condemned the humanists as unqualified for the determination of Christian doctrine, and attacked the Hebrew and Greek scriptures as unreliable in comparison with Jerome's translation, whether inspired or not. The Greeks were considered notoriously heterodox, while inveterate anti-Semitism overshadowed the handling of the "Hebrew truth": at best, philology could only be applied to the Latin tradition. Although divisions between the humanist and scholastic camps were far from neat, the Reformation inevitably intensified the climate of intolerance, rendering dialogue less audible amid noisy controversy, with print efficiently amplifying the polemical cacophony.

Early sixteenth-century humanists also demanded curricular reform. Petrus Mosellanus's *Oratio de variarum linguarum cognitione paranda* (*Oration on Obtaining Knowledge of the Various Languages*, 1518) was countered (together with swipes at Erasmus's *Annotationes*) by Jacques Masson (Jacobus Latomus, ca. 1475–1544), in the second book of his *De trium linguarum et studii theologici ratione dialogus* (*Dialogue Concerning the Three Languages and the Plan of Theological Study*, 1519). For Masson, Augustine's support for the learning of languages, when "the endless diversity of the Latin translators throw [the scriptures] into doubt" (*On Christian Doctrine* 2.11), was no longer pertinent, as the Vulgate, proved by tradition, was sufficient for exegesis, with scholastic commentary, rather than the philology of the humanists or the eloquence of the Fathers, ensuring that scriptural interpretation conformed to tradition and doctrinal orthodoxy (Rummel 1989, 1:79–87; François 2005). While some humanistically trained scholastic theologians like Maarten van Dorp (ca. 1485–1525) at Leuven publically migrated into the Erasmian fold, others, like Girolamo Aleandro (1480–1542), considered the textual, rhetorical, and historical practices of "the captious tribe of grammatists and poetasters" perverted displays of learning. The widely trained Alberto Pio (1475–1531), also alarmed by the appealing populism of Erasmus's "rhetorical theology," finally condemned Erasmus as having aided Luther, and in Book 10 of *Tres et viginti libri in locos lucubrationum variarum* (*Twenty-Three Books on the Topics of Various Studies*, 1531) defended scholastic method as divinely invented for handling scriptural obscurity, lauded Aristotle as a miracle of nature, and attacked Erasmus's anti-scholastic rhetoric (Minnich 2008). For Pio, the Vulgate's language was *minus Latina sed nota verba* ("less proper Latin, but familiar")—better for the grammar to be unorthodox than the thought (Pio 1529, 29r). He also countered the equation of wisdom with eloquence by asserting that language (*verba*) does not determine reality (*res*), but reality creates words: rational study of nature (philosophy) should inform revelation (theology). Likewise, Masson saw theology as conceptual, governing the interpretation of scripture rather than arising from it, a truth delivered in "words of no language" (Masson 1519, D1r).

Biblical Humanism and the Reformation

Luther's new understanding of the Pauline doctrine of salvation was not based on any textual correction made by the humanists. Nevertheless, his and Melanchthon's attacks on the scholastic understanding of justification would readily be associated with the humanists' criticism of theological authority, just as some humanists at first welcomed Luther's anti-scholastic stance. Overall, biblical humanists seem to have been no more disposed to convert to Protestantism than to remain Catholic, however much the humanistic emphasis on the purified text of scripture—from the Hebrew and Greek originals to faithful translations—mutated into the reformers' attack on unwritten verities and their demands for untrammeled access to the Word of God. Humanistic influence on Protestant exegesis and theology varied: Bucer's (Strasbourg) and Zwingli's (Switzerland) emphasis on the ethical (tropological) sense of scripture shows greater Erasmian influence than is evident in Luther's primary concern with the nature of Christ's sacrifice and what is imputed to believers through faith (McGrath 2012, 106). Zwingli's humanistic training informed his analysis of rhetorical figures of speech, especially *alloiosis* ("alteration"), *synecdoche*, and, as in the following example, *catachresis*, a figure of abuse. At Matthew 26.26, as Aramaic lacks the copulative verb ("to be"), Zwingli could renegotiate the relationship between "This" and "my body" as "signifies" rather than "is"—equivalence rather than identity—to argue for the commemoration of the historical event of Christ's sacrifice in the sacrament and thus against transubstantiation (Rex 2000, 63; McGrath 2012, 181–82).

For religious reformers, philology served theological needs, and the Fathers were judged according to their conformity to evangelical doctrine. Melanchthon's application of rhetorical analysis to biblical texts, although originating in humanistic training, sought to define "the principal topics of Christian teaching" chiefly from scripture to displace the scholastics' "theological hallucinations." Erasmus had developed the idea of commonplacing the key phrases and sentences from scripture under a set of headings (*loci theologici*), little nests for the fruits of reading, as he termed them. Melanchthon radically transformed Erasmus's idea of "theological topics" in his lecturing on Romans in 1519 and 1521, which resulted in the first evangelical systematic theology, *Loci communes theologici* (*Theological Commonplaces*, 1521). Rather than dispersing biblical texts under topical headings, Melanchthon interpreted Romans as Paul's writing in a new literary form, which Melanchthon dubbed the *genus didacticum* ("didactic genre"). This radically reorientated how the work should be read: for Melanchthon, Paul's *scopus* ("goal") of justification without merit or works determines the book's structure and language for the persuasive teaching of this doctrine. Melanchthon therefore extolled Paul's letter, essentially on theological grounds, as rhetorically and dialectically excellent, whereas Erasmus preferred to paraphrase Paul's off-putting style to make it more attractive and accessible to "pure Romans and adult Christians" (*CWE* 4:195–99). The Reformation thus confessionalized the energies and talents previously expended in humanist-scholastic skirmishes, drawing them into the imperatives of Catholic and Protestant doctrine and church discipline. Melchor Cano's highly influential *De locis theologicis* (*On Theological Topics*, 1563) in turn defended Catholic scholasticism and eschewed eloquence (Rummel 1995, 82), but also required engagement with the original biblical texts in order to counter the textual and philological arguments of opponents on their own terms (Book 2, chapters 12–15).

The affordability of Erasmus's Greek New Testament extended its influence, and it informed, defects and all, the Greek editions by Robert Estienne (1546, 1549, 1550, and 1551), who also drew on the superior (and costly) Complutensian text, and those of Théodore de Bèze (1565, 1582, 1588–1589, and 1598), who built on Estienne's editions using the so-called Codex Bezae and Codex Claromontanus. Enshrined by some as the *textus receptus* (the universally agreed version of the text), de Bèze's editions were defended with as much passion and unreasonable commitment as the Latin Vulgate continued to be in Catholic quarters (Metzger 1968, 106). Nor was the text of the Vulgate neglected. In 1528, Robert Estienne published the first of his much-improved critical editions; his 1540 edition was further collated with some thirty manuscripts for the *Biblia Latina ad vetustissima exemplaria castigata* (*Latin Bible, Corrected According to the Most Ancient Copies*, 1547), edited by Jean Henten (ca. 1500–1566) and reprinted several times by Plantin from 1559. A later Estienne edition provided the basis of the short-lived *Vulgata Sixtina* (1590, prepared under Pope Sixtus V) and the enduring revised edition, the *Vulgata Clementina* (1592, prepared under Pope Clement VIII; Hall 1963, 64–68).

Fundamental to the biblical scholarship of the Counter-Reformation was the Tridentine Decree (1546) underlining the authenticity of *haec ipsa vetus et vulgata editio* ("this ancient and vulgate edition"; Tanner 1990, 2:664–65); the focus was on improving the editions of the Vulgate and Greek Septuagint. Cano (2.13) repeated the charge that use of the Hebrew text rendered Christian exegesis dependent on Jewish learning. The Sixtine *Vetus Testamentum iuxta Septuaginta* (*Old Testament according to the Septuagint*, 1587), based on the manuscript Vaticanus Graecus 1209 discovered by Cardinal Antonio Carafa, became the *textus receptus*, and was reprinted in the London Polyglot (1657; Hall 1963, 58). Yet it was for later scholars to explore how the Septuagint could be used to criticize the Protestants' "inspired" *Hebraica veritas* ("Hebraic truth"), once the complex history of the Masoretic apparatus—including vowel points, pronunciation marks, and accents—which protected the text against corruption, was better understood. Christian Hebraism developed more vigorously in Protestant centers, especially after the 1559 (Roman) and 1564 (Tridentine) Indices of Prohibited Books outlawed the scholarship of Protestant Hebraists, although lectureships were established at Catholic and Protestant universities, which fostered a Christian scholarly culture independent of Jews and Judaism (Burnett 2012, 7–9). The turn by Christian Hebraists to the ancient authorities of Josephus and Philo, as well as to the Jewish religious texts, had signaled the departure from patristic authority. The deepening interest in the Old Testament drew scholars to the problems of sacred history and its relationship to ancient chronology. Joseph Justus Scaliger (1540–1609) and Isaac Casaubon (1559–1614) interpreted the Hebrew Bible and *Targumim* in light of the Mishnah and Talmud, commentaries on Jewish laws and customs, as philology began to give place to the investigation of routine cultural and social praxis (Shuger 1994, 31–32; Grafton and Weinberg 2011). The extended apparatus of the eight-volume Antwerp Polyglot (1569–1572), edited under Benito Arias Montano, similarly included treatments of ancient measures, coinage, architecture, clothing, as well as political geography and further fruits of the emerging oriental studies. The printing of the Gospels in Arabic (1591) added to the ever-richer comparative philology and reception history.

If the close of the sixteenth century saw no end to the religious controversy that stimulated and shaped biblical scholarship, the immense, nine-folio *Critici Sacri* (*Sacred Critics*, 1660), edited by John Pearson and others, sought common ground in both blending the key Latin works of humanists into rich commentaries and reissuing their treatises, so that works of Valla, Erasmus, Nebrija, Zúñiga, François Vatable, Münster, Fagius, Angelo Canini, Castellio, Johannes Drusius, Masius, Montano, Scaliger, Casaubon, Petrus Cunaeus, Kaspar Waser, Grotius, and many more, complemented Brian Walton's *Biblia Polyglotta*, the so-called London Polyglot (1653–1657). The London Polyglot and *Critici Sacri* arguably represent the final, monumental gathering together of the scholarship devoted to the literal and grammatical sense of the scriptures, offering, in the tradition of the polyglots of Alcalá, Antwerp, and Paris (the Paris Polyglot, edited by Guy Michel Lejay, was published in 1645), yet further enhanced fullness of scriptural meaning in the historical witnesses of Hebrew, Greek, Latin, Aramaic, Syriac, Arabic, Ethiopic, Samaritan, and Persian (Miller 2001, 465–68). Yet from Scaliger's revolutionary work on chronology onwards, the very preserve of sacred history began to transform the interpretation of scripture into the study of a text subject to historical analysis. Masius, in his commentary on Joshua (1574), planted the seeds for the more radical assertion of the Ezran authorship of the Pentateuch found in Thomas Hobbes's *Leviathan* (1651, Chapter 33.2–4), which argued, on the grounds of textual criticism and historical reasoning, that Moses could not be its author (Malcolm 2002). In the free-thinking Isaac Vossius (1618–1689), who lacked his father's respect for sacred text, we again arguably find the tipping point between "late humanism" and the radical criticism of the Bible associated with Spinoza (1632–1677) and the Enlightenment: the valuing of human reason over the traditions of textual authority, and the triumph of philosophy over theology and ecclesiastical *imperium* (Grafton 2012; Israel 2001, 449).

Suggested Reading

Relationships between biblical humanism and scholasticism are explored in Rummel (2008 and 1989). On the Old Testament, see Saebø (2008). Rummel (1995) handles the larger scope of humanist–scholastic relations in the Renaissance, and Hamilton (1996), humanists and the Bible. For New Testament scholarship in this period, see Bentley (1983), and for further issues of translation, Botley (2004). Pabel (2008) studies, through Jerome, the editing and printing of sixteenth-century patristic scholarship; more widely, see Backus (1996). For the exegetical dispute between Erasmus and Melanchthon, see Wengert (1998). For other work by the author relevant to this chapter, see Taylor (2010a and 2010b).

References

Backus, Irena, ed. 1996. *The Reception of the Church Fathers in the West: From the Carolingians to the Maurists*. 2 vols. Leiden: Brill.

Bentley, Jerry H. 1978. "Erasmus, Le Clerc, and the Principle of the Harder Reading." *Renaissance Quarterly* 31: 309–21.

———. 1983. *Humanists and Holy Writ: New Testament Scholarship in the Renaissance*. Princeton: Princeton University Press.

Botley, Paul. 2004. *Latin Translation in the Renaissance: The Theory and Practice of Leonardo Bruni, Giannozzo Manetti and Desiderius Erasmus*. Cambridge: Cambridge University Press.

———. 2010. *Learning Greek in Western Europe, 1396–1529: Grammars, Lexica, and Classroom Texts*. Philadelphia: American Philosophical Society.

Braden, Gordon, Robert Cummings, and Theo Hermans, eds. 2010. *The Oxford History of Literary Translation in English, Volume 2: 1550–1660*. Oxford: Oxford University Press.

Burnett, Stephen G. 1996. *From Christian Hebraism to Jewish Studies: Johannes Buxtorf (1564–1629) and Hebrew Learning in the Seventeenth Century*. Leiden: Brill.

———. 2012. *Christian Hebraism in the Reformation Era (1500–1660): Authors, Books, and the Transmission of Jewish Learning*. Leiden: Brill.

Celenza, Christopher S. 1994. "Renaissance Humanism and the New Testament: Lorenzo Valla's Annotations to the Vulgate." *Journal of Medieval and Renaissance Studies* 24:33–52.

Crane, Mark. 2010. "A Scholastic Response to Biblical Humanism: Noël Beda Against Lefèvre d'Etaples and Erasmus (1526)." *Humanistica Lovaniensia* 59:71–97.

De Jonge, Henk J. 1980. "Erasmus and the Comma Johanneum." *Ephemerides Theologicae Lovanienses* 56:381–89.

Delph, Ronald. 2008. "Emending and Defending the Vulgate Old Testament: Agostino Steuco's Quarrel with Erasmus." In Rummel 2008, 297–318.

De Petris, Alfonso. 1975. "Le teorie umanistiche del tradurre e *l'Apologeticus* di Giannozzo Manetti." *Bibliothèque d'Humanisme et Renaissance* 37:15–32.

Drysdall, Dennis L. 2012. "The Two Versions of Erasmus's *Apologia de In principio erat sermo* and the Role of Edward Lee." In *ACNL* 2012, 363–72.

Dunkelgrun, Theodor W. 2012. "The Multiplicity of Scripture: The Confluence of Textual Traditions in the Making of the Antwerp Polyglot Bible (1568–1573)." Ph.D. diss., University of Chicago. ProQuest (document ID 1040725740).

Erasmus, Desiderius. 1986. *Erasmus's Annotations on the New Testament; The Gospels; Facsimile of the Final Latin Text (1535) with All Earlier Variants (1516, 1519, 1522 and 1527)*. Edited by Anne Reeve. London: Duckworth.

———. 1990. *Erasmus' Annotations on the New Testament: Acts, Romans, I and II Corinthians: Facsimile of the Final Latin Text with All Earlier Variants*. Edited by Anne Reeve and Michael A. Screech. Leiden: Brill.

François, Wim. 2005. "*Ad divinarum rerum cognitionem*: Petrus Mosellanus and Jacobus Latomus on Biblical or Scholastic Theology." *Renaissance and Reformation* 29:13–46.

Grafton, Anthony. 2012. "Isaac Vossius, Chronologer." In *Isaac Vossius (1618–1689) Between Science and Scholarship*, edited by Eric Jorink and Dirk van Miert, 43–84. Leiden: Brill.

Grafton, Anthony, and Joanna Weinberg. 2011. *"I Have Always Loved the Holy Tongue": Isaac Casaubon, the Jews, and a Forgotten Chapter in Renaissance Scholarship*. Cambridge: Belknap.

Hall, Basil. 1963. "Biblical Scholarship: Editions and Commentaries." In *The Cambridge History of the Bible: The West from the Reformation to the Present Day*, edited by Stanley L. Greenslade, 38–93. Cambridge: Cambridge University Press.

Hamilton, Alistair. 1996. "Humanists and the Bible." In *The Cambridge Companion to Renaissance Humanism*, edited by Jill Kraye, 100–17. Cambridge: Cambridge University Press.

Hankins, James. 2003. "The Study of Greek in the Latin West." In *Humanism and Platonism in the Renaissance*, vol. 1, 273–92. Rome: Edizioni di Storia e Letteratura.

Israel, Jonathan I. 2001. *Radical Enlightenment: Philosophy and the Making of Modernity, 1650–1750*. Oxford: Oxford University Press.

Jarrott, Catherine A. L. 1964. "Erasmus' *In principio erat sermo*: A Controversial Translation." *Studies in Philology* 61:35–40.

Kessler-Mesguich, Sophie. 2008. "Early Christian Hebraists." In Saebø 2008, 254–75.

Kristeller, Paul O. 1961. *Renaissance Thought: The Classic, Scholastic and Humanist Strains*. New York: Harper & Row.

Lee, John A. L. 2005. "Demitrios Doukas and the Accentuation of the New Testament Text of the Complutensian Polyglot." *Novum Testamentum* 47:250–90.

Malcolm, Noel. 2002. "Hobbes, Ezra, and the Bible: The History of a Subversive Idea." In *Aspects of Hobbes*, 383–431. Oxford: Clarendon Press.

Manetti, Giannozzo. 1981. *Apologeticus*. Edited by Alfonso De Petris. Rome: Edizioni di Storia e Letteratura.

McGrath, Alister E. 2012. *Reformation Thought: An Introduction*. 4th ed. Chichester: Wiley-Blackwell.

Metzger, Bruce M. 1968. *The Text of the New Testament: Its Transmission, Corruption, and Restoration*. 2nd ed. Oxford: Clarendon Press.

———. 1975. *A Textual Commentary on the Greek New Testament*. London: United Bibles Society.

Miller, Peter N. 2001. "The Antiquarianization of Biblical Scholarship and the London Polyglot Bible (1653–57)." *Journal of the History of Ideas* 62:463–82.

Minnich, Nelson H. 2008. "Alberto Pio's Defense of Scholastic Theology." In Rummel 2008, 277–95.

Monfasani, John. 2008. "Criticism of Biblical Humanists in Quattrocento Italy." In Rummel 2008, 15–38.

Moss, Ann. 2003. *Renaissance Truth and the Latin Language Turn*. Oxford: Oxford University Press.

Nauta, Lodi. 2009. *In Defense of Common Sense: Lorenzo Valla's Humanist Critique of Scholastic Philosophy*. Cambridge: Harvard University Press.

O'Connell, Séamus. 2006. *From Most Ancient Sources: The Nature and Text-Critical Use of the Greek Old Testament Text of the Complutensian Polyglot Bible*. Fribourg: Academic Press; Göttingen: Vandenhoeck & Ruprecht.

Pabel, Hilmar M. 2008. *Herculean Labours: Erasmus and the Editing of St. Jerome's Letters in the Renaissance*. Leiden: Brill.

Pabel, Hilmar M., and Mark Vessey, eds. 2002. *Holy Scripture Speaks: The Production and Reception of Erasmus' Paraphrases on the New Testament*. Toronto: Toronto University Press.

Pio, Alberto. 1529. *Responsio accurata et paraenetica*. Paris: Josse Bade.

Price, David H. 2011. *Johannes Reuchlin and the Campaign to Destroy Jewish Books*. Oxford: Oxford University Press.

Rex, Richard. 2000. "Humanism." In *The Reformation World*, edited by Andrew Pettegree, 51–70. London: Routledge.

Rice, Eugene. 1985. *Saint Jerome in the Renaissance*. Baltimore: Johns Hopkins University Press.

Rummel, Erika. 1986. *Erasmus' Annotations on the New Testament: From Philologist to Theologian*. Toronto: Toronto University Press.

———. 1989. *Erasmus and His Catholic Critics*. 2 vols. Nieuwkoop: De Graaf.

———. 1995. *The Humanist-Scholastic Debate in the Renaissance and the Reformation*. Cambridge: Harvard University Press.

———. 2002. "Why Nöel Béda Did Not Like Erasmus' Paraphrases." In Pabel and Vessey, op. cit., 265–78.

———, ed. 2008. *Biblical Humanism and Scholasticism in the Age of Erasmus*. Leiden: Brill.

Saebø, Magne, ed. 2008. *Hebrew Bible—Old Testament: The History of Its Interpretation*. Vol. 2, *From the Renaissance to the Enlightenment*. Göttingen: Vandenhoeck & Ruprecht.

Schenker, Adrian. 2008. "From the First Printed Hebrew, Greek and Latin Bible to the First Polyglot Bible, the Complutensian Polyglot: 1477–1517." In Saebø, op. cit., 276–91.

Seidel Menchi, Silvana. 1987. *Erasmo in Italia (1520–1580)*. Turin: Bollati Boringhieri.

Shuger, Debora K. 1994. *The Renaissance Bible: Scholarship, Sacrifice, and Subjectivity*. Berkeley: University of California Press.

Stinger, Charles. 1977. *Humanism and the Church Fathers: Ambrogio Traversari (1386–1439) and Christian Antiquity in the Italian Renaissance*. Albany: State University of New York Press.

———. 1996. "Italian Renaissance Learning and the Church Fathers." In Backus, op. cit., 2:473–510.

Tanner, Norman P. 1990. *Decrees of the Ecumenical Councils*. 2 vols. London: Sheed & Ward; Washington, DC: Georgetown University Press.

Taylor, Andrew. 2010a. "Versions of the English Bible 1550–1660." In Braden, Cummings, and Hermans, op. cit., 120–40.

———. "The Translation of Biblical Commentary 1550–1660." In Braden, Cummings, and Hermans, op. cit., 155–63.

Trinkaus, Charles. 1970. *In Our Image and Likeness: Humanity and Divinity in Italian Humanist Thought*. 2 vols. Chicago: University of Chicago Press.

Valla, Lorenzo. 1505. *In Latinam Novi Testamenti interpretationem ex collatione Graecorum exemplarium Adnotationes*. Edited by Desiderius Erasmus. Paris: Iehan Petit.

———. 1970. *Collatio Novi Testamenti*. Edited by Alessandro Perosa. Florence: Sansoni.

Welte, Michael. 1999. "The Problem of the Manuscript Basis for the Earliest Printed Editions of the Greek New Testament." In *The Bible as Book: The First Printed Editions*, edited by Paul Saenger and Kimberly Van Kampen, 117–24. London: The British Library and Oak Knoll Press.

Wengert, Timothy J. 1998. *Human Freedom, Christian Righteousness: Philip Melanchthon's Exegetical Dispute with Erasmus of Rotterdam*. Oxford: Oxford University Press.

Wilson, Nigel G. 1992. *From Byzantium to Italy: Greek Studies in the Italian Renaissance*. London: Duckworth.

CHAPTER 20

....

CATHOLICISM

....

JASON HARRIS

In 1584, the vicar-general of Liège and nominee for the archbishopric of Antwerp, Laevinus Torrentius (1525–1595), a humanist scholar and Latin poet, wrote to the renowned philologist Justus Lipsius to remonstrate with him about his use of Stoic authors, rather than the Bible or patristic writers, as his model in his philosophical treatise *De Constantia* (*On Constancy*, 1584). The accusation that Lipsius wrote *quamquam elegantissime nimis tamen profane* ("though very elegantly, yet too profanely") because of his recourse to classical rather than Christian sources is one that may helpfully introduce some of the preferences and concerns exhibited by Catholic authors who wrote in Latin from the 1520s onwards (Lipsius 1983, 86–90). As Lipsius himself wrote of his critics at the beginning of the preface to the second edition of *De Constantia* (Lipsius 1585, A2):

> *Negant satis pie hoc argumentum a me tractatum; negant locis aliquot satis vere. Parum pie ideo: quia philosophum egisse tantum videor, inquiunt, nec inspersisse quae potui et debui e libris sacris.*

> They deny that I have handled my theme with sufficient piety; in some places, they deny that I am accurate enough. "Insufficiently pious" for this reason—that I seem only to have played the part of a philosopher, they say, and not to have sprinkled my work with what I could and ought to have taken from the holy books.

It would be easy to cite this alongside many other similar passages from the writings of Catholic authors in order to corroborate a stereotype of repressive religiosity that sterilized literary creativity. On the contrary, Lipsius's continued cultivation of classicism, despite his increasing recourse to religious topics later in his career, is typical of the broader intellectual scope of Catholic Latin in this period. Indeed, I hope to demonstrate in this chapter that the confessional pressures of the Counter-Reformation had many more positive than negative effects upon Catholic writing in Latin.

The present chapter surveys only Latin writings on religious subjects produced from ca. 1520 onwards by authors whose confessional allegiance was to the Church of

Rome, leaving secular poetry, oratory, and other genres to the chapters devoted to them elsewhere in this volume. Nevertheless, the corpus remains broad and differentiated, ranging from scholarly and devotional writings in which the articulation of confessional identity is of secondary importance, to works whose principal objective was to demarcate the boundaries of orthodoxy, to inculcate a specifically Catholic piety, or to extirpate the errors of alternative creeds. These diverse undertakings were brought to fruition through a still more variegated spectrum of approaches, yet some broad contextual and intellectual continuities can be discerned. This chapter begins with a consideration of the unique sacerdotal status of Latin within Catholicism, then surveys the broad features of the corpus as a whole—paying particular attention to the writings of Roberto Bellarmino (1542–1621) and Caesar Baronius (1538–1607)—before concluding with some observations upon the ways in which the varied character of this corpus finds expression in the Latinity of its authors.

LATIN AS THE CATHOLIC TONGUE

The first question I wish to explore is to what extent Catholics had a distinctively "Catholic" view of the Latin language. To a large degree, the early Reformation may be understood as a debate about the sacerdotal character of the church; accordingly, the Catholic Church's retention of Latin as the language of scripture and the liturgy became a key marker of confessional difference, and would, of course, remain so until the second half of the twentieth century, when the Second Vatican Council (1962–1965) instituted the practice of celebrating the liturgy in the vernacular. However, the distinctive hieratic use of Latin within Catholicism was not normally justified on the basis of any intrinsic quality of the language itself; indeed, arguments in favor of the retention of Latin in the liturgy and as the language of scripture focused, largely, upon historical and pragmatic considerations. The Tridentine decree as to the "authentic" character of the Vulgate translation of the Bible was defended with reference to this version's antiquity, its association with Jerome, the extent and reliability of its distribution in manuscript, and, by contrast, the supposed limitations in quality and quantity of the Greek and Hebrew textual traditions (Jedin 1961, 67–98). With regard to the use of Latin as opposed to the vernacular in the liturgy, Catholic scholars often alluded to the intrinsic dignity of the language, but typically argued that practical considerations be weighed carefully, such as the need for priests to be able to officiate in various countries, the difficulty of producing reliable translations, and the confusion that could arise from having different versions of the liturgy in every different locality. They also issued the warning (widely cited and contested by Protestant authors) that use of the vernacular might grant license to the ignorant to presume knowledge and, as a consequence, to propagate unto others their misunderstandings and heresies—witness the example of Johannes Eck's *De missa Latine dicenda* (*On the Need for Mass to be Said in Latin*) in the seventh edition of his *Enchiridion contra Lutherum* (*Handbook Against Luther*, 1536; Eck 1536, 239–245). Notwithstanding the pragmatic nature of these arguments, the use of Latin in a sacred context may have impressed some of the wider Catholic community with a sense of the language's inherent holiness; intimations of this may perhaps be gleaned from the use of Latin in charms, spells, and incantations, as also from its appearance as demonic speech emanating from the possessed during Catholic exorcisms (Sluhovsky 2007, 20, 54–5, 151, 195, 198, 201, and 207). By contrast, many Protestant attacks upon Catholicism interpret the retention of Latin as a sign either of superstition or of obfuscation (Scribner 2001, 246–50); for instance, English Puritan references to the "Romish" or "Popish" tongue often associate it with scholastic subtleties designed to obscure rather than elucidate meaning, as in the play *The Second Part of the Return from Parnassus*, first published anonymously in 1606 (Smeaton 1905, 32). Nevertheless, the central Protestant charge was that Catholic retention of a Latin Bible and liturgy was merely an instance of the clericalism designed to retain sacerdotal power and hide the diabolical character of Catholic doctrine, which accusation has less to do with Latin than with ecclesiological polemic.

One important consequence of the Catholic Church's retention of Latin worship was its concomitant investment in the education of its clergy in and through the medium of Latin. The slow but steady creation of seminaries in the wake of the Council of Trent (1545–1563) and the rapid expansion of the Jesuit school system transformed the educational foundation of the Catholic clergy. This process took time and evolved rather unevenly in different parts of Europe, yet expectations changed more rapidly, dragging the implementation of the reform proposals behind them. Thus, for example, when in 1584 the Irish Catholic writer Richard Stanihurst (1547–1618) satirized the attempt of uneducated rustics from Ireland to gain clerical preferment in Rome, he depicted them as attempting to use Latin to demonstrate their credentials, though the only phrase they could muster was, he reports, a quotation from the Vulgate Latin version of 1 Timothy 3.1: *Qui episcopatum desiderat, bonum opus desiderat* ("He who desires a bishopric desires a good work")—a self-serving attempt to reclothe their ambition as piety (Stanihurst 2013, 84–5). Implicit in Stanihurst's text and in others of the same kind is the notion that a high standard of Latin had come to be regarded as essential for anyone seeking a career in the clergy and that those who fell short of this were objects of ridicule. In the new seminaries established by the Council of Trent, Latin was to be the language of daily intercourse, and colloquial use of the vernacular was expressly forbidden. Perhaps inevitably, surviving evidence suggests that this aspiration was never fully attained, yet the emphasis upon conversational Latin proficiency among the priesthood reinforced the association of Catholicism with Latin, especially in the eighteenth and nineteenth centuries when spoken Latin rapidly declined outside the schoolroom in much of Protestant Europe. By the early seventeenth century, one hundred years of humanist polemic and fifty years of an organized institutional response ensured that all young Catholic priests would have had a good grounding in spoken and written Latin in accordance with reformed, classicizing standards. Perhaps as a consequence of this, a notable shift may be discerned in Protestant polemic. The pre-Reformation and early Reformation tendency to pillory ignorant priests for their failure to understand or correctly cite scriptural and liturgical texts largely disappeared. Thereafter, when

Protestants drew attention to Catholic use of Latin, it was either to attack the supposed attempt of the Catholic clergy to gain power through use of an auxiliary, sacerdotal language, or to lampoon scrupulous priests for being overly immersed in Latin formulae to the point of superstition, rather than mocking them for being ignorant of the language.

In this regard, the significance of the Jesuit schools cannot be overstated, and the wider contribution of members of the Society of Jesus to the promulgation of spoken and literary Latin in the early modern and modern period is unparalleled. The combination of scholastic and humanistic elements within the Jesuit curriculum created a particularly felicitous atmosphere for the production of Neo-Latin scholarship and literature across the full range of genres and disciplines. In schools run by the Society, and in others that sought to emulate their achievements, we can see the attempt to foster a culture of humane Latinity that went much further than the desire to produce an educated priesthood. The production of literature in and for these schools, particularly poetry and plays, stands out as one of the most striking developments within Catholic Latin culture. Although such literature had its counterpart within the school systems of Protestant Europe, the institutional commitment to retaining an international Latin-speaking clergy ensured the continuing vitality of Latin literary creativity within Catholic communities into the nineteenth century. Furthermore, outside the school system, the decision to compose literary works in Latin could, on occasion, take on a decidedly clerical character. A notable instance of this may be found in the case of Alessandro Piegadi's publication of seven Latin translations by Catholic authors from the eighteenth and nineteenth centuries of a passage from Dante on the eve of the poet's sexcentenary celebrations in 1865 (Piegadi 1864). In the context of *Risorgimento* cultural politics, presentation of the newly heralded national poet's work in the language of the clergy could be a powerful statement of clericalism, asserting the place of Dante within wider church tradition rather than as a champion of the vernacular. This perspective helps explain the editor's preface, which subtly draws the readers' attention to the parallel case of Mexico, where the church also felt embattled in the face of secularizing constitutional reform. Piegadi invents the story of a Mexican student Nonvrai ("Not Real") who studied in Italy and exchanged with the editor Latin verse by the celebrated Mexican poet Diego José Abad (1727–1779). The whole invented episode appears to be designed to provide a preemptive response to the forthcoming centenary in which Dante would be heralded as a critic of church abuses and a champion of national unity. More generally, for the Catholic Church, Latin served as an internationalizing force that transcended divergent regional pressures, much as it did within the Austro-Hungarian Empire in the same period. As active use of Latin both inside and outside the classroom diminished throughout Europe in the course of the nineteenth century, it retained a niche within Catholic institutions. This did not, of course, mean that Protestants associated Latin with Catholicism, but they did associate Catholicism with Latin. Correspondingly, when secular, and at times internationalist, initiatives from the late nineteenth century onwards attempted to rekindle the active use of Latin as a "living" spoken and literary medium, they tended to arise or find a home in Catholic countries, or to rely upon the support of Catholic institutions. A good example is that of Karl Heinrich Ulrichs (1825–1895; Numa Numantius), who, despite his Lutheran background and his activism for gay rights, spent the final years of his life in Italy, publishing a Latin journal (*Alaudae* [*Larks*]; also the name of a garrison raised by Caesar in Gaul) that sought to promote the international use of Latin as a living language (Stroh 2004), and that would ultimately be recast as the *Vox Urbis* (*Voice of the City*), published by the Catholic architect Aristide Leonori (Jenniges 2007, 8–11). However, the decision at the Second Vatican Council to embrace a new evangelism whose characteristic medium was to be the vernacular largely eradicated the active Latin community within the Catholic Church, though it never entirely disappeared and, indeed, received some support under Pope Benedict XVI, among whose last acts was the re-founding of a Latin institute in Rome to promote the active use of Latin within the church. Nevertheless, since the 1970s, the most successful initiatives in relation to active Latin use have arisen and been maintained outside the Catholic Church (for example, at the Universities of Heidelberg, Munich, Leuven, and Kentucky), perhaps marking the end of the historical period in which this was seen as largely the preserve of the Catholic clergy.

THE CORPUS OF CATHOLIC LATIN

Among the very first negative reactions to the work of Martin Luther and other early reformers was the objection that they ought not to debate theological matters in the vernacular. The success of the reformers' writings very soon ensured that Catholic theologians could not maintain this stance, at least in regard to theological polemic. Nevertheless, they reserved technical theological discussion for their Latin writings. The purposeful use of Latin to restrict readership to the scholarly sphere was not, of course, exclusive to Catholics or to religious topics, but it was a frequent target of Protestant criticisms, which, as already mentioned, often also associated the practice specifically with the use of scholastic rather than humanistic Latin. Although Protestant and Catholic scholars shared the language and intellectual framework of Aristotelianism that was taught in all universities throughout the early modern period, Protestant writers increasingly eschewed the linguistic formulations of late-medieval theologians, which, however, remained essential within the sphere of Catholic theological education and debate. In response to such critique, Catholic theological writings that addressed Protestant interlocutors typically deployed a greatly restricted vocabulary and a less obviously scholastic mode of argumentation, particularly when compared with, for example, the theological theses produced within universities. In the latter, the titles of which customarily indicated that they were written *ad mentem Duns Scoti* or *ad mentem Thomae Aquinatis* ("according to the mind of Duns Scotus"; "according to the mind of Thomas Aquinas"), scholastic Latinity survives with its vocabulary and word order intact, though its syntax is sometimes amended to classical norms, except in technical collocations. This technical discourse formed a distinct auxiliary register within the language, one that students were expected to learn and to speak at university. Nevertheless, for the most part, authors could successfully write in humanistic mode for a wider audience. The more accomplished writers, such as Eck and Bellarmino, exhibit no difficulty in switching register with genre, whether it be from scholastic instruction to rhetorical polemic, or from homily to epistolography, and so forth.

The rapid growth in the number of universities during the fifteenth and sixteenth centuries ensured that a large audience existed for technical theological and philosophical works; tens of thousands of such texts survive, ranging from single-sheet theses to multivolume tomes. This corpus has been very largely neglected by intellectual and cultural historians, with only the most prominent works by the most famous authors receiving any critical analysis, such as those by the Spanish Jesuit Francisco Suárez (Hill and Lagerlund 2012); yet it is these texts that offer the most distinctively Catholic use of Latin, both at the level of syntax and semantics, and at the level of broad cultural enterprise, reflecting the commitment of Catholic scholars to maintaining an intellectual discourse that bridged the linguistic gulf between the late Middle Ages and the early modern period. Among Protestant scholars, the range and application of such language was much more restricted because they had dispensed with many of the conceptual refinements upon which their Catholic counterparts relied.

Polemical theology, and many apologetic works, were cast in a rather different mold. Catholic theologians, like their Protestant antagonists, deployed the full range of humanist rhetoric to ridicule and vilify their opponents. Arguments *ad hominem* took as their model the tirades of Cicero's *Philippics*, often combining argumentation with accusations of effeminacy, degeneration, and monstrosity, further embellished with the language of late antique heresiology. Such writing is at its most stark when composed in commentary form, in which an opponent's work is quoted and rebutted line by line, resulting in repetitious name-calling and outraged exclamation, as in the case of the Jesuit writer Stephen White, who attacked the work of the aforementioned Richard Stanihurst in just this way (Harris 2009, 126–53). Nevertheless, while inter-confessional polemic of this period exemplified intellectual discourse at its most coarsely aggressive, it was largely devoid of actual obscenity, following, in this, the precepts of ancient rhetors. Scatological language is found, though perhaps with less frequency and force than in equivalent vernacular writings. Biting sarcasm and the full range of ancient invective are occasionally deployed in other kinds of academic dispute in this period, but it is in religious debate that they are most prominent. An indicative example may be adduced from the *Lutherus Thaumaturgus* (*Luther the Miracle Worker*) of the Swiss Jesuit Laurenz Forer (1580–1659), published in 1624 (Forer 1624, 164):

> *Porro non cygnum sed porcum potius Lutherum appellandum esse vel ex eo discas quod non modo plenus fuit* Cacodaemone, *sed etiam* Cacadaemone; *cuius canor (erubesco scribere) nihil fere aliud fuit quam faetor, paedor, stercus, oletum, latrina, lupanar, hara, et id genus alia Islebica aromata, quae passim reperies illius libris copiose aspersa, inspersa, et superspersa.*

Besides, Luther should not be called a "swan" but a pig, as you can see from the fact that he was not only full of an evil spirit, but of a dung-demon, whose "song" (I blush writing this) is nothing but the stink, stench, shit, filth, toilets, whorehouse, pigsty, and other smells of that kind from Eisleben, which you will find abundantly sprinkled, infused and poured throughout his books.

This was not, of course, the only manner in which writers tackled confessional differences. Pious indignation and stern censure, while appropriate for apologetics and polemic, had no place in, for example, homiletic or parenetic discourse. Thus, the *Homiliarius contra sectas* (*The Homilist Against the Sects*, 1536) of Johannes Eck, an author not unable to engage in verbal brawling, deploys exegesis and ratiocination to confute his opponents, focusing rather upon expounding Catholic doctrine than upon expressing scorn or disgust for their ideas, though even here he indulges in the occasional stinging insult.

Without doubt, the most important and influential Catholic controversial work (that is, a work that argues against Protestant theology) was the four-volume *Disputationes de controversiis Christianae fidei* (*Disputations on the Controversies of the Christian Faith*) of the Jesuit theologian Roberto Bellarmino (1581–1593). The significance of Bellarmino's work lay in its argumentative rigor, the seriousness with which it engaged Protestant arguments, and the tone it adopted (see Brodrick 1928 for an introduction to Bellarmino). Though the author shared earlier heresiologists' belief that the battle against heresy was the battle against the Antichrist, and that blind obstinacy and degeneration of morals were characteristic features of genuine heretics, he did not demonize his opponents, explaining in his preface that he would pass over such things in silence, or with only a warning at the outset that: *haereseos perversitatem tanto esse graviorem caeteris omnibus sceleribus atque flagitiis quanto communibus morbis magis est formidolosa et metuenda pestis* ("the wickedness of heresy is as much worse than all other crimes and outrages as the plague is more frightful and fearsome than more common diseases"; Bellarmino 1581–1593, Praefatio, n.p.).

Bellarmino's *Disputationes* are a model instance of the development of early modern dogmatic theology in response to the divergent teachings of the reformers. Their influence on both the substance and style of later Catholic debate was immense, though within the field of heresiology older manuals also remained current, such as the *Adversus omnes haeresos* (*Against All Heresies*, 1534) of the Spanish Franciscan Alfonso de Castro (1495–1558). Characteristic of all such works was the endeavor to situate recent arguments within the context of the anti-heresy writings of the early church fathers in order to demonstrate that Protestant ideas were not new and had long ago been refuted by figures of great authority. The extent to which such writings retained the scholarly deportment of Bellarmino's *Disputationes* varied according to the context of writing. Generally speaking, the more comprehensive and systematic the scope of a treatise, the more moderate its tone; by contrast, specific disputes tended to evoke more bilious approaches. Bellarmino himself was not above deploying the rhetoric of personal attack in his one-on-one debates; for instance, in his dispute with James I of England (Bourdin [2004] 2010).

The development of intra-confessional dogmatic theology was very much shaped by the rival theological schools associated with the religious orders, and the debates between them could at times become as acerbic as inter-confessional polemic. The best-known of these is the seventeenth-century battle between the Jesuits and the Jansenists in Belgium and France, which was in fact a series of controversies over both moral and dogmatic theology. The common theme was the contention that Jesuit teachings on grace and free will were defective and perhaps connected to insufficient moral rigor. To the extent that this debate represents a significant portion of the Neo-Latin patrimony of Catholic authors in this period, it must be regarded as part of the larger scholarly engagement with the writings of Augustine of Hippo, which can be seen to characterize the great majority of religious literature, both Catholic and Protestant, in the seventeenth century. Other less well-known but equally productive debates between Catholic writers include the Franciscan–Dominican dispute over the Immaculate Conception of Mary, the proto-quietist debate within the regular orders as to the proper approach to contemplative prayer, and a set of unrelated disputes between different national churches as to the identity of particular saints. A particularly lively instance of this last kind of dispute is the "Scotic debate" about saints identified in medieval sources as *Scoti* or as having come from *Scotia*—a name that originally referred to Ireland but subsequently, after dynastic cross-fertilization, designated Scotland. In an attempt to celebrate their own national church, which had been almost wiped out by the spread of Presbyterianism, Scottish hagiographers eagerly claimed Patrick, Brigid, Columba, and many other Irish saints of the Middle Ages as Scots. Irish hagiographers fought back bitterly, and the invective became so splenetic and indecorous that several works of hagiography on both sides ended up censured on the Index of Prohibited Books (Caulfield 2009). Nevertheless, much serious historical scholarship was scattered throughout these writings, and the debate played no small role in the development of Irish Catholic identity as a precursor to what would become, in subsequent centuries, a fully fledged Irish national identity. This is but one indication of the manner in which the corpus of early modern Catholic religious writing, though often devoted to abstruse points of controversy, can be of great value to literary and cultural historians as well as to those focused upon the history of ideas or religion.

The Scotic debate forms part of a larger body of Latin hagiography from the early modern period that was of great historiographical and ecclesiological importance. Protestant attacks upon the Catholic cult of saints had not only poured scorn upon the purported idolatry of miracles, relics, and pilgrimages, but had also questioned the historical veracity of Catholic tradition. From the 1570s onwards, a coalescence of diverse initiatives resulted in a remarkable historiographical revolution as Catholic scholars attempted to put the cult of saints on a firm historical footing. Alongside the efflorescence of new shrines, pilgrimage sites, canonizations, and cults, across Europe scholars began to investigate their own local saints, to gather and edit manuscripts, and to produce new critical accounts of their lives. Two projects are particularly worth noting in this regard. First, the six-volume compendium of saints' lives, *De probatis sanctorum historiis* (*On the Approved Histories of the Saints*), published in Cologne between 1570 and 1575 by the German Carthusian Laurentius Surius; second, its ultimate replacement, the multivolume *Acta Sanctorum* (*Acts of the Saints*) initiated by Heribert Rosweyde and Jean Bolland, and, after the first two volumes were printed in Antwerp in 1643, continued by their followers, the Society of Bollandists, down to the present day. These works are significant not only in their own right, but also because they became authorities for subsequent Catholic writers, the margins of whose books were littered with references to them. Indeed, for writers from the 1650s onwards, they are almost as important as the hagiographical *Legenda aurea* (*Golden Legend*) by the Italian Dominican Jacobus de Voragine (ca. 1230–1298) was for medieval authors.

Related to the revival of Catholic hagiography was the revision of the *Martyrologium Romanum* (*Roman Martyrology*), which was first printed in 1583 and subsequently redacted several times through the work of Caesar Baronius, before reaching a stable form in the 1630 edition published under the auspices of Pope Urban VIII (1568–1644). The martyrological tradition was especially important for the overseas missions and for frontier zones between Catholicism and Protestantism, where the reformers had produced their own martyrologies as a testimony to the integrity of their faith. Thus, in addition to devoting scholarship to past martyrs, Catholic scholars were equally concerned to gather and present information on contemporary martyrs, for both polemical and devotional purposes—see, for example, Book 3 of the *Analecta Sacra, Nova, et Mira* (*Sacred, New, and Wondrous Gatherings*) of David Rothe, which contained an extensive *processus martyrialis* ("procedure for recognizing martyrs"; Rothe 1619). These martyrologies are rich in detail about the lives of contemporary figures and the problems that the era of confessionalization presented for them, but they are also consciously crafted literary creations within the tradition of medieval martyrology, albeit recast in the light of the confessional imperatives of the early modern period. These works are pointedly intertextual, demonstrating the authenticity of the martyrdom through parallels with earlier exemplars, especially from patristic authors.

The story of the reception of patristic writings within the early modern period is, of course, in many ways the combined history of both the Catholic and the Protestant reformations. Perhaps as much textual space is devoted to the opinions and significance of patristic writers as to unmediated interpretation of the Bible itself. Certainly, Catholic books are filled with citations of patristic authorities, and Protestant interlocutors had equally to engage with these in order to rebut their opponents' arguments. Jerome, Ambrose, and Augustine are especially commonly cited, but later writers such as Gregory the Great (ca. 540–604) and even Bernard of Clairvaux (ca. 1090–1153) are also widely attested in Catholic works. Naturally, the choice of authorities is in part determined by the matter under discussion, though the first three authors mentioned tend to arise almost irrespective of the subject. Of particular importance in this respect is the intermediary role of exegetical handbooks such as those produced from 1614 onwards by the Flemish Jesuit Cornelius a Lapide (Cornelis Cornelissen van den Steen, 1567–1637), who provided a conspectus of patristic commentaries on all the books of the Bible apart from Job and the Psalms (e.g., on the Epistles of Paul [*Commentarii in omnes Pauli Divi epistolas*, 1614] or on the Pentateuch [*Commentarii in Pentateuchum*, 1616]).

Catholic writers used such works to guide their interpretation of biblical texts and to string together *catenae* ("chains") of allusions to diverse biblical passages that, following patristic tradition, they believed referred to one another or could be used to explain one another. Understanding how Catholic writers thought and composed their works through the exegetical tradition passed down to them in commentaries, the liturgy, and the homiletic tradition is key to understanding the implicit significations of their biblical and patristic citations. In this regard, the methodology for reading and interpreting early modern Catholic writings is quite distinct from that which must be applied to contemporary Protestant authors, whose works must be approached through related but distinct exegetical traditions, such as that pursued by Calvin (Puckett 1995).

Perhaps the most explicit evidence of the significance of the exegetical background to Catholic writing may be found in the extensive devotional literature of the Catholic Reformation. The litanies, liturgies, catechisms, festal publications, breviaries, books of hours, primers, and prayer books that flowed from the presses of printers like Christophe Plantin not only provide ample evidence of Catholic religiosity in this period, but also offer invaluable insight into the interpretative matrices of religious writers. In particular, the Latin liturgy is perhaps an underestimated influence upon the Latinity and biblical understanding of scholars who every day heard renderings of biblical passages within the predigested interpretative frameworks of its cyclical services. Much of the evidence of biblical phrasing and even syntax that appears from time to time in Catholic writers might best be attributed to this source, for the recurring texts of the liturgy were committed to memory to an even greater degree than the Bible itself. Devotional literature is saturated with the language of the liturgy. The genre is too rich, extensive, and diverse to identify one dominant figure, but the writings of Petrus Canisius (1521–1597) were especially highly admired, particularly his *De Maria Virgine* (*On the Virgin Mary*, 1577). Combining treatise, contemplation, verse passages, and woodcuts, it occupied a central place in the defense of Catholic Mariology and provided ample fuel for subsequent devotional writers. A particularly large number of publications stemmed from the rejuvenated Catholic confraternities that sponsored devotional works for their own benefit and also for the edification of school children. Emblem literature, lives of Christ, and mystical writing all flourished well into the eighteenth century. It is worth remarking that this literature exhibited a distinctive Latinity, often eschewing periodic construction, deploying instead the humble rhetorical register (*sermo humilis*) of biblical and hagiographical texts, but reveling in oxymoron, paradox, and the language of emptiness and yet infinity, as well as being richly inwoven with expressions from and allusions to the Psalter. It is also not insignificant that Catholic writers, particularly those from contemplative orders, sometimes switched to this mode of writing in the midst of, or as a prelude or postscript to, other kinds of texts. Something similar can be observed in Protestant vernacular writings, but among Latin authors it is perhaps more common among, if not exclusively characteristic of, Catholics.

Devotional poetry is, naturally, rather different in character, though it often shares with prose texts a tendency to contain extensive allusions to or borrowings from the Psalms. Marian poetry is particularly numerous, following on in the tradition of

Sannazaro's *De Partu Virginis* (*On the Virgin Birth*, 1526), but there is also a considerable amount of Catholic verse devoted to the infant Jesus, some of which may also have an educational function or origin. While I leave more detailed discussion of poetry to other chapters, it is worth mentioning here that Catholic writers also composed a large number of poems on scholastic themes in classical meters, many of which dealt with doctrinal matters. These verses were often characterized rather more by technical ingenuity than by literary felicity, but the genre was much practiced and evidently valued in the seventeenth century; a typical example is the poetry of the Irish Franciscan Bonaventure Baron (1610–1696; Baron 1645).

Perhaps the single most important Latin work on a religious topic by a Catholic writer in this period was the twelve-volume *Annales Ecclesiastici* (*Church Annals*) of the Italian Oratorian Caesar Baronius (Cesare Baronio), which were printed in Rome between 1588 and 1607 (Pullapilly 1975). As has already been emphasized, the historical dimensions of the confessional debate were of huge importance to Catholic scholars who wished to assert the unimpaired continuity of Catholic tradition. For heresiologists, hagiographers, martyrologists, and historians, Baronius offered the most authoritative reference point in contemporary scholarship as well as a thorough confutation of Protestant revisionism and propaganda such as that which had been presented in the so-called *Magdeburg Centuries* (formally entitled the *Ecclesiastica Historia* [*Church History*]) by the Magdeburg-based Croatian Lutheran Matthias Flacius Illyricus (1520–1575) and others between 1559 and 1574. The flaws of Baronius's work are evident from a modern critical standpoint. His apologetic purpose shaped his deployment of evidence, his limited knowledge of Hebrew and Greek severely restricted his research, he made mistakes in chronology, and he mistakenly treated spurious documents as authentic; nevertheless, his achievement was immense and his influence even greater. Among the accolades he received were a cardinalate in 1596 and the position of Vatican librarian the following year, and in 1605 he was very nearly elected pope, but was blocked by the Spanish faction. Aside from his numerous continuators, epitomators, and imitators, his significance may be gauged from the fact that he is one of the most widely quoted authors of the seventeenth century; for example, he provided the framework within which the hagiographical work of Jean Bolland was pursued, as may easily be seen from the citations in his *Acta Sanctorum* (1643).

From the perspective of Latinity or the genre of historiography, Baronius's influence is harder to gauge. His work reflects the increasing tendency among historians of the sixteenth century to reproduce source materials in the form of extensive quotation and reasonably specific referencing. He also adduces a wide range of secondary sources, particularly later commentators, to interpret events. These techniques, combined with the annalistic form, reduce the narrative flow of the text, which is also somewhat devoid of rhetorical color, so that horrendous tragedies and glorious events are both alike narrated with a studied neutrality of tone that is monotonous but not inelegant. Indeed, the style of the text varies in accordance with the nature of the sources. Thus, the first book of the *Annales*, which deals with the New Testament period, reads like an extended commentary upon the Bible, as particular passages are analyzed as historical record and then supplemented by the observations of patristic commentators. In subsequent books the approach is rather different, as the discourse often consists of a patchwork of quotations from other writers woven together in chronological sequence with a few connecting remarks in between. Nevertheless, Baronius is always present as an editorial force, molding his sources and his narrative into a lofty conception, the grandeur of which he not infrequently alluded to through humble supplications of the *caeleste numen* ("heavenly power") to provide him with the ability to raise his discourse to the appropriate level, as at the beginning of the third volume (Baronius 1588–1607, 3:1):

> *Haec autem adeo eximia et excelsa oratione digne persequenti, ut magnitudo postulat argumenti, divino opus esse auxilio intelligimus, quo veritatis recto tramite ipsa oratio haud haesitans secura ducatur.*

> But we perceive that anyone who is trying to pursue these matters with a discourse as remarkable and elevated as the magnitude of the subject demands must have recourse to divine aid, by which his discourse may be led without hesitation upon the straight path of truth.

Historiographically significant is the absence of Livy's history as a model for Baronius's work. Aside from the superficial parallels in annalistic form, Baronius deploys none of Livy's narrative technique, meticulously reproducing and documenting sources rather than confecting speeches or set-pieces of narrative ecphrasis. Even setting aside the matter of rhetorical coloring, his prose also lacks the versatility and dynamic flow of Livy's word order and discourse structure. The presence of more purple passages in his dedicatory epistles and at the opening and closing of some volumes suggests that the style of the main body of the work is a conscious choice rather than a defect in Baronius's literary capacity, though it would of course have been a yet more enormous undertaking to write consistently in an elevated style throughout the entire multivolume history. He was ready to deploy complex, contextualizing periodic constructions when he deemed this appropriate, as when describing a decisive moment at the Council of Certa (305 CE), when the church rejected the Donatists, a group of moral rigorists who argued that the validity of the sacraments was contingent upon the moral standing of the officiating priest (Baronius 1588–1607, 5:335):

> *Quod enim Donatistae episcopi in eadem collatione anno superiori victi penitus et confutati, non tantum non acquievissent, sed obstinatiores atque pugnaciores abscessissent, et publica vi alii grassati essent, et alii vero verbis et scriptis complura sparsissent mendacia, nempe corruptum a nostris fuisse iudicem, se vero ab eodem compressos neque loqui permissos, et alia id genus complura fingentes, quibus populus Donatista revocaretur, ne relicto schismate ad Ecclesiam Catholicam se transferret, sed contineretur in impietatis officio: res tanta haud dissimulanda, contemnandaque patribus visa est.*

> That the Donatist bishops, though thoroughly defeated and confounded at this same conference in the previous year, had not only not acquiesced, but had departed

more obstinate and more belligerent than before, and some had gone on the rampage using public forces, while others had spread about numerous lies by word of mouth and in writing, saying that the judge had been corrupted by our side, that they had in fact been oppressed by him and not allowed to speak, and making up many other things of this kind in order to hold back the Donatists, so that they would not, having left the schism behind, cross over to the Catholic Church, but would instead remain in the service of impiety—such proceedings the church fathers felt they could not ignore, but must condemn.

In sum, Baronius produced a standard reference work in appropriate style that answered the need of Catholic scholars to place on a firm historical footing their claims for the universality and continuity of Catholic tradition. The lack of rhetorical ostentation of his work was an argument for its sobriety and reliability, not a deficiency arising from incapacity. The actual limitations in his abilities, such as his insufficient knowledge of Greek, he quietly circumvented through use of translations and avoidance of matters inaccessible to him for linguistic reasons—a fault that would later be perceived and exposed by Isaac Casaubon in his attack upon the *Annales* (Casaubon 1614). Indeed, Baronius's work, supplemented by continuators and corrected by editors, continued in use down to the nineteenth century as an intertext and framework of interpretation for Catholic Latin writers on any subject pertaining to religion.

CATHOLIC STYLISTICS AND LATINITY

The enormous range of Catholic writing in Latin ensured that no single stylistic or linguistic preference would characterize the whole corpus. Furthermore, Catholic and Protestant writers inhabited the same linguistic world, so literary trends in one community very commonly had analogues or direct counterparts in the other. It is worth noting, for example, that the official Catholic ban on Erasmus's works by no means prevented Catholic writers from benefiting from Erasmian educational reforms, and the evidence of their Latinity suggests that his collection of proverbs, *Adagia*, for example, shaped Catholic Latin idiom every bit as much as it did the writing of Protestant authors. Where there is divergence between writers of different confessional allegiances, it is largely because of the material that they are writing about. Thus, for example, although some Protestant authors wrote in mystical mode using the *sermo humilis*, most Protestants influenced by mysticism or pietism deployed the vernacular to express their religiosity, and accordingly such devotional strains in Latin were much more common among Catholic writers. Likewise, as indicated above, although Protestants and Catholics shared the technical language of Aristotelian scholasticism, Catholic usage incorporated a wider range of late-medieval formulations as a consequence of the continuing intellectual discourses of Scotism and Thomism, both of which underwent an impressive revival in Catholic scholarly life during the sixteenth and seventeenth centuries, with significant consequences within the field of ethics and theories of identity (Campbell 2013).

The most difficult stylistic legacy to assess is that of the Jesuit educational system—difficult because of the pervasive breadth and depth of its influence, which extended far beyond members of the Society of Jesus. The moderate eclecticism of Jesuit Ciceronianism is not markedly different from that employed by many Protestant authors, though it is perhaps inevitably more greatly infused with locutions from the later church fathers. The writings of Antonio Possevino (1534–1611) might stand as an exemplar of a certain kind of urbane Jesuit Latinity. For instance, his *Moscovia* (*Moscow*, 1586) is an illustrative example of ethnography, within which can be discerned the linguistic vitality of Neo-Latin authors in describing cultures and phenomena not encountered by ancient writers. Similar linguistic resourcefulness is apparent in the Jesuit letters from overseas missions, in which may be found the use of periphrasis, neologisms, Grecisms, and glossing to adapt their classicizing Latin to the task of describing things for which there was no established Latin vocabulary. None of this was, of course, unique to the Jesuits, but those who benefited from the Jesuit education system were generally among the more adept writers, so that Jesuit Latinity might best be understood in terms of *the* quality (rather than *a* quality) of their writing. Nevertheless, this is the subject of much current research, and it is certainly possible that some distinctive patterns will be discerned in Jesuit Latinity; such as, for example, the decision of some Jesuit-educated Irish writers to spell their country's name *Ibernia* rather than *Hibernia* (Caulfield 2009).

Yet, as previously intimated, a consideration of Catholic Latinity must extend into the twentieth century, not merely to include the administrative use of Latin as the official first language of the Vatican (a circumstance that now results in Latin translation—rather than original composition—of official documents), but also to include the lexicographical and journalistic work of writers such as Karl Egger (1914–2003), whose compositions are of both lexicographical and stylistic interest (Egger 1986, 1990, and 1992–1997). The appearance of such writers in the twentieth century was a testimony to what is perhaps the most important aspect of Catholic Latinity in the early modern and modern period—that it had a practical function outside the sphere of education, affording employment opportunities to new language-learners. It was this that ensured the continued vitality among Catholics of active Latin use in speech and composition outside the classroom, and it was the gradual rise of the vernacular within the institution of the Catholic Church, vestiges of which can be seen long before the Second Vatican Council, that eventually removed this institutional support for living Latin as a community language for Catholics.

SUGGESTED READING

For general coverage, see the various chapters in Part VIII ("Latin and the Church") of *ENLW* (1:719–88), which include discussion of patristics and the Reformation. Still indispensable is *CNLS*, especially 2:288–97, on theology and related disciplines. Both broad perspectives and detailed case studies can be found in Fumaroli (1980). Hsia (1998) provides much of the more pertinent cultural and historical context. O'Malley et al. (2006) is a useful point of departure for consideration of the Jesuits' cultural impact. Pullapilly (1975) discusses Baronius's life and work. For Bellarmino, Brodrick (1928) is still a valuable source of biographical information.

References

Baron, Bonaventure. 1645. *Metra Miscellanea*. Rome: Grignanus.

Baronius, Caesar. 1588–1607. *Annales Ecclesiastici*. 12 vols. Rome: Typographia Vaticana.

Bellarmino, Roberto. 1581–1593. *Disputationes de controversiis Christianae fidei*. Ingolstadt: Sartorius.

Bourdin, Bernard. (2004) 2010. *The Theological-Political Origins of the Modern State: The Controversy between James I of England and Cardinal Bellarmine*. Translated by Susan Pickford. Washington, DC: Catholic University of America Press.

Brodrick, James. 1928. *The Life and Work of Blessed Robert Francis Cardinal Bellarmine, S. J.* 2 vols. London: Burns, Oates, and Washbourne.

Campbell, Ian. 2013. *Renaissance Humanism and Ethnicity Before Race: The Irish and the English in the Seventeenth Century*. Manchester: Manchester University Press.

Casaubon, Isaac. 1614. *De Rebus Sacris et Ecclesiasticis Exercitationes XVI ad Baronii Annales*. London: Norton.

Caulfield, David. 2009. "The Scotic Debate: Philip O'Sullivan Beare and His *Tenebriomastix*." In *Making Ireland Roman: The Latin Writing of Early Modern Ireland*, edited by Jason Harris and Keith Sidwell, 109–25. Cork: Cork University Press.

Eck, Johannes. 1536. *Homilarius contra sectas*. Ingolstadt: Alexander I. Weißenhorn.

Egger, Karl. 1986. *Sermo Latinus hodiernus: Acta diurna 1982–1985*. Rome: Libreria Editrice Vaticana.

———. 1990. *Omnia Dici Possunt Latine: Acta Diurna 1986–1989*. Rome: Libreria Editrice Vaticana.

———. 1992–1997. *Lexicon recentis Latinitatis*. 2 vols. Rome: Libreria Editrice Vaticana.

Forer, Laurenz. 1624. *Lutherus Thaumaturgus*. Dillingen: Rem.

Fumaroli, Marc. 1980. *L'âge de l'éloquence: Rhétorique et* res literaria *de la Renaissance au seuil de l'époque classique*. Geneva: Droz.

Harris, Jason. 2009. "The rhetoric of history: Stephen White's *Apologia pro innocentibus Ibernis*." In *Making Ireland Roman: The Latin Writing of Early Modern Ireland*, edited by Jason Harris and Keith Sidwell, 126–53. Cork: Cork University Press.

Hill, Benjamin, and Henrik Lagerlund. 2012. *The Philosophy of Francisco Suarez*. Oxford: Oxford University Press.

Hsia, Ronnie Po-Chia. 1998. *The World of Catholic Renewal 1540–1770*. Cambridge: Cambridge University Press.

Jedin, Hubert. 1961. *A History of the Council of Trent*. Vol. 2, *The First Sessions at Trent*. Translated by Ernest Graf. London: Nelson.

Jenniges, Volfgangus. 2007. "Vox Urbis (1898–1913) quid sibi proposuerit." *Melissa* 139:8–11.

Lipsius, Justus. 1585. *De Constantia*. 2nd ed. Antwerp: Plantin.

———. 1983. *Epistolae*. Vol. 2, *1584–1587*. Edited by Marcel A. Nauwelaerts with Sylvette Sué. Brussels: Paleis der Academiën.

O'Malley, John W., Gauvin A. Bailey, Steven J. Harris, and T. Frank Kennedy, eds. 2006. *The Jesuits II: Cultures, Sciences, and the Arts, 1540–1773*. Toronto: University of Toronto Press.

Piegadi, Alessandro. 1864. *Morte del Conte Ugolino, quadro di Messer Dante Allighieri, ritratto in metro latino dal giovane messicano Uguccione Nonvrai e da altri sei celebri autori.* Venice: Piegadi.

Puckett, David L. 1995. *John Calvin's Exegesis of the Old Testament.* Columbia: Westminster John Knox Press.

Pullapilly, Cyriac. 1975. *Caesar Baronius: Counter-Reformation Historian.* Notre Dame: University of Notre Dame Press.

Rothe, David. 1619. *Analecta Sacra, Nova, et Mira. De rebus Catholicorum in Hibernia pro Fide et Religione Gestis,* 3rd ed. Cologne: Rolinus.

Scribner, Robert. 2001. *Religion and Popular Culture in Germany (1400–1800),* edited by Lyndal Roper. Leiden: Brill.

Sluhovsky, Moshe. 2007. *Believe Not Every Spirit: Possession, Mysticism, and Discernment in Early Modern Catholicism.* Chicago: University of Chicago Press.

Smeaton, William Henry Oliphant, ed. 1905. *The Return from Parnassus.* London: J.M. Dent.

Stroh, Wilfried. 2004. *Alaudae. Eine lateinische Zeitschrift 1889–1895 herausgegeben von Karl Heinrich Ulrichs. Nachdruck mit einer Einleitung von Wilfried Stroh.* Hamburg: MännerschwarmSkript Verlag.

Stanihurst, Richard. 2013. *Great Deeds in Ireland: Richard Stanihurst's De Rebus in Hibernia Gestis.* Edited by John Barry and Hiram Morgan. Cork: Cork University Press.

....

CHAPTER 21

PROTESTANTISM

....

IRENA BACKUS

THIS chapter will focus particularly on the roles attributed to the vernacular and Latin in the spreading of the Reformation message in different contexts and also on the Latin training of some of the main reformers such as Martin Luther (1483–1546), Philipp Melanchthon (1497–1560), John Calvin (1509–1564), and Théodore de Bèze (1519–1605). Special attention will be paid to the use of Latin textbooks, ancient and contemporary, in Protestant schools and universities; to the different methods of teaching Latin to Protestant youth; and to the coexistence of Latin with the vernacular. The final part of the chapter will concern itself with the education system put into operation by the Zurich reformer Heinrich Bullinger (1504–1575). Bullinger does not focus his attention on the status of Latin, but his system tells us a lot about the importance and the nature of the Latin recommended, given that it can be examined in the light of the Latin training he received and the type of Latin training he passed on during his early years as head of the cloister school at Kappel near Zurich from 1523 onwards.

There have been no studies of the specific issue of whether Protestantism—be it Lutheran, Zwinglian, or Calvinist—contributed to the renewal and reshaping of Latin in the early modern era, tending instead to favor Hebrew and Greek as the authentic biblical languages. However, recent work on the Protestant Latin Bible (especially Gordon and McLean 2012) has shown that, along with its vested interest in vernacular Bible translations, Protestantism, especially in its Calvinist manifestation, did much to promote its own Latin Bible translations intended as a replacement of and an improvement upon the Vulgate. The three most representative examples are: Robert Estienne's (1503–1559) Latin Bible of 1557; Théodore de Bèze's Greek-Latin New Testament, corrected and supplemented with new annotations over its five editions in 1557 (Latin only, published with Estienne's Latin Bible), 1565, 1582, 1588, and 1598 (the latter four all in Greek and Latin; Backus 1980, 1–8); and Immanuel Tremellius's (1510–1580) and Franciscus Junius's (1545–1602) Old Testament, published between 1575 and 1579 and reprinted in 1580 (Austin 2007). De Bèze, significantly, juxtaposed his own Latin translation of the New Testament with the Vulgate, showing the exact nature of his corrections. De Bèze attributed the Vulgate to a *vetus interpres* ("ancient translator"), not to

Jerome, as he explained in his preface to Estienne's 1557 Bible. He did not believe that Jerome was actually the Latin translator of the Vulgate, because it was full of errors, too far removed from the Greek, and unworthy of Jerome, who would never have produced such a poor piece of scholarship (de Bèze 1962, 226):

> *Nam quod istam de qua agimus Hieronymo tribuitis cum summa illius infamia coniunctum esse res ipsa clamat, quia si ita esset, necesse est fateamur Hieronymum plurima eaque manifesta errata non animadvertisse.*

> But your attribution of this translation to Jerome is pure insult to him because, if this is so, we have to say that necessarily Jerome failed to notice so many obvious errors.

De Bèze's own Latin version relies mainly on Erasmus's; departures from Erasmus and the Vulgate are indicated and justified in marginal annotations. Naturally, de Bèze, in common with many other early modern scholars, was unaware that the Greek text on which the Vulgate rested was in many ways better founded than his own Byzantine or "Eastern" text, the more recent New Testament text found in the majority of the manuscripts. Although de Bèze owned two witnesses to the earlier "Western" text, one comprising the Gospels and Acts (D or Codex Bezae), and the other the Epistles (D* or the Codex Claromontanus), he only used these minimally when establishing his own text (Backus 1980, 1–15; Krans 2006, 227–36). His Erasmian-style Latin translation was closer to classical Latin and more elegant, but not more accurate, than the Vulgate. Acts 1.3 in the 1565 Greek-Latin version of the New Testament is just one example of de Bèze's translation (de Bèze 1565, 2):

> *Quibus etiam seipsum postquam ipse passus fuit repraesentarat vivum multis indubitatis signis per dies quadraginta conspectus ab eis et dicens quae ad regnum Dei spectant.*

> And after he passed away, he manifested himself to them as alive through many sure signs, and he was seen by them for forty days and spoke of things concerning the Kingdom of God.

Compare the simpler and less classical Latin of the Vulgate:

> *Quibus et praebuit seipsum vivum post passionem suam in multis argumentis, per dies quadraginta apparens eis et loquens de regno Dei.*

> After his Passion he presented himself to them showing by many proofs that he was alive, appearing to them over a period of forty days and speaking about the Kingdom of God.

Its greater concern with translating the Bible into Latin is one of the chief hallmarks of "Reformed" Protestantism, and a feature that distinguishes it from Lutheranism, but it is not the only one. This chapter will now focus on other perhaps slightly less well-known aspects of Protestantism and Neo-Latin.

NEO-LATIN AND LUTHERANISM

In Lutheran territories, Luther's German translation of the entire Bible (1521–1534) seems to have acted as a sign to those communities that no further Latin versions were required, and commanded wide attention from the start. Luther had received basic Latin training at the local schools in Mansfeld, then in Magdeburg, and finally at Eisenach. The three schools focused on the *trivium* (grammar, rhetoric, and logic); in other words, the standard medieval curriculum, which would have involved grammar based on that of Donatus, Aristotelian logic, and Boethian rhetoric, which was subordinated to logic. While Luther obviously mastered Latin, there was nothing in his early education to qualify him as a Latin innovator. However, as has been pointed out more recently by Carl P. E. Springer among others, Luther was bilingual in Latin and German and switched from one to the other in his *Tischreden* (*Table Talks*) and other writings (Springer 2007). His most outstanding contributions to the Latin language, however, were satirical verse compositions against his religious opponents, such as the verses against Simon Lemnius (1511–1550), the Latin poet of Swiss origin, sacked by Luther from his teaching post at the University of Wittenberg for dedicating his first published collection of poetry to the Roman Catholic Albrecht of Brandenburg, and the author of the famous *Monachopornomachia* (*The Battle of Monks and Whores*, 1539), a swingeing verse satire of Luther's, his disciples', and their wives' personal morality which appeared about a year after his sacking. Luther's verses against Melanchthon's one-time disciple and student are scatological but not without wit. The poem is entitled *Dysenteria Martini Lutheri in merdipoetam Lemchen* (*Martin Luther's Flux of Dysentery Against the Excremental Poet Lemnius*): its impact depends on its varied use of the Latin term *merda* ("excrement"), as the following example amply demonstrates (Luther 1883–2009, 2.4: 89–90):

> *Quam bene conveniunt tibi res et carmina, Lemchen!*
> *Merda tibi res est, carmina merda tibi.*
> *Dignus erat Lemchen merdosus carmine merdae,*
> *Nam vatem merdae nil nisi merda decet.*
> *Infelix princeps, quem laudas carmine merdae!*
> *Merdosum merda quem facis ipse tua.*
> *Ventre urges merdam, vellesque cacare libenter.*

Lemnius, how well what you do fits in with your verses. / What you do is excrement and so are the poems you write. / I found you worthy, O excremental Lemnius, of an excremental poem, / As only excrement is suitable for the singer of excrement. / Unfortunate is the prince whom you praise with your excremental song. / The excrement you fabricate makes him defecate. / You force your belly to spout excrement and you would like to defecate it freely.

Contrary to appearances, Luther was also capable of writing lyrical poetry in Latin, and we should distinguish here between Luther's sacred and profane poetry. Self-evidently, he thought that nothing to do with the divinity should serve as the object of mockery, as shown by his verses from the first-person perspective of the Teichel spring in Wittenberg, composed ca. 1544 (Luther 1883–2009, 1.35:605):

> *Qui mare, qui fontes, qui flumina cuncta creavit,*
>   *Me quoque iussit aquae particulam esse suae.*
> *Corpore sum parvo, scatebris exilibus ortus,*
>   *Magni me sed opus glorior esse Dei.*

He who created the sea, all rivers and their sources / Also commanded me to be small part of his waters. / My body is small; I take my beginnings from a thin gush, / But I glory in being the work of the great God.

The quatrain on the death of his daughter Magdalena written in 1542 is also to be placed in the category of sacred poetry (Luther 1883–2009, 2.5:185–86):

> *Dormio cum sanctis hic Magdalena, Lutheri*
>   *Filia et hoc strato tecta quiesco meo.*
> *Filia mortis eram, peccati semine nata,*
>   *Sanguine sed vivo, Christe, redempta tuo.*

I Magdalena the daughter of Luther am asleep here / And rest in peace covered with this thin layer over me. / I was the daughter of death, born from the seed of sin, / But O Christ I live again, redeemed by your blood.

What emerges quite clearly, however, is that Luther did not think that Latin should count as the language most suitable for the text of the Bible, even though it was perfectly suitable for biblical commentaries and theological treatises, as well as for poetry, obscene or sacred.

Be that as it may, it was not Luther but his colleague Philipp Melanchthon whose predilection for poetry and drama primed the pump for the outpouring of late humanist literature in Germany (1540–1620; Fleischer 1989). The appropriation of Neo-Latin for literary purposes by German Reformation circles completed the translation of the empire of the Neo-Latin language from Italy to Germany, which had been started by Konrad Celtis, who delivered in 1492 a famous speech to students at Ingolstadt in which he called on Germans to rival Italians in learning and letters. On stage and in the battle of the books, it put the Reformation on an equal footing with, and turned the tables on, Rome. At the same time, Melanchthon's humanism provided a key to scripture, replacing the one in the hand of the papacy. The rhetorical tradition united the Protestant poet, preacher, and playwright in a cultural communication system without which the Reformation would have remained a cry in the wilderness (Fleischer 1989). What Fleischer does not say in his article but what is generally an acknowledged fact is that Melanchthon was known as the "teacher of Germany" (*praeceptor Germaniae*) and that he had a major impact on German Protestant education (Walter 1999; Maag 1999; Seigel 1968; and, most influentially, Hartfelder 1889).

Melanchthon wrote numerous treatises dealing with education and learning in which he touched on the value of ancient letters. Here I shall examine two of them: namely, the lecture *De corrigendis adolescentiae studiis* (*On Improving the Studies of Young People*) delivered in 1518 (Melanchthon 1843, 15–25) and the oration *In laudem novae scholae* (*In Praise of the New School*) delivered in 1526 (Melanchthon 1843, 106–111). In the former, he outlines his views on literature as dealing with things that pertain to the knowledge of nature and also to the forming of manners; literature, moreover, teaches one to evaluate morals according to the correct criteria, since reading the writings of other people helps one to understand what humans are like. Melanchthon explicitly distinguishes the study of humanities (*artes*) from the study of God (*theologia*) while affirming that the two are inseparable, since reading ancient literature correctly and getting to the sources of Christian civilization leads inevitably to piety and understanding of Christ's message: *Atque cum animos ad fontes contulerimus, Christum sapere incipiemus* ("When we turn our minds to the sources, we shall begin to taste Christ"; Melanchthon 1843, 23). At the same time, he warns his students not to contaminate the sacred with alien literature, referring to Titus 2.7–8 where Paul orders Christians to have steadfast faith and not to contaminate Christian with pagan writings. In fact, according to Melanchthon, one of the medieval church's main lapses was that it failed to distinguish between the profane and the holy, between Aristotelian philosophy and Christian theology. The works of God cannot be compared with the works of man, he argues, for "the perfume of the ointments of the Lord is far sweeter than the aroma of human disciplines" (Melanchthon 1843, 23). While the mouths of men speak lies continually, all truth is from God. Nevertheless, since the "sacred things are the most powerful for the mind, work and care are necessary," one must be educated in order to understand God's word and his will in our lives. Therefore, *duce Spiritu comite artium nostrarum cultu ad sacra venire licet* ("with the Spirit as leader, and the cultivation of the arts as an ally, we may approach things sacred"; Melanchthon 1843, 23). In keeping with this principle, Melanchthon proposes to his students that he begin lecturing on Homer's epic poetry and Paul's letter to Titus. The role of Latin here is crucial, as it is only by speaking good, classically founded Latin that a human can show himself to be truly educated.

The address *In laudem novae scholae* was delivered upon the opening of a new school in Nuremberg in 1526. The city's civic leaders and merchants had responded to Luther's call to establish schools, and Melanchthon begins his speech by complimenting them on their action. *In Praise of the New School* deals with the role of classical education in preparing good citizens. In the well-constituted state, says Melanchthon, "the first task for schools is to teach youth, for they are the seedbed of the city" (Melanchthon 1843, 109). A liberal education is crucial for this task, as without it "there could be no good men, no admiration of virtue, no knowledge of what is honest, no harmonious agreements concerning honest duties, no sense at all of humanity" (Melanchthon 1843, 107). As in his inaugural lecture at Wittenberg, so here, too, Melanchthon alerts his audience to the value of studying history, literature, and philosophy for the cultivation of good citizens. Melanchthon encourages parents to look beyond the obvious but simple goal of getting a job. Virtuous and noble citizens, who seek to promote the well-being of the temporal realm in which they live, are those who have studied the subjects that teach them about social life. Thus Melanchthon asks how anyone can be a good civic leader if he has never read that literature in which is contained all thought on the ruling of cities. Going beyond the practical advantages granted by schooling, Melanchthon instructs parents to encourage their children to learn about virtues, ideas, and principles. Children who will best contribute to the state are those who understand the higher goals of their vocations.

Naturally, a very considerable part of Melanchthon's educational efforts was therefore devoted to writing textbooks of Latin grammar, dialectic, and rhetoric, all of which were a huge success and went through several editions in the author's lifetime and thereafter. They also influenced curricula in new Protestant academies (providing university-level education) such as Strasbourg and, somewhat later, Geneva. As regards his Latin grammar, it was intended for beginners and, like his other textbooks, underwent very numerous editions in his lifetime, the most authoritative being the Basel edition published by Oporinus in 1553. Melanchthon defines grammar as the science of speaking and writing correctly, as it teaches not just the parts of speech but also their genders, tenses, and inflections. He goes out of his way to make the explanations as simple as possible, often resorting to verse mnemonics, such as might also help Latin beginners nowadays. Here is just one example, a hexameter intended to help memorize the genders of third declension nouns ending in *–is* in the nominative and the genitive: *Mascula sunt panis, penis, crinis, cinis, ignis* ("The following are masculine: bread, penis, hair, ash, fire"; Melanchthon 1553, 54). Grammar is intended to give children a sure way of avoiding these and similar errors, and in Melanchthon's view, it constitutes the foundation of all the other arts. It is worth noting here that Melanchthon, following the model of Cicero, establishes close links between rhetoric and dialectic, which share the common foundation of Latin. As he put it, in his *Elementa rhetorices* (*Elements of Rhetoric*, 1531), *Tanta est dialecticae et rhetoricae cognatio vix ut discrimen deprehendi possit* ("Dialectic and rhetoric are so closely related that there is hardly any difference between them"; Melanchthon 1546, 10). Some, he goes on to say, are of the opinion that dialectic "explains things as they are" (*res nudas proponit*) whereas rhetoric adds to this eloquence "as a sort of dress" (*quasi vestitum*). Melanchthon is not fundamentally opposed to this view, but he prefers to consider rhetoric as a separate study, that of eloquence. However, granted that rhetoric concerns all realms of learning and is not just limited to law or similar matters, it cannot be separated from dialectic completely, the latter being in his view, the art of teaching (*ars docendi*). Referring to Cicero's example, he distinguishes the two disciplines as that of teaching (dialectic) and that of moving and compelling one's audience or interlocutors to a particular course of action (rhetoric). He gives the example of penance. When we want to teach someone what penance is, we use the definitions, propositions that are the staple of Aristotelian dialectic, such as predicables, categories, and so on. When we want to move someone to repentance, rhetoric is the appropriate tool, whether it be as an addition to dialectic or not (Melanchthon 1546, 10–11). In short, Melanchthon, although not the first writer to do so, was nonetheless the first Protestant writer who broke with the medieval tradition of Latin as learned language and the language of logic. He linked grammar, dialectic, and rhetoric, thus moving reasoning from its medieval strictly formal mode towards the mode of living communication in the Latin that closely approximated the classical model and broke with medieval Latin neologisms.

This method of reasoning, although it could be traced back to Cicero, found its clearest expression in Rudolphus Agricola (1444–1485) and in his textbook *De inventione dialectica* (*On Dialectical Invention*, 1479; Agricola 1997; Akkerman and Vanderjagt 1997). Indeed, Melanchthon recommends Agricola often in his writings, although he separates dialectic more clearly from rhetoric than his model did. As is well known, Agricola's *De inventione dialectica*, one of the most influential, if not *the* most influential, humanist manual of the fifteenth century, assimilated the art of dialectic to that of rhetoric (Agricola 1992). Argumentation for Agricola focused, not on truth or on definitions, predicables, categories, and so on, but on what might be said with reasonable probability (Nauta 2012, 190–92). Accordingly, Agricola focused on Aristotle's *Topics* (rather than on the *Organon*, the name given to Aristotle's six works on logic), and on Cicero, but also on the writings of classical historians, poets, and orators. Thus, for Agricola, dialectic was an open field; he considered it the art of finding whatever can be said with any degree of probability on any subject. Melanchthon's distinction was clearer, as we saw, in that he identified dialectic as the part of linguistic communication that dealt with definitions and explanations, while rhetoric appealed more directly to human feelings. Even so, both Agricola and Melanchthon, with their prioritizing of the *Topics* over the *Organon*, found themselves at the antipodes of the Aristotelian and Stoic models as described by Cicero in his *Topica* 6. They followed Cicero in rejecting the Stoic model of giving dialectic a more important role than rhetoric, choosing instead to link the two disciplines. Melanchthon was the first to give this model and its approach to Latin as living language of learned communication a Protestant identity.

Neo-Latin and Calvinism

Although the Melanchthonian paradigm did also exercise an influence on Calvinist territories, and although Melanchthon was much quoted as a Christian pedagogue and Latinist, there is not much evidence that his textbooks were necessarily standard at all educational institutions. Certain features of Calvinist education were particular to its conditions, circumstances, and the public it was trying to gain. Melanchthon certainly inspired Johannes Sturm (1507–1589), the founder of the Strasbourg gymnasium and Academy (Strasbourg University from 1621; Arnold 2009), and Sturm in turn inspired Calvin and his organization of school and university education in Geneva. However, all three educators had their own preoccupations as well. Like Melanchthon, Sturm, for his part, maintained that the medieval educational model was defective in several respects, but he demarcated himself from Melanchthon by his added criticism that the medieval system did not divide pupils according to age groups and degrees of knowledge already acquired. We can read this criticism in the educational *Prospectus* (*Viewpoint*) of Claude

Baduel (d. 1561), Sturm's colleague, the founder of the school and Academy at Nîmes in 1540, who became in 1555 a minister and subsequently professor of mathematics and philosophy at Geneva (Borgeaud 1900, 26). In collaboration with Baduel, Sturm put a new model into operation and founded the modern secondary school system with linguistic training as its priority. Sturm thought that Latin should be the language of learning and instruction, as he said in his discourse on visiting the school of Lauingen in 1564 (Sturm 1995, 246):

> We want youth—all of them, including those in the lowest grades—to have Latin conversations. We do not want teachers speaking to them in their native tongue, nor will it be necessary. . . . When boys enter school, when they play, when they walk together, when they are on the way to school, their language should be Latin or Greek. Let no one come here if he is going impudently to stray in this matter.

As regards Calvin, he self-consciously copied Sturm, incorporating some elements of Baduel's pedagogy, and adding to these an innovation: following his own Latin teacher, Maturin Cordier (1479?–1564), Calvin considered that more attention should be paid to teaching Latin as a second language after the vernacular. Sturm's views notwithstanding, for Calvin the relationship between Latin and the vernacular was not to be taken for granted, and the place of Latin as the intellectually superior language was no longer guaranteed. This is no doubt why Baduel differs from Sturm in that he actually proposes a specific curriculum for the learning of Latin as a second language for his Academy of Nîmes, which was strongly oriented towards secondary education. However, some teachers went further, most notably Maturin Cordier, teacher of Latin at the Collège de la Marche in Paris around 1523, where he numbered John Calvin among his pupils. Converted to the Reformation by the humanist printer Robert Estienne, Cordier fled from France around 1536–1537 and found refuge in Geneva, where Calvin, together with the French reformer Guillaume Farel (1489–1565), was in the process of putting his Reformation program into practice. Encountering strong opposition, the two reformers were banished from the city in 1538, and Cordier left at the same time, following Farel to Neuchâtel. In 1545 he accepted the offer to direct the recently founded Protestant college in Lausanne (which offered secondary- rather than the university-level education found at the academies). He remained there until 1559, retiring from the headmastership in 1557. In 1559, the Bernese authorities dismantled both sections of the Lausanne Academy, and Calvin took this opportunity to recall Cordier and several other teachers to Geneva (Le Coultre 1926; Crousaz 2012). It is now well known that Cordier was much concerned not just with the correct method of teaching Latin—which consisted in taking the pupil's mistakes as a point of departure and gradually guiding him to write pure classical Latin—but also with the fact that Latin sentences constructed by beginners should follow the grammatical structure of correct French. In the section on Latin proverbs in his *Principia Latine loquendi et scribendi* (*Rules of Speaking and Writing Latin*, 1557), Cordier frequently gives the French equivalents as well as literal translations of the Latin; for example, the proverb *Tu cantas ante festum* is annotated both by the literal *tu chantes devant la feste* ("you are singing [prematurely] before the beginning of the celebration") and by the more idiomatic *Tu cries noel devant qu'il soit venu* ("you are shouting 'it is Christmas' before it has come"). Cordier's *Colloques en faveur des enfans qui vont à l'escole* (*Dialogues for the Benefit of Schoolchildren*), initially composed in Latin (1564), was printed as a bilingual French–Latin edition in 1598 in Geneva. Given this edition's simplicity, reliance on common classical vocabulary, and Christian moral message, which its author managed to combine successfully with as many quotations and maxims as possible from non-Christian authors of antiquity (Cottret 1995, 26–29), it is not surprising that it was used as a Latin textbook in schools in French-speaking Switzerland until the nineteenth century (Crousaz 2012, 535). Cordier indeed considered that Latin should be taught as if it were a living language, and since his *Colloquia* (*Conversations*) were organized in ascending grades of difficulty, this made them accessible to students of all levels, as illustrated by the posthumous bilingual edition. In short, whatever we may think of his attempt at reforming the study of Latin, Cordier differed fundamentally from Melanchthon and Sturm in that he tried self-consciously to adapt Latin to contemporary French conversation instead of just assuming that it ought to become his students' first language.

Calvin put Cordier and Baduel's precepts into practice for the first time in 1541, when he was recalled from exile in Strasbourg to become the city's undisputed religious leader and submitted to the Council his projected church ordinances. In the paragraph devoted to the doctors "whom our Lord has instituted to govern his church," he pointed out that Geneva should establish a school or schools whose task it was to oversee and inculcate a solid education based on Christian principles. Granting that a knowledge of the Bible and theology is the most important acquisition in the realm of knowledge, Calvin thought nonetheless that a good grounding in the humanities was indispensable to all future theologians and ministers, which is why he wanted to found both a secondary school and a (university-level) theological Academy in Geneva on the model of Strasbourg and, to some extent, of Lausanne, intended not only for theologians but also for the future governing classes. Calvin's project was ready by 1541 but would not be fully implemented until 1559. The curriculum of the secondary school was very similar to Strasbourg's but was also inspired by Baduel's and Cordier's methodology of teaching Latin in conjunction with Christian morals. The youngest children in the seventh grade began by learning to read and write Latin and French; the sixth-graders learned the basis of Latin declension and conjugation; the following year, they were instructed in Latin syntax with Virgil's *Eclogues* as the textbook. The fourth-graders learned the refinements of syntax with the aid of the shortest and the simplest of Cicero's letters, as well as the art of translating into Latin and versification using Ovid's elegies as models. The fourth-graders also began to learn Greek which they were supposed to have mastered well enough by the following year to devote that to stylistic exercises in Greek and Latin. The two final years were devoted to the study of Greek and Latin authors and to the study of dialectic, where Cicero's *Paradoxes* and his speeches served as the set texts. Interestingly, students at this stage were expressly discouraged from learning rhetoric, a feature that distinguished the Genevan from the Strasbourg and the Melanchthonian paradigms (Borgeaud 1900, 28–38).

BULLINGER AND THE ZURICH MODEL

The Zurich reformer Heinrich Bullinger (1504–1575) did not give any indication of how Latin should be taught in his 1527 *Studiorum ratio* (*How to Study*; Bullinger 1987). However, his *Diary* does provide us with detailed information on how he learned Latin (Bullinger [1904] 1985). Moreover, as we shall see, his pedagogical activities at the Kappel school show us how he taught Latin and how he combined Latin and the vernacular.

In his *Von warer und falscher leer* (*Of True and False Learning*, 1527) Bullinger openly expresses his approval of Greek and Latin philologists, starting with Manuel Chrysoloras (ca. 1355–1415), the author of the first Greek grammar published in Western Europe, and moving on to Cardinal Bessarion and Theodorus Gaza, who, in his view, took up the task of renewing Greek studies in the same way that Lorenzo Valla, Niccolò Perotti, Ermolao Barbaro, Angelo Poliziano, and Filippo Beroaldo renewed the study of Latin. Bullinger has particular praise to spare for Valla's biblical endeavors, exaggerating vastly when he states that Valla was "the first after Jerome" to have translated the New Testament from Greek into Latin. Bullinger concludes that this was a clear sign from God that he had renewed the study of languages so that "his holy word would at last be well understood" (Staedtke 1962, 16–30 and 31). In the same work, Bullinger is more matter-of-fact about Erasmus (cited according to Staedke 1962, 34–35):

> The very learned Erasmus has, with incredible industry in both languages, Latin and Greek, treated the New Testament with particular rigor and fidelity. He was the first to translate it after Valla and Lefèvre d'Étaples. He drove, politely but with great force, barbarism, sophistry and scholasticism out of theology and led it back to the languages and the ancient Fathers. He also made their writings available to us in an elegant form, as did the very learned Beatus Rhenanus after him. It is therefore fitting that we should acknowledge very openly our gratitude to Erasmus for having been of great help to us and for his constancy and labors. However, we should thank God first from whom we have everything that we possess and whom we would no doubt make very angry if we spoke ill of the highly deserving Erasmus. May God preserve him for as long as he needs him.

This passage echoes the mechanics of Bullinger's own conversion after he abandoned the scholastics in favor of the church fathers and the Bible. However, more importantly, it shows us why the reformer erected the myth of Renaissance humanism, and therefore, implicitly, of its Latin, as the forerunner of the Reformation. In his view, the rediscovery of the ancient languages led to the emergence of literary criticism, which in turn permitted the revision of the biblical text, new translations, and a renewal of interest in the Fathers whose works, once available, showed up the *lacunae* in scholastic collections of patristic texts.

Despite his respect for the Italian education system, Bullinger never studied there himself. His own early education was based on grammar and Latin literature and could be considered humanist only insofar as a relatively small part of it was given over to the study of dialectic, but it differed from the humanist approach in including only a little Greek and no rhetoric. According to his *Diary* (started in 1541, and ended shortly before his death), he attended the Latin school in Emmerich between 1516 and 1519, which was under the influence of the German humanist Alexander Hegius of Deventer (ca. 1440–1498). Bullinger studied Latin grammar and literature: he mentions Donatus and Aldo Manuzio's grammars, and, as set reading, singles out selections from Pliny's, Cicero's, and Jerome's letters, as well as poems by Virgil, Horace, and Mantuan (1447–1516). The daily program included many grammatical exercises and much parsing; pupils were expected to speak Latin daily (*Perpetuo loquendum Latine*), to compose one Latin letter per week (*Singulis vero hebdomadis singulae formandae erant epistolae*); and Bullinger remembers the discipline as being severe (*Disciplina quoque adhibebatur severa*; Bullinger [1904] 1985, 2–3). His teachers were all impregnated by the spirit of Northern humanism filtered through the modern devotion (*devotio moderna*), which went back to Hegius, Murmellius, and others (Bullinger [1904] 1985, 3).

In other words, Bullinger's earliest education was not very different from that received by Erasmus at Deventer some twenty years earlier. However, it did not correspond to the ideal of humanist education as Erasmus conceived of it in *De recta pronuntiatione* (*On Correct Pronunciation*, 1528) and *De pueris instituendis* (*On Education for Boys*, 1529). As we know, Erasmus was against severe discipline, and advocated a wide curriculum for even the youngest schoolchildren, who were to acquire a thorough knowledge of Greek and Latin and rhetoric, the rudiments of dialectic, a thorough knowledge of geography, and a smattering of arithmetic, music, astrology, and medicine (Chomarat 1981, 1, 162–63). They were to be initiated, namely, in the seven liberal arts, geometry constituting the sole exception. This broad-based system was much more reminiscent of the Italian curriculum than the education Bullinger received (Grendler 1989).

After enrolling at the University of Cologne in 1519, the future reformer joined the *Bursa Montis* (Thomist college) where he was plunged into the medieval system in the full sense of the word. Indeed, judging by the *Diary* entry for July 8, 1519, he exclusively studied the logical works of Peter of Spain and some Aristotle (*Petri Hispani tractatus, Parva logicalia . . . Aristotelica quaedam*), as well as the textbook written by the college masters, *Copulata omnium tractatuum parvarum logicalium Petri Hispani tribus adiectis modernorum tractatibus* (*The Tying-Together of All the Short Treatises of Peter of Spain on Logic with Three Treatises by Modern Authors*, 1498; Bullinger [1904] 1985, 4). However, scholastic logic was not the sole object of academic attention at Cologne. It was only at this point that Bullinger turned to what he calls *humaniora studia*, which included lectures on Erasmus's *De copia* (*On Copiousness*), Agricola's *De inventione dialectica*, Cicero, Virgil, Paul's *Epistle to the Romans*, an introduction to Greek literature, and so on. At the same time, he read Quintilian, Pliny, Homer, and various writings of Erasmus for himself, and began composing letters, speeches, dialogues, and what he calls *fictas narrationes* ("fictional narratives"). Joachim Staedtke has reconstructed Bullinger's early attempts at reading and writing Latin, noting among other topics his interest in Prudentius and his own versified harmony of the Gospel accounts of the Passion, entitled *Passio domini nostri Jesu Christi* (*The Passion of Our Lord Jesus Christ*; Staedtke 1962, 261–92; Bullinger [1904] 1985, 7–10; Backus 2007).

In other words, Bullinger's *studia humanitatis* were filtered largely through German humanists and through Erasmus's works. He never produced any classical editions or commentaries worth a mention; his literary compositions never came to much; and the study of rhetoric never played much of a part in his education. However, there is no doubt that he was strongly influenced by the humanist method of reading, and that after his unhappy encounter with the scholastic methods of the *Bursa Montis*, he opted to study original works in their entirety and to analyze their language and style. Moreover, since turning to the *studia humanitatis* exposed him to Paul's *Epistle to the Romans* alongside pagan literature, he would have seen how reading scripture could also benefit from humanist methods of reading classical authors. As he says in the *Studiorum ratio* in 1527/8 (Bullinger 1987, 58):

> These studies [of profane letters] lead to the study of sacred letters, as is known to all those who have ever dealt with the holy scripture. . . . They also make men wise as they can seek sage counsel in them. This wisdom could be observed in the past in the Roman Senate, which assembled men that were extremely learned and very wise such as Cicero, Cato, Caesar, Portius, and others. The Senate did nothing rash, nothing it could be ashamed of, nothing imprudent or regrettable. Indeed these studies make you so wise that practically no aspect of knowledge in human affairs is anything but most familiar to you. They improve morals, they plant honesty and a love of what is good. They give an aversion to what is bad. They also make your household pleasant and charming. That is why they are called humanities and fine literature (*humanae et bonae litterae*).

Beyond the usefulness of profane studies for sacred letters, Bullinger makes the point that *bonae litterae* serve the purpose of making us into humans and inculcating the right values. In his view, we can only study scripture if we are good human beings, as he wrote in the *Studiorum ratio* in the chapter devoted to sacred letters (Bullinger 1987, 58):

> Those who practice the art of oratory, require that the orator be a good man as it is unseemly that such an honest skill resides in a wicked and dishonest heart. It is therefore all the more appropriate that we require from the candidates in holy scripture a spirit of devotion to God, a mind clear of all dirt, and morals which are exempt from all impurity.

These qualities, which all theology candidates must possess, are acquired via studying profane letters, which thus constitutes an integral part of becoming a true Christian. In his emphasis on man's humanity, which he sees as essential to his handling of matters divine, Bullinger, like Melanchthon, appeals directly to the humanist ethical model without emitting the caveats articulated by Maturin Cordier on the differences between pagan and Christian morality.

Bullinger's method for teaching Latin was full-fledged by the time he was nineteen years old and reached Kappel in January 1523. He did not abandon profane for sacred letters at that stage, but the Kappel program instead shows that he saw the two disciplines as mutually complementary. His elementary curriculum at Kappel has only Donatus's *Grammar* in common with the one he had followed as a schoolboy at Emmerich. Bullinger replaced the authors he had studied with Cato's distichs, a few books of the *Aeneid*, and several works by Erasmus. The latter included *De constructione octo partium orationis* (*Of the Construction of the Eight Parts of Discourse*, 1513) written by William Lily for St. Paul's School at John Colet's request, then revised by Erasmus, a manual of syntax known for its simplicity and for incorporating humanist principles into the basic rules of syntax elaborated by the ancient grammarians Priscian and Diomedes. Its chief feature was its anti-Aristotelianism: by according greater importance to the verb than to the noun in a Latin sentence, it weakened the central position of the concept of substance (Bullinger [1904] 1985, 7; Chomarat 1981, 1:267–90). Bullinger also used Erasmus's *Colloquies*, and his *De copia*. By replacing traditional textbooks and authors with humanist material, Bullinger simplified the task of learning Latin and made it more agreeable, fully in keeping with humanist principles (Bullinger [1904] 1985, 7–10; Bullinger 1991).

Of all the reformers we have examined, Bullinger shows the clearest evidence of Erasmus's direct influence, which did not stop him from lecturing in the vernacular on the Bible, as his Kappel writings show (Bullinger [1904] 1985, 10). Although he did inevitably have recourse to Melanchthon's theological writings, he does not seem to have been overtly influenced by the Wittenberger's grammatical, dialectical, and rhetorical literary works, although he shared Melanchthon's respect for antiquity as a source of moral values.

Conclusions

It is not easy to draw any general conclusions about Protestantism's input into and dependence on Neo-Latin. As I have argued, it was Melanchthon who first gave a Protestant identity to what was basically Ciceronian Latin adapted to contemporary circumstances, and to Agricola's model of reasoning. Melanchthon's influence, while wide, was not universal; we have seen that it bypassed Zurich, where Bullinger seems to have preferred to draw directly on Erasmus's Latin while retaining respect for Melanchthon's theological writings and sharing his high opinion of pagan values. Judging by his early attempts at writing verses on Christ's Passion, Bullinger was not averse to using Latin—not for scatological, satirical poetry as Luther did, but for sacred poetry and biblical adaptations. As for the Genevan paradigm, if we go by Maturin Cordier's example, Cordier's input was twofold: on the one hand, he took into account the fact that not Latin but French was his pupils' first language and adapted his textbooks accordingly; on the other, unlike Bullinger, he did not feel that classical learning automatically improved morality, and issued warnings about some of the pagan models. His manuals, accordingly, are characterized by a relatively large number of Christian examples, while not neglecting pagan authors altogether. If there is a general conclusion to draw, it is that Protestantism needed Latin, and humanist Latin particularly, to affirm itself as a serious alternative to Catholicism. While certain adaptations to the language and to Greco-Roman concepts of civilization were necessary, Latin alone, revised according to the humanist model, could provide the sort of weight and profile that would make the entire religious movement internationally conspicuous and give it a unity and a catholicity, both of which would be lost if Latin were replaced by a multitude of vernacular languages.

SUGGESTED READING

A standard reference for the work of Calvin, Melanchthon, and Zwingli is the *Corpus Reformatorum* (1834–) which currently runs to 108 volumes in Latin, French, and German. Hillerbrand (1996) is a useful reference work; see Springer (2014) for a recent survey. Scribner, Porter, and Teich (1994), Opitz (2013), and Selderhuis (2013) are collections relevant to this topic; Green (2009) contains several chapters on Latin in Protestant education. For early Protestantism in general, see Chadwick (2001); for Calvin, see (e.g.) Lane (1999); for Bullinger, see Gordon and Campi (2004). Bloemendal and Norland (2013) discuss Protestant school drama; Ohlemacher (2010) demonstrates the underestimated relevance of Latin for Protestant (Lutheran) catechesis.

REFERENCES

Agricola, Rudolphus. 1992. *De inventione dialectica libri tres.* Edited by Lothar Mundt. Tübingen: Niemeyer.

———. 1997. *Écrits sur la dialectique et l'humanisme.* Edited and translated by Marc van der Poel. Paris: Champion.

Akkerman, Fokke, and Arie J. Vanderjagt, eds. 1997. *Rodolphus Agricola Phrisius (1444–1485).* Leiden: Brill.

Arnold, Matthieu, ed. 2009. *Johannes Sturm (1507–1589): Rhetor, Pädagoge und Diplomat.* Tübingen: Mohr Siebeck.

Austin, Kenneth. 2007. *From Judaism to Calvinism: The Life and Writings of Immanuel Tremellius (1510–1580).* Aldershot: Ashgate.

Backus, Irena. 1980. *The Reformed Roots of the English New Testament: The Influence of Theodore Beza on the English New Testament.* Pittsburgh: Pickwick.

———. 2007. "Bullinger and Humanism." In *Heinrich Bullinger: Life—Thought—Influence,* edited by Emidio Campi and Peter Opitz, vol. 2, 637–59. Zurich: Theologischer Verlag.

Bloemendal, Jan, and Howard B. Norland, eds. 2013. *Neo-Latin Drama: Contexts, Contents and Currents.* Leiden: Brill.

Borgeaud, Charles. 1900. *L'Histoire de l'Université de Genève 1559–1956.* Vol. 1, *L'Académie de Calvin,* 1559–1798. Geneva: Georg.

Bullinger, Heinrich. (1904) 1985. *Diarium (Annales vitae) der Jahre 1504–1574*. Edited by Emil Egli. Basel: Basler Buch- und Antiquariatshandlung.

———. 1987. *Studiorum ratio*. 2 vols. Edited by Peter Stotz. Zurich: Theologischer Verlag.

———. 1991. *Theologische Schriften*. Vol. 2, *Unveröffentlichte Schriften der Kappeler Zeit*. Edited by Hans G. vom Berg, Bernhard Schneider, and Endre Zsindely. Zurich: Theologischer Verlag.

Chadwick, Owen. 2001. *The Early Reformation on the Continent*. Oxford: Oxford University Press.

Chomarat, Jacques. 1981. *Grammaire et rhétorique chez Érasme*. 2 vols. Paris: Belles Lettres.

Cottret, Bernard. 1995. *Calvin: Biographie*. Paris: Lattès.

Crousaz, Karine. 2012. *L'Académie de Lausanne entre Humanisme et Réforme (ca. 1537–1560)*. Leiden: Brill.

De Bèze, Théodore. 1565. *Jesu Christi Novum Testamentum Graece et Latine Theodoro Beza interprete*. Geneva: Stephanus.

———. 1962. *Correspondance*. Vol. 2, *1556–1558*. Edited by Fernand Auber, Alain Dufour, and Henri Meylan. Geneva: Droz.

Fleischer, Manfred. 1989. "Melanchthon as Praeceptor of Late-Humanist Poetry." *The Sixteenth Century Journal* 20:559–80.

Gordon, Bruce, and Emidio Campi, eds. 2004. *Architect of Reformation: An Introduction to Heinrich Bullinger, 1504–1575*. Grand Rapids: Baker Academic.

Gordon, Bruce, and Matthew McLean, eds. 2012. *Shaping the Bible in the Reformation: Books, Scholars and Their Readers in the Sixteenth Century*. Leiden: Brill.

Green, Ian. 2009. *Humanism and Protestantism in Early Modern English Education*. Farnham: Ashgate.

Grendler, Paul. 1989. *Schooling in Renaissance Italy*. Baltimore: Johns Hopkins University Press.

Hartfelder, Karl. 1889. *Philipp Melanchthon als Praeceptor Germaniae*. Berlin: Hofmann.

Hillerbrand, Hans J., ed. 1996. *The Oxford Encyclopaedia of the Reformation*. 4 vols. New York: Oxford University Press.

Krans, Jan. 2006. *Beyond What Is Written: Erasmus and Beza as Conjectural Critics of the New Testament*. Leiden: Brill.

Lane, Anthony N. S. 1999. *John Calvin: Student of the Church Fathers*. Edinburgh: T. and T. Clark.

Le Coultre, Jules. 1926. *Maturin Cordier et les origines de la pédagogie protestante dans les pays de langue française*. Neuchâtel: Université de Neuchâtel.

Luther, Martin. 1883–2009. *D. Martin Luthers Werke*. 127 vols. Prepared under various editors. Weimar: Böhlau.

Maag, Karen, ed. 1999. *Melanchthon in Europe: His Work and Influence Beyond Wittenberg*. Grand Rapids: Baker.

Melanchthon, Philipp. 1546. *Elementorum rhetorices libri duo*. Cologne: Gymnicus.

———. 1553. *Grammatica Latina*. Basel: Oporinus.

———. 1843. *Corpus Reformatorum*. Vol. 11, *Declamationes Philippi Melanchthonis usque ad annum 1552*. Edited by Karl G. Bretschneider. Halle: Schwetschke.

Nauta, Lodi. 2012. "From Universals to Topics: The Realism of Rudolph Agricola." *Vivarium* 50:190–224.

Ohlemacher, Andreas. 2010. *Lateinische Katechetik der frühen lutherischen Orthodoxie*. Göttingen: Vandenhoeck and Ruprecht.

Opitz, Peter, ed. 2013. *The Myth of the Reformation*. Göttingen: Vandenhoeck and Ruprecht.

Scribner, Bob, Roy Porter, and Mikulás Teich, eds. (1994). *The Reformation in National Context*. Cambridge: Cambridge University Press.

Seigel, Jerrold. 1968. *Rhetoric and Philosophy in Renaissance Humanism: The Union of Eloquence and Wisdom, Petrarch to Valla*. Princeton: Princeton University Press.

Selderhuis, Herman J., ed. 2013. *A Companion to Reformed Orthodoxy*. Leiden: Brill.

Springer, Carl P. E. 2007. "Martin's Martial: Reconsidering Luther's Relationship with the Classics." *International Journal of the Classical Tradition* 14:23–50.

——. 2014. *The Reformation*. In *ENLW*, 1:747–58.

Staedtke, Joachim. 1962. *Die Theologie des jungen Bullinger*. Zurich: Theologischer Verlag.

Sturm, Johannes. 1995. "For the Lauingen School." In *Johann Sturm on Education: The Reformation and Humanist Learning*, edited and translated by Lewis W. Spitz and Barbara Sher Tinsley, 199–254. St. Louis: Concordia.

Walter, Peter. 1999. "Melanchthon und die Tradition der *studia humanitatis*." *Zeitschrift für Kirchengeschichte* 110:191–208.

CHAPTER 22

....

POLITICAL ACTION

....

MARC LAUREYS

In this chapter, I will consider the role and function of Neo-Latin language and literature (and its constant recourse to the classical tradition) as an instrument of political power, more specifically for the representation, negotiation, and legitimization of political power, understood as a social practice pursued by various actors in a wide range of possible communicative contexts. In this sense, Neo-Latin is a medium of political communication, to be compared with ceremonial, ritual, and protocol, as well as (both permanent and ephemeral) architecture, monuments, works of art, or other kinds of ornaments, and even musical performances: like the linguistic medium of Neo-Latin, all these artistic resources were exploited as vehicles of a political message, meant to display and confirm, and, much less often, to subvert, societal structures and relations of power and authority. The oral and nonverbal, as opposed to written, variants of such ritualized communication have been studied for many years, above all in Münster, under the general label of "symbolic communication" (Althoff and Siep 2000; Stollberg-Rilinger 2004).

The most important actors, who laid the basis of this political communication in Latin during the early modern age, were Renaissance humanists who proved to be exquisite propagators of political power because of their specific linguistic, literary, and scholarly expertise, variously made serviceable for political action. Several humanists adopted political functions as statesmen, secretaries, or advisers, most often in secular or clerical courts, but also in republican settings. Many humanists also expressed their political ideas in their writings, not infrequently proffering different ideas at different stages of their careers, depending on the specific context or occasion at hand, which has sparked modern scholarly debate about the nature and degree of their political convictions, most famously in connection with civic humanism (Herde 1965; Seigel 1966; Baron 1967). Finally, they strove to educate the future political elite on the basis of their program of "humanist studies" (*studia humanitatis*), at first above all in their own schools, and later—as the influence of the humanist movement widened—in the existing system of secondary and higher education, too.

Political thought and action became closely associated with Renaissance humanism for another reason as well: ever since antiquity it had been intimately connected with or even subsumed under moral philosophy, which Renaissance humanists integrated into their canon of *studia humanitatis*. Over the course of the sixteenth and seventeenth centuries, humanist scholars gradually shifted the focus of political thought from the theory of the forms and functions of political structures to a description and analysis of political reality from the perspective of the political actor (e.g., Burke 1991). This change in orientation went hand-in-hand with a renewed interest in the ancient historians Tacitus (first–second centuries CE) and Polybius (second century BCE), who were felt to be expert guides in the hidden mechanisms and strategies of political power and government (the *arcana imperii* ["secrets of the empire"], as Tacitus had called them in his *Annals*, 2.36.1). In this context, the notion of prudence (*prudentia*), originally derived from Aristotle's *Nicomachean Ethics* 6 (1140a24–1145a11)—*phronēsis* (practical wisdom) as opposed to *sophia* (speculative wisdom)—and established by patristic authors as one of the cardinal virtues, encapsulated the necessary qualities and prerequisites of political action. Gradually, however, this concept of *prudentia* became associated ever more closely with the "reason of state" (*ratio status*) and entirely or partially dissociated from its original ethical background (Münkler 1998). Niccolò Machiavelli (1469–1527) was the first political thinker who radically disconnected ethics and politics and advocated a morally indifferent understanding of the reason of state. Justus Lipsius (1547–1606), in turn, proposed the idea of a "mixed prudence" (*prudentia mixta*), in which the balance between political pragmatism and morality may be adjusted according to specific circumstances.

Prudentia as a leading principle of political action was primarily designed for the absolute monarch and his acquisition and preservation of power. The principal institutional context of *prudentia* was, therefore, the early modern court and its hierarchies, regulations, competition, and intrigues. Here the early modern "politician" (*politicus*)—that is, adviser, emissary, or other official in a ruler's entourage—arose (Till 2003); it should be noted, though, that the term itself in this early modern sense, signifying a political and administrative elite in a court environment, suffered for a long time from negative connotations (Weber 2004). A crucial part of the political action in this context was communication between the ruler and his collaborators in his courtly household. Here again, Tacitus was advanced—most prominently by Justus Lipsius—as a model author who perfectly illustrated the techniques of "simulation" and "dissimulation" (*simulatio* and *dissimulatio*; Tacitus, *Annals* 4.71.3) as well as the characteristics of the "imperial conciseness" (*imperatoria brevitas*; Tacitus, *Histories* 1.18.2), all necessary qualities of successful political communication (Geitner 1992, 10–106; Jansen 1995). Designed as rules for communicative interaction in the political sphere, these principles spilled over into more general theories of conduct in a court environment or even "courteous" behavior in society at large; this crossover merely continued the tradition of a "rhetorical" conception of courtly conversation, manners, and etiquette, expressed in courtesy books ever since the late Middle Ages, but increasingly influential after the publication of works such as Baldassare Castiglione's *Cortegiano* (1528) and Giovanni della Casa's *Galateo* (1558) (Göttert 1988; Beetz 2012).

Renaissance humanists were certainly not the only contemporary theorists of political thought, nor can every political action in the period be explained through Renaissance humanism. Yet it is clear that new developments then in both the theory and practice of politics were triggered to an important extent by the intellectual and cultural renewal brought about by the humanist movement, and more specifically by its revalorization of the Latin language and the classical tradition.

LATIN LANGUAGE AND CLASSICAL LEARNING AS AN INSTRUMENT OF EARLY MODERN POLITICAL DISCOURSE

By placing the comprehensive restoration of classical Latin at the center of their program for educational and cultural renewal, humanists created the basis for associating Latin with a political and cultural ideology. Lorenzo Valla (1407–1457) offered the most famous Quattrocento praise of Latin in his *Elegantiae linguae Latinae* (*On How to Achieve Elegance in the Latin Language*, written in the 1440s): Valla claimed that

> peoples and nations have since long cast off the Roman Empire as a cumbersome burden; they considered its language, however, sweeter than all nectar, more splendid than all silk, and more precious than all gold and pearls, and kept it with them as a kind of god sent down from heaven. . . . So wherever the Roman language rules, the Roman Empire continues to exist. (Garin 1952, 596)

To Valla's mind, the universal supremacy of the language of Rome fully compensated for the loss of the political primacy of the city of Rome. Accordingly, he saw Latin as the cornerstone of an all-embracing cultural ideology.

The humanists' search for the perfect mastery of classical Latin soon led to a debate concerning the best style and the most valuable models, upon which almost no medieval Latin author had ever reflected (Leonhardt 2009, 186–200). But stylistic currents are not about style alone: classical authors were not merely literary models who displayed specific styles, forms, techniques, and concepts, their works also carried specific political and cultural notions. In two distinct phases of the early modern debate surrounding the best Latin style—Ciceronianism and Tacitism, respectively—the theory and practice of Latin was explicitly linked with political ideology.

For the High Renaissance papacy, the propagation of a Ciceronian standard of language and style in official documents and literary works was an integral part of their political ideology: the popes defined and fashioned themselves as the sole rightful heirs to the Augustan legacy, in which Cicero's writings had become the unrivaled standard for Latin prose. Cicero, who was felt to incarnate the perfect synthesis between eloquence (*eloquentia*) and wisdom (*sapientia*), had always received pride of place in the humanist canon of model authors. In the course of the fifteenth century, other stylistic models, such as Apuleius, and a more eclectic approach were advanced, but Cicero's preeminence was never fundamentally challenged. By the beginning of the sixteenth century, Roman humanists, such as Pietro Bembo (1470–1547) and Jacopo Sadoleto (1477–1547), who were closely linked to the papal curia, firmly established—along the lines suggested by Lorenzo Valla—the Ciceronian norm as a token of the cultural imperialism of the Renaissance papacy. Rather than opting for a Latinity nourished by various sources, they advocated a strictly Ciceronian style associated with the most prominent period of Roman culture, during which the foundations of its imperial power were laid. Early Christian authors, such as Lactantius and Augustine, had shown how Christian wisdom could be couched in Ciceronian diction and how Ciceronian Latin helped shape the cultural identity of Christianity (Hankins 2003). During the Counter-Reformation, scholars such as Pompeo Ugonio (d. 1614), professor of rhetoric at the Sapienza University in Rome, or the Jesuit Melchior Inchofer (1584–1648), who composed a *Historia sacrae Latinitatis* (*History of Sacred Latinity*, 1635), similarly saw Ciceronian Latin as a privileged ideological instrument, this time associated with Roman Catholicism. These authors saw a spiritual bond between the brilliance of pure Latin and its singular role as language of the church, and emphasized its continued cultivation as a necessary prerequisite for safeguarding the past legacy and future mission of Catholicism (Laureys 2000 and 2003).

From the late sixteenth through the late seventeenth century, Ciceronianism was challenged by Tacitism, a tradition sparked by close attention to the style and content of Tacitus's *Annals* and *Histories*. An earlier interest in Tacitus had already emerged among German humanists in the early sixteenth century who drew on Tacitus's *Germania* to construct their idea of a "German nation." In the more specific form first advanced by Justus Lipsius, however, Tacitism is a phenomenon in which style is linked with political concept. Convinced of a *similitudo temporum* ("resemblance of times") between Tacitus's era and his own, Lipsius drew his ideas about political ethics from Tacitus, who depicted in his historical writing *velut theatrum hodiernae vitae* ("as it were a spectacle of modern-day life"; Lipsius 1978, 256 [dedication of his commentary to Tacitus of 1581]). Lipsius was convinced that Tacitus's analysis of the turbulent times of the early principate could advise him how best to respond to the turmoils in his own time and instruct the ruling elite how to perform its public duties in challenging circumstances. Tacitus, moreover, taught not only how to behave and govern, but also how to speak: to Lipsius's mind, Tacitus's nervous and pointed style, marked by brevity (*brevitas*) and aphorisms (*sententiae*), fitted perfectly the political and moral ideas he wanted to convey (Laureys 2014a).

Strict Ciceronians and Tacitists serving in political offices or writing for the political elite were convinced that Latin carried a political message and was thus the most effective linguistic medium for the representation and legitimization of power, in its evocation not only of the literary, but also of the political legacy of classical Rome. But also beyond the Latin style, classical learning was exploited as a source of political wisdom and inspiration for political action. As basic reading techniques and strategies, Renaissance humanists developed, practiced, and taught a specific method for extracting relevant information from classical authors. In the humanistic school curriculum, students were trained to collect and store information by excerpting texts according to specific thematic categories and compiling this material in so-called commonplace-books (Moss 1996). Reading techniques thus became tools of both analysis and composition of texts. Using this pragmatic approach, moral *sententiae* and *exempla* pertaining to *virtus* ("virtue") and *prudentia*, for instance, could be methodically drawn from classical authors and conveniently reused in new texts; so reading and annotating such authors, particularly historians, helped prepare one for a career in politics. Gabriel Harvey, for instance, oriented his reading of Livy consistently towards political action (Grafton and Jardine 1990): in the marginalia of his copy of Livy, Harvey singled out political ideas, which he thought could be useful to those either holding or aspiring to a political, diplomatic, or military office. By absorbing ancient history and moral philosophy so systematically, an attentive reader was expected to distill from these authoritative texts political and moral lessons that would enable him to understand the rise and fall of world empires, shape his views of state and government, and master political tactics.

From the early Renaissance onwards, philological, antiquarian, and historical scholarship was put to political use. Renaissance humanists succeeded brilliantly not only in recovering antiquity as a golden age of wisdom and beauty, but also in convincing rulers throughout Europe of the political force of classical models and values. In addition, they demonstrated and taught valuable methodical skills, from mastering Latin and interpreting critically ancient sources, to showing literary and rhetorical virtuosity in written and oral communication.

Besides training elite pupils to become eloquent and virtuous statesmen, they also sought from the outset to make their mark in centers of political power by capitalizing on their own erudition and experience (Enenkel 2012a). The political dimension and potential of humanism appear as early as in the work of its first torchbearer, Petrarch (1304–1374), whose philological approach to the classical authors and new sense of the past paved the way for a revalorization of the classical legacy in early modern political thought. One specific example shows Petrarch demonstrating the subversive power of philological scrutiny in politics: when in 1360 the Emperor Charles IV asked Petrarch to verify the authenticity of the so-called *Henricianum*, a charter that purportedly placed Austria outside the jurisdiction of the German Empire due to privileges allegedly granted by Julius Caesar and Nero, Petrarch unmasked this document as a forgery (*Seniles* 16.5; Petrarch 2004–2010, 3:2106–21). Petrarch's exposure of the *Henricianum* clearly anticipated Lorenzo Valla's much more famous demolition of the "Donation of Constantine" about a century later. The penetrating force of humanistic scholarship was felt even more clearly in the political-religious conflicts of the sixteenth century, when, after the rise of the Protestant Reformation, two opposing camps both claimed a special relationship with the historical foundations of the Christian faith, which they were eager to document and analyze using a wealth of sources (e.g., Backus 2003; van Liere, Ditchfield, and Louthan 2012).

Humanistic learning, however, served more often to celebrate and consolidate rather than undermine political power. Towards the end of his life, Petrarch associated himself with Francesco da Carrara (1325–1393), Lord of Padua, and dedicated to him one of the later versions of his *De viris illustribus* (*On Illustrious Men*), which directly inspired the iconographic program of classical "uomini famosi" in the *sala illustrium virorum* ("hall of illustrious men") of Palazzo Carrara (1370s), and characterized Francesco himself as illustrious man, incorporating him into an ancient tradition of heroes and political role models (e.g., Donato 1985, 103–24). Similar forms of cooperation in a context of patronage and clientelism are legion throughout the Renaissance. Petrarch's historical writings celebrate the unique luster of Roman history, first presented to an Italian readership that Petrarch hoped would revive this magnificent tradition (Keßler 1978). Nearly all subsequent humanistic historiography was similarly meant as a guidebook for political action, based on the principles of classical Roman morality and inspired by the great protagonists of ancient history and their glorious achievements.

Petrarch's idea of Rome, therefore, is closely connected with a notion of the Italian nation as sole heir of ancient Rome's legacy, and diametrically opposed to foreign "barbarians," who never had had any part in Roman culture and needed to be repelled just as Roman ancestors once fought back Gauls, Goths, Huns, and others. This eminently humanistic construction of nationhood, defined on moral and cultural rather than ethnic grounds, was appropriated in various ways by Italian humanists of the fifteenth century and provoked the rise of nationalistic discourses north of the Alps from the early sixteenth century on (Hirschi 2005 and 2012, 119–211). In the multinational, multilingual Habsburg Empire, in turn, Latin helped construct a common political identity, against the background of the rise of national awareness and vernacular languages throughout the Habsburg lands; since the Holy Roman emperors saw and presented themselves as heirs of the ancient Roman imperial tradition, it was only natural for them to build their political ideology on the classical tradition (Tanner 1993; Burke 1999; Römer 2002; Klecker 2002).

In the course of the early modern age, more specialized applications of classical learning in a political context emerged: for instance, the Tacitist movement was furthered not only by innovative texts and studies, such as collections of political aphorisms and treatises on the reason of state, but also by "political commentaries" on the works of Tacitus. The first such commentary was published in 1581 by the Piemontese Carlo Pasquale (Charles Pascal, 1547–1625), who eventually allied himself with the French royal court of Henri III and Henri IV: Pasquale approached Tacitus not merely as a historiographer of the early principate, but above all as a political adviser who revealed governance's hidden workings and the techniques of political manipulation required to secure power in a challenging environment (Momigliano 1955). Such political commentators used their philological and historical knowledge to distill from Tacitus's writings political observations in compact maxims. In his commentary on Tacitus's *Annals*, Books 1–4, for example, Pasquale portrayed Tiberius as a prudent ruler who expertly managed to maintain power and control his subjects, even if he had to abandon moral principles sometimes; Pasquale's constant reference to Tacitus automatically sanctioned such principles of political conduct.

Antiquarianism, furthermore, which gradually evolved as an independent field of study, and first focused on the institutions, rites, and customs of classical, particularly

Roman, antiquity, always claimed a contemporary cultural and political relevance. In 1347, for instance, the Italian popular leader Cola di Rienzo (1313–1354) rediscovered a bronze tablet inscribed with the *Lex de imperio Vespasiani*, presented it to his fellow citizens in an elaborate ceremony, carefully staged in the Lateran basilica, and used it to affirm most vividly the unbroken continuity of the sovereign authority of the Roman people (e.g., Collins 2002, 41–48). Biondo Flavio (1392–1463) was the first to produce an extensive survey of antiquarian knowledge, especially in his *Roma triumphans* (*Rome Triumphant*, 1459), a far-reaching description and analysis of Roman civilization that concludes with an exaltation of the grandeur of the Roman Empire and the triumph of Roman culture. Through glorifying ancient Rome, Biondo implicitly urged his readers to connect with this illustrious tradition and reestablish its foundations; the political context of this in the wake of the fall of Constantinople to the Ottoman sultan Mehmed II (1453) should not be overlooked (Enenkel 2012b, 45–47). The political exploitation of antiquarian scholarship continued unabated during the sixteenth and seventeenth centuries: both antiquarian treatises, in which the notion of a "Rome triumphant" as a cultural model was explicitly or implicitly articulated, and collections of antiquities gathered by elites throughout Europe played a crucial role in the self-identification of sovereign rulers and their dynasties and other noble families (Walther 1998 and 2011; Wrede 2000).

TURNING RHETORIC INTO ACTION: THE PRAGMATICS OF POLITICAL DISCOURSE IN NEO-LATIN LITERATURE

Renaissance humanists not only provided classical learning to ruling powers so that they could augment their political messages with references to ancient Rome; many humanists also actively participated in political life as diplomats or secretaries, counselors, or tutors in princely or republican governments, and some of them managed to attain high political office, such as the chancellorship of the Florentine republic (Coluccio Salutati, Leonardo Bruni, Poggio Bracciolini, Carlo Marsuppini) or the papacy (Tommaso Parentucelli/Nicholas V, Enea Silvio Piccolomini/Pius II). Whereas alliances between humanism and politics took place predominantly in absolutist regimes under a system of court patronage, twentieth-century scholars have identified a variant of humanism carrying a specifically republican political orientation; namely, the civic humanism that developed in early fifteenth-century republican Florence, as it faced subordination to the Visconti regime in Milan. Civic humanism sought to restore the political ideals of republican Rome, drawing its inspiration from Cicero's statesmanship, who had struck a perfect balance between philosophical wisdom, oratorical and literary eloquence, and political commitment (Baron 1966). The concept of civic humanism, always associated primarily with Leonardo Bruni, has remained influential, but has nonetheless been modified by several later scholars (e.g., Hankins 2000), who have pointed out that even in Florence genuine "civic humanists" unequivocally committed to republican ideals were rare. Such critics of Baron's views have emphasized that we should not necessarily expect humanists to formulate their personal political convictions in writing, but that humanist literary practice, including that on politics, was dictated by stylistic and generic rules, and so humanist political communication was essentially rhetorical, intent on delivering whatever political message its author saw fit to convey. James Hankins, however, has urged us to look beyond the facile dichotomy of "civic humanist" and "professional rhetorician," when trying to settle the question of Bruni's "sincerity," and to consider both the political and rhetorical traditions within which Bruni was working (Hankins 2000, 159–78).

In their political action and communication, the humanists' distinctive hallmark in relation to non-humanist peers was their perfect mastery of a classically pure Latin language and their familiarity with antiquity's literary legacy. Ever since that time, authors had taken recourse to both pagan and Christian facets of the classical tradition to represent political power and authority. Strategic references to famous passages from Virgil's *Aeneid*, for example, started appearing in epics written in praise of rulers during late antiquity, and remained a constant feature of similar Latin poems in the medieval and early modern periods. From the later Middle Ages onwards, Claudian's (ca. 370–404 CE) various consulship panegyrics offered a model. Representations of the ideal sovereign drew on Latin texts such as Seneca's essay *De clementia* (*On Clemency*, 55–56 CE) or Pliny's panegyrical oration for the Emperor Trajan (100 CE). Allusions to Lucan's civil war epic *Pharsalia* (ca. 64–65 CE) could illustrate the dark sides of political ambition, often balanced against contrasting citations from Virgil's *Aeneid*. Classical stylistic and rhetorical principles were observed in the official correspondence of large, prestigious chanceries, which therefore helped establish literary guidelines for political communication, and ancient models often inspired how political power was evoked and analyzed in biographical or historiographical works.

Rhetoric connects the literary and political dimensions of humanism and the Neo-Latin works it inspired. As a canonical discipline of the *studia humanitatis*, rhetoric belonged to the humanists' privileged areas of competence, and their command of its theory and practice made them experts in political communication. As early as 1944–1945, Paul Oskar Kristeller (1905–1999) famously saw Renaissance humanists as "the professional heirs and successors of the medieval rhetoricians, the so-called *dictatores*" (Kristeller [1944–1945] 1979, 93), who followed the example of their medieval predecessors in teaching grammar and rhetoric in schools or serving as notaries or other public officials, entrusted with political, administrative, or legal duties, in princely and communal chanceries. Though never unanimously accepted, Kristeller's concept of the nature of Renaissance humanism has remained very influential, even if many scholars have correctly pointed out that early humanists down to the end of the fourteenth century continued medieval rhetorical traditions in their professional work and revived classical practice only in their personal writings. The tradition of the *dictatores* and the development of humanistic writing, therefore, do not seem to have proceeded in tandem, even if there are clear similarities between *dictatores* and humanists in terms of their professional occupations, their rhetorical practice in speech and texts, and their self- and community-fashioning within their own societies (Witt 2000).

By the early fifteenth century, at any rate, the humanists had redesigned political rhetoric to accord with the central concerns of their movement. Coluccio Salutati (1331–1406), chancellor of Florence, was the first humanist who managed to "fuse humanistic scholarship and political action" (Grafton 1991, 12). Salutati placed his humanistic interests squarely in the service of his city-state and helped define the political roles humanism could play. Political rhetoric soon came to be cultivated, not only by humanist men of letters (*litterati*), but also by a new political elite trained in humanist schools, and so new modes of political discourse, characterized in form and content by humanistic values, gained prominence throughout European chanceries and courts (e.g., Mack 2002).

This revalorization of rhetoric to serve political engagement informed speech as well as writing. The oral practice of humanist political rhetoric, more related to rhetoric's original function, has so far been less investigated than its literary expression. Both humanist political oratory and its medieval antecedents have only recently been (re)discovered as an independent research field (Haye 1999; Helmrath [2006] 2013c, 169–88; Feuchter and Helmrath 2008), whereas many scholars have published on the impact of rhetoric on humanist literary production (e.g., Murphy 1983). Oratorical practice is of course much harder to grasp, and can necessarily only be approached through written sources, which only indirectly and often imperfectly reflect the underlying communicative processes that went on during the delivery of a text. Transforming an oral performance into a written text might involve, not only extensive literary refashioning, but also translation from the vernacular into Latin. The oral and written dimensions of humanist political discourse, therefore, cannot be radically separated. Both categories, moreover, oscillate between discursive "persuasion" and ceremonial "celebration" (Bisson 1982), between counseling and *epideixis*, addressed either to individual rulers or to communities that could be defined by geographical, confessional, or professional criteria. The political functions of humanist rhetoric relate, in other words, to the deliberative and the epideictic genres, and barely touch on the judicial genre in which humanists seemed to take a merely theoretical interest. From the humanists' perspective, epideictic was the dominant branch of rhetoric, not least because this kind of speech (*genus dicendi*), focused on praise and blame, had always been associated with ethical concerns, as in Aristotle's *Rhetoric* 1.9 (1366a23–25). For Aristotle, praise was the logical response to a man's virtuous character and actions and could incite others to emulate him; both Aristotle and later rhetoricians repeatedly stressed the close connection between praise and advice, which extended epideixis into the deliberative and even the judicial genre, as in Aristotle's *Rhetoric* 1.9.35 (1367b37–39) and Quintilian's *Institutio oratoria*, 3.7.2 and 28. As rhetoric slowly invaded all literature, every author, not only the orator, participated in the propagation of moral values, and the relationship between literature's ethical dimension and an author's ensuing moral purpose gradually became universally accepted. In their revival of political rhetoric, too, humanists drew on these moral foundations of literary practice to express the norms and values of their political thought (Laureys 2014b).

Political oratory found its expression in orations, sermons, and letters. In many respects, humanist oratory not only recalled the political rhetoric of antiquity, but was also influenced by the medieval traditions of the *ars dictaminis* ("art of letter-writing"), *ars praedicandi* ("art of preaching"), and *ars arengandi* ("art of speech-making"); recent studies have helped clarify the nature of the impact of medieval rhetorical traditions on its Renaissance, and particularly humanist, counterparts (Witt 2000 and 2012). New developments also occurred from the early Renaissance onwards: discussions of peace and war, for example, and, more specifically, anti-Turkish Crusade propaganda, became so prominent that these practically generated their own literary tradition, manifest in sermons and orations (Hankins 1995; Mertens 1997a; Helmrath [2000] 2013b). Much more research is needed, however, on relationships between old and new institutional contexts for political oratory (councils, synods, churches, embassies, parliaments, courts, and universities) and on its functions and forms (Mertens 1997b). Cultural profiles of the individuals who practiced political oratory are only slowly beginning to emerge: several recent studies have illustrated, for instance, how important humanist schooling was in the formation of new "functional elites," who played an important role in politics (Mayer 1989; Petris 2002; L'Hospital 2013; Daniels 2013). Several rhetorical treatises paid renewed attention to the deliberative genre, and the question what the most suitable style of communication was for "politicians" in public service; some of these treatises' authors were simultaneously high-profile political actors and keen to meet the specific needs of others in their class. Carlo Pasquale not only developed a new kind of "political" commentary on Tacitus, as we have seen, but also wrote a treatise, *De optimo genere elocutionis* (*On the Best Style*, 1592), in which he explored the links between ancient Roman politics and literature, unsurprisingly highlighting the Tacitean style as the most appropriate idiom both for Tacitus's and Pasquale's own political contexts (Neumann 2013, 73–75). In the Rhineland, Jakob Omphalius (1500–1567), jurist and chancellor of the Electorate of Cologne, composed, besides several works on political government, the treatise *De elocutionis imitatione ac apparatu* (*On the Imitation and the Equipment of Style*, 1537), a style manual designed for practical use (Ahl 2004). In Paris, Charles du Moulin (1500–1566), jurist and lawyer at the Parlement de Paris, published in 1551 a commentary on the advocate Guillaume du Breuil's (d. 1344 or 1345) *Stilus curiae parlamenti* (*Style of the Parliament of Paris*, ca. 1330) elaborating on magistrates' rhetorical requirements (Fumaroli 1980, 436–39). In later surveys of stylistic theory, such as Johannes Gottlieb Heineccius's (1681–1741) widely used *Fundamenta stili cultioris* (*Foundations of a More Cultivated Style*, first 1719), the *stilus politicus sive civilis* ("political or civil style") became an established category, alongside the *stilus oratorius* ("oratorical style") (Heineccius 1756, 188-89).

Beyond political oratory, the humanists used many verse and prose genres for the purposes of political persuasion and celebration. Canonical sources like Virgil's *Aeneid* were not only appropriated by authors of Neo-Latin epic, but were also picked up in various other genres. One example of political instrumentalization of the *Aeneid* in different genres is the humanist pope Pius II's strongly autobiographical *Commentarii*, which both harken back to Caesar's Commentaries on the Gallic War and identify its author, Pius II (Enea Silvio Piccolomini, 1405–1464), with the epic hero (and his own namesake!) Aeneas, presenting his life through the prism of Rome's national epic (Enenkel 2008, 266–329). This focus on outstanding personalities and famous deeds rather than structures of power exemplifies how politically minded humanists exploited the classical tradition in literary texts, particularly in the earlier phase of humanism, reflecting aesthetic preferences as much as political concerns.

Since antiquity, the strong moralistic orientation of historiographical and biographical writing had made these forms highly suitable for the rhetoric of advice and praise; conversely, polemical writing deployed for the rhetoric of dissuasion and blame also developed out of classical models. European political conflicts, as well as the confrontation with the Ottoman Empire and Islam, were powerful catalysts for new forms of literary creativity. The potential of political drama was first probed by Albertino Mussato (1261–1329) in his *Ecerinis* (1315), dealing with the recent history of Ezzelino III da Romano (Latinized "Ecerinus," 1194–1259), the "tyrant of Padua"; many later humanists followed suit (e.g., Beyer 2008). Ulrich von Hutten (1488–1523) used his polemical dialogues as weapons in his fight against the Roman Church (Becker 2013). In his pioneering *Utopia* (1516), for which there are classical precursors (like Lucian) but no exact precedents, Thomas More (1478–1535) illustrated how powerfully contemporary structures and customs could be criticized under the guise of "utopian" writing (Baker-Smith 1991). The Menippean satire was rediscovered in early modern times and soon employed with similar subversive force (De Smet 1996). And Sebastian Brant (1457–1521) was one of the first humanists to exploit the new medium of the pamphlet for political purposes, creating innovative forms of propaganda for the Emperor Maximilian I (Wuttke [1976] 1996).

In terms of more strictly pragmatic kinds of political literature (as opposed to treatises of political theory), the long-standing "mirror for princes" tradition continued to thrive, and new kinds of texts also appeared. Justus Lipsius's *Politica* (*Politics*, 1589) and *Monita et exempla politica* (*Political Advice and Examples*, 1605), as well as Carlo Pasquale's "political" commentary on Tacitus condensed in brief adages, spawned a new tradition of collections of political aphorisms, predominantly inspired by Tacitus (De Bom 2011, 129–208). This Tacitean mode of compactly formulated political maxims, characterized by wit and brevity, also transferred to epigraphical writing which required the same literary qualities, *argutiae* (~ pithiness, wit and brevity combined). In 1678, Christian Weise (1642–1708), professor of poetry and eloquence at the University of Jena, published *De poesi hodiernorum politicorum sive de argutis inscriptionibus* (*On the Poetry of Modern-Day Political Affairs, or On Pithy Inscriptions*), an influential treatise on such "lapidary" sayings, which treats "witty inscriptions" as "modern political poetry," because, as Weise explains in his address to the reader, "nowadays notable judgments on affairs of state are commonly cast in this form" (Sparrow 1969, 107). Similarly condensed forms of political wisdom are found in contemporary collections of political emblems (*emblemata politica*).

The Secret of Neo-Latin's Success

Neo-Latin's role in political action is indissolubly connected with the humanists' promotion of Latin as a privileged language for political communication, always set against the double background of the appropriation of the classical legacy and the competition with the vernacular languages. Why, then, was this privileged status of Latin so successful? Which qualities made Latin stand out as a political idiom? Thomas Haye has asked this question of medieval diplomacy, and his five answers apply to a significant extent to Latin's status in the early modern period, too (Haye 2003). First, Latin was a "ubiquitous" language, omnipresent across European society for both oral and written communication. Second, Latin was a "prestige" language; communicating in Latin implicitly evinced the classical tradition, so that the speaker or writer could display his erudition, earn the political and social prestige that that learning guaranteed, and acknowledge his addressee or readership as equally cultured. Third, Latin was the dominant language of "written discourse," and remained as such well into the early modern period due to its central place in schooling and its consequent status as literary and scholarly language. Since oral communication in a political or diplomatic context was, as a rule, highly stylized, ritualized, and dependent on written formulae and set models, and was often prepared in writing before the actual delivery of the message, it was natural, particularly for this type of oral communication, to resort to that language in which these formulae and models had primarily been expressed. Fourth, Latin was a "neutral" language: since it was nobody's native language anymore, the use of this idiom guaranteed a linguistic equality among all parties involved in political and diplomatic exchanges and negotiations. Choosing any one vernacular would disturb that balance, and would both advantage its native speakers and imply that vernacular's political prestige. The choice of linguistic medium often provoked heated debate in international diplomacy, as at the Westphalian Peace congress in 1648 following the Thirty Years' War (Braun 2010, 187–378), and Latin's neutral quality also explains, for example, why the first-ever treaty signed between Russia and China, the Treaty of Nerchinsk (1689), was composed in Latin, and why Latin remained an official language in Hungary until 1848. And fifth, Latin was a "curial" language: until the seventeenth century, the papal curia not only organized the most sophisticated political protocol and ceremonial, a model for other early modern courts and chanceries, but also boasted the widest network of officials who maintained political ties with all European regimes. By establishing the standards for diplomatic practice, the curia's continuing use of Latin enhanced its status as a political and diplomatic language, even in regions that did not subscribe to the Roman Church's ideological reasons for claiming Latin as Catholicism's authentic language.

Over the course of the seventeenth century, the significance of these five factors gradually diminished, and by the early eighteenth century, Latin had definitively lost its status as European politics' and diplomacy's main language, overtaken by French as the next *lingua franca* (Fumaroli 2001).

Suggested Reading

Useful examples of a survey of Neo-Latin from a socio-pragmatic perspective are Ludwig (2003) and Burke (2004); see also Waquet (1998) and Leonhardt (2009). No comprehensive study of Neo-Latin "political action" exists; many of the studies referred to here fit under the heading "political communication," an increasingly important concept in early modern studies (e.g., Stollberg-Rilinger 2005; Schorn-Schütte 2006; Shapiro 2012), but hardly ever discussed in exclusively Neo-Latin terms. Analysis of political discourse as a network of language acts in a particular historical context—a research tradition founded by Quentin Skinner and J. G. A. Pocock—is mainly relevant to our topic in its discussion of political rhetoric (especially Skinner 1996) rather than its consideration of specialized idioms. For other work related to the contents of this chapter by the author, see also Laureys (2004, 2010, 2014a, 2014b).

References

Ahl, Ingmar. 2004. *Humanistische Politik zwischen Reformation und Gegenreformation: Der Fürstenspiegel des Jakob Omphalius*. Stuttgart: Steiner.

Althoff, Gerd, and Ludwig Siep. 2000. "Symbolische Kommunikation und gesellschaftliche Wertesysteme vom Mittelalter bis zur Französischen Revolution: Der neue Münsteraner Sonderforschungsbereich 496." *Frühmittelalterliche Studien* 34:393–412.

Backus, Irena. 2003. *Historical Method and Confessional Identity in the Era of the Reformation (1378–1615)*. Leiden: Brill.

Baker-Smith, Dominic. 1991. *More's Utopia*. London: HarperCollins Academic.

Baron, Hans. 1966. *The Crisis of the Early Italian Renaissance: Civic Humanism and Republican Liberty in an Age of Classicism and Tyranny*. Rev. ed. Princeton: Princeton University Press.

———. 1967. "Leonardo Bruni: 'Professional Rhetorician' or 'Civic Humanist'?" *Past and Present* 36:21–37.

Becker, Arnold. 2013. *Ulrichs von Hutten polemische Dialoge im Spannungsfeld von Humanismus und Politik*. Göttingen: V&R Unipress.

Beetz, Manfred, ed. 2012. *Rhetorik und Höflichkeit*. Special issue, *Rhetorik* 31. Berlin: De Gruyter.

Beyer, Hartmut. 2008. *Das politische Drama im Italien des 14. und 15. Jahrhunderts: Humanistische Tragödien in ihrem literarischen und funktionalen Kontext*. Münster: Rhema.

Bihrer, A., and E. Stein, eds. 2004. *Nova de veteribus. Mittel- und neulateinische Studien für Paul Gerhard Schmidt*. Munich and Leipzig: Saur.

Bisson, Thomas N. 1982. "Celebration and Persuasion: Reflections on the Cultural Evolution of a Medieval Consultation." *Legislative Studies Quarterly* 7:181–209.

Braun, Guido. 2010. *La connaissance du Saint-Empire en France du baroque aux Lumières, 1643–1756*. Munich: Oldenbourg.

Burke, Peter. 1991. "Tacitism, Scepticism, and Reason of State." In Burns and Goldie 1991, 479–98.

———. 1999. "Presenting and Re-Presenting Charles V." In *Charles V and His Time 1500–1558*. Edited by Hugo Soly and Wim Blockmans, 393–475. Antwerp: Mercatorfonds.

Burke, Peter. 2004. *Languages and Communities in Early Modern Europe*. Cambridge: Cambridge University Press.

Burns, James H., with Mark Goldie, eds. 1991. *The Cambridge History of Political Thought 1450–1700*. Cambridge: Cambridge University Press.

Collins, Amanda. 2002. *Greater than Emperor: Cola di Rienzo (ca. 1313–1354) and the World of Fourteenth-Century Rome*. Ann Arbor: University of Michigan Press.

Daniels, Tobias. 2013. *Diplomatie, politische Rede und juristische Praxis im 15. Jahrhundert: Der gelehrte Rat Johannes Hofmann von Lieser*. Göttingen: V&R Unipress.

De Bom, Erik. 2011. *Geleerden en politiek: De politieke ideeën van Justus Lipsius in de vroegmoderne Nederlanden*. Hilversum: Verloren.

De Smet, Ingrid. 1996. *Menippean Satire and the Republic of Letters, 1581–1655*. Geneva: Droz.

Donato, Maria M. 1985. "Gli eroi romani tra storia ed 'exemplum': I primi cicli umanistici di Uomini Famosi." In *Memoria dell'antico nell'arte italiana*, edited by Salvatore Settis, vol. 2, 95–152. Turin: Einaudi.

Enenkel, Karl A. E., and Jan Papy, eds. 2006. *Petrarch and his readers in the Renaissance*. Leiden and Boston: Brill.

———. 2008. *Die Erfindung des Menschen: Die Autobiographik des frühneuzeitlichen Humanismus von Petrarca bis Lipsius*. Berlin: De Gruyter.

———. 2012a. "Einleitung: Ideologische und politische Diskurse in der neulateinischen Literatur." In Enenkel, Laureys, and Pieper 2012, ix–xxvii.

———. 2012b. "The Politics of Antiquarianism: Neo-Latin Treatises on Cultural History as Ideology and Propaganda." In Enenkel, Laureys, and Pieper 2012, 43–64.

Enenkel, Karl, Marc Laureys, and Christoph Pieper, eds. 2012. *Discourses of Power: Ideology and Politics in Neo-Latin Literature*. Hildesheim: Olms.

Feuchter, Jörg, and Johannes Helmrath, eds. 2008. *Politische Redekultur in der Vormoderne: Die Oratorik europäischer Parlamente in Spätmittelalter und Früher Neuzeit*. Frankfurt: Campus.

Fumaroli, Marc, 1980. *L'âge de l'éloquence*. Geneva: Droz.

———. 2001. *Quand l'Europe parlait français*. Paris: Fallois.

Garin, Eugenio, ed. 1952. *Prosatori latini del Quattrocento*. Milan: Ricciardi.

Geitner, Ursula. 1992. *Die Sprache der Verstellung: Studien zum rhetorischen und anthropologischen Wissen im 17. und 18. Jahrhundert*. Tübingen: Niemeyer.

Göttert, Karl-Heinz. 1988. *Kommunikationsideale: Untersuchungen zur europäischen Konversationstheorie*. Munich: Iudicium.

Grafton, Anthony. 1991. "Humanism and Political Theory." In Burns and Goldie, op. cit., 9–29.

Grafton, Anthony, and Lisa Jardine. 1990. "Studied for Action: How Gabriel Harvey Read his Livy." *Past and Present* 129:3–51.

Hankins, James. 1995. "Renaissance Crusaders: Humanist Crusade Literature in the Age of Mehmed II." *Dumbarton Oaks Papers* 49:111–207.

———. 2000. *Renaissance Civic Humanism: Reappraisals and Reflections*. Cambridge: Cambridge University Press.

———. 2003. "The Popes and Humanism." In *Humanism and Platonism in the Italian Renaissance*, Vol. 1, 469–94. Rome: Edizioni di Storia e Letteratura.

Haskell, Yasmin, and Juanita Feros Rhuys, eds. 2010. *Latinity and Alterity in the Early Modern Period*. Tempe: Arizona Center for Medieval and Renaissance Studies.

Haye, Thomas. 1999. *Oratio. Mittelalterliche Redekunst in lateinischer Sprache*. Leiden: Brill.

———. 2003. "Die lateinische Sprache als Medium mündlicher Diplomatie." In *Gesandtschafts- und Botenwesen im spätmittelalterlichen Europa*, edited by Rainer C. Schwinges and Klaus Wriedt, 15–32. Ostfildern: Thorbecke.

Heineccius, Johann Gottlieb. 1756. *Fundamenta stili cultioris.* Leipzig: Fritsch.

Helmrath, Johannes. 2013a. *Wege des Humanismus: Studien zu Praxis und Diffusion der Antikeleidenschaft im 15. Jahrhundert.* Vol. 1. Tübingen: Mohr Siebeck.

——. (2000) 2013b. "Pius II. und die Türken." In Helmrath 2013a, 279–341.

——. (2006) 2013c. "Der europäische Humanismus und die Funktionen der Rhetorik." In Helmrath 2013a, 159–88.

Herde, Peter. 1965. "Politik und Rhetorik in Florenz am Vorabend der Renaissance." *Archiv für Kulturgeschichte* 47:141–220.

Hirschi, Caspar. 2005. *Wettkampf der Nationen: Konstruktionen einer deutschen Ehrgemeinschaft an der Wende vom Mittelalter zur Neuzeit.* Göttingen: Wallstein.

——. 2012. *The Origins of Nationalism: An Alternative History from Ancient Rome to Early Modern Germany.* Cambridge: Cambridge University Press.

Jansen, Jeroen. 1995. *Brevitas: Beschouwingen over de beknoptheid van vorm en stijl in de renaissance.* 2 vols. Hilversum: Verloren.

Keßler, Eckhard. 1978. *Petrarca und die Geschichte: Geschichtsschreibung, Rhetorik, Philosophie im Übergang vom Mittelalter zur Neuzeit.* Munich: Fink.

Keßler, Eckhard, and Heinrich C. Kuhn. 2003. *Germania Latina, Latinitas teutonica: Politik, Wissenschaft, humanistische Kultur vom späten Mittelalter bis in unsere Zeit.* 2 vols. Munich: Fink.

Klecker, Elisabeth. 2002. "Karl V. in der neulateinischen Habsburg-Panegyrik des 17. und 18. Jahrhunderts." In Kohler, Haider, and Ottner 2002, 747–66.

Kohler, Alfred, Barbara Haider, and Christine Ottner, eds. 2002. *Karl V. 1500–1558: Neue Perspektiven seiner Herrschaft in Europa und Übersee.* Vienna: Verlag der Österreichischen Akademie der Wissenschaften.

Kristeller, Paul Oskar. (1944–1945) 1979. "Humanism and Scholasticism in the Italian Renaissance." In *Renaissance Thought and Its Sources*, 85–105. New York: Columbia University Press.

Laureys, Marc. 2000. "The Pagan and Christian Legacy of Rome in Pompeo Ugonio's Oration *De lingua Latina.*" *Neulateinisches Jahrbuch* 2:125–53.

——. 2003. "Latin as Language of the Blessed: Melchior Inchofer on the Excellence and Dignity of the Latin Language." In Keßler and Kuhn, op. cit., 2:655–78.

——. 2004. "Das osmanische Reich aus der Sicht des Genueser Historikers Uberto Foglietta". In Bihrer and Stein 2004, 894–913.

——. 2010. "History and poetry in Philippus Meyerus's humanist Latin portraits of the prophet Mohammed and the Ottoman rulers (1594)". In Haskell and Feros Rhuys 2010, 273–299.

——. 2014a. "Latin Language and Style as an Instrument of Political and Cultural Ideology." In *ENLW* 2:1019–21.

——. 2014b. "Praise and Blame." In *ENLW* 2:1148–50.

Leonhardt, Jürgen. 2009. *Latein: Geschichte einer Weltsprache.* Munich: Beck.

Lipsius, Justus. 1978. *Epistolae.* Vol. 1, *1564–1583.* Edited by Aloïs Gerlo, Marcel A. Nauwelaerts, and Hendrik D. L. Vervliet. Brussels: Paleis der Academiën.

L'Hospital, Michel de. 2013. *Discours et correspondance: La plume et la tribune II.* Edited by Loris Petris with David Amherdt. Geneva: Droz.

Ludwig, Walther. 2003. "Latein im Leben: Funktionen der lateinischen Sprache in der Frühen Neuzeit." In Keßler and Kuhn, op. cit., 1:73–106.

Mack, Peter. 2002. *Elizabethan Rhetoric.* Cambridge: Cambridge University Press.

Mayer, Thomas F. 1989. *Thomas Starkey and the Commonweal: Humanist Politics and Religion in the Reign of Henry VIII.* Cambridge: Cambridge University Press.

Mertens, Dieter. 1997a. "'Europa, id est patria, domus propria, sedes nostra. . .': Zu Funktionen und Überlieferung lateinischer Türkenreden im 15. Jahrhundert." In *Europa und die osmanische Expansion im ausgehenden Mittelalter*, edited by Franz-Reiner Erkens, 39–57. Berlin: Duncker & Humblot.

———. 1997b. "Die Rede als institutionalisierte Kommunikation im Zeitalter des Humanismus." In *Im Spannungsfeld von Recht und Ritual: Soziale Kommunikation in Mittelalter und Früher Neuzeit*, edited by Heinz Duchhardt and Gert Melville, 401–21. Cologne: Böhlau.

Momigliano, Arnaldo. 1955. "The First Political Commentary on Tacitus." In *Contributo alla storia degli studi classici*, 37–59. Rome: Edizioni di Storia e Letteratura.

Moss, Ann, 1996. *Printed Commonplace-Books and the Structuring of Renaissance Thought.* Oxford: Clarendon Press.

Münkler, Herfried. 1998. "Staatsräson." In *Historisches Wörterbuch der Philosophie*, edited by Joachim Ritter, Karlfried Grunder, and Gottfried Gabriel, vol. 10, 66–71. Basel: Schwabe.

Murphy, James J., ed. 1983. *Renaissance Eloquence.* Berkeley: University of California Press.

Neumann, Florian. 2013. *Geschichtsschreibung als Kunst: Famiano Strada S.I. (1572–1649) und die ars historica in Italien.* Berlin: De Gruyter.

Petrarch, Francesco. 2004–2010. *Le senili.* Edited by Elvira Nota and translated by Ugo Dotti and Felicita Audisio. 3 vols. Turin: Nino Aragno.

Petris, Loris. 2002. *La plume et la tribune: Michel de L'Hospital et ses discours (1559–1562), suivi de l'édition du* De initiatione Sermo *(1559) et des* Discours de Michel de L'Hospital *(1560–1562).* Geneva: Droz.

Römer, Franz. 2002. "Zur Panegyrik in der Epoche Karls V." In Kohler, Haider, and Ottner, op. cit., 67–82.

Schorn-Schütte, Luise, ed. 2004. *Aspekte der politischen Kommunikation in Europa des 16. und 17. Jahrhunderts.* Munich: Oldenbourg.

———. 2006. *Historische Politikforschung: Eine Einführung.* Munich: Beck.

Seigel, Jerrold E. 1966. "'Civic Humanism' or Ciceronian Rhetoric? The Culture of Petrarch and Bruni." *Past and Present* 34:3–46.

Shapiro, Barbara J. 2012. *Political Communication and Political Culture in England, 1558–1688.* Stanford: Stanford University Press.

Skinner, Quentin. 1996. *Reason and Rhetoric in the Philosophy of Hobbes.* Cambridge: Cambridge University Press.

Sparrow, John. 1969. *Visible Words: A Study of Inscriptions in and as Books and Works of Art.* Cambridge: Cambridge University Press.

Stollberg-Rilinger, Barbara. 2004. "Symbolische Kommunikation in der Vormoderne: Begriffe—Forschungsperspektiven—Thesen." *Zeitschrift für Historische Forschung* 31:489–527.

———, ed. 2005. *Was heißt Kulturgeschichte des Politischen?* Berlin: Duncker & Humblot.

Tanner, Marie. 1993. *The Last Descendant of Aeneas: The Hapsburgs and the Mythic Image of the Emperor.* New Haven: Yale University Press.

Till, Dietmar. 2003. "Politicus." In *HWR* 6: 1422–45.

Van Liere, Katherine, Simon Ditchfield, and Howard Louthan, eds. 2012. *Sacred History: Uses of the Christian Past in the Renaissance World.* Oxford: Oxford University Press.

Walther, Gerrit. 1998. "Adel und Antike: Zur politischen Bedeutung gelehrter Kultur für die Führungselite der frühen Neuzeit." *Historische Zeitschrift* 266:359–85.

———. 2011. "Barocke Antike und barocke Politik: Ein Überblick." In *Welche Antike? Konkurrierende Rezeptionen des Altertums im Barock*, edited by Ulrich Heinen, vol. 1, 79–115. Wiesbaden: Harrassowitz.

Waquet, Françoise. 1998. *Le latin ou l'empire d'un signe, XVIe–XXe siècle*. Paris: Albin Michel.

Weber, Wolfgang. 2004. "Die Erfindung des Politikers: Bemerkungen zu einem gescheiterten Professionalisierungskonzept des 17. Jahrhunderts." In Schorn-Schütte 2004, 347–70.

Witt, Ronald G. 2000. *In the Footsteps of the Ancients: The Origins of Humanism from Lovato to Bruni*. Leiden: Brill.

———. 2012. *The Two Latin Cultures and the Foundation of Renaissance Humanism in Medieval Italy*. Cambridge and New York: Cambridge University Press.

Wrede, Henning. 2000. "L'Antico nel Seicento." In *L'idea del bello: Viaggio per Roma nel Seicento con Giovan Pietro Bellori*, edited by Evelina Borea and Carlo Gasparri, vol. 1, 7–15. Rome: Edizioni de Luca.

Wuttke, Dieter. (1976) 1996. "Sebastian Brant und Maximilian I. Eine Studie zu Brants Donnerstein-Flugblatt des Jahres 1492." In *Dazwischen: Kulturwissenschaft auf Warburgs Spuren*, vol. 1, 213–50. Baden-Baden: Koerner.

CHAPTER 23

....

GENDER

....

DIANA ROBIN

THE mastery of classical Latin and knowledge of its literary monuments provided a gateway for women into the learned salons, academies, universities, and the political forums of early modern Europe. During the same epoch, the *querelle des femmes*, the debate about female nature and gender difference, supplied the ideology for women's advancement. The *querelle*, which first appeared in late medieval France, launched an ideological war that found its expression in treatises, biographies, poetry, dialogues, plays, orations, and eulogies. Most of the early *querelle* texts were either Neo-Latin works or vernacular translations of such works. Among these, Boccaccio's Latin *De mulieribus claris* (*On Famous Women*, ca. 1361–1362), a compendium of over one hundred biographies of women from antiquity to his own time, has been called the founding text not only of the *querelle* but of Renaissance feminism itself (Benson 1992, 9; Ross 2009a, 1–2; Jordan 1990, 2; Campbell 2013, 361–79).

In the fifteenth century, three pathbreaking women writers entered the *querelle*: the classically educated courtier to King Charles V of France (1337–1380) Christine de Pizan (1365–ca. 1430); the Brescian humanist and Latinist Laura Cereta (1465–1499); and the Veronese humanist Isotta Nogarola (1418–1466). Both Pizan's allegory in dialogue form, *Le livre de la cité des dames* (*The Book of the City of Ladies*, 1405; Quilligan 1991) and Cereta's Latin letter to Bibolo Semproni, *De liberali mulierum institutione* (*In Defense of Liberal Education for Women*, ca. 1488; Cereta 1997, 72–80) borrow extensively from Boccaccio's *De mulieribus claris*. But their portrayals of his famous women differ markedly from his. Neither Pizan nor Cereta describe their subjects' sexual histories; nor do they portray Boccaccio's learned women as exceptions to their gender (Robin 1997). In Pizan's allegory, three female characters representing womanhood (Reason, Rectitude, and Justice) build a fortified city where women will be safe from misogynist attacks. In the *De liberali mulierum institutione*, Cereta represents her catalog of famous women as both a *generositas* (lineage) of female rulers, scholars, and poets from antiquity to the present and also as a *respublica mulierum* ("republic of women") unlike the masculine world of letters, the *respublica litterarum* ("republic of letters"; Cereta 1997, 74; 80n; Rabil 1981, 50, 101–2). Both Pizan and Cereta show in their works that, while women are by nature endowed with intelligence, knowledge is won through toil and engagement with the world. Nogarola responds differently to the *querelle* in her Latin dialogue with the Venetian governor of Verona, Ludovico Foscarini, *De pari aut impari Evae atque Adae peccato dialogus* (*Dialogue on the Equal or Unequal Sin of Adam and Eve*, 1451). The protagonist of her dialogue ("Isotta") does not deny that Eve, the archetypal woman, is guilty of *debilitas* ("weak-mindedness") by nature. Yet Isotta demonstrates such a command of her classical Greek and Latin sources in her dialogue with "Ludovico" that she easily proves herself her male combatant's equal—if not his superior (Nogarola 2004, 138–58; Fenster 2004, 58–77).

Renaissance European cities and courts were rife with misogynistic Latin treatises and verses. Under the influence of the learned noblewomen of the courts in Northern Italy, Latin-writing courtiers joined the *querelle*, publishing treatises in praise of women. Antonio Cornazzano dedicated his *De mulieribus admirandis* (*On Admirable Women*, 1467) to Duchess Bianca Sforza of Milan (Benson 1992, 36–37). Bartolomeo Goggio wrote his *De laudibus mulierum* (*On Praises of Women*) for his patron, Duchess Eleonora d'Aragona of Ferrara (Fahy 1965, 30–55; Gundersheimer 1980, 43–65). Also in Ferrara, Agostino Strozzi penned his *Defensio mulierum* (*A Defense of Women*, 1501) in honor of Margarita Cantelma, a friend of Isabella d'Este (Benson 1992, 44–45). In Germany, a contemporary of Strozzi and Goggio, Heinrich Cornelius Agrippa von Nettesheim (1486–1535), delivered a Latin oration on the superiority of women, *De nobilitate et praecellentia foeminei sexus* (*On the Nobility and Excellence of the Female Sex*, 1529) as the inaugural address at the University of Dôle (Agrippa 1996; Nauert 1999, 24–26).

In the later sixteenth and seventeenth centuries, the majority of defenses of women were written in the vernacular, although it is clear from their references to Latin and Greek works that their authors were steeped in classical learning (Labalme 1981, 81–109). In Venice, Lucrezia Marinella's (1571–1653) treatise *La nobiltà e l'eccellenza delle donne* (*On the Nobility and Excellence of Women*, 1601; Marinella 1999) was commissioned by the publisher Giambattista Ciotti to respond to Giuseppe Passi's misogynistic *I donneschi difetti* (*The Womanly Defects*, 1599; Cox 2008, 159). Moderata Fonte's (Modesta da Pozzo, 1555–1592) dialogue *Il merito delle donne* (*On the Worth of Women*, 1600; Fonte 1997) featured seven women discussing higher education for women, domestic economy, and the disadvantages of marriage for women, among other topics.

The themes of the *querelle des femmes* infused the poetry of later sixteenth-century writers in France. Poitiers was an important center of French women fluent in Greek and Latin literature and the issues of the *querelle*. The poet Louise Labé (ca. 1520–1566), who wrote a volume of Latin poetry now lost, and the mother and daughter poets Madeleine (Madeleine Neveu, 1520–1587) and Catherine des Roches (Catherine Fradonnet, 1542–1587), who also published dialogues, took up motifs from Boccaccio's *De mulieribus claris* in their works, situating themselves at the heart of the *querelle* (Larsen 2007, 110–11; des Roches and des Roches 2006, 42–43; Stevenson 2005, 194–95). Self-taught but sufficiently learned in Latin to become Michel de Montaigne's *amanuensis* and his *fille d'alliance* (spiritual daughter), Marie de Gournay (1565–1645) became a participant in the *querelle* with the Paris publication of her pro-woman treatise, *L'Égalité des hommes et des Femmes* (*The Equality of Men and Women*, 1622; Gournay 2002).

In seventeenth-century England as in France, women writers schooled in the Latin classics entered the *querelle*. Aemilia Lanyer (1569–1645), the daughter of a Venetian-born musician at the court of Elizabeth I, received a humanist education and schooling in Latin eloquence. Lanyer took up Eve's defense in her vernacular work *Salve Deus Rex Judeorum* (*Hail, God, King of the Jews*, 1611; Lanyer 1993). She prefaced the *Salve Deus* with eleven dedicatory poems, each addressed to a woman; in her biblical history, women occupied the central roles (Barrett-Graves 2007). Also expert at Latin grammar and rhetoric, the English Protestant poet Rachel Speght (b. 1597), joined the *querelle des femmes* with her polemical treatise, *A Mouzell for Melastomus* (1617; Speght 1996), in which she mocked misogynist attacks on women.

NEO-LATIN EDUCATION AND GENDER: FROM COURT SCHOOLS TO THE PUBLIC ARENA

Schooling in Latin and its literary legacy enabled women to play significant roles, not only in political discourse (the *querelle*), but also in such venues as the court schoolroom, the learned household academy, the literary salon, and the public forum—as opposed to the institutions of the church, state, and university, from which women were excluded.

In Italy, Gianfrancesco Gonzaga and Paola Malatesta, Marquis and Marquise of Mantua, hired the university-educated classicist Vittorino da Feltre (1378–1446) to establish a Latin school for their daughters and sons at court in 1423. Vittorino also taught them classical Greek, a language all but unknown in Europe until the fifteenth century (Woodward 1905, 29–92). In 1450, Duke Francesco Sforza and Duchess Bianca Maria Visconti of Milan brought in Vittorino's protégé Baldo Martorello and the Hellenist Constantinus Lascaris to teach Latin and Greek to their children, Galeazzo Maria and Ippolita Maria Sforza. When Ippolita married Alfonso, the son of King Ferdinand of Naples, her Latin tutor Martorello remained her secretary in Naples. Her trousseau included Cicero's *De senectute* (*On Old Age*), copied out in her own hand (Pellegrin 1955, 67).

In 1429, Duke Niccolò d'Este III of Ferrara employed the prominent humanist and Greek scholar Guarino da Verona (1374–1460) to create a palace school for his children modeled on the humanist school he founded in Verona (Grendler 1989, 126–29). The Este court school continued to be a model of Greek and Latin pedagogy under the aegis of Duchess Renée de France (1510–1574). The Latin and Greek orations, dialogues, and letters of the Protestant Olympia Morata (1526–1555), whose father Fulvio Pellegrino directed Renée's palace humanist school, were published posthumously in Basel (1558; Morata 2003). Numerous extant Latin letters and orations demonstrate that humanist schooling enabled the fifteenth-century noblewomen of Padua, Pesaro, Milan, and Cesena to act as respected political negotiators and representatives of their families (King and Rabil 1983, 34–44).

But fifteenth-century Italy also saw the entrance of non-patrician women into the public sphere as Latin writers and speakers. Among such women, Cassandra Fedele of Venice (1465–1558), Isotta Nogarola of Verona, and Laura Cereta of Brescia published in manuscript form not just single letters, but books of their collected Latin letters, orations, and dialogues. Fedele was tutored at home in Latin and Greek by the Servite friar Gasparino Borro. Nogarola and her siblings were also taught both ancient languages at home by the Veronese humanist Martino Rizzoni. Cereta was convent-schooled.

The mastery of the Latin letter form remained at the center of Renaissance humanist schooling, whether at the court school or in the household academy. Modeled on the writings of Cicero and the humanist canon of Roman writers, women's familiar letters (*epistolae ad familiares*) served as templates for the composition and public performance of their orations, dialogues, and other works. Cassandra Fedele regularly exchanged letters with Latin-writing friends, among whom were university students, professors, and theologians from Padua, Udine, Verona, Venice, Rimini, Brescia, Modena, and Florence. Since many of her correspondents knew one another, her book of 121 collected letters (1487–1521) constituted a virtual salon. She delivered her first public oration—on the true path to the good through philosophy—at the University of Padua in 1487 (published in various editions from 1487 to 1636). In a subsequent oration before the Venetian Senate, Fedele decried the joyless drudgery of most women's lives, urging them instead to seek *voluptas ac delectatio* ("pleasure and delight") in philosophical and literary studies (Fedele 1636, 207; Fedele 2000, 162):

> *quos quidem ipsas* [sc. *fructus*] *cum paululum degustarim mecumque reputarim, in eam—ultro abiecta atque exsecrata colo et acu mulierculae armis—procurri sententiam, etsi literarum studia nulla feminis praemia nullamque dignitatem pollicerentur atque praestarent, fuisse tamen cuique capessenda amplectendaque, ob eam solam voluptatem ac delectationem, quae inde eis* [text breaks off mid-sentence].

> Since I enjoyed a little of this [i.e. the profit deriving from literary studies] myself and reflected upon it, I spontaneously threw away and cursed the distaff and the needle, the weapons of a common little woman, and I soon came to the conclusion that even if the study of literature offered women no rewards or honors, they should nonetheless pursue and embrace such studies alone for the pleasure and enjoyment they [bring] to them.

In 1556, the Venetian Senate commissioned the then-nonagenarian Fedele to deliver her last Latin oration: in honor of Queen Bona Sforza of Poland, on her state visit to the Republic (Fedele 1636, 207–10; cf. Fedele 2000, 162–64).

As the early editions of their Latin letterbooks show, Isotta Nogarola and Laura Cereta developed similarly extended circles of humanist, Latin-eloquent colleagues, and family friends. Nogarola publicly debated with Ludovico Foscarini, the Venetian governor of Verona, in 1451 (Nogarola 1886, 2:187–216; Nogarola 2004, 145–58; King and Rabil 1983, 57–69). Subsequently Nogarola presented four major public addresses in

Latin: two of them lectures commissioned in 1453 by the Venetian patrician Ermolao Barbaro, Verona's newly appointed bishop (Nogarola 1886, 2:267–89; Nogarola 2004, 163–74). Nogarola composed her third oration for the international congress at Mantua convened by Pope Pius II in August 1459. In a call for the destruction of the Turkish state, Nogarola summoned the pope to war with the shrill and bloody rhetoric of the Old Testament prophet Habakkuk: *In fremitu conculcabis terram, in furore obstupefacies gentes . . . Percuties caput de domo impii, denudabis fundamentum eius* ("You, [Pius], will trample the land underfoot with a rumbling and you will stun nations with your rage. . . . You will cut off the head of the house of the impious man, and you will lay bare its foundations" [Nogarola 1886, 2:143–56; Nogarola 2004, 178–86]).

Laura Cereta lectured publicly in Brescia on a number of different topics during the years between her husband's early death and her own at the age of thirty (Rossi 1620, 196–200; Cereta 1640, vi–xvii; Rabil 1981, 22–23; Cereta 1997, 151–75). Her Latin lectures include the obligatory humanist discourse on fortune (Cereta 1640, 47–55; Cereta 1997, 153–58); a funeral oration on the death of a friend's baby daughter (Cereta 1640, 91–94; Cereta 1997, 158–60); and an excoriation of the brutality of the German invasion of Brescia in 1487 (Cereta 1640, 94–100; Cereta 1997, 161–64). Cereta's comic Latin dialogue *On the Death of an Ass*, which prefaces the only known autograph copy of her Latin letterbook, was clearly meant for public performance (Cereta 1997, 180–202).

In Spain, when Queen Isabella of Castile (1479–1504) came to the throne, she brought the Italian humanists Pietro Martire d'Anghiera (1457–1526) and Lucio Marineo Siculo (1460–1533) to her court to teach her five children Latin grammar and rhetoric. She established a humanist school for the daughters and sons of the nobility in the castle appointing as its director the Latinist Beatriz Galindo (1465–1534), who taught philosophy and medicine at the University of Salamanca. Isabella also corresponded with the then-famous Venetian Latinist Cassandra Fedele, hoping to bring her to the Spanish court as a scholar in residence (Fedele 2000, 18–23; Robin 2013, 384). When Isabella's daughter, Catherine of Aragon (1485–1586), married Henry VIII, the king of England, she brought her Latin tutor, Juan Luis Vives (1493–1540), to England. Accompanying Catherine to court in England, Vives published his treatise *De institutione foeminae christianae* (*On the Education of the Christian Woman*, 1524) in a translation by Richard Hyrde (d. 1528; Vives 1529; Vives 2002); eight more editions followed in the sixteenth century. Isabella's other daughter, Queen Maria of Portugal (1521–1577), appointed the classical scholar Luisa Sigea (1522–1560) to her court (Howe 2008, 44–45). Sigea was fluent not only in Latin and Greek but also in Hebrew, Syriac, and Arabic. Her major Latin poem, *Sintra*, was published posthumously in Paris in 1566. Learned Spanish women also wrote treatises. Beatriz Galindo wrote a commentary on Aristotle (Stevenson 2005, 384). Doña Oliva Sabuco de Nantes (1562–1622) authored two scientific works, titled *Nueva filosofia de la naturaleza del hombre* (*A New Philosophy of Human Nature*) and a treatise on the lymphatic system (Cruz and Hernández 2011, 7; Howe 2008, 130–34). Since Spanish noblewomen were generally fluent in Latin, they served as expert litigators and negotiators on behalf of their families (Nader 2004, 6). The sixteenth-century Mendoza clan exemplified the intellectual family in Renaissance Spain. The historian and bibliophile

Diego Hurtado de Mendoza and his siblings included in their literary circle the scholar poets Doña Magdalena Bobadilla (described as *doctissima in Latina*, "most learned in Latin"), the Latin poet Catalina Paz, and the humanist Doña Maria Pacheco, among others (Stevenson 2005, 208).

In sixteenth-century England, the royal court itself represented the cultural center and exemplar of humanist learning. Queen Elizabeth I (reigned 1558–1603) was admired for her ability to speak Latin *extempore*, her Latin letters, and her translation of Boethius's *Consolation of Philosophy*, among other Latin texts (Elizabeth I 2000). Elite families in sixteenth-century England schooled their daughters and sons in Latin and the humanist curriculum at home, in what Sarah Gwyneth Ross has called "household academies" (Ross 2009a, 53–94). Thomas More's (1478–1535) domestic academy included his four biological children (Margaret, Elizabeth, Cecily, and John) by his first wife Jane Colt; and his two wards (Margaret Giggs and Giles Heron). More's resident tutor, John Clement, became a family member when he married Giggs; More's ward Giles Heron joined the family by marrying Cecily More; and William Roper did the same when he married Margaret More (1504–1544). Other humanist family academies in England included Edward Seymour's (Duke of Somerset) daughters Anne, Margaret, and Jane Seymour, who published a book of Latin distichs on Marguerite de Navarre's death (1549; Stevenson 2005, 258–60). Sir Anthony Cooke's daughters Anne Bacon (1528–1610), Mildred Cecil (1525–1589), Elizabeth Hoby Russell (1540–1609), and Katherine Killigrew (1542–1583) were known for their Latin erudition and their interest in religious reform (Ross 2009a, 166–69; Robin 2013, 390–1). Anne Bacon translated into English John Jewel's Latin treatise on England's break with Rome (1564; Ross 2009a, 166–67). Mildred Cecil, wife of Elizabeth's chief advisor William Cecil, who spoke Latin fluently, translated from the Greek patristic authors (Stevenson 2005, 265–67). Jane Lumley Fitzalan (1536–1576) and Mary Fitzalan (1540–1557), the daughters of Henry Fitzalan, the twelfth Earl of Arundel, also received a humanist education in a More-style household academy; Jane Lumley was famous for publishing in manuscript (ca. 1555) the first English translation of Euripides's *Iphigenia at Aulis* (Ross 2009a, 84–87).

Seventeenth-century English women continued to distinguish themselves for their Latin erudition. Lucy Hutchinson (1620–1681) translated Lucretius's *De rerum natura* into English (Hutchinson 2011; Stevenson 2005, 392). The court emblematist Esther Inglis (1571–1624) illustrated and translated fifty volumes of Latin, Greek, and French poetry (Ross 2009b, 159–81), while the noted Latin teacher Bathsua Makin (1600–1676?) published a manual on pedagogy, *An Essay to Revive the Antient Education of Women* (Ross 2009a, 183–87, 240–1; Stevenson 2005, 376).

In France, the culture of Latinity still flourished in the sixteenth century, though no longer at the royal court. The home of the humanist scholar Jean de Morel (1511–1581), who married the poet and Latin scholar Antoinette de Loynes, became a hub for such Neo-Latin poets and members of the Pléiade as Ronsard, Du Bellay, Dorat, and Scévole de Sainte-Marthe. The Morels' three daughters, Camille, Lucrece, and Diane, were tutored from 1556 to 1562 by the Flemish diplomat and Latin poet Karel Utenhove (1536–1600) whom Sir William Cecil had served as a patron and friend (Campbell

2009; Stevenson 2005, 263–66). Utenhove's circulation of the Morel sisters' Latin verses brought them fame not only in France but in England as well (Campbell 2009).

Latin was spoken and the ancient authors were cultivated in the homes of the great Parisian scholar-publishers Charles and Robert Estienne (Broomhall 2002, 53–54). In such humanist households, the French women printers of Latin and Greek Charlotte Guillard and Esmonda Tusana were schooled (Stevenson 2005, 194; Broomhall 2002, 196, 226). Though intellectual women in sixteenth-century France did not write or publish in Latin, they read and translated works from both the Greek and Latin canons. The mother–daughter partners Madeleine and Catherine des Roches collaborated with the poet Louise Labé in a translation from the Greek of Longus's novel *Daphnis and Chloe* in 1578 (Stevenson 2005, 194–95), while Catherine des Roches published her translations of passages from Claudian's epic poem *De Raptu Proserpinae* (*The Rape of Proserpina*) in 1586 and Pythagoras's *Symbols* in 1583. Anna d'Este and Marguerite de Valois were among the very few French women who left collections of their Latin letters to posterity (Stevenson 2005, 281).

In seventeenth-century Germany, Latin was still the obligatory language for cultivated poetry (Stevenson 2005, 337). Humanist-schooled noblewomen in Germany included Katharina Ursula, Landgräfin von Hessen-Kassel (1593–1615), her sisters Anna (1617–1672) and Elisabeth von Baden-Durlach (1620–1692), Sophie Elisabeth von Braunschweig-Lüneburg (1613–1676), and Antonia von Württemberg (1613–1679), all of whom published and corresponded in Latin with learned men and women. Elisabeth von der Pfalz (1618–1680) exchanged letters with both Descartes and the Dutch Latinist Anna Maria van Schurman (Stevenson 2005, 343). Among other Latin-educated German women, Stevenson lists the Protestant polemicist Argula von Grumbach, the poet Euphrosine Aue (1677–1715) of Colberg, and Margaretha Sibylla von Einsiedel (1642–1690), the so-called "Misnian Minerva of Dresden," who studied Hebrew, Greek, mathematics, and theology in addition to Latin (Stevenson 2005, 346).

Humanism spread eastward in the fifteenth and sixteenth centuries to Buda, Cracow, and Prague. Beatrice of Aragon (1457–1508), daughter of King Ferdinand of Naples, was betrothed to King Matthias Corvinus of Hungary in 1475, arriving in Buda the following year. Steeped in the values of her father's learned academy in Naples led by the Neo-Latin poet Giovanni Gioviano Pontano (1426–1503), Beatrice encouraged her husband Matthias to build a Renaissance palace at Visegrád, to create an academy for scholars, and to assemble the Bibliotheca Corviniana, a library of over three thousand volumes, many of them rare Greek and Latin codices (Tanner 2008). Bona Sforza (1494–1557), granddaughter of Duke Galeazzo Maria Sforza of Milan and King Alfonso II of Naples, arrived in Poland as the second wife of Sigismund I in 1518. The celebration of their marriage was a major cultural event, with Italian and Polish Neo-Latin poets in attendance. Bona brought the humanist values of her father's Neapolitan court to Cracow; she played a leading role in the city's literary culture, the arts, architecture, and the university. Bona's learned daughter Catherine Jagelonska (1526–1583) left a number of letters in Latin (Fiszman 1988). In Prague, Elizabeth Jane Weston (1581–1612), the stepdaughter of the court alchemist to Emperor Rudolf II, published a book titled *Parthenica* (1608), which contained a large collection of her Neo-Latin poems and her Latin prose letters (Weston 2000; Stevenson 2005, 248–49). Alluding both to the epithet for the warrior princess Camilla in Virgil's *Aeneid* (11.483) and Poliziano's salute to Cassandra Fedele, *O decus Italiae virgo* ("O virgin, glory of Italy"), Weston fashioned herself as the *virgo Angla* ("English virgin")—though she married and had seven children (Fedele 1636, 155; Fedele 2000, 90–91, 102n).

Queen Christina of Sweden (1626–1686) read and wrote Latin, Greek, and all the modern European languages. Abdicating the throne in 1654, she moved with her renowned library of Greek and Latin classics to Rome, where she gathered a circle of humanists around her. Among her learned, Latin-writing contemporaries in Sweden were Catharina Bure (1601–1678); the daughter of King Gustavus Adolphus's tutor, Gräfin Maria Aurora von Königsmarck (1662–1728); and Sophia Elisabeth Brenner (1659–1730). An advocate for women's education, Brenner, who wrote and spoke Latin fluently, has been compared to Olympia Morata and Anna Maria van Schurman (Stevenson 2005, 357; on van Schurman, see also below).

THE CONVENT

Recent scholarship on convents has emphasized the ways in which Latin-schooled nuns in early modern Europe interacted with the worlds beyond their walls (Lehfeldt 2013, 12–31). Some studies have shown how highly educated convent women reshaped religious practice and ideology (Bornstein and Rusconi 1996). Scholars of monastic culture in sixteenth-century Milan and Florence have shed light upon the ways in which classically educated nuns utilized the convent as a power base to further their own interests and those of their families, even after enclosure during the Counter-Reformation (Baernstein 2002; Strocchia 2009). Convent women were similarly instrumental in promoting the literary, artistic, and musical life of their institutions and their cities (van Wyhe 2008; Evangelisti 2007; Weaver 2002; Monson 1992 and 1995).

By the sixteenth century, Latin was no longer a major staple of convent curricula in Continental Europe. Long gone were the legendary nuns and abbesses of the German High Middle Ages who wrote Latin poetry—Hildegard von Bingen (1098–1179), Mechthild von Magdeburg (ca. 1210–1282), Herrad von Landsberg (ca. 1125–1195), and Gertrud von Helfta (1256–1302). With the advent of the Reformation in cities such as Augsburg and Nuremberg, Latin correspondence was forbidden in some convents as in Nuremberg in 1503, for example (Stevenson 2005, 226). Nonetheless, the Nuremberg abbess of St. Clara, Charitas Pirckheimer (1467–1532), continued to exchange Latin letters and verses with Konrad Celtis, among other humanists—as did such other prominent non-convent women as Margarethe von Staffel of Rheingau (d. 1471), Ursula Canter of Groningen (before 1489–before 1516), and Margarethe Welser of Augsburg (1481–1552) who corresponded with Erasmus (Stevenson 2005, 229).

Unlike Northern Europe, Spain continued to offer noblewomen deemed unmarriageable such as Sor Teresa de Cartagena (ca. 1420–1460), who was deaf (Howe 2011, 125–26), the refuge of convent life. A descendant of a learned *converso* (the Spanish term for a convert to Catholicism from either Judaism or Islam) family, Cartagena entered the Franciscan monastery of Santa Clara in Burgos, Spain, and later transferred to the Cistercian monastery de las Huelgas in Burgos where she studied the Latin writings of Augustine and St. Jerome, subsequently composing her own autobiographical work, *Arboleda de los enfermos* (*Grove of the Infirm*; Howe 2008, 125–6). Similarly, Teresa Sánchez de Cepeda y Ahumada (later known as Saint Teresa of Ávila, 1515–1582), also the granddaughter of *conversos* expelled from Spain, was educated at the Augustinian convent of Nuestra Señora de Gracia in Ávila, where she read Cicero's *De officiis* and Virgil's *Georgics*. In 1535, she took vows as a nun of the Order of Our Lady of Mount Carmel (Bilinkoff 1989, 112–16). There in Ávila, Saint Teresa founded the first reform Carmelite convent in Spain as a school for nuns.

A number of classically educated Spanish women entered convents to devote themselves to study and writing in the seventeenth century (Robin 2013, 385–86). The most prolific among these, Sor Juana Inés de la Cruz (1651–1686), who was a scholar of classical Latin literature as well as scripture, published three volumes of her Spanish poetry and prose works (Kirk 2011, 139–57). Doña Valentina de Pinelo, the daughter of wealthy Genoese parents, entered the Augustinian convent of San Landro in Seville where she studied Latin and the Bible; she published a panegyric of Saint Anne in 1601 in Spanish, citing Latin literary texts as well as patristics and scripture (Perry 1990, 91–92). The Latin-learned Zaragozan nun Ana Francisca Abarca de Bolea (1602–1686) became the abbess of a Cistercian convent where she met with a circle of humanists (Cruz 2011, 4).

In Italy, Latin grammar and rhetoric were not obligatory components of the curriculum in fifteenth- and sixteenth-century convents—despite the voluntary monachization of women who were well known for their Latin style like Giulia Nogarola of Verona, Cecilia Gonzaga of Mantua, and Alessandra Scala of Florence (Stevenson 2005, 174). Several sixteenth-century convent-trained nuns published in Latin: Suor Barbara da Correggio (fl. 1556); Suor Battista Vernaccia (d. 1583); Domitilla Graziani, a Poor Clare of Perugia (d. 1580); and the Dominican Suor Lorenza Strozzi (1514–1591), who composed a book of Latin hymns in the lyric meters of Horace's *Odes* (1588; Stevenson 2005, 296–98). Certainly, a robust tradition of classically inflected vernacular theater has been documented in sixteenth- and seventeenth-century Italian convents (Weaver 2002, 108). Antonia Pulci Tanini (1452–1501), who entered a convent as an *ammantellata* (a third-order Dominican sister, not a nun), studied Latin at the cathedral school in Florence, though her five extant plays are in Italian (Weaver 2010, 3–4).

While few Latin-learned nuns lived in convents in Renaissance France, Claudine Scholastique de Bectoz (d. 1547), abbess at the convent of Saint Honorat-de-Tarascon in 1542, was legendary for her knowledge of Latin literature and her mastery of Latin prose. King François I and Marguerite de Navarre visited her at the convent at Saint Honorat. She is said to have written Latin poetry, but none of it survives (Stevenson 2005, 186). The Dominican nun Anne de Marquets (1533–1588) was the only other well-known Latin-literate nun in sixteenth-century France and was much admired by the Flemish Latin scholar and diplomat Karel Utenhove, who taught the humanist Jean de Morel's daughters. In England, convents were closed during the Reformation, although some were reestablished in Belgium, the Netherlands, France, and Portugal.

WOMEN IN UNIVERSITIES AND ACADEMIES

Three seventeenth-century women, the Parisian-born scholar Marie de Jars de Gournay (1565–1645), the Dutch polymath Anna Maria van Schurman from Utrecht (1607–1678), and the Venetian philosopher and theologian Elena Lucrezia Cornaro Piscopia (1646–1684), pioneered women's entrance into the academies and Universities of Continental Europe. All three were learned in Latin and other classical and modern languages. Van Schurman and Piscopia wrote and published in Latin, while Gournay read Latin but published her works in French. All three writers forged connections with one another as well as with the learned men of their era through their Latin correspondence. None of the three ever married; nor did they consider monachization a desirable alternative to marriage. Study and writing were their primary commitments.

Gournay was an outlier in France. She taught herself Latin and Greek at a time when France was practically the only country in Continental Europe where learned men and women published almost solely in the vernacular. Having translated Virgil, Tacitus, Sallust, Ovid, Cicero, and Diogenes Laertius (from the Greek) into French, Gournay became the trusted editor and *fille d'alliance* of Michel de Montaigne. Chiefly known for her two feminist treatises, *L'Égalité des hommes et des femmes* and *Le Grief des Dames* (*The Ladies' Complaint*, 1626), she never enrolled in any of the official learned academies, though she was an honored presence in academic and university circles. As a champion of the intellectual equality of the sexes, she corresponded with Anna Maria van Schurman and other intellectual women of her epoch (Gournay 2002; Stevenson 2005, 196–98).

Van Schurman was born in Cologne but lived most of her life in Utrecht (Schurman 1998). Her major Latin writings include her feminist treatise *Dissertatio de ingenii muliebris ad doctrinam et meliores litteras aptitudine* (*An Argument Concerning Women's Innate Capacity for Knowledge and Higher Learning*, 1641); and a philosophical discourse *On the End of Human Life*, the *De vitae termino* (1639). Her Latin, Greek, Hebrew, and French letters were published with her *Dissertatio*; she was also proficient in Chaldaic, Arabic, Ethiopian, Flemish, German, and Italian (Pal 2012, 94). Van Schurman, hidden by a curtain, attended classes at the new University of Utrecht. At the convocation of the university in 1636, she presented a Latin ode she had composed (Van Beek 2002, 3:286–87).

Cornaro Piscopia defended her dissertation at the University of Padua in 1678. The first woman in Europe to receive a doctorate in philosophy, Piscopia was inducted into several learned Italian academies: the Recovrati of Padua, the Erranti of Brescia, the Pacifici of Venice, the Infecondi and Dodonei of Rome, and the Intronati of Siena. Among her numerous writings, her Latin oration calling for the liberation of Vienna from the Turks (1683) demonstrated the power of an educated woman's voice. In the eighteenth century, a number of learned women followed in Piscopia's footsteps, earning their doctorates at universities in Italy (Stevenson 2005, 322–23).

When the prestigious Accademia dell'Arcadia was founded in Rome in 1690, several Latin-learned women were inducted, among them Anna Maria Ardoini, Maria Selvaggia Borghini, Diamante Patavina, Teresa Bandettini, Cristina Roccati, and Luisa Bergalli (Stevenson 2005, 313, 317, 319, 433–34). Bergalli (1703–1779), who managed the Sant'Angelo theater in Venice, published two editions of her translations of Terence's comedies (Venice 1726, 1731). In 1726, she brought out a two-volume historical anthology of 250 Italian women poets, the *Componimenti poetici delle piu illustri rimatrici d'ogni secolo* (*Poetic Compositions of the Most Prominent Female Versifiers of All Time*; Stewart 1994; Tassistro 1920; Mioni 1908).

Conclusion

As this chapter has shown, the rich culture of Latinity in palace and home schools, convents, and academies, produced a lasting tradition of classically trained women who fought to secure a place in the distinguished academies, institutions of higher learning, and universities that had excluded them. By the middle of the eighteenth century, women were not only entering these institutions; in Italy, women held university professorships in jurisprudence, philosophy, mathematics, anatomy, obstetrics, Greek, mechanics and hydraulics, among other disciplines (Stevenson 2005, 322–23). But educated women did not achieve these goals in isolation from one another; such women as van Schurman, Makin, and Bergalli reached out to one another. As van Schurman wrote to the then ninety-year-old Gournay to congratulate her on her fight for women's rights, together they were following a higher, more enduring cause (text and translation Stevenson 2005, 351):

> *Palladis arma geris, bellis animosa virago;*
>   *utque geras lauros, Palladis arma geris . . .*
> *I prae Gornacense decus, tua signa sequemur:*
>   *quippe tibi potior, robore, causa praeit.*

> You bear the arms of Pallas, virago courageous in war;
>   That you may wear the laurels, you bear the arms of Pallas. . .
> Go ahead, glory of Gournay, we will follow your standards,
>   Seeing that a cause superior in strength to yourself is leading the way!

Suggested Reading

On the ideology of gender and the culture of Latin see Campbell (2013); Ross (2009a); Allen (2002); Jordan (1990); and Woodbridge (1984). For historical surveys of European women writing Latin from antiquity to the eighteenth century, see Stevenson (2005); Churchill, Brown, and Jeffrey (2002); Cox (2008 and 2011); Robin (2013); and King and Rabil (1983). For women and Latin literacy in Spain, see Cruz and Hernández (2011) and Howe (2008). On convents and Latin culture, see Van Wyhe (2008); Evangelisti (2007); and Weaver (2002).

References

Agrippa, Heinrich C. 1996. *Declamation on the Nobility and Preeminence of the Female Sex.* Translated by Albert Rabil. Chicago: University of Chicago Press.

Allen, Prudence. 2002. *The Concept of Woman.* Vol. 2, *The Early Humanist Reformation, 1250–1500.* Grand Rapids: W. B. Eerdmans.

Baernstein, Renée. 2002. *A Convent Tale: A Century of Sisterhood in Spanish Milan.* New York: Routledge.

Barrett-Graves, Debra. 2007. "Lanyer, Aemilia Bassano (ca. 1569–1645)." In Robin, Larsen, and Levin 2007, 199–200.

Benson, Pamela J. 1992. *The Invention of the Renaissance Woman.* University Park: Pennsylvania State University Press.

Bilinkoff, Jodi. 1989. *The Avila of Saint Teresa.* Ithaca: Cornell University Press.

Bornstein, Daniel, and Roberto Rusconi, eds. 1996. *Women and Religion in Medieval and Renaissance Italy.* Translated by Margery J. Scheider. Chicago: University of Chicago Press.

Broomhall, Susan. 2002. *Women and the Book Trade in Sixteenth-Century France.* Burlington: Ashgate.

Campbell, Julie D. 2009. "Crossing International Borders: Tutors and the Transmission of Young Women's Writing." In Campbell and Larsen 2009, 213–28.

———. 2013. "The *Querelle des femmes.*" In Poska, Couchman, and McIver 2013, 361–79.

Campbell, Julie D., and Anne R. Larsen, eds. 2009. *Early Modern Women and Transnational Communities of Letters.* Farnham: Ashgate.

Cereta, Laura. 1640. *Epistolae.* Edited by Jacopo Filippo Tomasini. Padua: Sebastiano Sardi.

———. 1997. *Collected Letters of a Renaissance Feminist.* Translated by Diana Robin. Chicago: University of Chicago Press.

Churchill, Laurie J., Phyllis R. Brown, and Jane E. Jeffrey, eds. 2002. *Women Writing Latin: From Roman Antiquity to Early Modern Europe.* 3 vols. London: Routledge.

Cox, Virginia. 2008. *Women's Writing in Italy 1400–1650.* Baltimore: Johns Hopkins University Press.

———. 2011. *The Prodigious Muse: Women's Writing in Counter-Reformation Italy.* Baltimore: Johns Hopkins University Press.

Cruz, Anne J., and Rosilie Hernández, eds. 2011. *Women's Literacy in Early Modern Spain and the New World.* Burlington: Ashgate.

Des Roches, Madeleine, and Catherine Des Roches. 2006. *From Mother and Daughter: Poems, Dialogues, and Letters by les Dames des Roches.* Edited and translated by Anne R. Larsen. Chicago: University of Chicago Press.

Elizabeth I. 2000. *Collected Works*. Edited by Leah Marcus, Janet Mueller, and Mary Beth Rose. Chicago: University of Chicago Press.

Evangelisti, Silvia. 2007. *Nuns: A History of Convent Life, 1450–1700*. Oxford: Oxford University Press.

Fahy, Conor. 1965. "Three Early Renaissance Treatises on Women." *Italian Studies* 12:30–55.

Fedele, Cassandra. 1636. *Epistolae et orationes*. Edited by Iacopo Filippo Tomasini. Padua: Bolzetta.

———. 2000. *Letters and Orations*. Translated by Diana Robin. Chicago: University of Chicago Press.

Fenster, Thelma. 2004. "Strong Voices, Weak Minds? The Defenses of Eve by Isotta Nogarola and Christine de Pizan, Who Found Themselves in Simone de Beauvoir's Situation." In *Strong Voices, Weak History: Early Women Writers and Canons in England, France, and Italy*, edited by Pamela Joseph Benson and Victoria Kirkham. Ann Arbor: University of Michigan Press.

Fiszman, Samuel B. 1988. *The Polish Renaissance in Its European Context*. Bloomington: Indiana University Press.

Fonte, Moderata. 1997. *The Worth of Women*. Translated by Virginia Cox. Chicago: University of Chicago Press.

Gournay, Marie de Jars de. 2002. *Apology for the Woman Writing and Other Works*. Edited and translated by Richard Hillman and Colette Quesnel. Chicago: University of Chicago Press.

Grendler, Paul F. 1989. *Schooling in Renaissance Italy*. Baltimore: Johns Hopkins University Press.

Gundersheimer, Werner. 1980. "Bartolommeo Goggio: A Feminist in Renaissance Ferrara." *Renaissance Quarterly* 33:175–200.

Howe, Elizabeth T. 2008. *Education and Women in the Early Modern Hispanic World*. Aldershot: Ashgate.

———. 2011. " 'Let Your Women Keep Silence': The Pauline Dictum and Women's Education." In Cruz and Hernández, op. cit., 123–37.

Hutchinson, Lucy. 2011. *The Works of Lucy Hutchinson*. Vol. 1. Edited by Reid Barbour and David Norbrook. Oxford: Oxford University Press.

Jordan, Constance. 1990. *Renaissance Feminism: Literary Texts and Political Models*. Ithaca: Cornell University Press.

King, Margaret, and Albert Rabil, Jr. 1983. *Her Immaculate Hand: Selected Works by and about the Women Humanists of Quattrocento Italy*. Binghamton: Center for Medieval and Renaissance Studies.

Kirk, Stephanie L. 2011. "Women's Literacy and Masculine Authority: The Case of Sor Juana Inés de la Cruz and Antonio Núñez de Miranda." In Cruz and Hernández, op. cit., 139–57.

Labalme, Patricia H. 1981. "Venetian Women on Women: Three Early Modern Feminists." *Archivio Veneto* 5:81–109.

Lanyer, Aemilia. 1993. *Salve Deus Rex Judaeorum*. Edited by Suzanne Woods. New York: Oxford University Press.

Larsen, Anne. 2007. "Dames des Roches (Madeleine Neveu, 1520–1587); Catherine Fradonnet, 1542–1587)." In Robin, Larsen, and Levin 2007, 109–12.

Lehfeldt, Elizabeth A. 2013. "The Permeable Cloister." In Poska, Couchman, and McIver 2013, 12–31.

Marinella, Lucrezia. 1999. *The Nobility and Excellence of Women and the Defects and Vices of Men*. Translated by Anne Dunhill. Chicago: University of Chicago Press.

Mioni, Maria. 1908. *Una letterata veneziana del secolo XVIII*. Venice: Pellizzato.

Monson, Craig A, ed. 1992. *The Crannied Wall: Women, Religion, and the Arts in Early Modern Europe*. Ann Arbor: University of Michigan Press.

———. 1995. *Disembodied Voices: Music and Culture in an Early Modern Italian Convent*. Berkeley and Los Angeles: University of California Press, 1995.

Morata, Olympia. 2003. *The Complete Writings of an Italian Heretic*. Edited and translated by Holt N. Parker. Chicago: University of Chicago Press.

Nader, Helen. 2004. *Power and Gender in Renaissance Spain: Eight Women of the Mendoza Family, 1450–1650*. Urbana-Champaign: University of Illinois Press.

Nauert, Charles G. 1999. "Agrippa of Nettesheim, Heinrich." In *Encyclopedia of the Renaissance*, edited by Paul Grendler, vol. 1, 24–26. New York: Scribners.

Nogarola, Isotta. 1886. *Opera quae supersunt omnia*. Edited by Eugenius Abel. 2 vols. Vienna: Gerold et Socii.

———. 2004. *Complete Writings*. Translated by Margaret L. King and Diana Robin. Chicago: University of Chicago Press.

Pal, Carol. 2012. *Republic of Women. Rethinking the Republic of Letters in the Seventeenth Century*. Cambridge: Cambridge University Press.

Pellegrin, Elizabeth. 1955. *La Bibliothèque des Visconti et des Sforza, ducs de Milan, au XVe siècle*. Paris: Institut de Recherche et d'Histoire des Textes.

Perry, Mary Elizabeth. 1990. *Gender and Disorder in Early Modern Seville*. Princeton: Princeton University Press.

Poska, Allyson, Jane Couchman, and Katherine A. McIver, eds. 2013. *The Ashgate Research Companion to Women and Gender in Early Modern Europe*. Farnham: Ashgate.

Quilligan, Maureen. 1991. *The Allegory of Female Authority: Christine de Pizan's* Cité des Dames. Ithaca: Cornell University Press.

Rabil, Albert Jr. 1981. *Laura Cereta. Quattrocento Humanist*. Binghamton: Center for Medieval and Renaissance Studies.

Robin, Diana. 1997. "Woman, Space, and Renaissance Discourse." In *Sex and Gender in Medieval and Renaissance Texts: The Latin Tradition*, edited by Barbara Gold, Paul Allen Miller, and Charles Platter, 165–88. Albany: State University of New York Press.

———. 2013. "Intellectual Women in Early Modern Europe." In Poska, Couchman, and McIver, op. cit., 381–406.

Robin, Diana, Anne Larsen, and Carole Levin, eds. 2007. *Encyclopedia of Women in the Renaissance*. Santa Barbara: ABC-CLIO.

Ross, Sarah G. 2009a. *The Birth of Feminism: Woman as Intellect in Renaissance Italy and England*. Cambridge: Harvard University Press.

———. 2009b. "Esther Inglis: Linguist, Calligrapher, Miniaturist, and Christian Humanist." In Campbell and Larsen, op. cit., 159–81.

Rossi, Ottavio. 1620. *Elogi istorici de' Bresciani illustri*. Brescia: Bartolomeo Fontana.

Schurman, Anna Maria van. 1998. *Whether a Christian Woman Should Be Educated: And Other Writings from Her Intellectual Circle*. Translated by Joyce L. Irwin. Chicago: University of Chicago Press.

Speght, Rachel. 1996. *The Polemics and Poems of Rachel Speght*. Edited by Barbara Kiefer Lewalski. Oxford: Oxford University Press.

Stevenson, Jane. 2005. *Women Latin Poets*. Oxford: Oxford University Press.

Stewart, Paula. 1994. "Luisa Bergalli (1703–1779)." In *Italian Women Writers: A Bio-Bibliographical Sourcebook*, edited by Rinaldina Russell, 50–57. Westport: Greenwood Press.

Strocchia, Sharon. 2009. *Nuns and Nunneries in Renaissance Florence*. Baltimore: Johns Hopkins University Press.

Tanner, Marcus. 2008. *The Raven King: Matthias Corvinus and the Fate of His Lost Library*. New Haven: Yale University Press.

Tassistro, Carlotta E. 1920. *Luisa Bergalli Gozzi: La vita e l'opera sua nel suo tempo*. Rome: Bertero.

Van Beek, Pieta. 2002. "Alpha Virginum: Anna Maria van Schurman (1607–1679)." In Churchill, Brown, and Jeffrey, op. cit., 3:286–87.

Vives, Juan L. 1529. *A Very Fruitful and Pleasant Boke Called the Instruction of a Christen Woman*. Translated by Richard Hyrde. London: Thomas Berthelet.

———. 2002. *The Instruction of a Christen Woman*. Translated by Richard Hyrde and edited by Virginia W. Beauchamp, Elizabeth H. Hageman, and Margaret Mikesell. Urbana and Chicago: University of Illinois Press.

Van Wyhe, Cordula, ed. 2008. *Female Monasticism in Early Modern Europe*. Aldershot: Ashgate.

Weaver, Elissa B. 2002. *Convent Theatre in Early Modern Italy*. Cambridge: Cambridge University Press.

———. 2010. *Saints' Lives and Bible Stories for the Stage*. Edited and translated by James Wyatt Cook. Toronto: Iter, incorporating the Centre for Reformation and Renaissance Studies.

Weston, Elizabeth J. 2000. *Collected Writings*. Edited and translated by Donald Cheney and Brenda M. Hosington. Toronto: University of Toronto Press.

Woodbridge, Linda. 1984. *Women and the English Renaissance*. Urbana: University of Illinois Press.

Woodward, William H. 1905. *Vittorino da Feltre and Other Humanist Educators*. Cambridge: Harvard University Press.

CHAPTER 24

SOCIAL STATUS

FRANÇOISE WAQUET

In May of 1968, when Latin was officially removed from the first year of the *lycée* in France, the minister responsible justified the step by presenting teaching of the language as the preserve of "cultural heirs" ("héritiers de la culture") and as "an obstacle to democratization" ("un frein à la démocratisation"). In the egalitarian climate of the period, Latin was considered "bourgeois," and this was one of the reasons for its suppression. This symbolic episode shows that Latin was not just a school subject; it was a social tool. It raises a historical point about the conversion of a scholarly discipline, a body of knowledge, into a means of differentiation. We need to look back to discover how Latin acquired such a role in Western society; how it was used to draw a line between those who knew it and those who did not. Reserving knowledge of the language for a social elite and excluding lower classes from it reinforced its worth as a tool of differentiation. The status that Latin had acquired over time reveals itself again when girls, who had long been excluded, were permitted access to the language, not on intellectual, but on social grounds.

THE CONSTRUCTION OF A TOOL
OF DISTINCTION

It is fitting to start with the humanist school as it established itself during the classical revival in fifteenth-century Italy. At a time when any training beyond basic education was rare, school was an elite phenomenon, intended for elite children who were being prepared to carry out elitist roles. The teaching that a school was able to provide developed skills of acknowledged practical value for performing high-level civil or religious functions. However, this training carried a danger inherent to its own methods: there was a big risk that commenting on the ancient authors could be reduced to technical observations and that the text might disappear under an excess of scholarship. In fact, there were many cases during the last part of the fifteenth century in which masters and students could be found gratuitously flaunting their knowledge, smugly picking out the errors of Homer and Virgil and then arguing among themselves over the minutiae. Associated with such behavior, the humanist school strayed from its high educational ideal to end up merely training specialists or technicians.

In Italy, too, the elite then saw another model appear: that of the courtier. Baldassare Castiglione's *Libro del Cortegiano* (*Book of the Courtier*, 1528) taught that anyone living at court should always display *sprezzatura* ("studied carelessness"): he should "conceal all art and make whatever is done or said appear to be without effort and almost without any thought about it"; on the other hand, continued Castiglione, exposing the art "robs a man of all credit and causes him to be held in slight esteem" (Book 1, chapters 25–26; Castiglione 2002).

From the beginning of the sixteenth century in Italy, and then later elsewhere, one character who did reveal his art was roundly condemned: the pedant. This figure was ridiculed in numerous comedies, including *Il pedante* by Francesco Belo (1529), *Il candelaio* (*The Chandler*) by Giordano Bruno (1582), Edward Forsett's *Pedantius* (1581), then later *Le pédant joué* (*The Pedant Tricked*) by Cyrano de Bergerac (1654), and Molière's *Les femmes savantes* (*The Learned Ladies*, 1673). One of the traits which these satires invariably came back to was the pedant's penchant for excessive use of Latin, often of a particularly pompous variety, as well his deep concern to demonstrate a brand of learning that reveled in the details. These foibles appeared predominantly among regents and schoolmasters, moreover in "souls of little worth" ("âmes de bas aloi"), as Montaigne described them in his *Du Pédantisme* (*On Pedantry*) in the *Essais* (Montaigne 1962, 141). "Pedant" and "Latin" even came to be confused, as is evident in the expression "gens à latin" ("Latin people") coined by Molière to refer to pedants such as Trissotin in *Les femmes savantes*. It was not Latin itself that was the object of such mockery, rather a degeneration in its usage and notably an excessive fondness for citations and etymologies. This misuse of Latin was all the more ridiculous because it contrasted with the ideal of polite behavior among the ladies and gentlemen at court and then of the *mondains* (Stäuble 1991, 14–115; Royé 2008).

However, Latin was in no way driven out of fashionable society. It was actually integrated to some extent. The nobility considered a classical education crucial for fulfilling certain functions or for participating in courtly life: it was necessary to refine the taste and judgment of would-be patrons and to educate spectators so that they would be capable of decoding mythological references at court ballets and reading the Latin inscriptions at festivals. The goal, however, was not to turn the children of aristocrats into scholars. The erudite path, which required long years of study, was rejected. Preferred instead was a training based on translation, with the child working on political, historical, or military texts more suited to his requirements. This education was at first conducted at home, but things changed later with the appearance of the Jesuit colleges. In France, nobles sent their sons to these institutions. The duration of their studies reflected the career envisaged for them, either in the army or in the church. In this way, children received Latin instruction for varying lengths of time in the context of institutions that produced men of the world—it is worth bearing in mind that these colleges also taught the arts of the gentleman. In this way too, the noble education, far from rejecting Latin, integrated it, but in stripping it of everything that might make it pedantic (Motley 1990, 68–121). Latin, then, became a "noble" subject, regardless of whether the teaching in the colleges went into the minutiae.

Latin had become the symbol of society's upper-class education, and its increasing lack of real use—Latin would play an ever-smaller role in the future professional life—confirmed its symbolic function. This function lasted. For this reason we find numerous assertions in the nineteenth century that a classical education ought not produce Latinists. This is also the reason for the disdain in France and perhaps even more in England for the German philological approach, which was thought to turn students into specialists.

Under these conditions, Latin abandoned its scholarly leaning, which, in polite society, might have been fatal. In the process, it had changed its status. It was no longer purely useful or utilitarian knowledge, associated with professions lacking prestige. It was, for the elite who exposed their children to Latin in high doses, purely honorable knowledge, as Thorstein Veblen described it in his analysis of classical studies among the "leisure class" (Veblen 2007, 240–59). In this way, Latin "classified": it made the gentleman in England and the bourgeois in France; that is, it served to signal a person's belonging to a social class in which it was possible to spend money, time, and energy on acquiring knowledge that was not, in professional and economic terms, purely useful. It was part of a "culture of luxury" ("culture de luxe") in the words of the philosopher and sociologist Edmond Goblot (1925, 125).

These remarks summarize the opinions, current within society since the seventeenth century, on the need for Latin training among upper-class children. John Locke (1632–1704) was very clear on this point when he wrote: "Latin I look upon as absolutely necessary to a gentleman" (Locke 1823, 152). A century later, the English aristocracy, which had long looked down on the classics, had adopted different views altogether. An education without Latin was now inconceivable. Lord Chesterfield, in letters to his son, frequently insisted on a sure and steady training in Latin and on May 27, 1748, explained to him: "Classical knowledge, that is, Greek and Latin, is absolutely necessary for everybody; because everybody has agreed to think and to call it so" (Armstrong 1973, 130).

In France where, since the Revolution, no one talked of "the gentleman" anymore, and where, in the course of the nineteenth century, the demand had grown for teaching more adapted to the needs of modern society, even among the bourgeoisie, this same bourgeoisie, above all its richest components, kept teaching their children the classics. Latin and the elite went together. The words of contemporary commentators are revealing on this topic, such as the educationalist Monsignor Dupanloup's (1802–1878) statement to the National Assembly: "The ruling classes will always remain the ruling classes . . . because they know Latin" ("Les classes dirigeantes resteront toujours les classes dirigeantes . . . parce qu'elles savent le latin"; Prost 1968, 332).

Thus, Latin signified belonging to the ruling group. Conversely, the lack of any Latin skills indicated lower-class origins. "A man who does not smile knowingly at a citation from Homer or Virgil is a man condemned," noted Émile Zola. "That man is not one of ours, he has not polished school benches for ten years with the seat of his pants; he knows neither Greek nor Latin and that is enough to consider him one of the poor blokes" (Zola 1969, 239). One could not wish for a clearer expression of the distinction that Latin enforced. Zola's quote has its counterpart in an equally short passage by Paul Valéry. On the subject of teaching as it was in the France of 1945, he noted in his *Cahiers*: "it develops only what distinguishes (according to the conventions) a class and what allows a person to move or manoeuver within a restricted circle—like a password, because Greek and Latin are just a password. It is not a question of knowing them" (Valéry 1974, 1674).

Here we see a practice, often the only one, that demonstrates classical-language learning: adorning one's speech with a citation in Latin, without falling into pedantry. Being able to make appropriate citations in Latin was a distinguishing mark, a visible symbol of belonging to the world of cultivated people. For this reason, works such as Pierre Larousse's *Flore latine des dames et des gens du monde* (*Latin Pocket-Book for Ladies and Men of the World*, 1861) were published. It had at least six editions before 1914. At a time when French prose was peppered with Latin citations, this book offered itself as a type of "convenient and discreet translator" ("un traducteur commode et discret"), for those who had never learnt Latin or who had forgotten it, which they could consult without fear of making an error and above all without being humiliated (Larousse 1861, xxix–xxx). Now we understand the advice that in 1846 Andrew Amos gave to boys on their way into the trade professions: obtain some additional classical training. It would provide them with the social ease and respectability of gentleman, and, above all, it would save them the embarrassment that would befall them if, in urbane society, their ignorance of Latin should be uncovered because of a quotation (Clarke 1959, 170).

While Latin and the social elite were merging, some groups whose inclusion in that very elite was under threat passionately affirmed their dedication to classical studies as a way of preserving their social standing. The situation of the penniless gentry in Victorian England is revealing. In 1860, as part of a consideration of secondary teaching, the question arose over what sort of education to give to children according to their social class. The Schools Inquiry Commission of 1868 defined three types ("grades") of education according to the duration of schooling: "first grade" education, "which is to continue till 18 or 19"; "second grade" education, "which is to stop at about 16"; and "third grade" education, "which is to stop at about 14." Parents of "first grade" pupils, including the aristocracy, the gentry (rich or poor), professionals, and the clergy were not hostile to teaching innovations that gave a place to the sciences and modern languages, provided that they did not affect their children. For their own families, they wanted education to remain classical. This conservative attitude was particularly evident among members of the poorer gentry, for reasons that the Schools Inquiry Commission stated in very clear terms (Bamford 1967, 170–71):

> They would, no doubt, in most instances be glad to secure something more than classics and mathematics. But they value these highly for their own sake, and perhaps even more for the value at present assigned to them in English society. They have

nothing to look to but education to keep their sons on a high social level. And they would not wish to have what might be more readily converted into money, if in any degree it tended to let their children sink in the social scale.

Following the same logic, that powerful social bias in favor of the ancient language reappeared in France. Until the 1960s, it led the elite routinely to put their children into classical education and to consider a transfer into the Latin-less track a disgrace. The expression "descendre en moderne" ("going down to modern"), current at the time to describe the relegation of a child with a poor performance in the Classics track into the modern track, eloquently translated the fall in standards that the abandonment of Latin came to symbolize. The phrase had its counterpart in "monter en classique" ("going up to classic") to describe the opposite path that might be taken, albeit rarely, by a child who was gifted but who had been placed in the Latin-less track on account of his social background.

LATIN AS A SOCIAL BOUNDARY

Goblot, who associated Latin with a "culture of luxury," showed that at the same time it was a "barrier" that separated the different classes in society, effecting a "clear distinction ... between, on the one hand those who do not know Latin and on the other,—I will not say those who know it—but those who have learnt it" (Goblot 1925, 123). Incidentally, this remark targeted the poor skills of students of Latin as much in the seventeenth century as in the twentieth: the success of a few cannot conceal that the general level had consistently been low, despite long years of training (Waquet 1998, 157–82).

Humanist schools were schools for the elite, and Latin teaching, which was their principal concern, long remained an elitist subject. This was not least due to the fact that such an education was lengthy. This length already excluded the vast majority of children who, for obvious economic reasons, did not go further than the most elementary stage at school. Furthermore, over time, the establishments offering the most extensive education, such as the French collèges de plein exercice (which offered all the classes, as opposed to petits collèges offering only two to three classes), tended towards becoming elitist. They delegated the teaching of reading and writing skills to primary schools and thus created a clean break between elementary learning and teaching Latin. This led to an over-representation of the society's elite in the colleges, the strongholds of Latin: in the eighteenth century, the elite made up between two-thirds and four-fifths of their boarding pupils. As for the pupils who came from the town itself, social status determined the length of their studies: the majority of the nobles' sons and the sons of officials went on to the final class (called the "rhetoric class"), while only half of artisans' sons got that far.

Latin even came to distinguish between those who did and did not study it, between the rich and the poor in fact, within the classroom itself. The difference can be observed concretely in the classroom as arranged by Jean-Baptiste de La Salle (1651–1719), the founder of the Institute of the Brothers of the Christian Schools: the children "from a good background" ("de condition")—those who did Latin—were seated at tables located "in the most respectable part of the classroom" ("dans la partie la plus honorable de la classe"); they were thus separated from the poorer children, who were merely learning how to read and who were seated on simple benches (Lebrun, Vénart, and Quéniart 1981, 431).

This phenomenon of distinguishing between pupils went even further in the nineteenth century. The public schools in England, which were the Latin bastions *par excellence*, had an aristocratic recruitment if only because of their boarding fees. Latin, which reigned supreme, was occasionally used to maintain and reinforce their social exclusivity as well. Some of these schools were required, under the provisions of their foundation, to admit local children for free or for a nominal fee. To get around this awkward social arrangement, basic classes were dropped, so that a child must either have had a personal tutor or have gone through a fee-paying preparatory school to acquire the required amount of Latin to get into these exclusive institutions (Armstrong 1973, 143–44).

If the French *lycée* was more welcoming on a social level, it upheld through the teaching of Latin a distinction no less marked. The reorganization of the educational system under Napoleon set in place two tracks of teaching corresponding to the two social classes that made up society at the time: the bourgeoisie and the common people. This "ségrégation"—the official term—was based on Latin as well as on the payment of a special tax, called "rétribution." A directive of August 13, 1810, stated that: "All students admitted into an institution where Latin is taught will be subject to the *rétribution*" (Chervel 1993, 40). Throughout the nineteenth century, the *lycée* remained socially very even, and lower-class children made up the majority of the "modern" studies pupils in the twentieth century. In the mid-twentieth century, Latin still reflected social inequalities: in 1956, children of liberal professionals represented 12.6 percent of the students in the *lycées* doing classical studies, while the children of farmers and workers, who numbered almost double the population of the *lycées*, made up only 13.2 percent of Latinists (Ringer 1979, 330). In 1961–1962, the proportion of students who had done Latin in the faculties of arts at universities varied from 83 percent, for children of executives and professionals, to 41 percent for children of workers and farmers (Bourdieu and Passeron 1985, 26–27).

As well as marking off society's different classes, Latin also traced borders within the professional world, as the following examples from France make clear. Under the *Ancien Régime*, Latin made distinctions between related professions such as between the physician and surgeon. The pharmacists, in their desire not to be confused with grocers, advertised their knowledge of Latin. This use of Latin did not end with the Revolution, either. Under the Empire, during the reorganization of higher education, it was stipulated that for medicine, two of the five examinations that the candidate had to undergo must be in Latin; on the other hand, health officials took all of their examinations in French. Latin also distinguished a hierarchy in the engineering profession.

The increasing numbers of polytechnic students who had done the *baccalauréat*, that is to say who had done Latin, distinguished themselves not only from students studying arts and trades, who came from more modest social backgrounds, but also from their great rivals at the *École centrale* of whom 61 percent, on the eve of the First World War, had not studied the ancient language (Weiss 1984, 28). Latin had no use in these professions. It could not even claim to provide access to sources and to etymologies, which is what physicians could assert. It functioned as an indicator of social status. This emerges with particular clarity in the protests that German civil engineers staged against plans to open their profession to graduates from secondary schools that did not offer a classical education: they feared that the level of their profession would drop if Latin were abandoned as a prerequisite.

LATIN AS A SYMBOL OF SOCIAL EXCLUSION

Latin went on to become even more of an elite phenomenon as it was refused to those who tried to gain access to it from outside the ruling classes. The reasons behind this rejection belong to an idea of society in which each person has a role to perform according to his or her background. Consequently, there was no point in giving Latin to people who had absolutely no need of it on account of their backgrounds and who, ultimately, did not have a right to it; there was a great risk of ruining the providential equilibrium, of overturning the established order, or at least disturbing the current harmonious state of affairs. These reasons were clearly stated throughout the Europe of the *Ancien Régime*. Since children should be brought up in a way befitting their background and considering the role they were destined to play in society, Latin was of no use for the sons of artisans or shopkeepers; moreover, it might give these children aspirations above their station, aspirations that they would not be able to satisfy, leading to frustration and significant risk to society. The eighteenth-century reformers certainly considered it important to educate the people and respond to their demand for education; but this was to be limited to a basic level: learning to read and write, calculations, and some moral training. Latin was not a part of the program; it was explicitly excluded from it. A panorama of eighteenth-century Europe will make this evident.

The Spanish reformers considered Latin dangerous for the larger part of the population, as if it encouraged fanciful aspirations to inaccessible professions. Ultimately, it would lead to general weakness in the nation, and even riots; for the time being, it was identified as cause of the economic problems that were affecting the country by distracting hands and minds that would have been more naturally drawn to agriculture or engineering. In 1747, Ferdinand VI imposed a limit on the number of Latin schools, upholding a decree of Philip IV on the matter. From the beginning of the seventeenth century, Latin had already been considered responsible for the decline of Spain by the group of economic reformers known as *arbitristas*: it turned young people away from agriculture, crafts, and commerce and pressed them towards ecclesiastical or administrative careers, which were judged unproductive in economic terms. Indeed, Pedro Fernández Navarrete wrote in his *Conservación de monarquias* (*Preservation of the Monarchy*) of 1621 that the Latin schools, numbering more than 4,000, had had a hand in the decline of the kingdom's power (Kagan 1973, 301–2).

In Prussia, the "cameralists" thought that education should be *standesmäßig*—compatible with the role of the individual in the economic production and suitable for the occupation for which he was destined from birth. Among the poorer country folk, some instruction in reading and writing was enough; going any further than that encouraged their children to leave for the towns and so to swell the university proletariat, who were rendered unfit for manual labor and who, at the same time, were without the financial means to access official positions or liberal professions. Rulers, then, took action against this phenomenon. In Austria, Charles VI and then Maria Theresa gave only limited access to the *Gymnasien* to sons of craftsmen and farmers; in 1766, the empress declared in an edict that "not all children should be admitted to Latin schools, but only those of exceptional talent whose parents are sufficiently propertied to support them." In Silesia, Frederick II's officials reasoned in the same way. The education of farmers' sons had to respond to the economic imperative of working the land, as well as to worries over social discipline. Latin instruction for them was excluded on both accounts. Moreover, it was noted that Latin "only stimulates a desire to enter the priesthood, thereby destroying their natural inclination to practice the occupation of their fathers." In 1763, teaching Latin was forbidden in Silesia's rural schools. This measure was driven, once again, by the belief that Latin promoted arrogance and disobedience among the peasantry. The minister in charge of Silesia was clear on this point: various officials had assured him "that the most good-for-nothing, stubborn peasants in their districts are precisely those who have studied Latin." He was confirmed in this opinion by the archbishop of Breslau, who observed that "those peasants who have learned Latin . . . are in all respects the most disobedient" (van Horn Melton 1988, 114–19, 184–89).

In France, the craze among humble folk for having their children learn Latin was equally frowned upon. Louis Sébastien Mercier, in his *Tableau de Paris* (~ *Panorama of Paris*, 1781–1788), denounced the ambition of any petty bourgeois who could not himself read, to make a Latinist of his son, assuring him that "Latin leads to everything." But long years of school made the boy "a slacker who disdains any sort of manual work"; incapable, thereafter, of finding an administrative or clerical position, he would end up at home forever at the expense of his father. "The Latinist," Mercier continued, "does not know how to use his hands anymore, and it is then too late to take up a profession, and anyway this doctor who knows four lines of Cicero would not stoop to it." The demand for an education for the people to which Mercier, like others of his "enlightened" contemporaries subscribed, aimed at practical subjects and excluded Latin. Hence his call to the government to close the *collèges de plein exercice*, which were producing "a flood of slackers and loafers." In those institutions, there was a veritable "gangrene" that was eating away at the middle-classes, a "scourge" ("fléau") on the whole body of society (Mercier 1994, 1:205–8 and 1146–50; Chisick 1981, 135–53).

Similar remarks were made in Italy as well. In the competitions held by the Academy of Modena in 1772 and 1774 on the teaching of the lower classes, the contributors unanimously agreed that children from inferior backgrounds should be given an education befitting their status: therefore, they kept sons of craftsmen and farmers away from a Latin education, which, far from preparing them for a trade, only made them unhappy and useless in themselves as well as in society (Lucchi 1985, 39–52 and 78–80). Access to Latin was restricted, very concretely, by financial means. Latin teachers who were teaching in primary schools preparing children for secondary school could charge a monthly fee of twenty to twenty-five *soldi*, which excluded the children of peasants. In Piedmont at the end of the *Ancien Régime*, if secondary colleges were free, this was not the case for all primary schools, and the *settima* (then the transitional year between primary and secondary school) had to be paid for. Thus, Latin functioned as a deliberate filter, restricting access to secondary education for children thought unsuitable for it (Cigolini 1982, 1027–29).

Mutatis mutandis, the same arguments and the same processes were common throughout the nineteenth century. In France, the *lycée* functioned as means of social "segregation": it was a bastion of the bourgeoisie. Concern for the education of the lower classes went hand-in-hand with a refusal to allow them access to Latin: a classical education was considered incompatible with their social background; it rendered them unfit for the trades they were destined for by their birth, which, moreover, risked deep demoralization. Exclusion and differentiation only reinforced the prestige that was attached to Latin and the fascination it held for those who did not have access to it. Those excluded came to internalize the distinction that Latin created between social classes and between the different types of occupation. They brought their views into line with those of the authorities and the elite. From the end of the seventeenth century, the *petite bourgeoisie* were convinced that there could be no education without Latin. Locke remarked upon this phenomenon, specifically the craze among merchants and farmers for sending their children off to Latin school when they had neither the intention nor the means to make scholars of them (Locke 1823, 153):

> If you ask them, why they do this? They think it as strange a question, as if you should ask them why they go to church? Custom serves for reason, and has, to those that take it for reason, so consecrated this method, that it is almost religiously observed by them; and they stick to it, as if their children had scarce an orthodox education, unless they learned Lilly's grammar.

With such an early text (written in 1693), one might even ask whether the conviction of the lower classes might not have preceded that of the elite. Or, at least, whether it might not have played a large role in this complex process whereby some people's desire to imitate reinforced the need for differentiation among others.

In any case, Latin seemed a way to move beyond one's social status, to move up in society; this is what emerges from the texts cited above. The desire to move up in society using Latin endured: it can be seen at work in the United States during the 1890s and afterwards when working-class children went into secondary education in large numbers. They widely opted for classical subjects, and this preference increased over time: in the academic year 1889–1890, 35 percent chose Latin; in 1905, the percentage rose to 50 percent. The more educationalists sought to adapt the curriculum of these children to their requirements—not to say to their status—the more those children (or their parents) chose the traditional subjects. For them, secondary education meant Latin, not metalwork or sewing. Very quickly, educationalists saw a potential danger here and the risk that these children were harboring fanciful aspirations. They took pains, then, to turn them away from choosing Latin by pushing them towards practical subjects, better suited to their probable or apparent futures. They also reduced the amount of Latin available, while at the same time recommending it to those who had the means, above all financial, to continue their studies after secondary school (Nasaw 1979, 134–39 and 145).

Women's Long Road to Latin

It was principally for social reasons that access to Latin was refused to women for so long. Charles Rollin, rector of the University of Paris, was very clear on the subject. It was not a question of intellect ("sex, on its own, makes no difference in people's minds"), but was social: in a world governed by Providence, which defined each person's status and duties, women were not "destined to educate people, govern states, wage war, serve justice, plead cases or practice medicine; their share is within the home." For these domestic functions, Latin was useless; moreover, with the knowledge going hand-in-hand with it, it risked inciting unprecedented ambition, turning a woman away from her duties and leading towards disastrous consequences for her family as well as, ultimately, for society as a whole (Rollin 1734, 53–60).

With the exception of home schooling by scholars such as Gerardus Vossius, Tanneguy Lefèvre, or Charles Patin in the seventeenth century, who taught their daughters Latin, the teaching that girls received throughout the *Ancien Régime* was limited to morals, religion, the basics of reading, writing, counting, and handling a needle and thread. Things only changed very slowly, and, during the majority of the nineteenth century, a girl's education included no Latin, but subjects that prepared her for her future domestic functions. Although in Germany basic schooling for girls was more extensive and the literacy rate higher, access to the higher stages of learning was impossible for the large majority of the female population. Having the same education for the two sexes was considered unreasonable, as if it jeopardized "the foundations of the natural, and therefore inalienable, difference that the inequality is" (Hoock-Demarle 1991, 152; cf. Albisetti 1988, 18–19).

However, during the nineteenth century, Latin was gradually introduced into female education. It was done tentatively, in the form of optional courses or in schools for the elite, or in institutions designed to offer further education without preparing a student for a profession as such. This tendency arose earlier across the Atlantic than in Europe. But before Latin was offered as widely to girls as it was to boys—not forgetting that it was not equally available to all boys during the nineteenth century—there was a good deal of opposition. Just as in the past, arguments were based not on the girls' intellectual inferiority but on social reasons.

In France, secondary education for women, established in 1880, was intended to ensure stability within the households. It was supposed to help prevent a "divorce of intellect" ("divorce intellectuel") from developing between the educated husband and his uncultured wife. It was not, then, about giving girls an education that would prepare them for a profession; even less about making scholars of them. The type of teaching that was put in place was at the level, and above all in the spirit, of higher primary education (Mayeur 1977, 9–32). Latin came into the curriculum by way of electives and was limited to a certain period of time—"the short Latin" ("le latin court"). It was only in 1924 that public *lycées* offered the same Latin program to girls as they did to boys. This offer was, moreover, subject to payment. Moreover, it was on the basis of primarily social arguments that the supporters of Latin for girls, mostly Latin teachers, had fought and succeeded to bring about change. They showed that girls brought their "feminine" abilities to the study of Latin, which could only support their learning of the language; in particular, the fact that Latin was difficult reinforced that feminine quality of modesty. They focused on the maternal role for which the girls were destined: mastery of Latin would allow them to keep up with their sons' Latin studies, making them language "coaches" ("répétitrices"). More generally, Latin prepared them for their futures as house mistresses, as Léopold Druesnes, professor at the *lycée* in Lille and ardent advocate of Latin for girls, wrote in 1913:

> The qualities necessary for management of a household are ... reason, common sense, wisdom, method, a sense of order and rule. Well! All these qualities are precisely the qualities of the Latin mind and, in particular, of the Latin language. The Latin language is sensible, methodical and disciplined; it is an everlasting lesson in reason and common sense.

(Druesnes 1913, 250–52)

Conclusion and Further Thoughts

Since the seventeenth century at least, Latin had functioned as a means of social differentiation: it served to classify people as well as to reproduce and reinforce the structure of contemporary society. It is clear that today it no longer plays this role. However, some assign to it a new social, or sociopolitical, role. Latin, indeed just as Greek, is presented as a useful tool for integration into European society. "All young Europeans should be able to study an ancient language to return to their roots," asserted Jean-Pierre Levet, professor at the University of Limoges and president of Eurosophia (a European federation of Classics teachers in higher education), in an interview. This benefit applies *a fortiori* to children from immigrant backgrounds, for whom learning Latin means having the possibility to become a member of a national community; and Levet makes this explicit: "access to the ancient language and culture, means access to a deep understanding of the host country's culture and having an opportunity for integration" (Bernabeu 2007, 31).

Suggested Reading

The social status of Latin is not one of the areas of Neo-Latin studies that have received much attention, even though a considerable amount of information is available in work on the organization of Latin teaching and educational methods throughout the period (see the list of references below). For an overview of the topic in question from a Western perspective, see Waquet (1998). For the humanistic period, see Grafton and Jardine (1986). Burke (2004) provides a brief analysis of Latin as a factor of social inclusion. Royé's (2008) work on the pedant, principally from literary texts, allows us to pin this social figure down for the sixteenth to seventeenth centuries as the representation of inordinate use of Latin jargon. Waquet (2015), examines the social dimensions of girls' access to Latin.

[*Translated from the French by William Barton and the author.*]

References

Albisetti, James C. 1988. *Schooling German Girls and Women: Secondary and Higher Education in the Nineteenth Century*. Princeton: Princeton University Press.

Armstrong, John A. 1973. *The European Administrative Elite*. Princeton: Princeton University Press.

Bamford, Thomas W. 1967. *Rise of the Public Schools: A Study of Boys' Public Boarding Schools in England and Wales from 1837 to the Present Day*. London: Nelson.

Bernabeu, Laurence. 2007. "Les langues mortes n'ont pas rendu leur dernier souffle." *Valeurs mutualistes* 247:30–31.

Bourdieu, Pierre, and Jean-Claude Passeron. 1985. *Les Héritiers: Les étudiants et la culture*. Paris: Éditions de Minuit.

Burke, Peter. 2004. "Latin: A Language in Search of a Community." In *Languages and Communities in Early Modern Europe*, 43–60. Cambridge: Cambridge University Press.

Castiglione, Baldassare. 2002. *The Book of the Courtier*. Edited by Daniel Javitch and translated by Charles S. Singleton. New York: Norton.

Chervel, André. 1993. *Histoire de l'agrégation: Contribution à l'étude de la culture scolaire*. Paris: I.N.R.P., Éditions Kimé.

Chisick, Harvey. 1981. *The Limits of Reform in the Enlightenment: Attitudes Towards the Education of the Lower Classes in Eighteenth-Century France*. Princeton: Princeton University Press.

Cigolini, Maria T. 1982. "L'istruzione primaria in Lombardia nell'età delle Riforme." In *Economia, istituzioni, cultura in Lombardia nell'età di Maria Teresa*, vol. 3, *Istituzioni e società*, edited by Aldo De Maddalena, Ettore Rotelli, and Gennaro Barbarisi, 1025–37. Bologna: Il Mulino.

Clarke, Martin L. 1959. *Classical Education in Britain 1500–1900*. Cambridge: Cambridge University Press.

Druesnes, Léopold. 1913. "La jeune latiniste au foyer." *Bulletin de l'enseignement secondaire des jeunes filles* of *Revue universitaire* 22.2:250–52.

Goblot, Edmond. 1925. *La barrière et le niveau: Étude sociologique sur la bourgeoisie française*. Paris: Librairie Félix Alcan.

Grafton, Anthony, and Lisa Jardine. 1986. *From Humanism to the Humanities: Education and the Liberal Arts in Fifteenth- and Sixteenth-Century Europe*. London: Duckworth.

Hoock-Demarle, Marie-Claire. 1991. "Lire et écrire en Allemagne." In *Histoire des femmes en Occident*, vol. 4, *Le XIXe siècle*, edited by Geneviève Fraisse and Michelle Perrot, 147–67. Paris: Plon.

Kagan, Richard L. 1973. "Il latino nella Castiglia del XVII e del XVIII secolo." *Rivista storica italiana* 85:297–320.

Larousse, Pierre. 1861. *Flore latine des dames et des gens du monde, ou clef des citations latines que l'on rencontre fréquemment dans les ouvrages des écrivains français*. Paris: Larousse et Boyer.

Lebrun, François, Marc Venard, and Jean Quéniart. 1981. *Histoire générale de l'enseignement et de l'éducation en France*. Vol. 2, *De Gutenberg aux Lumières*. Paris: Nouvelle librairie française.

Locke, John. 1823. "Some Thoughts Concerning Education." In *The Works of John Locke*, vol. 9, 1–205. London: Tegg.

Lucchi, Piero. 1985. "La prima istruzione: Idee, metode, libri." In *Il catechismo e la grammatica*. vol. 1, *Istruzione e controllo sociale nell'area emiliana e romagnola nel '700*, edited by Gian P. Brizzi, 25–81. Bologna: Il Mulino.

Mayeur, Françoise. 1977. *L'Enseignement secondaire de jeunes filles sous la Troisième République*. Paris: Presses de la Fondation nationale des sciences politiques.

Mercier, Louis Sébastien. 1994. *Tableau de Paris*. 2 vols. Edited by Jean-Claude Bonnet. Paris: Mercure de France.

Montaigne, Michel de. 1962. *Essais*. Edited by Albert Thibaudet and Maurice Rat. Paris: Gallimard, Pléiade.

Motley, Mark. 1990. *Becoming a French Aristocrat: The Education of the Court Nobility, 1580–1750*. Princeton: Princeton University Press.

Nasaw, David. 1979. *Schooled to Order: A Social History of Public Schooling in the United States*. Oxford: Oxford University Press.

Prost, Antoine. 1968. *Histoire de l'enseignement en France, 1800–1967*. Paris: Armand Colin.

Ringer, Fritz. 1979. *Education and Society in Modern Europe*. Bloomington: Indiana University Press.

Rollin, Charles. 1734. *Supplément au traité de la manière d'enseigner et d'étudier les belles-lettres*. Paris: Veuve Estienne.

Royé, Jocelyn. 2008. *La Figure du pédant de Montaigne à Molière*. Geneva: Droz.

Stäuble, Antonio. 1991. *"Parlare per lettera": Il pedante nella commedia del Cinquecento e altri saggi sul teatro rinascimentale*. Rome: Bulzoni.

Valéry, Paul. 1974. *Cahiers*. Edited by Judith Robinson. Paris: Gallimard, Pléiade.

Van Horn Melton, James. 1988. *Absolutism and the Eighteenth Century of Compulsory Schooling in Prussia and Austria*. Cambridge: Cambridge University Press.

Veblen, Thorstein. 2007. *The Theory of the Leisure Class*. Edited by Martha Banta. Oxford: Oxford University Press.

Waquet, Françoise. 1998. *Le Latin ou l'empire d'un signe (XVIe–XXe siècle)*. Paris: Albin Michel.

———. 2015. "Latin for Girls: The French Debate." In *Learning Latin and Greek from Antiquity to the Present*. Edited by Elizabeth Archibald, William Brockliss, and Jonathan Gnoza 145–55. Cambridge: Cambridge University Press.

Weiss, John H. 1984. "Bridges and Barriers: Narrowing Access and Changing Structure in the French Engineering Profession, 1800–1850." In *Professions and the French State, 1700–1900*. Edited by Gerald L. Geison. Philadelphia: University of Pennsylvania Press.

Zola, Émile. 1969. *Œuvres complètes*. Vol. 13, *Chroniques et polémiques 1*. Edited by Henri Mitterand. Paris: Cercle du livre précieux.

PART III

COUNTRIES AND REGIONS

CHAPTER 25

···

ITALY

···

DAVID MARSH

LATIN POETRY

A survey of Neo-Latin literature in Italy may appropriately begin with compositions in verse. As Jacob Burckhardt famously wrote in his classic study *The Civilization of the Renaissance in Italy*, "Ultimately the chief pride of the humanists is their modern Latin poetry" (Burckhardt [1860] 1944, 152).

In Italy, pastoral poetry was one of the earliest and most popular genres to be revived. This rebirth began emblematically with the father of Italian literature, Dante Alighieri (1265–1321), who in 1320 sent two eclogues in reply to poems of Giovanni del Virgilio, a professor at Bologna (Grant 1965; Cooper 1977; Krautter 1983). In the next generation, the example of Dante and Giovanni del Virgilio inspired Petrarch (1304–1374) to compose a cycle of twelve allegorical eclogues that he called *Bucolicum carmen* (*Bucolic Poem*, 1346–1357; Berghoff-Bührer 1991; Petrarch 2001). In 1347, Giovanni Boccaccio (1313–1375) wrote a pastoral poem to his fellow poet Checco di Miletto Rossi (1320–1363), who replied in an eclogue; and he eventually assembled sixteen poems with the same title as Petrarch's collection (Grant 1965, 97–110; Cooper 1977, 38–42).

In the Quattrocento, themes and phrases borrowed from Virgil are evident in the eclogues of poets like Gregorio Correr (1409–1464; Correr 1991–1994) and Enea Silvio Piccolomini (1405–1464; Piccolomini 1994). In Bergamo, by contrast, the six eclogues of Giovanni Michele Alberto Carrara (1438–1490) offer vignettes of contemporary life (Carrara 1967). The second half of the Quattrocento produced a number of courtly pastorals: in Medicean Florence, the twelve eclogues of Naldo Naldi (1436–1513; Naldi 1974); and in the Ferrara of the Este, three eclogues by Tito Vespasiano Strozzi (1424–1505; Strozzi 1933) and the ten *Pastoralia* (*Pastorals*) of Matteo Maria Boiardo (1441–1494; Boiardo 1996).

Early Christians had interpreted Virgil's fourth eclogue as a prophecy of Christ's birth, and pastoral poetry had thereby acquired a religious dimension that was often exploited by Italian poets of the Renaissance. Among many other poems, the prolific Carmelite friar Battista Spagnoli "Mantuanus" (ca. 1448–1516)—writing in Mantua, and known in English simply as "Mantuan"—composed ten influential eclogues, several on religious topics (Grant 1965, 135–45; Cooper 1977, 107–1; *Poeti d'Italia, Adolescentia*). His first eclogue, titled *De honesto amore et felici eius exitu* (*On Honorable Love and Its Happy End*), opens with an elegant Neo-Virgilian exchange between shepherds with the allegorical names Fortunatus and Faustus:

FORTUNATUS: *Fauste, precor, gelida quando pecus omne sub umbra*
Ruminat, antiquos paulum recitemus amores...
FAUSTUS: *Hic locus, haec eadem sub qua requiescimus arbor*
Scit quibus ingemui curis, quibus ignibus arsi...

FORTUNATUS: Faustus, I pray you, while in this cool shade all our flock
Grazes, let us briefly recount our former loves. . .
FAUSTUS: This place, and this very tree beneath which we repose,
Knows with what grief I moaned, and what fires I burned. . .

Mantuan was soon widely admired and imitated for his combination of Virgilian elegance with the moral lessons also recurrent in his many poems on Christian themes.

Inspired by the Greek corpus known as the *Homeric Hymns*—first printed in Florence in 1488 by Chalcondyles—some humanists in Italy wrote poems that seem more pantheistic than Christian. In 1497, the Byzantine refugee Michael Marullus published four books of *Hymns to Nature*, twenty-one poems in hexameters and lyric stanzas that celebrate Greek deities in a philosophical strain (Marullus 2012). A decade later, the philosopher-prelate Giovanni Francesco Pico della Mirandola (1469–1533) published three *Heroic Hymns* (1507, 1511), which he provided with rich annotation and dedicated to his son Thomas. Some poets composed more orthodox poetry. The Benedictine historian and diplomat Zaccaria Ferreri (1479–1524) composed a collection of *New Ecclesiastical Hymns*—around seventy-five lyrics in classical meters celebrating various liturgical occasions. Dedicated in 1523 to Pope Clement VII, they were printed posthumously in Rome in 1525 (Stöve 1996; Philological Museum). The versatile poet Giuseppe Sporeni of Udine (ca. 1490–1562) wrote seventeen hymns in various meters (*Poeti d'Italia*). And in 1588 the Dominican nun Lorenza Strozzi (1514–1591) published 104 Latin hymns in Florence that demonstrate a mastery of lyric meters (Churchill, Brown, and Jeffrey 2002, 109–31).

Toward the end of the Quattrocento, two poets in Naples rivaled and even surpassed their contemporaries in Florence and Rome: Giovanni Pontano (1429–1503) and Jacopo Sannazaro (1458–1530). Both wrote excellent Latin poems, of which several are notable for their influence. Pontano's lament for his wife, *Melisaeus* (the eponymous character is an alter ego of Pontano), moved the Neapolitan Giano Anisio (1465/1475–ca.1541) to compose a homonymous eclogue mourning Pontano's death (Pontano 1948 and 2011; Anisio 2008). Inspired by the Bay of Naples, Sannazaro created five eclogues in a new pastoral genre, "piscatorial," in which fishermen replace the traditional shepherds and goatherds of antiquity (Sannazaro 1914 and 2009; Kennedy 1983; Kidwell 1993). The Neapolitan tradition culminates in the works of the prolific Jesuit poet Niccolò Partenio Giannettasio (1648–1715), who published several volumes of poetry, beginning with *Piscatoria et nautica* (*Piscatorial and Nautical Eclogues*, 1685; Grant 1965, 216–20), and continuing with two didactic poems—*Halieutica* (1689) on fishing, *Bellica* (1697) on war—and a cycle on the four seasons—*Aestates Surrentinae* (*Summers in Sorrento*, 1696), *Autumni Surrentini* (*Autumns in Sorrento*, 1698), *Ver Herculanum* (*Spring in Herculaneum*, 1704), and *Hyemes Puteolanae* (*Winters in Pozzuoli*)—which were collected in the posthumous edition titled *Annus eruditus* (*The Learned Year*, 1722; Tarzia 2000). Predictably, the Cinquecento spawned a great number of pastoralists: among the most elegant were the Venetian Andrea Navagero (1483–1529; Grant 1965, 140–43), and three poets of the Amalteo clan of Friuli: Girolamo (1507–1574), Giambattista (d. 1573), and Cornelio (1530–1603; Grant 1965, 150–55, 342–43; Philological Museum).

Toward the end of the Seicento, Tommaso Ravasini of Parma (1665–1715) published a dozen eclogues, many of them borrowing from the prolific Giannettasio, and most of them on Marian themes (Grant 1965, 283–89). In the mid-1690s, his exact contemporary, Tommaso Niccolò d'Aquino of Taranto (1665–1721) wrote a pastoral dialogue as his poetic ticket into the Accademia dell'Arcadia in Rome (D'Aquino 1984).

Although far less common than pastoral among Italian humanists, didactic poetry was by no means neglected. Despite the canonic precedent of Hesiod's *Works and Days* and its reworking in Virgil's *Georgics*, Latin poems on husbandry are surprisingly rare. By contrast, from the mid-Quattrocento, fragments of Cicero's translation of Aratus's *Phenomena*—reinforced by passages in Hesiod's *Theogony*—inspired humanist naturalists to write about astronomy. One of the first humanists to write didactic poetry was Basinio Basini of Parma (1425–1457), who composed two books of *Astronomica* (*Astronomical Matters*, 1455) largely based on Aratus (Cana 1970). In his brief life, Basinio also wrote various metrical epistles, twelve love elegies titled *Cyris* (the name of his mistress), and two works celebrating his patrons in Rimini: a thirteen-book *Hesperis*, celebrating Sigismondo Malatesta of Rimini (the title is derived from Hesperus, the "evening star, West," alluding to a dreamlike journey of Sigismondo westward beyond the boundaries of the real world), and the *Liber Isotteus* (*Book of Isotta*), three books of love elegies purportedly exchanged between Sigismondo and his mistress Isotta (*Poeti d'Italia*). His contemporary, the long-lived Giovanni Pontano, produced three works in the genre: *Urania* (1476), *Meteora* (*Celestial Phenomena*, 1490), and *De hortis Hesperidum* (*The Gardens of the Hesperides*, 1501). In 1536, Marcello Palingenio Stellato (ca. 1500–1551; Palumbo 2007) published twelve books on birth signs titled *Zodiacus Vitae* (*Zodiac of Life*; Palingenio Stellato 1996; *Poeti d'Italia*), which in 1561 was printed in an English translation by Barnabe Googe (1540–1594).

Ovid's calendar-poem *Fasti* in turn inspired at least four devotional works. Between 1480 and 1494, Lodovico Lazzarelli, already the author of two books *On the Images of the Pagan Gods* (1471), composed the monumental *Fasti Christianae Religionis* (*Calendar of the Christian Faith*), consisting of 17,380 lines in sixteen books (Lazzarelli 1991). Then, the first half of the Cinquecento produced the *Fasti* (1516) of Battista Spagnoli

("Mantuan"), the *Fasti sacri* (*Sacred Calendar*, 1547) of Ambrogio Fracco (b. 1480), and the *Fasti* (1553) of Girolamo Chiaravacci (ca. 1490–ca.1548; Ricciardi 1980)—poems that often reflect the Christian calendar (Miller 2003).

Among didactic poems, two stand out: the 1527 *De arte poetica* (*On the Art of Poetry*) of Girolamo Vida (1485–1566), a humanist bishop who also wrote a Latin epic about Christ (Vida 2009) and a poem *On the Game of Chess* (*De Scaccorum Ludo*, 1527; Philological Museum); and the 1530 *Syphilis* of Girolamo Fracastoro (1478–1553), whose eponymous hero gave the disease its modern name (*Poeti d'Italia*). Later didactic poems ranged far and wide. In 1543, the obscure schoolmaster and priest Giovanni Darcio of Venosa (1510–ca. 1554) published *Canes*, a poem on dogs in 294 hexameters, which was reprinted five times between 1582 and 1732 (Darcio 1994, 53). In 1591, Giordano Bruno (1548–1600) published three philosophical poems in Frankfurt: *De triplici minimo* (*The Threefold Smallest*), *De monade numero et figura* (*The Monad, Number, and Figure*), and *De innumerabilibus . . . seu de universo et mundis* (*The Innumerables . . . or The Universe and the Worlds*; Bruno 2000). Around 1700, the Jesuit poet Niccolò Partenio Giannettasio wrote two "military" didactic poems: eight books on naval battles (*Naumachica*) and fifteen books on wars (*Bellica*, noted above). Later in the eighteenth century, "enlightened" Latinists were again inspired to compose on scientific topics: witness Bernardo Zamagna, *Navis aeria* (*Airship*, 1768) on the Montgolfier balloon; and Giuseppe Maria Partenio, *Electrica* (1767) on electricity.

Epic poetry was famously revived by Petrarch, whose *Africa* won him a poet's laurels in 1341 but remained unfinished at his death. In the next century, his example inspired Maffeo Vegio to compose a thirteenth book of the *Aeneid*, as well as two religious poems, the *Antonias* on the life of St. Anthony of Egypt, and the *De vita et obitu Celestini papae V* (*The Life and Death of Pope Celestine V*; Vegio 2004). Predictably, the religious use of Latin epic soon expanded and flourished in an Italy faithful to the Roman Church. Among the most notable Christian epics are the 1526 *De partu virginis* (*The Virgin Birth*) of Jacopo Sannazaro (1458–1530), and the 1535 *Christiad* by Marco Girolamo Vida (1485–1566; Vida 2009). In a similar vein, the Jesuit Tommaso Ceva (1648–1737) in 1690 published nine books on the childhood of Christ titled *Jesus puer* (*Jesus as a Boy*; Gronda 1980; Ceva 2009), a work that was translated into German, French, and Italian.

The Crusades, real or imagined, inspired at least three epics: the *Carlias* (1480) of Ugolino Verino (1438–1516; *Poeti d'Italia*), the unfinished *Solymis* (on "Solyma," i.e., Jerusalem; Orth 2001) of Giovanni Maria Cattaneo (fl. 1500–1530), and the eleven-book *Syrias* (1591) of Pietro Angèli da Barga (1517–1596), who was inspired by Tasso's *Jerusalem Delivered*. The propagation of the faith abroad was also treated by the Jesuit Francesco Benci (1542–1594), who in addition to four books of poems (1590) published six books on *Five Jesuit Martyrs* (Venice 1591; Negri 1966).

Dynastic themes were not uncommon (Lippincott 1989). Ferreto de' Ferreti of Vicenza (ca. 1294–1337) eulogized Cangrande della Scala, the lord of Verona, in five books of hexameters *De Scaligerorum origine* (*The Origin of the Della Scala*; *Poeti d'Italia*). In 1455, the Sicilian notary Matteo Zuppardo wrote a brief epic, *Alfonseis* (2, 817 hexameters in ten books) in honor of Alfonso V of Aragon. This stylistically awkward work was inspired by the hope that Alfonso would lead a Crusade against the Turks, who two years earlier had taken Constantinople. In Milan, Francesco Filelfo narrated the exploits of Duke Francesco Sforza in the eleven books of his unfinished *Sphortias* (ca. 1450–1472). At Ferrara, Tito Vespasiano Strozzi composed a ten-book *Borsias* celebrating his Este patrons and their first duke, Borso d'Este (r. 1450–1471), in particular (Strozzi 1977; *Poeti d'Italia*). At Rimini, Basinio Basini of Parma wrote the *Hesperis* praising the exploits of Sigismondo Malatesta, mentioned above. Fabio Barignano of Pesaro (1532–1584) composed a *Gigantomachia* (*The Battle of the Giants*), an encomiastic poem in 3,500 hexameters celebrating his patrons of the Della Rovere family: Francesco, Lord of Pesaro, and Guidobaldo, Duke of Urbino.

Short epics on historical subjects were not uncommon (*Poeti d'Italia*). Ubertino Pusculo of Brescia (1431–1469) wrote *Constantinopolis*, recounting the fall of the Byzantine capital and his own capture. Paracleto Malvezzi (1408–1487) wrote four books of *Tarentina*, directed against Giovanni Antonio del Balzo Orsini, the Prince of Taranto, and describing the Turkish invasion of Otranto in 1480; and on the same topics, Marco Probo Mariano of Sulmona (1455–1499) dedicated a shorter poem, *Triumphus Hydruntinus* (*Triumph of Otranto*), to Alfonso, Duke of Calabria. A century later, Lorenzo Gambara (1506–1586) published, in four books, *De navigatione Christophori Columbi* (*The Voyage of Christopher Columbus*, 1583; Asor Rosa 1999; *Poeti d'Italia*).

A number of Latin poets chose to imitate the pseudo-Homeric mock epic *Batrachomyomachia*, which narrates in elevated verse a *Battle Between Frogs and Mice*. In 1448, the young Neapolitan poet Elisio Calenzio (1430–1503) composed the three-book *Croacus* featuring just such a conflict (the title is the name of the frog-king; Calenzio 2008). In Florence a generation later, Andrea Dazzi (1473–1548) composed a similar three-book epic, *Aeluromyomachia*, recounting a *Battle Between Cats and Mice* (Vivoli 1987).

Since antiquity, Greek mythology had provided matter for scholarly study and composition; and Ovid's *Metamorphoses* in particular was read, imitated, and "moralized," or interpreted in allegorical fashion. Giovanni Boccaccio compiled fifteen books he called *Genealogy of the Pagan Gods* (Boccaccio 2011); and Raffaello Regio (ca. 1440–1520) wrote an extensive commentary on the *Metamorphoses* (1493), which was often reprinted. In the Quattrocento, Marcantonio Aldegati, the Mantuan author of Latin elegies, composed a twelve-book *Gigantomachia*, a mythological narrative inspired by Ovid that includes praise of the Gonzaga family (excerpts in Bottari 1980; *Poeti d'Italia*). In a more Homeric vein, the Lombard prelate and statesman Francesco Sfondrati (1493–1550) composed a mythological epic in three books, *De raptu Helenae* (*The Abduction of Helen*), which was published with Jacopo Sadoleto's short epic *Quintus Curtius* (which in fact deals with the legendary Roman hero *Marcus* Curtius, 1559).

For satire, the classical models remained the Roman triumvirate of Horace, Persius, and Juvenal (Coffey 1976; Freudenburg 2005). Neo-Latin satire dates from the generation after Dante. Around 1350, Zanobi da Strada (1312–1361), a Florentine friend of Petrarch and Boccaccio, wrote a brief *Satyra in leguleium* (*Satire on a Pettifogger*), in which he denounces the animosity of a lawyer and caricatures the greed of the legal profession (Hortis 1879). In 1430, the young Venetian patrician Gregorio Correr composed his *Book of Satires*, which was praised even in the next century, by Pietro Bembo (Correr 1991–1994). The culmination of Quattrocento satire may be seen in the 10,000 lines of the 100 *Satyrae* of Francesco Filelfo (1398–1481; Filelfo 2005). Other satirists include the Florentine Lorenzo Lippi da Colle (1442–1485), who wrote five satires (Lippi da Colle 1978), and Gaspare Tribraco of Modena (1439–ca. 1471), whose nine satires date from 1459 to 1469 (Venturini 1970; Tribraco 1972).

Two Quattrocento collections of satires bear the Horatian title *sermones* ("conversations," in this context referring to hexameter satires): the four poems of the *Sermonum liber* (*Book of Satires*) of the Ferrarese poet Tito Vespasiano Strozzi, and the fifteen *Sermones obiurgatorii* (*Reproving Satires*) of Giovanni Michele Alberto Carrara of Bergamo (1438–1490; Carrara 1967). As a youth, Pierio Valeriano (1477–1558)—best known for his later work on hieroglyphics and Virgil—wrote a *Sermo de studiorum condicione* (*Satire on the Situation of Studies*), 343 hexameters dedicated to his teacher Nardino Celineo (Gaisser 1999; Valeriano 2010; Marsh 2013, 416). From 1650 to 1750, Jesuit writers were increasingly prominent in the field of satire, although the Jesuit plan of studies (*ratio studiorum*) did not mention Persius and Juvenal as suitable authors, and recommended Horace only for "select odes." As in other classical genres, Italian Jesuits were prolific Latin satirists: witness the 1672 *Specimen didascalici carminis et satyrae* (*Showcase of Didactic Poetry, and Satires*) of Giovanni Lorenzo Lucchesini (1638–1716), the twelve satires of Carlo d'Aquino (1654–1737), and the six satires of Giulio Cesare Cordara (1704–1785).

Most Latin poets in Italy wrote in various classical genres, with a predilection for eclogue, elegy, and epigram. To cite a typical case, Antonio Cortesi Urceo (known as Codro, 1446–1500), who studied in Ferrara, taught in Forlì, and became professor of Greek at Bologna, composed two books of *Sylvae* (~ miscellaneous poems, sketches), two satires, an eclogue, and a book of epigrams (Gualdo Rosa 1983).

Principally following the model of Ovid, elegiac poetry was central to the Latin tradition throughout the Middle Ages. We might date its humanistic revival from Coluccio Salutati's neo-Ovidian *Conquestio Phillidis* (*Complaint of Phyllis*), written in 1367 (*Poeti d'Italia*). But its real rebirth was inaugurated by the *succès de scandale* of the erotic *Hermaphrodite* by Panormita (Antonio Beccadelli, 1394–1471; Beccadelli 2010; Parker 2012). Besides this notorious work, the early Quattrocento produced a number of elegiac collections, including the *Angelinetum* (~ *Angela's Garden*, 1429) by Giovanni Marrasio of Noto (ca. 1400–1452; Tramontana 2008; *Poeti d'Italia*), and the *Cinthia* (ca. 1430) of Enea Silvio Piccolomini (*Poeti d'Italia*). The second half of the century is noted for the elegiac poetry of Cristoforo Landino's *Xandra* (1443–1458), Ugolino Verino's *Flametta* (1458–1463), Gabriele Altilio (ca. 1440–1502), and Tito Vespasiano Strozzi (*Poeti d'Italia*). Most of the Latin verse of Niccolò Perotti (1429–1480) and of Alessandro Braccesi (1463–1503) consists of elegiacs (*Poeti d'Italia*).

Pacifico Massimi (1400–ca. 1500) composed two sets of *Hecatelegia*—"hundred erotic elegies"—that were published in Florence in 1489 (Massimi 1986 and 2008). Exploiting a reference in Ovid to poems written by one Sabinus in response to Ovid's elegiac letters of heroines to their lovers (*Heroides*), Angelo Sani di Cure, calling himself "Sabinus," penned three such responding letters (1468)—Ulysses to Penelope, Demophoon to Phyllis, and Paris to Oenone—which were long printed with the authentic Ovidian corpus, and even translated into English by George Turberville (1567; Ovid 1996, 117–41 and 354–74). And Giovanni Darcio of Venosa composed an *Epistola Deidamiae ad Achillem* (*Letter of Deidamia to Achilles*, 272 verses in elegiacs) which was printed in Paris in 1543 (Darcio 1994).

Elegiacs were so popular and widespread that it is impossible to review the Italian poets in this genre with any sort of completeness. As typical of the early Cinquecento elegists we may cite three Northern Italian men of letters who wrote elegiacs and pastoral poetry (*Poeti d'Italia*): Baldassare Castiglione (1478–1529), famed for his Italian *Book of the Courtier*; his contemporary, Andrea Navagero; and the poet and philosopher Marcantonio Flaminio (1498–1550; Pastore 1997; Philological Museum).

The ruins of Rome inspired many poets, both Italians and foreign visitors, to reflect on human transience (Kytzler 1972). In the Quattrocento, we find a poem *De Roma* (*On Rome*) by Enea Silvio Piccolomini, and *De Roma fere diruta* (*On Rome Almost Destroyed*) by Cristoforo Landino (1424–1498). In the next century, Giano Vitale of Palermo (1485–1560) wrote elegiac meditations on the ruins of Rome, and Jacopo Sannazaro of Naples, a moving elegy on the ruins of Cumae (Marsh 1988).

The revival of classical lyric meters dates from the Quattrocento: two notable collections were Landino's eclectic *Xandra* and the more ambitious five books of *Odes* by Francesco Filelfo, who attempted to employ all the known Horatian meters. A century later, Pierio Valeriano published five books of *Amores* (*Loves*, 1549), which were followed the next year by a volume of *Hexameters, Odes, and Epigrams* (1550). But these are only a few prominent examples of the dozens of Italian odists who wrote from the fifteenth to the nineteenth century.

HUMANIST PROSE

In turning to humanist prose, we may again invoke the authority of Burckhardt: "There were two purposes . . . for which the humanist was as indispensable to the republics as to princes or popes, namely, the official correspondence of the State, and the making of speeches on public and solemn occasions" (Burckhardt [1860] 1944, 137). While such serviceable documents seldom attained a high level of elegance or originality, the rhetorical skills they required were easily transferred to more creative texts. In prose, the most influential models were the two great literary pioneers of the Italian Renaissance, Petrarch and Leonardo Bruni (1370–1444), both of whom composed biographies, histories, orations, treatises, and dialogues, and also collected their letters for publication.

Petrarch combined biography and history in his *De viris illustribus* (*On Illustrious Men*; Keßler 1978), while Bruni's *Historiae Florentini populi* (*History of the Florentine People*) established a new standard of classical style and political analysis (Bruni

2001–2007). Inspired by Bruni, Biondo Flavio (1392–1463) composed an ambitious history, the *Historiarum ab inclinatione Romani imperii decades* (*Decades of History from the Decline of the Roman Empire*, 1439–1452; Fubini 1968), which helped establish the concept and study of "medieval" Italy. Many humanists wrote historical memoirs based on their personal experience: witness Enea Silvio Piccolomini's *De gestis concilii Basiliensis commentarii* (*Notes on the Proceedings of the Council of Basel*) and *Commentarii* (*Notes*; Piccolomini 1967 and 2003). Later historians were sometimes less enthusiastic in recounting the annals of their cities. Pietro Bembo reluctantly undertook a history of Venice after the death of Andrea Navagero (Bembo 2007–2009); and the three-volume *Historia Neapolitana* (*Neapolitan History*, 1713) of Niccolò Partenio Giannettasio (1648–1715; Tarzia 2000) was largely plagiarized from the Italian work of Giovanni Antonio Summonte.

The personal side of history lay in biography, and beginning in the early Quattrocento, humanists who studied Greek tapped the rich mine of Plutarch's *Lives of the Greeks and Romans* (Pade 2007). In the Christian West, the lives of the popes inspired important projects, like the *Life of Pope Nicholas V* by Giannozzo Manetti (1396–1459; Manetti 2005) and the *Lives of the Popes* by Bartolomeo Sacchi (1421–1481), known as "Platina" (Miglio 1975; Platina 2008). Eventually scholars turned to the history of erudition, as in the 1643 *Portrait Gallery of Illustrious Men* (*Pinacotheca imaginum illustrium . . . virorum*) of Gian Vittorio Rossi (Janus Nicius Erythraeus, 1577–1647), 160 biographical sketches of contemporary men of learning and distinction (Philological Museum).

Beginning with Petrarch, Renaissance writers emphasized the social dimension of intellectual exchange in two genres, the dialogue and the epistle (Hempfer 2002; Worstbrock 1983). In antiquity, the philosophical dialogue, which had begun in Greek works by Plato and Xenophon, was later popularized in Latin by Cicero. The Quattrocento revival of the Ciceronian model began with Leonardo Bruni, who also translated works by Plato and Aristotle and composed a biography of Cicero. His example was followed in Latin dialogues by humanists like Poggio Bracciolini (1380–1459), Lorenzo Valla (1405–1457), and Giovanni Pontano (Marsh 1980; Pontano 2012). A satirical tradition of dialogue followed the model of the Greek sophist Lucian, who lampooned contemporary *mores* and classical myths in brief works that humanists were quick to translate and imitate beginning around 1400 (Marsh 1998). The Cinquecento in turn produced a variety of dialogues, often on literary themes, such as the 1551 *De poetis nostrorum temporum* (*The Poets of Our Time*) of Lilio Gregorio Giraldi (1479–1552; Giraldi 2011) and the 1561 *De dialogo* (*On the Dialogue*) of Carlo Sigonio (1524–1584).

As for epistles, formal letter-writing assumed special importance in the early Renaissance, when the rediscovery of Cicero's epistolary collections *To Atticus* and *Familiar Letters* inspired men of letters to revise and assemble their own correspondence for publication. Here, too, Petrarch and Bruni were in the forefront. Early in the Renaissance, the letters of Coluccio Salutati (1331–1406), chancellor of Florence from 1375, illustrated the complexities of civic politics in the late Trecento. His literary aspirations are evident from two early works written around 1367: his exercise in prose rhetoric, the *Declamation of Lucretia*, and his Ovidian poem, the *Complaint of Phyllis*. Later, as Peter Mack has observed, "Latin letter-writing manuals were among the most printed Renaissance works on rhetoric with about 900 editions of individual works published between 1460 and 1620" (Mack 2011, 228).

In the generation before Salutati "impersonated" the female voice of Lucretia, the virtues of famous women were being sung by their great advocate Giovanni Boccaccio (Boccaccio 2001). In the Quattrocento, Italian women began to participate ever more in the new learning of Renaissance humanism. The past twenty years have witnessed an explosion of editions and studies of women writers in Italy, whose publications by the sixteenth century far outnumbered those of their peers in the rest of Europe (Stevenson 2005, 141–76, and 279–323). To be sure, many wrote in the vernacular, but there are notable examples of treatises, letters, and poetry in Latin—and in a few cases even in Greek. The later Quattrocento produced scholars like Isotta Nogarola (ca. 1416–1466; Churchill, Brown, and Jeffrey 2002, 11–30), Cassandra Fedele (1465–1558; Churchill, Brown, and Jeffrey 2002, 55–82), and Laura Cereta (1469–1499; Churchill, Brown, and Jeffrey 2002, 83–108). And the next two centuries witnessed phenomenal poets like Olympia Fulvia Morata (ca. 1526–1555; Churchill, Brown, and Jeffrey 2002 133–66), Tarquinia Molza (1542–1617), Marta Marchina (1600–1642), and Elena Lucrezia Piscopia (1646–1684).

The tradition of Latin homilies and sermons dates from the earliest centuries of the Western Church, and it would be difficult to discern a clear break in content or style in the Renaissance. All the same, we may cite as emblematic the example of the Florentine philosopher Marsilio Ficino (1433–1499), who as an ordained priest (from 1473) delivered "Platonic sermons" in the Camaldolese church of Santa Maria degli Angeli (Allen, Rees, and Davies 2001). The rebirth of classical rhetoric in Renaissance Italy, which inspired numerous handbooks and treatises on the art of eloquence (Green and Murphy 2006; Mack 2011, 33–55) entailed the proliferation of humanist treatises on sermonizing (O'Malley 1979; Mack 2011, 257–78). In this genre, Italy offers such notable works as the *De rhetorica christiana* (*Christian Rhetoric*, 1574) of Agostino Valier (1531–1606), the *Divinus orator* (*Divine Orator*, 1595) of Ludovico Carbone (1545–1597; Moss and Wallace 2003), and the *Orator Christianus* (*Christian Orator*, 1612) of Carlo Reggio (1540–1612).

Another traditional genre was the Latin treatise, generally philosophical, scientific, or theological in nature, but here, too, there were humanist innovations. Besides his provocative dialogues on ethics, Lorenzo Valla fundamentally recast the principles of Aristotelian logic in his *Dialectical Disputations* (Mack 2011, 47–53; Valla 2012). Besides his Latin version of Plato and the Platonists, Marsilio Ficino (1433–1499) produced numerous treatises and commentaries expounding his conception of *religiosa philosophia* ("holy philosophy"). The controversial *On the Immortality of the Soul* (1516) of Pietro Pomponazzi (1462–1525), which distinguished philosophy from faith, was elaborated in the treatise *On the Human Mind* (1551) of Simone Porzio (1496–1554). Two similarly controversial works were philosophical treatises that challenged Aristotelian doctrines of dialectic and nature. In his *On the True Principles and True Method of Philosophizing* (1553), the ardent Ciceronian Mario Nizolio (1498–1576) rejected Platonic idealism and Aristotelian universals, insisting instead on grammar and rhetoric as the tools for studying reality. The *On the Nature of Things*

(1565) of Bernardino Telesio (1509–1588) replaced Aristotle's categories for natural phenomena with the poet's own sense-based criteria.

From earliest antiquity, apologues and parables offered a condensed form of literary edification, and the Quattrocento witnessed the rebirth of Aesopic fables in both Latin prose and poetry (Marsh 2004). The most notable prose fabulists were Gregorio Correr, Leon Battista Alberti (1404–1472), Bartolomeo Scala (1430–1497), and Lorenzo Astemio (ca. 1435–ca. 1505). Verse fables were composed in the same century by Leonardo Dati (1408–1472) and Francesco Filelfo (1398–1481), and in the next by Gabriele Faerno of Cremona (1510–1561; Faerno 2005).

In Italy, prose fiction in Latin often translated or imitated the famed tales of Boccaccio's *Decameron* (Marsh 2015). Occasionally, there were more original compositions. A prominent example is the *Story of Two Lovers* (1444) by Enea Silvio Piccolomini, which recounts an adulterous love affair in prose laden with echoes of classical poetry. The work enjoyed immense popularity: it was first published in Cologne in 1468, and by 1600 had been translated into Italian, French, German, Spanish, Polish, Hungarian, and English. Around the same time, Leon Battista Alberti included both Boccaccian tales and elaborate Aesopic fables in his *Dinner Pieces* (1430–1440), and composed a four-book allegorical novel titled *Momus* (1450). But the application of classical Latin to entertaining narrative, rather than edifying history, attracted few authors; and the early modern novel would develop almost exclusively in vernacular tongues. Emblematically, in the mid-seventeenth century, Gian Vittorio Rossi chose to set his Latin novel *Eudemia* (1645) in the age of Tiberius, and therefore could describe none of the baroque splendor or modern *mores* of contemporary Rome.

Renaissance authors also sought to revive ancient drama, which they knew through the Roman tragedies of Seneca and comedies of Plautus and Terence (Herrick 1960 and 1965). The earliest verse tragedy was Albertino Mussato's *Ecerinis* of 1315, a neo-Senecan tragedy about the tyrannical lord of Verona, Ezzelino III da Romano (Müller 1987; Grund 2011). Two generations later, Antonio Loschi of Vicenza composed the Senecan *Achilles* (ca. 1388; Grund 2011), while his Venetian contemporary Pier Paolo Vergerio (1370–1444) wrote a comedy, *Paulus*, in which the title character is tricked by his servant (ca. 1390; Grund 2005). In the early Quattrocento, the Lombard prelate Leonardo della Serrata (ca. 1405–1487) wrote a prose comedy called *Poliscena* (ca. 1433) that was often printed as a work of Leonardo Bruni (Nonni 1989); and the twenty-year-old Leon Battista Alberti composed an allegorical drama in prose titled *Philodoxus* (the speaking name of the protagonist, "Lover of Fame," 1424) that long passed for an ancient work written by one Lepidus (Grund 2005, 76–79). The Trecento tradition of North Italian playwriting continued in the early Quattrocento with Antonio Barzizza's Boccaccian comedy *Cauteraria* (*The Branded*, ca. 1425); Gregorio Correr's Senecan tragedy *Procne* (ca. 1429; Grund 2011); and Tito Livio Frulovisi's seven comedies (1429–1440; Frulovisi 1932; Arbizzoni 1998).

By the mid-sixteenth century, contemporary with the rise of the popular *commedia dell'arte* and the courtly *commedia erudita*, Jesuit institutions began to "produce"—that is, to compose and stage—Latin dramas as an instructional vehicle. They were typically based on biblical stories and the lives of saints, and after 1600, nourished the emerging musical form of sacred dialogue and oratorio (Smither 1977). In 1556, Gian Mario Simonetta of Naples published a volume of Latin works by Coriolano Martirano (1503–1557; Valeri 2008), a bishop of Cosenza who had begun his career under Clement VII in Rome and who later attended the Council of Trent. The dramatic works included eight tragedies and two comedies based on ancient models, as well as a tragedy titled *Christus patiens* (*Christ Suffering*); these were followed by verse translations of Homer's *Odyssey* Books 1–12, the *Batrachomyomachia*, and the *Argonautica* of Apollonius of Rhodes.

Our survey may fittingly conclude with two Italians who wrote Latin poetry of the highest quality and lived into the early twentieth century. Gioacchino Vincenzo Pecci (1810–1903), who joined the Jesuit order as a young man and was elected Pope Leo XIII in 1878, over the course of his long life wrote many Latin poems noted for their classical sophistication. Besides traditional hymns on saints and feasts, most of them are "occasional" poems devoted to contemporary friends; he also wrote topical poems about himself (including a deathbed meditation) and even two alcaic stanzas on a recent invention—*ars photographica*! His younger contemporary Giovanni Pascoli (1855–1912), best known as a poet in Italian, taught classical philology and wrote distinguished Latin poetry. Pascoli was a native of Romagna, the region of Italy renowned in the nineteenth century for its eminent Latinists; but he also won international fame when between 1892 and 1912 his Latin poetry was awarded twenty-six prizes by the Royal Academy of Amsterdam (Pascoli 1951, xvii–xxxiii). Besides five rustic poems (*Ruralia*) and some seventy-five epigrams, the majority of his *Carmina* treat Roman themes in collections devoted to political events (*Res Romanae* [*Roman Matters*]), literary history (*De poetis* [*On Poets*]), and Christian topics (*Poemata Christiana* [*Christian Poems*]).

This list of Pascoli's Latin poetry fittingly epitomizes the long tradition of Neo-Latin verse written in Italy from the late Middle Ages to the twentieth century. Over the centuries, Italian scholars reclaimed the subjects and sophistication of the Roman classics. The supremacy of Virgil in poetry and Cicero in prose led to a codification of those authors as models enforced by an increasingly regimented educational system. All the same, individual Italian humanists discovered new models and even new voices within the classical genres that defined the world of Latin composition.

Suggested Reading

ENLW contains several sections specifically on Italy by Fantazzi, Gahtan, and Kallendorf. Two useful anthologies that include a selection of Neo-Latin poetry written in Italy are provided by Nichols (1979) and MacFarlane (1980). Online resources include Italian Neo-Latin Poets (*Poeti d'Italia* in lingua latina): http://www.mqdq.it/mqdq/poetiditalia/indice_autori_alfa.jsp?scelta=AZ&path=autori, and the "Humanist

and Renaissance Italian Poetry in Latin" collection on the Perseus website: http://
www.perseus.tufts.edu/hopper/collection?collection=Perseus:collection:PDILL.   The
I Tatti Renaissance Library series (Harvard University Press) focuses on Neo-Latin
works written in Italy: for individual authors and titles discussed in this chapter, see the
references below.

References

Allen, Michael J. B., Valery Rees, and Martin Davies, eds. 2001. *Marsilio Ficino: His Theology,
His Philosophy, His Legacy*. Leiden: Brill.
Anisio, Aulo G. 2008. *Melisaeus*. Edited by Micaela Ricci. Foggia: Edizioni del Rosone.
Arbizzoni, Guido. 1998. "Frulovisi, Tito Livio." *Dizionario Biografico degli Italiani* 50:646–50.
———. 2005. "Lazzarelli, Ludovico." *Dizionario Biografico degli Italiani* 64:180–84.
Asor Rosa, Angela. 1999. "Gambara, Lorenzo." *Dizionario Biografico degli Italiani* 52:53–54.
Bausi, Francesco. 2000. "Geraldini, Antonio." *Dizionario Biografico degli Italiani* 53:321–23.
Beccadelli, Antonio. 2010. *Hermaphroditus*. Edited and translated by Holt Parker.
Cambridge: Harvard University Press.
Bembo, Pietro. 2007–2009. *History of Venice*. 3 vols. Edited and translated by Robert W. Ulery,
Jr. Cambridge: Harvard University Press.
Berghoff-Bührer, Margrith. 1991. *Das Bucolicum Carmen des Petrarca: Ein Beitrag zur
Wirkungsgeschichte von Vergils Eclogen*. Bern: Lang.
Boccaccio, Giovanni. 2001. *Famous Women*. Edited and translated by Virginia Brown.
Cambridge: Harvard University Press.
———. 2011. *Genealogy of the Pagan Gods: Books I–V*. Edited and translated by Jon Solomon.
Cambridge: Harvard University Press.
Boiardo, Matteo M. 1996. *Pastoralia*. Edited by Stefano Carrai. Padua: Antenore.
Bottari, Guglielmo. 1980. *Marcantonio Aldegati: Un poeta del Quattrocento*. Palermo: Il Vespro.
Bruni, Leonardo. 2001–2007. *History of the Florentine People*. 3 vols. Edited and translated by
James Hankins. Cambridge: Harvard University Press.
Bruno, Giordano. 2000. *Poemi filosofici latini*. Reprints edited by Eugenio Canone. La
Spezia: Agora Edizioni.
Burckhardt, Jacob. (1860) 1944. *The Civilization of the Renaissance*. Translated by Samuel G. C.
Middlemore. London: Phaidon Press.
Calenzio, Elisio. 2008. *La guerra della ranocchie: Croaco*. Edited by Liliana Monti Sabia.
Naples: Loffredo Editore.
Cana, A. 1970. "Basinio da Parma." *Dizionario Biografico degli Italiani* 7:89–98.
Carrara, Giovanni M. A. 1967. *Opera poetica, philosophica, rhetorica, theologica*. Edited by
Giovanni Giraldi. Novara: Istituto Geografico De Agostini.
Ceva, Tommaso. 2009. *Jesus puer*. Edited and translated by Felice Milani. Parma: Guanda.
Churchill, Laurie J., Phyllis R. Brown, and Jane E. Jeffrey, eds. 2002. *Women Writing Latin: From
Roman Antiquity to Early Modern Europe*. Vol. 3, *Early Modern Women Writing Latin*.
New York: Routledge.
Coffey, Michael. 1976. *Roman Satire*. London: Methuen.
Cooper, Helen. 1977. *Pastoral: Medieval into Renaissance*. Ipswich: D. S. Brewer.
Correr, Gregorio. 1991–1994. *Opere*. Edited by Aldo Onorato. 2 vols. Messina: Editrice Sicania.

D'Aquino, Tommaso N. 1984. *Galesus Piscator, Benacus Pastor: Egloga del poeta d'Arcadia Ebalio.* Edited by Felice Presicci. Manduria: Lacaita.

Darcio, Giovanni. 1994. *Canes, item Epistola Deidemiae ad Achillem, cum aliquot epigrammatis.* Edited and translated by Maria T. Imbriani. Naples: Edizioni Scientifiche.

Dizionario Biografico degli Italiani. 1960– . Various editors. Rome: Istituto Enciclopedia Italiana. http://www.treccani.it/biografie.

Faerno, Gabriele. 2005. *Le favole.* Edited by Luca Marcozzi. Rome: Salerno Editrice.

Filelfo, Francesco. 2005. *Satyrae.* Edited by Silvia Fiaschi. Vol. 1. Rome: Edizioni di Storia e Letteratura.

Freudenburg, Kirk, ed. 2005. *The Cambridge Companion to Roman Satire.* Cambridge: Cambridge University Press.

Frulovisi, Tito L. 1932. *Opera hactenus inedita.* Edited by C. W. Previté-Orton. Cambridge: Cambridge University Press.

Fubini, Riccardo. 1968. "Biondo, Flavio." *Dizionario Biografico degli Italiani* 10:536–59.

Geraldini, Antonio. 1924. *The Eclogues.* Edited by Wilfred P. Mustard. Baltimore: Johns Hopkins University Press.

Gronda, Giovanna. 1980. "Ceva, Tommaso," *Dizionario Biografico degli Italiani* 24:325–28.

Gualdo Rosa, Lucia. 1983. "Cortesi Urceo, Antonio, detto Codro." *Dizionario Biografico degli Italiani* 29:775–77.

Gaisser, Julia Haig. 1999. *Pierio Valeriano on the Ill Fortune of Learned Men: A Renaissance Humanist and His World.* Ann Arbor: University of Michigan Press.

Giraldi, Lilio G. 2011. *Modern Poets.* Edited and translated by John N. Grant. Cambridge: Harvard University Press.

Grant, W. Leonard. 1965. *Neo-Latin Literature and the Pastoral.* Chapel Hill: University of North Carolina.

Green, Lawrence D., and James J. Murphy. 2006. *Renaissance Rhetoric Short-Title Catalogue 1460–1700,* 2nd ed. Aldershot: Ashgate.

Grund, Gary R., ed. and trans. 2005. *Humanist Comedies.* Cambridge: Harvard University Press.

——, ed. and trans. 2011. *Humanist Tragedies.* Cambridge: Harvard University Press.

Hempfer, Klaus W., ed. 2002. *Möglichkeiten des Dialogs: Struktur und Funktion einer literarischen Gattung zwischen Mittelalter und Renaissance in Italien.* Stuttgart: Steiner.

Herrick, Marvin T. 1960. *Italian Comedy in the Renaissance.* Urbana: University of Illinois Press.

——. 1965. *Italian Tragedy in the Renaissance.* Urbana: University of Illinois Press.

Hortis, Attilio. 1879. *Studii sulle opere latine del Boccaccio.* Trieste: Julius Dase Editore.

Kennedy, William J. 1983. *Jacopo Sannazaro and the Uses of Pastoral.* Hanover: University Presses of New England.

Keßler, Eckhard. 1978. *Petrarca und die Geschichte: Geschichtsschreibung, Rhetorik, Philosophie im Übergang vom Mittelalter zur Neuzeit.* Munich: Fink.

Kidwell, Carol. 1993. *Sannazaro and Arcadia.* London: Duckworth.

Krautter, Konrad. 1983. *Die Renaissance der Bukolik in der lateinischen Literatur des XIV. Jahrhunderts: Von Dante bis Petrarca.* Munich: Fink.

Kytzler, Bernhard, ed. and trans. 1972. *Roma aeterna: Lateinische und griechische Romdichtung von der Antike bis in die Gegenwart.* Zurich: Artemis.

Lazzarelli, Ludovico. 1991. *Fasti Christianae religionis.* Edited by Marco Bertolini. Naples: M. D'Auria Editore.

Lippi da Colle, Lorenzo. 1978. *Satyrae V ad Laurentium Medicem.* Edited by Jozef IJsewijn. *Humanistica Lovaniensia* 27: 18–44.

Lippincott, Kristen. 1989. "The Neo-Latin Historical Epics of the North Italian Courts: An Examination of 'Courtly Culture' in the Fifteenth Century." *Renaissance Studies* 3:415–28.

Mack, Peter. 2011. *A History of Renaissance Rhetoric, 1380–1620.* Oxford: Oxford University Press.

Manetti, Giannozzo. 2005. *De vita ac gestis Nicolai Quinti summi pontificis.* Edited and translated by Anna Modigliani. Rome: Istituto storico italiano per il Medio Evo.

Marsh, David. 1980. *The Quattrocento Dialogue: Classical Tradition and Humanist Innovation.* Cambridge: Harvard University Press.

———. 1988. "Sannazaro's Elegy on the Ruins of Cumae." *Bibliothèque d'Humanisme et Renaissance* 50:681–89.

———. 1998. *Lucian and the Latins: Humor and Humanism in the Early Renaissance.* Ann Arbor: University of Michigan Press.

———. 2004. *Renaissance Fables: Aesopic Prose by Leon Battista Alberti, Bartolomeo Scala, Leonardo da Vinci, Bernardino Baldi.* Tempe: Arizona State University Press.

———. 2013. "Satire." In *ENLW* 1:413–423.

———. 2017. "Shorter Prose Fiction." In *NLL*, 308–21.

Marullus, Michael. 2012. *Poems.* Edited and translated by Charles Fantazzi. Cambridge: Harvard University Press.

Massimi, Pacifico. 1986. *Les cent élégies: Avec quatre élégies inédites.* Edited and translated by Juliette Desjardins. Grenoble: Éditions Littéraires et Linguistiques de l'Université de Grenoble.

———. 2008. *Les cent nouvelles élégies (Hecatelegium II).* Edited and translated by Juliette Desjardins Daude. Paris: Belles Lettres.

Miglio, Massimo. 1975. *Storiografia pontificia del Quattrocento.* Bologna: Pàtron.

Miller, John F. 2003. "Ovid's *Fasti* and the Neo-Latin Christian Calendar Poem." *International Journal of the Classical Tradition* 10:173–86.

Moss, Jean Dietz, and William A. Wallace. 2003. *Rhetoric and Dialectic in the Time of Galileo.* Washington, DC: Catholic University of America Press.

Müller, Hubert. 1987. *Früher Humanismus in Oberitalien: Albertino Mussato, Ecerinis.* Frankfurt am Main: Lang.

Naldi, Naldo. 1974. *Bucolica, Volaterrais, Hastiludium, Carmina varia.* Edited by W. Leonard Grant. Florence: Olschki.

Negri, Renzo. 1966. "Benci, Francesco." *Dizionario Biografico degli Italiani* 8:192–93.

Nonni, Giorgio. 1989. "Della Serrata, Leonardo." *Dizionario Biografico degli Italiani* 37:468–70.

O'Malley, John W. 1979. *Praise and Blame in Renaissance Rome: Rhetoric, Doctrine, and Reform in the Sacred Orators of the Papal Court, c. 1450–1521.* Durham: Duke University Press.

Orth, Peter. 2001. "Zur *Solymis* des Giovanni Maria Cattaneo." *Humanistica Lovaniensia* 50:131–41.

Ovid. 1996. *Ibis, Fragmenta, Ovidiana.* Edited and translated by Bruno W. Häuptli. Zurich: Artemis & Winkler.

Pade, Marianne. 2007. *The Reception of Plutarch's Lives in Fifteenth-Century Italy.* Copenhagen: Museum Tusculanum.

Palingenio Stellato, Marcello. 1996. *Le zodiaque de la vie (Zodiacus vitae).* Edited and translated by Jacques Chomarat. Geneva: Droz.

Palumbo, Margerita. 2007. "Manzoli (Manzolli), Pier Angelo (Marcello Palingenio Stellato)." *Dizionario Biografico degli Italiani* 69:294–98.

Parker, Holt N. 2012. "Renaissance Latin Elegy." In *A Companion to Roman Love Elegy*, edited by Barbara K. Gold, 476–90. Malden: Wiley-Blackwell.

Pascoli, Giovanni. 1951. *Carmina: Poesie latine*. Edited by Manara Valgimigli. Milan: Mondadori.

Pastore, Alessandro. 1997. "Flaminio, Marcantonio." *Dizionario Biografico degli Italiani* 48:282–88.

Petrarch, Francesco. 2001. *Bucolicum Carmen*. Edited and translated by Marcel François and Paul Bachmann. Paris: Champion.

Philological Museum: Bibliography of Neo-Latin Texts on the Web. Compiled by Dana F. Sutton. Available at http://www.philological.bham.ac.uk/bibliography/index.htm.

Piccolomini, Enea S. 1994. *Carmina*. Edited by Adrianus van Heck. Vatican City: Biblioteca Apostolica Vaticana.

———. 1967. *De gestis concilii Basiliensis commentariorum libri II*. Edited and translated by Denys Hay and Wilfrid K. Smith. Oxford: Oxford University Press.

———. 2003. *Commentarii rerum memorabilium*. Edited and translated by Margaret Meserve and Marcello Simonetta. Cambridge: Harvard University Press.

Platina, Bartolomeo. 2008. *Lives of the Popes*. Vol. 1, *Antiquity*. Edited and translated by Anthony d'Elia. Cambridge: Harvard University Press.

Poeti d'Italia in Lingua Latina. Compiled by Paolo Mastandrea, Manlio Pastore Stocchi, Roberta Cervani, and Alberto Cavarzere. Available at http://www.poetidialia.it.

Pontano, Giovanni. 1948. *Carmina: Ecloghe, elegie, liriche*. Edited by Johannes Oeschger. Bari: Laterza.

———. 2011. *Eclogues: Eclogae*. Edited by Hélène Casanova-Robin. Paris: Belles Lettres.

———. 2012. *Dialogues: Charon, Antonius*. Edited and translated by Julia Haig Gaisser. Cambridge: Harvard University Press.

Ricciardi, Roberto. 1980. "Chiaravacci, Girolamo." *Dizionario Biografico degli Italiani* 24:546–51.

Sannazaro, Jacopo. 1914. *Piscatory Eclogues*. Edited by W. P. Mustard. Baltimore: Johns Hopkins University Press.

———. 2009. *Latin Poetry*. Edited and translated by Michael C. J. Putnam. Cambridge: Harvard University Press.

Smither, Howard E. 1977. *A History of the Oratorio*. Vol. 1, *The Oratorio in the Baroque Era: Italy, Vienna, Paris*. Chapel Hill: University of North Carolina Press.

Stevenson, Jane. 2005. *Women Latin Poets: Language, Gender, and Authority, from Antiquity to the Eighteenth Century*. Oxford: Oxford University Press.

Stöve, Eckehart. 1996. "Ferreri, Zaccaria." in *Dizionario Biografico degli Italiani* 46:808–11.

Strozzi, Tito V. 1933. *Bucolicon liber*. Edited by József Fógel and László Juhász. Leipzig: Teubner.

———. 1977. *Die Borsias des Tito Strozzi*. Edited by Walther Ludwig. Munich: Fink.

Tarzia, Fabio. 2000. "Giannettasio, Nicola Partenio." *Dizionario Biografico degli Italiani* 54:448–49.

Tramontana, Alessandra. 2008. "Marrasio, Giovanni." *Dizionario Biografico degli Italiani* 70:706–11.

Tribraco, Gaspare. 1972. *Satirarum liber, dedicato al duca Borso d'Este*. Edited by Giuseppe Venturini. Ferrara: SATE.

Valeri, Elena. 2008. "Martirano, Coriolano." *Dizionario Biografico degli Italiani* 71:341–44.

Valla, Lorenzo. 2012. *Dialectical Disputations*. Edited and translated by Brian P. Copenhaver and Lodi Nauta. 2 vols. Cambridge: Harvard University Press.

Vegio, Maffeo. 2004. *Short Epics*. Edited by and translated by Michael Putnam. Cambridge: Harvard University Press.

Venturini, Giuseppe. 1970. *Un umanista modenese nella Ferrara di Borso d'Este: Gaspare Tribraco*. Ravenna: Longo.

Vida, Girolamo. 2009. *Christiad*. Edited and translated by James Gardner. Cambridge: Harvard University Press.

Vivoli, Carlo. 1987. "Dazzi, Andrea." *Dizionario Biografico degli Italiani* 33:184–86.

Worstbrock, Franz J., ed. 1983. *Der Brief im Zeitalter der Renaissance*. Weinheim: Acta Humaniora.

Valeriano, Piero. 2010. *L'infelicità dei letterati*. Edited and translated by Bruno Basile and Aniello Di Mauro. Naples: La Scuola di Pitagora.

CHAPTER 26

....

FRANCE

....

PAUL WHITE

THE French Renaissance was ambivalent about Neo-Latin. This ambivalence is explained partly by French writers' preoccupations during this period with the promotion of their own national language, and partly by the—perhaps related—preference of many French writers for Greek over Latin. The predilection for Greek went further than the Pléiade poets' championing of Greek models: some French writers wanted, in effect, to bypass Latin completely by arguing that the French language was a descendent of Greek. To some extent there was a "cultural cringe" in the face of (Tuscan) Italian with its established literary language, forms, and traditions, and its obvious continuities with Latin. At the same time, French writers asserted their own Neo-Latin identity. That the interests and agendas of French writers often went beyond the sphere of Neo-Latin does not mean that Latin was in any way undervalued in France in comparison with other European countries: rather, it was utterly taken for granted that Latin was the primary basis for and dominant medium of education, learned culture, and literary expression. By the start of the sixteenth century, the period generally taken to mark the beginnings of the French Renaissance, learned Latin culture in France already boasted a long history, and Latin was fully established as the language of the learned professions: law, medicine, and theology. A classicizing Latin, based on imitation of the "purest" ancient models, was championed by the early French humanists, and if the great humanist foundation that was the College of Royal Readers (Collège des lecteurs royaux) had to wait until 1534 for its first appointment in Latin eloquence (Sandy 2002, 3)—with royal readers in Greek and Hebrew having been appointed already in 1530—this was evidently not because Latin was seen as inferior, but because it was already comparatively so well established within institutions of learning.

FRENCH HUMANIST SCHOLARSHIP

....

Italian humanism influenced French Neo-Latin literature and learned culture through various channels. The city of Lyon, near the Italian border in east-central France, served as an important conduit, as well as being an important humanist center in its own right.

Moreover, the visits of major Italian humanists to Paris in the 1480s and 1490s galvanized Parisian humanist culture. French humanists began to make tours of Italian centers of learning as a major part of their intellectual formation. At the same time, the increasing availability of printed works by major Italian scholars and poets, whether imported from Italian presses or printed in Lyon and Paris, began to have an impact on French literary and learned culture. Still, during this early phase of French humanism, there was a strong sense in Paris that readerships in France were not yet sophisticated enough to appreciate the Italian new learning. Josse Bade (Jodocus Badius Ascensius, 1462–1535), one of the most prolific and influential scholar-printers of this period in France, presented the situation of Northern European learning in 1499 as that of an audience struggling to get to grips with the Italian scholarship: "at present not everyone is disposed [to discover] the innumerable literary luminaries that ornament all of Italy" (*lubet non omnibus sexcenta litterarum lumina Italiam late decorantia*); and even if the likes of the Italian Fausto Andrelini (ca. 1462–1518) had in this period been bringing humanist learning to Paris, there was still a lack of humanist teachers north of the Alps (see White 2013, 89, for a discussion of Bade's statement and its wider implications). Bade himself played a major role in promoting humanist Latin in France, and in printing the works of Italian writers: Lorenzo Valla, Angelo Poliziano, Marsilio Ficino, and particularly Filippo Beroaldo the Elder (1453–1505), the Bolognese humanist whose lectures in Paris in the late 1470s had enthused Robert Gaguin (1433–1501), a leading figure in the first generation of French humanists.

As well as educating readerships not yet accustomed to the new learning, promoters of humanist Latin in France would also have to contend with active resistance from the "bastion of scholasticism" (Moss 2003, 54), the University of Paris (founded in the mid-twelfth century), and in particular its Faculty of Theology: the Sorbonne. But in this first phase of the new learning's influence, the battle lines were not yet fully drawn: Beroaldo's lectures in the Sorbonne had been very well received; and the first important printing press whose output was almost completely humanist and classical—and completely Latin—had been established in the precincts of the Sorbonne. It was the project of two professors of the University of Paris, Guillaume Fichet (b. 1433) and Johann Heynlin (ca. 1425–1496), who were united in admiration for the Latin classics, particularly Cicero and Juvenal (Chartier and Martin 1989, 200). Motivated by the desire to promote a more classical Latinity along humanist lines, Fichet and Heynlin in 1469 invited three German printers, Martin Crantz, Ulrich Gering, and Michael Freiburger to set up a press in Paris. Rather than being the initiative of the printers themselves, the nature of the press's output was determined by the humanist scholars who provided the editorial and financial support (Hirsch [1960] 1978, 111–23).

In many ways, this was a false dawn for Latin humanism in France, which would await the coming of Guillaume Budé (1467–1540), "the first great classical scholar of France" (Reynolds and Wilson 1991, 172), to flourish. It was Budé's championing of the cause of a revival of learning in France that persuaded François I (1494–1547) to establish the Collège des lecteurs royaux in 1530. Because of his great erudition, and his efforts to promote their cause, French humanists looked to Budé as their figurehead; his central importance to their self-image is evidenced by their outraged reaction to a perceived slight on Budé's learning in Erasmus's *Ciceronianus* (*The Ciceronian*, 1528). Budé's influence on the character of French humanism was most notable in the domains of legal scholarship, antiquarianism, and the study of Greek: his annotations (1508 and 1526) on the *Pandects*, the digest of Roman law compiled for Justinian I in the sixth century, *De asse et partibus eius* (*The As and Its Parts*, on Roman coinage, 1515) and *Commentarii linguae Graecae* (*Notes on the Greek Language*, 1529) are each landmark works in their respective domains (Maclean 2005; Margolin 1984; La Garanderie 1995).

Budé's Latin style is difficult: the *De asse*, of which no modern translation exists at the time of writing, has been called by critics "prolix," "exuberant," and, less charitably, "more or less unreadable" (McNeil 1975, 27; Delaruelle 1907, 139). It had been considered difficult, too, by contemporary readers. Erasmus warned Budé that most readers would not be able to understand his Latin, and that even he, Erasmus, could not make sense of parts of it. He wrote in a letter to Budé, "you strain the sinews of your eloquence so much" (*sic intendas eloquentiae tuae nervos*) and compared him to the notoriously obscure Greek poet Lycophron and to the Oracle of Loxias (as the Greek oracle god Apollo was also called; La Garanderie 1967, 77–78). By contrast, Thomas More praised Budé's "careful choice of words," "well balanced sentences," and the "studied gravity of [his] diction" (McNeil 1975, 27); Christophe de Longueil (ca. 1488–1522), the French Ciceronian whom Erasmus attacked in the *Ciceronianus*, liked Budé's style and compared it to that of Thucydides (La Garanderie 1973, 348). It is surely significant that the most ready comparisons are to Greek authors: Budé's Latin is very Greek, a marker of the philhellenic character of much French neo-Latin humanism.

In the case of the *De asse*, obstacles to comprehension are at the levels of both style and terminology, and content—since this is a treatise on the more abstruse aspects of ancient Roman measures and coinage. The *De asse* also contains abundant annotations on various ancient texts, particularly Pliny the Elder. The text is full of long digressions, expressions of Budé's opinions about the political situation in France, including a long epilogue, part of it framed as a dialogue between Budé and his friend François Deloynes, full of philosophical reflections and Budé's ideas about French culture. Budé argued that France had the potential to equal or surpass Italy in learning, but that corruption and the pursuit of wealth had been a barrier to cultural improvement. The *De asse*'s anti-Italianism and its (not uncritical) patriotism—Budé's call for the French to establish a cultural identity independent of Italian influence—had a formative influence on later generations of promoters of French national culture and learning.

Bade, who first printed the *De asse* (1515), saw the opportunity to bring out a second edition little more than a year after the first, this time including some aids to reading. Bade's glosses supply both explanations of difficult vocabulary and some guidelines for reading Budé's style. Bade struggled to decipher some of Budé's more opaque metaphors, and he expressed some doubt about the interpretation of such expressions as Budé's saying of an unnamed cardinal (probably Georges d'Amboise [1460–1510]) that "he devoured the choking pear" (*anginarium pirum voravit*), supposing this to have to do with corruption of the highest ranks and the ambitious pursuit of offices. It is difficult to get a full sense of the texture of Budé's prose by excerpting passages, but the following sample gives some idea. It is taken from a section in which Budé criticizes the French military campaigns in the Italian peninsula. Budé here apostrophizes France (*Francia*), attacking implicitly the policies of Louis XII (1462–1515) and his first minister Georges d'Amboise (Budé 1516, 17r):

> *Sed quis te superum infensus ita praeposteram egit, ut choragis pastophoris pyrricham saltare velles? Videlicet nondum intelligebas nec rei nec famae tuae ita rationem habituros, quin quo iure quaque iniuria corollarium illud belli assequi conniterentur, primum venerandissimum, et ad extremum beatissimum; nullisque cancellis iudiciorum ambitionem perditam coerceri in iis hominibus posse, quos fretos vertice sacrosancto videmus iudices provocare digitis argutulis?*
>
> But what hostile god made you so perverse that you wished to dance a "Pyrrhic" led by priests? Did you not understand that they would take no account of your welfare or reputation, but rather endeavour, right or wrong, to bring about the consequence of war, [which they called] at first "most venerable" and then finally "most blessed"; and that in these men corrupt ambition could not be contained within any limits set by the courts; whom we see relying upon their sacred heads appealing to the judges with their nimble fingers?

The reader can make better sense of this by consulting the glossary supplied by Bade at the end of the volume. We are told that a *pyrrhica* is a dance with weapons; *choragus* means "dance-leader," a synonym of *praesul* (*praesul* also means "bishop"); *choragi pastophori* means the warmongering bishops and priests. Budé, then (Bade explains), "is showing that it is unbefitting and incongruous for priests to be the leaders of armed dances, that is, to preside over councils of war and to have command of the waging of war, and as it were to sound the war-trumpet for the combatants" (Budé 1516, 202r).

Juan Luis Vives (1493–1540) recommended that the *De asse* should be read by schoolboys—over-ambitiously, one cannot help but feel; although McNeil (1975, 26) relates that the work was indeed widely used as a textbook because it served as a treasury of classical quotations. The work was an immediate success with French readerships (Margolin 1984, 1). And Budé's style, though undeniably idiosyncratic, was in some ways characteristic of humanist Latin prose of sixteenth-century France: with the exception of Muret, whose elegant Ciceronian style was widely admired, the Latin—and indeed, vernacular—prose of French humanists was frequently marked by eclectic and profuse "Asiatic" stylistic tendencies (a term that had been used by Cicero to mark a contrast with the more sober "Attic" style; Castor and Cave 1984, xvi).

Budé's work had perhaps its furthest-reaching influence in the domain of legal scholarship. He initiated a trend in French humanism, that of restoration of the study of Roman law to its proper historical contexts. This is the so-called *mos gallicus*, the "French method" of legal study based on analysis of the original texts of Justinian, which was defined in opposition to the *mos italicus*, the "Italian method" based on the methods of the glossators and post-glossators (Maclean 2005, 15–16; Ducos 2002, 297). Legal humanism in sixteenth-century France centered on the University of Bourges, founded in the mid-fifteenth century by Louis XI (1423–1483), where the Italian scholar Andrea Alciati (1492–1550) taught for a relatively short time (1529–1532) but exerted a great influence on legal study in France by making philology central to the teaching of law. Alciati's followers, chief among them Jacques Cujas (1522–1590), were instrumental in carrying forward the "reformed" jurisprudence. The University of Bourges fomented reform in the religious sense, too: Jean Calvin (1509–1564) had been a student of Alciati.

The early proponents of humanism in France were not primarily interested in philology and textual scholarship: Robert Gaguin, Jacques Lefèvre d'Etaples (ca. 1455–1536), and even Budé, the figure in early French humanism who had the greatest impact in this area, did not see themselves primarily as textual critics. Later in the sixteenth century, though, it was French scholars who were at the cutting edge of this nascent discipline. By the 1560s, philological scholarship was dominated by France, and Paris in particular. The first French scholars to win international fame as textual critics were Adrien Turnèbe (1512–1565) for Greek, and Denis Lambin (1520–1572) for Latin. Succeeding them at the end of the century, Joseph Justus Scaliger (1540–1609)—son of Julius Caesar Scaliger (1484–1558), the Franco-Italian literary critic best known for his influential *Poetics* (1561)—made major contributions to textual criticism, historical scholarship, and chronology. Scaliger represents the high point of French philological scholarship, together with Isaac Casaubon (1559–1614), "a classical philologist of supreme skill and learning, whose name still adorns the critical apparatuses of a dozen classical authors" (Grafton and Weinberg 2011, 4).

No discussion of Latin humanism in France can omit the name of Petrus Ramus (Pierre de la Ramée, 1515–1572). Ramism, the culmination of attempts by mostly Northern European thinkers to redefine the relationship between rhetoric and dialectic, was a major force for the reform of education in the sixteenth century: it was responsible for loosening the grip of the classical rhetorical tradition on the humanist curriculum. All of Ramus's important texts, and those of his collaborator Omer Talon (ca. 1510–1562), were in Latin, at least until 1555, when he extended his teaching into the vernacular, and began to champion the vernacular languages (Mack 2011, 138). It may be the case, however, that this was mostly posturing and provocation on the part of Ramus: as the notes taken by his students show, he continued to teach in Latin (Magnien 2006, 54–55; cf. Meerhoff 2011). And if, as Ong argued, "Ramism is at the forefront of the vernacular movement in England, France, the Netherlands and Germany," the publication figures for Ramus's Latin textbooks speak of the continuing dominance of Latin in education and learned culture (Ong 1958, 14; cf. Sharratt 1976).

French scholars were at this time widely debating the question of whether French could rival Latin as a language of erudition and literature. Adrien Turnèbe insisted it could not. Turnèbe's nephew Etienne Pasquier (1529–1615) summarized his position in a 1552 letter:

> So then, it is in your view a waste of time and paper to express our thoughts in the vernacular, in order to communicate them to the public: since you think that our language is too base to accommodate noble ideas, but is meant only for the transaction of domestic affairs: and that any fine sentiment nurtured in the breast must be expressed in Latin. (quoted in Lewis 1998, 53)

Pasquier himself wished to question the assumption—he rehearsed the arguments of Du Bellay's 1549 *Deffence et illustration de la langue francoyse* (*Defense and Illustration of the French Language*)—that Latin was intrinsically more suited to literary, scholarly, and political discourse. Indeed, Latin had obvious shortcomings: echoing points raised by Erasmus in the *Ciceronianus*, Pasquier wrote: "I would add that the titles and honors of France, the military equipment, the terms of our everyday practices, in short half of everything that we make use of today, have changed and bear no relation to the language of Rome" (quoted in Demerson 2005, 295). This part of the debate had, in a sense, already been won: Latin was no longer the administrative, legislative, and bureaucratic language of the kingdom of France since the Ordinance of Villers-Cotterêts (1539) had established Parisian French as the language that would enable communication across the various dialects of the kingdom (Magnien 2006, 40–1).

Other French humanists challenged the preeminence of Latin from a different direction. The scholar-printer Henri Estienne (Henricus Stephanus, 1528–1598) championed Greek and French over Latin. In his *Traité de la conformité du françois avec le grec* (*Treatise on the Conformity of French with Greek*, 1566), intended partly as a riposte to the Roman humanist Lorenzo Valla's *Elegantiae linguae Latinae* (*Elegances of the Latin Language*, 1441), he argued that French had a much closer affinity with Greek than with Latin (although he did not go so far as some of his contemporaries—Jacques Périon, Léon Trippault—who claimed that the French language was actually derived from Greek). His *De la précellence du langage françois* (*Of the Preeminence of the French Language*, 1579) argued that French was superior as a literary language to Latin. Notwithstanding his preference for Greek and French, his Latin *oeuvre* was nevertheless substantial: as well as hundreds of Latin letters, poems, and lengthy prefaces, Estienne published numerous translations of Greek works into Latin (including verse translations of Anacreon, Theocritus, and the Greek Anthology, and an influential prose translation of Sextus Empiricus). His substantial output of original works in Latin included a trilogy of works engaging with debates on Latinity: *De Latinitate falso suspecta* (*On Some Wrongly Criticized Aspects of Latin*, 1576), *Pseudo-Cicero* (1577), and *Nizoliodidascalus, sive Monitor Ciceronianorum Nizolianorum* (*Master Nizolius; or, A Critique of the Nizolian Ciceronians*, 1578; the reference is to the Italian Ciceronian Mario Nizolio, 1498–1576). And although he put out only one *editio princeps* of a Latin work—as against eighteen first editions of Greek works—he edited and printed numerous classical Latin authors, his editions marking significant improvements in textual accuracy over those of his predecessors.

POETRY AND DRAMA

The positions taken up by the likes of Pasquier and Estienne in debates about language in no way precluded them from participation in Latin culture, and certainly did not stop them writing in Latin for the purposes of communication, prestige, and pleasure. Both wrote a good deal of highly accomplished Latin poetry.

The first major Neo-Latin poet of France was Jean Salmon Macrin (1490–1557). Salmon Macrin himself, together with a group of Latin poets in Lyon, was largely responsible for establishing this image of him as a French innovator and pioneer: he was, he claimed, the first French poet to imitate Horace and the Greek lyric poets (see, for example, his *Carmina* [*Poems*] 1.31, lines 41–48 and 57–60); and was vaunted in the poetry of Nicolas Bourbon (ca. 1503–ca. 1550) and others as the "French Horace." In fact, Salmon Macrin was not the first in France to write classicizing Latin poetry, nor even the first to write a Latin lyric collection in the manner of Horace: Petrus Burrus (1430–1504) probably has that distinction. Although, strictly speaking, Burrus was Flemish, he was educated in Paris, and all of his works were printed there. Salmon Macrin spent much of his life in service of the French court: during the 1530s he enjoyed the protection of Guillaume Du Bellay (1491–1543), an important patron to whom he dedicated his four books of *Carmina* (1530), and he won royal favor, serving as *valet de chambre* to François I from 1534. He wrote only in Latin, but his influence on French vernacular culture was significant also: his poetic *oeuvre* is often seen as an important site of mediation between the Neo-Latin poetry of the Italian Renaissance, and the great flourishing of vernacular poetry that was to come with the Pléiade. Salmon Macrin was also the first French poet to imitate extensively the style and tone of the love poems of Catullus, in the manner of Italian models such as Giovanni Pontano (1426–1503) and Michael Marullus (d. 1500). Neo-Catullan poets generally favored certain types of composition—the "kiss" poem, the playful epitaph for a pet, poems that were sensual and sometime obscenely sexual—and came to adopt a quite well-defined set of stylistic features: the use of diminutives, schemes of repetition, comparative expressions. With the work of Salmon Macrin, and with the Lyon publication of the *Basia* (*Kisses*, 1539) of Johannes Secundus, the Neo-Catullan style became popular in France. Studies of the development of this style demonstrate the extent to which French Neo-Latin and vernacular poetry mutually influenced one another in this period (Morrison 1955; Ford 1993 and 2013; Galand-Hallyn 1997). The city of Lyon was a particularly rich site of literary creativity in the first half of the sixteenth century. The works of Latin poets such as Jean Visagier (ca. 1510–1542), Nicolas Bourbon, and Etienne Dolet (1509–1546), for example, interconnected in various ways with the work of the great French poet Clément Marot (1496–1544), and the lines of influence went in both directions: from Latin to the vernacular, and *vice versa*.

Parallels and divergences in the development of Neo-Latin and French language poetry can be observed too in the work of the Pléiade, a group of French poets including Pierre de Ronsard (1524–1585) and Joachim Du Bellay (ca. 1522–1560). Du Bellay is the most prominent example of a Pléiade author who was also an important Neo-Latin poet. His Latin poems date from the latter part of his career; it may seem somewhat surprising that they exist at all, given his earlier injunction to aspiring French poets not to attempt to rival the ancients in their own languages. In the *Deffence et illustration de la langue francoyse*, he had famously characterized the Neo-Latin poetasters as *reblanchisseurs de murailles*, "whitewashers of walls," who prefer to transcribe Virgil rather than create something entirely new. He took them to task for trying to reconstruct the grandeur and excellence of ancient monuments from ruined masonry, declaring that nobody is capable of matching the forms given to the edifice of poetry by the ancient architects. When he published his Latin poetry at the end of his short career (1558), his views had evidently changed—as had the French literary landscape. Although Du Bellay does not in his Latin writing engage explicitly with the views he had earlier expressed in the *Deffence*, anxieties about imitation and self-expression feature prominently, and are subjected to careful scrutiny (see, e.g., his *Elegies* 1 and 7). His most direct engagement with the question of language choice comes in the poem *To the Reader* (*Ad lectorem*), which stands at the head of the book of epigrams. Here, Du Bellay imagines that the reader is shocked at his abandonment of his French "wife" (*nupta*), with whom he has fathered so many children, in favor of a Latin "mistress" (*domina*). How could he prefer a mistress to his wife? One is beautiful, responds the poet, but the other is more attractive (*Illa quidem bella est, sed magis ista placet*). In this erotically charged conception of poetic language, the point of the contrast between French wife and Latin mistress seems to be to link the Latin language with sensuality and pleasure—an odd association, given the emphasis elsewhere in the collection on the difficulty and labor involved in the composition of Latin verses. The French language is here characterized as a wife, but she is also a mother, and the "children" she and Du Bellay have produced together are his many poems in that language. The maternal character of France and the French language is an idea to be found frequently elsewhere in Du Bellay's work (most famously in the sonnet *France, mère des arts, des armes et des lois* [*France, Mother of the Arts, Arms, and Laws*]): French as the mother tongue, the natural language of the poet, is set in uneasy opposition to the artificiality and essential "otherness" of Latin.

Du Bellay's insistence on the unfamiliarity of Latin is part of a pose adopted by his poetic persona in the *Elegies*, which he composed, like his *Antiquitez de Rome* (*Roman Antiquities*) and *Regrets*, during his stay in Rome between 1553 and 1557. Like many Renaissance humanists, he made his career in court service, and his time in Rome was spent working at the papal court, as a secretary to his uncle Jean Du Bellay (1498–1560), a cardinal. The conceit of the collection is that this trip is an exile comparable to that suffered by Ovid, relegated to the shores of the Black Sea. Du Bellay writes in his elegy *Patriae desiderium* (*Longing for Home*; Du Bellay 1984, 65 and 67):

> *Annua ter rapidi circum acta est orbita Solis,*
> > *Ex quo tam longas cogor inire vias,*
> *Ignotisque procul peregrinus degere tectis,*
> > *Et Lyrii tantum vix meminisse mei,*
> *Atque alios ritus, aliosque ediscere mores,*
> > *Fingere et insolito verba aliena sono. . . .*
> *Sic teneri quondam vates praeceptor Amoris,*
> > *Dum procul a patriis finibus exul agit,*
> *Barbara (nec puduit) Latiis praelata Camoenis*
> > *Carmina non propriam condidit ad citharam.*

Three times the yearly revolution of the scorching Sun has completed its course since I was forced to undertake such a long journey and to live far away as a foreigner in a strange house; and to hardly remember my home, Liré; and to learn other customs, and other habits, and to compose in strange-sounding foreign words. . . . So once that bard, the teacher of tender Love, when he was living in exile far from the land of his home, composed foreign poems (and there was no shame in it) to a strange tune, preferring them to the Latin Muses.

The comparison here, in reference to Ovid's *Letters from Pontus* 4.13.17–22, is not without irony: Ovid was indeed ashamed to have to write in the Getic tongue, the "barbaric" language spoken in the land of his exile, rather than Latin; and his exile was a very real one. Du Bellay's inversion of the Ovidian situation (he chooses Latin as a foreign tongue whereas Ovid was forced to abandon Latin as his native language; "exile" *to* Rome versus exile *from* Rome) results in a sort of paradox: Du Bellay's use of Latin, as well as being a departure from his linguistic origins, is also "a return to cultural roots (those of ancient Rome and modern Italy)" (Tucker 1990, 15). Moreover, Latin is of course not as "foreign" to Du Bellay or to his French readership as he pretends. Du Bellay's self-presentation is shot through with ambivalence towards Latin and what it meant to write in Latin.

The Pléiade of course defined itself primarily as a movement to invigorate and, in Du Bellay's term, *illustrer* (~ "enrich") the French vernacular. At the same time, though, certain of its members and others in its orbit were working to pursue in Latin a project analogous to that of the Pléiade poets in French. In 1552, Marc-Antoine Muret (1526–1585) published his *Iuvenilia*, a collection of Latin poems in various genres in imitation of specific ancient models—Seneca for his tragedy *Julius Caesar*; Juvenal and Persius for his satires; and various combinations of multiple models for his elegies, epigrams, epistles, and odes—that was in many ways intended to stand as the Neo-Latin equivalent to the works of Pierre de Ronsard (1524–1585), Jean-Antoine de Baïf (1532–1589), and Du Bellay in French (Leroux in Muret 2009, 275). Muret in his preface stressed the need to do for Neo-Latin poetry in France what the members of the "Brigade" (as the Pléiade poets called themselves) had done for French. Those poets had, he affirmed, already brought French poetry to its pinnacle, or were about to do so (Muret 2009, 46). Latin, on the other hand, still lacked its great French poets: in 1552, Muret judged only Ausonius (who had been a native of Burdigala, the modern-day Bordeaux) among the ancients and Jean Salmon Macrin among the moderns to be worthy of mention. Further on he added the name of Jean Dorat. But he pointedly omitted to mention Théodore de Bèze (1519–1605), who had in 1548 published a collection very similar to Muret's *Iuvenilia* (the two collections were often bound together in later printings). De Bèze's *Poemata* (*Poems*), known later also as *Iuvenilia*, probably had a much greater influence in France than Muret and his friends would admit: relations between de Bèze and the Pléiade poets were precarious, and they frequently attacked each other in print (Smith 1995, 9). In any case, by 1552, de Bèze had largely disowned his early Latin poetry, converted to Protestantism, and left Paris for Geneva, where he would become the "pope" of Calvinism (Dufour 2006).

Jean Dorat (1508–1588), the great Hellenist scholar who in the 1540s had tutored members of the Pléiade at the Collège de Coqueret in Paris, and who continued to be a figure of central importance to the group, was an extremely prolific writer of Latin poetry. He was appointed by Charles IX (1550–1574) as the official royal poet for Latin. Ian McFarlane remarked that Dorat as *poeta regius* was doing in Latin what Ronsard, *poète du roi*, was doing in French (Demerson 1983, viii). Ronsard, incidentally, wrote next to nothing in Latin, and in shaping his public image he deliberately played down those Latin poems he had composed (Smith 1999b, 172). He wrote in an *Elegie* to Pierre L'Escot that Latin composition had been his first love as a youth, but, not being talented enough for it, he preferred to be first among poets in his own language than last among the Latins. Nevertheless, his French poetry reached a wider international readership in Latin translations, some of them done by Dorat (Smith 1999c; Ford 2013, 159).

Michel de Montaigne (1553–1592) judged that the best Neo-Latin poets that France produced in his age were Jean Dorat, Théodore de Bèze, George Buchanan, Pierre Mondoré, Michel de L'Hospital, and Adrien Turnèbe (*Essais* 1.17): Du Bellay he named only in the context of his French poetry. Of these, the most important so far unmentioned in this chapter are L'Hospital and Buchanan. Michel de L'Hospital (1507–1573) was a major political figure and patron as well as being an important Neo-Latin poet in his own right. He published very little in print during his lifetime, but was widely admired. L'Hospital exemplifies the political dimension of Neo-Latin poetry in France—he, along with others in his circle, used his poetry to advance the cause of religious toleration and irenism, particularly through strategies of dedication: he dedicated poems to prominent members of both Catholic and Protestant factions (Ford 2013, 215). During the Wars of Religion, which devastated France in the wake of the Reformation, Latin poetry was more likely to be used as an instrument of propaganda, as happened for example with Latin translations of poems by Ronsard (Smith 1999c, 213). But the composition and exchange of Latin poetry throughout this period could unite figures of diverse political and religious persuasions: the salon of Jean de Morel exemplifies this spirit of toleration. Among the figures who frequented it on both sides of the religious divide was George Buchanan (1506–1582), a Scot who spent much of his life in France. His poetic *oeuvre* is diverse, spanning secular and religious works (he was a convert to Protestantism). Particularly noteworthy are his tragedies (*Jephthes, Baptistes*) which he had composed to be performed by schoolboys, Montaigne among them, at the Collège de Guyenne in Bordeaux, and which were important models for the development of French humanist tragedy (Sharratt and Walsh 1983; Ford and Green 2009).

Latin humanist drama in sixteenth-century France was in the main composed by teachers and students in colleges (Lazard 1980; Ferrand 2013). Neo-Latin drama in France in the seventeenth century was largely the domain of Jesuit authors, and the latter half of the century produced more of it than any other period (Loach 2013, 113). Jesuit schools, like the humanist schools of the sixteenth century, encouraged pupils to put on public performances of these plays. Jesuit authors produced an abundance of Neo-Latin writing in all genres in this period, the best-known in the domain of poetry being René

Rapin (1621–1687). Rapin wrote sacred pastoral (*Eclogae sacrae*, 1659), georgic (the *Horti* [*Gardens*] of 1665), and epic (*Christus patiens* [*Christ Suffering*], 1674; Haskell 2003, 17).

SCIENCE AND PHILOSOPHY
IN SEVENTEENTH-CENTURY FRANCE

In the seventeenth century, the ascendency of French as a literary language continued apace, and although Latin continued to be used by both poetic and prose writers, it no longer held the dominant position it once had. More generally, seventeenth-century France saw the continued use of Latin for learned scientific and philosophical texts. The astronomer Pierre Gassendi (1592–1655) wrote mainly in Latin. The mathematician Marin Mersenne (1588–1648) called for the creation of an institution that would undertake to translate learned works into "the common tongue of Christian Europe, which is Latin" (Waquet [1998] 2001, 263). And it is often not fully appreciated that Descartes ("Cartesius," 1596–1650)—who was educated by the Jesuits—wrote his major works of philosophy, the *Metaphysical Meditations* (1641) and the *Principles of Philosophy* (1644), not in the French of the *Discours de la méthode* (*Discourse on Method*, 1637), but in Latin. Both of these works were only translated into French several years after their first Latin publication. The writing of the *Meditations* in Latin was presented by Descartes as a sort of precaution, a way of limiting access: he claimed to have been wary of exposing his ideas to a vernacular audience, lest the weak-minded misuse them (Descartes 1973, 7):

> *Viamque sequor . . . tam parum tritam atque ab usu communi tam remotam, ut non utile putarim ipsam in Gallico et passim ab omnibus legendo scripto fusius docere, ne debiliora etiam ingenia credere possent eam sibi esse ingrediendam.*

> I am following a path . . . so rarely trodden and so far from the usual ways, that I did not think it proper to explain it at length in French and in a language that can easily be read by everyone, lest weaker minds believe that they, too, could enter this path.

In addition to this motive of exclusivity—a traditional rhetorical move—the publisher's preface in the French edition of 1647 supplied another reason for Descartes's choice of Latin: in order to have his arguments heard, Descartes had to couch them in the idiom and terminology of the contemporary philosophical discourse; that is to say, the Latin of the doctors of the Sorbonne—an institution still seen by many, as it had been in the early sixteenth century, as the bastion of the scholastic establishment against the onslaught of new and progressive ideas. On the other hand, in a *Lettre-Préface* to the French translator of his *Principia*, Claude Picot (on whom, see Leroux 2012), Descartes presented the advantages of publication in French rather than Latin: that the work would be read by more people, and that it would be more easily understood. The second of these reasons is not just a restatement of the first: the reason why the French would be more easily understood than the Latin is not only that most readers lacked in Latin the facility of their mother tongue; it is that, for Descartes's purposes, Latin implied the Latin of the schools, an idiom all of its own, overburdened with jargon and terminology often abstracted to the point of meaninglessness. Descartes complained bitterly of the obscurantism of scholastic Latin, whose proponents aimed only to carry the point by confusing their interlocutors with disorientating language: they were like the blind man whose only way of beating a sighted man is to lead him into the depths of a dark cave. And in the *Discours de le méthode*, the choice to write in French was presented as utterly essential to the Cartesian philosophical project: the fresh perspective of those not educated in the Latin language tradition, unburdened and unprejudiced by those habits of mind, was more apt to understand by means of "pure natural reason."

Of course, Descartes still had to rely on Latin publication to reach as wide an international audience as possible and for corresponding with non-francophone colleagues. Latin remained the dominant language of science and philosophy, and indeed of diplomacy, and would continue to be so, at least until the end of the seventeenth century (Febvre and Martin [1958] 1976, 331). The statistics for books printed by French presses, which show a steady decline in the proportion of Latin works throughout the sixteenth century, present a very sharp decline in the second half of the seventeenth century, which persisted in the eighteenth (Waquet [1998] 2001, 81–82). The majority of books still being printed in Latin were works of theology and science, as well as textbooks, grammars, and dictionaries for use in schools and universities. French was well on the way to displacing Latin as the most widely used language in learned, literary, and political discourse.

SUGGESTED READING

The collections edited by Castor and Cave (1984), Sandy (2002), and Bury (2005) offer a variety of perspectives on Neo-Latin in France. Among French Neo-Latin poets, Du Bellay, Salmon Macrin, and the *sodalitium Lugdunense* (community of poets in Lyon) have attracted the most critical attention: see, for example, McFarlane (1959–1960), Demerson (1980 and 1984), Galand-Hallyn (1995, 1997, and 1998), and Bizer (1995). Philip Ford published widely on Neo-Latin in France, and Ford (2013) represents in many ways a summa of his work in this area. Grafton (1983–1993) remains an essential guide to French scholarship and its wider European context. Chartier and Martin (1989) and Lestringant and Zink (2006) are authoritative reference works containing a wealth of material about the fortunes of Latin in France.

REFERENCES

Bizer, Marc. 1995. *Imitation et conscience de soi dans la poésie latine de la Pléiade.* Paris: Champion.
Budé, Guillaume. 1516. *De asse et partibus eius.* Paris: Josse Bade.

Bury, Emmanuel, ed. 2005. *Tous vos gens à latin: Le latin, langue savante, langue mondaine*. Geneva: Droz.

Castor, Grahame, and Terence Cave, eds. 1984. *Neo-Latin and the Vernacular in Renaissance France*. Oxford: Clarendon Press.

Chartier, Roger, and Henri-Jean Martin, eds. 1989. *Histoire de l'édition française*. Vol. 1, *Le Livre conquérant: Du Moyen Âge au milieu du XVIIᵉ siècle*. Paris: Fayard.

Delaruelle, Louis. 1907. *Guillaume Budé: Les origines, les débuts, les idées maîtresses*. Paris: Champion.

Demerson, Geneviève. 1980. "Les Obsessions linguistiques de Joachim Du Bellay." In *ACNL* 1980, 512–27.

———. 1983. *Dorat en son temps: Culture classique et présence au monde*. Clermont-Ferrand: Adosa.

———. 1984. "Joachim Du Bellay, traducteur de lui-même." In Castor and Cave, op. cit., 113–28.

———. 2005. "Langue ancienne et nouveau monde." In Bury, op. cit., 295–308.

Descartes, René. 1973. *Oeuvres de Descartes*. Vol. 7, *Meditationes de prima philosophia*. Edited by Charles Adam and Paul Tannery. Paris: Vrin.

Du Bellay, Joachim. 1984. *Oeuvres poétiques*. Vol. 7, *Oeuvres latines: Poemata*. Edited by Geneviève Demerson. Paris: Société des textes français modernes.

Ducos, Michèle. 2002. "Legal Science in France in the Sixteenth and Seventeenth Centuries." In Sandy 2002, 297–313.

Dufour, Alain. 2006. *Théodore de Bèze: Poète et Théologien*. Geneva: Droz.

Febvre, Lucien, and Henri-Jean Martin. (1958) 1976. *The Coming of the Book: The Impact of Printing 1450–1800*. Translated by David Gerard. London: Verso.

Ferrand, Mathieu. 2013. "Humanist Neo-Latin Drama in France." In *Neo-Latin Drama in Early Modern Europe*, edited by Jan Bloemendal and Howard Norland, 365–414. Leiden: Brill.

Ford, Philip. 1993. "The *Basia* of Johannes Secundus and Lyon Poetry." In *Intellectual Life in Renaissance Lyon*, edited by Philip Ford and Gillian Jondorf, 113–33. Cambridge: Cambridge French Colloquia.

———. 2013. *The Judgement of Palaemon: The Contest Between Neo-Latin and Vernacular Poetry in Renaissance France*. Leiden: Brill.

Ford, Philip, and Roger Green. 2009. *George Buchanan: Poet and Dramatist*. Swansea: Classical Press of Wales.

Galand-Hallyn, Perrine. 1995. *Le "génie" latin de Joachim Du Bellay*. La Rochelle: Rumeur des Ages.

———. 1997. "Marot, Macrin, Bourbon: 'muse naïve' et 'tendre style.'" In *La Génération Marot: Poètes français et néo-latins (1515–1550)*, edited by Gérard Defaux, 211–40. Paris: Champion.

———. 1998. "Jean Salmon Macrin et la liberté de l'éloge." In *Cultura e potere nel Rinascimento*, edited by Luisa Secchi Tarugi, 515–29. Florence: Cesati.

Grafton, Anthony. 1983–1993. *Joseph Scaliger: A Study in the History of Classical Scholarship*. 2 vols. Oxford: Clarendon Press.

Grafton, Anthony, and Joanna Weinberg. 2011. *"I Have Always Loved the Holy Tongue": Isaac Casaubon, the Jews, and a Forgotten Chapter in Renaissance Scholarship*. Cambridge: Belknap.

Haskell, Yasmin. 2003. *Loyola's Bees: Ideology and Industry in Jesuit Latin Didactic Poetry*. Oxford: Oxford University Press.

Hirsch, Rudolf. (1960) 1978. "Printing in France and Humanism, 1470–1480." In *The Printed Word: Its Impact and Diffusion (Primarily in the 15th–16th Centuries)*, 111–23. London: Variorum.

La Garanderie, Marie-Madeleine de. 1967. *La Correspondance d'Erasme et de Guillaume Budé.* Paris: Vrin.

———. 1973. "Le style figuré de Guillaume Budé." In *L'Humanisme français au début de la Renaissance*, prepared by various editors, 343–55. Paris: Vrin.

———. 1995. *Christianisme et lettres profanes: Essai sur l'humanisme français (1515–1535) et sur la pensée de Guillaume Budé.* Paris: Champion.

Lazard, Madeleine. 1980. *Le Théâtre en France au XVIe siècle.* Paris: Presses Universitaires de France.

Leroux, Henri. 2012. *Claude Picot: Correspondant et ami mal connu de Descartes.* Paris: Editions Beaurepaire.

Lestringant, Frank, and Michel Zink, eds. 2006. *Histoire de la France littéraire.* Vol. 1, *Naissances, Renaissances: Moyen Âge–XVIe siècle.* Paris: Presses Universitaires de France.

Lewis, John. 1998. *Adrien Turnèbe, 1512–1565: A Humanist Observed.* Geneva: Droz.

Loach, Judi. 2013. "Performing in Latin in Jesuit-Run Colleges in Mid- to Late-17th-Century France: Why, and with What Consequences." In *The Early Modern Cultures of Neo-Latin Drama*, edited by Philip Ford and Andrew Taylor, 113–40. Leuven: Leuven University Press.

Mack, Peter. 2011. *A History of Renaissance Rhetoric, 1380–1620.* Oxford: Oxford University Press.

Maclean, Ian. 2005. *Interpretation and Meaning in the Renaissance: The Case of Law.* Cambridge: Cambridge University Press.

Magnien, Michel. 2006. "Le français et la latinité: De l'émergence à l'illustration." In Lestringant and Zink, op. cit., 36–77.

Margolin, Jean-Claude. 1984. "De la digression au commentaire: Pour une lecture humaniste du *De asse* de Guillaume Budé." In Castor and Cave, op. cit., 1–25.

McFarlane, Ian D. 1959–1960. "Jean Salmon Macrin (1490–1557)." *Bibliothèque d'Humanisme et Renaissance* 21:55–84, 311–49; and 22:73–89.

McNeil, David. 1975. *Guillaume Budé and Humanism in the Reign of Francis I.* Geneva: Droz.

Meerhoff, Kees. 2011. "Petrus Ramus and the Vernacular." In *Ramus, Pedagogy and the Liberal Arts*, edited by Steven J. Reid and Emma A. Wilson, 133–52. Farnham: Ashgate.

Morrison, Mary. 1955. "Catullus and the Neo-Latin Poetry of France Before 1550." *Bibliothèque d'Humanisme et Renaissance* 17:365–94.

Moss, Ann. 2003. *Renaissance Truth and the Latin Language Turn.* Oxford: Oxford University Press.

Muret, Marc-Antoine. 2009. *Juvenilia.* Edited by Virginie Leroux. Geneva: Droz.

Ong, Walter J. 1958. *Ramus: Method, and the Decay of Dialogue; from the Art of Discourse to the Art of Reason.* Chicago: University of Chicago Press.

Reynolds, Leighton D., and Nigel G. Wilson. 1991. *Scribes and Scholars: A Guide to the Transmission of Greek and Latin Literature*, 3rd ed. Oxford: Clarendon Press.

Sandy, Gerald N., ed. 2002. *The Classical Heritage in France.* Leiden: Brill.

Sharratt, Peter. 1976. "Peter Ramus and the Reform of the University: The Divorce of Philosophy and Eloquence?" In *French Renaissance Studies 1540–1570: Humanism and the Encyclopaedia*, edited by Peter Sharratt, 4–20. Edinburgh: Edinburgh University Press.

Sharratt, Peter, and Patrick Walsh, eds. and trans. 1983. *George Buchanan: Tragedies.* Edinburgh: Scottish Academic Press.

Smith, Malcolm. 1995. *Ronsard and Du Bellay versus Bèze: Allusiveness in Renaissance Literary Texts.* Geneva: Droz.

———. 1999a. *Renaissance Studies: Articles 1966–1994.* Geneva: Droz.

———. (1986) 1999b. "Lost Works by Ronsard." In Smith 1999a, 166–83.

———. (1988) 1999c. "Latin Translations of Ronsard." In Smith 1999a, 212–18.

Tucker, George H. 1990. *The Poet's Odyssey: Joachim du Bellay and the* Antiquitez de Rome. Oxford: Clarendon Press.

Waquet, Françoise. (1998) 2001. *Latin, or a Empire of a Sign*. London: Verso.

White, Paul. 2013. *Jodocus Badius Ascensius: Commentary, Commerce and Print in the Renaissance*. Oxford: Oxford University Press.

CHAPTER 27

THE BRITISH ISLES

ESTELLE HAAN

In the mid-nineteenth century Walter Savage Landor published a Latin essay in which he censured his contemporaries for attaching the nomenclature "dead" to "languages that are the only ones that will never die" ([*linguae*] . . . *quae solae sunt nunquam moriturae* (Landor 1847, 273). Landor, the last major English poet to compose Neo-Latin verse (Kelly 1974), acknowledged British Neo-Latin writing as a distinct category, whose preeminent authors (*principes*) he proclaimed to be the Scottish George Buchanan (1506–1582); the Welsh John Owen (1564–1622); and the English John Milton (1608–1674), Thomas May (1595–1650), and Thomas Gray (1716–1771; Landor, 1847, 290). He also reveals an alertness to the importance attached to Continental acclaim, describing Buchanan as one "whom Scaliger terms the god of literati" (*quem litteratorum deum appellat Scaliger*; Landor, 1847, 297). Landor's essay presents a seeming paradox: the value of Neo-Latin writing of the British Isles resides in its distinctive "Britishness," but also in its relationship to its Continental Neo-Latin peers and its classical Latin forebears.

Some two centuries earlier, a rather similar vision had been espoused by William Dillingham in his *Poemata varii argumenti* (*Poems on Various Subjects*, 1678). Here British Neo-Latin writing is recognized as distinct, but it is also juxtaposed with classical Latin poetry and with Continental Neo-Latin verse. As such, it is *both* ancient and modern, *both* national and Continental; its hybrid nature discernible in the volume's structure, content, and methodology (Haan 2010, 1–15). Thus Thomas More (1478–1535), George Buchanan, and Phineas Fletcher (1582–1650) take their place alongside Vida (1485–1566), Erasmus (1466–1536), de Bèze (1519–1605), and Grotius (1583–1645)—all now in the company of the classical authors Virgil, Manilius, and Lucan. Andrew Melville (1545–1622) and Thomas Reid (d. 1624) are both termed "Scots" (*Scoti*), while others are designated by their associated city: Phineas Fletcher of Cambridge (*Cantabrigiensis*); Vida of Cremona (*Cremonensis*); Erasmus of Rotterdam (*Roterodamus*), and so on. The volume is certainly showcasing British Neo-Latin, but also the lateral thinking of an Anglo-Latin poet and anthologist.

BRITISH NEO-LATIN: SOME LITERARY
TRENDS AND CRITICAL APPROACHES

Lateral thinking is central to an understanding of the literary history of Neo-Latin writing of the British Isles. Using "a language . . . which across the frontiers . . . could speak to a cultivated European audience" (Binns 1974, viii), the Neo-Latin author could cross geographical, linguistic, and ultimately chronological boundaries. This was rendered possible through epistolary correspondence, travel, study, teaching, and academic performance abroad (one need only think of Buchanan or Leland in Paris, Milton or Gray in Italy, or Addison in Vienna), and especially through intertextual engagement with classical and contemporary Latin works.

Like Dillingham and Landor, modern scholarship has come to recognize the distinctiveness of British Neo-Latin, while also acknowledging that it is much more than an insular product of the humanist pedagogical system in which it found its origins. This is reflected in the burgeoning of critical studies of, among others, Buchanan (McFarlane 1981; Ford 1982; Ford and Green 2009), Milton (Haan 1998a; Hale 2005; Haan 2012), Marvell (Haan 2003), Dillingham (Haan 2010), Gray (Haan 2000), Addison (Haan 2005a), and Bourne (Storey 1974; Haan 2007). Worthy of study in its own right, British Neo-Latin may also shed light upon an author's vernacular verse, whereby apparent code-selection is transformed into linguistic hybridity.

For example, Marvell's English poems *On a Drop of Dew* and *The Garden* find their literary and frequently their linguistic origins in his Neo-Latin poems (*Ros* [*Dew*] and *Hortus* [*Garden*]). A comparative reading of the Latin and its expanded vernacular counterpart serves to illuminate the reciprocity of Marvell's macaronic punning—and much more (Jaeckle 2001; Haan 2003, 57–94; Haan 2008). Likewise *Poems of Mr John Milton, Both English and Latin* (1645) may have a separate title-page and pagination for the respective "English" and "Latin" halves, but its carefully planned structure invites comparison between those two halves (Haan 2012, 141–65; Revard 2013). Milton's decision to adopt the vernacular is ironically articulated in a *Latin* poem (*Epitaphium Damonis* ll. 169–78; Milton 2014, 224), and in terms suggesting, not the abandonment, but the linguistic transformation, of Neo-Latin into a vernacular *Latinitas*. This would be realized in *Paradise Lost*, in the course of which the modern (Latinless) reader is, as I have argued elsewhere, surprised by syntax, seduced by the linguistic alterity of Latinity itself (Haan 2012, 167–98).

Less frequently noted is the fact that British Neo-Latin poets engaged with their Neo-Latin and vernacular peers at home and abroad. The structure and content of Milton's *Elegiarum liber* (*Book of Elegies*) may owe some debt to Buchanan's *Elegiarum Liber* (Haan 1997a), but it is also quasi-Chaucerian at times (Haan 2012, 71–75); his Latin poem to his father (*Ad patrem*) interacts with Neo-Latin verse tributes on the same subject by Alexander Gil, Jr. (Little 1950), and Hugo Grotius (Haan 1998b), while also presenting an "apology for poetry" in language reminiscent of Poliziano's *Nutricia* ([*Reward for Nursing*], 1486) and Vida's *De Arte Poetica* ([*On the Art of Poetry*], 1527; Haan 1995, 289–92). When Milton drew upon Italian collections associated with the addressees of his Neo-Latin works composed there (Haan 1998, 93–117 and 137–48), he also revealed a self-conscious sense of *Britannitas*: he proclaimed, in language evocative perhaps of John Leland's *Cygnea Cantio* (*Swan Song*, 1545), that England possessed her own poetic swans (*Mansus*, ll. 30–33; Milton 2014, 206–208), and announced epic plans for an *Arthuriad* (*Mansus*, ll. 80–84). In short, British Neo-Latin forever embodies, yet crosses, the permeable boundaries of space, language, and time.

It is a permeability that tends to be blurred as a consequence of the national compartmentalization characteristic of scholarly surveys of British Neo-Latin from Bradner (1940) through Binns (1990) to Houghton and Manuwald (2012). This approach is not conducive to a comparative analysis of text(s), sociocultural context(s), and intercultural (and indeed intracultural) exchange within and between four regions. And there is also a theoretical boundary that still needs to be crossed. Contrary to Binns's suggestion that Renaissance Latin poetry "does not stand up well to the techniques of literary criticism now in vogue" (Binns 1974, viii), the truth may lie in an independent formulation. Modern readings should be informed by an alertness to the nature of (a) the Renaissance concept of imitation (*imitatio*) as emulation (*aemulatio*) and (b) the complexities attendant upon intertextuality, since, after all, Neo-Latin is "the most intertextual poetry known to Europe" (Hale 1997, 12). Likewise a consideration of Latin translations of vernacular texts cannot adequately be undertaken without recourse to translation theory. For scholars of reception studies, it is difficult to imagine a more fertile ground for cultivation, while recent acknowledgement of the emerging female Neo-Latin voice in England (Hosington 2002 and 2006; Saunders 2002; Stevenson 2005, 255–75 and 368–94; Pal 2012, 142–76 and 177–205) facilitates future gendered readings.

Van Hal, commenting on current approaches to Neo-Latin, highlights the need for "the development of a more sophisticated, theoretical subdivision . . . more sensitive to the occurrence of . . . thematic overlapping, 'cross-fertilization' between genres" (Van Hal 2007, 354). The present, essentially selective, discussion is governed by a comparative reading through the lens of genre (and cross-fertilization between genres), rather than nation. Its aim is to facilitate an understanding of ways in which Latin served to bridge several types of divides or "spaces": (i) horizontal spaces (both physical and metaphorical) between four British regions; between Neo-Latin writers in Britain and their Continental predecessors and peers; between Latin and the respective vernacular(s); and (ii) vertical spaces (both chronological and cultural) between the Neo-Latin and the classical Latin text, and between the linear demarcations of "early modern," "Augustan," and "Romantic" retrospectively imposed by critics.

NATIONHOOD AND THE BRITISH
NEO-LATIN TEXT

Dillingham's collection paved the way for a series of Neo-Latin anthologies that would see print in seventeenth- and eighteenth-century England and Scotland. But the correlation between anthologizing and a self-conscious sense of nationhood may well trace its origins back to the early seventeenth-century *Delitiae* (a variant spelling of *deliciae*, "pleasures, charms") collections of Neo-Latin poetry published at Frankfurt separately and by country, each of whose titles proclaims its authors as pertaining to either Italy (1608), France (1609), Belgium (1612), or Germany (1612). That this practice was emulated in Britain is evident from the publication of the *Delitiae Poetarum Scotorum* (*The Charms of the Scottish Poets*, 1637), not without the articulation of geographical self-consciousness. In his dedicatory letter prefixed to the collection, Arthur Johnston notes how Buchanan has made illustrious "this furthermost corner of the earth, one lying virtually beneath the very pole of the universe" (*extremum hunc terrarum angulum, paene sub ipso mundi cardine iacentem*). Since Buchanan's death there has arisen, as it were, a countless army of poets, who rival those of the classical Augustan age. That sense of emulation, both chronological and geographical, is further conveyed in Johnston's *Musarum Elogia* (*Praises of the Muses*), but now, significantly, the rivals are both the classics of Augustan Rome and the Neo-Latin poets of modern Italy and France.

In seventeenth- and eighteenth-century England, collections of Neo-Latin verse by Italian poets were ardently matched by their British equivalents. Francis Atterbury's *Anthologia* of Latin-writing Italian poets (1684; revised and expanded in 1740 by Alexander Pope) was matched by the *Musarum Anglicanarum Analecta* (*Analects of the English Muses*, 1692), appearing again in 1699 (revised by Joseph Addison), 1714, 1721, 1741 (revised by Vincent Bourne), and 1761—an eighteenth-century best-seller. Uniting the various editions is a self-conscious aim to show that "Britons," far from being "utterly divided from the whole world" (*penitus toto divisos orbe Britannos*; Virgil, *Eclogues* 1.66), are joined to that world by virtue of their vibrant Neo-*Latinitas*. For example, the compiler of the third edition of 1714 offers the work in his Preface to the reader as one that mirrors "the more select Muses of the Italians and of the Scottish" (*selectiores Italorum Scotorumque Musae*), an *Anthologia* proffered to its readership by England (*Anglia*) "in case you might think that she herself is utterly divided from the literate world also" (*ne ipsam a literato etiam orbe penitus divisam putes*, A2r). The Virgilian sentiment concerning geographical remoteness is transformed into a caveat about an insularity that is potentially literary in essence. The preface to the 1717 edition compares its authors, not with Continental Neo-Latin poets, but with classical writers, overtly challenging readers who might be inclined to believe that the ancients alone were afforded access to the peak of Parnassus. For now "you may behold Richard Bathurst at Virgil's side" (*ad Virgilii latus Bathurstum spectes*, av). In short, Britons approximate the ancient Romans in terms of "the magnitude of genius as much as of empire" (*tam ingenii quam imperii magnitudine*, av).

Another type of anthology was that produced by the Universities of Oxford and Cambridge on royal occasions such as births, marriages, and deaths, the visit of a monarch to city or university, or the commemoration of another event (Binns 1990, 40–45; Hale 2005, 147–62; Goldring et al. 2014). These, however, were not exclusively royalist. The passing of a distinguished figure or university don could instigate an entire volume. Some volumes were bilingual, others multilingual; but Latin as linguistic medium was unquestionably predominant. An interesting aberration from the norm is the case of Milton. Though he was a talented student and composer of a substantial body of Latin writings during his Cambridge years (Hale 2005; Haan 2012, 55–93; Knight 2012a and 2012b), his Latin poems are nonetheless glaringly absent from university anthologies. His contribution of the vernacular *Lycidas* to the Cambridge *Iusta Edoardo King* (*Obsequies for Edward King*, 1638) pertains to his post-Cambridge years. His poem, the last and longest, is the jewel in that bipartite collection. Just one year later, however, he would compose a Neo-Latin pastoral, the *Epitaphium Damonis* (*Damon's Epitaph*, 1639; discussed further below), lamenting the death of Charles Diodati, himself a talented scholar and contributor of a Latin ode to an Oxford anthology, *Camdeni Insignia* (*Tributes to Camden*, 1624), on the death of the British antiquarian William Camden.

Nationhood and Neo-Latin Antiquarianism

Indeed, Camden assumes an important place within a tradition of British Neo-Latin antiquarian writing in which articulations of nationhood were frequently married to the mythological. His *Britannia* (1586), with its meticulous scrutiny of British topography and antiquities, sparked conflicting reactions across several regions. That it was poorly received in Scotland is attested by a now-lost work entitled *Nuntius Scoto-Britannus; or, A Paire of Spectacles for W. Camden, to looke upon North-Britain*, and by several Neo-Latin rebuttals, including a 1608 work by David Hume of Godscroft entitled *Camdenea* (*Matters Relating to Camden*; Vine 2012, 173). In England, by contrast, the aforementioned *Camdeni Insignia* would eulogize its now-deceased subject (d. 1623) in language typical of such university collections.

The mythological conception of the history of Britain, voiced by Geoffrey of Monmouth in his *Historia regum Britanniae* (*History of the Kings of Britain*), had been countered by Polydore Vergil in his *Anglica historia* (*English History*, published in three different versions, in 1534, 1546, and 1555). The controversy led the English poet and antiquarian John Leland to publish his *Assertio inclytissimi Arturii regis Britanniae* (*Assertion of the Most Renowned King Arthur of Britain*, 1544), a Neo-Latin defense of the Arthurian legend specifically directed against Polydore. The debate continued to rage, culminating perhaps in the *Historia Britanniae* (*History of Britain*, 1597–ca. 1607) of Richard White of Basingstoke. White's defense of the mythical history of Britain ran to some 1,000 pages, "attempt[ing] to reclaim 'the British history' for the Catholic tradition" (MacColl 2002, 245). One legendary tradition promulgated by Geoffrey was the purported Trojan origins of a Britain founded by Brutus, grandson of Aeneas. Milton, in implicit acknowledgement perhaps of the pro-Geoffrey cause, equates the city of London with Troy, and with Dardanus, one of Troy's mythical founders—*Tuque urbs Dardaniis Londinum structa colonis* ("And you, London, a city built by Dardanian settlers"; *Elegia prima*, l. 73; Milton 2014, 120)—while the English people constitute *Teucrigenas populos* ("Trojan-born peoples"; *In quintum Novembris*, l. 2; Milton 2014, 166). And as he articulates his plans for an *Arthuriad*, Milton couches the whole in Trojan terms (*Epitaphium Damonis*, ll. 162–63; Milton 2014, 224).

Much more explicit was the reaction in Wales, with several Neo-Latin writers leaping to Geoffrey's defense by presenting rebuttals of Polydore's stance. Foremost among these was Sir John Price, whose *Historiae Brytannicae Defensio* (*Defense of British History*, 1573) "remains one of the most important of the early writings of the Renaissance in Wales" (Davies 1981, 17). For David Powel (*De Britannica historia recte intelligenda* [*On the Right Understanding of British History*], 1585), however, historical accuracy could only be realized by rejecting the intransigence of both Polydore and Price. Scotland, too, saw attempts to demythologize history: John Major's *Compendium de gestis Scotorum* (*Compendium of the Deeds of the Scots*, 1521) was answered by Hector Boece's *Historia gentis Scotorum* (*History of the Scottish People*, 1527), the latter an important source for Buchanan's *Rerum Scoticarum historia* (*Scottish History*, 1582). A comparable scenario reared its head in Ireland in Stephen White's "systematic rebuttal" (Harris 2009, 127) of Gerald of Wales's *Topographia Hibernica* (*Irish Topography*, ca. 1188). White's reactionary *Apologia pro Ibernia* (*Defense of Ireland*, 1615) and *Apologia pro innocentibus Ibernis* (*Defense of the Innocent Irish*, ca. late 1630s) highlighted errors in the *Topographia*, criticizing its author's failure to differentiate between historical fact and fiction.

British Neo-Latin Poetry: Generic Continuity and Metamorphosis

If British antiquarian writing and its reception could shatter geographical, historical, and generic norms, so, too, could Neo-Latin poetry demonstrate the permeability of established boundaries, whether generic, geographical, linguistic, or chronological. This is particularly true of the British Neo-Latin pastoral, ode, and epigram.

British Neo-Latin pastoral evinces literary trends shared by England and Scotland, while raising intriguing questions about the interrelationships between Latin and the vernacular(s). This is encapsulated in the preface to William Dillingham's edition of Theodore Bathurst's Latin verse rendering of Spenser's *The Shepheardes Calendar* (1579) as *Calendarium Pastorale* (1653). The imagery is one of revitalization: Spenser, now "clad in a Roman toga" (*indutus. . . idem Romana toga*), seems "not so much to have been translated as to have been restored" (*non tam translatus, quam restitutus esse videatur*; A3v). Bathurst's Neo-Latin rendering is explicitly intended to illuminate, facilitate, and even embellish the vernacular original. The same claim is also made by Dillingham in regard to his own Latin renderings of Herbert's vernacular poetry (Haan 2010, 10–11).

While the history of Neo-Latin and vernacular pastoral has received scholarly attention (e.g., Grant 1965), there is still a need for a comparative study of the Italianate nature of pastoral experimentation in England and Scotland. Jacopo Sannazaro's fishermen's eclogues, *Piscatoriae* (1526; Kennedy 1983), had used political allegory to transform an Arcadian pastoral landscape into a Neapolitan seascape, thereby "inaugurat[ing] . . . throughout Europe . . . a rich and productive variant of pastoral poetry" (Hubbard 2007, 59). This methodology is replicated in the *Musae priores* (*Foremost Muses*; 1620) of the Scottish poet John Leech (fl. 1610–1624). Included under the subheading *Idyllia* are four groups of eclogues, one of which is piscatorial. Like Sannazaro, Leech employs allegory, but this time it is an allegory of praise, hymning King James and some thirty Scottish poets. Thirteen years later, England saw the publication of Phineas Fletcher's *Sylva Poetica* (*Poetic Miscellany*), *Eclogue* 3 of which is piscatorial, and in the same year (1633), his vernacular *Piscatorie Eclogues*, which owe no small debt to his Latin *Sylva* (Piepho 1984) and to Sannazarian Neo-Latin pastoral. Eighteenth-century England would witness an extended literary dialogue, a "pastoral debate" (Smith 2002) on the suitability or otherwise of a fisherman as pastoral protagonist, of fishing as pastoral occupation, and of the sea as pastoral domain.

Pastoral was reborn in other ways, too. Thomas Watson's *Amintae Gaudia* (*The Joys of Amyntas*, 1592), its title probably inspired by Tasso's pastoral play *Aminta* (performed 1573), allegorizes in *Eclogue* 6 a battle between Juno and Pluto as movements on a chessboard, thereby appropriating Vida's mock-heroic Neo-Latin *Scacchia Ludus* (*The Game of Chess*), which was well known in England from the late sixteenth century onwards (Haan 2010, 20). This contributed to the creation of a distinctively British Neo-Latin sub-genre in seventeenth- and eighteenth-century England: the Neo-Latin mock-epic sports poem (discussed further below), in which a pastoral *locus amoenus* is invaded and violated by the competitively bellicose other.

Neo-Latin pastoral could also serve as a means of celebration or lament. The *Daphn-Amaryllis* (1605) of the Scottish poet David Hume heralds the accession of James VI and I to the English throne. Andrew Aidie's *Pastoria* (*Pastoral Matters*, 1610) praises his fellow Scottish poets and historians, while also lamenting the vicissitudes of travel, *inter alia*. In England William Hawkins starkly unites the pastoral genre and a plague outbreak in his eclogue titled *Pestifugium* (*Escape from the Plague*, 1630). More formal laments were also expressed in pastoral terms. The death of Sir Philip Sidney inspired Neo-Latin pastorals by Thomas Watson and William Gager, among others (Baker-Smith 1986). But by far England's most accomplished Neo-Latin pastoral lament is John Milton's stunningly personal *Epitaphium Damonis*, on the premature death of his closest friend Charles Diodati, itself encapsulating and inscribing aspects of their bilingual (Greek and Latin) epistolary correspondence (Brown 2012), while also engaging with Theocritean and Virgilian intertexts (Campbell 1984; Hardie 2007; Haan 2012, 132–9 and 162–65). Latin once again unites two countries, enabling the poem to cross a continental frontier (and that quite literally, in that Milton would later send it from London to his erstwhile Florentine fellow-academician Carlo Dati; Haan 1998a, 55–56). Perhaps it also crosses a chronological frontier? The poem's voicing of grief and of a potentially homoerotic love (albeit exaggerated by Shawcross 1975), is Janus-like, casting a backward glance to the frequently homosexual content of classical Greek and Latin pastoral, but also looking forward to Thomas Gray's Neo-Latin writings to Richard West (Gleckner 1997; Haan 2000, 69–112) and perhaps to his famous vernacular *Elegy* (Curr 2002), and its Neo-Latin reception, the latter exemplified by a host of eighteenth- and nineteenth-century Latin translations (see Gibson, Wilkinson, and Freeth 2008).

The British Neo-Latin ode manifests itself across several of the regions and through several of the centuries under discussion. In Scotland it functioned as a somewhat surprising vehicle for "translation" whereby, in the case of George Buchanan's Psalm paraphrases, biblical material is clothed in a Neo-Horatian garb, and in language frequently evocative of the original context (Green 2000; Harrison 2012). In England, the Latin verse of such seventeenth-century vernacular poets as Herbert (Kelliher 1974; Knight 2012a), Marvell (Haan 2003, 19–56), and Cowley (Moul 2012) exemplifies the versatility with which Horatian alcaics and sapphics could be adapted to religious, university, royalist, and even botanical contexts. But perhaps it is in Anthony Alsop's fusion of wit, elegance, and satire that the Neo-Latin Horatian ode sees its most accomplished achievement (Money 1998). For other writers it continued to constitute the generic medium of communication, whether with literati (Joseph Addison to Edward Hannes and Thomas Burnett; Haan 2005b) or close friends (Thomas Gray's two Latin odes to Richard West; Haan 2000, 69–87 and 101–112). In the late eighteenth century, it could even be romanticized to describe an enthralling Hebridean landscape (Samuel Johnson's *Skia* [*Skye*] of 1773; Rudd 2012, 109–13).

Likewise, the Neo-Latin epigram staunchly prevails and seems to undergo a series of metamorphoses. The hugely popular epigrams of the Welsh poet John Owen (Harries 2005; Jansen 2009) demonstrate the heights that the genre could attain. Remarkable for their "inexhaustible wit" (Martyn in Owen 1976–1978, 1:13) and the universality of their truisms, Owen's epigrams would achieve acclaim across several centuries and countries, matched only by Buchanan's Neo-Latin corpus. Scotland saw the publication of, among others, John Leech's (1620) and Arthur Johnston's *Epigrammata* (1632). In England, the epigram could be employed for both satirical and encomiastic purposes: the former exemplified in the tradition of Neo-Latin epigrams on the 1605 "Gunpowder Plot" to blow up the Houses of Parliament in London (Haan in Fletcher 1996, xx–xxix) best epitomized perhaps by Milton's five anti-Catholic epigrams on the subject; the latter in his three eulogistic Latin epigrams on the Italian soprano Leonora Baroni (1611–1670). For several writers, most notably Thomas Campion, "epigram" seemed to function as an umbrella term for any type of short poem, as if in a reinterpretation of Scaliger's dictum in his *Poetics* (1561, Chapter 126) that "brevity" (*brevitas*) and "wit" (*argutia*) constitute the epigram's "essence" (*proprium quiddam*) and "soul" (*anima*). Of particular note is the emergence of the sacred epigram, which drew upon biblical material, exemplified by Richard Crawshaw's *Epigrammata sacra* (1634) in which "religious love [is] embedded in an English setting" (Larsen 1974, 119). The Neo-Latin epigrammatic tradition continued well into the eighteenth century and beyond, eventually culminating in Walter Savage Landor, with whose Latin essay this chapter commenced.

GENERIC REDISCOVERY

It is something of an irony that Neo-Latin epic of the British Isles, an appropriation of a form that assumed pride of place in the classical hierarchy of genres, has been misunderstood by some scholars. That the so-called failure of Abraham Cowley's *Davideis* (Ram 1969–1970) and his associated "epic reticence" (Dykstal 1991) can be countered by scrutiny of the later English books of the poem in relation to its Neo-Latin first book has been demonstrated by Hardie (2012). Bradner's comment that attempts at epic "failed to produce any single work of great importance in Latin" (Bradner 1940, 195) is misleadingly reductivist. For the meaning may lie in the attempts themselves: William Alabaster's (1567–1640) unfulfilled aspiration to compose an epic on Elizabeth I (of which he completed just one unpublished book); Andrew Melville's planned epic on Gathelus, the mythical founder of Scotland (which survives as a 150-line fragment); Patrick Panter's (ca. 1470–1519) incomplete epic on Sir William Wallace, which did at least see posthumous publication as *Valladios libri tres, opus inchoatum* (*The Epic of Wallace in Three Books, an Unfinished Work*, 1633). Were these epic false starts somehow connected to the choice of contemporary, near-contemporary, or quasi-historical subject matter (a question also discussed in Chapter 4)?

If so, that this was, however, achievable is demonstrated by three substantial seventeenth-century Neo-Latin epics, two of which pertain to Ireland, and the third to Scotland. The five-book epic *Ormonius* (1615) by the Irish Neo-Latin poet Dermot O'Meara takes as its subject the career of Thomas Butler, Earl of Ormond (Latinized "Ormonius"), who was still alive at the time of the poem's completion. This work merits close critical study for its skillful fusion of didactic and epic elements (O'Meara 2011, 25), its inventive transformation of the Ovidian theme of transformation, and its linguistic and thematic appropriation of Gaelic place-names and devices such as the Gaelic *Aisling* or female "dream" (O'Meara 2011, 34–36). It is Ireland, too, that can claim the existence, albeit in manuscript, of an anonymous Jacobite epic on the Williamite War (1688–1691), which may owe some debt to both Lucan and O'Meara, and is of much historical interest, not least in its presentation of brief vignettes of courageous Irish soldiers (Sidwell 2012). But it was Scotland that would produce what was in effect "the last Neo-Latin epic to be written in the British Isles" (Houghton 2012, 190): James Philp's *Grameid*. Albeit unfinished and unpublished, this five-book martial epic, tracing the initial skirmishes of the 1689 rising against William of Orange (led by John Graham of Claverhouse, hence the title *Grameid*), is of interest, not only as testimony to contemporary culture and sentiment, but also as an instance of an historical epicist's hyperbolic reinvention of Lucan and Virgil.

To some degree, the undeniable dearth of full-scale epic in England when compared to her comparator regions of Scotland and Ireland is compensated for by the flourishing of a tradition of the brief epic, noteworthy for its substitution of political and anti-Catholic subject matter for the conventional biblical material at the heart of this miniature genre (Lewalski 1966). Characteristic of this specifically Anglo-Latin genre, which first rears its head in the Elizabethan period and finds its zenith in the Jacobean, is its celebration of royal deliverance from Catholic conspiracy: the Spanish Armada (Thomas Campion, *Ad Thamesin* [*To the Thames*, 1595]); the plot of the Welsh spy William Parry (George Peele, *Pareus* [1585]); and most notably the Gunpowder Plot of 1605, the last of which engendered a cluster of "gunpowder epics" dating from just one year after the event (Francis Herring, *Pietas Pontificia* [*Papal Piety*]; Michael Wallace, *In serenissimi regis Iacobi liberationem* [*On the Liberation of the Illustrious King James*]) through 1611 (Phineas Fletcher, *Locustae vel Pietas Iesuitica* [*Locusts, or Jesuit Piety*, not published until 1627]) to 1626 (John Milton's *In quintum Novembris* [*On the Fifth of November*, published in 1645]; Herring 1992; Wallace 1993; Fletcher 1996). Common to all such works is their essential Virgilianism and their locating of the plot in Hell. Milton's poem reworks aspects of this tradition, but it also engages with Scottish Neo-Latin writings, chiefly George Buchanan's *Somnium* (*Dream*) and *Franciscanus* (*The Franciscan*), and also perhaps his Latin Psalm paraphrases: God the Father looks down, laughs at the conspiracy, and safeguards his people in language much closer to Buchanan's amplified renderings than to the Vulgate or the King James Version of the Bible. In a sense, then, the methodology of *In quintum Novembris* may mirror on a literary level that "inviolable treaty" (*inviolabile foedus*, l. 3; Milton 2014, 166), the union between the English and the Scottish achieved by King James and celebrated in the poem's opening lines.

The late seventeenth century saw the emergence of another peculiarly British subgenre of epic: the Neo-Latin mock-epic sports poem, whose reinvention of the games in Book 5 of the *Aeneid* may also have contributed to "an evolving mock-heroic form" (Bradner 1940, 221) in the eighteenth-century vernacular. The earliest example is probably Thomas Masters's *Mensa Lubrica* (1658; contained in the first edition of *Musarum Anglicanarum Analecta* of 1692) on the game of Shovel Board (the ancestor of the modern American game of shuffleboard). Likewise William Dillingham's *Suleianum* (in his *Poemata varii argumenti* of 1678) presents the sport of bowling as a Virgilian epic sports battle (Haan 2010, 17–37). The mock-epic potential afforded by other, rather less salubrious, "sports" and pastimes peppers the second edition of *Musarum Anglicanarum Analecta* of 1699, which includes mock-heroic poems on bull-baiting (Francis Knapp, *Taurus in Circo* [*The Bull in the Circus*]), cock-fighting (Joseph Freind, *Pugna Gallorum Gallinaceorum*), and bowling (Joseph Addison, *Sphaeristerium* [*Bowling Green*]). The last moves beyond Dillingham in its personification of the bowls as Roman wrestlers, anointed and glistening with oil as they run across the gym (*palaestra*, l. 9). Less explicitly Virgilian, it signals its classical intertext with greater subtlety and discernment

(Haan 2005a, 88–103). That the genre persisted well into the eighteenth century is attested to by the *Selecta poemata Anglorum* (*Selected Poems of the English*, 1744–1776), edited by Edward Popham, the first volume of which includes mock epics on handball (Arthur Bedford, *Lusus Pilae Palmariae* [*The Game of Handball*]) and on football (the anonymous *Pila pedalis*). A parallel vernacular tradition is perhaps best epitomized by Alexander Pope's mock-heroic depiction of a game of cards in Book 3 of *The Rape of the Lock*, lines 25–104, and especially lines 65–68:

> Thus far both armies to Belinda yield;
> Now to the Baron fate inclines the field.
> His warlike Amazon her host invades,
> Th' imperial consort of the crown of spades.

Neo-Latin didactic poetry seems to function as a literary and linear generic continuum through the three centuries of British Neo-Latin under discussion. Common to both Scottish and English poets is their recourse to the genre as a means of expounding or refuting contemporary astronomical or cosmological viewpoints, and their inventive implementation of Lucretian language. Comparative examination of representative examples from each century may serve to showcase this inventiveness.

In the case of Buchanan's five-book *De Sphaera* (*On the Sphere* [*of the World*], 1584; abbreviated *Sph.*), an incomplete didactic defense of the Ptolemaic (or geocentric) view of the universe as against the new Copernican (or heliocentric) view, the subject matter may have been contemporary, but the mode of expression constituted a "borrowed plumage" (Gee 2009) that was Lucretian even if the astronomical scheme posited was anti-Lucretian. Milton's *Naturam Non Pati Senium* (*That Nature Does Not Suffer Decay*, 1629; abbreviated *Nat.*), a rhetorical refutation of the widely debated concept of Nature's decay (Haan 1997b), fused the language of both Lucretius's *De Rerum Natura* (abbreviated *DRN*; e.g., *per inane* ["through the void," *Nat.* 53/*DRN passim*]; *machina mundi* ["machine of the world," *Nat.* 69/*DRN* 5.96]) and Buchanan (*singula perpetuum iussit servare tenorem* ["He ordained all things to observe their courses forever," *Nat.* 36]/*regia coeli . . . perpetuum servat solida et sincera tenorem* ["the heavenly palace. . ., stable and honest, observes the same course forever," *Sph.* 1.40–42]). At the close of the seventeenth century, England saw the emergence of a rather new sub-genre of didactic poetry celebrating the discovery of a scientific instrument. These works, characterized by an authorial stance of "simulated wonder" (Bradner 1940, 221), may evoke genuine wonder in the reader, not least in their felicitous appropriation of Virgilian didactic (the following examples are cited from the second edition of *Musarum Anglicanarum Analecta* of 1699). Thomas Bisse's *Microscopium* uses Virgilian hexameters to depict a world enlarged through the power of the microscope (Haan 2005a, 42–43). Joseph Addison's description of the barometer in *Barometri descriptio* both echoes and adapts the weather signs section of *Georgics* 1.351–513, only to show that such signs are provided by the barometer itself, rendering its user prepared in ways that surpass the Virgilian farmer (Haan 2005a, 30–49). In eighteenth-century England, the development of a Neo-Latin scientific/astronomical didacticism, due in part to the frequently abstract subject

matter prescribed for the "Tripos Verses" at Cambridge University (read out at graduation ceremonies by someone sitting on a *tripus*, a three-legged stool), is best epitomized
by Thomas Gray's *Luna habitabilis* (*The Habitable Moon*, on the topic set for the 1737
Tripos; Haan 2000, 35–50). There is something peculiarly modern, even "postmodern,"
about this pondering on imagined space, and here the space is an astronomical one—
that between the earth and the moon. Gray turns to Manilius and Lucretius only to substitute modern science for ancient speculation (the telescope's ability to "draw down" the
moon from the heavens), while indulging in fanciful speculations of his own: the moon
as a land awaiting colonization; an imaginary or imagined landscape linked to Earth by
a reciprocal gaze: that of the speaker and that of lunar inhabitants dwelling in a world
completely intelligible to us, a pseudo-Lacanian mirror image of the human self. Thus
could scientific invention be mirrored by generic inventiveness on the part of the Neo-
Latin poet.

Finally, Ovidian mock-didactic may assume a hitherto unnoticed place in the history of British Neo-Latin literature. It is a "truth" universally acknowledged by scholars
that Buchanan's bitterly anti-monastic *Franciscanus* (1566; McFarlane 1974; McFarlane
1981, 51–65; abbreviated *Franc.*) pertains to the genre of satire, and as such looks back
to Juvenal and Martial (Martyn 1976, 723; Martyn 1977, 135; McFarlane 1981, 54–6;
Crawford 2006, xxvi; Harrison 2012, 155). But the poem also evinces a sustained engagement with Ovid, particularly Book 1 of the *Ars Amatoria* (abbreviated *AA*), and the
didactic genre in general, thereby inviting a reappraisal of its generic status. Its mock-
didacticism manifests itself stylistically in its self-conscious emphasis on "admonition"
(*monere*: see *Franc.* 36, 67, 289, 405, 559, 754–5, 773, and 926) and "precept" (*praecepta*:
see *Franc.* 268 and 727) proffered, not by an *artifex* of Love (as in *AA* 1.7) to the incipi-
ent lover, but by a monk to the would-be novice. Generic awareness is likewise signaled
by recourse to didactic signposting, as in *principio* ("at the beginning," Virgil, *Georgics*,
4.8; Ovid *AA* 1.35; *Franc.* 93 and 292); *primum* ("first," *Georgics* 4.295; *Franc.* 234 and
438); *ergo* ("hence," *Georgics* 4.77 and 4.206; *AA* 1.455; *Franc.* 314); *nunc . . . expediam*
("now . . . I shall set out," *Georgics* 4.149–50; *Franc.* 228–32). Like Ovid, Buchanan imple-
ments, on a metaphorical level, traditional didactic subject matter: farming (e.g., *AA*
1.19; *Franc.* 301); fishing (e.g., *AA* 1.48; *Franc.* 116); fowling (e.g., *AA* 1.47; *Franc.* 454);
hunting (e.g., *AA* 1.45–46; *Franc.* 252), with the associated emphasis on "nets" (*retia*; e.g.,
AA 1.45; *Franc.* 56) and "snares" (*casses*; e.g., *AA* 1.392; *Franc.* 349), or the "noose"/"trap"
(*laqueus*; e.g., *AA* 1.646; *Franc.* 397); and bee-keeping (e.g., *AA* 1. 95–6; *Georgics* 4 *passim*), whereby the apportioning of such monastic duties as door-keeping and gardening
(*Franc.* 108–10) recalls the bees' division of labor in the hive (*Georgics* 4.158–68). But perhaps Buchanan's mock-didacticism (or more accurately his *mock* mock-didacticism) is
most daringly apparent in the erotically charged precepts issued to the novice (*Franc.*
372–99) on how to seduce his female victim(s). The clandestinely flirtatious (*AA* 1.139–
62 and 1. 569–606) is developed into a lecherous physicality (*Franc.* 374 and 377–8) and
a sexual violence (*Franc.* 545–58) against both the female domestic space and the female
body. This is rendered all the more shocking given the monastic status of the envisaged
perpetrator and the ironic appropriation of Ovid's synopsis (*AA* 1.101–32) of the rape of

the Sabine women. And as the poem nears its conclusion, the ritualistic precision of its failed exorcism (*Franc*. 852–906) seems to parody aspects of Virgil's account of the successful *bougonia* (*Georgics* 4. 295–314 and 550–58) whereby bees were resurrected from the carcass of a slaughtered bull.

The *Ars Amatoria* was in all likelihood the notorious *carmen*, which, Ovid claims (*Tristia* 2.207), was one of the two charges responsible for his banishment from Rome to the Black Sea. A fate not entirely dissimilar would dog Buchanan, as this anti-Franciscan mock-didactic poem would come back to haunt its Neo-Latin author with repercussions that would eventually lead the Scottish *litteratorum deus* (as described by Scaliger and Landor) to escape for his life across a continental divide.

Suggested Reading

On British Neo-Latin literature and culture, see Bradner (1940), Binns (1990), *CNLS* 1:164–76, and Burnett and Mann (2005). For the Irish humanistic context, see Millett (1976) and especially Harris and Sidwell (2009). For Scotland, see McFarlane (1981), Green (2012), Vine (2012), and Houghton (2012). For Wales, see Davies (1981 and 2012). On the Neo-Latin poetry of English poets, see Binns (1974) and especially Houghton and Manuwald (2012). For book-length studies of individual British Neo-Latin writers, see (on Milton) Haan (1998a), Hale (2005), Haan (2012); (on Marvell) Haan (2003); (on Dillingham) Haan (2010); (on Gray) Gleckner (1997), Haan (2000); (on Addison) Haan (2005a); and (on Bourne) Haan (2007). On female British Neo-Latin writers, see Stevenson (2005).

References

Baker-Smith, Dominic. 1986. "Great Expectation: Sidney's Death and the Poets." In *Sir Philip Sidney: 1586 and the Creation of a Legend*, edited by Jan Van Dorsten, Dominic Baker-Smith, and Arthur F. Kinney, 83–103. Leiden: Brill.

Binns, James W., ed. 1974. *The Latin Poetry of English Poets*. London: Routledge and Kegan Paul.

———. 1990. *Intellectual Culture in Elizabethan and Jacobean England: The Latin Writings of the Age*. Leeds: Francis Cairns.

Bradner, Leicester. 1940. *Musae Anglicanae: A History of Anglo-Latin Poetry 1500–1925*. New York: Modern Language Association of America.

Brown, Cedric C. 2012. "John Milton and Charles Diodati: Reading the Textual Exchanges of Friends." In Jones 2012, 107–36.

Burnett, Charles, and Nicholas Mann, eds. (2005) *Britannia Latina: Latin in the Culture of Great Britain from the Middle Ages to the Twentieth Century*. London: Warburg Institute.

Campbell, Gordon. 1984. "Imitation in *Epitaphium Damonis*." *Milton Studies* 19:165–77.

Churchill, Laurie J., Phyllis R. Brown, and Jane E. Jeffrey, eds. 2002. *Women Writing Latin: From Roman Antiquity to Early Modern Europe*. Vol. 3, *Early Modern Women Writing Latin*. New York: Routledge.

Crawford, Robert, ed. and trans. 2006. *Apollos of the North: Selected Poems of George Buchanan and Arthur Johnston*. Edinburgh: Polygon.

Curr, Matthew. 2002. *The Consolation of Otherness: The Male Love Elegy in Milton, Gray and Tennyson*. Jefferson: McFarland.

Davies, Ceri. 1981. *Latin Writers of the Renaissance*. Cardiff: University of Wales Press.

———. 2012. "*Est locus a castro declivi rupe recedens*: A Sense of Place in Some Latin Works from Glamorgan." In Houghton and Manuwald 2012, 208–29.

Dykstal, Timothy. 1991. "The Epic Reticence of Abraham Cowley." *Studies in English Literature* 31:95–115.

Fletcher, Phineas. 1996. *Locustae vel Pietas Iesuitica*. Edited and translated by Estelle Haan. Leuven: Leuven University Press.

Ford, Philip J. 1982. *George Buchanan: Prince of Poets*. Aberdeen: Aberdeen University Press.

Ford, Philip J., and Roger P. H. Green, eds. 2009. *George Buchanan: Poet and Dramatist*. Swansea: The Classical Press of Wales.

Gee, Emma. 2009. "Borrowed Plumage: Literary Metamorphosis in Buchanan's *De Sphaera*." In Ford and Green, op. cit., 35–58.

Gibson, Donald, Peter Williamson, and Stephen Freeth, eds. 2008. *Thomas Gray: Elegy in a Country Churchyard; Latin Translations 1762–2001*. Orpington: Holden Press.

Gleckner, Robert F. 1997. *Gray Agonistes: Thomas Gray and Masculine Friendship*. Baltimore: Johns Hopkins University Press.

Goldring, Elizabeth, Faith Eales, Elizabeth Clarke, and Jayne Elisabeth Archer, eds. 2014. *John Nichols's* The Progress and Public Processions of Queen Elizabeth I: *A New Edition of the Early Modern Sources*, 5 vols. Oxford: Oxford University Press.

Grant, William L. 1965. *Neo-Latin Literature and the Pastoral*. Chapel Hill: University of North Carolina Press.

Green, Roger P. H. 2000. "Davidic Psalm and Horatian Ode: Five Poems of George Buchanan." *Renaissance Studies* 14:91–111.

———. 2012. "George Buchanan, Chieftain of Neo-Latin Poets." In Houghton and Manuwald 2012, 142–54.

Haan, Estelle. 1992. "Milton's *In Quintum Novembris* and the Anglo-Latin Gunpowder Epic." *Humanistica Lovaniensia* 41:221–95.

———. 1995. "Milton's Latin Poetry and Vida." *Humanistica Lovaniensia* 44:282–304.

———. 1997a. "Two Neo-Latin Elegists: Milton and Buchanan." *Humanistica Lovaniensia* 46:266–78.

———. 1997b. "Milton's *Naturam Non Pati Senium* and Hakewill." *Medievalia et Humanistica* 24:147–67.

———. 1998a. *From Academia to Amicitia: Milton's Latin Writings and the Italian Academies*. Philadelphia: American Philosophical Society.

———. 1998b. "Milton's *Ad Patrem* and Grotius's *In Natalem Patris*." *Notes and Queries* 45:442–47.

———. 2000. *Thomas Gray's Latin Poetry: Some Classical, Neo-Latin and Vernacular Contexts*. Brussels: Latomus.

———. 2003. *Andrew Marvell's Latin Poetry: From Text to Context*. Brussels: Latomus.

———. 2005a. *Vergilius Redivivus: Studies in Joseph Addison's Latin Poetry*. Philadelphia: American Philosophical Society.

———. 2005b. "Twin Augustans: Addison, Hannes, and Horatian Intertexts." *Notes and Queries* 52:338–46.

———. 2007. *Classical Romantic: Identity in the Latin Poetry of Vincent Bourne*. Philadelphia: American Philosophical Society.

———. 2008. "From Neo-Latin to Vernacular: Marvell's Bilingualism and Renaissance Pedagogy." In *New Perspectives on Andrew Marvell*, edited by Gilles Sambras, 43–64. Reims: ÉPURE.

———. 2010. *Sporting with the Classics: The Latin Poetry of William Dillingham*. Philadelphia: American Philosophical Society.

———. 2012. *Both English and Latin: Bilingualism and Biculturalism in Milton's Neo-Latin Writings*. Philadelphia: American Philosophical Society.

Hale, John K. 1997. *Milton's Languages: The Impact of Multilingualism on Style*. Cambridge: Cambridge University Press.

———. 2005. *Milton's Cambridge Latin: Performing in the Genres 1625–1632*. Tempe: Arizona Center for Medieval and Renaissance Studies.

Hardie, Philip. 2007. "Milton's *Epitaphium Damonis* and the Virgilian Career." In Paschalis 2007, 79–100.

———. 2012. "Abraham Cowley's *Davideis: Sacri poematis operis imperfecti liber unus*." In Houghton and Manuwald 2012, 69–86.

Harries, Byron. 2005. "John Owen the Epigrammatist: A Literary and Historical Context." In *The Renaissance and the Celtic Countries*, edited by Ceri Davies and John E. Law, 19–32. Malden: Blackwell.

Harris, Jason. 2009. "A Case Study in Rhetorical Composition: Stephen White's Two *Apologiae* for Ireland." In Harris and Sidwell 2009, 126–53.

Harris, Jason, and Keith Sidwell, eds. 2009. *Making Ireland Roman: Irish Neo-Latin Writers and the Republic of Letters*. Cork: Cork University Press.

Harrison, Stephen. 2012. "George Buchanan: The Scottish Horace." In Houghton and Manuwald 2012, 155–72.

Herring, Francis. 1992. "Pietas Pontificia." Edited by Estelle Haan. *Humanistica Lovaniensia* 41:251–95.

Hosington, Brenda M. 2002. "Elizabeth Jane Weston (1581–1612)." In Churchill, Brown, and Jeffrey, op. cit., 217–46.

———. 2006. "Translation, Early Printing, and Gender in England, 1484–1535." *Florilegium* 23(1):21–52.

Houghton, Luke B. T., and Manuwald, Gesine, eds. 2012. *Neo-Latin Poetry in the British Isles*. London: Bristol Classical Press.

Houghton, Luke B. T. 2012. "Lucan in the Highlands: James Philp's *Grameid* and the Traditions of Ancient Epic." In Houghton and Manuwald, op. cit., 190–207.

Hubbard, Thomas K. 2007. "Exile from Arcadia: Sannazaro's Piscatory Eclogues." In Paschalis 2007, 59–77.

Jaeckle, Daniel. 2001. "Bilingual Dialogues: Marvell's Paired Latin and English Poems." *Studies in Philology* 98:378–400.

Jansen, Johannes. 2009. "The Microcosmos of the Baroque Epigram: John Owen and Julien Waudré." In *The Neo-Latin Epigram: A Learned and Witty Genre*, edited by Susanna de Beer, Karl A. E. Enenkel, and David Rijser, 275–99. Leuven: Leuven University Press.

Jones, Edward, ed. 2012. *Young Milton: The Emerging Author 1620–1642*. Oxford: Oxford University Press.

Kelliher, W. Hilton. 1974. "The Latin Poetry of George Herbert." In Binns, op. cit., 26–57.

Kennedy, William J. 1983. *Jacopo Sannazaro and the Uses of Pastoral*. Hanover: University Press of New England.

Knight, Sarah. 2012a. "*Juvenes Ornatissimi*: The Student Writing of George Herbert and John Milton." In Houghton and Manuwald, op. cit., 51–68.

Knight, Sarah. 2012b. "Milton and the Idea of the University." In Jones, op. cit., 137–60.

Landor, Walter S. 1847. *Quaestio quamobrem poetae Latini recentiores minus legantur*. In *Poemata et Inscriptiones*, 264–348. London: Moxon.

Larsen, Kenneth J. 1974. "Richard Crashaw's *Epigrammata Sacra*." In Binns, op. cit., 93–120.

Kelly, Andrea. 1974. "The Latin Poetry of Walter Savage Landor." In Binns, op. cit., 150–93.

Lewalski, Barbara K. 1966. *Milton's Brief Epic: The Genre, Meaning, and Art of* Paradise Regained. Providence: Brown University Press.

Little, Marguerite. 1950. "Milton's *Ad Patrem* and the Younger Gill's *In Natalem Mei Parentis*." *Journal of English and Germanic Philology* 49:345–51.

MacColl, Alan. 2002. "Richard White and the Legendary History of Britain." *Humanistica Lovaniensia* 51:245–57.

Martyn, John R. C. 1976. "George Buchanan: *Franciscanus*." In *ACNL* 1976, 720–46.

———. 1977. "Montaigne and George Buchanan." *Humanistica Lovaniensia* 26:132–42.

McFarlane, Ian D. 1974. "George Buchanan's *Franciscanus*: The History of a Poem." *Journal of European Studies* 4:126–39.

———. 1981. *Buchanan*. London: Duckworth.

Millett, Benignus. 1976. "Irish Literature in Latin, 1500–1700." In *A New History of Ireland*, vol. 3, *Early Modern Ireland*, edited by Theodore W. Moody, Francis X. Martin, and Francis J. Byrne, 561–86. Oxford: Clarendon Press.

Milton, John. 2014. *Shorter Poems*. edited by Barbara Kiefer Lewalski and Estelle Haan. Oxford: Oxford University Press.

Money, David K. 1998. *The English Horace: Anthony Alsop and the Tradition of British Latin Verse*. Oxford: British Academy.

Moul, Victoria. 2012. "Horatian Odes in Abraham Cowley's *Plantarum Libri Sex* (1668)." In Houghton and Manuwald, op. cit., 87–104.

O'Meara, Dermot. 2011. *The Tipperary Hero: Dermot O'Meara's* Ormonius *(1615)*. Edited and translated by David Edwards and Keith Sidwell. Turnhout: Brepols.

Owen, John. 1976–1978. *Epigrammatum libri*. 2 vols. Edited by John R. C. Martyn. Leiden: Brill.

Pal, Carol. 2012. *Republic of Women: Rethinking the Republic of Letters in the Seventeenth Century*. Cambridge: Cambridge University Press.

Paschalis, Michael, ed. 2007. *Pastoral Palimpsests: Essays in the Reception of Theocritus and Virgil*. Heraklion: Crete University Press.

Piepho, Lee. 1984. "The Latin and English Eclogues of Phineas Fletcher: Sannazaro's *Piscatoria* among the British." *Studies in Philology* 81:461–72.

Ram, Tulsi. 1969–1970. "Cowley and the Epic Poem: The Failure of the *Davideis*." *The Calcutta Review* 1:565–71.

Revard, Stella P. 2013. "The Design of the 1645 *Poems*." In Jones, op. cit., 206–20.

Rudd, Niall. 2012. "Samuel Johnson's Latin Poetry." In Houghton and Manuwald, op. cit., 105–24.

Saunders, Anne L. 2002. "Bathsua Makin (1600–1675?)." In Churchill, Brown, and Jeffrey, op. cit., 247–70.

Shawcross, John T. 1975. "Milton and Diodati: An Essay in Psychodynamic Meaning." *Milton Studies* 7:127–63.

Sidwell, Keith. 2012. "'Now or Never, Now and Forever': An Unpublished, Anonymous Jacobite Epic on the Williamite War (1688–1691)." In Houghton and Manuwald, op. cit., 250–67.

Smith, Nicholas D. 2002. "Jacopo Sannazaro's *Eclogae Piscatoriae* (1526) and the 'Pastoral Debate' in Eighteenth-Century England." *Studies in Philology* 99:432–50.

Stevenson, Jane. 2005. *Women Latin Poets: Language, Gender, and Authority from Antiquity to the Eighteenth Century*. Oxford: Oxford University Press.

Storey, Mark. 1974. "The Latin Poetry of Vincent Bourne." In Binns, op. cit., 121–49.

Van Hal, Toon. 2007. "Towards Meta-Neo-Latin Studies? Impetus to Debate on the Field of Neo-Latin Studies and its Methodology." *Humanistica Lovaniensia* 56:349–65.

Vine, Angus. 2012. "Spectacles from Scotland: Camden, Johnston and the *Urbes Britanniae*." In Houghton and Manuwald, op. cit., 173–89.

Wallace, Michael. 1993. "In Serenissimi Regis Iacobi Liberationem." Edited by Estelle Haan. In *Humanistica Lovaniensia* 42:368–401.

CHAPTER 28

THE GERMAN-SPEAKING COUNTRIES

ROBERT SEIDEL

GERMANIA: "GERMAN" AND "GERMANY" IN THE EARLY MODERN PERIOD

ALTHOUGH each of today's German-speaking countries has its own political, cultural, and indeed linguistic history and identity, the very idea of an area of German-speaking countries suggests a certain sense of shared language and tradition. To some extent, this sense is indebted to the Latin writings of humanists and their inclusive idea of a *Germania* defined by a common language and culture. Works discussing *Germania* from the fifteenth to the seventeenth century were composed in nearly every genre. The German arch-humanist Konrad Celtis, for example, followed Italian predecessors in planning a multimedia compendium, the *Germania illustrata* (*Germany Illuminated*), which aimed to establish a German nation as a cultural entity rather than as a confederacy of feudal estates (the more traditional conception). Celtis's cycle of elegies, the *Amores* (*Love Poems*, 1502), used the medium of love poetry to portray a unique topography of Germany as a cultural concept and, following the recent reception of Tacitus's *Germania*, to remind his readers frequently of the virtues of the ancient Germans. Similarly, the elevated form of the Horatian ode enabled reflections upon cultural values and national stereotypes throughout the period, from Celtis's *Ad Apollinem repertorem poetices ut ab Italis ad Germanos veniat* (*To Apollo, the Inventor of Poetry, That He May Come from the Italians to the Germans*, 1486) until the appearance of Jacob Balde's "German Odes" (1643, in *Silvae* 3.1–6; cf. Horace's *Roman Odes* in *Odes* 3.1–6).

In numerous volumes of *Heroides* (*Heroines*; Czapla in Weimar 1997–2003, 2:39–41), sixteenth-century authors such as Caspar Ursinus Velius, Georg Sabinus, and Johann Stigel used the Ovidian tradition of verse letters from abandoned women to their faithless lovers to express the laments of a sorrowful *Germania*. This *Germania* called upon her addressees, whether the emperor or the princes (her "sons") to work for unity in the face of crises that affected them all, such as the Turkish threat or confessional differences. The dramatist Nicodemus Frischlin (1547–1590), on the other hand, demonstrates that the cultural program of the Italian Renaissance, intended to regain the greatness of ancient Rome, took on a completely different meaning in a German context. For example, Frischlin's comedy *Julius Redivivus* (*Julius Revived*, 1585) has the two Romans, Cicero and Caesar, return to life to travel through modern Germany, portrayed as superior to its ancient predecessor and to contemporary surrounding nations not only in military terms, but also culturally by virtue of the "transfer of learning" (*translatio studii*). Singing the praises of this modern German nation is a central element of the comic plot.

Borrowing the ultimately Lucianic form of a dialogue with the dead, literary prose such as Ulrich von Hutten's *Arminius* (1529) also shaped German identity. Following Tacitus, this work forever stamped the collective German memory with the figure of Arminius, the prince of the Cherusci, as liberator of the fatherland. It goes without saying that the subject of *Germania* was explored in various expository writings, such as historical and geographical treatises. Such works variously assumed a more exhortative or a more encyclopedic character, as a comparison between Jakob Wimpfeling's *Germania* (1501) and Beatus Rhenanus's *Res Germanicae* (*German History*, 1531) demonstrates. Finally, in the early seventeenth century, Martin Opitz made the German language itself into a subject of the discourse of cultural patriotism with his Latin oration *Aristarchus sive de contemptu linguae Teutonicae* (*Aristarchus; or, On the Contempt for the German Language*; 1617), which formed only part of the author's lifelong effort to demonstrate the potential equality between the ancient idiom and the modern vernacular.

HUMANIST MANIFESTOS AND MOTIFS

The influence of the Italian Renaissance on German humanism can be seen as early as the middle of the fourteenth century in the *Kanzleihumanismus* ("chancellery humanism") at the court of Emperor Charles IV (1316–1378) in Prague. Other important early contexts are the reform Councils of Constance (1414–1418) and Basel (1431–1449), as German scholars increasingly established contacts within the ever-expanding European republic of letters. Yet it was only in the middle of the fifteenth century, when students from north of the Alps began traveling regularly to Italy, that Germans began to develop a feeling of cultural deficiency in comparison to humanist Italian scholars and poets. They reacted with an ambitious sense of competition, but also with a defiant appeal to supposedly unique German characteristics (such as alleged indigenous origins, freedom, imperial dignity) and with anger at the financial exploitation of the Germans by the church in Rome. With this cultural-patriotic amalgam came a number of calls for *studia humanitatis* ("humanist studies") and increased reflections on poetics (on early humanism generally, see Bernstein 2004a).

The most prominent champion of humanist educational ideals in the German cultural sphere was undoubtedly Konrad Celtis, who was also the first German poet laureate (*poeta laureatus*, crowned in 1487) and the founder of an early group of humanist scholars in Vienna, the Collegium poetarum et mathematicorum ("College of poets and scientists") in 1501. In the ode to Apollo previously mentioned, Celtis claimed a *translatio studii* by analogy with the ancient cultural transfer from Greece to Italy, asserting that the Muses had since furthered their transfer by traveling on from Italy to Germany. No less noteworthy was his inaugural lecture at the University of Ingolstadt, delivered when he was appointed professor of rhetoric and poetics. In this lecture, he argued for a wide-ranging education program that outlined all the foundational aspects of humanist apologetics and propaganda, from the individual's motives for scholarly activity (posthumous fame), to the political implications (*translatio studii* as a legitimization of the *translatio imperii*, the "transfer of empire" claimed by the Germans). Finally, in Celtis's *Ars Versificandi et carminum* (*Art of Versification and of Poems*, 1486) we have the first poetics by a German humanist. Though at its core it is only a textbook on meter, it also expresses contemporary views on poetry, such as poetry's capacity to express relevant knowledge appropriately (Robert 2007).

Over the course of the sixteenth and seventeenth centuries, treatises concerning poetics, rhetoric, and other liberal arts, and speeches in praise and in defense of poetry appeared, as well as (increasingly systematic) textbooks (Wels 2009), all of which forcefully asserted the claims of the German cultural nation to an equal—or, indeed, leading—role in Europe. Joachim Vadian undertook the writing of an early literary history in his extensive, multifaceted *De poetica et carminis ratione* (*On Poetry and the Nature of the Poem*, 1518), in which he highlighted the accomplishments of his teacher, Konrad Celtis, and of other countrymen. Although no German author produced comprehensive handbooks worthy of a Scaliger or a Vossius, more practical manuals such as Georg Fabricius's *De re poetica* (*Poetics*, 1556) found a large audience. Philipp Melanchthon's works (e.g., his *Elementa rhetorices* [*Elements of Rhetoric*], 1531; Classen 2003) became foundational everywhere the Protestant Reformation took hold. Somewhat later, Jesuit textbooks of poetics, such as Jacob Masen's *Palaestra eloquentiae ligatae* (*Arena of Poetic Eloquence*, 1654–1657; Burkard 2013), asserted their positions within the international publishing operations of the order.

Those writing in Latin in the early modern period, in Germany as in other countries, made full use of the humanistic concepts of "emulation" and "imitation" (*aemulatio* and *imitatio*). Ever since the stylistic dispute raised by Erasmus's *Ciceronianus* (*The Ciceronian*, 1528), but especially towards the end of the sixteenth century, anti-classicizing and pluralizing tendencies made themselves felt. These were manifest in the innovative, partially experimental lyrical poetry of Friedrich Taubmann (1565–1613) or Caspar von Barth (1587–1658), for example, as well as in later poetological theory on *argutia*, the baroque stylistic ideal of ingenious expression, such as Masen's *Ars nova argutiarum* (*New Art of Ingeniousness*, 1649). More and more, ambitious authors explored the intertextual potential of ancient models, using subtle and refined approaches to make points of contemporary significance. The *parodia Horatiana*

(~ *Horatian Pastiche*; Niehl 2006 and Robert 2006), to give but one example, uses the formal structure and thematic concepts of the conventional Horatian ode to examine a remarkable range of subjects, from religious propaganda (as a special case of *parodia Christiana*) to political appeals. Numerous lyric poets, and especially later humanists such as Paul Schede Melissus (1539–1602) and Johannes Adam (ca. 1570–after 1628) published such collections of Horatian parodies. If sometimes mannered, these and similar works attest to their authors' conviction that Latin, the ancient language, as well as the genres inherited from antiquity, are all perfectly capable of appropriately treating contemporary issues and of convincingly presenting readers with every manner of argument. Virtually all the conceptual decisions made by Latin authors since the sixteenth century must be understood in this context, whether they concern the book divisions of collections of lyric poetry (such as Celtis's four books of *Odes* and one book of *Epodes*, which mirrors Horace); the integration of specific paratextual elements (such as Melanchthon's Terentian prologues); or the use of Ciceronian—and, beginning in the later Renaissance, Tacitean—elements of style in literary prose (for the debate on Ciceronianism, see Robert 2011).

Learning and Its Rhetorical Foundations: Humanist Pedagogy

As it was throughout Europe, Latin was the undisputed language of choice for secondary and higher education well into the eighteenth century. Schools and universities produced a tremendous wealth of Latin works, from textbooks to highly specialized treatises, many of which still await systematic scholarly study. Due to the effectiveness of the reforms initiated by Melanchthon, the school systems in the Protestant territories were rigorously standardized. The Jesuit school ordinance, the *ratio studiorum* (*Plan of Studies*, which appeared in its definitive version in 1599), was, in turn, influenced considerably by the advances of the Protestants. This meant that a relatively homogenous education system in the German cultural sphere existed from the sixteenth century well into the early Enlightenment. Alongside the dominance of Latin as subject of study, medium of communication, and factual basis of knowledge, the pedagogical paradigm of this school system also entailed an almost natural connection between reading Latin authors and writing Latin texts. In other words, pupils and students were taught from the very beginning to produce proper and stylistically appropriate Latin in both verse and prose. In this context, too, specific teaching structures developed, each with its own exercises and drills, while the claims, successes, and failures of the education system were also subject to literary comment (on humanist pedagogy in general, see Kühlmann 2007a).

Aside from textbooks aimed at different educational levels, teachers and students alike had access to a rich variety of anthologies providing instructions and practical models for composing texts of their own. One prominent example is the *Progymnasmata* (*Preliminary Exercises*) by the late antique Greek instructor of rhetoric Aphthonios. Translated into Latin in the fifteenth century and expanded many times, the most popular version of this work in the German-speaking lands was the 1542 edition of the Marburg professor of rhetoric and poetics, Reinhard Lorichius. This work displays fourteen frequently required rhetorical and literary forms, from *fabula* ("fable") to *legislatio* ("law-giving"), together with a definition, examples, and manifold explanations and clarifications. The *Progymnasmata Latinitatis* (1588–1594) of Jacobus Pontanus contains brief dialogues, while the same author's *Attica bellaria* (*Attic Dessert*, 1615–1621) offers a mixture of minor literary forms. All these collections were used as stylistic examples, as were school colloquies written after the example of Erasmus's *Colloquia familiaria* (*Familiar Colloquies*, 1518), such as Hermann Schottenius's *Confabulationes tyronum literariorum* (*Conversations of Beginners in Literature*, 1525), printed in more than thirty editions.

Humanist educational initiatives were accompanied, from the very beginning, by treatises and pamphlets stressing the necessity of a solid school education for the progress and advancement of young people (e.g., Wimpfeling's *Adolescentia* [*Youth*], 1500). More powerful than any of these propagandistic writings, however, were the school dramas, which had broad public appeal, and in which the success and the failure of education were publicly displayed. A prominent example is Christopher Stymmelius's *Studentes* (*Students*, 1545), which represents both praiseworthy and reprehensible conduct through antagonistic protagonists. The Jesuits produced similar plays, such as Pontanus's *Ludus de instauratione studiorum* (*Play about the Renewal of Studies*, 1580). Educational curricula were themselves discussed and criticized onstage by prominent authors such as Frischlin (*Priscianus vapulans* [*Priscian Flogged*], 1578; Leonhardt 2008, 155–64) or, following closely in Frischlin's footsteps, Jakob Gretser with his trilogy *De regno humanitatis* (*The Kingdom of Humanism*, 1587–1590). Reworkings of the legend of Saint Catherine, such as Wolfgang Starck's *Catharina tragoedia* (1602), connect educational topics with the martyr dramas popular among Catholics: Catherine, the patron saint of education, is shown fighting her enemies with the weapons of rhetoric and triumphing in death.

Instruction in the composition of both prose and verse prepared students for writing formal political works, such as speeches of praise and valedictions, as well as occasional poetry for every conceivable event that might arise in their professional or private lives, such as anniversaries, weddings, and funerals. All these forms shared the goal of establishing an identity within the republic of letters or towards the outside world. A practice of the Wittenberg humanists, which gradually spread to the neighboring Protestant lands, was the keeping of autograph books (*alba amicorum*), in which one collected the (mostly poetic) entries of scholarly friends, and thereby documented for posterity the bonds between fellow students maintained over great distances of time and space (Schnabel 2011). The Königsberg theologian Michael Lilienthal described the origin and function of the custom of autograph books in the dissertation *De philothecis varioque earundem usu et abusu* (*Friendship Books and Their Various Uses and Abuses*, 1712).

RELIGION AND CONFESSIONALIZATION

Because of the close connection of Swiss and German scholars and poets with the Reformation, confrontations between various Protestant sects, and the significant Counter-Reformation activities of the Jesuits particularly, patterns of Christian argument and thought related to these differences influenced the German-speaking lands more strongly than most other areas of Europe. Formal theological discourses, as well as the writings that derived from them—dealing, for instance, with church politics, confessional polemics, and moral edification—used Latin whenever they were not (also) targeted at the uneducated part of the populace, as in the case of Luther's German translation of the Bible or vernacular Protestant sermons and hymns. Prominent examples include Melanchthon's statement of Protestant dogma, *Loci communes rerum theologicarum* (*Commonplaces in Theology*, 1521); the *Meditationes sacrae* (*Sacred Contemplations*, 1606) of Johann Gerhard; or the *Irenicum* (~ *Book of Peace*, 1614), written against the confessional strife of the late humanist period by the Palatinate theologian David Pareus. Theoretical compendia such as Johann Konrad Dannhauer's *Hermeneutica sacra* (*Sacred Hermeneutics*, 1654) attempted a systematic interpretation of sacred writing (Sdzuj 2011). Politically engaged treatises illuminate the connection between such specialist literature and satirical writing in verse and prose (Bernstein 2004c). A few years before the Reformation, to mention a prominent satirical example, the *Epistolae obscurorum virorum* (*Letters of Obscure Men*, 1515–1517) were written by a variety of authors, including Johannes Crotus Rubeanus and Ulrich von Hutten. Triggered by a contemporary dispute between the celebrated humanist Johannes Reuchlin and his scholastic opponents over the value of Jewish books, these letters mimic half-educated scholastics to ridicule Reuchlin's opponents and polemicize all kinds of moral and intellectual failure within the church. Willibald Pirckheimer dressed his attack on the Catholic Johannes Eck as a satirical dialogue (*Eccius dedolatus* [*Eck Planed Down*], 1520), in which Eck had his heresy removed through a number of extreme medical cures, inspired by the contemporaneous trepanations performed on the mentally deficient (to extract from their head what was thought to be a "stone of madness"). Similarly structured in dramatic scenes, though written in distichs, is Simon Lemnius's *Monachopornomachia* (*The Battle of Monks and Whores*, 1539), an obscene invective against Luther and his fellow reformers, portraying them as lecherous but impotent men unable to satisfy their wives. Johannes Major used his verse satire *Synodos avium* (*Synod of Birds*, 1557), in which the religious heirs of Luther are portrayed as bickering birds, to take up a Philippist position ahead of the inter-Protestant controversies on the horizon. Confessional polemical satire also came out of the anti-Reform camp, as, for instance, Johannes Atrocianus's *Nemo evangelicus* (*Evangelic Nobody*, 1528), notable for its dependence on Hutten's earlier verse satire, *Nemo* (*Nobody*, 1510).

Thomas Naogeorgus was the most prolific German satirist (see his *Satyrae, Satires,* of 1555), but he was even better known for his plays, especially *Pammachius* (~ [*The Pope*]

Who Fights Against Everything, 1538), a broad airing of grievances against the demonized papacy, the allegedly pernicious dealings of which, from the late antique period all the way up to the present, are depicted in every scene. Naogeorgus's *Mercator seu Iudicium* (*The Merchant, or Judgement*, 1539) attacks the Catholic doctrine of good works with a refashioning of the traditional motifs of the Everyman character, who must reconcile himself with God in the face of imminent death (Jeßing 2008). With his *Phasma* (*The Vision*, 1580; Kaminski 2008), Frischlin ostensibly wrote a pro-Lutheran drama, but in the process questioned all varieties of confessional dispute. Finally, in Johann Valentin Andreae's drama *Turbo* (*Whirlwind*; 1616), the title referring to the restlessness of the eponymous protagonist, the ideal of the simple discipleship of Christ was propagated against not only scholarship but also all confessional dogma. On the Catholic front, Jesuit theater was the most conspicuous dramatic instrument of religious propaganda (Valentin 2001). Today, however, many Jesuit plays, especially those by Jakob Bidermann, such as his famous piece about the haughty scholar, *Cenodoxus* (*Vainglorious*, the speaking name of the protagonist; 1602), are read less as instruments of indoctrination for the Counter-Reformation than as appeals for renewal within the church itself.

More numerous than the plays critical of church and educational systems were those that—as religious writings in the strictest sense of the word—brought biblical or legendary material onstage. While the Jesuits often focused on the lives of martyrs, political leaders, and military commanders (for the example of Belisarius, see Eickmeyer 2008), Protestant authors, following a suggestion Luther himself had made, dramatized overwhelmingly biblical, and largely Old Testament, material. Popular models were stories of idealized women such as Esther (e.g., Naogeorgus's *Hamanus*, 1543) or Susanna. Sometimes the practical applications of the drama would be mentioned in the title, as when Sixt Birck claimed that his *Judith* (1539) could "teach how arms ought to be taken up against the Turks" (*discitur, quomodo arma contra Turcam sint capienda*). The New Testament offered such popular tales as that of the Good Samaritan, the resurrected Lazarus (e.g., Johannes Sapidus's *Anabion sive Lazarus redivivus* [*Return to Life, or Lazarus Revived*], 1539), or the Prodigal Son. Among Catholic authors who were not members of a particular order, but who still dealt with biblical material, the Westphalian preacher Jakob Schöpper made a name for himself with critical dramas such as *Ectrachelistis sive Ioannes decollatus* (~ *The Man with the Broken Neck or John Beheaded*, 1546), encouraging reforms within the Catholic Church.

Aside from drama, religious literature also embraced other poetic genres, among which epic traditionally took pride of place. Although little noticed by literary historians until very recently, Protestant biblical epic was well known throughout German culture. Georg Aemilius's *Evangelia heroico carmine reddita* (*The Gospels in Heroic Verse*, 1549), for example, went through nine separate editions in less than a decade. Structurally similar to Virgil's *Aeneid*, Frischlin's epic, *Hebraeis*, first printed posthumously in 1599, covered the entire history of the people of Israel, from the beginning of the kingship under Saul to the destruction of Jerusalem. Ulrich Bollinger, editor of the *Hebraeis*, wrote a *Moseis* (1597), whose "pious" (*pius*) hero's characterization is even more dependent on the *Aeneid*. Andreas Gryphius, best known as a vernacular poet and playwright, also composed two Latin epics, about Herod and the *Olivetum* (*Olive Grove*) of 1646, which depicts Christ's Passion. Among Catholic compositions, Jakob Bidermann's *Herodias* (1622) dealt with the Bethlehem infanticide by King Herod, too.

Paraphrases of the Psalms were widespread among Protestants, including the followers of Luther (e.g., Eobanus Hessus's 1537 *Psalterium universum* [*Universal Psalter*]; Huber-Rebenich 2001), the Philippists, and the members of the Reformed movement. The Jesuits also freely made use of this genre, as in Niccolò Avancini's *Psalterium lyricum* (*Lyric Psalter*, 1696). The most versatile Protestant religious poet was the Saxon schoolteacher Georg Fabricius, whose *Poemata sacra* (*Sacred Poems*, 1567) deployed the various genres of late antique poetry to communicate religious truths and to help his readers acquire the practice of piety (*praxis pietatis*). Aside from Jakob Balde, Johannes Bissel was the most prominent Jesuit author who adapted, in various lyric forms, the entire thematic spectrum of religious poetry, including specifically Catholic subjects related to Mary and the legends of the saints, such as his *Deliciae veris* (*The Pleasures of Spring*, 1638; Kühlmann 2013). But most poetic genres, including, among other forms, verse letters, eclogues (for the Protestant context, see Mundt 2001), and even anacreontic poetry, such as Caspar von Barth's *Anacreon philosophus* (*Anacreon as Philosopher*, 1623), were put to religious use by both Protestants and Catholics.

Between Panegyric and Satire: Latin Literature in Its Social Context

Latin political writing embraced all geographical regions and literary forms. Whether conceptual or descriptive, panegyric or critical; whether aimed at the court or at the city; whether in verse or in prose; wherever the purpose was not to mobilize or entertain the masses (as in pamphlets, songs, and popular forms of instruction), Latin, with its capacity for intertextuality and carefully differentiated rhetoric, remained the medium of choice. The related disciplines of politics and law gave rise to such works as Ulrich Zasius's treatment of feudal law, *In usus feudorum* (*The Uses of Fiefs*, 1535); Johannes Althusius's compendium of political theory, *Politica methodice digesta* (*Politics Methodically Set Forth*, 1603); and Samuel Pufendorf's work on international law, *De iure naturae et gentium* (*The Law of Nature and Nations*, 1672). The political theory known as *Reichspublizistik* discussed the specifically German power-sharing relationship between the emperor and the estates of the Holy Roman Empire, as in Hermann Conring's *De Germanorum imperio Romano* (*The Roman Empire of the Germans*, 1644). Alongside such programmatic treatments were explicitly utopian political writings, such as Johann Valentin Andreae's *Christianopolis* (*The Christian City*, 1619). Among Catholic authors, Adam Contzen wrote both political theory (*Politica* [*Politics*], 1621) and a political novel (*Methodus doctrinae civilis* [*Method of Civil Doctrine*], 1628). Epic poetry, with its close association with imperial writers like Virgil and Claudian, and under the auspices of nascent territorial absolutism and the claims of the imperial dynasty to universal rule, served mainly panegyric purposes: one prominent example is the strongly pro-Habsburg *Austrias* (1516) of Riccardo Bartolini, an Italian resident at the imperial court in Vienna. The great historical events of the time naturally received epic treatment. From the wealth of epics about the wars with the Turks, I will mention only Balthasar Nusser's *De obsidione Viennae* (*The Siege of Vienna*, 1568), which represents the first Turkish siege of Vienna in 1529. Events specific to the German-speaking countries were also turned into heroic verse: Laurentius Pilladus of Lothringen depicted the 1525 Peasants' Rebellion, for instance, in his *Rusticias* (~ *Peasants' Epic*, 1548). Similarly, the Thirty Years' War was met with a plethora of reactions in the epic and panegyric vein. Julius Wilhelm Zincgref's brief *Epos ad Fridericum* (*Epic to Frederick*, 1619) and Opitz's *Oratio ad Fridericum regem Bohemiae* (*Speech to Frederick, the King of Bohemia*, 1620) praised the "Winter King" Frederick V, Elector of the Palatinate, in verse and prose respectively. Later works include Johann Nicolaus Sellius's *Cedrus Brandenburgica* (*Brandenburg Cedar*, 1688) on the occasion of the death of Frederick William, Elector of Brandenburg, and Renatus Karl von Senckenberg's *Carolina Cordaea* (*Charlotte Corday*, 1793), which recounts the murder of Charlotte Corday in revolutionary Paris.

In principle, all poetic forms could be injected with political content. In a collection of epigrams published in 1519, Hutten supported Emperor Maximilian I's struggle against the Republic of Venice. The Palatinate poet Paul Schede Melissus made use of the sophisticated Pindaric ode to honor Elizabeth I, who was greatly esteemed by Reformed Christians (*Ode Pindarica ad Elisabetham* [*Pindaric Ode to Elizabeth*], 1582), while the eclogues of Euricius Cordus (1514) and Joachim Camerarius (collected in 1568)—though formally recalling Virgil's *Eclogues*—voice critical reflections on the eve and aftermath of the Peasants' War. Verse satire was not only used to criticize political and ecclesiastical misdeeds; instead, authors such as Naogeorgus and Balde opposed the entire spectrum of vices typical at the time, as in Balde's *Satira contra abusum tabaci* (*Satire Against the Misuse of Tobacco*, 1657). Drunkenness and the crude manners both of the common people and of the lesser nobility were attacked vigorously as specifically German vices, against which any number of works were written in verse and prose. Alongside verse satire, literary prose forms also took up socially critical positions. Chief among these were satirical dialogues inspired by Lucian (second century CE), such as Hutten's *Phalarismus* (1517), polemicizing against a local tyrant; the playful title, *Phalarism*, means an "imitation of Phalaris," the Sicilian arch-tyrant of antiquity. Satirical prose also included ironic encomia and parodic disputations, a partial collection of which can be found, for example, in Caspar Dornau's *Amphitheatrum sapientiae Socraticae ioco-seriae* (*Amphitheater of Seriocomic Socratic Wisdom*, 1619). Among these can also be found such scandalous writings as the essay *Disputatio nova contra mulieres, qua probatur eas homines non esse* (*A New Disputation Against Women, in Which It Is Proven That They Are Not Human*, 1595), commonly attributed to Valens Acidalius.

Humanist political drama begins with Jakob Locher's *Tragedia de Thurcis et Suldano* (*Tragedy About the Turks and the Sultan*, 1497) in which exhortation for action in the Turkish war meets with a teleological interpretation of history. At the time of the Peasants' War, Schottenius's *Ludus Martius* (*War Play*, 1526) articulated an utopian vision of reconciliation. The struggles of the confessional period are reflected in plays dealing with the Thirty Years' War, but also, for instance, in Theodor Rhodius's *Colignius* (*Coligny*, 1614), in which the author, himself a Calvinist, dramatizes the heroic death of the leader of the French Huguenots, Admiral Gaspard de Coligny, in the Saint Bartholomew's Day massacre of tens of thousands of Huguenot Protestants throughout France. Catholic authors preferred to use historical or legendary examples to criticize political and social shortcomings, as did Jakob Keller in his *Mauritius* (*Maurice*, the Byzantine emperor; 1603), the first in a long series of Maurice plays on the Jesuit stage.

"Ego-Documents" and the Question of Literary Authenticity

It may seem bold to classify the humanists' carefully arranged and edited collections of poetry as "ego-documents", that is, as texts in which authors write about their own actions, thoughts, and feelings (the term was coined as *egodocumenten* in the mid-1950s by the Dutch historian Jacob Presser). Naturally, the poetic presentation of facts and events as well as the speaker's self-representation is constructed to a large extent, anchored in literary tradition and bound up in intertextual dialogue; nonetheless, a varying degree of autobiographical foundation and authenticity (not to be confused with immediacy or directness, which are scarcely to be expected) can always be assumed. While Celtis's *Amores* (1502) is a highly artificial construct in its use of the genre of love elegy to construct a cultural geography of *Germania* with philosophical and patriotic implications, other books of elegies might be less complex in structure but are more strongly aligned with the real-life experiences of their authors: examples include the sixteenth-century collections of the Swiss Simon Lemnius, the Hessian Petrus Lotichius Secundus, the Alsatian Jacobus Micyllus, and the Palatinate Johannes Posthius. In Lotichius's case, biographical elements from the young poet's participation in the Schmalkaldic War and his years of study in France and Italy are worked into the poems. Unlike much of Roman love elegy, his adventures with the *puella* or desired girl are only one topic among many, such as meetings with friends, experiences abroad, study, war, and all the different circumstances a learned poet might undergo in his life. Autobiographical references also appear in other genres, as in the epigrams of Cordus (collected in 1550) or in the *Anacreontics* (1570) of Johann Aurpach, with their many, varied references to daily bourgeois life. The extensive and very different bodies of lyric poetry by writers such as Melissus and Balde vary with regard to their authenticity as much as they do in their sociopolitical or intertextual references.

As examples, I will single out three genres, both because they have a strong claim to qualify as ego-documents and because they follow clearly discernible generic patterns

(Bernstein 2004b; Trunz 1995, 7–82). First is the *hodoeporicon*, or travel poem, which describes in narrative form the experiences of members of the republic of letters, whose studies often brought them to seats of learning both within and outside the German-speaking world (Wiegand 1984; Wiegand in Weimar 1997–2003, 2:62–64). These texts tend to make normative statements, as when they rank and evaluate a location that has been visited, mark out confessional positions, or (as in the special case of travelogues about Turkey) use the usual *topoi* about "barbarians." Among German humanists, who traditionally traveled frequently abroad, the *hodoeporicon* was disproportionately popular and widespread; many prominent poets as well as scholars of every confession composed such travel poems. Nathan Chytraeus and Nikolaus Reusner issued collections of texts by their contemporaries under the titles *Hodoeporica sive itineraria* (*Travel Poems, or Itineraries*, 1575) and *Hodoeporica sive itinera* (*Travel Poems, or Journeys*, 1580).

The explicitly autobiographical writings of the humanists had several ancient models in terms of genre, but no single pattern to follow. Formally divergent, partly in verse and partly in prose, they set themselves apart through their own specific forms of identity construction. The monk Johannes Butzbach conceived of his personal development as a journey, as the title *Odeporicon* (*Travelogue*, 1506) indicates; while the Alsatian (and later Swiss) reformer Johannes Fabricius Montanus (1565) stylized his life as a failure, imitating the model of Ovid and clearly contradicting the historical facts. Eobanus Hessus also compared himself to Ovid, though in a fictional epistle *To Posterity* (*Eobanus Posteritati*, 1514) he highlighted the accomplishments of the humanist generation, rather than a lack of success. The extensive *Philotheca* (literally, *Friendship Book*, 1645) by the quarrelsome philologist Kaspar Schoppe, the brief and fragmentary autobiographical sketch by the Nuremberg humanist Willibald Pirckheimer (ca. 1527), the various autobiographical efforts of the Austrian nobleman Sigmund von Herberstein (1486–1566) and the Rosicrucian Johann Valentin Andreae (1586–1654), all clearly demonstrate the heterogeneity of early modern autobiography.

The ego-document *par excellence* is the letter, which in this era was both a medium of communication and an instrument for shaping group identities. Guides to epistolography such as Erasmus's *De conscribendis epistolis* (*On Letter Writing*, 1522), were widespread. German humanists, too, from the earliest period (Celtis and Bebel) down to the time of Melchior Junius's *Scholae rhetoricae de contexendarum epistolarum ratione* (*Rhetoric Classes on the Art of Composing Letters*, 1587) made contributions to the history of this kind of Latin manual. The correspondence of numerous humanists remains, not only as autograph manuscripts or copies, but also in many cases in contemporary printed collections. Modern editions have focused on the letters of early humanists (e.g., Wimpfeling, Reuchlin, and Celtis) or the Reformers (such as Luther, Zwingli, and Melanchthon), while comparatively few collections from the Late Renaissance and baroque periods (e.g., those by Matthäus Rader, Martin Opitz, and Athanasius Kircher) have been similarly edited.

THE AUTUMN OF NEO-LATIN: SCHOLARSHIP, SCIENCE, AND ACADEMIC TEXTS

Somewhat later than in the neighboring Romance-speaking lands, but still detectably from the seventeenth century onwards, the production of Latin texts gradually gave way to vernacular works. As far as literary history is concerned, this transition occurred earlier in the Protestant than in the Catholic sphere; the writing of the Protestant Paul Fleming (1609–1640) represents one of the final Latin-language highpoints for that denomination, while Jesuit and Benedictine literature was overwhelmingly composed in Latin until well into the eighteenth century. Martin Opitz's *Buch von der Deutschen Poeterey* (*Book of German Poetry*, 1624), together with the language societies (Sprachgesellschaften) springing up in many cultural centers from the early seventeenth century onwards, provided the greatest impulse for this linguistic paradigm shift. In terms of social history, this shift is best understood as part of scholars' efforts to attain greater visibility in circles at court and among the urban bourgeoisie, while politically—at least in Protestant regions—it can be seen as a reaction against the international (and thus Latin-favoring) orientation of the Habsburg dynasty. Modern patterns of genre and style, such as Petrarchan lyric or *Gesellschaftslied* (popular polyphonic songs of the sixteenth to seventeenth centuries), were only rarely composed in Latin. Unlike most Catholic school drama, Protestant school drama began using the German language in the course of the seventeenth century (with important performances, e.g., in Breslau and Zittau) before finally disappearing altogether. Occasional poetry reached its highest number of compositions around 1700, though it soon gained a bad reputation due, among other reasons, to the poor quality of similar and increasingly popular works in German. Even if Latin poetry continues into the modern era to be written in the German-speaking countries, it has clung to only a niche existence since the middle of the eighteenth century. From this transitional period dates the two-volume collection edited by Johann Tobias Roenick, *Recentiorum poetarum Germanorum carmina Latina selectiora* (*Selected Latin Poems by Recent German Poets*, 1749–1751). There are also numerous Latin translations of German classics from the same period, such as *Carmina aliquot Goethii et Schilleri Latine reddita* (*Some Poems by Goethe and Schiller in Latin Versions*, 1833), whose publication was undertaken by such important figures (among others) as the philosopher and literary scholar Theodor Echtermeyer.

While in some practical branches of learning, a German-language alternative to the Latin production of the humanists had developed as early as the sixteenth century (e.g., in botanical dictionaries and in some alchemical and hermetic writings), Latin remained the normal language of publication in the academic disciplines of the seventeenth and eighteenth centuries, fully one or two generations longer than its reign in literature (Jaumann 2011). Some disciplines held fast to the Latin tradition throughout the eighteenth century, and in the realm of academic life—for example, dissertation writing—German only gradually gained the upper hand in the later nineteenth century. During the early Enlightenment, prominent authors such as the philosophers Gottfried Wilhelm Leibniz (1646–1716), Christian Thomasius (1655–1728), and Christian Wolff (1679–1754), as well as the natural scientist Johann Jakob Scheuchzer (1672–1733), published their works increasingly frequently in German or French, although Latin remained of almost equal value for them. Alexander Gottlieb Baumgarten's *Aesthetica* (*Aesthetics*, 1750–1758), the foundational document of the philosophical discipline of the same name, was published at a time when most scholarly theory appeared in German, and Christian Fürchtegott Gellert's treatise *Pro comoedia commovente* (*For a Sentimental Comedy*, 1751) was widely read in a German translation by Lessing. Among the representatives of classical German literature, only Friedrich Schiller could to some extent be reclaimed for Neo-Latin by virtue of his second medical dissertation *Tractatio de discrimine febrium inflammatoriarum et putridarum* (*The Difference Between Inflammatory and Putrid Fevers*, 1780). With the *Disquisitiones arithmeticae* (*Arithmetical Investigations*, 1801) of Carl Friedrich Gauß, the list of great Latin works by prominent authors in the German sphere ends right at the dawn of the nineteenth century.

Reference works, literary histories, and dissertations belong to that particular form of early modern Latin publications that are important today not only as subjects of academic analysis, but also as practical research tools. Examples of reference works would include Melchior Adam's collections of biographies of important humanist scholars, arranged according to the academic faculties of philosophy, medicine, theology, and law, in the series *Vitae Germanorum philosophorum / medicorum / theologorum / juresconsultorum et politicorum* (*Lives of German Philosophers* [1615] / *Doctors* [1620] / *Theologians* [1620] / *Lawyers and Politicians* [1620]). The often multivolume compendia of literary history (*historia litteraria*) have left a great deal of information about the careers of learned writers and their works, and also about the methodologies of the various fields of the research they conducted. In German cultural history, Daniel Georg Morhof's *Polyhistor sive de notitia auctorum et rerum commentarii* (*Polymath, or Notes on the Knowledge of Authors and Subjects*, first printed in 1688, later expanded many times) set the standard for this type of work. Early modern dissertations served as the basis for academic disputations and were disseminated widely in this form, particularly in the German-speaking countries, but also in the Netherlands and Scandinavia (Marti 2011). Quite different from modern doctoral dissertations (which, as we have mentioned, were also often published in Latin up until the end of the nineteenth century), their early modern counterparts were mostly composed by the chairmen of the disputation. They usually gave a detailed account of the state of contemporary debate on a specialized question and sometimes also theoretically engaged with their own academic purpose and context, as in the case of Johann Konrad Dannhauer's *Idea boni disputatoris* (*Idea of a Good Disputator*, 1629).

SUGGESTED READING

Schmidt (1999 and 2007) investigates the problematic issue of a "German cultural nation." The three-volume handbook by Adam and Westphal (2012) documents the multicentered nature of the Holy Roman Empire. Kühlmann (2007b), dividing the material into traditional genres, provides the most comprehensive overview of Neo-Latin literature in the German cultural sphere. Generally, both Protestant drama (for biblical drama, see Washof 2007) and Jesuit drama (Valentin 2001) were comparatively well researched; Glei and Seidel (2008) present some representative case studies. For poetry, see, for example, the edited volume by Czapla, Czapla, and Seidel (2003); shorter poetic works are well represented in the extensive collection of primary texts of Kühlmann, Seidel, and Wiegand (1997). The anthology by Heger (1975–1978) gathers many different genres. Research into early modern poetics has garnered a great deal of recent interest: see especially Müller and Robert (2007); Wels (2009); and Hintzen and Simons (2013). Relevant technical terms are concisely explained in Weimar (1997–2003). Füssel (1993) offers a good selection of author biographies; compare, too, the dictionary of Kühlmann (2008–2012). Important series with studies and editions valuable to Neo-Latin literature and the early modern period are *Frühe Neuzeit* (Berlin: De Gruyter), *NeoLatina* (Tübingen: Narr), *Bibliotheca Neolatina* (Heidelberg: Manutius), and *Noctes Neolatinae* (Hildesheim: Olms).

[*Translated from the German by Patrick Hadley.*]

REFERENCES

Adam, Wolfgang, and Siegrid Westphal, eds. 2012. *Handbuch kultureller Zentren der Frühen Neuzeit: Städte und Residenzen im alten deutschen Sprachraum.* 3 vols. Berlin: De Gruyter.

Bernstein, Eckhard. 2004a. "Vom lateinischen Frühhumanismus bis Conrad Celtis." In Röcke and Münkler 2004, 54–76.

———. 2004b. "Humanistische Standeskultur." In Röcke and Münkler 2004, 97–129.

———. 2004c. "Humanistische Intelligenz und kirchliche Reformen." In Röcke and Münkler 2004, 166–97.

Burkard, Thorsten. 2013. "Moralisierender jesuitischer Klassizismus: Jacob Masens *Palaestra eloquentiae ligatae.*" In Hintzen and Simons 2013, 81–109.

Classen, Carl J. 2003. "Neue Elemente in ihrer alten Disziplin: Zu Melanchthons *De Rhetorica libri tres.*" In *Germania Latina, Latinitas Teutonica: Politik, Wissenschaft, humanistische Kultur vom späten Mittelalter bis in unsere Zeit*, vol. 1, edited by Eckhard Keßler and Heinrich C. Kuhn, 325–73. Munich: Fink.

Czapla, Beate, Ralf G. Czapla, and R. Seidel, eds. 2003. *Lateinische Lyrik der Frühen Neuzeit: Poetische Kleinformen und ihre Funktionen zwischen Renaissance und Aufklärung.* Tübingen: Niemeyer.

Eickmeyer, Jost. 2008. "Der blinde Belisar—zwei Ausformungen einer exemplarischen Gestalt bei Jacob Bidermann SJ: Ein Baustein zur funktionalen Abgrenzung von Drama und heroischem Brief." In Glei and Seidel 2008, 201–31.

Füssel, Stephan, ed. 1993. *Deutsche Dichter der frühen Neuzeit (1450–1600): Ihr Leben und Werk.* Berlin: Erich Schmidt.

Glei, Reinhold F., and Robert Seidel, eds. 2006. *"Parodia" und Parodie: Aspekte intertextuellen Schreibens in der lateinischen Literatur der Frühen Neuzeit*. Tübingen: Niemeyer.

———, eds. 2008. *Das lateinische Drama der Frühen Neuzeit: Exemplarische Einsichten in Praxis und Theorie*. Tübingen: Niemeyer.

Heger, Hedwig, ed. 1975–1978. *Die deutsche Literatur: Texte und Zeugnisse*. Vols. 2.1–2, *Spätmittelalter, Humanismus, Reformation*. Munich: Beck.

Hintzen, Beate, and Roswitha Simons, ed. 2013. *Norm und Poesie: Zur expliziten und impliziten Poetik in der lateinischen Literatur der Frühen Neuzeit*. Berlin: De Gruyter.

Huber-Rebenich, Gerlinde. 2001. "Der lateinische Psalter des Eobanus Hessus und das Ideal der *docta pietas*." In Ludwig 2001, 289–303.

Jaumann, Herbert, ed. 2011. *Diskurse der Gelehrtenkultur in der Frühen Neuzeit: Ein Handbuch*. Berlin: De Gruyter.

Jeßing, Benedikt. 2008. "Zur Rezeption des *morall play* vom 'Everyman' in der neulateinischen und frühneuhochdeutschen Komödie: Georg Macropedius, Hans Sachs." In Glei and Seidel 2008, 87–99.

Kaminski, Nicola. 2008. "Polyglossie, Polysemie: zum konfessionspolitischen Standort von Nicodemus Frischlins *Phasma*." In Glei and Seidel 2008, 165–81.

Kühlmann, Wilhelm. 2007a. "Education in Early Modern Germany." In Reinhart 2007, 137–87.

———. 2007b. "Neo-Latin Literature in Early Modern Germany." In Reinhart 2007, 281–329.

———, ed. 2008–2012. *Killy Literaturlexikon: Autoren und Werke des deutschsprachigen Kulturraumes*. 2nd ed. 13 vols. Berlin: De Gruyter.

———. 2013. "Fiktionsironie und Autorbewusstsein in jesuitischer Barocklyrik: Zu Johannes Bisselius' SJ (1601–1682) *Deliciae Veris* (1638, 1640)." In Hintzen and Simons, op. cit., 163–82.

Kühlmann, Wilhelm, Robert Seidel, and Hermann Wiegand, eds. 1997. *Humanistische Lyrik des 16. Jahrhunderts: Lateinisch und deutsch*. Frankfurt: Deutscher Klassiker Verlag.

Leonhardt, Jürgen. 2008. "Frischlins *Priscianus vapulans* und die zeitgenössische Lateinkultur." In Glei and Seidel 2008, 155–64.

Ludwig, Walther, ed. 2001. *Die Musen im Reformationszeitalter*. Leipzig: Evangelische Verlagsanstalt.

Marti, Hanspeter. "Dissertationen." In Rasche 2011, 293–312.

Müller, Jan-Dirk, and Jörg Robert, eds. 2007. *Maske und Mosaik: Poetik, Sprache, Wissen im 16. Jahrhundert*. Berlin: Lit Verlag.

Mundt, Lothar. 2001. "Die sizilischen Musen in Wittenberg: Zur religiösen Funktionalisierung der neulateinischen Bukolik im deutschen Protestantismus des 16. Jahrhunderts." In Ludwig, op. cit., 265–88.

Niehl, Rüdiger. 2006. "Parodia Horatiana: Parodiebegriff und Parodiedichtung im Deutschland des 17. Jahrhunderts." In Glei and Seidel 2006, 11–45.

Rasche, Ulrich, ed. 2011. *Quellen zur frühneuzeitlichen Universitätsgeschichte: Typen, Bestände, Forschungsperspektiven*. Wiesbaden: Harrassowitz.

Reinhart, Max, ed. 2007. *Early Modern German Literature 1350–1700*. Rochester: Camden House.

Robert, Jörg. 2006. "Nachschrift und Gegengesang: Parodie und *parodia* in der Poetik der Frühen Neuzeit." In Glei and Seidel 2006, 47–66.

———. 2007. "Vor der Poetik—vor den Poetiken: Humanistische Vers- und Dichtungslehre in Deutschland (1480–1520)." In Müller and Robert, op. cit., 47–74.

———. 2011. "Die Ciceronianismus-Debatte." In Jaumann, op. cit., 1–54.

Röcke, Werner, and Marina Münkler, eds. 2004. *Hansers Sozialgeschichte der deutschen Literatur vom 16. Jahrhundert bis zur Gegenwart*. Vol. 1, *Die Literatur im Übergang vom Mittelalter zur Neuzeit*. Munich: Deutscher Taschenbuch Verlag.

Schmidt, Alexander. 2007. *Vaterlandsliebe und Religionskonflikt: Politische Diskurse im Alten Reich (1555–1648)*. Leiden: Brill.

Schmidt, Georg. 1999. *Geschichte des Alten Reiches: Staat und Nation in der Frühen Neuzeit 1495–1806*. Munich: Beck.

Schnabel, Werner W. 2011. "Stammbücher." In Rasche, op. cit., 421–52.

Sdzuj, Reimund B. 2011. "Die allgemeine Hermeneutik in der Frühen Neuzeit." In Jaumann, op. cit., 593–627.

Trunz, Erich. 1995. *Deutsche Literatur zwischen Späthumanismus und Barock: Acht Studien*. Munich: Beck.

Valentin, Jean-Marie. 2001. *Les jésuites et le théâtre (1554–1680): Contribution à l'histoire culturelle du monde catholique dans le Saint-Empire romain germanique*. Paris: Desjonquères.

Washof, Wolfram. 2007. *Die Bibel auf der Bühne: Exempelfiguren und protestantische Theologie im lateinischen und deutschen Bibeldrama der Reformationszeit*. Münster: Rhema.

Wels, Volkhard. 2009. *Der Begriff der Dichtung in der Frühen Neuzeit*. Berlin: De Gruyter.

Weimar, Klaus, ed. 1997–2003. *Reallexikon der deutschen Literaturwissenschaft*. 3 vols. Berlin: De Gruyter.

Wiegand, Hermann. 1984. *Hodoeporica: Studien zur neulateinischen Reisedichtung des deutschen Kulturraums im 16. Jahrhundert*. Baden-Baden: Koerner.

....

CHAPTER 29

IBERIAN PENINSULA

....

ALEJANDRO COROLEU AND
CATARINA FOUTO

PART 1: SPAIN

Alejandro Coroleu

As in other European countries, the rich literary corpus in Latin produced in Spain in the early modern period did not emerge in a setting in which Latin was the only written or spoken language. Rather, the development of Neo-Latin poetry, prose, and drama was inextricably linked to (and usually in competition with) the inevitable spread of the vernacular in all spheres of life. The most important space occupied by Latin, apart from the church, was in the universities. It was regarded as the best register of communication for scientific and academic purposes, and university regulations prescribed it as the official medium of instruction, inaugural orations, and drama. Lectures, particularly those on classical texts, theology, law, and philosophy, were supposed to be given in Latin, and consequently most textual commentaries and handbooks were published in that language. The purpose of the following section is to provide a conspectus of Neo-Latin literature in Spain between, roughly, 1475 and 1750. Given the close links between Renaissance humanism and Neo-Latin literature, there will be particular emphasis on the development of this body of texts in the sixteenth century and in the first half of the seventeenth century. I shall first pay attention to the cluster of scholarly disciplines fostered by humanists and then go on to discuss the Latin poetry, drama, and literary prose produced in Spain at the time. I shall also discuss a series of writings related to the enterprise of the Indies. The final section aims to examine the important role played by Latin as the language of political and cultural propaganda in early modern Spain.

Scholarly Disciplines

Like their other European counterparts, teachers and professors in Spain wrote much on Latin grammar, rhetoric, and eloquence. Of these figures, perhaps the most famous is Antonio de Nebrija (1444–1522), who taught at Salamanca and Alcalá de Henares. While lecturing at Salamanca, Nebrija wrote his first major work, the *Introductiones Latinae* (*Latin Introductions*), with a view to replacing the medieval grammars in use at the university (Rico 1978). First published in 1481, the *Introductiones* became a full-fledged handbook of Latin scholarship. Despite the numerous editions or reprints of the text that had appeared by the time of its author's death, the volume soon became the target of debates among fellow Latin masters such as Juan Maldonado (ca. 1490–1554) and Francisco Sánchez de las Brozas (1523–1600), professor of Greek and rhetoric at Salamanca. Maldonado's *Paraenesis ad politiores literas adversus grammaticorum vulgum* (*An Exhortation to Fine Letters Against the Crowd of Grammarians*, 1529) is a diatribe against Nebrija's methods, but also an exhortation to uphold humanist ideals (Asensio and Alcina Rovira 1980). Sánchez de las Brozas's *Minerva, seu de causis linguae Latinae* (*Minerva; or, The Causes of the Latin Language*, 1562) stands as one of the most outstanding Renaissance contributions to theoretical linguistics; in it, Sánchez upholds the autonomy of grammar and postulates a grammatical or syntactic linguistic system separate from logic. Like Sánchez de las Brozas, who also wrote treatises on rhetoric, Lorenzo Palmireno, professor of grammar, rhetoric, and Greek at Barcelona and Valencia, discussed issues of Latin style in his *Campi eloquentiae* (*Fields of Eloquence*, 1574), in which precepts of Latin composition are illustrated with the aid of lengthy vernacular examples (Maestre Maestre 1990, 125–227).

In the field of classical and biblical studies, Spain also produced distinguished scholars who, active in academia or in the development of the royal library of El Escorial, employed Latin in their work. Diego López de Zúñiga (1470–1531) was among those who attracted the attention of Cardinal Francisco Jiménez de Cisneros at the University of Alcalá. Inaugurated in 1498, the University of Alcalá applied the program of humanism to its curriculum and to the study of scripture (Sáenz-Badillos 1990). As early as 1508, Jiménez himself initiated a great project of biblical scholarship, which resulted in the publication in 1522 of the six volumes of the renowned Complutensian Polyglot Bible, thus called from Complutum, the Latin name of Alcalá de Henares. Out of a desire to defend the Latin Vulgate version of the Bible and the Western Christian orthodoxy, in 1520, Zúñiga prepared a series of critiques against Erasmus, which were collected in his *Annotationes contra Erasmum Roterodamum in defensionem translationis Novi Testamenti* (*Annotations Against Erasmus of Rotterdam in Defense of His Translation of the New Testament*, Rummel 1988, 1:145–77). Another expert employed at the university by Cisneros, Hernán Núñez de Toledo, taught rhetoric and Greek at Alcalá and Salamanca. His lectures on Seneca, Pomponius Mela, and Pliny the Elder led directly to three major commentaries, published in 1529, 1543, and 1545. In the field of classical studies, Juan Luis Vives not only produced his major work, *De tradendis disciplinis* (*On Education*, 1531), a critical synthesis of classical knowledge, but also wrote commentaries on Cicero, Virgil, and Augustine. Trained in the intellectual tradition of the Italian Renaissance, Juan Ginés de Sepúlveda (ca. 1490–1573) produced translations of Aristotle and Alexander of Aphrodisias. Last but not least, Benito Arias Montano (1527–1598), librarian of El Escorial, was an outstanding translator of and commentator on biblical texts, and the Jesuit Juan Luis de la Cerda (ca. 1558–1642) was the author of a highly influential commentary on the works of Virgil, in which "he combines erudite antiquarianism with occasional displays of another kind of exegesis—contemporary cultural and ideological commentary" (Laird 2002, 171).

Dealing largely with politics and with the consequences of moral decisions in a rhetorical manner, in the Renaissance, history came to form a fundamental part of the curriculum and thus began to be treated for the first time as an autonomous discipline. These developments were strongly reflected in Spain, and an important part of the Spanish Neo-Latin literature that flourished from the end of the fifteenth century was historiographical. Theoretical reflection on history was the subject of Nebrija's *Divinatio in scribenda historia* (*An Examination into the Writing of History*, 1509) and of the *De historiae institutione* (*The Principles of History*, 1557) of the philosopher Sebastián Fox Morcillo, and Nebrija also initiated the scientific study of ancient Roman and pre-Roman Spain through his researches on the toponymy of Greek and Roman chorographers and the vocabulary of Roman law. This culminated in the important work of Antonio Agustín on the text of the *Pandects*, and the material on Roman antiquities gathered together in his *De legibus et senatus consultis* (*The Laws and the Decrees of the Senate*) and *De Romanorum gentibus et familiis* (*The Tribes and Families of the Romans*), both published in 1592. Furthermore, several Spanish historians working in Latin chose to write biographies of famous men as a way of reflecting on cultural history. The antiquary and historian Pere Miquel Carbonell is the author of the *De viris illustribus Catalanis* (*The Illustrious Men of Catalunya*, 1476), a collection of fifteen biographies aimed at mapping out the state of Latin literature in the Catalan-speaking lands at the time (Vilallonga 1993, 63–72). For his part, Alfonso García Matamoros charted in his *De asserenda Hispanorum eruditione* (*Vindication of Spanish Erudition*, 1553) the development of Latin letters in Spain from Roman times to his own day, work that would later be carried forward by Nicolás Antonio in his *Bibliotheca Hispana vetus* (*Old Spanish Library*, 1696) and *Bibliotheca Hispana nova* (*New Spanish Library*, 1672), books that laid the foundations for the study of our present subject.

Poetry, Drama, and Literary Prose

From the last two decades of the fifteenth century, Neo-Latin poetry written in Italy was widely read in Spain, and the poems of Michele Verino, Battista Mantuano (commonly known in the English-speaking world as "Mantuan"), Publio Fausto Andrelini, and Angelo Poliziano were printed on Spanish presses, with or without commentaries, as early as 1489 (Alcina Rovira 2000). As an example, the broad circulation of Poliziano's Latin verse, best represented by his four *Silvae* (here ~ *Sketches*), is reflected in their publication in Alcalá around 1515 and in Salamanca in 1554 (Coroleu 2001). The Salamanca edition is of particular importance, as it includes an elaborate commentary by Sánchez de las Brozas, whom we have already encountered. This popularity reflected the fact that fifteenth-century Italian Neo-Latin poets were broadly incorporated into the Spanish educational curriculum in the early years of the following century, as Spanish scholars, lecturers, and teachers followed their European counterparts in exploiting the pedagogical possibilities offered by a poetic corpus of Christian classics. Juan Luis Vives's advice to include Mantuan and Poliziano among the texts employed for the teaching of poetry (*De tradendis disciplinis* 3.6) is in this respect an excellent testimony to how these poets' works came to assume canonical status in school and university courses throughout sixteenth-century Spain.

The reading and teaching of Italian Neo-Latin poets in classrooms, and the circulation of erudite commentaries on them, soon encouraged native imitations. Alvar Gómez de Ciudad Real, for example, modeled his epic poem *Thalichristia* (perhaps from Greek *thallō* ["bloom"], and hence *Narrative of the Blooming of Christ*, 1522) on Jacopo Sannazaro's *De partu Virginis* (*The Virgin Birth*). Similarly, Juan Sobrarias, editor of Verino, and the Valencian Joan Baptista Anyés imitated Verino and Mantuan, respectively, in their *Distichs* (1516) and *Egloga de nativitate Christi* (*Eclogue on the Birth of Christ*, 1527). As for Poliziano, his Latin poetry was widely imitated, for instance in the *Silva de laudibus poeseos* (*Sketch on the Praise of Poetry*, ca. 1525) of Juan Angel González, professor of poetry at Valencia, which was modeled on the *Nutricia* (*Reward for Nursing*), one of Poliziano's *Silvae*. The culmination of Neo-Latin verse in Spain was the religious poetry of Arias Montano, represented by his *Humanae salutis monumenta* (*Monuments of Human Salvation*, 1571) and *Hymni et saecula* (*Hymns and Generations*, 1593), indebted in equal measure to the verse of Horace and of Marcantonio Flaminio (Rekers 1972). On a par with their classical predecessors, at the turn of the seventeenth century, Latin poets of the previous century like Jaime Juan Falcó or Juan de Verzosa came to be regarded as literary authorities. They played a significant role in the controversies aroused by the obscure poetry of Luis de Góngora (1561–1627), and were commended by Baltasar Gracián in his influential encyclopedia on the baroque theory of wit, *Agudeza y arte de ingenio* (*Wit and the Art of Inventiveness*) of 1648. Yet by that time, despite the high prestige accorded to it by literary theoreticians of the age, Neo-Latin poetry had, for some years, bowed to the strength of its vernacular counterpart.

The combination of school practice and familiarity with classical authors and Italian humanist models was likewise central to the development of Neo-Latin drama in Spain. The universities' prescriptions regarding the performance of school dramas in Latin, together with the publication of Plautus, Terence, and humanist comedies like Leon Battista Alberti's *Philodoxeos fabula* (*Play about Philodoxus*, written after 1424 and published in Salamanca in 1502), contributed to the flourishing of Latin theater on school and university stages. Despite the strict regulations regarding the performance of drama in Latin, the vernacular was also very often present on the stage. Most Jesuit writers, for example, employed Latin or Spanish in the same play according to the social and cultural status of the different characters involved. Moreover, the aristocratic audience who gathered to see school plays were not expected to understand the texts in the original, and had in fact to be supplied with vernacular summaries. This detail might account for the fact that, for example, Juan de Mal Lara decided to undertake a translation of his own—now lost—play *Locusta* shortly after it was first staged at Salamanca in 1548. The first generation of Neo-Latin playwrights included Maldonado, author of the comedies *Hispaniola* (*The Spanish Woman*) and *Eremitae* (*The Hermits*), and, above all, Juan Pérez or Petreius, a lecturer at Alcalá who produced Latin versions of four Italian plays by Ludovico Ariosto and Alessandro Piccolomini. Around the mid-sixteenth century, the practice was taken over by Jesuits such as Miguel Venegas and Pedro Pablo Acevedo, who wrote tragedies in elevated Latin verse as prescribed by Jesuit regulations on the theater (Picón 1997).

The acceptance of classical and fifteenth-century Italian humanist genres also shaped the development of Latin prose genres by Spanish authors in the sixteenth century. Particularly popular were letters and dialogues, which constituted a pleasurable way of disseminating knowledge and an effective strategy for the presentation of opinions (Gómez 1988). Letters functioned as a means to discuss business, to express friendship, and above all to communicate scholarly information, and Latin writers such as Pere Miquel Carbonell, Alfonso de Palencia, Juan Luis Vives, Juan Ginés de Sepúlveda, Pere Joan Oliver, and Antonio Agustín all discussed their ideas in epistolary form (Gómez Moreno 1994, 179–96). Works in which reflection on theoretical or contemporary issues is placed within a dialogue framework are exemplified by some of Juan Luis Vives's dialogues, particularly his *De Europae dissidiis et bello turcico* (*The Discords of Europe and the Turkish War*, 1526) and *De veritate fidei Christianae* (*The Truth of the Christian Faith*, 1543); Bernardino Gómez Miedes's *De sale* (*On Salt*, 1572); Pedro Sánchez Ciruelo's *Disputatorius dialogus* (*Disputative Dialogue*, 1498); and Fox Morcillo's *De regni regisque institutione* (*The Principles of Kingdom and Kingship*, 1556). Neo-Latin writers also declaimed orations in praise of their humanist ideals or of their university or discipline, notably Nebrija's *De vi ac potestate litterarum* (*The Strength and Vigor of Letters*, 1486), Juan de Brocar's *Oratio paraenetica* (*Exhortatory Speech*, 1521), and Francesc Dassio's *De scientiarum et academiae Valentinae laudibus* (*Praise of Science and the University of Valencia*) of 1547 (Rico 2002, 163–94).

THE ENTERPRISE OF THE INDIES

Alongside general narratives on Spanish history, works by early modern Neo-Latin historiographers were also devoted to contemporary events. The issue that received the most attention from historians of the period was, without doubt, the exploration of the Americas and the political and religious treatment of the native Indians (Pagden 1986).

The legitimacy of the conquest of the New World came to dominate the intellectual atmosphere of early modern Spain. It was discussed in a series of scholarly and historiographical texts, such as the *De Indis recenter inventis* (*The Recent Discovery of the Indies*, 1539) by the Dominican Francisco de Vitoria, and the *De natura novi orbis* (*The Nature of the New World*, 1588) by the Jesuit José de Acosta. The controversy was also central to one of the most original pieces of prose writing composed in Latin in sixteenth-century Spain, Juan Maldonado's *Somnium* (*Dream*), which was published in 1541. Modeled on Cicero's *Somnium Scipionis* and combining narration and dialogue, Maldonado's text consists of a first-person account of a dream in which he travels to the Moon and to the heaven of Mercury, finally to land on American soil, where he describes an ideal society organized along essential Christian principles. In his depiction of Indian society, Maldonado invents a state of affairs that reflects a stage in the Conquest long past in some areas by his time. He is therefore able to use this society both as an illustration of what had actually gone wrong in his eyes, and as a nostalgic example of a lost opportunity to establish a truly Christian society that would combine the best of Christianity with the idealized state of innocence of the Indians. Complementary to the society depicted on the Moon, the American territory is, in this respect, not so much a perfect and finished society as a *tabula rasa* free from corruption, from which a harmonious society could have been built.

Maldonado's critical overtones in his *Somnium* contrast with the optimistic view conveyed in his *Oratiuncula habita Lucanalibus* (*A Brief Speech Held on the Day of Saint Luke*), a short piece published in Burgos in 1549, in which the author approached at greater length the subject of Indian society. An inaugural lecture delivered in Burgos in 1545, the *Oratiuncula* declares an ultimate confidence in the absolute value of Western civilization as contained in the humanist program of education and in the Christian project of universal conversion. The Indians, although depicted as barbarians lacking a real control over their environment due to their ignorance of arts and learning, appear, however, as the demonstration of the universal capacity of human beings to achieve human dignity by means of education. Indeed, on arriving in the Americas, the Spaniards—explains Maldonado in his *Oratiuncula*—found barbarian peoples, "naked and unaware of the existence of law." Years later, however, in the newly discovered territories, there were almost as many Christians as in Europe. Some of them had even devoted themselves to art and thought. Excellent proof—concludes Maldonado—"that the Indians did not lack talent but culture, not willingness to learn but preceptors and teachers" (60v).

The conquest of North, Central, and South America and the debate over the right of Europeans to enslave and subjugate the indigenous inhabitants of the New World were also the subject of a work completed by Juan Ginés de Sepúlveda in 1545 in dialogue form and entitled *Democrates secundus, sive de iustis causis belli apud Indios* (*Second Democrates; or, On the Just Conquest of the Indians*). The text was a response to the Dominican Bartolomé de las Casas, who three years earlier had written a fierce critique of Spanish colonialism in the New World. According to Sepúlveda, the brutish behavior, cannibalism, and paganism of the Indians made them slaves by nature to their

Spanish masters. Drawing on Aristotle's ideas on natural slavery discussed in the first book of the *Politics*, Sepúlveda concluded that war against the indigenous inhabitants of America was just, on the grounds that they had violated natural law and were barbarous by nature. In 1548, two of the most prominent theologians from the University of Salamanca, Melchor Cano and Bartolomé Carranza, were asked by the Spanish Crown to examine Sepúlveda's pamphlet. Given its inflammatory tone and the arguments employed by Sepúlveda, the *Democrates secundus* was denied the royal license, without which no book could legally be printed in Spain. Convinced that Las Casas was ultimately responsible for that decision, Sepúlveda pressed his case with the Council of Indies, which in August 1550 organized a debate between the two men. Although there was no formal outcome to the affair, the theologians refused to change their minds about Sepúlveda's work. Irrespective of the subversive nature of the text, the *Democrates secundus* is—together with Maldonado's pieces discussed above—an excellent example of how early modern Latin written in Spain was not a dead language, but one capable of discussing some of the most burning philosophical, religious, and political issues of the age.

POLITICAL AND CULTURAL PROPAGANDA

From the last decade of the fifteenth century onward, Latin was invaluable to the ruling circles of the Spanish monarchy, which employed it to frame the image of their empire during the period of expansion and conquest in Europe and the New World. The unification of Aragon and Castile under the so-called Catholic monarchs, Ferdinand and Isabella, and the discovery of America in 1492 reinforced the interest of the Crown in building an official historiography, which, through the use of Latin as a tool of communication, aimed at an international readership and forged a sense of political unity. As Spain began to enter into hegemony in Italy and the New World, a concerted effort to disseminate the history of the country took place under the patronage of the Spanish Crown (Tate 1996). In 1545, Sancho de Nebrija decided to publish in Granada a collection of four fifteenth-century partial historical narratives in Latin that are crucial for a better knowledge of Spanish history. As well as the *Rerum a Ferdinando et Elisabe . . . gestarum decades duae* (*Two Decades on the Deeds of Ferdinand and Isabella*) of Sancho's father Antonio de Nebrija, the volume included Rodrigo Ximénez de Rada's *De rebus Hispaniae* (*History of Spain*), Alfonso de Cartagena's *De regibus Hispaniae* (*The Kings of Spain*), and the *Paralipomenon Hispaniae* (~ *Lost Chronicles of Spain*) of the bishop of Girona, Joan Margarit. Dedicated to the future Philip II, Sancho's compilation was a clear attempt to put into the public domain a cluster of basic texts of the history of Spain written in the previous century. Aimed, through the choice of Latin, at both a local and an international readership, it also served a political function. The primary theme of the authors included was Spain's cultural and political precedence over other European nations. A Flemish scholar active at Salamanca, Jan Was, wrote *Rerum Hispaniae memorabilium annales* (*The Annals of Memorable Deeds of Spain*, posthumously printed in 1577). As Was himself acknowledged in the preface to his work, his intention was to reach beyond the frontiers of Spain in order to communicate with the rest of Europe. Presented as a scholarly history of Spain in Latin, aiming to educate the foreigner, Was's *Annales* dealt with all Spanish history, including ecclesiastical history, which he believed had not been properly treated in previous works.

Latin continued to play an important role in the construction of cultural identity when Spain's authority in Europe was waning. In the last two decades of Charles III's reign (1759–1788), a sense of national and cultural identity was forged, which, significantly, coincided with fierce criticism of Spain from abroad. Latinity (and Spanish Latinity in particular) was alleged by eighteenth-century Spanish writers as evidence of the cultural prestige of their country (Coroleu 2005). Interest in Latin humanism was crucial to the reassessment of sixteenth-century Spain as the Golden Age of Spanish literature. This is best represented by the work of the savant Gregorio Mayans y Siscar (1699–1781) and of Francisco Cerdá y Rico (1739–1792). An index of the Spanish books in Latin held in his own library, Mayans's *Specimen bibliothecae Hispano-Majansianae* (*Indication of the Spanish Library of Mayans*, 1753) constitutes a succinct history of Latin letters in Spain since the time of Nebrija. As for Cerdá, his *De Hispanis purioris Latinitatis cultoribus* (*Spanish Authors Writing Pure Latin*, 1781) discusses Latin literature in Spain from the late fifteenth century to the author's own day, thus intending to demonstrate the cultural continuity between the sixteenth and the eighteenth centuries. In his work, Cerdá held up Spanish Neo-Latin writers as examples of classical control and scholarly excellence, and as authors—he claimed—who bore comparison not only with their ancient predecessors but also with their contemporary European counterparts. Underlying Cerdá's catalog of early modern Latin writers is therefore a conscious program aimed at championing the literary heritage of his nation in the light of strong criticism of Spain's cultural belatedness.

PART 2: PORTUGAL

Catarina Fouto

The contribution of Portuguese intellectuals to the history of European early modern culture has been consistently overlooked. One of the principal reasons for this phenomenon is the fact that critical approaches to the history of early modern Portuguese culture have systematically excluded the significant corpus of Neo-Latin works written in this period. Yet the existence of a vibrant vernacular literature in Portugal developed side by side with Neo-Latin. The best evidence of the dynamic interaction between the two is the progressive enrichment of the Romance literary language favored by the reading of classical writers and the humanistic education, and, ultimately, the valorization of the vernacular as the language of the Portuguese Empire. In the wake of a renewed interest in the critical edition and translation of Neo-Latin works by Portuguese writers, this survey will begin by contextualizing the implementation and development of Neo-Latin in Portugal. The second part will chart the development of Neo-Latin prose, poetry, and drama in Portugal.

Contextualizing Neo-Latin
in Portugal

The idea that Portugal was a marginal cultural space has increasingly been questioned. Recent critical studies have emphasized that Portugal was part of the network of scholarly circulation within the European republic of letters (Enenkel and Berbara 2012). The incunabula and humanist editions in Portuguese public, private, religious, and school libraries clearly indicate that the feeble editorial activity in the country was compensated for by easy access to the European book market. Also, for many Portuguese Neo-Latin writers, spending some years abroad opened up the doors to important European printing centers, and publishing abroad was crucial to many of these individuals' success. Finally, as will be seen below, the works of these intellectuals and their reception in Europe show the fruit of sustained cultural exchange with the elite of European humanism (Earle 2009).

The beginning of Neo-Latin writing in Portugal owes much to cultural contact with Italy (Martins 1989), and can be traced back to the late fifteenth century when the Sicilian Cataldo Siculo (who corresponded with Pontano, Filelfo, and Battista Guarino) arrived in Portugal at the request of King John II (Ramalho 1988). The hesitant start of Portuguese humanism gave way to a period of intense cultural reform in the first half of the sixteenth century. From the very beginning, patronage was limited to the royal family and a handful of members of the high clergy and high aristocracy (namely the ducal houses of Braganza and Aveiro). The royal scholarships granted to Portuguese young men to study abroad were the first decisive step, followed by the transfer of the university from Lisbon to Coimbra in 1537. The creation of the Colégio das Artes in Coimbra (staffed by intellectuals like George Buchanan, André de Gouveia, Vinet, Fabrice, and Grouchy) and other colégios like Braga and Évora (where the Flemish Nicolas Cleynaerts and Jan Was taught) sealed this period of cultural renewal (Brandão 1948–1969; Da Silva Dias 1969). Contrary to the claims consistently made, Portuguese intellectuals continued to travel abroad after the handover of the Colégio das Artes to the Jesuits in 1555, merely avoiding cultural centers involved in religious wars. Furthermore, if it is true that Inquisitorial censorship became more active from the 1550s (making access to foreign books harder and delaying the publication process) and Tridentine orthodoxy gained ground in the country (Rodrigues 1981), this did not prevent a steady increase in the publication of books by Portuguese intellectuals both in their homeland and abroad. The political crisis that followed the death of King Sebastião at Ksar-el-Kebir (1578) and the Iberian Union (1580–1640) did not destabilize the rhythm of publication. However, similarly to what was happening elsewhere in Europe, Neo-Latin started to lose its prestige as a language of scholarly and intellectual production in Portugal in the 1630s, coinciding with the aftermath of the collapse of the scholarly book market in Europe brought about by the Thirty Years' War.

Neo-Latin Writing in Portugal

Unsurprisingly, the majority of Portuguese Neo-Latin works is closely linked to the institutional world of the university. The best early example of the development of humanist ideals is Estêvão Cavaleiro's *Nova grammatices Mariae matris Dei Virginis ars* (*New Art of Grammar of Mary, the Virgin Mother of God*, 1516), which rejects traditional teaching and aligns itself with the new Latinity of Lorenzo Valla and Antonio de Nebrija (see Part 1 in this chapter). André de Resende's *Erasmi encomium* (*Praise of Erasmus*, 1531) is a landmark in the defense of the humanist ideals followed by a younger generation of intellectuals (Sauvage 1971; Martins 1973), and significant, too, are the university and occasional speeches delivered by scholars such as Cataldo, Resende, and Pedro Perpinhão (*Orationes*, 1587). There are only a few echoes in Portugal of the heated—in other parts of Europe—debate about the stylistic ideal of Ciceronianism, but some references to it can be found in Cleynaerts's correspondence written in Portugal. In fact, Portuguese authors tended to align themselves with the ideals of eclectic *imitatio* (Torres 1982a).

If it is true that Portuguese intellectuals relied mainly on the foreign book market and did not produce philological editions (Osório 1975–1976), there is evidence of interest in this type of activity elsewhere, in prefatory texts, historiographical works (especially Resende's *De antiquitatibus Lusitaniae* [*On the Antiquities of Portugal*], 1593), and in the personal correspondence of humanists. Overseas, Aquiles Estaço distinguished himself as an accomplished poet, but also as the editor of Horace, Catullus, Cicero, Tibullus, and Suetonius. There were, however, numerous Neo-Latin commentaries; for instance, on Quintilian (António Pinheiro, 1538); Pliny the Elder (Martim de Figueiredo, 1529); Hippocrates, Galen, and Dioscorides (by the Jew João Rodrigues de Castelo-Branco, known as "Amatus Lusitanus"; Andrade, Torrão, and Costa 2013); and the influential corpus of commentaries on Aristotle by a number of scholars from the University of Coimbra between 1592 and 1606. The works of Tomé Correia, who developed his career abroad, are the best example of the contribution of Portuguese Neo-Latinists in the field of poetics: *De poematis genere quod epigramma vulgo dicitur* (*The Genre of Poetry Usually Called Epigram*, 1569) and *De antiquitate, dignitateque poesis et poetarum differentia* (*The Antiquity and Dignity of Poetry and the Difference Between Poets*, 1586).

Portuguese theologians were among the most widely read in Europe: Gaspar do Casal, Francisco Foreiro, Jerónimo de Azambuja, Bartolomeu dos Mártires, and Diogo Paiva de Andrade attended the Council of Trent (1545–1563) and actively contributed to the fight against heresy—which often meant Protestantism and Erasmianism combined (Fouto, forthcoming). The most prominent theologian *cum* scholar of this time, however, was Jerónimo Osório, who gained a reputation with his critique of Machiavelli's condemnation of the church (*De nobilitate civili et Christiana* [*Civil and Christian Nobility*], 1542), and later contended with the English lawyer and humanist Walter Haddon on the subject of the restoration of Catholic faith in England (*De religione* [*On Religion*], 1567).

Portuguese Neo-Latinists also attracted the attention of the European public in a different domain: contemporary historiography. Livy proved to be the principal model for these writers. While the Portuguese were eager to show the world the extent of their achievements overseas (royal commissions were frequent), the European audience was avid for information on unknown, distant and exotic places, peoples, and customs. André de Resende published his *Epitome rerum gestarum in India a Lusitanis* (*Summary of the Deeds of the Portuguese in India*, 1530) in Leuven; and Damião de Góis (Hirsch 1967; Torres 1982b) followed in his footsteps with *Commentarii rerum gestarum in India citra Gangem a Lusitanis anno 1538* (*Notes on the Deeds of the Portuguese in India on This Side of the Ganges*, 1539); *Fides, religio moresque Aethiopum* (*Faith, Religion, and Customs of the Ethiopians*, 1540); and *Deploratio Lappianae gentis* (*Lament over the Lapps*, 1540). Jerónimo Osório was later commissioned to translate Góis's vernacular account of the reign of King Emmanuel: his monumental *De rebus Emmanuelis regis Lusitaniae . . . gestis* (*The Deeds of Emmanuel, King of Portugal*) appeared in 1572. The development of history as an autonomous discipline in this period was consolidated by the honing of philological and critical approaches to sources, as is illustrated, for instance, by the works of André Resende and Jan Was.

Attention was also given to the writing of cultural and literary history. The eight volumes of the *Corpus illustrium poetarum Lusitanorum qui Latine scripserunt* (*Corpus of Famous Portuguese Poets Who Wrote in Latin*, abbreviated *CIPL*, 1745–1748), compiled by António dos Reis and Manuel Monteiro, constitute the best example of this. We should note that a significant part of the body of Neo-Latin poetry composed in Portugal circulated only in manuscript (as did vernacular poetry), and it is thanks to works such as *CIPL* (and the vernacular *Bibliotheca Lusitana* [*Portuguese Library*] by Diogo Barbosa Machado, 1741–1758) that it is now possible to present an overview of Neo-Latin literature in Portugal. The small number of printed editions of lyric poetry does not imply a lack of creative impulse or the existence of a limited national readership with insufficient command of the language: in 1579–1580, the poet Pedro Sanches dedicated to another Neo-Latinist, Inácio de Morais, an epistle known as *Carmen de poetis Lusitanis* (*Poem on Portuguese Poets*), which documents the variety of genres cultivated at the time and celebrates the poetic achievements of approximately fifty sixteenth-century Neo-Latinists. Their writings show the reading and assimilation of classical and early Christian authors (Horace, Virgil, Ovid, Statius, Seneca, Cicero, Plutarch, Juvenal, Martial, Catullus, Prudentius, and Claudian) as well as contemporary writers (particularly Poliziano, Sannazaro, Mantuan, Angeriano, Erasmus, and Vida). Among the best examples of the sophistication and variety of the lyric poetry composed in this period are the works of Portuguese writers living abroad, like Aquiles Estaço (*Silvae* [here ~ *Poetic Miscellany*], 1549), Henrique Caiado (*Aeglogae et silvae et epigrammata* [*Eclogues, Silvae, and Epigrams*], 1501), and Diogo Pires (*Carmina* [*Poems*], 1545; André 1992). Among other equally accomplished writers who returned to their homeland, and whose poetry was printed, were André de Resende (e.g., *De vita aulica* [*Life at Court*], 1533), Diogo de Teive (*Epodes*, 1565), and Jerónimo Cardoso (*Elegies*, 1563). A significant part of the lyric corpus is made up by occasional poetry, but there are equally excellent examples of satire, for instance Aires Barbosa's *Antimoria* (*Anti-Folly*, 1536), which engages directly with Erasmus's *Praise of Folly*; didactic and moral poetry such as Diogo Pires's *Cato Minor* (1592; Andrade 2005); and religious poetry: Prudentius, for instance, served as a model for both Resende's *Vincentius Levita et martyr* (*Vincent the Deacon and Martyr*, 1545), with a commentary by the author, and for Teive's vast collection of hymns (Book 2 of his *Epodes*), a good example of lyric production in Tridentine Portugal.

Religious themes were also recast in epic poems (Urbano 2005), as in Jorge Coelho's allegorical *De Patientia Christiana* (*Christian Patience*, 1540), and a number of epics inspired by Marco Girolamo Vida concern the lives of important members of the Jesuit order, including António Durão's *Ignatias* (1635) on Ignatius of Loyola, and Bartolomeu Pereira's *Paciecis* (1640) on the Portuguese Jesuit Francisco Pacheco. Contemporary historical events were equally celebrated in epic poems: Cataldo had inaugurated Portuguese epic in about 1490 with his *Arcitinge* on the Portuguese conquests, in 1471, of Arzila and Tanger in modern-day Morocco; he was followed by Diogo Paiva de Andrade, whose *Chauleis* (1628) commemorates the victory in the siege of the Indian fortress of Chaul in 1593. Yet another epic, José de Anchieta's *De gestis Mendi de Saa* (*The Deeds of Mem de Sá*, 1563), represents the war among European imperial powers against the backdrop of the exotic Brazilian landscape (Mem de Sá was a governor general of Portuguese Brazil). In the seventeenth century, at the time of the Dual Monarchy, Camões's vernacular epic poem *Os Lusíadas* (*The Lusiads*, i.e., The Portuguese) was translated into Latin Virgilian hexameters, first by Tomé de Faria (1622), and then by André Baião (1625).

Neo-Latin drama also flourished in Portugal within the educational system. Seneca was by far the most influential model, and although Latin translations of Euripides were available, it seems that his work left no discernible mark. The Colégio das Artes was the cradle of a vibrant Neo-Latin tradition, and even the vernacular tragedy *Castro* by one of its distinguished pupils, António Ferreira (1528–1569), was deeply influenced by classical and humanist theater. Teive's biblical plays *David* and *Iudith* (now lost) were celebrated, and his *Ioannes Princeps* (1554) about João Manuel, Prince of Portugal, is a rare example of tragedy commemorating a *contemporary* historical subject. Though written in Latin, the themes of Jesuit school plays were nothing like classical drama: lengthy and requiring big casts, they combined spectacle and a good deal of moralizing. Among the best Jesuit playwrights active in Portugal were Luís da Cruz, who wrote, for instance, *Sedecias* (1570) on the Jewish King Zedekiah, and the Spaniard Miguel Venegas, who wrote *Saul* (1559). A preference for contemporary subjects developed greatly in the seventeenth century, and often religious, mythological, and historical themes offered the possibility of commenting on contemporary political affairs: Lucas Pereira's dramatic eclogue *Geryon* (performed in Coimbra 1612) recasts the Portuguese struggle for independence in a conflict opposing Hercules and the oppressor Geryon; after independence had been regained, *Eduardus* (1650?) by Diogo Paiva de Andrade openly mourns the death of the brother of the new Portuguese king, John IV, in prison under the orders of the Spanish king, Philip IV.

With regard to prose writing, philosophical and moral dialogue was particularly favored by humanists, and Portugal is no exception: Osório's works such as *De gloria* (*On Glory*, 1549) were widely read, and the *Duarum virginum colloquium de vita aulica et privata* (*Colloquy of Two Virgins Concerning Courtly and Private Life*, 1552) was signed by one of the most accomplished female Neo-Latin writers, Luisa Sigea, who had earlier gained fame with the poem *Sintra* on the place of that name near Lisbon (posthumously published in 1566). The *De platano* (*The Plane Tree*, 1527) by João Rodrigues de Sá de Meneses intersperses the apology of humanist ideals with an erudite discussion on this type of tree. Letters were, of course, a privileged means of communication and are of great significance for the study of the cultural, intellectual, and scholarly debates among the Portuguese elite. The prose letters of Damião de Góis and Cleynaerts offer a unique insight into the everyday life of these intellectuals. A quite different, yet fine example of baroque Neo-Latin can be seen in the prophetic work of the Jesuit António Vieira: his treatise *Clavis prophetarum* (*The Key of the Prophets*, left incomplete due to the author's death in 1697) is influenced by millenarianism, and was written at a time when the use of Latin was in sharp decline.

In the eighteenth century, the use of Latin was virtually nonexistent outside academia: the didactic poems *De sacchari opificio* (*The Production of Sugar*) by Prudêncio do Amaral and *De rusticis Brasiliae rebus* (*Brazilian Agriculture*), by José Rodrigues de Melo's (published together in Rome 1781), are good examples of the final flourish of Neo-Latin, a last testimony to its potential to constantly adapt itself to new realities. In this respect, Iberian intellectuals were the first responsible for its expansion at a truly global scale.

SUGGESTED READING

Spain: Some material in this part is based on Coroleu (2014). Generally on Neo-Latin in Spain, see Moralejo (1980). Alcina Rovira (2000) provides a comprehensive catalog of poetry in the sixteenth and seventeenth centuries; for the influence of the Neo-Latin movement on the native Latin tradition, Gómez Moreno (1994); for the Latin output of humanists connected to the circle of Alcañiz and to other territories within the Crown of Aragon in the sixteenth century, Maestre Maestre (1990). On Montano and the Library of El Escorial, see Rekers (1972); for the project of the Complutensian Polyglot Bible, Sáenz-Badillos (1990); for the evolution of Neo-Latin literature in the Catalan-speaking lands in the fifteenth century, Vilallonga (1993). On Latin texts related to the enterprise of the Indies, see Pagden (1986); on the role of Latin in eighteenth-century Spain, Coroleu (2005). The reader will find specific studies on Neo-Latin in sixteenth-century Spain in the proceedings of the Alcañiz colloquia "Humanismo y pervivencia del mundo clásico," and specialist journals, such as *Calamus Renascens, Euphrosyne, Faventia,* and *Veleia.*

Portugal: HISLAMPA and Martins (1986) contain essential bio-bibliographical information on Iberian Neo-Latinists. Surveys of Neo-Latin in Portugal can be found in Albuquerque (1984); Aubin (2006); *Congresso internacional* (2002); and Tannus (2007). On Ciceronianism, see Torres (1982a); on poetics and rhetoric, Castro (1984). Neo-Latin drama is discussed in detail in Frèches (1964) and Pinho (2006). Matos (1991) offers comprehensive analysis of historiography. A brief survey of lyric poetry is Briesemeister (1980). There is no systematic study of Portuguese Neo-Latin prose or epic and lyric poetry: the reader will find specific studies in collections of essays (e.g., Ramalho (1988–1998), proceedings of international colloquia, critical editions, monographs devoted to specific authors, and specialist journals, such as *Humanitas, Euphrosyne, Arquivos do Centro Cultural Português, Ágora, Clássica-Revista Brasileira de Estudos Clássicos,* and *Calíope-Presença Clássica.*

References

Alcina Rovira, Juan F. 2000. "Poesía neolatina y literatura española en los siglos XVI y XVII." In *ACNL* 2000, 9–28.

Albuquerque, Luís de, ed. 1984. *L'Humanisme Portugais et l'Europe.* Paris: Fondation Calouste Gulbenkian; Centre Culturel Portugais.

Andrade, António. 2005. "O *Cato Minor* de Diogo Pires e a poesia didáctica do século XVI." Ph.D. diss., University of Aveiro.

Andrade, António, João Torrão, and Jorge Costa, eds. 2013. *Humanismo, Diáspora e Ciência (séculos XVI e XVII)—Estudos, Catálogo, Exposição.* Oporto: Biblioteca Pública Municipal do Porto and Universidade de Aveiro.

André, Carlos. 1992. *Mal de ausência: O canto do exílio na lírica novilatina portuguesa do século XVI.* Lisbon: Minerva.

Asensio, Eugenio, and Juan F. Alcina Rovira. 1980. *Paraenesis ad litteras: Juan Maldonado y el humanismo español en tiempos de Carlos V.* Madrid: Fundacíon Universitaria Española.

Aubin, Jean. 2006. *Le latin et l'astrolabe.* Vol. 3, *Études inédites sur le règne de D. Manuel I—1495-1521.* Paris: Fondation Calouste Gulbenkian; Centre Culturel Portugais.

Brandão, Mário. 1948–1969. *A Inquisição e os Professores do Colégio das Artes.* 2 vols. Coimbra: Oficinas da Atlântida.

Briesemeister, Dietrich. 1980. "Sur les origines de la poésie néolatine au Portugal dans la première moitié du XVIe siècle." *Roczniki Humanistyczne* 26:45–61.

Castro, Aníbal P. de. 1973. *Retórica e teorização literária em Portugal: Do humanismo ao neoclassicismo.* Coimbra: Centro de Estudos Românticos.

Congresso internacional do humanismo português. 2002. Lisbon: Centro de Estudos Clássicos.

Coroleu, Alejandro. 2001. "Poliziano in Print: Editions and Commentaries from a Pedagogical Perspective (1500–1560)." *Cahiers de l'Humanisme* 2:191–222.

———. 2005. "Latinity, Literary History and Cultural Prestige in Eighteenth-Century Spain." In *The Role of Latin in Early Modern Europe: Texts and Contexts II*, edited by Gerhard Petersmann and Veronika Oberparleiter, 132–43. Salzburg: Berger und Söhne.

———. 2014. "Neo-Latin Literature – Spain: The Long Sixteenth Century." In *ENLW* 2:1112–14.

Da Silva Dias, José S. 1969. *A política cultural da época de D. João III*. 2 vols. Coimbra: Universidade de Coimbra.

Earle, Thomas F. 2009. *Portuguese Writers and English Readers: Books by Portuguese Writers Printed Before 1640 in the Libraries of Oxford and Cambridge*. Oxford: Oxford Bibliographical Society.

Enenkel, Karl A. E., and Maria Berbara. 2011. *Portuguese Humanism and the Republic of Letters*. Leiden: Brill.

Fouto, Catarina B. Forthcoming. "Antierasmismo." In *Dicionário dos Antis: A Cultura Portuguesa em Negativo*, edited by José Eduardo Franco. Lisbon: Imprensa Nacional; Casa da Moeda.

Frèches, Claude-Henri. 1964. *Le théâtre neo-latin au Portugal (1550–1745)*. Paris: Nizet.

Gómez, Jesús. 1988. *El diálogo en el Renacimiento español*. Madrid: Cátedra.

Gómez Moreno, Angel. 1994. *España y la Italia de los humanistas: primeros ecos*. Madrid: Gredos.

Hirsch, Elisabeth. 1967. *Damião de Góis: The Life and Thought of a Portuguese Humanist*. The Hague: Nijhoff.

HISLAMPA: Hispanorum Index Scriptorum Latinorum Medii Posteriorisque Aevi. 1993. Lisbon: Imprensa Nacional; Casa da Moeda.

Laird, Andrew. 2002. "Juan Luis de La Cerda, Virgil, and the Predicament of Commentary." In *The Classical Commentary: History, Practices, Theory*, edited by Roy K. Gibson and Christina S. Kraus, 171–203. Leiden: Brill.

Maestre Maestre, José M. 1990. *El humanismo alcañizano del siglo XVI: Textos y estudios de latín renacentista*. Cádiz: Servicio de Publicationes, Universidad de Cádiz.

Martins, Isaltina das Dores F. 1986. *Bibliografia do Humanismo en Portugal no Século XVI*. Coimbra: Instituto Nacional de Investigação Científica.

Martins, José V. de P. 1973. *Humanismo e Erasmismo na cultura portuguesa do século XVI*. Paris: Fondation Calouste Gulbenkian; Centre Culturel Portugais.

———. 1989. *Humanisme et Renaissance de l'Italie au Portugal: Les deux regards de Janus*. Lisbon: Fundação Calouste Gulbenkian.

Matos, Luís de. 1991. *L'Expansion Portugaise dans la littérature latine de la Renaissance*. Lisbon: Fundação Calouste Gulbenkian.

Moralejo, José Luis. 1980. "Literatura Hispano-Latina." In *Historia de las literaturas hispánicas no castellanas*, edited by José M. Díez Borque, 94–137. Madrid: Taurus.

Osório, Jorge A. 1975–1976. "Crítica e Humanismo no Renacimento." *Humanitas* 27–28:23–52.

Pagden, Anthony. 1986. *The Fall of Natural Man: The American Indian and the Origins of Comparative Ethnology*. Cambridge: Cambridge University Press.

Picón, Vicente, ed. 2007. *Teatro escolar latino del siglo XVI: La obra de Pedro Pablo Acevedo S.I.* 2 vols. Madrid: UAM Ediciones.

Pinho, Sebastião T. de, ed. 2006. *O Teatro neolatino em Portugal, no contexto da Europa*. Coimbra: Imprensa da Universidade de Coimbra.

Ramalho, Américo da C. 1988. "Literatura Novilatina em Portugal entre 1485 e 1537." In *Congresso internacional: As humanidades greco-latinas e a civilização do universal*, 171–80. Coimbra: Instituto de Estudos Clássicos.

Ramalho, Américo da C. 1988–1998. *Para a História do Humanismo em Portugal*. 2 vols. Coimbra: Instituto Nacional de Investigação Científica.

Rekers, Bernard 1972. *Benito Arias Montano, 1527–1598*, London: Warburg Institute.

Rico, Francisco. 1978. *Nebrija frente a los bárbaros: El canon de gramáticos nefastos en las polémicas del humanismo*. Salamanca: Universidad de Salamanca.

———. 2002. *El sueño del Humanismo: De Petrarca a Erasmo*. Barcelona: Destino.

Rodrigues, Manuel A. 1981. "Do humanismo à Contra-reforma em Portugal." *Revista de Historia das Ideias* 6:125–76.

Rummel, Erika. 1988. *Erasmus and His Catholic Critics*. Nieuwkoop: De Graaf.

Sáenz-Badillos, Ángel. 1990. *La filología bíblica en los primeros helenistas de Alcalá*. Estella: Verbo Divino.

Sauvage, Odette. 1971. *L'Itinéraire érasmien d'André de Resende: 1500–1573*. Paris: Fondation Calouste Gulbenkian; Centre Culturel Portugais.

Tannus, Carlos A. K. 2007. "Um olhar sobre a literatura novilatina em Portugal." *Calíope: Presença Clássica* 16:13–31.

Tate, Robert B. 1996. "The Rewriting of the Historical Past: *Hispania et Europa*." In *Historical Literature in Medieval Iberia*, edited by Alan Deyermond, 85–103. London: Queen Mary and Westfield College.

Torres, Amadeu. 1982a. "Damião de Góis e o pensamento renascentista: Do ciceronianismo ao eclectismo." *Arquivos do Centro Cultural Português* 17:3–40.

———. 1982b. *Noese e crise na epistolografia Latina goisiana*. Paris: Fondation Calouste Gulbenkian; Centre Culturel Portugais.

Urbano, Carlota M. 2005. "Epopeia novilatina e hagiografia: alguns exemplos em Portugal." *Humanitas* 57:383–402.

Vilallonga, Mariàngela. 1993. *La literatura llatina a Catalunya al segle XV*. Barcelona: Curial Ed. Catalanes.

....

CHAPTER 30

THE LOW COUNTRIES

....

DIRK SACRÉ

In this chapter, I will first trace the historical outlines of humanism in the Low Countries and then survey several genres of Neo-Latin writing. It should be kept in mind that "Low Countries" is a convenient term comprising today's Netherlands, Belgium, and Luxembourg, but they did not overlap precisely with this area during the medieval and early modern periods. In the fifteenth century, most of the region discussed in this chapter was under Burgundian rule. The Burgundian Netherlands became the Habsburg Netherlands when Duchess Mary of Burgundy, married to Maximilian I of Austria, died in 1482. After 1556, when Philip II acceded to the Spanish throne, the territories were called the "Spanish Netherlands." The revolt of the Northern parts (roughly today's Netherlands) against Spain led to the Republic of the Seven United Provinces (1581). The Southern parts remained under Habsburg rule, suffering territorial losses in the European wars, mainly to France. Thus, in the second half of the seventeenth century, cities like Arras, Lille, Cambrai, Saint-Omer, Béthune, Bailleul, Valenciennes, and the university city of Douai (1667) became French; culturally, however, many of these regions remained strongly linked with Flanders. In humanist Latin, "Belgium" was the most common name for the Low Countries. In my own account, I use "Netherlands" sometimes synonymously with "Low Countries" (which is literally "Nether-Lands").

HUMANISM IN THE LOW COUNTRIES

....

The Low Countries entered into contact with Italian Renaissance humanism early on, mainly through the initiative of a few individuals and initially without far-reaching or long-lasting consequences (generally, see IJsewijn 1975; Tournoy 2007; Heesakkers et al. 2008). This situation changed in the fifteenth century. The Brethren of the Common Life (in whose schools the young Erasmus received his first education) improved the quality of their Latin teaching by focusing to a greater extent on the precise understanding of texts and acquainting themselves with new manuals from Italy; under their influence, the Latin schools increasingly thrived in both the North and the South. Among the moneyed Italian families in Bruges, we find individuals collecting classical texts and maintaining contact with Italian humanists: Carlo Gigli, for instance, was an acquaintance of Enea Silvio Piccolomini's (1405–1464), who would become Pope Pius II. In 1425, the region's first university was founded, in Leuven. The new university attracted a number of wandering Italian scholars looking for professorial posts, who for their part developed the new ideals in their new environment. A prominent student from the early years of Leuven University was Rudolphus Agricola (1444–1485; Kühlmann 1994), from Baflo near Groningen; according to Erasmus, the first person to have brought a breath of better literature from Italy to the Netherlands. His treatise *De inventione dialectica* (*On Dialectical Invention*, 1479), combining rhetoric and dialectic and rejecting scholastic logic, was an epochal work that was reissued time and again. A number of Christian schools and institutions followed suit. From the 1450s on, for instance, humanist manuscripts were eagerly collected in the abbey of Park, near Leuven. It was here that Erasmus, in 1504, discovered Lorenzo Valla's *Adnotationes in Novum Testamentum* (*Notes on the New Testament*, final redaction in the 1450s). Erasmus published these *Notes*, which applied textual criticism to the New Testament, a year later. Moreover, printing shops like Rodolphus Loeffs's and Dirk Martens's started to spread the works of Italian humanists and to make their new teaching manuals available.

Under the influence of Erasmus and the enthusiastic friends and confrères of his youth, things developed even more rapidly. The Rotterdam humanist (Enenkel 2010, with further literature) devoted his life to the task of popularizing Latin and Greek literature: after the example of the Italian humanists, he broadened the hitherto-narrow canon of authors studied to embrace all pagan and Christian writers from antiquity; made the texts of Cicero, Seneca, Jerome, Cyprian, Lactantius, and many others available in better editions with helpful annotations; and translated Greek authors such as Euripides, Lucian, and Plutarch into Latin. Erasmus, an advocate of Christian humanism, had an ultimate goal to make people better: that is, to help them live a better Christian life. For that they needed a sound knowledge of the ancient masters of wisdom, both pagan and Christian. Not surprisingly, then, Erasmus saw it as his task to approach the patristic authors and the Bible in the same way as he dealt with pagan authors. In that spirit he issued his *Novum Instrumentum* (*New Instrument*, 1516), a groundbreaking edition of the New Testament that was encouraged by the critical attitude Valla had displayed towards the Vulgate.

At the same time, Erasmus supplied his contemporaries with tools that enabled them to compete with the best writers and scholars abroad. His educational program led him to compose such works as the *Adagia* (*Proverbs*, first printed in 1500, later expanded several times), a collection of more than four thousand proverbial Greek and Latin expressions with commentaries, and such innovative and popular treatises as *De ratione studii* (*Method of Study*, 1511), *De duplici copia verborum et rerum* (*Copiousness in Both Words and Thoughts*, 1512), and *De conscribendis epistolis* (*Letter Writing*, 1522). He wrote the immensely popular *Colloquia familiaria* (*Familiar Colloquies*, 1518) as a manual of elegant Latin speech for every occasion, and published a summary of Valla's

Elegantiae linguae Latinae (*Elegances of the Latin Language*, written in the 1440s), one of the bibles of humanism. Erasmus's writings were meant for a wider audience, not just for an exclusive inner circle of specialists or young schoolboys; hence, he turned almost everything he wrote into a piece of literature, composed in an elegant, compelling, often witty style, free of the restraints of strict Ciceronianism as represented in Italy, for instance, by Pietro Bembo. Erasmus even derided the inappropriate, anachronistic endeavors of purist Ciceronians in his satirical dialogue *Ciceronianus* (*The Ciceronian*, 1528). He peppered his writings with polemical stabs at scholastic writing, as well as at uncritical interpretations of the ancients and *idées reçues* that could not stand the test of criticism. This led to conflicts with traditionalists in theology and other fields, which demanded much of his time, especially in his later years, but which also attracted the world's attention to his character and ideas and helped him become the major intellectual figure of his age. Through his extraordinarily wide network, and thanks to his literary talent, Erasmus would spread his ideas across Europe. In the Netherlands, the Collegium Trilingue ("trilingual college," 1518), an institution rather loosely connected to Leuven University, which implemented Erasmus's ideals, attracted large numbers of students until the end of the century (De Vocht 1951–1955). From Leuven the humanist movement rapidly spread throughout the Low Countries. Humanist centers developed in Bruges and in the region of Artois in the South, and, in the North, in Zeeland, Amsterdam, and elsewhere.

The rise of the Protestant Reformation and the ensuing religious conflicts deeply affected the country and had an impact on its culture, hence also on humanism and Latin literature. The gradual split into two camps sometimes forced humanists into the role of spokesman for one or the other: one thinks of the pressure exerted by Pope Leo X (r. 1513–1521) on Erasmus, urging him to write against Luther, or later, by Paul V (r. 1605–1621) on Lipsius, in both cases with a view to putting their knowledge at the service of the "good" (Roman Catholic) cause. The Spanish monarchy's intolerance of Protestants (and the burden of taxation it imposed on the Low Countries) led to a major rebellion against the Spanish king and thus to armed hostilities afflicting the region from the 1560s onwards; in the end, the Spanish re-established their control over the Southern Netherlands, imposed the Catholic religion, and repressed dissidents. The so-called fall of Antwerp in 1585 marked this Spanish reconquest of the South and the de facto independence of the Northern provinces, which would rapidly and almost completely adopt Protestantism. In the South, the economic crisis and the end of religious tolerance led to a genuine brain drain, mostly towards the North, where the Seven United Provinces were moving towards the golden age of their economic, intellectual, literary, and artistic life. In the Spanish South, typically humanist activities lost ground to a rather narrower vision of Latin scholarship and creativity. After the official independence of the North (1648), the cultural gap between the North and the South would become more and more striking; in the field of post-humanist scholarship and Neo-Latin literature, the South would be definitively surpassed by the North.

During the troubles of the second half of the sixteenth century, both confessional camps reinforced their positions with their own intellectual strongholds. In the South, the Spanish king had a second Catholic university founded at Douai (1562), which was run in part by the Jesuits; the new university attracted students coming mainly from the francophone parts of the country and from West Flanders, but there was also a colony of English and French youth. In the field of humanist studies, Douai remained a somewhat peripheral establishment with limited importance, except for the years from 1593 to 1635, when the chair of Latin and Greek was occupied by the Bruges humanist Andreas Hoius, an admirer of Justus Lipsius, a poet, dramatist, historian, and accomplished philologist (Sacré 1993). In the North, Janus Dousa (1545–1604), who had studied in Leuven and Paris and was an eminent Latin poet, an historian, and a good friend of Justus Lipsius's, was the pivotal figure in the effort to found a new university for the Reformed population. Established in Leiden in 1575, it could boast eminent professors attracted from the South, from France, and from Germany, including Justus Lipsius (1547–1606), Bonaventura Vulcanius (1538–1614), Joseph Scaliger (1540–1609), and Daniel Heinsius (1580–1655). Oriental studies, which would become one of the glories of Leiden, were initiated with Franciscus Raphelengius (1539–1597), who taught Hebrew and prepared a *Lexicon Arabicum* (*Arabic Dictionary*, 1613).

From the last decades of the sixteenth century on, Justus Lipsius dominated the scene, just as Erasmus had prevailed in the first half of the century (Morford 1991). Lipsius was a brilliant classicist and also issued a few productions of creative literature, such as his *Satyra Menippea: Somnium* (*The Dream: A Menippean Satire*, 1581), mocking incautious textual criticism. As was not unusual at the time, many of his antiquarian studies or commentaries aimed to bridge the gap between the ancients and the moderns: thus his *De militia Romana* (*The Roman Military*, 1595; a commentary on Polybius) was conceived as a manual of early modern warfare. Lipsius was moreover an outstanding connoisseur of ancient philosophy, especially of Stoicism, and wrote some philosophical works of his own, in which he tried to reconcile pagan and Christian wisdom and to deploy it for his own times, most successfully in his *De Constantia* (*On Constancy*, 1584; Papy 2004). In the same vein, his *Politica* (*Politics*, 1589), a very influential but also controversial work, in which he drew his materials from ancient and modern sources such as Machiavelli, was meant as a kind of "mirror for princes" for his suffering country, in which he also dealt with the tricky question of the relationship between state and religion. As a stylist (Deneire 2012), Lipsius had a remarkable impact: like Erasmus, he adopted an un-Ciceronian, eclectic style, combining features taken from pre-classical and post-classical authors, especially Seneca and Tacitus, and later writers, too; and he strove for a pointed, sharp style and a pregnant, often surprising or even puzzling, brevity. For at least half a century, this peculiar Lipsian style had its admirers and followers, but also its severe critics; for instance, among the Jesuits, who were more in favor of a moderately Ciceronian style. Lipsius's occasional verse, though not the work of a truly inspired poet, was nevertheless read and imitated during his lifetime and afterwards, so that we find many a Neo-Latin poet in the Low Countries adopting his archaic or post-classical lexicon, and *recherché* metrical features.

Though Leiden remained the intellectual center of the Northern Netherlands until the end of the period we are dealing with, it was soon flanked by a number of outstanding Latin schools, some of which were promoted to the rank of university by the local authorities, thus strengthening the scholarly and literary impetus given by the nucleus at Leiden. Whereas no new universities were founded in the South between 1562 and the nineteenth century, a fair number of institutions were established in the North, such as the Universities of Franeker (1595), Groningen (1614), and Utrecht (1636), and the semi-universities or "Athenaea" at, for instance, Harderwijk (1599) and Amsterdam (1632).

In the South, Leuven remained an important center of humanism and Neo-Latin literature, but gradually the intellectual center shifted to Antwerp, where many renowned printers were at work, among them Christophe Plantin (ca. 1520–1589) and his heirs, whose beautiful editions made the Plantin press the most prestigious printing and publishing house of the Netherlands during the last quarter of the sixteenth and the first decades of the seventeenth century. Its manager in this period, Balthasar Moretus (1574–1641), a former pupil of Lipsius, collaborated with artists such as Peter Paul Rubens for the illustration of his editions. The Plantin family acted as printers to the Catholic world (though Plantin had a branch office in Leiden for some years) and collaborated with the Jesuits. Antwerp was also home to the omnipresent Jesuit order, which soon came to dominate educational and literary fields. During the seventeenth century, the main scholarly project undertaken in the South was in fact launched by the Antwerp Jesuits: the *Acta Sanctorum (Deeds of the Saints)*, the famous scholarly edition of the Saints' lives, whose first volumes were published by Jean Bolland (1596–1665). The project was continued for more than three hundred years by the so-called Bollandists, and supplements are being published to this day (Peeters 1961).

In the new climate prevailing in the Southern Netherlands, scholarship dealing with the major heathen authors of antiquity declined in importance. In the North, in contrast, humanism and Neo-Latin literature continued to prosper, albeit with some ups and downs, until the end of the eighteenth, although the impact of humanist and Latin culture on society diminished gradually. The Northern Low Countries had their own important publishing houses now, which were also centers of learning, such as Blaeu's and the Elzeviers' at Amsterdam. The importance of Northern humanism, as opposed to the stagnation in the South, became apparent in the work of such pivotal figures as Hugo Grotius (1583–1645), Gerardus Joannes Vossius (1577–1649), Daniel Heinsius with his son Nicolaus (1620–1681), and Petrus Scriverius (1576–1660). All these humanists had very large networks of contacts, and some of them published their selected correspondences.

Drama

Neo-Latin drama in the Low Countries began to flourish in the Latin schools of such cities as Ghent and Bruges in the South, and Utrecht and Amsterdam in the North (Bloemendal 2013a; IJsewijn 1981); moreover, it was promoted at university, particularly at the Faculty of Arts in Leuven and in Douai. In the North, where the first university in Leiden was only founded in 1575, Latin drama does not seem to have enjoyed great popularity as part of academic life, but playwrights active around Leiden University would revitalize drama in the Senecan vein—among them Heinsius and Grotius. Contrary to some other countries, no courtly theater in Latin developed in the Low Countries. The pedagogical and moral potential of dramatic texts and performances was soon recognized by the religious orders involved in the education of youth, such as the Oratorians, Augustinians, and Jesuits. The Society of Jesus was an especially fervent defender of Latin drama as a means of increasing the linguistic skills of pupils, endowing them with moral and religious lessons, and teaching them to perform in public (Proot 2007). Dramatic performances had started on a modest scale during the last quarter of the fifteenth century, almost simultaneously with their establishment in Germany. After a first phase, in which Roman comedy was adapted for the stage, soon a good number of original comedies were written. From the 1550s on, original tragedies would follow. A good and early example of a comedy is the *Vinctus* (*Bound*, 1522) of Petrus Nannius, who became a professor at Leuven's Collegium Trilingue but wrote this piece, a prose comedy written in a Plautine style, while he was still teaching in Gouda. Macropedius's *Aluta* (1535) staged the eponymous protagonist, a drunken country woman depicted in Plautine language: such village farces enjoyed a definite popularity. The Plautine and Terentian tradition was continued far into the seventeenth century, as the Jesuit Martin du Cygne's *Comoediae XII phrasi cum Plautina tum Terentiana concinnatae* (*Twelve Comedies Made in Plautine and Terentian Language*, 1679) demonstrate. However, the free atmosphere and loose morality (not infrequently, scenes were situated in brothels) of the early sixteenth century gradually disappeared during the second half of the century, as the atmosphere became more austere and decorous moral conduct was increasingly stressed. Gradually, biblical themes (and, less commonly, classical figures or modern themes) were introduced. Several authors wrote, for instance, about the biblical story of the Prodigal Son, such as, in The Hague, Gnapheus with *Acolastus* (*The Licentious One*, 1529) and, in 's-Hertogenbosch, Macropedius with *Asotus* (*The Lost One*, staged ca. 1507).

A number of plays explored serious issues with contemporary relevance. From the later sixteenth century onwards, the reader can observe the confessional stands of the playwrights, either Catholics such as Cornelius Schonaeus and Georgius Macropedius in the North or the Jesuits in the South, or Reformed authors such as Gulielmus Gnapheus. Some authors would even rewrite their plays after having shifted camp, such as Jacob van Zevecote, an Augustinian friar from Ghent who finished his career as a teacher in Harderwijk in the North. Furthermore, the revolt in the Netherlands inspired historical drama: thus Daniel Heinsius's famous tragedy *Auriacus sive Libertas saucia* (*Orange; or, Liberty Wounded*, 1602) deals with the murder of the Prince of Orange (1584) and the latter's opposition to the Spanish king, from an undoubtedly biased point of view. In the South, local saints and the martyrs of the Catholic Church would be put onstage. The Luxembourger Nicolaus Vernulaeus (1583–1649), a professor at Leuven University and an internationally renowned dramatist, for instance, wrote several such dramas, though he also issued a tragedy on Henry VIII; an anonymous drama entitled *Sanctus Martyr Thomas Morus* (*The Saint and Martyr Thomas More*) is preserved in the library of Arras (MS 174).

There is good reason to assume that plays in the vernacular—especially the Dutch ones produced in many cities by the "rhetoricians' chambers" (*rederijkerskamers*)—and those in Latin influenced each other (Bloemendal 2013b). Themes regularly treated in the vernacular were also staged in Latin. The famous *Everyman* (*Elckerlijc*), for instance, was well received in Latin, with such plays as Macropedius's *Hecastus* (*Everybody*) and *Homulus* (*Little Man*, both 1539). Conversely, *Adam in ballingschap* (*Adam in Exile*, 1664), considered a masterpiece of the most famous Dutch playwright, Joost van den Vondel, was in fact a vernacular adaptation of *Adamus exul* (*Adam in Exile*, 1601), a Latin drama written by Hugo Grotius. Examples of later Latin drama would be the two Joseph tragedies of the Antwerp Jesuit Jacobus Libens (1603–1678), which were included in the well-known anthology *Selectae PP. Societatis Jesu tragoediae* (*Selected Tragedies of Fathers of the Society of Jesus*), published in Antwerp in 1634. Latin drama, however, seems to have died out rapidly after the suppression of the Jesuits in 1773.

POETRY

The focus of this section will be on the two forms of poetry in which the Low Countries excelled, lyric and elegy. Neo-Latin poetry in the Netherlands (Ellinger 1933; Peerlkamp 1838) quickly reached a level comparable to that of the best Latin poets from the neighboring countries and even from Italy. Lyric and elegiac poetry was brought to full perfection relatively early on by a young genius, Johannes Secundus (1511–1536), the son of the President of the Great Council at Mechelen (Schäfer 2004; Murgatroyd 2000; Secundus 1899). Secundus's cycle of *Basia* (*Kisses*), based upon Catullus's Poems 5 and 7 and their Neo-Latin imitations and adaptations, influenced both later Neo-Latin and vernacular poets throughout Europe over almost two centuries. His elegiac cycles, too, and especially his love poems, stand out in their formal impeccability and their inspired approach. Elegy 1.8, for instance, which introduces a rather rare theme, the wedding of the beloved, Julia, to another man, was only superficially inspired by humanist models; Nature and the elements rise in resistance against the wedding, exemplified by the superb final lines (19–20): *Praecipitantur aquae; mare pendet in aere densum; / ignibus excussis dissiluere poli* ("Water is hurled down, in the air hangs a solid sea; / the heavens have been split apart by the thunderbolts thrown"). Johannes Secundus had two brothers who were also gifted poets, Nicolaus Grudius (1504–1570) and Hadrianus Marius (1509–1568), both involved in the posthumous publication of their brother's verse. Together, they were the "three Belgian brothers" (*tres fratres Belgae*), undoubtedly the most famous Latin poets the Netherlands have ever produced (Guépin 2000). But Johannes's influence proved to be especially lasting, both in the vernaculars and in Latin. Representatives of the French Pléiade imitated his poems, just as did Latin poets like

George Buchanan and Marc-Antoine Muret. The same applies to the Bruges poet Janus Lernutius, who in his *Carmina* (*Poems*, 1579) issued a cycle of *Basia* and another one of *Ocelli* (*Little Eyes*). During the seventeenth century, love poetry was hardly compatible with the intellectual climate of the South, and Secundus's influence faded away, but in the North he remained an important model until the end of the eighteenth century. The years from 1575 to 1619 in Leiden have been designated as a period of "Secundomania" (van Dam 2000), with such important poets as Janus Dousa, Bonaventura Vulcanius, Hugo Grotius, and Daniel Heinsius. In fact, one perceives the presence of Secundus as late as the eighteenth century; for instance, in Janus van den Broucke's elegant *Poemata* (*Poems*, 1741).

From the later sixteenth century on, a new stylistic fashion becomes apparent in the Latin poetry of the North, but even more so in the South: under the influence of Justus Lipsius, archaic and post-classical words and uncommon expressions were accumulated in verses stuffed with erudite references. Both in the North, where Janus Dousa, Lipsius's good friend, had adopted these mannerisms, and in the South, some poets reacted against this and returned to the classical models. Daniel Heinsius, for instance, in Leiden, and Nicolas de Bourgogne (1586–1649) in Ghent, are free from the excesses that had surfaced before. Some authors, however, would follow peculiar models: Caspar Barlaeus (1584–1648), who was very famous as an epic poet during his lifetime, formed his rather turgid style after the example of the late-antique poet Claudian; and the famous bilingual poet Constantijn Huygens (1596–1687) developed an unparalleled, but very effective style in his numerous epigrams and other poems, with an often unseen order of the words, lexical and syntactic liberties, and an omnipresent play on words (Huygens 2003).

In the early seventeenth century, many Latin poets were active in the vernacular, too. Humanists like Erycius Puteanus (1574–1646) in the South, and Grotius and Daniel Heinsius in the North wrote Dutch verse as well and developed a Latin-like style in the vernacular, thus giving an impetus to the flowering of poetry in the national language; Heinsius's Dutch poetry also had a tremendous influence on German poetry (Aurnhammer 2008). On the other hand, Latin translations were an important means for vernacular poets to reach an international audience; thus Jacob Cats, one of the most successful Dutch poets of the seventeenth century, dreamt of a simultaneous publication of his Dutch poetry and a Latin translation of it; he himself contributed a Latin version (1644) of a piece from his Dutch *Trou-ringh* (*Wedding Ring*, 1637; Sacré 2009).

In the course of the seventeenth century, and especially in its second half, the Latin cultures of the North and the South seem to have undergone a different evolution, which accounts for a rather sterile Latin poetry in the eighteenth-century South, and a remarkably flourishing Latin Muse in the North; one does not get the impression that there was much interaction between the two parts of the Low Countries. The Southern poets increasingly limited themselves to either religious and devout poetry, or to anagrammatic and other playful types of poems with little substance. Only the Jesuits (but not all of them) seem to have been able to maintain a high artistic level; the Latin poets of the "Flemish" province of the Jesuits were generally recognized to be the best ones of their times. Above all, the "three Belgian Fathers" (*tres Patres Belgae*) should be mentioned here: three Jesuits from West Flanders whose reputation remained unchallenged for two centuries: Gulielmus Becanus from Ypres (1608–1683) whose eclogues and elegies, for instance on the young Jesus, stand out due to their classical purity after the fashion of Tibullus and Ovid; Jacques van de Walle (1599–1690) from Kortrijk, the most ambitious of the three, but, in spite of his pure style, the most unimaginative in his mostly epic-style poems interlarded with erudition; and Sidronius de Hossche from Diksmuide (1596–1653), without any doubt the most moving and the most gifted member of this triad, especially in his pious elegies, conspicuous for their Ovidian ease and elegance, which have not lost anything of their attractiveness, and which have been read and reissued from Spain to Mexico, and even translated into Armenian. They impressed Fabio Chigi (1599–1667), the later Pope Alexander VII, himself a good poet and a connoisseur and collector of Neo-Latin poetry, to such a degree that he repeatedly wrote that he wanted to have every single line written by de Hossche in his library (Sacré 1996).

The Latin poetry of the North did not decline at all, not even during the eighteenth century. In fact, it would be hard to find many parallels for the formal qualities displayed by a large number of Latin poets such as Johan van Broekhuizen (1649–1707) and Pieter Burman the Younger (1714–1778), who nowadays is somewhat known for his conflicts with the German philologist and excellent Latin poet Christian Adolf Klotz (1738–1771). Peerlkamp (1838) was rightly proud of Holland's poets of the second half of the eighteenth century; in Europe, only Italy and Croatia, I would say, could compete with the Netherlands in this field. It is no coincidence that the international contest for Neo-Latin poetry that existed from 1843 until 1978, the *Certamen Hoeufftianum*, named after its sponsor, the jurist and prolific Latin poet Jacob Hendrik Hoeufft (1756–1843), had its seat at Amsterdam and that several Latin poets from Holland were awarded prizes there, whereas no Belgian Latinist ever obtained the most prestigious distinctions at that contest.

Although poets from the Low Countries could not achieve lasting international fame outside their lyric and elegiac poetry, they were of course active in practically every genre and produced some noteworthy works. To mention just a few examples of hexameter poetry: among the more interesting specimens of epic is Georgius Benedictus's *De rebus gestis illustrissimi principis Guilielmi, comitis Nassovii* (*The Deeds of the Illustrious Prince William, Duke of Nassau*, 1586), eulogizing William of Orange. In the related didactic genre, Bartholomaeus Latomus's *Bombarda* (*Cannon*, 1536), which explains how cannons are made and describes their devastating powers, is one of the first didactic poems on technical inventions (Melchior and Loutsch 2009). One of the most admired didactic poems was Daniel Heinsius's *De contemptu mortis* (*The Contempt of Death*, 1621), modeled after Virgil's *Georgics* and clearly anti-Lucretian in content; it stressed the immortality of the soul and the fact that Christ had triumphed over death for man's sake; famous is the long section on soldiers, who should be prepared to die for their fatherland—clearly a topic suitable to the circumstances of the Thirty Years' War. When Neo-Latin poetry was at its zenith in the Low Countries, an Antwerp refugee in Heidelberg, Janus Gruterus, produced an interesting anthology of his countrymen's best products, the *Delitiae C poetarum Belgicorum huius superiorisque aevi illustrium* (*The Charms of One Hundred Famous Belgian Poets of This and the Preceding Century*, 1614).

PROSE

This final section surveys only a few important elements of the enormous production of Neo-Latin prose literature in the Low Countries. To begin with rhetoric, Latin oratory remained important until the end of the eighteenth century. In the seventeenth century, specialized institutions were incorporated into the universities and Athenaea to improve the Latin rhetorical skills of youngsters. In the South, Puteanus founded a *Palaestra bonae mentis* ("gymnasium of the good mind") in Leuven, supported by the government, which held oratorical exercises on a regular basis; in the North, and following an example that seems to have existed already in Lipsius's times, Petrus Cunaeus (1586–1638) established a similar Collegium Oratorium ("Rhetoric College"), while at the Amsterdam *Athenaeum illustre* ("distinguished Athenaeum") Petrus Francius (1645–1704) at the end of the seventeenth century focused more on the actual delivery of speeches than on composing them. The oratorical tradition in the schools of the North must have been quite strong: until deep in the nineteenth century, the best pupils, on finishing their secondary school training, would deliver a Latin speech in a city hall; by that time, the tradition had nearly died out in the South. Some collections of academic orations written and delivered by students under the direction of illustrious professors became lasting successes and rhetorical models, such as the *Rhetorum collegii Porcensis orationes* (*Speeches from Orators of the College of the Pig*), elaborated under Vernulaeus at Leuven, and reissued (and enlarged) time and again between 1614 and 1721.

To give a few practical examples: inaugural speeches or orations held during the academic year were a genre that possessed an almost unlimited range of possibilities. The oration David Ruhnken delivered at Leiden University in 1761 and entitled *De doctore umbratico* (*The Secluded Doctor*) is a brilliant, highly elegant attack against pedantry in the scholarly world. If one bears in mind the extraordinary vogue of Latin verse in the North, one will not be surprised that these speeches, following a tradition that had originated in Italy (one thinks of Poliziano), were often delivered in verse instead of prose. Especially in the South, it seems, orators (such as Puteanus and Vernulaeus in the seventeenth century) would also practice the genre of "sacred oration" (*oratio sacra*), related to that of the sermon or homily, but clothed in a more classical and more solemn dress. The flexibility of the genre is furthermore illustrated by the fact that Juan Luis Vives, before lecturing on Cicero's *Dream of Scipio*, charmed his audience with the delivery of a funny *Somnium Vivis* (*Dream of Vives*, 1520). So did Petrus Nannius (ca. 1496–1557) when he interrupted his Leuven course on the *Aeneid* to hold a witty speech, as a kind of supplement to underworld matters as narrated by Virgil. Rhetorical entertainments such as Vives's dream and Nannius's speech could also be regarded as examples of shorter Latin fiction. For longer fiction, I can refer only to the curious *Legenda aurea continens acta, gesta et cabriola leonis Belgici* (*The Golden Legend, Containing the Accomplishments, Deeds, and Capriols of the Belgian Lion*, 1791) of Jean Van Heeze from Bruges. This work, written in an almost macaronic language (recalling the sixteenth-century *Letters of Obscure Men*), is a satire against religious opponents in the turmoil of the late eighteenth century; its author was a priest who had been suspended, was opposed to the ideas of the French Revolution, and supported the Austrian emperor.

The related genre of Menippean satire was cultivated with much success in the Netherlands (De Smet 1996). Examples include Lipsius's *Satyra Menippea* of 1581, mentioned above; Puteanus's popular *Comus* (from the eponymous hero, the ancient god of revelry; 1608), a satire against gluttony which was translated into Dutch and French and might have influenced John Milton's *Comus* of 1634 (Verbeke 2010); and Daniel Heinsius's *Hercules tuam fidem* (*By Hercules!* 1608), attacking the life and works of the controversial classicist Kaspar Schoppe. Fiction is also represented by another branch of eloquence, the declamation, which thrived in the Low Countries; thus Juan Luis Vives composed *Declamationes Sullanae* (*Sullan Declamations*, 1520), a collection of invented speeches on the abdication of the Roman dictator Sulla; the best-known specimen in this genre is, of course, Erasmus's *Praise of Folly* (1511), framed as a paradoxical declamation (Trapman 2014, with further literature).

Various literary dialogues or treatises constitute important contributions to the ethical, philosophical, political, and, more generally, to the intellectual debates of the time. Until the end of the Ancien Régime and even beyond, they were often written in the academic language that was Latin: thus, to adduce only one late example, the former slave Jacobus Elisa Johannes Capitein (1717–1747), born in Ghana but educated in Holland, contended that Christian freedom and slavery were not incompatible in his *Num libertati Christianae servitus adversetur necne* (*Whether or Not Slavery Conflicts with Christian Freedom*, 1742; Parker 2010). To return to the golden age of Northern humanism, Vives's *De subventione pauperum* (*Supporting the Poor*, 1526) was an influential contribution to the debate on public relief of the poor and elicited more than one comparable work in the Netherlands; no less important were his *De institutione feminae Christianae* (*The Education of the Christian Woman*, 1524); his *De officio mariti* (*The Duties of a Husband*, 1529); his *De anima* (*On the Soul*, 1538), a very original treatise in the field of psychology; and his *De tradendis disciplinis* (*On Education*, 1531), a penetrating analysis of the sciences, their decay in Vives's times, and the way they should be practiced (generally Noreña 1970).

Historiography was treasured by many humanists. Quite often, historians would deal with the remote or recent history of their country or with local history. Thus Reynier Snoy (ca. 1477–1537), a friend of Erasmus's, wrote one of the first humanist histories in the Low Countries: his *De rebus Batavicis* (*Batavian History*), however, was not published until 1620; it was a first attempt at writing in a humanist Latin, and the author was aware of the fact that he had been unable to achieve the "elegance of Sallust or the pure speech of Livy." A popular example of regional history was the Frisian Ubbo Emmius's *Rerum Frisiacarum historia* (*History of Frisia*, 1616). Local history, which was many a time combined with the description of the city or region under consideration, and with accounts of the character of their inhabitants or their merits in art, literature, and other fields, tended to paint a flattering picture; this is clear, for instance, in Lipsius's *Lovanium* (*Leuven*, 1605) or in Carolus Scribani's *Antverpia* (*Antwerp*, 1610) and *Origines Antverpiensium* (*The Origins of the Antwerpers*, 1610). Examples of similarly patriotic national histories would be Hugo Grotius's *Parallelon rerumpublicarum . . . libri* (*Parallels Between Commonwealths*, written in 1602, published only in 1801–1803), a praise of the culture and the character of the Dutch in comparison with the ancient Greeks and Romans; and his *De antiquitate reipublicae Batavicae* (*The Antiquity of the Batavian Commonwealth*, 1610), defending on historical grounds an aristocratic regime in the Northern provinces (Grotius 2000).

Related to local or national historiography are descriptions of the current state of the Low Countries, their regions or cities (often containing a sketch of their history), and the (mostly laudatory) bio-bibliographies of their most renowned inhabitants. Within this area fall, for instance, Antoon Sander's *Flandria illustrata* (*Flanders Illustrated*, 1641–1644), Aubert Le Mire's *Elogia Belgica* (*Belgian Praises*, 1609), Frans Sweerts's *Athenae Belgicae* (*Belgian Athens*, 1628), Valerius Andreas's *Bibliotheca Belgica* (*Belgian Library*, 1623), and Jean-François Foppens's *Bibliotheca Belgica* (1739). National pride was also present in some works on the history of languages, especially in the debates on the most ancient language (the *Ursprache*): thus, the Antwerp humanist Joannes Goropius presented Dutch as the oldest and most perfect language in his *Origines Antwerpianae* (*Origins of Antwerp*, 1569), whereas in the North, Abraham Van der Myle would stick to the traditional priority of Hebrew, but would contend in his *De lingua Belgica* (*The Belgian Language*, 1612) that Dutch came in second, a work that advocates the cultivation of that later vernacular (Van Hal 2011).

Often, works of history have to be considered in clusters, as they were written in reaction to each other. The numerous works written on the religious conflicts and the Dutch Revolt in the sixteenth and seventeenth centuries often polemicized about the question of which party could claim to be fighting a "just war" (*bellum iustum*): Johannes Sleidanus's anti-Catholic *Commentarii de statu religionis et rei publicae Carolo V. Caesare* (*Notes on the Situation of Religion and State Under the Emperor Charles V*, 1555), for example, led to a Catholic rebuttal by the German Carthusian Laurentius Surius (*Commentarius brevis* [*Brief Notes*], 1566), supplemented by Michael von Isselt (*Commentarius* [*Notes*], 1586). Many shorter monographs on recent events or local wars, or on the deeds of a ruler were published as well. A friend of Erasmus's, Willem Hermansz, for instance, wrote an *Olandiae Gelriaeque bellum* (*The War Between Holland and Gelderland*, 1506–1508), while Hugo Grotius ventured his *Grollae obsidio* (*The Siege of Groenlo*, 1629), on the Dutch conquest of the small town of Groenlo in 1627. Sometimes, Latin authors from the Low Countries would also deal with the history of distant or remote regions. Grotius, in his *De origine gentium Americanarum* (*The Origin of the American Peoples*, 1642–1643), contended that the Native Americans were descended from Scandinavians and some other people who had settled there after 500 CE.

With these historical works we may connect the accounts of humanists and diplomats who for some years lived abroad and described what they had witnessed there. The most fascinating specimens might well be Nicolaes Cleynaerts's (1493–1542) posthumously published letters (1550, expanded 1566), written on his travels in Morocco and offering an interesting description of the city of Fez (Roersch 1940–1); the letters of the diplomat Ogier Ghislain de Busbecq on his stays in Turkey (*Legationis Turcicae epistolae* [*Letters of the Turkish Mission*], 1581–1589), which contain, among other things, his discovery of the funerary inscription of the Emperor Augustus in Ankara (the *Res gestae Divi Augusti* [*The Deeds of the Divine Augustus*]; Arrighi 2011); and Jean-Baptiste Gramaye's *Diarium rerum Argelae gestarum* (*Diary of the Events in Algiers*, 1623), which recounts his abduction by pirates, his captivity at Algiers, and his liberation (Ben Mansour 1998).

In the field of technical and scientific literature, we find a wealth of Latin works, written in various registers of style, from polished or highbrow to low-key and unadorned Latin. Many of these products reached an international audience or were pioneering works in their domains. It would be impossible, however, to give an adequate survey of them here, so I must limit myself to arousing the curiosity of readers by mentioning some of the Low Countries' most outstanding works. *De humani corporis fabrica* (*The Fabric of the Human Body*, 1543), by Andreas Vesalius, laid the foundation for modern anatomy (Vons and Velut 2014). In the field of botany, Lipsius's friend Carolus Clusius (1526–1609) discussed tulips for the first time (Egmond, Hoftijzer, and Visser 2007). The Jesuits, who had established the teaching of mathematics in the South, contributed to the flourishing of astronomy. Ferdinand Verbiest, a Flemish Jesuit who became the astronomer to the Chinese emperor, demonstrated the superiority of occidental astronomy in his *Astronomia Europaea* (*European Astronomy*, 1687; Verbiest 1993), which also included other sciences such as optics and mechanics. Another Jesuit, Leonardus Lessius (1554–1623), contributed to the development of early modern economic thought (Van Houdt 1998). As one of the most important cartographers in early modern history, Gerard Mercator (1512–1594) is still famous for his "atlases"—he was the first to use the word for collections of maps (Crane 2002).

Suggested Reading

For both the history of humanism (IJsewijn 1975 and 1988) and Neo-Latin literature (IJsewijn 1988; *CNLS* 1:148–63) in the Low Countries, various studies and surveys by Jozef IJsewijn remain fundamental, but they have to be complemented with more recent studies on, for instance, the contribution of the North or the activities of Italian humanists in the South. Brief surveys of Neo-Latin and the classical tradition in the Low Countries can be found in Deneire (2014), Heesakkers et al. (2008), and Tournoy (2007). A recent and rich chapter on Neo-Latin drama is Bloemendal (2013a). For the history of Neo-Latin poetry, Ellinger (1933) is still readable, though a modern survey is needed; a more recent contribution is Heesakkers (1995). We need more studies of (sub)genres like Smeesters (2011) on the *genethliacon* ("birthday poem"). There is no broad, well-documented story of early modern Latin prose in the Low Countries.

REFERENCES

Arrighi, Dominique. 2011. *Écritures de l'ambassade: Les* Lettres turques *d'Ogier Ghiselin de Busbecq.* Paris: Champion.

Aurnhammer, Achim. 2008. "Daniel Heinsius und die Anfänge der deutschen Barockdichtung." In *Daniel Heinsius: Klassischer Philologe und Poet*, edited by Eckard Lefèvre and Eckart Schäfer, 329–45. Tübingen: Narr.

Ben Mansour, Abd el Hadi. 1998. *Alger XVIe–XVIIe siècle: Journal de Jean-Baptiste Gramaye, "évêque d'Afrique."* Paris: Cerf.

Bloemendal, Jan. 2013a. "Neo-Latin Drama in the Low Countries." In *Neo-Latin Drama: Contexts, Contents and Currents*, edited by Jan Bloemendal and Howard B. Norland, 293–364. Leiden: Brill.

———. 2013b. "Similarities, Dissimilarities and Possible Relations Between Early Modern Drama and Drama in the Vernacular." In *The Early Modern Cultures of Neo-Latin Drama*, edited by Philip Ford and Andrew Taylor, 141–57. Leuven: Leuven University Press.

Crane, Nicholas. 2002. *Mercator: The Man Who Mapped the Planet.* London: Weidenfeld & Nicholson.

Deneire, Tom. 2012. "The Philology of Justus Lipsius's Prose Style." *Wiener Studien* 125:189–262.

———. 2014. "Neo-Latin Literature—The Low Countries." In *ENLW* 2:1096–98.

De Smet, Ingrid A. R. 1996. *Menippean Satire and the Republic of Letters 1581–1655.* Geneva: Droz.

De Vocht, Henry. 1951–1955. *History of the Foundation and the Rise of the Collegium Trilingue Lovaniense 1517–1550.* 4 vols. Leuven: Publications Universitaires.

Egmond, Florike, Paul G. Hoftijzer, and Robert P. W. Visser, eds. 2007. *Carolus Clusius: Towards a Cultural History of a Renaissance Naturalist.* Amsterdam: Koninklijke Nederlandse Akademie.

Ellinger, Georg. 1933. *Geschichte der neulateinischen Lyrik in den Niederlanden vom Ausgang des fünfzehnten bis zum Beginn des siebzehnten Jahrhunderts.* Berlin: De Gruyter.

Enenkel, Karl. 2010. "Erasmus, Desiderius." In *The Classical Tradition*, edited by Anthony Grafton, Glenn W. Most, and Salvatore Settis, 327–30. Cambridge: Belknap Press.

Grotius, Hugo. 2000. *The Antiquity of the Batavian Republic with the Notes by Petrus Scriverius.* Edited and translated by Jan Waszink. Assen: Van Gorcum.

Guépin, Jean P. 2000. *De Drie Dichtende Broers Grudius, Marius, Secundus in brieven, reisverslagen en gedichten.* Groningen: Styx.

Heesakkers, Christiaan L. 1995. "De Nederlandse muze in Latijns gewaad: De bestudering van de Neolatijnse poëzie uit de Noordelijke Nederlanden." *Tijdschrift voor Nederlandse Taal- en Letterkunde* 111:142–62.

Heesakkers, Christiaan L., Gilbert Tournoy, Dirk Sacré, Eric M. Moormann, Rudi Van der Paardt, and F. Decreus. 2008. "Netherlands and Belgium." In *Brill's New Pauly, Classical Tradition*, vol. 3, 1060–1139. Leiden: Brill.

Huygens, Constantijn. 2003. *Mijn leven verteld aan mijn kinderen.* 2 vols. Edited by Frans R. E. Blom. Amsterdam: Prometheus.

IJsewijn, Jozef. 1975. "The Coming of Humanism to the Low Countries." In *Itinerarium Italicum*, edited by Heiko A. Oberman and Thomas A. Brady, Jr., 193–301. Leiden: Brill.

———. 1981. "Theatrum Belgo-Latinum: Het Neolatijns toneel in de Nederlanden." *Mededelingen van de Kon. Academie voor Wetenschappen, Letteren en Schone Kunsten van België, Klasse der Letteren* 43:71–114.

————. 1988. "Humanism in the Low Countries." In *Renaissance Humanism: Foundations, Forms and Legacy*, vol. 2, edited by Albert Rabil, 156–215. Philadelphia: University of Pennsylvania Press.

Kühlmann, Wilhelm, ed. 1994. *Rudolf Agricola 1444–1485. Protagonist des nordeuropäischen Humanismus, zum 550. Geburtstag.* Bern: Lang.

Melchior, Myriam, and Claude Loutsch, eds. 2009. *Humanistica Luxemburgensia: La Bombarda de Barthélemy Latomus; Les Opuscula de Conrad Vecerius.* Brussels: Latomus.

Morford, Mark. 1991. *Stoics and Neostoics: Rubens and the Circle of Lipsius.* Princeton: Princeton University Press.

Murgatroyd, Paul, ed. 2000. *The Amatory Elegies of Johannes Secundus.* Leiden: Brill.

Noreña, Carlos G. 1970. *Juan Luis Vives.* The Hague: Nijhoff.

Papy, Jan. 2004. "Lipsius's (Neo-)Stoicism: Constancy between Christian Faith and Stoic Virtue." In *Grotius and the Stoa*, edited by Hans W. Blum and Laurens C. Winkel, 47-72. Assen: Van Gorcum.

Parker, Grant. 2010. "Can the Subaltern Speak Latin? The Case of Capitein." In *Latinity and Alterity in the Early Modern Period*, edited by Yasmin Haskell and Juanita Feros Ruys, 241–58. Tempe; Turnhout: Arizona Center for Medieval and Renaissance Studies; Brepols.

Peerlkamp, Petrus H. 1838. *De vita, doctrina et facultate Nederlandorum qui carmina Latina composuerunt*, 2nd ed. Haarlem: Loosjes.

Peeters, Paul. 1961. *L'oeuvre des Bollandistes.* Brussels: Palais des Académies.

Proot, Goran. 2007. "Het schooltoneel van de jezuïeten in de Provincia Flandro-Belgica tijdens het ancien regime (1575–1773)." Ph.D. diss., Antwerp University.

Roersch, Alphonse, ed. 1940–1. *Correspondance de Nicolas Clénard.* 3 vols. Brussels: Palais des Académies.

Sacré, Dirk. 1993. "Andreas Hoius en Justus Lipsius (met een onbekende brief aan Lipsius)." *Handelingen van de Koninklijke Zuidnederlandse Maatschappij voor Taal- en Letterkunde en Geschiedenis*, 47:269–92.

————, ed. 1996. *Sidronius Hosschius (Merkem 1596–Tongeren 1653) jezuïet en Latijns dichter.* Kortrijk: Stedelijke Openbare Bibliotheek.

————. 2009. "A Missing Link: An Overlooked Letter of Jacob Cats to Caspar Barlaeus." In *Syntagmatia: Essays on Neo-Latin Literature in Honour of Monique Mund-Dopchie and Gilbert Tournoy*, edited by Dirk Sacré and Jan Papy, 595–603. Leuven: Leuven University Press.

Schäfer, Eckart, ed. 2004. *Johannes Secundus und die römische Liebeslyrik.* Tübingen: Narr.

Secundus, Johannes N. 1899. *Basia: Mit einer Auswahl aus den Vorbildern und Nachahmern.* Edited by Georg Ellinger. Berlin: Weidmann.

Smeesters, Aline. 2011. *Aux rives de la lumière: La poésie de la naissance chez les auteurs néo-latins des anciens Pays-Bas entre la fin du XVe et le milieu du XVIIe siècle.* Leuven: Leuven University Press.

Tournoy, Gilbert. 2007. "Low Countries." In *A Companion to the Classical Tradition*, edited by Craig W. Kallendorf, 237–51. Malden: Blackwell.

Trapman, Johannes. 2014. "Erasmus—The Praise of Folly." In *ENLW* 2: 974–75.

Van Dam, Harm-Jan. 2000. "Second et la poésie néo-latine des Pays-Bas au XVIe siècle." In *La poétique de Jean Second et son influence au XVIe siècle*, edited by Jean Balsamo, Pierre Laurens, and Perrine Galand-Hallyn, 169–184. Paris: Belles Lettres.

Van Hal, Toon. 2011. "Reviving the Old Teutonic Language: An Unpublished Preface by Abraham Mylius Retrieved in Gottfried Wilhelm Leibniz's Heritage." *Lias* 38:129–47.

Van Houdt, Toon. 1998. "Tradition and Renewal in Late Scholastic Economic Thought: The Case of Leonardus Lessius (1554–1623)." *The European Journal of Medieval and Early Modern Studies* 28:51–73.

Verbeke, Demmy. 2010. "'Condemned by Some, Read by All': The Attempt to Suppress the Publications of the Louvain Humanist Erycius Puteanus in 1608." *Renaissance Studies* 24:353–64.

Verbiest, Ferdinand. 1993. *The Astronomia Europaea of Ferdinand Verbiest, S.J. (Dillingen, 1687)*. Edited and translated by Noël Golvers. Nettetal: Steyler.

Vons, Jacqueline, and Stéphane Velut, eds. 2014. "La Fabrique *de Vésale et autres textes*." Available at http://www3.biusante.parisdescartes.fr/vesale/debut.htm.

CHAPTER 31

··

SCANDINAVIA

··

ANNIKA STRÖM AND PETER ZEEBERG

THE HISTORICAL BACKGROUND

HUMANIST culture reached the Scandinavian countries around 1500. At that time, the entire area was united in the so-called Union of Kalmar under the Danish kings, including all the three medieval kingdoms of Denmark, Norway, and Sweden. This union, however, was unstable, and at the beginning of the 1520s, the Swedes broke away to form an independent kingdom. For the remainder of the period discussed in this chapter, the political landscape of Scandinavia comprised two kingdoms: Sweden, including Finland; and Denmark-Norway (a union that lasted until 1814), incorporating Iceland, Greenland, and the Faroe Islands. The Danish kings' realm included Schleswig and Holstein, where the kings ruled as dukes.

During the first century or so after the dissolution of the union, Denmark-Norway was dominant, a prosperous and powerful country, while Sweden was only gradually finding its feet. But during the earlier seventeenth century, beginning with the Swedish success and Danish disasters in the Thirty Years' War (1618–1648), the balance tipped: consequently, during most of the seventeenth century and the start of the eighteenth, Sweden was an important European power, while Denmark-Norway became impoverished and ceded important provinces to Sweden, especially the Scanian provinces in what is now southern Sweden. This political development was reflected in national cultural activities: while Latin writing flourished in Denmark-Norway in the sixteenth century, Sweden's golden age occurred in the second half of the seventeenth century.

Until the end of that century, Latin played a prominent role in Scandinavia. The vernaculars were used as administrative languages, and were introduced in the wake of the Protestant Reformation into church for the mass and liturgy, and favored by religious writers. But the breakthrough for the Scandinavian vernaculars as literary languages came over the course of the seventeenth century, and only in the eighteenth century did scholars start to publish in the vernaculars. The exception was

Iceland, which from the Middle Ages onwards had a strong vernacular literary tradition, although in Iceland, too, Latin writing flourished until well into the eighteenth century.

The progress of humanism in the Nordic countries came to be closely associated with the advance of the Lutheran Reformation. Most of the prominent Lutheran reformers studied with Luther and, especially, with Melanchthon at the university in Wittenberg, where they received a thorough humanist education. That said, the first phase of Nordic humanism predates the Reformation. In Denmark, the reign of Christian II (1513–1523) witnessed the first initiatives to promote humanist culture, including humanist Latin. The humanist Christiern Pedersen published a series of Latin works for a Danish readership in Paris in 1510–1514, which included the first Latin–Danish dictionary and the first edition of Saxo's *Gesta Danorum* (*Deeds of the Danes*, ca. 1200), a major medieval work praised by Erasmus for its exquisite classical Latin. In the early sixteenth century, too, the Carmelite monk Poul Helgesen advocated a reformed Catholic line in a series of works significantly inspired by Erasmus. Helgesen's most famous work is the so-called *Chronicon Skibyense* (*The Chronicle of Skibby*, ca. 1534), an unfinished historical work with a heated account of the religious struggles seen from a Catholic point of view—the title, devised and given by later scholars, stems from the fact that the manuscript was found in the church of Skibby in North Zealand. In Sweden, the main figures of this first humanist phase were the Roman Catholic archbishops Johannes Magnus and Olaus Magnus, who both wrote important works on the history of Sweden, as we shall see. But humanism's main breakthrough came with the Reformation, which resulted in markedly different developments in each of the two realms. In Sweden, the Reformation began around 1527, but it only gathered momentum gradually and encountered several relapses. In Denmark-Norway, the Reformation happened overnight in 1536, and was implemented by the so-called Church Ordinance of 1537. The development of humanism differed accordingly, in that Latin literature flourished in Denmark-Norway from the middle of the sixteenth century, while in Sweden a similar development was only seen in the first half of the seventeenth century, coinciding with the general strengthening of Swedish economics and political power. Research into Neo-Latin literature has roughly followed the same lines: in Denmark and Norway, research has concentrated on the early period, up to the beginning of the seventeenth century, while in Sweden and Finland the focus has been on the second half of the seventeenth and the beginning of the eighteenth centuries.

Denmark-Norway

In Denmark-Norway, the Reformation was carried through as the result of a civil war. Collaborating closely with the Wittenberg reformers, especially Philipp Melanchthon, the victorious King Christian III implemented the Church Ordinance of 1537, which organized not only the new church but also an entirely new educational system based on Melanchthon's Saxon pedagogy. The law ordained that there should be a Latin school in every town in the realm, and for these new institutions, a new and thoroughly humanist curriculum was therefore devised. Likewise, the university in Copenhagen was reopened with a new Lutheran humanist curriculum: its primary aim was to educate clergymen for the new reformed church, but students also had many opportunities for further studies abroad, primarily at Wittenberg and other German universities. The Reformation subsequently ushered in a marked consolidation of the Latin education system. In Iceland, on the other hand, the Reformation met serious opposition, which only finally ended with the decapitation of Bishop Jón Arason in 1550. From the last half of the sixteenth century onwards, all bishops in Iceland were educated at the university of Copenhagen and had close connections with Danish intellectual circles.

The result of the ambitious reformed educational program soon became clear. Throughout the second half of the century, humanist literature, not least poetry, thrived. To give a few examples: at the very beginning of the 1550s, several collections of poetry were published in Wittenberg by the two friends Hans Frandsen (1532–1584) and Hans Sadolin (1528–1600). A fine stylist who excelled in lyric poetry, Sadolin wrote and published Latin poetry throughout his life and was crowned *poeta laureatus* by the king in 1570. His *Epithalamion* for Frandsen's marriage (1566) is a charming masterpiece, and his occasional poetry for the royal family set high standards for the form. Another instance is the work of Erasmus Laetus, who published in 1560 a collection of pastoral poems (*Bucolica*; Zeeberg 2010), again printed in Wittenberg. The book contains a dedication to King Frederik II written by Melanchthon himself, and constitutes a highly ambitious example of how Danish students brought a new culture home from Wittenberg. A central topos is the allegorical description of the spread of humanism known as *translatio Musarum* ("transfer of the Muses"): the Muses who once lived in Greece and Rome have wandered to the Germanic lands, and are invited to live on a famous hill just outside Copenhagen. The new king is hailed as the leader of the new movement, and the poet presents himself as a prospective court poet: a new Virgil in the service of King Frederik as a new Augustus. Laetus succeeded, and over the following fifteen years he published many epic and didactic poems, dedicated to a series of European monarchs and rulers. Laetus also represents similar themes in a more historical occasional work, his extraordinarily personal eyewitness description of the birth and baptism of Prince Christian (1577), which describes the baptism as the final confirmation of the Reformation (Laetus 1992). Sixteenth-century Latin authors in Denmark-Norway were acutely conscious that they were part of a new movement in which Reformation and humanism went hand in hand, and the government shared this perception. During this period, Scandinavian Neo-Latin literature was heavily influenced by developments in Germany, given that most writers studied in Wittenberg or at other Lutheran universities, and their works therefore emanated from German literary milieux. But in the following century, travel and different influences increased, and the Netherlands in particular became important.

SWEDEN

In Sweden and Finland, education was available in the schools that taught the *trivium* and in gymnasia on both sides of the Baltic Sea. But there, unlike in Denmark-Norway, the Reformation only gradually took root and was not accompanied by an educational program. The University of Uppsala had been founded in 1477, but at the height of the Reformation it was all but closed down, and so, lacking the chance for an indigenous education, Swedish and Finnish students were sent to the universities in northern Germany (esp. Greifswald, Rostock, and Wittenberg). Finnish reformers, including the future bishop of Åbo (in Finnish, Turku) and highly influential writer Michael Agricola (ca. 1510–1557), were sent to Wittenberg and subsequently initiated Neo-Latin literature in Finland. This vogue for peregrination to foreign universities meant that educational ideas from Continental Europe such as Melanchthon's and Erasmus's pedagogical programs came to the notice of Scandinavian scholars, and were successively introduced and used in schools and universities. In the latter part of the sixteenth century, curricula were drawn up for elementary schools, the education at Uppsala University was awakened, and the Collegium Regium ("Royal College") was founded in Stockholm in 1576 by King Johan III. The Latin language and the study of classical authors once again assumed a central position in the curriculum. During these years, much occasional poetry—that is, epithalamia and epicedia—was produced by Swedish students at foreign universities. One of the most widely known authors was Laurentius Petri Gothus, a professor of Greek and later archbishop in Uppsala, who left behind three poetical works: *Strategema Gothici exercitus* (*The Stratagem of the Gothic Army*, 1559), *Aliquot Elegiae* (*Several Elegies*, 1561), and *Urbs Stockholmia* (*The City of Stockholm*, 1561), the first specimens of Latin poetry from Sweden. Another early example is Sylvester Johannis Phrygius (1572–1628), who became known as the semi-official poet of the royal family: his early works apparently introduced the literary fashions of Continental humanism into Sweden, and represent political tension in the Sweden of their time (Phrygius 2007).

The seventeenth century and the first half of the eighteenth witnessed Latin's most flourishing period as a literary language in Sweden. Several factors brought about this phenomenon: first, Sweden's rise to political, economic and military power was essential, since it created the need to educate the men who would lead the country in this period of expansion, as members of the nobility were now needed as Latin-literate administrators and diplomats. Swedish education, as we have seen, was deeply influenced by the ideas of humanism, and institutions of learning, starting with elementary schools and gymnasia, flourished during the seventeenth century. The University of Uppsala continued to expand, and new universities were founded in Dorpat (Tartu, Estonia) in 1632, Åbo (Turku) in 1640, and Lund in 1668. During the reign of Queen Christina (1632–1654), many learned men from the Continent came to the royal court and participated in the literary and intellectual propagation of humanist ideas: these included such luminaries as Isaac Vossius, Nicolaus Heinsius, René Descartes, Johannes

Schefferus, Hugo Grotius, and Samuel von Pufendorf. Latin was used for poetry but also for oratory and scientific enquiry, and came to dominate the entire educational system.

CENTERS OF LEARNING

The universities were the main centers of Neo-Latin culture. But there were also a number of other institutions and cultural milieux important for the burgeoning of Latin literature: The Collegium Regium was founded in Stockholm in 1576 by King Johan III with the goal of bringing Sweden back to Catholicism. While under the direction of the Norwegian Jesuit Laurentius Nicolai (Lars Nilsson, also known by the nickname *Kloster-Lasse* ["Abbey-Lasse"], 1538–1622), the school's main field of study was theology. Nicolai was evicted due to strong Lutheran opposition, and the Collegium thereafter became a Ramist center until it was closed in 1593 and its professors moved to the University of Uppsala. In Denmark, the school for young noblemen at Sorø was promoted to an Academy in 1623, and several important scholars were appointed professors. Among them were the philologists and historians Johannes Meursius (1579–1639) and Stephanus Johannis Stephanius (1599–1650), and the poet and mathematician Johann Lauremberg (1590–1658), who wrote a Latin satire on young noblemen's lack of interest in learning.

From 1576 to 1597, the astronomer Tycho Brahe (1546–1601) ran a research institute, *Uraniborg*, on the island of Hven in the Sound north of Copenhagen. This institution, lavishly funded by the government, played a decisive part in the development of modern science. Himself a member of the highest aristocracy, Brahe gathered both academics and noblemen around him in a sophisticated milieu where science, art, philosophy, and Latin poetry went hand in hand, presumably inspired by contemporary learned academies in Italy. His own Latin poetry was mainly written as part of his self-representation and appeared, for instance, as paratexts in his books or as inscriptions in his palace. An all-pervasive theme is Brahe's private version of the *translatio Musarum* topos: Urania, the muse of astronomy, is a refugee, rejected all over Europe, but now—at long last—she has found a home at Uraniborg. The most eloquent reflection of the exalted intellectual context of Uraniborg is Tycho's 600-line verse letter *Urania Titani* (*Urania to Titan*) modeled on Ovid's *Heroides*, a shrewd psychological portrait of a loving woman by means of alchemical and astrological imagery (Zeeberg 1994).

Other learned milieux developed in towns with cathedrals and Latin schools. One typical example was Oslo, which in the years around 1600 enjoyed a thriving intellectual culture centered around Bishop Jens Nilssøn (1538–1600) and the *lector theologiae* Halvard Gunnarssøn (ca. 1550–1608). Gunnarssøn's many works (e.g., versifications of world history, biblical history, and Norwegian history) are mostly meant for schoolroom use. Apart from such pedagogical writing, and both prose and verse works of theology, the Oslo humanists excelled in occasional poetry: particularly remarkable is Jens Nilssøn's lengthy, moving poem on the death of his daughter (*Elegidion in obitum filiolae suae Catharinae* [*Elegy on the Death of His Daughter Karine*], 1581; Nilssøn 2004). In Iceland, the main literary centers were the two cathedrals and their schools at Skálholt and Hólar. Works written there were for the most part concerned with Icelandic topics, including histories of Iceland, descriptions of the country, and Latin translations of old Norse literature. A similar important milieu could be found in the provincial town of Ribe in southern Jutland (Denmark) where the historians Hans Svaning (1503–1584) and Anders Sørensen Vedel (1542–1616) held prebends as dean at the cathedral, while the Danish playwright Peder Hegelund (1542–1615) was school master and later bishop, and the Latin poet Johannes Amerinus (ca. 1550–1605) was a district physician.

All over Scandinavia, Latin kept its position as the only language used in academic contexts until the first half of the eighteenth century. All teaching beyond the most basic level was conducted in Latin, and all scholarly writing—not least the huge bulk of dissertations written in the period—was in Latin. These dissertations explored and presented knowledge and science. Their contents (e.g., European politics, language, and the character of different provinces, towns, peoples, manners, and customs) reflect the learned culture of the time and scientific traditions. We can observe, therefore, how thinkers such as Copernicus, Descartes, Hobbes, Rousseau, and Kant were introduced and received in Scandinavia, as well as the impact exerted by classical and medieval texts on the region. Beyond the contents as such, university dissertations also had a social and representative function, most clearly visible in the dedications and gratulatory poetry that frequently accompany the main text.

We cannot know to what degree Latin was actually *spoken* in these institutions of learning, but the minutes from the professors' meetings at the University of Copenhagen around the turn of the seventeenth century seem to indicate that both Latin and the vernacular were spoken and to a large degree mingled (Zeeberg, forthcoming). Latin was preferred for academic and Danish for non-academic topics, but in both cases a high frequency of code-switching occurred. We observe a similar phenomenon in the private calendar notes written by Bishop Peder Hegelund in Ribe, Denmark, through the second half of the sixteenth century, which also suggest that the amount of Latin depended on the environment: during Hegelund's years as a student, the notes were almost exclusively in Latin, while over the years he spent in a provincial town, the amount of vernacular usage increased. But Latin stayed dominant overall (Skafte Jensen 2004, 93–124). Letters between scholars, of course, were nearly always written in Latin.

POETRY AND OCCASIONAL LITERATURE

Given that Latin in the early modern period was a group-defining language, much of Neo-Latin literature, and especially poetry, had social functions; it defined and maintained learned milieux, positioned its authors in relation to their patrons, or sometimes fulfilled both functions. This resulted in a large amount of occasional literature, but it also had similar functions in other fields. Perhaps the most common genre in this regard was the elegy, and especially elegiac letters: Ovid's exile poetry, especially his *Epistulae ex Ponto*, was fundamental to the school curriculum, not least because it did not offend Lutheran morals. The earliest books of poetry found in the Danish region are nearly all collections of elegiac letters addressed to friends, teachers, and (potential) patrons. Hans Frandsen's *Elegiarum liber primus* (*First Book of Elegies*, 1554), for example, written while the poet was studying in Wittenberg, consists of nineteen elegies, nearly all of them addressed to friends or patrons at home. The collection is tightly structured: the first half is directed to teachers and patrons and the second half to family and friends; each friend is placed between two family members, giving us a portrait of the young poet within his social frame.

Another Danish group of friends defined themselves in poetry during the first part of the seventeenth century. The group centered around Bertel Knudsen Aquilonius (1588–1650) and included Henrik Albertsen Hamilton (b. ca. 1690) and Aquilonius's former headmaster, the court poet Willich Westhovius (1577–1647). Aquilonius described his social network in a variety of genres besides elegiacs, such as mixed-meter lyric poetry and in hendecasyllables, often combined with ardent praise of Denmark and the island of Zealand. In the same period Zacharias Lund published a collection of charming elegiac love poems, *Juvenilia* (1634). His manuscripts testify to a lifetime's work of creating and constantly revising his poetical oeuvre (Skafte Jensen 2004, 125–63).

The seventeenth century was a very prolific period for poetry in Sweden. Dubbed the "father of Swedish poetry," Georg Lilia, who was later ennobled and took the name Stiernhielm, is an important early example. Lilia wrote the famous Swedish didactic epic *Hercules* (1647). Some later examples also deserve to be mentioned. Andreas Stobaeus, professor of poetry, was a copious poet (although little of his work was printed), as well as a man with an encyclopedic knowledge of history. The bulk of Stobaeus's *oeuvre* consists of poems for disputations, short poems dedicated to prominent men, panegyrical poems, and orations in hexameters such as *Augur Apollo* (*Apollo the Seer*), and *Optatae pacis spes rediviva* (*Renewed Hope for the Wished-for Peace*, 1710; Stobaeus 1994). Olof Hermelin (1658–1709) was probably the most influential Swedish poet of the century. Apart from official Latin polemics, he also left behind poems and letters and an autobiography in Latin elegiac couplets. Looking to Horace and Ovid as models, Hermelin produced elegant, beautiful poetry. Gunno Eurelius Dahlstierna (1661–1709) was also an important writer of Latin poetry and had a solid knowledge of the classical heritage. His later style was, however, very ornate and witty, a Swedish example of the "Marinism" fashionable on the Continent.

Throughout the period, occasional literature, typically in the form of poetry and orations, was written for private events (weddings, funerals), academic ones (promotions, dissertations), and public events such as royal weddings and coronations. Such work can be seen as part of an official duty, bestowing credit on the author as well as the addressee. This kind of writing was taught as part of the school curriculum, mainly modeled on Menander Rhetor's late-antique treatises on epideictic genres and on contemporary Northern European poetics, especially those by Scaliger, Pontanus, Correia, and Vossius (Ström 1994).

In Denmark-Norway, a favorite genre for occasional literature was the pastoral, which offered rich possibilities for variation and creativity. A fine example is Johannes Pratensis's *Daphnis* (1563), written for the wedding of the hymn writer Hans Thomesen. Pratensis consciously places his poem in the bucolic setting Laetus had created (discussed above), and imitates Virgil's eighth eclogue to celebrate the happy occasion against the gloomy background of impending war (Zeeberg 2008). Another eclogue entitled *Daphnis* is found in Halvard Gunnarssøn's *Akrostichis* (*Acrostic*, 1606), an ambitious collection of poems (of which only the first is really an acrostic) for the centenary of Christian IV's accession to the throne (Kraggerud 1991). In the seventeenth century, occasional poetry abounded. Very little research has been done on the Danish material, but a case study of Latin, Danish, and German poetry published at the introduction of absolutism in Denmark-Norway in 1660 has shown a fundamental difference between Latin and vernacular material: the Latin texts, written for an educated elite, tended to present precise analyses of different political perspectives on a given event, which are not found in the vernacular texts (Olden-Jørgensen 1996).

Early examples of Swedish occasional poets in Latin are Petrus Michaelis Ostrogothus (d. 1580) and Ericus Jacobi Skinnerus (d. 1597). Two families who produced much occasional poetry in the seventeenth century are those of Jonas Columbus and his sons Johannes and Samuel, and the Prytz brothers (Nils, Erik, and Johan). Petrus Lagerlöf (1648–1699) is also considered an important person for the development of poetry and language in the seventeenth century; his writing consists mainly of occasional poetry in Latin, and his works were later collected in the volume *Orationes et programmata ac carmina varia* (*Speeches, Programs, and Miscellaneous Poems*, 1780).

The tradition of classical rhetoric, acquired directly from ancient sources and from the work of contemporary scholars in Continental Europe, was omnipresent in Scandinavian education and Neo-Latin writing of the period. Rhetorical handbooks were produced in eastern Scandinavia in particular, and several prominent scholars of rhetoric can be found in the region. One important person in the development of rhetoric at the University of Uppsala was Johan Skytte (1577–1645), who, among many other activities, created the "Skytteanus" Chair in Eloquence and Politics at Uppsala in 1622. Several Continental scholars significant for the Scandinavian rhetorical tradition held the post, including Johannes Simonius, the first Professor Skytteanus in Uppsala, who wrote *De locorum topicorum usu* (*The Use of Commonplaces*, 1627); Johannes Loccenius (1598–1677); and Johannes Freinsheimius (1608–1660). Johannes Schefferus took over the chair of Professor Skytteanus in 1648, and is best known for his *De stylo* (*On Style*, 1653), later expanded to *Gymnasium styli* (*Gymnasium of Style*, 1657), which focuses on the so-called *progymnasmata*, or exercises in style and rhetoric.

At the University of Åbo/Turku, too, texts of this kind were both printed and extensively used, as chiefly facilitated by the professor of eloquence. The first to be mentioned is Johannes Terserus, who wrote a treatise on basic rules of rhetoric, *Breviarium Rhetoricae* (*Concise Rhetoric*, 1647). Martin Miltopaeus, who held the chair between 1660 and 1679, left behind the extensive work *Institutiones oratoriae* (*Education of the Speaker*, 1669), a series of twenty-two dissertations on rhetoric, containing basic rhetorical theory (*inventio* and *dispositio*) and copious quotations from classical authors. Miltopaeus's successor, Daniel Achrelius (1644–1692), himself a renowned orator, was the author of *Oratoria sive manducatio ad Romanam eloquentiam libellus* (*Oratory; or, Short Introduction to Roman Eloquence*, 1687) and *Epistolarum conscribendarum forma et ratio* (*System and Method of Letter-Writing*, 1689), the latter work combining advice for letter-writing and the use of *progymnasmata* (Sarasti-Wilenius 2000).

HISTORIOGRAPHY

After the dissolution of the Union of Kalmar, the relationship between Sweden and Denmark-Norway was one of constant nationalistic rivalry, which often resulted in literary feuds. Historiographical writing in Latin clearly reflected this tension. Denmark's national classic was Saxo's medieval *Gesta Danorum*, which won European renown when the *editio princeps* was published (1514) and presented Denmark as a powerful nation with a long history; Saxo's list of kings reaches back to times as distant as those offered for the origins of Rome. The publication of the *Gesta Danorum* directly prompted the *Historia de omnibus Gothorum Suenonumque regibus* (*History of All the Gothic and Swedish Kings*), written by the last Roman Catholic archbishop of Uppsala, Johannes Magnus, composed in the 1530s during Magnus's exile in Rome, and printed posthumously in 1554 by his brother Olaus Magnus, himself the author of the ethnological work *Historia de gentibus Septentrionalibus* (*History of the Nordic Peoples*, 1555). Magnus's history deliberately outdid Saxo's. He traced the origins of the Swedes back to the descendants of Noah, making Noah's grandson Magog the eponymous forefather of the Goths. The claim that Sweden was the original homeland of the Goths had already been advanced by the fifteenth-century historian Ericus Olai, but the so-called Gothicist tradition became a dominant trend in Swedish historiography for several centuries thanks to Magnus's book. One of the book's central (and contentious) themes is the denigration of Denmark and the Danes, who according to Magnus are the descendants of criminals deported from Sweden. The Union of Kalmar is described as Danish despotism, and the book ends with a long speech *contra Danos* ("against the Danes"). The works of the Magnus brothers gained an international reputation, and although they were written by a former (Catholic) enemy, the Swedish kings embraced Johannes's history as an authoritative legitimization of the new independent monarchy. This naturally demanded an answer from the Danes, as Danish diplomats soon realized, and the result was the historian Hans Svaning's *Refutatio calumniarum cuiusdam Joannis Magni Gothi* (*Refutation of the Slander of a Certain Johannes Magnus Gothus*, 1560–1561). As an appendix, Svaning included his history of King Hans (1483–1513), depicting the Union with Sweden from a Danish perspective.

Svaning also wrote an history of Denmark, most of which is now lost, and which was rejected by the government in 1579. Svaning's history was presumably rejected because of a prohibition against defamatory writings between the two countries that formed part of the peace treaty after the Seven Years' War (1563–1570). The prohibition was observed—except in times of war. During the Kalmar War (1611–1613), for example, the Uppsala professor Johannes Messenius published a belated answer to Svaning's *Refutatio calumniarum* entitled *Retorsio imposturarum* (*Rejection of the Deceits*, 1612). Over the half century following the rejection of Svaning's history, the Danish authorities made many attempts to commission a new history of Denmark in Latin, but these proved unfruitful until the 1630s, when two were commissioned from the Dutchmen Johannes Isacius Pontanus (1571–1639) and Johannes Meursius (1579–1639; Skovgaard-Petersen 2002). Before that, however, the chancellor Arild Huitfeldt (1546–1609) had produced an authoritative history of Denmark in Danish, which he explicitly presented as a preliminary work upon which a Latin work could be based.

The Gothicist tradition was pursued by other authors. Johannes Bureus (1568–1652) was the first director-general of the Swedish Central Board of National Antiquities (*antiquarius regius*). His prime interest was in runic inscriptions, which he collected in Latin works to form the basis for an antiquarian movement that grew throughout the seventeenth century, a time when research into languages was considered as a means of tracing a people's origins. Bureus was also interested in the Kabbalah, later became a member of the Rosicrucian order, and eventually merged rune studies with esoteric thinking, attributing mystical meanings to the runes. Around the same time, Danish runic inscriptions were also collected by Ole Worm (1588–1654). During the seventeenth century in Finland, Gothicism was promoted in several historiographical works. Particularly well known is the *Epitome descriptionis Sueciae, Gothiae, Fenningiae* (*Brief Description of Sweden, Gothland, and Finland*, 1650), written by Michael Wexionius Gyldenstolpe, a professor at Turku Academy; the work describes the history and geography of Sweden and Finland, tracing the origins of the people back to a biblical pedigree. Professor Petrus Bång contributed with an ecclesiastical history of the ancient Swedes, *Priscorum Sveo-Gothorum ecclesia seu historia ecclesiastica de priscis Sveo-gothicae terrae colonis* (*The Church of the Ancient Swedes; or, Ecclesiastical History of the Ancient Settlers in the Swedish-Gothic Land*, 1675). The most famous historiographer and panegyrist of Finland was, however, Daniel Juslenius, a professor of Greek and Hebrew in Uppsala and bishop of the Eastern Diocese of Finland. His most important works in the field of history are two dissertations on Finnish history and topics, *Aboa vetus et nova* (*Old and New Turku*, 1700) and *Vindiciae Fennorum* (*Defense of the Finns*, 1712). The Gothicist trend culminated in the great work of Olof Rudbeck the Elder, *Atland* or *Atlantica* (*Atlantis*, 1677–1702), who identified Sweden as the mythical Atlantis and established the Swedish language as that of Adam. Rudbeck's work was written in Swedish and only later translated into Latin, soon becoming famous but also attracting criticism from people such as Johannes Schefferus.

Parallel to these mythological and Gothicist traditions, a new trend emerged that concentrated on existing source material. The main figure in Icelandic humanism, Arngrímur Jónsson (1568–1648), translated Icelandic sagas into Latin for the use of Danish historians, and wrote several historical books, including an ambitious history of Iceland based on this material (*Crymogaea*, a Greek translation of "Ice-Land," 1609). In

1665, Peder Hansen Resen published the first standard edition of the *Edda*, with translations into both Latin and Danish. And in 1689 came *Antiquitates Danicae de causis comtemptae a Danis adhuc gentilibus mortis* (*Danish Antiquities About the Reasons Why Death Was Despised by the Danes When They Were Still Pagan*). This is a history of Old Norse (termed "Danish") culture based on Icelandic manuscript material, written by Thomas Bartholin in collaboration with the Icelander Árni Magnússon, who was the main force in a large-scale project to collect Icelandic manuscripts and bring them to Copenhagen. This trend culminated with the *History of Norway* (*Historia Rerum Norvegicarum*, 1711) by the Icelander Thormod Torfaeus, which collects vast amounts of saga material within a Latin rewriting.

In eastern Scandinavia, the writing of history based on source material was initiated by Messenius, who wrote, for instance, *Scondia Illustrata* (*Description of Scandinavia*, 1616); Messenius used medieval sources and therefore shed much light on Swedish cultural life, art, and literature as opposed to earlier mythological historiography. Other renowned historiographers within this trend were Johannes Schefferus and Samuel von Pufendorf (a native German, active in Sweden). Schefferus wrote several historiographical works such as *Lapponia* (*Lapland*, 1673); *De antiquis verisque Regni Sueciae insignibus* (*The Ancient and True Insignia of the Kingdom of Sweden*, 1679–1680); and *Suecia Literata* (*Literature of Sweden*, 1680), Sweden's first literary history. Pufendorf's main contributions were *Commentarii de rebus Suecicis* (*Notes on Swedish Affairs*, 1686) and *De rebus de Carolo Gustavo gestis* (*The Deeds of Charles Gustav*, 1696). In Finland, much later on, Henrik Gabriel Porthan, professor of eloquence in Åbo/Turku, discarded the ideas of the biblical origin of the Finns and showed that they actually had migrated from Russia to Finland, using reliable methods and sources; for instance, in a dissertation on the Finnish language and its origins entitled *De praecipuis Dialectis Linguae Fennicae* (*The Main Dialects of the Finnish Language*, 1801).

Nationalist Propaganda in Latin Verse

The national trends of historiography can also be observed in other prose, and especially in verse writing. After 1523, when Sweden gained independence from Denmark, it became important to establish it as a powerful nation in its own right; the date also marks Sweden's move from being a medieval society to becoming a more modern country. However, Sweden lacked home-grown writers, and therefore had to import talented authors from the Continent to write Swedish propaganda in Latin. Two such authors were the Germans Jacob Ziegler (ca. 1470/1471–1549) and Georg Norman (d. 1552/1553); they excelled at writing eloquent prose texts, manifestos, and letters that depicted the cruelty of Danish tyranny and of the Danish King Christian II. Poetry was also used to deliver propaganda, such as that of the German Henricus Mollerus (1528–1567), who celebrated past kings in Swedish history like Karl Knutsson Bonde (d. 1470) and the elder Sten Sture (d. 1503).

The Seven Years' War (1563–1570) was accompanied by a literary feud conducted both in Latin and in several vernaculars, contingent on the readership being targeted. Among the contributors was King Eric XIV of Sweden, who wrote several (unpublished) orations in Latin against the Danes (Eric XIV 2003). As mentioned above, the postwar peace treaty included a prohibition against defamatory writings between the two countries. The conciliatory impulse is clearly illustrated in a poem by the Dane Johannes Amerinus in celebration of the treaty: his *Ecloga nova et festiva de pacis foedere* (*Novel and Festive Poem on the Peace Treaty*, 1573), is a generically experimental poem, half eclogue and half epic, and 806 lines in length. In Amerinus's *Ecloga*, shepherds recount the history of the war in a dramatic epic style: this includes catalogs of ships and warriors, and gods as protagonists, which makes it possible to blame the war gods (and mercenary soldiers) for the war instead of the actual kings and countries involved. In the following year, the court poet Erasmus Laetus wrote a history of Denmark in the form of an epic entitled *Res Danicae* (*The History of Denmark*, 1574), an official, cautious version. But in 1573, Laetus had published a Virgilian epic on the establishment of the Union of Kalmar, entitled *Margaretica* (*Tales of Margaret* after Queen Margaret of Denmark, the founder of the union). *Margaretica* blatantly breaches the peace terms, showing the fight against Swedish villains, who happen to be unreliable drunkards, by heroic Danes. Laetus depicts Queen Margaret's founding of a union that proved so hated in Sweden as a historic, God-given task comparable to Aeneas's task in the *Aeneid*. Both poems were published abroad (in Frankfurt), but with the subtle difference that while the *Res Danicae* had official approval manifest in its dedication to the Danish king, *Margaretica* was dedicated to Elizabeth I of England.

The seventeenth century saw a series of Danish defeats in wars with Sweden. During the 1650s, central provinces in both Denmark and Norway were ceded to Sweden and were never reconquered. Nonetheless, some Danish successes could be found, and some could be enlarged to a size fit for epic poetry. The versatile court poet Willich Westhovius wrote a poem on a minor victory in 1611; the epigrammatist Henrik Harder composed an epic on the siege of Copenhagen in 1658–1659, *Hafnia Liberata* (*The Liberation of Copenhagen*); and Ole Borch, a medical professor, literary historian, and prolific Latin poet, celebrated a skirmish during the same siege, *Amagria Vindicata* (*The Defense of Amager*, an island opposite Copenhagen). Neither *Hafnia Liberata* nor *Amagria Vindicata* was printed at the time, but they were both included in Frederik Rostgaard's anthology of Danish Neo-Latin poetry, *Deliciae quorundam poetarum Danorum* (*The Charms of a Number of Danish Poets*, 1693). As late as the 1720s, several epics on topics from the wars with Sweden were composed. During the latter part of the seventeenth century, both prose and poetry were written in order to enhance the status of Sweden and its kings, especially after the successes of Charles XII. Several of the established Latin poets of Sweden at the time, mostly well-known professors at Uppsala or Lund, excelled in writing propagandistic poetry to celebrate his achievements in the war. Johan Bergenhielm, professor of history at Uppsala, published a large amount of Latin poetry. He is most famous for his dramatic play on the outbreak of the Nordic war, *Cento satyricus in hodiernos motus Septentrionis* (*A Satirical Cento on the Present-Day Disturbances in the North*, 1700), which describes in the voices of various European monarchs the actions of the enemies of the Swedish state and uses phrasing from classical authors such as Cicero, Sallust, Virgil, Ovid, and Lucan.

At the beginning of the Great Northern War, the Swedish victory in the Battle of Narva (now Estonia) against Russia in 1700 provided the subject for many orations and poems. The royal historiographer Olof Hermelin was given the task of writing official Latin polemics against Sweden's enemies, and he served as Minister of Propaganda until the Swedish defeat of Poltava (now Ukraine) in 1709. He penned several poems celebrating Charles XII (e.g., *In sceptrum Caroli XII* [*On the Crowning of Charles XII*], 1697) and the victory of Narva (*Narva Moscorum clade nobilitata* [*Narva, Ennobled by the Defeat of the Muscovites*], 1700). Magnus Rönnow was an orientalist, imperial translator (*translator regni*), and renowned poet. He wrote mainly eulogies to Swedish ruling families and noblemen, but also a long poem, *On the Victory at Narva* (*In victoriam Narvensem*, 1701). He also published several polemic verses such as the anti-Danish *Hercules Genuinus, Carolus Duodecimus, Magnae Scandinaviae Imperator* (*The Genuine Hercules, Charles XII, Emperor of Great Scandinavia*, 1706), reserving the name of Hercules for Charles XII.

The contents and themes chosen for these propagandistic poems are of course very patriotic, taking the past as a point of departure. The classical theme of the Golden Age (*aureum saeculum*) as found, for instance, in Virgil, Horace, and Ovid, is used to draw a parallel with the present age. The king is compared to the kings and heroes of antiquity and even presented as surpassing them in virtue. The concept of eternal fame is used to extol the king and place him among the celestial bodies; this theme is also seen in the frequently used metaphor of the king as the sun, often elaborated in allegorical form. Charles XII is frequently described as a lion (*leo polaris*, "polar lion"; *Suecus leo*, "Swedish lion"). The poems are characterized by their Christian ethos and frequently emphasize the king's piety. To glorify their country's past, these authors use the ideas of Gothicism: they evoke an idealized history by calling, for example, the Swedes *Gothi*, and by dating the nation's origins back to the descendants of Noah (Rönnow 2010).

The Eighteenth Century

From the beginning of the eighteenth century onwards, the vernacular tongues took over from Latin. New groups of Latin-less readers emerged, especially among the rising middle class. Both in Denmark-Norway and in Sweden, the roles of the languages were passionately discussed from various perspectives, not least from the utilitarian viewpoint that learning and its benefits should not be kept from a wider public. Among those staunchly opposing this view was the groundbreaking scientist and ardent Latinist Carl Linnaeus (1707–1778). The academies of science, founded in 1739 (Sweden) and 1742 (Denmark), nonetheless, published their papers in the vernacular, not in Latin. At this time, the use of Latin became restricted to university contexts, and over the following hundred years, it disappeared from the universities, too: teaching in the vernaculars had become common by 1800, and by 1850, Latin was no longer used even for dissertations.

The Norwegian Ludvig Holberg (1684–1754), who was a professor in Copenhagen, personified both the final phase of Neo-Latin literature and the rise of the vernacular. As a playwright and writer of essays, he imported French and English genres, molded a new literary Danish language to them, and also communicated learned matters to a broader public in Danish works of history, natural law, and moral philosophy. But at the same time, he published important works in Latin: memoirs, epigrams, and the novel *Nicolai Klimii iter subterraneum* (*Niels Klim's Underground Journey*, 1741), a satirical and philosophical novel about travels to remote countries in the vein of Swift's *Gulliver's Travels* (1726). Holberg's choice of Latin for this work was primarily motivated by the internationality of his intended readership. Soon after the publication of the novel, however, it was also translated into several European vernaculars.

In Sweden, the scientist, philosopher, theologian, and Christian mystic Emanuel Swedenborg published all his works in Latin. He also wrote patriotic poems about political and military events of the day; for instance, *Festivus applausus* (*Festive Applause*, 1710), which depicts a victory over Danish troops; another *Festivus applausus* on the return of Charles XII to Sweden from Turkey; *Ludus Heliconius* (*A Play on Mount Helicon*, 1714/1715); and *Camena Borea* (*The Muse of the North*, 1715), a plea for peace (Swedenborg 1995). In Finland, Henrik Hassel and Carl Fredrik Mennander participated in the quarrel of the ancients and the moderns. Hassel wrote a dissertation *De praesenti reipublicae literariae flore* (*The Present-Day Flowering of the Republic of Letters*, 1754) which extolled the moderns to the great detriment of the use of the ancient sources, imitation of the classics, and consequently, the use of the Latin language. Hassel further threatened the Latin language in his (Latin!) *De linguis eruditis* (*The Learned Languages*, 1748), in which he questions using Latin for learned writing.

In the later eighteenth century, yet another reorientation in scholarship took place. German "New Humanism" (*Neuhumanismus*) played off its preference for the Greek world and language against the Roman world and Latin. This movement further damaged the image of Neo-Latin literature after the orientation towards the moderns that had taken place in the previous century. An important representative of *Neuhumanismus* in Finland was Henrik Gabriel Porthan (1739–1804). As he was a professor of eloquence, however, his work also promoted Latin rhetoric and a knowledge of the classical authors among his students.

Suggested Reading

The standard history of Scandinavian Neo-Latin literature is Skafte Jensen (1995). Helander (2004) provides a comprehensive examination of Latin as a literary language, primarily based on Swedish seventeenth-century material. Detailed descriptions of many Neo-Latin printed works can be found in the *Database of Nordic Neo-Latin Literature* at *http://www.uib.no/neolatin/*. Recent research in Scandinavian Neo-Latin has been recorded in a series of articles (titled *Recent Work on Nordic Neo-Latin Literature*) by Karen Skovgaard-Petersen and Peter Zeeberg in the journal *Symbolae Osloenses*, volumes 72 (1997), 76 (2001), 79 (2004), and 85 (2011).

References

Eric XIV. 2003. *Oratio de iniusto bello regis Daniae anno 1563 contra regem Sueciae Ericum 14 gesto*. Edited and translated by Magnus Karlsson. Stockholm: Almqvist and Wiksell.

Helander, Hans. 2004. *Neo-Latin Literature in Sweden in the Period 1620–1720: Stylistics, Vocabulary and Characteristic Ideas*. Uppsala: Uppsala Universitet.

Kraggerud, Egil, ed. 1991. *Kongehyllest: Skrifter av J. J. Wolf og H. Gunnarssøn*. Oslo: Universitetsforlaget.

Laetus, Erasmus. 1992. *Erasmus Laetus' skrift om Christian IVs fødsel og dåb (1577)*. Edited and translated by Karen Skovgaard-Petersen and Peter Zeeberg. Copenhagen: Det Danske Sprog- og Litteraturselskab; Reitzel.

Nilssøn, Jens. 2004. *Biskop Jens Nilssøns latinske skrifter*. Edited by Egil Kraggerud and translated by Mette H. Berg. Oslo: Universitetsforlaget.

Olden-Jørgensen, Sebastian. 1996. *Poesi og politik: Lejlighedsdigtningen ved enevældens indførelse 1660*. Copenhagen: Museum Tusculanum Press.

Phrygius, Sylvester J. 2007. *The Early Latin Poetry of Sylvester Phrygius*. Edited and translated by Peter Sjökvist. Uppsala: Uppsala Universitet.

Rönnow, Magnus. 2010. "Selected War Poetry." Edited and translated by Elena Dahlberg. Licentiate thesis, Uppsala University.

Sarasti-Wilenius, Raija. 2000. *Noster eloquendi artifex: Daniel Achrelius' Latin Speeches and Rhetorical Theory in Seventeenth Century Finland*. Helsinki: Sarasti-Wilenius.

Skafte Jensen, Minna, ed. 1995. *A History of Nordic Neo-Latin Literature*. Odense: Odense University Press.

———. 2004. *Friendship and Poetry: Studies in Danish Neo-Latin Literature*. Edited by Marianne Pade, Karen Skovgaard-Petersen, and Peter Zeeberg. Copenhagen: Museum Tusculanum Press.

Skovgaard-Petersen, Karen. 2002. *Historiography at the Court of Christian IV (1588–1648): Studies in the Latin Histories of Denmark by Johannes Pontanus and Johannes Meursius*. Copenhagen: Museum Tusculanum Press.

Stobaeus, Andreas. 1994. *Two Panegyrics in Verse*. Edited and translated by Maria Berggren. Uppsala: Uppsala Universitet.

Ström, Annika, ed. 1994. *Lachrymae Catharinae: Five Collections of Funeral Poetry from 1628*. Stockholm: Almqvist and Wiksell.

Swedenborg, Emanuel. 1995. *Ludus Heliconius and Other Latin Poems*. Edited and translated by Hans Helander. Uppsala: Uppsala Universitet.

Zeeberg, Peter. 1994. *Tycho Brahes Urania Titani: Et digt om Sophie Brahe*. Copenhagen: Museum Tusculanum Press.

Zeeberg, Peter. 2008. "Virgilian Imitation in Johannes Pratensis' Latin Pastoral *Daphnis* (Copenhagen 1563)." *Symbolae Osloenses* 83:96–103.

———. 2010. "The *Bucolica* (1560) of Erasmus Laetus." In *ACNL* 2010, 839–45.

———. Forthcoming. "Andre sprog i Danmark: Latin." In *Dansk Sproghistorie*, Vol. 5, edited by Ebba Hjorth et al. Copenhagen.

CHAPTER 32

....

EAST-CENTRAL EUROPE

....

CRISTINA NEAGU

Now that Latin has long ceased being an international *lingua franca*, its relative longevity in East-Central Europe might seem surprising. France had abandoned all official use of Latin in 1539 by the Ordinance of Villers-Cotterêts, while in England the much earlier Statute of Pleading (1362) required court proceedings to be in English (Ostler 2007, 294). Elsewhere in Europe, commerce opted for the vernaculars as early as the thirteenth century, and national government, local administration, and law soon followed. In Poland and Hungary, however, all such official business was conducted in Latin until the very end of the eighteenth century, and in some spheres, Latin functioned as an official language well into the nineteenth century: in Hungary, for example, national mining industry regulations printed as late as 1831 in Bratislava were still written in Latin. One reason for this long-lasting retention might be that an absence of clear-cut national divisions characterized Central and Eastern Europe in this era, so Latin constituted a much-needed common language; closeness of ruling dynasties and alliances as well as the Ottoman threat meant that borders kept shifting and histories were frequently shared. IJsewijn, for one, argues that when focusing on the area now occupied by countries such as Poland, the Czech Republic, Slovakia, the former Yugoslavia, Hungary, and Romania, the student of Neo-Latin must forget all modern frontiers (*CNLS* 1:214).

Linking ethnicity to existing boundaries has never been straightforward in this part of the world, which included the historic kingdoms of Hungary, Bohemia, and Poland, the principality of Transylvania, and the easternmost parts of the Holy Roman Empire during the early modern period. In such a fragmented world, the hold of a language, whether Latin or the vernaculars of various ethnic groups, differed substantially. In Poland, for example, several languages coexisted: Poles, Lithuanians, Ruthenians, Armenians, Jews, Germans, Dutch, Muslims, and even Scots all lived together in relative harmony. Hungary, similarly, included a mixture of Hungarians, Slovaks, Jews, Romanians, Germans, and Romany people. Until as late as the end of the First World War, we do better to describe the region, not in terms of nation-states defined by ethnicity and language, but as a complex conglomeration of coexisting smaller entities shaped by distinct traditions. The rich tapestry of vernaculars eventually had a powerful impact on the rise of individual nations within this deeply fractured and diverse political and administrative structure. The influence of Latin as the language of the church, scholarship, politics, and culture was differently unifying, bringing together these different strands of interest, all linked with the study and imitation of the classics. Observing more purposefully the norms of a language associated with formal perfection inevitably affected the shaping and dissemination of ideas, not least because such a wide range of users across almost all areas of post-medieval culture in this part of the world—men of letters, poets, scientists, clergymen, physicians, diplomats, lawyers—tapped into Latin's abundant resources.

Intellectual Migration

To understand the intellectual dynamics of this region, we need to start by looking at how Neo-Latin expression preoccupied authors in different areas of cultural activity. The ideals of Italian humanists who advocated the adoption of ancient Latin literary and linguistic conventions to reinstate a cultural preeminence lost after the fall of Rome traveled quickly to the far ends of the Continent, and during the later fifteenth century, Hungary, Poland, and the Austrian and Czech lands were among the first countries north of the Alps to emulate Italian Renaissance culture (Almási 2009, 24). Humanists traveled both out of and towards Italy, and for most, such travel became synonymous with archival archaeology whereby they recovered previously unavailable classical texts that became central to humanistic studies (*studia humanitatis*). The pursuit of knowledge and ambitions for a more elevated career turned most humanists into frequent travelers.

In the Czech territories (Bohemia, Moravia, and Slovakia), the first contact with Italian humanism dates back to the mid-fourteenth century. Johannes Noviforensis (German: Johannes von Neumarkt; Czech: Jan ze Středy), chancellor to Emperor Charles IV, is considered responsible for Petrarch's 1365 visit to Prague, as we know from extant and revealing correspondence between the two men. Petrarch's side of the correspondence focuses on education, and on the idea that the court could be a favorable medium for disseminating scholarship, while Noviforensis's letters show how in tune the two men were and how intellectually refined the court in Prague was at that time (Špička 2010, 30). Petrarch's high regard for a land so far from Roman luxury is not surprising, given that Charles IV's reign (1346–1378) is remembered as the "Golden Age" of Bohemia, when Prague was a flourishing imperial capital and an increasingly enticing center of learning, with a university (founded in 1378), an ever growing number of spectacular buildings, and an impressive manuscript production. An excellent example of an achievement by local *scriptoria* is the *Liber viaticus*, a traveling breviary containing psalms, hymns, and ceremonies for feasts throughout the year, commissioned around 1360 by Noviforensis, whose official position enabled him to support thriving manuscript production. Now held in the Knihovna Národního Muzea (National Museum

Library) in Prague (XIII A 12), the *Liber viaticus* is just the most famous of many examples that illustrate the sophistication of Renaissance Bohemian book production.

The lure of Prague stirred the interest of many later humanists, including the prolific and versatile Enea Silvio Piccolomini (1405–1464). Piccolomini was a first-class historian, deeply immersed in regional politics as papal legate and later as Pope Pius II. Piccolomini's *Historia rerum Friderici III imperatoris* (*History of the Emperor Frederick III*, 1452–1458) helps us understand the wider context of the events he discusses, while his *Historia Bohemica* (*Bohemian History*, 1458), one of the most important Renaissance sources of information about the region, reflects his interest in the Czech lands, as does his *De Europa* (*Europe*, 1458), an ambitious unfinished cosmography that describes the geographical, ethnographic, and historical characteristics of Europe and Asia in which Piccolomini effectively first puts the East-Central European regions on the map for the West (Piccolomini 2001). He began this study by focusing on the kingdom of Hungary, viewing its survival as essential to avoiding conflict with the Ottoman Empire. Before Piccolomini, other Italian humanists had also become involved in Hungarian affairs. The acquaintance of Pier Paolo Vergerio the Elder (1370–1444) with the region was to prove lasting, since he settled in Hungary from 1418 until his death. His brief was to reorganize the chancellery according to humanistic principles, but he did much more, and under his influence Hungarian scholars gained a chance to form close contacts with humanist circles in Italy, which became particularly well-established at the courts of Buda, Cracow, and Prague. During the reign of King Matthias Corvinus (1440–1490) at the court of Buda, for instance, among the most charismatic foreign figures present were Antonio Bonfini (1434–1503) and Francesco Bandini (d. after 1490). Bandini acted as an architectural advisor to the king and (as a close associate of Marsilio Ficino) tried to establish a "Platonic Academy"; Bonfini's *Rerum Ungaricarum decades* (*Decades of Hungarian History*, finished in 1497, but only published between 1543 and 1568) constitutes one of the main sources of information regarding early Hungarian and East European history.

The pursuit of foreign contacts started at the Habsburg court of Vienna but was similarly in vogue at their court in Prague. By the 1570s, Habsburg tolerance had brought prosperity throughout the empire, and the court of the Holy Roman Emperor Maximilian II (1527–1576) became a magnet, not only for German-speaking intellectuals, but also for Italians, French, and Dutch, hosting humanists such as Hugo Blotius and Justus Lipsius, the Milanese artist Giuseppe Arcimboldo, the composer Philippe de Monte, the English mathematician John Dee, and the natural philosophers Carel Fabritius and Carolus Clusius. Rudolf II (1552–1612) seamlessly continued Maximilian's patronage, beginning his reign with the bold gesture of moving his court from Vienna to Prague. Like his father, the new emperor brought into his service European artists, architects, scientists, philosophers, and humanists, among whom were Bartholomeus Spranger, Adriaen De Vries, Jacob Hoefnagel, Tycho Brahe, Johannes Kepler, Erasmus Habermehl, Jost Bürgi, and Giordano Bruno. To illustrate the centrality of Prague, a print circulated widely during the sixteenth century that depicted Europe as a queen with her head in Iberia, arms in Italy and Jutland, and dress billowing eastwards; Spain outlines her crown, Sicily and Denmark her orb and scepter, and Bohemia, tellingly, stands in the place of her heart (Evans 2006, 76).

Scholarly networks developed fast in all directions. Strong immigration facilitated by princely courts and religious liberty, particularly in Poland and Transylvania, was counterbalanced by the emigration of young men to attend Italian, German, Swiss, and French universities, especially Ferrara and Padua. Padua's academic reputation was so elevated that in 1574, the Habsburg candidate for the Polish throne promised to send the sons of a hundred noblemen to study there at his own expense. Among the many Polish students who studied at Padua were Nicolaus Copernicus, Klemens Janicki, Stanislaus Hosius, and Jan Kochanowski; the equally impressive list of Hungarian and Croatian intellectuals includes Janus Pannonius, Andreas Dudith, Johannes Sambucus, Stephanus Brodericus, Ferenc Forgách, Nicolaus Istvánffy, and Antonius Verantius (Almási 2009, 47).

The Aristocratization of Learning

In East-Central Europe more than anywhere else, perhaps, Latin made its way into the nobility. Aristocratic families constituted up to ten percent of the population: although they enjoyed many privileges, the nobility also developed a sense of public duty, educated their youth, took keen interest in current affairs, and traveled widely. The Bohemian baron Bohuslav Hasištejnský of Lobkovice (Hassenstenius; 1462–1510), the young nobleman Zdeněk Brtnický z Valdštejna (1581–1623), Mihály Forgách (d. 1603), Baron of Ghymes, and the Moldavian prince Dimitrie Cantemir (1673–1723) are just a few examples of highly educated, well-traveled aristocrats who wrote in creative, expressive Latin. Like most of his educated contemporaries, Hasištejnský studied at Bologna and Ferrara, and in 1482, he became a doctor of law. A restless, inquisitive spirit, he traveled extensively; of his journeys, those to the Holy Land and Egypt are perhaps the most spectacular, although not documented in detail. Hasištejnský was a successful essayist, a prolific poet, and an author of philosophical prose. Among his many writings are *Ad sanctum Venceslaum* (*To St. Wenceslas*; Hasištejnský 2006, 23–30), a satire on Bohemian national life, and *De situ Pragae* (*The Region of Prague*, Hasištejnský 1969, 1–12), a well-documented topographical and historical work about Prague and its inhabitants.

Works focusing on descriptions of peoples, lands, and regions are numerous, although Neo-Latin scholarship has yet to discuss these in depth (*CNLS* 2:335). Travel writing had always been popular in this region. During the late fifteenth and sixteenth centuries, authors such as Martin Kabátník (d. 1503), Oldřich Prefát of Vlkanova (1523–1565), and Kryštof Harant of Polžic (1564–1621) wrote accounts of their journeys, and a very accomplished manuscript travel diary was kept by Zdeněk Brtnický. This diary covers the years 1597–1603 and begins with the narrator's studies at Strasbourg, then describes his journey to France, the Netherlands, England, Switzerland, Germany, Austria, and Italy. Another writer interested in travel was Baron Mihály Forgách, whose *Oratio de peregrinatione et eius laudibus* (*Speech on Traveling and Its Merits*, Wittenberg, 1587) is indebted both to the rhetorical technique of the Roman politician Marcus Junius Brutus (ca. 85–42 BCE; as described by Cicero in *Brutus*) and to Justus Lipsius's advice to profit from a so-called *peregrinatio academica* ("scholarly pilgrimage") and the association with *viri illustres* ("illustrious men"). Forgách wrote passionately about this advice and followed Lipsius's suggestion to the letter. Forgách, like most of his contemporaries, had attended famous universities (Strasbourg and Wittenberg). The relatively high proportion of university attendees among the East-Central European nobility and their exceptional mobility suggest their desire to validate their status, in reaction to the growing competition from lower-born contemporaries who successfully used their learning to occupy ever more powerful political and ecclesiastical administrative positions (Almási 2009, 54).

The Moldavian prince Dimitrie Cantemir, a prolific and original philosopher, historian, composer, musicologist, linguist, and ethnographer, was a rather special case who arrived late on the scene. Cantemir's native Moldavia was slow to join the republic of letters and, apart from the talented poet Johannes Sommer (1542–1574), there were not many other writers from that region one could mention. Most of the Moldavian population spoke a Romance language (Romanian) as in neighboring Wallachia, but Latin was not the first choice of written language: Church Slavonic tended to be used in official documents, and literature mainly opted for the vernacular. Cantemir was a remarkable exception: sophisticated and learned, he was what one might call a quintessential man of the Enlightenment. Unusually, however, his education began in the heart of the Ottoman Empire in Constantinople, where the historian and cartographer Meletios Mitrou, the future archbishop of Athens (1661–1714), introduced the young man to the latest trends in philosophy, historiography, sciences, and the works of Flemish chemist and physician Jan Baptist van Helmont (1580–1644). Cantemir's thoroughly "Western" education in the Ottoman Empire may seem odd, but contemporary sources reveal a distinctly open intellectual environment where conversational Latin was frequently used (Uță-Bărbulescu 2011, 10–12).

Cantemir returned to Moldavia a deeply original scholar. His political reign was short and unsuccessful, but as a man of letters he was widely admired in scholarly circles, and elected as a member of the Berlin Academy. His abundant corpus in Latin, Romanian, Turkish, and Russian reveals strains of Leibnizian rationalism, Byzantine philosophizing, and, crucially, a profound understanding of Islamic Ottoman culture (Nemoianu 1990, 593). His best-known work is *Incrementorum et decrementorum aulae Othmannicae historiae* (*Histories of the Growths and Diminutions of the Ottoman Court*; 1714–1716; Cantemir 2002), which became the main Continental source for Ottoman history. Unexpectedly, given its popularity, it circulated only in manuscript until Nicholas Tindal's English translation was printed in London in 1734–1735. Also much admired was Cantemir's *Descriptio Moldaviae* (*Description of Moldavia*, 1716; Cantemir 2006), a complex chorographical monograph that offers a rigorous and precise portrait of Moldavia. The book's novelty of detail is hugely interesting, but it is the quality of Cantemir's Latin that makes it exciting: it flows smoothly and naturally, recalling the modulations of his mother tongue, and the influence of Romanian is particularly noticeable when the author becomes emotional in his Latin account. He uses the pronoun *unus* as an indefinite article, frequently changes the gender of nouns, and favors a distinctly un-classical Latin syntax, all of which practices suggest a specific vernacular behind his Latin (Nicolae 2012, 776).

CULTURAL NATIONALISM

The popularity of geography and topography, exemplified by Cantemir's *Descriptio Moldaviae*, is unsurprising, given the impact of the voyages of exploration on European culture. Even so, a great number of chorographies were written in East-Central Europe, and the further we look from well-known cultural centers towards the periphery, the higher the concentration of chorographical works. These authors took advantage of a genre in vogue to publish attractive works of both descriptive and historical geography that focused on a complex, little-known region, always so prone to conflict and misunderstanding.

An interesting example is the sixteenth-century debate over Dacia's Roman heritage, which reflects the general humanist project to appropriate the classical past in which either the negation or the affirmation of a people's Latin legacy generally confirmed the author's sense of superiority. More than one ethnic group fought for the title: the area occupied by the Romans in northern Dacia was inhabited by three ethnic groups—Saxons, Magyars, and Wallachs—who all vigorously claimed a share in this ancient heritage, and each claimed to have the oldest roots. In 1591, for instance, Albert Huet (Hutterus), *Comes Saxonum* (Count of the Saxon nation), addressed a speech to the Prince of Transylvania and his counselors in which he stated that the first nation of Transylvania was the Saxon, originating from the Goths and the Dacians (Almási 2010, 102). Hutterus was just one in a series of humanists to elaborate on the idea, and Caspar Peucer (1525–1602)—probably influenced by Transylvanian students in Wittenberg—seems to have been the most widely read. Peucer claimed that the arrival of the Saxons in Transylvania during the reign of Charlemagne was no more than a tale, and that they actually arrived much earlier (Almási 2010, 102–3). According to the Magyar claim, Hungarian history started with Attila the Hun and his victorious encounter with the Romans; János Thurozi's *Chronica Hungarorum* (*Chronicle of the Hungarians*, 1488) sees in Attila a glamorous forebear of Matthias Corvinus, a popular line also exploited by Miklós Oláh (Nicolaus Olahus), Miklós Zrínyi, and later Mátyás Bél. Two hundred years before humanists took center stage, the identity of the Hungarians in Transylvania and elsewhere was developed into a full-fledged mythology in a chronicle written by Simon of Keza (1282–1285), which traced Attila's origins to the Scythians, a legendary people deemed by some (even as late as the nineteenth century) to be the original inhabitants of Africa, the builders of the pyramids, who, legends say, migrated towards the Black Sea and settled in Thracia (Klaniczay 2011, 183). So compelling was this story, and so pure the pedigree it alleged, that we see many supporters of a *Hungarus* identity even among the Transylvanian Saxons (Almási 2010, 103 and n. 47).

This brings us to the third nation claiming Dacian origin: the Wallachs, whose case was mainly developed abroad. Italians were among the first humanists to refer to the survival of Trajan's colonists, starting with Poggio Bracciolini in the mid-fifteenth century. Poggio was closely followed by Biondo Flavio, who elaborated on Poggio's statement that "the Dacians or Wallachs claim to have Roman origins." Biondo wrote: "I was delighted to hear them speaking and hear that when they did it in the common and ordinary manner of their people, their dialect reminded me of a rustic and ungrammatical Latin" (Almási 2010, 107). By far the most influential author on the question of the Wallachs' Roman origins was Piccolomini: in his *De Europa*, discussed above, he was the first to claim that the name "Wallachus" originated from "Flaccus," the commander of the Roman army who seized the land from the Dacians (Almási, 2009, 108).

Humanism as "Patria"

The abundance of chorographies and chronicles relates directly to the region's turbulent history. Whole countries became increasingly an endangered borderland of the Ottoman Empire, especially after the Battle of Mohács in 1526, a singularly decisive event in which the army led by King Louis II of Hungary and Bohemia was annihilated by that of Sultan Suleiman "the Magnificent," and which led to the long-lasting partition of Hungary between the Ottoman Empire, the Habsburg monarchy, and the Principality of Transylvania. In its wake, a once-rich, powerful kingdom became unrecognizable: the cream of Hungarian nobility perished, and the establishment collapsed, never to recover. Hungarian humanists were exiled all over Europe, and while Italy's lure was still powerful, it was increasingly Vienna and figures like Konrad Celtis (1459–1508) which attracted the new generation of East-Central humanists. The philosophy of Celtis and his followers, based on the assimilation of Neo-Platonism, had a strong impact upon such scholars as the Silesian Caspar Ursinus Velius (1493–1539), historian to Emperor Ferdinand I; and Johannes Alexander Brassicanus (ca. 1500–1539), who, like Velius, taught Greek at the University of Vienna. The most notable Hungarians in the circle around Celtis were Miklós Oláh (1493–1568); his successor as archbishop of Esztergom, Antonius Verantius (1504–1573); Stephanus Brodericus (ca. 1471–1539), bishop of Szerém and author of an eyewitness history of the Battle of Mohács; and Johannes Sambucus (1531–1584).

All these men lived through political shockwaves and religious turbulence, as well as at a time when Erasmian ideas profoundly influenced Europe's intellectual climate. Denied the safety of a homeland, much of this generation was in self-imposed exile for long periods. Seeking a home outside the borders of what was once their country, they ended up recovering the idea of *patria* in both their writings and their actions. If the idea of a ruling elite imbued with culture was characteristic of fifteenth-century Hungarian humanism, the early sixteenth century fostered a more acutely politically aware generation. Exile and hardship created a nostalgia for what was increasingly perceived as a realm of security, a golden age, which though no longer attainable, was not forgotten. What this realm of security required was reflection and clarity, manifest, among other things, in a noticeable literary shift from the lyrical to the narrative in the literature produced following Mohács (Birnbaum 1986, 60–61).

During this period of displacement, manuscripts on the history of Hungary produced by authors at King Matthias's court started to appear in print. To take just a few examples, the first three decades of Antonio Bonfini's history of Hungary were only published in 1543 through the editorial efforts of the Transylvanian Martin Brenner, having previously circulated only in manuscripts (of which five have survived). In the 1543 edition, the last part of Bonfini's work, describing the times of Matthias Corvinus, was missing, but by 1561, there was a real urgency about editing the complete Bonfini: the project had become highly politicized, due to the interests of patrons such as Tamás Nádasdy (the Hungarian Palatine), Ferenc Révai (the Deputy Palatine), Ferenc Forgách (bishop of Várad), and Antonius Verantius. The correspondence of the Hungarian humanist Sigismundus Torda (Gelous, d. 1569) with the Basel publisher Johannes Oporinus illuminates these efforts: Torda was keen to publish the whole of Bonfini's work, but ultimately it was Johannes Sambucus who finally printed it, in 1568.

Besides the publication of works originally written during Matthias's reign, there was also a trend for producing new historical accounts of fifteenth-century accomplishments. One of the first was Miklós Oláh's bipartite work *Hungaria-Athila* (*Hungary-Attila*). The *Hungaria* lingers—across nineteen chapters—on the beauty, wealth, and glory of Matthias's age. Although composed during 1536 and 1537, when the humanist was becoming an ever more influential figure at Queen Mary's court in Brussels, no edition of *Hungaria* appeared until 1735, when Mátyás Bél (1684–1749) published it in his *Adparatus ad historiam Hungariae* (*Provision for a History of Hungary*). The delay in printing *Athila* is less striking, since Johannes Sambucus included it in his celebrated edition of Bonfini's *Rerum Ungaricarum decades* of 1568. This is a monumental edition comprising not only Bonfini's first thirty books (previously published by Brenner) but also another ten books issued by the Transylvanian printer Gáspár Heltai (d. 1574) in 1565 (Neagu 2003, 204–5). Sambucus's edition also included texts from manuscripts owned by Révai and Forgách, as well as his own continuation of Bonfini's treatise providing details from the Jagellonian period (1496–1526), and Stephanus Brodericus's account of the Battle of Mohács. Taken for granted by most while the Hungarian kingdom was still basking in its days of glory and political stability, fifteenth-century cultural achievements began to be treasured almost obsessively when they became part of Hungary's past. Filtered through the eyes of the new generation, these achievements acquired a meaning capable not only of helping restore Hungarian self-confidence, but also of creating something resembling a resistance movement. By looking deep into a world that was disappearing before their eyes, sixteenth-century East-Central European scholars instinctively assumed the role of new image-builders. Significantly, and perhaps paradoxically, since this trend ultimately led to modern nationalism, most chorographies and chronicles produced in this part of the world were written in Latin until as late as the nineteenth century.

IMITATION, PROPAGANDA, AND FREEDOM OF EXPRESSION

Neo-Latin in this region flowered relatively late and, at first glance, with little original-ity. Much of this writing seemed to follow conventional principles, taking for granted Latin's primacy as a means of elegant expression and of recreating the virtues of classical civilization. Latin writing expanded despite the growth of the vernaculars (Evans 1979, 26), and the vogue for verse was an especially notable trend. Important poets include the Bohemian laureate Kaspar Brusch (1519–1559); Laurentius Corvinus (1465–1527), a Silesian scholar and one of the finest poets of the early Renaissance; Johann Michael Lange (1664–1731), another Silesian, professor of theology and, like Brusch, poet lau-reate in the Holy Roman Empire; the court poet of Emperor Rudolf II, Jiří Carolides (1579–1612); and the many exceptional Polish poets, among whom are Johannes Dantiscus (1485–1548), Klemens Janicki (1516–1543), Sebastianus Klonowicz (Acernus, 1542–1602), and Simon Simonides (1558–1629).

A member of King Sigismund I's diplomatic service and the first Polish poet laure-ate, Dantiscus was mentioned frequently in contemporary accounts as a congenial courtier and a great admirer of Erasmus, with whom he corresponded (Bietenholz and Deutscher [1985–1987] 2003, 377). His poems include early confessions of love, reli-gious verse, epigrams, epitaphs, and political panegyrics. His panegyrics include *Soteria* (1518; the title, used by Statius in *Silvae* 1.4, could be paraphrased as "gifts given upon the recovery from illness or escape from danger"); formally conceived as classical imitation, however, the poem reflects Dantiscus's present context in its address to Sigmund von Herberstein (1486–1566), a nobleman and fellow diplomat recovering from a difficult mission in the service of Maximilian I. Dantiscus compares von Herberstein to Ulysses, for example, but also focuses on contemporary events and complex policies. Markedly different from Dantiscus in his composition of highly strung and more personal poetry is Klemens Janicki. Janicki wrote numerous classically inspired epigrams, epitaphs, and *stemmata* (poems on coats of arms), but particularly favored elegy, as exemplified by his *Tristia* (*Sorrows*, 1541), a collection of ten elegies inspired by Ovid's *Tristia*. Deeply per-sonal and direct, strikingly elegant in style, Janicki's *Tristia* is the work of one of the most gifted writers of the Renaissance and one of the last of the Polish humanist poets to write only in Latin. The later sixteenth century in Poland was increasingly characterized by the steady cultivation of the vernacular as a literary language, a phenomenon indebted both to the impact of the Reformation and to the emergence of popular post-humanist culture. The first great Polish-language poet Jan Kochanowski (1530–1584), however, also continued to write in Latin. His impressive *oeuvre* includes Horatian odes (*Lyrica*), epigrams (*Foricoenia* [*Outdoor Celebrations*]), occasional poems, and four books of erotic elegies that place him within the tradition of Callimachus and Propertius (*CNLS* 1:242).

In Hungary, we discover another poet who escaped the constraints of his homeland and became, under the classical name of Janus Pannonius (1434–1472), a poet whose talent and controversial political career have always kept him in the limelight. His poems give readers an unprecedented view of the multifaceted world he inhabited as a writer and statesman. While he was studying in Italy, his name was usually associated with panegyrics and a lively, often irreverent, series of epigrams outstanding for their ingenuity and formal brilliance. After returning to Hungary in 1458, however, he embraced the elegiac mode with increasing pathos (Pannonius 1784, especially 279 and 286–96). Increasingly, he wrote as a rhetorician, not just because of the elegance of his style, but also as a means to persuade and to encourage others to become politically engaged; his writings functioned as a channel of creative energy for the humanist as a citizen (*vir civilis*) engaged in the exercise of duty.

THE PRACTICAL RELEVANCE OF LEARNING

The cult of the *Stammbuch* or *liber amicorum* ("friendship book") illustrates patterns of cultivated exchange in the second half of the sixteenth century. These autograph albums, including entries from friends encountered on one's travels, flourished particularly in the Germanic lands and Central Europe. Superficially formal, the surviving *Stammbücher* nonetheless reveal much about the movements, reading patterns, and preferred authors of educated society, and include a wide range of locations from provincial backwaters to exciting cosmopolitan centers. Latin predominates, but vernacular entries also regularly occur. Browsing through a typical album such as that of the Moravian nobleman Zdeněk Brtnický z Valdštejna, we learn that he studied first in Silesia, and then at Strasbourg, where his companions included a wide cross-section of compatriots. To complete his education, he traveled through the Netherlands, England, France, and Italy, and his album records, among others, the names of Justus Lipsius (1547–1606), Joseph Scaliger (1547–1609), Giulio Pace (1550–1631), and Hugo Grotius (1583–1645). Interpersonal dialogue within the *respublica litteraria* was commonplace, but the intensity with which East-Central European humanists applied themselves to networking was impressive: from the pragmatic documentation of fairly random encounters in their autograph albums, to the art of letter writing and letter collecting, they ensured that long-sought-after meetings were not forgotten. A deeply self-conscious breed, these humanists did everything they could to escape provincialism (Evans 1979, 29–31). Reading through their copious works, it strikes us as true for most of them that the practical relevance of learning was one great concern.

Examining an author like the Moravian-born Jan Amos Comenius (1592–1670), for instance, it is difficult to pick out a single guiding principle characteristic of a system of thought best described as full of obscurities and apparent contradictions. On one hand, Comenius was a theologian enamored with metaphysics and imbued with the speculative spirit of the seventeenth century; but on the other, most of his books focus on pedagogy, the field in which he made his most significant intellectual contribution. One of the first to support lifelong and equal opportunity learning, Comenius advocated a form of universal instruction that included poor children and women. He argued for the need for logical thinking and teaching based on the natural movement from simple to complex concepts (Comenius 1657, 43):

Nec ulla sufficiens dari potest ratio, cur sequior sexus (ut de hoc peculiariter aliquid moneam) a sapientiae studiis (sive Latinis litteris, sive sermone patrio tradendis) omnino excludendus sit.

Nor can any good reason be given why the weaker sex (to give a word of advice on this point in particular) should be excluded from the pursuit of knowledge (whether in Latin or in their mother tongue).

Comenius's vision for a democratic education was bold, especially in the context of a deeply troubled and war-stricken contemporary Europe. Related to this egalitarian impulse, Comenius also apparently introduced the pictorial textbook: his eye-catching *Orbis sensualium pictus* (*World of the Senses Depicted*), written during his stay in Transylvania in 1650, is divided into 150 chapters on a range of subjects, illustrated by woodcuts. Its innovative format compresses into a unified presentation of pictures and text an essential knowledge of the world: each image portrays an aspect either of nature or human society in language simple enough for a child starting its study. The book had a huge impact: originally published in Latin (1657), it was quickly translated into German, and the first quadrilingual edition (Latin, German, Italian, and French) appeared in 1666. A Czech translation was added in 1685 to make another quadrilingual edition (with Latin, German, and Hungarian). The first of several English editions appeared in 1659, translated as *Visible World* by Charles Hoole, a London schoolmaster, and the book continued to be printed in other countries until a final school edition was published in Prague in 1845.

Meanwhile, the imperial court in Prague was one of the most colorful and intellectually stimulating places in Europe, and it managed to preserve a degree of unity despite religious schisms, wars, and opposing theories. At Rudolf's court, Protestants and Catholics saw themselves as a recognizably single body of cosmopolitan scholars and artists (Evans 1979, 3), and this resulted in an unhindered pursuit of knowledge that expanded on the inherited picture of wisdom, confronting certainties with the evidence of discoveries that were themselves subjected to criticism as scholars became immersed in the wish to reform and to debate method and constructed systems. Much discussed at Rudolf's court were magic, astrology, alchemy, Neo-Platonism, and the Kabbalah. Art, philosophy, and the practice of science also flourished, as Rudolf brought into his service some of the most important European artists, architects, scientists, philosophers, and humanists, creating a powerhouse of Renaissance thinkers who were open to uncomfortable truths and opted to reconcile opposites whenever possible.

Latin scientific works are among the most important publications in this region during the sixteenth century. In the open-minded atmosphere of Rudolf's court, a groundbreaking book like Nicolaus Copernicus's *De revolutionibus orbium coelestium* (*The Revolutions of the Heavenly Spheres*, 1543), which appeared at the end of his life, was not only not forbidden in Prague, but was freely discussed. Copernicus's quiet existence was puzzling, because by the early 1540s, a summary of his ideas was already in print, facilitated by a young Austrian-born mathematician, Georg Joachim Rheticus (1514–1574). In 1539, Rheticus had visited Copernicus, who, swept along by the young man's enthusiasm, allowed Rheticus to pass his theory on to the learned world as an informative communication Rheticus addressed to Johannes Schöner, the *Narratio prima* (*First Account*), which was quickly printed twice, in Gdańsk (1540) and Basel (1541). Despite the revolutionary nature of the argument, Rheticus's unusual preview of heliocentrism went almost unnoticed, but the lack of response did not stop Copernicus from worrying about voicing his ideas, since their reception, in religious circles particularly, concerned him deeply. Although very different in nature, both Rheticus's *Narratio* and the introduction of *De Revolutionibus* wisely and tactically present the system as a hypothesis, which may explain why it had such an easy reception. Its specialized audience clearly held it in high esteem: documented copies belonged to many illustrious scholars, such as Giordano Bruno (1548–1600), Tycho Brahe (1546–1601), Galileo Galilei (1564–1642), and Johannes Kepler (1571–1630), all of whom engaged extensively with Copernican theory in their own Latin writing.

We move to another Latin-writing scientist from the region, Kepler, whose influential three-volume work written in Prague, the *Epitome astronomiae Copernicanae* (*Epitome of Copernican Astronomy*, 1618–1621) effectively proved Copernicus's hypothesis to be true and consequently made a major contribution to the birth of modern science. Using Tycho Brahe's observations from the last few decades before the invention of the telescope, Kepler discovered the laws of planetary motion—that a planet moves in an ellipse with the sun and thereby sweeps equal areas in equal time, and finally that a mathematical relationship exists between the size of a planet's orbit and the speed with which it travels around the sun, confirming that there must be a force in the sun that drives the planets relative to their distance from the sun, which Newton later identified as gravity. All of this revolutionary thought stemmed from Copernicus's work in Frombork (Fromborg), a small town in northern Poland, where he dared to postulate the existence of a heliocentric system. At the glamorous court of Rudolf II in Prague, Kepler was the first to understand correctly and quantitatively how the planets move.

The work Copernicus did at Frombork shows that one need not always look to well-established centers like Rudolf II's Prague or Matthias Corvinus's Buda for extraordinary cultural activity. Similarly, Oradea, an unassuming Transylvanian town, also harbored greatness, and among its many assets was a very special capitulary school that, at its height, was overseen by János Vitéz (1408–1472) and included Janus Pannonius and Miklós Oláh among its students. The school's lively intellectual climate also attracted well-established scholars like Paolo Vergerio, whose involvement in regional culture we have already discussed; as well as Filippo Podocataro, a Greek poet and Guarino's former student at Ferrara; and Gregory of Sanok (1403–1477), the Polish humanist and free-thinking archbishop of Lwów (modern-day Lviv in Ukraine). As archbishop of Oradea in modern-day Romania, Vitéz had also helped found a famous astronomical observatory: he commissioned Georg Peuerbach, professor of astronomy and mathematics at the University of Vienna (1423–1461) to create the *Tabulae Waradienses* (*Oradean Tables*), which helped calculate the eclipses of the moon and the sun and became the standard manual of European astronomers for two centuries. Completed by around 1459, the *Tabulae* were still used (although critically) by Tycho Brahe and survive in several manuscript copies. Two, copied by Peuerbach's former student and one of the most widely respected astronomers of his time, Johannes Regiomontanus (1436–1476), are especially precious (Venice, MS lat. 342; Nuremberg, Cent. V 57), and the work was also beautifully printed in a version edited by Georg Tannstetter (1514).

CONCLUSION

East-Central European Neo-Latinity, through its often unexpected trends and trail-blazing figures, has had a profound impact on European civilization. Almost all of the most influential and visionary works written here were published in Latin, from Comenius's ideas about equal opportunities in education, to Copernicus's heliocentric universe and Kepler's laws of planetary motion. Much of this region's Latin writing seems to push at conventional frontiers, do away with inherited ideas, and try new ground. To return briefly to Kepler as a fruitful example: not only did he prove Copernicus right and pave the way for Newtonian physics, but he also appears to have come up with the first work of science fiction, the *Somnium* (*Dream*, 1634). Here Kepler imagines a journey to the moon where space travelers stand on its surface and see the earth rotating slowly above them. The protagonist of this narrative uses his mother's spells to leave the earth; he speculates on the mountains, valleys, craters, climate, and possible inhabitants of the moon. In a strange coincidence, the original concept of rocket propulsion also came from this part of Europe: in a manuscript written between 1529 and 1569, discovered in the archives of Sibiu (MS Varia II 374), another small Transylvanian town, the author Conrad Haas (1509–1576) described delta stabilizing fins, bell nozzles, bundling, and using liquid fuel, thus introducing innovative concepts about rocket science at a time when nothing like this existed.

As for exploring uncharted territories, during the nineteenth century, another mathematician from distant Transylvania began to develop the basic ideas of hyperbolic geometry in Latin. János Bolyai (1802–1860) wrote to his father Wolfgang on November 3, 1823, that he had "created a new, another world out of nothing." The younger Bolyai had developed a complete system of non-Euclidean geometry, and in 1831, he published the *Appendix scientiam spatii absolute veram exhibens* (*Appendix Explaining the Absolutely True Science of Space*); "Appendix" referred to the conception of Bolyai's work as an addendum to his father's book on geometry, *Tentamen iuventutem studiosam in elementa matheseos . . . introducendi* (*Attempt to Introduce the Studious Youth to the Principles of Mathematics*), to which it was in fact appended a year later, in 1832. Bolyai's discovery was acknowledged by Carl Friedrich Gauß (1777–1855), and it helped free mathematicians to study abstract concepts irrespective of any possible connection with the physical world.

Original and exciting as they continue to be, most of these works are either little known or completely obscure today. Paradoxically, the language in which they were written, which was supposed to make them universally accessible, has rendered them unreadable by the majority. Although, as we have seen, Latin remained the official language of the region until the nineteenth century, in practice fewer and fewer people could read and write it fluently. But given the often extraordinary nature of these works, it is time to re-engage. New scholarship might target the highly innovative works of figures such as Johannes Sambucus and Georg Peuerbach, or those whom, for reasons of space, we could not discuss in the present essay, like Georgius de Hungaria (1422–1502) and Johannes Honterus (1498–1549), who all exemplify the originality and style characteristic of a region that, although remote, fragmented, and torn by conflicts, was also distinctly European, an iconic frontier whose geography, history, folklore, and cultural expression all invite further attention.

Suggested Reading

Among the best general references accounting for specific developments within the cultural idiom of Central and Eastern Europe Neo-Latinity are Almási (2009) and Birnbaum (1986). Basic information about aspects regarding historical developments and geographical diffusion of Neo-Latin is provided by IJsewijn (1990). A number of studies discuss literary trends within specific regions, such as Glomski (2007); comprehensive modern editions of individual authors include Cantemir (2002) and Hasištejnský (1969–1980). To understand the historical context of this region characterized by its ever-shifting frontiers and political alliances, a very good introduction is Evans (1979). For other studies by the author related to the contents of this chapter, see Neagu (2003, 2012).

References

Almási, Gábor. 2009. *The Uses of Humanism: Johannes Sambucus (1531–1584), Andreas Dudith (1533–1589), and the Republic of Letters in East Central Europe.* Leiden: Brill.
———. 2010. "Constructing the Wallach 'Other' in the Late Renaissance." In *Whose Love of Which Country? Composite States, National Histories and Patriotic Discourses in Early Modern East Central Europe*, edited by Balázs Trencsényi and Márton Zászkaliczky, 91–129. Leiden: Brill.

Bietenholz, Peter G., and Thomas B. Deutscher, eds. (1985–1987) 2003. *Contemporaries of Erasmus: A Biographical Register of the Renaissance and Reformation.* Toronto: University of Toronto Press.

Birnbaum, Marianna. 1986. *Humanists in a Shattered World: Croatian and Hungarian Latinity in the Sixteenth Century.* Columbus: Slavica Press.

Cantemir, Dimitrie. 2002. *Incrementorum et decrementorum aulae Othman(n)icae sive Aliothman(n)icae historiae a prima gentis origine ad nostra usque tempora deductae libri tres.* Edited by Virgil Cândea and Dan Sluşanschi. Timişoara: Editura Amarcord.

———. 2006. *Descriptio antiqui et hodierni status Moldaviae.* Edited by Dan Sluşanschi. Bucharest: Institutul Cultural Român.

Comenius, Jan A. 1657. *Opera Didactica Omnia.* Amsterdam: Laurentius de Geer.

Evans, Robert J. W. 1979. *The Making of the Habsburg Monarchy 1550–1700: An Interpretation.* Oxford: Clarendon Press.

———. 2006. *Austria, Hungary, and the Habsburgs: Essays on Central Europe, c. 1683–1867.* Oxford: Oxford University Press.

Glomski, Jaqueline. 2007. *Patronage and Humanist Literature in the Age of the Jagiellons.* Toronto: University of Toronto Press.

Hasištejnský, Bohuslav. 1969–1980. *Epistulae.* Edited by Jan Martínek and Dana Martínková. 2 vols. Leipzig: Teubner.

———. 2006. *Opera poetica.* Edited by Marta Vaculínová. Munich: Saur.

Klaniczay, Gábor. 2011. "The Myths of Scythian Origin and the Cult of Attila in the Nineteenth Century." In *Multiple Antiquities—Multiple Modernities: Ancient Histories in Nineteenth Century European Cultures,* edited by Gábor Klaniczay, Michael Werner, and Ottó Gecser, 183–210. Frankfurt: Campus.

Neagu, Cristina. 2003. *Servant of the Renaissance: The Poetry and Prose of Nicolaus Olahus.* Bern: Lang.

———. 2012. "The Power of the Book and the Kingdom of Hungary during the Fifteenth Century." In *Humanism in Fifteenth-Century Europe,* edited by David Rundle, 147–74. Oxford: Medium Aevum.

Nemoianu, Virgil. 1990. "Mihai Şora and the Traditions of Romanian Philosophy." *The Review of Metaphysics* 43:591–605.

Nicolae, Florentina. 2012. "The Influence of the Romanian Language in *Vita Constantini Cantemyrii, Cognomento Senis, Moldaviae Principis.*" In *ACNL* 2012, 767–78.

Ostler, Nicolas. 2007. *Ad Infinitum: A Biography of Latin.* New York: Walker.

Pannonius, Janus. 1784. *Poemata.* Utrecht: Bartholomeus Wild.

Piccolomini, Enea S. 2001. *De Europa.* Edited by Adrianus van Heck. Vatican City: Biblioteca Apostolica Vaticana.

Špička, Jiří. 2010. "Francesco Petrarca Travelling and Writing to Prague's Court." *Verbum: Analecta Neolatina* 12:27–40. Available at http://www.verbum-analectaneolatina.hu/pdf/12-1-02.pdf.

Uţă-Bărbulescu, Oana. 2011. *Latinis litteris operam navare: Despre traducerea surselor latine şi integrarea lor în "Scara a numerelor şi cuvintelor streine tâlcuitoare."* Bucharest: Editura Universităţii din Bucureşti.

CHAPTER 33

COLONIAL SPANISH AMERICA AND BRAZIL

ANDREW LAIRD

> Whereas the "Westerner" is a mere intruder in most of the cultures he has devastated, in the New World he is also a component—and an important one—in the person of mixed identity (mixed not just in the racial sense of course). The "Western Tradition" is not the entire tradition of the New World, but it is its tradition *as well*.
>
> —Roberto Fernández Retamar, *Martí en su (tercer) mundo*, Havana 1965

> I want Latin for the Left, because I see no advantage in letting go of conquests already attained.
>
> —Alfonso Reyes, *Discurso por Virgilio*, Mexico City 1930

In the wake of the conquest and colonization of the Americas, Spanish soon came to be the *lingua franca* for the different ethnic groups in Spain's territories, as Portuguese did in Brazil. Latin, on the other hand, remained the preserve of small elites—of Europeans and of "creoles," as Spaniards and Portuguese born in the colonies have come to be known. Following an overview of the role of Latin in early modern Ibero-America, this chapter will focus on two situations in which select groups used the language in their writing to affirm their identity and protect their interests: in the mid-1500s, when some acculturated members of the indigenous nobilities in central Mexico petitioned the Spanish crown in Latin; and during the later 1700s, when creole Jesuits produced a rich corpus of Latin literature to draw attention to their distinctive heritage as Spanish Americans.

THE STATUS AND USES OF LATIN

From the time of the voyages of discovery, debates about the Americas and the status of their peoples were conducted in Latin. That testifies less to Latin's reach than it does to the relatively theoretical nature of those Renaissance debates. Thus the first official

"Protector of the Indians," Fray Bartolomé de las Casas (ca. 1484–1566), addressed his works to humanists and scholars—although the fact that he also wrote about the destruction of the Indies in the vernacular shows that he recognized the importance of reaching a wider readership. Some years before the controversy between Las Casas and Juan Ginés de Sepúlveda about the rights of Indians came to a head in Valladolid in 1550–1551 (Lupher 2003, 43–149), Fray Julián Garcés anticipated Las Casas by citing classical sources to argue for the humanity of the peoples of Mexico in his *De capacitate et habilitate gentium* (*The Capacity and Aptitude of Native Peoples*, 1537; Laird 2014a). That treatise, the first work written in the Americas to be published in Europe, prompted a papal bull in the same year affirming that "Indians" were true human beings and should not be killed or enslaved—although the bull was soon rescinded.

Later Latin writings from the Americas about the condition of the native populations were also remote from historical praxis: in his *Speculum coniugiorum* (*A Mirror for Marriages*, 1556), Fray Alonso de la Vera Cruz examined from a philosophical perspective the problems posed by the polygamous marriages of Mexican converts to Christianity; Juan de Solórzano de Pereira, a judge in the high court of Lima, considered the natives' place in the Spanish Empire in the *De Indiarum iure disputatio* (*Disputation on Law in the Indies*, 1629); and another jurist in Peru, Diego de Avendaño, expressed pro-Spanish sympathies in the *Thesaurus Indicus* (*Indian Treasury*, 1668–1686).

The first guides to preaching in the New World written in Latin were far more disengaged from practice than the vernacular works on the subject. Las Casas's *De unico vocationis modo omnium gentium ad veram religionem* (*The Only Way of Calling All Peoples to the True Religion*, ca. 1540) *prima facie* maintained that rhetoric and dialectic appealed to the Indians' opinions and intellect, but the treatise was really devised to influence and persuade European readers. The *Rhetorica Christiana* (*Christian Rhetoric*, 1579), by the Franciscan missionary Diego Valadés, incorporated anecdotes about the natives of Mexico and their conversion, which were illustrated by the author's own engravings, but Valadés's six-part work was largely modeled on the six books of Fray Luis de Granada's *Ecclesiastica rhetorica* (*Ecclesiastical Rhetoric*, 1576) and was published as a conventional rhetorical textbook in Italy (Abbott 1996). In contrast, the *De procuranda Indorum salute* (*How to Secure the Indians' Salvation*, 1588) was based on direct observation. The Jesuit author, José de Acosta, who had traveled extensively in Mexico and Peru, urged missionaries to understand the beliefs and the languages of those whom they sought to convert.

While humanist Latin learning had defined the European Renaissance by shaping or challenging structures of political and religious authority, Latin was mainly the language of scripture, liturgy, and the Roman Catholic Church in the New World, where it did not serve statesmen and aristocrats, but the religious orders and newly founded universities that sought to secure their standing with the papacy and the courts of Spain and Portugal. The circulation of books and establishment of centers of learning, however, meant that there were also scholars and readers among the laity. Latin soon acquired a position in many ways comparable to the one it had in Iberia, operating in tandem with vernacular writing (Kagan 1974, 31–61).

There was scant opportunity for patronage and little place for the researches into pagan Greco-Roman antiquity that had been conducted in Italy or even in Spain. Some churchmen and educators in the New World nonetheless were familiar with a wide range of classical and Italian humanist texts that would continue to influence American Latin and vernacular literature (Osorio Romero 1980). The Dominicans and Franciscans who accompanied the conquistadors to the Caribbean in the 1490s, to Mexico in the 1520s, and to South America in the decade after that, had absorbed Erasmus's prescriptions for a Latin education along with his practical theology (Bataillon 2007, 715–24).

Book production and distribution can offer an indication of fundamental trends in the use of Latin in the American colonies—although there was no printing in Brazil until 1808, when the court of John VI of Portugal was moved from Lisbon to Rio de Janeiro (Hallewell 1982). A study of print culture in sixteenth-century Mexico City (García Icazbalceta 1954)—a press was established there in 1538—shows that of the 179 known titles printed between 1539 and 1600, twenty-nine (roughly a fifth) were in Latin. All twenty-nine volumes were either reprints of European texts on canon law, conventual rules and missals, or new educational works—on grammar, rhetoric, scholastic philosophy, poetry, and medicine. Advertisements for *quaestiones*, oral examinations, confirm that lectures and examinations at the Royal University of Mexico were conducted in Latin, as they would be in Lima and other Spanish American institutions, all of which were modeled on the University of Salamanca (Rodríguez Cruz 1977). The books in Spanish (which often contained accomplished Latin verse epigraphs) were religious manuals, *artes* or manuals of indigenous languages, and vocabularies. Those works, though written in the vernacular, still highlight the importance of Latin: Latin grammar provided the framework for the missionaries' studies of Amerindian languages (Percival 2004).

The fact that Fray Juan de Zumárraga, the first bishop of Mexico, adorned with classical quotations an urgent letter he wrote in 1529 about the abuses of the first acting government of New Spain (García Icazbalceta 1947, 4:99–102) shows that Latin literary learning could be displayed even in a situation of some gravity. Zumárraga's pupil Fray Cristóbal Cabrera addressed prose letters and *extempore* verse epistles in Latin to fellow missionary friars in Mexico during the 1530s and remarked that he rarely read or wrote in the vernacular (Gallardo 1866, 164–65). Others composed Latin poems, including some lengthy bucolic works (Osorio Romero 1989, 253–86) and two historical epics. The first, *De gestis Mendi de Saa* (*The Deeds of Mem de Sá*, 1563), by the Jesuit José de Anchieta, celebrated the Portuguese governor general Mem de Sá's successful campaigns in Brazil against both the heathen practices of the natives and the incursions of French Protestants (McGinness 2014). The second heroic poem, *Austriaca sive Naumachia* (*John of Austria's Deeds; or, The Sea Battle*, 1580), which related the Christian defeat of the Ottomans in the Battle of Lepanto (1571), was composed by Francisco de Pedrosa, who held the chair of grammar in the Cathedral of Guatemala (Fernández de la Cotera Navarro 2003).

Over the sixteenth century, the use of Latin diminished in the Iberian colonies as it did in the Iberian peninsula. The perceived need to train native preachers and catechists in the language was dispelled altogether after the 1545 session of the Council of Trent had enjoined preaching in vernaculars (*vulgares linguae*)—primarily in order to combat Protestant influence in Europe. The arrival in the New World of the Jesuits, who reached Brazil in 1549, Peru in 1568 and New Spain in 1572, consolidated the use of Latin in higher education, but it was thereafter confined mainly to universities and colleges. In 1599, the Society of Jesus adopted the *ratio studiorum* ("system of study")—a curriculum of classical authors that provided the foundation for most Latin writing in the Americas over the seventeenth and eighteenth centuries.

Students were frequently required to prepare dissertations on scholastic philosophy. Antonio Rubio's *Logica Mexicana* (*Mexican Logic*, 1605) and the commentaries on Aristotle's logic and Duns Scotus that Fray Jerónimo de Valera published in Lima were notable works from the early 1600s (Redmond 1972, 84–85; Hampe Martínez 1999, 47–99). By the mid-1700s, Jesuit colleges in New Spain were accommodating the new science and elements of Enlightenment scientific thought: Francisco Javier Clavijero set out an atomic theory in his unpublished *Physica particularis* (*Particle Physics*, ca. 1750); Diego José Abad went further in harmonizing Cartesian thought and Gassendi's atomism with Aristotelian philosophy in his *Nascitura Philosophia* (*Philosophy About to Be Born*, 1754–1756; Beuchot 1998, 138–73).

The Society of Jesus attached great importance to training in eloquence, known as *informatio ad eloquentiam*. Original textbooks of rhetorical theory printed in Peru and Mexico include Pablo José de Arriaga's *Rhetoris Christiani partes septem* (*Seven Parts of the Christian Orator*, 1619); Baltázar López's *Rhetorica* (*Rhetoric*, 1632); Tomás González's *Summa totius rhetoricae* (*Compendium of All Rhetoric*, 1646) and *De arte rhetorica* (*The Art of Rhetoric*, 1646; generally Abbot 1996; Osorio Romero 1980). Latin oratory flourished in colleges and seminaries: Rafael Landívar in Guatemala and Jose Manuel Peramás in Paraguay were among the many Jesuits who wrote funeral orations and eulogies in Latin, which were published after being delivered (Laird 2006, 95–113; Fraschini, Suárez, and Sánchez 2009, 23–74). The convention of presenting funeral orations in Latin continued in Mexico well into the nineteenth century (Osorio Romero 1976, 209–16).

From the later 1600s, verse panegyrics of the Virgin Mary of Guadalupe were published in New Spain. According to a popular creole tradition, the Virgin had appeared to an indigenous Mexican, Juan Diego, in 1531 (Brading 2001). The earliest examples of such works in Latin show that her initially controversial cult came to appeal to an erudite scholarly echelon as well as to the rank and file: José López de Abilés's *Poeticum viridarium* (*Poetic Pleasure Garden*, 1669) related the Virgin's apparition in elegiac couplets, while Bernardo Ceinos de Riofrío's *Centonicum Virgilianum Monimentum* (*Virgilian Centonic Monument*, 1680) was a cento, a medley of hexameter verses from Virgil, on the same theme. Riofrío's composition was prefaced with an original epyllion, *Aulica synodus Musarum* (*Courtly Assembly of the Muses*), by Bartolomé Rosales, which staged Virgil announcing to Mercury his reincarnation in the New World (Laird 2010, 222–23). José Villerías y Roelas, a clerk in Mexico City educated by Jesuits, composed an epic entitled *Guadalupe* (1724), drawing from a wide range of European Latin and vernacular models.

The poem describes how, after the Spanish conquest of Mexico, the Virgin of Guadalupe confounded the designs of the infernal Pluto and the Aztec goddess Tonantzin, who had conspired to oust Christians from New Spain (Laird 2010). A shorter and simpler narrative poem, José Mariano de Iturriaga's *Californias* (1734), praised the achievements of the Jesuit missionary Juan María de Salvatierra in Baja California.

There was an equally wide range of Jesuit Latin literature from Brazil, but didactic poetry has received most attention: Prudêncio do Amaral's *De sacchari opificio* (*The Production of Sugar*) and *De rusticis Brasiliae rebus* (*Brazilian Country Life*) by the Portuguese-born José Rodrigues de Melo were published in Rome in 1781 (Fonda and Rocha Rodrigues 1975). De Melo followed the four-book division of Virgil's *Georgics*: Books 1 and 2 treated the cultivation and uses of manioc; Book 3 husbandry; and Book 4 on the inspirational qualities of nicotine recalled Virgil's implicit association between honey and poetry in the fourth *Georgic*. An anonymous manuscript poem has also survived, *Brasilienses Aurifodinae* (*Brazilian Gold Mines*), completed in Italy in the early 1760s (Brito Mariano 2010). These poets did not question the necessity of using slaves for the various forms of production they describe: the unwavering bigotry shown towards Africans and native Brazilians in these works, though disconcerting, is not remarkable. What is more surprising is that none of the Portuguese or creole Jesuits from Brazil were provoked by European criticisms of the New World and its inhabitants. In contrast, nearly all the Latin works written by their *confrères* banished from Spain's dominions would be directed to this end, of which there will be further discussion below.

The expulsions of the Jesuits from the Portuguese and Spanish colonies meant that Latin, long confined to universities and seminaries, abruptly ceased to serve as a scholarly or literary medium for the elites. While insurgent statesmen came to compare Aztecs and Incas to Greeks and Romans and would use classical *exempla* to glamorize their struggle for independence (Earle 2007), the liberal and often secular tendencies of the new ruling classes in the emerging nations led to a questioning of the value of a Latin education altogether (Osorio Romero et al. 1991, 59–68).

LATIN AND THE NATIVE NOBILITY IN POST-CONQUEST MEXICO

Indigenous students were excluded from the universities in Spanish America as they were from the Jesuit colleges and academies in Brazil. But as early as 1517, Bartolomé de las Casas had argued that Indians should be taught Latin as well as Spanish—a view that would still be held by Solórzano y Pereira a century later. Latin must have been taught to native children in Peru in the mid-1500s for the Inca Garcilaso de la Vega to have been able to draw from Blas Valera's (1545–1597) now lost *Historia occidentalis* (*History of the West*), a major source for Garcilaso's own *Comentarios reales de los Incas* (*Royal Commentaries of the Incas*, 1609; MacCormack 2007, 192).

Some instruction in Latin was regarded as essential for the indigenous catechists and interpreters who were being trained to assist in the conversion of peoples in the New World, and the Franciscans' teaching initiative began in 1513 with the education of Taino children in Hispaniola (Kobayashi 1985, 160–62). Fray Martín de Valencia, who led the first group of friars to reach Mexico in 1524, taught the alphabet and Latin to Indian children for ten years in Tlaxcala, and Peter of Ghent founded the College of San José de los Naturales in Mexico City in 1527 after teaching native pupils in the nearby town of Texcoco (Motolinía 2001, 180). A decade later, Fray Julián Garcés, bishop of Tlaxcala, remarked that indigenous youths who had learned to write Latin were able to "know and speak it more elegantly than young Spaniards" (*nostris pueris elegantius Latine sciant atque loquantur*; Laird 2014a, 209).

But a catechist, Amerindian or not, would not need to write Latin or speak it *extempore*: an object of this more advanced instruction was to consolidate the faith of the newly Christianized peoples by providing their children with a scholarly education. A telling parallel in peninsular Spain was Charles V's royal decree of November 1526 ordaining that a boarding school for the sons of converted Muslims be attached to the Royal College of Santa Cruz, in Granada. Bishop Zumárraga invoked that very precedent in a letter he wrote to the king and emperor (Kobayashi 1985, 103) in the year after the inauguration in January 1536 of the Imperial College of Santa Cruz at Tlatelolco, near Mexico City. Thus the purpose of the college's foundation was never, as many historians have supposed, to train a native clergy, but to establish a gubernatorial class of judges and rulers, drawn primarily from the Nahua elite and imbued with Christian humanist principles.

The printing of Christian doctrines and prayer books in Amerindian languages in Mexico and Peru shows that translation *from* Latin was the main outcome of the natives' acquisition of the language. Pablo Nazareo of Xaltocan, though a native and a layman, was rector of the College of Santa Cruz de Tlatelolco. He explained in a 1561 letter to Philip II that he "toiled to the utmost night and day, to translate into [his] mother tongue the Gospels and Epistles which are read in church over the course of the entire year" (*Sic noctes diesque summopere laboravi ut, quae per anni totius discursum in Ecclesia leguntur, Evangelia et epistolas in linguam maternam traducerem*; Laird 2014b, 160). The most important long-term consequence of the indigenous scholars' training in Latin was not their contribution to the canon of colonial Latin literature, but the preservation or creation of texts in their own language. Fray Bernardino de Sahagún regularly signaled his debt to native Latinists in Tlatelolco for their assistance with the compilation of his ethnographic histories of pre-Hispanic Mexico, which were presented in Nahuatl and Spanish (León-Portilla 2002, 144). Other early written texts in the Mexican language, including the poems known as the *Cantares mexicanos* (*Mexican Songs*) and the *Çaçanillatolli ynquitlali ce tlamatini ytoca Esopo* (*Fable Discourses Composed by the Wise Man Named Aesop*) show, to varying degrees, evidence of the Nahuas' capacities as readers and translators of Latin (Bierhorst 1985; Kutscher 1998).

Nearly all the known writings actually in Latin by Amerindian authors were by alumni of Tlatelolco. Most were petitions to the Spanish crown for titles, pensions, and restitution of lost land, either for the authors themselves or for the communities they led. They show a wide range of learning, citing classical and Christian sources. A letter written by the rulers of Azcapotzalco to Philip II, for example, contains a lengthy quotation from Cassius Dio as well as an adage derived from Virgil (Laird 2011, 303):

> *Audaces enim fortuna iuvat, timidosque repellit. Ad haec ausum non minimum praestat id quod litteris est proditum, nimirum principes non Christianos solum, verum et ethnicos in suos subditos fuisse mites, benignos, clementes, eosdemque in suis querellis aut quibusvis petitionibus lubentissime audisse. Cuius rei argumento est Hadrianus imperator, et is pro multis unus sufficiet, qui transiens in itinere a muliere quadam rogatus ut eam audiret, cum respondisset sibi otium non esse, audivit ab ipsa muliere: Noli ergo imperare. Tum conversus aequissimo animo eam audivit.*

Fortune helps the bold and drives back those who are fearful [cf. Virgil, *Aeneid* 10.284]. Daring this is very well supported by what is shown in literature: there is no doubt that not only Christian princes but pagan ones too have been lenient, kind and merciful to their own subjects and very willing to hear their complaints or suits of every kind. The Emperor Hadrian is proof of this principle and this one figure will serve for many. During a journey he was asked by a certain woman for an audience: when he replied that he did not have time, he heard her reply "In that case, do not be an emperor." At that he was more than prepared to listen to her [cf. Cassius Dio 69.6].

The use of such *exempla* was recommended by Erasmus in his widely circulated prescriptions on epistolography. The Nahuas who wrote in Latin could thus imbue their letters with a deeper texture, deploying classical or biblical references that might be meaningful to their addressees. On the other hand, they had little knowledge of Spanish literature or culture with which to embellish their appeals, and there were in any case no manuals on writing letters in Spanish.

The native authors also used classical analogies implicitly or explicitly in order to draw attention to their distinctive traditions and identities. A letter to the Holy Roman Emperor Charles V in 1552 explains that the Nahuas were not a single people (Laird 2014b, 157):

> *Has Indias antiquis in temporibus fuisse divisas in tres partes nimirum Mexicum, Tlacubam, et Tetzcocum atque ex consequenti tres dominos seu rectores habuisse qui dominabantur aliorum populorum circumiacentium.*

In former times these Indies were divided into three parts, namely Mexico, Tlacopan, and Texcoco, as a consequence they had three lords or rulers who also ruled the other peoples situated nearby.

The echo here of Caesar's tripartite division of Gaul in *Gallic Wars* 1.1 (*Gallia est omnis divisa in partes tres*; "All Gaul is divided into three parts") may have been a kind of *captatio benevolentiae* to the Emperor Charles, who is hailed in this text as "Caesarean majesty" (*Caesarea maiestas*) or "most invincible Caesar" (*Caesar invictissime*).

As well as providing genealogical and chronological information about their respective polities, the writers explained the meanings or etymologies of Mexican names, often using structures and idioms characteristic of Nahuatl courtly speech in their Latin prose. Other texts by Mexican Latinists surviving from the sixteenth century include the *Libellus de medicinalibus Indorum herbis* (*Little Book of the Indians' Medicinal Herbs*, 1552), a translation of a native herbal; and a trilingual vocabulary of Spanish, Latin, and Nahuatl, compiled by an unknown indigenous scribe (Laird 2014b, 152–55).

Few Latin writings by indigenous people outside New Spain have come to light. The anonymous *Planctus Indorum Christianorum in America Peruntina* (*The Lamentation of Christian Indians in Peruvian America*, ca. 1750), which was suppressed by the Inquisition and deplored the Spaniards' conduct towards the natives of Peru, is a possible example that may have been written by Calixto de San José Túpac Inga. The achievements of native scholars constitute a very small fraction of the Latin writings produced in the sixteenth to eighteenth centuries.

LATIN AND THE EXPRESSION OF CREOLE IDENTITY

Throughout the colonial era, the Spanish crown had long regarded its interests as best served if economic and political control of its territories remained in the hands of native Spaniards. Thus Spanish Americans (often referred to as *criollos* or creoles), deprived of self-determination and the benefits of their own labor, could no longer be identified with peninsular Spaniards. Nor were they disposed to see themselves as the inheritors of their countries' pre-Hispanic past, for fear of relinquishing the privileges and powers they did have over the native populations—privileges that were justified, however speciously, by the triumph of Christianity over paganism in the New World (Knight 2002, 202–331).

The Jesuit intelligentsia became the principal *porte-parole* for a dissatisfied but highly conservative creole class. The religious elite came to articulate pride in a distinctive legacy that was both Spanish and American, in a succession of disputes that might be termed "culture wars"—long before any intimation of future political struggles. Vernacular authors had long expressed pride in their American *patria*, but by the 1700s, Latin was a vehicle for expression of creole identity at a time when its popularity as a language was sharply declining in Europe: a succession of factors over the course of the eighteenth century accounts for this.

A challenge to the cultural hegemony of peninsular Spain came from Mexico City in the early 1740s when scholars responded roundly to the claims about the Americas made by a renowned Spanish antiquarian, Manuel Martí, Dean of Alicante, in a letter in which he advised a young man against pursuing his studies in the New World (Martí 1738, 2:38–39):

Quo te vertes apud Indos, in tam vasta litterarum solitudine? Quem adibis, non dicam
magistrum, cuius praeceptis instituaris, sed auditorem? Non dicam aliquid scientem,
sed scire cupientem? Dicam enucleatius a litteris non abhorrentem? Ecquosnam evolves
codices? Equas lustrabis bibliotecas? Haec enim omnia tam frustra quaeres, quam qui
tondet asinum vel mulcet hircum.

Why do you look to the Indies, a great literary wasteland? To whom will you turn?—
I won't say "which teacher will instruct you?" but whom will you find even to listen
to you? I won't say "will you find anyone who knows anything?" but will you even
find anyone who *wants* to know anything? In a nutshell: will you find anyone who
doesn't recoil from the study of literature? What documents will you unscroll? What
libraries will you consult? You'll search for all these things with as much success as
someone who tries to shave an ass or milk a he-goat.

Juan Gregorio de Campos y Martínez rebutted these remarks in the *Oratio apologetica*
(*Defense Speech*, 1746): the volume also contained a Latin letter from the rector of the
Royal University of Mexico to Philip V protesting against Martí's calumny. The devastating impact on New Spain's intellectual class of a few sentences in an occasional letter may seem surprising, but it can be explained: Manuel Martí was one of the greatest
antiquarians of his age in Europe—and he had also finalized the canonical *Bibliotheca*
Hispana vetus (*Old Spanish Library*, 1696), a Latin bio-bibliography of Iberian authors
from antiquity to the 1400s, initiated by Nicolás Antonio. The *Bibliotheca*, still a vital
resource for historians of Spanish literature, confirmed Martí's reputation. His authoritative status as a classical scholar best accounts for the creoles' refutations of his claims
being made in Latin (Laird 2012, 249–51).

The most prominent counter to the Dean of Alicante's disparaging remarks was an emulation of his *Bibliotheca Hispana vetus*: the *Bibliotheca Mexicana* (*Mexican Library*) by Juan José
Eguiara y Eguren, the first and only volume of which appeared in 1755. This was a projected
bio-bibliographical catalog in Latin of authors in New Spain and other colonies, from the
time of the Conquest until the year of its publication. Eguiara wrote several *anteloquia* ("prefaces") to the work that extolled the Aztec "antiquities" of Mexico and praised the achievement of indigenous as well as creole authors. Though never completed, the *Bibliotheca*
Mexicana was one of the most ambitious Latin works ever undertaken in the Americas.

Charles III's Bourbon Reforms of 1759–1788 strengthened the crown's hold over
Spain's territories, further reducing their autonomy and increasing fiscal revenue from
their populations. But the most disruptive measure was the expulsion in 1767 of the
Jesuits, most of whom settled in the Italian Papal States, before their Society was dis-
solved altogether by a papal decree in 1773 (Batllori 1966; Guasti 2006). Had the creole
Jesuits not been forced into exile, many of their Latin works might never have been published or even written. Their achievements, especially those of the emigrés from New
Spain, were impressive. Unlike Eguiara y Eguren's generation, they sought a readership
not merely in Spain, but all over Europe.

These Jesuits were motivated by a barrage of polemics about the New World from
Enlightenment philosophers, scientists, and historians. The *Recherches philosophiques*

sur les Américains (*Philosophical Investigations on the Americans*, 1768) by the Dutch philosopher Cornelius de Pauw commended the works of Newton, Descartes, Locke, and others, and held that no such books had come from America—a charge that would have been galling to scholars like Clavijero and Abad, who had long embraced the "New Science" and atomism. Drawing upon the French naturalist George-Louis Leclerc Buffon, De Pauw had also maintained that indigenous Americans were an inferior species of mankind, claiming that the achievements of their civilizations had been fabricated by the Spaniards. Similar opinions were expressed in Guillaume Thomas Raynal's *Histoire Philosophique des deux Indes* (*Philosophical History of the Two Indies*, 1770) and William Robertson's *History of America* (1777).

In response to such conjectural historiography, the exiled former Jesuits swiftly produced vernacular works emphasizing the importance of evidence and first-hand observation; for instance, Clavijero's celebrated study of pre-Hispanic Mexico, *Storia antica del Messico* (*Ancient History of Mexico*, 1780). But not all the emigrés could write in Italian, and many of their contributions to the eighteenth-century "dispute of the Americas" were in Latin: that dispute was, after all, a reprise of a debate in that language two centuries earlier, in which Julius Caesar Scaliger had maintained that the Indies were barren and uninhabitable, in a ferocious response to Girolamo Cardano's encyclopedic work of natural philosophy, *De subtilitate* (*On Subtlety*, 1550; Cañizares Esguerra 1999).

José Manuel Peramás, a Catalan who had worked in the Jesuit province of Paraguay, challenged the arguments of De Pauw and Raynal in his account of the Jesuit missions to the Guarani Indians, *De administratione Guaranica comparata ad rempublicam Platonis commentarius* (*Memorandum Comparing the Guarani Administration to Plato's Republic*, 1793). Peramás's *Annus patiens* (*Year of Suffering*, 1768), recording the events following his expulsion from America, likewise stressed the importance of witness. So, too, did the Guatemalan poet Rafael Landívar in the preface to his *Rusticatio Mexicana* (*Mexican Country Life*, 1781, extended version 1782): "I relate those things which I have seen and those that have been told to me by eyewitnesses [*testes oculati*]." The subject matter of Landívar's didactic poem—the natural wonders, culture, and production of Mesoamerica—suggests that his work was also an answer to Buffon and De Pauw (Laird 2006, 51–53).

Spanish and creole legacies were celebrated in epic poems published in Italy, such as Andrés Diego de la Fuente's *Guadalupana imago* (*The Guadalupan Image*, 1773) on the divine painting of the Virgin of Guadalupe, and Francisco Javier Alegre's short epic *Alexandrias*, which implicitly paralleled Alexander the Great's capture of Tyre to Cortés's taking of the Aztec capital of Tenochtitlan, and ended with an imprecation to the Mexican Virgin (Laird 2006, 28–9). Abad's ambitious heroic poem on theology in forty-three books, *De Deo Deoque homine* (*God and God as Man*, 1780; Abad 1974), also described the Virgin (42.613–19) and featured the *flos Mexiceus*, the Mexican passion flower, in an account of Christ's nativity (23.109). These authors called attention to their Spanish American provenance in other ways: Abad sometimes adopted the pseudonym *Selenopolitanus*, "citizen of the Moon" because the name "Mexico" meant "Place of the Moon" in Nahuatl; Alegre identified himself as "Mexican" (*Mexicanus*) or as *Americanus Veracrucensis* ("an American from Veracruz").

The proliferation of texts in Latin by the creole exiles was not in spite of the championing of the vernacular as a medium by progressive *savants* in France and elsewhere, but because of it. The *Encyclopédiste* Jean D'Alembert's challenge to the role of Latin was more nuanced than is often realized: D'Alembert had recognized Latin's usefulness as a *lingua franca*, but his *Réflexion sur l'harmonie des langues* (*Reflections on the Harmony of Languages*, 1767) had promoted the vernacular on the basis that no modern author could write Latin well. That led Giambattista Roberti, a Venetian Jesuit and academician, to maintain that Italians alone could write Latin properly (Kerson in Abad 1991, 363). Thus the Spanish Americans in Italy felt compelled to prove their proficiency in Latin as well as to demonstrate its utility. Francisco Javier Alegre, for example, published a translation of all of Homer's *Iliad* (1776) into Latin hexameters, explaining in his preface that Latin usage would always be subject to regional variation.

Diego José Abad followed Alegre by invoking Livy's "Patavian" Latin as a precedent for the *peregrinitas* or "foreignness" of his own style in a reply to Roberti, entitled *Dissertatio ludicro-seria de Latinitate exterorum* (*A Playful and Serious Discourse on the Quality of Latin of People from Abroad*, 1778). Abad concurred with Roberti's defense of Latin as a universal language of knowledge: Latin transcended time and space as the basis for all forms of scientific, humanistic, and theological understanding (Laird 2012, 240). His defense of his compatriots' Latinity and of their intellectual capacities was an answer, not only to Roberti, but also to the claims of Buffon and De Pauw that the climate of a region determines the intelligence and capacities of its inhabitants (Abad 1991, 396–97):

> *Si quod multi existimant verum esset, qui sub mitiore caelo nascuntur, eos ut plurimum mitiore quoque praeditos esse ingenio, atque ad omnia promptiore et meliore, oportebat profecto Mexicanos esse mortalium ingeniosissimos, quandoquidem caelum nacti sunt indulgentissimum ... Nusquam non aliquot ingenio praestantissimi; nusquam non aliquot ingenio praestantissimi; nusquam item non aliquot stupidi et male ingeniati, ut Plautino verbo utar, nascuntur.*

> If it were true, as many believe, that those who are born under a milder climate are usually endowed with a milder disposition, better prepared for all situations and more capable, indeed Mexicans would have to be the most ingenious of mortals since they enjoy a most indulgent climate. . . . Everywhere, there are a few men of outstanding genius; likewise everywhere there are some stupid and, to use Plautus's term, meanly gifted individuals.

The defense of Latin and the defense of the Americas were related concerns. A very clear demonstration of this was provided by another former Jesuit from New Spain, Manuel Fabri (1737–1805), who exhorted his younger countrymen to master Latin in order to make known the natural riches of their homeland (Abad 1974, 66):

> *Agite igitur, Mexicani juvenes, in idque totis viribus incumbite, ut puram tersamque Latinitatem, e Tulliano potissimum fonte caeterisque aetatis aureae Principibus petitam, serio et constanti studio multorumque annorum labore et perseverantia*

possideatis. Id enim a vobis in primis carissima Patria expectat, ut quas in eius sinum opes plenis natura manibus profudit, pretiosiores apud exteras gentes efficiatis.

Rise up then, Mexicans in your prime, and apply all your strength to this: to lay claim, after endless hard study and years of steadfast toil, to a pure and succinct Latinity, taken from the spring of Cicero and the other great men of the Golden Age. For your most beloved *Patria* expects this from you above all, that you render all the more precious among foreign peoples the treasures which Nature's bountiful hands have poured forth into her bosom.

The late eighteenth century might be regarded as the *floruit* of Latin literature for Ibero-America, especially New Spain. But the *belle-lettrisme* in this period was always ideological: works that appeared to be purely literary or religious served a further purpose. Thus José Manuel Peramás's epic about Columbus, *De invento novo orbe inductoque illuc Christi Sacrificio* (*The Discovery of the New World and the Introduction There of Christ's Sacrifice*, 1777), was written to quash propaganda critical of the Spanish conquest (Arbo and Laird 2015). The defamation of Spain and of the Christianization of the Americas, which came to be known as the "Black Legend," had originated in sixteenth-century Italy and was revived by Voltaire and Montesquieu before being endorsed later in the Enlightenment by Raynal, Robertson, and other historians (Guasti 2006, 372–73). Moreover, Peramás's very choice of Columbus as a subject betrayed his own Spanish pan-Americanism (Batllori 1966, 353, 584): the great admiral's legacy had never been confined to the Caribbean—and Mexico and South America were given considerable prominence in his poem. The emigrés' responses to Enlightenment criticisms of the Americas would continue to resonate, shaping and influencing later currents of creole patriotism, which eventually led to independence (Brading 1991), but the former Jesuits in Europe were themselves a conservative and close-knit group. For all that they strongly identified themselves with the particular areas of the New World they had left behind, the views and the interests they defended so vigorously were primarily their own.

Conclusion

Walter Benjamin's often quoted adage that "there is no document of civilization which is not at the same time a document of barbarism" (Benjamin 1969, 256) could well be applied to the impressive range of Latin rhetorical and philosophical treatises, chronicles, epistles, dialogues, and poetry from the vast region now known as Latin America. Such a corpus cannot be considered in isolation from politics, race, or class, since its production depended on the economic exploitation of peoples who derived little tangible benefit from the intellectual advances made within universities and elite religious institutions. It is also telling that while the rights and legacies of "Indians" were recurrently addressed in Latin writing from the sixteenth to eighteenth centuries, the use of black slaves in the New World was rarely challenged, and the vast population of *mestizos* (people of mixed-race origin) barely ever mentioned.

Recent histories of Latin in Spanish America have often approached their subject anachronistically in terms of *national* history, conceived in terms of nation-states that had not yet come into existence when most Latin texts were being produced (Méndez Plancarte 1945; Rivas Sacconi 1949; *CNLS* 1:296–310; Hanisch Espíndola 1991; Osorio Romero et al. 1991). Such narratives have also effaced the differences between the exclusive practice of humanism in the colonial era and the more inclusive pursuit of classical studies in recent times. In his influential essay, *Discurso por Virgilio* (*A Discourse through Virgil*, 1931), the Mexican Alfonso Reyes provided a rationale for such a tendency: he argued that to abandon the patrimony of Latin after it had served as a literary and intellectual medium for three centuries was tantamount to prescribing the abolition of human knowledge, when the political ideal of education should be to bring everyone up, not down, to an equal level.

It remains the case that the Latin output of Brazil and Spanish America should not be misconceived as being multicultural in its provenance—it has to be understood as a creole legacy. Latin's relative inaccessibility thus distinguished it from the languages of Spanish and Portuguese, which were soon imposed on many different ethnic groups. But, like those Romance vernaculars, Latin, for all that it was European in origin, no longer belonged only to Europe. The Latin works written in the Americas or by creoles in exile constitute *de facto* an American legacy. Recognition of the literary and scholarly interest of that corpus is important, but its texts need to be interrogated and examined critically as productions of the dominant elites if they are properly to inform a pluralist and inclusive intellectual history of colonial Latin America.

Suggested Reading

Laird (2014c) is a diachronic account of Latin writing in Spanish America and Brazil from the sixteenth to twentieth centuries, citing further sources, bibliographies and catalogs of manuscripts. The two earlier surveys, Menéndez Pelayo (1911) and *CNLS* (1:296–310), are eclectic but discuss some authors and texts in detail. There are studies of traditions in particular regions, including New Spain-Mexico (Briesemeister 2002; Osorio Romero et al. 1991), New Granada-Colombia (Rivas Sacconi 1949), Charcas-Bolivia (Eichmann Oehrli 2003; Barnadas 2005), Peru (Hampe Martínez 1999; Helmer 2013), La Plata-Argentina (Fraschini, Suárez, and Sánchez 2009), and Chile (Hanisch Espíndola 1991).

References

Abad, Diego J. 1974. *Poema heroico*. Edited and translated by Benjamin Valenzuela. Mexico City: Universidad Nacional Autónoma de México.

———. 1991. *Dissertatio Ludicro-Seria*. Edited and translated by Arnold Kerson. *Humanistica Lovaniensia* 40:357–422.

Abbott, Don P. 1996. *Rhetoric in the New World: Rhetorical Theory and Practice in Colonial Spanish America*. Columbia: University of South Carolina Press.

Arbo, Desiree, and Andrew Laird. 2015. "Columbus, the Lily of Quito and the Black Legend: The Context of José Manuel Peramás' Epic on the Discovery of the New World, *De invento novo orbe inductoque illuc Christi Sacrificio* (1777)." *Dieciocho* 38.

Barnadas, Josep M. 2005. *Ensayo bibliográfico sobre el Latín en Bolivia*. La Paz: Plural.

Bataillon, Marcel. 2007. *Erasmo y España*. Translated by Antonio Alatorre. Mexico City: Fondo de Cultura Económica.

Batllori, Miguel. 1966. *La cultura hispano-italiana de los jesuitas expulsos: Españoles, hispano-americanos, filipinos, 1767–1814*. Madrid: Gredos.

Benjamin, Walter 1969. "Theses on the Philosophy of History." In *Illuminations*, edited by Hannah Arendt and translated by Harry Zohn, 253–64. New York: Schocken.

Beuchot, Mauricio. 1998. *The History of Philosophy in Colonial Mexico*. Translated by Elizabeth Millán. Washington, DC: Catholic University of America.

Bierhorst, John, ed. and trans. 1985. *Cantares Mexicanos: Songs of the Aztecs*. Stanford: Stanford University Press.

Brading, David A. 1991. *The First America: The Spanish Monarchy, Creole Patriots and the Liberal State 1492–1867*. Cambridge: Cambridge University Press.

———. 2001. *Mexican Phoenix: Our Lady of Guadalupe: Image and Tradition Across Five Centuries*. Cambridge: Cambridge University Press.

Briesemeister, Dietrich. 2002. "El latín en la Nueva España." In *Historia de la literatura mexicana*, vol. 2, *La cultura letrada en la Nueva España*, edited by Georges Baudot and Raquel Chang-Rodríguez, 524–48. Mexico City: Siglo Veintiuno.

Brito Mariano, Alexandra de. 2010. "New World 'Ethiopians': Slavery and Mining in Early Modern Brazil through Latin Eyes." In *Latinity and Alterity in the Early Modern Period*, edited by Yasmin Haskell and Juanita Feros Ruys, 201–20. Tempe: Arizona Center for Medieval and Renaissance Studies.

Cañizares Esguerra, Jorge. 1999. "New World, New Stars: Patriotic Astrology and the Invention of Indian and Creole Bodies in Colonial Spanish America, 1600–1650." *American Historical Review* 104:33–68.

Earle, Rebecca. 2007. *The Return of the Native: Indians and Myth-Making in Spanish America, 1810–1930*. Durham: Duke University Press.

Eichmann Oehrli, Andrés. 2003. "El latín en Charcas-Bolivia (1580–1825)." In *América Latina y lo Clásico*, edited by A. Giuseppina Grammatico, G. Antonio Arbea, and Luz M. Edwards, vol. 2, 178–217. Santiago de Chile: Universidad Metropolitana de Ciencias de la Educación.

Fernández de la Cotera Navarro, Patricia. 2003. "Paganismo y Cristianismo en la *Austriaca siue Naumachia* de Francisco de Pedrosa." *Calamus renascens* 4:49–66.

Fonda, Enio A., and Mirtes Rocha Rodrigues. 1975. "*De sacchari opificio carmen*: Um poema e dois autores." *Revista de Letras* 17:107–16.

Fraschini, Alfredo E., Marcela A. Suárez, and Luis A. Sánchez, eds. 2009. *Literatura neolatina en el Río de La Plata: Antología bilingüe*. Villa María: Universidad Nacional de Villa María.

Gallardo, Bartolomé José. 1866. *Ensayo de una biblioteca española de libros raros y curiosas*. Vol. 2. Madrid: Manuel Tello.

García Icazbalceta, Joaquín. 1947. *Don Fray Juan de Zumárraga, primer obispo y arzobispo de México*. Edited by Rafael Aguayo Spencer and Antonio Castro Leal. 4 vols. Mexico City: Porrúa.

———. 1954. *Bibliografía mexicana del siglo XVI*. 2nd ed. by Agustín Millares Carlo. Mexico City: Fondo de Cultura Económica.

Guasti, Niccolò. 2006. *L'esilio italiano dei gesuiti spagnoli: Identità, controllo sociale e pratiche culturali (1767–1798)*. Rome: Edizioni di Storia e Letteratura.

Hallewell, Laurence. 1982. *Books in Brazil: History of the Publishing Trade*. Metuchen: Scarecrow Press.

Hampe Martínez, Teodoro, ed. 1999. *La tradición clásica en el Perú virreinal*. Lima: Universidad Nacional Mayor de San Marcos.

Hanisch Espíndola, Walter. 1991. *El latín en Chile*. Santiago: Biblioteca Nacional.

Helmer, Angela. 2013. *El latín en el Perú colonial: Diglosia e historia de una lengua viva*. Lima: Universidad Nacional Mayor de San Marcos.

Kagan, Richard. 1974. *Students and Society in Early Modern Spain*. Baltimore: Johns Hopkins University Press.

Knight, Alan. 2002. *Mexico: The Colonial Era*. Cambridge: Cambridge University Press.

Kobayashi, José M. 1985. *La educación como conquista: Empresa franciscana en México*. 2nd ed. Mexico City: Colegio de México.

Kutscher, Gerdt, ed. and trans. 1998. *Aesop in Mexiko: Die Fabeln des Aesop in aztekischer Sprache*. Edited by Gordon Brotherston and Günther Vollmer. Berlin: Gebr. Mann.

Laird, Andrew. 2006. *The Epic of America: An Introduction to Rafael Landívar and the* Rusticatio Mexicana. London: Duckworth.

———. 2010. "The *Aeneid* from the Aztecs to the Dark Virgin: Virgil, Native Tradition and Latin Poetry in Colonial Mexico from Sahagún's *Memoriales* to Villierías' *Guadalupe* (1724)." In *A Companion to Vergil's* Aeneid *and Its Tradition*, edited by Joseph Farrell and Michael C. J. Putnam, 217–38. Chichester: Wiley-Blackwell.

———. 2011. "Aztec Latin in Sixteenth-Century Mexico: A Letter from the Rulers of Azcapotzalco to Philip II of Spain, February 1561." *Studi Umanistici Piceni* 31:293–314.

———. 2012. "Patriotism and the Rise of Latin in Eighteenth-Century New Spain: Disputes of the New World and the Jesuit Construction of a Mexican Legacy." *Renæssanceforum* 8:231–62.

———. 2014a. "Humanism and the Humanity of the Peoples of the New World: Fray Julián Garces, *De habilitate et capacitate gentium*, Rome 1537." *Studi Umanistici Piceni* 34:183–225.

———. 2014b. "Nahuas and Caesars: Classical Learning and Bilingualism in Post-Conquest Mexico; An Inventory of Latin Writings by the Native Nobility." *Classical Philology* 109:150–69.

———. 2014c. "Latin America." In *ENLW* 1: 821–32.

León-Portilla, Miguel. 2002. *Bernardino de Sahagún: First Anthropologist*. Translated by Mauricio J. Mixco. Norman: University of Oklahoma Press.

Lupher, David A. 2003. *Romans in a New World: Classical Models in Sixteenth-Century Spanish America*. Ann Arbor: University of Michigan.

MacCormack, Sabine 2007. *On the Wings of Time: Rome, the Incas, Spain and Peru*. Princeton: Princeton University Press.

Martí, Manuel. 1738. *Emmanuelis Martini, ecclesiae Alonensis decani, epistolarum libri duodecim*. 2 vols. Amsterdam: Wetstein and Smith.

McGinness, Anne B. 2014. "Between Subjection and Accommodation: The Development of José de Anchieta's Missionary Project in Colonial Brazil." *Journal of Jesuit Studies* 1:227–44.

Méndez Plancarte, Gabriel. 1945. *Los fundadores del humanismo mexicano*. Bogotá: Instituto Caro y Cuervo.

Menéndez Pelayo, Marcelino. 1911. *Historia de la poesia Hispano-americana*. (2 volumes) Madrid: Librería General de Victoriano Suárez.

Motolinía, Toribio. 2001. *Historia de los Indios de la Nueva España*. Edited by Edmundo O'Gorman. Mexico City: Porrúa.

Osorio Romero, Ignacio. 1976. *Tópicos sobre Cicerón en México*. Mexico City: Universidad Nacional Autónoma de México.

———. 1980. *Floresta de gramática, poética, y retórica en Nueva España (1521–1767)*, Mexico City: Universidad Nacional Autónoma de México.

———. 1989. *Conquistar el eco: la paradoja de conciencia criolla*. Mexico City: Universidad Nacional Autónoma de México.

Osorio Romero, Ignacio, Tarsicio Herrera Zapién, Mauricio Beuchot, Salvador Díaz Cintora, and Roberto Heredia Correa. 1991. *La tradición clásica en México*. Mexico City: Universidad Nacional Autónoma de México.

Percival, W. Keith. 2004. "Nebrija's Linguistic Oeuvre as a Model for Missionary Linguistics." In *Studies in Renaissance Grammar*, 15–29. Aldershot: Ashgate.

Redmond, Walter B. 1972. *Bibliography of the Philosophy in the Iberian Colonies of America*. The Hague: Nijhoff.

Rivas Sacconi, José M. 1949. *El latín en Colombia: Bosquejo histórico del humanismo colombiano*. Bogotá: Instituto Caro y Cuervo.

Rodríguez Cruz, Agueda M. 1977. *Salamantica Docet: La Proyección de la Universidad de Salamanca en Hispanoamérica*. Salamanca: Universidad de Salamanca.

CHAPTER 34

···

NORTH AMERICA

···

JEAN-FRANÇOIS COTTIER,
HAIJO WESTRA, AND JOHN GALLUCCI

PART 1: NEW FRANCE

Jean-François Cottier and Haijo Westra

To provide a first impression of the history of Neo-Latin literature in North America, we must begin with the Latin writing of New France, which, alongside texts written in the vernacular, accompanied the French presence in this immense territory. In what concerns us here, the area is limited to its Canadian part, from the valley of the Saint Lawrence River between Quebec and Montreal (then called "Canada," and which now corresponds to the province of Quebec) and Acadia (now Nova Scotia and northern Maine). Such an undertaking might perhaps seem paradoxical now, since today, as in the seventeenth century, New France is perceived as a vast wilderness, populated by Indians to be converted, zealous missionaries, and fur traders—all people quite removed from the concerns of the republic of letters (Bapst 2013, 65–86).

However, the harvest of Latin texts is plentiful and touches on the same areas as vernacular literature. Indeed, the Latin material sheds new and important light on all of the vernacular genres: reports, travel accounts, history, and annals, as well as on spiritual, scientific, linguistic, and liturgical texts. Besides, the very use of the language of the church and schools indicates a deep connection with written culture, and provides human evidence that cannot be ignored. Consulting the library catalog of the library of the Jesuit Father Pierre Potier, for instance, reveals that more than half of his books were in Latin (see below for more on this author). Alongside the theological and classical texts we might expect, there are also numerous modern works written in Latin (Potier 1996).

The Latin writing of New France flowed largely from the pens of missionaries, in particular the better-educated among them: the Jesuits. Some of these texts have since been translated into French and others into English. A great number of them were published (and/or translated) in Reuben Gold Thwaites's large collection (1896–1901), which was continued and expanded with a large amount of unedited material, but without facing translation, in the edition of Lucien Campeau (1967–2003).

On the present-day province of Quebec more specifically, projects such as *Archéologie du littéraire au Québec*, led by Bernard Andrès and dedicated to the literature produced and circulated in Quebec from the Conquest to the turn of the nineteenth century, help us better understand the birth and development of literature and intellectual history in Quebec. Similarly, the various recent literary histories and, above all, Marc André Bernier's (1997) research on rhetoric, as well as that of Yvan Lamonde (1980) on philosophy and its teaching in Quebec in the eighteenth and nineteenth centuries, allow us to evaluate the position and role fulfilled by Latin in Quebec's educational system. Thanks to these works, and other examinations of books and older libraries, we have better knowledge today of book collections and archives, and it has become easier to identify works written or published in Latin. Other studies have also analyzed various aspects of teaching in Quebec. They allow us to better contextualize the topic, as in the case of the Séminaire de Québec, the Jesuit education, or the teaching of the Sulpicians. There probably remain very many manuscripts and works to be discovered in the heritage collections (Cottier 2010 and 2012). We are only at the very beginning of a real rediscovery of this literature.

The "Jesuit Relations" and Allied Material

Written in the form of letters addressed to the General in Rome, and typically attributed to the Superior in Quebec City as the sender, the so-called Jesuit Relations chronicle the state of the missions to different indigenous peoples over a one- or two-year period. These reports are the origins of many further scholarly, scientific, and literary explorations of the New World by the Fathers of the Society of Jesus. The first Relation, dated January 31, 1612, was written by Pierre Biard (Campeau 1967–2003, 2:203–25; for translation, see Biard 2003), the Jesuit in charge of the first (unsuccessful) mission to Acadia. Biard's letter includes geographic and ethnographic descriptions, as well as the activities, accomplishments, difficulties, and prospects of the enterprise. His report was printed (exceptionally, without any changes) in the *Litterae annuae* (*Annual Records*), the in-house journal of the Society in which similar reports from missions around the world were published, and reflects the unmediated observations of the missionary in the field, including the first encounter of a Jesuit with the native peoples of Canada, particularly the Micmac (Mi'kmaq) of Nova Scotia. Biard's style, except for the epistolary address, is straightforward and descriptive, with few subordinate clauses or figures of style, and is designed to be clear and informative. Some of the ethnographic vocabulary appears borrowed from classical authors, without explicit attributions. Trained in the Jesuit colleges, and often former teachers of Latin themselves, the missionaries had absorbed and internalized the ethnographic register of classical Latin authors, poets as well as prose authors, and their descriptions of faraway places and peoples, especially the nomadic peoples of antiquity. They projected this background onto their encounter with North American indigenous peoples. At the same time, their classical learning gave them access to a wider and more nuanced vocabulary when referring to indigenous peoples: Biard refers to the latter as *populi* ("peoples"), *gens* ("tribe, people"), *natio* ("nation"), *gentiles* ("non-believers"), *indigenae* ("natives"), *incolae* ("inhabitants"), *sylvatici* ("men of the forests"), *sylvicolae* ("forest dwellers"), and *barbari* (non-Europeans, non-believers; and to refer to foreign custom as in: *ut barbarum*). The publication—mostly in censored and edited form—of these Latin Relations in the *Litterae annuae* (a project that proved unsustainable over time) suggests that they were intended for the benefit of other members of the Society, missionaries in particular, but their Latinity made them accessible as well to a learned international audience, occasionally through a separate reprint by a commercial printing house.

However, the Latin texts had a more limited audience, and their reception could not compete with the success of the Relations written in French by the Superior in Quebec City and addressed to the Provincial in France. Censored for content and edited for language and style, the French Relations became a printing success with a broad lay public upon publication by Cramoisy in Paris, and served to generate support for the endeavor. The Latin Relation was not a mere translation of the French, as in the case of the Latin Relation for the year 1640 written by René Ménard (Campeau 1967–2003, 4:532–54), even though it provides a partial summary of the French Relation by Paul Le Jeune. Ménard, a recent arrival to America, had been a college teacher of literature and rhetoric and employed an ambitious vocabulary, using the Early Christian term *ethnici* ("gentiles") to refer to indigenous persons, and spelling it *aethnici* in his archaizing zeal. In addition to the annual reports on all missionary activity by the Jesuits of New France, there were reports on the individual missions, some of which are powerful documents in their own right, such as the two Latin accounts of the destruction of the Huron missions by Paul Ragueneau, dated March 1 and May 1 of 1649. The May account is particularly striking for the emotional engagement it expresses, albeit tersely, and is unequaled in its Latinity by any of the other Superiors, according to the most recent editor of these documents (and the source of this overview), Lucien Campeau (1967–2003, 7:459–65; 500–20). The Latin texts have their own expressive value in addition to their unique ethnographic frame of reference, which can only be fully grasped if one reads the documents in the original language.

A similarly dramatic account was written by Isaac Jogues: his *Epistola Patris Isaaci Jogues in Nova Francia* (*Letter of Father Isaac Jogues from New France*), dated August 5, 1643 (Campeau 1967–2003, 5:592–625), details his tormented stay with the Iroquois and provides the first description of their way of life and language. Jogues produced an account of a missionary's state of mind *in extremis*, yet keeps a coherent chronological order and describes his own initial hesitation as to whether to write in French or Latin: his long absence from Europe has caused him difficulty in composing both in the vernacular and in the scholarly language. He eventually chooses Latin because he recalls biblical quotations in that language, and because of the personal and spiritual content of his epistle, but he apologizes in advance for offending both against the laws of grammar and against the rules of his office after eight years of service in the field.

A special form of allied material is the necrology. Once a missionary died, a necrology or eulogy provided a retrospective of his career, writings and activities, at home and abroad; for example, the *Vita et mors* (*Life and Death*) of René Ménard by Paul Ragueneau (Campeau 1967–2003, 9:552–57). Such an account might include a description of the individual's religious visions and experiences, as in the case of Jean de Brébeuf, with extracts in French and Latin by Paul Ragueneau. Another important source for individual careers is contained in the annual catalogs of the Mission of New France prepared by the Superior to be sent to the Jesuit headquarters in Rome, detailing the disposition of personnel over the missions to the individual nations. From 1660, we possess annual reports by François de Laval, the Jesuits' candidate for bishop of Quebec, written with great precision and economy (Campeau 1967–2003, 9:429–39).

The greatest number of the substantial body of Latin documents in the context of the Relations, however, consists of short letters, extending to a maximum of a couple of pages in modern editions and typically dealing with a limited number of items in as many paragraphs in a terse, business-like style. Correspondents included the Superior in Quebec City, the Provincial in France, the General of the Society in Rome, as well as missionaries in the field. The period covered is mainly 1611–1762, from the first, abortive mission to the East Coast (1611–1613) and the settlement at Quebec City in 1625, to the fall of New France and the suppression of the Society by the English during the Seven Years' War (1756–1763). Most of the extant originals are held at the Archivum Romanum Societatis Iesu in Rome (esp. Codex Gal. 10 and 110: *Missio Canadensis*) and in the archives of the Jesuit province of Paris, now at Vanves.

Historiography

The first history of the mission to New France is by François Ragueneau, entitled *Monumenta historica missionis Novae Franciae ab anno 1607 ad 1637* (*Historical Records of the Mission to New France from the Year 1607 until 1637*; Campeau 1967–2003, 3:409–463). This account by the Jesuit Superior in Quebec covers the early settlement of the Society at Quebec City and the missions to the Hurons and the Montagnais (Innu). Its style is more elaborate than that of a report: a historiographically ambitious work, it also displays a deep personal involvement with its subject matter and an interest in the geography of the valley of the Saint Lawrence River. Ragueneau also wrote a description of the massive earthquake that shook the region in 1663, based on a vernacular account by Charles Simon that is no longer extant. Although the Latin version includes some classical phrasing, there appears to be no direct link with descriptions of similar phenomena in antiquity by authors like Pliny the Elder and Seneca (Thwaites 1896–1901, 48:182–223).

The first history of Canada, *Historiae Canadensis seu Novae Franciae libri decem ad annum usque Christi MDCLVI* (*History of Canada or New France in Ten Books until the Year of Christ 1656*), was commissioned by the Society and written by an officially designated Jesuit historian, François Ducreux (Ducreux 1951–1952). In his preface, Ducreux provides the first self-conscious reflection on—and justification of—his new, North American subject matter as worthy of being recounted. He rejects the secular humanist *arbitrium* ("judgment") as to what constitutes an appropriate historical narrative as determined by classical models and esthetic criteria, and confronts such an approach with a series of arguments drawn from the New Testament, notions of progress, rival esthetic principles, and the usefulness of the genre of missionary history for those involved in the same endeavor elsewhere. Ducreux claims to have interviewed missionaries returning from Canada, but his account is clearly based on the French Relations. Published in Paris by the king's printer, Sébastien Cramoisy, who also printed the French Relations, Ducreux's book seems to have had a wide reception, and may even have been initially intended for the teaching of history in the Jesuit colleges.

A much later treatise on Canada and the customs of its native peoples, based on early missionary accounts, *De regione et moribus Canadensium seu barbarorum Novae Franciae* (*The Land and the Customs of the Canadians or Barbarians of New France*), was written by Joseph de Jouvancy as part of a more ambitious history of the Society (Dionne 2012), and published separately in Rome in 1710. Jouvancy's work occupies a prominent place in the first volume of the nineteenth-century edition of the Jesuit Relations by Thwaites, along with its English translation (Thwaites 1896–1901, 1:239–97). Both Ducreux and Jouvancy were experts on the language curriculum of the Jesuit colleges, and sophisticated Latinists who had internalized classical authors' esthetic principles and stylistic practices, which resulted in a more complex syntax and a more elaborate vocabulary, with distinctive classical echoes. In effect, Ducreux and Jouvancy rewrote their vernacular sources, modifying the reports from the field in content, form, and expression. Moreover, never having set foot in Canada, these two historians lacked the personal experience of living with indigenous people, resulting in generalizing, negative assessments signaled by the frequent pejorative use of the term "barbarian" (*barbarus*).

SCIENTIFIC WRITING

Also written in Latin in New France were the scientific works of two eighteenth-century Jesuits, the Belgian Pierre Potier (1708–1781), and the Frenchman Jean-Baptiste de La Brosse (1724–1782). Thirty-eight of Potier's manuscript notebooks survive in various archival collections: many of the notebooks merely contain course notes, but others are more extended treatises, on the Huron language in particular. Included among the notebooks, too, are lecture notes that give us a good idea of what interested Potier and demonstrate his sound classical learning. The Jesuit archives in Montreal preserve twenty-four notebooks of linguistic studies, of which five are dedicated to Huron. Four of those were written in Latin. The Jesuit Jean-Baptiste de La Brosse was a former professor of Latin and humanities and was the author of a Latin-Montagnais dictionary, a *Liber Superstitionum* (*Book of Superstitions*), now lost, an *Animadversiones* (*Observations*) and *Annotationes* (*Notes*), a philosophy course, mission records—which have been published by Léo-Paul Hébert (1973 and 1994)—and a catalog of the Tadoussac Amerindians (*Catalogus generalis totius Montanensium gentis; General Catalog of the Whole Montagnais People*; Hébert 1982). La Brosse was also the author of a Latin–Abenaki dictionary and a Montagnais grammar in Latin (Cottier and McKenzie, forthcoming).

We should also mention works that were not actually written in New France but discuss it, either as a whole or in part. German theologian Jonas Conrad Schramm, for instance, published *De philosophia Canadensium populi in America septentrionali balbutiente dissertatio* (*Dissertation on the Stammering Philosophy of the Canadian People in North America*, 1707; Étarian 1983), which explores at length the then-very-popular travelogues of the Baron de Lahontan (1703). Finnish botanist Pehr Kalm, who visited New France during the summer of 1749 (Kalm 1977), wrote a travelogue that interweaves (often Latin) botanical observations with more general reflections on the country he was discovering. Relevant to our consideration of the Latin in New France is the fact that Kalm, who was well-educated in the humanities and expressed himself confidently in Latin, delighted in emphasizing that the French Canadians did not know Latin, and even suspected that the bishop of Quebec was a poor Latinist. However, behind the criticism of that bishop—the Frenchman Henri-Marie Dubreuil de Pontbriand of Quebec, former pupil of the Jesuit Collège de la Flèche and teacher at the Sorbonne—lies the mockery of a Catholic bishop by a Protestant minister, rather than a necessarily accurate picture of the situation.

Spiritual Writing and Poetry

Although Relations, historiography, and science dominated the Jesuit writing in New France, the fact that the first Latin text from this region that appeared in print was a spiritual work characterizes the religious impulse of the mission. The *Affectus amantis Christum Iesum* (*Emotion of a Lover of Christ*; Chastellain 1999) was written by Pierre Chastellain in Huronia between 1641 and 1646. The book was completed on September 29, 1646, and was printed in France by Denis Béchet. The *Affectus* must have been retrieved in 1648, shortly before the annihilation of the Hurons by the Iroquois; it outlines, in its author's words, the "first fruit of a field recently cleared" and offers a personal synthesis of missionary practice and the great mystical inspiration of the Christian tradition in the form of spiritual exercises spread over a week. Chastellain composed it during the period when he was head of the central Jesuit residence of Saint-Marie, near the river Wye, which had a great deal of cultural and religious influence in his time.

Few in number, the significance of the poetic works related to New France lies in the way their European authors imagined a new world and in their subsequent rereading and rewriting of their classical models. The only poem written by an eyewitness is a short Virgilian cento drawn from Book 1 of the *Aeneid* specifically, and identifying the disastrous state of the Jesuit mission in about 1650 with the lot of the Trojans (Westra 2010). The earliest extended treatment of the mission, Ovidian in inspiration and featuring an ambivalent poetic description of the country by a personification of Canada, was published as part of the *Franciade* by the Jesuit Laurent Le Brun in 1639 (O'Brien 2012). The panegyrical *Metamorphosis* of Etienne de Carheil provides insight into the poet's preoccupations prior to his missionary activity among the Cayugas (Smeesters 2012). Well before the arrival of the Jesuits in New France, the young Hungarian poet Stephanus Parmenius composed a description of Newfoundland (1583) that demonstrated his horror of the wilds (Quinn and Cheshire 1972).

CONCLUSION

This overview has highlighted texts that we know exist but have only rarely been studied and have almost never been properly edited or translated: the work still to be done on Neo-Latin writing in New France is considerable. When such research is conducted, much new material will no doubt be unearthed, which will contribute substantially, not only to our understanding of the cultural history of New France, but also to the contemporary history of Europe and of France in particular. Equally importantly, this work will also improve our knowledge about the priests who dreamed of building a new society, taking with them a worldview informed by Catholicism and based on a humanistic culture centuries old.

PART 2: NEW ENGLAND

John Gallucci

Within the English-speaking regions of North America in the seventeenth and eighteenth centuries, we find a varied corpus of Neo-Latin writing. From entries in private journals to academic oratory, from *theses* and *quaestiones* ("investigations") required of the university student to original poetical compositions published in books, magazines, and newspapers; from theological treatise to scientific communication with Enlightenment Europe, these texts form an imperfectly known chapter in early American cultural history. Yet far from being a passive moment in the *translatio studii* ("transmission of learning"), the composition of Neo-Latin in the emerging United States constitutes an original linguistic and literary vein.

POETRY

New England, Pennsylvania, and Virginia seem to form the major regions where the writing of Latin verse developed, but texts from all regions of the developing colonies are found. Foundational for the study of this poetry is Leo M. Kaiser's anthology of American Neo-Latin verse (Kaiser 1984) and his earlier "Census" of American Latin verse (Kaiser 1981). Subjects of this poetry include the topography of the New World, the celebration of nature, descriptions of Native Americans, and the theme of the advancement of American civilization. "Indeed, American poets seem to have felt that they might write on any subject at all, often with that degree of intimacy" associated with Renaissance poets (Kaiser 1981, 207).

Poets whose names deserve to be mentioned specifically include William Morrell, who wrote *Nova Anglia* (*New England*, 1625), with its descriptions of Native Americans: *Sunt etenim populi minimi sermonis et oris / austeri, risusque parum saevique superbi* ("They are in fact a people of little speech and of stern appearance; they laugh little and are fierce and haughty"; Kaiser 1984, 6). Nathaniel Gardner of Boston's South Grammar School described his teaching day in a poem conventionally titled *The (Latin) Teacher* (1754), highly praised by several scholars: *Surgunt, ecce, scholae, collegia, templa per urbes / saevities qua olim late imperitaverat agris* ("Behold, where harsh barbarity was lord over the fields, schools, colleges, temples arise through the cities"; Kaiser 1984, 68; Shields 2007, 450). John Beveridge of Philadelphia, also a teacher of Latin and friend of Gardner's, wrote and published his *Epistolae familiares et alia quaedam miscellanea* (*Letters to Friends and Some Miscellanea*) in 1765. One Neo-Latin poem was written by a Native American, a student at Harvard named Eleazar (Kaiser 1984, 33–34). While most of the writers anthologized were from the English-speaking colonies or states, one finds in the eighteenth and nineteenth centuries a number of French poets, such as Stephen Theodore Badin, ordained in Maryland as the first Catholic priest in the United States. His *Sanctissimae Trinitatis laudes et invocatio* (*Praise and Invocation of the Most Holy Trinity*) was published in Louisville, Kentucky, in 1843. The anonymous *Sibyllae Americanae Genethliacum Ludovico XVII* (*Birthday Poem of the American Sibyl for Louis XVII*), published in Philadelphia in 1782, celebrated the birth of King Louis XVI's first son.

Two collections of poetry were composed for official purposes. The accession of George III of England was celebrated by the publication in 1761 of the volume *Pietas et gratulatio collegii Cantabrigiensis apud Novanglos* (*Affection and Congratulation of the College of Cambridge in New England*), with verse in Greek, Latin, and English. In Virginia, as stipulated in the statutes of the founding of the College of William and Mary, students offered Latin verses of their own composition to the governor of Virginia over a number of years (Counsell 1930).

A fitting complement to Kaiser's work is Gilbert L. Gigliotti's unpublished doctoral dissertation "Musae Americanae: The Neo-Latin Poetry of Colonial and Revolutionary America" (1992). This, the first extended study of American Neo-Latin poetry, fully justifies the author's claim that American Neo-Latin poetry is a form of "artistic expression" (18). Overall, the extent of the Neo-Latin poetry written shows that for educated Americans, as for educated Englishmen, "contemporary Latin poems were part of [one's] normal reading" (Binns 1990, 2–3, 114; Monaghan 2005, 12).

THEOLOGY AND ACADEMIC WRITING

A rich variety of Neo-Latin prose from this region exists. Kaiser's second "Census" (Kaiser 1982) lays an essential foundation. Broadly speaking, theological works predominate in the earlier periods, with scientific works and medical dissertations coming to the fore in the eighteenth century. Among the earliest Latin writings from North America is the *Relatio itineris in Marilandiam* (*Report About the Voyage to Maryland*) by the Jesuit Andrew White of 1633. Recently edited in an exemplary edition (White 1995), this brief but fascinating travel narrative contains, among other valuable passages, a discussion of the Native Americans White met and befriended. A number of related Latin texts about the colony of Maryland include White's *Declaratio coloniae domini baronis de Baltamore in Terra Mariae* (*Declaration of Lord Baltimore's Colony in Maryland*) and documents pertaining to land tenancy and ownership (Hughes 1908). Latin writings from French Jesuit missionaries in the Illinois and Louisiana territories are gathered in Thwaites's (1896–1901) important collection of the Jesuit Relations.

In New England, one finds several theological works. An early theological work by John Norton, the *Responsio ad totam quaestionum syllogen a . . . Domino Gulielmo Apollonio . . . propositam* (*Answer to the Whole Set of Queries Brought Forth by Mr. William Apollonius*, 1648), was, according to Kaiser (1982, 168), "the first book written in Latin in America." The Puritans Increase Mather and his son, Cotton Mather, wrote in Latin, and the latter includes Latin prose (e.g., the *Statuta, leges, et privilegia . . . collegii Harvardini; Statutes, Laws, and Privileges of Harvard College*) and verse in his English *Magnalia Christi America; The Glorious Works of Christ in America*, 1702). The Reverend John H. Livingston, a president of Queen's College (now Rutgers University in New Jersey), studied theology in Utrecht and learned Latin with such diligence that he "could speak the Latin almost as readily as his native tongue" (Gunn 1829, 161). In New York in 1785, he published *Oratio inauguralis de veritate religionis Christianae* (*Inaugural Speech on the Truth of the Christian Faith*).

The fundamental importance of Latin in school and university curricula and academic life, especially in the seventeenth century, is well known. At Harvard, some compilations of Cartesian logic were prepared in Latin, including William Brattle's *Compendium logicae secundum principia D. Renatii Cartesii* (*Compendium of Logic according to the Principles of René Descartes*, 1735; Kennedy 1990). Samuel E. Morison's history of

Harvard College includes much material in Latin and allows one to see the extent to which Latin was used both within and without the curriculum. Of particular interest is the Latin address to his benefactors by Caleb Sheeshahteaumuck, the first Native American to graduate from Harvard (Morison 1936, 1:355). A number of college presidents delivered Latin prose orations as part of various academic ceremonies. Speeches by Urian Oakes (1631–1688; Kittredge and Morison 1935) and John Leverett (1662–1724) of Harvard; by the Reverend Samuel Johnson (1696–1772) of King's (Columbia) College, and by Ezra Stiles (1727–1795) of Yale College are interesting sources for the history of education in America. Of especial interest is Ezra Stiles's *Oratio inauguralis* (*Inaugural Speech*) of 1778, in which he outlines an *encyclopaedia scientiarum* ("encyclopedia of learning"), beginning from the vernacular and classical languages, and moving on to the natural sciences, and finally on to philosophy and theology. The speech contains references to Linnaeus and to Benjamin Franklin, who *fluidi electrici energiam et stupendam vim legesque philosophice explicuit et demonstravit* ("explained and demonstrated scientifically the laws and energy and tremendous force of electrical fluid," p. 11; in 1755 Stiles delivered another Latin speech in Franklin's honor, who received an honorary degree from Yale). Ezra Stiles reveals a remarkable catholicity in calling for the study of literature written in the Arabic language, arguing that if one gives so much time and labor to learning the languages of ancient Greece and Rome in order to read *centum plusve minusve volumina librorum* ("a hundred volumes, more or less, of books"), then—*a fortiori*—*quanto utilius et optatius, ex una lingua Arabica congerere vel acquirere posse innumerabilium virorum eruditissimorum labores, Europaeis in omni fere genere scribendi antecellentium* ("how much more useful and desirable, from a single Arabian language, to be able to gather or acquire the labors of countless learned men, who excel the Europeans in almost every kind of writing"; pp. 7–8). A Latin speech by John Blair Smith, the first president of Union College, in Schenectady, New York, likewise deserves mention. This locale had been for generations an outpost on the American frontier, and in his *Oratio inauguralis de institutione iuventutis* (*Inaugural Speech on the Education of Youth*) of 1796, we find, alongside a traditional commitment to the importance of higher learning, signs of a new American frontier.

Scientific Treatises

In the realm of the natural sciences, one finds a relatively large body of Neo-Latin American writing. The history of American botany includes connections with Neo-Latin literature through the correspondence of various American scientists with Linnaeus and other Europeans. The scientist, surveyor, and statesman Cadwallader Colden (1668–1776), lieutenant governor of the province of New York; the botanist John Bartram (1699–1777) of Pennsylvania; the Virginian John Clayton (1694–1773); the classical scholar James Logan (1674–1751), secretary to William Penn; and the botanist

Henry Muhlenberg (1753–1815) all wrote in a scientific Latin that participated in the "learned networks in natural history" (Shields 2007, 450–51).

Colden corresponded with Linnaeus (Colden 1843, 29–30), who addressed him as a *vir illustris* ("distinguished man") and published some of Colden's botanical observations in the *Acta societatis regiae scientiarum Upsaliensis* (*Proceedings of the Royal Society of Science in Uppsala* 1743, 81–136; 1744–1750, 47–82) under the title *Plantae Coldenghamiae in provincia Noveboracensi Americes sponte crescentes* (*Plants Growing Spontaneously at Coldenham in the Province of North America*). Colden's daughter, Jane Colden, would become an important scientist in her own right, and had some knowledge of Latin (Harrison 1995, 22). Clayton sent botanical specimens to the Dutch botanist Johannes Fredericus Gronovius (1686–1762), who published them in his Latin treatise *Flora Virginica* (*Virginian Flora*) in 1762, so that, as he stated in his dedicatory note, he might communicate these findings "to the learned world". John Bartram, friend to Pehr Kalm, learned enough Latin to use Linnaeus's system (Stetson 1949). Henry Muhlenberg, also of Pennsylvania and a "botanical pioneer" (Smith 1962) also used Latin in his publications. A text published posthumously in 1817, his *Descriptio uberior graminum et plantarum calamariarum Americae Septentrionalis indigenarum et cicurum* (*Copious Description of Grasses and Reed-Like Plants, Both Indigenous and Cultivated, of North America*, 1817), contains a Latin preface by its editor.

Most important of these scientific writers was James Logan, a major figure in early American cultural and scientific life. His library, the "greatest of all American colonial libraries" (Tolles 1955, 418), led to the development of Philadelphia as a center for scientific study. Besides being the author of several fine Latin poems (Kaiser 1984, 43–45), Logan published several scientific works in Latin: the *Experimenta et meletemata de plantarum generatione* (*Experiments and Exercises on the Generation of Plants*, 1739; edition and translation in Lokken 1972, 81–88); and a work on optics, *Demonstrationes de radiorum lucis in superficies sphaericas remotius ab axe incidentium a primario foco aberrationibus* (*Concerning the Aberrations from the Primary Focus of the Light Rays Which Fall on Spherical Surfaces Farther from the Axis*, 1741; edition and translation in Lokken 1972, 46–60). In New England, John Winthrop, professor of natural science at Harvard College, authored a Latin poem connecting the transit of Venus to George III's accession to the English throne (1760; Kaiser 1984, 140), and he also wrote in Latin a treatise, *Cogitata de Cometis* (*Reflections on Comets*), which Benjamin Franklin presented to the Royal Society in London in 1767. Benjamin Franklin's own letters on electricity were translated into Latin: of this translation only fragments have been identified (Van der Pas 1978).

Latin was also the language used for medical theses in early America: for example, William Stokes's *Tentamen medicum inaugurale* (*Inaugural Medical Essay*, 1793), on asphyxia, which he dedicated to Thomas Jefferson. A Latin oration that has been called a "pivotal document *sui generis* in the annals of American medical history" was delivered in 1768 by John Lawrence to celebrate the graduation of the first class of American medical students from the College of Philadelphia (Dietrich 1953).

It is here that one should mention Francis Daniel Pastorius (1651–1720), the founder of Germantown, Pennsylvania, "a man with a compulsion for accumulating information," a "polyhistor," in the words of one of his editors (Pastorius 1982, 1). Pastorius was also the author of a Latin letter (Goebel 1904) that, in the words of Anthony Grafton, is a "charming" text that "adumbrates . . . the ethnographic writings of men such as Lafitau and Lahontan and their successors" and even "seems to belong to the new travel writing of the eighteenth and early nineteenth centuries" (Grafton 2011, 28–29).

Epitaphs, Inscriptions, and Biography

Leo M. Kaiser collected a number of Latin epigraphs and inscriptions for his *Corpus inscriptionum Graecarum Latinarumque Americae* (*Corpus of Greek and Latin Inscriptions from America*; Kaiser 1955–1956, 69). These important texts form a veritable "Who's Who" of American scholars and leaders in the colonial and republican periods. It is fitting to cite here a portion of the epitaph of Ezechial Cheever, a teacher his whole life and headmaster of the Boston Latin School for over thirty years, author of a work of Latin accidence that remained in use in schools for over a century, and teacher of Cotton Mather, who delivered his funeral oration in 1708 and who may have composed this epitaph: *grammaticus, a quo, non pure tantum, sed et pie, loqui . . . didicerunt qui discere voluerunt* ("a teacher of grammar, from whom they who wished to learn, learned to speak not only with purity, but with piety"; Kaiser 1955–1956, 143).

A special motif in American Neo-Latin writing is the person and life of George Washington, the first President of the United States. In the nineteenth century, two writers wrote lengthy Latin biographies of this Founding Father. In Ohio, Francis Glass, a schoolteacher, published his *Georgii Washingtonii . . . Vita* (*Life of George Washington*) in 1835. In 1836, in Charleston, South Carolina, William Lance published his *Georgii Washingtonis Vita*. At the turn of the century, Joseph Willard, President of Harvard, delivered in 1800 a *Concio brevis* (*Brief Speech*) commemorating the recently deceased Washington. A number of Latin diplomas were awarded to Washington (Kaiser 1966).

Private Journals

We also have evidence that Latin was used privately, for personal communication. Many writers made Latin entries in their journals and diaries, such as Cotton Mather and Samuel Sewall. A 1645 Latin letter from Samuel Winthrop to his father, John Winthrop, Esq., at Boston, has been edited (Winthrop 1891–1892). Journals and letters also contain some interesting references to the practice of speaking Latin. The Virginian William Byrd II noted in his diary on November 11, 1709, that: "my wife quarreled with Mr. Dunn and me for talking Latin and called it bad manners" (Byrd 1963, 48).

The American War of Independence also manifested itself in Latin. Ezra Stiles recorded speaking Latin with the French general Rochambeau, who was then in command of the French forces fighting with the American Patriots: "October 7. I conversed with the General [de Rochambeau] in Latin. He speaks it tolerably" (Stiles 1901, 2:473). John Lewis, tutor at Yale College, wrote to Ezra Stiles of a recent innovation in the technology of warfare, known to history as the submarine *Turtle*. The venerable tutor emphasized that circumstances rendered his description of this invention necessarily incomplete: "I have this moment parted with Mr. Bushnel; *hic homo est machinae inventor ... Accurate discribere illam valde mirificam machinam ob hostes non licet, neque possum si vellem*" ("this man is the inventor of a machine. ... . Because of the enemy's presence, I am not allowed to describe in detail that marvelous machine, nor can I, if I wished to"; Stiles 1916, 530–31 and 1901, 1:600). Ezra Stiles's diary also referred to a certain Miss Lucinda Foot (Stiles 1901, 3:102–3). Examining this intelligent young lady, he found her "well fitted for the Freshmen class," but due to her sex (*sexus ratione*) she was not admitted. Stiles wrote for her in Latin a "Certificate or Diploma on Parchment" (Stiles 1901, 3:103) and may have continued to tutor her privately (Lutz 1996). There are other instances of women learning Latin (Monaghan 2005, 368; Stevenson 2005, 396).

CONCLUSION

As we follow the evolving frontiers of the young American Republic from New England to New York and New Jersey; to Pennsylvania, Maryland, and Virginia, and further westwards to Kentucky and beyond, we see that the Latin language was used as a living language for purposes of genuine communication at many levels. To be sure, this corpus remains relatively modest when measured against its contemporary developments in Great Britain, Europe, and elsewhere in the New World. Yet if the varied and disparate corpus of Neo-Latin in America makes any summary difficult, it also demonstrates how flexible the classical idiom could be. This same diversity suggests future lines of inquiry. Many of these texts have been subordinated and cited only glancingly in traditional disciplines—literature, history—within early American studies, and scholars are only beginning to see how they might be valued for their own sakes. As Gigliotti (1992, 6) fittingly writes, though, the result of closer study of Neo-Latin writing in America "could modify the understanding of our literary history."

SUGGESTED READING

New France: As only a very few Latin texts from New France have been studied by scholars to date, readers are referred to the monumental editions of the Jesuit Relations by Thwaites (1869–1901) and Campeau (1967–2003), as well as to the two special issues of the journal *Tangence* (Cottier 2010 and 2012). Especially useful for research in this field is the critical bibliography of Laflèche (2000). Two representative Latin authors available in good modern editions are Ducreux (1951–1952) and Potier (1996). Deslandres (2003) provides an excellent overview of life in New France.

New England: Space precludes the inclusion of a complete listing of Leo M. Kaiser's numerous groundbreaking articles and editions of American Neo-Latin prose and verse. His bibliographies of Neo-Latin prose and verse are to be complemented by reference to the *Evans Series of Early American Imprints*, which lists over six hundred titles in Latin. Gummere's *The American Colonial Mind and the Classical Tradition* (1963), the work of a classicist, shows the value of a knowledge of Latin in understanding of early American culture.

REFERENCES

Bapst, Patrick. 2013. "Alter orbis litterarum, ou Une littérature coloniale historicisée: Le statut des textes latins dans le contexte missionnaire de la Nouvelle-France (1608–1763)." Mémoire de maîtrise, University of Lausanne. Serveur académique lausannois (ID Serval: serval: BIB_S_000000019665).

Bernier, Marc A. 1997. "La conquête de l'éloquence au Québec: La *Rhetorica in Seminario Quebecensi* (1774) de Charles-François Bailly de Messein." *Voix et Images* 66:582–98.

Biard, Pierre. 2003. *The Jesuit Mission in Acadie and Norembègue*, 1611–1613. Translated by George Topp and William Lonc. Halifax: Lonc.

Binns, James W. 1990. *Intellectual Culture in Elizabethan and Jacobean England: The Latin Writings of the Age.* Leeds: Francis Cairns.

Byrd, William. 1963. *The Great American Gentleman William Byrd of Westover in Virginia: His Secret Diary for the Years 1709–1712.* Edited by Louis B. Wright and Marion Tinling. New York: G.P. Putnam's Sons.

Campeau, Lucien, ed. 1967–2003. *Monumenta Novae Franciae.* 9 vols. Rome: Institutum Historicum Societatis Jesu.

Chastellain, Pierre. 1999. *L'âme éprise du Christ Jésus ou Exercices d'amour envers le Seigneur Jésus pour toute une semaine.* Translated by Joseph Hofbeck. Montreal: Guérin.

Colden, Cadwallader. 1843. *Selections from the Scientific Correspondence of Cadwallader Colden with Gronovius, Linnaeus, Collinson, and Other Naturalists.* Edited by Asa Gray. New Haven: Hamlen.

Cottier, Jean-François, ed. 2010. *À la recherche d'un signe oublié: Le patrimoine latin du Québec et sa culture classique.* Special issue, *Tangence* 92.

———. ed. 2012. *Nova Gallia: Recherches sur les écrits latins de Nouvelle-France.* Special issue, *Tangence* 99.

Cottier, Jean-François, and Marguerite McKenzie, eds. and trans. Forthcoming. *Jean-Baptiste de La Brosse: Montanicae linguae elementa (1768).*

Counsell, E. M. 1930. "Latin Verses Presented by Students of William and Mary College to the Governor of Virginia in 1771–1772, 1773, and 1774." *The William and Mary Quarterly* 10:269–74.

Deslandres, Dominique. 2003. *Croire et faire croire: Les missions françaises au XVIIe siècle,* Paris: Fayard.

Dietrich, Herbert J. 1953. "Oration on the Birthday of Medical Honors in America, by John Lawrence, 1768." *Transactions and Studies of the College of Physicians of Philadelphia* 25:41–52.

Dionne, Fannie. 2012. "De regione et moribus Canadensium seu Barbarorum Novae Franciae: Les 'Barbares de Nouvelle-France,' texte anonyme (1616) édité par Joseph de Jouvancy (1710)." Mémoire de maîtrise, University of Montreal. Papyrus: Institutional Repository (Permalink: http://hdl.handle.net/1866/8777).

Ducreux, François. 1951–1952. *The History of Canada or New France*. Edited and translated by James B. Conacher and Percy J. Robinson. Toronto: The Champlain Society.

Étarian, Anne-Marie. 1983. "La philosophie balbutiante des Canadiens." In *Sur Lahontan*, edited by Réal Ouellet, 73–97. Quebec: L'Hêtrière.

Gigliotti, Gilbert L. 1992. "Musae Americanae: The Neo-Latin Poetry of Colonial and Revolutionary America." Ph.D. diss., Catholic University of America. ProQuest (document ID 304010787).

Goebel, Julius. 1904. "Zwei unbekannte Briefe von Pastorius." *German-American Annals* 2:492–503.

Grafton, Anthony. 2012. "The Republic of Letters in the American Colonies: Francis Daniel Pastorius Makes a Notebook." *The American Historical Review* 117:1–39.

Gummere, Richard M. 1963. *The American Colonial Mind and the Classical Tradition: Essays in Comparative Culture*. Cambridge: Harvard University Press.

Gunn, Alexander. 1829. *Memoirs of the Rev. John H. Livingston*. New York: Rutgers Press.

Harrison, Mary. 1995. "Jane Colden: Colonial American Botanist." *Arnoldia* 55.2:19–26.

Hébert, Léo-Paul, ed. 1973. *Le troisième registre de Tadoussac: Miscellaneorum liber (1691–1758)*. Quebec: Presses de l'Université du Québec.

———, ed. 1982. *Le quatrième registre de Tadoussac: Magnus liber*. Quebec: Presses de l'Université du Québec.

———, ed. 1994. *Le registre de Sillery (1638–1690)*. Quebec: Presses de l'Université du Québec.

Hughes, Thomas. 1908. *History of the Society of Jesus in North America: Colonial and Federal*. Vol. 1.1, *Documents nos. 1–140 (1605–1838)*. London: Longmans, Green, and Co.

Kaiser, Leo M. 1955–1956. "Latin Epitaphs for CIGLA." *The Classical Journal* 51:69–80 and 141–44.

———. 1966. "The Latin Diplomas of George Washington." *The Classical Journal* 61:198–201.

———. 1981. "A Census of American Latin Verse." *Proceedings of the American Antiquarian Society* 91:197–299.

———. 1982. "Contributions to a Census of American Latin Prose, 1634–1800." *Humanistica Lovaniensia* 31:164–189.

———. 1984. *Early American Latin Verse, 1625–1825: An Anthology*. Chicago: Bolchazy-Carducci.

Kalm, Pehr. 1977. *Voyage de Pehr Kalm au Canada*. Translated by Jacques Rousseau, Guy Béthune, and Pierre Morisset. Montreal: P. Tisseyre.

Kennedy, Rick. 1990. "The Alliance Between Puritanism and Cartesian Logic at Harvard, 1687–1735." *Journal of the History of Ideas* 51:549–72.

Kittredge, George L., and Samuel E. Morison. 1935. "Urian Oakes's Salutatory Oration: Commencement, 1677." *Publications of the Colonial Society of Massachusetts* 31:405–36.

Laflèche, Guy. 2000. *Bibliographie littéraire de la Nouvelle-France*. Laval, Quebec: Singulier.

Lamonde, Yvan. 1980. *La philosophie et son enseignement au Québec (1665–1920)*. Montréal: Hurtubise.

Lokken, Roy N., ed. 1972. "The Scientific Papers of James Logan." *Transactions of the American Philosophical Society* 62:1–94.

Lutz, Cora E. 1996. "Ezra Stiles and the Education of Women." *The Yale University Library Gazette* 71:49–55.

Monaghan, E. Jennifer. 2005. *Learning to Read and Write in Colonial America*. Worcester: University of Massachusetts Press.

Morison, Samuel E. 1936. *Harvard College in the Seventeenth Century*. 2 vols. Cambridge: Harvard University Press.

O'Brien, Peter. 2012. "*La Franciade* de Le Brun: poétique ovidienne de l'exil en Nouvelle-France." In Cottier 2012, 35–60.

Pastorius, Francis D. 1982. *Deliciae Hortenses or Garden-Recreations and Voluptates Apianae*. Edited by Christoph E. Schweitzer. Columbia: Camden House.

Potier, Pierre. 1996. *Les écrits de Pierre Potier*. Edited by Robert Toupin. Ottawa: Presses de l'Université d'Ottawa.

Quinn, David B., and Neil M. Cheshire, eds. 1972. *The New Found Land of Stephen Parmenius: The Life and Writings of a Hungarian Poet, Drowned on a Voyage from Newfoundland, 1583*. Toronto: University of Toronto Press.

Shields, David S. 2007. "Eighteenth-Century Literary Culture." In *The Colonial Book in the Atlantic World*. Vol. 1, *A History of the Book in America*, edited by Hugh Amory and David D. Hall, 434–76. Chapel Hill: University of North Carolina Press.

Smeesters, Aline. 2012. "La métamorphose d'Étienne de Carheil." In Cottier 2012, 61–79.

Smith, C. Earle. 1962. "Henry Muhlenberg: Botanical Pioneer." *Proceedings of the American Philosophical Society* 106:443–60.

Stetson, Sarah P. 1949. "The Traffic in Seeds and Plants from England's Colonies in North America." *Agricultural History* 23:45–56.

Stevenson, Jane. 2005. *Women Latin Poets*. Oxford: Oxford University Press.

Stiles, Ezra. 1901. *The Literary Diary of Ezra Stiles, D.D., LL.D. President of Yale College*. 3 vols. Edited by Franklin B. Dexter. New York: Charles Scribner's Sons.

———. 1916. *Extracts from the Itineraries and Other Miscellanies of Ezra Stiles, D.D., LL.D., 1755–1794, with a Selection from His Correspondence*. Edited by Franklin B. Dexter. New Haven: Yale University Press.

Tolles, Frederick B. 1957. *James Logan and the Culture of Provincial America*. Boston: Little, Brown, and Co.

Thwaites, Reuben Gold, ed. 1896–1901. *The Jesuit Relations and Allied Documents: Travels and Explorations of the Jesuits Missionaries in New France, 1610–1791; The original French, Latin and Italian Texts, with English Translations and Notes*. 73 vols. Cleveland: Burrows.

Van der Pas, Peter. 1978. "The Latin Translation of Benjamin Franklin's Letters on Electricity." *Isis* 69:82–85.

Westra, Haijo. 2010. "Références classiques implicites et explicites dans les écrits des Jésuites sur la Nouvelle-France." In Cottier 2010, 27–37.

White, Andrew. 1995. *Voyage to Maryland (1633): Relatio itineris in Marilandiam*. Edited and translated by Barbara Lawatsch-Boomgaarden. Wauconda: Bolchazy-Carducci.

Winthrop, Robert C. 1891–1892. "Samuel Winthrop to His Father." *Proceedings of the Massachusetts Historical Society* 7:13–15.

CHAPTER 35

···

ASIA

···

NOËL GOLVERS

LATIN, understood as Western civilization's main language of cultural expression from Roman antiquity until the early modern period, might seem rather foreign to the idea of "Asia," in terms of geography, culture, and imagination. Indeed, despite some vague ancient literary references (Ferguson 1978), sporadic Antonine numismatic discoveries, some reports on medieval Franciscan journeys to and through central Asia such as the Flemish monk Willem van Ruysbroeck's *Itinerarium* (1253–1255), and some rare fourteenth-century Franciscan epitaphs in China, Latin was absent from central- and far-eastern Asian lands until the sixteenth century. Following the Portuguese expansion in the Far East, however, particularly in India, Japan, and China, Jesuits and members of other religious congregations gradually penetrated these countries, entering China from Macau (China was also known, from ca. 1600, as the "Middle Kingdom"). Although the Jesuits were very active across all of these parts of the Far East, the focus of this chapter will be on how the Jesuits, as the most outspoken representatives of humanistic culture in the region, brought that culture to the Chinese in particular, using Latin to introduce China to the West while assimilating some native Chinese traditions and cultural heritage into their humanist worldview. This chapter will consider how that purpose was accomplished, its results, and how Latin's presence there developed.

THE PRESENCE OF LATIN BOOKS
AND LIBRARIES

The Jesuits, as representatives of the humanistic culture exemplified by their pedagogical manual the *ratio studiorum* (*Plan of Studies*, 1599), introduced Western concepts, books and libraries to the Far East, bringing books in particular into circulation among their Western colleagues to help with their spiritual life, preaching, and teaching, as well as their intellectual duties. These books also facilitated the intensive and extensive translation and publication program started by the Sicilian Jesuit Niccolò Longobardo (1559–1654) around 1611, which initially mainly relied on Aristotelian sources, but later expanded what we might think of as the "apostolate of the press," given how effectively the medium of print could spread religious doctrine, to every field of Western science. In the case of China, some 4,100 early modern texts survive as remnants of the Jesuit libraries predating the suppression of the order in 1773: approximately 65 percent of these works are in Latin, and the rest are in several European vernaculars (Verhaeren 1949). This is only a small part of the books that actually circulated across two and a half centuries (Golvers 2012b and 2013). In any case, Latin printed books constituted a significant number and served in turn as the sources for approximately 1,000 Chinese works, some of which are translations from Latin, but most of which incorporate Latin into Chinese-language works.

COMPREHENSIVE REPORTS

The Jesuits wrote copiously about their experiences in China, Japan, and India, recording their observations of new anthropological, geographical, historical, and cultural facts in reports, letters, and treatises of all kinds, which they then sent to inform both the Society's center in Rome, and Jesuits in other important provincial centers. Of these works, some were printed and some circulated in manuscript: these were stored in European (Jesuit and, later, public) archives and formed an important foundation of contemporary European knowledge of this "new" part of the world. Such interest perhaps reached its cultural culmination in the eighteenth-century fashion for *chinoiserie*. The first-hand information included in these works was mostly a byproduct of reporting on the mission's progress, but it often also led to separate writing on related topics. Wide-ranging cultural information, interwoven with linguistic observations, resulted in some large-scale compilations produced in Europe: some were published in Latin, such as Athanasius Kircher's *China Illustrata* (*China Illustrated*, 1667), Theophilus Siegfried Bayer's *Museum Sinicum* (*Chinese Museum*, 1730), and Etienne Fourmont's *Meditationes Sinicae* (*Chinese Meditations*, 1737).

As the mission operated in a secular context, reports on the progress of the mission were also expected to contain digressions on political, social, and sometimes also military and cultural backgrounds, if such information was thought necessary for making well-considered strategic decisions. Therefore, the *Litterae annuae*—annual records or "yearly letters" sent from each individual mission post and eventually grouped within the larger report from a given province—contain many observations that stray beyond the specific terms of the mission, and turn the "letters" into first-hand sources for contemporary regional Chinese history (Dehergne 1980 and 1982). Sometimes such "letters" grew into monograph-sized studies, as we shall see. Through the *Litterae annuae*, an important, prolific channel of information on the Asian "New World" was created: reporting to the central Jesuit authorities, Latin was their main language. Copies made either by local *amanuenses* in Macau, in Rome, or in other provincial centers circulated among the Jesuit colleges, and were seen as edifying reading material to stimulate young Jesuit novices to imitate the missionaries in Asia. Many of these works were subsequently printed, distributed throughout Europe—mostly after what Antoine Brou has described as a *toilette littéraire*, a "literary tidying-up" (Brou 1934)—and collected in Jesuit and other libraries. Occasionally the information they contained was incorporated into more general compilations, either in Latin or the European vernaculars. Latin compilations include Matteo Ricci's and Nicolas Trigault's *De Christiana expeditione apud Sinas* (*On the Christian Mission Among the Chinese*, 1615) and the magisterial syntheses by an anonymous author (perhaps the Tyrolean Jesuit Martino Martini [1614–1661]) on the basis of the annotations of his Portuguese fellow father António de Gouveia, entitled *Progressus et incrementum fidei ac Christianae religionis apud Sinas* (*Progress and Growth of the Faith and the Christian Religion Among the Chinese*; Japonica-Sinica 107). Although the *Progressus* was never printed, it is written in fine Latin with complex periods and sophisticated sentence structure. Later, another work of an equally high literary standard, the *Collectanea historiae Sinensis ab anno 1641 ad annum 1700* (*Collected Papers of Chinese History from 1641 to 1700*; Japonica-Sinica 104–5, I–II; 109–111) was composed by the Lithuanian Jesuit and penitentiary of St. Peter's (a function at the papal court), Thomas Ignatius Dunyn-Szpot (1643–1713). This work also exists in an abbreviated, updated version: both versions relied on the materials sent from China to the General of the Society's headquarters in Rome. Never printed, they were filed in the order's archive (*tabularium*), which can be consulted now either in the Archivum Romanum Societatis Iesu or in the Biblioteca Nazionale Centrale Vittorio Emanuele II in Rome.

More episodic in form, more focused on particular contemporary moments, and often widely read and translated, were the treatises that reported on specific phases of seventeenth-century history or formed temporary "accounts" of the mission, such as Martino Martini's *De bello Tartarico historia* (*History of the Tartarian War*, 1654), the first European eyewitness report on the Manchu conquest of China, which ran to twenty-four consecutive editions. Another example is the *De Bello Eruthano* (*On the Zunghar War*, 1697; Japonica-Sinica 149, 318) on the expeditions of the Kangxi Emperor against the Zunghar people (Latin *Eruthani*, a people from the westernmost province of Mongolia), which was written by the then-Superior of the Jesuits in China, Antoine Thomas, and never published. Similar episodes from contemporary history, and especially their consequences for the Chinese church, were described in the German Jesuit Adam Schall von Bell's *Historica narratio de initio et progressu missionis Societatis Jesu apud Sinenses* (*Historical Narrative About the Beginning and Progress of the Jesuit Mission Among the Chinese*, 1665; Schall 1942). Other examples include Giandomenico Gabiani's *Incrementa Sinicae ecclesiae* (*The Growth of the Chinese Church*, 1673) which relies on oral testimonies and diaries by other Jesuits in China like the Sicilian Lodovico Buglio (1606–1682) and the Flemish Ferdinand Verbiest (1623–1688) to describe the persecution of Christianity during the early years of the regency of the Manchu commander Gūwalgiya Oboi (1610–1669) between 1665 and 1667; Prospero Intorcetta's *Compendiosa narratio de statu missionis Chinensis ab 1581–1669* (*Compendious Narrative About the State of the Chinese Mission from 1581–1669*; 1672), and François de Rougemont's *Historia Tartaro-Sinica nova* (*New Tartarian-Chinese History*, 1673).

Similar reports were printed in China through the xylograph or woodcut process, then distributed in great quantities through the Jesuit network in Catholic Europe: these include some particularly important letters by Ferdinand Verbiest in the 1670s, such as his *Epistola ad socios Europaeos* (*Letter to European Fellow Fathers*, August 15, 1678), which describes the dramatic situation of a mission immobilized but full of expectations, torn between spectacular growth and a lack of missionaries, and emphasizes also how future candidates in Europe might be more appropriately prepared for the mission, including a defense of the modern scientific methods. Verbiest's *Epistola ad regem Alphonsum VI* (*Letter to King Alfonso VI* [*of Portugal*]; September 1 and 7, 1678) confirmed the loyalty of the Jesuit mission towards the Bragança dynasty and the *Padroado* (the patronage association between Portugal and the Holy See), and his *Epistola ad Innocentium XI* (*Letter to* [*Pope*] *Innocent XI*; August 15, 1678) again stressed how significant the successes of Western astronomical science had proved to be for the progress of the mission, as well as the importance of creating a Chinese liturgy. Another remarkable document, which describes the restoration of the Jesuit mission in the late 1660s and 1670 at the end of the Oboi Regency, is *Innocentia victrix* (*Innocence Victorious*, 1671), a series of documents in which the Chinese characters and Latin translation and commentaries are printed xylographically: a striking example of the successful symbiosis of Latin and Chinese in the context of the Jesuit mission. Several of these xylographical texts were afterwards reprinted and sometimes translated in Western pamphlets (such as the Verbiest letters), or assimilated into larger-scale publications, such as António de Gouveia's work and *Innocentia victrix*, quoted in full in the famous hagiographic collection of the *Acta Sanctorum* (*Deeds of the Saints* [vol. *Propylaeum Maii*, 1685–1688]).

In addition to all these narrative sources, there are also some more statistically based catalog-like works that explain the position of the Chinese church: among these are Martino Martini's *Brevis relatio de numero et qualitate Christianorum apud Sinas* (*Short Relation About the Number and Nature of Christians Among the Chinese*; 1654; Martini 1998); and the continuation of a Chinese bio-bibliography of European Jesuits in the century following the arrival of Francis Xavier (1581–1681), Philippe Couplet's *Catalogus Patrum Societatis Jesu* (*Catalog of the Fathers of the Society of Jesus*, 1686), which is important for reconstructing the Jesuits' literary activities and translates into Latin all the titles of the Chinese books the fathers authored. The *Catalogus Patrum* relied on Latin epigraphic monuments, of which only the bilingual, Sino-Latin tombstone inscriptions of the churchyard of Zhalan and its French counterpart, both in Beijing, survive (Malatesta and Zhiyu 1995). Many stories taken from these sources provided the materials for European Latin compositions about the heroic role of the China missionaries. One of the most popular instruments of such European propaganda was the Latin or vernacular Jesuit school theater: several plays about Chinese subjects were performed in the German-speaking lands, for example (Valentin 1986, 976), while drama about the mission to Japan was also presented at the English College in Saint-Omer (France; Takenaka and Burnett 1995).

Also mission-related but not written in an historical vein are a series of apologetic writings that were mainly prompted from the 1660s onwards by some influential anti-Jesuit publications. The first such critique was *Instructiones ad munera apostolica rite obeunda* (*Instructions for the Proper Performance of Apostolic Duties*), published in 1669 in Ayutthaya (Siam) by François Pallu (1625–1684) of the Paris-based Société des Missions Etrangères, founded in the early 1660s. The *Instructiones* sharply condemned the Jesuit mission in China's methodology, particularly its use of *media humana* ("humane means") like mathematics, music, and arts. The second work to provoke Jesuit apologetic writings was Domingo Fernández Navarrete's *Tratados* (*Treatises*, 1676) on various Chinese affairs. During the so-called "Canton detention" (1665–1671), when the main core of European missionaries was put under house arrest, waiting to be deported from China, some Jesuits present (especially Jacques Lefaure, Prospero Intorcetta, and Francesco Brancati) produced well-argued and voluminous responses to the situation. Brought back to Europe in 1700, these manuscripts were stripped of their Chinese characters and published in Paris in 1701, then distributed both within and outside Europe.

Later on, many other "apologies" (in this case, defenses of the Jesuit position) were composed within the context of the seventeenth-century Chinese Rites Controversy, in which Jesuit, Dominican, and Franciscan missionaries debated which Confucian or Chinese imperial rituals were compatible with Roman Catholic practice. These disputes addressed, among many other topics, the use of mathematics, and especially the interpretation of particular Chinese rites and terms. The controversy led to a thorough study of and philological research into Chinese texts of the (Neo-)Confucian tradition; some of the authors involved in the controversy, especially Francesco Saverio Filippucci (1632–1692) and Kilian Stumpf (1655–1720), turned out to be very sharp textual analysts of Chinese canonical texts. Their writings, while fundamentally related to the Catholic Church, are also important documents in the history of the Western understanding of Chinese philosophy and language. In fact the complex, important series of works about the Chinese Rites Controversy written by European authors would benefit considerably from further study.

SCIENCE

The Jesuit reports that focus on scientific activities tend to offer a more general perspective on contemporary Chinese history. Some cover the journey to China, such as the Bohemian Jesuit astronomer Wenceslas Pantaleon Kirwitzer's *Observationes cometarum anni 1616 in India Orientali factae* (*Observations of Comets Made in 1616 in Eastern India*, 1620), and, much later, François Noël's *Observationes mathematicae et physicae in India et China factae . . . ab anno 1684 usque ad annum 1708* (*Mathematical and Physical Observations Made in India and China . . . from 1684 to 1708*, 1710). Particularly exemplary are the book-length reports by Verbiest on the successes of the "scientific"—that is, the astronomical and mathematical—method to consolidate the Jesuit mission and its impact on the Chinese, such as his *Astronomia Europaea* (*European Astronomy*, 1687), which distills the earlier reports entitled *Astronomiae apud Sinas restitutae Mechanica* (*The Mechanics of* [*Our*] *Astronomy After Its Restitution in China*, 1676) and *Compendium Latinum* (1677; Golvers 2003). The "mathematical" instruction of future candidates for the China mission is described in the two-volume *Synopsis mathematica* by Antoine Thomas (1685). Most other reports on the achievements of the European Jesuits in China in astronomy and related fields remained in manuscript, but some had more of an impact when they were inserted into other, more comprehensive, printed works: Verbiest's text of *Astronomia Europaea*, for example, was inserted into Leibniz's *Novissima Sinica* (*Latest Chinese News*, 1697), through which the "icon" of the Jesuit mathematician in China became widely promulgated throughout Europe.

Related to this phenomenon were the many copies of Chinese-Manchu *Eclipse Maps* (*Typi eclipsis*), which were circulated in Europe, with an appended Latin title-page and translation, to prove the success of the Jesuit mission in the field of astronomy. It is worth briefly explaining the difference between the Chinese and Manchu languages exemplified by such works: since the Manchu Conquest in 1644, Manchu had been the language of the ruling Qing dynasty as spoken at court and by ruling politicians, and several Jesuits preferred it to Chinese because of its relative "easiness": Manchu lacked the sophisticated literary history that any serious study of Chinese texts would necessitate. While on the subject of narrative descriptions of scientific projects, especially cartography, we should mention Antoine Thomas's manuscript *De dimensione unius gradus orbis terrae* (*On the Measurement of One Degree of the Terrestrial Meridian*, 1702; Bosmans 1926), as well as many other maps and atlases. Many letters from Jesuits in China to fellow fathers in Europe contain much information on these achievements, continuing the two-way scholarly correspondence between the continents, and requesting recent observations, books, and instruments, but members of the "inner circle" of the Society were the only readers of most of these letters. That said, some scientific observations carried out in China were communicated to other European scholars, assimilated into publications such as Leibniz's, but also into works written across Europe of a more general nature, such as Etienne Souciet's *Observations* (1732), Bayer's *Museum Sinicum* (1730), Melchior dalla Briga's *Scientiae eclipsium* (*Science of the Eclipses*, 1744), and Maximilian Hell's *Observationes astronomicae* (*Astronomical Observations*, 1768). Jesuit scientific observations also appeared in new learned periodicals, such as the *Acta Eruditorum*, which Leibniz and Otto Mencke founded in Leipzig in the early 1680s. Beijing became an important link in a European network of communication between hubs like St. Petersburg (in the work of the Academia Imperialis co-founded by Leibniz and Tsar Peter I, which was particularly active between 1730 and 1755), Paris, London, and Lisbon (Golvers 2012).

Such networks' intense activity helped integrate this part of the Far East into contemporary scholars' understanding of the wider world. Very little of the correspondence was published, but one notable exception was the *Epistolium* (1630) of Johann Schreck

(Johannes Terrentius; 1576–1630), a German Jesuit working in China in the 1620s: Schreck's technical question posed in it about the calculation of the Chinese calendar was published together with Johannes Kepler's (1571–1630) answer. With the Jesuits of Ingolstadt as intermediaries, Johannes Kepler answered instead of Galileo Galilei, who was apparently not interested. Another example of correspondence is that between Athanasius Kircher (1602–1680) and other Jesuits about questions to do with science in China, published by Andreas Müller as *De invento Sinico epistolae* (*Letters on the Chinese Invention*, ca. 1676: the title refers to Müller's apparent invention of a "key" to facilitate the learning of the Chinese language).

After more general depictions in comprehensive vernacular works by authors like the Portuguese Jesuit Alvaro Semedo (1586–1658), among others, Chinese geography was definitively introduced to European readers through Martino Martini's *Novus Atlas Sinensis* (*New Chinese Atlas*, 1655; Martini 2002). Martini offers a detailed description of the fifteen Chinese provinces and their administrative subdivisions, and presents for each the orography and hydrography, human resources, and some natural and cultural marvels and wonders. Martini relied partly on personal experience and partly on native written sources. The fifteen provincial maps which accompany his account were copied from preexisting Chinese models, then largely adapted by their engravers (including the celebrated Dutch cartographer Johann Blaeu) to contemporary Western cartographic norms. Through its use of such sources (unfortunately, mostly only indicated in general terms), and its splendid maps, liveliness stemming from direct observation, taste for colorful and picturesque detail, comparisons made from time to time with oddities in contemporary Europe, and, last but not least, its elegant Latin style, Martini's book rendered a previously semi-mythical Chinese and Far Eastern world in its real proportions in its encyclopedic depiction of many of China's onomastic, geographical, administrative, economic, and demographic aspects. Martini showed at the same time the identity of medieval "Cathay" (as Marco Polo, for one, called China) and contemporary "China," which was also discussed in the Dutch orientalist Jacob Golius's *De regno Catayo* (*The Kingdom of Cathay*), appended to Martini's work. Unsurprisingly, the *Novus Atlas Sinensis* immediately became a commercial success, going through many reprints and translations, and remaining the main source of information about Chinese geography and anthropology, natural resources (particularly mining), and many other aspects until the mid-eighteenth century, when the French cartographer Jean Baptiste Bourguignon d'Anville's new maps of China appeared.

A parallel enterprise, also authored in Latin, was undertaken by the Polish Jesuit Michael Boym (1612–1659), which arrived in Europe almost simultaneously with Martini's *Atlas*. Boym's work, however, remained in manuscript, probably due to a decision by the Jesuit authorities, and so only fragments of his *Atlas imperii Sinarum* (*Atlas of the Empire of the Chinese*) are preserved (Szczesniak 1953). Most of the many other cartographical works were in Chinese (in the Manchu language, discussed above). As well as atlases and maps, Latin travelogues were also produced, such as Johann Grueber's (1623–1680) description of his passage through Tibet (Lhasa; Wessels 1924), and Verbiest's two "Tartary" letters of 1682 and 1683, written while he was in the train of the Kangxi Emperor. These were the first descriptions published in Europe of these remote areas, characterized by their topographical accuracy, ethnographic interest, and a true sense of the "spectacular," which caused Grueber's and Verbiest's works to be changed from their original epistolary form into popular, much-read travelogues, which were soon printed in Latin and translated into several vernaculars. Several other similar travelogues also appeared, such as Antoine Thomas's long manuscript description of his journey on foot through the Indian subcontinent, *Status Indiae Orientalis* (*The Character of East India*, 1681; Japonica-Sinica 18, 487–95), which gives a detailed topographical and demographical description of the coastal areas of India, especially its different kinds of people.

In written geographical works and maps, natural history was foregrounded. Chinese natural history was the main focus of the work of the aforementioned Johann Schreck, a former member of the Accademia dei Lincei (1611) who arrived in China in 1619. His botanical work—collecting, cataloguing, describing, and identifying native plants—is mainly known through his unpublished correspondence with several European scholars, especially Johann Faber (1574–1629), a German physician, collector, and botanist based in Rome. Revealing its classical model, a significant collection of descriptions of Chinese plants was called *Plinius Indicus* (*Indian Pliny*), a manuscript that survived until either the end of the seventeenth or the middle of the eighteenth century in the Portuguese college at Beijing, but is now lost. Other first-hand descriptions, along with observations on fauna, were articulated in Boym's *Flora Sinensis* (*Chinese Flora*, 1656), most probably a spinoff of Boym's aborted cartographic project; the work describes not only several (mainly south Chinese) plants, but also some local animals, and includes illustrations on the hand-colored provincial maps. Carl Linnaeus's (1707–1778) interest in botany was mainly stimulated by the medical uses for Eastern plants. New botanical discoveries in the Far East had reached Europe since the very early days of the Portuguese presence, which then circulated through Portuguese networks throughout Europe. One related work, for instance, was Andreas Vesalius's *Epistola de radicis Chinae usu* (*Letter on the Use of China Root*, 1546), which introduced this plant to European scholars.

Another aspect of Chinese culture to which the Jesuits were introduced was traditional medicine. Although they themselves relied on Western medicine and possessed a large medical library, converted Chinese physicians informed them about Chinese medicine, and, probably with those physicians' help, they made a serious effort to promote some elements of Chinese medicine in Europe, particularly pulse diagnostics, as evidenced by Andreas Cleyer's *Specimen medicinae Sinicae* (*Specimen of Chinese Medicine*, 1682), and Michael Boym's *Clavis Medica ad Chinarum doctrinam de Pulsibus* (*Medical Key According to the Teachings of the Chinese on the Pulse*, 1686). *Medicamenta simplicia quae a Chinensibus ad usum medicum adhibentur* (*Simple Drugs Used by the Chinese*, 1682), a work on Chinese phyto-pharmacology containing some 289 prescriptions, was also printed.

History, Politics, and Philosophy

Reporting back on a mission so firmly embedded in contemporary Chinese politics and culture inevitably also involved dealing with many sociological and political factors. Local religious and philosophical beliefs, as well as the Chinese governmental structure, created idiosyncratic conditions to which the mission needed to adapt itself and therefore become acceptable to the Chinese educated class. Engagement with that class was profoundly important to the Jesuits because of the Society's long-held perception that instruction and literacy, books, libraries, and their own century-old cultural heritage had an enormous impact on social and political life. Given the shared emphasis placed on books and education by the Jesuits and the Chinese educated class, the late-humanist Jesuits considered China the mission closest to their own educational institutions, and thought themselves the most appropriate priests and teachers to carry out the mission to the East. Although many Jesuits probably had a rather superficial knowledge of Chinese culture and language, acquired on arriving at the *Colégio de Madre de Deus* in Macau and during their instruction there, several others, especially those permanently residing in Beijing (who were known as "the Court Jesuits"), acquired through their own intensive study (and helped by Chinese converts) a thorough knowledge of many aspects of Chinese traditional culture. These men then reported on that knowledge in their written works, either on subjects chosen almost at random, in separate chapters of more general studies like the vernacular works by the Portuguese Alvaro Semedo (1586–1658), Gabriel de Magalhães (1610–1677), and the French Louis Daniel le Comte (1655–1728), or in monographs dedicated to a particular topic. They often wrote in Latin, their studies being particularly intended for wider distribution in European Jesuit circles, both to help future candidates prepare for the mission, and, indirectly, to educate other scholars about the East.

Ancient Chinese history and chronology (in the familiar form of year-by-year annals) was of great interest to Martino Martini and to Philippe Couplet. Between 1640 and 1650, Martini studied native Chinese historical texts intensively, although he rarely provided the author and title of his sources, and in Amsterdam in 1658, his *Sinicae historiae decas prima* (*First Decade of Chinese History*) was published, owing a strong stylistic debt to Livy. The *Decas* describes Chinese dynastic history from its mythical beginnings (in 2852 BCE) up to Christ's birth, structured according to a chronological timeline and divided into dynasties and individual emperors, which closely follows Martini's Chinese sources. Probably as a result of his use of a Chinese model, an abundance of superficially Latinized Chinese names and a very terse style render Martini's Latin in the *Decas* very different from the rich Latin diction of his *De bello Tartarico historia* and *Novus Atlas Sinensis*. More research into the European dissemination of the *Decas* needs to be done, but it was most likely rarely consulted, perhaps because of its relative lack of stylistic elegance and the fact that it is overloaded with obsolete Chinese names. In any case, a *Decas secunda* (which Martini had prepared by 1654–1655) was never published, and the manuscript has apparently been lost. By contrast, we can hardly overestimate the impact of Martini's *Decas* as the first attempt to base European historiography on China on reliable native sources and as proof that the origins of Chinese historical records went further back than biblical chronology. In its challenge to traditional biblical chronology derived from the Vulgate, the *Decas* sparked an intense debate between European chronographers as to whether the Septuagint (based on ancient Greek versions of Jewish sources) or the Vulgate was most authoritative in its chronology. Martini's version of Chinese history was taken up by Philippe Couplet, a Jesuit from the Spanish Netherlands, who wrote, among other things, the *Tabula chronologica monarchiae Sinicae iuxta cyclos annorum LX* (*Chronology of the Chinese Monarchy According to Sixty-Year Cycles*; 1686), which included dynastic tables from 2952 BCE to 1683 CE.

Contemporary scholars also pondered whether events mentioned in the Bible were echoed in the Chinese sources, such as the Flood described in Genesis 6–9, and the eclipse said to have happened on Golgotha during the Crucifixion. Any parallel would allow scholars to compare Western and Chinese chronological systems, and the debate raged across a strenuous epistolary back-and-forth between Chinese and European scholars, only occasionally surfacing in publications like Bayer's *De eclipsi Sinica*; 1718), discussing a Chinese record of a solar eclipse that some thought to have happened at Jesus's death. In the eighteenth century, it was mainly French Jesuits such as Joseph de Moyrac de Mailla (1669–1748) who continued studies of Chinese history and chronology, but these were printed in French rather than in Latin.

At the center of the sociopolitical organization of Chinese life was philosophy, particularly Confucianism, which consisted of a corpus of canonical texts known by Latinate contemporaries as the *Tetrabiblion Sinense* (*Four Chinese Books*), accompanied by a galaxy of commentaries and related studies. When the Jesuits arrived in China and organized the instruction of the new candidates, they relied on these texts, in their Neo-Confucian variants, to study Chinese. Translations into European languages were also produced and circulated among the Jesuit students and scholars in Macau from the time of the Italian Jesuits Michele Ruggieri (1543–1607) and Matteo Ricci (1552–1610). Building on this initial phase, the Portuguese Inácio da Costa (1603–1666) embarked on a systematic project for translating the four basic texts into Latin, accompanied by translated passages from relevant commentaries as well as Jesuit observations on the texts. After da Costa's death, the project was developed by Prospero Intorcetta, supported by the Austrian Christian Herdtrich (1625–1684), also known for a superior Latin-Chinese dictionary, and two fathers from the Flandro-Belgian province, Philippe Couplet and François de Rougemont. The project's first publications were Intorcetta's *Sapientia Sinica* (*Chinese Wisdom*, 1662) and *Sinarum scientia politico-moralis* (*The Political-Ethical Knowledge of the Chinese*, 1672). After a long, complex process of revision and copying, the manuscripts, originally intended for publication in Amsterdam, were printed in Paris as *Confucius Sinarum philosophus* (*Confucius, the Philosopher of the Chinese*, 1687), and presented a text and commentaries of only three of the canonical texts. The fourth text (*Mencius*) was omitted, as were the Chinese characters for technical reasons to do with typesetting. We can compare this well-considered selection with the manuscript itself, now held in the Bibliothèque nationale de France (MS. Lat. 6277/1 and 2; Golvers 1998; Meynard 2011). The text of *Confucius Sinarum philosophus*, together with a series of shorter texts, introduced Confucius to late-humanist European intellectual discourse along with a kind of Sinophilia, although Intorcetta's unpublished prefatory letter makes it clear that the target readers were to be Jesuit students and mission candidates. Other later attempts to translate the Confucian corpus were undertaken by François Noël, in his *Sinensis imperii libri classici Sex* (*Six Classic Books of the Chinese Empire*, 1711), containing all four books, including *Mencius* and two other related texts, and his *Philosophia Sinica* (*Chinese Philosophy*, 1711).

LINGUISTICS, LITERATURE, AND PRINTING

Knowledge of the Chinese language was a priority and necessity for missionaries as well as a source of curiosity for the European public, whether in its "official" form (Mandarin or *guanhua*) the language of courtly and intellectual discourse, or in its regional variants. Many signs of aversion to the Chinese language exist; some Jesuits, such as Verbiest in 1678, held the conviction that, because of its monosyllabic structure and lack of inflection, Chinese could not be adequately described according to (classical Latin) grammatical terms and categories (Verbiest 1938). Nonetheless, learning Chinese, and to a lesser extent Manchu, was compulsory for Jesuit missionaries, and instruction started as soon as they arrived in Macau. The first Latin-language description of Chinese is Martino Martini's *Grammatica linguae Sinensis* (*Grammar of the Chinese Language*, 1652–1653; Paternicò 2013), a description of the Chinese language that takes as its starting point the categories of Renaissance Latin grammar as set out by Johannes Despauterius (1480–1520) and Manuel Álvares (1526–1582). Martini's grammar largely simplifies and distorts the proper character of the Chinese linguistic system, and was probably only intended as a propaedeutic course to instruct young Jesuits in Europe before they left for China. The fact that the book was not published at the time and only attached in print to a few copies of the 1696 edition of Mélchisedec Thévenot's *Relations des divers voyages curieux* (*Reports of Various Curious Travels*) may not be due to problems in printing the characters or the tones, but rather to some reluctance about spreading knowledge of the language outside the Society and subsequently risking the loss of a "monopoly" on access to native Chinese sources. Working at the same time, but apparently unaware of Martini's initiative, Ferdinand Verbiest, himself a recent student of Manchu in 1676–1677, composed a grammatical description of this "language of the ruling class," the *Elementa linguae Tartaricae* (*Elements of the Tartarian Language*). Like Martini's Chinese grammar, Verbiest's Manchu grammar was conceived from the perspective of a Latin author and also aimed at future candidates for the China mission. Verbiest's autograph manuscript, which reached Europe in around 1684, is now lost, but the text has been rescued through its insertion in Thévenot's *Relations* of 1696, albeit without the *alphabetarium* of 1,400 Manchu characters, which was still present in the library of the Jesuit Collegio Romano in the mid-nineteenth century (Aalto 1976 and 1977), but was subsequently lost.

Emergent lexicography can be seen in numerous attempts to compose a bilingual dictionary of Latin (or Portuguese, or French) and Chinese. Numerous testimonies referring to the composition and consumption of such works exist, and most may have been composed for use within a limited circle of users, perhaps within a local residence like Canton during the 1665–1671 Detention. As far as we know, the sources refer only once to a printing project for a general Chinese–Latin dictionary, and its completion seems to have been thwarted by the death of Christian Herdtrich, a well-known lexicographical talent, in 1684. All copies that arrived in European collections were in manuscript and got buried in private collections, so contemporary scholars lost the opportunity to read them. Later efforts to present a partial or more comprehensive grammatical description of the Chinese language, based on Jesuit materials, were published by Theophilus Siegfried Bayer in the *Museum Sinicum*, but more comprehensive were Etienne Fourmont's *Meditationes Sinicae* (*Chinese Mediations*, 1737) and Joseph de Prémare's *Notitia linguae Sinensis* (*Knowledge of the Chinese Language*, 1831). Despite their lack of any direct experience of the country, other European scholars sought a "key to Chinese" (*clavis Sinica*), such as Christian Mentzel, Andreas Müller, and Leibniz, who published in Latin several monographs on aspects of the Chinese language, which mostly relied (either directly or indirectly) on Jesuit materials (Mungello 1985, 174–246).

When we survey these attempts, we need to realize how complicated the problem of describing and teaching Chinese in a humanist context was. First, transliteration and transcription presented problems, since, following Matteo Ricci's work, several consecutive and different systems had been developed, each of which proposed sophisticated solutions for rendering the "five tones" of the Chinese language. Second, there was the difficulty of morphologically adapting Chinese words and names to fit Latin as an inflected language. Third, there was the issue of transposing foreign terms into a completely different language system. As a result, studies about the origin and nature of Chinese script were often associated with the pressing early modern debate about the existence of a "universal" or "original" language, as well as the study of Egyptian hieroglyphs, as in Gottlieb Spitzel's *De re literaria Sinensium commentarius* (*Commentary on the Literature of the Chinese*, 1660), and in an anonymous chapter entitled "De Sinarum literis" ("The Chinese Letters") in the manuscript of *Confucius Sinarum philosophus* (Lundbaek 1988).

For many years, all Latin texts produced in China and in other Eastern nations like Japan were printed in Europe, but the Jesuits clearly desired a Western-style printing press that could function well in the East. The first such press was used in Goa (1587–1588) and Macau (1588–1590) before it reached its final destination in Amacusa, Japan. It was employed to publish Juan Bonifacio's *Christiani pueri institutio* (*The Education of a Christian Boy*, 1588) and Duarte de Sande's *De missione legatorum Iaponensium ad Romanam curiam . . . dialogus* (*Dialogue on the Mission of the Japanese Ambassadors to the Roman Curia*, 1590; De Sande 2009). Other products were printed on the Chinese xylograph press, especially in Beijing (Boxer 1947). A request, which followed logically, to implement the *ius censendi* (right to censor) within China was not really successful.

LATIN BETWEEN EAST AND WEST

So far, we have described Latin as the vehicle used in European communication between Asia and Europe. While the *lingua franca* for the Portuguese mission was of course Portuguese, and, as we would expect, French for the French mission, Latin was used both to make contact with the central Jesuit authorities in Rome (Gaubil 1970, 261), and to make scholarly reports to European institutions. At the same time, the immersion in the Chinese environment is sometimes said to have produced a loss of command of Latin and even of one's grasp of the vernacular. Although this may have been true in some cases, in others it shows the working of the Ovidian topos of displacement, as Verbiest clearly demonstrates.

For communication within Asia, especially in China, Latin was mainly used in liturgical, diplomatic, and educational contexts. From the very beginning of the Jesuit mission, Latin was the "second vernacular" of the liturgy after Chinese, despite manifest problems such as the pronunciation of the sacred language, for instance (Verbiest 1938). That said, every serious attempt to promote Chinese—and this was a main aspect of the Rites Controversy previously mentioned—as a substitute for Latin within the Chinese liturgical context failed. Latin's role in diplomatic exchange emerged when the Jesuits made contact with various foreign embassies, such as the English embassies led by men like George McCartney (1737–1806) in the eighteenth century, and the official Russian legacies led by Nicolae Milescu (1636–1708) and others. Several Latin works survive from this exchange, such as the correspondence Verbiest sent to Tsar Alexis of Russia in 1676, along with the accompanying *Astronomiae mechanica*, now preserved as manuscripts in Athens (Golvers and Nicolaidis 2009). Significant, too, is the Sino-Russian Treaty of Nerchinsk (1689): the Latin text was the original version of this pact, which settled the contemporary conflicts at the Russian–Chinese border (Sebes 1961).

Finally, Latin's undisputed position in both liturgy and diplomacy prompted the Jesuits to teach Latin to their most reliable Chinese assistants. This took place in most of the main Jesuit colleges, especially Macau (Pina 2011), Hangzhou, and Beijing (Gaubil 1970). As one result, Chinese who had mastered Latin were able to inform the Dutch politician and maritime authority Nicolaas Witsen (1641–1717) as he prepared his magisterial work *Noord en Oost Tartarye* (*North and East Tartary*, 1705). Other Chinese who had learned Latin were selected to accompany Jesuits on their journey back to Europe, such as Michael Shen Fuzong (ca. 1658–1691), a Qing convert who came to Europe with Philippe Couplet and instructed the English orientalist Thomas Hyde at the University of Oxford in Sinological matters. Others received instruction in the Collegio de' Sinesi in Naples, which had been sanctioned by the pope in 1732 and became an important

European center for the study of oriental languages (Fatica 2006); these men were deeply "classicized" when they returned to China.

Didactic materials were prepared for those who were taught Latin in China, which prove that this instruction, however scant the evidence might be, was more than accidental. Most important among these pedagogical tools was Joseph de Prémare's unpublished Latin grammar for Chinese learners, *De Romana lingua dialogus* (*Dialogue About the Roman Language*). Dictionaries were also translated, like Pierre Danet's *Dictionnaire françois et latin* (*French–Latin Dictionary*, 1685) translated into Chinese by Jean-Placide Hervieu and into Manchu by Dominique Parrenin. Often the result of this Latin instruction was only the imitation of Latin liturgical formulae, but a number of Chinese came to speak and write Latin actively. Among the few extant testimonials are the Latin letters that Michael Shen Fuzong wrote to Thomas Hyde from London, the Latin diary of André Ly (Ly 1906), and several recently edited *testimonia* or witness accounts sent by Chinese Christians to Rome.

CONCLUSION

The penetration of Latin into China from the mid-sixteenth century onwards was entirely linked to the (Jesuit) mission in the footsteps of the Portuguese *descobrimentos* ("discoveries"). Latin was the language of the majority of Western books and scientific communications, of the reports addressed to the Roman ecclesiastical authorities, and—despite all efforts to create a Chinese liturgical language—of the liturgy. Latin was taught to Chinese converts, mostly privately, although several attempts at a more systematic school instruction were made. As a consequence of the mission's extremely difficult situation—its cultural isolation, its permanent lack of staff and resources, its overloaded program—writing was limited to non-fictional topics related to the function of the mission, its context (including topics such as geography and science), and strategies to be adopted for its implementation. In fact, only a few poems, by Jesuits such as the German Adam Schall von Bell, the Belgian Antoine Thomas, and the Frenchman Jean-François Foucquet, survive, and only three of Schall's poems, published in his *Historica relatio de ortu et progressu fidei orthodoxae in regno Chinensi* (*Historical Report on the Start and Progress of the Right Faith in the Chinese Kingdom*, 1672), were printed. The most convincing testimonies of a more widespread Latin written culture in early modern China are some rare bilingual documents, such as xylograph printings like *Innocentia Victrix*, the text of the Treaty of Nerchinsk, and the steles of the Jesuit graveyard in Zhalan (Beijing). More recently, after the Maoist revolution and the expulsion of the Christian missions in 1950, Latin has begun to be taught again in China. It has found many enthusiastic students, not only in some of the national universities, but also in some private institutes, such as the recently founded Academia Latina in Beijing.

Suggested Reading

For an overview of the topic, see Standaert (2001, 2003). For an identification of the main European *dramatis personae*, see Dehergne (1973). On the linguistic aspects of "romanization," see Golvers (1995), and on the "romanization" systems, see Dudink (2001). For a detailed description of Latin and other Western books on China, see Löwendahl (2008–2012). Dudink and Standaert's Christian Chinese Texts database is also useful. For other work by the author relevant to this chapter's contents, see Golvers (1992, 2010).

References

Aalto, Penti. 1976. "The *Elementa Linguae Tartaricae* by Ferdinand Verbiest, S.J." In *Tractata Altaica Denis Sinor sexagenario optime de rebus Altaicis merito dedicata*, edited by Walter Heissig and John R. Krueger, Felix J. Oinas, and Edmond Schütz, 1–10. Wiesbaden: Harrassowitz.

———. 1977. "The *Elementa Linguae Tartaricae* by Ferdinand Verbiest, S.J., Translated." *Zentralasiatische Studien* 11:32–120.

Bosmans, Henri. 1926. "L'oeuvre scientifique d'Antoine Thomas de Namur, S.J., vice-président effectif et président intérimaire de l'Observatoire de Péking (1644–1709) [2me partie]." *Annales de la Société Scientifique de Bruxelles* 46:154–81.

Boxer, Charles R. 1947. "Some Sino-European Xylographic Works, 1662–1718." *Journal of the Royal Asiatic Society* 79:199–215.

Brou, Antoine. 1934. "Les jésuites sinologues de Pékin et leurs éditeurs de Paris." *Revue d'Histoire des Missions* 2:551–66.

Dehergne, Joseph. 1973. *Répertoire des Jésuites de Chine de 1552 à 1800*. Rome: Institutum Historicum Societatis Iesu.

———. 1980. "Les Lettres annuelles des missions jésuites de Chine au temps des Ming (1581–1655)." *Archivum Historicum Societatis Iesu* 49:379–92.

———. 1982. "Lettres annuelles et sources complémentaires des missions jésuites de Chine (suite)." *Archivum Historicum Societatis Iesu* 51:247–84.

Dudink, Ad. 2001. "Western Transcriptions of Chinese." In Standaert 2001, 260–85.

Dudink, Ad, and Nicholas Standaert. *Chinese Christian Texts Database* (1552–ca. 1840). Available at http://www.arts.kuleuven.be/info/eng/OE_sinologie/CCT.

Fatica, Michele, ed. 2006. *Matteo Ripa e il collegio dei cinesi di Napoli (1682–1869)*. Naples: Università degli studi di Napoli "l'Orientale."

Ferguson, John. 1978. "China and Rome." In *Aufstieg und Niedergang der römischen Welt*, vol. 2.9.2, *Politische Geschichte (Provinzen und Randvölker: Rom und der Ferne Osten)*, edited by Hildegard Temporini, 581–603. Berlin: De Gruyter.

Gaubil, Antoine. 1970. *Correspondance de Pékin: 1722–1759*. Edited by Renée Simon. Geneva: Droz.

Golvers, Noël. 1992. "Scientific literature in Latin by the Jesuits in XVIIth-century China". *Revista de la Academia Colombiana de Ciencias Exactas, Fisicas y Naturales* XVIII:389–402.

———. 1995. "The Latin Treatises of F. Verbiest, S. J., on European Astronomy in China: Some Linguistic Observations." *Humanistica Lovaniensia* 44:305–67.

Golvers, Noël. 1998. "The Development of the *Confucius Sinarum philosophus* Reconsidered in the Light of New Material." In *Western Learning and Christianity in China: The Contribution and Impact of Johann Adam Schall von Bell, S.J. (1592–1666)*, vol. 2, edited by Roman Malek, 1141–64. Nettetal: Steyler.

——. 2003. *Ferdinand Verbiest, S.J. (1623–1688) and the Chinese Heaven.* Leuven: Leuven University Press.

——. 2010. "From Propertius's 'Laudes Italiae (Romae)' to 17th century Jesuit 'Laus Sinarum'. A new aspect of Propertius's reception." *Humanistica Lovaniensia* 59:213–221.

——. 2012a. "'Savant correspondence' from China with Europe in the 17th–18th Centuries." *Journal of Early Modern Studies* 1(1):21–41.

——. 2012b. *Libraries of Western Learning for China: Circulation of Western Books Between Europe and China in the Jesuit Mission (ca. 1650—ca. 1750).* Vol. 1, *Logistics of Book Acquisition and Circulation.* Leuven: Leuven University Press.

——. 2013. *Libraries of Western Learning for China.* Vol. 2, *Formation of Jesuit Libraries.* Leuven: Leuven University Press.

Golvers, Noël, and Efthymios Nicolaidis. 2009. *Ferdinand Verbiest and Jesuit Science in 17th Century China: An Annotated Edition of the Constantinople Manuscript (1676).* Athens; Leuven: Institute for Neohellenic Research; F. Verbiest Institute.

Japonica-Sinica Collection. Archivum Romanum Societatis Iesu, Rome.

Löwendahl, Björn. 2008–2012. *China Illustrata Nova: Sino-Western Relations, Conceptions of China, Cultural Influences and the Development of Sinology Disclosed in Western Printed Books, 1477–1877.* 3 vols. Hua Hin: Elephant Press.

Lundbaek, Knud. 1988. *The Traditional History of the Chinese Script from a Seventeenth Century Jesuit Manuscript.* Aarhus: Aarhus University Press.

Ly, André. 1906. *Journal d'André Ly, prêtre chinois, missionnaire et notaire apostolique, 1746–1763.* Edited by Adrien Launay. Paris: A. Picard et Fils.

Malatesta, Edward, and Gao Zhiyu, eds. 1995. *Departed, yet Present: Zhalan, the Oldest Christian Cemetery in Beijing.* Macau; San Francisco: Instituto cultural de Macau; Ricci Institute.

Martini, Martino. 1998. *Opera Omnia.* Vol. 2, *Opere minori.* Edited by Giuliano Bertuccioli, Trento: Università degli Studi di Trento.

——. 2002. *Opera Omnia,* Vol. 3, *Novus Atlas Sinensis.* Edited by Giuliano Bertuccioli. Trento: Università degli Studi di Trento.

Meynard, Thierry. 2011. *Confucius Sinarum Philosophus (1687): The First Translation of the Confucian Classics.* Rome: Institutum Historicum Societatis Iesu.

Mungello, David E. 1985. *Curious Land: Jesuit Accommodation and the Origins of Sinology.* Stuttgart: Steiner.

Paternicò, Luisa. 2013. *When the Europeans Began to Study Chinese: Martino Martini's Grammatica Linguae Sinensis.* Leuven: F. Verbiest Institute.

Pina, Isabel. 2011. *Jesuitas chineses e mestiços da missão da China.* Lisbon: Centro Cientifico e Cultural de Macau.

De Sande, Duarte. 2009. *Diálogo sobre a missão dos embaixadores japoneses à Cúria Romana,* edited and translated by Américo da Costa Ramalho and Sebastião Tavares de Pinho. 2 vols. Coimbra: Impresa de Universidade de Coimbra.

Schall, Adam. 1942. *Lettres et mémoires.* Vol. 1, *Relation historique.* Edited by Henri Bernard. Tientsin: Hautes Etudes.

Sebes, Joseph. 1961. *The Jesuits and the Sino-Russian treaty of Nerchinsk (1689): The Diary of Thomas Pereira, S.J.* Rome: Institutum Historicum Societatis Iesu.

Standaert, Nicolas, ed. 2001. *Handbook of Christianity in China.* Vol. 1, *635–1800.* Leiden: Brill.

———. 2003. "The Transmission of Renaissance Culture in Seventeenth-Century China." *Renaissance Studies.* 17:367–91.

———. 2013. *Chinese Voices in the Rites Controversy: Travelling Books, Community Networks, Intercultural Arguments.* Rome: Institutum Historicum Societatis Iesu.

Szczesniak, Boleslaw. 1953. "The Atlas and Geographic Descriptions of China: A manuscript of Michael Boym (1612–1659)." *Journal of the American Oriental Society* 73:65–77.

Takenaka, Masahiro, and Charles Burnett. 1995. *Jesuit Plays on Japan and English Recusancy.* Tokyo: The Renaissance Institute.

Valentin, Jean Marie. 1986. *Le Théâtre des Jésuites dans les pays de langue allemande. Répertoire chronologique des pièces répresentées et des documents conservés (1555–1773).* Stuttgart: Hiersemann.

Verbiest, Ferdinand. 1938. *Correspondance de Ferdinand Verbiest de la Compagnie de Jésus (1623–1688), directeur de l'observatoire de Pékin.* Edited by Henri Josson and Léon Willaert. Brussels: Palais des Académies.

Verhaeren, Hubert. 1949. *Catalogue de la bibliothèque du Pé-t'ang.* Beijing: Imprimerie des Lazaristes.

Wessels, Cornelius. 1924. *Early Jesuit Travellers in Central Asia, 1603–1721.* The Hague: Martinus Nijhoff.

General References

Sarah Knight and Stefan Tilg

Each chapter contains a section titled "Suggested Reading" and a list of references cited: we refer readers to individual chapters for specific bibliographical recommendations. What follows here is a list of general aids to the reader: the majority are print sources, but we also suggest some resources valuable to Neo-Latin researchers that are now available online. We do not aim to give an exhaustive list but rather to provide select references especially useful for readers orientating themselves within the research field, and for further study. Given the inherently interdisciplinary nature of Neo-Latin studies discussed in our introduction, a list of titles touching on Neo-Latin topics would in some sections of this bibliography (e.g., those on journals and book series) virtually amount to a list of all titles dealing with the early modern world. We therefore focus on titles dealing exclusively with Neo-Latin literature and language.

Neo-Latin Studies: Surveys and Methodology

Some earlier twentieth-century surveys of Neo-Latin are still valuable, such as Don C. Allen's "Latin Literature" (*Modern Language Quarterly* 2 [1941]: 403–20) or Karl O. Conrady's "Die Erforschung der neulateinischen Literatur: Probleme und Aufgaben" (*Euphorion* 49 [1955]: 413–45). Today, however, the first point of access will typically be one or all of the major reference works described in our introduction: the second edition of the *Companion to Neo-Latin Studies* (CNLS), the *Encyclopaedia of the Neo-Latin World* (ENLW), the volume *Neo-Latin Literature* (NLL), and our own Handbook. These works either contain reflections on the discipline, as in Demmy Verbeke's "History of Neo-Latin Studies" in *ENLW* 1:905–20, or refer to numerous smaller-scale surveys. Particularly reader-friendly is the illustrated catalog edited by James Hankins, "The Lost Continent: Neo-Latin Literature and the Rise of Modern European Literatures; Catalog of an Exhibition at the Houghton Library, 5 March–5 May 2001" (*Harvard Library Bulletin* 12 [2001]: 1–92). A substantial methodological dialogue between a number of leading scholars in the field can be found in Hans Helander, "Neo-Latin Studies: Significance and Prospects" (*Symbolae Osloenses* 76 [2001]:5–102). The growing methodological self-awareness of Neo-Latin studies is also attested to by articles like Toon Van Hal's "Towards Meta-Neo-Latin Studies? Impetus to Debate on the Field of Neo-Latin Studies and Its Methodology" (*Humanistica Lovaniensia* 56 [2007]:349–65) and by the different approaches taken by contributors to edited volumes such as Marc van der Poel's *Neo-Latin Philology: Old Tradition, New Approaches* (Leuven: Leuven University Press, 2014).

Journals and Proceedings

The leading journal of Neo-Latin is *Humanistica Lovaniensia*, founded as a series of monographs and editions in the late 1920s and revived as a journal in 1968 by Jozef IJsewijn. Digitized versions of all pre-2000 volumes are now available on the website http://upers.kuleuven.be/en/free-ebooks. Since 1999, the *Neulateinisches Jahrbuch: Journal of Neo-Latin Language and Literature* has also been an important research forum. For other journals not exclusively dedicated to Neo-Latin studies but containing a great deal of Neo-Latin material, see Demmy Verbeke's article "Neo-Latin Journals" in *ENLW* 2:1057–58.

The International Association for Neo-Latin Studies has organized tri-annual conferences in different locations across Europe and North America since 1971. These conferences are the largest and best-known events in the world of Neo-Latin studies, typically attended by several hundred scholars. Many of the papers delivered there are published in the conference proceedings, whose general title, *Acta conventus Neo Latini* (*Proceedings of the Neo-Latin Conference*), is followed by the Latinized name of the place in which a given conference was held. The first volume of 1973, for instance, is called *Acta conventus Neo-Latini Lovaniensis* (*Proceedings of the Neo-Latin Conference Held in Leuven*); the 2012 volume is called the *Acta conventus Neo-Latini Upsaliensis* (*Proceedings of the Neo-Latin Conference Held in Uppsala*). These volumes are a treasure trove of Neo-Latin studies in their entire chronological and thematic extension. The research platform *Iter: Gateway to the Middle Ages and Renaissance* has digitized the *Acta* from 1979–1994 and made them freely available at https://archive.org/details/IterProject.

Book Series

Several book series now exist that are dedicated exclusively to Neo-Latin. Some of these tend to publish Neo-Latin editions with vernacular translations and commentary, while others mainly publish monographs or collections of essays. The series *Supplementa Humanistica Lovaniensia* publishes editions, monographs, and essay collections (mainly in English); as with the journal *Humanistica Lovaniensia*, digital copies of all pre-2000 volumes are freely available at http://upers.kuleuven.be/en/free-ebooks. Other important series are the Anglo-Dutch initiative *Bibliotheca Latinitatis Novae*, which has published editions of Latin texts (with facing English translations) of, for instance, John Barclay's *Icon Animorum; or, The Mirror of Minds*, Justus Lipsius's *Politica*, and several others. Specializing in monographs, edited collections (mainly German-language), and editions is the *NeoLatina* series published by Gunter Narr. *Noctes Neolatinae: Neo-Latin Texts and Studies*, published by Georg Olms, was conceived as a supplement to the *Neulateinisches Jahrbuch* and focuses on editions and monographs. Published by Harvard University Press, the *I Tatti Renaissance Library* includes Latin texts and English translations of works written by Italian humanists.

Bibliographical Aids

A good starting point for current developments is the bibliographical appendix (*Instrumentum Bibliographicum*) of the journal *Humanistica Lovaniensia*, listing recent publications in the field according to a number of categories (e.g., genres, authors, regions). *The Year's Work in*

Modern Language Studies, published by the Modern Humanities Research Association, has also started to include a section on Neo-Latin.

For larger collections of titles, including older ones, we recommend two ambitious projects in particular: the *Bibliographie Internationale de l'Humanisme et de la Renaissance* attempts to identify all relevant publications from 1965 onward, and includes a wealth of Neo-Latin titles; it is now also available as a searchable database under the title *International Bibliography of Humanism and the Renaissance*. The *Iter Bibliography* at http://www.itergateway.org/resources is also a convenient database of studies covering the European Middle Ages and Renaissance from 400–1700.

Systematic bibliographies of certain research topics can often be found in specialized articles, monographs, and edited volumes. The best general advice to a reader wanting to find these publications is to check one of the major reference works for Neo-Latin studies (*CNLS, ENLW, NLL*, and this Handbook), which will lead to many further references for a given topic.

ANTHOLOGIES AND COLLECTIONS OF TEXTS

Besides printing the Latin text, the titles listed chronologically below provide a general introduction, individual introductions to authors and texts, and notes. Unless otherwise stated, they also contain a facing translation in a modern European language. We list here only collections presenting a variety of authors from different countries: references to more geographically specific collections can often be found in the chapters in our "Part III: Countries and Regions". Generally, very few prose anthologies exist; the only larger, more recent, and internationally oriented example is Springhetti (1951). Finally, we would like to draw attention to the "Anthology of Neo-Latin Texts" contained in Jozef IJsewijn's first edition of the *Companion to Neo-Latin Studies* (1977, 312–54). Although never published separately, and omitted from the second edition of the *Companion* (1990–1998), this anthology provides a delightful and balanced selection from both poetry and prose (without translations).

- Emilio Springhetti. 1951. *Selecta Latinitatis scripta auctorum recentium (saec. XV–XX) (Selected Latin Writings by Later Authors, Fifteenth to Twentieth Centuries).* Rome: Pontifical Gregorian University [without translations].
- Pierre Laurens, ed. 1975. *Musae reduces: Anthologie de la poésie latine dans l'Europe de la Renaissance (The Return of the Muses: An Anthology of Latin Poetry in Renaissance Europe).* 2 vols. Leiden: Brill [more comprehensive than Laurens 2004 but less focused on lyric poetry].
- Fred J. Nichols, ed. 1979. *An Anthology of Neo-Latin Poetry.* New Haven: Yale University Press.
- Alessandro Perosa and John Sparrow, eds. 1979. *Renaissance Latin Verse: An Anthology.* London; Chapel Hill: Duckworth; University of North Carolina Press [without translations].
- Ian D. McFarlane, ed. 1980. *Renaissance Latin Poetry.* Manchester: Manchester University Press.
- James J. Mertz, John P. Murphy, and Jozef IJsewijn, eds. 1989. *Jesuit Latin Poets of the 17th and 18th centuries: An Anthology of Neo-Latin Poetry.* Wauconda: Bolchazy-Carducci.
- Andrée Thill, Gilles Banderier, and Marc Fumaroli, eds. 1999. *La Lyre jésuite: Anthologie de poèmes latins (1620–1730) (The Jesuit Lyre: An Anthology of Latin Poems, 1620–1730).* Geneva: Droz.
- Pierre Laurens, ed. 2004. *Anthologie de la poésie lyrique latine de la Renaissance (An Anthology of Latin Lyric Poetry of the Renaissance)* Paris: Gallimard [less comprehensive than Laurens 1975 but more focused on lyric poetry].

Many more texts, including prose and drama, are collected online. The single most important reference here is Dana F. Sutton and Martin Wiggins's resource *The Philological Museum* (http://www.philological.bham.ac.uk/), divided into two parts: the first part, "Library of Humanistic Texts," is a collection of online editions with introduction, English translation, and notes; the second part, "Bibliography of Neo-Latin Texts on the Web" attempts to catalog all primary Neo-Latin texts available online, either as scanned images or as full-fledged editions. At the time of writing, this bibliography contains almost 50,000 entries. Among regional projects, the electronic collection of Croatian Latin authors (CroALa) at http://www.ffzg.unizg.hr/klafil/croala/ deserves particular mention because it shows how a full text database can be combined with sophisticated search functions.

DICTIONARIES AND GLOSSARIES

Most Neo-Latin texts can be read with a dictionary of classical Latin, and many new coinages are easy to understand on the basis of classical Latin and the vernacular languages. Sometimes, however, new words remain obscure, and in technical contexts, especially, these may obstruct proper understanding of a whole text. Neo-Latin aids do not normally consider words that are extensively glossed in classical dictionaries, but focus instead on new and divergent material. It must be said, however, that Neo-Latin lexicography is still in its infancy, and we do not yet possess a comprehensive dictionary. The best specialized reference to date is an online resource, Johann Ramminger's *Neulateinische Wortliste* (*Neo-Latin Word List*; http://ramminger.userweb.mwn.de), which is continuously updated. For Renaissance prose in particular, René Hoven's *Dictionary of Renaissance Latin from Prose Sources* (2nd ed., Leiden: Brill 2006) is also worth recommending. The *Anglo-Latin Wordbook* at http://reed.utoronto.ca/wordbook/ collects the vocabulary glossed in the "Records of Early English Drama" series. In addition, each volume of the journal *Humanistica Lovaniensia* contains also an *Instrumentum Lexicographicum* in which new word forms and coinages are described.

A number of more specialized dictionaries have also been published, such as Leo F. Stelten's *Dictionary of Ecclesiastical Latin* (Peabody: Hendrickson 1995) and William T. Stearn's *Botanical Latin* (3rd ed., North Pomfret: David and Charles 1983). Readers interested in the Latin words for modern vocabulary such as "campsite" (*campus tentorius*) or "flirtation" (*amor levis*) should consult Karl Egger's *Lexicon recentis Latinitatis* (*Dictionary of Modern Latin*, 2 vols., Vatican City: Libreria Editrice Vaticana 1992–1997).

Last but not least, Adriano Cappelli's *Dizionario di abbreviature latine ed italiane* (*Dictionary of Latin and Italian Abbreviations*, first published in 1899) has helped generations of students cope with abbreviations found both in manuscripts and in early Neo-Latin printed works.

HISTORIES OF LATIN

The last fifteen years have seen a renewed interest in Latin as a linguistic, literary, and cultural force from antiquity to the present day. This interest manifests itself in a number of histories of Latin, aimed at the general reader rather than a specialist audience. All of these accounts dedicate longer sections to Neo-Latin and point out the vitality of Latin during the early modern period:

- Joseph Farrell. 2001. *Latin Language and Latin Culture*. Cambridge: Cambridge University Press 2001.
- Tore Janson. (2002) 2004. *A Natural History of Latin*. Translated by Merethe Damsgård Sørensen and Nigel Vincent. New York: Oxford University Press.
- Nicholas Ostler. 2007. Ad Infinitum: *A Biography of Latin and the World It Created*. London: Harper.
- Jürgen Leonhardt. (2009) 2013. *Latin: Story of a World Language*. Translated by Kenneth Kronenberg. Cambridge: Belknap.

More specialized and focusing on the social functions of Latin as a subject of classical education in the early modern and modern periods is Françoise Waquet's *Latin, or the Empire of a Sign* (1998). Translated by John Howe. London: Verso, 2001.

INDEX

Note: For works, see the names of individual authors. On the whole, we have only indexed anonymous works, but when a Neo-Latin or classical work is mentioned frequently (e.g. Thomas More's *Utopia*, Virgil's *Aeneid*), we have indexed that separately under the name of the author.

Abad, Diego José, 316, 528, 534, 535
Abelard, Peter, 279
Abenaki language, 546
Abilés, José López de, 528
Åbo. *See* Turku (Åbo), Academy of
academic journals
    Acta Eruditorum, 266, 562
    Journal des Sçavans, 266
    Nova Acta Eruditorum, 266
    Philosophical Transactions of the Royal Society, 266
academies. *See also under individual places*
    "household," 365, 366, 368
    "Platonic," 511
Accademia degli Erranti (Brescia), 373
Accolti, Benedetto, 155
Acevedo, Pedro Pablo de, 114, 465
Achrelius, Daniel, 501
Acidalius, Valens, 453
Acosta, José de, 466, 526
Adam, Johannes, 448
Adam, Melchior, 457
Addison, Joseph, 428, 430, 434, 436, 437
Adriani, Marcello Virgilio, 271
Aemilius, Georg, 451
Aeschylus, 110
Aesop, 404, 530
Afonso VI (king of Portugal), 560
Africa, 63, 106, 290, 514, 529
Agricola, Michael, 496
Agricola, Rudolphus, 123, 129, 335, 339, 478
Agrippa, Heinrich Cornelius, 364
Aidie, Andrew, 433
Alabaster, William, 61, 110, 435
Albert VII (archduke of the Spanish Netherlands), 139
Alberti, Leon Battista, 211, 234–35
    De commodis litterarum atque incommodis, 234, 238–39, 240, 242

    Della famiglia, 27
    Dinner pieces, 404
    Momus, 27, 207, 404
    Philodoxus, 89, 464
Albertus Magnus, 305
Albrecht of Brandenburg, 331
Albucasis, 281
Albumasar, 280, 284
Alcabitius, 280, 284
Alcalá de Henares, University of, 282, 300, 462
alchemy, 3, 257, 263, 264, 267, 369, 456, 497, 519
Alciati, Andrea, 79, 415
Aldegati, Marcantonio, 399
Aldrovandi, Ulisse, 269
Aleandro, Girolamo, 306
Alegre, Francisco Javier, 60, 63, 534–35
Alexander VI (pope), 107
Alexander of Aphrodisias, 463
Alexander of Hales, 305
Alexander of Villedieu, 221–22, 226, 227, 228
Alexander the Great, 63, 82, 194, 534
Alexis (tsar of Russia), 569
Alfonso the physician, 300
Alfonso II (king of Naples), 365, 369, 399
Alfonso V (king of Aragon), 64, 153, 399
al-Ghazali. *See* Ghazali, al-
Alhazen, 281
Alighieri, Dante, 3, 27, 254, 316, 395
    Divine Comedy, 62
allegory, 303, 363, 399, 404, 472, 505
    in drama, 88–89, 91, 93, 94, 96, 106, 108, 111, 112, 115
    in pastoral, 395, 396, 433
Allesch, Gerd, 78
allusion. *See* intertextuality
Alpago, Andrea, 290
Alpetragius, 281
Alpini, Prospero, 290

Alsop, Anthony, 83–84, 434
Alstedt, Johann Heinrich, 145
Althusius, Johannes, 452
Altilio, Gabriele, 400
Álvares, Manuel, 567
Amalteo family, 397
Amaral, Prudêncio do, 473, 529
Amaseo, Romolo Quirino, 27
Amatus Fornacius: amator ineptus, 211
Amboise, Georges d', 413–14
Ambrose, Saint, 303, 305, 321
American War of Independence, 553
Americas (continents), 183, 465–67, 488, 525–26,
    532–35. *See also* Latin America; North
    America
  indigenous peoples
    Abenaki (*See* Abenaki language)
    Hurons, 543, 544, 545–46
    Incas, 191–92, 529
    Iroquois, 543
    Montagnais, 544 (*See also* Montagnais
      language)
    Nahuas, 530–32 (*See also* Nahuatl language)
Amerinus, Johannes, 498, 504
Ammianus Marcellinus, 20
Amos, Andrew, 382
Anacreon, 49–50, 416, 452, 454
anatomy. *See* medicine
Anchieta, José de, 472, 527
Andreae, Johann Valentin, 96, 188–89, 451, 452, 455
Andreas, Valerius, 488
Andrewes, Lancelot, 243
Angèli da Barga, Pietro, 58, 398
Angeriano, Girolamo, 471
Anghiera, Pietro Martire d', 159, 367
Anglo-Dutch War (Second), 81
Anyés, Joan Baptista, 464
Amsterdam, 479, 485
  Athenaeum, 481
  Royal Academy, 405
Andrelini, Publio Fausto, 412, 463
Anisio, Giano, 202, 396
Anne (duchess of York), 81
Anne (queen of England), 208
Anne, Saint, 371
Annius of Viterbo, 152, 158
anticlassicism, 89, 91–93, 94, 96, 99, 447
antiquarianism. *See* historiography
Anthony, Saint, of Egypt, 63, 397
Antonia (princess of Württemberg), 369
Antonio, Nicolás, 463, 533
Antwerp, 481

Anwykyll, John, 32
Aphthonius, 120, 131, 449. *See also* oratory;
    progymnasmata
Apollonius of Perga, 266
Apollonius of Rhodes, 64, 405
apologetic writing
  Catholic, 318–19, 323, 561
  humanistic, 176, 298, 300, 301, 302, 305, 447, 473
  political, 143, 159–60, 432, 533
Apuleius, 184, 185, 186, 194, 348
Aquilonius, Bertel Knudsen, 499
Aquinas, Thomas, Saint, 145, 146, 296, 301, 305
  Thomism, 258, 317, 325, 339
Arabic language, 279–91, 480. *See also* oriental
    studies
  dictionaries, 289, 480
  grammar books, 288
  philosophical terms, 256–57
  scientific writing, 267, 270, 271, 550
  translation into Hebrew, 281
  translation into Latin, 112, 249–50, 255, 265,
    267, 270, 271, 281–82, 295, 308
Aramaic language, 288, 299–301, 306, 308.
    See also Bible
Arason, Jón, 495
Arator, 66
Aratus, 64, 397
Archimedes, 265, 270
architecture, 90, 308, 345, 369, 417–18, 511
Arcimboldo, Giuseppe, 511
Ardoini, Anna Maria, 373
Aretino, Pietro, 90
Arias Montano, Benito, 308, 463, 464
Ariosto, Ludovico, 22, 90, 210, 465
Aristotle
  anti-Aristotelianism, 341
  Aristotelianism, 143–45, 242–43, 249, 265, 266,
    317, 325, 331, 333, 334–35, 558
  commentaries on, 112, 257, 266, 270, 271, 279,
    281–82, 283–84, 367, 470, 528
  De Anima, 257, 271, 283–84
  Historia animalium, 268, 270–71
  Nicomachean Ethics, 251, 254, 346
  Organon (logical works), 237, 335, 339
  Poetics, 103, 112–13, 201
  Politics, 136, 144, 254, 467
  Rhetoric, 120–21, 127, 353
  translations of, 171, 251, 254, 266, 270, 402, 463
arithmetic. *See* mathematics
Armenian language, 485
Arriaga, Pablo José de, 528
Arthur (legendary king of Britain), 157, 429, 431–32

Asia, 2, 7, 114, 268, 511, 557–70. *See also* China; India; Japan; Manchus; Tibet
Astemio, Lorenzo, 404
astrology
  academic study of, 263, 264, 339, 519
  Arabic sources, 257, 280, 282–85, 288, 290
  represented in literature, 67, 188, 190, 497
  zodiac, 201, 397–98
astronomy
  academic study of, 179, 263, 267, 270, 272, 421, 497, 520–21
  Greek sources, 267, 270
  Jesuit, 489, 560, 561–62, 569
  represented in literature, 58, 64, 67, 84, 397, 437–38, 497
Athanasius, Saint, 295, 303
Atlantis, 502
atlases. *See* cartography
Atrocianus, Johannes, 450
Atterbury, Francis, 430
Attila, 154, 514
Aue, Euphrosine, 369
Augurelli, Giovanni Aurelio, 202, 204
Augustín, Antonio, 463, 465
Augustine, Saint
  academic study of, 3, 371
  commentaries on, 463
  views on language, 17, 305, 348
  theology, 138, 170, 295, 303, 320, 321
Augustinians, 482
Augustus (Roman emperor), 51–52, 59, 347, 489, 495
Ausonius, 419
Aurpach, Johann, 454
Austen, Jane, 180
Austria. *See also* German language; Habsburg dynasty
  Henricianum, 349
  historiography, 158
  represented in literature, 65–66, 191, 453
  schools, 386
autobiography. *See* biography
autograph books, 449, 518
Avancini, Niccolò, 114
Averroes. *See also* Arabic language
  commentaries on Aristotle, 249–50, 254, 271, 279
  criticism of, 280, 281, 286
  medical works, 282, 287
  philosophy, 280, 283–84
  translations of, 112, 249–50, 271, 281–82
Avicenna, 279, 280, 283, 285, 286, 287, 288.
      See also Arabic language
  Canon of Medicine, 279, 281, 282, 286, 290

Ávila, Saint Teresa of, 371
Azambucha, Jerónimo de, 470
Azpilcueta, Martin de, 146
Aztecs, 529, 533

Bachmann, Christian, 96
Bacon, Anne, 368
Bacon, Francis, 250, 273
Bacon, Roger, 279
Bade, Josse, 200, 412, 414
Badin, Stephen Theodore, 548
Baduel, Claude, 335–36
Baïf, Antoine de, 419
Baião, André, 472
Balde, Jakob, 44, 204, 209, 445, 452, 453, 454
Bandettini, Teresa, 373
Bandini, Francesco, 511
Bång, Petrus, 502
"barbarians," 154, 156, 157, 220, 419, 455, 466, 543, 545, 548
Barbaro, Ermolao, 253, 271, 338, 367
Barberini, Maffeo, 189, 190
Barbosa, Aires, 472
Barclay, John, 187
  Argenis, 42, 184, 189–91, 195, 196
  Euphormionis Lusinini Satyricon, 184, 189–91, 205–6, 210, 211
Barignano, Fabio, 399
Barlaeus, Caspar, 484
Baron, Bonaventure, 323
Baroni, Laura, 434
Baronius, Caesar, 160, 162, 314, 321, 323–25
baroque, 129, 162, 178, 404, 447, 455, 464, 473
Barth, Caspar von, 50, 205, 447
Barthélemy de Loches, Nicolas, 109
Bartholin, Caspar, 266
Bartholin, Thomas, 179, 503
Bartolini, Riccardo, 60, 65–66, 453
Bartram, John, 550–51
Barzizza, Antonio, 404
Basel, University of, 267
Basil, Saint, 296, 305
Basini, Basinio, 64, 397, 399
Bathurst, Richard, 430
Bathurst, Theodore, 432
Baumgarten, Alexander Gottlieb, 457
Bayer, Theophilus Siegfried, 558, 562, 566, 567
Bayle, Pierre, 250
Baynard family, 75
Baynard, Ann, 209
Beatrice of Aragon, 369
Bebel, Heinrich, 455

Becanus, Gulielmus, 485
Beccadelli, Antonio (Panormita), 400
Bectoz, Claudine Scholastique de, 371
Béda, Noël, 241, 304–5
Bedford, Arthur, 427
Beedom, Thomas, 36
Beijing. *See under* China.
Bél, Mátyás, 514, 516
Belgium. *See* Low Countries
Bell, Adam Schall von, 559, 570
Bellarmino, Roberto, 143, 314, 317, 319
Belo, Francesco, 380
Belon, Pierre, 290
Bembo, Pietro, 131, 156, 348, 400, 402, 479
Benci, Francesco, 207, 398
Benedict XVI (pope), 317
Benedictines, 104, 396, 456
Benedictus, Georgius, 485
Benešić, Damjan, 202
Benningh, Jan Bodecher, 206
Berard, Stephen, 195
Bérault, Jean, 210
Bergalli, Luisa, 373
Bergenhielm, Johan, 207, 211, 504
Berlaimont, Noël de, 31
Bernard of Clairvaux, 321
Beroaldo, Filippo, 185, 338, 412
Berosus, 152
Bessarion, Basilios, Cardinal, 270, 338
Beveridge, John, 548
Bèze, Théodore de, 240, 242, 420, 427
    Ad Serenissimam Elizabetham Angliae
        Reginam, 34
    biblical scholarship, 307, 329–30
    Epistola magistri Passavantii, 206
    Iuvenilia, 78, 419
    Triumphale carmen, 42
Biard, Pierre, 542
Bible, 295–309. *See also* Arabic language;
        Aramaic language; Greek language;
        Hebrew language; Syriac language
    Antwerp Polyglot, 299, 308
    Arabic Gospels, 308
    Complutensian Polyglot, 298, 299, 300–1, 307,
        308, 462
    epics based on, 66, 435, 451–52
    King James (Authorised Version), 436
    London Polyglot, 308
    Masorah, 299, 301, 308,
    Mishnah, 308
    New Testament, 94, 323, 330, 338, 339, 478, 545, 566
        Acts, 330

Greek New Testament, 296–99, 300–3, 307
    John, 297, 303
    Latin translation, 296–99
    Luke, 304
    Matthew, 297, 301, 304, 306
    Paul, 298, 303, 304, 306, 307, 315, 321, 333, 339–40
    Peter, 302
    Revelation, 303
    Syriac, 299
Old Testament, 205, 298–300, 305
    Daniel, 154
    Ecclesiastes, 205
    Ezra, 309
    Genesis, 566
    Habakkuk, 367
    Hebrew Old Testament, 299–300
    Isaiah, 299
    Job, 321
    Joshua, 308
    Psalms, 41, 42, 44–45, 298, 321, 322, 396,
        434, 436, 452, 510
    Song of Songs, 44
Paris Polyglot, 308
Pentateuch, 299, 301, 309, 321
plays based on, 94–95, 109–10, 111–12, 113, 115, 451
Protestant (Protestant Latin Bible) Latin Bible, 329
rediscovery of biblical manuscripts, 297–98,
        301, 302–3, 307, 308, 330
Septuagint, 298–301, 307, 566
Talmud, 308
Targums, 299, 308
Torah, 299
translations, 17, 18, 295–309, 296, 329–30,
        338, 530
    Psalms, 44–45, 434, 436
Vulgate, 17, 236, 295–98, 303, 314, 315, 329–30,
        436, 566. *See also* Jerome, Saint
Bidermann, Jakob, 114, 451, 452
bilingualism. *See also* macaronic writing;
        multilingualism
    in authorial career, 28–29, 243, 250, 265–66,
        273, 331, 431
    in education, 336–37, 498
    in poetry, 36
    in printed works, 558, 560
Billingsley, Henry, 265
biography. *See also* diaries; letters
    Arabic authors, 285–87
    autobiography, 42, 168, 174, 176, 192, 194, 204,
        286–87, 355, 371, 454–55
    biographical dictionaries, 287
    George Washington, 552

learned men, 457
   missionaries, 544
   necrology, 544
Birck, Sixt, 451
Birckman, Arnold, 79
Birken, Sigmund von, 210
Bisse, Thomas, 437
Bissel, Johannes, 189, 452
Blaeu family, 418, 563
Blégny, Nicolas de, 201
Blommaerts, Jan, 290
Blotius, Hugo, 511
Bobadilla, Magdalena de, 368
Boccaccio, Giovanni, 395, 399, 400
   Decameron, 90, 96, 185, 404, 405
   On famous women, 363–64, 403
Boccalini, Traiano, 211
Bock, Hieronymus, 268, 272
Boece, Hector, 159, 432
Boerhaave, Herman, 273
Boethius, 104, 251, 256, 331, 368
   Consolation of Philosophy, 225, 226
Boétie, Etienne de la, 204
Bogislaw X (duke of Pomerania), 107, 158
Bohemia, 185–86, 208, 510–12. *See also*
   East–Central Europe
Boiardo, Matteo Maria, 395
Boileau-Despréaux, Nicolas (Boileau), 210, 211
Bolea, Ana Francisca Abarca de, 371
Bolland, Jean, 321, 323, 481
Bollinger, Ulrich, 451
Bologna, University of, 237–39
Bolyai, János, 521
Bolyai, Wolfgang, 521
Bomberg, Daniel, 299
Bonaventure, Saint, 305
Bonde, Karl Knutsson, 503
Bonfini, Antonio, 157, 158, 511, 516
Bonifacio, Juan, 568
Bonin, Just, 201
Borch, Ole, 504
Borghini, Maria Selvaggia, 373
Borro, Gasparino, 366
Bosau, Helmold von, 158
Bošković, Ruđer Josip, 267
botany
   academic study of, 263, 268, 269, 270, 271, 274,
      283, 290, 456, 489, 546, 550–51, 564
   taxonomy, 266, 274, 456
Botero, Giovanni, 143
Botello de Moraes y Vasconcelos, Francisco, 199
Botner, Damian, 80

Botta, Bartolomeo, 66
Botticelli, Sandro, 172
Bourbon, Nicolas, 417
Bourges, University of, 414–15
Bourgogne, Nicolas de, 448
Bourne, Vincent, 428, 430
Boyle, Robert, 265–66
Boym, Michael, 563, 564
Braccesi, Alessandro, 400
Braga, Colégio of, 469
Bragança (Braganza) dynasty, 469, 560
Brahe, Tycho, 47, 179, 267, 497, 511, 520, 521
Brancati, Francesco, 561
Brandolini, Aurelio, 298
Brant, Sebastian, 28, 107, 211, 355
Brasavola, Antonio Musa, 268, 283
Brassicanus, Johannes Alexander, 515
Brattle, William, 549
Brazil. *See* Latin America
Brébeuf, Jean de, 544
Brenner, Martin, 516
Brenner, Sophia Elisabeth, 370
Brethren of the Common Life, 477–78
Breuil, Guillaume du, 354
Breydenbach, Bernhard von, 289
Brie, Germain de, 74
Briga, Melchior dalla, 562
Brigid, Saint, 320
Britannico, Giovanni, 200
British Isles, 17, 22, 11, 204, 427–39. *See also*
   England; Ireland; Scotland; Wales
Brocar, Juan de, 465
Brodericus, Stephanus, 512, 515, 516
Broekhuizen, Johan van, 485
Brothers of the Christian Schools, 384
Broucke, Janus van den, 484
Bruges, 478, 479
Brunfels, Otto, 271
Bruni, Leonardo
   civic humanism, 135, 351–52
   historiography, 153–55, 156, 401
   letters, 174, 402, 403
   views on language, 15, 124, 249, 252–52, 255,
      257, 260, 298
Bruno, Giordano, 250, 254, 260, 380, 398, 511, 520
Brusch, Kaspar, 517
Brutus (legendary founder of Britain), 157, 432
Bruyerin, Jean-Baptiste, 282
Bucer, Martin, 306
Buchanan, George, 430, 439
   academic career, 234, 235, 240, 241, 428, 469
   drama, 109, 113, 240, 420

Buchanan, George (*cont.*)
  historiography, 432
  poetry, 204–5, 241–42, 428, 436, 437, 438, 484–84
  Psalm paraphrases, 45, 434, 436
Budé, Guillaume, 125, 241, 412–14
Buffon, George-Louis Leclerc, 534, 535
Bugenhagen, Johannes, 158
Buglio, Lodovico, 559
Bugnot, Gabriel, 196
Buonaccorsi, Filippo, 156
Bulkeley, Peter, 74
Bullinger, Heinrich, 329, 338–41
Buonamici, Lazzaro, 255, 259
Burckhardt, Jacob, 233, 395, 401
Bure, Catharina, 370
Bureus, Johannes, 502
Bürgi, Jost, 511
Burman, Pieter (the Younger), 485
Burnett, Thomas, 434
Burrus, Petrus, 417
Burton, Robert, 3, 242
Busbecq, Ogier Ghislain de, 176, 489
Butler, Thomas (earl of Ormond), 61, 435
Butzbach, Johannes, 455
Byrd, William, II, 552
Byzantine Empire, 266, 330, 396, 454, 513.
    See also Constantinople

Cabrera, Cristobál, 527
Caesarius, Johannes, 123
Caesar, Julius, 67, 92, 158, 317, 349, 446
  Gallic Wars, 218, 355, 531
  represented in literature, 109, 110, 419
Caiado, Henrique, 472
Calderón de la Barca, Pedro, 115
Calenzio, Elisio, 399
Calixtus III (pope), 107
Callimachus, 301, 518
Calonymos, Calonymos ben, 249
Calphurnius, Franciscus, 286
Calvin, Jean, 28, 126, 190, 228, 322, 329, 336, 415
  Calvinism, 45, 126, 178, 335–37, 419, 454
Cambridge, 427
  University of, 274, 287, 437–38
    Christ's College, 243
    Clare Hall (now Clare College), 81
    drama, 90–91, 92, 109, 110, 244, 315
    Emmanuel College, 81
    Magdalene College, 82
    poetry, 35, 47, 81–83, 235, 237, 243–45, 431

St. John's College, 81, 82
    Trinity College, 244
Camden, William, 158, 159, 431
Camerarius, Joachim, 453
Camões, Luis de, 472
Campanella, Tommaso, 187, 250, 255, 257
Campano, Giovanni Antonio, 42
Campion, Thomas, 46–47, 48, 434
Campos y Martínez, Juan Gregorio, 533
Canada. *See under* North America: New France
Canini, Angelo, 308
Canisius, Petrus, 322
Cano, Melchor, 307, 467
Cantelma, Margarita, 364
Cantemir, Dimitrie, 512
Canter, Ursula, 370
Capitein, Jacobus Elisa Johannes, 487
Carafa, Antonio, 308
Carafa, Diomede, 136
Carbonell, Pere Miquel, 463, 465
Cardano, Girolamo, 285, 534
Cardoso, Jerónimo, 472
Carheil, Etienne de, 547
Carlos (prince of Asturias), 146
Carolides, Jiři, 517
Carr, Joseph, 82
Carranza, Bartolomé, 467
Carrara dynasty
    Francesco da, 138, 350
    Giovanni Michele Alberto, 202, 395, 400
    Ubertino, 58, 63
Cartagena, Alfonso de, 467
Cartagena, Teresa de, 371
cartography, 156, 489, 511, 513, 562–64
Casal, Gaspar do, 470
Casas, Bartolomé de las, 466–67, 526, 529
Casaubon, Isaac, 201, 206, 308, 325, 415
Cassius Dio, 531
Castiglione, Baldassare, 124, 345, 380, 401
Castellio, Sebastian, 303, 308
Castro, Alfonso de, 319
Cataldo Siculo, Aquila, 469, 470, 471
Catherine of Alexandria, Saint, 298, 449
Catherine of Aragon (queen of England), 367
Cato, Marcus Porcius 152
Cats, Jacob, 35–36, 484
Cattaneo, Giovanni Maria, 398
Catullus, 41, 44, 47–50, 73, 77, 417, 470, 471, 483
Caussin, Nicolas, 114, 122
Cavaleiro, Estêvâo, 470
Cavendish, Margaret, 209

Cecil, Mildred, 368
Cecil, William, 368
Celestine I (pope), 17
Celestine V (pope), 398
Celineo, Nardino, 400
Celsus, 270
Celtic language, 17
Celtis, Konrad, 108, 332, 370, 447, 515
    Amores, 45–46, 445, 454
    Ars versificandi et carminum, 446
    De situ et moribus Norimbergae, 158
    founder of *Collegium poetarum et
        mathematicorum*, 447
    Germania illustrata, 158, 445
    letters, 455
    odes and epodes, 445, 447, 448
censorship
    Catholic, 79, 469, 543, 569
        Index of Forbidden Books,
            211, 308, 320
    of historiography, 501–2
    Protestant, 370
cento, 51, 140, 207, 528, 547
Cerceau, Jean-Antoine du, 210
Cerda, Juan Luis de la, 463
Cerdá y Rico, Francisco, 468
Cereta, Laura, 363, 366, 403
Cerri, Antonio, 201
Cervantes, 114
Ceva, Tommaso, 398
Chalcondyles, Demetrios, 396
Champier, Symphorien, 285, 286
Charlemagne, 62, 96, 154, 285, 514
Charles II (king of England), 81
Charles III (king of Spain), 468, 533
Charles IV (Holy Roman Emperor), 349, 446, 510
Charles V (Holy Roman Emperor), 136, 137, 143,
    267, 530, 531
Charles V (king of France), 363
Charles VI (Holy Roman Emperor), 386
Charles VIII (king of France), 107, 173
Charles IX (king of France), 420
Charles X Gustav (king of Sweden), 60
Charles XII (king of Sweden), 504, 505, 506
Chastellain, Pierre, 546–47
Chaucer, Geoffrey, 33, 428
Chauvin, Étienne, 250
Cheever, Ezechial, 552
chemistry. *See under* science
Chiaravacci, Girolamo, 398
Chigi, Fabio, 485

China, 2, 356, 557–70. *See also* Chinese language;
        Manchus
    Beijing, 562, 565, 569 , 570
        college, 564, 569
    Hangzhou, College of, 569
    printing in, 560, 568–69
Chinese language. *See also* Manchu language
    dictionaries, 566, 568, 570
    study of, 562, 567, 570
    translations into Chinese, 558, 570
    translations into Latin, 560, 566–67
Chorier, Nicolas, 211
chorography. *See under* historiography
Chrestien, Florent, 201
Christian II (king of Denmark), 494, 503
Christian III (king of Denmark), 494–95
Christian IV (king of Denmark), 495, 500
Christina (queen of Sweden), 370, 496
Chrysoloras, Manuel, 338
Chrysostom, John, Saint, 296, 297, 303, 305
"chymistry". *See under* science
Chytraeus, Nathan, 206, 455
Cicero, 87, 92, 153, 446
    Brutus, 14, 161, 513
    Ciceronianism, 130, 402
        Christian Ciceronianism, 16–17, 295, 348
        Jesuit, 326, 348, 480
        in letters, 131
        in literary histories, 161
        in oratory and rhetoric, 121, 224
        in political writing, 136–40, 347–48,
        in prose style, 20–22, 186, 226, 271, 303, 347,
            405, 413, 414, 447, 448, 470, 479, 480, 536
        Protestant, 341
    commentaries on, 463
    De inventione, 224, 335
    De officiis, 143, 225, 371
    De senectute, 225, 365
    ethics, 124, 141, 351
    Laelius de amicitia, 19, 225
    letters, 167–69, 170, 173, 218, 337, 339, 366, 403
    Paradoxa Stoicorum, 225, 337
    Philippics, 318
    Pro Archia, 218
    Pro rege Deiotaro, 218
    rhetorical writing, 14, 20, 108, 120, 124, 218, 334, 366
    Somnium Scipionis, 63, 225, 466, 486
    Topica, 335
    Tusculan Disputations, 174
Cinzio, Giambattista, 201
Ciotti, Giambattista, 364

Ciruelo, Pedro Sánchez, 465
Cittadella, Pietro, 202
Clapmarius, Arnold, 140
Clavijero, Francisco Javier, 528, 534
Claudian, 22, 58, 352, 369, 452, 471, 484
Claudius (Roman emperor), 205
Claus, Anton, 98
Clayton, John, 550–51
Clement VII (pope), 66, 396, 405
Clement VIII (pope), 307
Clement XIV (pope), 69, 114
Clement, John, 368
Cleyer, Andreas, 564
Cleynaerts, Nicolas, 469, 470, 473, 489
Clusius, Carolus, 176, 489, 511
Cochlaeus, Johannes, 158
Coelho, Jorge, 472
Coimbra
    Colégio das Artes, 469, 472
    University of, 109, 240, 469, 470
Colden, Cadwallader, 550–51
Colden, Jane, 551
Coleridge, Samuel Taylor, 190
Colet, John, 21, 125, 341
Coligny, Gaspard de, 454
colleges, 211, 240. See also under individual places
Collegium Trilingue. See Alcalá de Henares,
        University of; Leuven
Cologne, 79, 320, 354, 372
    University of, 284, 339–40
colonialism, 465–67, 525–37, 541–53, 557–70
Colonel, Pablo, 300
Colt, Jane, 368
Columba, Saint, 320
Columbus, Christopher, 58, 399, 536
comedy, 87–99, 186, 404–5, 482
    comicotragedy, 87
    farce, 89–90, 91, 92, 96, 482
Comenius, Jan Amos, 518–19, 521
commentaries. See also under individual authors
    medical, 283
    philosophical works, 249, 257, 265, 270, 271,
        281, 283–84, 367
    patristic, 296–97, 321–22, 323–24
    political, 350
    rabbinical, 295, 299
Commines, Philippe de, 162
commonplace books, 53, 131, 139–42, 348–49
Concini, Concino, 190
Confucianism, 561, 566–68
Connibert, 92
Conring, Hermann, 452

Constantinople, 171, 266, 295, 296, 396, 513
    fall of (1453), 2, 59, 295, 351, 399
Contarini, Gasparo, 135
Contzen, Adam, 143, 452
convents, 175, 250, 285, 366, 370–72, 373, 527
converts to Christianity, 371
    in China, 564–65, 569–70
    Jewish, 189, 299, 300
    in Mexico, 68–69, 526
    Muslim, 288, 290, 300, 530
    in New France, 541
Cooke, Anthony, 368
Copenhagen
    siege of, 60, 504
    University of, 495
Copernicus, Nicolaus, 179, 267, 437, 498, 512, 520, 521
Cordara, Giulio Cesare, 400
Corday, Charlotte, 453
Cordier, Maturin, 336–37, 340, 341
Cordus, Euricius, 268, 453, 454
Cornazzano, Antonio, 90, 364
Corneille, Pierre, 114
coronation of poets, 63, 105, 170, 447, 495
Correggio, Barbara da, 371
Correia, Tomé, 470, 499
Correr, Gregorio, 106, 110, 202, 395, 400, 404
Cortese, Paolo, 296
Cortés, Hernando, 534
Corvinus, Laurentius, 517
Corvinus, Matthias (king of Hungary), 157, 369,
        511, 514, 516, 520
Costa, Inácio da, 566
Cotton, John, 74
Councils of the church
    Basel, 295, 446
    Certa, 324
    Constance, 446
    Constantinople, 296
    Ferrara-Florence, 295
    Nicaea, 296
    Trent, 315, 405, 470. See also
        Counter-Reformation
        Tridentine decree, 307, 314
    Vienne, 295
Counter-Reformation, 2, 93, 237, 313–26, 348,
        370, 398
    biblical scholarship, 307–8
    drama, 93, 111–13
Couplet, Philippe, 560, 565, 566, 569
Cousturier, Pierre, 305
Cowley, Abraham, 43, 92, 434, 435
Cowper, William, 190

Cramer, Daniel, 96
Crantz, Martin, 412
Crasso, Niccolò, 211
Crawshaw, Richard, 435
creoles, 525, 532–37
Cressolles, Louis de, 123
Croatia, 485, 512. *See also* East–Central Europe
Cromwell, Oliver, 81, 135, 244
Crusades, 155, 354, 398, 399
Crusius, Thomas Theodor, 124
Cruz, Juana Inés de la, 371
Cruz, Luís da, 114, 472
Cujas, Jacques, 415
Cunaeus, Petrus, 205, 308, 486
Cygne, Martin du, 482
Cyprian, Saint, 303, 478
Cyrano de Bergerac, Savinien, 380
Czech language
    textbooks, 31
    translations from Latin, 519
Czech territories, 509, 510–11. *See also* Czech
    language; East-Central Europe

D'Abano, Pietro, 271
D'Alembert, Jean, 535
D'Anville, Jean Baptiste Bourguignon, 563
D'Aquino, Carlo, 400
D'Aquino, Tommaso Niccolò, 397
D'Aragona, Eleonora, 364
Dahlstierna, Gunno Eurelius, 499
Dantiscus, Johannes, 517
Darcio, Giovanni, 398, 401
Daneau, Lambert, 141–42
Danet, Pierre, 570
Danish language
    translations into, 503
    vernacular works, 506
Dannhauer, Johann Konrad, 450, 457
Dares Phrygius, 105
Dassio, Francesc, 465
Dati, Agostino, 223, 226
Dati, Carlo, 434
Dati, Leonardo, 106, 404
Dazzi, Andrea, 399
Dedekind, Friedrich, 206
Dee, John, 265, 511
De Libera, Alain, 259–60
Della Casa, Giovanni, 346
Del Medigo, Elia, 281
Della Rovere family, 399
Deloynes, François, 413
Demetrius, 120

Demosthenes, 120, 153, 244
Denmark, 159, 494. *See also* Danish language;
    Scandinavia
Descartes, René, 496
    bilingualism, 28, 250, 265, 273, 421–22
    letters, 179, 369
    philosophy, 258–59, 266, 498, 528, 534, 549
Deshoulières, Madame, 209
Despauterius, Johannes, 567
Deventer Academy, 228, 339
devotio moderna, 175, 339
Deza, Diego de, 301
dialectic. *See* logic
dialogues, 31–32, 129–30, 206–7, 253, 268, 337,
    363–64, 367, 402
diaries, 338–39, 489, 512, 547, 552–53, 559, 570
dictionaries. *See under individual languages and
    fields of study*
didactic poetry, 57–58, 61, 62, 64, 67, 203, 206, 437
Diego, Juan, 528
Dillingham, William, 427, 428, 432, 436
Diodati, Charles, 431, 433–34
Diogenes the Cynic, 203
Diogenes Laertius, 372
Diomedes, 103, 126, 341
Dionysius of Halicarnassus, 120
Dioscorides, 265, 271–72, 280, 470
Diophantus, 267
diplomacy, 422, 569
    Italian, 64, 105, 142, 351
    writing by diplomats, 142, 144, 178, 289–90,
        356, 396, 488–89, 496–96, 517
Disticha Catonis, 224, 341
Dôle, University of, 364
Dolet, Etienne, 417
Dominicans, 320, 466, 527, 561
Donation of Constantine, 296, 349. *See also* Valla,
    Lorenzo
Donatus, 17, 87, 103, 126, 217, 220, 324–25, 331,
    339, 341
Donne, John, 210
Dorat, Jean, 368, 419, 420
Dornau, Caspar, 207, 453
Dorp, Maarten van, 305
Douai, University of, 480
Dousa, Janus, 203, 207, 480, 483
drama. *See* comedy; Jesuits; tragedy; schools;
    universities
Drant, Thomas, 210
Dringenberg, Ludwig, 228
Druesnes, Léopold, 389
Drury, William, 92–93

Drusius, Johannes, 308
Dryden, John, 210
Du Bellay, Guillaume, 417
Du Bellay, Jean, 204
Du Bellay, Joachim, 27, 45, 75–78, 192, 368, 416, 417–19
Dubois, Jacques, 282
Dubreuil de Pontbriand, Henri-Marie, 546
Ducas, Demetrius, 300
Ducreux, François, 545
Dudith, Andreas, 512
Dugonics, András, 195
Duns Scotus, John, 257, 259, 317, 325, 528
Dunyn-Szpot, Thomas Ignatius, 559
Dupanloup, Félix Antoine Philibert, 381
Duport, James, 82, 235, 236, 243
Durão, António, 472
Dürer, Albrecht, 172
Dutch language
    textbooks, 31–32
    translations from Latin, 210–11, 487
    translations into Latin, 273, 484
    works adapted in Latin, 483
    works adapted from Latin, 483
    vernacular works, 484

East-Central Europe, 237, 509–22. *See also* Bohemia; Croatia; Czech territories; Hungary; Poland; Romania; Slovakia; Transylvania; Wallachia
Echtermeyer, Theodor, 456
Eck, Johannes, 207, 314, 317, 319, 450
Eckhart, Meister, 254
education. *See* academies; colleges; schools; universities; *under individual countries, languages, and fields of study*
Edward VI (king of England), 237
Egger, Karl, 326
Eguiara y Eguren, Juan José, 533
Egypt, 287, 289–90, 512
    hieroglyphs, 400, 568
Einsiedel, Margaretha Sibylla von, 369
Eleazar, 548
Elizabeth I (queen of England), 237, 365, 504
    in historiography, 159
    as Latinist, 368
    in poetry, 34, 47, 61, 80, 435, 453
Elisabeth (countess Palatine), 369
Elisabeth (margravine of Baden-Durlach), 369
Elzevier (family of Dutch printers), 481
emblems, 35–36, 79–80, 142, 322, 355, 368
Emilio, Paolo, 157

Emmerich, 339, 341
Emmius, Ubbo, 158, 487
Engerd, Johann, 59
England, 368, 427–39. *See also* English language
    Gunpowder Plot, 59, 244, 434, 436
    schools, 74, 125–26, 381–84
    universities, 237, 242–45
English language
    bilingualism, 29, 30–36, 192, 243, 244, 273, 274
    influenced by Latin, 91, 252
    Statute of Pleading, 509
    textbooks, 31–32
    translations from Latin, 32, 33, 43, 77, 84, 93, 173, 189, 210, 266, 273, 367, 368, 397, 401, 404, 513, 519
    translations into Latin, 43, 195, 255, 273, 432–33, 434, 551
    vernacular works, 6, 42, 244, 256, 265–66
    works adapted from Latin, 487
Enlightenment, 203, 309, 513, 528, 533, 536
Ennius, 63
epic poetry, 57–69, 435. *See also* Bible
    Christian, 398–99, 421, 451–52, 472
    epyllion (brief epic), 62, 68, 436, 528
    mock epic, 235, 399, 433, 436–37
    political, 354, 452–53, 504, 527, 528–29
    vernacular, 244
Epicureanism, 265, 266
epigrams, 194, 400, 432, 434–35, 517, 518. *See also* Martial; occasional poetry
    collections of, 73–80, 206
epigraphy. *See* inscriptions
epistolography. *See* letters
epitaphs, 74, 77, 82, 417, 428, 431, 432, 433, 517, 552, 557. *See also* inscriptions
epyllion. *See under* epic poetry
Erasmus, Desiderius, 2, 269, 427, 470, 471, 477, 478–79, 515
    Adagia, 325, 478
    biblical scholarship, 296–97, 300, 301–6, 307, 308, 330, 338
    Christian humanism, 108, 174–76, 478, 527
    Ciceronianus, 20–21, 131, 161, 173, 413, 416, 447, 479
    Colloquia familiaria, 341, 449, 478
    Compendium rhetorices, 126
    criticism of, 127–28, 300, 301, 462
    De conscribendis epistulis, 127–28, 173, 455, 478, 531
    De duplici copia, 127, 339, 341, 478
    De pueris instituendis, 339
    De ratione studii, 20, 125, 126, 478
    De recta pronuntiatione, 339
    educational program, 325, 339–41, 496, 527

Institutio principis Christiani, 136–37
    Latin style, 21, 22, 413
    letters, 173–76, 370, 517
    poetry, 201
    Praise of Folly, 8, 130, 207, 472, 487
Eric XIV (king of Sweden), 504
erotic writing, 46–47, 400, 438, 499, 518
    Amores, 45, 46, 47, 48, 401, 445, 454
    Basia, 48, 50, 73, 417, 483, 484
    Catullan, 48–49, 50, 417, 483
    homoerotic, 434
    matrimonial, 46, 80, 418
Erpenius, Thomas, 288–89, 290
Ertl, Anton Wilhelm, 191
essay, 506, 512
    literary critical, 120, 427, 435
    epistolary, 168, 174, 178
    pedagogical, 241, 368
    philosophical, 256–57
    Plutarchan, 136
    satirical, 453
    Senecan, 104, 113, 352
Estaço, Aquiles, 470, 472
Este dynasty, 61, 395, 399
    Alfonso II d', 203
    Anna d', 369
    Borso d', 399
    Isabella d', 364
    Leonello d', 64, 65
    Niccolò d', 365
Estienne, Henri, 49–50, 369, 416
Estienne, Robert, 299, 307, 329, 336, 369
ethics. *See also* Aristotle; *under*
        philosophy: moral
    academic study of, 237, 251–52, 254, 306, 325,
    in literature, 108, 184, 200
    in politics, 145, 346, 348, 353,
    in rhetoric, 127, 129, 152, 340, 353
Ethiopic language, 308
Eton College, 80
Euclid, 265, 270, 521
Eugene IV (pope), 207
Euripides, 201, 368, 472, 478
Évora, Colégio of, 469
Evrard of Béthune, 227
Exner, Balthasar, 142
Ezzelino III da Romano, 104–5, 355, 404

Faber, Johann, 564
Fabius Pictor, Quintus, 152
Fabri, Manuel, 535
Fabrice, Arnould, 469

Fabricius, Georg, 447, 452
Fabricius Montanus, Johannes, 455
Fabritius, Carel, 511
Facio, Bartolomeo, 161
Fadella, Marco, 286
Faerno, Gabriele, 404
Fagius, Paul, 299, 308
Falcó, Jaime Juan, 204, 208, 464
Faletti, Girolamo, 203
Fano, Cristoforo da, 209
Farce de Maître Pathelin, 91–92
Farel, Guillaume, 336
Faria, Tomé de, 472
Farley, Robert, 36
Fedele, Cassandra, 366, 367, 370, 403
Feltre, Vittorino da, 365
Ferdinand I (Holy Roman Emperor), 515
Ferdinand I (king of Naples), 365, 369
Ferdinand II (king of Aragon), 107, 467
Ferdinand VI (king of Spain), 385
Fernández Navarrete, Domingo, 561
Fernández Navarrete, Pedro, 386
Ferrara
    court literature, 61, 64, 364, 395, 399, 400
    court school, 365
    medical humanism, 283
    University of, 512
Ferreira, António, 472
Ferreri, Zaccaria, 396
Ferreti, Ferreto de', 398
Fichet, Guillaume, 412
Ficino, Marsilio, 172, 249, 250, 255, 403–4, 412, 511
fiction. *See* prose fiction
Filelfo, Francesco
    fables, 404
    letters, 171–72, 174, 469
    odes, 42, 401
    satires, 202, 203, 204, 206, 211, 400
    Sphortias, 61, 399
Filippucci, Francesco Saverio, 561
Finland. *See also* Finnish language; Scandinavia
    history and education, 494, 495, 496
    Latin writing, 502, 503, 506
Finnish language, 503
Firmianus, Petrus. *See* Zacharie de Lisieux
Firmicus Maternus, 67
Fitzalan, Henry (earl of Arundel), 368
Fitzalan, Jane. *See* Lumley, Jane
Fitzalan, Mary, 368
Folengo, Teofilo, 207
Foreiro, Francisco, 470
Fiera, Baptista, 209

Fitzherbert, Thomas, 143
Flacius Illyricus, Matthias. *See Magdeburg Centuries*
Flaminio, Marcantonio, 45, 218, 401, 464
Flavio, Biondo, 155–56, 158, 161, 351, 402, 515
Flayder, Hermann, 96
Fleming, Paul, 456
Fletcher, Phineas, 427, 433, 436
Florence
    certame coronario, 106
    court literature, 395
    civic humanism, 351–52
    historiography, 154–55, 402
    literary history, 181
    Neo-Platonism, 172–73
    represented in literature, 106
    schools, 217, 218
Florus, Hercules, 108
Fonte, Moderata, 364
Foot, Lucinda, 553
Foppens, Jean-François, 488
Forer, Laurenz, 318
Foresti, Jacopo Filippo, 160, 285–86
Forgách, Ferenc, 512, 516
Forgách, Mihály, 512–13
Forsett, Edward, 96, 380
Foscarini, Ludovico, 364, 366
Foucquet, Jean-François, 570
Fourmont, Etienne, 558, 568
Foxe, John, 95, 96
Fox Morcillo, Sebastián, 136, 463, 465
Fracco, Ambrogio, 398
Fracastoro, Girolamo, 57, 398
France, 411–22, 477, 541–47. *See also* French language
    literary production in, 61, 364–65, 368–69, 371–72, 430
    Revolution, 79, 381, 384, 453, 487
    satire of, 209
    schools, 221, 336–37, 341, 379–90
    wars of religion, 207, 420
France, Renée de, 365
Francesco da Buti, 222, 226, 228
Franciscans, 204, 320, 438–39, 527, 530, 557, 561
Franckenau, Georg Franck von, 201
Francis Xavier, 58, 560
Francius, Petrus, 486
François I (king of France), 371, 412, 417
Frandsen, Hans, 495, 499
Franklin, Benjamin, 550, 551
Frederick (prince of Wales), 78
Frederick II (Holy Roman Emperor), 105
Frederick II (king of Denmark), 495

Frederick II (king of Prussia), 386
Frederick III (Holy Roman Emperor), 511
Frederick V (Elector Palatine), 453
Frederick William (Elector of Brandenburg), 453
Freiburger, Michael, 412
Freind, Joseph, 436
Freinsheimius, Johannes, 500
French language
    dictionaries, 570
    influenced by Latin, 19
    bilingualism, 27–28, 31–32, 35, 192
    Ordinance of Villers-Cotterêts, 416, 509
    textbooks, 31–32
    translations from Latin, 79, 173, 189, 210, 211, 254, 272, 336–37, 398, 404, 420–21, 487, 519, 543
    translations into Latin, 92, 195, 211, 273, 543
    vernacular works, 256, 265–66, 274, 356, 422, 534–44
Freytag, Georg Wilhelm, 289
Frischlin, Nicodemus, 66, 92, 96, 110, 204, 446, 449, 451
Frisi, Paolo, 220
Froben, Johannes, 174
Froschauer, Christoph, 269
Frulovisi, Tito Livio, 89, 404
Fuchs, Leonhart, 280, 283
Fuente, Andrés Diego de la, 534
Fuss, Johann Dominicus, 1

Gabiani, Giandomenico, 559
Gager, William, 110, 433
Gaguin, Robert, 157, 159, 173, 412, 415
Galen, 267, 270, 280, 282, 285, 287, 470
Galilei, Galileo, 23, 28, 179, 265, 267, 272–73, 520, 563
Galindo, Beatriz, 367
Galland, Pierre, 242
Gambara, Lorenzo, 399
Gameren, Hannard van, 204
Garcés, Julián, 526, 530
Gardner, Nathaniel, 548
García Matamoros, Alfonso, 463
Garissoles, Antoine, 59
Gart der Gesundheit, 268
Gassendi, Pierre, 421, 528
Gathelius (legendary founder of Scotland), 435
Gaubius, Hieronymus David, 273
Gauß, Carl Friedrich, 457, 521
Gaza, Theodorus, 270, 338
Geldenhouwer, Gerard, 203
Gellert, Christian Fürchtegott, 457
gender, 363–73
    and Latin literacy, 36, 255, 388–89, 553
    matriarchy, 193–94

querelle des femmes 363–65
satire, 209–10, 453
women Latin writers, 74, 363–73, 403, 429
Geneva
    Academy of, 126, 334, 336–37
    schools, 335, 337
Geoffrey of Monmouth, 157, 431–32
Geoffrey of Vinsauf, 222, 223, 226
geography. *See also* historiography:
    chorography; travel
    academic study of, 218, 308, 339
    Greek sources, 265, 270
    written works, 158–59, 161, 446, 454, 502, 511,
      514, 542, 544, 563–64, 570
geometry. *See* mathematics
George III (king of England), 548, 551
George, Saint, 82
Georgius of Hungary, 522
Gerald of Wales, 21, 432
Geraldini, Antonio, 396
Gerard of Cremona, 282
Gerhard, Johann, 450
Gering, Ulrich, 412
German language, 445–57
    bilingualism, 29, 331
    dictionaries, 456
    influenced by Latin, 254
    textbooks, 31
    translations from Latin, 79, 93, 173, 195, 210,
      211, 269, 273, 398, 404, 457, 519
    translations into Latin, 107, 211, 272, 456
German-speaking countries, 88, 445–57. *See also*
    Austria; Germany; German language;
    Switzerland
    autograph books, 518
    chorography, 158
    concept of nationhood, 348, 445–46
    school drama, 97–98, 109, 560
Germany, 1. *See also* German language;
    German-speaking countries
    humanism, 332, 446–49
    Neuhumanismus, 506
    Peasants' War, 107, 453–54
    schools, 228, 385, 386, 388
    universities, 145, 207–8, 240, 250, 495, 496, 512
Gessner, Conrad, 179, 268–70
Ghazali, al-, 249
Ghistele, Cornelis van, 210
Giannettasio, Niccolò Partenio, 58, 397, 398, 402
Gilbert, Balthasar, 121
Giggs, Margaret, 368
Gigli, Carlo, 478

Gil, Alexander, Jr., 429
Gillis, Peter, 174
Gilson, Étienne, 258
Giovio, Paolo, 161–62
Giphanius, Obertus, 203
Giraldi, Lilio Gregorio, 402
Giselinus, Victor, 178
Giustiniani, Agostino, 288
Glass, Francis, 552
Glisson, Francis, 257
Gnapheus, Guilielmus, 94–95, 482
Goclenius, Rudolph, 250, 257
Goedaert, Johannes, 273
Godeau, Michel, 211
Goggio, Bartolomeo, 364
Góis, Damião de, 471, 473
Golius, Jacob, 287, 288, 289, 563
Gomaer, François, 44
Gómez de Ciudad Real, Alvar, 464
Gómez Miedes, Bernardino, 465
Góngora, Luis de, 464
Gonzaga dynasty
    Cecilia, 371
    Ercole, 281
    Gianfrancesco, 365
González de Dios, Juan, 199, 200
González, Juan Angel, 464
González, Tomás, 528
Googe, Barnabe, 397
Goropius, Joannes, 488
Gospels. *See* Bible
Goths, 350, 501, 502, 504, 514
Gott, Samuel, 189
Göttingen, University of, 27
Gournay, Marie de, 364–65, 372, 373
Gouveia, André, 469
Gouveia, António de, 559, 560
Gozzi, Gasparo, 218
Gracián, Baltasar, 464
Graham, John, 435
Gramaye, Jean-Baptiste, 489
grammar books. *See also* schools; *under*
    individual languages
    ancient, 14, 16, 17–18, 341
    humanist, 32, 126, 302, 334, 462
Granada, Luis de, 526
Grangier, Bonaventure, 204
Gratiolo, Andrea, 282
Gravina, Vincenzo, 203
Gray, Thomas, 428, 434, 438
Graziani, Domitilla, 371
Great Northern War, 207, 504–5

Greek Anthology, 50, 73, 74, 416
Greek language, 228, 250. *See also* Bible
    academic study of, 17, 28, 119–20, 136, 144, 153,
        171, 218, 228, 244, 283–84, 295–97, 337–39,
        365, 411, 413, 415–16, 478
    grammar books, 295, 338
    poetry, 35, 41, 43, 50, 73, 80, 81, 83, 206
    prose fiction, 184, 190–91
    translation into Latin, 19, 23, 130, 151–52, 188,
        249, 253, 255–59, 265–68, 270–72, 296, 535
Gregory XIII (pope), 160
Gregory, Saint (the Great), 321
Gregory of Sanok, 521
Gregory, David, 84
Grenan, Bénigne, 211
Gretser, Jacob, 97, 449
Grimald, Nicolas, 109
Grimm, Jacob, 27
Gronovius, Johannes Fredericus, 179, 551
Grosseteste, Robert, 251, 260
Grotius, Hugo, 481, 497, 518
    biblical scholarship, 308
    historiography, 488
    letters, 178
    poetry, 427, 429, 484
    political writing, 146
    tragedies, 112–13, 482, 483
    translator of Theocritus, 84
Grouchy, Nicholas de, 469
Grudius, Nicolaus, 483
Grueber, Johann, 563–64
Grumbach, Argula von, 369
Gruterus, Janus, 142, 485–86
Gryphius, Andreas, 115, 451–52
Guarini, Guarino, 234, 241
Guarino, Battista, 124, 234, 469
Guarino da Verona, 174, 222, 226, 228, 365, 520–21
Guarna, Andrea, 94
Guicciardini, Francesco, 162
Guillard, Charlotte, 369
Guillén de Brocar, Arnao, 300
Guise, Charles de (cardinal of Lorraine), 204–5
Gunnarsøn, Halvard, 497, 500
Gunpowder Plot. *See under* England
Gustavus Adolphus (king of Sweden), 59, 370
Guyenne, Collège de, 240, 420
Guyet, François, 206
Gwinne, Matthew, 96, 110
Gyldenstolpe, Michael Wexionius, 502

Haas, Conrad, 521
Habermehl, Erasmus, 511

Habsburg dynasty. *See also* Austria; Holy
    Roman Empire
    court as intellectual center, 511
    Latin and political identity, 350, 456
    represented in literature, 65–66, 191, 453
Haddon, Walter, 471
Hadrian of Canterbury, 17
hagiography, 115, 151, 160, 320–21, 323, 560
    Acta Sanctorum, 320, 560
    De probatis sanctorum historiis, 320
    drama, 405
Haimendorff, Christoph Fürer von, 289
Hall, Joseph, 188
Hamilton, Henrik Albertsen, 499
Hannes, Edward, 434
Harant, Kryštof, 512
Harder, Henrik, 60, 504
Harvard College, 549–50
Harvey, Gabriel, 349
Harvey, William, 267
Hasištejnský (Hassenstenius), Bohuslav, of
    Lobkovice, 208, 512
Hassel, Henrik, 506
Havre, Jan van, 203
Hawghe, Walter, 75
Hawkins, William, 433
Hayneccius, Martin, 92
Hayyim, Jacob ben, 299
Herberstein, Sigmund von, 517
Hebrew language. *See also* Bible
    academic study of, 295, 299–301, 306, 308, 323,
        329, 411, 480, 488, 502
    grammar books, 299
    translation from Arabic, 281–82, 288
    translation into Latin, 249, 255–56, 281,
        298–300, 305
Heerkens, Gerhard Nicolaas, 203, 209
Heeze, Jean Van, 487
Hegelund, Peder, 498
Hegius, Alexander, 228, 339
Heidegger, Martin, 241, 255, 259
Heineccius, Johannes Gottlieb, 354
Heinsius, Daniel, 480, 481
    commentary on Horace's *Satires*, 200–201
    De contemptu mortis, 485
    Hercules tuam fidem, 205, 487
    poetry, 484
    tragedies, 112–13, 482
    translator of Theocritus, 84
    Virgula divina, 205
Heinsius, Nicolaus, 481, 496
Hell, Maximilian, 562

Helfta, Gertrud von, 370
Helgesen, Poul, 494
Heliodorus, 183–84, 190, 191
Helmont, Jan Baptist van, 513
Heltai, Gáspár, 516
Hennegrave, Antoine, 211
Henri II (king of France), 350
Henri III (king of France), 350
Henrietta Maria (consort of Charles I of England), 81
Henrietta (daughter of Charles I of England), 81
Henry VIII (king of England), 3, 187, 367, 483
Henry Frederick (prince of Wales), 35
Henry Frederick (Elector Palatine), 34
Henry of Settimello, 161, 224
Henten, Jean, 307
Herberstein, Sigmund von, 455
Herbert, George, 41, 51–52, 433, 434
Herder, Johann Gottfried, 1, 27
Herdtrich, Christian, 566, 567
Hermannus Alemannus, 112
Hermansz, Willem, 488
Hermelin, Olof, 499, 505
hermetic writing, 249, 266
Hermogenes, 120
heroic poetry. See epic poetry
Heroides. See letters: verse letters; under Ovid
Heron, Giles, 368
Herring, Francis, 436
Hervieu, Jean-Placide, 570
Hesiod, 243, 397
Hessus, Helius Eobanus, 47, 452, 455
Hevelius, Johannes, 267
Heynlin, Johann, 412
Hilary, Saint, 305
Hildegard of Bingen, Saint, 370
historiography, 125, 130, 151–62, 350, 467–68, 471, 487–89, 501–3, 544–45
    antiquarianism, 155–56, 162, 350–51, 413, 431–32, 463, 480, 502, 532, 533
    chorography, 156, 158–59, 161, 431–32, 463, 513–15, 517
    chronicles, 151, 154, 158, 160–62, 285–86, 494, 514, 515, 517, 536
    chronology, 154, 161, 308, 323, 415, 532, 565, 566
    ecclesiastical, 160–61, 308–9, 323
Hippocrates, 280, 287, 470
Hobbes, Thomas, 28, 146, 179, 250, 255, 309, 498
Hobson, Thomas, 244
hodoeporicon. See under travel
Hoefnagel, Jacob, 511
Hoeufft, Jacob Hendrik, 485

Hogg, William, 205
Hoius, Andreas, 480
Holberg, Ludvig, 73, 506
    Nicolai Klimii iter subterraneum, 183, 184, 192–94, 195
Holland. See Netherlands
Holonius, Gregorius, 111
Holy Land, 512. See also Crusades; Jerusalem
Holy Roman Empire. See also Habsburg dynasty
    Latin and political identity, 28, 274, 350
    translatio imperii, 153, 350, 447
Holyday, Barten, 210
Homer 105–6, 169, 207, 244, 333, 339, 399, 400, 405
    Homeric Hymns, 396
    Iliad, 58, 60, 66, 168, 535
    Odyssey, 58, 168, 405
Honerdus, Rochus, 113
Honterus, Johannes, 522
Hoole, Charles, 519
Horace, 17, 20, 169, 225, 339, 446, 464, 470, 471, 499
    Ars poetica, 112, 218, 225
    Epistles, 169, 206, 208
    Epodes, 41, 53, 448
    Odes, 22, 42, 43, 44, 45, 50, 51–52, 80, 218, 371, 400, 417, 434, 445, 448, 463, 517
    Satires, 95, 199, 200, 201, 203, 204, 206, 210, 218, 400
Horák, Jan, 95
Hosius, Stanislaus, 512
Hossche, Sidronius de, 485
Hrotsvitha of Gandersheim, 88
Huet, Albert, 514
Huguenots, 190, 207, 454. See also France
Huitfeld, Arild, 502
Hume, David, 431, 433
humor. See comedy; satire; wit
Hungarian language
    translations from Latin, 404, 519
    vernacular works, 195
Hungary, 509–22. See also Hungarian language
    historiography, 157, 511, 514, 516
    Latin and political identity, 28, 356
    represented in literature, 195
Huns, 157, 350
Hutchinson, Lucy, 368
Hutten, Leonard, 94
Hutten, Ulrich von, 206, 355, 446, 450, 453
Huygens, Constantijn, 178, 179, 484
Hyde, Thomas, 569, 570
Hyginus, 64
hymns, 42, 44, 371, 405, 510. See also Bible; Homer
Hyrde, Richard, 367

Ianua, 220–21, 226
Iberian peninsula, 270, 300, 461–73.
　　See also Portugal; Spain
　reconquista, 270
　Iberian Union, 469–70
Ibn Ḥallikān, Aḥmad ibn Muḥammad, 287
Iceland, 493–94, 495, 498. See also Icelandic
　　language; Scandinavia
Icelandic language, translations into Latin,
　　498, 502–3
Ignatius of Loyola, 59, 113–14, 206, 210, 472.
　　See also Jesuits
illustrations, 201, 271, 289, 291, 481, 519, 526, 564
　pictorial textbooks, 519
imitatio, 123, 127, 129–31, 201, 238, 354, 418–19, 429,
　　447, 464
Inchofer, Melchior, 348
India, 191, 471–72, 557, 558, 561, 564
Inglis, Esther, 368
Inglot, William, 75
Innocent XI (pope), 560
inquisition, 240, 272, 301, 469, 532. See also
　　censorship
inscriptions, 75, 160, 380, 489, 497, 552, 560.
　　See also epitaphs
　literary genre, 82, 355
　querelle des inscriptions, 28
　runic, 502
intertextuality, 321, 428, 429, 447–48, 454
　in epic poetry, 58, 60, 64,
　in lyric poetry, 51–52
　in martyrology, 428
　in satire, 210
Intorcetta, Prospero, 559–60, 561, 566–67
Ireland, 17, 21, 320, 326, 432, 435–36. See also
　　British Isles; English language
Irenaeus, 303
Isabella I (queen of Castile), 367
Isidore of Seville, 104
Islam, 280, 286, 288, 290, 291, 300, 355, 371, 513.
　　See also Muslims
Isocrates, 136
Isselt, Michael von, 488
Istanbul. See Constantinople
Istvánffy, Nicolaus, 512
Italian language, 395–405
　models for Latin literature, 62
　translations from Latin, 255, 398, 404, 519
　translations into Latin, 96, 142, 143, 185, 211,
　　255, 272–73, 290, 316, 404
　Italy, 395–405
　concept of nationhood, 350

model of Renaissance humanism, 411–12,
　　445–46, 477–78, 510–11
　schools, 217–29, 371, 387
　universities, 237, 238–39, 283–84, 373
Iturriaga, José Mariano de, 68–69, 529
Iuvencus, 66

Jackson, James, 81
Jacobites, 84, 435
Jagiellonian dynasty, 516
　Catherine, 369
James, Saint, 107
James I (king of England; also James VI of
　　Scotland), 159, 189, 240, 319, 433, 436
James II (king of England), 84
　Williamite War, 435
Janicki, Klemens, 45, 512, 517
Jansenism, 320
Japan, 2, 557, 568
Jefferson, Thomas, 551
Jerome, Saint, 321, 371. See also Bible
　Against Jovinian, 210
　Ciceronianism, 16–17
　De viris illustribus, 161
　editions, 303, 478
　letters, 173, 339
　Vulgate, 17, 22, 295, 296, 305, 314, 329–30
Jerusalem, 66, 67, 189, 289, 398–99
Jesuits. See also Counter-Reformation; missions,
　　religious; *under individual authors*
　Bollandists, 481
　criticism of, 205–6, 210, 320, 436, 532–36
　drama, 92–93, 96–98, 113–15, 405, 420, 451, 454,
　　465, 472, 482–83, 560–61
　Latin style, 326, 480
　litterae annuae, 542–43, 558–59
　poetics, 447
　poetry, 44, 60, 62, 74, 79, 400, 452, 472, 484–85,
　　527, 528–29, 547, 570
　political thought, 143, 146
　ratio studiorum, 114, 126, 242, 400, 448, 528, 557
　Relations, 542–44
　represented in literature, 59, 68–69, 189, 206,
　　210, 399, 436, 472, 529
　rhetoric, 121, 526, 528
　schools, 59, 74, 126, 264, 315–16, 326, 380,
　　448, 549
　science, 489, 528, 534, 545–46, 550–52,
　　560, 561–64
　textbooks, 447–48, 527
　theology 318–20, 321, 473, 546
Jewel, John, 368

Jiménez de Cisneros, Francisco, 462
João Manuel (prince of Portugal), 108, 472
Jogues, Isaac, 543
Johan III (king of Sweden), 496, 497
John II (king of Portugal), 469
John III (king of Portugal), 108
John IV (king of Portugal), 473
John VI (king of Portugal), 527
Johnson, Samuel (author and lexicographer), 434
Johnson, Samuel (Reverend), 550
Johnston, Arthur, 430, 434
Jonson, Ben, 43, 48
Jónsson, Arngrímur, 502
Joseph II (Holy Roman Emperor), 220
Josephus, 308
journals. See academic journals; diaries
Jouvancy, Joseph de, 545
Judaism, 66, 189, 298, 299, 308, 450, 451, 470, 509
Julius II (pope), 203
Junius, Franciscus, 329. See also Bible
Junius, Melchior, 131, 455
Jupiter (Jean de Clacy), 227, 228
Juslenius, Daniel, 502
Justinian I (Byzantine emperor), 162, 412, 413, 414
    Pandects, 413, 463
Juvenal, 194, 199–212, 412, 471
    in education, 225, 400
    imitation of, 82, 95, 186, 241–42, 419, 438

Kabátník, Martin, 512
Kabbalah, 299, 502, 519
Kalm, Pehr, 546, 551
Kant, Immanuel, 261, 498
Kangxi Emperor, 559, 564
Kappel, school of, 329, 338, 340–41
Katharina Ursula (landgravine of
        Hessen-Kassel), 369
Keckermann, Bartholomaeus, 145
Keller, Jakob, 454
Kepler, Johannes, 179, 267, 285, 511, 520, 521, 563
Ker, Anne, 36
Ker, Robert, 36
Killigrew, Katherine, 368
King, Edward, 244, 431
King, William, 206
Kircher, Athanasius, 455, 558, 563
Kirwitzer, Wenceslas Pantaleon, 561
Kitzscher, Johann von, 107
Klonowicz, Sebastianus, 517
Klose, Ernst Gottlieb, 1
Klotz, Adolf, 485
Knapp, Francis, 436

Kochanowski, Jan, 512, 517
Königsmarck, Maria Aurora von, 370
Krantz, Albert, 158
Krolikiewicz, Jan Maximilian. See Poniński, Antoni
Kromer, Martin, 159
Kunić, Rajmund, 84
Kyber, David, 272

Labé, Louise, 209, 364, 369
La Brosse, Jean-Baptiste de, 545–46
Lactantius, 104, 303, 348, 478
Laetus, Erasmus, 495, 500, 504
La Fresnaye, Vauquelin de, 210
Lagerlöf, Petrus, 500
Lahontan, Louis Armand de, 546, 552
Lambin, Denis, 415
Lampridio, Benedetto, 43
Lance, William, 552
Landino, Cristoforo, 42, 44, 45, 59, 401
Landívar, Rafael, 62, 528, 534
Landor, Walter Savage, 427, 428, 435, 439
Landsberg, Herrad von, 370
Landshut, War of the Succession of, 65
Lane, Edward William, 289
Lange, Johann Michael, 517
Lanyer, Aemilia, 365
Lapide, Cornelius a, 321
Larousse, Pierre, 382
La Salle, Jean-Baptiste de, 384
Lascaris, Constantinus, 365
Lascaris, Giano, 253, 255, 259
Latin language. See also under scholasticism:
        scholastic Latin
    barbarisms, 22, 253, 257–58, 260, 282, 291, 338
    grammar books, 32, 218–27, 334, 339
    medieval Latin, 1–2, 13–24, 186, 270, 279, 281–82, 335
    spoken, 21, 31–33, 93, 221, 233, 236, 264, 315–17,
        369, 498, 513, 553
    vocabulary
        medieval Latin, 19
        Neo-Latin, 22–23, 24
        philosophical, 256–58
    vulgar Latin, 14–19
Latomus, Bartholomaeus, 485
Latin America, 189, 525–37. See also Portuguese
        language; Spanish language
    Brazil, 472, 527, 528, 529
    Spanish America
        Baja California, 68–69, 529
        Mexico, 28, 68, 316, 525, 526, 527, 529–36
        Paraguay, 534
        Peru, 183, 191, 526, 528, 529, 530, 532

Lauremberg, Johann, 209, 497
Lausanne, Academy of, 336, 337
Laval, François de, 544
law, 452, 526
    academic study of, 236, 251, 264, 288, 373, 512
        legal oratory, 121, 128, 334
        university course, 221, 227, 239, 263
    canon, 235, 239, 527
    Latin style, 19, 354
    legal profession, 30, 91, 128, 202, 204, 239, 400
    natural law (*ius naturale*), 145–46, 467, 506
    Roman law, 105, 112, 139, 152, 413–15, 463
Lawrence, John, 551
Lazzarelli, Lodovico, 396, 397
Le Brun, Laurent, 547
Le Comte, Louis Daniel, 565
lectures, 242, 366–67, 412, 461, 527, 545–46
    medical, 263, 267–68
    on language and literature, 288, 308, 339,
        462, 464
    pedagogical, 333, 447, 466
    philosophical, 145, 263, 271
Ledesma, Miguel, 282
Lee, Edward, 304
Leech, John, 433, 434
Lefaure, Jacques, 561
Lefèvre d'Etaples, Jacques, 241, 304, 415
Lefevre, Tanneguy, 388
Legge, Thomas, 109
Legrand, Antonius, 188
Le Roy, Albert, 203
Leibniz, Gottfried Wilhelm, 3, 255, 256, 261, 457,
    513, 562, 568
Leiden, University of, 211, 267, 287, 480, 481, 482
Leipzig, University of, 80
Le Jay, Gabriel, 96
Lejay, Guy Michel, 308
Le Jeune, Paul, 543
Leland, John, 428, 429, 431
Le Mire, Aubert, 177, 488
Lemnius, Simon, 95, 331, 450, 454
Lenard, Alexander, 195
Leo X (pope), 60, 66, 203, 281, 290, 479
Leo XIII (pope), 405
Leo Africanus, 290–91
Leoniceno, Nicolò, 283
Leonori, Aristide, 317
Lepanto, Battle of, 527
Lernutius, Janus, 484
L'Escot, Pierre, 420
Lessius, Leonardus, 146, 489
Leto, Pomponio, 90

letters, 167–80, 366, 403, 455, 465, 473, 518, 531,
    562. *See also* Jesuits: litterae annuae *and*
    Relations; *under individual authors*
    guides to letter writing, 127–28, 173, 177, 455, 501
    letterbooks, 74–75, 366, 367
    letter-essays, 168, 174, 178
    satirical, 206, 450
    self-fashioning in, 167–69, 171, 174, 176–77
    verse letters, 42, 45, 47, 169, 206, 397, 401,
        418–19, 445, 452, 455, 497, 498–99, 527
Leuven
    Collegium Trilingue, 300, 479
    University of, 478
Leverett, John, 550
Levita, Elias, 299
Lewis, John, 553
L'Hospital, Michel de, 206, 420
Libanius, 120
Libens, Jacobus, 483
liber amicorum. *See* autograph books
liberal arts, 119, 124, 126, 339, 447. *See also studia
    humanitatis*
    trivium, 235, 331, 496
Lilia, Georg, 499
Lilienthal, Michael, 449
Lily, William, 341
Linnaeus, 266, 269, 274, 505, 550–51, 564
Lippi da Colle, Lorenzo, 202, 400
Lipsius, Justus, 479, 511, 513, 518
    edition of Seneca, 137
    letters, 125, 176–78, 179,
    Lipsianism, 21, 480, 484
    Lovanium, 488
    political writing, 135–36, 139–41, 144, 346, 348,
        355, 480
    Somnium (*Satyra Menippea*), 196, 205, 210, 480, 487
    Stoicism, 176, 177–78, 313, 480
litterae annuae. *See under* Jesuits
liturgy, 297
    bilingual, 32
    in China, 560, 569, 570
    Greek, 301
    Latin, 2, 16, 18, 19, 314, 315, 322, 526, 569, 570
    Mass, 314, 493
    poetry, 396
    vernacular, 314, 493, 569
Livingston, John H., 549
Livy, 151, 153, 154, 324, 349, 471, 487, 535, 565
Locatello, Boneto, 286, 287
Loccenius, Johannes, 500
Locher, Jakob, 28, 107, 211, 453
Locke, John, 381, 387

Loeffs, Rodolphus, 478
Logan, James, 550–51
logic
    academic study of, 290, 296, 462, 478
        controversies, 240–42
        Latin terminology, 251–52
        in schools, 221, 227–28,
    Aristotelian, 227, 237, 331, 334–35, 339, 403, 528
    Averroian, 282
    Cartesian, 549
    Ramist, 122–23, 240–42, 244
Lombard, Peter, 296, 305
Lombardelli, Orazio, 236
London
    represented in literature, 47, 432
    St. Paul's School, 125, 341
Longueil, Christophe de, 413
Longinus. *See* Pseudo-Longinus
Longobardo, Niccolò, 558
Longolius, Christophorus, 21
Longus, 369
López, Baltázar, 528
López de Zúñiga, Diego, 300, 304, 308, 462
Lorichius, Reinhard, 449
Loschi, Antonio, 105, 404
Louis II (king of Hungary and Bohemia), 515
Louis XI (king of France), 415
Louis XII (king of France), 414
Louis XIII (king of France), 191
Louis XIV (king of France), 62, 191
Louis XVI (king of France), 548
Louis XVII (king of France), 548
Lovati, Lovato de', 13, 21, 104
Low Countries, 34, 74, 80, 88, 173, 203, 477–89.
        See also Dutch language; Netherlands
Loynes, Antoinette de, 368
Lucan, 58, 67, 225, 352, 427, 435, 436, 505
Lucchesini, Giovanni Lorenzo, 203, 400
Lucian, 187, 200, 355, 402, 453
    Dialogues of the Dead, 446
    paradoxical encomium, 200, 207, 453
    translations into Latin, 3, 206, 478
Lucilius, 199, 200, 203, 207
Lucretia, 403
Lucretius, 58, 368, 436–38, 485
Ludovicus Sanctus of Beringen, 168
Lumley, Jane, 368
Lund, Zacharias, 499
Luther, Martin, 329–42
    criticism of, 95, 111, 304, 314–15, 317, 318–19,
        450–51, 479
    letters, 455

Lutheranism, 112, 126, 160, 204, 304, 330,
        331–35, 452, 494–95
    poetry, 331–32
    theology, 2, 115, 237, 300, 304, 306–9, 450
    Tischreden, 29, 331
Luxembourg. *See* Low Countries
Lwów (Lviv), 521
Ly, André, 570
Lycophron, 413,
Lydgate, John, 33
Lyon, 172, 286, 411–12, 417
Lysias, translations of, 171

macaronic writing, 30–33, 92, 99, 207–8, 428, 465,
        487. *See also* bilingualism; multilingualism
Macau, Colégio de Madre de Deus, 565, 569
Machado, Diogo Barbosa, 471
Machiavelli, 90, 142, 143, 162, 346, 471, 480
    Machiavellianism, 142–43
Macrin, Salmon, 204, 417, 419
Macrobius, 20, 184
Macropedius, Georgius, 8, 91, 92, 93, 482, 483
Madruzzo dynasty, 59
Magalhães, Gabriel de, 565
Magdalen College School, 32
Magdeburg Centuries, 160, 323, 331
Magdeburg, Mechthild von, 370
Magnus, Johannes, 494, 501
Magnus, Olaus, 494, 501
Magnússon, Árni, 503
Major, Johannes, 450
Major, John, 432
Major, William, 210
Makernesse, William, 81
Makin, Bathsua, 368, 373
Malatesta dynasty, 397, 399
    Paola, 365
    Sigismondo, 64, 397
Maldonado, Juan, 462, 465, 466, 467
Mal Lara, Juan de, 465
Malpighi, Marcello, 266
Malvezzi, Paracleto, 399
Manardo, Giovanni, 179, 283
Manchu language, 562, 563, 467–68, 567, 570
    translations into Latin, 562
    translations into Manchu, 570
Manchus, 559. *See also* China
Manetho, 152
Manetti, Giannozzo, 296–99, 402
Manilius, 58, 67, 427, 438
Manso, Giovanni Armonio, 105
Mantino, Jacob, 281

Mantuan, Battista Spagnoli, 339, 395–96, 398, 463, 464, 471
Manzini della Motta, Giovanni, 105
Manuzio, Aldo, 112, 172, 300, 339
Manuzio, Paolo, 176
maps. *See* cartography
Marchina, Marta, 403
Margaret I (queen of Denmark), 504
Margarit, Joan, 467
marginalia, 30–31, 33, 141, 151, 207, 268, 297, 321, 330, 349
Maria of Aragon (queen of Portugal), 367
Maria Manuela (princess of Portugal), 146
Mariana, Juan de, 136
Mariano, Marco Probo, 399
Maria Theresa (archduchess of Austria), 386
Marinella, Lucrezia, 364
Marineo Siculo, Lucio, 157
Marius, Hadrianus, 483
Marot, Clément, 417
Marquets, Anne de, 371–72
Marrasio, Giovanni, 400
Marsuppini, Carlo, 351
Martens, Dirk, 174, 478
Martí, Manuel, 532
Martial, 20, 48, 53, 73, 74, 79, 438, 471
Martianus Capella, 20, 88
Martini, Martino, 559, 560, 563, 565–66, 567
Martirano, Coriolano, 110, 405
Mártires, Bartolomeu dos, 470
Martorello, Baldo, 365
martyrs
    martyrology, 321, 323
    represented in literature, 44, 88, 97, 98, 111, 114–15, 399, 449, 451, 472, 482–83
Marullus, Michael, 42, 396, 417
Marvell, Andrew, 428, 434
Mary, Virgin, 47, 59, 68–69, 113, 304, 320, 322–23
    of Guadalupe, 528–29, 534
Mary I (queen of England), 237
Mary II (queen of England), 84
Mary of Austria (Mary of Hungary), 516
Mary of Burgundy, 477
Masen, Jacob, 98, 447
Masius, Andreas, 299, 308
Massa, Nicolò, 286–87
Massimi, Pacifico, 400
Masson, Jacques, 305, 306
Masters, Thomas, 436
mathematics. *See also* Euclid; science
    academic study of, 2–3, 263, 266, 272, 489, 520–22, 561–62

Arabic sources, 257, 270, 283, 284–85, 288, 290
    arithmetic, 267, 339, 457
    geometry, 265, 339, 521–22
    Greek sources, 267, 270
    vernacular tradition, 265–66, 272–73
Mather, Cotton, 549, 552
Mather, Increase, 549
Mattioli, Pietro Andrea, 271
Maupertuis, Jean-Baptiste Drouet de, 210
Maurice (Byzantine emperor), 454
Maury, Jean, 211
Maximilian I (Holy Roman Emperor), 65, 355, 453, 517
Maximilian II (Holy Roman Emperor), 511
Maximus, Valerius, 142, 255
Mayans y Siscar, Gregorio, 468
May, Thomas, 67, 427
McCartney, George, 569
Medici dynasty, 272, 395
    Cosimo de', 171
    Lorenzo de', 172
medicine, 263–74
    academic study of, 251, 257
        debates, 243
        dissertations and orations, 457, 551
        university courses, 221, 227, 237, 239, 263, 267, 384
    anatomy, 209, 267, 287, 373, 489
    Arabic sources, 279, 281–82, 283, 285, 287, 288, 290
    Chinese, 564
    letters, 179
    represented in literature, 30, 43–44, 57, 81–83, 201, 204, 207–8, 209, 243, 398, 450
    vernacular writing about, 265, 268
Mehmed II (Ottoman sultan), 351
Mehus, Lorenzo, 161
Melanchthon, Philipp, 329–42
    educational program, 2, 228, 332–35, 337, 340, 448, 494–95, 496
    letters, 455
    rhetorical writing, 123, 126, 129, 307, 332–35, 447
    theology, 108, 306–7, 332, 341, 450
Melkites, Christian, 287
Melville, Andrew, 52, 427, 435
Mem de Sá, 472, 527
Menander, 94
Menander Rhetor, 499
Ménard, René, 543, 544
Mennander, Fredrik, 506
Mendoza dynasty, 367–68
    Diego Hurtado de, 368

Menippean satire. *See* satire
Mencke, Otto, 562
Mentzel, Christian, 568
Mercator, Gerard, 489
Mercier, Louis Sébastien, 386
Merian, Maria Sibylla, 273
Mersenne, Marin, 421
Messenius, Johannes, 502, 503
Mesue, 279, 282, 283, 288
metaphysics. *See* philosophy
meter, 41–54. *See also* Scaliger, Julius
    Caesar: *Poetics*
  free verse, 82
  neglected, 88, 89
  polymetra, 42, 499
  textbooks, 43, 130–31, 447
Mexico. *See under* Latin America
Meursius, Johannes, 497, 502
Mey, Guilelmus de, 210
Mezzo, Tommaso, 90
Michelangelo, 172
Michel de Marbais, 227
Micraelius, Johannes, 250
Micyllus, Jacobus, 454
Milan, 155
  court literature, 61, 171, 399
Milescu, Nicolae, 569
Miletto Rossi, Checco di, 395
Milich, Jacob, 286, 287
Milne, Alan Alexander, 195
Milton, John, 487
  academic career, 47, 235, 243–44, 431
  bilingualism, 28, 53–54, 192, 244, 428
  Latin poetry, 243–44, 427, 428–29, 431–32, 434
    Elegies, 45, 47, 243–44, 428–29, 432
    Epitaphium Damonis, 428, 431, 432, 433–34
    In quintum Novembris, 243–44, 432, 436
    Naturam non pati senium, 243, 437
    Ode to John Rouse, 43
Miltopaeus, Martin, 500
Mirandola, Gianfrancesco Pico della, 131, 173
Mirandola, Giovanni Pico della, 173, 249, 252–53,
    256, 260, 287, 299, 396
mirrors for princes. *See* political writing
missions, religious
  Asia, 321, 326, 557–70
  Ireland, 17
  Latin America, 68–69, 321, 326, 525–37
  Middle East, 288, 290
  North America, 541–53
Mitrou, Meletios, 513
  mnemonics, 222, 227, 334

Modena, Academy of, 387
modistic grammar.
    See under scholasticism
Moerbeke, William of, 112
Mohács, Battle of, 515–16
Moldavia, 513–14
Molière, 30, 115, 380
Molina, Luis de, 146
Mollerus, Henricus, 503
Molza, Tarquinia, 74, 403
Monardes, Nicolas, 268
Monavius, Jacob, 44
Monck, George (Duke of Albemarle), 81–83
Mondoré, Pierre, 420
Monmori Parasitosycophantosophistae
    Apochytrapotheôsis, 205
Montagnais language, 546
Montaigne, Michel de, 364, 372
  addressee of Latin writing, 204
  Essais, 176, 241, 255, 380, 420
  Latin education, 109, 236, 240, 241
Montanus, Petrus, 203, 208, 209
Monte, Philippe de, 511
Monteiro, Manuel, 471
Monte Simoncelli, Balduino de, 207
Montenay, Georgette de, 35–36
Montesquieu, 162, 180, 536
Montpellier, University of, 267
Morais, Inácio de, 471
moral philosophy. *See* ethics;
    philosophy: moral
Morata, Olympia, 365, 370, 403
More, Thomas, 2–3, 28, 73–74, 368, 413,
    427, 482–83
  Utopia, 73, 184, 187–89, 206, 355
Morel, Camille de, 368–69
Morel, Diane de, 368–69
Morel, Jean de, 368–69, 372, 420
Morel, Lucrece de, 368–69
Moretus, Balthasar, 481
Morhof, Daniel Georg, 121, 129, 131, 457
Morison, Samuel, 549–50
Morisot, Claude-Barthélemy, 191
Morocco, 472, 489
Morrell, William, 548
Moscow, 187, 326
Mornay, Philippe de, 30–31
Mosellanus, Petrus, 305
Moulin, Charles du, 354
Moyrac de Mailla, Joseph de, 566
Muhlenberg, Henry, 550–51
Müller, Andreas, 563, 568

multilingualism, 29–37, 251, 259, 431, 519. *See also* bilingualism; macaronic writing
    dictionaries, 31
    textbooks, 31–33
Münster, Sebastian, 299–300, 308
Muratori, Ludovico Antonio, 220
Muret, Marc-Antoine, 109, 110, 140, 176, 204, 414, 419, 484
Murmellius, Johannes, 339
music, 172
    in education, 339, 561
    sacred, 41–42, 51–53, 75, 405
Muslims, 288, 289, 290, 509, 530. *See also* Islam
Mussato, Albertino, 104–5, 115, 355, 404–5
Myle, Abraham Van der, 488

Nabod, Valentin, 283, 284–85
Nádasdy, Tamás, 516
Nahuatl language, 534
    influenced by Latin, 530
    translations from Latin, 530
    translations into Latin, 532
Naldi, Naldo, 395
Nannius, Petrus, 207, 482, 486
Naogeorgus, Thomas, 95, 109, 110, 115, 204, 450–51, 453
Naples, 155, 397, 402
    Academy of, 369
    Collegio de' Sinesi, 569–70
Napoleon, 384
nationalism. *See also* political writing; propaganda
    clerical, 316
    criticism of, 174–76
    historiography, 158–59, 413, 431–32, 487–88, 501–3, 514–17
    in poetry, 445, 446, 503–5
    and Roman empire, 347–48, 350–51
    and vernaculars, 274, 411
Native Americans. *See* Americas (continents): indigenous peoples
natural history, 263, 264, 266, 267, 268–270, 274, 290, 550–51, 564. *See also* botany; philosophy; zoology
natural philosophy. *See* science
Nau, Sébastien (or Jean), 210
Navagero, Andrea, 42, 397, 401, 402
Navarre, Marguerite de, 368, 371
Nazareo, Pablo, 530
Nazianzen, Gregory, Saint, 296
Nebrija, Antonio de, 300, 308, 462, 463, 465, 467, 468, 470

Nebrija, Sancho de, 467
Needham, Peter, 195
Nepos, Cornelius, 218
Nero (Roman emperor), 105, 137, 205, 349
Netherlands, 122, 139, 210, 372, 566. *See also* Dutch language; Low Countries
New Spain. *See* Latin America
New World. *See* Americas (continents)
Newton, Isaac, 3, 23, 179, 266, 273, 520, 521
Nicholas V (pope), 151, 296, 351, 402
Nicholas of Cusa, 255
Nicholas of Lyra, 295
Nicolai, Laurentius, 497
Nicolaus the Sophist, 120
Nicocles (king of Salamis), 136
Nifo, Agostino, 249
Nilssøn, Jens, 497
Nîmes, Academy of, 336
Nizzoli (Nizolio), Mario, 21, 403, 416
Noël, François, 567
Nogarola, Giulia, 371
Nogarola, Isotta, 363–64, 366, 403
Nolte, Johann Friedrich, 22–23
Norman, Georg, 503
North America, 2, 7, 74, 135, 541–53. *See also* English language; French language
    New England, 547–53
    New France, 541–47
    United States of America, 7, 388, 548
Norton, John, 549
Norway, 73, 493, 494–95. *See also* Scandinavia
notaries, 221, 227, 352, 399
novel, novella. *See* prose fiction
Noviforensis, Johannes, 510
Nugent, Thomas, 22
numismatics, 156, 157, 557
Núñez, Hernan de Toledo, 300, 462
Núñez, Pedro Juan, 121
Nuremberg, 158, 333, 370
Nusser, Balthasar, 453

Oakes, Urian, 550
Oberammergau Passion Play, 109
Oboi, Gûwalgiya, 559
    Oboi regency, 560
occasional poetry, 42, 449, 498–501, 518
Octavian. *See* Augustus (Roman emperor)
Odasi, Tifi, 207
odes, 83, 171, 434. *See also* Celtis; Filelfo; Horace; Pindar
Oecolampadius, Johannes, 299
Oláh, Miklós, 514, 515, 516, 520

Olai, Ericus, 501
Old Norse language. *See* Icelandic language, translations into Latin
Oldenburg, Henry, 179
Oliver, Pere Joan, 465
O'Meara, Dermot, 21, 22, 61, 435
Omphalius, Jakob, 354
Opitz, Martin, 446, 452, 455, 456
Oporinus, Johannes, 334, 516
Oppian, 58
Oradea, 520, 521
oratory, 119–31, 403, 486, 528. *See also imitatio*; schools; universities
  and philosophy, 253, 334–35, 404, 405, 478
  political, 351–54
  progymnasmata, 120, 123, 131, 449, 500, 501
  sacred, 122, 403, 526 (*see also* preaching)
  satirical, 207
  in schools, 218, 222, 224
  textbooks, 121–23, 126–31, 222, 224, 334–35, 354, 403, 447, 500–1, 526, 528
Oresme, Nicole, 272
oriental studies, 279–91, 299, 308, 480, 505, 557–70. *See also* Arabic language; Asia
Origen, 303, 304, 305
Orosius, 154
Orphic hymns, 41, 42, 52, 243
Orsini del Balzo, Giovanni Antonio, 399
Orta, Garcia da, 268
Oslo, 497
Osório, Jerónimo, 471, 473
Ostrogothus, Petrus Michaelis, 500
Ottoman empire, Ottomans. *See also* Constantinople
  conflict with Christian Europe, 172, 355, 509, 511, 515
  education, 288, 513
  represented in historiography, 513
  represented in dialogues, 465
  represented in literature, 107, 191, 399, 445–46, 451, 453, 527
  represented in oratory, 354, 367, 373
  represented in travel accounts, 280, 289, 455, 489
Otranto, Battle of, 399
Oudin, François, 62
Overbury, Thomas, 190
Ovid, 45, 372, 400, 455
  Amores, 76
  Ars Amatoria, 438–39
  Epistulae ex Ponto, 47, 244, 418–19, 499
  Fasti, 68, 397
  Heroides, 401, 445, 497

  Metamorphoses, 58, 64, 106, 185, 218, 399, 435
    in schools, 224, 337
  Tristia, 218, 517
Owen, John, 78, 427, 434
Oxford, University of, 35, 81, 84, 88, 237, 274, 287, 569
  anthologies of verse, 35, 81, 431
  Balliol College, 210
  Christ Church, 94, 95
  drama, 90, 94, 109, 110

Pace, Giulio, 518
Pacheco, Francisco, 204, 206, 208–9, 210, 472
Pacheco, Maria, 368
Padua
  Accademia degli Infiammati, 253
  Accademia degli Recovrati, 373
  early humanism in, 13, 104–5, 115, 355
  University of, 237, 267, 373, 512
Pagninus, Sanctes, 298–300
Paiva de Andrade, Diogo, 470, 472, 473
Palencia, Alfonso de, 465
Palingenio Stellato, Marcello, 397–98
Palladius (bishop), 421
Pallini, Girolamo, 210
Pallu, François, 561
Palmireno, Juan Lorenzo, 92, 462
Paludanus, Peter, 305
Paman, Henry, 81
panegyrical writing, 59, 171, 235, 352, 452–54, 499. *See also* patronage; political writing; propaganda
  religious, 69, 371
Pannonius, Janus, 512, 518, 520
Panormita. *See* Beccadelli, Antonio (Panormita)
Panter, Patrick, 435
Panvinio, Onofrio, 160
Paré, Ambroise, 265
papacy, 95, 110, 153, 160, 347–48, 402, 450–51, 560, 569. *See also under individual popes*; Vatican
  papal curia, 155, 170, 348, 356, 568
  Pontifical Academy for Latin, 317
Pappus, 267
Paracelsus, 265
Paraguay. *See under* Latin America
Parentucelli, Tommaso. *See* Nicholas V (pope)
Pareus, David, 450
Paris, 411–22
  Colleges, 211, 240–42
    Collège de l'Ave Maria, 240, 242
    Collège de Coqueret, 420

Paris (*cont.*)
  Collège du Mans, 240
  Collège de la Marche, 336
  Collège Mazarin, 121
  Collège de Navarre, 91, 237
  Collège de Presles, 240
  Collège Royal, 240, 283, 287, 288,
    300, 411–12
  Collège de Sainte Barbe, 109, 240, 241
  Parlement de, 354
  represented in literature, 209, 234, 241, 354,
    386, 453
  Royal Academy of Sciences, 266
  schools, 221, 226
  University of, 227, 237–38, 240, 412
    Sorbonne (Faculty of Theology), 412, 421
Parry, William, 436
Parkhurst, John, 75
Parmenius, Stephanus, 547
Parrenin, Dominique, 570
Partenio, Giuseppe Maria, 368
Pascoli, Giovanni, 405
Pascal, 179
Pasquale, Carlo, 350, 354, 355
Pasquier, Etienne, 415–16
Passi, Giuseppe, 364
pastoral poetry, 395–97, 421, 431, 432–34, 453, 473,
    495, 500, 504
  in Virgilian career, 57, 65
Pastorius, Francis Daniel, 552
Pastorius, Joachim, 125
Patavina, Diamante, 373
Patin, Charles, 388
Patrick, Saint, 320
patristic writing, 295–312, 313, 319, 321–22, 323–34,
    338, 346, 478
Patrizi, Francesco, 136, 250
patronage, 53, 58–61, 153, 171–72, 242–43, 498–99,
    527. *See also* panegyrical writing;
    political
  writing; propaganda
Paul III (pope), 281
Paul V (pope), 189, 479
Paul of Venice, 283
Paul, Saint. *See* Bible
Pauw, Cornelius de, 534, 535
Paz, Catalina, 368
Pearson, John, 308
Pecci, Gioacchino Vincenzo, 405
Pedersen, Christiern, 494
Pedrosa, Francisco de, 527
Peiresc, Nicolas-Claude Fabri de, 179

Pelagianism, 303, 304
Pellegrino, Fulvio, 365
Pellicanus, Conrad, 299
Penn, William, 550
Peramás, Jose Manuel, 528, 534, 536
Peregrinatio Aetheriae, 17
Pereira, Bartolomeu, 472
Pereira, Lucas, 473
Pérez, Juan, 90, 465
periochae, 97, 98
Périon, Jacques, 416
Perotti, Niccolò, 20, 222, 223, 226, 228, 338, 401
Perpinhão, Pedro, 470
Persian language, 308
Persius, 199, 200, 203, 210, 225, 400, 419
Peru. *See under* Latin America
Peter of Spain, 339
Peter I the Great (tsar of Russia), 562
Peter of Ghent, 530
Peter Martyr. *See* Anghiera, Pietro Martire d'
Petrarch, 1, 13, 260, 295–96, 349–50
  Africa, 60–61, 62–63, 398
  bilingualism, 53–54
  Bucolicum carmen, 395
  Canzoniere, 456
  Ciceronianism, 130, 138
  drama, 88–89
  letters, 88, 167–70, 176, 280, 402–3, 510
    verse letters, 42
Petri, Laurentius Gothus, 496
Petronius, 184, 200, 205–6
Peucer, Caspar, 514
Peuerbach, Georg, 521, 522
Phaedrus, 218
Philadelphia, College of, 551
Philip II (king of Spain), 160, 467, 530
Philip IV (king of Spain), 385, 473
Philip V (king of Spain), 533
Philippe I (duke of Orléans), 68
Philippe II (of Chartres; duke of Orléans), 68
Philo, 308
philosophy, 249–61. *See also* Arabic language;
    Chinese language; Greek language;
    Hebrew language
  bilingualism, 265–66
  dictionaries of, 250, 258
  in letters, 172–73, 175–78
  metaphysics, 249, 250–51, 257, 258, 259, 290,
    421, 519
  moral, 124, 151, 152, 175, 346, 349 (*see also*
    ethics)
  philhellenism, 255

political (*see* political writing)
  represented in poetry, 58, 204, 243
  represented in prose fiction, 185, 187, 193, 205–6
  scholastic (*See* scholasticism)
  taxonomy, 250, 256–58
  translations of philosophical works, 249–61,
    421–22, 566–67
  vernacular, 255–56, 265
Philip, James, 435
Phrygius, Sylvester Johannis, 496
physics. *See* science
Piccolomini, Alessandro, 90, 465, 478
Piccolomini, Enea Silvio, 124, 395, 478, 511
  Chrysis, 89
  Cinthia, 45, 400–401
  Commentarii, 355, 402
  De gestis concilii Basiliensis, 402
  De Europa, 511, 514
  Historia Bohemica, 158, 511
  Historia de duobus amantibus, 184, 185–86, 404
  Historia rerum Friderici III imperatoris, 511
  letters, 173, 174
  as pope (Pius II), 171, 351, 367
Picot, Claude, 421
Piegadi, Alessandro, 316
Pietro d'Abano, 285
Pietro da Isolella, 221, 226, 228
Pilladus, Laurentius, 453
Pindar, 41, 42–43, 44, 45, 453
Pinelo, Valentina de, 371
Pio, Alberto, 306
Pirckheimer, Charitas, 370
Pirkheimer, Willibald, 207, 450, 455
Pires, Diogo, 472
Pisani, Ugolino, 89–90
Piscopia, Elena Lucrezia Cornaro, 372–73, 403
Pitcairne, Archibald, 84
Pius II (pope). *See* Piccolomini, Enea Silvio
Pius III (pope), 113
Pizan, Christine de, 363
Plantin, Christophe, 307, 322, 481. *See also*
  printing
Platina. *See* Sacchi, Bartolomeo
Plato, 144, 172, 243, 249, 250–51, 252, 253, 256,
    265–66, 402
  Laws, 136
  Neo-Platonism, 172–73, 266, 403–4, 515, 519
  Republic, 136, 187, 534
  Timaeus, 270
  translations into Latin, 172, 249, 270, 402
Plautus, 20, 88, 89, 91, 99, 108, 239, 404, 482
  Amphitruo, 107

editions, 90, 464
  vocabulary, 22, 535
Pléiade, 368, 417–19, 420, 483
Pliny the Elder, 209, 268, 270, 413, 462, 470, 564
Pliny the Younger
  Panegyricus, 352
  letters, 168, 173, 176, 339
Plutarch, 171, 471, 478
  Lives, 153, 402
  Moralia, 136
  translations of, 171, 478
Podocataro, Filippo, 520–21
poetics, 398, 446–47, 470, 499. *See also* Aristotle;
    Scaliger; Vida
Poggio Bracciolini, Gian Francesco, 135, 174, 298,
    351, 402, 515
  Facetiae, 186
  historiography, 155
  letters, 171
Poitiers, 364
Poland, 509–10, 512, 517, 520. *See also*
    East-Central Europe; Polish language
  Latin works about, 159, 205
Pole, Reginald, 143
Polish language
  textbooks, 31
  translations from Latin, 404
political writing, 135–46, 345–56, 452. *See also*
    apologetic writing; Jesuits: political
    thought; patronage; panegyrical writing;
    propaganda
  civic humanism, 135, 345–46, 351–52
  mirrors for princes, 135–46, 234, 480
  monarchical writing, 135
  reason of state, 143, 346, 350
  republican writing, 135, 138, 147, 154–55,
    351–52, 552
Poliziano, Angelo, 412, 471
  Latin style, 260
  letters, 171, 174
  poetry, 45, 73, 79, 370, 429, 463–64, 486
  scholarship, 256–57, 300–301, 338
Polo, Marco, 563
Polybius, 153, 346
polyglot writing. *See* multilingualism
Pomerania, 107, 158
Pomponazzi, Pietro, 253, 255, 403
Pomponius Mela, 462
Poniński, Antoni, 205
Pontano, Giovanni, 136, 196, 369, 469
  dialogues, 207, 402
  poetry, 42, 45, 46, 48, 67, 73, 396, 417

Pontanus, Jacob, 449, 499
Pontanus, Johannes Isacius, 158–59, 502
Pope, Alexander, 77, 430, 437
Popham, Edward, 437
Porphyrio, Pomponius, 206
Porée, Charles, 98
Porta, Giambattista della, 90, 91
Porthan, Henrik Gabriel, 503, 506
Portugal, 468–73, 525, 527, 557, 560, 564, 570.
    See also Latin America: Brazil;
    Portuguese language
  universities, 469
Portuguese language
  textbooks, 31
  translations into Latin, 471, 472
  vernacular works, 268, 537, 569
Porzio, Simone, 403
Possevino, Antonio, 326
Postel, Guillaume, 287, 288
Posthius, Johannes, 454
Potier, Pierre, 541, 545–46
Powel, David, 432
Prague, 369, 510–11, 519–20
Prasch, Johann Ludwig, 184, 194, 195
Prasch, Susanna, 194
Pratensis, Johannes, 500
Prato, Felice da, 299
preaching, 34, 119, 125, 186, 354, 403, 450, 486
  Latin and vernacular, 122
Prefát, Oldřich, 512
Prémare, Joseph de, 568, 570
Presbyterianism, 320
Price, John, 432
printing, 265, 269, 271, 369, 411–12, 422
  Arabic type, 287–88
  Bible, 299, 300
  in China, 560, 567–69
  in Latin America, 527
Priscian, 120, 220, 341
Procopius, 154
progymnasmata. See under oratory
propaganda. *See also* nationalism; panegyrical
    writing; patronage; political writing
  Crusades, 354
  political, 107, 154, 158, 159–60, 345, 355, 467–68,
    503–5, 517–18, 536
  religious, 59, 114, 323, 448, 451, 560
  war, 34, 420
Propertius, 45, 47, 60, 518
prose fiction, 129, 183–95, 205, 486–87, 502–3
  chivalric, 62, 92
  novella, 185–86

roman à clef, 189–90, 191–92
  romantic, 190, 194
  satirical, 187–88, 189–90, 192, 196
  somnia, 196, 466 (*see also* Lipsius, Justus)
  utopian, 187–89, 193, 466
proverbs, 34, 131, 186, 205, 269, 336, 355. *See also*
    Erasmus: *Adagia*
Prudentius, 41, 44, 50, 224, 339, 471, 472
Psalms. *See* Bible
Pseudo-Dionysius, 296
Pseudo-Longinus, 120
Pseudo-Quintilian, 120
Ptolemy, 265, 270, 280, 284–85, 437
Pufendorf, Samuel, 146, 452, 497, 503
Puritanism, 52, 315
Pusculo, Ubertino, 399
Puteanus, Erycius, 27, 178, 211, 484, 486, 487
Puttenham, George, 44
Pythagoras, 243, 369

Quarrel of the Ancients and the Moderns, 506
querelle des femmes. See under gender
Qing dynasty, 562, 569. *See also* Kangxi Emperor
Quintianus Stoa, Giovanni Francesco, 44,
    110, 113
Quintilian, 20, 108, 124, 125, 126, 169, 224, 242,
    258, 339, 353
  commentaries on, 470
  and declamation, 120, 128

Rabe, Jacob, 204
rabbinical tradition, 300
  commentaries, 295, 299
  Masorah, 299, 301
Rabelais, François, 28, 242
Rader, Matthäus, 455
Radulphus Brito, 227
Ragueneau, Paul, 543, 544
Raimondi, Giovan Battista, 288
Ramus, Petrus, 3, 122–23, 235, 240, 241, 415, 497
  Ramism, 244, 415
Randolph, Thomas, 43
Raphael, 172
Raphelengius, Franciscus, 480
Rapin, René, 67, 420–21
Rashi, 295
ratio studiorum. See under Jesuits
Rauwolf, Leonard, 290
Ravasini, Tommaso, 397
Ray, John, 269
Raynal, Guillaume Thomas, 534, 536
Rede, Edward, 75

Reformation, Protestant 2, 3, 329–42.
    See also Counter-Reformation
    biblical scholarship, 306–9
    and drama, 93, 95, 111–13, 115, 450–51
    and historiography, 160, 349
    and humanist education, 237, 264, 329–42, 447,
        479, 494–95
    represented in literature, 67, 450–51
    and vernaculars, 236, 329–42, 493, 517
Regio, Raffaello, 399
Regiomontanus, Johannes, 521
Régnier, Mathurin, 210
Reid, Thomas, 427
Reis, António dos, 471
Remigius, 104
Renouard, Antoine-Augustin, 79
Resen, Peder Hansen, 502–3
Resende, André de, 470, 471, 472
Restić, Junije Antonio, 203, 206,
Reuchlin, Johannes, 91–92, 95, 299, 303, 304,
        450, 455
Reusner, Nikolaus, 455
Révai, Ferenc, 516
Reyes, Alfonso, 537
Rhazes, 279, 280, 285, 287, 288
Rhenanus, Beatus, 446
Rheticus, Georg Joachim, 520
rhetoric. *See* oratory
Rhetores Latini Minores, 12
Rhetoric to Alexander, 120
Rhetoric to Herennius, 120, 224
Rhodius, Theodor, 454
Ribe, 498
Ricci, Matteo, 559, 566, 568
Riccioli, Giambattista, 285
Rich, Henry (earl of Holland), 243, 244
Richard of Middleton, 305
Rienzo, Cola di, 351
Rigault, Nicolas, 205
Rimini, court literature, 397, 399
Riofrío, Bernardo Ceinos de, 528
Ritter, Georg, 80
Rizzoni, Martino, 366
Robert, Claude, 162
Robert (king of Naples), 63, 170
Roberti, Giambattista, 535
Robertson, William, 536
Robortello, Francesco, 112
Roccati, Cristina, 373
Roches, Catherine de, 364, 369
Roches, Madeleine de, 364, 369
Rococciolo, Francesco, 202

Rodrigues de Castelo-Branco, João, 470
Rodrigues de Melo, José, 473, 529
Rodrigues de Sá de Meneses, João, 473
Roenick, Johann Tobias, 456
Roillet, Claude, 109
Rojas, Fernando de, 108
Rollin, Charles, 388
Romania, 509. *See also* Romanian language;
        Transylvania; Wallachia
    Dacians, 514–15
Romanian language, 513, 514
Romani da Fabriano, Ludovico, 105
Rome
    academies
        Arcadia, 203, 373, 397
        Dodonei, 373
        Infecondi, 373
        Lincei, 564
        Romana, 90
    as political model, 347–48, 350–51
    represented in literature, 67, 196, 205, 206, 401,
        404, 418–19
Rönnow, Magnus, 505
Ronsard, Pierre de, 238, 368, 416, 419, 420
Ronssaeus, Balduinus, 179
Roper, William, 368
Rosales, Bartolomé, 528
Rossi, Gian Vittorio, 196, 206, 402, 404
Rostgaard, Frederic, 60, 504
Rosweyde, Heribert, 321
Rothe, David, 321
Rottkirchen, Jacobus von, 79
Rougemont, François de, 560, 566
Rouse, John, 43
Rousseau, Jean-Jacques, 498
Rowling, J.K., 195
Royal Academy of Sciences (Paris), 266. *See also*
        academic journals
Royal Society (London), 179, 266–67. *See also*
        academic journals
Rubeanus, Johannes Crotus, 450
Rubens, Peter Paul, 481
Rubio, Antonio, 528
Rudbeck, Olof (the Elder), 502
Rudolf II (Holy Roman Emperor), 369–70, 511,
        517, 519–20
Ruel, Jean, 271, 283
Ruggieri, Michele, 566
Ruggle, George, 30, 91
Ruhnken, David, 486
Ruiz de Villegas, Hernán, 204
Ruprecht of the Palatinate, 65

Russell, Elizabeth Hoby, 368
Russia, 356, 569

Saavedra Fajardo, Diego de, 142
Sabino, Angelo. *See* Sani di Cure
     ("Sabinus"), Angelo
Sabinus, Georg, 445
Sabuco de Nantes, Oliva, 367
Sacchi, Bartolomeo, 136, 161, 402
Sadoleto, Jacopo, 348, 399
Sadolin, Hans, 495
Sagan, Françoise, 195
Sahagún, Bernardino de, 530
Saint-Omer, College of, 114, 560–61
Sainte-Marie among the Hurons, 546–47
Sainte-Marthe, Scévole de, 368
saints. *See* hagiography; *under individual names*
Salamanca, University of, 145–46, 467, 527
Sallust, 106, 151, 225, 373, 487, 505
salons, 209, 250, 363, 365, 366, 420
Salutati, Coluccio, 105, 295, 351, 353
     letters, 167, 402
     poetry, 400
Salvatierra, Juan María, 68–69, 529
Samaritan language, 308
Sambucus, Johannes, 157, 512, 515, 516, 522
Sanadon, Noël Étienne, 48–49
Sanches, Pedro, 471
Sánchez de las Brozas, Francisco, 462, 463
Sande, Duarte de, 568
Sander, Antoon, 488
Sani di Cure ("Sabinus"), Angelo, 401
Sannazaro, Jacopo, 60, 203, 396, 398, 401, 433, 464, 471
Sapidus, Johannes, 451
Sarbiewski, Casimir, 43
satire, 95, 129, 199–212, 241, 331, 438, 453. *See also*
     Horace; Juvenal; Lucian; Persius; prose
     fiction: satirical
     Menippean satire, 183, 184, 191, 199–201, 203,
     205–8, 355, 487
satyr-play, 200–201
Satyra in poetastros O-c-enses, 208
Santeuil, Jean-Baptiste de, 210
Saxo Grammaticus, 494, 501
Scala, Alessandra, 371
Scala, Bartolomeo, 155, 404
Scala dynasty
     Antonio I della (lord of Verona), 105
     Cangrande I della (lord of Verona), 105, 399
Scaliger, Julius Caesar
     Exotericae exercitationes, 534
     Latin style, 257

Poetics, 43, 73, 112, 130, 200, 434–35, 499
poetry, 43, 204, 427
Scaliger, Joseph Justus, 176, 178, 205, 308, 415,
     480, 518
Scandinavia, 183, 274, 457, 488, 493–506. *See also*
     Denmark; Norway; Sweden
Schede Melissus, Paul, 448, 453, 454
Schedel, Hartmann, 285
Schefferus, Johannes, 123, 496–97, 500, 502, 503
Scheuchzer, Johann Jakob, 457
Schiller, Friedrich, 457
Schmalkaldic League, 159
Schmalkaldic War, 454
scholasticism. *See also* Aristotle; Latin
     language: medieval Latin; Spanish
     Scholasticism
     and Catholicism, 307, 315, 316, 317, 325
     grammar, 222, 227, 228
     satirized, 450
     scholastic Latin, 1–2, 251–54, 255–61, 264,
     282–83, 325
     criticism of, 249, 254, 264, 270–71, 305,
     317, 422
     Sorbonne, 412, 421
     thought, 295–96, 298, 303–7, 338–40, 528
Scholier, Pieter, 203
schools, 217–29, 379–90, 477–78. *See also* Jesuits;
     under individual places and fields of study
     Catholic, 59, 74, 126, 236, 241, 264, 315–316, 322,
     326, 380
     convent, 371
     court, 365–66
     drama in, 89, 92, 93–94, 96–98, 108–9, 449, 481–82
     establishment of, 125–26, 333, 335, 336, 337, 341,
     448, 480–81, 495, 496, 497, 530
     exercises, 42, 74, 123, 130–31, 222, 336–37, 448–9
     Latin spoken at, 236, 315–16
     legislation, 122
     medieval, 200
     oratory at, 125, 333–34, 353, 354, 486
     Ottoman, 288
     Protestant, 2, 74, 126, 315, 329, 331
     textbooks, 334–35, 337, 339, 341, 448
     teaching anthologies, 1, 186, 448–49
Schonaeus, Cornelius, 92, 94–95, 482
Schöner, Johannes, 520
Schopenhauer, Arthur, 27
Schoppe, Kaspar, 178, 205, 455, 487
Schöpper, Jakob, 109, 451
Schottenius, Hermann, 107, 449, 453
Schramm, Jonas Conrad, 546
Schreck, Johann, 562–63, 564

Schweitzer, Heinrich, 266
Schurman, Anna Maria van, 369, 370, 372, 373
science, 179, 263–74, 367, 398, 414, 520–22, 551.
    See also astrology; astronomy;
    mathematics; medicine
  chemistry, 201, 263, 273, 513
  "chymistry," 263, 264, 265, 267
  natural philosophy, 237, 263–66, 270, 273,
    290, 534
  physics, 266, 284, 521, 528
  scientific instruments, 272, 437–38, 520
  taxonomy, 264, 266, 274
  textbooks, 266
  translations, 265–66
    from Greek into Latin, 270–72
    from Latin into vernaculars, 272–73
Scipio Africanus, 63
Scotland, 320, 431. *See also* British Isles; English
    language
  historiography, 159, 432
  poetry, 434–36
Scribani, Carolus, 143, 488
scribes, 239, 297, 301, 302, 304, 532
scripture. *See* Bible
Scriverius, Petrus, 481
Scudéry, Madeleine de, 184
Scythians, 157, 195, 514
Sebastião I (king of Portugal), 469
Second Scholastic. *See* Spanish Scholasticism
Secundus, Johannes, 45, 47, 48, 73, 79, 417, 483–84
Secundus, Petrus Lotichius, 41, 454
Sedulius, 66
Segni, Bernardo, 254
Selden, John, 146
Sellius, Nicolaus, 453
Semedo, Alvaro, 563, 565
seminaries, 315. *See also* theology; universities
Semproni, Bibolo, 363
Senckenberg, Renatus Karl von, 453
Seneca the Elder, 120
Seneca the Younger, 169, 471
  Apocolocyntosis, 205
  commentaries on, 462
  correspondence with Paul (spurious), 296
  De clementia, 352
  editions of, 478
  Epistulae morales, 130, 168, 177–78
  Naturales quaestiones, 270
  Senecanism, 21, 136–39, 480
  Stoicism, 177–78
  tragedies, 41, 44, 91, 97, 104–13, 225, 404, 419,
    472, 482

Senguerdius, Wolferdus, 266
Septimius Severus (Roman emperor), 16
Sepúlveda, Juán Ginés de, 463, 465, 466–67, 526
Serapion, 290
Sergardi, Lodovico, 203
sermons. *See* preaching
Serrata, Leonardo della, 404
Settano, Quinto, 210
Seven Years' War, 502, 504, 544
Severinus, Marcus, 267
Sewall, Samuel, 74, 552
Sextus Empiricus, 416
Seymour family, 368
Sfondrati, Francesco, 399–400
Sforza dynasty, 61, 399
  Bianca, 364, 365
  Bona (queen of Poland), 366, 369
  Francesco, 171, 365, 399
  Galeazzo Maria, 365, 369
  Ippolita Maria, 365
Shakespeare, William, 98
Sheeshahteaumuck, Caleb, 550
Shen Fuzong, Michael, 569, 570
Sibylline Oracles, 301
Siculo, Lucio Marineo, 367
Sidney, Philip, 433
Siena, 155
  Accademia degli Intronati, 373
Sigea, Luisa, 211, 367, 473
Sigismund I (king of Poland), 369, 517
Sigismund (Holy Roman Emperor), 185, 186
Sigonio, Carlo, 27, 129, 156, 160, 161–62, 402
Silius Italicus, 68
Simon, Charles, 544
Simon of Keza, 514
Simonet de Villeneuve, C., 67–68
Simonetta, Gian Mario, 405
Simonides, Simon, 517
Simonius, Johannes, 500
Simons, Joseph, 114
Sinology. *See* Asia; China; Manchus; oriental studies
Sixtus V (pope), 307
Skinnerus, Ericus Jacobi, 500
Skytte, Johan, 500
slavery, 187, 188, 467, 487, 526, 529, 536–37
Sleidan, Johann, 159–60, 488
Slovakia, 509, 510. *See also* East-Central Europe
Smith, John Blair, 550
Snoy, Reynier, 487
Soarez, Cyprianus, 129
Soave, Francesco, 219
Sobrarias, Juan, 464

social class, 219, 379–90, 530, 532, 536, 565, 567
Solinus, 270
Solórzano de Pereira, Juán de, 526, 529
Sommer, Johannes, 513
Soncino, Joshua Solomon, 299
Sophie Elisabeth (duchess of
          Braunschweig-Lüneburg), 369
Sophocles, 74
Soresi, Pier Domenico, 219
Sorø, Academy of, 497
Sotades, 211
Soto, Domingo de, 145
Souciet, Etienne, 562
Souterius, Daniel, 34
South America. *See* Latin America
Sozinus, Marianus, 186
Spain, 461–68. *See also* Latin America; Spanish
          language
     arbitristas, 385–86
     Black Legend, 536
     enterprise of the Indies, 465–67
     Jesuits, 69
Spanish language
     dictionaries, 532
     models for Latin literature, 108
     textbooks, 31
     translations from Latin, 79, 404, 465
     translations into Latin, 142
     vernacular works, 210
Spanish Scholasticism, 145–47
Speccius, Christoph, 96
speculative grammar. *See under* scholasticism
Speght, Rachel, 365
Spenser, Edmund, 432–33
Speroni, Sperone, 253, 255
Spiegel, Jakob, 60
Spinoza, Baruch, 250, 309
Spitzel, Gottlieb, 568
Sporeni, Giuseppe, 396
Spranger, Bartholomeus, 511
Squire, Robert, 93
St. Andrew's, University of, 235, 240
St. Bartholomew's Day Massacre, 205, 242, 454.
          See also France: wars of religion
Staffel, Margarethe von, 370
Stanhope, Philip Dormer, (earl of Chesterfield), 381
Stanihurst, Richard, 21, 315, 318
Starck, Wolfgang, 449
Stobaeus, Andreas, 499
Statius, 58, 471, 517
Stockholm, Collegium Regium, 496, 497
Stay, Benedict, 58

Steuco, Agostino, 300
Stephanius, Stephanus Johannis, 497
Stephanus, Henricus. *See* Estienne, Henri
Stephanus, Robertus. *See* Estienne, Robert
Stephen (king and patron saint of Hungary), 157
Stiblinus, Caspar, 188
Stigel, Johann, 445
Stiles, Ezra, 550, 553
Stoicism, 104, 139, 265, 266, 313, 335. *See also*
          Lipsius; Seneca the Younger
Stoicus vapulans, 89, 96
Stoke, William, 551
St. Petersburg, 562
Strada, Zanobi da, 202, 399
Strasbourg, 209, 306, 337
     gymnasium (later academy), 126, 334, 335
Strozzi, Agostino, 364
Strozzi, Lorenza, 371, 396
Strozzi, Tito Vespasiano, 46, 61, 202, 395, 399, 400
Stuart dynasty, 84
Stuart, Elizabeth, 34
students (*See under* universities)
studia humanitatis
     based on Cicero and Quintilian, 124
     and ethics, 174, 333, 339–40, 345–46
     and patriotism, 446
     and travel, 510
     treatises on, 125
Stumpf, Kilian, 561
Sture, Sten (the Elder), 503
Sturm, Johannes, 108, 111, 113, 121, 123, 126,
          136, 335–37
Stymmelius, Christoph, 93–94, 449
Suarez, Francisco, 146, 318
Suetonius, 470
Suleiman I the Magnificent (Ottoman sultan), 515
Sulla, 154, 487
Sulpicia, 209
Summonte, Giovanni Antonio, 402
Surius, Jean, 114
Surius, Laurentius, 321, 488
Surlet, Jean de Chokier de, 142
Svaning, Hans, 498, 501–2
Swammerdam, Jan, 273
Sweden, 493–506. *See also* Swedish language
     Thirty Years' War, 189, 493
Swedish language
     translations from Latin, 94, 211
     translations into Latin, 502
Swedenborg, Emanuel, 506
Sweerts, Frans, 488
Swift, Jonathan, 192, 193, 506

Switzerland, schools 126, 337. *See also* Bullinger; Calvin; Zwingli
Syriac language, 295, 299, 308, 367, 372. *See also* Bible

Tacitus, 120, 140, 151, 158, 346, 354, 372, 480
  Annals, 141, 346, 348, 350,
  Germania, 158, 348, 445, 446,
  Histories, 141, 346, 348
  Tacitism, 21, 139–42, 143, 177, 347–49, 355, 448
Talon, Omer, 415
Tanini, Antonia Pulci, 371
Tannstetter, Georg, 521
Tarabotti, Arcangela, 209
Tasso, Torquato, 398–99
Taubmann, Friedrich, 447
Taylor, Joseph, 83
Teive, Diogo de, 107, 472
Telesio, Bernardino, 404
Terence, 20, 87, 90, 91, 99, 404, 448
  Andria, 33, 34
  Adelphoe, 218
  in education, 32, 34, 107, 225, 464
  Hecyra, 15
  imitation of, 20, 88–89, 92, 94, 482
  translation into vernaculars, 32, 33, 373
Terserus, Johannes, 500
Tertullian, 305
textbooks. *See* schools; *under individual fields of study*
Textor, Ravisius, 91
theater. *See* comedy; Jesuits; tragedy; schools; universities
Theocritus, 84, 416, 434
Theodore of Tarsus, 17
Theodosius (Roman emperor), 16
Theodulus, 224
theology, 295–309, 313–26, 329–42. *See also* Bible; Counter-Reformation; Reformation; scholasticism
  academic study of, 145–46, 227, 549–50
  and historiography, 160
  and Latin style, 29, 260, 264, 422, 450
  and literature, 52–53, 78, 108, 111, 188–89, 207, 461
Theon, 120
Theophrastus, 270–71
Theophylactus, 297
Thessaliensis, Kempo, 209
Thévenot, Mélchisedec, 567
Thilo, Valentin, 129
Thirty Years' War, 59, 189, 356, 453, 454, 470, 485, 493

Thomas à Kempis, 175
Thomas, Antoine, 559, 562, 564, 570
Thomasius, Christian, 457
Thomesen, Hans, 500
Thou, Jacques-Auguste de, 110, 161–62
Thucydides, 151, 413
Thurozi, János, 514
Tiberius (Roman emperor), 350, 404
Tibet, 563
Tibullus, 45, 470, 485
Timanthes, 177
Timpler, Clemens, 123
Tindal, Nicholas, 513
Titian, 172
Tittelmans, Franz, 304
Tlatelolco, College of Santa Cruz, 530–31
Toledo, Francisco de, 146
Torda, Sigismundus, 516
Torfaeus, Thormod, 503
Torrentius, Laevinus, 313
Tortelli, Giovanni, 285
Tosetti, Lello di Pietro Stefano dei, 170
Tottel, Richard, 109
Tournet, Jean, 210
tragedy, 91–92, 99, 103–15, 201, 404–5, 420
  tragicomedy, 87, 107, 110, 115
Trajan (Roman emperor), 352, 515
translatio studiorum, 259–60, 547
translation, 251–52. *See also* bilingualism; multilingualism; *under individual languages and fields of study*
  from Latin into vernaculars, 29, 32–33, 122, 185, 530
  from vernaculars into Latin, 28, 31, 122, 326, 421
Transylvania, 509, 512, 514–15, 516, 519, 520, 521
Trapezuntius, Georgius, 121, 129, 270
travel, 178, 433, 510
  accounts, 189, 289–90, 489, 512–13, 546, 549, 563–64, 567
  in verse, 455
Traversari, Ambrogio, 161, 296
Treaty of Nerchinsk, 356, 569, 570
Tremellius, Immanuel, 329. *See also* Bible
Tribraco, Gaspare, 202, 400
Trigault, Nicolas, 559
Trinitarianism, 301
Trippault, Léon, 416
Trithemius, Johannes, 161
trivium. *See* liberal arts
Tschudi, Ägidius, 158
Tucci, Stefano, 114

Turberville, George, 401
Turkey, Turks. *See* Ottoman Empire, Ottomans
Turku (Åbo), Academy of, 502
Turnèbe, Adrien, 240, 241–42, 415, 420
Tusana, Esmonda, 369

Ubaldini, Roberto, 190
Ughelli, Ferdinando, 162
Ugonio, Pompeo, 348
Ukraine, 521
Ulrichs, Karl Heinrich, 316–17
Union of Kalmar, 493, 501, 504
United States of America. *See under*
    North America
universities, 233–45, 290, 308, 317–18, 372–73, 412,
    461, 512. *See also* schools; lectures; *under*
    individual places and fields of study
  anthologies of verse, 35, 80–83, 431, 548
  association with Latin, 28–29, 233, 236, 250,
    263–65, 267, 273–74, 317, 422, 461, 470,
    495, 505–6, 528
  biblical scholarship (*See* Bible)
  disputations, 145, 233, 234, 236, 240–42,
    243–44, 296, 453, 457
  dissertations, 1, 28, 145, 193, 233, 373, 449, 457,
    498, 499, 506, 528
  drama, 88, 90–91, 93, 108–9, 113, 234,
    464, 481–82
  establishment of, 300, 335, 337, 412, 462, 469,
    478, 479, 480–81, 482, 486, 495–97,
    510, 526
  examinations, 457, 527, 547
  faculty structure, 237, 240, 263, 267, 412, 457
  foreigners at, 237, 446, 469, 478, 480, 494, 495,
    496, 512–13, 514, 569
  literary production at, 47, 59, 192, 193, 207–8,
    331, 434, 437–38, 496, 498, 548
  medieval inheritance, 145, 221, 259–60,
    265, 305, 317, 339, 412, 462 (*see also*
    scholasticism)
  new posts at, 280, 287, 288, 300, 308, 500
  notes, 415, 498, 545–46
  oratory, 27, 59, 121, 129–30, 332, 354, 364, 366,
    447, 465, 470, 486, 500, 551
  rituals, 52, 83, 274, 550
    graduation, 438
  students, 233–45, 264, 316, 512
    accommodation of, 237–240
    instructions for, 234, 236, 243–45
    exclusion, 529, 536
    miseries of, 92, 207–8, 238–39, 241, 242

represented in literature, 89, 92–94, 98,
    207–8, 316, 449
  social status of, 233, 237–38, 384
  speaking Latin, 21, 233, 236, 264
Uppsala, University of, 496, 500
Uraniborg, 497
Urban VIII (pope), 43, 45, 206, 321
Urceo, Antonio Codro, 208, 400
Urfé, Honoré d', 184
Utenhove, Karel, 368–69, 372
utopias. *See under* prose fiction

Vadian, Joachim, 447
Valadés, Diego, 526
Valdštejna, Zdeněk Brtnický z, 512
Valencia, Martín de, 530
Valera, Blas, 529
Valera, Jerónimo de, 528
Valeriano, Pierio, 208, 400, 401
Valerius, Cornelius, 177
Valerius Flaccus, 58
Valerius Maximus, 225
Valéry, Paul, 382
Valla, Giorgio, 112, 287
Valla, Lorenzo
  biblical scholarship, 296–99, 301, 302, 308, 338, 478
  Dialecticae disputationes, 252, 258, 403
  dialogues, 402
  and *Donation of Constantine*, 349
  Elegantiae linguae Latinae, 20, 23, 126, 347–48,
    416, 478–79
  humanism, 174, 255, 412
  translation from Greek, 151
  views on Latin, 2, 14, 15, 16, 20, 22, 249, 470
Valois, Marguerite de, 369
Varro, 199, 205
Vatable, François, 308
Vatican, 326. *See also* censorship;
    Counter-Reformation; Inquisition;
    papacy; *individual popes*
  Second Vatican Council, 314, 317, 326
Vazquez de Menchaca, Fernando, 146
Vedel, Anders Sørensen, 498
Vega, Garcilaso de la, 529
Vega, Lope de, 114
Vegio, Maffeo, 62–63, 67, 398
Velius, Caspar Ursinus, 445, 515
Venegas, Miguel, 465, 472
Venice
    Accademia degli Pacifici, 373
    historiography about, 155, 156, 402

Vera Cruz, Alonso de la, 526
Verardi, Carlo, 107
Verardi, Marcellino, 107
Verbiest, Ferdinand, 489, 559, 560, 561–62, 564, 567, 569
Vegara, Juan de, 300
Verantius, Antonius, 512, 515, 516
Vergerio, Pier Paolo, 89, 124, 174, 234, 241, 404, 511, 520
Vergil, Polydore, 157, 158, 431–32
Verino, Michele, 463, 464
Verino, Ugolino, 62, 398, 400
Vernaccia, Battista, 371
vernacular. *See also* translation; *individual languages*
    defenses of, 3, 27–29, 416, 417–18
Verne, Jules, 192
Vernulaeus, Nicolaus, 144, 482, 486
Verona, school of, 365
Verzosa, Juan de, 464
Vesalius, Andreas, 179, 489, 564
Vico, Giambattista, 162
Vida, Marco Girolamo, 57, 66, 398, 427, 429, 433, 471, 472
Vieira, António, 473
Vienna, 511, 515
    Collegium poetarum et mathematicorum, 447
    siege of (1529), 453
    siege of (1683), 191, 373
Vimercato, Francesco, 283–84
Vinet, Elie, 469
Villegas, Jerónimo de, 210
Villerías y Roelas, José, 528
Virdung, Michael, 110
Virgil
    Aeneid, 64, 65, 66–67, 69, 194, 436, 531
        as political model, 59, 60, 65, 352, 354–55, 436, 452–53, 495, 504, 505, 547
        as structural model, 66, 110, 168, 451
        supplements to, 63, 67–68, 398, 486, 528
    as career model, 57–58, 65
    in centos, 207, 528, 547
    commentaries on, 60, 463
    Eclogues, 65, 218, 337, 395, 453
    in education, 17, 218, 220, 224–25, 244, 337, 339, 341
    Georgics, 57, 58, 65, 67, 218, 371, 397, 437–39, 485, 529
    Latin style, 20, 21–22, 57–59, 64, 395, 396, 405, 436, 537
Virgilio, Giovanni del, 395
Virginia, College of William and Mary, 548

Virtus vindicata, sive Polieni Rhodiensis satyra, 208
Visagier, Jean, 417
Visconti dynasty, 351
    Bianca, 365
    Filippo Maria, 171
Vitale, Giano, 401
Vitalian, Pope, 17
Vitéz, János, 520–21
Vitoria, Francisco de, 146, 466
Vitruvius, 90
Vittorino da Feltre, 174
Vives, Juan Luis
    dialogues, 486
    letters, 173, 465
    pedagogy, 121, 204, 184, 207, 367, 414, 463, 464, 487
    political writing, 487
    Somnium, 196, 486
Vlatten, Johann von, 174
Voltaire, 98, 115, 162, 250, 536
Vondel, Joost van den, 115, 483
Voragine, Jacobus de, 321
Vossius, Gerardus, 73, 121, 122, 129, 178, 388, 481, 499
Vossius, Isaac, 309, 496
Vries, Adriaen De, 511
Vulcanius, Bonaventura, 480, 483

Waldstein, Baron. *See* Valdštejna, Zdeněk Brtnický z
Wales, 78, 432. *See also* British Isles; English language
Wallace, Michael, 436
Wallace, William, 435
Wallachia, 513, 514–15
Walle, Jacques van de, 485
Walton, Brian, 308
war. *See* American War of Independence; Anglo-Dutch War (second); France: wars of religion; Germany: Peasants' War; Great Northern War; Landshut: War of the Succession of; propaganda: war; Schmalkaldic War; Seven Years' War; Thirty Years' War; William III: Williamite War
Waser, Kaspar, 308
Washington, George, 552
Was, Jan, 467–68, 469, 471
Watson, Thomas, 109, 433
Webbe, Joseph, 33
Weiditz, Hans, 271
Weise, Christian, 355
Welser, Margarethe, 370

Wenzenberg, Battle of, 65
West, Richard, 434
Westhovius, Willich, 499, 504
Westminster School, 74
Weston, Elizabeth, 74, 369–70
Westphalia, Peace of, 356. *See also* Thirty
  Years' War
White, Andrew, 549
White, Richard, 432
White, Stephen, 318, 432
Widmanstetter, Johann Albrecht, 287, 299
Wieringa, Nicolaas Jachirides, 210–11
Wigglesworth, Michael, 74
Willard, Joseph, 552
Willem van Ruysbroeck, 557
Willes, Richard, 29, 34
William I (prince of Orange), 482, 485
William III (king of England), 84, 208, 435
  Williamite War, 435
William of Auxerre, 305
William of Conches, 104
William of Ockham, 305
Willich, Jodocus, 123
Willughby, Francis, 269
Wimpfeling, Jakob, 136, 228, 446, 449, 455
Winthrop, John, 551
Winthrop, Samuel, 552
wit
  argutia, 73, 355, 434–35, 447, 464
  educational purpose, 74, 128, 486
  Facetiae, 186, 196, 206
  linguistic play, 30, 33–34, 77
  satirical, 98, 192, 201, 207, 209, 331, 479
Witsen, Nicolaas, 569

Wittenberg
  autograph books, 449
  represented in literature, 95, 332
  University of, 126, 494, 495, 496, 514
Wittgenstein, Ludwig, 251
Wolff, Christian, 256, 261, 457
Worm, Ole, 502
Woverius, Johannes, 176
Wright, James, 77

Xenophon, 136, 146, 153, 402
  translations of, 171
Ximénez de Cisneros, Francisco, 300, 301
Ximénez de Rada, Rodrigo, 467

Zabarella, Jacopo, 257
Zacchia da Vezzano, Laudivio, 105
Zacharie de Lisieux, 184
Zamagna, Bernardo, 398
Zamora, Alfonso de, 300
Zasius, Ulrich, 452
Zeidler, Johannes, 80
Zeidler, Michael, 80
Zevecote, Jacob van, 482
Ziegler, Hieronymus, 111
Ziegler, Jacob, 503
Zincgref, Julius Wilhelm, 453
Zola, Émile, 381–82
zoology, 266, 274
Zrínyi, Miklós, 514
Zumárraga, Juan de, 527
Zunghar people, 559
Zurich, 338–41
Zwingli, Ulrich, 126, 306, 455